The African American Experience

The African American Experience

JOE WILLIAM TROTTER, JR.

Carnegie Mellon University

HOUGHTON MIFFLIN COMPANY

Boston   New York

〜

To my students, past and present

Carnegie Mellon University
Pittsburgh, Pennsylvania

University of California
Davis, California

University of Minnesota
Minneapolis–St. Paul, Minnesota

Tremper Senior High School
Kenosha, Wisconsin

Editor in Chief: Jean L. Woy
Senior Development Editor: Frances Gay
Senior Project Editor: Christina M. Horn
Production/Design Coordinator: Jodi O'Rourke
Senior Cover Design Coordinator: Deborah Azerrad Savona
Manufacturing Manager: Florence Cadran
Senior Marketing Manager: Sandra McGuire

Cover design: Nina Wishnok/Dynamo Design
Cover image: Jacob Lawrence, *Builders #4.* New Orleans Museum of Art.

PART OPENER PHOTO CREDITS: *Part I:* New York Public Library; *Part II:* Library of Congress; *Part III:* Chicago Historical Society; *Part IV:* Harper's Weekly; *Part V:* National Archives; *Part VI:* AP Photo/Beth A. Keiser.

Text credits appear on page A-72, which constitutes an extension of the copyright page.

Printed in the U.S.A.

Library of Congress Catalog Card Number: 00-1338859

ISBN: 0-395-75654-5

2 3 4 5 6 7 8 9-QF-05 04 03 02 01

CONTENTS

BOXES

MAPS AND ILLUSTRATIONS

TABLES

PREFACE

The *African American Experience* is rooted in the recent maturation of African American studies as a scholarly field. Over the past three decades, scholars have revamped our understanding of race, class, culture, and power in U.S. and African American history. Yet popular perceptions of African Americans reflect certain enduring stereotypes and erroneous notions about African American life and history. In the mainstream media, portraits of African Americans continue to revolve around images of poor and working-class blacks as economically improvident, culturally impoverished, devoid of viable family life, isolated from community, and largely passive in the face of dehumanizing social conditions. In contrast, this book shows how African Americans developed their own notions of work, family, culture, and power and forged their own distinct community. The black poor, working-class, and business and professional people created a broad range of multiclass institutions that not only fueled the African American struggle for cultural autonomy but also established a foundation for the ongoing struggle for political freedom and economic emancipation.

While this study rejects portraits of the black community as internally fragmented and incapable of acting in its own best interests, it rejects the idea that racism overwhelmed difference, transformed the black population into a homogeneous mass, and suppressed internal dissent. This book builds on research in African American social, working-class, and women's history and probes both class and gender conflicts within the black community. Poor and working-class blacks were by no means passive participants in middle-class or elite-led community-building activities. They challenged the moral injunctions of their elite counterparts and pioneered in the development of unique cultural forms such as the blues and gospel. Similarly, black women questioned the most blatant manifestations of gender inequality within the black community. They built their own auxiliaries and pushed for change within black civic, religious, civil rights, and political organizations. By showing how black life unfolded within diverse groups and regions and how it changed over time, this book also treats the black experience as a dynamic, multifaceted, historical process from its African beginnings through the onset of the twenty-first century.

As African Americans navigated internal social conflicts and forged collective responses to class and racial inequality, they also gained the support of a small but in-fluential roster of white allies. These included abolitionists during the antebellum years, radical Republicans during the emancipation period, and freedom marchers during the modern civil rights era, to name a few. Such recurring patterns of inter-racial cooperation offered hope that America could create a more just and inclusive society. Still, both the promise and limits of American democracy persist as the cur-tains open on a new century.

This book is divided into six interrelated parts, each covering a major phase in African American life and history. Part I (Chapters 1–2) traces the black experience from its African roots to enslavement in the Latin American and Caribbean colonies of Portugal, Spain, France, and England. By discussing the multiracial na-ture of slavery in the Old World, Part I concludes that the rise of race-based slavery was the product of historical developments on a global scale. Focusing on the en-slavement of blacks in British North America, Part II (Chapters 3–6) describes the transition from a relatively flexible system of indentured servitude during the early seventeenth century to bondage "for life" during the late seventeenth and eigh-teenth centuries. It also analyzes regional differences and concludes with a discus-sion of the promise and limits of the American Revolution and life in the new republic for African Americans.

The development of African American life in the antebellum South is the sub-ject of Part III (Chapters 7–10). This section discusses work, housing, and living conditions in a variety of urban and rural settings; the development of slave culture, family, community, and forms of resistance; and the growth of a free black popula-tion, the rise of abolitionism, and the coming of the Civil War. Part III also de-scribes how African Americans helped to transform the Civil War into a struggle for their own liberation.

Part IV (Chapters 11–14) discusses the triumphs and disappointments of eman-cipation. It shows how newly emancipated blacks won and then lost the franchise; won and then lost a measure of control over their own land and labor; and won and then lost a coterie of white allies. At the same time, these chapters show how African Americans forged new forms of culture, community, and political activism and resisted the rise of Jim Crow, disfranchisement, and mob violence.

The African American struggle for freedom escalated during the era of the Great Migration, the Great Depression, and the two world wars, which are the subjects of Part V (Chapters 15–19). African Americans built new institutions and launched new cultural, civil rights, and political movements. The NAACP, the National Ur-ban League, the Garvey movement, the Communist Party, and the Congress of In-dustrial Organizations all helped to establish a foundation for the modern civil rights movement and the rise of the Second Reconstruction during the 1950s and 1960s, as discussed in Part VI (Chapters 20–23). Part VI explores not only the rise of massive nonviolent direct action struggles but also the Black Power movement, the decline of the Second Reconstruction, and the emergence of new African American movements for social change during the 1990s. By the turn of the twenty-first century, African Americans struggled to redefine what it meant to be black in an increasingly multiracial nation and world.

Reinforcing the foregoing treatment of black life and history, *The African American Experience* includes special features designed to deepen the reader's understanding of the subject. Distributed at appropriate points throughout the text are more than one hundred photographs; statistical tables, maps, and charts; special full-color inserts displaying artifacts and artwork; and boxed excerpts of primary sources. The Appendix contains tables that show population growth, urbanization, and suburbanization, as well as excerpts from more than a dozen documents—key civil rights laws, executive orders, and Supreme Court decisions. By providing a visual image of African American life over time and by telling the story in the voices and language of the people who lived during different periods of the nation's history, these documents and artwork enable readers to imagine times and experiences quite different from their own. An extensive Chronology of significant events also appears at the end of the book, to enable readers to review the sequence of events. These pages are tinted at the edges for ease of reference.

Because historical knowledge and interpretation require an understanding of diverse viewpoints, this book provides brief historiographical critiques of available scholarship. These "Changing Historical Interpretations" boxes pinpoint areas of controversy on key topics, issues, and periods in African American history—the origins of African slavery, the emergence of African American culture, Reconstruction, the rise of Jim Crow, the development of black urban communities, and the origins of the modern civil rights movement. By introducing readers to major controversies in African American life and history, these succinct essays encourage students to ponder how and why commonly agreed-on facts often produce widely divergent interpretations. This unique feature allows students to explore how historians think, conduct their research, and interpret the black experience.

As always, I am indebted to numerous institutions, staff, colleagues, friends, and relatives for helping to make this book possible. At Carnegie Mellon University, I wish to thank Steve Schlossman, head of the Department of History; Peter Stearns, former dean of the College of Humanities and Social Science; Gail Dickey, business manager; Elaine Burrelli, administrative assistant; Robin Dearmon Jenkins, Ph.D. candidate; colleagues Tera Hunter and Joel Tarr; members of the advisory board of the Center for Africanamerican Urban Studies and the Economy (CAUSE); and the offices of the president and provost. For encouraging my research, writing, teaching, and work with CAUSE, I also appreciate the current and past support of the Mellon Bank Foundation, the Maurice Falk Medical Fund, the Ford Foundation, and collaborative schools and colleagues in the Midwest Consortium for Black Studies.

Moreover, this book was completed while I was a Fellow at the Center for Advanced Study in the Behavioral Sciences (CASBS), Stanford, California. I am grateful for the financial support provided by the Andrew W. Mellon Foundation. At CASBS, I benefited from the critical insights of Center Fellows Portia Maultsby, Michael Fultz, Edward Ayers, Michael Johnson, Sara Berry, and Jitka Maleckova. For providing a forum for the discussion of my ideas for the book, especially Chapter 10, I am indebted to James Grossman and participants in the Newberry Library Seminar in Social History in Chicago.

At other universities, I am indebted to friends Earl Lewis, University of Michigan, Ann Arbor; Quintard Taylor, University of Washington, Seattle; Julie Saville, University of Chicago; Elias Mandala, University of Rochester; Laurence Glasco, University of Pittsburgh; Stephanie Shaw, Ohio State University, Columbus; Henry Louis Taylor Jr., State University of New York, Buffalo; James and Lois Horton, George Washington University, Washington, D.C.; Clarence Walker, University of California, Davis; Irwin Marcus, Indiana University, Pennsylvania; Darlene Clark Hine, Michigan State University; and Nellie McKay and other members of the Midwest Consortium for Black Studies. And I would like to thank the following reviewers who gave very helpful critiques and advice on the manuscript at various stages in the process: Mia Bay, Rutgers University; Nemata Blyden, University of Texas at Dallas; Stephanie Cole, University of Texas at Arlington; Selika Ducksworth-Lawton, University of Wisconsin—Eau Claire; Roy E. Finkenbine, University of Detroit—Mercy; Thelma Wills Foote, University of California, Irvine; Paul Harvey, University of Colorado; Larry E. Hudson Jr., University of Rochester; Ben Keppel, University of Oklahoma; Elias Mandala, University of Rochester; Edna Greene Medford, Howard University; Tiffany Ruby Patterson, Binghamton University; W. Bryan Rommel-Ruiz, Colorado College; Clarence E. Walker, University of California, Davis; and Michael R. West, College of the Holy Cross.

I also wish to extend a special thanks to the editors and staff of Houghton Mifflin Company for the careful attention given to this book. I am especially grateful to Jean Woy, Vice President and Editor in Chief, and her predecessor, Sean Wakeley, for their firm confidence in this project. For effectively steering this book through various phases of the production process, I also thank Frances Gay, Senior Development Editor; Christina Horn, Senior Project Editor; and Sharon Donahue, photo researcher. Indeed, it has been a real pleasure working with and learning from these publishing professionals.

For providing inspiration as well as community-based forums, documents, books, and memories of the postindustrial North-to-South migration, I thank my brothers and sisters, and nieces and nephews, especially Otis and his wife, Dotsie; my sister, Voncille Hines; my niece, Marva Ann Williams; and my nephews, Greg Harris and Carson Trotter III. Most important, however, I am indebted to my wife, LaRue. In addition to her love and ongoing spiritual support, LaRue offered unyielding faith and confidence in this book. Finally, for inspiring my teaching, challenging my ideas, and sustaining my faith in the educational enterprise, I am grateful to my students. These include not only undergraduate students and the high school students whom I first taught, but also numerous graduate students—Steve Tripp, John Hinshaw, Ancella Livers, Donald Collins, Liesl Miller Orenic, Matthew Hawkins, Trent Alexander, Charles Lee, Susannah Walker, Tywanna Whorley, and Robin Dearmon Jenkins, to name only a few. To them, I dedicate this book with a great deal of appreciation and respect for sharing their remarkable insights into the human condition.

Joe William Trotter Jr.
Pittsburgh, Pennsylvania

PART I

The African American Experience in Global Perspective: Prelude to a New World

The African American experience had its roots in the gradual globalization of the world's people. Like Asian, Latino, and European immigrants, African Americans were part of the great transatlantic migration of people from the Old World. Unlike other ethnic and nationality groups, however, African Americans entered the New World in chains. Yet their enslavement was by no means inevitable. Before the arrival of Europeans on the west coast of Africa during the fifteenth and sixteenth centuries, Africans had developed their own independent economic, social, and political systems. In addition to the ancient kingdoms of Egypt and Ethiopia in North and East Africa, the medieval kingdoms of Ghana, Mali, and Songhay had emerged in West Africa. Although the spread of the Sahara Desert in ancient times had disrupted the geographical unity of the continent and stimulated the emergence of sharp regional differences, the development of trans-Saharan transportation and trade networks joined Africans together across regions and promoted the vigorous transfer of goods, people, and ideas, including the spread of Islam into West Africa and the export of gold and human captives to North Africa and the Mediterranean.

In the meantime, during the medieval crusades, Europeans gained knowledge of sugar production following their capture of the Islamic territories of the eastern Mediterranean and North Africa. On their Mediterranean sugar plantations, Europeans initially enslaved Arabs, Africans, and eastern and southern Europeans. Only gradually did the plantation system spread to the islands off the northwest coast of Africa and then to the New World, where Europeans acquired a predominantly African labor force. Despite the heroic efforts of Africans to resist enslavement and retain their freedom, Europeans gradually instituted a color- or race-based system of human bondage and set the principal context for the first four hundred years of black life in the New World. As a backdrop for understanding this process in British North America, Part I analyzes the development of independent precolonial African societies; the rise of a multiracial system of bondage in the Mediterranean world; and finally the emergence of African bondage in the New World colonies of the Caribbean and Latin America.

CHAPTER 1

◡

Before the Atlantic Crossing

Western images of Africa have changed tremendously over time, but certain perceptions endure. Despite the remarkable, though tedious and slow, climb of African nations toward independence and democracy during the late twentieth century, no contemporary image of Africa is more pervasive than the portrait of starving men, women, and children in the drought- and civil war–stricken countries of East Africa and the Sahel. The image of Africa as a land of economic hardship, starvation, and political turmoil has a long history. Between 2500 and 2300 B.C., the major rivers of the Sahara gradually evaporated, forcing inhabitants of the river valleys to move farther north and south. As Europeans entered Africa in search of a better life and riches for themselves during modern times, they often seized on these harsh conditions as a rationale for their enslavement and colonization of African peoples. They argued that an even worse fate had confronted blacks in their own land and at their own hands. In short, Europeans denied that Africans could come to grips with their own problems. On the contrary, as this chapter will demonstrate, precolonial Africans adapted to changing social, cultural, and environmental conditions by creating numerous states and social systems—Egypt and Ethiopia in the northeast, the trans-Saharan trade network in the northwest, and a succession of West African kingdoms from Lake Chad in the east to the Atlantic Ocean in the west. By assessing the transformation of African societies during the ancient period, we will be able to better understand the many forces that gave rise to the African American experience in the New World.

NORTHEAST AFRICA

Before 2500 B.C., the Sahara was a highly fertile land capable of supporting a variety of plant, animal, and human life. The Sahara river system flowed unbroken

2

from Lake Chad in the east, southwest into the Benue-Niger Rivers, and thence to the Atlantic Ocean. Moreover, from west to east, numerous mountainous rivers replenished this inland system of waters, giving rise to vibrant Stone Age fishing communities. Remains of harpoons, fishhooks, and decorative wavy-line clay pottery offer evidence of a thriving culture in this region. Farther east, Sahara tributaries added to the river systems of the Nile Valley and Ethiopian highlands. Given the pre–Saharan Desert history of this continent, it is no wonder that recent archaeologists have located some of the most impressive early remains of human life in Africa.

Ancient Egypt

The emergence of the Sahara Desert presented Africans with new and enduring challenges to human survival and development. As the wet phase of the Sahara came to an end, settlements on the edge of the Nile Valley gradually moved inland along the naturally irrigated floodplains of the Nile River. Egyptians depended increasingly on the annual overflow of the Nile River, which owed its existence to its tributaries, the White Nile and Blue Nile (and Atbara), the latter originating in the highlands of Ethiopia (see map). Each year, heavy rains and floods inundated these rivers, bringing into the Nile Valley new dark, fertile soils. All along the Nile Valley, farming communities depended on these annual deposits of fresh land and water from thousands of miles away. It was this remarkable phenomenon that led the Greek historian Herodotus to describe Egypt as the "miracle" or "gift" of the Nile River.

The fertility of the Nile Valley gave rise to a series of small agricultural communities along its banks. These small communities soon developed into a number of local states, which in turn formed the foundation for the emergence of the Upper and Lower kingdoms of Egypt. Under the leadership of Narmer, or Menes, Upper and Lower Egypt united into a single kingdom sometime between about 3000 B.C. and 2850 B.C., setting in motion one of the longest-lasting cultures in human history.

Several overlapping periods of stability and instability punctuated ancient Egyptian history: the Old Kingdom (3100–2180 B.C.); the First Intermediate period (2180–2080 B.C.); the Middle Kingdom (2080–1640 B.C.); the Second Intermediate period (1640–1570 B.C.); and the New Kingdom (1570–1090 B.C.). During the New Kingdom era, Egypt established a large standing army and extended its territorial control over Palestine and Syria in the northeast, to parts of Nubia in the south, and to key trade routes down the Red Sea into the "Land of Punt" on the Somali coast of East Africa.

Closely interconnected with the rise of the centralized Egyptian state were significant developments in religion, culture, and science. Ancient Egyptians believed in many gods, each of which had its own shrine or temple. Egyptian gods represented different aspects of nature, including the sun god, Re; the god of wind, Amun; and others representing different forms of animal life. During the Middle Kingdom, the gods of wind and sun were combined into Amun-Re, the official

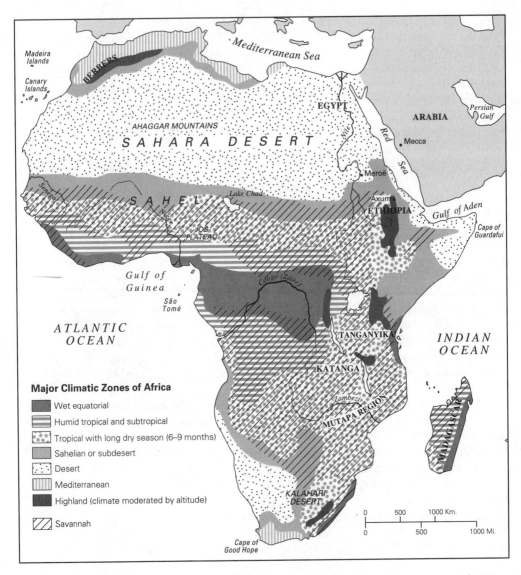

Vegetation Zones, Modern Africa. Before the emergence of the Sahara Desert between 2500 and 2300 B.C., West and East Africa were connected by a system of inland waterways. The spread of the Sahara created conditions for the emergence of significant regional differences in modern Africa.

state god. Over time, the pharaohs, or rulers, of ancient Egypt claimed power over the rains and floods and increasingly linked their authority to the gods themselves. At the same time, Egyptians created the world's first annual twelve-month calendar of 365 days, as well as an instrument for measuring the rise and fall of the Nile and the techniques that underlay the building of the pyramids. Moreover, hieroglyphics (a combination of pictures and sound symbols inscribed on papyrus, a form of paper) and hieratics (a cursive form of hieroglyphics) recorded the political and administrative activities of the kings and bureaucrats and constituted the earliest written history of Africa and of the world.

Nile Valley farmers, workers, and slaves or captives provided the basis of Egyptian wealth, political influence, and cultural development. Referred to as the "living dead," captives made up between 10 and 13 percent of the total population during ancient times. Because Egyptian bondage was not tied to skin color or race, captives included dark-skinned Nubian peoples from the south and light-skinned Semitic and Mediterranean people from the north. Nile Valley farmers and workers—captive and free—produced food surpluses for royal and noble households and labored on huge irrigation projects, temples, and royal tombs. Over a period of 1500 years, Egyptian pharaohs directed the building of over seventy pyramids. Khufu, or Cheops, the Great Pyramid, was the largest and most renown of the royal tombs, built for the first pharaoh of the 4th Dynasty. In the fifth century B.C., the Greek historian Herodotus described the human costs of pyramid making:

Cheops . . . drove them [the Egyptian people] into the extremity of misery. . . . To some was assigned the dragging of great stones from the stone quarries in the Arabian mountains as far as the Nile; to others he gave orders, when these stones had been taken across the river in boats, to drag them, again, as far as the Libyan hills. . . . The people were afflicted for ten years of time in building the road along which they dragged the stones. . . . The pyramid itself took twenty years in the building.

The pharaohs also employed craftsmen and artists to adorn the walls and columns of their palaces and tombs. During the 1920s, archaeologists uncovered the tomb of King Tutankamun, still preserved with its various contents after over thirty centuries. By contrast, the poor were buried in simple graves with few worldly possessions to speed them on their journey.

Although rural peasants and captives faced inequality and exploitation, they did not accept their position without protest and appeals for social justice. In "The Tale of the Eloquent Peasant," a text from the First Intermediate period, a peasant appealed to the king for justice. After a large landowner had seized his property through illegal means, the farmer wrote:

Leader free of greed, great man free of baseness, destroyer of falsehood, creator of rightness, who comes at the voice of the caller! When I speak, may you hear! Do justice, oh praised one, who is praised by the praised; remove my grief, I am burdened. Examine me, I am in need.

The pharaoh recognized the justice of the man's cause and recompensed him with the goods of the dishonest steward.

Poor people also expressed their dissatisfaction with inequality by raiding the tombs of the elites, by making appeals for freedom and release from bondage, and by running away. Records from the late ancient period show how owners of runaway bondsmen and -women employed agents authorized to imprison, beat, and return their possessions, but the problem persisted.

Egyptian women were subordinated to their men, but their position also reflected their class and social status. Some women in royal families became powerful figures and made an indelible imprint on Egyptian history. Queen Hatshepsut (c. 1504–1482 B.C.), for example, was at first named regent on behalf of her stepson, but she soon took power by skillfully manipulating the gender system. Claiming to be the son of the god Amun, she received the crown as "king" of Egypt. During her reign, she selected able military and administrative advisors and built an elaborate temple at Thebes. Cut deep into rock walls, the temple included multiple rooms of artistic carvings and writings that celebrated her reign. Although existing historical scholarship is clearer on the role of Queen Hatshepsut and women in royal households, we must not assume that peasant and captive women were passive.

Beginning around 1100 B.C., Egypt faced increasing attacks from outside. In succession, the Greeks (332 B.C.), Romans (30 B.C.), and Arabs (after A.D. 622) conquered Egypt and helped to reorient its culture toward Greco-Roman, Christian, and then Islamic ideas and social practices. By the early tenth century A.D., Egypt had become a predominantly Islamic country. Islamic unity in Egypt and on the Arabian Peninsula was short-lived, however. The Shi'ites, an Islamic reform group in Baghdad, criticized established groups for corruption and violation of the principles of the Koran. Under the influence of Shi'ites in North Africa, the Fatimid dynasty, aided by a small army recruited from a group of people in northwest Africa called Berbers, gained control of Egypt and much of North Africa in A.D. 950. As the so-called Berber soldiers left the army and became part of Egyptian society, Islamic rulers replenished their ranks by importing Turkish captives from north of the Mediterranean (around the Black Sea region) and blacks from south of the Sahara. Whereas the black bondsmen served as foot soldiers, the Turkish captives, called Mamluks, became part of a highly disciplined cavalry of horsemen armed with bows, arrows, and iron swords.

With the end of the Fatimid dynasty in A.D. 1171, the Turkish soldier Salah al-Din ibn Ayyub (known as Saladin in European history) ascended to power and founded the Ayyubid dynasty. Under the Ayyubid dynasty, the Mamluks received extensive opportunities to earn their freedom, become army commanders, and acquire land. In A.D. 1250, the Mamluks established two dynasties that governed Egypt until the Ottoman Turks conquered Egypt in 1517. The Ottomans overpowered the Mamluk horsemen with new instruments of warfare, including firearms and cannon.

Nubia

Egyptian history unfolded in close connection with the Nubian peoples to the south and east. Under direct Egyptian rule between 1500 and 1000 B.C., Nubians adopted many aspects of Egyptian language, religion, and writing and in turn influenced the Egyptian institution of kingship/pharaohs. After 1000 B.C., Nubians developed a politically independent state known by the Egyptians as Kush. As the power of Kush increased, however, in 730 B.C. the state invaded and conquered Egypt, establishing what became known as the 25th, or Ethiopian, Dynasty.

Nubian control of Egypt came to an end with the Assyrian invasion of Lower Egypt in about 678 B.C. Kushite leaders abandoned Egypt and established a new kingdom farther south along the upper Nile, first at Napata and then permanently on the island of Meroe, between the Nile and Atbara Rivers. At Meroe, the interplay of Egyptian and indigenous cultural influences created a unique culture. Meroites developed their own writing script, added their own local gods to the pantheon of Egyptian gods, and modified their pyramids and burial tombs to reflect their own perspectives (Meroite pyramids were small and flat topped, rather than large with pointed tops).

In A.D. 350, the kingdom of Aksum on the Eritrean coast invaded Meroe and promoted the spread of Christianity in the region. However, by A.D. 800, under the impact of Islam, Aksum had lost control of its trade to the Indian Ocean, and the capital was moved deep into the interior of the Ethiopian central highlands. During the twelfth century, a new Zagwe dynasty displaced the old Aksumite line of kings and ushered in an aggressive period of expansion. The Zagwe kings extended

Pyramids of Meroe. Unlike the Egyptian pyramids, the pyramids of Meroe were small with flat tops rather than large with pointed tops. *Werner Forman Archive/Art Resource, N.Y.*

Ethiopia's influence farther south of Lake Tana to Gojjam and the Shoan Plateau, where it came into conflict with the Muslim states of the Awash Valley. At the Battle of Shimbra-Kure in 1529, Muslims defeated the Ethiopian army and controlled southern Ethiopia for the next six years.

In the meantime, Ethiopian rulers not only had maintained contacts with the declining Christian, or Coptic, church of Egypt but also had reestablished linkages with Mediterranean Christendom. Building on these contacts with European Christendom, the Ethiopian emperor eventually appealed to Christian Europe for help in dispelling the Muslims. Portugal responded with a small, well-armed contingent of troops. Although scholars now doubt that Portuguese support was necessary, in 1543 the combined Ethiopian-Portuguese armies defeated the Muslims, and Ethiopia regained its footing as a Christian nation on the African continent.

The history of ancient Ethiopia and Egypt suggests that African societies were always in flux. They were the products of ongoing interactions between peoples of diverse regions, cultures, and institutions. Such interactions were constantly formed and reformed to meet new needs and circumstances. It is also clear that changes in the natural and man-made environment helped to shape the ongoing formation and re-formation of African societies. Although the emergence of the Sahara Desert would hamper interactions between different parts of the continent and foster distinct regional differences, Africans retained contacts with each other and other parts of the world by developing innovations in agriculture, manufacturing, transport, and trade. The history of northwest Africa and the rise of the trans-Saharan trade reflected these processes.

NORTHWEST AFRICA AND THE TRANS-SAHARAN TRADE

Like Egypt and Ethiopia, northwest Africa experienced the impact of Christendom and Islam. Although the original inhabitants of this area referred to themselves as Imazighen, meaning "the noble" or "freeborn," the Greeks called them Libyans, and the Romans and later the Arabs referred to them as Berbers, the term that is now most commonly used.

In 146 B.C., the Romans conquered Carthage, the most significant independent state in this region, and renamed it "Africa," a name that would eventually refer to the entire continent. The Romans soon extended their control over the North African kingdoms of Numidia and Mauritania to the west. By A.D. 711, however, the Arabs had gained control of North Africa from Egypt in the east to Morocco on the Atlantic coast. In the coastal towns and cities such as Carthage (later renamed Tunis), Arabs set up farms using war captives from northern, central, and southern Africa. At the same time, the Islamic state levied tribute, or taxes, on peoples in the highlands and along the edges of the desert to the south.

Even as Arabs conquered and enslaved African peoples, however, they carried out an aggressive program to convert subject peoples to Islam and consolidate their hold over the region. Arab leaders recruited North Africans into the military, exposed them to the Islamic faith, and provided opportunities for movement up in the hierarchy of the empire. North Africans slowly adopted the Muslim faith, but they did so on their own terms. Islam gained its strongest and most orthodox foothold in the cities, whereas rural inhabitants slowly incorporated Islam into their traditional religious beliefs and practices. Even in the coastal cities and towns, North Africans reshaped Islam to fit their own circumstances. In the conflict between Baghdad and rival factions of Islam, for example, North Africans sided with the dissenting Shi'ite movement and resisted centralized authority.

North Africa served as the major conduit for the spread of Islam into West Africa south of the Sahara. As North Africans converted to Islam in rising numbers, they perceived their non-Muslim black West African neighbors as culturally inferior. Advocating strict observance of Islamic law and holy war against "infidels," the Almoravids, a new Islamic state in northwest Africa, launched holy wars against their rivals to the north and south. By A.D. 1054, the Almoravids not only had taken Awdaghust from the West African kingdom of Ghana but also had conquered the desert town of Sijilmasa, much of the northern coast, and southern Spain. Although the Almoravid empire would collapse under the weight of internal and external conflicts during the thirteenth century, it helped to spread Islamic culture, mosques, and centers of learning throughout North and West Africa.

In addition to conquest, the expansion of the trans-Saharan trade network stimulated the spread of Islam into West Africa. Before about A.D. 300, the trans-Saharan trade was largely a regional affair. It involved the exchange of desert salt, donkeys, and horses for food from the agricultural regions to the north and south. During the third and fourth centuries A.D., the introduction of the camel among nomads of the northern Sahara by the Romans transformed the trans-Saharan trade into an international trade network. The camel's capacity to store fat and water enabled it to travel twice the time and distance of short pack-oxen and horses. Under the impact of this new form of desert transport, new trading settlements emerged north and south of the Sahara, and products from sub-Saharan Africa entered the Mediterranean world in growing numbers.

By the early sixteenth century, several major caravan routes accounted for the bulk of this trade. One route stretched from Timbuktu to Sijilmasa via Taghaza near the Atlantic coast; a second reached the Mediterranean from Gad via Tadmekka; another route connected the Lake Chad and Kanem-Bornu area to Tunis via the desert town of Ghat; and still another extended from Lake Chad to Tripoli and Cairo via the Fezzan (see map). Although North Africans (mainly the Sanhaja in the west and Tuareg in the central and southern Sahara) controlled transport across the desert, trading communities on each end of their routes exercised decisive power. The principal West African import was salt from Saharan salt mines like the one at Taghaza in the center of the western Sahara. Other imports included a variety of manufactured products from Europe via the Mediterranean—cloth, metal, cooking utensils, jewelry, copper, and weapons. Conversely, West Africans exported gold from mines at Bambuk, Bure, and the Akan forests; agricultural,

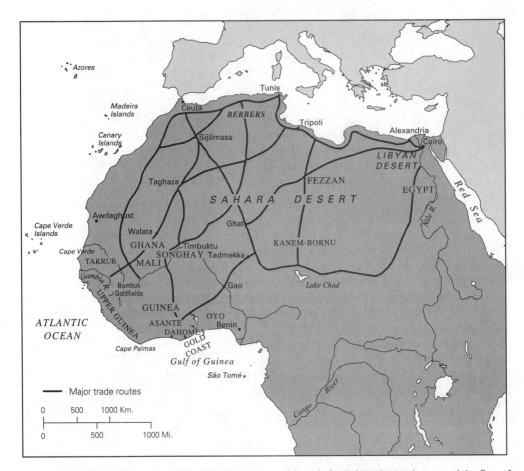

Trans-Saharan Trade Network and West African States. Although the Sahara Desert hampered the flow of trade and ideas among parts of the African continent, the introduction of the camel during the third and fourth centuries A.D. stimulated the rise of an extensive international trade network, which linked West and southern Africa to East and northern Africa.

animal, and forest products, including ivory, gum, and kola nuts; and growing numbers of human captives taken in wars with neighboring ethnic groups.

Between A.D. 900 and 1400, nearly 3.4 million African captives entered the markets of North Africa and the Mediterranean (see table). Many of these slaves were women headed for the harems and households of the Muslim world. Others, in substantial numbers, were young boys targeted for service as eunuchs in the same Islamic lands. Still others, as we will see in Chapter 2, were bound for European sugar plantations in the Mediterranean. Until the sixteenth century, whites from European countries also became captives in Islamic households, serving alongside

Estimated Numbers of the Trans-Saharan Slave Trade		
Period	Annual Average	Total
650–800	1,000	150,000
800–900	3,000	300,000
900–1100	8,700	1,740,000
1100–1400	5,500	1,650,000
1400–1500	4,300	430,000
1500–1600	5,500	550,000
1600–1700	7,100	710,000
1700–1800	7,100	715,000
1800–1880	14,500	1,165,000
1880–1900	2,000	40,000
Total		7,450,000

Source: William D. Phillips, Jr., *Slavery from Roman Times to the Early Transatlantic Trade* (Minneapolis: University of Minnesota Press, 1985), p. 87. Reprinted with permission.

Africans as eunuchs, concubines, and domestics. More so than Christians and Europeans, it was Muslims, Arabs, and diverse African nationality groups themselves who controlled the trans-Saharan trade and determined the course of West African history during the medieval period.

WEST AFRICA

Although the long-term spread of the Sahara Desert had undercut farming communities in the region, a thriving agricultural economy had emerged by the medieval period. In the savannah grasslands just below the Sahel (the Arabic word for "border,") on the southern edge of the Sahara Desert, farmers not only raised sheep, goats, and a few cattle, but also produced cereal crops like millet and sorghum, as well as cotton and sesame. Farther south, in the forest zone, hunters, gatherers, and fishermen pursued earlier forms of making a living. They collected their food from wild leaves, roots, and berries and hunted small animals. At the same time, the forest people built on their knowledge of the growing cycles of certain root, fruit, and tree crops and pioneered in the development of vegeculture. They gradually domesticated various types of gourds and calabashes, as well as oil and sophia palms. Cereal production and cattle herding played little role in the agricultural development of the forest region because of the tsetse fly, which transmitted the cattle-killing disease called *nagana*. A form of "sleeping sickness," *nagana* made it difficult for cows and horses to survive in the region.

Along with the expansion and diversification of the agricultural sector, West Africans developed centers of cotton and cotton textiles, sheep raising and woolen cloth, and iron production. Until recently, scholars assumed that iron-making techniques spread into West Africa from the kingdom of Meroe, south of Egypt. Although most scholars now seem to believe that such processes reached West Africa via Carthage, some argue that West Africans discovered iron-making processes independently of outside influence. In any case, ironworks arrived early in West Africa. Remains from the Nok culture of central Nigeria (c. 280–180 B.C.) suggest the earliest and most advanced use of iron-making technology in West Africa. Building on their earlier history of clay modeling, the Igbo-Ukwo developed the fine art of bronze casting. Over the next millennium, ironworks spread widely through West Africa and formed the basis for more efficient agriculture, warfare, and hunting techniques, which in turn stimulated population growth, new artistic forms, and large territorial and political units.

Iron making represented a major technological achievement. Although metals like copper and tin required a relatively simple process of smelting or melting metal from its ore (that is, metal-bearing rock), iron extraction entailed a complex chemical process. Because the iron was chemically intermixed with its ore, craftsmen had to carefully execute a number of steps in the production of iron. First, as suggested by archaeological evidence, mainly large slag heaps and metal products from ancient times, West Africans constructed two types of iron-smelting furnaces—one a trench dug below the ground and the other a circular clay structure built several feet above the ground. Second, they carefully selected the proper proportions of ore, crushed hardwood, charcoal, and sometimes a flux substance such as lime to aid the smelting process; workers meticulously layered these ingredients in the oven. Third, iron workers then fired the furnace, using bellows to pump air into the structure, which increased the heat and facilitated the chemical process necessary for smelting. Fourth, after a certain number of hours, workers opened the furnace and raked out red-hot iron (crude iron). Finally, after the crude iron had been extracted, the product required frequent reheating and hammering to remove impurities and prepare it for forging into useful weapons, tools, or implements.

West Africans became not only skilled iron workers but also leather, cloth, wood, copper, brass, gold, and, to some extent, silver craftsmen. Over time, these craftsmen concentrated in specialized villages where they intermarried with each other and passed their skills on from one generation to the next. Among the various crafts, the metal workers were most revered, while the leather workers seemed least valued. Some scholars describe these occupational specialties as "castes," midway in status between free persons and slaves. As we will see below, the various craft workers played a key role in the development of West African religious and cultural life.

The intensification of agriculture, manufacturing, and the trans-Saharan trade stimulated the political, social, and cultural transformation of West African society. Small, village-based, West African communities increasingly united to form larger state systems. In turn, Ghana, Mali, and Songhay emerged as the major kingdoms of medieval West Africa. The development of these kingdoms reveals not only the impact of technological, economic, and political change but also patterns of ethnic diversity, conflict, and cooperation among West African peoples.

State Formation, Politics, and the Economy

The rise of West African kingdoms coincided with the expansion of the trans-Saharan trade from about the fourth century A.D. through the medieval period. The kingdom of Ghana, the first of these centralized states to gain prominence, had its roots in the expansion of the Soninke peoples. Well-armed with iron swords and spears and mounted on horses received from Saharan traders, the Soninke expanded their dominion over less-organized neighboring groups and resisted the onslaught of Islamic North Africans. By the mid-eleventh century, as alluded to earlier, Ghana had enclosed Awdaghust, one of the most important Islamic trading centers in the southwestern Sahara, and had extended its boundaries from just east of Takrur and Bambuk to the upper Niger River in the west (see map on page 10).

Situated midway between desert sources of salt and the goldfields of Bambuk on the upper Senegal River, the Soninke served as middlemen in the trans-Saharan trade. Soninke merchants bought gold from the Bambuk miners in exchange for salt, linen, and other manufactured items from northwest Africa. They then sold gold to Muslim traders at the capital city of Kumbi-Saleh, where they received new supplies of salt and goods for another round of trade with the gold miners farther south. The Ghanaian king not only extracted agricultural surplus from the outlying rural areas but also imposed double duties on salt: once when it entered the area from the Sahara and again on re-export to the goldfields. The king also extracted all the large gold nuggets for the royal treasury and permitted only the remainder to enter the trade network.

Taxation of the salt trade and the extraction of gold nuggets not only enriched West African rulers but also stimulated the emergence of new merchant groups. The Wangara and Dyula, for example, facilitated the integration of the far-flung empires into a tightly interconnected West African trade network. These merchants traveled throughout West Africa and stimulated intraregional as well as international trade. Closely related to the trade activities of the Wangara and Dyula was the increasing use of the cowrie shell from the Indian Ocean as a medium of exchange in the West African economy. Although use of the cowrie shell strengthened intraregional trade and taxation, international trade continued to revolve around salt, gold, and, to some extent, war captives.

As Islam penetrated deeper into West Africa and as Ghana in turn conquered Islamic outposts, the king employed literate Muslim administrators to systematize tax collection and oversee international trade. Muslims instituted elaborate accounting procedures and helped royal officials extract enormous surplus from the African peasantry. As we will see, Islamic officers would influence not only the economic life of West African kingdoms but its religious and cultural life as well.

The Ghanaian king exercised substantial direct and indirect control over the population. Partly by holding the sons of local leaders hostage at his court, the king gained compliance from local elites. Although Ghana did not have a standing army, for example, the king could raise an army of over two hundred thousand men on short notice. The Ghanaian army sometimes raided neighboring ethnic groups and sold captives to Muslim traders. A late-eleventh-century report described such raids by the kingdom of Ghana: "The people of Ghana make raids on the land of Barbara [probably Bambara] and Anima. . . . These people have no iron and fight only with clubs of ivory. For this reason the people of Ghana overcome them, for they fight with swords and spears."

Although Ghana incorporated Muslims into its administrative structure, the Islamic Berbers resented Soninke domination. Under the leadership of Yahya ibn Umar and his brother Abu Bakr, the Sanhaja joined the Almoravid movement and waged war against Ghana. The Almoravids reconquered Awdaghust during the 1050s, as noted above, and plundered the Ghanaian capital of Kumbi-Saleh in A.D. 1076. Soon thereafter, Ghanaians converted to Islam in rising numbers, and the kingdom gradually declined. By A.D. 1300, as new trans-Saharan trade routes emerged to the east and the new Bure goldfields opened to the south and west, Ghana lost its control of the trans-Saharan gold trade from the western Sudan.

Closely related to the decline of Ghana was the rise of Mali as the second great West African kingdom. Mali had its origins in the same forces that led to the decline of Ghana, namely the opening up of the new Bure goldfields in the woodland savannah country to the south, and the development of new trans-Saharan trade routes farther east of Awdaghust. The opening of new goldfields and trade routes enabled the Soninke and Malinke peoples of the south to assert their independence. During the early 1200s, the Sosso, a branch of Soninke, established a new state independent of former Ghana and extended their influence over most of old Ghana as well as their southern neighbors the Malinke.

Under the leadership of Sundiata (also called Sundjata), several small Malinke lineages formed an alliance and resisted the authority of the new Soninke-based Sosso state. The Malinke defeated the Sosso army at Kirina near modern Bamako and brought several Soninke peoples under their control. Shortly thereafter, the Malian empire built its capital at Niani, located in the savannah country of the upper Niger Valley near the Bure goldfields. The empire of Mali soon extended from the edges of the forest zone in the southwest, through the savannah territories of the Malinke and southern Soninke, to the Sahel of the ancient Ghanaian kingdom. Mali incorporated and moved well beyond the boundaries of the old Ghanaian kingdom. At its height in the 1300s, Mali stretched from the Atlantic Ocean south of Senegal to the Songhay capital of Gao on the east side of the middle bend of the Niger River, including the city of Timbuktu, originally established by northwest Africans as a trading center and grazing settlement for livestock. To the south, Mali incorporated the goldfields of Bure and Bambuk, and along the Sahel, it extended from the Atlantic east to Walata and Tadmekka.

Like Ghana, Mali relied on literate Muslims to administer the kingdom. Unlike Ghana, however, Mali established a large standing army to facilitate defense as well as compliance from peoples in outlying areas. More so than Ghana, Mali exploited its broader, more fertile, and diverse farming communities, which produced sorghum and millet in the savannah, rice in the regions of the Gambia and Niger

Rivers, and camels, sheep, and goats in the more arid Sahelian grasslands. As long as local rulers collected and forwarded tribute to the capital, Malian kings allowed traditional rulers to maintain their authority, which they claimed as an entitlement for themselves and their descendants.

Following a series of internal dynastic struggles, Mali declined during the late fifteenth century. By the early 1500s, Mali had lost most of its non-Malinke population and was composed mainly of its small original Malinke homelands. Located on the eastern bend of the Niger River, the Songhay posed the most formidable challenge to the Malian state. As early as the ninth century, Songhay had emerged as a single state, with its capital at Kukiya. Although farmers, hunters, and fishermen of diverse ethnic groups inhabited the area, the Sorko fishermen dominated the region. Using their mastery of the river, these people developed trading routes along the territory upstream toward the Niger bend, including the city of Gao, which emerged as the chief trans-Saharan trade route of the central and eastern Sahara.

As Mali declined during the fifteenth century, Songhay expanded its cavalry and increasingly transformed its trading vessels into war canoes. Under the leadership of Sonni Sulayman Dandi and his successor, Sonni Ali the Great (1464–1492), Songhay captured Timbuktu and extended the empire's control north to the desert town of Taghaza, east to Agades, west to the Senegal River, south to below the Niger River, and deep into Mossi territory, where Songhay forces launched periodic raids and sold war captives to Muslim traders. Songhay reached its peak under the reign of Muhammad Ture, also known as Askiya Muhammad (1493–1528). Unlike Mali and Ghana, whose territory spread widely from west to east, the kingdom of Songhay extended more narrowly north and south along the Niger River. Its authority revolved around control of the Niger River and its surrounding peasant communities. Songhay replaced local traditional rulers with royal officials. These officials could not claim hereditary rights to their posts and were dependent on the king for their authority. The centralization of authority in turn put more distance between the king and the masses of the people.

Although Ghana, Mali, and Songhay represented the chief West African kingdoms during the medieval period, other important states came to prominence at the same time. Located near the Atlantic coast in the Senegal Valley, Takrur was one of the earliest of these West African states. Some scholars suggest that Takrur may have antedated Ghana as an early trading state. At about the same time that Takrur expanded in the Senegal Valley, the state of Kanem emerged in the region northeast of Lake Chad. Beginning around A.D. 900, several Kanuri-speaking pastoralist groups banned together under a single dynasty known as the Sefawa. Early on, the state exhibited Islamic influences, and by the late eleventh century, the Kanuri-speaking Sefawa had set up a new Islamic dynasty in Kanem. As Kanem fell during the fourteenth century, one of its principal tributaries, Borno, exerted its independence. Located to the southwest of the empire, Borno established its own trade networks across the Sahara and succeeded in transforming Kanem into a tributary state. Although a series of peasant revolts hampered the expansion of Borno, the state strengthened its position by importing enough horses and firearms from

North Africa to outfit a cavalry of three thousand troops. Armed with new weapons, Borno undercut the volume of trade flowing through the kingdom of Songhay and retained its position in the region through the eighteenth century.

Important West African kingdoms and states also emerged west of Borno and south of the savannah grasslands. Between A.D. 1000 and 1200, the Hausa city-states developed west of the kingdom of Borno. Based on a combination of agriculture, manufacturing, and trade, the principal Hausa states were Gobir, Katsina, Zazzau, and Kano. Although all of these states were important trade centers, Kano craftsmen became especially well known for their weaving, cloth dyeing, and leatherworks. Kano products not only reached other parts of West Africa but also entered the Mediterranean trade of North Africa and Europe. Although no single Hausa state emerged and consolidated the others into a single empire, these states nonetheless represented key links in the trans-Saharan trade and the spread of Islam into West Africa. Similarly, the principal forest states, the Yoruba kingdoms of Ife and Benin, emerged during the eleventh and twelfth centuries A.D. Extending from the borders of the savannah into the region to the south, Ife and Benin produced a substantial agricultural surplus—a range of root and cereal crops as well as domestic animals—that supported ruling elites, court craftsmen and artists, and significant urbanization. By the fifteenth century, Benin had evolved into a large walled city.

Although a large number of highly organized states had emerged in West Africa by the eve of the Atlantic slave trade, other metalworking agricultural communities remained small and less formally organized. Some analysts have referred to these as "stateless" societies. Small, family-based villages of subsistence farmers were widespread in the savannah and forest regions of West Africa. These communities cultivated crops for home consumption and local or intervillage trade rather than for long-distance trade. As such, they escaped taxes levied on products that entered the international trade network. Unlike the large states, these small communities settled internal difficulties locally, usually in family groups without bureaucratic structures. These small communities also developed mechanisms for banding together to defend themselves from external attacks but usually disbanded after such dangers had subsided. Although the so-called stateless societies had their own ideas about governance, they were not completely isolated from international influences. Such communities provided an initial lineage foundation for ethnic-based states like the early Soninke and Malinke, which in turn spearheaded the rise of Ghana, Mali, and Songhay.

Social, Religious, and Cultural Life

Socioeconomic and cultural life in West African states was highly stratified. Most kingdoms were comprised of three major groups: nobles, freeborn or commoners, and captives. Kings, administrators, merchants, and army commanders inhabited the best residences, wore the best clothing, and adorned themselves with the most expensive jewelry. Moreover, on their death, their graves were often marked by imposing tombs.

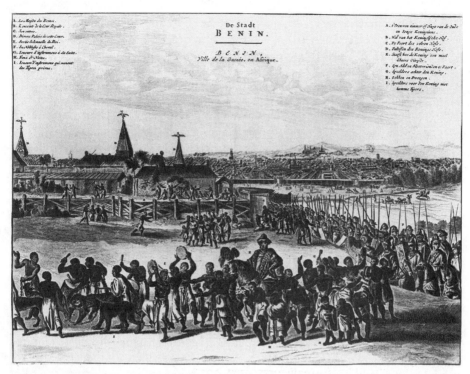

By the fifteenth century, the Yoruba kingdom of Benin had evolved into a large walled city. Here a Dutch artist captures the city in the seventeenth century. *Corbis*

Social stratification was most pronounced in the urban centers. The capital of ancient Ghana, Kumbi-Saleh, was divided between its Islamic center and its royal African sector. The former received Arab and North African merchants and housed Muslim mosques, whereas the latter housed the king and his court, about six miles away. In between were the stone and wooden structures of the Soninke people; outlying residents apparently lived mainly in houses of less durable construction. In Mali and Songhay, patterns of social inequality were even more pronounced than they were in Ghana.

Mali and Songhay maintained large standing armies, and army officials became important residents at the royal court. Composed of a small elite corps of horsemen and contingents of foot soldiers, the army not only played a role in securing the empire against external attacks but also collected taxes on trade, extracted monetary tribute from surrounding rural provinces, and maintained farms with the forced labor of captives. Merchants also figured prominently at the king's court, trading their products and enriching themselves in the process. During the reign of Askiya Muhammad, the Moroccan Leo Africanus observed life at Gao, the capital of Songhay, accenting the place of merchants and soldiers:

> The houses there are very poor, except for those of the king and his courtiers. The merchants are exceedingly rich. . . . Here is a certain place where slaves are sold, especially on those days when the merchants are assembled. . . . The king of this region has a certain private palace where he maintains a great number of concubines and slaves; and for the guard of his own person he keeps a sufficient troupe of horsemen and footmen.

The various royal pilgrimages to Mecca also symbolized the concentration of wealth at the top of West African society. Mansa Musa, Mali's most renowned ruler, made his famous pilgrimage to Mecca in 1324–1325. He arrived in Egypt with a hundred camel loads of gold, which he distributed so freely that the value of gold in Cairo dropped precipitously. During his pilgrimage to Mecca, Askiya Muhammad's caravan included an escort of five hundred cavalry and one thousand infantry, as well as three hundred thousand pieces of gold, a third of which were distributed as gifts in Islamic cities along the way.

Scholars are reluctant to generalize about gender differences in West African societies because there were significant differences in the roles of men and women from place to place and from one ethnic group to another. Some societies were matrilineal and conferred important power on women. Other societies, probably most, were not only patrilineal but also polygynous, with men empowered to take more than one wife and to exercise fundamental control. In matrilineal systems, the offspring belonged to the family of the mother, whose oldest brother served as the head of the family. Conversely, in patrilineal arrangements, the father served as head of the family and exercised parental authority and responsibility for the children. The arrival of Islam reinforced patrilineality and polygyny but limited the number of wives to four. Support for polygyny was widespread, although in practice only the elite could afford to support multiple wives.

Despite significant variations in gender practices from one society to another, salient gender differences were apparent in the economic and social life of West Africa during the period. Men normally cleared the land and cultivated crops for the market and international trade, whereas women raised food crops for family and communal subsistence. Even in the practice of skilled crafts such as weaving, men produced such goods largely for the wider regional and international market, whereas women produced for home consumption. Thus, women invariably dominated local trade markets, whereas men traveled widely and controlled international trade. Moreover, as in so many societies elsewhere, women shouldered the bulk of domestic work, tending children, cooking, and cleaning.

Along with the gender division of labor, most societies linked state power closely to military service and excluded women. Still, women in West African societies devised ways for influencing the state, politics, and culture of the region. Most African states placed considerable power in the hands of royal families. Specifically, they established the practice of designating "electing families" and "enthroning families." The former decided who within the royal household should be enthroned, whereas the latter could accept or veto the selection. Thus, women in royal families were in an excellent position to voice their opinions and to influence the affairs of state, including arranging succession to the throne. Since queen mothers and queen sisters had intimate knowledge of the king's health and were the first to know of his death, they played important roles in matters of succession to the throne. Succession often precipitated crises and heated struggles among the elite and required delicate handling.

Enslavement was no doubt the most important manifestation of inequality in West African society. West African societies not only exported bondsmen and -women but also used them in the regional economy as domestics, concubines, soldiers, and agricultural workers. Captives also served as skilled labor on construction projects, in the manufacture of cloth, and in the mining and processing of gold, copper, and salt. In the salt-mining town of Taghaza, captives constructed the principal buildings of the town from blocks of salt secured from the mines. Moreover, bondsmen took on great symbolic as well as practical value. West African kings sometimes gave captives as gifts to secure "loyal" subjects, and to Islamic officials to indicate piety and commitment to the Koran. When the first Muslim missionary arrived in the kingdom of Kanem, for example, the ruler showered him with gifts of one hundred captives, camels, and silver coins.

Like other aspects of West African society, slavery was a highly gendered experience. The large North African demand for women in their harems and as domestics led to large numbers of women in the trans-Saharan trade. Yet it was men who were usually designated for sale outside West Africa; women and children were used in households within the area. On one occasion, the Arab scholar Ibn Battuta described bondswomen in West African households: "During Ramadan I saw many of them . . . in the house of the sultan, each one brings his food carried by twenty or more of his slave girls, they all being naked." The practice of selling men far away from their region of origin and enslaving their women and children hampered resistance movements, but captives nonetheless sought freedom by running away, self-purchase, and service in the army or state bureaucracy.

Although West African societies were stratified along class and cultural lines, they developed some beliefs and practices that helped to mitigate conflict, ease tensions, and create unity. Through ongoing historical and cultural interactions, West Africans of diverse ethnic and cultural backgrounds developed a core of beliefs and practices that helped to distinguish and unify them as a region. Certain underlying understandings and perspectives on the natural and spirit worlds characterized their world view. Although they might not agree on the precise significance of twin births, for example, most imbued such births with supernatural significance. Despite the payment of tribute by agricultural villages, to take another example, land was a community resource and could not be alienated or owned outright by an individual.

West African bondsmen and -women gained access to freedom and a level of upward mobility. Some of the provincial governors of the kingdom of Mali were slaves. When disputes weakened the dynasty, slave men sometimes occupied the throne, as did Sakura the freed slave (c. 1300) and Sandiki (1387–1388). Such opportunities for people at the bottom of society, particularly slaves, led some contemporary Arab observers to comment on and exaggerate the sense of justice among African rulers.

The Negroes possess some admirable qualities. They are seldom unjust, and have a greater abhorrence of injustice than any other people. The sultan (the musa) shows no mercy to any one guilty of the least act of it. There is complete security in their country.

The Spanish Muslim al-Sharishi also painted an idyllic portrait of captive women in royal households:

God has endowed the slave girls there with laudable characteristics, both physical and moral, more than can be desired: their bodies are smooth, their black skins are lustrous, their eyes are beautiful, their noses well shaped, their teeth white, and they smell fragrant.

African religious traditions played a key role in bridging as well as fomenting social cleavages. West Africans believed in one god, the creator, but their ideas differed from Islam and Christianity. They held that the original mover was no longer active in shaping human affairs. Rather than an ongoing moral force for good or evil, God set the stage for human action, retired from active duty, and allowed human beings to shape their own destinies. Supernatural forces did play a role in day-to-day life, but they were not intrinsically good or evil.

West Africans recognized at least two distinct sets of supernatural beings. One group included the spirits of the ancestors who watched over the descendants of specific lineages or ethnic groups. Africans believed that the spirit of a deceased relative could influence the life of the family. The spirits of the dead had to be handled with care through prayer, sacrifice, and ritual. Since the spirits of the ancestors would live on after death, funeral rites also figured prominently in religious practices. Such rites served to create solidarity within families, lineages, and ethnic groups. A second group of spirits were more universal in their work. These spirits were not the property of any one family, ethnic, or lineage group. By controlling aspects of nature—thunder, lightning, death, and disease, for example—their duties cut across ethnic, class, and social lines. The number of such spirits varied from one West African society to another, but almost everywhere professional or semi-professional religious leaders, both men and women, emerged to provide instructions on how to press these "gods" into service.

Several forms of ritual observance emerged as the principal way to put the individual or congregation in touch with the gods. Rituals included sacrifice (of animals and sometimes humans), spirit possession, music, dance, and prayer. Along with such rituals, most West African societies used divination. This religious practice was different from those attached to specific gods or spirits. Employing amulets, talismans, and other magical devices, the diviners advised individuals on the spirit world and answered questions about the future, misfortune, death, sickness, and witchcraft.

Malinke religious traditions illustrate the close connection between the material and spiritual worlds of West African peoples. The Malinke believed that the "spirits of the land" determined the success of their harvests. According to their origin story, the earliest farmers in the area negotiated with the spirits to ensure successful

The West African city of Timbuktu became a major center of Islamic education and learning during the reign of Mali's Mansa Musa. Following a period of decline, it was also revitalized under Songhay's Askiya Muhammad. *New York Public Library. Astor, Lenox and Tilden Foundations*

crops. The village head, *mansa* in Malinke, represented the most direct descendant of the first generation of farmers and thus the most viable link to the ancient "spirits of the land." Thus, the *mansa* combined both spiritual and secular authority and power. By persuading local *mansas* to cede their power to him, Sundiata, the first emperor of Mali, became the *mansa* of all the Malinke people. He combined at an even higher level of organization both spiritual and secular authority.

Following Sundiata's reign, most of the Malian rulers were Muslim. Islam had a powerful influence on the culture of royal officials and merchants in the towns and cities. In Egypt, on his pilgrimage to Mecca, Mansa Musa recruited a Muslim architect who returned to Mali and designed mosques. Mansa Musa also sent Sudanese scholars to North African universities to study, and by the end of his reign, the West African city of Timbuktu had itself become a major center of Islamic education and learning. Although Timbuktu would decline during the fall of Mali, it was revived and expanded under the control of Songhay during the reign of Askiya Muhammad. The Moroccan Leo Africanus described the city of Timbuktu during its period of revival:

The rich king of Tombuto [governor of Timbuktu] has many articles of gold, and he keeps a magnificent and well furnished court. When he travels anywhere he rides upon a camel which is led by some of his noblemen. . . . Here there are many doctors, judges, priests, and other learned men, that are well maintained at king's cost. Various manuscripts and written books are brought here out of Barbarie and sold for more money than any other merchandise.

Even as rulers like Mansa Musa and Askiya Muhammad made pilgrimages to Mecca and promoted Islamic culture, they recognized the need to adapt Islam to African conditions. Most Africans lived in the countryside and maintained their traditional beliefs, which challenged certain Islamic ideas about marriage and the family. Islam permitted men up to four wives, for example, but indigenous African societies allowed as many as a man could attract. Whereas the Islamic rulers of Songhay accepted marriage between a free man and a slave woman, or between a slave man and a free woman, as legitimate, most West African peasant societies accepted the former but rejected the latter. Moreover, although Islam promoted literate culture, most Africans continued to pursue and enrich their own oral traditions.

Art, music, dance, and storytelling permeated West African society and culture. African metal, cloth, wood, and leather workers not only were skilled in fashioning material culture but also were key communicators of oral traditions, beliefs, and ideas. The crafts themselves were invariably imbued with deep religious significance. Among the Bambara, for example, only blacksmiths or woodworkers could cut down large old trees, believed to be inhabited by the gods. More importantly, archaeological evidence suggests that West African craftspeople and artists developed their own aesthetic principles. Their decorative, ornamental, and intricate designs of furniture, jewelry, cloth, tombs, and buildings convey unique ideas about beauty.

West African artistic practices withstood the new designs ushered in by the arrival of Islam. The most outstanding evidence of artwork from the ancient period comes from the kingdom of Benin. The bronze and terracotta heads from Ife and Benin offer powerful evidence of African aesthetics. Such art also reflects African beliefs about the social order, including the notion that the king represented the fusion of both divine and earthly power. The cultural productions of Ife and Benin are best known because the British looted Benin City in 1897 and shipped its massive artworks back to England.

Integral to each craft were musicians, storytellers, and griots. Craftsmen not only made a variety of musical instruments—the drum, guitar, harp, flute, zither, and xylophone—but also used instruments to accompany an even wider variety of songs—religious, work, dance, recreational, and others. Described as "antiphonal" and highly "rhythmic," songs with or without instrumental accompaniment represented the major form of African music. African songs and dances served a variety of purposes, both religious and secular, although the line between the religious and worldly was quite blurred in West African culture.

Oral traditions contained the most outstanding literary achievements of West Africans during the period. The epic bards—the "griots," or oral historians—

This seventeenth-century bronze plaque from Benin City shows the Oba and his assistants. © *The British Museum, London*

emerged at the center of West African literary and cultural life. As a group, they were well regarded and ranked high with the metal workers in status. It was the griots who gave life to one of the most famous epics in West African society—the Sundiata *fasa* ("praise song in honor of jata"). Named after the Malian king, the jata epic recalls the struggle between the Malinke and the Soninke states, which gave rise to the kingdom of Mali. According to Ibn Battuta, Malian bards regularly recited the story honoring the great deeds of the king and his predecessors. Over twenty versions of the epic exist, but all agree on the basic ordering of events. Rich with folklore and tales relating to jata's childhood as well as his exploits as a leader of the nation, the jata epic helped to reinforce important aspects of West African ideas, beliefs, and social practices (see box).

Written nearly a century after Sundiata's reign during the Islamic era, the epic also demonstrates the way that West Africans sought to reconcile their beliefs in the "spirit of the land" with the spread of Islam. In some versions of the epic, for example, the character Bilali Bounama heads the descent lists of ancestors. Bounama is described as both a companion of the prophet Muhammad and the original founder of the Manding lineage—that is, Sundiata's branch of the Keitas, the direct descendants of the Prophet's helpers. Some griots even suggest that Muhammad himself was born just one day before Bilali.

SOURCES FROM THE PAST

Griot Djeli Mamoudou Kouyaté Narrates the Sundiata Fasa, n.d.

We are now coming to the great moments in the life of Sundiata. The exile will end and another sun will arise. It is the sun of Sundiata. Griots know the history of kings and kingdoms and that is why they are the best counsellors of kings. Every king wants to have a singer to perpetuate his memory, for it is the griot who rescues the memories of kings from oblivion, as men have short memories.

Kings have prescribed destinies just like men, and seers who probe the future know it. They have knowledge of the future, whereas we griots are depositories of the knowledge of the past. But whoever knows the history of a country can read its future.

Other peoples use writing to record the past, but this invention has killed the faculty of memory among them. They do not feel the past any more, for writing lacks the warmth of the human voice. With them everybody thinks he knows, whereas learning should be a secret. The prophets did not write and their words have been all the more vivid as a result. What paltry learning is that which is congealed in dumb books!

I, Djeli Mamoudou Kouyaté, am the result of a long tradition. For generations we have passed on the history of kings from father to son. The narrative was passed on to me without alteration and I deliver it without alteration, for I received it free from all untruth.

Listen now to the story of Sundiata, the Na'Kamma, the man who had a mission to accomplish.

At the time when Sundiata was preparing to assert his claim over the kingdom of his fathers, Soumaoro was the king of kings, the most powerful king in all the lands of the setting sun. . . . But Soumaoro was an evil demon and his reign had produced nothing but bloodshed. Nothing was taboo for him. His greatest pleasure was publicly to flog venerable old men. He had defiled every family and everywhere in his vast empire there were villages populated by girls whom he had forcibly abducted from their families without marrying them. . . .

. . . Soumaoro proclaimed himself king of Mali by right of conquest, but he was not recognized by the populace and resistance was organized in the bush. Soothsayers were consulted as to the fate of the country. The soothsayers were consulted as to the fate of the country. The soothsayers were unanimous in saying that it would be the rightful heir to the throne who would save Mali. This heir was "The Man with Two Names." The elders of the court of Niani then remembered the son of Sogolon. The man with two names was no other than Maghan Sundiata.

Source: D. T. Niane, *Sundiata: An Epic of Old Mali* (London: Longmans, 1965), pp. 40–45. The abridged version of *Sundiata: An Epic of Old Mali* is published by joint permission of Pearson Education Limited and Présence Africaine, owners of the original copyright. All rights reserved.

On the other hand, West African bards invoked the name of Surakata as their own collective progenitor and reinforced the effort to blend Islamic and indigenous African beliefs. According to oral traditions, Surakata was initially an infidel who pursued Muhammad with the intent to kill him. After failing his mission on several occasions, Surakata had a change of heart. Impressed by Muhammad's extraordinary power, he converted to Islam and became a staunch believer and supporter of the Prophet. Surakata soon accompanied Muhammad into battle with his enemies. At the Battle of Kaybura, one of Muhammad's most renowned campaigns, Surakata became the father of later bards by singing the praises of Muhammad and encouraging victory over his enemies.

As suggested by the translation of the Sundiata epic, only slowly did Africans and their Islamic allies collaborate in the translation of African oral traditions into written form. Although the technical difficulties of translating the varieties of African tongues into written symbols were formidable, other examples of this effort include Es Sadi's history of the Sudan, *Tarikh-es-Soudan,* and Kati's *Tarikh-El-Fettach.* By undertaking the difficult and often painful task of reconciling Islam with their own indigenous beliefs, West Africans demonstrated their ability to forge new cultural forms that gave unity and cohesiveness to their lives.

~

THE AFRICAN EXPERIENCE WAS DEEPLY rooted in the transformation of the Sahara from a rich agricultural land of many rivers into a desert covering about one-third of the continental landmass. Although the desert would not bar interactions between different parts of the African continent, it did help to create distinct regional differences between West Africa south of the Sahara, Egypt, and northwest Africa. The history of these regions not only reveals the immense contributions, strengths, and achievements of diverse African peoples and cultures but also highlights the myriad challenges that they faced before the advent of European expansion and the emergence of the international slave trade. Although war, exploitation, and even human bondage were integral aspects of African history, these forms of inequality and social conflict would take on new and different meanings in the confrontation with European traders, armies, and nation-states. Driven as they were by a strong capitalist ethos, Europeans would heighten indigenous forms of inequality and usher in new ones. These issues are explored in Chapter 2.

CHAPTER 2

~

Transatlantic Trade, the Plantation System, and Black Labor

During the fifteenth century, the rise of unified states, wealth, capital, and innovations in sailing technology transformed the role of Europeans in international trade networks. The new technology enabled Europeans to sail around the west coast of Africa, dispense with North African middlemen, and sell their products directly to West Africans in exchange for gold. Although Europeans initially sought the riches of West African gold mines and the luxury goods of the Indian Ocean trade, they soon realized that the new maritime technology produced other possibilities. Their position on the West African coast provided opportunities to sell shipping services to Africans, establish coastal settlements, and gain access to new labor supplies. European merchants not only transported goods from one continent to another but also soon carried goods from one part of the West African coast to another, including bound labor for their own sugar plantations in the Mediterranean and on islands off the coast of northwest Africa.

As sugar plantations spread across the Atlantic Ocean to the New World, the demand for Africans escalated and soon supplanted indigenous and European sources of labor. After rising slowly during the sixteenth century, the number of Africans rapidly increased and became the predominant labor force during the seventeenth and eighteenth centuries. African labor fueled the production of the major cash crops as well as the mining of precious metals. Sugar, tobacco, rice, coffee, cotton, silver, and gold figured prominently in the lives of New World blacks, who faced harsh working conditions, constraints on family and cultural life, and stiff punishment for infractions of plantation discipline and rules of comportment. Although the forces unleashed by the imperatives of capitalist production curtailed their choices, African peoples would nonetheless play a key role in shaping their own experiences over time and space. Focusing on Caribbean and Latin American societies, this chapter examines the Old World origins of New World bondage, the transition from a mixed to an African labor force, and the development of enslaved African American communities, cultures, politics, and forms of resistance.

THE OLD WORLD ROOTS OF NEW WORLD BONDAGE

The Atlantic system of bondage had its roots in the development of Mediterranean sugar plantations. During the medieval crusades, Europeans adopted sugar-producing techniques when they conquered the Islamic countries of the eastern Mediterranean and North Africa. Following their expulsion from these areas by the Muslims, Europeans carried their knowledge of sugar to the islands of Cyprus and Sicily and to southern Spain and Portugal. Sugar production required a combination of agricultural and manufacturing skills, huge amounts of capital, and a large labor force for planting, weeding, harvesting, and refining. European merchants and manufacturers provided capital and managerial knowledge, but the local population proved inadequate to meet the labor demands of the crop.

The Mediterranean Model

Unable to secure a free labor force among regional farmers, the Mediterranean sugar industry gradually turned toward bound labor. Sugar planters purchased Europeans from the northern and eastern seaports of the Black Sea, captives from wars between Christians and Muslims, and Africans from the trans-Saharan trade. Notably, although northern European slaves had made the transition to various forms of serfdom by the late medieval era, enslaved whites from southern and eastern Europe continued to supply the labor needs of sugar plantations alongside Africans, Arabs, and Muslims. Sugar planters developed techniques of closely supervised gang labor, attention to profits, and social subordination that would later inform the spread of the plantation system along the west coast of Africa and in the New World.

The decision to import Africans to the New World was partly a product of past practices and conditions in Europe as well as on the Mediterranean sugar islands. The English word *slave* soon developed cognates in all western languages: *esclave* in French, *esclavo* in Spanish, *escravo* in Portuguese, *schiavo* in Italian, and *Sklave* in German. As early as 1479, the Spanish government authorized Portugal to sell slaves within its borders. The port at Seville soon emerged as the primary center for the sale of humans to European countries. On the Spanish mainland, the trading cities of Cádiz, Málaga, Cartagena, and Granada also imported significant numbers of captives. Although Africans were the predominant group, the Spanish enslaved Arabs, mainly Muslims, and after 1500, a few Amerindians. Some contemporaries compared enslaved Africans and Muslims in Seville to "a giant chessboard containing an equal number of white and black chessmen." These cities employed blacks in a wide range of common labor and domestic service jobs as well as in silver mines. Other Africans worked in soap factories and municipal granaries and as longshoremen, retail sellers, and assistants for shopkeepers and merchants. Although Africans worked in a variety of jobs on the European mainland, the Mediterranean sugar industry claimed the bulk of their labor.

The plantation system spread slowly outward from the Mediterranean to the islands off the coast of northwest Africa. As early as 1335, the Genoese merchant Lanzaroto Malocello aroused European interest in the Canary Islands. The Pope assigned the islands to the crown of Castile (later Spain) in 1344, and the Treaty of Alçacovas in 1479 further confirmed the Spanish claim. More importantly, in the Treaty of Tordesillas, two years after Columbus's first voyage to America, Portugal and Spain agreed to a line of demarcation that ceded to Spain control of all land in the New World (with the exception of Brazil), and to Portugal, dominion over West Africa and islands of the Atlantic Ocean (except the Canaries). The Canary Islands provided not only an environment for the profitable production of dyestuffs such as orchil and another popular dye called "dragon's blood," but also captives for sale in the Mediterranean slave markets and for a nascent Canary Island sugar industry. Europeans subsequently used the Canaries as a staging ground for occupying other islands, such as Madeira and the Azores, and establishing beachheads on the coastal mainland of West Africa itself.

The Mediterranean sugar islands established a model for the development of the plantation system and helped to set in motion the largest forced migration of human beings in world history. The Portuguese and Spanish took the lead in peopling the coastal islands with African labor. Between 1433 and 1488, Portuguese mariners used ocean wind patterns to navigate the western coast of Africa. Such knowledge—mainly recognition that ocean wind patterns tended to be circular—soon enabled them to inch their way along the west coast of Africa and in time sail around the Cape of Good Hope to East Africa as well. After reaching the Senegal River in 1444, the Portuguese established trade relations with the gold-producing portion of the Guinea Coast called the Gold Coast, a fort at El Mina, and sugar plantations on the islands of Madeira, Príncipe, and São Tomé. As Europeans opened up new plantations off the coast of Africa, they turned increasingly toward labor from sub-Saharan Africa. Before the turn of the sixteenth century, Portugal imported to its island colonies some 500 to 1,000 Africans per year.

During the sixteenth century, the sugar industry spread across the Atlantic to the New World. In 1502, the Spanish imported their first Africans to work on sugar plantations in Hispaniola (later named Saint-Domingue under the French and called Haiti following independence). The crown limited this early trade in human beings to Christians born in Spain or baptized or naturalized there. In 1518, the Spanish government reversed this policy and granted *ascientos* (licenses) for the transport and sale of people directly from Africa to the New World; but only in 1595 would the crown limit its contract to one carrier, the Portuguese. The annual number of Africans rose from about 2,000 in the sixteenth century to an average of about 80,000 in the 1780s. After declining during the 1790s, the number rose to a new peak in the 1840s. Despite American and European legislation outlawing the international slave trade after 1808, it persisted through the 1870s. Although historians disagree on the precise figures, they agree that no less than 10 million Africans landed alive in the Americas during the era of the slave trade (see figure). Another 2 million Africans died in the so-called Middle Passage (see page 36) en route to the New World.

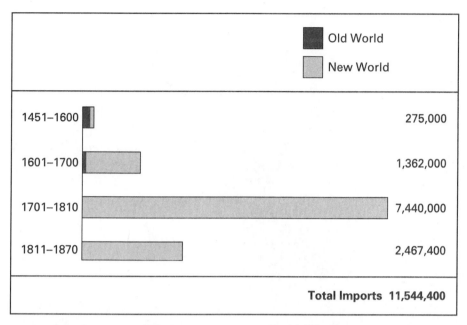

	Old World	
	New World	
1451–1600		275,000
1601–1700		1,362,000
1701–1810		7,440,000
1811–1870		2,467,400
	Total Imports 11,544,400	

Imports of Africans by Time and Region. The earliest Africans entered the Spanish and Portuguese colonies of the New World during the sixteenth century, but the numbers remained relatively small until the seventeenth and eighteenth centuries. By the end of the international slave trade, over 11 million Africans had entered the Americas, but only about 5 percent of these reached British North America. *Source: Data from Orlando Patterson,* Slavery and Social Death: A Comparative Study *(Cambridge, Mass: Harvard University Press, 1982), p. 162. Adapted from* Time on the Cross: The Economics of American Negro Slavery, *by Robert William Fogel and Stanley L. Engerman. Copyright © 1974 by Robert William Fogel and Stanley L. Engerman. Used by permission of W. W. Norton & Company, Inc.*

The Portuguese dominated the initial phases of trade with West Africa, but the Spanish, English, French, and Dutch soon made legal and extralegal inroads on Portuguese interests. With three thousand miles of African coastline, however, most countries could not police the huge West African trade, and monopolistic efforts soon broke down. By the eighteenth century, independent shippers carried the bulk of slaves to the New World, and piracy against the shipping of other nations steadily increased. Using their base on the Canary Islands, the Spanish regularly conducted secret raids on Portuguese strongholds. During the 1560s, before the British became major actors in the slave trade, the Englishman John Hawkins launched three raiding expeditions against the Portuguese in West Africa (see map). Hawkins not only forcibly seized Africans from rival ships but also fomented war between indigenous factions to increase the number of bondsmen and -women at his disposal.

Portugal faced its most serious threat from the Dutch. During the 1630s and 1640s, the Dutch took the Portuguese ports of São Jorge da Mina, Angola, and Arguin. Although Portugal would regain much of its colonial territory, including Angola, it permanently lost Mina and other Gold Coast ports. After 1650, the English

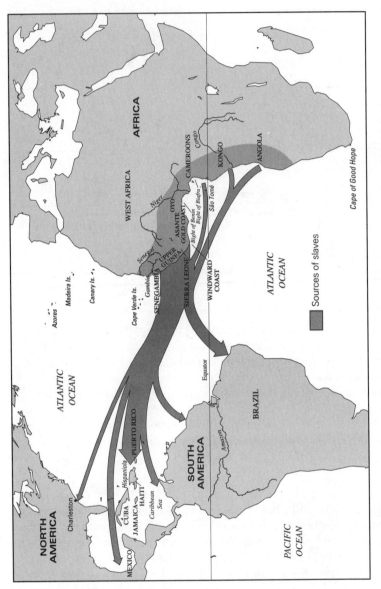

Origins and Destinations of Africans Enslaved in the New World. Blacks arrived in the Americas from a variety of West African locations—including Senegambia, Upper Guinea, and the so-called Gold Coast—but the Niger Delta region (and Cameroons) became the most consistent source of captives shipped to the New World over time.

and French would undermine both Portuguese and Dutch influence. As early as 1677, the French captured Gorée (the former Portuguese El Mina) from the Dutch, and the English established a series of forts and made inroads on Dutch control of the Gold Coast. Sweden, Denmark, and Germany followed suit with their own drives for a piece of the West African trade.

European Traders, African States, and Captives

Wherever Europeans gained a foothold in the African trade, they initially deferred to African heads of state and merchant elites for both health and military reasons. Although Africans and Europeans shared similar diseases and immunities, yellow fever and certain strains of malaria were especially deadly for Europeans. New arrivals to the West African coast suffered mortality rates as high as 25 to 50 percent in the first few months. When the Portuguese sent a fleet of twenty ships to enforce its will on the Jolof state in 1590, disease undercut its force, and resistance from African peoples defeated the effort. The heavy mortality cost of conducting business on the west coast of Africa, along with proud, independent, and determined African peoples, discouraged European forays inland.

European raids on African peoples also met staunch and determined military resistance. When a Portuguese war ship arrived in the Senegambian region in 1446, African ships met and attacked the vessel, killing most of its crew. A year later, a Danish sailor and most of his contingent lost their lives when an African ship intercepted their craft near the island of Gorée. When the Portuguese sought to impose their handpicked successor on the kingdom of Kongo, the people rose up and drove the Portuguese south toward Angola. Europeans of different national backgrounds soon recognized the power of indigenous residents and sought to arrange lucrative trading agreements with their leaders.

African states placed a number of legal and technical constraints on European traders. According to a Dutch commercial guide from the mid-seventeenth century, European traders provided gifts and taxes to African leaders in a variety of states along the so-called Slave Coast area. At Allada, for example, prospective European buyers presented offerings not only to the king and merchants but also to entertainers, food venders, and interpreters. Once Europeans met such gift-giving requirements, African officials opened the market to them with the promise of protection.

The sources of African captives varied from place to place and over time. Some areas supplied few people to the European market; others faced drastic depopulation; and still others supplied captives for a period and then dropped out of the slave trade network altogether. Although the kingdom of Benin first attracted the attention of Europeans and became well known on the continent, it supplied relatively few people for the international trade. Between 1516 and the late 1600s, the king of Benin restricted the sale of captives and then banned the export of humans entirely. The embargo was lifted during the early 1700s, when the kingdom faced internal disputes and civil war, but the trade from Benin remained small, even during the height of the slave trade during the late eighteenth century. By the early nineteenth century, Benin no longer supplied captives to the international market, although human exports from the larger area called the Bight of Benin continued.

During the sixteenth century, Senegambia emerged as one of the earliest and most important exporters of people from Africa. Located on the shores of the Senegal and Gambia Rivers, this area supplied nearly one-third of all human exports during the period. Senegambia also represented a pointed example of how Europeans diverted the earlier trans-Saharan trade in people to the Atlantic coast. As soon as the Portuguese reached the Senegal region, they tapped northward-bound caravans for bondsmen and -women, exporting some 700 to 1,000 per year. With the opening of markets north of the Gambia River, such exports rose after about 1456 to an estimated 1,200 to 2,500 per year. Closely associated with the breakup of the Jolof empire into a number of smaller states, captives from the Senegambia would decline as the region regained political, military, and social stability during the seventeenth century.

Upper Guinea and Sierra Leone were also important sources of black labor during the sixteenth century. Like Senegambia, these areas supplied about one-third of the total exports. In the southern part of the region, around the present-day Sierra Leone, ancestors of the Bullom, Temne, Limba, and other ethnic groups referred to by Europeans as Sape were inundated by a people called Mane. The conflict between the Mane and the Sape resulted in the sale of many people until the early seventeenth century. Once social relations between the Mane and Sape stabilized,

Enslaved Africans march overland to forts on the West African coast. *The Library Company of Philadelphia*

however, this area contributed even fewer captives than the Senegambia. To the east of Sierra Leone and Upper Guinea was an area known to Europeans as the Windward Coast. Subdivided into what Europeans called the Grain Coast on the east and the Ivory Coast on the west, this area produced few bondspeople for sale in the international trade network.

The so-called Gold Coast had the highest concentration of European trading posts and military personnel. The Portuguese, Dutch, English, Danes, Swedes, and Germans all built forts along the Gold Coast. Yet until the end of the seventeenth century, Europeans valued the area more for its gold than its labor. Indeed, the Dutch and Portuguese sometimes discouraged the trade in humans, fearing interference with the gold trade, but several developments slowly converged to transform European interest in the area from gold to people: the increasing labor demands of sugar plantations in the Old and New World; the spread of interethnic warfare among West African peoples; and the emergence of new coastal slave-trading states. Together the Gold Coast state of Asante and the Bight of Benin states of Dahomey and Oyo emerged as key suppliers of humans to European traders.

Under the leadership of Osei Tutu, the Asante kingdom was founded in the 1670s. By the early 1700s, Asante had conquered the Akan states of Denkyera and Akwamu, among others, and had pushed the boundaries of the Asante nation, an area covering most of present-day Ghana, from the forest on the coast to the savannah on the north. Initially, Asante's ruling elites depended on unfree labor to produce gold for sale in exchange for European firearms and North African salt, cloth, and other products. By the 1680s, however, the trade in people had increased to 75 percent of the total value of exports from the region. Organized into a centralized state around 1650, Dahomey also gradually turned toward the sale of captives as a means of territorial expansion. Under the leadership of King Agaja, Dahomey captured the coastal states of Allada and Quidah during the 1720s and increased its contacts with Europeans and the human trade. In exchange for firearms from Europeans over the next two decades, Dahomey provided increasing numbers of captives for the international trade. Before Dahomey could fully consolidate its hold over conquered territories, the state of Oyo to the north became a major supplier of captives, reaching its peak as an exporter during the 1780s. Yet to exert its independence of Oyo and to strengthen its hand as a state, Dahomey intensified its involvement with the trade in people. Under the leadership of Tegbesu (1740–1774) and other rulers, the Dahomean armies systematically raided neighboring peoples for sale to Europeans.

The Niger Delta and the Cameroons provided the most continuous supply of captives over time. Beginning around the late seventeenth century, Africans in this area devised an elaborate commercial organization that increased the number of bondspeople. According to recent scholars, this area, also known as the Bight of Biafra, supplied more captives per mile of African coastline or rural hinterland than any other part of the continent. In the Niger Delta and Cameroons, the Ijo and Efik increased their regional trade activities, but they depended on other groups to establish connections with long-distance trade and transport of people from the interior. The Akwa and the Aro, both trading groups with strong religious credentials

SOURCES FROM THE PAST

1785

Diary of Antera Duke, an Efik Slave Trader

26.9.1785

About 6 a.m. at Aqua Landing; it was a fine morning so I went down to the landing and after 5 o'clock Esin and I went on board the Opter but Esin went away before me. . . .

27.9.1785

About 6 a.m. at Aqua Landing; it was a fine morning. We hear that Tom Salt or Captain Andrew's people are fighting with Combesboch's long boat. Captain Opter, the Captain of the tender, and Combesboch's Captain of the tender went down the river in the long boat to look for the boat which the Combesboch people had taken from his mate, and they got away with goods for fifteen slaves. So Tom Salt or Captain Andrew fought with the Captains and the people got the Captain out of the boat (?). One captain took thirty-two men and one woman from them and brought them back. . . .

3.10.1785

. . . so I got together goods for Calabar Antera to go to Cameroons. Soon after that we three put our heads together and settle what we think to do and at 7 o'clock at night I put the things in Egbo Young's big canoe and at midnight I sailed to go to Curcock. . . .

10.10.1785

At about 5 a.m. in Curcock town; it was a fine morning so I went down to the landing. I gave Andam Curcock goods for one slave to live at his place. At three o'clock after noon I saw our Boostam canoe come down with five slaves and yams. At the same time I sailed away home with the slaves in my canoe and there were three small canoes besides mine. . . .

14.12.1785

About 5 a.m. at Aqua Landing; there was a great morning fog; I went down to the landing to put yams in [my] canoe. After 8 o'clock we went down in three big canoes, I, Esin, and Egbo Young with 32 slaves. So he kept 25 slaves and about 6,000 yams. He dashed (gave) us three great guns. Some time after 8 o'clock at night we went aboard Captain Fairweather whose tender went away with 250 slaves and two tons [of palm-oil].

Source: Daryll Forde, ed., *Efik Traders of Old Calabar: Containing the Diary of Antera Duke.* Copyright © 1956. Published by Oxford University Press for the International African Institute.

as diviners, emerged as the principal suppliers of people from the interior. When their spiritual pronouncements as keepers of the famous Aro-chuku Oracle called for punishment by sacrifice to the gods, victims were often spared for sale into human bondage (see box).

Although Europeans depended on developing trade relations with African traders and heads of state to meet their demand for unfree labor, they did not forgo opportunities to raid African villages, aggravate internal rivalries, and increase the number of captives. Portuguese behavior in the Kongo and Angola offers an extreme illustration of this process. Early on, the Portuguese launched their own raiding parties and deliberately fomented interethnic strife to gain their objectives. When the Portuguese landed in the area in 1483, they initially deferred to the authority of King Nzinga Nkuwu, who converted to Christianity and was baptized into the Catholic church. Moreover, the king solicited and received Portuguese support in driving back a challenge from the surrounding Tio peoples. Within a decade, however, in order to man their sugar plantations on the island of São Tomé, the Portuguese slowly and then rapidly launched slave raids on Kongo villages. In 1493, the king of Portugal authorized settlers on São Tomé to engage in the human trade. By 1507, an estimated 2,000 captives worked on the island's sugar plantations, and another 5,000 to 6,000 were held for reexport elsewhere. Although some of these people came from other parts of West Africa, 50 percent or more came from the Kongo region of central Africa.

Portuguese slave-raiding activities soon ensnared members of the royal family and weakened the king's authority. As a result of Portuguese influence, first the Kongo, then Angola, and later Matamba and Kasanje became the principal suppliers of people to the Portuguese New World plantations in Brazil. Although some scholars suggest that these areas were already involved in internal slave-trading operations before the arrival of the Portuguese, only the coming of Europeans incorporated these Africans into the international slave trade network.

Integral to the rise of the trade in human beings was the emergence of Afro-European communities on the west coast of Africa. Mixed Afro-Portuguese communities emerged in Upper Guinea, in Sierra Leone, and on the Cape Verde Islands. Although the Portuguese government used Cape Verde Islands as a base for organizing trade with Senegambians, many Portuguese individuals defied official policy and moved onto the mainland, then intermarried with Africans. Although they retained their identity as Portuguese and Catholics, their descendants were mixed in appearance and Luso-African in culture. By the early 1600s, the Afro-Portuguese made up the principal trade community on the coast and up the Gambia River. These people slowly developed a new lingua franca, or creole, that permitted communication between Europeans and a wide range of African language groups. Similarly, on the Senegal River, an Afro-French community developed at St. Louis. Unlike the Afro-Portuguese, however, these people were the product of intense language and cultural interactions more than of actual intermarriage between Africans and the French. A similar process of linguistic and cultural interchange took place in the English areas of influence. The African Philip Quaque of Cape Coast, for example, was educated in England. Later ordained as an Anglican priest, he married an Englishwoman and returned to Cape Coast Castle, where he served as the fort's official chaplain. For his part, the Englishman Richard Brew spent thirty years among Africans on the Gold Coast and established a prominent Anglo-African family in the area. The emergence of mixed communities suggested that European notions of African or black inferiority would become most pronounced in the New World as human bondage itself escalated.

The Process of Enslavement

Enslavement was a dehumanizing and painful process. It involved capture and movement to the Atlantic coast, the ocean passage to the Americas, and disembarkation and settlement in the New World. The journey began with capture on the West African coast, where men and women were chained together and forced to make the trip along inland waterways and overland to the European forts and trading ships. Captives were often passed on from one group of indigenous traders to another until they reached the coastal slave-trading states. Usually victims of wars deep in the interior, such people had already suffered what one recent scholar calls "social death," the loss of connection to their original community. Since war captives were traditionally put to death, captivity created a new status that ensured physical survival but divorced people from their place in a culture that confirmed their existence as human beings.

The historical record is replete with stories of escape attempts and mutinies, but few were successful. Upon reaching the coast, survivors were housed together with others from diverse locations within West Africa. Invariably overcrowded and disease ridden, these holding areas, maintained by African heads of states, merchants, and European trading firms, served as the staging ground for international shipment. Following intense and demeaning physical inspection, European slave traders made their selections, settled on a price with African middlemen, and marked their charges with hot branding irons. An eighteenth-century observer described the procedure in the kingdom of Dahomey:

> As the slaves come down to Fida [Dahomey] from the inland country, they are put into a booth or prison, built for that purpose, near the beach, all of them together; and when the Europeans are to receive them, they are brought out into a large plain, where the [ships'] surgeons examine every part of every one of them, to the smallest member, men and women being all stark naked. Such as are allowed good and sound, are set on one side [and] . . . marked on the breast with a red-hot iron, imprinting the mark of the French, English or Dutch companies, that so each nation may distinguish their own.

It often took several days and sometimes weeks to secure a sufficient number of captives to embark for the Americas. In the meantime, captives had to endure an additional round of indignities and poor living conditions. They were either returned to holding areas on shore or brought on board European ships to await the arrival of new shipments. Depending on how far afield the traders had traveled, new arrivals sometimes brought diseases and epidemics, causing sickness and even death for those already selected as fit for the transatlantic voyage. When the ship had reached its quota of cargoes, human and material, it embarked on the journey to the Americas, the so-called Middle Passage, the most destructive aspect of the trade in human beings. The ocean passage received its Eurocentric name from the second leg of an intercontinental trade network that included, first, movement from Europe to Africa and, finally, return to Europe after dispatching human cargoes in the colonies of America. For Africans, of course, it was the "first passage" from their continental home.

In preparation for the overseas trip, people were stripped naked, chained together, and tightly packed in highly confining compartments. Although some slavers, as such ships were called, utilized "loose packing" techniques, most followed the principal of maximum capacity. People were chained close together and forced to lie down on layers of shelving with little room for sitting up straight or moving about. For the next several weeks, bondsmen and -women suffered some of the most inhumane conditions known in human history. In the hot, humid, cramped, foul-smelling holds of ships, those positioned on the lower decks had to endure not only their own vomit, urine, and feces but the trickling down from others above them. Seeking to ensure the maximum number of survivors, ship captains often stocked a variety of foods for the voyage, but such supplies often proved insufficient beyond bare survival.

Although colonial authorities placed limits on the number of human beings each ship could carry, captains routinely ignored such regulations. Contemporary accounts repeatedly described the maladies or "fevers" that accompanied the slave ships, including yellow fever, smallpox, and dysentery. Epidemics sometimes broke out and decimated an entire cargo. More often, as much as a third of human exports lost their lives at sea. As the Portuguese cleric Alonso de Sandoval put it, the African bondsmen and -women were

packed so closely in such disgusting conditions, and so mistreated, as the very ones who transport them assure me, that they come by six and six, with collars around their necks, and these same ones by two and two with fetters on their feet, in such a way that they come imprisoned from head to feet, below the deck, locked in from outside, where they see neither sun nor moon, [and] that there is no Spaniard who dares to stick his head in the hatch without becoming ill, nor to

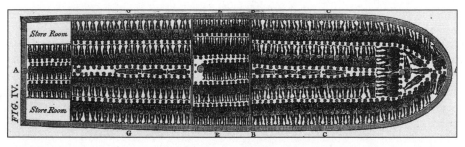

This detailed sketch of a slave ship demonstrates the tight, unsanitary, and dehumanizing packing methods. *Peabody Essex Museum, Salem*

SOURCES FROM THE PAST

1756

The Enslavement of Olaudah Equiano

I have already acquainted the reader with the time and place of my birth. My father, besides many slaves, had a numerous family, of which seven lived to grow up, including myself and a sister, who was the only daughter. As I was the youngest of the sons, I became, of course, the greatest favourite with my mother, and was always with her; and she used to take particular pains to form my mind. . . . One day, when all our people were gone out to their works as usual, and only I and my dear sister were left to mind the house, two men and a woman got over our walls, and in a moment seized us both; and, without giving us time to cry out, or make resistance, they stopped our mouths, and ran off with us into the nearest wood. Here they tied our hands, and continued to carry us as far as they could, till night came on, when we reached a small house, where the robbers halted for refreshment, and spent the night. . . . The next day proved a day of greater sorrow than I had yet experienced; for my sister and I were then separated, while we lay clasped in each other's arms: it was in vain that we besought them not to part us: she was torn from me, and immediately carried away, while I was left in a state of distraction not to be described. . . .

The first object which saluted my eyes when I arrived on the coast was the sea, and a slave-ship, which was then riding at anchor, and waiting for its cargo. . . . I now saw myself deprived of all chance of returning to my native country, or even the least glimpse of hope of gaining the shore, which I now considered as friendly; and I even wished for my former slavery, in preference to my present situation, which was filled with horrors of every kind, still heightened by my ignorance of what I was to undergo.

Source: The Interesting Narrative of Olaudah Equiano, or Gustavus Vassa, the African (London, 1789), I:46–48.

remain inside for an hour without the risk of great sickness. So great is the stench, the crowding and the misery of that place . . . that most arrive turned into skeletons.

Captured and sold into slavery in 1756, the African Olaudah Equiano (Gustavus Vassa), from the Niger Ibo region of West Africa, left a vivid description of his feelings on reaching the coast and entering the slave ship (see box). His description also demonstrates how the pain of separation from home led some Africans to desperate responses—refusal to eat and efforts to end their lives by jumping overboard:

Quite overpowered with horror and anguish, I fell motionless on the deck and fainted. . . . I now saw myself deprived of all chance of returning to my native country. . . . I became so sick and low that I was not able to eat. . . . One day

Olaudah Equiano. This engraving was printed in his 1789 autobiography. Equiano left one of the earliest and most detailed descriptions of the enslavement of Africans in the Americas. *Library of Congress*

when we had a smooth sea and a moderate wind, two of my wearied countrymen who were chained together . . . preferring death to such a life of misery, somehow made through the nettings and jumped into the sea, immediately another quite dejected fellow . . . also followed.

Once Africans reached America, another round of indignities ensued. When the ships anchored, they were met by colonial merchants, slave traders, and government officials charged with inspecting the cargo to determine if any illegal goods were aboard. In Spanish America, the government set limits on the number of people allowed on a ship, depending on the size and condition of the ship. Although officials charged with such duties invariably took bribes and overlooked infractions of the law, they routinely met slave ships and conducted a perfunctory inspection. They required the unloading of captives into small boats waiting alongside the ship, counted the slaves, and then reloaded them on board the seagoing vessel. Following the legal inspection, the captain took charge of the cargo and arranged the transfer of captives to local wholesalers. These agents conducted their own minute inspection of the Africans' physical conditions, paying close attention to their eyes, teeth, limbs, and sexual organs, with particular interest in signs of venereal disease. After completing this inspection, merchants transferred captives to nearby warehouses or encampments, where they were allowed to eat, clean up, receive some medical attention, and rest in preparation for sale locally. Survivors of the Middle Passage were about to embark on their new lives in a new world.

THE CARIBBEAN AND LATIN AMERICA

The African American experience in the New World unfolded within the larger context of European colonization of America. In 1492, the Genoese mariner Christopher Columbus landed in America and claimed the land for the Spanish empire. Two years later, the Spanish initiated colonization of the Caribbean on the island of Hispaniola. Within less than four decades, Spain also conquered the Aztec empire in the high-lying valley of Mexico and extended Spanish dominion over Incan peoples of Peru on the mainland of South America. The Portuguese soon followed suit with the exploration of Brazil around 1500, although Portugal's colonization of the area would not begin in earnest until 1532. Before long, the Dutch, French, and English also colonized portions of the New World in their own interests. Yet on the basis of linguistic, archaeological, and historical evidence of African artistic styles, facial features, and words in ancient Amerindian cultures (such as the Olmec of Mexico at Laventa), such scholars as Leo Wiener and, more recently, Ivan Van Sertima have forcibly argued that Africans came to the New World before Christopher Columbus and the aggressive expansion of Europe. These scholars accept that African boat-making skills and knowledge of ocean currents were considerable and that some of their crafts were durable enough to make the Atlantic crossing. Even so, most Africans entered the New World with Europeans.

Transition to African Labor

From the outset, African labor, knowledge, and skills helped to advance the European conquest of the New World. Although scholars now doubt that Pedro Alonzo Nino, a pilot on Columbus's first voyage, was black, Africans did accompany Columbus on his second voyage in 1493–1494 and also accompanied Balboa to the Pacific Ocean in 1513, Cortez to Mexico in 1519–1520, and Pizarro to Peru in the 1530s. More important, as on the west coast of Africa, gold and labor propelled the initial European settlement of America. Beginning in 1495, the Spanish government required Hispaniola's indigenous Arawak ages fourteen through seventy to pay tribute in gold and agricultural produce. When Amerindians deserted their villages in large numbers rather than deliver payments to Spanish officials, indigenous farmlands deteriorated, malnutrition spread, and Native Americans died in growing numbers. The Dominican friar Bartolomé de Las Casas estimated that more than 3 million original inhabitants of Hispaniola died through starvation, over-work, and disease between 1494 and 1508. In his report on the declining Arawak population, de Las Casas reported: "Who of those born in future centuries will be-lieve this? I myself who am writing this and saw it and know most about it can hardly believe that such was possible."

As the population declined, the demands on survivors escalated, adding to the mortality rate in a vicious circle. The cycle repeated itself as Europeans moved from one island to the next. In 1511, the Arawak and Caribs in Puerto Rico responded to forced labor in the mines by rising up and killing nearly eighty Spanish settlers. In the Bahamas, where no precious metals could be found, Europeans focused on the indigenous Lacayans as a source of slave labor for Hispaniola and to some extent Puerto Rico. According to one contemporary observer, Peter Martyr (1493–1525), the Bahamas lost 40,000 inhabitants in less than five years. Although the sea crossing was quite short, many died en route. Spanish ships, Martyr wrote, could sail "without compass or chart, merely by following for the distance between the Lacayan Islands and Espaniola . . . the trace of those Indian corpses floating in the sea, corpses that had been cast overboard by earlier ships."

Although the colonists were especially preoccupied with gold, they soon discov-ered the promise of profits in agriculture, particularly sugar production. In 1500, the Spanish crown sponsored an expedition of over three thousand men, charging them with stimulating Spanish settlement in the Caribbean islands. In 1515, the surgeon Ganzalo de Vellosa employed sugar planters from the Canary Islands to set up a sugar mill on Hispaniola. Two years later, the first full-fledged sugar mill opened in Spanish America. By 1527, Hispaniola had twenty-five working mills, which exported increasing volumes of sugar to Europe.

Following its establishment in Hispaniola, sugar production soon spread to Puerto Rico, Jamaica, Barbados, and Brazil. As early as 1624, the Dutch directed their trade activities toward the Portuguese sugar region of northeastern Brazil. Be-tween 1636 and 1645, Dutch traders took control of the Pernambuco region and introduced sugar-producing techniques based on the Madeira model from the northwest coast of Africa. Under Dutch control, Brazil became the leading pro-ducer of sugar for the European market and replaced the sugar islands off the west coast of Africa in importance. Like the Spanish, the Portuguese initially exploited the labor of indigenous residents, and, like the Spanish, they faced staunch Amerindian resistance. After defeating the Tupinamba in Bahia around 1549, the Portuguese pressed these people into work on the sugar plantations. By the late six-teenth century, Brazil's bound workers were mostly Tupinamba and other rural in-digenous peoples.

Under the impact of European colonization, diseases, and sugar production, the indigenous population continued to decline. The cleric de Las Casas became a staunch reformer on behalf of Amerindians. Emphasizing the suffering of indige-nous inhabitants, he recommended the substitution of African for Amerindian slave labor. Indeed, the Spanish government outlawed the use of Amerindians in the sugar-refining houses by the late 1500s, emphasizing the large numbers of deaths that occurred among indigenous workers. As a consequence of the declining Amerindian population, planters turned toward alternative sources of labor. European indentured servants (called *engagés* in French) partly filled the labor needs of the Caribbean islands during the early years but proved insufficient and difficult to retain over the long haul. The number of servants shipped from the single port of Bristol to the West Indies rose from nearly 1,500 in 1654–1659 to about 1,800 in 1660–1669. Thereafter, the numbers dropped to a little more than 700 in the 1670s, and to less than 450 during the 1680s.

A variety of factors militated against the large-scale employment of white servants. First and most importantly, European servants had legally enforceable agreements for a specified term of service, usually three to four years in English colonies and thirty-six months in French settlements. When they ended their term of service, they were also entitled to a portion of land and resources for establishing themselves as free men. Thus, their obligations to work on sugar plantations were limited. European indentured servants also faced abuses from their employers, which in turn undermined efforts to recruit additional workers. Moreover, as the sugar industry expanded, large planters took increasing amounts of the best land out of circulation, leaving free workers fewer opportunities to carve out farms for themselves and their families.

As planters found it increasingly difficult to exploit European and Amerindian labor, the importation of Africans increased dramatically. Stretching from Cuba in the northwest to Trinidad near the Venezuelan coast, the Caribbean islands imported an estimated 4 million Africans, about 40 percent of all Africans brought to the Americas during the entire transatlantic slave trade. African imports soon transformed the major sugar-producing islands into black majorities. By 1560, an estimated 12,000 to 13,000 Africans inhabited Hispaniola, compared with about 1,000 whites. Hispaniola had also become the major port for the transshipment of blacks to other islands.

As early as 1530, Puerto Rico had some 2,292 Africans, compared with only 327 Europeans. In 1645, before the transition from tobacco to sugar in Barbados, there were 5,680 blacks to 18,130 whites, mostly indentured servants looking forward to gaining access to their own land and bound labor. By the 1670s, Africans had become a majority; and by 1690, they made up 60,000 of the colony's 80,000 inhabitants. Over the next century, the enslaved black population would outnumber free whites by four to one.

Jamaica's transformation was even more dramatic than that of Barbados. The African population rose from 1,300 in 1658, to 40,000 in 1698, and to over 200,000 during the eighteenth century. This represented an increase from less than 25 percent to over 90 percent of the total population. By the mid-eighteenth century, huge black majorities also existed on the islands of Antigua, Montserrat, St. Thomas, and Guadeloupe. Although it would be later and less complete than elsewhere, during the nineteenth century Cuba would experience a similar transformation.

In smaller numbers, Africans also reached the mainland of Spanish America. During the colonial era, from the sixteenth through the early nineteenth century,

Africans played a prominent role in the economies of Mexico (New Spain), Panama, and Peru. The Spanish imported an estimated 100,000 Africans into New Spain during the entire colonial period. Most of these Africans came between 1570 and 1610 and worked in a variety of jobs: on sugar plantations in Morelos, Pueblo, and Veracruz; in the silver mines of the northern region; and in the urban centers of Mexico City, Guadalajara, Querétaro, Valladolid, Antequera, and Puebla. By the end of the colonial period, Africans and their descendants made up 60 percent of the inhabitants of Panama, where they worked in the transshipment of goods between the Atlantic and Pacific Oceans. According to available evidence, the number of Africans probably equaled the number of whites in Peru in 1604; however, by the late eighteenth century, the number of Africans had dropped to less than 1 percent. Quito and New Granada (now Ecuador and Colombia) also imported African labor.

Only the Portuguese colony of Brazil surpassed the Caribbean islands in the number of Africans imported to the New World. Brazil imported an estimated 5 million Africans between the 1530s and the mid-nineteenth century. Its annual slave imports rose from an average of about 2,000 during the sixteenth century; to 13,000 a century later; and to a peak of 60,000 during the eighteenth century. African imports into Brazil remained high through the mid-nineteenth century. In relatively rapid succession, Brazil employed enslaved blacks to produce first sugar, then gold, and finally coffee.

As the sugar boom peaked in the first half of the seventeenth century, the discovery of gold in the Brazilian highlands stimulated new demands for African labor. Mine owners imported over 1 million Africans into the mining districts of Minas Gerais, Mato Grosso, and Goias. Although some blacks came from the declining sugar regions of Pernambuco, imports directly from Africa reached an estimated 7,000 to 15,000 per year. In all, nearly 2 million Africans entered Brazil during the mining boom, which peaked by the mid-eighteenth century. During the 1780s, the Brazilian economy rebounded from a hard recession and grew steadily for nearly 150 years. Although mining never recovered, sugar production rebounded, and coffee emerged during the nineteenth century as the new boom crop. Located south of the mining district in the rural hinterlands of Rio de Janeiro, coffee producers imported the largest percentage of new Africans. During this period, African imports peaked at about 38,000 per year during the 1840s. Following the country's ban on slave imports in 1850, the old sugar areas of the northeast became principal suppliers of black labor to the coffee growers.

Work and Social Conditions

New World bondsmen and -women deployed a range of skills that greatly enhanced their value to owners. In Brazil, for example, large numbers of skilled miners arrived from the Portuguese-influenced Costa da Mina (located between the Bight of Benin and the Windward Coast), where they had acquired knowledge of pick-and-shovel methods for working in dangerous gold-mine pits. In Mexico, too, the Spanish imported Africans to work in the most skilled as well as common laborer jobs in the mining and refining of silver.

More important, sugar was the mainstay of Caribbean and much of Latin American economies, and it built directly on the skills that Africans had acquired in their homelands. Planters carefully selected captives from the sugar-producing Canary Islands and São Tomé. Africans not only supervised Amerindian field hands, instructing them in the clearing, planting, weeding, harvesting, and transporting of cane to the mills and refinery plants, but also played a key role in setting up machinery, constructing buildings, and carrying out the technical operations in the refining process. In the mills, skilled hands placed the plant between rollers, which squeezed juice from the cane into large containers. The juice was then poured into large cauldrons and boiled down to separate impurities from the syrup. After extensive boiling in rooms that became extremely hot and steamy, the syrup was poured into clay molds, where it dried into the standard sugar loaf. The final step involved crating and shipping to market.

Sugar, coffee, and mining did not exhaust the range of jobs that captives occupied. They also worked on cattle ranches and cultivated ginger, indigo, cacao, and tobacco. Moreover, throughout the Caribbean and Latin America, blacks lived in the major cities and worked as carpenters, blacksmiths, barbers, and retail sellers as well as laborers in household, commercial, and governmental establishments and on public works. As suggested by the history of blacks in Brazil, the work experiences of captives also varied considerably over time. When sugar production declined in the northeast, for example, blacks gained greater access to skilled jobs as artisans and opportunities to earn income. Some of these Africans and Brazilian-born blacks gained sufficient resources to purchase their freedom. As sugar planters lost their edge in the market, bondsmen and -women also seized more control over their time, including opportunities to tend their own subsistence crops and sell surpluses in nearby towns or to neighboring plantations.

Enslaved men and women shared some but not all work experiences. From the beginning to the end of the transatlantic trade, plantation owners purchased disproportionately more men than women and children. Available statistics suggest that men outnumbered women three to one. During the entire period, women made up only 36 to 38 percent of Africans entering the Caribbean on Dutch, Danish, and British ships. The sex ratio for grown men and women was about 187 males to every 100 females. For children the ratio was an estimated 193 boys per 100 girls. Planters and colonial officials frequently alleged that women were "useless in field labor," but recent scholarship undermines this proposition. Planters invariably purchased women with an eye for their use in field or common labor, whereas they purchased men with both skilled and unskilled work in mind. Even when they captured women from other ethnic groups outside their own district, West African states emphasized keeping women and children at home. Between 1791 and 1798, women made up only about 38 percent of all adult Africans transported from West Africa in English ships. An almost identical ratio characterized the numbers of male and female children on such ships (see table).

Age and Sex of Africans Carried from the West Coast in English Ships, 1791–1798			
African Region	Men	Women	Boys	Girls
Senegambia	4,319	2,143	817	519
Sierre Leone	517	243	55	29
Windward Coast	4,526	2,414	383	215
Gold Coast	2,539	1,321	188	117
Bight of Biafra	14,375	10,971	435	384
Bight of Benin	304	189	9	10
Congo-Angola	11,596	6,144	968	509
Unknown	10,113	5,822	992	556
Total	48,289	29,247	3,847	2,339

Source: Claire C. Robertson and Martin Klein, eds., *Women and Slavery in Africa* (Madison: University of Wisconsin Press, 1983), p. 31. Reprinted by permission of The University of Wisconsin Press.

As we will see, given the actual burdens that planters placed on black women as workers, had the market produced more women, certainly planters would have purchased them. When the prices of men and women are compared without regard to skill levels, the prices of males average about 10 to 20 percent more than for women. Conversely, when analysts control for skills, the price differential virtually disappears, suggesting that planters valued men and women about equally as general field hands. Indeed, because men were widely dispersed in skilled and miscellaneous laboring jobs, contemporary scholarship shows that women were overrepresented in the field labor forces of most New World plantations. In Jamaica, for example, women made up 54 percent or more of field hands on sugar and coffee plantations during the late eighteenth and early nineteenth centuries. Women worked extensively clearing, planting, weeding, and harvesting the key staple crops.

Gender differences were closely linked to emerging color and cultural cleavages within the enslaved population. Even before blacks left the west coast of Africa, they had witnessed the slow spread of mulatto populations among the coastal traders. In America, interracial mixing continued and even intensified over time. A small elite, mainly the product of unequal and exploitative sexual relations between white men and black women, gained increasing status among slaves as well as free blacks. In Brazil and Haiti, for example, a large middle strata of mixed peoples— mulattos, mestizos, and others—stood between enslaved blacks and European ruling elites. Within the middle tier, the color line per se blurred as education, money, family background, occupation, and other criteria took on significance. Some free blacks could move among whites of the same class background on a relatively equal basis. To explain this phenomenon, the Portuguese coined the term *dinheiro embranquece*, or "money whitens," and one recent historian has called the color dimension of this process the "mulatto escape hatch." To be sure, such terms exaggerate the privileges of color and economic position among blacks, enslaved and free alike, but they nonetheless underscore the rise of socioeconomic and cultural differences within the African American population.

As the plantation system spread through the New World colonies, the distinction between American-born and African-born blacks also slowly emerged. Almost everywhere, over time, planters favored American-born, or "seasoned," blacks over African-born, or "saltwater," blacks. In Brazil, new Africans from abroad were called *bocal* (*bozal* in Spanish). Whites perceived the *bocal* as ignorant of European culture and backward looking. Compared with American-born Creoles (*crioulo* in Portuguese; *criollo* or *ladino* in Spanish), who were knowledgeable and relatively trusted components of the enslaved labor force, the newcomers faced greater restrictions on their movement and expressions. Indeed, the old Africans and African Americans frequently looked down on and ridiculed the new blacks.

Despite the emergence of significant internal distinctions within the enslaved population, African and African American men, women, and children shared the horrors of slavery together. With the transition to an all-African labor force, malnutrition, disease, and death took a rising toll on all blacks. Once planters made the decision to use enslaved Africans, they believed that it was cheaper to import new workers than to maintain the health and longevity of existing ones. Although sugar planting and refining required important skills and knowledge, it was difficult, dangerous, and life-threatening work. A mistake in the sugar-refining process not only would ruin the product but also could result in a serious injury, a loss of limbs, or severe burns. With temperatures sometimes soaring to over 120 degrees Fahrenheit, the mill houses exposed captives to lung disorders and other infectious diseases. Available statistics show that young Africans who arrived in the American sugar regions died at a rate nearly twice that of those who stayed at home.

Working conditions in the mining districts were even more hazardous than those in sugar production. Miners who worked in the placer mines in river streams stood for long periods of time in cold water, whereas pick-and-shovel miners faced the dangers of cave-ins, rock slides, and rising water. Although contemporary observers sometimes referred to domestics as pampered servants, life in the big house was also difficult. Household workers were on call around the clock and were frequently whipped for minor infractions. When they resisted harsh conditions in the house, domestics were often condemned to hard labor in the field. When two Bahia female house slaves challenged their master's authority, they were demoted from domestics to field hands and repeatedly whipped until they both died a short time later.

Planters and their overseers and managers imposed a strict regimen on all blacks. As noted earlier, harsh conditions on plantations in the Caribbean and Latin American colonies prevented Africans from becoming a self-reproducing population until the nineteenth century. Physical brutality for minor and major infractions was also common. Although the government specified offenses and penalties, planters could easily sidestep regulations and punish captives well beyond the letter of the law. In Spanish and Portuguese law, penalties for runaways escalated with each of-

Whipping of a female slave in the Caribbean. The portrait was titled "Flagellation of a Female Samboe Slave"—that is, a slave with one black and one white parent. *James Ford Bell Library/University of Minnesota*

fense, ultimately leading to the death sentence. A four-day absence brought fifty lashes; eight days brought one hundred lashes and "an iron shackle of twelve pounds, on one foot for two months"; four months' absence and evidence of involvement with *cimarrónes* (organized communities of fugitives) brought two hundred lashes; and "absence of more than six months and the committing of some offense, whether or not with the *cimarrónes,* was punishable by death." Punishment for runaways also included hangings, castration, and other forms of mutilation, including the pouring of hot molten fat or pitch on a captive's naked body. To paraphrase one commentator, the captive's life was often "nasty, brutish, and short."

Although the transition to sugar and Africans produced similar conditions from one colony to the next, it would be a mistake to assume that there were no differences among the colonies. Indeed, there were important legal and cultural differences between the Iberian and British colonies. In the Iberian colonies, blacks could legally marry, own property, purchase their freedom, and even seek redress against abusive owners before the church and state. Moreover, Portuguese and Spanish colonies seemed less riveted to a racially divided world based on skin color. Some people of color would gain access to the government, society, and culture of the dominant groups. Conversely, British colonial law defined bondsmen and -women as chattel without any rights that owners were bound to respect. Still, in practice, the treatment of captives tended to converge across national boundaries, based on particular demographic, economic, and social factors. Wherever captives touched down in the New World, they experienced a hard life. In Spanish, British, and Portuguese America, bondage was a tough form of inequality. It created superprofits for white elites and helped to underwrite the economic development of Europe and the Americas. Within this exceedingly exploitative and inhumane context, however, Africans would forge a New World culture that would enable them to survive, maintain their dignity, and devise new forms of resistance.

SLAVE CULTURE, POLITICS, AND RESISTANCE

Africans responded to bondage by creating new cultures, families, communities, and forms of resistance. As noted earlier, when Africans arrived in the New World, they shared certain underlying understandings and perspectives on the human, natural, and spirit worlds. Based on centuries of interactions between African peoples of diverse ethnic and nationality backgrounds, these understandings helped to lay the foundation for the development of new African American cultures. Although the large numbers of Europeans and Amerindians would curb this process on the mainland, it would emerge clearly and forcefully in the Caribbean and Brazil, where Africans made up huge majorities and successfully blended their Old World cultures with New World ideas and beliefs.

Beginning with the Middle Passage, people from diverse backgrounds forged new bonds. "Shipmates," survivors of the overseas journey, acquired a new sense of kinship and began the arduous process of rebuilding their lives in the New World. Recognition of their common experience helped to link men, women, and children of African descent to each other throughout the New World spiritually, culturally, and physically. As discussed earlier, on the west coast of Africa, diverse ethnic and language groups had already made the transition to a creole lingua franca that enabled them to communicate with different groups of Europeans as well as each other. This language was especially well developed in Portuguese areas and had moved forward in Dutch, English, and French zones. Whereas in Africa, the lingua franca was a second language, in America the new Creole language became the principal tongue, which blacks passed on to their children.

At the same time that Africans struggled to build a new system of communication through language, they also developed New World music, songs, dance, dress, and other forms of aesthetic expression. Contemporary observers frequently commented on black music as part of festivals and funerals. Hans Sloane, a visitor to Jamaica in 1688, recorded the lyrics and music of songs in Koromanti and Angolan. When colonial officials sought to limit the captives' practice of their own language in Brazil, Africans petitioned the crown to permit them to sing songs in "the Angolan idiom." Although authorities condemned and outlawed drums in some colonies as subversive instruments, blacks refashioned new percussion instruments out of New World materials and adapted their dance traditions to the new environment and music. In the 1640s, for example, the Dutch artist Ekhout painted a dancing scene that included a band with African percussion instruments, some with designs identified with line and lozenge motifs from central Africa.

Closely intertwined with their growing ability to communicate with each other and forge new cultural forms across nationality lines, Africans took their first steps toward creating new families and communities. Despite the unequal sex ratios, the number of black children born and raised in New World societies gradually increased, adding to the Creole population. On certain plantations, conditions were more favorable for family and community life than others. In the French colony of Guadeloupe, for example, a 1680 survey revealed that over 70 percent of enslaved people lived in family groups, either formally or informally. Similarly, during the seventeenth century, Barbados planters imported equal numbers of men and women, which enabled Africans to form families early on. Moreover, enslaved people often gained access to provision grounds to grow their own food and to modest materials to construct their own houses, which provided additional opportunities to structure their family and community life. Although this so-called peasant breach was designed to help planters defray the costs of maintaining captives, Africans took hold of these opportunities and turned them into perquisites that planters would later find difficult to deny.

The development of African American culture drew on both African and European ideas. Few planters could avoid importing large blocs of Africans from the same ethnic or nationality group. With an estimated 15,000 imports a year arriving from Angola between 1620 and 1623, Brazil offers the most pointed example of this process. But other places also received ethnic clusters. On the well-documented Remire estate of French Guiana, the largest group came from Allada, with the remainder almost equally divided between Angola and the northern part of Senegal. Out of twenty-four married couples on the Remire estate, twelve came from the same nationality group and two from the same village. Some were already married before they reached the Americas. The Kalabari bondsman Quanbom and his wife, Aunon, were bought and sold together and remained together on the Remire estate. Without formal sanction by church or state, enslaved men and women developed familial commitments to each other, to their children, and to extended kin. When planters respected such unions, these relationships endured over long periods of time. Within these family units, men and women defined roles for themselves and their children and instilled values, attitudes, and knowledge that would enable them to build broader and more inclusive communities.

Religion played a key role in African efforts to build families and sustain their New World culture. Contrary to popular and some scholarly perceptions, some Africans had already confronted the Christian challenge to their indigenous beliefs before arriving in America. Although Africans and Europeans had different systems of religion, they shared some key elements, particularly the notion that there existed two worlds—this material one and a spiritual, otherworldly one, knowledge of which required divine revelation. The close correspondence between African cosmologies, emphasizing multiple "gods," and Catholicism, stressing multiple saints, facilitated the adoption of Christianity. Still, as with their earlier response to Islam, Africans adapted Christianity to their own world views.

Rather than simply adhering to European gods, Africans found ways to retain beliefs associated with their own deities—from Senegambia, Reboucou; from Allada, Boudou, or Vodu; and from Angola, Gambi, or Nzambi. The emergence of an informal African priesthood helped to give substance to their faith. Under the guidance of their own spiritual leaders, African Americans rejected European beliefs in ancient or limited revelations based on biblical scriptures. On the contrary, perhaps even more so than their forebears, they believed that God was repeatedly revealed to living human beings.

Europeans sometimes accepted African ideas but more often condemned and feared them as the work of Satan. Colonial officials often questioned the work of African diviners as "an implicit or explicit pact with the devil." Although some blacks would create a new religion out of African and Catholic forms, others would virtually reconstruct their Old World religion on American soil. In Brazil, for example, the heavy and sustained importation of Yoruba people into northeastern Brazil enabled Africans to develop a distinctive Afro-Brazilian religion called Candomble. By the early nineteenth century, some free blacks regularly returned to Africa to renew their contacts with the ancestral spirits that characterized their New World beliefs. In Angola, as Europeans gained a strong foothold, they condemned some indigenous priests to captivity in the New World for challenging certain Euro-Christian beliefs. Portuguese church officials sentenced the head priest of Matamba to slavery in Brazil during the late 1600s. In a sense, even before leaving home, some Africans had already worked to remake European gods in their own image. On arrival in America, for example, the same Matamba priest mentioned above was condemned for spreading the same beliefs among blacks in Brazil and ordered back to Africa. Throughout large parts of the Caribbean and Latin America, Africans insisted on the integrity of their beliefs as diviners and people possessed by the spirit of God.

As their familial, religious, and communal bonds with each other grew, Afro–New World blacks also gave their ideas broader institutional expression. By the early seventeenth century, African Americans had formed organizations that buried their members, staged festivals and celebrations, and held informal elections of officials to preside over enslaved black communities. In Brazil, blacks elected kings and queens over the larger community and governors and lesser officials to help administer the affairs of each nation (or ethnic group). Although Brazilian authorities withheld formal recognition of these structures, their informal influence on Brazilian and African American society was considerable. These efforts informed African participation in mainstream organizations like the Catholic broth-

Family of Negro Slaves from Loango, c. 1792. Although the illustration reflects certain idealistic and stereotypical notions about slaves in the Caribbean, it nonetheless shows that Africans built new families in the Americas. *James Ford Bell Library/University of Minnesota*

erhoods, especially the well-known Brotherhood of Our Lady of the Rosary. As early as 1693, a Colombian captive expressed surprise that a colonial official would ask him

> if he knew that the Negroes of the Arara, Mina, and other newly arrive[d] [*bozales*] nations [*castas*] have their kings, governors, and captains, and if they meet in their councils [*cabildos*] to deal with the problems of their nation or caste, and have their parties and festivities in which they join together.

Although most captives resisted bondage within the context of the plantation system, others sought permanent and immediate release from the slavery regime. Throughout the Americas, Africans escaped as individuals and as groups. Fugitives offered planters their most common problem. In a study of criminal cases in Peru between 1560 and 1650, running away was the largest single category of offenses

(270 cases), with theft (81), assault (72), and murder (36) comprising the next three most common infractions of colonial slave codes. Although some blacks absconded for short periods of time, seeking to gain concessions for better treatment, others resolved to be free or die.

The mountainous topography of the Caribbean and Latin American colonies provided ample opportunities for escape. Runaway communities emerged almost everywhere in the Caribbean and Latin America: in Jamaica, Hispaniola, Cuba, Mexico, Panama, Puerto Rico, and Brazil, to name a few. Variously called Maroon, *cimarrón, quilombo,* and *mocambo* communities in English, Spanish, and Portuguese America, respectively, these communities of escaped slaves were especially prominent in Jamaica and Brazil. As early as the seventeenth century, Jamaican Maroons controlled outposts in the eastern and western mountains of the colony. Despite repeated attempts of the Spanish and the English (after 1655) to destroy these enclaves, the Maroons not only retained their autonomy but also launched raids on nearby plantations, freed captives, and in general kept colonial authorities and owners on edge. Conceding defeat in 1739, English officials signed a peace treaty with the runaways. The treaty recognized the freedom of Maroons, granted them title to the land, and exempted them from taxes. For their part, the runaways agreed to cease raids on plantations and to return further fugitives to owners. Hispaniola, Cuba, Mexico, and Surinam authorities also signed peace treaties with powerful Maroon communities.

Maroon settlements offered Africans opportunities to recreate their own beliefs, culture, and notions of community. African ideas and social organization informed Palmares, the largest and most renown Brazilian *quilombo.* Established in the backlands of Pernambuco in northeastern Brazil, Palmares persisted for nearly the entire eighteenth century. Runaways installed a king, raised their own food, developed extensive fortifications, and deployed a large military force to protect the establishment from outside attack. Although Brazilian authorities overpowered and destroyed the settlement in 1794, such establishments persisted elsewhere in Brazil and the Caribbean until the advent of emancipation.

Rebellions emerged as the most overt and violent form of resistance. In 1522, the earliest recorded African revolt erupted on the island of Hispaniola, on the plantation of the governor, Admiral Diego Columbus (son of the explorer). Some forty Africans killed nine whites before a mixed force of Amerindians and Spanish put the revolt down. Spanish authorities blamed the revolt on *ladinos* (Christianized blacks from Spain) and *gelofes* (Islamized Africans, who also came to Hispaniola via Spain). The Spanish government decreed that no more *ladinos* or *gelofes* would be sent to America.

As the black population increased, colonial authorities frequently reported "plots," real and imagined, to overthrow their rule: in Mexico City (1537 and 1609), in Cartagena (1693), and in Barbados (1649, 1675, and 1692), to name a few. Following the brutal suppression of the 1692 plot, authorities reported few conspiracies in Barbados during the eighteenth century. Then, in 1813, enslaved Barbadians launched a desperate attack. During three days of violence, some fifty whites lost their lives. For their part, nearly a thousand blacks died in the fighting and the mass executions that followed. At the same time, Jamaican bondsmen escalated their attacks on the plantation system. Their efforts culminated in the famous Christmas Revolt of 1831, which precipitated passage of the general Emancipation Act in 1833. Although planters and other colonial elites no doubt exaggerated certain plots to revolt, the ubiquity of resistance suggests widespread planter insecurity as well as the African Americans' determination to free themselves from bondage.

The most renowned and successful revolt occurred in the French colony of Saint-Domingue (formerly Hispaniola under Spanish authority), where blacks outnumbered whites nearly fourteen to one. As elsewhere, black culture, community, and religious traditions informed the revolt. Under the initial leadership of a bondsman named Boukman, described as a voodoo priest and Maroon from Jamaica, enslaved blacks assembled at the Mourne Rouge, a mountain overlooking a heavily forested area. Boukman urged captives to return to their own god of liberation and social justice:

> The God who created the sun which gives us light, who rouses the waves and rules the storm, though hidden in the clouds, he watches us. He sees all that the white man does. The God of the white man inspires him with crime, but our god calls on us to do good works. Our god, who is good to us, orders us to revenge our wrongs. He will direct our arms and aid us. Throw away the symbol of the god of the whites, who has so often caused us to weep, and listen to the voice of liberty, which speaks in the hearts of us all.

Blacks rose up against their French captors on August 22, 1791. After Boukman's death early on in the struggle, Toussaint L'Ouverture, a former overseer, took up the banner. Following nearly twelve years of bloody warfare, blacks declared their independence and changed the island's name from Saint-Domingue to Haiti. Blacks gradually gained control over the island, adopted a new constitution, and extended citizenship to all residents without regard to race or color, but only after the French lured Toussaint into a trap and shipped him off to prison in France did blacks declare their independence. Following Toussaint's imprisonment, African Americans completed the work of independence under the leadership of Jean Jacques Dessalines. They pushed Napoleon's troops off the island and became the second republic in the Western Hemisphere. Although Haiti inspired fear and hatred in planters, it inspired hope among captives throughout the Americas.

∾

THE ENSLAVEMENT OF AFRICAN PEOPLES was a complicated and difficult process. Europeans discovered that slave raids on African villages were perilous undertakings. Both the military might of African states and the West African disease environment posed formidable obstacles to European designs. Rather than risk alienating indigenous inhabitants and endangering their own lives, Europeans initially confined their activities to the coast and negotiated with African peoples and their leaders for material and human cargo. Before falling prey to European slave raiders themselves, African statesmen and commercial elites sold people captured in interethnic wars with their enemies rather than members of their own nationality groups. Still, the enslavement of Africans in the New World was not a foregone conclusion. It was accompanied and even preceded by the coerced labor of indigenous Indian people and white indentured servants, but these sources of forced labor were relatively short-lived. Although the transition to enslaved African labor varied from place to place and over time, Africans gradually forged New World families and communities and resisted human bondage. This process gained its most powerful expression in Brazil and the Caribbean, but it also characterized life in Mexico, Peru, and other places on the Spanish mainland. Although Africans in British North America would share much with their Latin and Caribbean counterparts, their experiences and responses to bondage would take on unique characteristics. The beginnings of African American life in North America are examined in Chapter 3.

PART II

Enslavement, Revolution, and the New Republic

1619–1820

Part I discussed the rise of an enslaved African labor force in the European colonies of the Caribbean and Latin America. Part II explores similar but contrasting developments in British North America. In 1619, when the first Africans landed in Jamestown, Virginia, indentured servitude rather than enslavement for life defined the system of labor in British North America. Some of the earliest black residents gained their freedom and imported their own black and white servants under the colonies' "headright system," which encouraged settlement by offering free men fifty acres of free land for each new worker brought into the colony. By the late 1600s and early 1700s, however, this labor system came to a close when the British colonies instituted new laws condemning Africans to servitude *durante vita*—"for life." Borrowing from the Caribbean experience, colonial legislators also instituted "black codes" and sought to redefine Africans as property, or "things," by excluding them from the "rights of Englishmen."

Like their Caribbean and Latin American counterparts, African Americans in British North America resisted enslavement in myriad ways. Before making the shift to perpetual enslavement, blacks often joined forces with white indentured servants and sought to escape from servitude together. As the colonies defined blacks as bondspeople in perpetuity, African Americans intensified their efforts to build families and communities as a foundation for diverse forms of resistance, including flight, rebellion, and plots to rebel. In the wake of the American Revolutionary War, African Americans heightened their struggle for freedom by participating in mass demonstrations and protests leading to the break with England and the creation of the new republic.

Although the American Revolution failed to abolish human bondage, it stimulated the growth of the free black population and established a new philosophical context for the African American struggle for freedom. Part II examines the arrival of African Americans in the British colonies; their shift from a somewhat fluid system of servitude to a color-conscious system of bondage for life; the development of African American culture and changing forms of resistance to enslavement; and the growth of the free black population in the wake of the American Revolution and the rhetoric of the "rights of man."

CHAPTER 3

∽

The Transition to African Labor

As suggested in Chapter 2, a variety of international and local forces shaped the African experience in the New World. These forces represented the complicated interaction of historical changes in Europe, America, and Africa. The results, however, were never predetermined. They depended on the volition, culture, and politics of African peoples, as well as the vagaries of international relations, geography, and economics during the expansion of commercial capitalism. African peoples in Latin America and the Caribbean played a key role in shaping their own experience over time and space, but the forces unleashed by the imperatives of capitalist production limited their choices. This chapter examines similar though quite different processes in British North America, where black life also had its earliest beginnings in Spanish conquest and settlement of the region.

AMBIGUOUS BEGINNINGS

The first Africans came to North America with Spanish-speaking explorers who pushed northward from the Caribbean into the Gulf of Mexico, Florida, and the south Atlantic coast. As early as 1526, Africans were part of Lucas Vásquez de Ayllón's settlement of nearly five hundred people on the future site of South Carolina. Two years later, another contingent of blacks entered the Tampa Bay region with Pánfilo de Narváez. When the indigenous people violently resisted their settlement, the Spanish-speaking African Estebanico (Estebán, or Stephen) was one of the few survivors. A skilled linguist, Estebán played a major role in the small party's escape and remarkable eight-year transcontinental journey across the southwest from Florida to Mexico City, the capital of New Spain. As the Spanish officer Alvar Núñez Cabeza de Vaca later recalled, Estebán "was constantly in conversation [with indigenous peoples], finding out about routes, towns, and other matters we wished to know." In search of the fabled Seven Cities of Cíbola, which were reputed to have streets and houses adorned with gold, Estebán later died on a return expedition to the area around Arizona and New Mexico.

Other Africans accompanied Francisco Vásquez de Coronado into the southwest and Hernando de Soto into the southeast. By 1565, Africans also helped the Spanish establish St. Augustine, Florida, the first permanent non-Indian settlement in North America. Before the British established their settlement at Jamestown in 1607, nearly 100 Africans inhabited St. Augustine, which served as an outpost to protect Spanish ships from European pirates. Although most of these Africans were men, the wealthiest settlers reported a handful of African and mulatto women among their servants and slaves.

From the beginning of Spanish settlement of North America, Africans resisted enslavement by running away and joining forces with the indigenous peoples. Ayllón's

Although most Africans arrived in British North America, the first settlement emerged in Spanish America. This is a modern illustration of the free black settlement of Gracia Real de Santa Teresa de Mose, located about two miles north of St. Augustine. *Courtesy of Florida Museum of Natural History, Fort Mose Exhibition*

SOURCES FROM THE PAST

1619

John Rolfe
Describes the
First Africans
to Arrive in
Virginia

In May [1619] came in the *Margaret of Bristoll*, with foure and thirty men, all well and in health; and also many deuout gifts: and we were much troubled in examining some scandalous letters sent into *England*, to disgrace this Country with barrennesse, to discourage the aduenturers, and so bring it and vs to ruine and confusion. Notwithstanding, we finde by them of best experience, an industrious man not other waies imploied, may well tend foure akers of Corne, and 1000. plants of Tobacco; and where they say an aker will yeeld but three or foure barrels, we haue ordinarily foure or fiue, but of new ground six, seuen, and eight, and a barrell of Pease and Beanes, which we esteeme as good as two of Corne, which is after thirty or forty bushels an aker, so that one man may prouide Corne for fiue; and apparell for two by the profit of his Tobacco. . . .

The 25. of *Iune* [1619] came in the *Triall* with Corne and Cattell all in safety, which tooke from vs cleerely all feare of famine; then our gouernour and councell caused Burgesses to be chosen in all places, and met at a generall Assembly, where all matters were debated [that were] thought expedient for the good of the Colony, and Captaine *Ward* was sent to *Monahigan* in new *England*, to fish in May, and returned the latter end of May, but to small purpose, for they wanted Salt. The *George* also was sent to *New-found-land* with the Cape Merchant: there she bought fish, that defraied her charges, and made a good voyage in seuen weekes.

About the last of August [1619] came in a dutch man of warre that sold vs twenty Negars: and *Iapazous* King of *Patawomeck*, came to Iames towne, to desire two ships to come trade in his Riuer, for a more plentifull yeere of Corne had not beene in a long time, yet very contagious, and by the trechery of one *Poule*, in a manner turned heathen, wee were very iealous the Saluages would surprize vs.

Source: Captain John Smith, *Works,* 1608–1631, ed. Edward Arber (Westminster, U.K.: Archibald Constable and Co., 1895), Part II: 540–543.

colony in the southeast collapsed soon after blacks set fire to several buildings and escaped into surrounding Indian territory. Because Africans ran away and allied with Amerindians, Spanish authorities frequently complained that blacks were the "worst enemies we can have."

Black life in North America originated in the non-English parts of the continent, but the British colonies absorbed the vast majority of Africans and their descendants. England also set the principal socioeconomic, political, and cultural parameters of African American life during the colonial era. The first Africans entered the region via ships engaged in piracy against the Spanish colonies in the Caribbean. In 1619, a "Dutch man-of-war" dispatched the initial group of 20 Africans in the English settlement of Jamestown, Virginia (see box). Over the next two decades, the black population increased slowly, rising to no more than 170 by 1640.

SOURCES FROM THE PAST

1655

The Virginia Court Awards Anthony Johnson, a Former Slave, Custody of His Slave Property

The deposition of Captain Samuel Goldsmith taken (in open court) 8th of March Sayth, That beinge at the howse of Anthony Johnson Negro (about the beginninge of November last to receive a hogshead of tobacco) a Negro called John Casor came to this Deponent, and told him that hee came into Virginia for seaven or Eight yeares (per Indenture) And that hee had demanded his freedome of his master Anthony Johnson; And further said that Johnson had kept him his servant seaven yeares longer than hee ought. . . . Further this deponent saith That mr. Robert Parker and George Parker they knew that the said Negro had an Indenture (in on Mr. Carye hundred on the other side of the Baye) And the said Anthony Johnson did not tell the negro goe free The said John Casor would recover most of his Cowes of him; Then Anthony Johnson (as this deponent did suppose) was in a feare. Upon this his Sonne in lawe, his wife and his 2 sonnes perswaded the said Anthony Johnson to sett the said John Casor free. more saith not

Samuel Goldsmith

This daye Anthony Johnson Negro made his complaint to the Court against mr. Robert Parker and declared that hee deteyneth his servant John Casor negro (under pretence that the said Negro is a free man). The Court seriously consideringe and maturely weighinge the premisses, doe fynde that the said Mr. Robert Parker most unjustly keepeth the said Negro from Anthony Johnson his master as appeareth by the deposition of Captain Samuel Goldsmith and many probable circumstances. It is therefore the Judgement of the Court and ordered That the said John Casor Negro forthwith returne unto the service of his said master Anthony Johnson, And that mr. Robert Parker make payment of all charge in the suit, also Execution.

Source: Warren M. Billings, ed., *The Old Dominion in the Seventeenth Century: A Documentary History of Virginia, 1660–1689* (Chapel Hill: University of North Carolina Press, 1975), pp. 155–156.

Although 1619 marked the beginnings of African life in British North America, the arrival of blacks also signaled the rise of a multiracial, but unfree, labor force. Merchant elites sought labor from a variety of sources, including Amerindians, Europeans, and Africans. Thus, the first generation of Africans shared a subordinate status with white indentured servants and substantial ambiguity in their social status. Some could demand payment for their labor, gain their freedom, legally marry, own property, and even import servants of their own, including white ones (see box). Anthony Johnson arrived in the colony in the 1620s. Two decades later, Johnson had imported five servants for his own use and owned 250 acres of land under the colony's headright system, which rewarded with fifty acres of free land persons who brought workers into the colony. Another black man, Richard Johnson, apparently no relation to Anthony, imported two white servants and received one hundred acres of land. Another black received five hundred acres for importing a total of eleven people. These early Africans used their access to land and freedom to initiate the building of black families. By the 1650s, for example, Anthony Johnson had married Mary, described as "a Negro woman" who had entered the colony in 1622. The couple's household soon included no fewer than four children, who later inherited the family's wealth.

Early colonial Africans also gained substantial access to English courts of law, partly because of the Africans' conversion to Christianity and growing familiarity with European culture. In 1624, for example, John Phillip, described as "a negro Christened in *England* 2 years since," testified in the Virginia court against a white man. At about the same time, the Virginia court mandated that the "negro caled by the name of *brase* [apparently a sailor] shall belonge to *Sir Francis Wyatt, Governor etc.,* As his servant"; the court also ordered that another black, possibly the same "brase," receive "monthly for his labor forty pownd waight of good marchantable tobacco for his labor and service so longe as he remayneth" with Lady Yeardley, wife of the former colonial governor. Such evidence suggests that Africans who entered North America during the first years were not "slaves for life." Some apparently arrived as free men and remained so. Others served a period of years and then gained their freedom. Still others faced a long period of servitude that covered the balance of their lives, but this fate also greeted some white servants as well.

Although indentured servitude offered opportunities for freedom, it was nonetheless a form of unfree labor marked by unequal class relations and economic exploitation. Earlier forms of European labor exploitation conditioned the rise of indentured servitude in England and later in North America. Until the onset of European expansion overseas, English society had recognized a condition known as villeinage. Defined as hereditary servitude passed on from father to son by law, villeinage deprived Englishmen of their freedom and subjected them to the arbitrary will of the "lords of the land." The villein (servant) and his family had few property or contractual rights and could be bought and sold with or without the land on which they worked. Once the legal, hereditary, or customary practice of villeinage declined, however, the British government instituted the system of indentured servitude, which reinforced old patterns of inequality. Although the system represented a voluntary agreement between free people, indentured servants could also be bought and sold to the highest bidders and "transferred like movable goods or chattels."

Indentured servitude in America was even harsher than its English counterpart. Separated by distance from relatives, friends, and English law, New World servants faced substantial abuse. Whereas servants entered annual or short-term contracts in England, most contracted for as much as seven years in the colonies of North America, where they often served for more than seven years and sometimes for life. Colonial law permitted masters to increase the length of service for a variety of offenses, particularly running away and theft. In Lancaster County, Virginia, for example, a white servant, Christopher Adams, escaped from his master for six months. When later captured by authorities, the man received a stiff penalty in the Virginia court: three years' additional service—one year for the time away, another for the crop that he would have produced, and another for the expenses involved in his recovery. Since white indentured servants frequently stole food and held communal feasts in the woods near plantations, persons found guilty of hog killing faced a year of additional service to the owner and a year of service to the informer. A third offense could result in death. Women servants often had additional years added to their term for pregnancy during the period of their indenture. In one case, when a woman became pregnant and delivered a child, the colonial court added two years' service to her contract.

Colonial court records are replete with cases of mistreatment of white servants by white masters. In 1623, one white Virginia servant, Thomas Best, wrote: "My master Atkins . . . hath sold me for a £150 sterling like a damnd slave." As early as 1614, John Rolfe reported that: this "buying and selling of [white] men and bodies" had already become a scandal in the colony. Captain John Smith also protested the "extortion and oppression" of men who sold "even men, women and children for who will give most." An extreme case involved John and Alice Proctor and their servants Elizabeth Abbott and Elias Hinton, who died after a series of beatings, administered by the Proctors as well as by other servants. A colonial official counted five hundred lashes inflicted on the girl at one time and warned Proctor that he might as well kill her and be done with it. A woman, Alice Bennett, examined the girl's body and found it riddled with holes and sores. Witnesses said that Proctor beat Hinton to death with a rake. Yet there is no evidence that the perpetrators of these abuses were punished by law.

Indentured servitude subordinated whites as well as blacks, but the system took its greatest toll on Africans. From the outset of British settlement in North America, most whites arrived with written contracts and recourse to courts of law, whereas the first Africans were literally "sold" to the colonists in exchange for "vitualles." Colonial records regularly reported ships arriving in Virginia to sell Africans in exchange for commodities like tobacco as well as food. Although whites lay legal claim to better treatment and specified periods of service, Africans soon confronted laws and social practices that permitted servant holders to claim their labor for an indefinite period of time. In 1640, for example, Maryland passed a statute specifying that "all persons who were imported without indentures [are] to serve four years (slaves [that is, blacks] excepted)." Thus, despite fluidity in their early encounter with the Chesapeake labor system, blacks faced the brunt of new and existing European forms of labor exploitation.

As early as the mid-1620s, the exploitation of African labor took on increasingly racial overtones. In 1624 and 1625, Virginia conducted two censuses that revealed the subordination of Africans within a larger context of unfree labor. In 1624, none of the twenty-two blacks enumerated had last names, and almost 50 percent had no names at all. The 1625 census offered more complete data for whites than the earlier one, including age and date of arrival of ships, but failed to record similar information for Africans. Moreover, blacks were usually placed at the end of such lists along with Amerindians. By 1627, the will of George Yeardley, governor of Virginia (1619–1621, 1626–1627), offered an even clearer separation of blacks from whites. Yeardley equated Africans and European servants with things rather than persons, but he further identified blacks as a separate category: to his heirs, he left "goode debts, chattels, servants, negars, cattle or any other thing." In Yeardley's mind, blacks occupied a status just above cattle and just below other white servants.

The increasing legal and social separation of black and white laborers escalated over time. In 1639, a Maryland civil rights statute reflected the gradual emergence of extended servitude and even slavery for Africans: "All the inhabitants of the province of Christian standing (slaves excepted) to enjoy full liberties and rights of Englishmen." A year later, the Virginia court sentenced white and black fugitives to different terms of service for running away from their master. A Dutchman and a Scotsman received an added year of service, whereas the African, John Punch, received a sentence of servitude for life. Until the 1630s and 1640s, the colonial statutes usually dealt with all persons defined as "unfree" or servant labor. Now such laws started to recognize distinctions between enslaved Africans and other unfree workers. Moreover, until this time, the terms used to describe unfree labor ("Irish Slave," "Negro Servants," and "Negars") were quite ambiguous.

Changing gender and sexual relations also underscored the increasing racialization of servitude. By the 1630s, the Chesapeake colonies had started to tax the field labor of black women, whereas before, the state had taxed all male labor, excluding that of both black and white women. At the same time, Virginia and Maryland instituted new constraints on interracial sex and marriage. On 17 September 1630, the Virginia court sentenced a white man, Hugh Davis, to a sound whipping "before an assembly of Negroes and others for abusing himself to the dishonor of God and shame of Christians, by defiling his body in lying with a negro" (presumably a woman). In 1640, another white man had "to do penance in church according to laws of England, for getting a negroe woman with child and the woman whipt." During the early 1650s, a white man won a slander suit for the statement that "he had a black bastard in Virginia."

Despite growing social restrictions on interracial sexual relations, such relationships persisted. Indeed, since black children took the status of their fathers in early colonial Chesapeake society, for awhile the free black and mulatto population increased faster than the white population. Some whites feared and sought to reverse this process. In the meantime, however, the number of children resulting from the unions of free and servant white women and black men also markedly increased. Because these children took the status of their fathers, who were invariably servants or slaves, some planters actually sanctioned and even encouraged these interracial relations. They gained not only access to the future labor of young children but also an extension of the mother's term of service, ostensibly to cover the labor lost during pregnancy.

The enslavement of Africans was also related to the impact of Europeans on Amerindian society. As in the Caribbean and Latin America, the arrival of the English provoked widespread resistance among the indigenous people. In Virginia, for example, Europeans encountered a powerful "confederacy" of some six indigenous ethnic groups. In 1622 and again in 1644, Amerindians attacked the Virginia colony, killing some eight hundred people. In the second attack, however, the war dragged on for two years, and the colonists turned the tide. By 1646, the Virginia assembly was describing the Indians as "driven from the townes and habitations, lurking up & downe the woods in small numbers." Warfare, combined with the onslaught of European diseases, particularly smallpox, reduced the indigenous population from an estimated eight or nine thousand in 1607 to fewer than two thousand during the 1660s. Coupled with growing restrictions on the exploitation of white labor, the declining indigenous population offered an additional rationale for the enslavement of African people. Over the next half century, British North America would define Africans as "slaves for life."

EXPANSION AND CONSOLIDATION OF AFRICAN SLAVERY

As resistance, warfare, and disease undermined the labor potential of indigenous people, and as white indentured servants gained their freedom and occupied their own land, the British colonists intensified their search for African labor. By the onset of the American Revolution in 1775, nearly 300,000 Africans had entered the British colonies of North America. Most of these blacks came from the Senegambia, Sierra Leone, Windward Coast, Gold Coast, Bight of Biafra, and Angola regions of West and central Africa (see table). During the first third of the eighteenth

Africans Imported into British North America, by Origin				
	Percent of Slaves by Identifiable Origin Imported By—			
Coastal Region of Origin	(1) Virginia 1710–1769	(2) South Carolina 1733–1807	(3) British Slave Trade 1690–1807	(4) Speculative Estimate, All Imported into North America (%)
Senegambia	14.9	19.5	5.5	13.3
Sierra Leone	5.3	6.8	4.3	5.5
Windward Coast	6.3	16.3	11.6	11.4
Gold Coast	16.0	13.3	18.4	15.9
Bight of Benin	—	1.6	11.3	4.3
Bight of Biafra	37.7	2.1	30.1	23.3
Angola	15.7	39.6	18.2	24.5
Mozambique-Madagascar	4.1	0.7	*	1.6
Unknown	—	—	0.6	0.2
Total	100.0	100.0	100.0	100.0

*Included in Angola figure.
Source: Philip C. Curtin, The Atlantic Slave Trade: A Census (Madison: University of Wisconsin Press, 1969), p. 157. Reprinted by permission of The University of Wisconsin Press.

century, these Africans experienced a preponderance of men over women, widespread disease, and high death rates. Thereafter, however, as the ratio of women to men gradually improved and the death rate declined, the black population rose from less than 70,000 in 1720, to an estimated 236,400 in 1750, to nearly 500,000 in 1770. The tobacco- and rice-producing regions of the Upper and Lower South, respectively, claimed the vast majority of these Africans. In rapid succession, between 1660 and the early 1700s, the British colonies codified the enslavement of Africans and their descendants as *durante vita,* or "slaves for life."

The Chesapeake Region

The legal transformation of Africans into slaves for life gained its first and sharpest articulation in the Upper South, or Chesapeake, region—in the colonies of Virginia and Maryland, both of which border the Chesapeake Bay (see map). Virginia passed its statute in 1661, followed by Maryland three years later:

> Bee itt Enacted . . . That all Negroes or other slaues already within the Prouince And all Negroes and other slaues to bee hereafter imported into the Prouince shall serue Durante Vita[.] And all Children born of any Negro or other slaue shall be Slaues as their ffathers were for the terme of their liues [.]

At the same time, the colonies blocked earlier avenues to freedom, including conversion to Christianity, mastery of European language and culture, and access to land and labor through the headright system. In 1670, the Virginia legislature prohibited blacks from importing white servants. "No negro . . . though baptised and enjoyed their own freedom shall be capable of any such purchase of Christians [that is, whites]." By the early 1700s, colonial legislators also redefined offspring of blacks by the status of their mother, rather than the status of their father. Although white women gained some protection from unscrupulous efforts to enslave their children, black women now faced the prospects of unwanted children by free white men. Such practices enabled planters to retain access to black women while curtailing interracial sexual relations among their wives and daughters. The Maryland statute explicitly stated that the new law aimed at "divers freeborne English women forgettfull of their free Condicon and to the disgrace of our Nation doe intermarry with Negro Slaues."

Once the Chesapeake codified Africans as slaves for life, the importation of Africans dramatically increased. In 1680, about 4,600 blacks lived in the Chesapeake. Two decades later the black population had trebled, rising to 13,000, almost all of whom were enslaved people. By 1770, Africans and their descendants numbered about 200,000. They made up about a third of the total population, more than two-thirds of all laborers, and nearly all agricultural workers. Whereas the first generation of blacks had arrived primarily from the West Indies and included substantial numbers of women as well as men, the new wave came directly from Africa and was predominantly male. Between 1700 and 1740, for example, African-born men made up about 50 to 75 percent of the estimated 54,000 blacks imported into

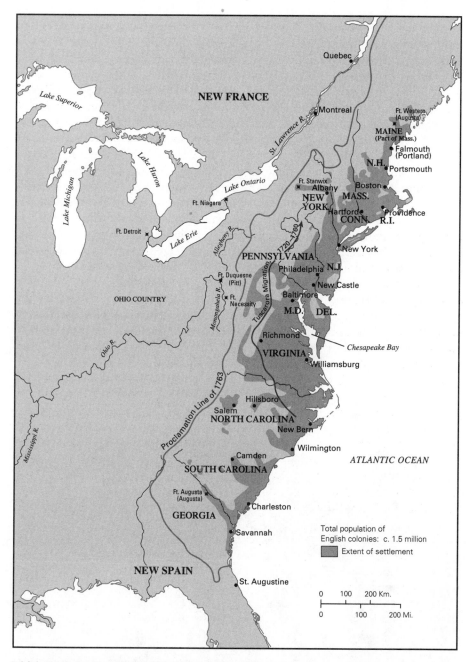

British North America, Eighteenth Century. The Chesapeake colonies of Virginia and Maryland claimed the largest concentration of Africans by the 1770s. Although blacks constituted about a third of the total Chesapeake population and only about 5 percent of the northern colonies, they made up a much larger percentage of the total in the Deep South, where they became a majority in South Carolina and in the low-country areas of Georgia.

Virginia and Maryland. Men outnumbered women by a ratio of nearly two to one, and black women found it impossible to sustain the African American birthrate. Only during the 1740s would African Americans gradually overcome the sexual imbalance and develop a self-sustaining population.

As in the Caribbean, once Africans survived the Middle Passage and arrived in the Chesapeake, they faced the rigors of New World bondage. They were sold to the highest bidders, stripped of their African names, and dispersed across work units of various sizes. As in other New World slave societies, life in the Chesapeake revolved around staple production, namely tobacco. A delicate crop, tobacco required strenuous labor and meticulous care. Under the strict supervision of overseers, gangs of slaves sowed the seeds during late winter or early spring in specially prepared beds. Thereafter, they tended the small plants until they were ready for transplanting to the tobacco fields. At the appropriate moment, when a spring or early summer rain occurred, the plants were carefully removed from their beds and transplanted. Blacks had to work feverishly to complete the job before the ground dried and destroyed the small seedlings.

Following transplanting, tobacco cultivation entered its peak growing season between June and August. Most new Africans arrived in the Chesapeake during this period, when the crop demanded consistent hoeing, weeding, and plowing. Workers then confronted the difficult chores of harvesting and preparing the plant for market. These processes involved cutting stalks close to the ground and transporting

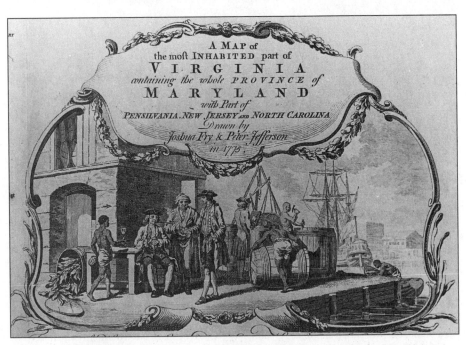

Shipping tobacco along the shores of the Chesapeake, Virginia Tobacco Wharf, 1775. *Yale University Art Gallery*

bundles to well-ventilated tobacco houses, where plants were hung for curing. After curing, Africans carefully sorted the cured stalks by quality and then stripped the tobacco leaves from the stalk. Finally, they bound, pressed, and prepared the crop for shipping. Tobacco cultivation was a difficult and arduous process that frequently strained "every nerve" of the bondsmen and -women, but life and labor were even more difficult in the Lower South, where rice production predominated during the colonial era.

The Lower South

African labor emerged later in the Deep South colonies of South Carolina and Georgia than it did in the Chesapeake. In 1670, the first Africans entered the British Lower South with planters who migrated from the island of Barbados. The Lower South bypassed the period of ambiguity that marked the rise of slavery in the Upper South. From the outset, the proprietors used Barbados as a model for the establishment of plantation labor in South Carolina. As one spokesman put it, "Negroes and other servants" were "fitt for such labor as wilbe there required." Between 1706 and the coming of the American Revolution, South Carolina imported an estimated 95,000 blacks. Unlike in the Chesapeake, however, South Carolina's black population became a majority. As early as 1708, Africans made up over 50 percent of the colony's total population of 9,580. In 1720, the number of Africans reached an estimated 12,000, compared with about 7,000 whites. By the 1750s, blacks made up nearly 40,000 of the colony's 65,000 people.

Although African bondage emerged from the beginning of South Carolina's history, the character of slavery and the use of black labor nonetheless changed over time. Until the 1720s, life for Africans and African Americans was less rigid than it would become. Since most of these early arrivals came in small groups from the West Indies, some were already American born and had mastered elements of the English language, customs, and culture. On arrival in early colonial South Carolina, blacks lived on small farms and worked closely with landowners, who produced mainly for the West Indian market. Since black and white men frequently found themselves on opposite ends of a sawbuck, one historian has described early colonial South Carolina as years of "sawbuck equality."

South Carolina whites acknowledged the value of Africans to the development and protection of the land. They depended on Africans for understanding of the local geography, climate, and topography, all of which resembled West Africa more than the English countryside. Africans identified useful flora and fauna, accenting what to avoid as poisonous and what to use for food, beverage, and medicine. Since the colony feared invasion by the Spanish, French, and Indians, colonial officials also drafted bondsmen during war times and regularly enlisted them into the militia. Black soldiers fought in every major war that faced the early colony. As late as 1708, the colonial governor reported on

the whole number of the militia of this province, 950 white men, fit to bear arms . . . to which might be added a like number of negro slaves, the captain of

As suggested by this advertisement, South Carolina planters took special care to import Africans knowledgeable in rice cultivation. Although Lower South slaves died in disproportionately large numbers until the late eighteenth century, this ad also reveals efforts to prolong the life of bondsmen. *Library of Congress*

TO BE SOLD on board the Ship *Bance-Island*, on tuesday the 6th of *May* next, at *Ashley-Ferry*; a choice cargo of about 250 fine healthy

NEGROES,

just arrived from the Windward & Rice Coast. —The utmost care has already been taken, and shall be continued, to keep them free from the least danger of being infected with the SMALL-POX, no boat having been on board, and all other communication with people from *Charles-Town* prevented.

Austin, Laurens, & Appleby.

N. B. Full one Half of the above Negroes have had the SMALL-POX in their own Country.

each company being obliged by act of Assembly, to enlist, train up, and bring into the field for each white, one able slave armed with a gun or lance, for each man in his company.

Moreover, another contemporary observer wrote that the law "gives every one of those his freedom, who in time of an invasion kills an enemy." When Virginia offered to send white soldiers to South Carolina in exchange for black women, South Carolina authorities rejected the offer, saying that it would be "impracticable" to deprive black men of their women. Such an act, they believed, "might have occasioned a Revolt."

During the early to mid-eighteenth century, South Carolina made the transition from a mixed economy of small farming and cattle raising for the West Indian market to increasing dependence on rice production and international trade. As in the pioneer phase, African knowledge of rice cultivation as well as their labor played key roles in the success of the Deep South economy. Many Africans entered the low country of colonial South Carolina with knowledge of rice planting, hoeing, processing, and cooking techniques. They planted rice in the spring by creating a hole in the ground with the heel of their foot, planting the seed, and then covering it with their foot. Africans also influenced the use of the mortar-and-pestle method of cleaning and processing rice. Like their West African counterparts, South Carolina blacks, usually women, placed small amounts of grain in a wooden mortar (made from the upright trunk of a pine or cypress tree). They then beat the grain with long wooden clubs or pestles "with a sharp edge at one end for removing husks and a flat tip at the other for whitening the grains."

As rice plantations rapidly expanded, the colony entered a new and more intense era of labor exploitation, and the quality of black life deteriorated. Even more so than for tobacco, rice cultivation required grueling labor in unhealthy surroundings. From the beginning, blacks worked in damp swamplands, but the introduction of floodgates for irrigating the rice fields intensified the health hazards that they faced. Irrigation required extensive ditch digging and long periods of standing and work in stagnant water. Yet unlike tobacco planters, rice producers adopted the task, rather than the gang, system of labor and permitted blacks to set their own pace, as long as they performed a set number of specified tasks. Moreover, rice planters allotted small parcels of land to bondsmen and -women for their own subsistence use and gave them limited access to marketing outlets for their goods. Africans and their American-born descendants would later elaborate the system of tasks and access to small plots of land into important instruments of resistance against the system of slavery itself. By completing their tasks early, they managed to carve out time for themselves for cultivating their own crops, participating in the market economy, and increasing their level of autonomy.

The task system, small garden plots, and marketing opportunities were insufficient to allay the harsh impact of rice production. South Carolina blacks experienced not only intense suffering through the imposition of rice cultivation but also greater demographic imbalance, disease, and mortality than their Chesapeake counterparts. African men outnumbered women, reaching nearly 130 men to every 100 women in some places by the late 1720s. Moreover, although planters imported 15,000 new Africans between 1734 and 1740, the black population rose from about 26,000 to only 40,000 during the same period, suggesting a high death rate among the slave population. This pattern resembled the Caribbean, where planters often "worked slaves to death" because they could rely on cheap sources of new workers from the transatlantic slave trade. Only slowly would South Carolina's black population become self-sustaining, as we will see, following the imposition in 1741 of a prohibitive tax on the importation of new Africans after the Stono Rebellion of 1739.

The rapid growth of rice plantations also shaped the early history of Georgia. Although the colony of Georgia emerged during the early 1730s, it did not adopt slave labor until the mid-1750s. Georgia had its origins as a "philanthropic enterprise," designed by English elites to reform elements of the nation's "criminal classes." The trustees believed that slavery would compromise efforts to create a class of virtuous, hard-working, small landholders. Thus, colonial statutes initially prohibited the importation and use of slaves. Following the failure to attract white workers in sufficient numbers during the 1740s and under growing pressure from South Carolina planters who wished to expand their area of rice cultivation, the British Parliament permitted the introduction of human bondage. After passage of the new law in 1750, planters from neighboring South Carolina flooded into Georgia to set up rice plantations using enslaved African labor. By the eve of the

As rice plantations rapidly expanded during the early eighteenth century, the Lower South entered an intense period of labor exploitation. This photo shows slaves at work in rice fields.
Library of Congress

Revolution, the colony's black population had increased to about 15,000, roughly 50 percent of the total (see box).

Africans not only played a role in the Deep South colonies of British North America but also accompanied the French settlement of Louisiana. As the British pronounced blacks slaves for life, the French colonized the Louisiana territory with African labor. By 1718, a French company under the leadership of the Scotsman John Law laid out the city of New Orleans and encouraged the importation of slave labor. By 1750, the colony had a population of about 10,000, nearly 50 percent enslaved blacks. Owing primarily to African labor, Louisiana would become a major sugar-producing region with a decidedly Caribbean pattern of African bondage.

Although tobacco and rice dominated the working lives of blacks in the mid-eighteenth-century colonial south, African slaves worked in a variety of occupations. Alongside rice cultivation, Deep South planters also produced indigo as a major cash crop. In North Carolina, the production of turpentine, pitch, and other naval stores from the rich pine forests represented major profits in the employment of black labor. For its part, the Chesapeake became an important source of slave-produced wheat crops as well as tobacco. Similarly, despite its growth as a sugar-producing area, from the outset Louisiana employed Africans to produce indigo,

CHANGING HISTORICAL INTERPRETATIONS

The Controversy over the Origins of Slavery

The enslavement of Africans in the Americas is a subject of ongoing scholarly and popular debate. Although current scholarship shows how African bondage emerged from a complicated series of global demographic, economic, social, cultural, ideological, and political developments, the debate initially churned around a set of sharply but narrowly drawn issues: Was African slavery the consequence of racist attitudes and behavior among Europeans? Was it a result of economic necessity in a New World of bountiful land and natural resources but few workers? Did it emerge from the time that Africans first set foot on British/Amerindian soil? Did it develop later? Did it represent continuity with a similar status among Africans on the continent?

Until about the mid-twentieth century, most professional historians, mainly whites, followed the lead of U. B. Phillips, the leading scholar on African bondage in the United States. In the view of these historians, American slavery rescued blacks from an even harsher bondage in their own land. In the meantime, African American scholars like W. E. B. Du Bois and Carter G. Woodson countered the racist interpretation of black bondage. In books, and in articles published in magazines and journals like the *Crisis* and the *Journal of Negro History,* these scholars emphasized the role of whites and white racism in establishing and perpetuating human bondage. With the advent of the modern civil rights movement during the 1950s and 1960s, these scholars' ideas and interpretation gained increasing support among white historians, culminating in Winthrop Jordan's *White over Black* (1968). Jordan concluded that racial prejudice and cultural and psychological factors interacted with certain material forces to set in motion "a cycle of Negro debasement"—that is, a race-based system of human bondage. The debate nonetheless continued, albeit on somewhat different terrain.

As early as the 1940s, the West Indian historian Eric Williams foreshadowed the rise of a different interpretation. In 1944 Williams wrote his path-breaking study of African bondage, *Capitalism and Slavery.* He complained that scholars too often equated slavery with black people, racism, and the existence of color prejudice. In his view, this correlation was wrong: "Slavery was not born of racism: rather, racism was the consequence of slavery. Unfree labor in the New World was brown, white, black, and yellow; Catholic, Protestant and pagan." In other words, Williams forcefully argued that slavery had economic roots. Although Williams's book gained few adherents in the early aftermath of World War II, his emphasis on economic factors experienced a revival in the wake of Jordan's *White over Black.*

Several historians of Africa and the African American experience—the late Guyanese scholar Walter Rodney, John Thornton, Peter Wood, Daniel Littlefield, and most recently Ira Berlin, among others—not only emphasized the role of European capitalism but also demonstrated how African bondage varied from place to place, over time, and by gender. Most importantly, however, these studies accent the hand that Africans took in shaping the institution of human bondage on the continent as well as in the New World. By emphasizing the interplay of people from Europe, Africa, and the Americas, this scholarship has important implications for current efforts to understand the multiracial nature of inequality in our own times. Research on the enslavement of blacks reminds us again that the African American experience opened on a global stage.

tobacco, rice, cotton, and forest products. In addition to the lowliest labor-intensive jobs in the colonial economy—collectors and dispensers of refuse, loaders and haulers of all kinds of commodities, builders of roads and canal passages—African Americans occupied a variety of skilled positions on plantations and farms as well as in cities. As noted in the table, Robert Carter's Chesapeake plantations employed enslaved blacks in a wide range of skilled occupations.

Virginia landowner George Mason also employed bondsmen as carpenters, coopers, sawyers, blacksmiths, tanners, curriers, shoemakers, spinners, weavers, knitters, and even whiskey makers. Mason's huge plantation provided timber and charcoal for the carpenters, coopers, and blacksmiths while his cattle, sheep, and orchards supplied skins, hides, wool, and fruit for his tanners, curriers, shoemakers, weavers, spinners, and distillers. As Mason's son later recalled, "It was very much the practice with gentlemen of landed and slave estates . . . to employ and pay but few [free white] tradesmen." White craftsmen, however, would gain a stronger foothold in the North, where blacks made up only a small percentage of the total population. Nonetheless, as we will see, northern blacks concentrated disproportionately in the port cities of Philadelphia, Boston, and New York, where they also entered a relatively broad range of occupations.

Occupations of Male Bondsmen on Robert Carter's Chesapeake Plantations, 1733	
Agricultural	
Field hands	74
Drivers	13
Family farmers	0
Total	87
Semiskilled	
Servants	0
Sawyers	3
Carters	2
Boatsmen	1
Total	6
Craftsmen	
Carpenters and coopers	6
Others	1
Total	7
Grand Total	**100**

Source: Adapted from Allan Kulikoff, *Tobacco and Slaves: The Development of Southern Cultures in the Chesapeake, 1680–1800* (Chapel Hill: University of North Carolina Press, 1986), p. 385. Copyright © 1986 by the University of North Carolina Press. Used by permission of the publisher.

The North

As the African American population reached a majority in the Deep South and an estimated one-third in the Chesapeake, it also gradually increased in the New England and middle colonies. As late as 1770, Africans and their descendants made up less than 5 percent of the total population in the northern colonies. Yet slavery emerged earlier in the North than in the Deep South. In 1626, the Dutch initiated the institution of African slavery in the North when New Amsterdam landowners imported enslaved Africans from the Dutch West Indian colony of Curaçao. After the British took over the colony and renamed it New York in 1664, they sanctioned and extended the institution of human bondage. The number of blacks in the colony increased from 2,000 during the early 1700s to about 10,000 (10 to 15 percent of the total) on the eve of the American Revolution.

Although New York contained the largest concentration of Africans and their American descendants in the North, other middle colonies and New England augmented the number of blacks in the region. Almost from the beginning of their arrival in New England, Africans faced the prospects of legal enslavement. Indeed, the New England colonies legalized slavery earlier than their southern counterparts. In 1641, Massachusetts enacted its Body of Liberties, which sanctioned both slavery and indentured servitude:

> There shall never be any bond slaverie, villinage or captivitie amongst us, unless it be lawfull Captives taken in just warres, and such strangers as willingly sell themselves or are sold to us. And these shall have all the libertieis and Christian usages which the law of God established in Israell concerning such persons doth morally require. This exempts none from servitude who shall be Judged thereto by Authoritie.

Until relatively recently, scholars assumed that a strong abolitionist sentiment undercut the growth of slavery in the North. As early as February 1688, the Germantown, Pennsylvania, Mennonites issued their historic protest against the African slave trade. During the eighteenth century, the New Jersey Quaker John Woolman would emerge as perhaps the most renowned of the Quaker advocates of abolition. Yet Massachusetts, Rhode Island, Connecticut, New Jersey, and, despite its early antislavery pronouncements, Quaker Pennsylvania enslaved significant numbers of blacks. Although relatively few blacks entered the northern colonies as compared with the South, the number of northern blacks nonetheless increased from under 2,000 in 1690, to just over 14,000 in 1720, to nearly 50,000 by 1770. The port cities of Philadelphia, Boston, Portsmouth (New Hampshire), and Newport attracted disproportionate numbers of blacks in their respective states: about 20 percent of Pennsylvania's total black population; 30 percent of that of Massachusetts and New Hampshire; and 50 percent of Rhode Island's.

By the 1770s, the wealthiest urbanites belonged to the slaveholding class—nearly 70 percent in Boston and Philadelphia. Small shopkeepers and artisans also owned a handful of slaves, giving one contemporary visitor the impression that "every" house in Boston had "one or two" slaves.

Engraving of enslaved blacks at work in New Amsterdam, c. 1642–1643. *I. N. Phelps Stokes Collection, Miriam and Ira D. Wallach Division of Art, Prints and Photographs, New York Public Library, Astor, Lenox and Tilden Foundations*

As elsewhere in British North America, the first wave of blacks entered the northern colonies from the West Indies. This pattern persisted until the 1740s, when wars on the continent limited the supply of white indentured servants. The number of white laborers also declined as earlier servants completed their indentures, moved west, and sought land of their own. Consequently, for the first time in the history of the northern colonies, landowners and merchants imported large numbers of blacks directly from Africa. Before 1741, for example, 70 percent of New York's black population came from the West Indies or other mainland sources. By 1750, the pattern had reversed itself—an estimated 70 percent of blacks now came directly from Africa, whereas only 30 percent arrived from the West Indies or other places in British America. From the outbreak of the Seven Years' War in 1756 through the early 1760s, Quaker merchants also imported rising numbers of Africans into Pennsylvania. In 1762 alone, some 500 enslaved blacks entered the Philadelphia region.

As the northern colonies increased their reliance on African labor, the earlier demographic balance between men and women broke down. Sex ratios shifted from a relatively equal distribution of black men and women to nearly two or three men to every woman. Black death rates also escalated, rising during the 1750s and

1760s to an estimated 60 per 1,000 persons in Boston and Philadelphia, compared with less than 30 per 1,000 for whites. Despite increasing northern participation in the international trade in human beings, however, this phenomenon was short-lived and involved far fewer people than those imported into the plantation economies of the Upper and Lower South. By the 1770s, northern whites turned again to European labor, and the African-born population declined.

Although their numbers were small compared with those of the Upper and Lower South, enslaved blacks nonetheless played an important role in the economy of New England and the middle colonies. They lived and worked on small farms, in coastal cities, and on large commercial farms, where they sometimes made up 50 percent of the labor force. The densest areas of black settlement included southern New England, Long Island, and northern New Jersey. The area around Narra-gansett Bay in Rhode Island and northern New Jersey included substantial estates with twenty or more bondsmen and -women, used to provide meat and agricul-tural crops for the West Indian sugar islands. Whereas black women worked as dairy maids and domestics of various kinds, these large estates employed black men in a wide variety of jobs, including work as stock minders, herdsmen, or "cowboys."

In some areas of northern New England, the Hudson Valley, and Pennsylvania, blacks made up as much as 25 percent of the work force. They worked not only in the wheat fields but also in the houses of their masters as domestics. However, since white indentured servants made up an estimated 75 percent of the total work force, some scholars argue that Africans were valued as much as status symbols as for la-bor in the wheat fields and houses of the colonial North. In their wills, for exam-ple, landowners often listed "slaves" among expensive clocks, jewelry, carriages, and other luxury goods of high value, rather than among livestock, implements, or farm tools. Few southern plantations recorded blacks in this way.

Other northern blacks worked in highly capitalized rural and urban industries. Located in the northern hinterlands, colonial tanneries, saltworks, and iron fur-naces employed significant numbers of captive black workers. In these rural indus-tries, Africans often made up the majority of workers classified as skilled and unskilled. Iron masters, the largest employers of industrial slaves, were sometimes the largest slaveholders in parts of Pennsylvania, New York, and New Jersey. As early as 1727, Pennsylvania iron masters expressed their dependence on black labor when they petitioned the colonial legislature to reduce the tariff duties on slaves so that they could keep their furnaces in operation.

In addition to doing housework (cooking, cleaning, tending gardens, and run-ning errands for their owners), enslaved urban blacks labored in a wide range of general labor and manufacturing pursuits as teamsters, stockmen, dock workers, draymen, and sailors, on the one hand, and as shipyard, sail factory, and rope walk workers on the other. Although some employers supplemented bound labor with free white hands, others relied entirely on wage-earning slaves. According to William Penn, enslaved blacks were better than white servants, "For then . . . a man has them while they live"—that is, for life.

Although urban elites were the principal slaveowners in the North, urban bondsmen and -women lived in the least desirable, overcrowded, and unhealthy ur-ban quarters. Seaport bondsmen and women occupied back rooms, lofts, closets, and back alleys. As a result of such overcrowding, some northern owners discouraged childbearing among blacks. One New Yorker advertised the sale of a cook, "because she breeds too fast for her owners to put up with such inconvenience." Others considered children of black women an added expense and sometimes gave them away. Such pressures on black women to curtail childbearing placed a severe strain on black urban families, which included few children.

Partly because of limitations on space, northern blacks gained opportunities to live outside the master's household and to hire their own time in the wage labor market. In exchange for a fixed amount of their earnings, slaveowners allowed them to dispose of a portion of their income as they saw fit. Self-employed slaves not only filled a variety of occupations in a diversified economy but also gained substantial control over their work, including the selection of employers and the opportunity to save money toward the purchase of their own freedom. As we will see, urban slavery also stimulated the rise of a small free black population. Still, although a disproportionate number of northern blacks worked in urban areas and in rural industries, most lived and labored on northern farms.

LEGAL DIMENSIONS

As the enslavement of Africans expanded in practice and in law, colonial officials adopted systematic "slave codes." Chesapeake legislators borrowed from the Caribbean slave codes and became a model for other colonies. Based on color and African origins, the slave codes played a key role in colonial efforts to control the movement and behavior of Africans and later African Americans. Such codes suppressed the human and civil rights of Africans and redefined them as property. The new laws eliminated the right of Africans to bear arms, engage in commerce, own property, move from place to place, or seek legal redress of their grievances in courts of law. Other provisions prohibited enslaved people from beating drums, assembling in large groups, or gaining legal sanction for their marriages, family, and community life.

The new colonial slave codes also covered a variety of specific offenses and established levels and types of punishment. Chesapeake legislators defined murder, rape, and repeated cases of theft as capital offenses for bondsmen, punishable by hanging. For robbing a house or store, blacks could receive sixty lashes by the sheriff and be placed in the pillory—with their ears nailed to posts and even severed from their heads. Lying, disobedience, or intransigence resulted in whipping, maiming, or branding. Such laws supported the master's right to implement strict disciplinary measures, including the killing of slaves deemed intransigent. In 1669, for example, Virginia passed "An act about the casual killing of slaves." The law stated:

> Be it enacted and declared by this grand assembly, if any slave resist his master (or other by his masters order correcting him) and by the extremity of the correction should chance to die, that his death shall not be accompted Felony, but the mas-

ter (or that other person appointed by the master to punish him) be acquit from molestation, since it cannot be prepensed malice (which alone makes murther Felony) should induce any man to destroy his own estate.

As the size of the black population increased in the Deep South, whites feared the growth of a black majority and soon passed some of the most stringent slave codes known to British North America. South Carolina planters and colonial officials repeatedly complained that the growing numbers of blacks enabled them "to drink, quarrel, fight, curse and swear, and profane . . . resorting in great companies together, which may give them an opportunity of executing any wicked designs." Accordingly, the South Carolina assembly not only deprived

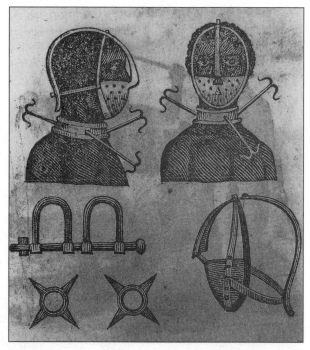

Plantation owners sometimes employed muzzles to control the communication of slaves with each other. Such devices also deprived the slave of food and water. *Library of Congress*

blacks of the right to bear arms, assemble, and move from place to place but also subjected them to the close regulation of their personal lives, including forms of dress. In the Negro Act of 1735, the South Carolina assembly limited the types of clothing that blacks could wear, arguing that African Americans wore "clothes much above the condition of slaves, for the procuring whereof they use sinister and evil methods." In order to enforce these restrictions, the colonial legislature strengthened the slave patrols, making it mandatory that every able-bodied white male take responsibility for regulating the behavior of blacks. South Carolina planters also provided a model for Georgia's legal and extralegal discipline of black labor. Southerners reinforced the slave codes with the whip, leg irons, chains, and even muzzling devices designed to control the slaves' communication with others as well as to restrict their intake of food and drink.

Although the African population of the North was smaller than that of the South, northern statutes also limited African people's movement and their ability to peaceably assemble, bear arms, and defend themselves from attacks by hostile whites. As early as 1656, Massachusetts excluded blacks from militia service. By 1705, New York had enacted the death penalty for any slave caught traveling alone forty miles from Albany. In 1705–1706, New England colonies prohibited blacks from "striking a white person." Violators could be whipped severely at the discretion of local magistrates. In 1730, Connecticut passed a similar but more stringent law that permitted the whipping of blacks who "attempted to strike" a white person. At the same time, municipalities reinforced colonial statutes by passing their own supplementary measures. Boston prohibited blacks from carrying a stick or cane or "any other thing of that nature" that might "be fit for quarrelling or fighting," and South Kingstown, Rhode Island, supplemented the colony's ban on the sale of "spirits" to slaves by prohibiting the sale of "cider" to bondsmen and -women as well.

Northern slave codes were nonetheless somewhat less stringent than those of the Upper and Lower South, where the law more often prescribed the death sentence, maiming, and dismemberment for certain slave offenses. Indeed, as early as 1656, New England legislatures prescribed the death penalty for any slaveowner who "willfully killed his servant or slave," although there is little evidence of convictions under the law. Among northern colonies, only Massachusetts instituted a law prohibiting interracial sexual relations. As the historian Lorenzo J. Greene noted, the Puritan colonies of New England promoted marriages and stable family among slaves:

> All the New England colonies required that wedding banns be read either at three public meetings or be posted in a public place at least fourteen days before the wedding. These regulations applied to black as well as white persons, slaves as well as freemen.

Moreover, northerners also prohibited the emancipation of old or infirm bondspeople without the posting of bonds to ensure their social welfare, but it does not follow that the law was uniformly upheld in practice.

Despite differences between the North and South, slave codes underscored a central paradox of human bondage—that is, how to treat human beings as property and at the same time recognize their humanity and make them responsible for their own behavior. The system of slavery posed problems because it sought to combine "things" and "humans" into a single category. Despite the legislative definition of Africans as property or chattel and the legalization of their sale in a commercial economy, the law recognized Africans as moral beings capable of discriminating between right and wrong. As such, the law burdened blacks with the liabilities and responsibilities of life in a human and civil society but denied them the immunities and privileges of membership in such communities. In other words, unlike bondage in West Africa, the European system of bondage recognized the enslaved person's humanity as a means of punishment and discipline, designed to reinforce the property rights of slaveholders. This irreconcilable paradox would mark the black experience from the rise of human bondage in the colonial period through the emancipation era of the mid-nineteenth century.

⤳

BY THE EVE OF THE AMERICAN REVOLUTION, the enslavement of Africans had expanded and consolidated on mainland British America. Although Africans initially shared a subordinate status with Native Americans and white indentured servants, they soon faced the full brunt of racial inequality. After a period of ambiguity in the Chesapeake region, colonial authorities defined Africans as slaves "for life." Virginia and Maryland not only systematically deprived Africans of human and civil rights in their own territory but also provided a precedent for the subsequent expansion of the plantation system and African labor into the Deep South. Although the northern colonies failed to develop an extensive plantation system, they gradually increased their participation in the buying and selling of human beings and used African labor in a variety of rural and urban pursuits. They also instituted slave codes and intensified the extralegal control of Africans and their American descendants. Such laws and social practices demonstrated certain continuities in the experience of bondsmen and -women across regional, generational, and class lines, but they were more severe in the South than in the North. Although African knowledge, technology, and labor enabled Europeans to survive and later profit from New World plantations, Africans and their American descendants would also use their African culture, beliefs, and ideas to resist social injustice in the new land.

CHAPTER 4

⤚

Responses to Bondage

Despite the enactment of stringent slave codes and forms of labor discipline, Africans and their American descendants were by no means passive in the face of enslavement. From their settlement at Jamestown in 1619 through the late seventeenth century, blacks in the Chesapeake region responded to bondage within the context of indentured servitude. During this period, Africans frequently ran away with white indentured servants, but the escalation of the international slave trade and the transformation of Africans into slaves for life disrupted this earlier pattern of cooperation and changed the context of black resistance. By the mid-eighteenth century, increasing numbers of blacks worked on large diversified plantations that housed owners, overseers, and a mixture of American- and African-born blacks. Building on both their African background and American experience, blacks gradually developed a new culture and forms of resistance. The emergence of New World families and communities not only enabled blacks to survive the rigors of bondage but also established the foundation for individual and collective struggles against the system of slavery itself. The development of African American culture and acts of resistance were by no means unproblematic, however. In addition to navigating the rough terrain of intercolonial and European-Amerindian wars, African Americans had to overcome their own internal cleavages and social conflicts.

THE EMERGENCE OF AFRICAN AMERICAN CULTURE AND COMMUNITIES

Key to the rise of African American culture and communities was the emergence of new modes of communication and new beliefs about the spirit and material worlds. North American blacks elaborated on a process of language and culture formation that had its beginnings on the west coast of Africa. Certain underlying characteristics of West African languages facilitated the emergence of New World linguistic and cultural forms. As the captive Olaudah Equiano revealed in his recollections, blacks from different language groups could understand each other: "One of my fellow prisoners spoke to a countryman of his, about the horses, who said they were the same kind they had in their country. I understood them, though they were from a distant part of Africa."

Language and Religion

A distinctive African American language emerged most clearly in the South Carolina and Georgia Sea Islands, where blacks made up a majority of the colonial population. In 1740, a South Carolina woman offered a reward for return of "a Negro fellow named Pierro but commonly stiles himself Peter." Pierro, or Peter, the owner claimed, "spoke English, French, and Dutch." Fifteen years later, a group of South Carolina runaways "spoke English, French, Spanish, and German." Arabic was also spoken by some blacks in the Carolinas. Some captives, such as the Muslim Job Ben Solomon, were literate in Arabic. Solomon has been called "the

Job Ben Solomon, the Islamic slave who gained his freedom and returned to his home in West Africa. *By permission of the Houghton Library/Harvard University*

SOURCES FROM THE PAST
1734

Job Ben
Solomon
Writes His
Way Out of
Slavery (as
described by
Thomas
Bluett)

Job, who is now about 31 or 32 years of age, was born at a town called
Boonda [Bondu] in the county of Galumbo (in our maps Catumbo) in
the kingdom of Futa in Africa; which lies on both sides the River Senegal, and on the south side reaches as far as the River Gambia.

In February, 1730, Job's father hearing of an English ship at Gambia
River, sent him, with two servants to attend him, to sell two Negroes, and
to buy paper, and some other necessaries; but desired him not to venture
over the river, because the country of the Mandingoes, who are enemies
to the people of Futa, lies on the other side. Job not agreeing with Captain Pike (who commanded the ship, lying then at Gambia, in the service of Captain Henry Hunt, brother to Mr. William Hunt, merchant, in
Little Tower-street, London) sent back the two servants to acquaint his
father with it, and to let him know that he intended to go farther. Accordingly having agreed
with another man, named Loumein Yoas, who understood the Mandingoe language, to go
with him as his interpreter, he crossed the River Gambia, and disposed of his Negroes for some
cows. As he was returning home, he stopped for some refreshment at the house of an old acquaintance; and the weather being hot, he hung up his arms in the house, while he refreshed
himself. Those arms were very valuable; consisting of a gold-hilted sword, a gold knife, which
they wear by their side, and a rich quiver of arrows, which King Sambo had made him a present of. It happened that a company of the Mandingoes, who live upon plunder, passing by at
that time, and observing him unarmed, rushed in, to the number of seven or eight at once, at
a back door, and pinioned Job, before he could get to his arms, together with his interpreter,
who is a slave in Maryland still. They then shaved their heads and beards, which Job and his
man resented as the highest indignity; tho' the Mandingoes meant no more by it, than to make
them appear like Slaves taken in war. On the 27th of February, 1730, they carried them to
Captain Pike at Gambia, who purchased them. . . .

. . . By him he was carried to Maryland, and sold to a planter, with whom Job lived about
a twelve month . . . ; at the end of which time he had the good fortune to have a letter of his
own writing in the Arabic tongue conveyed to England. This letter coming to the hand of Mr.
Oglethorpe, he sent the same to Oxford to be translated; which, when done, gave him so much
satisfaction, and so good an opinion of the man, that he directly ordered him to be bought
from his master, he soon after setting out for Georgia. Before he returned from thence, Job
came to England; where being brought to the acquaintance of the learned Sir Hans Sloane, he
was by him found a perfect master of the Arabic tongue, by translating several manuscripts and
inscriptions upon medals: he was by him recommended to his Grace the Duke of Montague,
who being pleased with the sweetness of humour, and mildness of temper, as well as genius and
capacity of the man, introduced him to court, where he was graciously received by the Royal
Family, and most of the nobility, from whom he received distinguishing marks of favour.
After he had continued in England about fourteen months, he wanted much to return to his

CONTINUED

native country, which is Bundo (a place about a week's travel over land from the Royal African Company's factory at Joar, on the River Gambia) of which place his father was High-Priest, and to whom he sent letters from England. Upon his setting out from England he received a good many noble presents from her most Gracious Majesty Queen Caroline, his Highness the Duke of Cumberland, his Grace the Duke of Montague, the Earl of Pembroke, several ladies of quality, Mr. [Samuel] Holden, and the Royal African Company, who have ordered their agents to show him the greatest respect.

Source: Thomas Bluett, *Some Memoirs of the Life of Job, the Son of Solomon the High Priest of Boonda in Africa* (London: Richard Ford, 1734), pp. 9–53. Also appears in Philip D. Curtin, ed., *Africa Remembered: Narratives by West Africans from the Era of the Slave Trade* (Madison: The University of Wisconsin Press, 1968), pp. 33–55.

fortunate slave" because he was able to draft a letter in Arabic explaining his predicament, a letter that resulted in his being bought out of bondage and returned to his West African home (see box).

British slaveowners deliberately withheld aspects of their language from blacks. They viewed "proper" English as an "emblem of civilization" and white superiority. They camouflaged its secrets from bondsmen by "accent, tone, diction, and vocabulary." Thus, eighteenth-century Chesapeake advertisements for runaways frequently emphasized the inability of Africans to understand English. Moreover, as early as 1740, South Carolina prohibited the teaching of slaves to write, and Georgia later prohibited the teaching of slaves to read or write. Such prohibitions, however, strengthened the resolve of some blacks to learn to "talk to books," as they perceived many whites could do.

As Africans from different regions interacted with each other and Europeans, their New World language gradually emerged as the first, or "creolized," language of American-born blacks. Early Africans spoke a pidgin comprised of words from English, African, and to some extent Spanish, Portuguese, and Amerindian languages. By the mid-eighteenth century, fugitive ads revealed the slow growth of black English in the region. In 1745, a Virginia advertisement declared that "Sambo" could speak English "so as to be understood." Ten years later, another Virginian reported that his "Angola Fellow" spoke "very good English, as he was imported young." In the Sea Islands, blacks perfected the Gullah language of South Carolina and the Geechee dialect of Georgia. After the 1730s and 1740s, the Gullah language became the dominant language of Sea Island blacks. It also became the language through which new Africans gained access to English, while reinforcing Gullah's indigenous roots. In varying degrees, African American culture influenced language formation in the Upper South and North as well as the Deep South. Indeed, African terms like *goober, tote, gumbo, banjo, yam, okra,* and *juke,* among others, entered the language of the region and nation. Whites increasingly made the distinction between the Africans' acquisition of "good standard English" on the one hand and "good black English" on the other. As one historian notes, however, black English was a product of "ingenuity," not of ignorance, "and it served its function well."

Early African American English was largely a spoken rather than a written language. When asked if he could read, one South Carolina bondsman remarked that he "would rather choose hereafter to practice the good he could remember." As in Africa, folklore played a key role in the language training of black children, who learned not only ways to survive the system of bondage but also certain subtle and not so subtle means to resist the harsh demands of the slave regime. Folk tales clarified and confirmed the social and cultural values of African Americans, instilled a sense of morality, and painted a picture of proper behavior. Conversely, the process of curtailing the slave's access to literacy and formal English inadvertently facilitated the use of an alternative strategy of resistance—that is, the deliberate misapprehension of instructions. Captives regularly evaded orders under the pretense that they did not understand English. In short, blacks who failed to learn formal English as well as those who mastered English used language as weapons of resistance.

Despite the difficulties of acquiring access to formal English, a few blacks gradually gained recognition for their literary skills. Africans gained greater access to education and literacy in the northern than in the southern colonies and gradually made an impact on the literature of the region. In 1760, the slave Jupiter Hammon of Long Island, New York, wrote "An Evening Thought: Salvation by Christ with Penitential Cries." Although Hammon's verse is regarded as the earliest known poem of an American-born black, Phillis Wheatley would become the most renown of the early black writers in British North America. Born in Senegal around 1753–1754, Wheatley was sold to the Boston merchant and tailor John Wheatley in 1761. Seven years later, at about age fourteen, she wrote "An Address to the Atheist." Five years later, a London publishing house released her *Poems on Various Subjects, Religious and Moral.* Her writings demonstrated not only her facility with the English language but also her firm commitment to Christianity. In perhaps her most famous verse, she wrote:

> Twas mercy brought me from my *Pagan* land,
> Taught my benighted soul to understand
> That there's a God, that there's a *Saviour* too:
> Once I redemption neither sought nor knew.

Unlike Phillis Wheatley and Jupiter Hammon, most African Americans expressed themselves through oral communication. Moreover, their language reflected the blending of African and European words and linguistic styles.

African American language and oral traditions facilitated the spread of New World black culture. As in Africa, religion occupied a pivotal place in this process. Seventeenth-century West Africans came from a variety of religious backgrounds, including Islam and Christianity as well as various indigenous religions. Yet, as in language, they shared core ideas about the spirit, natural, and social worlds. As noted in Chapter 1, West African blacks believed that spirits inhabited the bodies of human beings. At death, the spirit left the body for a broader spiritual realm

AN

Evening THOUGHT.

SALVATION BY *CHRIST*,

WITH

PENETENTIAL CRIES:

Composed by Jupiter Hammon, a Negro belonging to Mr Lloyd, of Queen's-Village, on Long-Island, the 25th of December, 1760.

SALVATION comes by Jesus Christ alone,
  The only Son of God ;
Redemption now to every one,
  That love his holy Word.
Dear Jesus we would fly to Thee,
  And leave off every Sin,
Thy tender Mercy well agree ;
  Salvation from our King.
Salvation comes now from the Lord,
  Our victorious King ;
His holy Name be well ador'd,
  Salvation surely bring.
Dear Jesus give thy Spirit now,
  Thy Grace to every Nation,
That han't the Lord to whom we bow,
  The Author of Salvation.
Dear Jesus unto Thee we cry,
  Give us thy Preparation ;
Turn not away thy tender Eye ;
  We seek thy true Salvation.
Salvation comes from God we know,
  The true and only One ;
It's well agreed and certain true,
  He gave his only Son.
Lord hear our penetential Cry :
  Salvation from above ;
It is the Lord that doth supply,
  With his Redeeming Love.
Dear Jesus by thy precious Blood,
  The World Redemption have :
Salvation comes now from the Lord,
  He being thy captive Slave.
Dear Jesus let the Nations cry,
  And all the People say,
Salvation comes from Christ on high,
  Haste on Tribunal Day.
We cry as Sinners to the Lord,
  Salvation to obtain ;
It is firmly fixt his holy Word,
  Ye shall not cry in vain.
Dear Jesus unto Thee we cry,
  And make our Lamentation :
O let our Prayers ascend on high ;
  We felt thy Salvation.

Lord turn our dark benighted Souls ;
  Give us a true Motion,
And let the Hearts of all the World,
  Make Christ their Salvation.
Ten Thousand Angels cry to Thee,
  Yea louder than the Ocean.
Thou art the Lord, we plainly see ;
  Thou art the true Salvation.
Now is the Day, excepted Time ;
  The Day of Salvation ;
Increase your Faith, do not repine :
  Awake ye every Nation.
Lord unto whom now shall we go,
  Or seek a safe Abode ;
Thou hast the Word Salvation too
  The only Son of God.
Ho ! every one that hunger hath,
  Or pineth after me,
Salvation be thy leading Staff,
  To set the Sinner free.
Dear Jesus unto Thee we fly ;
  Depart, depart from Sin,
Salvation doth at length supply,
  The Glory of our King.
Come ye Blessed of the Lord,
  Salvation gently given ;
O turn your Hearts, accept the Word,
  Your Souls are fit for Heaven.
Dear Jesus we now turn to Thee,
  Salvation to obtain ;
Our Hearts and Souls do meet again,
  To magnify thy Name.
Come holy Spirit, Heavenly Dove,
  The Object of our Care ;
Salvation doth increase our Love ;
  Our Hearts hath felt thy fear.
Now Glory be to God on High,
  Salvation high and low ;
And thus the Soul on Christ rely,
  To Heaven surely go.
Come Blessed Jesus, Heavenly Dove,
  Accept Repentance here ;
Salvation give, with tender Love ;
  Let us with Angels share.

F I N I S.

Jupiter Hammon's "An Evening Thought" is considered the earliest poem by an American-born black. *New-York Historical Society* where it combined with those of the ancestors. Spirits, including those of the ancestors, were quite active and could influence the course of life on earth. Since West Africans believed that spirits inhabited not only the bodies of human beings but inanimate objects as well, they employed a variety of ritual and magical practices—the wearing of amulets or charms, for example—to gain favor. Such beliefs gave rise to a plethora of African American healers, conjurers, priests, and magic workers who served as intermediaries between the spirits, the individual, and the group.

Although the international slave trade disrupted the institutional structures of West African religious traditions, the memory of African beliefs and social practices influenced New World black culture and forms of resistance. During the early colonial years, black religion reflected the interplay of African beliefs and white resistance to the conversion of slaves. Many slaveholders believed that Christianity would bestow human rights on blacks and undermine the system of bondage, whereas others believed that the religious instruction of bondsmen and -women would require valuable time away from labor in the fields, shops, and households of their masters. Converts to Christianity would no longer be able to work on Sunday, depriving masters of material returns on their investment.

Other Christian slaveowners opposed slave conversion on racial grounds. In 1748, for example, the Swedish botanist Peter Kalm traveled through the British colonies and reported:

> They [masters] are partly led by the conceit of its being shameful, to have a spiritual brother or sister among so despicable a people, partly by thinking that they should not be able to keep their Negroes so meanly afterwards; and partly through fear of the Negroes growing too proud, on seeing themselves upon a level with their masters in religious maters.

In South Carolina, some white Anglican parishioners "resolved never to come to the Holy Table" while slaves were "rec[eive]d there." A white woman was even more direct. She asked her minister: "Is it possible that any of my slaves could go to heaven, & must I see them there?"

The rise of Afro-Christianity was not only hampered by white resistance to slave conversion but also undercut by the reorientation of Christian precepts to justify the enslavement of Africans. In New England and the northern colonies no less than in the Upper and Lower South, Christian ministers repeatedly exhorted blacks to be obedient to their masters. In 1727, for example, Bishop Gibson of London assured slaveholders that conversion to Christianity did not alter the status of slaves:

> The Freedom which Christianity gives, is a Freedom from the Bondage of Sin and Satan, and from the Dominion of Men's Lusts and Passions and inordinate Desires; but as to their *outward* Condition, whatever that was before whether bond or free; their being baptized and becoming Christians makes no manner of change in it.

White ministers not only preached obedience, discipline, and hard work in the interests of slaveowners but also segregated black members, refused them a voice in church governance, and adopted the belief that slavery was part of "God's plan" for the conversion of "African heathens."

As religious thinkers, theorists, and theologians sanctioned the holding of human property, growing numbers of planters permitted the proselytization of their slaves. In 1724, in the Chesapeake, three Anglican clergymen in Prince George's County, Maryland, reported that they preached to the enslaved people and baptized both children and adults, particularly the American born. In 1731, another Prince George's minister emphasized that he not only baptized blacks "where perfect in their catechism" but also "visit[ed] them in their sickness and married them when called upon." In 1706, the Anglican Francis Le Jau embarked on his ministry among the poor whites, Indians, and Africans of Charlestown, South Carolina. In New England, the Congregationalist ministers John Eliot and Cotton Mather spearheaded the movement to convert Africans to the Puritan faith. Eliot warned masters to attend to their duty of Christianizing the slaves "lest the God of Heaven, out of mere pity, if not justice unto those unhappy blacks, be provoked unto a vengeance which may not without honor be thought upon." Similarly, in his treatise *The Negro Christianized,* Cotton Mather argued forcefully that slaves were "men and not beasts" and that "there is a reasonable soul in all of them."

Such proselytizing work reinforced rather than challenged the owners' property rights in slaves. Thus few blacks accepted the earliest Euro-American brand of Christianity. The number of formal converts to Christianity remained minimal, particularly in the Deep South. In 1720, following eleven years of service in St. Thomas Parish, South Carolina, one Anglican minister reported baptizing only eight or nine black converts out of some eight hundred slaves. After five years' service, in 1728 another South Carolina minister baptized none of the fifteen hundred blacks in St. John's Parish. In the Chesapeake region, the Maryland minister Thomas Bacon suggested that most of the baptized African Americans adopted only the outward signs of Christianity, "as if they had remained in the . . . countries from whence their parents had been first imported." In 1724, William Tibbs of St. Paul's Parish, Baltimore County, Maryland, reported that most blacks refused instruction. In 1741, another white minister lamented that blacks rejected Christianity because of "the Fondness they have for their old Heathenish Rites, and the strong prejudice they must have against teachers from among those, whom they serve so unwillingly." In New England, despite substantial proselytizing among blacks, an estimated 50 percent of blacks remained unconverted by the late colonial period. Blacks who did convert to Christianity expected freedom in this world and the next. Thus, masters' fears that Christian teachings might undermine bound labor had a basis in fact.

From the outset of their encounter with Christianity, blacks expressed the view that slavery was incompatible with Christian beliefs. Once enslaved people received baptism, planters regularly complained of "the untoward haughty behavior of those Negroes who have been admitted into the Fellowship of Christ's Religion." In 1723, a New York minister complained that "some [slaves] have under pretense of going to catechizing taken opportunity to absent from their masters service many days." A South Carolina minister reported that some baptized slaves "became lazy and proud, entertaining too high an opinion of themselves, and neglecting their daily labor." In 1731, James Blair, an Anglican church official, reported from Virginia that "when they [slaves] saw that baptism did not change their status they grew angry and saucy, and met in the nighttime in great numbers and talked of rising." Six years earlier, in South Carolina, authorities blamed "secret poisonings and bloody insurrection" on recent converts to Christianity.

Under the impact of the Great Awakening during the 1730s and 1740s, a new brand of white Christianity attracted the attention of blacks. White ministers like Jonathan Edwards and George Whitfield inaugurated a series of revivals. These ministers called the old formalized Anglican and Congregational faiths into question. Emphasizing "regeneration" and "conversion," Edwards and other revivalists believed that stimulating the emotions helped to prepare people to receive God's grace. Such ministers also downplayed theological training and placed primacy on the conversion experience "as evidence of salvation." As a result, more African Americans turned to Christianity than before.

Methodist and Baptist denominations emerged at the forefront of the evangelical movement. These sects stressed piety over theology, emotions over dogma, and the inspired spoken word, or preaching, over learned clerical wisdom. It was this form of religious worship that most appealed to blacks and poor whites and transformed the role of Christianity in the lives of African Americans. Contemporary observers frequently commented on the reception that white evangelical preachers received among the enslaved. In South Carolina, one observer noted how blacks encouraged one Methodist preacher:

> There was a peculiar *unction* that descended upon the preacher in the presence of these sable children of Africa. While they were not good judges of rhetoric, they were excellent judges of good preaching, and by their prayers and that peculiar magnetism which many have felt and none can explain the power of the Holy Ghost seemed often present in the preacher and the hearer.

New England blacks also responded enthusiastically to the new preachings. In November 1741, the Reverend Eleazer Wheelock described reactions to one of his sermons in Taunton, Massachusetts:

> Preached there . . . one or two [blacks] cried out. Appointed another meeting in the evening. . . . I believed 30 cried out; almost all the negroes in town wounded, 3 or 4 converted. A great work in town. . . . Col. Leonard's negro in such distress that it took 3 men to hold him. I was forced to break off my sermon before I had done, the outcry was so great.

Evangelical ministers regularly reported "a great many groaning and crying out."

The evangelical movement had perhaps its greatest impact on African Americans in the Chesapeake. In 1755, two white Baptists initiated the first evangelical mission to blacks on William Byrd's plantation in Mecklenburg County, Virginia. At about the same time, in Hanover County, Virginia, nearly a thousand blacks converted to evangelical Protestantism. According to the Presbyterian minister

Samuel Davies, African Americans understood not only "the important doctrines of the Christian Religion, but also a deep sense of things upon their spirits, and a life of the strictest Morality and Piety." Still, even the Baptists and Methodists would soon accommodate to the system of human bondage and short-circuit the full incorporation of Africans into the "brotherhood of man" and "fatherhood of God."

Whether under the influence of the formal Congregationalist and Anglican churches on the one hand and the new revivalist Methodist and Baptist bodies on the other, African Americans developed their own distinctive beliefs and practices, a blend of their African traditions with New World ideas. White observers often commented on the different forms of worship among blacks as compared with those of whites. In the Chesapeake, one eighteenth-century observer reported that "their religious services are wild, and at times almost raving." Another said that "they commonly are more noisy in time of preaching than the whites, and are more subject to bodily exercise, and if they meet with any encouragement in these things, they grow extravagant." The evangelical use of the psalmody, in which a lead singer read aloud line by line the words of a song, not only enabled blacks to learn new songs but also allowed them to adapt their African singing style of "call and response" to New World Christianity. As one Virginia observer put it:

> I cannot but observe . . . that the Negroes, above all the human species I ever knew, have an ear for music, and a kind of ecstatic delight in Psalmody; and there are no books they learn so soon, or take so much pleasure in, as those used in that part of the divine worship.

Family and Community

African American kinship and family formation also revealed the impact of Old and New World ideas on African American life. Africans from diverse ethnic groups perceived kinship as the principal means of organizing relations between individuals and groups. West African societies incorporated a variety of people from outside the immediate family and developed an elaborate kinship system. Because New World slaveholders denied black families legal recognition and subjected them to breakup by sale and sexual exploitation, African ideas helped enslaved blacks to sustain notions of kinship and to survive labor, social, and sexual tyranny. At the same time, African Americans gradually made the transition to European-type monogamous families.

As the ratio of men to women evened out, growing numbers of black men and women lived in household units with spouses and children. As early as 1733, for example, over 50 percent of the blacks on Robert "King" Carter's Virginia plantation lived as families with husband, wife, and children. And one study shows that on four large Chesapeake plantations between 1759 and 1775, over 53 percent of slave children under ten years of age lived with both parents (see table). This process emerged more slowly in the Deep South colonies of Georgia and South Carolina but surfaced much earlier in the northern colonies. In 1659, New

African American Slave Household Structure on Four Large Plantations of the Chesapeake, 1759–1775					
	Percentage Occupying, by Age				
Household Type	Males, 15+ (*N* = 189)	Females, 15+ (*N* = 158)	Children, 0–9 (*N* = 224)	Children, 10–14 (*N* = 99)	Overall (*N* = 670)
Husband-wife	3	4			2
Husband-wife-children	37	42	53	46	45
Mother-children	2	19	25	10	15
Father-children	7	0	7	6	5
Siblings	5	3	5	9	5
Mother-children-other kin	3	11	6	10	7
Other extended	3	4	2	5	4
No family in household	40	18	2	15	18
Total	**100**	**101**	**100**	**101**	**100**

Source: Adapted from Allan Kulikoff, *Tobacco and Slaves: The Development of Southern Culture in the Chesapeake, 1680–1800* (Chapel Hill: University of North Carolina Press, 1986), p. 370. Copyright © 1986 by The University of North Carolina Press. Used by permission of the publisher.

England court records showed black men and women living as man and wife. By the early 1700s, such instances became even more prominent. New England authorities regularly recorded the marriages of enslaved blacks by both clergymen and magistrates. Moreover, such couples had to publicize their intentions before marriage. In early November 1700, for example, the city of Boston published the banns of "Charles Negro & Peggee Negro." Two weeks later the same city recorded the intentions of "Semit Negro & Jane Negro."

African Americans valued their families and pressured owners to respect the sanctity of their marriages. On some occasions, their protests forced owners to sell families intact or not at all. In April 1751, for example, the slaveholder Isaac Roberts of Philadelphia advertised the sale of a black family but warned prospective buyers that he was "not inclined to sell them separate." Some colonial era blacks made it known that they would "spill" their "last drop of blood" rather than see their families separated.

Although nuclear-type families slowly increased over time, African Americans continued to validate certain African forms of family life. As recent scholars note, although polygyny was not a universal practice in West African societies, it did inform New World black responses to family life. During the eighteenth century, for example, despite the dearth of African women on Maryland's Eastern Shore, some male slaves lived with more than one woman. In 1713, the Reverend John Sharp reported from New York that some male slaves could not cement Christian marriages because of "polygamy contracted before baptism where none or neither of the wives will accept a divorce." In 1738, Boston's Elihu Coleman complained that Yankees allowed blacks "to take husbands and wives at their pleasure, and then leave again when they please, and then take others again as fast and as suddenly as they will and then leave them again." Although white contemporaries and some historians later described such practices as evidence of promiscuity, and even animal-like breeding, such practices also reveal the complicated transformation of African marriage and family patterns under the impact of New World slavery and racial oppression.

Naming practices offer additional evidence of African influences on black families. Africans brought to the New World a tradition of naming male and female children after the day of the week on which they were born: Cudjo (Monday), Quashee (Sunday), Quaco (Wednesday) for males; and, for females, Cuba (Wednesday), Phibbi or Phiba (Friday), and Abba (Thursday). When one South Carolina slaveowner died, his estate listed a variety of African names among the enslaved— Allahay, Assey, Cumbo, Cush, Quash, Quashey, Rinah, and Sambo, to name a few. Moreover, blacks often named their sons after their fathers but seldom named daughters after mothers, as whites frequently did.

African American language, religion, and family formation underlay the gradual rise of New World slave communities and the emergence of new black aesthetics and leisure time activities. The interplay of African ideas and certain European cultural traditions shaped New World slave music, dance, art, and celebrations. Unlike Europeans, however, Africans and their American descendants blurred the distinction between the sacred and the secular. Music and dance marked African American work and play as well as worship. Groups of blacks performed both spiritual and secular songs as they toiled in the fields, rowed boats, loaded goods, and dug ditches. Closely intertwined with music, sometimes described by whites in positive terms as "sweet chants," were rhythms and styles of dance, particularly the African ring dances, which facilitated interaction between the individual and the group. Songs, music, and dance not only lifted the spirits of the enslaved and enabled them to endure bondage but also informed bondsmen and -women of secret meetings, conveyed helpful information to runaways, and served the larger cause of resistance. It was partly the subversive potential of African American culture that led several colonies to outlaw the beating of drums during the colonial era.

Africans also used their own notions of aesthetics and taste to modify Euro-American forms of dress, food, furnishings, and even architecture. Although slaveowners determined the types and quality of fabrics, foods, and building materials that blacks had at their disposal, Africans introduced their own food crops—including yams, okra, sesame seeds, and peanuts—and used their own ideas about beauty and seasoning to change the look of European clothing and the taste of New World dishes. African Americans preferred heavily seasoned foods and clothing of bright colors and contrasting patterns, which European elites considered gaudy and distasteful. Moreover, using African-style mud walls and thatched roofs, blacks often constructed and furnished their own dwellings in Virginia, South Carolina, and Georgia. In some cases, their aesthetic principles and styles influenced the architecture of buildings constructed for planters' use, as suggested by the conical-roofed powder house built in Clarke County, Virginia. Blacks also employed African motifs, designs, and techniques in their basket weavings and pottery. Although African Americans also gradually adopted European dress styles,

A conical-roofed powder house at Greenway Court, Clarke County, Virginia, c. 1750. The roof's style suggests the impact of African culture on southern architecture. *Library of Congress*

planters hampered this process by passing laws restricting the types of clothing that enslaved blacks could wear.

Annual festivals or carnivals provided occasions for the most public display of African American culture. These public expressions of black culture gained perhaps their greatest prominence in the northern colonies. In New York, African Americans celebrated Pinkster Day; in New Jersey, General Training Day; and in New England, Election Day. African Americans used these occasions to display their stylish dress, enjoy music and dance, drink, eat, and play games such as "Paw Paw" or "Props," a West African gambling game that became popular among whites as well as blacks. Although owners permitted slaves to take a holiday for these events, African Americans also used these festive occasions to critique the injustices of white society under the guise of satire. At the same time, they elected their own black "kings," "governors," and other lesser officials and established an internal system of rules and behavior. Although whites ridiculed the notion of black elected officials, blacks crowned such officials with a great deal of influence within the enslaved community. Indeed, influential whites gradually came to rely on such kings and governors to obtain "settlements and adjustments, and arrange many matters in their relations with the negroes."

FROM DAY-TO-DAY RESISTANCE TO OPEN REBELLION

African American culture, family, and community life reinforced and intensified resistance to slave labor. Community and leisure time activities enabled blacks to participate in numerous acts of resistance, ranging from day-to-day skirmishes with slaveowners and overseers to overt rebellion. After completing the dreaded Middle Passage and time on Caribbean plantations, Africans responded to bondage in the households, shops, and fields of British North America.

Workplace and Economic Struggles

As in religion, language, and aesthetics, Africans brought their own notions of work to North America and resisted efforts to exploit their labor and deny their humanity. Although West African ideas about work were not monolithic, most Africans brought to the New World rural work habits and rhythms governed by the seasons rather than the clock. They were accustomed to cycles of intense labor followed by periods of relaxation. As such, like European indentured servants and other white workers, they faced criticism from white elites, who complained that Africans practiced "slovenly" work habits. As blacks became slaves for life, however, such criticisms took on increasingly racial overtones. During the early to mid-eighteenth century, the Virginia planter Landon Carter wrote, "Where the General is absent . . . Idleness is Preferred to all business." On another occasion, he stated, "Negroes tyre with the Continuance of the same work." And at another point, he said, "I can't make my people work or do anything." During the late eighteenth century, George Washington made similar complaints, urging his overseers to guard against permitting blacks to set the work pace. As he put it, some overseers, finding "it a little troublesome to instruct the Negroes" in systematic work habits, adopted the "slovenly" labor practices of the slaves.

Although slaveowner complaints represented rising stereotypes about black people as "lazy" and "unwilling" to work, they also suggest African resistance to forced labor. Africans not only slowed the work pace but also resisted European technology designed to increase productivity. On Maryland's Eastern Shore in 1747, for example, visitor Edward Kinner reported that "you would really be surpriz'd at their Perseverance; let an hundred Men shew him how to hoe, or drive a Wheelbarrow, he'll still take the one by the Bottom, and the other by the Wheel." During the same period, when Dorchester, Massachusetts, imported Africans to work excavating a hill, the Africans transported the dirt away in baskets or trays on their heads. When slaveowners introduced wheelbarrows, seeking to improve efficiency, according to one contemporary source, the laborers at first hampered the effort by placing the "barrows on their heads." Although Europeans and later historians frequently ridiculed Africans as "backward" and "lazy," such criticisms failed to acknowledge the efforts of blacks to shape the work process to their own advantage.

Africans and their descendants were not uniformly hostile to European technology and mechanisms for improving productivity, however. Because Deep South and some Upper South planters adopted the task system, slaves also gradually turned the new technology—especially iron plows and wheeled carts—to their advantage. They used the new implements to hasten the completion of assigned tasks and increase time for work and leisure for themselves. Similarly, some people made themselves even more valuable to their owners by acquiring indispensable skills, which gave them a greater measure of freedom within the context of bondage. In advertisements for the sale of slaves, owners frequently stressed the skills of black artisans. In December 1742, a South Carolina woman offered to sell "A Fine young Negro man, born in this county, . . . brought up to the Ship Carpenter's trade." Two weeks later, another slaveowner presented "A likely Negro Fellow to be sold, . . . a Ship Carpenter and Wheelwright by Trade." Although black women had fewer opportunities for gaining artisan skills, they sometimes expanded their margin of options by mastering a variety of household and field tasks. The *South Carolina Gazette,* on 1 February 1739, advertised the sale of a black woman "fit either for the Field or House, being used to both." More importantly, the ad stated that the woman could "milk very well, wash and iron, dress vituals, and do anything that is necessary to be done in the House."

African Americans who hired out their own time had the greatest opportunities for expanding the margin of freedom. Planters frequently complained that the hired slaves took work "clandestinely about town, and thereby defrauded [their] master of several sums of money." In South Carolina, one master reported that "A Negroman named Lancaster, commonly known about the town for a white washer, and fisherman, has of late imposed upon his employers, and defrauded me of his wages; I do therefore advertise all persons not to employ the said Lancaster, without first agree with me."

Despite prohibitions on their participation in commercial pursuits for profit, African Americans constructed an extensive underground economy. By the 1720s, enslaved people sold a variety of goods and services to Europeans and to each other through an extensive network of informal contacts. Europeans kept this network and practice alive by eagerly capitalizing on the lower costs enslaved people were obliged to offer. In 1721, the governor of South Carolina urged that "a sufficient provision be made against trading with Negroes, or other Servants, & Slaves, and receiving anything from them." By 1734, Charleston officials accused blacks of cornering the market on certain products. When slave crops entered Charleston, South Carolina, black women took charge of the urban marketing operation. These women developed a reputation for their bargaining skills within and outside the slave community. Although Virginia and Maryland planters relied on slaves to take products to market and to shop for plantation wares in nearby towns and cities like Baltimore, Norfolk, and Alexandria, they reported that such trade provided blacks opportunities for "defrauding" them of their money. Blacks gained some commercial opportunities because some whites were ashamed to sell certain products, especially chickens. One Virginia writer asked: "Pray why is a fowl more disgraceful . . . in the sale of it at market, than a pig, lamb, a mutton, a veal, a cow or an ox." Another Virginia observer described blacks as "the general chicken merchants," an occupation based partly on widespread theft. In New York, the Geneva Club, a group of enslaved blacks, transformed theft and the sale of illegal goods into a thriving business.

Closely intertwined with the underground economy and various forms of work slowdowns, running away represented the colonial blacks' most powerful form of resistance to human bondage. From the vantage point of slaveowners, fugitives also represented the most damaging theft of the master's property. Following the decline of white indentured servitude, the number of black runaways increased dramatically. Colonial officials and slaveowners regularly reported the names, ages, and sexes of runaways and advertised for their return. From the founding of the *South Carolina Gazette* in 1732, owners advertised for the recovery of fugitives. Although the proportion of runaways as a percentage of imports seldom exceeded 5 percent,

Runaways as Proportion of Imports to Colonial South Carolina			
Date	Imports	Runaways	Percentage
1735–39	11,849	512	4.32
1740–49	1,563	619	39.60
1750–59	15,912	847	5.32
1760–69	20,810	1,037	4.98
1770–75	20,808	844	4.05
Total	**70,943**	**3,862**	**5.43**

Source: Daniel C. Littlefield, *Rice and Slaves: Ethnicity and the Slave Trade in Colonial South Carolina* (1981; reprint, Urbana: University of Illinois Press, 1991), p. 162. Copyright © 1991 by Daniel C. Littlefield. Used with the permission of the University of Illinois Press.

the absolute number of runaways steadily increased between 1735 and 1770, rising from 512 at the outset of the period to over 1,000 near the end (see table).

Although American-born men, artisans, and those with a proficiency in English stood the best chance of permanent escape, most escapees were field hands. Between 1736 and roughly the American Revolution, an estimated 1,500 notices of runaways appeared in newspapers published in the Upper South cities of Williamsburg, Richmond, and Fredericksburg. These notices described 1,138 men and 142 women, mostly American-born rather than African-born blacks. On 21 November 1745, the *Virginia Gazette* offered a typical example of such runaway ads:

> RUN AWAY about the First Day of *June* last from the Subscriber, living on *Chickahominy* River, *James City* County. A Negro Man, short and well-set, aged between 30 and 40 Years, but looks younger, having no Beard, is smooth-fac'd, and has some Scars on his Temples, being the Marks of his Country; talks pretty good *English*; is a cunning, subtile Fellow, and pretends to be a Doctor. It is likely, as he has a great Acquaintance, he may have procur'd a false Pass. Whoever brings him to me at my House aforesaid, shall have two Pistoles Reward, besides what the Law allows.

In the New England and the middle colonies, too, slaveowners regularly advertised for the recovery of runaways. In 1718, a Rhode Islander advertised in the *Boston News Letter:*

> Ran away from his master Charles Dickinson of Boston-neck in Kingstown, in Narragansett in Rhode Island Colony, a Negro man aged about 25 years.... Who shall take up said Negro and convey him to his Master above said, or advise him so that he may have him again shall be fully paid for the same.

In 1738, a New Hampshire minister offered three pounds sterling for the recovery of a fugitive. Similarly, in 1749, a Massachusetts owner promised "a reasonable reward and all necessary charges" for the return of a runaway. Although some runaways eluded capture and others were returned to owners and punished for their infraction, others chose death over return. In Coventry, Rhode Island, for example, one fugitive "cut his own throat and soon after expired" rather than return to bondage. Suicide, however, was rarely employed as a mode of resistance.

Poison, Arson, and Revolt

Blacks not only resisted by running away, participating in the underground economy, and slowing down the work pace. They also employed poisoning, arson, and revolts or conspiracies to revolt against owners and overseers. As discussed earlier, African Americans had extensive knowledge of plants and their medicinal properties. Indeed, some blacks gained freedom or other rewards for introducing whites to various cures and antidotes for poisoning. The *South Carolina Gazette* reprinted one bondsman's poisoning antidotes for more than thirty years. As the system of bondage tightened, however, blacks also turned such knowledge on their masters. By the early 1770s, for example, the Virginia court convicted and executed growing numbers of enslaved people for poisoning whites. Similarly, although South Carolina made poisoning a felony offense in the Negro Act of 1740, such occurrences persisted. In 1761, the *Gazette* reported that "the Negroes have again began the hellish practice of poisoning."

Along with reports of poisoning, enslaved blacks burned naval stores, houses, grain storage facilities, and especially barns. Colonial newspapers regularly reported barns burning "down to the Ground, and all that was in [them]." Barn burning increased markedly during the harvesting and marketing seasons between October and January. In 1732, the *South Carolina Gazette* exclaimed:

> I Have taken Notice for Several years past, that there has not one Winter elapsed, without one or more Barns being burnt, and two Winters since, there was no less than five. Whether it is owning to Accident, Carelessness or Severity, I will not pretend to determine; but am afraid, chiefly to the two latter.

Arson was particularly destructive in the towns, with their densely settled populations, frame buildings, and poor water supplies and provisions for fighting fires. In November 1740, a fire broke out in Charleston and raged out of control for six hours, destroying an estimated three hundred houses and new town fortifications. Property losses reached an estimated 250,000 pounds sterling.

Whether the fires were set by blacks or not, they were repeatedly blamed for arson. During the early 1720s, a Boston official accused blacks of setting a rash of fires. As he put it, such fires were "designedly and industriously kindled by some villainous and desperate Negroes." Indeed, some of the most serious cases of arson as a form of revolt broke out in New York. In 1712, New York blacks and some Native Americans responded to "some hard dosage . . . received from their masters" and vowed "to destroy all the whites in the town." The conspirators set fire to an outhouse, and when whites responded to the blaze, they killed nine persons before soldiers put down the revolt. In the revolt's aftermath, colonial authorities burned several members of the group alive at the stake while breaking another on the wheel.

In 1741, when several fires erupted on the night of 28 February, white elites concluded that a slave plot was underway. Authorities soon arrested some 150 persons, including 25 poor whites. Penalties fell most heavily on the 134 blacks brought to trial. Authorities burned 13 of these blacks alive, hanged another 18, and deported 70 to the West Indies. Only about 33 blacks were discharged and cleared of charges.

Colonial era responses to bondage gained their most violent expression in the Stono Rebellion in South Carolina. In 1733, Spanish officials at St. Augustine, Florida, encouraged the revolt when they offered freedom to any slaves who deserted the British rice plantations. Encouraged by these actions as well as their own expanding numbers, on 9 September 1739, about twenty blacks gathered at the Stono River, twenty miles from Charleston, and launched a full-scale rebellion. Under the leadership of an Angolan slave named Jimmy, they raided a store for weapons and ammunition and turned southward toward Georgia and St. Augustine. They not only burned several houses and killed some twenty white occupants but also secured more guns, supplies, and slave recruits, which swelled their numbers to over fifty people. After marching over ten miles from their point of departure, they stopped on a field to regroup. As they relaxed, danced, and beat drums to attract additional recruits, armed whites mounted a counterattack and overwhelmed the group. In addition to killing as many of the rebels as possible, they cut off the heads of the dead men and mounted them on posts along the road. Some rebels nonetheless escaped and remained at large for several weeks. Only a month later would colonists report that "the rebellious Negros are quite stopt from doing any further Mischief, many of them [an estimated forty to fifty] having been put to the most cruel Death."

Although some blacks rebelled against the authority of the state, others used the state as an instrument of their liberation. As early as 1661, Emanuel Pieterson, a free black man, and his wife, Reytory, petitioned the New Netherlands court for the freedom of a young black man named Anthony. The petitioners explained that Anthony, whom they had adopted and reared at their own expense, was the orphaned child of free black parents and prayed that "he may be declared by your noble honors to be a free person." The court granted their request and saved Anthony from enslavement. In 1675, Phillip Corven petitioned the Virginia court for his freedom. According to Corven, his emancipation had been guaranteed in the will of his deceased mistress. The will specified that Corven would serve the woman's cousin for eight years after her death; at that time, he would gain his freedom, along with "three barrels of corne and a sute of clothes." Corven's petition stated that he had been sold to another master, "contrary to all honesty and good conscience with threats and a high hand," and twenty years added to his service. In 1726, Peter Vantrump sought his freedom before the General Court of North Carolina, describing himself as "a Free Negro" who "at his own voluntary disposal . . . hired himself" to employers," but on the latest occasion a North Carolina employer held him in bondage against his will: "Your complainant often told the Sayd porter that he was not a Slave but a free man yet nevertheless the Sayd porter now against all right now pretends your complainant to be his Slave and hath held and used him as Such." Despite the desperate pleas of Vantrump and Corven, the state denied their requests for freedom. Yet their petitions demonstrated how some blacks sought to use the law as a tool in their own struggle for freedom.

In their petitions for freedom, African American bondsmen and -women gradually gained moral support from a few whites. In 1688, the Mennonites of Germantown, Pennsylvania, issued the earliest protest against slavery in the English-speaking colonies of North America. The Germantown meeting condemned the "traffic" in human bodies and urged members to stop "robbing and stealing" other people for profit. The statement also concluded that blacks had "as much right to fight for their freedom as you have to keep them slaves," but few Quakers followed the lead of the Germantown meeting during the late seventeenth and early eighteenth centuries. By the 1750s, however, such antislavery sentiment had slowly expanded, as evidenced in New Jersey Quaker John Woolman's famous pamphlet "Some Considerations on the Keeping of Negroes: Recommended to the professors of Christianity of every Denomination." Woolman urged Quakers to bring their antislavery practices in line with their antislavery beliefs. In 1758, the yearly meeting voted to exclude Quaker slaveholders and slave merchants from a voice in the business of the church. The order also rejected slaveholders' financial contributions to the congregation's upkeep. In 1766, the Philadelphia school teacher and abolitionist Anthony Benezet also published an influential antislavery tract, "A Caution and Warning to Great Britain and Her Colonies, in a Short Representation of the Calamitous State of the Enslaved Negroes in the British Dominions." Although such pronouncements did little to diminish the spread of slavery, they did form an important ideological support for the African American struggle against bondage. They also suggested that the struggle against slavery would proceed with a few white allies.

INTER- AND INTRAETHNIC RELATIONS

African American culture and forms of resistance not only were influenced by their confrontation and interactions with Europeans but also were shaped by the widespread interaction of African Americans and Native Americans. From the outset of the colonial era through the eve of the Revolution, blacks and indigenous people developed oscillating relationships characterized by both hostility and friendliness. In Bacon's Rebellion of 1676, African Americans not only helped lower- and middle-class whites challenge the unjust authority of colonial elites but also joined rabidly anti-Indian whites in raids on Indians in Virginia and Maryland. After the rebellion collapsed, eighty enslaved blacks and thirty white indentured servants refused to surrender but were later captured and returned to bondage and servitude. The rebellion also resulted in an act in 1676 that empowered soldiers who had captured Indians to "reteyne and keepe all such Indian slaves or other Indian goods as they either have or hereafter shall take." In 1682, the Virginia assembly provided for the enslavement of Amerindians for life. Indeed, for a while the numbers of Indian slaves expanded along with those of African slaves.

During the eighteenth century, most Africans and their descendants continued to fight alongside whites in European-Indian conflicts. On the one hand—for example, in South Carolina's Yamasee War (c. 1715)—colonial officials enlisted large numbers of blacks to fight against indigenous Americans. On the other hand, some

Amerindians, notably members of the Creek and Cherokee nations, became "slave catchers." They regularly rounded up runaway slaves for profit and returned them to owners. On some occasions, planters charged the indigenous groups like the Creeks with "robbing and plundering us of our Slaves and Goods" in order to return them later for rewards. In 1728, an English agent reported that Indians "have now a Negro belonging to a Man at Pan Pan who has run away from his master and has been catch'd several times and still gets away."

Although most blacks fought alongside whites, they sometimes fought on both sides of Indian-European wars. As early as 1690, New Jersey officials uncovered an African-Indian plot to "cut off" the English and "save none but the Indians and Negroes." In the Tuscarora War of 1711–1712, Native Americans not only captured and tortured some blacks along with whites but also harbored runaways, who eventually intermarried with members of the group and later took part in wars against its enemies. In 1735, the South Carolina assembly reported that "Several Slaves have made their Escape from these Province and very probably are sheltered and protected by the Tuskerora Indians." Blacks also played a major role in Native American trade networks, which officials discouraged and drove deeper underground. In addition to disrupting black-indigenous trade networks, colonial authorities also moved to disrupt social relations between African Americans and Indians by passing legislation to "prevent any Negroe from taking a Wife among the Free Indians, or Free Indians from taking a Slave a Wife."

The emergence of African American culture and responses to bondage were complicated by interactions with Europeans and Amerindians and by the interplay of blacks from different cultural, gender, and class backgrounds as well (see box). The development of the African American slave community was by no means monolithic, smooth, or unproblematic. Blacks from different strata of West African society experienced varied adjustments and responses to New World bondage. Slaveowners often identified enslaved upper-class Africans as the major source of their problems with African labor. European colonial officials frequently complained that such people were "nursed up in luxury and ease, and wholly unaccustomed to work." Since many slaves arrived in North America via the West Indies, slaveowners paid particular attention to the assessments of Caribbean slaveowners like Captain John Stedman of the Dutch colony of Surinam. During the eighteenth century, Stedman reported:

> I have seen some instances of newly imported Negroes refusing to work, nor could promises, threats, rewards nor even blows, prevail; but these had been princes or people of the first rank in their native country . . . whose heroic sentiments still preferred instant death to the baseness and miseries of servitude.

In Virginia one slaveowner, Hugh Jones, agreed that enslaved members of the African aristocracy made the worst slaves:

> Those Negroes make the best slaves that have been slaves in their own country; for they that have been kings and great men are generally lazy, haughty, and obstinate; whereas the others are sharper, better humored, and more laborious.

CHANGING HISTORICAL INTERPRETATIONS

The Slave Culture Debate

Closely interrelated with the controversy over the origins of slavery, discussed in Chapter 3, is the dispute over the fate of African culture under the impact of widespread human bondage in North America. Pro-slavery, segregationist, and racist interpretations of African American history emphasized the inferiority of African culture. According to leading white scholars, slavery served a positive function. It introduced an "inferior people" to the "civilizing processes" of western culture. In this view, the persistence of African culture in the New World, not slavery or racial subordination, restricted black participation in the fruits of European civilization and democratic institutions.

Conversely, antislavery, integrationist, and liberal writers condemned slavery as an inhumane institution that sought to transform human beings into "things." However, although antiracist scholars agreed on the destructive nature of slavery for African people, they offered contrasting interpretations of black culture.

During the inter–World War years, W. E. B. Du Bois and the anthropologist Melville Herskovits argued that important facets of African culture survived the transatlantic crossing. According to these analysts, African culture had a positive impact on the creation of a unique African American culture in the New World. This culture enabled blacks to preserve their humanity under the trying circumstances of bondage, and later Jim Crow, as free but unequal citizens.

On the other hand, E. Franklin Frazier, one of the most influential black sociologists of the period, accented the destruction of African cultural norms in the vortex of the international slave trade and the rapid spread of the plantation system through the American South. In 1939, Frazier published his classic *The Negro Family in the United States*. He argued that the institution of slavery not only destroyed the African language, ideas, beliefs, and social practices but also hampered enslaved blacks' acquisition of the rudiments of western culture, including viable forms of family and kinship relations.

In the aftermath of World War II, a growing number of scholars and public policy experts adopted Frazier's interpretation of African American culture and family life. This scholarship peaked with the publication of Daniel Patrick Moynihan's *The Negro Family: The Case for National Action* (1965). Moynihan and others argued that "the slave was totally removed from the protection of organized society," was "totally ignorant of and completely cut off" from the past, and possessed "absolutely no hope for the future."

To be sure, Frazier, Moynihan, and others counteracted prevailing racist interpretations of slave culture. They accented the ways that color- or race-based slavery undercut the humanity of African people and forged a brutal context for the development of African American life. Yet, by overlooking the precise ways that African Americans survived the horrors of human bondage, such scholars and public policy experts reinforced certain stereotypes about black responses to slavery and racial subordination.

CONTINUED

Beginning with John Blassingame's groundbreaking study *The Slave Community* (1972), growing numbers of scholars (most notably Herbert Gutman in *The Black Family in Slavery and Freedom* [1976]) resuscitated the ideas of Herskovits and Du Bois. They stressed the ways that blacks built on their African experiences to create a new African American culture and forged a variety of subtle and not so subtle forms of resistance to enslavement.

Similar to recent scholarship on the origins of slavery controversy, contemporary research underscores African American culture creation as a dynamic historical process. The development of New World black culture entailed the autonomous activities of Africans themselves as well as their ongoing socioeconomic, demographic, cultural, and political interactions with Europeans and Amerindians. In recent years, however, scholars like Deborah Gray White, Jacqueline Jones, and Brenda Stevenson have emphasized the role that women as well as men played in developing African American culture and families and against what odds.

Perhaps even more so than the origins debate, the culture contest carries huge import for contemporary forms of inequality and efforts to redress racial injustice. Contemporary historical scholarship underscores the ongoing intersections and separations of African American ideas, beliefs, and social practices on the one hand and those of Euro-Americans on the other. Current social movement activists, leaders, teachers, and public policy makers might well learn from these insights.

The Muslim captive Job Ben Solomon, discussed earlier, had not only participated in the sale of Africans before his capture but also agreed to continue the practice in exchange for his freedom.

Like other aspects of black life, the African background also conditioned gender differences within the African American community. In societies like eighteenth-century Gambia, women carried out the consistent, heavy, and laborious farming and household chores. In some cases, "the men were occupied for only about two months of the year, at seed time and harvest . . . but for the rest of the year they hardly seemed even to bother to hunt or fish." As noted in Chapter 1, women were highly valued as childbearers and agriculturists in African societies. Thus, the preponderance of men over women was a consequence not merely of European demand for males, but of African societies' restrictions on who could be enslaved. In the New World, black women continued to combine field and household labor, whereas few enslaved men performed domestic chores. Moreover, as planters adopted new technology, moved from hoe to plow, and diversified the production of farm crops, men dominated work with the new tools and learned a wider variety of skills and jobs beyond field labor. For their part, women continued to hoe by hand, often concentrating on areas that the plows missed. Only domestic service in the planters' households relieved women of field work. Even here, planters preferred to use young girls and elderly women for such household duties.

The division between African-born and American-born blacks also represented an important source of difference within the slave community. The American-born, or "seasoned," Africans instructed the "new Negroes," took the lion's share of skilled jobs, and gained opportunities for mobility beyond the master's household and plantation. Before sex ratios evened out, American-born black men also took a disproportionate share of available black women as spouses. As the African population increased, planters elevated the American-born blacks of earlier years to favored status. In the Chesapeake, the American-born concentrated in the established Tidewater region, whereas the new Africans occupied the harsh and quite isolated Piedmont frontier, where they had relatively fewer contacts with whites or with the most highly Americanized portions of the black population. Similarly, South Carolina's plantation majority developed in substantial isolation from whites and the highly assimilated African American population in and around Charlestown. Here, efforts to create a new African American language and culture entailed substantial internal conflict and turmoil. Africans who turned to European forms of reading sometimes faced ridicule from others, for example. When one European minister trained a few baptized blacks for missionary work among the slaves, he soon reported "some Profane men who laught at their Devotions." Another minister reported simply that "all other slaves do laugh at them."

Unlike in the Chesapeake and early Deep South colonies, the line between the American- and African-born was less sharply drawn in the northern colonies. Seasoned Africans from the West Indies and American-born blacks dominated the northern black population. During the 1740s and 1750s, however, the rapid upsurge of new imports revitalized African elements of northern black culture and modified the previous salience of European forms. By the eve of the American Revolution, a new and more Africanized black culture had emerged in the North.

≈

FROM THEIR SETTLEMENT AT JAMESTOWN through the late seventeenth century, blacks in North America responded to bondage within the context of indentured servitude. During the late seventeenth and early eighteenth centuries, however, the transformation of Africans into "slaves for life" undermined the multiracial nature of the labor force while introducing new cultural tensions and social conflicts among Africans and their American-born descendants. Despite such difficulties, as the African slave trade declined and blacks made the transition to a self-reproducing population, the gap between African- and American-born blacks closed considerably. By the eve of the American Revolution, African American culture and slave communities gradually took shape in British North America. These processes gained potent expression in African American language, family life, religion, leisure time activities, and diverse modes of resistance, ranging from subtle day-to-day conflicts with overseers and plantation owners to open protests and rebellion against the system of bondage itself. In the meantime, as the ideas of the American Revolution—liberty, equality, and citizenship—gained momentum among white colonists, African Americans prepared to launch a more overt, articulate, and concerted effort to win their own freedom. This story is told in Chapter 5.

CHAPTER 5

~

African Americans and the
American Revolution

Following the conclusion of the French and Indian War in 1763, the relations between the colonies and Great Britain deteriorated. The British imperial government imposed new taxes and tightened control over colonial commerce. As the new restrictions took effect, the colonies increasingly resorted to revolutionary ideology to justify their resistance. White colonists protested against what they called the British Parliament's effort to "enslave" them. Their ideas of revolution rested on the premise that human beings had certain "natural" and "inalienable rights" to freedom that were given to them at birth. As the colonists filled the air with cries of "liberty" against "tyranny," enslaved and free blacks, particularly in the northern colonies, not only joined street demonstrations but also participated in the first military engagements between the colonial forces and the imperial army. Their efforts played an important role in the American Declaration of Independence in 1776.

Although African Americans supported the independence movement, the colonists soon defined the revolutionary struggle in racist terms and barred blacks from the Continental army. Blacks clearly understood this contradiction between the colonists' insistence on freedom for themselves and their enslavement of Africans and African Americans. As whites excluded blacks from the struggle for national liberation, African Americans employed the rhetoric of the Revolution to buttress their own fight for freedom. For blacks, bond and free, however, the road to liberation was not necessarily synonymous with support for the American revolutionaries. Following rejection by the American forces, large numbers of enslaved people escaped from the plantations and took refuge behind British lines. Only then, as the British welcomed blacks into their ranks, did the colonists drop the racial bar and enlist blacks in the revolutionary struggle.

BLACK RESISTANCE, ANTISLAVERY SENTIMENT, AND THE BEGINNINGS OF THE REVOLUTION

From the Stamp Act crisis of the 1760s through the mid-1770s, African Americans took advantage of the revolutionary struggle and raised their own chants for "Liberty." Although contemporary whites like Henry Laurens of South Carolina interpreted the words of African Americans as "thoughtless imitation," blacks soon demonstrated the deep meaning that freedom held for them. In November 1773, a group of enslaved Virginians held a "secret meeting" to select a leader to guide their participation in the war. When the Virginian James Madison heard of their efforts, he exclaimed that the "revolutionary rhetoric" and growing resistance of slaves "should be concealed as well as suppressed." At about the same time, a South Carolina legislator complained that "it was already known, [the slaves] entertained ideas that the present contest was for obliging us to give them their liberty."

Freedom Petitions and Resistance Activities

African American use of republican ideology emerged most forcefully in the northern colonies, where blacks lodged a rising number of freedom petitions with colonial officials. In 1773, enslaved Bostonians delivered emancipation petitions to General Thomas Gage, commander in chief of the British forces in North America; to the governor of the Massachusetts Bay Colony; and to the Massachusetts General Court. In one case, a group of blacks petitioned for freedom, exclaiming that "a Grate Number of Blacks" were "held in a state of slavery within the bowels of a free and christian country." Another group petitioned the governor for permission to work for themselves one day a week and to use their earnings to purchase themselves. The petitioners expected "great things from men who have made such a noble stand against the designs of their *fellow men* to enslave them." Such petitions not only invoked the principles of "liberty" but also underscored the point with references to the Bible: "We desire to bless GOD, who loves Mankind, who sent his Son to die for their Salvation, and who is no Respecter of Persons (see box)."

During the war years, black men and women escalated their petition drive for freedom. The language of such petitions became even more forceful. In Pennsylvania, when conservatives sought to limit their freedom, blacks petitioned the legislature in no uncertain terms: "We fear we are too bold, but our all is at stake. The grand question of slavery or liberty is too important for us to be silent—it is the momentous passion of our lives; if we are silent this day, we may be silent forever." In January 1777, Massachusetts blacks based their demand for freedom on the same principles that led to the break with England, pleading that the principle of liberty "pleads stronger than a thousand arguments." Two years later, in Portsmouth, New Hampshire, some nineteen blacks asked that "the name of slave may not more be heard in a land gloriously contending for the sweets of freedom." Portsmouth blacks also proclaimed that "the God of nature gave them life and freedom, upon

SOURCES FROM THE PAST

— 1773

Africans in Boston Petition the Governor for Relief

PROVINCE OF THE MASSACHUSETTS-BAY.

To his Excellancy THOMAS HUTCHINSON, Esq; Governor;

To the Honorable His Majesty's Council, and

To the Honorable House of REPRESENTATIVES in General Court assembled at BOSTON, the 6th Day of January, 1773.

The humble PETITION of many SLAVES, living in the Town of BOSTON, and other Towns in the Province, is this, namely,

That your Excellency and Honors, and the Honorable the Representatives would be pleased to take their unhappy State and Condition under your wise and just Consideration.

We desire to bless GOD, who loves Mankind, who sent his Son to die for their Salvation, and who is no Respecter of Persons; that he hath lately put it into the Hearts of Multitudes on both Sides of the Water, to bear our Burthens, some of whom are Men of great Note and Influence; who have pleaded our Cause with Arguments which we hope will have their weight with this Honorable Court.

We presume not to dictate to your EXCELLENCY and Honors, being willing to rest our Cause on your Humanity and Justice; yet would beg leave to say a Word or two on the Subject.

Although some of the Negroes are vicious, (who doubtless may be punished and restrained by the same Laws which are in Force against other of the King's Subjects) there are many others of a quite different Character, and who if made free, would soon be able as well as willing to bear a Part in the Public Charges; many of them good natural Parts, are discreet, sober, honest, and industrious; and may it not be said of many, that they are virtuous and religious, although their Condition is in itself so unfriendly to Religion, and every moral Virtue except *Patience*. How many of that Number have there been, and now are in this Province, who have had every Day of their Lives imbittered with this most intolerable Reflection, That, let their Behaviour be what it will, neither they, nor their Children to all Generations, shall ever be able to do, or to possess and enjoy any Thing, no, not even *Life itself*, but in a Manner as the *Beasts that perish*.

We have no Property! We have no Wives! No Children! We have no City! No Country! But we have a Father in Heaven, and we are determined as far as his Grace shall enable us, and as far as our degraded contemptuous Life will admit, to keep all his Commandments: Especially will we be obedient to our Masters, so long as GOD in his sovereign Providence shall *suffer* us to be holden in Bondage. . . .

We humbly beg leave to add but this one Thing more: We pray for such Relief only, which by no Possibility can ever be productive of the least Wrong or Injury to our Masters; but to us will be as Life from the dead.

Signed, FELIX
1773

Source: Deirdre Mullane, ed., *Crossing the Danger Water: Three Hundred Years of African-American Writing* (New York: Doubleday, 1993), pp. 32–33.

the terms of most perfect equality with other men. That freedom is an inherent right of the human species."

Blacks also hoped to alleviate the poverty of their children and ensure their freedom. A Connecticut petition referred to "the miserable conditions" of children "who are training up, and kept in preparation, for a like State of Bondage and Servitude as their parents." In Boston, Belinda petitioned for the freedom of her daughter as well as her own. Belinda decried the injustice of slavery and the exploitation of her labor:

> The face of your petitioner is now marked with the furrows of time, and her frame feebly bending under the oppression of years, while she, by the laws of the land, is denied the enjoyment of one morsel of that immense wealth, a part whereof hath been accumulated by her own industry, and the whole augmented by her servitude.

The petitioner urged the general court to provide a living allowance "out of the estate of Colonel Royall [her owner], as will prevent her, and her more infirm daughter, from misery in the greatest extreme." Another black woman suggested that she would continue to work "most agreeable" for herself and her family if placed "on terms of freedom."

African Americans not only petitioned governmental bodies but also participated in street demonstrations and overt encounters with imperial authorities. In 1770, they took part in the street fighting that became known as the Boston Massacre. In the violent encounter between British soldiers and colonists, the black sailor Crispus Attucks lost his life. Part African and part Nantucket Indian, Attucks was a runaway slave who worked on ships and in a local rope factory. When the English government increased the number of troops stationed in Boston, soldiers sometimes supplemented their pay by taking civilian jobs. This practice undercut the livelihood of black and white workers like Attucks, who blamed British officials for widespread suffering among his fellow workers. In a letter to the governor, Attucks also warned, "You will hear further from us hereafter."

Under the leadership of Crispus Attucks, a multiracial group of working people marched against the British military guard at the Custom House on King Street. Attucks urged the group to "attack the main-guard," or as he exclaimed, "strike at the root." Ignoring the fact that Attucks was over forty years old at the time, one contemporary observer described the group as "saucy boys, negroes and mulattoes, Irish Teagues and outlandish jacktarrs." When British soldiers finally fired into the crowd, Attucks was the first of four colonials to die in the revolution that transformed the thirteen colonies into an independent nation. At the funeral services for fallen victims of English tyranny, white Bostonians honored the dead without regard to the color line. As the *Massachusetts Gazette* reported, "all the Bells tolled a solemn Peal," and the townsmen laid Attucks to rest with his white compatriots "in one vault in the middle burying ground."

In the throes of social conflict, black women also found a militant voice. When the earl of Dartmouth, the king's representative in North America, arrived in

British troops fire on Crispus Attucks and other demonstrators in the confrontation that became known as the Boston Massacre. *Bettmann/Corbis*

Boston in August 1772, the black poet Phillis Wheatley expressed hope that he would fight tyranny:

No more *America*, in mournnful strain
Of wrongs, and grievances unredress'd complain,
No longer shall thou dread the iron chain,
Which wanton *Tyranny* with lawless hand
Has made, and with it meant t' en-slave the land.
Should you, my lord, while you peruse my song,
Wonder from whence my love for *Freedom* sprung,
Whence flow these wishes for the common good,
By feeling hearts alone best understood,
I, young in life, by seeming cruel fate,
Was snatch'd from *Afric's* fancy'd happy seat:
What pangs excruciating must molest,
What sorrows labour in my parent's breast?
Steel'd was that soul and by no misery mov'd

That from a father seiz'd his babe belov'd
Such, such my case. And can I then but pray
Others may never feel tyrannic sway?

Whereas during the 1760s, Wheatley had written, "Twas mercy brought me from my Pagan Land," she now concluded: "Such, such my case. And can I then but pray / Others may never feel tyrannic sway?"

Three years later, black women supported colonial military encounters with British forces. In early 1775, when British commander General Thomas Gage sent officers from Boston to explore the roads of Suffolk and Worcester, they encountered a black woman cook in a local tavern. The woman understood and discouraged their plans, as suggested by the report of a British officer:

At first she was very civil, but afterwards began to eye us very attentively . . . when we observed to her that it was a very fine country, upon which she answered so it is, and we have brave fellows to defend it, and if you go up any higher you will find it is so.

Fearing for their lives, the British officers "resolved not to sleep there that night."

Black men fought in the first battles of war. They served in early regiments from Connecticut, Rhode Island, New Hampshire, New York, Virginia, and especially

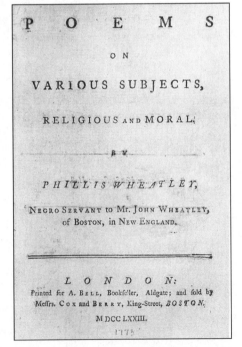

A London publisher released Phillis Wheatley's collection of poems, with this portrait, in 1773.
Left: Boston Athenaeum; Right: American Antiquarian Society

Massachusetts, which early on accepted black volunteers for its "minutemen" and militia units. Some historians describe the slave Prince Easterbrook as "the first to get into the fight" at the Battles of Lexington and Concord on 19 April 1775. At the Battle of Bunker Hill in Boston, according to contemporary sources, the black soldier Cuff Whittemore "fought to the last, and when compelled to retreat, though wounded . . . he seized the sword [of a British officer] slain in the re-doubt. . . . He served faithfully throughout the war, with many hair-breadth scrapes from sword and pestilence." Also, at the Battle of Bunker Hill, another black man, Peter Salem, received credit for killing a British officer, one Major Pit-cairn: "A negro man belonging to Grotan, took aim at Major Pitcairn, as he was ral-lying the dispersed British troops, & shot him thro' the head. . . ."

Following the Battle of Bunker Hill, fourteen white Massachusetts officers petitioned the legislature to recognize the valor of another black rebel, Salem Poor. "In the person of this said Negro," the petition stated, "centers a brave and gallant soldier." General John Thomas, commander of a brigade in Boston, later described black soldiers as "in General, Equally serviceable with other men, for Fatigue & in action; many of them have proved themselves brave." In Virginia, a free black, William Flora, and an anonymous bondsman participated in the Battle of Great Bridge. The bondsman rendered invaluable service as a spy, while Flora "was the last sentinel that came into the breast work" and "did not leave his post until he had fired several times . . . amidst a shower of musket balls [from the British]."

The homefront activities of black men and women reinforced the exploits of black soldiers. As the Virginian Edmund Randolph noted, black women "could handle deadly weapons" and joined their men in Maroon settlements in the swamps of South Carolina, Georgia, and parts of North Carolina. In December 1774, in St. Andrew Parish, Georgia, six black men and four women owned by Captain Morris made a desperate bid for freedom. They not only killed the over-seer and his wife but also murdered or wounded neighboring plantation owners and members of their families. Similarly, in the summer of 1775, in St. Bartholomew Parish, South Carolina, several preachers, including two black women, confessed that they planned "to take" their freedom by "killing the whites." In Wilmington, North Carolina, authorities uncovered a conspiracy to emancipate slaves from Beaufort, Pitt, and Craven Counties. According to reports, under the leadership of a bondsman named Merrick, blacks planned to "fall on and destroy the family where they lived, then to proceed, from House to House (burn-ing as they went) until they arrived in the Back Country."

In the North and South, enslaved blacks often defied the law and met in secret religious meetings before sunrise and after sunset. In these secret gatherings, black ministers sometimes preached to "Great crowds of Negroes" in their own language and style, telling them that "Our Lord . . . was about to alter the World & set the Negroes Free." In Savannah, the black preacher named David spoke for many when he declared that he "did not doubt, but God would send Deliverance to the Negroes, from the power of their Masters as he freed the Children of Israel from Egyptian Bondage." In 1782, the New York minister and writer Jupiter Hammon published a sermon entitled "A Winter Piece." In this sermon, Hammon supported the quest for freedom in this world:

> My Brothers, many of us are seeking temporal freedom, and I wish you may obtain it; remember that all power in heaven and on earth belongs to God. . . . But how art we to forget that God spoke these words, saying, I am the Lord thy God, which brought thee out of the house of bondage.

At another point, Hammon echoed the rights-of-man movement:

> That liberty is a great thing we may know from our feelings, and we may likewise judge from the conduct of the white people in this war. . . . I must say that I have hoped that God would open up their eyes, when they were so much engaged for liberty, to think of the state of the poor blacks.

Antislavery Sentiment

As African Americans deepened their resistance activities, the contradiction between their enslavement and the struggle for national liberation loomed large. Some white revolutionary leaders gradually recognized the contradiction and spoke out against human bondage. As early as the 1760s, James Otis of Boston had expressed the belief that blacks and whites, born in America, "are free born by the law of nature." In August 1772, Benjamin Franklin wrote from England to the Quaker Anthony Benezet: "I am glad to hear that the disposition against keeping Negroes grows more general in North America. Several pieces had been lately printed here against the practice, and I hope in time it will be taken into consideration and suppressed by the legislature." In October 1773, the *Pennsylvania Chronicle* was even more direct. "While we persist in the practice of enslaving Africans," the editor exclaimed, "our mouths ought to be shut entirely as to any duties or taxes which Great Britain may see cause to lay upon us."

In 1774, the Continental Congress voted to outlaw the continuation of the slave trade and sanctioned a boycott against those who continued the practice. Although some states, such as Pennsylvania, imposed prohibitively high tariffs on the traffic, Connecticut and Rhode Island outlawed it altogether. According to the Rhode Island law, "Those who are desirous of enjoying all the advantages of liberty themselves should be willing to extend personal liberty to others." In a similar vein, the *New Jersey Gazette* proclaimed that "the man who only abhors tyranny when it points to himself . . . is altogether unworthy of the esteem of the virtuous, and can never . . . merit the confidence of a free people." Likewise, in the *Massachusetts Spy,* the Worcester County committee of correspondence denounced the institution of slavery and resolved to use its influence toward "emancipating the NEGROES." In New York, the young attorney John Jay warned that if the new nation failed to free blacks, then "her own prayers to Heaven for liberty will be impious."

WHEREAS the NEGROES in the counties of Briftol and Worcefter, the 24th of March laft, petitioned the Committees of Correfpondence for the county of Worcefter (then convened in Worcefter) to aflift them in obtaining their freedom.   THEREFORE,
In County Convention, June 14th, 1775.
RESOLVED, That we abhor the enflaving of any of the human race, and particularly of the NEGROES in this country. And that whenever there fhall be a door opened, or opportunity prefent, for any thing to be done toward the emancipating the NEGROES; we will ufe our influence and endeavour that fuch a thing may be effected,   *Atteft.* WILLIAM HENSHAW, Clerk.

Antislavery resolution of the Worcester County Committee of Correspondence. *American Antiquarian Society*

After putting down the slave revolt of 1774, slaveholders of St. Andrew Parish, Georgia, adopted an antislavery resolution. The signatories declared their intention "to show the world that we are not influenced by any contracted or interested motives, but a general philanthropy for all mankind." The resolution condemned slavery as an unnatural practice and then promised "to use our utmost endeavors for the manumission of our Slaves in this Colony." In his "A Summary View of the Rights of British America" (1774), the Virginian Thomas Jefferson condemned Britain for perpetuating the slave trade and slavery. In his early draft of the Declaration of Independence, Jefferson elaborated upon this antislavery theme. According to Jefferson, the King had waged "cruel war against human nature itself, violating its most sacred rights of life and liberty in the person of a distant people, who never offended him, captivating and carrying them into slavery in another hemisphere, or to incur miserable death in their transportation thither." (See the Documents section.) Although slaveholders rejected this passage and Jefferson deleted it from the final draft of the Declaration of Independence, it demonstrated how some whites moved toward antislavery ideas during the struggle with England. In April 1775, the abolitionist movement gained even greater articulation when Anthony Benezet, Thomas Paine, and several Quakers met at a tavern in Philadelphia and formed the Society for the Relief of Free Negroes Unlawfully Held in Bondage. Nearly a decade later, the society became the Society for Promoting the Abolition of Slavery, Relief of Free Negroes Unlawfully Held in Bondage and for Improving the Condition of the African Race.

Some white women also spoke out against slavery. The countess of Huntingdon in England and Sarah Osborne of Newport, Rhode Island, played crucial roles in the spread of abolitionist ideas. As promoters of the evangelical faith and religious and educational activities, these women influenced blacks like Bristol Yamma, John Quamine, Newport Gardner, and Osborn Tanner as well as white ministers like Ezra Stiles and Samuel Hopkins of Newport. These women had a lot to do with the forthright words of men like Reverend Hopkins, who warned that "if we continue in this evil practice . . . have we any reason to expect deliverance from the calamities we are under?" Abigail Adams of Boston expressed best the revolutionary sentiment of white women when she wrote to her husband, John: "It always appeared a most iniquitous scheme to me to fight ourselves for what we are daily robbing and plundering from those who have as good a right to freedom as we have." As such sentiments took hold, some slaveholders freed enslaved blacks before joining the Continental army. One Connecticut slaveowner freed his slaves, declaring, "I will not fight for liberty and leave a slave at home."

Exclusion from the Military

Despite the spread of antislavery sentiment and the participation of blacks in the early skirmishes of the war, colonists soon rejected the participation of blacks as soldiers. In May 1775, the Massachusetts Committee on Public Safety prohibited the enlistment of "any deserter from the ministerial army" as well as "any stroller, negro, or vagabond." Another enunciation of the decree barred "Negroes, Boys unable to bear Arms nor Old men unfit to endure the Fatigues of the Campaign." The commonwealth's new militia act excluded "Negroes, Indians and Mulattoes." Washington, the Continental army, and other New England and mid-Atlantic states followed suit: Rhode Island, Connecticut, Pennsylvania, Delaware, New Jersey, and New York. The language of such statutes varied, but the end result was the same. As the New York statute put it, "All bought servants during their Servitude shall be free from being listed in any Troop or Company within this Colony." After a brief period of debate, the colonies decided to bar all blacks, enslaved and free, from armed service. The order also called for the expulsion of blacks already under arms. Only the vigorous protests of black soldiers allowed them to serve out their terms.

As white authorities would do later during the Civil War, colonial officials offered conflicting reasons for excluding blacks. Some argued that white soldiers would resist serving alongside blacks, whom they considered "inferior." Others argued that blacks were "cowardly" and would not fight. Still others maintained that armed blacks would take revenge against whites. In Maryland, by the fall of 1775, authorities reported that "the insolence of the Negroes in this country is come to such a height, that we are under a necessity of disarming them which we affected [sic] on Saturday last. We took about eighty guns, some bayonets, swords, etc." For their part, the antislavery friends of blacks argued that it was improper or wrong to ask blacks to spill blood for a cause that would not result in their own freedom. The Massachusetts Committee on Public Safety argued that the use of bondsmen was "inconsistent with the principles that are to be supported, and reflect dishonor on this colony." Above all, however, slaveowners perceived the enlistment of blacks as a threat to their property investment.

As the struggle for liberty intensified, slaveholders increased rather than lessened their vigilance and repression of African Americans. Southern colonists set up special committees to investigate rumors of slave insurrections, formed new militia companies, and increased their efforts to apprehend suspects in revolts or plots to revolt. Throughout the war, planters continued to execute enslaved blacks for insurrectionary activities, both real and imagined. In Virginia, in April 1781, authorities tried and convicted Jack, a bondsman, for robberies, attempted poisoning, and "Engaging and Enlisting several Negroes to raise in Arms and Join the British, the said Jack to be their Captain." Before his execution, Jack managed to escape, freeing a number of other "slaves, deserters, and Tories" in the process. He remained at large for several weeks before being captured and apparently put to death. In the same year, the Virginia court found another slave, John Taylor's Billy, guilty of waging war against the state. The court sentenced Billy "to be hanged by the neck until dead and his head to be severed from his body and stuck up at some public cross road on a pole." Although Billy received a reprieve from the governor, others were not so lucky.

Not all enslaved blacks took advantage of the opportunity to desert their owners. One slaveowner reported that "not one of them left me during the war . . . although they had had great offers." Even when captured by the British, according to the same slaveholder, "they always contrived to make their escapes and return home." The British offered "clothes," "money," and "freedom" to a Virginia bondsman, William Hooper, who pretended to accept the offer but later deserted and rejoined his owner some seventy miles away. Other blacks stayed put and became virtually free people on their owners' land. In South Carolina, blacks often produced and sold crops for their own benefit. In some cases, when an overseer sought to exert his authority, blacks paid no attention to his orders, or as some owners reported, they showed "no subjection" to the overseer's commands.

SHIFTING MILITARY POLICIES AND THE RECRUITMENT OF BLACK TROOPS

Although African American resistance was by no means limited to the conditions ushered in by the revolutionary struggle, the growing conflict between England and the colonists opened up new possibilities for freedom. British officials took advantage of the colonists' efforts to protect their property rights in slaves. On one occasion, General Gage warned South Carolina planters that their opposition to the Crown might mean "that your rice and indigo will be brought to market by Negroes instead of white people." After seizing the city of Williamsburg for the English Crown in the spring of 1775, Lord Dunmore threatened to emancipate the enslaved people and "reduce the City of Williamsburg to ashes." On 7 November 1775, he dropped the threat and issued a proclamation promising slaves of rebels freedom in exchange for service in the British army. Dunmore's proclamation stated in part:

> I do hereby further declare all indented servants, negroes, or others, (appertaining to rebels,) free, that are able to bear arms, they adjoining His Majesty's Troops, as soon as may be, for the more speedily reducing the Colony to a proper sense of their duty, to His Majesty's Crown and dignity.

Similarly, as the war unfolded and spread from the North and Upper South into the Deep South, British officials expanded on Dunmore's strategy. On 30 June 1779, the commander in chief of the British army, Henry Clinton, issued the Philipsburg Proclamation, which extended freedom to blacks in exchange for participation in the military forces.

British Recruitment

The Philipsburg and Dunmore Proclamations were by no means humanitarian or emancipationist policies. They were military measures designed to bring the recalcitrant colonies into line. Before Lord Dunmore issued his famous edict, for example, African Americans had offered "to join him and take up arms." Dunmore not only dismissed their overture but also threatened "severe" reprisals against them should they "renew their application." Dunmore's proclamation applied to able-bodied slaves of "rebels" only, leaving slaves of loyalists in chains. In addition, the Philipsburg Proclamation stipulated that blacks captured behind enemy lines would be sold for the profit of their captors.

Despite limitations, British military policies increased opportunities for blacks to escape from rebel plantations. African Americans had already increased their perception of England as an ally when the English court delivered its ruling in the famous Somerset case of 1772. James Somerset had been purchased in Virginia, but his master later took him abroad, where Somerset escaped after two years on English soil. Through the intervention of the English abolitionist Granville Sharp, Somerset gained his freedom on English soil, where, the chief justice argued, the free "law of England" overruled the institution of slavery. This ruling encouraged many North American blacks, and some took dramatic and direct steps to test its promise. Described as a "cunning, artful, sensible Fellow," a Georgia house servant named Bacchus forged a pass, assumed the name John Christian, and headed for a "Vessel bound for Great Britain, from knowledge he has determined of Somerset's case." As early as June 1775, when Dunmore abandoned Williamsburg and took refuge aboard the ship *Fowey* at Yorktown, he added black runaways to his fleeing contingent of three hundred white soldiers. Following his proclamation, however, some sources suggest that some two hundred runaways joined Dunmore "immediately" and that another hundred followed within a week.

By early December 1775, the British had armed three hundred blacks. They outfitted them in military uniforms with the words "Liberty to Slaves" inscribed across the breast. The governor dubbed these soldiers Lord Dunmore's Ethiopian Regiment. Before the New Year, black soldiers fought at the Battle of Kemp's Landing, where they pushed the revolutionaries back and captured two of their commanding officers. In the Battle of Great Bridge, however, the revolutionary forces, which also included enslaved and free blacks, forced the governor's troops to retreat. Although Dunmore would abandon his Chesapeake landbase by August 1776, he retained naval operations along the coast. Chesapeake planters soon transported blacks, their families, and other valuables inland away from the coast, where English ships offered asylum to runaways and launched raids on nearby plantations. Chesapeake authorities also increased the number of militia companies charged with stopping "the Negros flocking down from the interior parts of the country" to British lines. Despite such precautions, blacks continued to desert the plantations of Virginia and Maryland. In February 1777, British ships reported receiving an estimated 3,000 runaways from the tobacco counties of Virginia. After the Philipsburg decree and the opening of the Deep South campaign, South Carolina and Georgia also reported growing numbers of fugitives. By war's end, some 15,000 to 20,000 blacks had deserted to British lines. Some 800 to 1,000 of these blacks served as soldiers in the British army. As one report stated, they were not "enticed" but "came as freemen and demanded protection." They often presented themselves, saying that "they came for the King." Some expressed the belief that "the War was come to help the poor Negroes."

Some northern blacks also joined loyalists and resisted the patriots. The black contingents, however, generally disappeared with the retreat of the British. In late 1775, a small number of loyalist blacks supplemented the 561 blacks in Boston. By early 1776, when the British departed, they took their "company of Negroes" with them. In New York, however, the British occupied the state for most of the war and recruited blacks as teamsters and members of the "Light Dragoons." In New Jersey, a black man named Tye led a group of loyalists in attacks on plantations and liberated enslaved blacks and white indentured servants.

Revolutionary Enlistment of Black Troops

As enslaved and free blacks defected to British lines in rising numbers, the revolutionaries dropped racial barriers and enlisted blacks into the military. Washington became convinced that the outcome of the war hinged on "which side can arm the Negroes the faster." Moreover, white draftees remained low, and desertion among whites had become a major problem. An estimated one-third of white American troops deserted during the course of their service. In the Deep South, turnover among the troops was especially large, requiring about four hundred thousand enlisted men to maintain only thirty-five thousand men in active duty. Furthermore, the Continental army faced increasing reverses on the battlefield. Key military defeats at Forts Washington and Lee forced the Continental army to retreat across the state of New Jersey. Under the impact of these military setbacks, one historian concludes that "the Continental Army dissolved like a morning fog."

As early as 1777, when the Continental Congress set troop quotas for the various states, the racial bar started to fall. Military officials in the northern, mid-Atlantic, and Upper South states ignored state laws and informally admitted blacks to the military. At the same time, states gradually modified their legal ban on blacks. By October 1777, the Connecticut legislature had exempted from military service any two white men who secured one able-bodied substitute, without regard to "color or status." Another Connecticut statute exonerated from financial responsibility any slaveholder who manumitted his or her slaves. This law not only encouraged masters to free blacks but also encouraged bondsmen to enlist in military service in exchange for freedom.

By 1781, most northern states had passed laws permitting whites to send enslaved men to fight on their behalf. Rhode Island declared "free" any slave who enlisted and passed muster. The state compensated slaveowners and then requested reimbursement from the Continental Congress. Most northern states compensated masters about $400 and promised the bondsmen freedom and a bounty of $50 upon discharge from military service. In lieu of cash, however, New York provided a sizable land grant to any master who enrolled an able-bodied slave into the armed forces for a period of three years. A white officer applauded the change, writing in his journal that "the Negro can take the field instead of his master, and therefore no regiment is to be seen in which there are not Negroes in abundance, and . . . among them are able-bodied and strong fellows." Some states used historical precedent to justify their decision. As Rhode Island officials put it: "History affords us frequent precedents of the wisest, freest and bravest nations having liberated their slaves, and enlist them as soldiers to fight in defence of their country." In a letter to Washington, one northern governor exclaimed that it was "impossible" to "recruit our battalions in any other way."

Upper South states also enlisted black troops. Between the summer of 1780 and the spring of 1781, Maryland authorized the enlistment of enslaved and free blacks. One officer urged the governor to reconsider the execution of a young black convicted of crime, because "he is young healthy and would make a fine soldier." Some Virginians also contemplated, then dropped, plans to raise a regiment of 750 slaves. One advocate declared: "I am of the opinion that the Blacks will make excellent soldiers—indeed experience proves it." Another attacked the opposition: "As to the danger of training them to Arms—tis the child of distempered imagination. There are some people who are forever frightening themselves with Bugbears of their own Creation." But planters feared an economic loss and refused to put the patriot cause above their material interests. As one planter put it, "The price if paid . . . is not equal to the value of a healthy, strong young negro man." Many Virginia slaveholders, as one observer stated, "considered it unjust, sacrificing the property of a part of the community to the exoneration of the rest." Although Virginia banned the enlistment of slaves, it opened its ranks to free blacks.

As northern and Upper South states enabled slaveowners to escape military service by enlisting slaves and free blacks, Deep South states used slaves as an incentive to attract whites to the revolutionary army. South Carolina and Georgia offered slaves as gifts to reward high-ranking officers, pay expenses, and entice poor whites into the military. In April 1781, some South Carolina military officials offered slave bounties by rank: private (one adult slave servant), a colonel (three adult slaves and a child servant). Since these bounties were usually predicated on raiding loyalist property and taking of slaves, they often fell short of their promise and left many white enlisted men and officers disgruntled. Consequently, some slave raids included the property of patriots as well as loyalists.

Although Deep South states rejected the direct use of black troops, the Continental Congress eventually approved the use of black troops, enslaved and free. Like state governments, the central government promised bondsmen freedom and a cash bounty following the war. By 24 August 1778, the Continental army listed some 755 blacks distributed among fourteen brigades. By war's end, an estimated 5,000 blacks had served in the revolutionary army. Contemporary observers soon reported growing numbers of blacks among the white troops. African American soldiers had adopted such surnames as Freeman, Freedom, Liberty, and Free. Many of these blacks represented direct substitutes for whites seeking to elude military service. In New Fairfield, Connecticut, a black man substituted for Jonathan Giddings. In Newark, New Jersey, a slave named Cudjoe served for his master. In Anne Arundel County, Maryland, a slave named Anthony substituted for a Thomas Johnson Jr. In North Carolina, when military officials caught the white deserter William Kitchen, he produced a slave to serve out his time. In another case, a New Jersey man purchased Samuel Suffin for the express purpose of fulfilling his military obligation.

AFRICAN AMERICANS IN THE REVOLUTIONARY FORCES

Black soldiers performed the hard labor and drudgery tasks for fellow white troops as well as officers. Military records are replete with references to blacks as laborers, orderlies, or semidomestic servants. They transported supplies, repaired roads, erected fortifications, dug graves, cooked, washed, and cleaned encampments. White soldiers detested such duties and insisted that blacks perform them wherever and whenever possible. In June 1777, the quartermaster general at Ticonderoga formed a black regiment of "constant fatigue men." In addition to fatigue duty, African Americans became personal servants of white officers. William Lee, Washington's assistant, was perhaps the most renowned. In addition to seven years before the war, Lee served Washington through the entire war years and for twenty years thereafter. Lee is pictured in the background of Washington's famous portrait at West Point in 1780. Similarly, the free black Agrippa Hull, formerly a servant of the evangelist Jonathan Edwards, enlisted in the Massachusetts brigade of General John Paterson, whom he served as an orderly for two years of the war. After leaving the service of Paterson, Hull performed similar duties for the Polish commander Kosciuszko. Another black soldier, Prince Whipple, served as a bodyguard to General Whipple, an aide to George Washington.

George Washington and his assistant, William Lee. This 1780 portrait is by John Trumbull. *Canvas 91.4 × 71.1 cm. Metropolitan Museum of Art. Bequest of Charles Allen Munn, 1924. Accession #24.109.88*

Labor Battalions and Hired Bondsmen

Although Virginia, South Carolina, and Georgia barred the use of slaves as soldiers, slaveowners nonetheless hired or leased blacks to the military. Hired bondsmen worked at the garrisons, in military hospitals and munitions plants, and on the construction of roads and forts. In Virginia, hired blacks performed a variety of duties with the Lancaster District Minutemen and the Second Regiment. In South Carolina, hired slaves erected the double-walled fort at Sullivan's Island and prepared the outworks for the mounting of thirty cannon. Enslaved men erected these structures with such skill that the British assault on the fortress failed. Hired bondsmen also added to the munitions supply when they removed lead ornaments from public buildings, melted them down, and manufactured bullets.

In the North and South, military officials compelled some African Americans to work on defense projects against their will. In March 1776, New York empowered military officials to command the labor of all slaves and free blacks. The law required blacks to appear at a central locale, with all the shovels, axes, hoes, picks, and other tools that they could muster. The city and county of New York compelled blacks to work around the clock on fortifications. Whereas one-half of white male inhabitants were required to work on the Long Island defense project, all blacks were so ordered.

When southerners failed to cooperate in providing hired slave hands, volunteers, or draftees to the military, legislators authorized the impressment of slave laborers against their owners' will. As early as November 1775, Georgia impressed one hundred blacks to erect barriers around the arsenal in Savannah. Two years later, the state passed a comprehensive law requiring slaves to work building forts and other public works to defend the state. Almost from the outset of hostilities, South Carolina also empowered military authorities to take able-bodied black men as pioneers and laborers. When Charleston faced the threat of a British invasion in 1780, military officials forced black men into work on building fortifications. Only a note from the governor excused any slave from duty. If masters failed to comply, their slaves were taken by force.

Infantry, Cavalry, and Artillerymen

Although most blacks served in labor battalions, the intensification of hostilities pressed them into a variety of military occupations, including duty as drummers, infantry, cavalry, and artillerymen. Jabez Jolly, William Nickens, and "Negro Bob" were drummers in the Massachusetts, Virginia, and South Carolina regiments, respectively. In Goochland County, Virginia, the free black John Banks served for two years in the cavalry. This branch of the service involved extraordinary expenses in the maintenance of horses and equipment. The cavalry recruited few poor whites or blacks. As part of the Third Pennsylvania Artillery Regiment, another African American, Edward Hector, distinguished himself as one of a few black artillerymen. The Pennsylvania legislature later rewarded Hector for protecting his horses and ammunition wagon from capture by the enemy. The Georgia legislature rewarded the former slave Austin Dabney for similar artillery service.

Black soldiers helped to purchase American freedom with their lives and limbs in numerous battles and encampments. In addition to the early battles of Lexington, Concord, and Bunker Hill, their service included engagements at Saratoga, Ticonderoga, and Valley Forge. In 1776, Prince Whipple and Oliver Cromwell were at the oars of the boat that transported Washington across the Delaware River to attack the British forces in New Jersey on Christmas Eve. Black soldiers were also present at the final great battle of the war at Yorktown. Although most blacks fought alongside whites, there were three black units: the First Rhode Island Regiment, a Massachusetts company dubbed the Bucks of America, and the Black Brigade of Saint-Domingue. A white army surgeon later remarked that the black soldiers "discharged their duties with zeal and fidelity."

Under the command of Colonel Christopher Greene, the First Rhode Island Regiment engaged the enemy at the Battle of Rhode Island. Composed of a core of ninety-five ex-slaves and thirty-five freedmen, the Rhode Island unit drove the British and their mercenary Hessian troops back in three separate attacks upon their encampment. According to one observer, the Hessian colonel asked permission to change command and go to New York, because he "dared not lead his regiment again to battle, lest his men shoot him for having caused so much loss." The French general Lafayette later described the battle as "the best fought action of the war."

The Rhode Island regiment also fought at Red Bank, Points Bridge, and Yorktown. One contemporary traveler reported that the Rhode Island regiment "is the most neatly dressed, the best under arms, and the most precise in its maneuvers." Indeed, throughout the war, the Rhode Island unit received credit for serving with "efficiency and gallantry." For its part, the Black Brigade, called the Frontages Legion after its French commander, was made up of some 545 black volunteers. Described by the *Paris Gazette* as "colored: volunteer Chasseurs, Mulattoes, and Negroes," the Saint-Domingue blacks helped to save American forces from annihilation in the siege of Georgia during the fall of 1779. Two of these soldiers, Henri Christophe and Martial Besse, received wounds but returned to Saint-Domingue and later became leaders in the Haitian Revolution. Although there is little direct evidence on Boston's black unit, the Bucks of America, John Hancock presented the regiment a banner "bearing his initials" as a "tribute to their courage and devotion throughout the struggle."

In addition to the regular rigors of war, black troops fought under special burdens. They faced antiblack attitudes and social practices within and outside the armed forces. Although some whites, such as Alexander Hamilton, argued that the "natural faculties" of blacks were equal to whites, others, such as Thomas Jefferson, continued to question their valor and intelligence. As Hamilton put it, whites insisted on believing things about blacks that were "founded neither on reason nor in experience." White officers sometimes expressed the greatest disdain for the black troops under their charge. One captain in the Continental army wrote home to his wife that the "nasty lousy appearance" of his black troops was enough "to make one sick of the service." In contrast to its policy with white soldiers, the government denied black soldiers regular pay during the duration of the war. Moreover, most whites served in special volunteer units and state militia, which offered short terms of three, six, nine, or twelve months of service, close to home. Conversely, blacks served mainly in the Continental army, with tours of three years or more. Although a few blacks, such as Thomas Hall of Philadelphia, served close to home during their enlistment, most African Americans traveled long distances from their families and communities of origin.

Compared with their attempts to join the army, blacks faced less resistance to enlistment in the navy. When war broke out, African Americans had already established a long tradition as seamen in colonial navies. In the major port cities of Boston, Baltimore, Philadelphia, New York, and Charleston, among others, black sailors were a vital part of the various state navies as well as the Continental navy. Like their army counterparts, they served primarily in the labor and service departments as "cabin boys," "powder boys," body servants, cooks, general laborers, and stevedores. In addition, the navy employed large numbers of black pilots, particularly on small crafts designed to navigate the inland rivers. In January 1777, for example, one slaveowner sent two of his enslaved pilots to the Maryland Council to be used to transport goods and men along the Chesapeake Bay. The man described his "two sailor negroes" as "fine fellows as ever crost the sea" and urged the council to take good care of them. In Virginia, the black pilot Caesar of Hampton later received his freedom for piloting the "armed vessels of this state during the . . . war years." His exploits included steering the schooner *Patriot* and capturing the British supply vessel *Fanny*. Following the war, Captain James Barron of the navy of Virginia recalled the contributions of black sailors Harry, Cupid, and Aberdeen. Barron believed that these "coloured men, in justice to their merits should not be forgotten."

In South Carolina, as in Virginia, the state authorized the hiring of enslaved blacks on boats at Charleston, Stono Inlet, Georgetown, and Beaufort. The state compensated owners for work performed as well as for any injury or death. The South Carolina navy also purchased its own blacks for labor on the docks and in shipyards. In May 1777, the South Carolina navy purchased a man named Titus for 700 pounds sterling, and at about the same time, it bought two other black men for work in the rope walk. The navy also advertised for such bondsmen in newspapers. One advertisement in the *South Carolina Gazette* announced: "The Commissioners of the Navy are in want of a Number of Negro ship carpenters or caulkers; any person having such to hire by the year are desired to apply."

James Forten would become one of the most renowned black veterans of the revolutionary navy. A free black of Philadelphia, Forten was the son of an African captive. He received some education at the school of the antislavery Quaker Anthony Benezet. At age fifteen, he became a powder boy on a privateer vessel named *Royal Louis*. Under the command of Stephen Decatur Sr., the ship faced defeat at the hands of the English frigate *Amphyon*. Forten and other black and white sailors were taken prisoner. Although most blacks were sold into the West Indies, Forten escaped that fate when the son of a British sea captain took an interest in his welfare. After serving seven months aboard a British prison ship, preferable to being sold in the West Indies, Forten escaped and returned to Philadelphia.

African Americans also served the revolutionary forces as spies, messengers, and guides. When the French major general Lafayette arrived in Williamsburg, Virginia, in March 1781, he received invaluable assistance from James, a bondsman belonging to William Armstead of Kent County. James spied on the movement of the British units under the command of Benedict Arnold and used his knowledge of the Portsmouth region to deliver clandestine letters to other spies operating in or near the British lines. Lafayette later wrote that James "properly acquitted himself with some important communication I g[a]ve him . . . his intelligence from the enemy's camp were industriously collected and more faithfully delivered." For his service, the Virginia assembly granted James his freedom and a pension.

If James was the most well known of the black spies in the service of the revolutionary army, he was not alone. The bondsman Saul Matthews also worked as a spy in the Portsmouth area. He entered the British lines on several different occasions and provided useful information on British troop movements up and down the James River. In March 1783, the South Carolina legislature freed a man named Antiqua, as well as his wife and child, for securing information on "the enemy's movements and designs." Supplementing the formal efforts of spies like James, Saul Matthews, and others was an informal network of enslaved blacks who delivered important information to military officials on a regular basis. Since the British also sent black spies into rebel territory, these networks could be used to deceive as well as to inform.

Blacks in the British Forces

The British army, like the revolutionary forces, employed blacks mainly in labor battalions. More so than the revolutionary forces, however, the British gained their greatest productivity from southern blacks. In Savannah and Charleston, blacks worked on British fortifications, transported supplies, and labored as skilled carpenters, coopers, wheelwrights, and blacksmiths. African Americans also served as foragers, spies, guides, messengers, and soldiers for the British army. In defense of Savannah against the French and Saint-Domingue forces, a black guide steered a much-needed contingent of British reinforcement troops around enemy lines. According to one source, the black guide eluded the revolutionary forces by taking the British troops over land previously covered only "by bears, wolves and runaway Negroes." When General Cornwallis moved north from Charleston across North Carolina into Yorktown, Virginia, during the last days of the war, blacks raided plantations and confiscated food and supplies for the imperial army. In the Savannah area, the British armed an estimated two hundred blacks in 1779; by June 1781, another two hundred blacks served at the fort in Augusta. In the defense of Savannah against rebel American and French troops, Georgia governor James Wright credited blacks with saving the city: "They contributed greatly to our defense and safety." The *Virginia Gazette* also wrote that "a greater number of sailors, marines, militia and armed blacks accounted for the rebels' retreat."

Blacks were even more prominent in the British navy. They represented a mixture of fugitives, forced laborers, and hired "property" of loyalist slaveowners. Like their revolutionary counterparts, these men were considered invaluable. When Dunmore abandoned his landbase and took refuge aboard ship, blacks deserted to his ranks via water. The British incorporated these ex-slaves into its navy as pilots and crewmen. When Virginia rebels captured the pilot boat *Hawk Tender,* its crew included two blacks. The British praised black pilots like Joseph Harris, a runaway. "I think him too useful to His Majesty's service to take away," a naval officer wrote. "He is well acquainted with many creeks in the Eastern Shore, at York, James River, and Nansemand, and many others." In July 1775, Governor Lord William Campbell of South Carolina hoped to outmaneuver the rebels by taking on black pilots. Officials described one black pilot as "by far the best Pilot in this Harbour, and has marks of his own by which he will carry any vessel in spite of what they [patriots] can do." When the British launched its attack on Charleston, enslaved black men piloted three frigates—the *Byron,* the *Sphinx,* and the *Acteon*—up the channel.

Although blacks used the rift between the colonies and England to fight for their own liberation, it was an exceedingly difficult task. If the war offered new opportunities for enslaved and free blacks to fight for their own freedom, it also presented new perils and disruptions in their lives. Indeed, as one historian notes, African Americans stood between "two fires," and many were victimized by both sides of the war. In 1776, for example, after the British launched a series of raids on revolutionary forces in Georgia, the colonists retaliated by attacking loyalist forces and confiscating large numbers of enslaved people, whether they desired to leave or not. In a counterattack, the loyalists organized small guerrilla raids on rebel property and duplicated the process. The British, no less than American forces, asserted their right to sell, hire out, or employ blacks for their own profit. Commanders frequently instructed their subordinates to "sell a Negro to help provide for yourself," "to sell them, and buy shoes for your corps." In short, the imperial army and navy were not only havens for black fugitives but also instruments in the extension of African bondage as well.

When Cornwallis entered Yorktown, where the war officially ended, some four to five thousand blacks accompanied him. They served in capacities similar to those they had known on the plantations, mainly as cooks and laborers for white soldiers, officers, and their women. One officer recalled that "every officer had four to six horses and three or four Negroes, as well as one or two Negresses for cook and maid. Every soldier's woman was mounted and also had a Negro and Negress on horseback for her servants." In the last days of the war, to conserve on food and supplies, Cornwallis expelled large numbers of black refugees from the camp. As the Hessian officer Johann Ewald reported: "We had used them to good advantage . . . and set them free, and now, with fear and trembling, they had to face the reward of their cruel masters." Although Cornwallis surrendered on 19 October 1781, the fighting continued intermittently until the Treaty of Paris was signed in 1783.

An estimated one hundred thousand people left North America in the wake of the American Revolution. Most of these exiles were blacks—loyalist free blacks or slaves of loyalist slaveowners. The majority of these immigrants departed from three American ports—Savannah, Charleston, and New York—and the Spanish port of St. Augustine. Some moved to England; others to Canada, especially Nova Scotia; and others to the West Indies. Still others returned to West Africa. The war itself had witnessed the use of black soldiers from the French colony of Saint-Domingue, which for years had maintained a black militia. As these African Americans established black communities in other parts of the world, they would not only expand the scope of the African diaspora but also spread revolutionary ideas about liberty, equality, and social justice.

≈

THE REVOLUTIONARY WAR SET THE STAGE for the transformation of African American life. Although enslaved and free blacks fought and served on a discriminatory and unequal basis, they adopted the language of "liberty" and sought to transform the Revolution into a struggle for their own liberation. They decried racial limitations on their rights and pushed for a more inclusive, nonracist definition of the independence movement. As their freedom struggle intersected with the rising labor and military demands of war, they achieved partial victory when first the British and then the revolutionary government dropped racial barriers and enlisted blacks into the armed forces. As a result of their part on the fields of battle, some five thousand black soldiers would gain their freedom. Yet, even as the new nation made good on its promise to some blacks, it failed to live up to its revolutionary creed and abolish the institution of slavery. Both the promise and limits of the revolution would become apparent during the early postwar years. African American life in the early republic is the subject of Chapter 6.

~

Race, Republicanism,
and the Limits of Democracy

In the wake of the American Revolution, African Americans gained new hope for the future. The Revolution not only stimulated the manumission movement and growth of the free black population but also modified some of the harshest features of slave codes and unleashed a powerful ideology of freedom, rights, and equality. Enslaved and free blacks would use the new ideas to reinforce their efforts to end the system of human bondage. Before African Americans could make good on the promise of the Revolution, however, they faced the intensification of racist ideology, extension of the international slave trade, and new restrictions on the small free black population.

Limitations on the rights-of-man movement for African Americans were inextricably interwoven with growing class conflicts among whites. Middle- and working-class whites exhibited dissatisfaction with elite domination of the new nation's economy and polity. In their view, the Revolution enriched large landowners and merchants at the expense of the small yeoman farmers. Their discontent gained violent expression in Shays's Rebellion of 1786. Commercial elites rallied their forces, put down the revolt, and called for a new constitutional convention in 1787. The new federal constitution that they adopted not only represented the triumph of a class-biased republic but also strengthened the institution of slavery as a race-based system of labor exploitation and social relations. Still, enslaved and free blacks would repeatedly invoke revolutionary ideas to buttress their efforts to end slavery and gain their own independence.

FREE BLACKS AND THE PROMISE OF THE REVOLUTION

The Revolutionary War represented the beginning of a new era in African American history. As the revolutionary states established independent constitutions, they adopted the rhetoric of the "rights of man," encouraged freedom suits, and passed gradual manumission statutes (see box). In 1780, Pennsylvania initiated the process of gradual manumission when it outlawed the perpetual enslavement of black people. Specifically, the law stipulated that any person born to slave parents after 1780 would be free on their twenty-eighth birthday. Between the early 1780s and 1804, Connecticut, Rhode Island, New York, and New Jersey enacted similar statutes. In 1783, for its part, the Massachusetts Supreme Court concluded that slavery was "inconsistent with our own conduct and constitution [adopted in 1778]" and set the slave Quok Walker free. Two years after the famous Quok Walker case, the court outlawed slavery by judicial decree.

Antislavery Sentiment and the Second Great Awakening

Although southern states rejected gradual emancipation legislation, they did entertain freedom suits, eased the process of individual manumission, and allowed slaveowners to free blacks by will or by deed. Except for North Carolina, which limited emancipation to persons performing "meritorious service" for the state, southern states revoked their bans on private acts of manumission. The new state constitutions of Delaware, Maryland, Kentucky, North Carolina, and Tennessee went a step further and enfranchised free blacks on the basis of the same property qualifications that governed the voting of free white men. As such laws took effect, some slaveholders emancipated captives and sought to reconcile their practice with their belief in "liberty for all." A Virginian reported: "I cannot satisfy my conscience . . . to have my negro slaves separated from each other, from their husbands and wives." A Maryland slaveowner freed her slaves because human bondage contradicted "the inalienable rights of Mankind." In Kentucky, an emancipator said simply that slavery "was inconsistent with republican principles . . . which declare that all men are by nature equally free." Although most manumissions took place in the Upper South, Deep South planters also freed some of their slaves. Unlike their Upper South counterparts, however, Deep South planters usually freed the products of their own interracial sexual relations with black women.

The manumission movement was reinforced by the Northwest Ordinance of 1787, the expansion of antislavery societies, and the evangelical sentiment unleashed by the Second Great Awakening. The Northwest Ordinance prohibited slavery north of the Ohio River, in what was known as the Northwest Territory—the states of Ohio, Indiana, Illinois, Wisconsin, and Michigan. Although such states would develop antiblack policies that limited the in-migration of free blacks, they also became important sources of antislavery sentiment and support for the underground railroad, which aided fugitives fleeing southern bondage for the North. In varying forms, antislavery societies in New York, Massachusetts, and Virginia envisioned the complete abolition of slavery. Ministers and teachers like Samuel Hopkins of Rhode Island and St. George Tucker of Virginia advocated individual manumission of blacks as "a matter of Christian conscience."

In 1785, the Second Great Awakening emerged in the James River, Virginia, area. Similar to the Great Awakening of the 1730s and 1740s, this religious movement reinforced the emancipation process. Evangelicals merged antislavery

SOURCES FROM THE PAST

1783

Virginia Emancipates Slaves for Military Service During the American Revolution

An act directing the emancipation of certain slaves who have served as Soldiers in this State, and for the Emancipation of the Slave Aberdeen.

I. Whereas it hath been represented to the present General Assembly, that during the course of the war, many persons in this State had caused their slaves to enlist in certain regiments or corps raised within the same, having tendered such slaves to the officers appointed to recruit forces within the States, as substitutes for free persons whose lot or duty it was to serve in such regiments or corps, at the same time representing to such recruiting officers that the slaves, so enlisted by their direction and concurrence, were freemen; and it appearing further to this Assembly, that on the expiration of the term of enlistment of such slaves, that the former owners have attempted again to force them to return to a state of servitude, contrary to the principles of justice, and to their own solemn promise;

II. And whereas it appears just and reasonable, that all persons enlisted as aforesaid, who have faithfully served agreeable to the terms of their enlistment, and have thereby of course contributed towards the establishment of American liberty and independence, should enjoy the blessings of freedom as a reward for their toils and labors;

Be it therefore enacted, That each and every slave who, by the appointment and direction of his owner, hath enlisted in any regiment or corps raised within this State, either on Continental or State establishment, and hath been received as a substitute for any free person whose duty or lot it was to serve in such regiment or corps, and hath served faithfully during the terms of such enlistment, or hath been discharged from such service by some officer duly authorized to grant such discharge, shall, from and after the passing of this act, be fully and completely emancipated, and shall be held and deemed free, in as full and ample a manner as if each and every [one] of them were specially named in this act. . . .

III. And whereas it has been represented to this General Assembly, that Aberdeen, a negro man slave, hath labored a number of years in the public service at the lead mines, and for his meritorious services is entitled to freedom; *Be it therefore enacted,* That the said slave Aberdeen shall be, and he is hereby, emancipated and declared free in as full and ample a manner as if he had been born free.

Source: Hening's Statutes at Large of Virginia, 1783, in Deirdre Mullane, ed., Crossing the Danger Water: Three Hundred Years of African-American Writing (New York: Doubleday, 1993), pp. 37–38.

religious traditions with the new revolutionary ideology and used it to promote the abolitionist movement. With the arrival of the English minister Thomas Coke in 1784, English and northern white religious leaders entered the Chesapeake region with their "revitalized notions of the brotherhood of man." Coke strongly urged Methodists to "emancipate their Slaves." Although Coke would soon modify his position on emancipation under pressure from influential slaveholders, the Methodist church adopted antislavery principles, declaring slavery "contrary to the laws of God, of men, and of nature, and that it was hurtful to society and contrary to the dictates of conscience and pure religion." In 1785, Baptists pursued a similar course when representatives from various churches condemned hereditary slavery as "contrary to the word of God." By 1790, the Virginia Baptists also endorsed the use of the state "to extirpate the horrid evil [slavery] from the land and pray Almighty god, that our Honorable Legislature may have it in their power, to proclaim the general jubilee, consistent with the principles of good policy." Although North Carolina limited manumission to those showing evidence of "meritorious service" to the state, Quakers regularly violated the law and became trustees of slaves liberated by non-Quaker masters.

In 1787, the English abolitionist and potter Josiah Wedgwood carved this cameo for the London Society for the Abolition of Slavery. This symbol of bondage would become widely known in America, with both male and female versions in use by the eve of the Civil War. *Library of Congress*

The belief that all people were equal in the sight of God struck a deep chord in the hearts and minds of African Americans. Between the end of the American Revolution and the early nineteenth century, thousands of Methodist and Baptist churches admitted blacks. By 1800, black Methodists sometimes outnumbered white parishioners in the churches of Maryland and South Carolina. When the revival movement erupted, one master lamented that his bondsman Sam

> was raised in a family of religious persons, commonly called Methodists, and has lived with some of them for years past, on terms of perfect equality. . . . The refusal to continue him on these terms . . . has given him offense, and is the sole cause of his absconding.

During the 1780s and 1790s, the black Methodist minister Harry Hosier, usually called "Black Harry," traveled with white itinerant ministers Coke, Asbury, Garrettson, and Whatcoat. In Maryland and Virginia, "Black Harry" preached to both enslaved and white audiences.

African Americans made up an even greater proportion of Baptist congregations than of Methodist ones. Until the early 1800s, black and white worshippers also shared the same buildings and frequently seated themselves as they pleased. As late as 1792, in Charles City, Virginia, free black men voted on church affairs along with other "free male members" of the congregation. In some cases, enslaved preachers were so effective among white as well as black congregations that whites helped them gain their freedom. In North Hampton, Virginia, white Baptists raised money and purchased the freedom of Jacob Bishop. In Roanoke, Virginia, a white congregation bought the freedom of a man named Simon, stating that "we think him ordained of God to preach the gospel."

In Charleston, South Carolina, blacks not only outnumbered whites but also controlled the finances, discipline, and roster of delegates to quarterly conferences. In Tennessee, as late as 1806, the Baptist church permitted "Black Brethren . . . [to] enjoy the same liberty . . . as white members have and do enjoy." Moreover, black and white preachers headed interracial churches and often shared the same pulpit. In Gloucester County, Virginia, the black minister William Lemon pastored the predominantly white Petsworth Baptist Church. He also served as a delegate to the local Baptist Association meetings between 1797 and 1801. In Fayetteville, North Carolina, the black Methodist minister Henry Evans, a shoemaker by trade, organized the city's first Methodist church and preached to a mixed congregation of blacks and whites until his death in 1810. In the Deep South, black ministers also preached to white congregations, especially in Georgia, where Andrew Bryan, Jesse Peters, and David George addressed white as well as black audiences.

Growth of the Free Black Population

As the manumission movement gained momentum, the promise of the Revolution found its greatest expression in the rise of the free black population. Most of the 5,000 blacks who served in the Continental army soon gained their freedom. Through natural increase and immigration, among other sources, the free black population increased from negligible numbers at the onset of the American Revolution to 60,000 in 1790 and to nearly 234,000 in 1820. Most of this increase occurred during the first two decades after the war, when the free black population rose by an estimated 70 to 80 percent. By the early 1800s, free blacks made up nearly 10 percent of the black population and about 5 percent of all free people in the South, particularly the Chesapeake region, which claimed over 134,200 free blacks, compared with about 20,150 in the Deep South. Free people of color made up a faster-growing component of the southern population than enslaved and free whites. Although most free blacks lived in the rural South, the free black population was disproportionately northern. By 1820, nearly 42 percent (about 99,280) of all free blacks lived in the North.

The rapid growth of the free black population reinforced the flight from bondage in the postwar years. Fugitives now included blacks who had military experience on the side of both British and American forces. In Massachusetts, for example, along with Felix Cuff, a Revolutionary War veteran, a group of blacks ran away from their owners and took refuge in a cave called Devil's Den, in a snake-infested area in the town of Waltham called "Snake Hill." These Maroons defended themselves from outside attack and eventually gained their freedom. Virginia and North Carolina slaves escaped into the Dismal Swamp, where they erected a Maroon community, replete with agriculture, livestock, and a system of governance and physical defense. The group remained intact through the early 1790s. In Georgia and South Carolina, bands of blacks retained their arms from the war years and used them to establish new runaway camps in the swamps of the lower Savannah River. Fugitives cleared swampland, erected houses, planted rice fields, and set up elaborate fortifications to protect the settlement from invasion. After securing their location in the spring of 1787, some one hundred armed men not only attacked plantations on both sides of the Savannah River but also assaulted two militia companies of Georgia state troops. Under the leadership of "Captain Cudjoe" and "Captain Lewis," these men called themselves "the King of England's Soldiers." Only the combined forces of Georgia state troops and Indians destroyed the settlement. According to the commanding officer of the Georgia militia, the leaders of these Lower South fugitives "are the very fellows that fought, and maintained their ground against the brave lancers at the siege of Savannah."

In the wake of the Haitian Revolution in 1792, free black émigrés moved into South Carolina and Georgia in rising numbers. Since these free black immigrants had opposed the slave revolt and sided with the French, they were forced to flee for their lives when enslaved blacks rose up and drove slaveowners off the island. The Haitian revolt also played a key role in the U.S. acquisition of the Louisiana Territory in 1803. As blacks broke the French grip on their key Caribbean stronghold, Napoleon found it difficult to hold on to the vast North American territory and sold it to the United States for a pittance, and without regard for the indigenous peoples in the region. The Louisiana Purchase brought nearly 10,500 free blacks into the union. As with the Haitian refugees, the French- and Spanish-speaking free blacks of Louisiana had sided with slaveowners in the area and occupied a privileged position. In the Upper South, too, the number of Haitian immigrants increased. "Within a few weeks" of Haitian immigration, a Virginia resident wrote to the governor that several blacks had "eloped from their master's plantations."

Cities offered the greatest opportunities for runaways to make good their escape. In 1795, a Virginia owner reported that his bondsman had "inquired very particularly" about the way to Philadelphia because "he heard Negroes were free there." The growth of free black urban communities enabled rising numbers of enslaved blacks to forge certificates and "pass for free men." Planters frequently advertised that fugitives were probably bound for places where they had friends and relatives who would "conceal and assist them." Bordered by three slave states, Pennsylvania attracted large numbers of free blacks and fugitives from the Upper South. Philadelphia's free black population increased by nearly 210 percent between 1790 and 1800 and by another 50.4 percent the following decade. New York experienced 83.5- and 54.3-percent increases during the same periods. Though less dramatically, Boston's black population rose by 53.3 and 26.4 percent in these decades. The percentage of northeastern blacks living in cities increased from roughly 12 to 17 percent in 1790 to nearly 30 percent by 1820 (see tables).

Blacks as Percentage of Total Population, 1790

New England		Upper South	
Maine	0.6%	Delaware	21.6
New Hampshire	0.6	Maryland	34.7
Vermont	0.3	Virginia	40.9
Massachusetts	1.4	North Carolina	26.8
Rhode Island	6.3	Kentucky	17.0
Connecticut	2.3	Tennessee	10.6
Middle States		**Lower South**	
New York	7.6	South Carolina	43.7
New Jersey	7.7	Georgia	35.9
Pennsylvania	2.4		

Source: Ira Berlin, *Slaves Without Masters: The Free Negro in the Antebellum South* (New York: The New Press, 1974), p. 23. Data from U.S. Bureau of the Census.

Growth of Enslaved and Free Black Population, 1790–1820

	1790	1800	1810	1820
Slave	697,624	893,602	1,191,362	1,538,022
Free	59,557	108,435	186,446	233,634
Total	**757,181**	**1,002,037**	**1,377,808**	**1,771,656**

Source: Negro Population, 1790–1915 (1918; reprint, New York: Arno Press, 1968), p. 53. Data from U.S. Bureau of the Census.

Although cities like New York, Boston, and Philadelphia claimed the largest concentration of free northern blacks, Baltimore, Alexandria, Richmond, Petersburg, and Norfolk accounted for the bulk of free blacks in the Upper South states of Maryland and Virginia. In the Deep South, Savannah, Charleston, and New Orleans registered the largest numbers of free people of color in Georgia, South Carolina, and Louisiana. Urban officials often complained that "large numbers of free blacks flock from the country to the towns." As whites moved to the rural western frontier as the site of new opportunities, African Americans moved to the urban frontier in rising numbers.

The expansion of black families and kin networks underlay and reinforced urban population growth. A growing proportion of runaway advertisements listed blacks as belonging to family units that linked them to urban and rural places. In 1803, one newspaper advertisement sought to recover a forty-five-year-old runaway. According to the ad, the woman had a husband at the plantation of Hugh Wilson, esq., James Island, has relatives at the plantation of the Rev. Dr. Frost, Goosecreek and has a son at the plantation of Doctor Jones, in the same parish; she is well known in the city, probably she may make for Georgetown, being well acquainted there.

When one enslaved mechanic continued to run away to visit the plantation where his wife resided, a Maryland master promised to "purchase his wife if her master will sell her at a reasonable price." Planters regularly reported blacks absconding through a complicated network of families and friends, as indicated by the following phrases: "related to a family of negroes, who lately obtained their freedom"; "went off in company with a mulatto, free fellow named Tom Turner, who follows the water for a living"; "several relations will conceal and assist him to make his escape." For their part, new African runaways also utilized communal and kin networks forged in Africa and on slaveships. Newspapers frequently listed new arrivals as members of the same runaway parties. Unlike blacks in the prewar period, who came from a variety of West African sources, most of the new Africans came from the Angolan region and facilitated the process of African American culture and community formation. Advertisements seeking their recovery reiterated the point: last observed with "fellow of the same country"; "supposed to be secreted by some of his country people"; were "purchased out of same ship."

Black Family Life

Although slavery subordinated black family life to the imperatives of profits, such calculations sometimes encouraged slave families as a means of promoting the natural increase of the black work force. Thomas Jefferson and other planters encouraged their overseers to maintain sexually balanced work forces—"half men & half women." Jefferson stated that he regarded "a woman who brings a child every two years as more valuable than the best man on the farm. What she produces is an addition to capital, while his labor disappears in mere consumption." Jefferson also approved slave marriages but sought to limit them to his own plantation: "There is nothing I desire so much as that all the young people on the estate should intermarry with one another and stay home. . . . They are worth a great deal more in that case than when they have husbands and wives abroad." On Charles Carroll's large estate in Annapolis, Maryland, an estimated two-thirds of enslaved blacks under fifteen years old lived with both parents.

Chesapeake black families also extended outward from "intimate ties of blood" to encompass aunts and uncles, nephews and nieces, cousins, and grandparents. Of 128 blacks on Carroll's home plantation, all but 30 belonged to such extended kin groupings. A similar pattern characterized Thomas Jefferson's Bear Creek Quarter in Bedford County, Virginia. Low-country planters also expressed an increasing preference for American-born blacks "in large families" rather than "gangs" of African-born blacks separated from their families. The proportion of African-born blacks in South Carolina's population had dropped from 45 percent on the eve of the war to between 10 and 20 percent by 1820. While only about one-third of a sample of low-country estates listed blacks living in family units on the eve of the Revolution, the proportion had increased to four-fifths by the early 1800s.

Although the system of bondage subordinated black families to the imperatives of profit, African Americans imbued such units with their own familiar and communal meanings. Bondsmen and -women worked to vouchsafe the family from sale and arbitrary breakup. Enslaved blacks repeatedly petitioned planters for permission to move to another plantation to be with a spouse and their children. Conversely, they also asked planters to purchase family members from other places and reunite broken families. Although it often took them five to ten years to purchase a single slave, free blacks dedicated their lives to purchasing the freedom of others. Between 1792 and 1805, the freeman Graham Bell of Petersburg, Virginia, bought and liberated nine people. Another free black, the barber John C. Stanly of North Carolina, not only purchased his wife and children in 1805 but also, over the next thirteen years, liberated nineteen slaves, one of them a brother-in-law. The free black woman of Washington, D.C., Althea Tanner, bought her own freedom as well as that of twenty-two relatives and friends.

African American naming practices also underscored the significance of extended kinship networks. Enslaved children often received the names of deceased relatives. On the Charles Carroll plantation, the majority of blacks received the names of blood relatives. Such naming practices reinforced ties between the past and present, which enabled slaves to transmit cultural values and establish the groundwork for building the larger African American community. Slaves used their families not only to transmit cultural values about kinship and community but also to pass on what historians have referred to as slaves' "most valuable property: their skill." In both the Upper and Lower South, slave parents, men and women, invariably taught their children the same skills that they had acquired. In the Chesapeake, Sam, a slave of C. C. Pinckney, passed his skills as carpenter to his oldest son, Anthony. On the Carroll estate, the cooper Joe trained both of his sons in the trade of barrel making. Similarly, black women taught their female children specialized skills, such as midwifery, as well as knowledge of a variety of household tasks. Such work experiences not only enabled some blacks to purchase their freedom but also in turn enabled free people of color to earn a living, gain access to resources, and purchase loved ones out of bondage.

In contrast to the prerevolutionary period, when few northern blacks lived in two-parent households, they now moved toward the establishment of separate independent households free of interference from their masters. As late as 1790, only one of every three Boston blacks lived in their own independent households. By 1820, an estimated 84 percent of Boston blacks lived in autonomous households. Similarly, in Philadelphia, 50 percent of blacks lived in white households in 1790, but by 1820 some 75 percent were living in their own households. This process was much slower in New York, where emancipation came late and most free blacks continued to live in white households. In New York, consequently, the independent households of single male or female adults were almost nil, whereas they made up 7 to 8 percent of such households in Philadelphia and Boston. By 1820, most northern black households had at least one adult male and one adult female. The ratio of black households with adult men and women ranged from 76 percent in Boston, to 79 percent in Philadelphia, to 81 percent in New York. Since black mortality rates were usually two to three times those of whites, northern black families also had a lower ratio of children per adult than whites. In 1820, children made up about 35 percent of Philadelphia's white population, compared with under 30 percent of the blacks. The ratios were even lower in Boston and New York.

As in the South, the meaning of family for northern blacks also emerged clearly in naming practices. The prerevolutionary generation had African, Anglicized African, classical, and even place names: Cuffee, Quash, and Cudjoe; Caesar, Pompey, and Cato; York, London, and Jamaica. The new generation shed the old names and donned new ones, many with biblical, mainstream English, and artisan derivations: forenames such as Elizabeth, Sarah, Abraham, Isaac, Jacob, Daniel, David, and Joseph, and surnames such as Mason, Cooper, Carpenter, Johnson, Brown, Smith, Williams, and Thomas. However, northern blacks assiduously avoided taking the names of the most prominent slave-owning white families, such as Wharton, Shippen, and Dickinson.

Occupational Opportunities in the Early Republic

Freedom opened up new occupational opportunities for African Americans, and by the early 1800s, some had secured jobs as painters, poets, authors, astronomers, entertainers, and merchants. The Bostonian Paul Cuffee and the Philadelphian James Forten Sr. emerged as the most prominent of the early American black merchants. Born on the Massachusetts island of Cuttyhunk, Cuffee was the seventh of the ten children of a formerly enslaved father and a Native American mother. During the Revolutionary War, Cuffee established a successful whaling and coastal fishing business. Cuffee's business activities expanded during the early years of the republic, his fleet of ships sailing not only to the Caribbean but also to such European countries as Sweden, France, and Russia. Cuffee's fortune enabled him to buy land and to play a major role in the early establishment of black institutions. He also became an early pioneer in the efforts to resettle African Americans in Africa when he gained approval from the British government to trade with Sierra Leone, established on the west coast of Africa as a haven for emancipated blacks from the English-speaking parts of the New World. For his part, James Forten developed a successful sail-manufacturing business. Following his escape from a British ship during the Revolutionary War, he returned to Philadelphia and took a job in a sail-making firm owned by a free black named Robert Bridges. Following Bridges's retirement in 1798, Forten purchased the business. Over the next three decades, he hired both black and white workers and amassed a fortune of $100,000. Like Cuffee, Forten also used his resources to support community-building and antislavery activities.

Although some blacks like Cuffee and Forten developed successful business enterprises, the skilled trades represented the most significant opportunities for free blacks in early America. Such opportunities were most pronounced in the Deep South, where planters manumitted only a few bondsmen and -women, usually

Paul Cuffee became not only a renowned entrepreneur but also a pioneer in the resettlement of African Americans in Africa. *Library of Congress*

with kinship ties, and helped them to establish a foothold in the economy. In cities like Charleston, Savannah, and New Orleans, free blacks gained access to jobs as masons, carpenters, cartwrights, shoemakers, tailors, and butchers, among others. In the Upper South, too, a few white planters assisted free blacks to gain a footing in the economy as skilled craftsmen or landowners. The Virginia planters George Washington and Robert Carter provided some blacks small plots of land, access to firewood, opportunities to hire their wives and children for pay, apprenticeship training, and aid for the aged and infirm. Carter, and to some extent Washington, also enabled some blacks to become tenant farmers, with agreements to give them a specified amount of the produce or profits, along with opportunities to hire their own workers to produce crops. Such free black tenant farmers invariably hired free blacks. One planter reported good results with black tenantry, or sharecropping, as it would later be called: "I am the gainer . . . and they seem to be happy and cheerful and do more than twice the labour than when they were in a state of bondage, and make themselves a comfortable livelihood."

AFRICAN AMERICANS AND THE LIMITS OF DEMOCRACY

Despite substantial progress, African Americans faced a tough battle turning the Revolution to their benefit. Although freedom provided new economic opportunities, most free blacks and fugitives gained jobs at the bottom of the postrevolutionary economy. They worked mainly as general laborers, domestics, and personal service workers. A 1795 Philadelphia census listed 41 percent of free black men as "unskilled" laborers, sawyers, and whitewashers. Another 12 percent worked as domestic or personal servants or waitingmen and coachmen. Others worked as mariners (10 percent), artisans (12 percent), professionals (5 percent), and proprietors, hucksters, craters, bakers, and grocers (21 percent). About one-third of free black women worked as retailers and boardinghouse keepers, and 50 percent labored as laundry- or washerwomen.

For some free blacks, emancipation ushered in not upward but downward occupational mobility. In 1816, another Philadelphia census revealed a decline in professional positions and a rise in domestic and personal service. As long as blacks with skills remained enslaved, masters had a stake in their profitable employment, either in their own households or shops or as hirees elsewhere. When these skilled blacks gained their freedom, however, they faced stiff competition from enslaved artisans as well as free whites. As a result, they were often forced out of their trades or made to work at much lower wages than their enslaved and free white counterparts. Consequently, whites from diverse class backgrounds, including merchants, landowners, and artisans, exploited free black labor.

Restrictions and Racial Hostility

From the outset, despite the manumission movement, southern states established stiff restrictions on free blacks. Virginia law stipulated that free blacks could be sold into slavery for failing to pay their taxes. Maryland decreed that such people would have property rights, but not all "the rights of free men." Moreover, when the Haitian revolt sent thousands of West Indians into the South, whites welcomed white French émigrés but resisted the in-migration of blacks. All along the southeastern seaboard except Virginia, southern states erected barriers against the black émigrés. When black immigrants continued their trek into ports like Charleston and Savannah, whites held mass meetings and sent angry petitions to legislatures demanding an end to the influx. For its part, the city of Savannah barred any ship that had docked in Saint-Domingue from its harbor.

African Americans not only faced restrictions in the South but also confronted barriers in the North. Although abolitionism gained support among influential whites, the gradual emancipation movement was insufficient to guarantee the full citizenship rights of ex-slaves. Moreover, New York (1799) and New Jersey (1804) enacted gradual emancipation laws later than elsewhere. In New Jersey, the number of enslaved actually increased between 1790 and 1800. More importantly, northern states imposed racial restrictions on the "right to vote and hold office," on marriage, and on in-migration from other states. In 1800, Boston invoked a state law against the settlement of free blacks from other countries and ordered the deportation of 240 free blacks from the city. Most of these blacks were from Rhode Island, New York, Philadelphia, and the Caribbean. Despite the decline of slavery in the North, one contemporary traveler remarked that "chains of a stronger kind still manacled their [free blacks'] limbs, from which no legislative act could free them; a mental and moral subordination and inferiority, to which tyrant custom has here subjected all the sons and daughters of Africa."

Although the Northwest Ordinance prohibited slavery north of the Ohio River, blacks also confronted racial hostility in the old northwest (Ohio, Indiana, Illinois, Wisconsin, and Michigan). Northern journalists and political leaders referred to free and enslaved blacks alike "as depraved and ignorant a set of people as any of their kind." On one occasion, for example, the Ohio legislature reported free blacks as "more idle and vicious than slaves" and urged strong measures to prevent their migration into the state. Similarly, an Indiana Supreme Court judge opposed the migration of what he called "a low ignorant, degraded multitude of free blacks." Free blacks, the Indiana Colonization Society argued, "add nothing to the strength, and little to the wealth" of the state and nation. As nonslaveholding whites moved into the territories in rising numbers, they were exceedingly hostile to slavery. They believed that the use of enslaved blacks would spawn a large free black population, which would in turn compete with whites for land and other resources. Moreover, according to northern whites, southerners released their most troublesome and unproductive blacks onto the Northwest Territory. Thus, antislavery sentiment, intertwined with antiblack beliefs, hampered the in-migration of free blacks.

The state constitutions and laws of the Northwest Territory contained discriminatory provisions against free blacks. In 1804, the Ohio legislature passed a law requiring free blacks and mulattoes to provide proof of their freedom on entering the state. In 1807, Ohio intensified such restrictions by prohibiting free blacks and mulattoes from settling in the state unless they posted a $500 bond to guarantee their ability to support themselves. In 1815, Indiana passed a law imposing a $300 annual poll tax on all adult black and mulatto men. For its part, the federal government reinforced state and local restrictions against free blacks. Congress regularly admitted new states into the union—both north and south of the border—with explicit restrictions against free blacks in their constitutions. The federal government also limited naturalization and the acquisition of citizenship to "foreign whites" (1790), restricted enlistment into the federal militia to white men (1792), eliminated blacks from service as U.S. mail carriers (1810), and disfranchised free blacks in the nation's capital (1820).

By the War of 1812 and its aftermath, most whites perceived free blacks as a problem. Southern slaveholders viewed free blacks as a threat to the institution of slavery, while northerners viewed them as economic competitors and a threat to their Euro-American cultural way of life. Thus, popular opinion in both the North and South coalesced around efforts to transport free blacks out of the country. In 1817, this new viewpoint gained organized expression when a group of influential whites—including John Randolph, Francis Scott Key, and Richard Rush—founded the American Colonization Society and sought ways to resettle free blacks on African soil.

The racial limitations of the Revolution were intertwined with class conflicts among whites. Highlighting the conservative character of the new polity was Shays's Rebellion, which broke out among farmers in western Massachusetts in 1786. Under the leadership of the Revolutionary War veteran Daniel Shays, these farmers rebelled against eastern bankers and merchants who passed the high cost of living in the new nation on to the medium-sized and small landowners and the poor. Although some blacks like Prince Hall of Boston volunteered to help put down the rebellion, other blacks like Tobias Green of Plainfield, Aaron Carter of Colrain, and Moses Sash of Worthington joined white farmers in their resistance movement. According to contemporary court records, Moses Sash, described as a farmer and laborer, was not only a participant in the uprising but also "a Captain & one of Shaises [Shays's] Council." In contrast to the single indictment handed down on the white participants in the rebellion, the court returned two indictments against Sash. Whereas both Sash and the whites were indicted for "disorderly, riotous & seditious" behavior "by force of arms," Sash was additionally indicted for "fraudulently, unlawfully & feloniously" stealing two guns. Although Governor John Hancock eventually pardoned most of the participants, Shays's Rebellion precipitated growing fear among the nation's small elite that lower-class whites might undermine the independence and sovereignty of the new nation. It was partly this fear, as well as the persistence of slavery as a labor system, that led to the creation of a new federal constitution.

The New Constitution and Defense of Slavery

In 1787, representatives of the thirteen states met in Philadelphia and drafted a new, more centralized constitution. The new document made substantial concessions to slaveowners and reinforced African and African American bondage. In his *Notes on the State of Virginia,* published in the same year, Thomas Jefferson articulated the racial ideology of the new nation that justified the perpetual enslavement of blacks on American soil. According to Jefferson, not slavery but blacks degraded whites and undermined the strength of the nation. In his view, African Americans were an inferior people—in color, culture, physique, intelligence, and morality. More specifically, Jefferson concluded that blacks were "in memory . . . equal to the white; in reason much inferior; . . . and in imagination . . . dull, tasteless, and anomalous . . . never yet could I find that a black had uttered a thought above the level of plain narration."

The new constitution underscored the triumph of racialist thought in the nation-building process. Specifically, the founding document expanded southern representation in Congress by counting slaves as three-fifths of a person; guaranteed the extension of the international slave trade for twenty years, or until 1808; and mandated the return of fugitive slaves who escaped across state lines. In 1793, Congress also passed the Fugitive Slave Act, which authorized slaveowners to enter free territory and seize runaway slaves. Since the law denied alleged fugitives an opportunity to prove their status, it made free blacks no less vulnerable to enslavement than escaped bondsmen and -women. (See the Documents section.) In short, the new republic justified the perpetual enslavement of Africans on American soil.

The international slave trade played a pivotal role in limiting the promise of the Revolution. As the prospective deadline for the termination of the international slave trade drew near, southern planters augmented their enslaved work forces with fresh "imports from Africa and the Caribbean." Between the end of the Revolution and the end of the slave trade, an estimated 100,000 Africans entered the human flesh markets of the United States; most of these arrived after 1790. In 1807, Congress banned the international slave trade; violaters of the ban could be fined $800 and given various prison terms. Any person convicted of outfitting slaveships was subject to even stiffer penalties, including a $2,000 fine. In the early aftermath of the law, however, most states did little to enforce the ban on slave imports. As historian John Hope Franklin has noted, "The first underground railroad was not that carried on by the abolitionists to get the Negro slaves to freedom but the one carried on by merchants, and others to introduce more Negroes into slavery."

Until the early 1800s, the western lands of Kentucky and Tennessee received most of their slave labor from the Chesapeake, while the international slave trade supplied the Deep South states of South Carolina and Georgia. Thereafter, the Chesapeake supplied the slave labor demands of the Upper and Lower South. In the decade between 1810 and 1820, an estimated 137,000 blacks left the Chesapeake for the frontier south, most moving into the southwestern states of Mississippi and Alabama. In rapid succession, cotton lands opened in western, central, and southern Georgia, Alabama, Mississippi, and Louisiana. Before the United States could take the western lands and initiate cotton production, however, it had to confront Amerindians, defeat them, and push them farther west. In 1814, Andrew Jackson's frontier army attacked the Creek nation and forced concessions from the Chickasaw, Choctaw, and Cherokee nations. These concessions enabled white settlers to spread across the "rich virgin soil" known as the "black belt." By the 1810s, southerners moved toward a vigorous defense of slavery as a "positive good" in the enrichment of the white commonwealth.

Other southerners defended slavery as "a necessary evil" in the social control of what they called "an inferior people." Accordingly, as the demand for slave labor increased, southern states established new restrictions against free blacks. New state constitutions or amendments disfranchised blacks except in Tennessee and North Carolina; at the same time, Virginia, Georgia, Kentucky, Maryland, North Carolina, and South Carolina barred free black migrants or made their entrance difficult by bond and other requirements. In 1806, Virginia went a step further and required any newly manumitted blacks to leave the state. To enforce these provisions of the law and control the interstate movement of free blacks, southern states also initiated a complicated system of registration and passes. These laws not only allowed authorities to imprison indigent or vagrant free blacks but also prohibited their participation in commercial activities. By the early 1800s, Georgia and Mississippi reinstituted bans against freeing slaves and made emancipation a prerogative of the state legislature rather than of individual masters. According to one angry Virginia planter, "A man has almost as much right to set fire to his own building though his neighbor['s] is to be destroyed by it, as to free his slaves." Whites regularly harassed free blacks and deprived them of their freedom, including permitting enslaved blacks to testify against free people of color (but not against whites). Moreover, although officials of slaveholding states publicly condemned the kidnapping of free blacks for sale and reenslavement, hundreds of blacks lost their freedom through the operation of kidnapping rings, particularly in the Delaware-Virginia area.

As southerners moved increasingly toward a defense of slavery as either a "necessary evil" or a "positive good," the nascent southern antislavery movement declined. By 1820, it had failed to penetrate the Deep South and held only a tenuous grip on Virginia and Maryland. In the new western states of Kentucky and Tennessee, slaveholders also successfully resisted the establishment of abolitionist societies. As early as the 1790s, southern legislators in Virginia and Maryland had passed new laws restricting the ability of abolitionists and blacks to lodge freedom suits, mainly by instituting new prohibitively high court costs. The Virginia assembly even barred abolitionists from service on freedom suit juries while permitting hostile slaveowners to serve. Similarly, as early as 1793, southern Baptists and Methodists had revoked their antislavery decrees and reconciled their brand of evangelicalism with the system of bondage. In 1797, the Roanoke Baptist Association barred free blacks from the church's business meetings. Most churches now practiced some form of racial discrimination, including separate seats for blacks (enslaved and free) and whites. In an extreme case, a Virginia church painted its benches for African Americans black. Others relegated blacks to back rows, corners, or galleries.

The new racial order did not entirely preclude interracial cooperation. In early 1791, Secretary of State Thomas Jefferson approved Benjamin Banneker's appointment as "scientific assistant" to Major Andrew Ellicott, the presidential appointee to survey the District of Columbia as the location of the nation's capital. Banneker

Benjamin Bannaker's
PENNSYLVANIA, DELAWARE, MARYLAND, AND VIRGINIA
ALMANAC,
FOR THE
YEAR of our LORD 1795;
Being the Third after Leap-Year.

BANNAKER.

PHILADELPHIA:
Printed for WILLIAM GIBBONS, Cherry Street

The black astronomer, mathematician, and farmer Benjamin Banneker produced a widely acclaimed almanac and also served on the commission that planned the nation's capital in Washington, D.C. Benjamin Banneker was the grandson of an enslaved African named Banna Ka, who later became known as Bannaky, a name passed on to Banneker's father, Robert Bannaky. No doubt the spelling *Bannaker,* which appears on the almanac above, represents another change in the family's surname before it became Banneker. *American Antiquarian Society*

played a key role in the location of the White House, Treasury, and other public buildings. In March 1791, the *Georgetown Weekly Ledger* reported that Ellicott was "attended by *Benjamin Banneker,* an Ethiopian, whose abilities, as a surveyor, and an astronomer, clearly prove Mr. Jefferson's concluding that race of men were void of mental endowments, was without foundation." A certain level of cooperation also persisted among blacks and working-class whites. Some planters continued to report blacks running away with white servants, while others complained that runaway slaves and poor whites collaborated in defrauding masters of their property: "It is suspected those two fellows have joined themselves together again, and . . . that it is their design for Peter to be sold as often as they find it convenient if either of them is in need of money." Sometimes white women joined runaway slaves, including men who were the fathers of their children. One enslaved man, Jacob, escaped with an Irish woman, Betty Larkey, and their mulatto son.

THE RISE OF BLACK INSTITUTIONS: CIVIL AND HUMAN RIGHTS STRUGGLES

Despite evidence of collaboration across racial lines, such efforts were insufficient to offset the increasing coalescence of whites around notions of black inferiority. Consequently, African Americans heightened their own independent struggle for freedom. Their efforts gained sharp expression in the growth of protest movements, community-building activities, and plots against the institution of bondage itself. From the outset of the postrevolutionary era, African Americans rejected notions of racial inferiority by founding their own institutions and launching their own struggles for equal rights. In the summer of 1791, Benjamin Banneker, astronomer, mathematician, and creator of almanacs, countered Thomas Jefferson's racist assessment of African American abilities on two levels. On the one hand, Banneker based his case on the brotherhood of man and the fatherhood of God:

> One universal Father hath . . . not only made us all of one flesh, but . . . without partiality afforded us all the Same Sensations, and endued us all with the same faculties . . . however diversified in Situation or colour, we are all of the Same Family, and Stand in the Same relation to him.

On the other hand, he based his arguments on the rhetoric of the Revolution:

> Sir, Suffer me to recall to your mind that time . . . in which you clearly saw into the injustice of a State of Slavery.

On 17 October 1787, Boston blacks petitioned the state legislature for equal access to education. Under the leadership of Prince Hall—the Barbados-born black Revolutionary War veteran, minister, and fraternal order leader—the petition stated that blacks shouldered their share of the taxes and should

> have the right to enjoy privileges of free men. . . . But [we] . . . now receive no benefit from the free schools in the town of Boston, which we think is a great

grievance, as by woful experience we now feel the want of a common education. . . . We therefore pray . . . same provision may be made for the education of
our children. And in duty bound we pray.

In December 1793, the South Carolina legislature received a petition that stated
that the excessive taxes levied on the state's free blacks made their lives "but a small
remove from Slavery. . . . In confidence therefore . . . We do most humbly pray,
That your Honours would condescend to take the distressed Case of your Petitioners into your wise consideration, and Vouchsafe to Grant them such relief." Another petition decried the extraordinary hardship imposed on free black "widows
with large families, & women scarcely able to support themselves, being frequently
followed & payment extorted by your tax gatherers."

In 1797, free blacks moved their protests from the local to the national level.
Precipitating the increasing nationalization of the freedom struggle was a North
Carolina law providing for the reenslavement of any free black manumitted without approval of the state. Four North Carolina free blacks—Jacob Nicholson,
Jupiter Nicholson, Joe Albert, and Thomas Pritchett—migrated to Philadelphia
and soon filed a petition with the president, Senate, and House of Representatives.
Their petition, widely regarded as the first presented by blacks to the Congress of
the United States, not only appealed for help against North Carolina but also
protested the federal Fugitive Slave Act. Rather than ruling on the petition, however, the U.S. Congress voted fifty to thirty-three to reject the petition without consideration of its merits.

African American Churches, Schools, and Fraternal Orders

As whites ignored the appeals of free blacks for citizenship rights and social justice,
African Americans embarked on their own community-building activities. African
American churches, schools, fraternal orders, and mutual benefit societies gradually
increased (see box). Against the determined opposition of whites, free and enslaved
blacks gradually broke ranks with white bodies and established their own churches.
Independent black churches first emerged in the cities of Charleston, Augusta, and
Savannah. Urban blacks took advantage of their greater geographical, economic,
and social mobility and founded separate black churches between 1773 and 1775.
On the eve of the Revolution, a white Baptist minister named Palmer preached
among the enslaved people of Silver Bluff, near Savannah. Under the impact of
Palmer's preaching, eight slaves, including David George and his wife and Jesse
Galphin (or Jesse Peter), converted to the Baptist faith. Shortly thereafter, David
George, George Liele, Jesse Galphin, and Andrew Bryan emerged as gifted exhort-
ers of the early black Baptist faith.

When George Liele and David George left the country during the British evacu-
ation, it was men like Galphin and Bryan who shouldered the burden of building
the black Baptist church in the war's aftermath. In 1793, Galphin spearheaded the
formation of the First African Church of Augusta, Georgia. One white contemporary
described Galphin's countenance as "grave, his voice charming, his delivery good."

SOURCES FROM THE PAST

1802

John Marrant
Reports His
Conversion to
Evangelical
Christianity

I, JOHN MARRANT, born June 15th, 1755, in New York, in North America wish these gracious dealings of the Lord with me to be published, in hopes they may be useful to others, to encourage the fearful, to confirm the wavering, and to refresh the hearts of true believers. My father died when I was little more than four years of age, and before I was five my mother removed from New York. . . . Some time after I had been in Charlestown, as I was walking one day, I passed by a school, and heard music and dancing, which took my fancy very much, and I felt a strong inclination to learn the music. . . . I became master both of the violin and of the French horn, and was much respected by the gentlemen and ladies whose children attended the school, as also by my master. This opened to me a large door of vanity and vice, for I was invited to all the balls and assemblies that were held in the town, and met with the general applause of the inhabitants. I was a stranger to want, being supplied with as much money as I had any occasion for; which my sister observing, said, "You have now no need of a trade." I was now in my thirteenth year, devoted to pleasure, and drinking in iniquity like water; a slave to every vice suited to my nature and to my years. The time I had engaged to serve my master being expired, he persuaded me to stay with him, and offered me anything, or any money, not to leave him. His entreaties proving ineffectual, I quitted his service, and visited my mother in the country; with her I staid two months, living without God or hope in the world, fishing and hunting on the Sabbath-day. Unstable as water I returned to town, and wished to go to some trade. . . . One evening I was sent for in a very particular manner to go and play for some gentlemen, which I agreed to do, and was on my way to fulfill my promise; and passing by a large meetinghouse I saw many lights in it, and crowds of people going in. I enquired what it meant, and was answered by my companion, that a crazy man was hallooing there; this raised my curiosity to go in, that I might hear what he was hallooing about. He persuaded me not to go in, but in vain. He then said, "If you will do one thing I will go in with you." I asked him what that was? He replied, "Blow the French horn among them." I liked the proposal well enough, but expressed my fears of being beaten for disturbing them; but upon his promising to stand by and defend me, I agreed. So we went, and with much difficulty got within the doors. I was pushing the people to make room, to get the horn off my shoulder to blow it, just as Mr. Whitefield was naming his text, and looking round, and, as I thought, directly upon me, and pointing with his finger, he uttered these words, "Prepare to meet thy God, O Israel." The Lord accompanied the word with such power that I was struck to the ground, and lay both speechless and senseless near half an hour. When I was come a little too, I found two men attending me, and a woman throwing water in my face, and holding a smelling-bottle to my nose; and when something more recovered, every word I heard from the minister was like a parcel of swords thrust into me, and what added to my distress, I thought I saw the devil on every side of me. I was constrained in the bitterness of my spirit to halloo out in the midst of the congregation, which disturbing them, they took me away; but finding

CONTINUED

I could neither walk or stand, they carried me as far as the vestry, and there I remained till the service was over. When the people were dismissed Mr. Whitefield came into the vestry, and being told of my condition he came immediately and the first word he said to me was, "Jesus Christ has got thee at last."

Source: John Marrant, *Narrative* (London: Plummer, 1802). This document is also available in Dorothy Porter, ed., *Early Negro Writing, 1760–1837* (Boston: Beacon Press, 1971), pp. 429–432.

Moreover, the minister said, Galphin understood "the mysteries of the kingdom." For his part, Bryan preached to both blacks and whites in Savannah and its surrounding area. Before Bryan could secure the independence of Savannah's First African Baptist Church, however, he and his congregation faced violent opposition from local whites. Bryan himself suffered whippings and imprisonment on two different occasions, but he and his congregation stood firm. On one occasion, according to one report, Bryan "told his persecutors that he rejoiced not only to be whipped, but *would freely suffer death for the cause of Jesus Christ.*" By 1812, Bryan's Savannah African Baptist Church had splintered twice, giving rise to the Second and Third African Baptist Churches in the city. Independent black Baptist churches spread even more rapidly through the Upper South and the new western states of Kentucky and Missouri.

Although the decentralized structure of the Baptist denomination enabled black churches to expand rapidly, independent black Methodist churches also increased. The black Methodist movement was especially strong in the North. Under the leadership of Richard Allen and Absalom Jones, African Americans formed independent African Episcopal churches in Philadelphia. Born a slave in Philadelphia in 1760, Allen converted to Methodism at age seventeen. For several years he traveled through parts of Delaware, Pennsylvania, and New Jersey, working as a general laborer and preaching the gospel before returning to Philadelphia in 1786. When members of the white St. George's Church forced blacks from their seats to make room for whites, Richard Allen and the slave-born Absalom Jones spearheaded the formation of black Episcopal churches. By 1794, under the leadership of Allen, Philadelphia blacks had built and dedicated Bethel African Methodist Episcopal Church. At the same time, under the leadership of Jones, Philadelphia blacks formed St. Thomas Episcopal Church. Within one year after opening its doors, St. Thomas claimed a membership of over 400. By the onset of the War of 1812, St. Thomas had 560 members, and Bethel had soared to over 1,270. In 1816, free black African Methodist Episcopal church leaders from Maryland, Pennsylvania, Delaware, and New Jersey convened in Philadelphia and formed the independent African Methodist Episcopal (AME) church.

If southern whites resisted independent black churches, they were even more hostile to independent black schools and fraternal orders. In Richmond, Virginia,

Richard Allen, a founding leader of the African Methodist Episcopal church. *Bettmann/Corbis*

when Christopher McPherson sought to establish a black school, authorities jailed him and then committed him to the Williamsburg Lunatic Asylum. When blacks sought a charter for a Masonic order, they were repeatedly denied by the American order. Still, African Americans soon established their own Masonic orders and schools. In Baltimore, for example, the Sharp Street AME church soon doubled as "a school for the education of black children of every persuasion." Similarly, as early as 1787, when white citizens rejected their application for a charter, black masons turned to England and gained approval to set up an African Masonic lodge. They gained authority to administer mutual benefit funds, conduct processions, and perform burial rites.

Under the leadership of Prince Hall of Boston, the new Masonic order not only formed the foundation for mutual support and fellowship but also established, along with the church, a training ground for black leadership. By 1791, Prince Hall became the "Provincial Grand Master of North America and Dominions and Territories there unto belonging." The movement spread rapidly to other northern cities. Since the white Masonic orders of Europe and America turned to ancient Egypt as well as the Greeks and Romans for guidance, African Americans found the order's rituals and beliefs especially appealing. In 1787, at the same time that Boston blacks formed the Masonic order, Philadelphia blacks gained the cooperation of Quakers and formed the Free African Society, designed to offer mutual aid, leadership training, and charity work to "the free *Africans* and their descendants." Members of the Free African Society later formed Philadelphia's first independent black churches. Blacks repeatedly expressed their kinship with Africa in their institution-building activities: benefit societies, such as the Angolan Society, the Angola Beneficial Association, the Sons of Africa, the African Female Benevolent Society, and the Male African Benevolent Society; and schools and businesses, such as the African School, the Friends African School, and the African Insurance Company, to name a few.

Urbanization and Resistance Movements

The emergence of black institutions was the consequence not merely of racial discrimination in white institutions but also of the increasing spatial concentration of blacks in the urban environment. By 1820, Charleston and New Orleans had black majorities, and blacks made up a disproportionately large percentage of other southern cities like Savannah, Louisville, Mobile, and Norfolk. In the North, predominantly black clusters gradually emerged in cities like Philadelphia, Boston, and New York. From the early postrevolutionary years, for example, blacks in Philadelphia gradually increased their numbers in two separate parts of the city. The oldest cluster formed in the northern part of the city, in the North and South Mulberry wards, a poor district that also housed Irish and German working-class families. A new area also opened in the southern part of the city, encompassing the Cedar and Locust wards and the western section of the South ward. As realtors erected low-rent tenements in this area, it also attracted grow-

Andrew Bryan, a pioneer Baptist minister and founder of the First African Baptist Church of Savannah. *The Granger Collection, New York*

ing numbers of free blacks and fugitive slaves. The black population in this area rose from 265 free blacks in 1790 to nearly 4,200 in 1820. Blacks also moved into West Southwark and Moyamensing, an area south of the Cedar ward community. Although some blacks continued to live in the old northern location, by 1820 over three-fifths of all blacks in the city lived in the southern part of the city, in the Locust and Cedar wards, West Southwark, and Moyamensing. Blacks also gradually concentrated in certain sections of other cities.

Increasing urbanization also fueled Gabriel Prosser's plot to rebel, the most prominent manifestation of black resistance in the aftermath of the American Revolution. In the summer of 1800, enslaved blacks planned an assault on the city of Richmond. Beginning around April, several bondsmen—mainly urban artisans, blacksmiths, coopers, weavers, carpenters, and shoemakers—took advantage of their ability to travel to and from the various plantations to plan the rebellion. Over a period of several months, enslaved blacks participated in a mass organizing campaign. Although it is not clear who originated the idea, the blacksmith Gabriel Prosser, or Prosser's Gabriel, as he was called, soon emerged as the principal leader. According to recent scholarship, Gabriel headed the plot because of his extraordinary skill at making decisions, delegating tasks, and attending to details "to avert the strong possibility of disaster." Gabriel also exhibited a keen awareness of the growing class conflict among whites, which, like the Revolution itself, suggested

As the free black population expanded in the wake of the American Revolution, it faced exclusion and discrimination in virtually every aspect of American life. Free blacks especially resented the participation of Christian churches in this system of racial inequality and responded by setting up their own independent churches in the urban centers of both the North and South. This lithograph shows the edifice and parishioners of the African Episcopal Church of St. Thomas, Philadelphia, 1829. *The Historical Society of Pennsylvania,* A Sunday Morning View of the African Episcopal Church of St. Thomas in Philadelphia. *Lithograph by William L. Breton, 1829 (Accession #Bb862 B756)*

new possibilities for blacks to obtain their freedom. As plans for the revolt took shape, Gabriel and his two brothers locked hands and affirmed that "here are our hands and hearts. We will Wade to our Knees in blood sooner than fail in the attempt." The revolt failed when a heavy storm washed out roads, bridges, and access routes to the city. In the meantime, someone had leaked word about the conspiracy. Officials soon arrested several bondsmen, and within one month, authorities completed trials and hanged twenty-seven African Americans, including Gabriel Prosser. Twenty conspirators were acquitted and another seven pardoned.

Before authorities discovered the plan, enslaved blacks had organized their numbers over six counties and several cities. Gabriel claimed a force of 10,000 men ready to join the revolt, but other contemporary estimates put the number at 1,000 to 3,000. Under Gabriel's leadership, recruiters had fanned out over the area, asking prospective participants if they wished to join "a society to fight the white people for [their] freedom." One recruit later recalled his endorsement of the plan. When asked if he was a recruit, he replied: "By God I am. . . . I will fight for my freedom as long as I have breath and that is as much as any man can do." Under a banner reading "Death or Liberty," the men planned to arm themselves with guns, knives, and clubs; meet at a bridge on the outskirts of Richmond; kill all whites except Quakers, Methodists, and others associated with the abolitionist movement; and force slaveowners to liberate their slaves. If the owners resisted, the armed band would move into the countryside, organizing blacks for a general revolt against the entire system. Thus, despite its failure, the Virginia plot demonstrated the new role that the Revolution, work skills, and increasing urbanization would play in African American political struggles during the late eighteenth and nineteenth centuries.

Although enslaved and free blacks devised a variety of strategies for combating the institution of slavery and racial oppression, their efforts would remain insufficient. As the demand for slave labor escalated alongside a more intense and hostile racial climate, it not only reinforced and extended the institution of slavery and undercut the growth of the free black population but also aggravated internal conflicts within the free black population and between bond and free blacks. Color divisions emerged as one of the most potent conflicts within the free black community. The free black population had been disproportionately light-skinned but was now increasingly black. In the North and Upper South, slaveowners manumitted blacks with little regard to color differences and blood ties. The arrival of large numbers of Haitian refugees and the acquisition of Louisiana, however, reinforced the number of light-skinned blacks, particularly in Charleston, Savannah, and New Orleans. In Charleston, South Carolina, color conflict gained institutional expression in the creation of the Brown Fellowship Society during the 1790s. The society limited "its membership to free brown men only" and barred dark-skinned blacks, who later established their own society of dark men.

The West Indians were also people of considerable skills and wealth. As artisans, landowners, and slaveowners, their presence helped to instill class consciousness as well as color consciousness into social relations. In the West Indies, these people often held the balance of power between the enslaved and planters and frequently sided with planters in squashing slave revolts. A similar pattern prevailed in Louisiana, where free people of color secured the right to bear arms and participated in the wars of the region against Native Americans, other European powers, and even enslaved blacks. As such, European policymakers sought their help not only as allies in intercolonial and Indian wars but also as potential allies in their struggle to put down slave rebellions.

When the United States took control of Louisiana, officials at first sought to weaken the black militia. In the wake of the huge slave rebellion in St. John the Baptist Parish in 1811 and the War of 1812, however, Louisiana approved and strengthened the free black militia. Drawing on their earlier history in the colony, free blacks volunteered to help put down the rebellion of 1811. The state governor,

William C. C. Claiborne, accepted the offer, placed free blacks under white officers, and armed them against the bondsmen. After two weeks of warfare, the governor reported that the free blacks had "performed with great exactitude and propriety." A year later, the legislature approved and recognized the free black militia of Louisiana. These free blacks would play a key role in Andrew Jackson's defense of the city of New Orleans during the British invasion. Their service enabled free people of color to resist the further erosion of their status by white American officials. A similar experience greeted free blacks in Mobile and Natchez. In these areas, whites would sometimes say that "there is . . . all the difference between a free man of color and a slave, that there is between a white man and a slave."

∽

AFTER A VERY HOPEFUL BEGINNING during the early years of the republic, African Americans faced increasing limitations on their lives. Despite the growth of the free black population as the most visible symbol of the fruits of the Revolution for African Americans, the architects of the new nation elaborated on its racist design. African Americans faced the extension of the international slave trade through 1808, the expansion of bondage into the new western territories, and the intensification of racist ideology, which justified the institution of slavery and the denial of full citizenship to free blacks. Although free and enslaved blacks experienced substantial internal conflicts, they acknowledged their common interests and participated in individual and collective struggles for full citizenship rights for themselves, their families, and their communities. They appealed not only to the Declaration of Independence but also to the principles of evangelical religion. They repeatedly urged authorities to remove a variety of disabilities confronting enslaved and free blacks alike. Although blacks gained significant white support during the postwar years, white assistance had dissipated by the early 1800s. Only during the acceleration of the cotton kingdom during the 1820s and 1830s would blacks gain a growing number of white supporters. These efforts would culminate in the rise of a militant abolitionist movement, the Civil War, and the emancipation of some 4 million people during the 1860s. Part III examines these developments.

The Antebellum Era, Expansion of Cotton Culture, and Civil War
1820–1865

By the early nineteenth century, technological changes and the opening of new agricultural land in the Deep South had intensified the demand for slave labor. By effectively and cheaply separating cotton fiber from its seed, the cotton gin enabled cotton to become the United States's leading industry. Cotton dominated the nation's foreign exports and fueled the early industrialization of Great Britain and the northern United States, including the early industrial towns of Lowell and Waltham, Massachusetts. As huge profits from the production of cotton rolled into the South and the nation, it became apparent that African American labor stood at the center of the nation's wealth and economic well-being. Accordingly, a vigorous internal slave trade developed. Nearly a million blacks experienced forced migration from the Upper South states of Virginia and Maryland to the booming cotton states of Georgia, South Carolina, Alabama, Mississippi, and Louisiana.

Seeking to stabilize the enslaved African American labor force, large landowners increasingly combined what some analysts have called the "hard" and "soft" sides of labor discipline—that is, stiff restrictions on African American movement, cultural expression, and manumission, coupled with improvements in material conditions, including food, clothing, and shelter. Although such antebellum labor practices introduced a certain ambiguity into the lives of some blacks, the measures failed to create the desired pliant black work force. On the contrary, enslaved people used their improved material conditions to strengthen their families and forge new communal links, with each other on the one hand and with the free black population on the other. Their efforts involved not only greater communication from plantation to plantation but also closer relations between town and country as well as between regions.

The African American struggle against slavery gradually gained the support of influential white abolitionists and culminated in the coming of the Civil War. Enslaved and free blacks joined the Union forces and helped to transform the war between the states into a war for their own liberation. Part III focuses on the rapid spread of cotton production; the internal slave trade and the forced migration of blacks from the Upper to the Lower South; and the role of enslaved and free blacks in the advent and outcome of the Civil War.

~

CHAPTER 7

Under the Lash: Migration, Work, and Social Conditions

The late antebellum years witnessed the triumph of cotton as the South's and the nation's dominant growth industry. Like sugar, tobacco, and rice farming, cotton agriculture imposed its own technological, locational, and skill requirements and helped to transform African American life and labor. More specifically, large-scale cotton production stimulated the geographical reorientation of the black population from the Upper to the Lower South, the growth of a vigorous domestic slave trade, and the urban and industrial use of bondsmen and -women. As planters increased their dependence on black labor, however, they instituted new slave codes and social policies designed to stabilize black work forces. The new policies reflected what some historians call the "hard" and "soft" sides of human bondage.

On the one hand, planters took steps to improve the physical well-being of enslaved people. New laws not only redefined "the willful, malicious, and deliberate killing of slaves" as murder but also required slaveowners to provide "necessary" food, clothing, housing, and medical care for their bondsmen and -women. On the other hand, planters strengthened laws regulating slave movement, assembly, and self-expression, including new restrictions on reading, writing, and preaching. The coupling of material improvements and harsh disciplinary procedures established a new and more complicated context for the growth of African American culture and communities. Still, African American bondsmen and -women were by no means deceived by the growing complexities of the plantation system. They would use their access to improved material conditions to wage an ongoing battle against disciplinary measures, making it impossible for planters to fully stabilize the work force.

COTTON AND THE JOURNEY TO THE DEEP SOUTH

The confluence of a number of national and international changes established cotton as a new foundation for the nation's wealth. In England, revolutionary changes in the textile industry—that is, new spinning and weaving machines—cheapened the production of cotton fabrics and created huge demands for raw cotton. At the same time, northern states rapidly set up their own textile mills and created their own demand for cotton. Manufacturers had long recognized the value of cotton, but technological obstacles precluded use of the fiber on a massive scale. The difficulty of separating the cotton fiber from its seed represented a major barrier that made the production of cotton an extremely slow, labor-intensive, and costly enterprise. The fibers clung to the seed so firmly that they had to be cut or torn away by hand. This was particularly true for short-staple cotton, which grew in the interior, as compared with long-staple sea island cotton, which grew in the low-lying coastal areas of Georgia and South Carolina.

During the 1790s, when inventors like Eli Whitney perfected the cotton gin, which effectively separated fiber from seed, growing numbers of planters shifted out of rice, indigo, and tobacco into cotton production. The cotton gin enabled planters to expand the production of cotton beyond the coastal areas of Georgia and the Carolinas into the interior, where short-

At the gin house: blacks feed raw cotton into a ginning machine. Eli Whitney's technological innovation effectively separated cotton fiber from its seed and stimulated huge demands for slave labor. *Schomburg Center for Research in Black Culture/The New York Public Library*

staple cotton predominated. Cotton soon emerged at the center of southern and U.S. economic growth. Production rose from less than 300,000 bales in 1820, to over 700,000 bales in 1830, to over 2 million in 1850, to nearly 4.5 million in 1860. Cotton not only dominated the nation's foreign exports but also fueled the early industrialization of the North as textile mills opened in New England cities like Lowell and Waltham, Massachusetts.

The rapid rise of the "cotton kingdom" involved the painful relocation of blacks from the older Chesapeake and southeast coastal regions to the southwest. In the aftermath of the American Revolution through the early nineteenth century, Upper South tobacco planters and Deep South rice growers faced soil exhaustion, declining productivity, and a shrinking demand for slave labor. In Virginia, the price for an able-bodied male field hand increased from $350 during the early nineteenth century to $1,000 in 1860. By contrast, in New Orleans, the price of the same hand rose from $1,000 to $1,500. Although black women and children sold for much less than men, their value on the market also increased.

As the demand for slave labor escalated, nearly 1 million blacks migrated under the lash from the Upper to the Lower South. The Deep South states of Georgia, South Carolina, Alabama, Mississippi, and Louisiana absorbed the bulk of this black population movement. Between 1820 and 1860, although enslaved blacks continued to make up about one-third of the total southern population, they now lived mainly in the Deep South. In Georgia, Louisiana, and Alabama, African Americans made up over 40 percent of the total population, ranging from about 330,000 to 460,000 people in each state. In South Carolina and Mississippi, they were a majority. By 1860, nearly 60 percent of the estimated 4 million blacks lived in the Deep South (see map).

The Increasing Demand for Slave Labor

Under the impact of growing demands for slave labor, many planters adopted a "breeding" mentality. According to the writer and observer Frederick Law Olmsted, planters "commonly esteemed" black women less for their "laboring qualities" than for their procreative potential. One Virginia planter stated that his women were "uncommonly good breeders" and that he "never heard of babies coming so fast as they did on his plantation." Most importantly, he said, "every one of them . . . was worth two hundred dollars . . . the moment it drew breath." As an added incentive to childbearing black women, some planters freed them after they had given birth to ten to fifteen children. On one occasion, in an estate settlement case, a Tennessee court prohibited the sale of an enslaved woman because she was "so peculiarly valuable for her physical capacity of childbearing." It would be unjust, the court ruled, to deprive the heirs of her "service."

Some men were also valued for their sexual prowess. Ex-slave Elige Davison of Virginia recalled: "I been marry once 'fore freedom with home weddin', Massa, he bring some more women to see me. He wouldn't let me have jus' one woman. I have 'bout fifteen and I don't know how many children. Some over a hundred, I's sho'." Texas-born ex-slave Jeptha Choice recalled: "When I was young they took care not to strain me. . . . [I] was in demand for breedin'." According to Choice, his master "used strong healthy" men "to stand the healthy" black girls. A few traders specialized in the so-called fancy girl market—that is, mulatto women who served as house servants and prostitutes.

Traders frequently expressed an interest in buying "all likely and handsome fancy girls." Often described as "bright" or "brown skinned," such females sold for as much as 30 percent more than field women. Despite emphasis on the "fancy girl" market, breeding, and procreative potential, black women and men were highly valued for both their productive and reproductive capabilities. Moreover, as we will see, having children was part of the familial, cultural, and value systems of enslaved blacks themselves.

The rising demand for black labor stimulated a thriving domestic trade in human beings. Numerous small traders entered the field and worked aggressively to build up "their stock." According to a recent study, rural "grassroots" traders dominated the domestic slave trade. During the 1850s, over ninety-seven "documented" slave-trading firms operated in South Carolina alone. Interchangeably

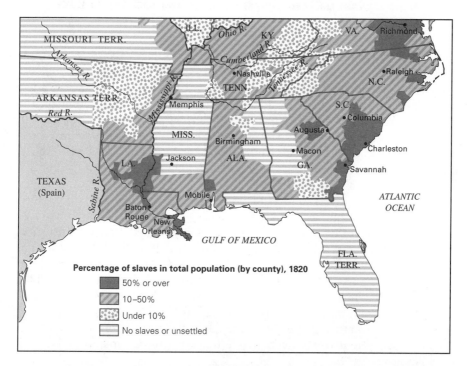

Percentage of slaves in total population (by county), 1820

- 50% or over
- 10–50%
- Under 10%
- No slaves or unsettled

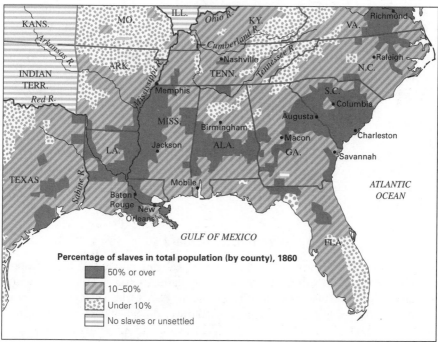

Percentage of slaves in total population (by county), 1860

- 50% or over
- 10–50%
- Under 10%
- No slaves or unsettled

Distribution of the U.S. Slave Population, 1820 and 1860. Under the impact of cotton production, the center of African American population shifted from the Upper South states of Maryland and Virginia to Deep South states like Georgia, Alabama, and Mississippi. By the beginning of the Civil War, the Deep South states claimed over 60 percent of all blacks in the United States.

referred to as "Negro traders," "slave traders," or "Negro speculators," such firms spread deep into the countryside, where owners and agents attended estate and execution sales and worked hard to locate private owners who desired to sell "a few Negro slaves." An advertisement of the firm of Clinkscales and Boozer on the North Carolina–Virginia border urged planters "having such property to sell . . . to bring them to us, or drop a line to us and we will come and see them." In a letter to a fellow trader, a South Carolinian wrote, "I have just met Mr. Barr from Alabama. He tells me prime fellows are worth [$]1050."

In addition to small traders, the domestic trade gave rise to huge urban-based slave-trading firms. Upper South and border cities like Richmond, Baltimore, Washington, and Norfolk became the key export centers, while Deep South cities like Charleston, New Orleans, Memphis, and Montgomery became the principal importers. Large traders included Austin Woolfolk of Baltimore; Seth Woodruff of Lynchburg; Hart and Davis, also of Lynchburg; and Franklin and Armfield of Alexandria, Virginia. Large firms deployed substantial capital and transformed the internal slave trade into an elaborate business with specialized functions. They employed their own sales and marketing forces, built their own holding facilities, and launched intense advertising campaigns. Franklin and Armfield, one of the earliest, largest, and most elaborately developed slave-trading firms, also maintained its own fleet of slavers.

Slave traders invariably advertised for large numbers of young blacks. Their business correspondence repeatedly emphasized that "persons having young slaves for sale will find this a favorable opportunity to sell." Although traders made some purchases "upon a short credit," they usually emphasized "cash" payments. On one occasion, the firm of Austin Woolfolk advertised for three hundred blacks ages thirteen to twenty-five: "Persons having such to sell shall have cash, and the highest prices. . . . Liberal commissions will be paid to those who will aid in purchasing for the subscriber." Such cash transactions sometimes included the sale of people by the pound, especially children. One trader wrote to his brother that he "would be willing and glad to [pay] for plough boys 5 or 6 dollars per pound. If the boy is very likely and weys 60 to 90 or 100—may be gone. If you can get Ned's boy at 7 per pound take him." The trader also instructed his brother to buy "likely girls" for slightly less per pound.

Migration Southward

African Americans entered the Deep South by water, land, and rail. Water transport included coastwise vessels down the Atlantic or "flatboats and steamers" on inland river systems. The journey from the Chesapeake to New Orleans was the principal component of the coastwise trade (see map). Many of these blacks left from Alexandria, Virginia, home of Franklin and Armfield, whose advertisements announced the array of ships available for carrying people to the Crescent City. On one occasion, the company announced the availability of the brigs *Tribune*, *Uncas*, and *Franklin*. In a visit to the firm in 1835, Ethan Allen Andrews, a Latin teacher from New Haven, Connecticut, reported that

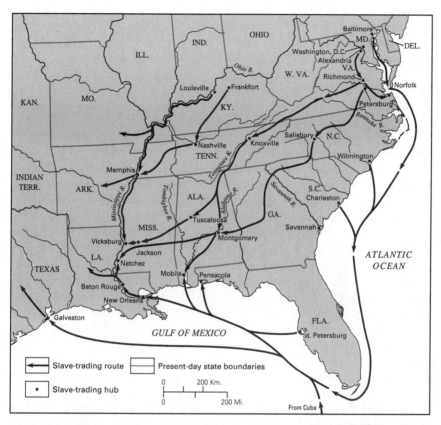

Principal Routes of the Internal Slave Trade, 1810–1860. Key to the redistribution of the black population from the Upper South to Lower South was the emergence of an extensive internal slave-trade network. Enslaved African Americans from the declining tobacco-growing areas of the Chesapeake entered the cotton-producing region by rail, water, and overland transportation, often on foot.

the number of slaves, now in the establishment, is about one hundred. They are commonly sent by water from this city to New Orleans. Brigs of the first class, built expressly for this trade, are employed to transport them. The average number, sent at each shipment, does not much exceed one hundred and fifty, and they ship a cargo once in two months.

Some observers described the coastal trade as an extension of the Middle Passage. In 1834, following a tour of one slaver, a visitor reported that

the hold was appropriated to the slaves, and is divided into two apartments. The after-hold will carry about eighty women, and the other about one hundred men.

> On either side [of the hold] were two platforms running the whole length; one raised a few inches, and the other half way up the deck. They were about five or six feet deep. On these the slaves lie, as close as they can be stowed.

Partly because of fear of revolt, some blacks entered the Deep South under even tighter controls. In January 1830, for example, one group of Norfolk blacks arrived in New Orleans "bolted down to the deck." Nonetheless, for most African Americans the relatively short journey along the eastern seaboard was less harrowing than the long Middle Passage from West Africa.

The Mississippi, Ohio, Missouri, and Alabama Rivers figured prominently in the inland transport and sale of people. Inland rivers produced their own tales of suffering and pain. According to William Wells Brown, an ex-slave, traders on the Mississippi, from St. Louis to New Orleans, confined bondsmen and -women to a "large room on the lower deck . . . men and women promiscuously—all chained two by two." During the 1840s, the traders Hughes and Downing transported people from Kentucky down the Ohio and Mississippi Rivers to Natchez. The partners placed their human cargo "on deck of the steamboat . . . chained two by two." In his recollection of sale down the Alabama River, the educated ex-slave Sella Martin later wrote: "In our journey of five months down the banks of the Alabama river, from Montgomery to Mobile in that state, I saw sights of suffering and wrongdoing, the remembrance of which makes me shudder as I write."

"Sale down river" entered the consciousness of blacks as an awful prospect. As a disciplinary measure to control slaves who remained behind, Upper South planters routinely threatened bondsmen and -women with sale to the cotton plantations in the southwest, the Georgia rice swamps, or the Louisiana sugar district. One bondsman later recalled that

> the traders was all around, the slave-pen at hand, and we did not know what time any of us might be in it. Then there were the rice-swamps, and the sugar and cotton plantations; we had had them held before us as terrors, by our masters and mistresses, all our lives. We knew about them all; and when a friend was carried off, why, it was the same as death, for we could not write or hear, never expected to see them again.

In his autobiography, Frederick Douglass later recalled the painful sale of a Maryland man to a Georgia trader. After the man offended his master with remarks about "mistreatment" and "hard work," "he was immediately chained and handcuffed. Without a moment's warning," according to Douglass, "he was snatched away, and forever sundered, from his family and friends, by a hand more unrelenting than death."

Although many blacks reached the Deep South cotton region by water, most traveled overland. Ex-slaves frequently recalled their sale and transport in caravans numbering more than fifty enslaved people (see box). Traders harnessed the women together with halters, similar to the ones used to restrain horses, and linked the men together with long chains and iron neck collars, which were padlocked. According to a former Maryland bondsman, the men were also "handcuffed in pairs,

---

1847

Fugitive William Wells Brown Describes the Domestic Slave Trade

On our arrival at St. Louis I went to Dr. Young [Brown's owner], and told him that I did not wish to live with Mr. Walker any longer. I was heart-sick at seeing my fellow-creatures bought and sold. But the Dr. had hired me for the year, and stay I must. Mr. Walker again commenced purchasing another gang of slaves. He bought a man of Colonel John O'Fallon, who resided in the suburbs of the city. This man had a wife and three children. As soon as the purchase was made, he was put in jail for safe keeping, until we should be ready to start for New Orleans. His wife visited him while there, several times, and several times when she went for that purpose was refused admittance.

In the course of eight or nine weeks Mr. Walker had his cargo of human flesh made up. There was in this lot a number of old men and women, some of them with gray locks. We left St. Louis in the steamboat Carlton, Captain Swan, bound for New Orleans. On our way down, and before we reached Rodney [Mississippi], the place where we made our first stop, I had to prepare the old slaves for market. I was ordered to have the old men's whiskers shaved off, and the gray hairs plucked out where they were not too numerous, in which case we had a preparation of blacking to color it, and with a blacking brush we would put it on. This was new business to me, and was performed in a room where the passengers could not see us. These slaves were also taught how old they were by Mr. Walker, and after going through the blacking process they looked ten or fifteen years younger; and I am sure that some of those who purchased slaves of Mr. Walker were dreadfully cheated, especially in the ages of the slaves which they bought.

We landed at Rodney, and the slaves were driven to the pen in the back part of the village. Several were sold at this place, during our stay of four or five days, when we proceeded to Natchez. There we landed at night, and the gang were put in the warehouse until morning, when they were driven to the pen. As soon as the slaves are put in these pens, swarms of planters may be seen in and about them. They knew when Walker was expected, as he always had the time advertised beforehand when he would be in Rodney, Natchez, and New Orleans. These were the principal places where he offered his slaves for sale.

Source: The Narrative of William Wells Brown: A Fugitive Slave (Boston, 1847), pp. 41–45.

---

with iron staples and bolts, with a short chain about a foot long uniting the hand-cuffs and their wearers." According to Charles Ball, who later experienced bondage in both the Upper and Lower South, "The poor man to whom I was ironed, wept like an infant when the blacksmith, with his heavy hammer, fastened the ends of the bolts that kept the staples from slipping from our arms." As for Ball himself, he added, "I felt indifferent to my fate. It appeared to me that the worst that could come had come and that no change of fortune could harm me."

Yoked together, men, women, and children often walked for miles, and for several weeks, before reaching their destination. Such caravans averaged on foot between twenty and twenty-five miles per day. One coffle traveling from Richmond to Natchez took forty-four days. Another traveling from Pittsylvania County, Virginia, took seven weeks. Still another from Yancyville, North Carolina, to Hinds County, Mississippi, took about thirty days. Catherine Beal, a former slave, recalled parts of her trip from Richmond to Macon, Georgia. "Late in the even's we stretched the tents and cooked and spread out blankets an' slept. Then after breakfas', bout sunup we start travelin' again." In 1834, the British author and geographer George W. Featherstonhaugh offered a similar but more detailed description of another overland coffle in western Virginia:

> Just as we reached New River . . . we came up with a singular spectacle. . . . It was a camp of . . . about three hundred slaves . . . who had bivouacked the preceding night *in chains* in the woods. . . . The female slaves were, some of them, sitting on logs of wood, whilst others were standing, and a great many little black children were warming themselves at the fires of the bivouac. In front of them all, and prepared for the march, stood, in double files, about two hundred male slaves, *manacled and chained to each other*.

Although most blacks entered the Deep South by land or water, some came by rail "on the cars," as the journey was called. In 1856, according to a northern visitor to the South, "every train going south has slaves on board . . . twenty or more, and [has] a 'nigger car,' which is generally also the smokers' car, and sometimes the luggage car." In February 1859, the *Petersburg Express* reported on the "SLAVE EXODUS"—"the car allotted to servants [slaves] on the Richmond and Petersburg

Overland coffles usually harnessed women together with halters, similar to ones used to restrain horses, and linked the men together with long chains and iron neck collars, which were padlocked. In this illustration, the carpenter and artist Lewis Miller depicts a less-regimented scene of slaves bound from Virginia to Tennessee. *Abby Aldrich Rockefeller Folk Art Center, Williamsburg, Virginia, Accession #1978.301.1*

Railroad was filled to such an extent that one of the spring bars over the track broke down, without, however, producing any harm." In 1848, a Boston newspaper described preparations for the transport of enslaved people from a Washington, D.C., railroad depot: "Quite a large number of colored people gathered round one of the cars. . . . I found in the car towards which they were so eagerly gazing fifty colored people some of whom were nearly as white as myself." In some cases, the railroads transported blacks to waterfronts, where they were then transferred to boats or ships.

Most African Americans entered the Deep South via the domestic slave trade, but some came via the underground international slave trade. Southwestern states regularly violated the ban on African imports until the eve of the Civil War. An estimated 54,000 Africans entered the country after 1808. In 1839, rather than insisting on enforcement of the ban, President Van Buren proposed an amendment to reopen the slave trade. Such a change, he said, would help to preserve the "integrity and honor of our flag." Other American statesmen and lawmakers were less easily persuaded. In the same year, for example, the Cuban slaver *Amistad* sailed into Long Island Sound near Culloden Point, carrying fifty-three Africans and two Spaniards. Under the leadership of Joseph Cinque, a member of the Mende ethnic group in the region of Sierra Leone, the Africans had overpowered the vessel's crew near Havana, Cuba. Although the rebels had killed the captain and another white man, they had also released all but two members of the crew and allowed them to go ashore. The African rebels had ordered the Spanish navigators to set sail for Africa, but the ship sailed into U.S. waters. The U.S. Supreme Court heard the case and set the men free. According to Justice Storey, "Upon the whole, our opinion is . . . that the said negroes be declared free, and be dismissed from the custody of the court."

Although the U.S. Supreme Court set the *Amistad* Africans free, by the 1850s, the movement for legalization of the international slave trade escalated. As late as 1859, the *Texas State Gazette* attacked the ban on the overseas trade as a violation of "every principle of justice" and "free trade." "The same reason which would induce us to approve a high protective tariff," the editor concluded, "leads us to protest against the fanatical laws passed to prohibit the African slave trade." Deep South planters feared that the increasing sale of blacks into the Lower South would transform the Upper South into hostile antislavery territory. In the *Montgomery Advertiser*, one pro-slave advocate declared that "free labor will necessarily take the place of slave labor, and when [it] preponderates . . . they will become antislavery states."

Although Upper South and northern states defeated such proposals, the underground trade remained a significant part of the slave labor system until the Civil War. Baltimore shipbuilders played a major role in building slavers for the international trade. The city became famous for its "fast, seaworthy clippers." The clippers sailed to ports around the world but were perhaps best known in the slave ports of Africa. The *Amistad*, for example, was a speedy Baltimore-built schooner. New York, Boston, and New Orleans merchants were also involved in the people trade. In June 1858, these cities accounted for all but one of twenty-two vessels captured and detained by the British navy for participation in the illegal slave trade, which some captains took few precautions to conceal. In 1859, the *Clothilde*, the last known slave ship to dock in a U.S. port, entered Mobile, Alabama. The ship carried nearly 130 West African men, women, and children.

Whether blacks arrived in the Deep South via the domestic or international trade, they usually arrived exhausted, ragged, hungry, and often sick. Nonetheless, the traders enthusiastically announced:

> Just arrived, with a choice lot of VIRGINIA and CAROLINA NEGROES, consisting of plantation hands, blacksmiths, carpenters, cooks, washers, ironers, and seamstresses, and will be receiving fresh supplies during the season.

Traders also used the language of advertising to describe their holding pens. In New Orleans, one trader described his facility as a "large and commodious showroom." Ex-slaves often recalled how the traders "instructed" the bondsmen and -women "how to show ourselves off." Traders ordered people to "talk up," "look spry," and even "sing." On such occasions, the food improved, the overt discipline eased, and the hard task of enlisting bondspeople in the business of selling themselves commenced. As one ex-slave put it, "When he go to sell a slave, he feed that one good for a few days, then . . . makes 'em look like they been eating plenty meat and such like and was good and strong and able to work."

Stories of the auction block were integral to the narratives of ex-slaves and the travelers' accounts of whites who visited the region. James Martin, an ex-Virginia slave, later recalled the details of the auction block for black men, women, and children. According to Martin, the traders put people "in stalls like the pens they use for cattle." Referring to black men as "Bucks" and women as "Wenches," the auctioneer supervised the bidding with "a big black snake whip and pepperbox pistol in his belt."

> The overseer yells, say, you bucks and wenches, get in your hole. Come out here. Then, he make 'em hop, he makes 'em trot, he makes 'em jump. How much, he yells, for this buck? A thousand? Eleven hundred? Twelve hundred dollars? Then the bidders makes offers accordin' to size and build.

In 1853, William Chambers, a Scotsman, reported an auction in Richmond, Virginia:

> "Sale is going to commence—this way gentlemen" . . . with her infant at the breast, and one of her girls at each side . . . "Well, gentlemen . . . here is a capital woman and her three children, all in good health—What do you say for them? Give me an offer?"

As with the early development of tobacco, rice, and sugar plantations, the first wave of Deep South enslaved migrants prepared the cotton plantations for cultivation and human habitation. They cut down trees, removed stumps, and burned brush. They constructed "big houses," slave quarters, barns, stables, and gin houses. During this phase of settlement and work, planters preferred a preponderance of able-bodied single young men and women. When newly arrived émigrés entered the expanding southwest, the "old planters" advised them "to buy none in families, but to select only choice, first rate, young hands from 14 to 25 years of age (buying no children or aged negroes)." After completion of this pioneering phase, the sex ratio evened out, and African Americans embarked on the actual work of cultivating the new crop.

PLANTATION, INDUSTRIAL, AND URBAN WORK

Cotton cultivation required extensive plowing, hoeing, and picking. In the spring, blacks plowed the ground, sometimes with double mule teams; opened "drills," or light furrows, in the cotton beds; and sowed the seed. During the hot and humid summer months, they repeatedly "chopped" cotton with heavy hoes to remove weeds and grass until the plants were large enough and secure enough to stand on their own and be "laid by"—that is, until the plant could grow and flower into ripened bolls. From September through December, bondsmen and -women moved the cotton crop from field to gin house to buyers. In this phase of the work process, African Americans picked, ginned, pressed, and loaded cotton onto wagons for shipment. Enslaved cartmen, horsemen, and boatmen transported the product over land and water to market. Beyond the fields, blacks repaired fences, houses, and barns; cut, gathered, and stored firewood; raised hogs; canned vegetables; and cured meat.

As cotton cultivation expanded, rice, sugar, and, to some extent, tobacco growers added cotton to their repertoire of crops. On his travels through the Deep South, Captain Basil Hall of the British navy noted the frequent combination of rice and cotton cultivation in the coastal areas of South Carolina and Georgia. On one South Carolina rice plantation, he observed that "this plantation, at the time [of] our visit [during the 1820s], consisted of 270 acres of rice, 50 of cotton, 80 of Indian corn, and 12 of potatoes. . . ."

In Louisiana, the sugar district competed quite closely with cotton for black labor. Firms frequently advertised explicitly for "NEGROES suited to the New Orleans market." During the late 1850s, for example, one trader advertised in the Charleston area: "500 NEGROES WANTED, WILL PAY MORE THAN ANY OTHER PERSON, FOR NO. 1 NEGROES suited for the New Orleans market." In the 1830s, another advertisement stated: "Fellows will be preferred with proper certificate for the New Orleans market." When the New Orleans sugar district advertised for women, it specified young "girls 16–20 heavy set and very smart, suitable for shipping purposes." Another trader lamented: "I am sorry that I have not got any good negroes on hand that will suit the New Orleans market. . . . Likely young men such as I think would suit the New Orleans market are very hard to find and also stout young women." In Louisiana's sugar district, some 68 percent of the blacks were males, compared with about equal percentages of men and women in the cotton district. In his enslavement on a Louisiana cotton plantation, Solomon Northrup later reported that his master hired him out on sugar plantations in the area "during the season of cane cutting and sugar-making" because of his "inability in cotton-picking."

Division of Labor on Plantations

Most antebellum blacks lived and labored on large plantations with twenty or more enslaved blacks. Whether they specialized in rice, tobacco, sugar, or cotton, large slaveowners concentrated on marketing, finance, and general management and hired overseers to supervise the day-to-day details of the plantation labor force. Overseers, usually poor whites, worked on annual contracts, with an annual income that ranged from as low as $100 to a high of $1,200 plus a house, food, and a slave as a personal servant. According to the instructions of one Mississippi planter:

> The overseer will never be expected to work in the field, but he must always be with the hands. When not otherwise engaged in the employers business and must do everything that is required of him, provided it is directly or indirectly connected with the planting or other pecuniary interests of the employer.

In other words, owners charged overseers with keeping daily records of plantation activities, making oral and/or written reports, and serving as guardian of the employer's property.

Although some overseers received good reports, most did not. Both employers and bondspeople regularly lodged complaints against overseers. A Virginia planter declared that the overseers were "the curse of [the] country, sir, the worst men in the community." A Mississippi planter described the majority of overseers as "passionate, careless, inefficient men, generally intemperate, and totally unfitted for the duties of the position." An ex-slave from Ashland, Kentucky, recalled "floggings and abuse" by "cruel overseers." A Missouri ex-slave referred to the various overseers on his plantation as "hard men, real devils."

The management hierarchy not only separated enslaved people from owners and overseers but also instituted divisions among the enslaved. Owners appointed drivers to conduct the direct supervision of other blacks. As a designated "head driver," some blacks were sometimes exempt from direct labor in the field, equipped with a horse and whip, and required to set the work pace for others. One South Carolina planter defined the duties of the drivers:

> . . . under the Overseer, to maintain discipline and order on the places . . . to be responsible for the quiet of the negrohouses, for proper performance of tasks, for bringing out the people early in the morning, and generally for immediate inspection of such things as the Overseer only generally superintends.

African American drivers occupied a precarious place in the plantation command system. If they pushed the enslaved people too hard, they invited the wrath of their fellow bondsmen and -women. If production lagged, they confronted the prospect of getting a flogging themselves and falling back into the ranks of field hands. In a letter to John H. Cocke, the owner of plantations in Virginia and Alabama, one driver, George Skipwith, described how difficult it was to discipline the black labor force. After he whipped one field hand for slowing down the work pace, the man then rallied other blacks against the driver. As the driver related, "He came up to the house to our preacher and his family because he knoed they would protect him in his rascality."

Despite such difficulties, some drivers developed effective managerial skills. A South Carolina planter, William Elliott, entrusted his plantations to two black "servants," who gained his approval to borrow and loan money in his name. Such practices breached the law; and, on one occasion, authorities fined Elliott for failing to retain a white overseer on his place. According to Olmsted, some planters employed white overseers "as a matter of form." Some female household workers and field hands also obtained supervisory positions. One ex-slave, Louis Hughes, recalled that each plantation had a slave "fore-woman who . . . had charge of the female slaves and also the boys and girls from twelve to sixteen years of age, and all the old people that were feeble." In Mississippi, another enslaved black later recalled a "colored woman as foreman."

As suggested by the use of drivers and forewomen, African Americans experienced substantial occupational differentiation and hierarchy. Beneath drivers was a broad range of craftsmen—carpenters, blacksmiths, weavers, and coopers, among others. Artisans occupied an even more pivotal role in the labor force than supervisors. Planters frequently valued skilled men more highly than drivers: Perry-Driver, $900; Jack Cooper, "good hand," $1,000; Pleasant Carpenter, "fine Negro," $1,000; and Moses Engineer, "good Negro," $1,000. Below these skilled craftsmen was a tier of field and household specialists—male plowmen, butlers, valets, and coachmen on the one hand, and female cooks, nurses, midwives, laundresses, seamstresses, and manufacturers of household items like soap and candles on the other. Finally, at the bottom were the general field hands, household laborers, and personal servants. As individuals, they were the least valued of all workers. Yet, as a group, the antebellum plantation economy turned on their labor. By 1860, an estimated 60 to 75 percent of enslaved men and women worked as field hands. In the field itself, planters often divided their work force into "full hands," able-bodied males in their prime working ages; "three-quarter hands," women, older children, and some older male workers; and "half hands," younger children, partially disabled men, and pregnant women. Owners subdivided field labor into "plow gangs," mainly men, and "hoe" gangs, which included the majority of men and women.

The gender division of labor was less sharply drawn among enslaved men and women than it was among plantation owners, their families, and white employees. With the exception of skilled craftsmen, large numbers of black women performed the same range of jobs as black men. They plowed fields, worked in hoe gangs, dug ditches, and picked cotton. Planters frequently remarked that black women could "do plowing very well & full well with the hoes" and were "equal to men at picking." Hoeing was backbreaking labor in the antebellum South, partly because the hoes were made out of heavy pig iron and were "broad like a shovel." One ex-slave recalled that manufacturers made the hoes heavy so that they fell hard, but the biggest problem "was lifin 'em up."

Although most women were classified as three-quarter hands, a substantial number ranked as full hands. In some cases, they were among the leading pickers on their place. On a Virginia plantation, Susan Mabry picked 400 to 500 pounds of cotton a day. An average worker picked 150 to 200 pounds per day. In eastern Georgia, Emily Burke observed men and women plowing "side by side and day after day." According to her observations, "the part the women sustained in this [otherwise] masculine employment, was quite as efficient as that of the more athletic sex." Another observer said that he saw no "indication that their sex unfitted them for the occupation." Although men usually did the heaviest lifting, hauling, and digging, some women routinely participated in these tasks as well. Ex-slave women from Mississippi and Georgia recalled that women "split rails . . . just like a man . . . split wood jus' like a man." The child of one black woman recalled that her mother was "strong an could roll and cut logs like a man, and was much of a woman."

Work Experiences on Plantations

Whether enslaved blacks worked on tobacco, rice, sugar, or cotton farms, their experiences varied somewhat by the size of units, the labor and skill requirements of different crops, and the principal mode of organizing work assignments. Although most blacks cultivated large plantations with twenty bondspeople or more, most slaveowners held fewer than ten blacks. Indeed, many slave-owning families owned fewer than five. On these small units, enslaved people worked under the direct supervision of their owners, who often drove plows and wielded hoes, while the owners' wives performed a variety of household tasks. According to one white South Carolina youth who grew up in a small slaveholding family, his mother "ran a spinning wheel, wove cloth, did her own cooking and milked cows," while his father "plowed, drove the wagon, and made shoes." Even when they could afford to delegate tasks to blacks and withdraw from the field, small owners often found it necessary to enter the field to work alongside bondspeople to save the crop. Observers often noted how such planters would "temporarily forget their pride" when illness or weather conditions created a shortage of hands.

The work experiences of black bondsmen and -women also varied by the skill requirements of different staples. In their autobiographical writings, ex-slaves regularly reported variations in the labor demands of the different crops. According to Charles Ball, who worked on plantations in both the Chesapeake and the Deep South, "the tasks" in the tobacco fields of Maryland and Virginia were not as excessive as those in the cotton region, nor was "the press of labour so incessant throughout the year." In his view, "the utmost rigor of the system" of bondage greeted slaves "on the cotton plantations of Carolina and Georgia, or the rice fields which skirt the deep swamps and morasses of the southern rivers." Rice production involved an intricate system of banks, ditches, flooding, and drainage, all highly labor intensive and hazardous to the health of workers. Similarly, as suggested in Chapter 2, sugar production involved not only its own seasonal agricultural cycle of plowing, planting, and harvesting but also the extensive heat, ditch digging, and drainage of water from the sugar houses. Tobacco was somewhat less labor intensive than rice, sugar, and cotton, but it still required sustained and strenuous manual labor. Tobacco workers not only had to plow and plant but also had to carefully transplant small budding plants from one cultivated field to another.

If the labor requirements of rice and sugar produced greater physical hardships for workers than tobacco or cotton production, the mode of organizing work assignments evened the score considerably. Although planters frequently used a mixture of "gang" and "task" systems, rice and sugar planters employed the task system more widely than their tobacco or cotton counterparts. The task system assigned enslaved workers a specific number of "daily tasks" and required their satisfactory completion. As Olmsted observed in eastern Georgia and South Carolina:

> Nearly all ordinary and regular work is performed *by tasks*. . . . For instance, in making drains in . . . clean meadow land, each man or woman of the full hands is required to dig one thousand cubic feet; in swampland . . . the task for ditches is five hundred feet [200 feet in a strong cypress swamp] . . . in hoeing rice, a certain number of rows, equal to one-half or two thirds of an acre.

At the end of a task, overseers and drivers inspected and approved the work before releasing bondsmen and -women from their day's labor. Partly because planters allotted small garden plots to blacks for their own use during "off time," enslaved people preferred the task system. After completing assigned tasks, they used their remaining time as they saw fit, including working their own fields, hunting, fishing, or enjoying a measure of leisure. One ex-slave woman recalled the possibilities of greater autonomy under the task system: "Oh, no, we was nebber hurried. . . . Master nebber once said, 'Get up an' go to wok', an' no oberseer effer said it, neither. . . . Oh, no we was nebber hurried."

In contrast, the "gang" system placed large numbers of workers in one group under close supervision of an overseer or driver. In a contemporary description of the gang system, the Englishman James Silk Buckingham underscored what enslaved people called work from "can see 'til can't." According to Buckingham:

> The slaves are all up by daylight; and every one who is able to work, from eight or nine years old and upwards, repair to their several departments of field labor. They do not return to the houses either to breakfast or dinner; but have their food cooked for them in the field. . . . They continue that at work til dark. . . . Absence from work, or neglect of duty, was punished with stinted allowance, imprisonment, and flogging.

The ex-slave Solomon Northrup, who was kidnapped in New York and sold into slavery in the Deep South, reinforced the same point. For him, there was "no such thing as rest." On the Louisiana plantation where he lived and worked,

> the hands are required to be in the cotton field as soon as it is light in the morning, and, with the exception of ten or fifteen minutes, which is given them at noon to swallow their allowance of cold bacon, they are not permitted to be a moment idle until it is too dark to see, and when the moon is full, they often times labor till the middle of the night.

Under the lash of the whip, "gang" laborers had few incentives to work harder or faster. The harder they worked, the more planters and overseers expected. At each phase of the agricultural cycle, especially during the harvest season, blacks faced a vigorous work regimen. After a day's work, according to Northrup, cotton hands faced a fearful moment at the gin house, where planters and overseers weighed the cotton and punished those considered unproductive. Whether they produced too little or a lot, he said, they approached the gin house in fear. As Northrup put it, "If it falls short in weight, . . . he knows that he must suffer. And if [he] has exceeded it by ten or twenty pounds, in all probability his master will measure the next day's task accordingly." Although blacks preferred the task system, the heavy labor demands of planters made both the task system and the "gang" system unpleasant. They were both slave labor systems that enabled masters to appropriate the fruits of black labor.

Urban and Industrial Slavery

Although slavery was fundamentally an agricultural labor system, it was not limited to the countryside or to farming. Alongside the expansion of southern plantations was the growing use of slave labor in rural industries and cities. Urban and industrial slavery was more flexible and diverse in its labor requirements than plantation slavery. Industrial bondspeople gained opportunities to arrange contracts with employers, compete with white workers, and move from one industrial site to another. Consequently, some contemporary observers (and later scholars as well) suggested that slavery could not survive in the urban environment. In 1848, a Kentucky observer reported that "slavery exists in Louisville and St. Louis only in name." In New Orleans, at about the same time, a visitor remarked that slavery is by "nature eminently patriarchal and altogether agricultural . . . it does not thrive . . . when transplanted to cities." Frederick Douglass later remarked that "slavery dislikes a dense population."

By the late antebellum years, enslaved blacks had declined as a percentage of the urban population in most cities. By 1860, with nearly 28,000 blacks, Baltimore had the largest concentration of blacks of any southern city, but most of them were free people of color. Between 1820 and 1860, except for Richmond—and for some decades, Mobile—women also outnumbered urban bondsmen, partly because of the high demand for female domestic servants, and partly because plantation-based buyers outbid their urban counterparts for the higher-priced male slaves.

Although enslaved people declined as a percentage of the population in antebellum cities, their absolute numbers actually increased. Between 1820 and 1860, Richmond's bound population experienced the most dramatic growth, rising from under 4,400 in 1820 to about 11,700 in 1860. Savannah's enslaved population rose less rapidly, from nearly 3,100 in 1820 to over 7,700 in 1860. In New Orleans, Charleston, Louisville, and Mobile, the population of bondsmen experienced substantial growth during the first half of the period but declined thereafter. Despite the decline, however, by 1860, Charleston and New Orleans had the first (13,900) and second (13,400) highest number of urban enslaved blacks, respectively.

Urban slavery suggests that human bondage was quite adaptable to a variety of settings. During slack periods in the agricultural cycle, planters hired or leased their slaves to a variety of employers. The system of "hiring out" augmented the ranks of urban and industrial bondsmen. Most cities designated a "hiring day" when planters came to town to rent or hire bondspeople to employers seeking to increase their own free white, black, or mixed labor forces. Although the hiring-out system existed throughout the South, it was most prominent in the Upper South, where

Virginia planters alone hired out some 15,000 enslaved people per year during the 1850s. Planters and prospective employers not only came together in town on hiring days but also placed advertisements in local newspapers, participated in public auctions, arranged private deals, and even used specialized hiring and rental agencies like Richmond's P. M. Tabb and Son.

Southern elites regularly touted the virtues of industrial slavery. In 1859, the New Orleans *Daily Picayune* predicted global success for the industrial South, based on its low transportation costs, abundant raw materials, and slave labor: "With raw material growing within sight of the factory; with slave labor that, under all circumstances and at all times is absolutely reliable . . . manufactured fabrics can be produced so as to compete successfully with the world." In Richmond, a tavern advertised for "fifteen men" and "three or four boys." A coach repair shop advertised for "six strong, active, intelligent, coloured boys, for a term of not less than five years." Another firm assured owners that their hired bondsmen would be "well fed, well clothed and well treated."

Bondsmen and -women frequently expressed a preference for the hiring-out system. It provided substantial latitude in negotiating working and living conditions, movement across the urban landscape, and opportunities to accumulate cash. In some cases, labor agreements involved negotiations around marriage and family. In a letter to a man who owned the husband of his hired woman, the owner of Virginia's Cloverdale Iron Furnace wrote, "We have hired the wife of your boy Nathan, and he is anxious that we should hire him—we are willing to take him at the rate of $125 per year." The owner approved the deal, but the employer made it clear that the details should be discussed with Nathan: "Talk with him about it and if you conclude to let him [come], . . . send him on as soon as possible."

Enslaved urban blacks also insisted on contracts that protected them from some of the most dangerous jobs, especially in the coal and iron industry. In 1825, one owner told an ironmaster that "his bondsman says that working in the furnace is ruinous to his eyes therefore I do not wish him to work there against his will." Similarly, another owner informed an employer about his "man Will"—emphasizing that he did not want Will "to work in the ore or blowing rock as he has been so much injured by it and he is very dissatisfied at it—but he is willing to work at anything that thear is not so much danger." Still another employer consented to let "my boy George . . . work at the blacksmith trade" but added emphatically, "I want you to understand me fully, I do not want him to work at the ore bank."

As the system of hiring out became more lucrative, planters permitted growing numbers of enslaved blacks to hire themselves. Artisans were the most numerous of these self-hirees. These included carpenters, coopers, blacksmiths, masons, shoemakers, cabinet makers, painters, tailors, seamstresses, and mechanics, particularly in cities of the Deep South. Contemporary descriptions of these artisans frequently employed terms like "first rate" and "excellent." Although many of these enslaved men negotiated year-long contracts, others arranged short seasonal or even shorter-term agreements. Such people gained access to resources and economic opportunities that sometimes allowed them to purchase their own freedom. Since southern states placed stiff constraints on manumission, some of the hirees became "free slaves" who worked unsupervised by owners that still retained legal title to their person. Accordingly, many whites abhorred the hiring-out system. Some newspaper editors complained that such practices "weakened the close connection of master and servant" and undercut "the respect which the servant should entertain for the master." One South Carolina committee investigated the issue and concluded that "the evil is he buys the control of his own time from his owner. . . . He avoids the discipline and surveillance of his master and is separated from his observation and superintendance."

Despite such protests, the hiring-out system was a lucrative arrangement. It served the needs of diverse parties and persisted through the antebellum era. As hired, leased, or corporately owned blacks, African Americans worked in a broad range of jobs in southern industries. Slave labor fueled the rise of southern lumber, naval stores, coal, railroad, textile, tobacco, and iron companies. By 1860, hundreds of enslaved blacks cut, loaded, and transported hardwood, cypress, oak, and pine to sawmills, where they not only hauled, stacked, and loaded finished slabs for transport to market but also fired and operated the steam engines. Forestry workers learned and executed the techniques of "girdling" trees, collecting resin, and manufacturing tar and turpentine products. At the same time, some 2,000 enslaved men entered "the darkest abode of man" to load and transport coal to manufacturing sites. As owners instituted boilers, steam-powered elevators, and water pumps, enslaved miners also operated the new equipment. Bondsmen also mined gold in Georgia, North Carolina, and Virginia—before the Comstock lode opened in California—and salt in the Kanawha Valley of western Virginia and eastern Kentucky.

In addition to rural-based industries like coal, lumber, and salt, African American bondsmen and -women worked in a plethora of jobs in the manufacturing, commercial, and transportation sectors of the urban economy. Slave labor fueled the construction of southern railroads like the Richmond and Fredericksburg, the Richmond and Petersburg, the New Orleans Pontchartrain Railroad Company, and the South Carolina Railway, among others. In a letter to one large slaveowner, an official of the Virginia and Tennessee Railroad hoped "to hire a lot of hands for the ensueing year to work upon the Rail road." The company also promised to "feed and clothe [slaves] well and treat hands with the utmost degree of humanity in every respect." In this case, the company's agent expressed desperation: "Give me a trial and I will warrant satisfaction." Railroad workers represented an important bridge between blacks in the rural-industrial, urban, and plantation sectors of the economy. Enslaved blacks served not only as general laborers, porters, and baggage and freight handlers but also as repairmen, firemen, and mechanics.

Antebellum industrialists also employed slave labor in textile mills, tobacco factories, and iron mills. By 1860, southern cotton and woolen industries employed some 5,000 slaves. Although some textile manufacturers started to replace blacks with free white labor during the 1850s, the southern textile industry had its origins in slave labor. After visiting one of the most well known of these establishments, the Saluda mill in South Carolina, a visitor reported:

We had the gratification recently of visiting this factory situated on the Saluda River, near Columbia [S.C.], and of inspecting its operations. It is on the slave-labor, or anti-free soil system; no operators in the establishment but blacks. The superintendent and overseers are white, and . . . principally from the manufacturing districts of the North, and although strongly prejudiced on their first arrival at the establishment against African labor, from observation and more experience they all testify to their equal efficiency, and great superiority in many respects.

Enslaved blacks also made up the work force of textile mills in Georgia, Florida, Mississippi, and Alabama. In some of these factories, bondsmen, -women, and children worked alongside white operatives.

The most prominent case of urban-industrial slavery emerged in the antebellum Chesapeake. By 1850, Richmond, Petersburg, and Lynchburg tobacco manufacturers owned, hired, or leased over 6,000 captive people. At the same time, an estimated 7,000 enslaved men labored in the ironworks of Maryland and Virginia. In the tobacco mills, different groups of workers carried out a series of interlocking assignments. One group separated the product leaf by leaf; another group arranged the leaves in layers and applied an "extract of licorice"; another group "rolled the [leaves] into long, even rolls, and then cut them into [tobacco] plugs of about four inches in length"; and, finally, another group packaged, loaded, and shipped the finished product.

Formed in 1836, Richmond's Tredegar Iron Works emerged as the South's leading manufacturing firm. Initially the company employed a mixed labor force of enslaved blacks and free whites. In 1847, however, when white workers walked out to protest the training and hiring of skilled blacks, the company dismissed the whites and turned to a slave labor force, except for "Boss men." In the iron plants, enslaved men not only did the hot, heavy, and dirty tasks of cleaning the plant and lifting and hauling the ore, but also performed the skilled jobs of puddling, heating, and rolling the iron ore into bars for market. As recent historians of the Tredegar Iron Works note, the proprietor selected a small core of bondsmen for skilled training. He depended on these men to train others, often their sons and/or other relatives and friends, for specific jobs in the ironworks. Moreover, the owner instituted an overwork system that allowed bondsmen to work beyond the specified ten-hour day to earn money for their own personal use.

Urban industries did not exhaust the use of slave labor. A variety of private and public sector agencies purchased, rented, or hired slave labor. These included churches, hospitals, social welfare institutions, and municipal governments. Southern municipalities employed enslaved blacks not only to clean streets and collect garbage but also to build and repair bridges, roads, waterlines, and other aspects of the city's physical infrastructure. Under close supervision and often in chains, blacks worked on these projects as hired slaves and also as convicts punished for infraction of slave codes. Deep South cities—Savannah, New Orleans, and Charleston—depended more heavily on slave labor for public works than their Upper South counterparts. In Savannah and Charleston, for example, enslaved firemen headed engine teams as well as serving as bucket and axe men. Municipal officials often praised these slave fire units as "efficient" and "well-managed" fire companies. In New Orleans, the city paid an estimated $30,000 per year to cover the costs of hired slaves. Such costs suggest that owners managed to profit from hiring out their bondsmen to public as well as private employers.

Although urban bondsmen and -women worked in a variety of jobs, most worked as general laborers and as household and personal servants. Men worked mainly as carriage drivers, draymen, wagoners, roadmen, refuse collectors, gardeners, messengers, and couriers of packages and letters. For their part, women cooked food, washed clothing, cleaned houses, and performed countless chores within and outside the home, including nursing children, caring for the sick and aged, and going to market. Such household workers were constantly on call. Whether performed by black men or women, general labor and household work was designated by elites as "menial service." A New Orleans doctor stated: "They are ever at the elbow . . . behind a table, in hotels and steamboats, ever ready, brush in hand, to brush the coat or black the shoes, or to perform any *menial service* which may be required." Yet, even here, the language of "menial service" camouflaged the enslaved black's mastery of a certain set of skills and know-how. Only indirectly, when they complained about the "difficulty" of "getting good service," did elites acknowledge the skills of general laborers.

Slavery in the West

Slavery not only characterized African American life in the antebellum South but also marked the experiences of blacks in the westward movement. In varying degrees, slavery extended into the states and territories of Texas, Kansas, Oregon, Utah, California, and the land of diverse Indian nations. The state of Texas had few blacks in 1840, but an estimated 200,000 by 1860. Although blacks cultivated the state's cotton crop, they also played a pivotal role in the state's expanding cattle industry. By 1860, some scholars suggest that African Americans made up the majority of the state's cowboys. The Mormon territory of Utah also legalized the institution of slavery but counted less than 30 slaves among its 59 black residents in 1860.

Some Native Americans also sanctioned the institution of human bondage. When the Indian removal treaties pushed Native Americans west during the 1830s, the Cherokee, Choctaw, Chickasaw, Creek, and Seminole held African Americans in bondage. Slave labor helped to alleviate the suffering of some Native American elites on their infamous Trail of Tears, which symbolized the "white man's" destruction of the "red man's" way of life. An estimated 175 slaves died on the journey west with the Cherokee. On the trail itself, African Americans served some Native Americans as cooks, nurses, and even night watchmen during encampments. On reaching their destination, Native American elites employed slave labor to reestablish themselves on the new western land.

Under the protection of federal law, the five Indian nations established their own plantation economy. In 1838, for example, George Lawer left northwest Georgia with 30 enslaved blacks. Within half a year, he had resettled in the Western Cherokee Nation and soon reported several hundred acres of farmland under cultivation with slave labor. By 1860, the five Indian nations held an estimated 7,000 African Americans in bondage, making up about 14 percent of the total population. As in the South, these blacks carried out a broad range of tasks, including the cultivation of corn, rice, and cotton crops.

Although other western states and territories outlawed human bondage, white settlers from Washington to New Mexico routinely violated the law. In 1852, for example, a Kentuckian in California wrote home to his father that "although the law made it impossible to hold a slave . . . longer than the present year . . . no one, will put themselves to the trouble of investigating the matter." Consequently, some 300 enslaved blacks worked in the goldfields of the state, and others worked in household service and general labor. After the Oregon Territory banned slavery, one territorial representative reported bondsmen in Benton, Lane, Polk, and Yamhill Counties. Still, compared with the antebellum South, slavery failed to gain a firm foothold in the West, partly because elites had access to abundant sources of co-erced Mexican and Indian labor.

BONDAGE, LAW, HEALTH, AND LIVING CONDITIONS

As the demand for slave labor diversified as well as increased in the antebellum South, planters took steps to stabilize their work forces. Slave states instituted new laws and social policies designed to improve the physical treatment of bondsmen and -women while tightening restrictions on African American access to freedom of movement, culture, and political expression. By the late antebellum period, most southern states prohibited "the willful, malicious, and deliberate killing of slaves," as well as "branding," "mutilation," and "starvation." The codes redefined the "malicious killing" of slaves as murder and prescribed the same penalty as murder of a free white person. Although the codes varied somewhat from state to state, they resembled the Alabama Code of 1852, which stated:

> The master must treat his slave with humanity, and must not inflict upon him any cruel punishment. Any person who with malice aforethought causes the death of a slave, by cruel whipping or beating, or by any inhuman treatment or by the use of any weapon in its nature calculated to produce death, is guilty of murder in the first degree.

The Alabama Code further mandated that owners provide a slave "with a sufficiency of healthy food and necessary clothing; cause him to be properly attended during sickness, and provide for his necessary wants in old age."

Antebellum southern courts sometimes found owners and overseers guilty of brutality or murder of blacks. During the late 1840s, a South Carolina court convicted an owner of starving his slaves. When the defendant appealed the ruling, the state Supreme Court upheld the conviction. At about the same time, a North Carolina court sentenced an owner to death for the murder of his female slave. The man had repeatedly beat the woman "with clubs, iron chains, and other deadly weapons, time after time; burnt her; [and] inflicted stripes . . . which literally excoriated her whole body."

Beyond changes in the law, some planters took practical steps to improve the physical well-being of enslaved people. Slave management literature proliferated. In magazines, newspapers, and journals, slaveowners regularly exhorted each other to provide clean, sanitary, dry, and warm slave quarters; hire physicians; and vary the diet of the enslaved. In 1836, in a letter to the *Southern Agriculturist*, one planter wrote: "*Cleanliness* is a matter which cannot be too closely attended to. Every owner should make it a rule to appoint a certain day in the week; for reviewing his negroes and their habitations, to see that both are clean and in good order." In 1856, a Virginia planter recommended that slave quarters "be built of plank, have large glass windows, and good chimneys, and should be elevated at least two feet above ground." Since most owners provided slave homes beyond sight of the "big house," one planter recommended "a coat of paint" and "some cheap ornamental cornice," which "makes a very pretty house and obviates the necessity for sticking the negro cabin out [of] sight of the mansion."

Not all slave housing was miserable. Some enslaved blacks lived in relatively good quarters. By the late antebellum years, on some of the largest and most productive plantations, owners replaced barns, sheds, and lofts with somewhat better wooden cabins. In Work Projects Administration (WPA) interviews, ex-slaves later recalled a mixture of one-, two-, three-, and even four-room houses. Olmsted described a Georgia village of some thirty tenement houses representing the upper end of slave quarters:

> Each cabin was a framed building, the walls, boarded and white-washed on the outside, lathed and plastered within, the roof shingled; forty-two feet long, twenty-one feet wide, divided into two family tenements, each tenement divided into three rooms—one, the common household apartment . . . each of the other [bedrooms].

Bondsmen and -women also gained access to small garden plots, which they used to raise corn, peas, squash, and sometimes sweet potatoes. Such garden vegetables supplemented their regular diet of corn and pork. One ex-slave wrote that "every plantation" had gardens, "patches, as they are called . . . in which they plant corn, potatoes, pumpkins, melons, etc. for themselves." As suggested by their diary entries, large planters and mistresses also exhibited a growing interest in the health of blacks: "I walked over to the quarters this morning before breakfast, to see a sick woman, found her quite sick." "Aunt Olivia went . . . to the quarters, found one of [the] negroes very sick." "On yesterday we [had] 16 grown negroes lying up—today 14." Partly through such housing, health, and nutritional improvements, the enslaved population increased by 23 to 30 percent each decade from 1820 through 1860.

Despite changes in the material conditions of enslaved blacks and their increasing life expectancy, their housing, health, clothing, and living conditions remained inadequate. Since most worked on plantations with large numbers of other blacks, their living quarters were more densely populated than the housing of rural whites. Whereas planters, small farmers, and poor whites lived in widely scattered rural households, blacks often occupied three-, ten-, or thirty-family communities. Josiah Henson, an ex-slave from Maryland, reported:

Most slaves lived in inadequate quarters, but their housing did vary from place to place. At the "model" Oak Lawn, Louisiana, plantation, the "Negro Quarters" included forty-two units. *From* Frank Leslie's Illustrated Newspaper, *6 February 1864. General Research Division, New York Public Library*

We [were] lodged in log huts, and on the bare ground. Wooden floors were an un-known luxury. In a single room were huddled, like cattle, ten or a dozen persons, men, women, and children. . . . The wind whistled and the rain and snow blew in through the cracks. . . . Here were the children born and the sick neglected.

In Georgia, according to Fanny (Frances Anne) Kemble, the well-known British ac-tress and wife of a southern plantation owner, overseers also made it difficult for en-slaved women to maintain clean quarters:

This morning I paid my second visit to the infirmary. . . . The poor woman Har-riet . . . was crying bitterly. . . . She and old Rose informed me that Mr. O___ [the overseer] had flogged her that morning for having told me that the women had not time to keep their children [and quarters] clean.

Ella Johnson, an ex-slave from the South Carolina Piedmont, recalled that enslaved people lived in "just little old one-room log cabins," usually with two windows and wooden floors, but other "poor old slaves had just the bare ground for a floor." The ex-slave Bill Homer of Louisiana recalled that the slave quarters comprised "fifty one-room cabins and dey was ten in a row and dere was five rows. De cabins was built of logs and had dirt floors and a hole where a window should be and a stone fireplace for de cookin' and de heat." An ex-slave from Georgia recalled "chimblies made of sticks and red mud. Dem chimblies was all de time catchin' fire." In Al-abama, another ex-slave reported, "Us have cabins of logs . . . with one room and one door and one window hole." J. L. Tims of Mississippi remembered, "We lived in an old log house. It had one window, one door, and one room."

Although planters clothed their personal servants and household workers in the best garments, they usually cut costs in dressing the field hands and industrial bondsmen. Many planters relied on enslaved women to produce "homespun" gar-ments for blacks, whereas others allotted small amounts for cheap northern fabrics called "negro cloth."

Enslaved blacks often suffered from acute respiratory and intestinal diseases. Respiratory diseases ranged from bad colds and sore throats to influenza, pneumo-nia, tuberculosis, and diphtheria. These diseases were especially widespread during the winter months when blacks inhabited poorly ventilated and unhealthy quar-ters. Planters frequently complained that "myself & several of the colored people have bad colds," or "hands & children have suffered very much from colds—in fact cold has been quite an epidemic."

Intestinal diseases increased during the summer months, when people spent more time outdoors in direct contact with the earth. Inadequate disposal of human waste and contaminated water led to epidemics of cholera, dysentery, diarrhea, ty-phoid, and hepatitis. According to one South Carolina physician, blacks usually en-tered "the open air for the calls of nature, in all kinds of weather." A Richmond physician later recalled how the accumulated piles of human waste were "regularly [but not often enough] scraped up, and hauled off to enrich the land" as "night soil."

Winter and summer, enslaved people faced the ravages of intestinal parasites. These worms affected the lungs, liver, blood vessels, gallbladder, vagina, anus, and skin. A recent study estimates that 30 percent of Virginia slaves "harbored worms during their lifetimes." These included tapeworms, associated with eating poorly cooked meat; roundworms, related to poor sanitation; and hookworms, which entered the body through contact with the ground. Barefoot, field workers and ditch diggers were especially vulnerable to the hookworm.

African Americans also suffered from sexually transmitted diseases, mainly syphilis and gonorrhea; various types of tumors, especially those afflicting the skin and bones; and mental disorders. Slaves with the latter were described in historical accounts as "deranged," "slightly deranged," or "lunatic" or as having "fits of insanity." Moreover, plantation blacks endured countless everyday mishaps that injured and sometimes even killed them: runaway mule teams and overturned carts, kicks from mules, and cuts and bruises from axes, scythes, and pitchforks. On one occasion, a 260-pound field hand jumped eight feet from a hay loft onto a sharpened pitchfork concealed under the hay below. Only miraculously did he survive the wound to his stomach.

Urban and industrial bondsmen and -women faced special health hazards, as they lived and labored under even more congested and unsanitary conditions than their rural brothers and sisters. When one Virginia slaveowner moved his family and enslaved blacks from the farm to a house in town, over twenty blacks died, as well as a few of his own family members. According to a report of the man's friend, crowded and unsanitary conditions precipitated the epidemic: "The lot was small, and back yard so much crowded with out houses, and trees, as to exclude the sun almost entirely. The cellars of course must have been exceedingly damp, and in them the Negroes lodged." Epidemics of cholera hit the city of Richmond in 1832, 1834, 1849, and 1854. Poor whites and especially blacks suffered disproportionately from such outbreaks. In the Norfolk, Virginia, cholera epidemic of 1832, an estimated 75 percent of the victims were blacks, who "lived in *low* damp places, in the basements of houses, in cellars and in kitchens without floors."

Among various ailments, specific occupational hazards compounded the medical difficulties of industrial bondsmen: lung disease afflicted tobacco workers; rock falls, deadly gases, and explosions injured and killed miners; and hot molten metal burned and damaged the skin and eyes of iron workers. Only in yellow fever epidemics, as a result of immunity provided by their sickle cell trait, did blacks have lower death rates than whites. In 1821, Norfolk whites made up 81 percent of yellow fever deaths. In Portsmouth, Virginia, in 1855, whites made up over 90 percent of such deaths.

Enslaved women and children experienced unique health problems. Females suffered recurring menstrual pain, discomfort, and often severe damage to their reproductive system. They regularly complained of amenorrhea, or "lack of menstrual flow"; excessive bleeding between menstrual cycles; and complications from both benign and malignant tumors. The plight of these women was often noted by visitors to southern plantations. "The first morning I was on the estate," wrote one visitor to a Mississippi plantation, "an old negro woman came into the room and said to him [the owner], 'Dat gal's bin bleedin' agin dis mornin'; 'How much did she bleed?' 'About a pint, sir.'" Moreover, childbearing women faced more life-threatening cases of puerperal (childbed) fever and prolapsed uterus than their

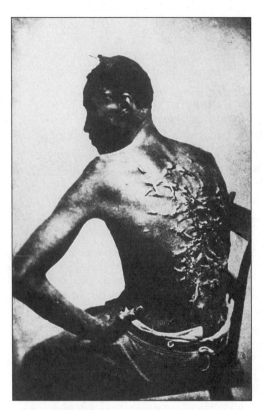

Floggings represented an ongoing source of pain for bondsmen and -women. Such whippings not only broke the flesh but also damaged internal organs. *Corbis*

white counterparts. For their part, children not only faced the full range of childhood diseases—including mumps, measles, and chickenpox, among others—but also suffered sickness or death more often than white children from neonatal tetanus (caused by improper umbilical cord procedures at birth); worms (partly from eating dirt); and "smothering," "overlaying," or "suffocation" (now referred to as sudden infant death syndrome), which afflicted babies between two weeks and four months old. Although antebellum physicians frequently referred to the death of black children who were "overlaid by the wearied [slave] mother, who sleeps so dead a sleep as not to be aware of the injury to her infant," most enslaved children died from serious medical complications during early infancy.

Although women and children faced special health conditions, their well-being was inextricably interwoven with that of black men. Floggings represented both a symbolic and concrete link in the living conditions of all bondspeople. Whippings not only constituted an ongoing source of pain and discomfort but also undermined the physical well-being of enslaved people. Floggings broke the flesh, weakened the physical constitution, and made the recipients vulnerable to disease. Overseers and drivers used a variety of whips: a narrow strip of tough cowhide, a whipcord, or a cat-o'-nine-tails, all of which left deep gashes in the skin. Others employed paddles or broad leather straps, which did not remove the skin with each lash but nonetheless caused blisters and often damaged internal organs. Plantation records, advertisements, and medical reports noted the impact of repeated whippings on the bodies of enslaved people. One male had "numerous scars and extensive callous ridges on his back, constituting permanent injury." Another man had "numerous scars, from severe whipping, over almost every part of his body." Still another was described as "very feeble, badly used, and much whipped."

In an unusual case, the governor of Virginia commuted the sentence of five hundred lashes on the back of a bondsman. A physician persuaded him that repeated floggings, even when punctuated by periods of cessation, left the "skin more sensitive to pain" and subjected the slave to intense "constitutional suffering" and damage to the entire body. As one ex-slave recalled after a whipping, "You be jes' as raw as a piece of beef an' hit eats you up. He loose yore [labor] an' you go to house no work done dat day." One female ex-slave recalled the beating of her brothers: "I can' never forgit how my massa beat my brothers cause dey didn' wuk. He beat 'em so bad dey was sick a long time." Following a brutal whipping, one hundred lashes on his bare back, Josiah Henson's father was a changed man:

> . . . previous to this affair my father . . . had been a good-humoured and light-hearted man, the ringleader in all fun at corn-huskings and Christmas buffoonery. His banjo was the life of the farm . . . but from this hour he became utterly changed. Sullen, morose, and dogged . . . no fear or threats of being sold to the far south—the greatest of all terrors to the Maryland slave—would render him tractable.

White mistresses also wielded the whip, especially against women. According to the recollections of one ex-slave, when one mistress got sick after drinking water and eating food served by an enslaved woman named Alice, she accused the woman of trying to poison her:

> She sez dat Alice done try ter pizen her. Ter sho yo' how sick she wuz, she gits out of de bed, strips dat gal ter de waist an' whip her wid a cowhide till de blood runs down her back. Dat gal's back wuz cut in gashes an' de blood run down ter 'er heels.

The injured woman was chained down until she recovered from the whipping and then sold to slave traders in Richmond. Harriet Jacobs later described her day-to-day fear of a jealous mistress (see box). As Frederick Douglass recalled: "A mere look, word, or motion—a mistake, accident, or want of power—are all matters for which a slave may be whipped at any time."

Planters and overseers supplemented whippings with a range of inhuman devices for inflicting punishment. While some planters built penitentiaries on the plantations to confine people for certain offenses, others continued to force enslaved people to wear eleven- to fourteen-pound iron bells and horns fastened and padlocked around their heads. One Kentuckian punished blacks by floggings, after which he placed them in the smokehouse. William Wells Brown recalled, "He made a fire of tobacco stems, which soon set me to coughing and sneezing." Moses Roper, who was enslaved in the Carolinas and Georgia, described how his owner, his son, and his brother each gave him 150 lashes which "ploughed up" his back. With his "back ploughed up by lashes," Roper recalled that his owner then poured tar on his head "and set it on fire . . . the pain which I endured was the most excruciating, nearly all my hair having been burnt off." Mistresses also supplemented the rawhide with other instruments of corporal punishment. As Lewis Clarke, a Kentucky bondsman, recalled, his mistress

> could relish a beating with a chair, the broom, tongs, shovel, shears, knife-handle, the heavy heel of her slipper, or a bunch of keys; her zeal was so active in these

SOURCES FROM THE PAST

1861

Harriet Jacobs Describes Life with an "Unprincipled Master and a Jealous Mistress"

I would ten thousand times rather that my children should be the half-starved paupers of Ireland than to be the most pampered among the slaves of America. I would rather drudge out my life on a cotton plantation, till the grave opened to give me rest, than to live with an unprincipled master and a jealous mistress. The felon's home in a penitentiary is preferable. He may repent, and turn from the error of his ways, and so find peace; but it is not so with a favorite slave. She is not allowed to have any pride of character. It is deemed a crime in her to wish to be virtuous.

Mrs. Flint possessed the key to her husband's character before I was born. She might have used this knowledge to counsel and to screen the young and the innocent among her slaves; but for them she had no sympathy. They were the objects of her constant suspicion and malevolence. She watched her husband with unceasing vigilance; but he was well practised in means to evade it. . . .

I had entered my sixteenth year, and every day it became more apparent that my presence was intolerable to Mrs. Flint. Angry words frequently passed between her and her husband. He had never punished me himself, and he would not allow any body else to punish me. In that respect, she was never satisfied; but, in her angry moods, no terms were too vile for her to bestow upon me. Yet I, whom she detested so bitterly, had far more pity for her than he had, whose duty it was to make her life happy. I never wronged her, or wished to wrong her; and one word of kindness from her would have brought me to her feet.

After repeated quarrels between the doctor and his wife, he announced his intention to take his youngest daughter, then four years old, to sleep in his apartment. It was necessary that a servant should sleep in the same room, to be on hand if the child stirred. I was selected for that office, and informed for what purpose that arrangement had been made. . . . During the day Mrs. Flint heard of his new arrangement and a storm followed. I rejoiced to hear it rage. . . .

. . . The fire of her temper kindled from small sparks, and now the flame became so intense that the doctor was obliged to give up his intended arrangement.

I knew I had ignited the torch, and I expected to suffer for it afterwards; but I felt too thankful to my mistress for the timely aid she rendered me to care much about that. She now took me to sleep in a room adjoining her own. There I was an object of her especial care, though not of her especial comfort, for she spent many a sleepless night to watch over me. . . . At last, I began to be fearful for my life. It had been often threatened; and you can imagine, better than I can describe, what an unpleasant sensation it must produce to wake up in the dead of the night and find a jealous woman bending over you. Terrible as this experience was, I had fears that it would give place to one more terrible.

Source: Harriet Jacobs, *Incidents in the Life of a Slave Girl* (1861), ed. Jean Fagan/Yellin (Cambridge, Mass.: Harvard University Press, 1987).

barbarous inflictions, that her invention was wonderfully quick, and some way of inflicting the requisite torture was soon found.

Despite the enactment of new laws prohibiting brutality to slaves, southern courts rarely convicted whites, particularly owners, of brutality against blacks. Bondsmen and -women could not initiate legal proceedings on their own behalf or testify against whites. As the Louisiana Code of 1824 put it, "The [slave] . . . cannot be a party in any civil action, either as plaintiff or defendant, except he has to claim or prove his freedom." Even when planters were brought up on charges of brutality or neglect of enslaved people, they dominated local juries and exonerated each other. In some of the most brutal cases, judges often took the position that "the power of the master must be absolute to render the submission of the slave perfect." Moreover, when the state put an enslaved person to death for committing a capital crime, it compensated the owner for loss of property. In Alabama, for example, the law stated:

> Whenever on the trial of any slave for a capital offense, the jury returns a verdict of guilty, the presiding judge must cause the same or another jury to be impaneled, and sworn to assess the value of such slave. . . . The owner of such slave . . . is entitled to receive . . . one-half the amount assessed by the jury, to be paid out of the fund assessed for that purpose.

In effect, the law defined most crimes against blacks as property crimes against whites. Slaveowners usually initiated such cases against an employee, lessee, or overseer of enslaved blacks. These men sought compensation for monetary damages to "their property." The enslaved person's "right" to live in a humane and safe environment played little role in such proceedings.

Although planters now provided blacks more medical treatment than before, such medical care left much to be desired. Preferred remedies for all kinds of ailments included "bleeding" and/or "vomiting," dangerous practices that undermined the body's constitution and damaged the health of the enslaved. Moreover, southern medical schools waged concerted campaigns to attract bondspeople and poor whites to their clinics. Under the guise of providing free or low-priced medical treatment, medical school clinics attracted enslaved blacks, compiled extensive records, and conducted outright experiments. Enslaved women served as subjects of early cesarean operations, and men and women were subjects of experimental vaccines and numerous operations designed to demonstrate certain procedures to young medical students. Abuse was widespread. On one occasion, when a master sent his slave to a local medical school for treatment of a leg ulcer caused by a burn, the surgeon amputated the man's leg, "just to let students see the operation, and bring the doctor, as well as the medical college . . . into notice." The editor of a leading medical journal denounced the procedure as unnecessary and the doctor as "heartless." Black cadavers represented a big business in cities like Richmond, which supplied the University of Virginia Medical School with "specimens" for "teaching purposes."

Slaves became the subject of ruthless medical experiments in antebellum hospitals. In some cases, they apparently benefited from "professional" medical care, but in too many cases they suffered more from their ailments. This sketch shows a man who apparently benefited from the treatment, but many others died. *Special Collections and Archives, Tompkins-McCaw Library, Virginia Commonwealth University*

Policies designed to discipline and control the slave work force took precedence over those aimed at improving the enslaved people's physical well-being. Accordingly, planters intensified their call for the vigorous enforcement of laws "on the books," including prohibitions on bondsmen and -women possessing guns, walking with canes, beating drums, blowing horns, and possessing liquor. The definition of crimes as well as prescribed punishments continued to differ radically for enslaved blacks and free whites. For the enslaved, capital crimes included murder, manslaughter, rape, and even attempted rape of a white woman; rebellion and attempted rebellion; and arson, robbery, and poisoning. Blacks could also suffer death for "striking" a white person. Since the demand for slave labor was so great, few enslaved people faced imprisonment or the death penalty, however. Whippings continued to be the most common form of punishment for blacks.

As antebellum southern states reinforced former restrictions, they also added new ones. They not only prohibited teaching enslaved people to read, write, or preach but also outlawed the practice of employing bondspeople in printing offices and giving them access to books and pamphlets. Planters, public officials, and religious leaders increasingly argued that it was not necessary for blacks to read the Bible to find salvation. One religious publication said, "Millions of those now in heaven never owned a bible." The prohibitions on black preachers and literacy were closely related to tightening definitions of "unlawful assembly" among bondsmen, which now included as few as five people. Other aspects of the codes prohibited slaves from administering drugs to whites or practicing medicine among blacks other than on the home plantation. A Tennessee judge declared: "A slave under pretense of practicing medicine . . . might convey intelligence from one plantation to another, of a contemplated insurrectionary movement; and thus enable the slaves to act in concert." In addition to the old laws requiring "submission" to the master's will, the new regulations and judicial interpretations aimed to control every "gesture, facial expression, or tone" of the bondsperson's interaction with whites. A North Carolina judge said, "insolence" could be construed as "a look, the pointing of a finger, a refusal or neglect to step out of the way, when a white person is seen to approach." The judge believed such acts performed by enslaved people violated "the rules of propriety, and if tolerated, would destroy that subordination, upon which our social system rests."

Southern cities and towns elaborated on the state codes and added their own regulations. They enacted strict curfew laws; required enslaved people to live in with their masters or employers; and took even greater steps to regulate their deportment and interactions with whites in public places. When blacks and whites met on the streets of Richmond, both law and custom required blacks to "step aside." Charleston prohibited enslaved people from swearing, smoking, or making "joyful demonstrations." Southern cities defined black communal activities as "disorderly" and prohibited the "shouting and dancing . . . and assemblies . . . of slaves and free Negroes in the streets and other [public] places."

Compared with the antebellum South, slave codes and social practices varied more widely in the antebellum West. Texas developed both law and customs that paralleled other parts of the antebellum South. Austin, Galveston, and Houston developed elaborate legal and extralegal restrictions on bondspeople. In 1855, an Austin ordinance outlawed the association of "any white man or Mexican" with enslaved blacks and empowered the city authorities to "control" and supervise the conduct, carriage, "demeanor and deportment of any and all slaves" within the city limits. For their part, although the Mormons approved the institution of slavery and blocked blacks from full fellowship in the church, the Utah "slave code" and church officials accented the responsibilities and duties of the slaveholders to enslaved people's material well-being. As such, they limited the ability of slaveowners to bring blacks into the territory. Among the Native Americans, the Cherokee instituted stiff slave codes that barred black-Indian marriages and expressed the "strongest color prejudice," while the Seminoles provided substantial opportunities for enslaved blacks to own livestock, bear arms, and pursue greater autonomy in day-to-day living.

The federal government reinforced the enslavement of antebellum blacks. In 1820, northern and southern states approved the Missouri Compromise, which admitted Missouri into the union as a slave state in exchange for the admission of Maine as a free state. The Missouri question had sparked some of the most acrimonious sectional debate since the nation's formation. It was the crisis over Missouri and slavery that prompted the aging Thomas Jefferson to write, "This momentous question . . . like a fire bell in the night, awakened and filled me with terror." The Missouri Compromise violated the Northwest Ordinance of 1787, which banned slavery northwest of the Ohio River. As a slave state, Missouri drove a wedge between the "free states" of Illinois, Indiana, and Ohio on the one hand and the far western states and territories on the other. Still, the Missouri Compromise established a firm ban on slavery north of 36°30' north latitude.

In 1846, as the nation waged war with Mexico, the U.S. Senate rejected the Wilmot Proviso, which called for a ban on "involuntary servitude" or "slavery" in any territory gained as a result of military conquest. Four years later, Congress strengthened the Fugitive Slave Act. Although the new law called for the suppression of the slave trade in Washington, D.C., it actually strengthened the hand of slaveholders, allowing them and their representatives to enter northern states and apprehend fugitives. Since alleged fugitives had no recourse to due process of law, the law encouraged the capture of free blacks as well as runaways.

Despite the ban on slavery north of 36°30' in the Missouri Compromise, the Kansas-Nebraska Act of 1854 disrupted that arrangement. The new law permitted slavery to spread well above the restricted boundary. As pro- and antislavery whites rushed into the territory to determine the outcome of its status as a state, violence erupted and helped to set the stage for the growing sectional conflict that would lead to the Civil War. In 1857, when the Missouri black Dred Scott sued for his freedom, the U.S. Supreme Court ruled that blacks "were not intended to be included, under the word citizens in the Constitution, and can therefore claim none of the rights and privileges which that instrument provides for and secures to citizens of the United States." As Chief Justice Roger B. Taney put it, blacks had "no rights that whites were bound to respect." Two years later, the U.S. attorney general also ruled that enslaved people were not citizens and therefore could not receive patents for their inventions. Until then, some enslaved blacks had gained official recognition of their inventions, notably Norbert Rillieux of Louisiana and Henry Blair of Maryland, who had received patents for sugar refining equipment and mechanical corn harvesters, respectively. The Dred Scott case, the fugitive slave law, recurring political compromises, and prohibitions on slave inventions all revealed how the federal government no less than southern state and local governments reinforced the institution of human bondage.

$\sim$

BY THE LATE ANTEBELLUM YEARS, the profits, power, and prestige associated with the plantation system underlay the transformation of African American life and labor. The growth of the antebellum economy entailed the spatial relocation of the black population from the Chesapeake to the Deep South, expansion of the internal slave trade, and the diversification of black labor. African Americans not only continued to cultivate sugar, tobacco, and rice but also added cotton cultivation and a variety of urban-industrial pursuits to their repertoire of skills. In other words, black bondsmen and -women not only helped to build the plantation system but also fueled the growth of southern cities and industrialization. Although planters introduced new policies designed to stabilize their enslaved work forces, stabilization was an incomplete process. As we will see in Chapter 8, black bondsmen and -women would use their improved physical conditions to build families, strengthen the bonds of community, and counteract the debilitating impact of bondage on their lives.

~

Community, Culture, and Resistance

The antebellum era ushered in more complex conditions for the development of African American life. Enslaved families and communities fragmented under the impact of the domestic slave trade, the difficult journey to the Deep South, and the double crush of old and new restrictions on their geographical mobility, literacy, speech, and assembly. To some extent, however, these forces were counteracted by the end of the international slave trade and the expansion of a self-reproducing black population. African Americans used the gradual improvements in their living conditions, diet, and health care to deepen their efforts to build families, cement bonds of community, and resist the impact of bondage on their lives. Bondsmen and -women carefully evaluated the benefits of material improvements against the pain of social injustice and rejected the notion of paternal kindness. One ex-slave spoke for many when he exclaimed:

> Kind! I was dat man's slave; and he sold my wife, and he sold my two chill'en. . . . Kind!, yes, he gib me corn enough, and he gib me pork enough, and he neber gib me one lick wid de whip, but whar's my wife?—Whar's my chill'en? Take away de pork, I say; take away de corn, I can work and raise dese for myself; but gib me back de wife of my bossom, and gib me back my poor chill'en as was sold away.

Bondsmen and -women defied both formal and informal restrictions on their lives and pushed for the liberation of themselves, their families, and the enslaved community. Rooted deeply in African American ideas about work, family, God, and social justice, antebellum resistance included a broad range of day-to-day confrontations with masters, mistresses, and overseers, as well as outright rebellion and plots to rebel. Although the struggle for freedom entailed significant internal conflicts along cultural, status, and gender lines, black bondsmen and -women not only made common cause with each other on plantations, farms, and industrial sites of the Upper and Lower South but also joined free and unfree urban blacks to fight for the abolition of slavery and the freedom of all African Americans.

JUDEO-CHRISTIAN/AFRICAN IDEAS AND THE BLACK FAMILY

During the antebellum years, Judeo-Christian ideas of monogamy and the nuclear family gained increasing ground among African Americans. Couples announced "marriage plans" with masters' consent and scheduled "weddings" where planters or enslaved or white preachers officiated. Plantation ministers stressed biblical prohibitions against "pre-marital sexual intercourse, adultery, fornication, and the separation of mates." Southern Protestants encouraged enslaved blacks to memorize such passages as

> Thou shalt not commit adultery. . . . He who looketh on a woman, to lust after her, hath committed adultery with her already in his heart. . . . St. Paul saith, fornication and all uncleanness, let it not be once among you. . . . Let every man have his own wife, and every woman her own husband.

Despite such pronouncements, over and over again former bondsmen and -women recalled how their marriage ceremonies stopped short of the important Christian phrase "What God has joined together let no man put asunder." By 1860, according to recent scholarship, a majority of antebellum blacks lived in double-headed households composed of husband, wife, and children. Enslaved men and women also had most of their children by the same mate. On the Good Hope Plantation of South Carolina, seventy-three of ninety enslaved men and women had all of their children by a single partner. Only four women out of this sample had children by more than two men, and in each case they settled into a permanent union with the third. On the eve of the Civil War, a study of Nelson County, Virginia, revealed that 31 percent of African American marriages had lasted more than twenty years. On sample plantations in Tennessee, Mississippi, and Louisiana, planters broke up an estimated 32 percent of marriages by the callous sale of mates, but the remaining 68 percent were considered "unbroken" over a long period of time.

Although enslaved families gravitated toward the Euro-American model, it was an incomplete process. Partly because the institution of human bondage often ignored gender differences, black men and women developed more cooperative and reciprocal relations than white planters, their families, and employees. In the master's household, for example, childrearing responsibilities seldom fell on the shoulders of white men, and white women usually escaped hard field labor or outside work. Conversely, black men and women often subverted these roles. When the owner sold Charles Ball's mother from her Maryland home to a Georgia trader, his father and grandfather stepped in and raised him. When enslaved women and mothers ran away, men often filled their shoes. When one slave woman, Betty Guwn, accompanied her mistress away from the plantation for long seasonal vacations, her husband took care of the family, including taking the children "to the field" and watching over them during working hours.

Unlike free white families, black married men and women often lived apart. As one ex-slave put it, there were two types of slave marriages: those on the "home" plantation and those "abroad," where men and women lived on separate units. Oscar Rogers recalled how his father used to visit the family only one day a week, but "he came early and stay till bedtime." When men with abroad marriages visited their wives without passes, they risked severe whippings. Millie Barber recalled how patrollers caught her father on her mother's place without a pass. "They stripped him right befo' mammy and give him thirty-nine lashes." Since married women remained subject to the unwanted advances of white men, some men preferred abroad marriages to avoid witnessing the sexual abuse of their wives and children. When federal officials interviewed black women after the Civil War, they frequently recalled unwanted sexual relations and rape by white men, using such phrases as "he made me mean" and "he took away my shame."

Although a plethora of circumstances could break up marriages and families, African Americans devised their own sanctions for families and defined appropriate roles for men, women, and children. "You see," a Virginia ex-slave said, "God made marriage" but "white men" made the law. In their familial relations with wives and children, black men sought to "provide and protect." During their off-time, men hunted, built furniture, and worked small garden plots to enhance the diet and comfort of their families. Men who performed these tasks, the former bondsman William Green recalled, became "great men in the family and the quarters." When black women faced punishment from overseers or masters, enslaved men frequently interceded with masters and overseers to "put de whippin'" on them instead of their wives. Despite risk of life or limb, some black men took extraordinary steps to protect their wives from abusive masters and overseers. One ex-slave, Josiah Henson, recalled:

> I can remember the appearance of my father one day with his head, bloody and his back lacerated . . . his right ear had been cut off close to his head. He received a hundred lashes on his back. He had beaten the overseer for a brutal assault on my mother, and this was his punishment.

When another man sought to untie his wife from a whipping post, the overseer shot and killed him.

Enslaved women also worked for the well-being of their families. They made, mended, and washed clothing; manufactured candles, soap, and dye; and raised, prepared, preserved, and cooked food. One ex-slave remembered: "My mother . . . could do everything. She cooked, washed, ironed, spun, nursed and labored in the field. She made as good a field hand as she did a cook." Some women also hunted and fished. Frederick Douglass recalled that his grandmother was not only a good nurse but also "a capital hand at making nets for catching shad and herring." Betty Brown of Arkansas testified: "My mamma could hunt good as any man. . . . She'd have 'coon hides n' deer n' mink, n' beavers, lawd." Women also improved the taste of food through creative cooking. African Americans regularly recalled their mother's or grandmother's "hoe" or "ashcakes," which required considerable skill. According to one ex-slave:

> She'd take a poker before she put the bread in and rake the ashes off the hearth down to the solid stone or earth bottom, and the ashes would be banked in two hills to one side and the other. Then she would put the batter down on it; the

batter would be about an inch thick and about nine inches across. She'd put down three cakes at a time and let 'em stay there till the ashes were firm—about five minutes on the bare hot hearth. They would almost bake before she covered them up. Sometimes she would lay down as many as four at a time. The cakes had to dry before they were covered up, because if they were wet, there would be ashes in them when you would take them out to eat. She'd take her poker then and rake the ashes back on top of the cakes and let 'em stay there till the cakes were done. . . . Then she'd rake down the hearth gently, backward and forward, with the poker till she got down to them and then she'd put the poker under them and lift them out. That poker was a kind of flat iron. It wasn't a round one. Then we'd wash' em off like I told you and they be ready to eat. . . . Two-thirds of the water used in the ash cake was hot water, and that made the batter stick together like it was a biscuit dough. She could put it together and take it in her hand and pat it out flat and lay it on the hearth. It would be just as round! That was the art of it!

Enslaved families enabled black men and women to demonstrate their love for each other, offer each other and their children a modicum of protection, and initiate the young into the intricacies of human bondage and resistance. It was in the black family and community that children first learned how to express their humanity, while training the tongue "to remain silent" and "mask" innermost thoughts in the larger world of plantation masters, overseers, and slave patrols. In the quarters, according to William Wells Brown: "The slave . . . is brought up to look upon every white man as an enemy to him and his race." Such discipline was necessary for both their own and their parents' protection. The ex-slave Elijah P. Marrs stated: "Mothers were necessarily compelled to be severe on their children to keep them from talking too much." Since black children played with white children until they reached nine or ten years of age, they sometimes said things to white children that got their parents into trouble. As Marrs further noted, "Many a poor mother has been whipped nearly to death on account of their children telling white children things." At the same time, enslaved parents instructed their children on modes of direct resistance. W. H. Robinson's father instructed him "to die in defense" of his mother. According to the testimony of a Tennessee woman, her mother instilled into her a sense of resistance to abuse. "Ma fussed, fought, and kicked all the time. I tell you, she was a demon. She said that she wouldn't be whipped, and when she fussed, all Eden must have known it." She instilled the same fighting spirit into her daughter; "I'll kill you, gal, if you don't stand up for yourself. . . . Fight, and if you can't fight, kick; if you can't kick, then bite."

Although enslaved children expressed the greatest admiration and respect for the authority of their parents, they soon learned the limits of their parents' power to protect them from mistreatment by overseers, planters, and members of plantation households. Jacob Stroyer recalled the first time that he was whipped by a white person:

This was the first time I had been whipped by anyone except father or mother, so I cried out in a tone as if I would say, this is the first and last whipping you will give me when father gets hold of you . . . but soon found my expectation blasted, as father very coolly said to me "Go back to your work and be a good boy, for I cannot do anything for you."

Moses Grandy described how his mother resisted the sale of her children:

> I remember well my mother often hid us all in the woods to prevent masters selling us. . . . After a time the master would send word to her to come in, promising he would not sell us. But at length persons came who agreed to give the right price. . . . My mother frantic with grief resisted their taking her child away; she was beaten and held down; she fainted.

When she regained consciousness, her children were gone.

Enslaved families not only initiated the young into an oppressive slave society but also worked to provide a protective fold for their growth and development. As Grandy's story demonstrates, however, their best efforts often failed. Thus, black

South Carolina, 1862. This photo reflects the value of family in the lives of slaves, despite much abuse and the absence of legal protection. *Bettmann/Corbis*

families continued to rely on certain African notions of kinship. Black men, like their white counterparts, initiated courtship and searched for wives on and off the plantation, but they drew on African aspects of their American culture and transformed European courting, marriage, and childbearing patterns. In Maryland and Virginia, as in some West African societies, some black men formally presented the woman with a brass ring as a sign of a proposal for marriage. If she accepted the ring, the woman became his wife. In like manner, in Georgia, after a period of courtship, the man visited a woman's cabin, roasted peanuts in the ashes, and, while eating, proposed marriage. If the woman agreed, they went to his cabin and became man and wife.

"Jumping the broom" was perhaps the most widespread African marriage ritual practiced by African Americans. Customarily, a relative or close friend from both the man's and the woman's side of the family held opposite ends of the broom, placing it about a foot off the ground. After the couple jumped together across the broom, they became husband and wife. Georgian Sheldrick Waltour recalled that he and his wife "jumped the broom" after the preacher "say de blessin' on us" but "befo' de feastin' begin." Josephine Anderson of Florida stated that the broom ritual "seals de marriage, and at de same time brings . . . good luck. Brooms keep hants away."

African culture influenced not only marriage rituals but also the actual types of families that blacks built on antebellum plantations. Rather than being simple units of husband, wife, and children, enslaved families embraced extended kin. These networks involved uncles, aunts, grandparents, and even nonrelatives—that is, "fictive kin"—in childrearing responsibilities. Numerous blacks later remembered the role of grandparents in their lives. Georgia Baker recalled that her grandfather took care of her and her siblings while their parents worked in the fields. Perry Jemison related that her grandmother was named "Snooky" and her grandfather "Anthony," and they both played an important role in her life as a child. In his recollections of slavery days, Austin Grant reported that his grandfather used "to tell us things, to keep the whip off our backs." When Ellen Thompson's father was sold and her mother later died, her grandmother took care of her with the aid of her uncles. When Mingo White of Alabama was sold away from his family, his father's friend stepped in and took care of him: "The only carin' that I had or ever known anything about was given me by a frien' of my pappy. His name was John White. My pappy tol' him to take care of me for him."

Under the impact of antebellum bondage, certain African ideas about sex and sexual relations also persisted. As recent scholars note, enslaved women adhered to notions of motherhood that were deeply rooted in the African past. As in many West African societies, bondswomen considered motherhood a nearly "sacred" act. Thus, for many, "a marriage was not considered consummated until after the birth of the first child." Consequently, enslaved blacks rejected white society's notion of prenuptial intercourse and out-of-wedlock motherhood as "evil." In so doing, they modified "guilt-laden" Euro-American sexual mores, yet at the same time enslaved mothers worked diligently to protect their young daughters from premature maternal responsibility.

RELIGION, MUSIC, AND LEISURE TIME ACTIVITIES

The transformation of the black family was closely intertwined with changes in African American religious beliefs and practices. During the 1820s and 1830s, planters placed growing restrictions on African American organized religious activities. As discussed in Chapter 7, blacks found it exceedingly difficult to pursue their own modes of worship, particularly following Nat Turner's rebellion in 1831 (see page 203). After Turner's insurrection, for example, a new Mississippi statute stated: "It is unlawful for any slave, free Negro, or mulatto to preach the gospel upon pain of receiving thirty-nine lashes upon the naked back of the . . . preacher." When blacks defied the law, ex-slave West Turner of Virginia said, "Den dey would rush in an' start whippin' and beatin' de slaves unmerciful, saying that 'You ain't got no time to serve God. We bought you to serve us.'"

During the early 1840s, southern Methodists and Baptists split from their northern counterparts over the issue of slavery. After parting ways with northern abolitionist congregations, rising numbers of planters now believed that it was "safe" to proselytize the enslaved. Some planters built "small chapels" or "praise houses" for slaves and hired white ministers to supervise their services, whereas others gradually incorporated blacks into segregated sections of white congregations. Black membership in the Methodist denomination rose from 94,000 in 1840 to 207,000 in 1860. When we add the number of blacks served by missionaries and Sunday schools, the number of black Methodists reached over 453,300. Although the Baptists expended fewer resources proselytizing among enslaved people and kept less systematic statistics, the number of black Baptists also dramatically expanded. In 1846, the Southern Baptist Association reported 150,000 black members. By 1860, an estimated 400,000 blacks belonged to southern Baptist churches. The number reached 600,000 with the addition of blacks attending Baptist Sunday schools. Other denominations—Presbyterian, Episcopalian, Church of Christ, Lutheran, and Quaker—also swelled the ranks of black Protestants by several thousands. In some Baptist and Methodist churches, blacks made up 20 to 40 percent of the total and were often the majority.

In these biracial churches, enslaved blacks received heavy doses of the "Pauline" scriptures. First Corinthians 7:21 represented the key message for slaves: "Let every man abide in the same calling wherein he was called. Art thou called servant? Care not for it. . . ." Ex-slave Henry Bibb recalled the same passages. "Servants be obedient to your masters,—and he that knoweth his master's will and doeth it not shall be beatin' with many stripes;—means that God will send them to hell, if they disobey their masters." Plantation ministers also prohibited the use of musical instruments and what they called "secular dancing" in religious services.

African American Religious Beliefs and Practices

Bondsmen and -women detested the self-serving sermons and restrictions on the physical expression of their beliefs in plantation churches. In his comments on the

Pauline scriptures, one ex-slave remarked that "this kind of preaching has driven thousands into infidelity . . . they cannot believe or trust in such a religion." Thus, blacks pushed for their own independent forms of worship. Since white ministers often appointed enslaved preachers, gave them special passes, and permitted them to travel widely from plantation to plantation, carrying the message to the black community, blacks gained an extraordinary opportunity to worship in their own way. The Baptist minister Reverend John Jasper of Virginia emerged as one of the most renowned of the enslaved antebellum preachers. In the Richmond-Petersburg area of Virginia, whites and blacks acknowledged the fame of Reverend Jasper from about 1830 through the antebellum years. The son of an enslaved field hand father and household servant, Jasper migrated to Richmond from rural Virginia, where he had also worked as a field hand. According to Jasper's biographer, "He marshalled the Scriptures with consummate skill, and built an argument easily understood" by his illiterate hearers, and "yet so compact and tactful was he, that his most cultured hearers bent beneath his force." By the eve of the Civil War, as whites turned toward seminary-trained ministers and curtailed the emotional style of the Great Awakening, African Americans retained the earlier forms and in some ways elaborated on them. Blacks continued to punctuate sermons with verbal responses: "Yes, glory! That's it, hit him again! . . . Yes, sweet Lord! Yes, sir!" Under the influence of enslaved ministers like Jasper, one observer reported, blacks worked "themselves up to a great pitch of excitement, in which they yell and cry along, and finally shriek and leap up, clapping their hands and dancing."

As the Methodist denominations penetrated southern plantations, they silenced slave instruments of music, such as the banjo and the fiddle, and prohibited "secular dancing." In place of previous musical and dance forms, blacks built on their African heritage and created the "ring shout." Charles Lyell, a visitor to the South Carolina and Georgia sea islands offered one of the earliest descriptions of the ring shout:

> At the Methodist prayer meetings, they are permitted to move round rapidly in a ring, joining hands in token brotherly love, presenting the right hand and then the left, in which manner, I am told, they sometimes contrive to take enough exercise to serve as a substitute for the dance.

Among the Gullah, such shouts took place after the regular service and benediction. Moreover, although they sang Baptist and Methodist hymns during regular service, blacks sang only their spirituals during the ring shout.

Even as enslaved blacks worshipped under white supervision or with planters' permission, they also carved out underground churches called "brush arbors" or "hush harbors." According to ex-slave Amanda McCray, "The grass never had a chance ter grow for the troubled knees that kept it crushed down." In these settings, away from the watchful eye of masters, African Americans introduced their own interpretation of evangelical Protestantism and transformed it to meet their own needs. Whereas slaveowners exhorted blacks to obey their masters, blacks emphasized the scriptures that proclaimed all people "equal in the eyes of God." As a result of their deep belief that the Bible held the key to their own liberation, some enslaved people defied the ban on learning to read so that they could read the Bible.

Even as enslaved blacks worshipped under white supervision, they also carved out underground churches called "brush arbors" or "hush harbors," where they worshiped as they pleased, conducting their own baptismal, marriage, and burial rites. Here they conduct a funeral. *The Historic New Orleans Collection, accession no. 1960.46*

One ex-slave, William McWhorter, recalled: "Dey jus' beat 'em up bad when dey catched 'em studin', readin', and writin'." Still, McWhorter continued, "some dat wanted larnin' so bad dey would slip out at night and meet in a deep gully whar dey would study by de light'ood torchers . . . and if dey was lucky enough 'til dey larned to read de Bible, dey kept it a close secret."

Although some planters gradually permitted the distribution of Bibles to enslaved blacks, most continued to withhold the written word. Even so, blacks who could not read gained access to the Bible through the oral transmission of memorized biblical stories. As one Beaufort, South Carolina, ex-slave woman exclaimed:

Oh! I don't know nothing! I can't read a word. But, oh! I read Jesus in my heart, just as you read him in de book. . . . I read him here in my heart just as you read him in de Bible. O, . . . my God! I got Him! I hold him here all de time! He stay with me!

Another ex-slave stated simply: "I reckin somethin' inside just told us about God and that there was a better place hereafter."

"Brush arbors" underscored not only the restrictions on bondspeople in biracial Christian churches but also the persistence of unique African religious expression among African Americans. In these unsupervised settings, blacks replenished the African aspects of their culture and reinforced the growth of distinct African American religious beliefs and practices. Underground black preachers also conducted baptisms, weddings, and funerals. In his narrative, Charles Ball of Maryland recalled the influence of African practices on funeral rites in the Upper South. Ball described in substantial detail the funeral of an enslaved child whom he helped to inter:

> Its father buried with it, a small bow and several arrows; a little bag of parched meal; a miniature canoe, about a foot long, and a little paddle, (with which he said it would cross the ocean to his own country), [a] small stick, with an iron nail, sharpened and fastened into one end of it; and a piece of white muslin, with several curious and strange figures painted on it in blue and red, by which he said, his relatives and countrymen would know the infant to be his son, and would receive it accordingly, on its arrival amongst them. . . . [He] cut a lock of hair from his head, threw it upon the dead infant, and closed the grave with his own hands. He then told us the God of his country was looking at him, and was pleased with what he had done.

Ideas and practices described as "voodoo-like" also persisted. Afro-Christians believed in herbalism, ghost lore, witchcraft, fortune telling, and especially conjuring, the belief that one person could cause harm to another through supernatural practices. A Virginian, Duncan Gaines, recalled the practice in antebellum Virginia: "There was much talk of voodism and anyone ill for a long time without getting relief from herb medicine was thought to be 'fixed' or suffering from some sin that his father had committed." Thus, the conjurers, root doctors, or voodoo doctors competed with slave preachers and retained substantial influence in the enslaved community. Their influence rested on their ability to "fix" and undo "fixes." According to Henry Bibb, "The remedy is most generally some kind of bitter root; they are directed to chew it and spit towards their masters when they are angry with slaves. At other times they prepare certain kinds of powders, to sprinkle about their master's dwellings." Although such practices gained expression in the Upper South, they were most prominent in the Deep South states of South Carolina, Georgia, and Louisiana.

Some conjurers developed the admiration, fear, and respect of all on the place. William Wells Brown recalled how the conjurer Dinkie lived independent of blacks and whites. Fellow blacks, overseers, and masters alike left Dinkie alone. "No one interfered with him. . . . Dinkie hunted, slept, was at the table at meal time, roamed the woods, went to the city, and returned when he pleased." Since so many conjurers endured the whip like other slaves, some argued that only blacks could be conjured. When their medicine failed, however, conjurers sometimes blamed the victim for failing to follow instructions. When one man complained after receiving a whipping despite following the conjurer's advice, the conjurer told him: "I gi' you a runin' han' [a charm that would give the possessor swiftness]! Why didn't yer

1. Slave Drum, Virginia (c. 1645).
From the outset of their enslavement, Africans used their Old World experience to fashion a new culture in the Americas. Modeled after similar drums in West African society, this drum suggests the impact of African culture on black life in colonial America. Because Africans used drums for both leisure and resistance activities, colonial assemblies came to outlaw their use.

2. *The Old Plantation* (c. 1800). Although this watercolor by an unknown artist was found in South Carolina, its precise origins and meaning are uncertain. The most recent interpretation is that the scene represents a double-wedding ceremony with participants playing instruments and wearing clothes that suggest a mixture of West African and European styles.

3. Pieced Quilt, Beaver Dam Plantation, Hanover County, Virginia (late 18th century).
This is the earliest known slave-made quilt in the United States. On southern plantations, black women became skilled quilters, and they perfected designs and juxta-
posed colors that reflected their own aesthetic values and tastes.

**4. Shotgun House, New
Orleans (mid-19th century).**
The shotgun house (so called
from the saying that a bullet
fired at the entrance would
travel uninterrupted out the
back door) represents the chief
African American contribution
to American vernacular architecture. Black migrants from
the Caribbean islands of Haiti
and Cuba brought the design
to New Orleans and Charleston
during the early 1800s.

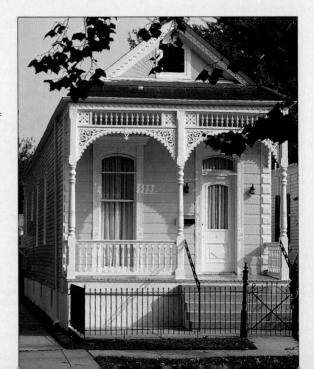

5–6. Dutreuil Barjon, Sleigh Bed (c. 1835), and Peter Bentzon, Footed Cup (c. 1820). African Americans not only worked as general laborers in the fields and factories of the antebellum South but also practiced a number of skilled crafts that offered them greater prospects for purchasing their freedom. Barjon, a free black who made this French-style bed, was trained by the New Orleans free black Jean Rousseau. Similarly, as early as the 1790s, the free black Peter Bentzon opened his own silversmith shop in Philadelphia. In addition to the unadorned vase-like cup shown here, art historians have identified at least eight other pieces produced by Bentzon.

7. Joshua Johnson, *Portrait of a Gentleman* (1805–1810). Joshua Johnson, a resident of Baltimore, is the earliest known professional painter of African descent in the United States. Although Johnson's principal clientele consisted of white elites, he also painted black subjects. The African Methodist Episcopal minister Daniel Coker is the subject of this portrait.

8. Robert S. Duncanson, *The Land of the Lotus Eaters* (1861). A self-taught landscape artist, Duncanson became the first black to gain international recognition for his paintings. After receiving a commission from a wealthy Cincinnati entrepreneur, his reputation soared. Although Duncanson's best-known work is *Blue Hole, Flood Waters, Little Miami River* (1851), his international stature was most closely identified with *Lotus Eaters*.

Photo 1: © The British Museum; **Photo 2:** Abby Aldrich Rockefeller Folk Art Center, Williamsburg, Virginia, Acc. #1935.301.3; **Photo 3:** Valentine Museum, Richmond, Virginia; **Photo 4:** Mitchel Osborne Photography; **Photo 5:** Center for African American Decorative Arts; **Photo 6:** Philadelphia Museum of Art. Purchased with the Thomas Skelton Harrison Fund and partial gift of Wynard Wilkinson; **Photo 7:** Reproduced by permission of the American Museum in Britain, Bath; **Photo 8:** Oil on Canvas. The Royal Collections, Sweden. Photo by Alexis Daflos.

run?" For his part, Bibb gave up the practice when it failed to protect him from a whipping and, most importantly, when it failed to win him the love of his favorite girl:

> One of these conjurers, for a small sum, agreed to teach me to make any girl love me that I wished. After I paid him, he told me to get a bull frog, and take a certain bone out of the frog, dry it, and when I get a chance I must step up to any girl whom I wished to make love me, and scratch her somewhere on her naked skin with this bone, and she would be certain to love me, and follow me in spite of herself; no matter who she might be engaged with, nor who she might be walking with . . . so when I got a chance, I fetched her a tremendous rasp across her neck with this bone, which made her jump. But in place of making her love me, it only made her angry with me. She felt more like running after me for thus abusing her, than she felt like loving me.

Spirituals and Slave Songs

The growth of African American spirituals reinforced the unique features of black religious culture. Central to this process was the "Chosen People" idea. Some ex-slaves recalled songs involving the refrain "Heaven will be my home," partly because they were convinced that their masters would not be there. As one ex-slave recalled, "This is one reason I believe in a hell. I don't believe a just God is going to take no such man as that [her master] into his kingdom." Over and over again, enslaved blacks sprinkled the lyrics of their songs, as later collected by white witnesses, with phrases affirming their belief that they were "children of God," "born of God," "the people of God," or "the people of the Lord." Spirituals left no doubt that blacks believed in a life after death: "to the promised land I'm bound to go"; "I walk the heavenly road"; and "Heaven shall be my home." Blacks also developed their share of sad songs: "rollin'" through "an unfriendly world"; "trouble" in mind; this world is "a hell to me"; and "feeling like a motherless child." Such songs demonstrated that slavery was indeed an incredibly cruel experience, but bondsmen and -women repeatedly bounced back from such sentiments with words of triumph and optimism. Numerous lyrics expressed feeling like "an eagle" and the ability to bear on wings and "fly, fly, fly." Although white Christians held similar beliefs, such ideas took on a different and more profound meaning when uttered by enslaved African Americans.

The creation of slave songs was a dynamic social and cultural process. African Americans adopted white hymns and folk songs but changed the words, musical structure, and mode of performance to fit their own vision—for example, by using African call-and-response patterns, which linked the individual to the larger collectivity or community. Songs also represented what some analysts call "communal recreation," which meant that enslaved people constantly reworked old songs into new versions. In 1845, a white traveler through the South remarked that blacks "leave out old stanzas, and introduce new ones at pleasure. You may, in passing from Virginia to Louisiana, hear the same tune a hundred times, but seldom the same words accompanying it." When later asked where they got their songs, ex-slaves emphasized the spontaneous and communal nature of the process. One collector of such songs later recorded the response of one black woman:

> We'd all be at the "prayer house" [on] de Lord's day, and de white preacher he'd splain de word and rid whar Exekiel done say—Dry bones gwiner lib ergin. . . . I'd jump up dar and den hollar and shout and sing and pat, and dey would all catch de words and I'd sing it to some ole shout song I'd heard 'em sing from Africa, and dey'd all take it up and keep at it, and, keep addin to it, and den it would be a spiritual.

Religion not only offered blacks hope for life beyond the suffering of this world but also instilled confidence that power relations could change in their lifetime. Some songs went straight to the heart of physical suffering on this earth: "No more rain, no more snow, No more cowskin on my back!" Their songs also indicated a fervent wish to change power relations: "Glory be to God that rules on high." Accordingly, African American songs and oral traditions accented Old Testament stories of the weak overcoming the strong: Pharaoh and the Israelites—"did not old Pharaoh get lost . . . get lost . . . get lost in the Red Sea?"; Daniel and the lion's den—"O' my Lord, delivered Daniel. . . . Why not deliver me too?"; and many others —"did not" the Lord deliver "Jonah from de belly of de whale" and "de Hebrew children from de fiery furnace?" Although the New Testament's "Prince of Peace" appealed to African Americans, they sometimes portrayed Jesus as an Old Testament warrior. Mounted on a horse with sword in hand, Jesus engaged in combat with Satan as a champion of the weak. "Ride on, King Jesus," one song stated, "No man can hinder thee."

African American cultural creations revealed the blurring of lines between the spiritual and the secular, between work, worship, and play. In addition to the "praise houses" and "brush arbors," slaves created, recreated, and sang their songs on boats, in the fields, and in the quarters. "Michael Row the Boat Ashore," "Lay This Body Down," and "Brudder, Don' Git Weary" all were quite explicitly work songs with strong spiritual content:

> Brudder, don' git weary,
> Brudder, don' git weary,
> Brudder, don' git weary,
> Fo' de work is most done.
> De ship is in de harbor, harbor, harbor
> De ship is in de harbor, To wait upon de Lord . . .
> 'E got 'e ca' go raidy, raidy, raidy
> 'E got 'e ca' go raidy, Fo' to wait upon de Lord.

Leisure Time Activities

Although African American cultural activities blurred the distinction between work and leisure, by the late antebellum years enslaved blacks claimed a slightly wider margin of off-time activities than before. In addition to Saturday and Sunday, leisure time included Easter, the Fourth of July, Whitsuntide, New Year's Day, and especially Christmas. Lasting from no less than three up to twelve days, Christmas represented the chief seasonal celebration, with gift giving, merriment, and inter-plantation visitations. Off-time activities blended songs, music, dance, food, beverages, and storytelling. One slaveowner reported: "I have a fiddle in my quarters and though some of my good brethren in the church would think hard of me, yet I allow dancing; ay I buy the fiddle and encourage it." A Mississippi planter related:

I have a good fiddler, and keep him well supplied with catgut.* . . . [He] plays for the negroes every Saturday night until 12 o'clock. They are exceedingly punctual in their attendance at the hall, while Charley's fiddle is always accompanied with Ihurod on the triangle, and Sam to "pat."

According to one historian of African American dance, Africans used the "motor-muscle memory of the various West African ethnic groups," to create new African American dances: the buzzard lope, breakdown, pigeon wing, cakewalk, Charleston, "set de flo," and snake hips. Dance routines also reinforced African culture by use of the "fiddler-caller," who instructed the dancers to execute steps, which varied in complexity and separated the best from the average. The ex-slave Mark Chaney, from Mississippi, related how his father, an African-born slave, taught him how "to dance like dey did in Africa." In 1838, William B. Smith described a "beer dance" on one Prince Edward, Virginia, plantation:

The banjo man, was seated on the beer barrel, in an old chair. *Tumming* his banjo. . . . Before him stood two athletic blacks, clapping [juba]† to the notes of the Banjor. . . . The rest of the company, male and female were dancers. The clappers rested the right foot on the heel, and its clap on the floor was in perfect unison with the notes of the Banjor and palms of the hands on the corresponding extremities. The dancers having the most . . . flexible contortions of the body and limbs, that human imagination can devise.

African Americans continued to improvise the making as well as the playing of musical instruments. Mark Chaney recalled how his father made his own "fiddle outa pine bark." Wash Wilson, who experienced slavery in Texas and Louisiana, recalled:

Dere wasn't no music instruments. Us take pieces of a sheep's rib or cow's jaw or a piece of iron, with a old kettle, or a hollow gourd and some horse-hair to make de drum. Sometimes dey'd git a piece of tree trunk and hollow it out and stretch a goat's or sheep's skin over it for de drum. Dey'd take de buffalo horn and scrape it out to make de flute. Den dey'd take a mule's jawbone and rattle de stick 'cross its teeth.

* Catgut: a tough cord usually made from sheep intestines, used for instrument strings.
† Juba: an African-inspired dance characterized by handclapping, foot stomping, and slapping of hands against the body.

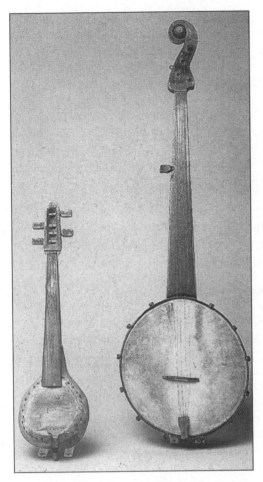

Although African Americans gradually adapted their Old World culture to New World conditions, at the same time they continued to build on their African heritage, such as by using gourds and animal hides to craft banjos. *The Blue Ridge Institute & Museum/Blue Ridge Heritage Archives of Ferrum College, Ferrum, Virginia*

Despite such improvisation, the repertoire of instruments played by enslaved people spanned a broad spectrum, including fifes, flutes, mouth bows, quills (a flutelike instrument usually made from a reed), accordions, French horns, and pianos, as well as the more widespread banjo, of African origins, and fiddle, acquired from poor whites.

Although consumption of alcoholic beverages required the approval of owners, African American dances included plenty of food and alcoholic drinks. The "beer dance" earlier described by Smith included one man holding "in his right hand a jug gourd of persimmon beer, and in his left, a dipper or water gourd, to serve the company while two black women were employed in filling the fireplace, six feet square, with larded persimmon dough." John Crawford of Mississippi later recalled how his grandfather manufactured alcoholic beverages for enslaved blacks: "Grandpappy used to own a still which was ran by grandpappy's friend Billy Bush. . . . They made whiskey out of corn and made whiskey out of peaches. They made apple cider and grape wine and dandelion wine and alder (elderberry) wine." "At the parties and at Christmas," Crawford said, blacks "got plenty of whiskey."

African Americans not only used their off-time to sing, dance, eat, play music, and drink but also used these occasions to tell stories and extend their oral traditions. According to Chaney, his father often placed him on his knee and told him "all 'bout when he lived in Africa . . . Dat Good Ole Land." The trickster figure—involving the ordeal of the smaller and weaker Brer Rabbit outsmarting the larger and stronger Brer Fox or Brer Wolf—occupied a key position in black folk tales. The Rabbit tales were especially prominent in the low country of Georgia and South Carolina, where Brer Rabbit repeatedly outsmarts his foes in stories like the famous "tarbaby" tale. In these tales, enslaved African Americans approved such practices as theft from the master's cupboard as a means of redressing economic exploitation and inequality. As such, these tales also helped to set the stage for more overt forms of resistance to bondage.

DAY-TO-DAY RESISTANCE, REBELLION, AND ATTEMPTS TO REBEL

Antebellum black families, religion, and leisure time activities established the cultural foundations for slave resistance. Even more so than in the early years of the nineteenth century, black resistance spanned the spectrum from day-to-day encounters in the fields, households, and shops of slaveowners to overt revolts and plots to revolt. The historical record is replete with examples of enslaved men and women who took courageous stances against abuse. Early in life, Frederick Douglass, the son of an enslaved woman and a white father, determined to be a free man. Born around 1818 in Talbot County, Maryland, Douglass resisted the routine and discipline of slave labor by age sixteen. When his owner sent him to a professional "Negro Breaker," a person specializing in whipping and subduing slaves for a fee, Douglass not only resisted the "Negro Breaker" but also won the fight. He later wrote: "I was a changed being after that fight. I was nothing before, I was a man now." When an overseer tried to whip Lucy Perry, she said: "De minute he grabs me I seize on ter his thumb an' I bites hit ter de bone." Another ex-slave, Martha Brady, "knocked" an overseer "plum down," when he said something that "he had no bizness to say." One woman shamed an overseer when she fought him "for a whole day and stripped him naked as the day he was born." On one occasion, according to the testimony of another woman, her mother's temper "ran wild."

> For some reason Mistress Jennings struck her with a stick. Ma struck back and a fight followed. Mr. Jennings was not at home and the children became frightened and ran upstairs. For half hour they wrestled in the kitchen. Mistress, seeing that she could not get the better of ma, ran out in the road, with ma on her heels. In the road my mother flew into her again. The thought seemed to race across mother's mind to tear mistress clothing off her body. She suddenly began to tear Mistress Jennings' clothing off. She caught hold, pulled, ripped and tore. Poor mistress was nearly naked when the storekeeper got to them and pulled ma off.

Still, "Ma" refused to accept a whipping for her actions when the mistress's husband returned home. She was then permanently hired out to work away from her home plantation.

Resistance in the Fields and Factories

Antebellum slave resistance gained its most powerful manifestations in the fields. Planters repeatedly complained about field hands breaking farm tools, injuring work animals, and sabotaging crops. According to Olmsted, planters increased the weight and durability of tools like hoes, and substituted mules for horses, because enslaved blacks frequently destroyed tools, injured draft animals, and ruined crops to slow the work pace.

Such tools as we [northerners] constantly give our [free white] laborers, and find our profit in giving them, would not last a day in [the South]. . . . So, too, mules are . . . substituted for horses [because] . . . horses cannot bear the treatment that they *must* get from negroes.

One planter, John Hammond, suspected outright sabotage: "I find [hoe-hands] chopping up cotton dreadfully and begin to think that my stand has every year been ruined in this way."

Blacks frustrated the efforts of overseers and planters to keep them at work non-stop. A Virginia planter angrily recorded in his diary that "hands wont work unless I am in sight." On one plantation, a contemporary observer noted:

The overseer rode among them, on a horse carrying in his hand a raw hide whip, constantly directing and encouraging them; but . . . as often as he visited one line of the operations the hands at the other end would discontinue their labor, until he returned to ride toward them again.

More so than men, women of childbearing age had great latitude in feigning illness as a means of slowing down the work pace. Since planters highly valued black children, they were somewhat more solicitous of black women's complaints of illness. One planter complained that such women

don't come to the field and you go to the quarters and ask the old nurse what's the matter and she says, "Oh, she's not fit to work sir"; and . . . you have to take her word for it . . . and you dare not set her [to] work; and so she will lay up till she feels like taking the air again, and plays the lady at your expense.

When field hands gained the cooperation of drivers, their resistance was most effective. Solomon Northrup, a driver on a Louisiana plantation, developed a technique for feigning the whipping of bondsmen:

Practice makes perfect, truly; and during my eight years' experience as a driver, I learned to handle the whip with marvelous dexterity and precision, throwing the lash within a hair's breadth of the back, the ear, the nose, without, however, touching either of them . . . they would squirm and screech as if in agony, although not one of them had in fact been even grazed.

Black bondsmen and -women also undermined the system through theft and the sale of stolen property. In addition to planters and farmers, who reported theft of garden crops, poultry, and pork, urban and industrial slaveowners recorded the loss of a broad range of products. One rice miller reported that his product "had been much exposed to plunder." In Virginia, the manager of William Weaver's ironworks informed the owner: "I had a notion of comeing down tomorrow evening . . . but I am afraid if I leave here they will steal the place. They come very near it while I am here." At the Tredegar Iron Works, slaves sometimes stole bar iron, which they exchanged for consumer goods. In 1830, in the goldfields, the *Niles Register* reported that blacks stole valuable amounts of gold dust by conceal-ing it "in their hair." According to one contemporary "anonymous" informer, at night African Americans watched for slow-moving trains, boarded them, and threw off what they could." In the train yards, the informer also stated, while railroad agents slept, bondsmen would "take off what they wanted . . . and I have no doubt but hundreds of dollars worth of lost goods go in this way." When a fire destroyed the facilities of one railroad company, blacks saved "nearly all of their plunder" but allowed the "company's tools, supplies, and property to burn!"

Enslaved people not only took goods, slowed down the work pace, destroyed property, injured livestock, and feigned sickness but also sometimes inflicted in-juries on themselves and committed suicide and infanticide. Ex-slaves recalled how some women took their own lives as well as the lives of their children. An ex-Kentucky slave, Lewis Clarke, remembered how one "slave mother took her three children and threw them into a well, and then jumped in with them, and they were all drowned." A mother of thirteen children reportedly killed each one of her off-spring in infancy rather than have them grow up in bondage. According to reports, the woman belonged to an extraordinarily cruel and brutal master who had, among other atrocities, cut off six of the woman's toes for various offenses. In 1837, in Co-lumbia, South Carolina, when the owner severely whipped one man for an offense that he did not commit:

> As soon as the flogging was over, the slave went into the back yard, where there was an axe and a block, and struck off the upper half of his right hand. He went and held up the bleeding hand before his master, saying, "You have mortified me, so I have made myself useless."

On a Georgia rice plantation, an enslaved man named London drowned himself when the overseer threatened him with a whipping.

Runaways and Fugitives

Rather than taking such desperate measures as self-inflicted injuries, suicide, and infanticide, a growing number of enslaved men and women resisted by running away. Recent scholarship offers a careful profile of the fugitives, derived mainly from newspaper advertisements for the capture and return of such runaways. First, although fugitives were disproportionately young, skilled men, the advertisements show people of all ages, sexes, and skill levels. Second, most runaways traveled short distances and returned after a few days, but permanent fugitives had the greatest impact on the plantation regime. Third, fugitives usually left alone, in twos, or in small groups of three or four. Fourth, whereas most Upper South runaways headed north, Deep South fugitives continued to escape, as earlier, into the nearby swamps, seeking to establish themselves in Maroon communities on land away from owners' control. Fifth, whatever their destination, fugitives depended on the confidential support of family and friends, at the home plantation and throughout their route. Finally, although precipitating incidents included whippings, denial of marriage requests, sale of family members, and intensification of the work regimen, running away was deeply rooted in the accumulated abuses of the slave system.

Fugitives devised a variety of creative ways of escaping bondage. The legendary Henry "Box" Brown had himself crated and shipped from Richmond, Virginia, to freedom in Philadelphia. Similarly, the enslaved woman Lear Green had herself packed into a sailor's chest and transported from slavery in Maryland to freedom in Pennsylvania. Some blacks also subverted gender and racial conventions to gain their freedom. In 1848, the woman Ellen Craft, a seamstress, disguised herself as a man and escaped with her husband, William, a cabinetmaker, from Macon, Georgia, to Philadelphia:

> "Now William," said Ellen, "listen to me and take my advice, and we shall be free in less than a month." "Let me hear your plans, then," said William. "Take part of your money and purchase me a good suit of gentlemen's apparel, and when the white people give us a holiday, let us go to the North. I am white enough to [pass] as the master, and you can pass as my servant."

When William replied, "But you are too short," Ellen requested a pair of high-heeled boots and a "very high hat." When William said, "But your face is smooth, you do not have a beard," Ellen said, "I could bind up my face in a handkerchief . . . as if I was suffering dreadfully from the toothache, and then no one would discover

Slaves devised a variety of techniques for escaping bondage. Henry "Box" Brown, shown here, and Lear Green literally crated and "shipped" themselves to freedom. *Library of Congress*

the want of beard." When William asked, "But how will you sign your name, they will surely detect you then," Ellen replied that she would bind her right hand, place it in a sling, and pretend that she could not write. After such persuasive responses, William conceded that the plan could work and the couple agreed to take the perilous journey to freedom. They arrived in Philadelphia on Christmas morning.

Frederick Douglass and Harriet Tubman became the most well known of the antebellum runaways. At age nineteen, Douglass escaped from a Baltimore shipyard and made his way to New Bedford, Massachusetts. For her part, Harriet Tubman, a field hand, escaped from the Eastern Shore of Maryland. As a child, she recalled that she "prayed to God to make me strong and able to fight." In 1849, a few years after her marriage to John Tubman, a free man, Harriet and her brothers faced the prospect of sale away from their home plantation. After she failed to convince her husband and brothers to join her, Harriet escaped without them. By walking at night and hiding out by day, she finally reached Pennsylvania. When she touched free soil, she later recalled, "I looked at my hands to see if I was the same person. Dere was such a glory ober everything, de sun came like gold throu de trees, and ober de fields, and I felt like I was in heaven." After a period of euphoria, loneliness set in. As Tubman recalled, the most painful part of freedom was the absence of her family:

Harriet Tubman, the famous conductor on the underground railroad, as a relatively young woman. *Library of Congress*

> I had crossed de line of which I had long been dreaming. I was free; but dere was no one to welcome me to de land of freedom, I was a stranger in a strange land, and my home after all was down [in] de old cabin quarter, wid de ole folks and my brudders and sisters.

At this point, Harriet made a "solemn resolution": "I was free, and dey should be free also; I would make a home for dem in de North, and de Lord helping me, I would bring dem all here." True to her resolution, Harriet made nearly twenty trips into slave territory and led out six of her brothers, their wives, fiancés, nieces, nephews, and finally her elderly parents. For her daring exploits on behalf of her people, Tubman became known by many as "the Moses," or "deliverer," of her people.

Although most fugitives left their owners individually or in small groups, some escaped in large contingents. In July 1845, some seventy-five enslaved blacks from three Maryland counties organized a mass movement toward the Pennsylvania line. Near Rockville, Maryland, whites caught and surrounded the blacks, killing several and recapturing about thirty-one. Three years later, authorities fought another party of seventy-five fugitives near the Ohio River in Kentucky. Although the fugitives fought back, nearly all were killed or recaptured. In Mississippi, a similar effort failed in 1850 when heavily armed whites forced the group to surrender. Large group escapes posed extraordinary risks, but African Americans continued to establish Maroon communities in the swamps and mountains of the antebellum South. In 1827, a group of whites reported a substantial community of runaways at the fork of the Alabama and Tombigbee Rivers. The group had two cabins and were about to build a fort when the settlement was "attacked" and, after a "severe" show of resistance, "conquered." As late as 1856, when whites attacked a Maroon camp in North Carolina, blacks fought back, killing one of their attackers and urging the whites "to come on, they were ready for them again." The most prominent case of black resistance occurred in the Seminole wars of 1835 to 1842, when enslaved people played an important role in the military conflict between U.S. authorities, planters, and the Seminole nation. A black named Abraham served as an effective interpreter and comrade to the Indians. One General Jesup overstated the case: "The negroes rule the Indians and it is important that they should feel themselves secure: if they should become alarmed and hold out, the war will be renewed." The war ended only when federal authorities guaranteed blacks land in the southwest.

Revolts and Rebellions

Individual and collective armed struggle constituted recurring themes in the antebellum blacks' quest for freedom. Southern planters exhibited growing fear of being "murdered" by enslaved people. In 1853, a Texan reported that such murders were "painfully frequent." At about the same time, a Louisiana newspaper reported that "the growing frequency of many murders have taken place, by negroes upon their owners." A Florida editor also recorded "another instance of the destruction of the life of a white man by a slave." In 1852, after the governor commuted the death sentence of an enslaved man convicted and sentenced to hang for the murder of an overseer, the *Richmond Dispatch* editorialized: "We think that full protection should be guaranteed to the overseers in the tobacco factories, by law, against the attacks of turbulent hands." One rice miller feared an enslaved carpenter, Jack Savage. He described Savage as "always giving trouble . . . [and] was the only Negro ever in our possession who I considered capable of murdering me, or burning my dwelling at night."

The most significant antebellum revolts and plots to revolt broke out in Charleston, South Carolina, in 1822 and in Southampton, Virginia, in 1831. In 1822, Denmark Vesey, a free black carpenter, preached against the slaveholders. Inspired by the example of Haiti as a black republic, Vesey and his compatriots made plans to capture the city of Charleston, confiscate its shipping, burn the city to the ground, and set sail for the West Indies. Before Vesey and other black bondsmen could make good on their plans, another slave revealed their intent to authorities. In the wake of the plot's discovery, some thirty-five blacks were executed and another thirty-seven sold out of the state.

In 1831, Nat Turner's rebellion broke out in rural Virginia. An enslaved preacher, carpenter, and trusted carriage driver on the plantation of Joseph Travis, Nat had also learned to read and write. During his childhood, he had received encouragement from his parents and the slave community, who considered him a gifted child who would someday become a prophet (see box). Turner later recalled his growing sense of mission:

> In my childhood a circumstance occurred which made an indelible impression on my mind. . . . Being at play with other children, when three or four years old, I was telling them something, which my mother overhearing, said it happened before I was born. . . . Others being called on, were greatly astonished, knowing that these things had happened, and caused them to say, in my hearing I surely would be a prophet, as the Lord had shown me things that had happened before my birth. And my father and mother strengthened me in this my first impression, saying in [my] presence, I was intended for some great purpose.

At one point, Turner escaped from his master's plantation and remained at large for nearly two months before he voluntarily returned. Before leading the slave revolt, he asked the Lord for a sign. When an eclipse of the sun took place, Turner took that as his cue to rebel.

On 21 August 1831, Turner and a small group of enslaved blacks broke into his master's house and killed the entire family. The group then marched toward the county seat. Their numbers increased to nearly seventy as they marched. Within twenty-four hours, Nat Turner's rebellion had claimed the lives of fifty-nine whites: ten men, fourteen women, and thirty-five children. In their effort to put down the revolt and in the brutal reprisals afterward, whites killed some one hundred black men, but Turner eluded authorities for nearly two months before he was captured and put to death. Turner's rebellion reflected the ways that the abuses of slavery came together in the Upper South and gained expression in a violent revolt under the leadership of a Christian, literate, and skilled bondsman.

Following Vesey's conspiracy and Nat Turner's revolt, southern states increased their surveillance and repression of African American activities. The number of whites serving in slave patrols and state and local militia increased. Because such revolts coincided with the expansion of the abolitionist movement, as we will see later, southern states made it a felony "to say or do anything" that might foment rebellion. Such laws prohibited "the publication, circulation, and promulgation of abolition doctrines," revealing the deep-seated fears that whites had of slave rebellion. When asked if white masters feared insurrections, one ex-slave replied: "They live in constant fear upon [this] subject. . . . The least unusual noise at might alarms them greatly. They cry out 'What is that?' Are the boys all in?"

Despite the resistance activities of Turner, Vesey, fugitives, and countless black men and women, stereotypes of the "docile slave" endured. Southern novelists, journalists, ministers, planters, and later racist historians diligently crafted the antebellum male as "Sambo" and the black woman as "Jezebel" or "Mammy." In planters' eyes, black men were faithful, humorous, musical, and docile, whereas women were deeply religious, asexual, and loyal beings who placed the affective and

SOURCES FROM THE PAST

1831

Nat Turner Discusses His Motives for Leading a Revolt of Enslaved Blacks

Sir,—you have asked me to give a history of the motives which induced me to undertake the late insurrection, as you call it—To do so I must go back to the days of my infancy, and even before I was born. I was thirty-one years of age the second of October last, and born the property of Benjamin Turner, of this county. In my childhood a circumstance occurred which made an indelible impression on my mind, and laid the groundwork of that enthusiasm which has terminated so fatally to many, both white and black, and for which I am about to atone at the gallows. It is here necessary to relate this circumstance. Trifling as it may seem, it was the commencement of that belief which has grown with time, and even now, sir, in this dungeon, helpless and forsaken as I am, I cannot divest myself of. Being at play with other children, when three or four years old, I was telling them something, which my mother, overhearing, said it had happened before I was born. I stuck to my story, however, and related some things which went, in her opinion, to confirm it. Others being called on, were greatly astonished, knowing that these things had happened, and caused them to say, in my hearing, I surely would be a prophet, as the Lord had shown me things that had happened before my birth. And my mother and grandmother strengthened me in this my first impression, saying, in my presence, I was intended for some great purpose, which they had always thought from certain marks on my head and breast. . . .

I was not addicted to stealing in my youth, nor have ever been; yet such was the confidence of the Negroes in the neighborhood, even at this early period of my life, in my superior judgment, that they would often carry me with them when they were going on any roguery, to plan for them. Growing up among them with this confidence in my superior judgment, and when this, in their opinions, was perfected by Divine inspiration, from the circumstances already alluded to in my infancy, and which belief was ever afterwards zealously inculcated by the austerity of my life and manners, which became the subject of remark by white and black; having soon discovered to be great, I must appear so, and therefore studiously avoided mixing in society, and wrapped myself in mystery, devoting my time to fasting and prayer.

By this time, having arrived to man's estate, and hearing the Scriptures commented on at meetings, I was struck with that particular passage which says, "Seek ye the kingdom of heaven, and all things shall be added unto you." I reflected much on this passage, and prayed daily for light on this subject. As I was praying one day at my plough, the Spirit spoke to me, saying, "Seek ye the kingdom of heaven, and all things shall be added unto you.". . .

. . . Knowing the influence I had obtained over the minds of my fellow-servants—(not by the means of conjuring and such-like tricks—for to them I always spoke of such things with contempt), but by the communion of the Spirit, whose revelations I often communicated to them, and they believed and said my wisdom came from God,—I now began to prepare them for my purpose, by telling them something was about to happen that would terminate in fulfilling the great promise that had been made to me. . . .

Source: From "The Confessions of Nat Turner," as recorded by Thomas R. Gray, in Deirdre Mullane, ed., *Crossing the Danger Water: Three Hundred Years of African-American Writing* (New York: Doubleday, 1993), pp. 88–96.

This sketch from an anti-abolitionist publication offers graphic details of Turner's rebellion: (1) Turner attacking a white mother and her children; (2) Turner's master, Mr. Travis, being attacked; (3) Captain John T. Barrow defending himself while his wife escapes; and (4) the militia pursuing Turner and the other rebels. *Library of Congress*

material needs of the plantation household above their own. Such stereotypes ignored the complex personalities, strategies, and ideas that shaped black responses to bondage. Indeed, as the foregoing evidence and recent scholarship suggest, planters invented "Sambo" and "Mammy" to counteract slave resistance and wipe out models of male and female strength and sexuality.

Planters expressed an ongoing fear of "rebellious slaves" who secured firearms, raided plantations, burned buildings, and killed white men, women, and children. Thus, as historian John Bassingame notes, they had a deep-seated need to believe in Sambo to reassure themselves that their fragile system of bondage was secure. Similarly, in the case of black women, some planters worried about the implications of the expanding mulatto population, which reflected the frequency of interracial sex and the often turbulent relationships between white men and women in their own households. Accordingly, planters invented Mammy to counteract their own self-serving stereotype of the black woman as Jezebel—that is, a woman driven by her "libido" or sex, who presumably threatened the "purity" of the white race. At the same time, planters' notions of Mammy and Jezebel enabled them to continue to deny black women the "benefit" of femininity as defined for white women under the rubric of the "cult of true womanhood" or the "Victorian lady." Moreover, contemporary white images of black women provided little room, positive or negative, for resisters like Harriet Tubman and countless others (see box).

Although late antebellum black culture nourished a powerful resistance movement, enslaved blacks nonetheless experienced significant social cleavages. As the number of African-born blacks decreased, other divisions became more prominent within the enslaved community. Occupational, cultural, color, and gender differences undercut black unity. Economic and status tensions were most acute between drivers and general field hands. Because drivers carried the whip and used it to increase production, ex-slaves regularly recalled the driver as "mean as the devil." Henry Cheatam of Mississippi recalled how the driver brutally beat his mama and his pregnant aunt. Consequently, Cheatam vowed "to kill" the driver "if it was de last thing I ever done." Although black culture blurred the line, enslaved people experienced growing tensions between spiritual and secular cultural orientations. In his narrative, the ex-slave Henry Bibb, who lived and labored in Kentucky and Louisiana, complained that many blacks violated the Sabbath. As he put it, "Those who make no profession of religion resort to the woods in large numbers on that day to gamble, fight, get drunk, and break the Sabbath."

Gender conflicts were even more problematic than cultural ones. Although enslaved men and women took risks to protect each other and their children, they also had disagreements and fights. In 1838, for example, on one plantation, a man beat his wife, locked her up, and prevented her from attending New Year's festivities. When her husband, Jim, hit her in the head with an iron poker, one Louisiana woman refused to tell her master how she received "the knot on her forehead." Other enslaved women, however, resisted such abuse. An ex-slave, Anna Baker, later learned why her mother had run away and left her children: "It was 'count o' de slave drivers. Dey kep' a-tryin' to mess 'roun wid her an' she wouln' have nothin' to do wid 'em." In 1859, a Mississippi slave was convicted and sentenced to death for raping a ten-year-old female slave, but the judge reversed the decision and released the man, claiming that "there is no act which embraces either the attempted or actual commission of a rape by a slave on a female slave." A year later, the Mississippi legislature made it a crime punishable by death or whipping for a black man to rape or attempt to rape a black female under age twelve. This law underscored the precarious position of black women and girls within the African American community as well as within southern society. Finally, color consciousness also increased among antebellum blacks. As we will see in Chapter 9, such consciousness favored mulattoes over blacks for the most skilled and supervisory jobs, which offered greater opportunities for self-purchase and freedom.

~

DESPITE THE DESTRUCTIVE IMPACT OF SLAVERY on their lives, antebellum blacks took advantage of improved physical conditions to strengthen their families, extend

SOURCES FROM THE PAST

1849

Harriet Tubman Walks to Freedom

What was to become of the slaves on this plantation now that the master was dead? Were they all to be scattered and sent to different parts of the country? Harriet had many brothers and sisters, all of whom with the exception of the two, who had gone South with the chain-gang, were living on this plantation, or were hired out to planters not far away. The word passed through the cabins that another owner was coming in, and that none of the slaves were to be sold out of the State. This assurance satisfied the others, but it did not satisfy Harriet. Already the inward monitor was whispering to her, "Arise, flee for your life!" and in the visions of the night she saw the horsemen coming, and heard the shrieks of women and children, as they were being torn from each other, and hurried off no one knew whither. . . .

And so without money, and without friends, she started on through unknown regions; walking by night, hiding by day, but always conscious of an invisible pillar of cloud by day, and of fire by night, under the guidance of which she journeyed or rested. Without knowing whom to trust, or how near the pursuers might be, she carefully felt her way, and by her native cunning, or by God given wisdom, she managed to apply to the right people for food, and sometimes for shelter; though often her bed was only the cold ground, and her watchers the stars of night.

After many long and weary days of travel, she found that she had passed the magic line, which then divided the land of bondage from the land of freedom. But where were the lovely white ladies whom in her visions she had seen, who, with arms outstretched, welcomed her to their hearts and homes. All these visions proved deceitful: she was more alone than ever; but she had crossed the line; no one could take her now, and she would never call any man "Master" more.

Source: Sarah H. Bradford, *Harriet Tubman: The Moses of Her People* (1869, 1886; reprint, New York: Citadel Press, 1991).

the boundaries of community, and resist the most debilitating influences of human bondage. From the foundation of evolving African American culture and social practices, antebellum black men and women mounted a broad range of individual and collective protests against the institution of slavery. African American family, culture, and forms of resistance not only demonstrated the creative blending of African and Euro-American ideas but also challenged and exploded certain erroneous stereotypes about the character of black people. Despite its severity, the institution of human bondage destroyed neither the slaves' "creative instincts" nor their "thirst" for freedom and independence. Indeed, despite their own internal social conflicts and cleavages, enslaved and free blacks would play key roles in the growth of the abolitionist movement, the coming of the Civil War, and emancipation.

CHAPTER 9

∽

Free Blacks, Abolitionists, and the Antislavery Movement

B y 1860, the African American population included a half million free blacks. Although free people of color made up only a tiny fraction of the total, they had a disproportionately large impact on the development of antebellum African American culture, communities, and politics. According to some scholars, the socioeconomic and political experiences of free blacks foreshadowed the future of all blacks in the wake of the Civil War and emancipation. In both the North and South, antebellum free people of color could legally marry, own property, and establish their own institutions. As America moved toward the enfranchisement of working-class and poor white men, however, free black men and women faced economic exploitation, disfranchisement, segregation, and the intensification of the colonization movement, which aimed to transport free people of color to Africa and secure the United States as a republic of slaves and free whites. Although free blacks lived and labored on the precarious borders of antebellum slave society, they were by no means quiescent. They deepened their own institution-building and political activities; strengthened their ties with their enslaved kinfolk and sympathetic white allies; and pushed for the abolition of slavery and the acquisition of full citizenship.

URBANIZATION, WORK, AND THE ECONOMY

As the cotton kingdom expanded and the enslaved population increased, free blacks found it exceedingly difficult to hold their own. Northern and southern journalists and political leaders repeatedly described free blacks as "lazy," "ignorant," and more "depraved" than slaves. Their very presence challenged slavery and notions of white superiority in the North and South. Consequently, both white elites and working-class whites devised a variety of mechanisms for limiting the growth of the free black population. By the 1850s, most southern states had either prohibited manumission altogether or required blacks to leave the state on receiving their freedom. Only the states of Delaware, Missouri, and Arkansas permitted newly emancipated blacks to remain in the state. For their part, the new midwestern states also limited the settlement of free blacks within their borders. An Ohio legislator exclaimed that "the United States were designed by the God in Heaven to be governed and inhabited by the Anglo-Saxon race alone[!]" Accordingly, the states of the old northwest—Ohio, Indiana, Illinois, Michigan, and Iowa—all established laws requiring free blacks to post bonds (as much as $500) before they could legally take up residence. In 1851, such antiblack sentiment culminated in the adoption of a new Indiana state constitution that barred blacks from settlement altogether. According to Article 13, "No negro or mulatto shall come into, or settle in the State, after the adoption of this constitution."

Growth of the Free Black Population

Hostile public opinion and legal constraints undercut the growth of the free black population. Until the 1820s, the number of free blacks had increased at a faster rate than that of enslaved blacks or whites. By 1840, however, the free black population was growing more slowly than both other groups. During the two decades before the Civil War, it increased by 12 percent, as compared with an increase of over 23 percent for bondspeople and whites. The impact of legal and extralegal restrictions on the growth of the free black population was most prominent in the Deep South states of Mississippi, Georgia, South Carolina, and Louisiana. Although these states accounted for well over 50 percent of the total black population, only about 13 percent of the total free black population lived there.

Despite its declining growth rate, the free black population nonetheless continued to increase. Between 1820 and 1860, the number of free blacks rose from about 233,500 to more than 488,000 (see table). Although these numbers were almost equally divided between North and South, most free blacks lived in the southern slave states. The natural increase of the free black population was added to by blacks who continued to gain freedom through manumission, running away, and self-purchase. In 1845, a Baltimore official exclaimed: "With all the restrictions which legislation has imposed on manumission, they still go on. . . . It may be taken for certain that they will go on; that nothing can stop them." Similarly, a Louisiana slaveholder complained that the manumission of enslaved blacks had "become notorious." According to this commentator, "The policy jury invariably yields to the wishes of the master, and enables him . . . to grant the emancipation." Public officials and opinion leaders also regularly complained that fugitives swelled the numbers of free blacks. In Richmond, one journalist noted the many "runaways in this neighborhood who have escaped detection by misrepresenting their condition." In 1834, the mayor of New Orleans said that slaves "crowd in the city, hide, and make our city a den" of free blacks and "mulattoes."

Self-purchase was an exceedingly difficult route to freedom. By the late antebellum years, the high price of slaves made it almost prohibitive for blacks to purchase themselves or for free blacks to purchase loved ones. When a Tennessee free black sought to purchase his wife, the owner responded: "No sum of money would induce me to part with Sarah. . . . The price is so enormously high in the country

U.S. Free Black Population, 1820–1860

	1820	1830	1840	1850	1860
United States	233,504	319,599	386,303	434,449	488,070
North	99,281	137,529	170,728	196,262	226,152
South	134,223	182,070	215,575	238,187	261,918
Upper South	114,070	151,877	174,357	203,702	224,963
Lower South	20,153	30,193	41,218	34,485	36,955

Percent Increase, 1810–1860

	1810–1820	1820–1830	1830–1840	1840–1850	1850–1860
United States	25.2%	36.9%	20.9%	12.5%	12.3%
North	27.0	38.5	24.1	15.0	15.2
South	24.0	35.6	18.4	10.5	10.0
Upper South	21.2	33.1	14.8	16.8	10.4
Lower South	42.1	49.8	36.5	−16.3	7.2

Proportion of Blacks Who Were Free, 1820–1860

	1820	1840	1860
United States	13.2%	13.4%	11.0%
North	83.9	99.3	100.0
South	8.1	8.0	6.2
Upper South	10.6	12.5	12.8
Lower South	3.5	3.1	1.5

Source: Ira Berlin, *Slaves Without Masters: The Free Negro in the Antebellum South* (New York: Oxford University Press, 1974), pp. 136–137. Reprinted by permission of the author.

that I could not replace such a one as her." Still, the process of self-purchase added to the roster of free blacks. In New Orleans, for example, free blacks filed over 30 percent of the formal petitions for manumission between 1827 and 1852. In 1834, an estimated 1,129 of Cincinnati's nearly 1,500 blacks had known slavery. Well over a third had purchased their own freedom, at a cost of $215,522, or about $450 per person. In Kentucky, the experiences of the ex-slave Free Frank reveal the long arduous process of self-purchase in the lives of one family. The process started in 1817, with Frank's purchase of his wife at $800, and continued through 1857, with the purchase of Frank's sons, daughters, and finally grandchildren (see table).

Migration to Urban Centers

Difficult conditions in the rural South stimulated the increasing urban migration of free blacks. In the plantation and rural-industrial areas of the South, the lives of free blacks were tightly interwoven with the experiences of their enslaved counter-

Free Frank Family Members Purchased, 1817–1857			
Date of Purchase	Name	Relationship to Free Frank	Price
1817	Lucy	Wife	$800[1]
1819	Free Frank		800[2]
1829	Frank Jr.	Son	2,500 (est.)[3]
1835	Solomon	Son	500[4]
1843	Sally [Sarah]	Daughter	950[5]
By 1850	Juda [Judah, Julia]	Daughter	4,380 (est.)[6]
	Commodore	Grandson	
	Permilia	Granddaughter	
	Louisa	Daughter-in-law	
By 1856	Calvin	Grandson	3,030[7]
	Calvin	Grandson	
	Robert	Grandson	
	Lucy Ann	Granddaughter	
By 1857	Charlotte	Granddaughter	993.61[8]
	Child of Charlotte	Great Grandchild	
	Child of Charlotte	Great Grandchild	

1. Pulaski County Real Estate Conveyances, Book 3: 228; Certificate of Good Character for Free Frank, Sept. 7, 1830, Free Frank [McWorter] Papers; *Atlas Map of Pike County*, p. 54.
2. Pulaski County Real Estate Conveyances, Book 4: 138; Certificate of Good Character for Free Frank, Sept. 7, 1830, Free Frank [McWorter] Papers; *Atlas Map of Pike County*, p. 54.
3. Pulaski County Real Estate Conveyances, Book 7:55–56.
4. Ibid., Book 8: 199–200.
5. Ibid., Book 12: 379–80.
6. *Pike County Atlas*, p. 54; John E. McWorter to Rev. P. B. West, Aug. 31, 1919, mimeographed; Arthur McWorter to Thelma McWorter Kirkpatrick [Wheaton], Jan. 1937; and Thelma Elise McWorter, "Free Frank of Pike County, Ill." (Chicago, *ca.* 1937, mimeographed), all in Free Frank [McWorter] Papers.
7. Pike County Circuit Court Records, *Solomon, Exr. of Frank McWorter* v. *Lucy McWorter widow et al.* (1857), case no. 8850.
8. Pike County Inventories, Appraisements, Bills, etc., 1866–1869, pp. 28–29, Pike County Courthouse, Pittsfield, Ill.
Source: Juliet E. K. Walker, *Free Frank: A Black Pioneer on the Antebellum Frontier* (Lexington, Ky.: University of Kentucky Press, 1983) p. 162. Copyright © 1983 University of Kentucky Press. Reprinted by permission of the publisher.

parts. They worked alongside enslaved blacks as boatmen, fishermen, farm hands, and wage laborers in a variety of rural industries, including turpentine, lumber, coal, and ironworks. Although some rural free blacks practiced skilled crafts, most found jobs as general laborers. As in the postwar years, some worked the land in exchange for a share of the crop. Free black tenants often found themselves indebted to the landlords at the end of each season and day of reckoning. As with the crop-lien system of the early emancipation years, many of these rural free blacks pledged ungrown crops to secure credit for living expenses, supplies, and equipment for raising the next crop. As a result of these oppressive conditions, rural free blacks moved into cities in rising numbers. Moreover, rural employers often housed free blacks with slaves that they owned, hired, or leased. Thus, the health and living conditions of many rural free blacks were indistinguishable from those of bondsmen and -women. According to available statistics, an estimated 25 percent of rural free blacks resided in housing provided by employers, whereas others took up residence on marginal land, in housing of poor construction and few amenities. According to one contemporary source, most of their houses were "small" and "very tattered." In 1836, one observer reported that "the emancipated negroes generally leave the country, and congregate in the cities and larger towns." By the eve of the Civil War, over 33 percent of southern free blacks and virtually all of their northern kinsmen lived in cities, compared with only 5 percent of slaves, and little more than 15 percent of southern and northern whites. In other words, antebellum free blacks became the most highly urbanized component of the U.S. population. The vast majority of northern free blacks lived in New York, Philadelphia, Boston, Chicago, Cincinnati, Providence, New Haven, and a few smaller urban centers, while southern free blacks concentrated mainly in Baltimore, Richmond, New Orleans, Charleston, Memphis, Mobile, Natchez, and Vicksburg. Free blacks were not only disproportionately urban, as in earlier years, but predominantly light-skinned and female as well. By 1860, women outnumbered men by 100 to 92. Conversely, slaves had a nearly even ratio of men to women.

Manumission and self-purchase favored light-skinned black men and women, frequently the relatives of white landowners. In 1860, the U.S. Census reported an estimated 36 percent of free blacks as "mulattoes," compared to only about 10 percent for slaves. Even when slaveowners refused to emancipate their offspring by black women, they often provided such children with special training, privileges, and contacts that enabled them to purchase their own freedom. Such practices were especially prominent in the Deep South, where persons of mixed racial backgrounds made up about 75 percent of the total free black population. Although some Upper South owners also liberated members of their kin group, declining economic opportunities to use bound labor in the tobacco region of the Upper South opened the door of emancipation to both enslaved dark and light-skinned blacks. Thus, the complexion of the free black population was much darker in the Upper South and northern states than it was in the Deep South.

Free blacks encountered stiff barriers to gaining a foothold in the urban economy. As long as employers could lease, purchase, or hire slaves, they often preferred bondsmen and -women over free blacks. In the Upper South city of Baltimore, for example, the free black population dwarfed its slave counterpart, but employers vigorously advertised for slave labor. In 1840, one employer advertised for servants to wash, iron, and cook but mandated that "they be SLAVES/FOR LIFE." Another employer sought a black porter for his grocery store, emphasizing that a slave was "preferred." Numerous other Baltimore employers appealed for black workers under the rubric "slaves preferred." Compared with free blacks, enslaved people had fewer rights, which permitted employers to exercise greater control over the work force. Indeed, some owners hired out their slaves as a disciplinary measure and urged lessees to apply "the whip" generously. Since, legally, free blacks could walk away from such arrangements, many employers saw them as less desirable workers than slaves.

Free African Americans not only faced competition from their enslaved brothers and sisters but experienced resistance from poor landless white wage earners as well. White workers constantly complained that free people of color depressed their standard of living by working for less. In Petersburg, Virginia, for example, white workers stated: "We consider the Negro mechanic a curse on our working interest in as much as they nearly monopolize work at reduced prices." White artisans and working men detested working alongside blacks. As a white St. Louis dock worker put it, "I despise working by the side of a negro. . . . They are the worst class on the levee . . . a slur on our employment." In the same city, a white artisan exclaimed that "craftsmen and other laborers have an undoubted right to strike for higher wages . . . that is when they are white men. Color of course gives a different complexion to these rights."

In the North, free blacks faced a similar, and in some ways more hostile, environment. As German and Irish immigrants poured into northern cities during the 1830s and 1840s, they took a growing share of artisan and general labor jobs. Before departing his home in Virginia, one free black artisan "expected to find the people of color in free New York far better off than those in Virginia." He was disappointed to find, however, that "many of the skilled tradesmen" that he knew from the South had become "cooks and waiters" in New York. In 1827, a black newcomer to Cincinnati also described his disappointment on arriving in the city:

> I thought upon coming to a free state like Ohio I would find every door thrown open to receive me, but from the treatment I received by the people generally, I found it little better than in Virginia. . . . I found every door was closed against the colored man in a free state, excepting the jails and penitentiaries.

Similarly, when Frederick Douglass, a skilled ship caulker, arrived in New Bedford, Massachusetts, he reported that "every white man would leave the ship . . . if I struck a blow at my trade." Although some northern white abolitionists encouraged the employment of black artisans, blacks repeatedly complained that "we have among us carpenters, plasterers, masons, etc., whose skills as workers is confessed and yet they find no employment not even among [white] friends." European immigrants also barred blacks from the relatively well-paying carting trade. Carters transported a variety of goods, including firewood and manure, which required a "dirt carter's" license.

As competition between free blacks, slaves, and white workers intensified, however, whites defined certain jobs in racial terms and opened the door to the employment of free blacks. In conversations with northern visitors, southern whites repeatedly confirmed that "no white man would ever do certain kinds of work . . . and if you should ask a white man . . . he would get mad and tell you he wasn't a nigger." The South Carolina slaveowner Edward Laurens admitted that whites "degraded" certain occupations by employing blacks and discouraged young white men "whose spirit and highmindedness we endeavor almost daily to incite" from entering "the arena with them." In Cincinnati, a local editor believed that the "evils of slavery . . . infected" the city and relegated blacks to "certain kinds" of labor "despised as being the work of slaves."

Employment Opportunities for Free Blacks

General labor, household, and domestic service occupations emerged at the core of "Negro work." Such jobs required heavy lifting, loading, carrying, and cleaning. In fifteen antebellum northern and southern cities, over 60 percent of free black men worked in jobs defined as unskilled, semiskilled, and personal service. Such jobs tended to become more prominent as one moved from the Deep South to the Upper North. By the 1850s, for example, only 17 percent of free black men in New Orleans and 21 percent in Charleston occupied such jobs, compared with 58 percent in Louisville, 69 percent in St. Louis, 67 percent in Cincinnati, 77 percent in Pittsburgh, 73 percent in New York, and 77 percent in Boston.

Although employers and white workers stereotyped certain jobs as black labor, such jobs varied by region, city, and skill. In New Orleans and Charleston, blacks dominated the barbering, carpentry, masonry, blacksmithing, tailoring, and shoemaking trades. Norfolk, Richmond, and Louisville blacks also gained a substantial footing in the skilled crafts as well as the better-paying laboring jobs like carters or draymen. White workers controlled the drayman job in cities like Baltimore and St. Louis, but blacks dominated the same job in Norfolk, Virginia, and took a large proportion of such jobs in other southern cities. Although blacks in northern cities gained a foothold in the barber trade, few worked in the skilled trades or the more lucrative laboring jobs like draymen. During the late 1830s, for example, the New York *Colored American* urged the mayor to stop discrimination against black carters. According to the editor, city inspectors routinely denied blacks licenses to enter the trade. For their part, white carters reinforced such discrimination by physically assaulting the few black draymen who worked in the city with or without licenses.

In each city and region, free black women gained employment primarily as household or domestic service workers. Whereas free black men often entered freedom as skilled artisans, few black women started their lives with prospects for making a living beyond jobs as "seamstresses," "washers," and "cooks." Young black males, particularly in the South, gained apprenticeships with a variety of skilled craftsmen. A study of Petersburg, Virginia, shows that the city clerk regularly recorded black "boys" as apprentices to carpenters, coopers, bricklayers, painters, blacksmiths, bakers, and barbers, but the options for "girls" were so few that the clerk seldom recorded them. In the urban North and South, available evidence suggests that the majority of free black women worked as domestics in the homes of white employers.

The lowly occupational position of free black women had substantial consequences for the livelihood of free black families. Although the majority of free blacks, like slaves, lived in double-headed households, the number of female-headed families increased over time. In Boston, for example, the percentage of free black families headed by couples decreased from about 66 percent to 60 percent during the 1850s alone. Although only 11 percent of Cincinnati's black households were headed by women in 1830, the figure had doubled by 1860. In the urban South, Petersburg and Charleston, for example, the percentage of families headed by women sometimes exceeded those headed by men. Thus, the poor economic position of free women of color symbolized severe suffering for growing numbers of urban blacks. Yet we must not conclude that such free black families were necessarily "unstable." As one study of Charleston, South Carolina, notes, for example: "The census manuscripts provide data which suggest that the female-headed families were stable."

Restrictions on the entrepreneurial activities of African Americans reinforced their lowly position in the antebellum economy. Southern states undercut the establishment of black taverns by prohibiting free blacks from manufacturing, transporting, and selling alcoholic beverages. In 1833, when the Kentucky legislature set a new minimum of $40 for acquisition of liquor licenses to be issued by the city of Louisville, it excluded free people of color from the privilege. The Louisville city council reinforced the state statute by prohibiting free blacks from opening grocery stores, important outlets for the sale of alcoholic beverages during the period. St. Louis, Charleston, and Washington, D.C., enacted similar restrictions on free black participation in the sale of alcoholic drinks. In 1836, Washington enacted the most comprehensive restrictions. It prohibited free blacks as well as agents of free blacks from keeping "any tavern, ordinary, shop, porter cellar, refectory, or eating house of any kind, for profit or gain." Based on the notion that free blacks represented a channel for the sale of stolen agricultural produce, several southern cities outlawed the licensing of free blacks as "a Hawker, huckster, or peddler." In the North, white competitors accomplished a similar exclusion of blacks by informal means.

Free people of color were not entirely victimized by their position in the economy. They took jobs at the bottom of the labor force and challenged white rhetoric about their "improvidence," "depravity," and "ignorance." As discussed earlier, African Americans used such work not only as a route to their own freedom but also as a vehicle for securing the freedom of loved ones. By the late antebellum years, they also organized their own labor unions and fought to secure their jobs. On the Baltimore docks, for example, free blacks gained a monopoly on work and resisted white efforts to drive them out. Indeed, after white workers moved to exclude blacks, African Americans rallied and excluded the whites, turning the docks into a predominantly black occupational enclave. Similarly, in 1850, New York City blacks formed the American League of Colored Laborers. The ALCL not only aimed to organize skilled black workers but also promoted the training of black youth in mechanical and agricultural pursuits and advocated the establishment of independent black businesses. According to the Reverend Charles B. Ray, a black New York minister and newspaper editor, these black men and women had "the proper materials in their character to become industrious, economical, and reputable citizens."

Black Entrepreneurs and Property Holders

Some free blacks sidestepped constraints and became entrepreneurs and substantial property holders. They parlayed their general labor, household, and craft skills into businesses catering to black and white clients. In Philadelphia, the sailmaker James Forten accumulated more than $100,000 around the docks of the city. The most successful of these black entrepreneurs, however, catered to an elite white clientele, as grocers and proprietors of hotels, restaurants, and especially barbershops. In Boston, Peter Howard became one of the city's most well-known proprietors of a black barbering and hairdressing business. In San Francisco, William Alexander

Elizabeth Hobbs Keckley, ex-Virginia slave and dressmaker who later designed dresses for First Lady Mary Todd Lincoln.
Moorland-Spingarn Research Center, Howard University

Leidesdorff became a prominent merchant and land speculator who bequeathed property worth $1.5 million to his heirs. In 1850, Cincinnati listed the value of black property holdings at $1,317,000. Out of eighty-eight African Americans who held property of $1,000 or more, close to half worked as laborers, stewards, butlers, and cooks. Three of Cincinnati's most renowned residents and property holders were Richard Phillips, a huckster ($13,000); Joseph J. Fowler, another huckster ($18,000); and John G. Gaines, a stevedore ($3,000).

Antebellum free black entrepreneurs also included several women. In New York City, Free Love Slocum, Paul Cuffee's sister, operated an import-export business; in Philadelphia, Grace Bustil Douglass operated a millinery shop; in Washington, D.C., Elizabeth Keckley, a Virginia-born ex-slave, became perhaps the most renowned antebellum black female entrepreneur when she established a successful dressmaking business. Her fame later soared when she designed and made dresses for First Lady Mary Todd Lincoln. Moreover, black property ownership was not exclusively a male affair. In 1850, women made up 31.1, 16.9, and 10.5 percent of black property holders in Louisville, Cincinnati, and Pittsburgh, respectively.

African American property holders offered inspiring stories of individual and group success and entrepreneurship. The barber trade provided black men their most promising opportunities to earn a living, purchase real estate, and increase their standing in antebellum cities. The black editor William Dabney later celebrated the mid-nineteenth-century black barber and barbershop:

Barber shops were the greatest places for gossip and the white customers were generally well informed as to the doings of Negro society. The Negro barber, as a workman, was an artist. The razor in his hands became an instrument that made sweet melody as it charmed away the grass that grew on facial lawns.

In both northern and southern cities, blacks operated leading downtown barber-shops that catered to the city's elite. In Cincinnati, the barber William W. Watson received his freedom in 1832. Within less than a decade he owned his own barbershop and bathhouse that catered to a predominantly white clientele in the Central Business District. He also owned two brick houses and lots within the city and another 560 acres of farmland in nearby Mercer County, bringing his property holdings to an estimated $5,500. In her rationale for *Uncle Tom's Cabin*, Harriet Beecher Stowe, who lived in Cincinnati during her research for the book, named Watson and five other former bondsmen as examples of the race's capacity for "conquering for themselves comparative wealth and social position by their strength of character, energy, patience and honesty."

Black entrepreneurial activities and property ownership were not unmixed blessings. In the Deep South, black wealth included enslaved people as well as land and other material possessions. In Charleston, by 1850, some 371 free people of color paid taxes on real estate valued at more than $1 million. At the same time, New Orleans free blacks owned property estimated at $15 million. This property included bondsmen, -women, and children. In Louisiana, Cyprian Ricard owned 91 slaves, Charles Rogues owned 47, and Marie Metoyer owned 50. As early as 1830, in Louisiana, ten free blacks owned 50 or more enslaved people—that is, enough to qualify as large planters. Although the number of such holdings dropped to six by 1860, free black slaveholders owned 492 people, averaging about 82 persons per unit. Even more so than the free black population itself, all of these large planters were mulattoes. The wealthiest, Auguste Dubuclet of Iberville Parish, owned real property valued at $200,000, including a total of 1,200 acres of land and 94 slaves. In the Sumter District of South Carolina, William Ellison was also a large planter and slaveholder. He received his freedom at age twenty-nine and soon became a gin manufacturer, selling his product to local planters, who sometimes incurred debts with the free black entrepreneur. Ellison later purchased a house from the governor of the state and owned over 60 enslaved people. Until the 1850s, Ellison and his family occupied a privileged position within antebellum South Carolina society.

Although some blacks purchased slaves for profit, others, probably most, purchased people as a means of liberating family members and friends. As suggested above, by the 1830s and 1840s, southern states had largely outlawed the emancipation of slaves by will or deed. Thus, African American slaveholding also included the purchase of friends and kin, especially spouses and children, who, though enslaved, actually lived as free people of color. In other words, although mid-nineteenth-century black elites owed their livelihood to white clients, their lives were closely intertwined with those of black workers and the poor.

As mulatto and dark-skinned blacks alike gained a foothold in the economy, their industriousness did not insulate them from racist attacks. On the contrary, their progress sometimes generated as much resistance and hatred as their alleged intemperance and improvidence. In 1834, an English visitor remarked that whites discussed African American self-help and improvements "with a degree of bitterness that dictated a disposition to be more angry with their virtues than their vices." In 1841, a white working man exclaimed that "white men . . . are naturally indignant . . . when they see a set of idle blacks dressed up like ladies and gentlemen, strutting about our streets and flinging the 'rights of petition' and 'discussion' in our faces." Such attitudes underlay a variety of practices that curtailed the rights of all blacks and helped to forge bonds across intraracial class and color lines. In 1844, for example, one mulatto leader, John Gaines of Cincinnati, rejected the idea of a separate school for mulatto children: "This I anticipate would be fraught with evil consequences. . . . It would not only divide the colored children, but create prejudices too intolerable to be borne."

DISFRANCHISEMENT, SEGREGATION, AND EXCLUSION

Free blacks not only faced restrictions on their role as producers but bore constraints on their access to citizenship as well. White men from diverse ethnic backgrounds—including growing numbers of Irish and German immigrants and their children—gained the franchise and participated in an expanding democratic polity, while federal, state, and local laws and social practices denied free blacks full citizenship rights. Both northern and southern states increasingly blurred the distinction between enslaved and free blacks. Whereas free blacks had retained the vote in North Carolina, Pennsylvania, and New York before 1820, disfranchisement of free blacks became nearly universal during the 1820s and 1830s. In 1837–1838, the Pennsylvania constitutional convention restricted voting to white males twenty-one years of age or older. Until then, African American men had voted in Philadelphia, Pittsburgh, and elsewhere in the state. For its part, New York instituted a high property requirement and blocked most free blacks from the vote. By 1860, only four states—Maine, New Hampshire, Vermont, and Massachusetts—allowed free blacks unrestricted access to the franchise. At the same time that northern states restricted the franchise, they also limited the rights of free blacks to testify in courts against whites, serve in the militia, marry across racial lines, and even petition their government. In 1839, the Ohio legislature redefined the right of petition as a privilege for free blacks, proclaiming that blacks and mulattoes

> who may be residents within the State, have no constitutional right to present their petitions to the General Assembly for any purpose whatsoever, and that any reception of such petitions on the part of the General Assembly is a mere act of privilege or policy and not imposed by any expressed or implied power of the constitution.

The line between slavery and freedom was even less distinct in the South. In 1834, a Tennessee lawyer declared that the "interests and associations" of free blacks "are identified and blended with the slave, and what is for the benefit of one is for the benefit of the other." Although whites paid fines and served prison terms for a variety of offenses, free blacks, like slaves, endured the whip "well laid on" their bare backs. Like bondsmen, free blacks also faced death for crimes like manslaughter, arson, rebellion, and rape of a white woman; searches of their person and homes without warrants; and reenslavement for violation of vagrancy laws. Moreover, southern states jailed free blacks who entered their ports as seamen. Although the U.S. Supreme Court declared such detention laws unconstitutional in 1823, southern states ignored its ruling and continued to incarcerate black sailors. Some northern free blacks like Solomon Northrup were captured and enslaved as a result of such practices.

The fortunes of free blacks ebbed and flowed with the fortunes of the enslaved. In the wake of Nat Turner's rebellion, Virginia prohibited meetings for teaching free blacks to read, North Carolina prohibited free blacks from preaching, and Maryland made it a felony for free blacks to "call for, demand or receive abolition papers." During the 1850s, federal policies also highlighted and reinforced the link between the lives of enslaved and free blacks. The Fugitive Slave Act of 1850 not only undercut the fugitive network but also weakened the free black community by increasing penalties for persons aiding and abetting runaways. On the pretense of apprehending runaways, slave catchers and kidnappers regularly raided free black communities, seeking to entrap free as well as runaway blacks for sale in the domestic slave trade. Similarly, in the Dred Scott case of 1857, the U.S. Supreme Court undermined the liberty of free blacks as well as the enslaved. As Chief Justice Roger B. Taney declared, America was a white republic, with black people having "no rights that whites were bound to respect." (See the Documents section.)

Antebellum America not only weakened the legal status of free blacks but also restricted their access to the housing market. As early as the 1830s, white realtors and homeowners mobilized to prohibit free blacks or mulattoes "from purchasing or holding real estate" within city limits. In Boston, when a free black family made plans to move into a white neighborhood, residents threatened to destroy the structure before allowing blacks to move in. By 1860, the index of segregation showed increasing housing segregation along color lines. Such segregation was much higher in the North than in the South. In order to create an even residential distribution of blacks and whites, a higher percentage of northern blacks would have had to change their current address than would southern blacks: Boston, 61.3; Chicago, 50.0; and Cincinnati, 47.9, compared with Nashville, 43.1; New Orleans, 35.7; and Charleston, 23.2. Southern free blacks continued to live in as domestics, occupied general labor jobs, and, as a population, scattered more widely across the urban landscape than their northern counterparts. Whites often described the growing spatial concentration of northern blacks in such pejorative terms as Bucktown (Cincinnati), Little Africa (New York and Cincinnati), Hayti (Pittsburgh), and Nigger Hill (Boston).

Realtors and landlords regularly charged poor black and white tenants exorbitant rent for dilapidated and unhealthy properties, but blacks faced the brunt of such economic exploitation. One northern journalist stated, "Heaven preserve the shanties . . . and supply proprietors with tenants from whom the rent can be screwed." According to contemporary observers like George C. Foster, free blacks lived in "lofts," "garrets," "cellars," "blind alleys," "narrow courts," and "abandoned land." Such homes were poorly heated during the winter, too hot during the summer, and without proper water and sewer facilities at all times. During periodic outbreaks of diseases like cholera, free blacks suffered disproportionately. In 1832, when an epidemic of cholera hit Baltimore, the first wave of 500 deaths included

104 blacks, some 92 of them free blacks. During the 1850s, in New Haven, Connecticut, a contemporary observer reported that "vice close to their homes was a menace . . . housing was scarce, and colored people were not wanted as tenants." Like their southern urban counterparts, blacks in New Haven also had much higher death rates than whites: between 1830 and 1850, the city's black death rate per 1,000 persons was about 37 to 38, as compared with 15 to 21 for whites.

As free blacks faced difficulties gaining decent housing, they also confronted increasing restrictions on their access to public accommodations. Restaurants, theaters, hotels, and boarding houses routinely barred African Americans or served them on a segregated and unequal basis. By the onset of the Civil War, free blacks were so thoroughly segregated in the institutional life of the nation, including cemeteries, that a northern observer concluded that racial prejudice "haunts its victim wherever he goes, in the hospitals where humanity suffers, in the churches where he kneels to God, in the prisons where he expiates [his] offenses, in the graveyards where [he] sleeps the last sleep."

Discriminatory educational policies proved most damaging to free blacks' attempts to expand opportunities for their children. Antebellum southern states and cities—including Charleston, New Orleans, Baltimore, Louisville, and Washington, D.C.—all excluded free black children from the public schools. In the North, however, following protests from the black community, state legislatures gradually established segregated schools for free blacks and whites. Still, the struggle for education was an uphill battle in the urban North. In 1831, when a committee of white abolitionists proposed to build an interracial manual labor institution of higher education in New Haven, whites used both "lawful" and unlawful means to defeat the proposal. They not only held mass demonstrations against the school but also violently attacked the homes of black and white abolitionists. The most vicious attack on free black education emerged in Canterbury, Connecticut. In 1833, when the black student Sarah Harris requested enrollment in an all-white private girl's school, Prudence Crandall, the Quaker school teacher, admitted her. Parents immediately protested the presence of Harris by removing their children from the institution. Crandall responded by transforming her school into an academy for young women of color. Under pressure from white residents, the state legislature ruled against the establishment of a school for nonresident blacks. When Crandall defied the injunction, she was arrested, convicted, and jailed. After release from jail "on a technicality," Crandall resumed her school, but whites soon closed it down by smashing windows and setting fire to the facility.

Although the American Colonization Society (ACS) declined in the face of widespread free black opposition, it remained the most potent symbol of organized racial hostility against antebellum free people of color. As the nation opened its doors to rising numbers of German and Irish immigrants, the ACS worked hard to rid the country of free blacks. In 1847, it spearheaded the formation of Liberia as an independent nation and urged the federal government to use its surplus revenue to colonize free blacks in Africa. Although the organization's charter called for voluntary emigration of free blacks, such policies increased pressure on free blacks to move. Members regularly expressed their belief that free blacks and whites could not peacefully coexist in the democratic polity.

The antiblack sentiment that fueled ACS efforts to secure a peaceful and lawful removal of free blacks led others to adopt violent methods to secure the same goals. In the South, the patrols regularly conducted midnight raids on the homes of free blacks and threatened inhabitants with bodily harm if they did not leave the region. When free blacks complained of such attacks, authorities advised them to "leave the state." Some of the most destructive attacks on free blacks occurred in northern cities. By 1850, working-class and immigrant whites had launched violent attacks on free black communities in Providence, Boston, Pittsburgh, Washington, D.C., New York City, Cincinnati, and Philadelphia. These riots not only resulted in numerous physical injuries and death but also left black homes, churches, schools, and other institutions in ruins, forcing some free blacks to leave the country for Canada and, to some extent, Africa.

In Cincinnati, the Queen City, African Americans faced riots in 1829, 1836, and 1841. During an economic downturn and the hot summer months of August and September 1841, racial violence erupted when whites attacked black churches and businesses on Sixth and Broadway. Unlike most antebellum riots, African Americans selected Major J. Wilkerson, a twenty-eight-year-old "self-made man of color," to organize an armed defense of the community. For a while, heavily armed black men pushed the white mob out of their community, leading to white as well as black casualties, but whites were able to regroup, move an iron cannon into place, and fire on the black area. When officials finally declared martial law, guardsmen and mobsters herded black people into the square at Sixth and Broadway. Although many had posted bond for their release, they were detained. Authorities arrested some three hundred black men, who were violently attacked by members of the mob en route to jail. Before the mob spent its energy, additional attacks on black homes, churches, and businesses took place. In the wake of the riot, the value of black private property holdings dropped by an estimated $150,000.

INSTITUTIONS, CULTURE, AND POLITICS

As African Americans confronted racial hostility in the antebellum city, they increased their institution-building activities. Black religious, fraternal, and mutual benefit societies dramatically expanded. With only a few churches in 1820, by 1860 northern blacks reported 192 African Methodist Episcopal (AME), 46 AME Zion, 75 Baptist, 21 Presbyterian, and 2 Episcopal churches. Among the AME churches alone, New Orleans, Boston, Cincinnati, Providence, and St. Louis reported 2 to 3; Louisville, Brooklyn, and Pittsburgh, 4 to 6; New York, 7; Philadelphia, 9; and Baltimore, 10, the largest number of any city in the United States. Baltimore's free black Methodist churches included 5 regular Methodist, 3 AME, 1 AME Zion, and 1 Methodist Protestant church. Southern churches claimed the bulk of black church membership among both the Methodists and Baptists. Moreover, in the South, members of regular Methodist churches outnumbered AME members by nearly three to two in such cities as Baltimore. Between 1851 and 1863, membership in the largest black Baptist churches in the North ranged from

The Largest Black Baptist Churches, North and South, 1851–1863		
Church	Year	Membership
North		
African, Boston, Massachusetts	1851	110
Abyssinian, New York City, New York	1860	440
Ebenezer, New York City, New York	1855	108
Zion, New York City, New York	1851	378
First African, Philadelphia, Pennsylvania	1859	268
Shilo, Philadelphia, Pennsylvania	1859	303
Union, Philadelphia, Pennsylvania	1859	359
Chillicothe Baptist, Chillicothe, Ohio	1845	<u>181</u>
Total		**2,144**
South		
First African, Petersburg, Virginia	1851	1,635
Gillfield, Petersburg, Virginia	1851	1,361
First African, Richmond, Virginia	1859	3,160
Second African, Richmond, Virginia	1859	1,029
Springfield, Augusta, Georgia	1863	1,711
First African, Savannah, Georgia	1862	1,815
Second Colored, Savannah, Georgia	1862	1,146
First African, Lexington, Kentucky	1861	<u>2,223</u>
Total		**14,080**

Source: Mechal Sobel, *Trabelin' On: The Slave Journey to an Afro-Baptist Faith.* Copyright © 1988 by Princeton University Press. Reprinted by permission of Princeton University Press.

just over 100 to nearly 450, compared to a southern range of about 1,150 to 3,160 (see table).

At the same time, under the leadership of Richard H. Gleaver, deputy grand master of the African Independent Grand Lodge, the black lodge movement spread from Boston, Philadelphia, and New York into the states of the Midwest, Upper South, and Deep South. By the 1850s, the black lodge movement had reached Cincinnati, Pittsburgh, St. Louis, Washington, D.C., Louisville, Baltimore, and New Orleans. As early as 1838, in Philadelphia alone, free blacks maintained some 100 lodge and benefit societies, with nearly 75,000 members. The lodges had paid out $14,200 in benefits to members and reported $10,000 in their treasuries.

Black newspapers and journals also proliferated. In 1827, African Americans published their first newspaper, *Freedom's Journal,* in New York. Under the editorship of the Presbyterian minister Samuel Cornish and John Russwurm, *Freedom's Journal* placed the struggle against slavery and the fight for full citizenship rights at the top of its agenda. Although it was a short-lived publication, it nonetheless helped spearhead the development of black journalism. Within two months after the paper ceased publication in March 1829, Cornish initiated another short-lived paper, the *Rights of All.* In 1836, however, he teamed with journalist Philip Bell, who would later leave the city for the West, and the minister Charles B. Ray of New York to launch the *Colored American* (originally the *Weekly Advocate*), which became the longest-running antebellum black publication. Like *Freedom's Journal*, it heightened the struggle against slavery in the South and discrimination in the North. Other antebellum black publications followed suit: David Ruggle's *Mirror of Liberty*, the nation's first black magazine, in New York City; Benjamin Robert's *Anti-Slavery Herald* in Boston; Henry Highland Garnet and William H. Allan's *National Watchman Clarion* in Troy, New York; Martin R. Delany's *Mystery* in Pittsburgh; William H. Day's *Aliened American* in Cleveland; and Philip Bell, Mifflin W. Gibbs, and J. H. Townsend's *Pacific Appeal* in San Francisco, to name a few.

Samuel Cornish, New York minister and founder of *Freedom's Journal*, the nation's first black newspaper. In 1836 Cornish also helped to launch the *Colored American*. *The Granger Collection*

Searching for an "American" Identity

In their community-building activities, free blacks retained a consciousness of their "African" roots, but the colonization movement forced them to reconsider their self-designation. African Americans now scrupulously avoided the term *African* while searching for a way to claim "America" without denying their "African" origins. As suggested by the new black publications and institutions, free blacks experimented with a variety of alternatives—"oppressed American," "aliened American," "people of color," and "colored American." In 1844, for example, a group of Louisville blacks broke from the white First Baptist Church and founded the Second Colored Baptist Church. The African Baptist Church of Boston became the "First Independent Church of the People of Color." According to the church publication, "The name African is ill applied to a church composed of American citizens." Likewise, according to the editors of the *Colored American,* they adopted this newspaper title because "we are Americans—colored Americans." As Cornish further put it, "Many would rob us of the endeared name 'Americans,' a distinction more emphatically belonging to us than five-sixths of this nation, one that we will never yield."

As free people of color searched for an "American" identity, they also gravitated toward middle-class, Euro-American definitions of gender roles. Over and over again, free black publications promoted the idea that women were "the gentler sex," "naturally" more moral, more loving, and more caring than men. Indeed, some free blacks believed that sharper gender distinctions helped counteract racial stereotypes, justified emancipation, and smoothed the path to full citizenship. In an 1839 article, the *Colored American* drew the gender line starkly:

Man is strong—Woman is beautiful
Man is daring and confident—Woman is defferent and unassuming
Man is great in action—Woman in suffering
Man shines abroad—Woman at home
Man talks to convince—Woman to persuade and please
Man has a rugged heart—-Woman a soft and tender one
Man prevents misery—Woman relieves it
Man has science—Woman taste
Man has judgement—Woman sensibility
Man is a being of justice—Woman an angel of mercy

For their part, black women reinforced certain aspects of the male-dominant idea of gender roles. In the struggle against racial inequality, they believed that it was their duty to "encourage and support the manhood" of their men as "tough and protective" providers for their families and communities. Mary Shadd Cary, a teacher in various schools in New York and Pennsylvania, offers an extreme example. When she moved to Canada during the turbulent 1850s, she soon became the first black female editor in North America with the formation of the *Provincial Freeman*. In addition to promoting the settlement of U.S. free blacks in Canada, the paper vigorously promoted full citizenship for black Canadians. Yet Shadd initially camouflaged her identity as a woman. As such, she revealed her ambivalence about women transcending "woman's sphere" and entering the man's "public sphere." Still, despite the adherence of free blacks to certain aspects of the prevailing gender paradigm, the dynamics of racial and class inequality undercut such notions in practice. As noted earlier, unlike their white counterparts, free black women worked outside the home in large numbers. And as we will see later, they also played key roles in the abolitionist movement and the struggle for full citizenship rights. They developed these roles at a time when most white women were strictly chastised for public speaking and advocacy work.

Black Writers and Artists

Along with black newspapers and magazines, free black men and some women published their life stories. These included the life histories of William Wells Brown (1847), Henry Bibb (1849), Solomon Northrup (1853), and Harriet Jacobs (*Incidents in the Life of a Slave Girl*, published under the pseudonym Linda Brent in 1861). Slave narratives represented the most distinctive African American contribution to antebellum American literature. They highlighted not only the brutalities of slavery but also the ingenuity and courage of African Americans, who devised a variety of strategies (especially escape) for resisting the rigors of human bondage and affirming their humanity. In her narrative, Harriet Jacobs described the plight of the young slave girl who struggled to retain her sense of womanhood in the face of tyranny:

I entered upon my fifteenth year—a sad epoch in the life of a slave girl. My master began to whisper foul words in my ear. . . . No matter whether the slave girl be as black as ebony or as fair as her mistress. In either case, there is no shadow of law to protect her from insult, from violence, or even from death.

Jacobs related how she turned away from her owner "with disgust and hatred," because he "tried his utmost to corrupt the pure principles" of womanhood that her grandmother had instilled. Like other ex-slaves, she also recounted her escape to the North: "I was . . . faint in body, but strong of purpose. I did not look back upon the old place, though I felt that I should never see it again." Jacobs also described the escape of a young male slave, under the rubric "The Slave Who Dared to Feel Like a Man." On the eve of his escape Benjamin explained to her that "he was no longer a boy and everyday made his yoke more galling." The narratives of ex-slave men were even more direct. Henry Bibb, for example, crafted his narrative as a "testimony on record against this man-destroying system."

Free blacks also produced their first dramatic works and plays during the antebellum era. In 1821, the black businessman Allen Royce opened the African Grove, America's first black theater in New York City. Two years later, the Grove staged Henry Brown's "The Drama of King Shotaway," considered the first play presented by a black playwright on the U.S. professional stage. This play, about a slave revolt on the Caribbean island of St. Vincent, helped to launch the career of James Hewlett, a West Indian–born black who played the lead role. Ira Alridge, an African-born ex-slave from Maryland, also received his early stage training at the Grove. Alridge would soon gain international renown for his portrayal of Shakespeare's Othello.

Poems, novels, and historical works rounded out the intellectual accomplishments of antebellum free blacks. The free black woman Frances Ellen Watkins Harper (1854), AME bishop Daniel A. Payne (1850), and the North Carolinian George Moses Horton (1829) all produced their own volumes of poetry during the period. Although Horton remained enslaved, his owners gave him latitude to write and sell his poems, which were widely read by northern free blacks and whites in abolitionist papers like the *Liberator*. In 1853, William Wells Brown followed up the narrative of his life with the first novel by a black American author, *Clotel, or, The President's Daughter* (1853), and a play, *The Escape, or, A Leap for Freedom* (1858). In 1859, Harriet E. Wilson published *Our Nig, or, Sketches from the Life of a Free Black*, the first novel by an African American woman. Historical and social studies included works by Rev. J. W. C. Pennington, *A Text Book of the Origin and History of the Colored People* (1841); Martin R. Delany, *The Condition, Elevation, Emigration and Destiny of the Colored People of the United States* (1852); and William Cooper Nell, *Colored Patriots of the American Revolution* (1855) and *Services of Colored Americans in the Wars of 1776 and 1812* (1855).

Taken together, these antebellum black writers and artists were deeply religious and used their pen as an instrument of liberation. Over and over again, they emphasized the "fatherhood of God" and the "brotherhood of man" and challenged popular beliefs about the white man's "manifest destiny" to subjugate peoples of color. Rev. J. W. C. Pennington condemned slavery and color prejudice as a sickness that abhorred the truth and threatened to carry "the total nation down to a state of refined heathenism." In her poem "Bury Me in a Free Land," the poet

1854

Free Black Poet Frances Ellen Watkins Harper Decries Slavery

Bury Me in a Free Land

Make me a grave where'er you will,
In a lowly plain, or a lofty hill;
Make it among earth's humblest graves,
But not in a land where men are slaves.

I could not rest if around my grave
I heard the steps of a trembling slave;
His shadow above my silent tomb
Would make it a place of fearful gloom.

I could not rest if I heard the tread
Of a coffle gang to the shambles led,
And the mother's shriek of wild despair
Rise like a curse on the trembling air.

I could not sleep if I saw the lash
Drinking her blood at each fearful gash,
And I saw her babes torn from her breast,
Like trembling doves from their parent nest.

I'd shudder and start if I heard the bay
Of bloodhounds seizing their human prey,
And I heard the captive plead in vain
As they bound afresh his galling chain.

If I saw young girls from their mothers' arms
Bartered and sold for their youthful charms,
My eye would flash with a mournful flame,
My death-paled cheek grow red with shame.

I would sleep, dear friends, where bloated might
Can rob no man of his dearest right;
My rest shall be calm in any grave
Where none can call his brother a slave.

I ask no monument, proud and high,
To arrest the gaze of the passers-by;
All that my yearning spirit craves,
Is bury me not in a land of slaves.

Source: Patricia L. Hill, ed., *Call and Response: The Riverside Anthology of the African American Literary Tradition* (Boston: Houghton Mifflin Company, 1998), p. 352.

Frances Watkins Harper proclaimed: "I could not rest if I heard the tread / Of a coffle gang. . . . I could not sleep if I saw the lash" (see box). In William Wells Brown's play *The Escape*, Glen and Melinda escaped from the labor and sexual abuse of the plantation regime. On reaching their new home in Canada, Glen recalled how he fought the overseer and made the blood "flow freely. . . . It was a leap for freedom."

The Abolitionist Movement and the Underground Railroad

Using their culture and community institutions as a springboard for organization, planning, and strategy, free blacks fought for full citizenship rights and the abolition of slavery. During the 1830s and 1840s, blacks held a series of national conventions in Philadelphia, Buffalo, and Cleveland. Until the 1850s, each of these conventions condemned the ACS effort to transport free blacks to Africa. Black delegates took their stand on the Declaration of Independence and the Preamble of the Constitution: "The latter guarantees in letter and spirit to every freeman born in this country all the rights and immunities of citizenship."

Frederick Douglass and Sojourner Truth emerged as perhaps the most renowned black spokespersons for the peaceful abolition of slavery and the extension of equal rights to free blacks. Shortly after arriving in New Bedford, Massachusetts, Douglass became a full-time agent of the Massachusetts Anti-Slavery Society and spoke out against slavery throughout New England. He soon became such an articulate speaker and debater that some white abolitionists feared that his credibility as a former slave would be compromised. Consequently, under substantial pressure from his white allies, Douglass wrote the *Narrative of the Life of Frederick Douglass* (1845), which revealed important details of his life as a fugitive. On the book's release, Douglass fled to Europe, where he stayed and lectured for two years. In 1846, with the aid of friends, he purchased his freedom, returned to the United States, and two years later launched the *North Star* as a new organ of abolitionism. The paper advocated greater influence for blacks in the abolitionist movement, waged a stronger fight against slavery in the South, and promoted a more diligent struggle against racial discrimination in the North. In the first issue of the *North Star*, Douglass addressed one editorial to white friends and another to blacks. To white friends, he wrote:

It is neither a reflection on the fidelity, nor a disparagement of . . . our [white] friends . . . to assert what common sense affirms and only folly denies; that the man who has suffered the wrong is the man to demand redress—that the man struck is the man to cry out—and that he [who] has endured the cruel pangs of slavery is the man to advocate liberty.

To enslaved and free blacks, he wrote:

We solemnly dedicate the *North Star* to the cause of our long oppressed and plundered fellow countrymen. . . . Giving no quarter to slavery of the South, it will hold no truce with oppressors at the North. While it shall boldly advocate emancipation for our enslaved brethren, it will omit no opportunity to gain for the nominally free, complete enfranchisement. Every effort to degrade you or your cause . . . shall find in it a constant, unswerving and inflexible foe.

Sojourner Truth and Harriet Tubman were the two most famous black women of the nineteenth century. Whereas Tubman was a southern-born slave who later escaped to freedom in the North (discussed in Chapter 8), Truth was a New York–born slave who gained her freedom under the state's Emancipation Act of 1827. Seeking to draw a line between her slave past and freedom, Isabella Baumfree changed her name to Sojourner Truth in June 1843. In a conversation with the Quakers James and Lucretia Mott, she said:

> The Lord gave me Sojourner because I was to travel up an' down the land showin' the people their sins an' bein' a sign unto them. Afterward I told the Lord I wanted another name 'cause everybody else had two names; and the Lord gave me Truth, because I was to declare the truth to the people.

Indeed, Truth became one of the most energetic itinerant ministers of her day. She regularly preached against slavery in the South, social injustice in the North, and women's rights. Historian Nell Painter has recently demonstrated that Sojourner Truth's "And Ar'n't I a Woman?" speech, delivered at the Akron, Ohio, Woman's Rights Convention in 1851, was the invention of her white feminist comrade Frances Dana Gage. Still, as Painter concludes, Gage's Truth "triumphs scholarship" as a symbol of Truth's life and struggle against slavery, racism, and sexism: "Look at me! Look at my arm! I have plowed, and planted, and gathered into barns, and no man could head me! And ar'n't I a woman? . . ." (see box on page 230).

This engraving shows Frederick Douglass as a young man. Douglass launched the *North Star* on 28 July 1848. The paper sought a stronger role for blacks in their own struggle for freedom. *By permission of the Houghton Library, Harvard University*

Even as Douglass, Truth, and others vigorously promoted the message of "moral suasion," there were other powerful dissenting voices calling for the forceful and "violent" overthrow of the "peculiar institution" of slavery. In 1829, two years before Nat Turner's rebellion, David Walker, a free black clothier who had moved from North Carolina to Boston, issued his famous pamphlet *Walker's Appeal.* In this militant abolitionist document, Walker urged slaves to rise up and "throw off the yoke" of bondage. At the same time, he exhorted free blacks to stay put and fight: "Let no man of us budge one step. . . . America is more our country, than it is the whites—we have enriched it with blood and tears."

Following Walker's death in 1830, Maria W. Stewart formulated and directed a similar message to enslaved and free blacks. She also declared her readiness to die in the interest of black liberation. On one occasion she urged blacks to affirm their birthright as "true born" Americans and demand their citizenship. Although she faced constraints and complaints from within the black community, she insisted that neither gender nor color should bar black women from speaking out

Sojourner Truth, c. 1870. In June 1843, Isabella Baumfree changed her name to Sojourner Truth and became one of the most outspoken proponents of abolition and women's rights. She continued to be active during the Civil War and Reconstruction years. *National Portrait Gallery, Smithsonian Institution, Washington, D.C./Art Resource, N.Y.*

on behalf of the race. "What if I am a woman? . . . It is not color of skin that makes the man or the woman, but the principal formed in the soul." In a convention held in Buffalo in August 1843, Garnet, Ray, and other New York and Detroit blacks endorsed the Liberty Party and violent defense of their rights if necessary. As Garnet put it, "You cannot suffer greater cruelties than you have already. Rather die freemen than live to be slaves." A year later, one delegate urged the gathering to "let blood flow without measure—until our rights are acknowledged or we [have] perished from the earth."

The struggle for social justice spread well beyond the doings of the most renowned black spokespersons. The fight for freedom was a grassroots social movement that involved numerous ordinary working-class free and enslaved blacks. By the 1850s, free blacks had organized an elaborate underground escape network designed to free fugitives by aiding their escape farther north or by concealing their residence within local black communities. The "underground railroad" depended on the cooperation of large numbers of free blacks. For example, since slaveowners regularly passed through Ohio Valley cities like Cincinnati, Pittsburgh, and

SOURCES FROM THE PAST

1851

Sojourner Truth Addresses the Ohio Women's Rights Convention

Well, children, where there is so much racket there must be somethin' out o'kilter. I think that 'twixt the Negroes of the North and the South and the women at the North, all talkin' 'bout rights, the white men will be in a fix pretty soon. But what's all this here talkin' 'bout?

That man over there say that women needs to be helped into carriages, and lifted over ditches, and to have the best place everywhere. Nobody ever helps me into carriages, or over mud-puddles, or give me any best place! And ar'n't I a woman? Look at me! Look at my arm! I have ploughed, and planted, and gathered into barns, and no man could head me! And ar'n't I a woman? I could work as much and eat as much as a man—when I could get it—and bear the lash as well! And ar'n't I a woman? I have borne thirteen children, and seen 'em mos' all sold off to slavery, and when I cried out with my mother's grief, none but Jesus heard me! And ar'n't I a woman?

Then they talk about this thing in the head; what's this they call it? ["Intellect," whispered some one near.] That's it honey. What's that got to do with women's rights or Negro's rights? If my cup won't hold but a pint and yours holds a quart, wouldn't you be mean not to let me have my little half measure full?

Then that little man in black there, he says women can't have as much rights as men, 'cause Christ wasn't a woman! Where did your Christ come from? Where did your Christ come from? From God and a woman! Man had nothin' to do with Him.

If the first woman God ever made was strong enough to turn the world upside down all alone, these women together ought to be able to turn it back, and get it right side up again! And now they is asking to do it, they better let 'em. 'Bliged to you for hearin' me, and now ole Sojourner hasn't got nothin' more to say.

Akron, Ohio, May 29, 1851

Source: Address by Sojourner Truth to the Ohio Women's Rights Convention. Adapted from Marius Robinson, *Pittsburgh Saturday Visitor,* 7 June 1851.

Evansville, black hotel and riverboat employees reported on the arrival of planters and slave catchers, informed slaves of their opportunities for gaining freedom, and facilitated contact with conductors. In June 1848, blacks working at the Pittsburgh Merchants Hotel helped two female slaves escape from a visiting planter. In early August 1841, a letter from a Cincinnati fugitive informed his enslaved wife and her friends that black boatmen would guide them to abolitionists and freedom. For their part, numerous black women joined Anti-Slavery Sewing Society circles, which produced clothing for runaways and aided their escape from bondage. These free African American men and women took great pride in their resistance activities. The free black Cincinnati agent John Hatfield reported, "I never felt better pleased with anything I ever did in my life, than in getting a slave woman clear, when her master was taking her from Virginia."

Whether blacks called for peaceful and voluntary abolition, violence, or the intensification of the underground railroad, the struggle for liberation was by no means an all-black affair. The most well-known white allies and abolitionists included William Lloyd Garrison, Harriet Beecher Stowe, and John Brown. In 1831, Garrison issued the opening number of the *Liberator,* declaring: "I will be as harsh as truth and as uncompromising as justice. . . . I am in earnest—I will not equivocate—I will not excuse—I will not retreat a single inch—and I WILL BE HEARD." At about the same time, blacks and whites formed new antislavery societies: the New England Anti-Slavery Society (1832), the American Anti-Slavery Society (1833), and the American Moral Reform Society (1835), the latter of which aimed to link abolitionism with the evangelical reform and temperance movements. These organizations reinforced the struggle against slavery at the state and local levels. In 1842, for example, when the U.S. Supreme Court's ruling in *Prigg v. Pennsylvania* weakened the underground railroad, several states passed personal liberty laws prohibiting state participation in the apprehension of fugitives.

In the wake of the Fugitive Slave Act of 1850, northern whites escalated their efforts on behalf of free blacks and bondspeople. In Boston, the abolitionist minister Theodore Parker warned blacks against "kidnappers and slave catchers." In the Christiana Riot of 1851, Pennsylvania's free blacks and their white allies killed one slave catcher and mortally wounded another. All parties in the incident were later tried and acquitted. Although opponents destroyed Crandall's school and the New Haven project for free blacks, discussed earlier, interracial institutes of education developed and succeeded in other states: the Oneida Institute near Utica, New York; Lane Seminary and College in Cincinnati; the short-lived Noyer Academy in Canaan, New Hampshire; New York Central College in McGrawville, New York; and Oberlin Collegiate Institute in northern Ohio. Black schools like New York's African Free School provided students to these new interracial abolitionist institutions, which offered advanced training for future black leaders like Henry Highland Garnet, Alexander Crummell, and Charles Reason.

In 1852, Harriet Beecher Stowe published *Uncle Tom's Cabin.* The novel highlighted the evils of slavery and generated widespread white support for the abolitionist cause. This outpouring of white support culminated with John Brown's attack on the federal arsenal at Harpers Ferry, Virginia. On 16 October 1859, under Brown's leadership, thirteen whites and five blacks aimed to capture the arsenal, arm slaves, and lead a war of liberation. The five blacks included Lewis Sheridan Leary and Dangerfield Newby, killed during the attack; John Anthony Copeland and Shields Green, both captured and hanged along with Brown; and Osborne Perry Anderson, who escaped. Although Brown's effort failed, it confirmed for many African Americans that a war of liberation was possible and that some whites were prepared to pay the supreme price for their freedom. John Rock, the free black Bostonian, dentist, and lawyer, said: "Sooner or later the clashing of arms will be heard in this country. . . . The black man's service will be needed . . . to strike a genuine blow for freedom . . . [with a] power which white men will be bound to respect."

Inter- and intraracial solidarity was difficult to achieve. Free blacks repeatedly complained that white abolitionists viewed them as "exhibits" rather than as "advocates" for their own liberation. They also criticized their white counterparts for

John Brown, a Connecticut minister, and thirteen of the men (including three of his sons) who joined his effort to liberate slaves by armed force. On 16 October 1859, the group attacked the federal arsenal at Harpers Ferry, Virginia. Brown was hanged along with other members of his party, including two blacks. *Division of Political History, Smithsonian Institution*

using blacks as service personnel or "colored mail-wrappers" and denying them leadership positions. Despite intense class and ethnic fragmentation among whites over the slavery issue, they rallied around notions of white superiority, citizenship, and republicanism. Thus, most white abolitionists were willing to go only so far in their defense of black rights. At the same time, African Americans confronted a variety of internal conflicts among themselves.

Differences of Color, Class, Gender, and Ideology

Class, color, gender, cultural, ideological, and political differences threatened racial solidarity. Light-skinned blacks gained economic and political opportunities and privileges denied to their darker-skinned counterparts. During the 1840s, on two occasions, for example, the Ohio State Supreme Court sanctioned the right of mulattoes to vote, arguing that they were not "Negroes." When Democrats gained control of the Ohio legislature and passed a law in 1850 disfranchising anyone with a "distinct and visible admixture of African blood," the Ohio Supreme Court again defended mulatto men, insisting that the law could not disfranchise males with over 50 percent of white ancestry. Family relations reinforced such color divisions. Between 1850 and 1860, in a survey of eight cities, 82 percent of the men listed as "black" were married to women listed as "black," whereas 87 percent of those listed as "mulattoes" had spouses who were also "mulattoes."

Educated, propertied, and skilled black elites also sought to revamp the behavior of their working-class counterparts. As the free black Baptist and Methodist churches expanded, they sought to curb the earlier emotional style of black worship. Bishop Richard Allen and Daniel Coker of the AME church urged free blacks to contain the emotional outcry that characterized tent meetings, where "shouting, ring-dancing, and groaning" gained free expression in Methodist revival services. Even more so than church services, elites condemned working-class black music, dance, drinking, gaming, and leisure time activities. Working-class blacks patronized the illegal "cookshops" and "groggeries." In Richmond, Virginia, according to a police report of one shop, "The house has four rooms on the first floor . . . the first was used as a grocery, the second as a bar room, the third as a snack room, and the fourth as a kitchen." Black customers visited the shop to drink, dance, play cards, throw dice, and enjoy the company of the opposite sex. Although the police regularly raided such places and middle-class blacks condemned them as detrimental to the health of the community, large numbers of working-class blacks kept them in business.

Paradoxically, at the same time that middle-class and elite blacks sought to suppress certain aspects of black culture, whites developed mechanisms for imbibing those very elements of African American life. Urban whites formed minstrel companies and adapted black songs for white audiences. Performing in "blackface," white performers like Thomas Dartmouth "Daddy" Rice popularized stereotypical black rural images like "Jim Crow" and his urban counterpart, "Zip Coon." By 1850, the most well-known minstrel companies—the Virginia Minstrels and the Christy Minstrels—regularly performed at some of the leading theaters of the nation and Europe. Although some blacks, like the dancer and musician William Henry Love, toured with early minstrel companies, blacks were largely excluded from these jobs, which enabled whites to observe and absorb black culture while defending themselves against its full impact.

African American women played a key role in the community life of free blacks. They made up the bulk of church members and spearheaded the formation of a plethora of antislavery societies, temperance unions, sewing circles, and mutual aid and benefit societies. In Philadelphia, for example, women made up more than three-fifths of the membership of mutual aid societies, although male societies maintained the largest treasuries and paid the highest benefits. Women also swelled the ranks of black political and civil rights conventions. Yet black women were often disfranchised within the black community. During the early 1840s, in Boston, for example, the Reverend Jehial C. Beman, minister of the AME Zion church, dismissed Julia Foote from the congregation when she refused to stop holding services and preaching to women in her home. Foote later joined three other AME women denied the privilege of preaching and protested at the AME's annual Philadelphia conference. Following the negative response to their protests, Foote launched her career as an independent preacher and traveled widely across the northern states of New England and the mid-Atlantic. In Philadelphia, following her husband's death in 1823, the free black woman Zilpha Elaw also became an itinerant Methodist preacher. Over the next fifteen years, she traveled widely through New England and the middle states, made at least two trips to the South, and preached for five years in England.

Free black women were not only denied access to the pulpit as ministers in established black churches but also refused a voice on key political matters. They did not, however, accept these constraints without a fight. At one of the early conventions, black women passed and delivered a resolution to the men: "Where as we the ladies have been invited to attend the Convention and have been deprived of a voice, which we the ladies deem wrong and shameful. Therefore, resolved, That we will attend no more after tonight, unless the privilege is granted." As a result of the women's protest, the men introduced and passed a resolution "inviting the ladies to share in the doings of the Convention." Indeed, unlike most of their white counterparts, leading black spokesmen offered growing support to the women's movement. When the predominantly white advocates of women's rights held their famous Seneca Falls Convention in 1848, Frederick Douglass was the only male to speak out in support of women's suffrage. Similarly, the black nationalist Martin Delany not only encouraged the presence of female delegates at the black conventions but also endorsed the right of women to gain equal access to education. In his view, "The potency and respectability of a nation . . . depends entirely upon the position of their women."

Free blacks also faced important ideological and political differences. They fought slavery and the American Colonization Society in different ways. As noted above, not all free black leaders adhered to Douglass's mode of abolitionism, emphasizing as he did "moral suasion" and close cooperation between black and white abolitionists. In 1840, the abolitionist movement split when William Lloyd Garrison supported full female participation. Many whites withdrew from the American Anti-Slavery Society and formed the American and Foreign Anti-Slavery Society. The new organization opposed Garrison's pro-woman, antichurch, and antigovernment stance. Although Douglass and leading black Boston and Philadelphia abolitionists like Charles Lenox Remond and Robert Purvis remained loyal to Garrison, New Yorkers like Cornish, Garnet, and others gradually rejected Garrison's prohibition on party politics. In New York, some blacks continued to vote and used their leverage to fight remaining restrictions on the franchise. African Americans also increasingly questioned Garrison's pacifist tactics, particularly as black communities faced increasing mob attacks. The New York–based *Colored American* called on blacks to "die virtuous martyrs in a holy cause" of self-defense, emancipation, and enfranchisement.

After fighting against the colonization movement for more than three decades, however, substantial numbers of free blacks moved toward an emigration position during the turbulent 1850s. Martin R. Delany emerged as the most forceful spokesperson for such ideas. Born in Charlestown, Virginia, around 1812, Delany had moved to western Pennsylvania with his family by the 1820s. In Pittsburgh, between 1843 and 1847, Delany published a newspaper, the *Mystery*. He also co-edited the *North Star* with Frederick Douglass. In 1849, Delany and Douglass parted ways as Delany moved increasingly toward a black nationalist stance. Delany advocated pride in blackness, independent action, and gradually emigration to a new homeland. In 1852, he first advocated movement to some part of the Caribbean or South America before targeting the Niger Valley of West Africa as a promising new site of African American return to Africa. Similarly, in 1858, the Reverend Henry Highland Garnet of Troy, New York, formed the African Civilization Society and sought "to establish a grand center of Negro nationality from which shall flow the streams of commercial, intellectual, and political power which shall make colored respected everywhere." Garnet emphasized "giving the Gospel to Africa, and thus render obedience unto the [divine] command of our Lord Jesus Christ to go into all the world and preach the Gospel to every creature." For his part, Delany also said that Africa would be "civilized and enlightened" as a result of the African American search for independence in Africa. As such, these nineteenth-century black nationalists also exhibited certain New World cultural biases toward Africa and its people.

By the late 1850s, even Frederick Douglass despaired of abolitionist protest. As early as 1849, he expressed sympathy for the use of violence. He now asked, "Who dare say that the criminals deserve less than death at the hands of their long-abused chattels?" In 1859, he also supported John Brown's plans to launch a violent attack on slaveholders in the South. When word reached Douglass that Brown's effort had failed and that federal authorities had ordered his arrest, Douglass fled to Canada and then to England. Shortly before the outbreak of the Civil War, Douglass moved toward the emigration idea. He decided to investigate Haiti as a site for black settlement. Although he chartered a boat and wrote an editorial announcing the proposed trip, he postponed his plans in the wake of news that southern whites had fired on the federal forces at Fort Sumter and that civil war seemed imminent. Douglass wrote, "Since this article upon Haiti was put to type . . . we find ourselves in circumstances which induce us to forego a much desired trip to Haiti, for the present." Douglass would soon turn his attention to the recruitment of black soldiers for the Union army. In taking up this work of liberation, he would also conclude that "the World" had not seen "a nobler and grander war than that which the loyal people of this country are now waging."

∼

ANTEBELLUM FREE BLACKS TOOK JOBS at the bottom of the urban economy and transformed them into instruments of freedom for themselves, relatives, and friends. Still, they faced significant internal conflicts and social differences. Free blacks catering to white clients amassed resources, power, and prestige that enabled them to protect themselves better than their working-class, poor, and enslaved counterparts. Such internal differences were not only economic but also social, cultural, and political. Although some free blacks supported spirited worship services; leisure time dancing, gambling, and drinking; and even violence in the fight for their rights, others called for formal modes of worship and leisure; temperance; and "moral suasion" to secure their rights. Despite such differences, however, racist notions of republicanism undercut the opportunities and rights of all blacks—enslaved and free, men and women—and reinforced racial solidarity across status lines. Although African Americans gained the support of white abolitionists, such support was insufficient to overturn the system of slavery and transform free blacks into citizens. Only the events of the Civil War and the rapid expansion of industrial capitalism would bring blacks more fully into the economy and polity as citizens as well as producers. Building on their antebellum communities, ideas, and strategies for social change, African Americans would play a key role in their own emancipation during the Civil War years, the subject of Chapter 10.

CHAPTER 10

⁓

The Civil War and the Struggle
for Freedom

lthough slavery was a pivotal factor in the coming of the Civil War, African Americans faced an uphill battle transforming the war into a struggle for their own freedom. Like southern slaveholders, northern whites perceived blacks as inferior, socially and biologically. They not only initially rejected blacks for military service but also respected southerners' claims to "property rights" in slaves. Accordingly, when federal forces first arrived in the South, they returned fugitives to their owners and helped to curb black resistance. For their part, the Confederate states used slave labor to supply their armed forces with food, medical supplies, and services, including labor on defense installations and munitions plants, which enabled the Confederacy to achieve victories on the battlefield. Consequently, federal officials gradually dropped restrictions on the employment of black labor and the recruitment of black troops. The shift in federal policy was related not only to reverses on the battlefield but also to the activism of African Americans themselves. Enslaved black men and women deserted the plantations in rising numbers while at the same time their free black counterparts, particularly in the North, waged a militant campaign to end restrictions on the recruitment of black troops. Thus, federal policy changed under the combined impact of defeat on the battlefield and growing black resistance to bondage.

Once recruited, black soldiers fought in nearly five hundred battles, many of them major engagements. The growing political and military participation of blacks hastened the defeat of the Confederacy, the abolition of slavery, and the rise of a free black wage-earning working class. Still, despite their display of valor on the battlefield, African Americans fought under extraordinary hardships and forms of discrimination. They not only served in segregated units under white officers but also faced discrimination in recruitment procedures, assignments, pay, and aid to their families. Black women and children and the aged and infirm endured the brunt of deprivation on the home front and in fugitive or contraband camps organized by the federal government. These forms of inequality transcended the institution of slavery. They were also related to persistent patterns of discrimination against free blacks in the North and South. Consequently, during the war years,

African Americans not only mobilized against the institution of slavery but also waged a consistent struggle against the denial of full citizenship rights to free blacks, including the franchise and equal access to public accommodations.

WHITE ATTITUDES TOWARD BLACKS IN THE NORTH AND THE SOUTH

In November 1860, the election of Abraham Lincoln as president helped to precipitate the Civil War and the emancipation of some 4 million enslaved African Americans. Although the Republican Party disavowed any intention of emancipating slaves, or interfering with the institution where it existed, Lincoln's victory reinforced southern fears that their future and the institution of slavery were imperiled. A month later, South Carolina seceded from the Union. By February 1861, Mississippi, Alabama, Georgia, Texas, Louisiana, and Florida had followed suit. Southern secessionists established the Confederate States of America, selected Jefferson Davis as president, and chose Montgomery and later Richmond as its capital city. Although the slaveholding Upper South and border states of Missouri, Kentucky, Maryland, Delaware, and later the new state of West Virginia remained in the Union, the states of Virginia, Tennessee, and North Carolina joined the Confederacy. Thus, even before Lincoln delivered his inaugural address and took the reins of government in March 1861, the slaveholders had already challenged his authority to run the country. In his inaugural address, Lincoln not only reiterated his aim to "save the Union" but also held the line on the spread of slavery into the new territories west of the Mississippi River. His stand, along with southern obstinacy, set the stage for the bloodiest war in the nation's history. The collision came on 12 April 1861, when the Confederate states launched an attack on Fort Sumter in Charleston Harbor.

Recruitment of Black Troops

Despite Republican victory in the election of 1860 and the swift advent of the Civil War thereafter, northerners initially rejected blacks as soldiers and citizens. Much like southern whites, they defined the war as a white man's war. When Ohio blacks petitioned Governor David Tod for permission to raise a black regiment, he replied: "Do you not know . . . that this is a white man's government; that white men are able to defend and protect it?" At the local level, when Cincinnati blacks planned public demonstrations to support the Union's war effort, municipal officials prohibited such meetings. Even the staunchest northern Unionists believed that the enlistment of black troops would violate the "accepted mode of warfare" and prove "shocking to our sense of humanity." According to one midwestern Republican senator, "Negro warfare" would unleash "all the scenes of desolation attendant upon savage warfare." Similarly, a border state congressman exclaimed that the use of black troops would belittle "the manhood of 20 millions of [white] freemen."

According to public officials, white soldiers would refuse to volunteer if forced to serve with blacks; if drafted, they would desert. A northern white soldier confirmed such beliefs when he exclaimed that the use of black troops "will raise a rebellion in the army that all the abolitionist(s) this Side of hell could not stop." Moreover, the soldier further stated that the "Southern People are rebels to the government but they are White and God never intended a nigger to put white people Down."

At the same time that some whites expressed the belief that blacks would fight "savagely," shock white sensibilities, and undermine the manhood of white soldiers, others argued that blacks were too timid and would not make good soldiers. As late as September 1862, President Lincoln himself declared: "If we arm them . . . I fear that in a few weeks the arms would be in the hands of the rebels." Conversely, some whites feared that blacks would serve honorably and as such make claims for equal treatment. A northern congressman declared: "If you make him the instrument by which your battles are fought, the means by which your victories are won . . . you must treat him as a victor is entitled to be treated, with all decent and becoming respect." Like southern whites, most northerners rejected this prospect. Indeed, by remaining loyal to the Union, northern whites hoped to contain slavery where it existed and to maintain the status quo for free blacks.

At the outset of the war, federal officials not only rejected blacks as soldiers but also repeatedly reassured "loyal southerners" that their "property right" in slaves would be "scrupulously protected." In his 1861 Independence Day speech, Lincoln reiterated the resolve of Union forces to preserve the institution of slavery among loyal pro-Union southerners. At the same time, Congress adopted the so-called Crittenden resolution. Put forward by the Kentucky congressman John J. Crittenden, the resolution reassured southerners that the North only hoped to "preserve the Union." Military officials soon reinforced such pro-slavery pledges of the president and the Congress. When General Benjamin F. Butler took his post in Maryland, he loudly proclaimed the services of the U.S. Army to put down any evidence of slave rebellion and bar fugitives from Union lines. Similar pronouncements were issued by General William S. Harney, Department of the West; General Robert Patterson, at Harpers Ferry; General George B. McClellan, in western Virginia; General Henry W. Haller, in Missouri and western Kentucky; General Don Carlos Buell, in central Kentucky; and General Dix in Maryland.

Accordingly, when federal troops first moved into the South, Union generals returned enslaved blacks to their owners. General Harney stated: "I should as soon expect to hear that the orders of the Government were directed towards the overthrow of any other kind of property as of this [in] negro slaves." When McClellan took command of the Army of the Potomac and fought against slave-built fortifications, he retained his conviction that neither "confiscation of property . . . [n]or forcible abolition of slavery, should be contemplated." As late as February 1862, as Hallers forces entered Tennessee and then the Mississippi area, he reiterated the doctrine of noninterference with the institution of human bondage: "Let us show to our fellow citizens . . . that we come to crush out rebellion . . . [and that] they shall enjoy . . . the same protection of life and property as in former days."

Blacks in the North

Restrictions on black participation in the military were closely intertwined with restrictions on the civil rights of free blacks in the North and South. As discussed in Chapter 9, at the outset of the Civil War, free blacks endured a variety of civil disabilities. Not only did they enjoy few citizenship rights in the South but they also could not testify against whites in the courts of Indiana, Illinois, Iowa, California, and Oregon. With the exception of Massachusetts, northern and western states also barred blacks from jury service. Although most New England and midwestern states accepted blacks into the public schools along with whites, the major cities of Pennsylvania, New Jersey, and southern Ohio established segregated and "unequal" public schools for black and white children. Only five states (Vermont, Massachusetts, Maine, Iowa, and New Hampshire) permitted blacks to vote on an equal footing with whites. Free blacks also faced increasing residential segregation as well as discrimination in hotels and restaurants and on streetcars. In Philadelphia and other northern cities, streetcar companies either excluded blacks altogether or forced them to ride on the outside platform, rain or shine, in heat or cold.

Despite the tight labor market and increasing wartime demand for workers, northern blacks found it exceedingly difficult to enter skilled jobs, expand their entrepreneurial activities, and enter the professions. Even in Boston, where blacks enjoyed a broader range of civil rights than African Americans elsewhere, they were nonetheless circumscribed. As the black Boston attorney John Rock stated:

> We are colonized in Boston. It is five times as difficult to get a home in a good location in Boston as it is in Philadelphia, and it is ten times more difficult for a colored mechanic to get employment than in Charleston. Colored men in business in Massachusetts receive more respect, and less patronage than in any place that I know of. In Boston, we are proscribed in some eating houses, many of the hotels, and all the theatres but one.

For their part, laboring black men could scarcely "keep soul and body together." Moreover, several northern states retained their so-called black laws, which made it illegal for free blacks to settle within their borders without posting a security bond. Periodically, law officers sought to enforce these laws. When they did, some blacks faced reenslavement. In 1863, the state of Illinois convicted eight blacks of entering the state illegally and sold seven into "temporary" enslavement to pay their fines. Northern hostility gained its most violent expression in the New York draft riot of 1863. The Draft Act of 1863 permitted wealthy white men to buy their way out of military service by employing a substitute or by paying a $300 fee. In the summer of 1863, hundreds of working-class New Yorkers took to the streets, attacking African Americans as the most visible and vulnerable symbol of their discontent with the federal government. As we will see, such working-class resistance generated support for the recruitment of blacks to alleviate the demand for white soldiers.

Blacks in the South

In the meantime, the Confederacy not only used enslaved blacks as body servants, cooks, orderlies, and gravediggers but also employed slave labor to build roads, erect fortifications, and transport war supplies. On the home front, black bondsmen and -women continued to cultivate the principal crops of southern agriculture, which supplied their own subsistence needs, white families, and the military. Indeed, some wartime planters encouraged blacks more so than before to grow their own food crops and sell the surplus where possible, while others turned their old and incapacitated blacks out to fend for themselves. At the same time, as the northern states blockaded southern ports and cut off access to northern textile-manufacturing products, planters extended the production of cotton fabrics for military and domestic consumption. Black women often bore the brunt of these new productive activities. According to a formerly enslaved woman on a South Carolina plantation, "My old missus made me weave to make clothes for the soldiers till 12 o'clock at night & I was so tired & my own clothes I had to spin over night." Moreover, industrial bondsmen provided a bulwark in the production of southern weapons of war. In Richmond, Virginia, the Tredegar Iron Works, the Confederate's leading industrial firm, employed nearly six thousand slaves during the Civil War.

To meet the growing manpower needs of the Confederacy, slaveowners increased work loads, floggings, and even death as disciplinary procedures. Even more so than before, runaways became a special target of punishment. Planters en-

This engraving shows the lynching of an African American man, William Jones, at the corner of Clarkson and Hudson Streets during the New York Draft Riot of 1863. *New-York Historical Society*

listed the services of the Confederate troops to execute fugitives recaptured from Union ranks. In one affidavit, collected by the Freedmen's Bureau, a Maryland owner "confessed that in August 1861 he had murdered one of his slaves, Jack Scroggins, by whipping him to death for having escaped to the Federal lines." In South Carolina, a group of Confederate scouts disguised themselves as Union soldiers and approached an enslaved man named Harry and asked him to lead them to Confederate hideouts. When Harry led them to a Confederate encampment, they summarily hanged the man as a "traitor."

Since men outnumbered women and children as runaways, planters leveled brutal reprisals against the families of fugitives. In Kentucky, a black woman recalled how her master's son whipped her "severely" when she refused to do some work that she "was not in a condition to perform." According to her testimony, the man beat her in the presence of his father, who had instructed his son to tie her down and give her "a thousand lashes." On a Georgia plantation, one owner bound the feet of his cook in leg irons: "She had to drag herself around her kitchen all day, and at night she was locked into the corn-house." Faced with the prospects of brutal retaliation, some enslaved people urged white southerners to beat the "Yankees," whereas others volunteered their services as personal servants and even arms bearers for the Confederacy. In New Orleans, for example, some free blacks took up arms as part of the Confederate Louisiana Native Guard. As we will see later, however, as the Union army penetrated the South and defeated Confederates, these units would later join the Union army.

EARLY AFRICAN AMERICAN RESPONSES TO THE WAR

As northern whites excluded blacks from the military and southern whites sought to mobilize them against their own interests, African Americans worked to transform the war into an instrument of their own liberation. In the North, African Americans protested their exclusion from Union forces through letter writing campaigns, newspaper editorials, mass meetings, and resolutions to public officials. Over and over again, they insisted that they were U.S. citizens, that they would fight, and that the war itself was a "divinely inspired" conflict to end human bondage. In a letter to General J. S. Negley, African Americans in Pittsburgh and western Pennsylvania exclaimed:

> We consider ourselves American citizens. . . . [A]lthough deprived of all political rights, we yet wish the government of the United States to be sustained against the tyranny of slavery, and are willing to assist in any honorable way or manner to sustain the present administration.

As citizens, free blacks petitioned legislators to remove the word *white* from militia laws and allow blacks to take up arms against the rebels. As one Massachusetts petition put it, "Such a distinction is anomalous to the spirit of justice and equality pervading all the other laws of the commonwealth. . . . We desire to be recognized by the laws as competent to and worthy of defending our homes and the government that protects these homes." In a letter to the *Daily Atlas and Bee* (19 April 1861), Boston blacks predicted that their services would be needed and that they would fight when the time came: "The colored man will fight,—not as a tool, but as an American patriot. He will fight most desperately, because he will be fighting against his enemy, slavery."

In New York, a convention of blacks exclaimed that "ordinary means, such as Reason, Justice [and] Patriotism" had failed and that "more effective remedies ought now to be thoroughly tried in the shape of warm lead and cold steel, duly administered by two hundred thousand black doctors." Accordingly, blacks organized their own drilling companies, as they often put it, "to the end of becoming better skilled in the use of fire-arms; so that when we shall be called upon by the country, we shall be better prepared to make a ready and fitting response." African Americans also believed that their fight for freedom had the support of "the highest authority" in the "universe." As John Rock, the Boston attorney, put it in a speech:

> I think I see the finger of God in all this. Yes, there is the handwriting on the wall: I came not to bring peace, but the sword. Break every yoke, and let the oppressed go free. I have heard the groans of my people, and am come to deliver them.

Another prospective enlistee, William H. Carney, revealed that he had "a strong inclination" to prepare for the ministry, but when the country called for men, he said that he "could best" serve his God by "serving my country and my oppressed brothers."

Between 1861 and 1862, African Americans offered their services to the War Department in no uncertain terms. In April 1861, Jacob Dodson, a janitor in the U.S. Senate chambers, wrote that "some three hundred" reliable "colored citizens" desire to enter the service for the defense of the [capital] City." Dodson also vouched for his own military qualifications: "I have been three times across the Rocky Mountains with Fremont and others." In Battle Creek, Michigan (October 1861), the black physician G. P. Miller sought permission to raise "five to ten thousand free men to report in sixty days to take any position that may be assigned us." If his men were rejected for regular units, Miller offered them to fight as guerrillas, "if armed and equipped by the government." In Canada, black fugitives offered to return to the United States "as soldiers in the Southern parts during the Summer season, or longer if required." In a letter to the governor of Ohio, Cleveland blacks were even more emphatic:

> We heartily offer you two or more regiments of colored men for that purpose [guarding rebel prisoners] and we will assure you that no one of them shall escape; and we will discharge any duty imposed upon us as soldiers and appertaining to camp duty. And, in our judgment, we could not offer any more severe rebuke to the rebel master.

As northern blacks held mass meetings, passed resolutions, and launched letter writing campaigns, southern blacks "voted for freedom with their feet." In rising numbers, fugitives left the Confederate states and moved into Union territory. As during the revolutionary era, they heightened their resistance to slavery by running away and joining the ranks of the enemy army. When federal forces defeated Confederates in the

SOURCES FROM THE PAST

1863

Testimony on the Number of Fugitives Entering Union Lines After the Emancipation Proclamation

[Fortress Monroe, Va.] May 9, 1863

Question   How many of the people called contrabands, have come under your observation?

Answer   Some 10,000 have come under our control, to be fed in part, and clothed in part, but I cannot speak accurately in regard to the number. This is the rendezvous. They come here from all about, from Richmond and 200 miles off in North Carolina. There was one gang that started from Richmond 23 strong and only 3 got through. . . .

Question   In your opinion, is there any communication between the refugees and the black men still in slavery?

Answer   Yes Sir, we have had men here who have gone back 200 miles.

Question   In your opinion would a change in our policy which would cause them to be treated with fairness, their wages punctually paid and employment furnished them in the army, become known and would it have any effect upon others in slavery?

Answer   Yes—Thousands upon Thousands. I went to Suffolk a short time ago to enquire into the state of things there—for I found I could not get any foot hold to make things work there, through the Commanding General, and I went to the Provost Marshall and all hands—and the colored people actually sent a deputation to me one morning before I was up to know if we put black men in irons and sent them off to Cuba to be sold or set them at work and put balls on their legs and whipped them, just as in slavery; because that was the story up there, and they were frightened and didn't know what to do. When I got at the feelings of these people I found they were not afraid of the slaveholders. They said there was nobody on the plantations but women and they were not afraid of them. One woman came through 200 miles in Men's clothes. The most valuable information we received in regard to the Merrimack and the operations of the rebels came from the colored people and they got no credit for it. I found hundreds who had left their wives and families behind. I asked them "Why did you come away and leave them there?" and I found they had heard these stories, and wanted to come and see how it was. "I am going back again after my wife" some of them have said "When I have earned a little money." "What as far as that?" "Yes" and I have had them come to me to borrow money, or to get their pay, if they had earned a months wages, and to get passes. "I am going for my family" they say. "Are you not afraid to risk it?" "No I know the Way." Colored men will help colored men and they will work along the by paths and get through. . . .

Source: Testimony Before the American Freeman's Inquiry Commission, 9 May 1863. This document appears in Ira Berlin et al., *Free at Last: A Documentary History of Slavery, Freedom, and the Civil War* (New York: The New Press, 1992), pp. 107–110.

Battle of Vicksburg in the summer of 1863, they brought the Mississippi River valley under increasing control, and slaves flocked to Union encampments. By war's end, some five hundred thousand fugitives had moved within Union lines (see box).

The perils of escape fell especially hard on black women. Since they had primary responsibility for large numbers of children, fewer black women escaped than men.

Compared with the prewar years, growing numbers of black women now escaped in family and even community groups. The disruption of war made the prospects of holding on to their children and living among other kin less promising. An enslaved Missouri woman wrote to her husband: "They are treating me worse and worse every day. Our child cries for you." Still, she assured her husband, "Do not fret too much for me for it wont be long before I will be free." Two years into the war, a seventy-year-old Georgia woman led some twenty-two of her children and grand-children to freedom. The woman and other kin boarded a flatboat and traveled some forty miles down the Savannah River to federal forces. In careful detail, Elizabeth Botume, a northern teacher, described the flight of another woman, who escaped

with her hominy pot, in which was a live chicken, poised on her head. One child was on her back with its arms tightly clasped around her neck, and its feet about her waist, and under each arm was a smaller child. Her apron was tucked up in front, evidently filled with articles of clothing. Her feet were bare, and in her mouth was a short clay pipe. A poor little yellow dog ran by her side, and a half-grown pig trotted on before.

In another instance, when a Louisiana owner shot and killed the child of one woman as she escaped, she insisted on bringing the dead child into Union lines "to be buried . . . *free.*"

Black runaways took a toll on the southern economy and forced a reorientation of Confederate labor and military policies. Whereas planters largely volunteered the use of slaves during the early war years, they soon resisted the contribution of

The line between fugitives and refugees blurred as the war escalated and thousands of blacks left the plantations. Here a group of fugitives ford the Rappanhannock River, Virginia, in July or August 1862, following the Second Battle of Bull Run. *Library of Congress*

bondsmen to the war effort. Southern state militia faced a difficult time recruiting men. As one frustrated official put it, "If there is any more men taken out of this county . . . we may as well give it to the negroes . . . now we have to patrol every night to keep them down." At the same time, as casualties mounted, nonslave-holding whites resented the disproportionate burden of the war effort that fell on them. Consequently, in October 1863, the Confederacy passed a new law that allowed the government to take slaves from their owners for military use. At about the same time, the Confederacy instituted new tax laws that permitted the government to confiscate farm animals and implements in lieu of monetary payments. Such activities angered slaveholders, who increasingly relocated their blacks to the interior, not only to escape the encroachment of Union forces but also to elude the Confederate impressment agents. This process, known as "refugeeing" slaves, further disrupted black families and communities and stimulated even more escapes. When one Georgetown, South Carolina, owner moved enslaved people inland, he soon reported twenty-one of his men leaving "to join the Yankees."

FEDERAL POLICY AND THE ENLISTMENT OF BLACKS

Although black bondsmen and -women increasingly voted for freedom with their feet and undercut the Confederate labor force, only slowly did federal officials turn to the use of blacks as laborers and then soldiers. Before African Americans became combatants on behalf of the Union, they served the war effort in a variety of nonmilitary and semimilitary activities as laborers, spies, scouts, and guides. An estimated two hundred thousand free blacks worked as teamsters, cooks, carpenters, nurses, scouts, and general laborers on a plethora of wartime projects. When federal forces captured and occupied territory along the coast of North Carolina in late 1861 and early 1862, black men built federal forts at New Bern; the upper end of Roanoke Island; and Washington, North Carolina. Vincent Colyer, an agent of the Brooklyn YMCA and superintendent of the organization's poor relief in North Carolina, reported that "these three forts were our chief reliance for defense against the rebels, in case of an attack; and have since been successfully used for that purpose by our forces under Major-Generals Foster and Peck, in the two attempts which have been made by the rebels to retake Newbern." Colyer also described the broad range of other tasks that blacks performed as stevedores, blacksmiths, coopers, wheelwrights, and bridge builders: "The large rail-road bridge across the Trent was built chiefly by them, as were also the bridges across the Batchelor's and other Creeks, and the docks at Roanoke Island and elsewhere."

Behind Union lines, blacks often worked in large gangs under strict supervision of foremen, with insufficient rations, clothing, rest, and medical care. At a post in southern Louisiana, one northern officer stated that his "cattle at home" were "better cared for than these unfortunate persons." Black laborers invariably took jobs that white soldiers detested—that is, "cleaning cesspools, scrubbing privies, and policing grounds." Few black military workers received wages. Instead they received in-kind payments of clothing and food. In loyalist territory, many never received direct compensation at all; instead, military officers issued checks for black labor to slaveowners. One northern employer said that such practices made him "ashamed to look a negro in the face."

The employment of black labor behind Union lines was by no means limited to the South. Some northern municipalities coerced blacks into service on military installations, particularly in southern Ohio. In Cincinnati, according to a governor's report, city officials forced black men to work on fortifications:

> The police acting in concert and in obedience to some common order, in a rude and violent manner arrested the colored men wherever found—in the street, at their places of business, in their homes and hurried them to a mule pen on Plum Street, and thence across the river to the fortifications, giving them no explanation of this conduct and no opportunity to prepare for camp life.

When General Lewis Wallace (later author of *Ben Hur*) received word of these abusive tactics, he demolished the camp and set up headquarters for the voluntary recruitment of the "Black Brigade." On the brigade's discharge after three weeks of intensive labor, Colonel Dickerson praised them for having "labored faithfully, building miles of roads, rifle pits and magazines, and clearing acres of forest land."

The distinction between combat and noncombat laborers blurred considerably in practice. Black men were often asked to pick up arms and defend Union encampments. Captain James B. Tolbert, head of a contraband camp at Pine Bluff, Arkansas, described the "armed services" of black nonmilitary personnel:

> Fifteen of them had arms; and were ordered to hold the point along the river; which they did throughout the action, some of them firing as many as 30 rounds, and one actually ventured out and captured a prisoner. Their total loss is five killed and twelve wounded.

Noncombat laborers not only took up arms behind Union lines but also performed the dangerous tasks of spies, scouts, and guides for federal troops. One observer reported from North Carolina:

> In this work they were invaluable and almost indispensable. They frequently went from thirty to three hundred miles within the enemy's lines; visiting his principal camps and most important posts, and bringing us back important and reliable information. . . . They were pursued on several occasions by bloodhounds, two or three of them were taken prisoners; one of these was known to have been shot, and the fate of the others was not ascertained.

Black men exploited certain stereotypes of their character to become effective spies. In Virginia, Allan Pinkerton, chief of the U.S. Secret Service, reported on the techniques of the spy John Scobell. In addition to being able to read and write, according to Pinkerton, Scobell had "what seemed an inexhaustible stock of negro plantation melodies . . . [and] a charming variety of Scotch ballads, which he sang with a voice of remarkable power and sweetness." More importantly, Pinkerton concluded:

Possessing the talents which he did, I felt sure, that he had only to assume the character of the light-headed, happy darky and no one would suspect the cool-headed, vigilant detective, in the rollicking negro whose aim in life appeared to be to get enough to eat, and a comfortable place to toast his shins.

In successful raids on their camps, Confederate officials frequently complained that "the guides of the enemy are nearly always free negroes and slaves."

As the Union faced difficulties subduing southern rebels on the battlefield, they turned to black soldiers to help prosecute the war and alleviate hardships on whites. Rather than appeal to the justice of black enlistment, northern whites often expressed the desire for black troops in racist terms. Samuel J. Kirkwood, the governor of Iowa, not only urged the use of blacks to fill "menial labor" assignments but also exclaimed: "When this war is over . . . I shall not have any regrets if it is found that a part of the dead are *niggers* and that *all* are not white men." During the war years, a racist poem, presumably by an Irish immigrant, reflected working-class white sentiment. According to the poem, "Sambo's Right to Be Kilt," it was appropriate to allow blacks to die in the place of whites:

Some tell us 'Tis a burnin shame to make the Naygers Fight;
An' That The Thrade [threat] of bein Kilt
Belongs but to the White;
But as For Me, Upon my Soul:
So Liberal are we here,
I'll Let Sambo be murthered instead myself
On every day in the year.

Shortly after General Butler announced his intention to aid slave catchers in Maryland, he reversed himself when he took command of Fortress Monroe in the Virginia Tidewater region in the summer of 1861. As blacks deserted the plantation and moved into his lines, Butler secured permission from the general in chief and the secretary of war to retain such fugitives as "contraband" of war. In August 1861, Congress legalized Butler's policy with passage of the First Confiscation Act, which undercut the Confederate war effort by making "all property" used to support the war "subject of . . . capture wherever found." The law included bondsmen and -women who had been "employed in or upon any fort, navy yard, dock armory, ship, entrenchment, or in any military or naval service." Only in July 1862 did Congress pass the Second Confiscation Act, which proclaimed all slaves owned by southern rebels "forever free of their servitude." At the same time, Congress passed the Militia Act, which allowed federal authorities to use enslaved blacks for "any military or naval service for which they may be found competent." For such service, black men and their families would receive their freedom.

In September 1862, Lincoln issued his preliminary Emancipation Proclamation, which became official on New Year's Day of 1863. Whereas the preliminary edict referred to compensated emancipation and the desirability of exporting free blacks to Africa or some other territory outside the United States, the official order dropped such considerations and affirmed the liberation and recruitment of enslaved blacks into the Union military as key goals. Although the Emancipation Proclamation exempted slaves in the loyal border states and loyalist enclaves of southern territory, it set in motion a set of policies that undermined slavery everywhere. The proclamation specified the use of blacks "to garrison forts, positions, stations, and other places, and to man vessels." (See the Documents section.) In the fall of 1863, the War Department issued General Order #329, which authorized the systematic recruitment of slave men—even in the loyalist border state strongholds of Maryland, Kentucky, Missouri, and Delaware—based on compensated emancipation. Along with the continuing activity of African Americans on their own behalf, federal policy now helped to transform the Civil War into a war of liberation for enslaved and free blacks.

Federal authorities, blacks, and their white abolitionist allies wasted little time pushing the enlistment of black soldiers. As early as January 1863, the secretary of war authorized the state of Massachusetts to raise a black regiment. Massachusetts quickly advertised for black men:

> To Colored Men—Wanted. Good men for the 54th Regiment of Massachusetts Volunteers of African Descent, Col. Robert G. Shaw. $100 bounty at the expiration of term of service. Pay $13.00 a month and State Aid to families. All necessary information can be obtained at the office, corner of Cambridge and North Russell Streets—Lieut. J. W. M. Appleton—Recruiting Officer.

Other northern states—Pennsylvania, Connecticut, and Ohio—soon followed suit. Three months later, the War Department sent General Lorenzo Thomas, adjutant general of the army, to the Mississippi Valley to carry out a full-scale recruitment of black troops in the South. In May 1863, the Union escalated the recruitment of blacks by establishing the Bureau of Negro Troops in the War Department. Although state regiments like the Massachusetts Fifty-Fourth and Fifty-Fifth were quite significant, most black soldiers served as part of the federal U.S. Colored Troops.

Despite the vigorous "fight to fight," recruitment was not easy. Blacks were not eager to give their lives without guarantees that joining the war would indeed purchase the freedom of their people. When recruitment agents first entered black communities, black leaders often complained that not more than ten or twelve men showed an interest. According to one report, as the war dragged on, northern blacks, like northern whites, showed a waning interest in fighting:

> At the beginning of the War . . . every man you met wanted to go to War, but now when they know that hard fighting is to be done, hardships to be suffered and privations endured, it is rather difficult, in fact impossible to get their courage screwed to the fighting pitch.

One Ohio black said simply, "I have no inclination to go to War."

Since the war had absorbed growing numbers of young able-bodied white men, some northern African Americans had gradually improved their economic position by taking jobs that paid much higher wages than before. In addition to expanding employment in established general labor occupations—in hotels, boarding houses, barbershops, restaurants, freight depots, and commercial outlets—the war produced new opportunities in government- and military-related services. Although some free blacks, as noted earlier, faced coercion on these projects, others were able to use them to their advantage. In November 1861, for example, the Washington correspondent of the *Anglo-African* newspaper reported the positive economic impact of the war on blacks in the District of Columbia:

> This being the seat of war all classes here are benefitted by it. Five hundred men find employment each day in the Quartermaster's department. . . . Business of every kind for males has increased fully ten per cent. . . . Three or four thousand men are employed at cutting wood in Virginia around the different fortifications, and on the northern front of Washington. Laundresses are doing a fine business. They have the exclusive wash of entire regiments and the families of U.S. officers; also for the hospital inmates. Many females are securing a comfortable livelihood by peddling little notions around the different camps. In a word, we are all doing well as far as employment is concerned. None need be idle.

Understandably, then, as wartime employment improved for some blacks, they were reluctant to give up their jobs for the uncertainties of military training and warfare. Frustrated with such reluctance on the part of free northern blacks, a white Bostonian declared that "the blacks here are too comfortable to do anything more than talk about freedom." The increasing recruitment activities of black leaders like Martin R. Delany, John Mercer Langston, Henry Highland Garnet, Frederick Douglass, and Mary Ann Shadd Cary helped to change the picture. Frederick Douglass captured the urgent tone of black recruits when he exclaimed:

> There is no time to delay. The tide is at its flood that leads on to fortune. From East to West, from North to South, the sky is written all over Now or Never.

In his recruiting efforts Douglass also appealed to notions of manhood and self-respect:

> Liberty won by white men would lose half its luster. Who would be free themselves must strike the first blow. Better even die free, than to live slaves.

In Nashville, Tennessee, one black leader urged "every able bodied descendent of Africa to rally to arms, for arms alone will achieve our rights." The speaker also identified war with the will of God: "God will rule over our destinies. He will guide us, for he is the friend of the oppressed and downtrodden. The God of battles will watch over us and lead us."

In August 1863, Mary Ann Shadd Cary became the first official woman recruiter for the Union army. Soon thereafter, according to William Still, Cary recruited black men in the West and brought them to Boston: "Her men were always considered the best lot brought to headquarters. Indeed, the examining surgeon never failed to speak of Mrs. Cary's recruits as faultless." In Still's view, Cary's recruitment efforts proved the truth of the old adage, that "it takes a woman to pick out a good man." Other black women—particularly Harriet Jacobs and Josephine

Ruffin—served as unofficial recruiters. By vigorously recruiting black men for military service, these black women demonstrated that they perceived their gender interests in racial terms. Similarly, black men envisioned their fight as a "divinely inspired" way to gain their citizenship, defend their manhood, and retain their integrity. Following a Washington, D.C., meeting where the recruiter stressed the connection between liberty, manhood, honor, and self-respect, 140 black men enlisted in the Union army. As the speaker put it, "When we show that we are men, we can then demand our liberty, as did the revolutionary fathers—peaceably if we can, forcibly if we must."

Under the impact of such vigorous recruitment efforts, growing numbers of black men joined the Union army. After deciding that he could best serve his God by serving his country and liberating slaves, one recruit, William H. Carney, spoke for many when he said, "The sequel is short—*I enlisted for the war.*" In the North, nearly 75 percent of military-age black men soon volunteered for military service, but Union forces recruited their first black regiments in South Carolina, Louisiana, and Kansas. Even before Lincoln's proclamation, the exigencies of war had led to the gradual recruitment of southern blacks. As early as May 1862, General Hunter, commander of the Department of the South, defied War Department orders and recruited the First Regiment of South Carolina Volunteers. Although the War Department forced Hunter to disband most of these units, one company remained active through the entire war. In Kansas (August 1862), General Lane also violated federal guidelines and recruited over five hundred black troops. When the federal government changed its policy toward blacks, the Kansas Colored Volunteers became the first black regiment raised in a free state.

In Louisiana, General Butler pursued a similar policy. He mustered free and enslaved blacks into the First, Second, and Third "Native Guards," with their own black officers. Butler presumably recruited only "free blacks," but he actually ignored the distinctions between slaves, fugitives, and free blacks. In late August 1862, Secretary of War Stanton approved the arming of some five thousand black volunteers in the Department of the South. The order required the emancipation of all male slaves, as well as their wives and their children, who volunteered their service. Accordingly, federal officials initiated the recruitment of the First South Carolina Volunteers at Port Royal. Under the command of the white officer Thomas Wentworth Higginson, an abolitionist and friend of John Brown, the unit received official status as part of the Union army in January 1863. With the exception of the Massachusetts Fifty-Fourth and Fifty-Fifth, all black soldiers entered the federal service as part of the U.S. Colored Troops.

In July 1864, the federal government allowed northern states to meet their draft quotas by recruiting southern slaves and free blacks. The enlistment of black troops soared. By war's end, an estimated 180,000 blacks had served in Union forces. Most of these blacks came from the border and southern states: Kentucky, Delaware, Maryland, and Missouri, 42,000; Tennessee, 20,000; Louisiana, 24,000; Mississippi, 18,000; the remaining Confederate states, 37,000; and all northern states, about 38,000, but this figure represented about three times the proportion of blacks in the total eligible northern population pool. As black men in the Union blue penetrated Confederate territory, they took the initiative, urging blacks to desert the plantations and become part of their liberating forces. Hundreds of enslaved blacks left their owners and marched to Union encampments, where black men were inducted into the military and their families organized into contraband labor camps.

ON THE BATTLEFIELD AND THE FIGHT WITHIN THE FIGHT

Black soldiers fought in an estimated 450 battles. Nearly 40 of these were major engagements, including the Battles of Port Hudson, Milliken's Bend, and Fort Wagner. In these engagements, as in the Revolutionary War, African Americans received praise for valor. In May 1863, two Louisiana regiments of ex-slaves and free blacks attacked Confederate forces at Port Hudson on the lower Mississippi River. Although the assault failed, black soldiers proved their mettle by repeatedly defying enemy artillery fire. According to contemporary historian and ex-slave William Wells Brown:

> Six charges in all were made. . . . Shells from the rebel guns cut down trees three feet in diameter, and they fell, at one time burying a whole company beneath their branches. . . . Seeing it to be a hopeless effort . . . the troops were called off. But had they accomplished anything more than the loss of many of their brave men? yes: they had. . . . [T]he undaunted heroism, and the great endurance of

Although most African American soldiers served in labor battalions, here a group of black Union soldiers, recruited in Tennessee, man an artillery battery. *Chicago Historical Society*

the negro, as exhibited that day, created a new chapter in American history for the colored man.

The white general Nathaniel P. Banks later reported: "The severe test to which they were subjected, and the determined manner in which they encountered the enemy, leaves upon my mind no doubt of their ultimate success." The government, Banks concluded, "will find in this class of troops effective supporters and defenders." Another white officer, in charge of engineers, reported that his "prejudices with regard to negro troops have been dispelled by the battle. . . . The brigade of negroes behaved magnificently and fought splendidly. . . . They are far superior in discipline to the white troops, and just as brave."

Milliken's Bend produced similar results. At this installation on the Mississippi River just above Vicksburg, black soldiers turned back a Confederate assault with furious bayonet charges. In a letter to his aunt, a white captain, M. M. Miller of Galena, Illinois, described the bravery of black soldiers:

> I never more wish to hear the expression, "the niggers won't fight," come with me 100 yards from where I sit, and I can show you the wounds that cover the bodies of 16 as brave, loyal and patriotic soldiers as ever drew bead on a Rebel. The enemy charged us so close that we fought with our bayonets, hand to hand. . . . It was a horrible fight, the worst I was ever engaged in—not even excepting Shiloh. . . . I can say for them that I never saw a braver company of men in my life.

In July 1863, the Massachusetts Fifty-Fourth Colored Troops attacked Fort Wagner in the Charleston, South Carolina, harbor. Under the command of the white colonel Robert G. Shaw, black troops launched charge after charge. Despite heavy artillery fire that cut "wide swaths" out of their ranks, black troops fought their way into the fort, where Shaw was killed. Despite the death of their commander, the Fifty-Fourth continued to overpower their enemy. Only the failure of white troops to come forward forced them to retreat. About 250 of the 600 black men who launched the attack lost their lives (some accounts say 1,500 blacks died). Lewis Douglass, the son of Frederick Douglass, participated in the attack. He later wrote to his future wife:

> Dear Amelia: I have been in two fights, and am unhurt. I am about to go in another I believe to-night. Our men fought well on both occasions. The last was desperate we charged that terrible battery on Morris Island known as Fort Wagener. . . . This regiment has established its reputation as a fighting regiment not a man flinched, though it was a trying time. Men fell all around me. A shell would explode and clear a space of twenty feet, our men would close up again, but it was no use we had to retreat, which was a very hazardous undertaking. How I got out alive I cannot tell, but I am here. . . . Remember if I die I die in a good cause.

An estimated 10,000 blacks served in the U.S. Navy. As early as September 1861, the navy accepted the enlistment of blacks. As in the army, black naval personnel were initially restricted to the bottom ranks as "first class boys." By 1862, however, the navy opened the rank of seaman to blacks and thus provided more mobility for black naval recruits than for their army counterparts. Still, although blacks served in a wide range of naval occupations, they were barred from the rank of petty officer. Nonetheless, blacks made up nearly 25 percent of the country's naval forces. Robert and John Smalls of South Carolina became the most renowned black naval heroes when they delivered the Confederate vessel *Planter* to Union forces in May 1862. As Confederate officers slept ashore, the Smalls and seven other enslaved men, along with their wives and children, steered the craft out of Charleston Harbor into the waters patrolled by the Union navy. It was a daring feat. On the one hand, the crew had to carefully navigate past enemy guns by flying the Confederate flag. On the other, before the Union navy could fire on and sink the craft, the Smalls' party had to lower the Confederate colors and hoist a white flag of surrender. For this accomplishment, Robert Smalls received an appointment in the Union navy.

Both black civilians and black enlisted men aided the operations of the Union navy in southern waters. They served as cooks, stewards, and laborers. They also joined raids on nearby plantations, stole supplies, and liberated slaves. According to an account by George W. Reed, a black sailor aboard the U.S. gunboat *Commodore Reed*:

> Our crew are principally colored; and a braver set of men never trod the deck of an American ship. We have been on several expeditions recently. . . . At first, there was a little prejudice against our colored men going on shore, but it soon died away. We succeeded in capturing 3 fine horses, 6 cows, 5 hogs, 6 sheep, 3 calves, an abundance of chickens, 600 pounds of pork, 300 bushels of corn, and succeeded in liberating from the horrible pit of bondage 10 men, 6 women, and 8 children. The principal part of the men have enlisted on this ship.

Indeed, according to recent historians, black seamen played a "primary" role in the success of the federal navy during the Civil War.

Similar to their part in antebellum resistance movements, black women enhanced the struggle for freedom. In Vienna, Virginia, Lucy Carter served as a spy for the Sixteenth New York Cavalry. In 1862, Susie Baker King Taylor escaped from bondage with her family and joined the Union encampment at St. Catherine's Island in South Carolina. She then moved to Camp Saxton in Beauford, South Carolina, where she became a laundress and nurse for Company E. She later described the suffering that she sought to relieve:

> About fo[u]r o'clock, July 2, the charge was made. . . . When the wounded arrived . . . the first one brought in was Samuel Anderson of our company. He was badly wounded. Then others of our boys, some with legs off, arm gone, foot off, and wounds of all kinds imaginable.

Aided by the white southern abolitionist Elizabeth Van Lew of Richmond, the ex-slave Elizabeth Bowser infiltrated the Confederacy by serving as a domestic in the household of President Jefferson Davis. Pretending illiteracy and partial insanity, Bowser gathered crucial information. She not only read letters and dispatches from the Confederate war front but also absorbed details from conversations during dinner time and conferences.

Sojourner Truth and Harriet Tubman also continued their abolitionist activities during the Civil War years. In her Battle Creek, Michigan, home, Truth went from door to door collecting food for Michigan's First Colored Regiment, stationed at Camp Ward in Detroit. In 1864, Truth moved to Washington, D.C., where she served as a nurse to soldiers and aided refugees and their families. In Washington, Truth also met the seamstress Elizabeth Keckley, who later lost a son in action, and helped to form the Contraband Relief Association (CRA). An organization of black women, the CRA assisted former slaves who flooded into the District of Columbia during the Civil War. Black women spearheaded such relief efforts throughout the urban North and the Union-occupied areas of the South. Their efforts on behalf of black bondsmen and -women were especially important because federal authorities at first avoided responsibility for the families of blacks who deserted plantations and entered Union lines as laborers and later as soldiers. The government initially relied on civilian superintendents of northern black and white churches and benevolent societies to do this work. Contraband relief societies distributed food, clothing, bibles, schoolbooks, and medical supplies to fugitives in Union-occupied territory. Yet, like most northerners and federal officials, these aid societies believed that any aid to freedmen and -women should be temporary, because they feared that "charity" would create a permanently dependent class of black poor. Thus, the activities of black women supplemented and even tempered the often harsh judgments and practices of these white allies.

For her part, Harriet Tubman served as a spy and military scout. Some contemporaries described Tubman as "the head of the intelligence service in the Department of the South." Others described her as "the only American woman to lead troops black and white on the field of battle, as she did in the Department of the South." Tubman traveled widely throughout the war zone, General David Hunter having issued her a pass authorizing her to go "wherever she wishes to go." The pass also allowed her "free passage, at all times, on all government transports." Because she was dark-skinned, wore a bandanna, and seemed to fit the "Mammy" stereotype, her effectiveness as a spy was even greater. In July 1863, the Boston Commonwealth reported her conspicuous role in Colonel James Montgomery's attack on Confederate forces along the Combahee River in South Carolina:

> Col. Montgomery and his gallant band of 300 black soldiers, under the guidance of a black woman, dashed into the enemy's country, struck a bold and effective blow, destroying millions of dollars worth of commissary stores, cotton and lordly dwellings, and striking terror into the heart of rebeldom, brought off near 300 slaves and thousands of dollars worth of property, without losing a man or receiving a scratch. It was a glorious consummation.

The Boston paper also reported: "Many and many times she has penetrated the enemy's lines and discovered their situation and condition, and escaped without injury, but not without extreme hazard."

African Americans served the Union cause against great odds. They faced discrimination in modes of recruitment, pay, military occupations, and aid to their wives, widows, and children. Although most blacks volunteered their services, some entered the military against their will. Federal officials and municipal authorities often arrested black men, offering them enlistment in the military as an option to prison. In Helena, Arkansas, one contemporary observer reported that recruiting officers came among blacks and forcibly "carried away . . . the Best men leaving some families without any men to assist them." In Louisville, a black soldier offered a sworn testimony that federal officers coerced him into service:

> When Col. Glenn wanted me to enlist he had me brought up to his office. I told him I did not want to enlist. Lt. Col. Glenn asked me "What in hell was the reason," I did not want to go. He then turned a round to the Sergeant who stood close by and told him to "take this damned nigger to jail," that I was but a "dam[n]ed Secesh [secessionist] nigger anyway." I then replied, "Well rather than go to jail I will join." I was mustered at Louisville by Capt. Womack.

In another case, a Lexington slaveowner requested the arrest and enlistment of a bondsman who had refused to serve him any longer "and affirms that he is as free as I am."

Discrimination in the Military

On entering the Union ranks, African Americans received unequal pay, restrictions on promotions, and maltreatment by white officers in the racially segregated units. Although the Militia Act stipulated the payment of rations and $10 per month (minus $3 for clothing) to black enlistees, white privates received $13 per month plus a $3.50 clothing allowance. Federal authorities also levied a special tax on the pay of black soldiers for the care of their dependents but exempted whites. Moreover, with the exception of the Louisiana "Native Guards," fewer than one hundred African Americans received the rank of commissioned officer. Black men gained such offices mainly as chaplains and surgeons, outside the chain of command. Even so, as commissioned and noncommissioned officers, they received the same pay as privates.

Black men endured not only unequal pay and restrictions on their access to officer slots but excessive fatigue duty as well. On one occasion, Charles P. Bowditch, a captain in the Massachusetts Fifty-Fourth, wrote: "The negroes are kept at work digging trenches, hauling logs and cannon, loading ammunition, etc. . . . They keep us at work pretty steadily. I have been on fatigue duty about thirty hours out of the last seventy." On another occasion, Bowditch wrote that blacks were also ordered "to lay out camps, pitch tents, dig wells, etc. for white regiments who have lain idle until the work was finished for them." In December 1863, General Daniel Ullman, commander of the Louisiana Corps de'Afrique, complained to the Senate

Military Committee that blacks were not only given excessive fatigue duty but also outfitted with inferior equipment as soldiers:

> Since I have been in command such has been the amount of fatigue work thrust upon the organization that it has been the utmost difficulty that any time could be set aside for drill. . . . Then, again I have been forced to put in their hands arms almost entirely unserviceable, and in other respects their equipments have been of the poorest kind. . . . I assure you that these poor fellows are deeply sensible to this gross injustice.

Although the War Department would issue orders barring discrimination in fatigue duty in June 1864, such unequal practices nonetheless continued through the war years.

Black men also faced the greatest risks of injuries and loss of life in combat. A third of black enlisted men, nearly double the rate of whites, were listed as dead or missing by war's end. These figures were not only the product of discrimination behind Union lines but also the result of southern attitudes and policies toward black soldiers. The Confederacy defined blacks as insurrectionists against the state, a capital offense. Although recent scholars argue that the Confederacy failed to implement this policy in practice, Confederate officers and their men nonetheless carried out special punitive measures against blacks, compared with those against white Union soldiers. The Fort Pillow Massacre became the most infamous example of wartime racial injustice. Located on the Mississippi River, Fort Pillow was garrisoned by some 570 Union troops, nearly 50 percent blacks.

Under the command of General Nathan Bedford Forrest, Confederate troops attacked and captured Fort Pillow on 16 April 1864. According to a congressional committee, Confederate soldiers massacred an estimated 300 troops, mainly blacks. When the congressional committee later interrogated twenty-one black survivors of the massacre, they uniformly recalled the shooting and killing of men "in cold blood" after they had surrendered. According to the testimony of one survivor, when one Confederate officer urged the men to stop killing the blacks, another officer rebuked him, saying "Damn it, let them go on; it isn't our law to take any niggers prisoners; kill every one of them." In an editorial of the Fort Pillow tragedy, the *Christian Recorder* partly blamed the federal government for its unequal treatment of black soldiers:

> We say, emphatically, that the massacre, at Fort Pillow, has been invited by the tardiness of the government and the action of Congress. While they have professed to regard every man wearing the U.S. uniform, as being equal in theory, they have acted towards the black soldiers, in such a way, as to convince the confederate government that they, themselves, do not regard the black soldiers as equal to the white. The rebels have taken advantage of this equivocation, to commit just such horrible butchery as that at Fort Pillow.

Following Fort Pillow, however, blacks fought with even greater determination. Some even called for an avengement of Fort Pillow: "Swear anew never to cease fighting. . . . [Make] a rebel bite the dust for every hair of those three hundred of our black brethren massacred at Fort Pillow." Thus, as one white soldier from Pennsylvania put it in a letter back home, "The Johnies [Confederate soldiers] are not as afraid of us as they are of the Mokes [black troops]. When they charge they will not take any prisoners, if they can help it. Their cry is, 'Remember Fort Pillow.'"

Union officials also neglected and even mistreated the families of black soldiers. Although black women served the war effort as laundresses, cooks, seamstresses, and nurses, the wartime demand for able-bodied men far outstripped the demand for women. Thus, black women, children, the elderly, and the infirm swelled the ranks of refugees. Military officers and philanthropic groups alike identified black women with "vice and disease"—"a curse" to the soldier as well as to themselves. Some officers enacted draconian measures. In the fall of 1864, for example, Major General Foster, commander of the Union army in South Carolina, ordered "the arrest and forced labor" of black women without any visible means of support. Foster also barred such women from visiting their kinsmen in army camps. Arguing that their presence slowed troop movements and threatened the outbreak of epidemics, military authorities destroyed the encampments of black women and their families outside Fort Nelson, Kentucky.

Enslaved women also faced rape and sexual abuse at the hands of Union as well as Confederate soldiers. According to one eyewitness account, at Fortress Monroe in Virginia, four Union soldiers

From the early years of the war, black women served Union forces as nurses, cooks, and camp servants. On the far right we see a black woman, identified as Mrs. Fairfax, who served as chief cook in the Union camp of General Fitz John Porter, Army of the Potomac, Harrison's Landing, Virginia, August 1862. *Library of Congress*

went to the house of two colored men (father and son-in-law). Two of them seized a colored woman in the front yard, each in turn gratifying his brutal lusts, while the other stood guard with sword and pistol. The other two went to the house, one stopping at the door to stand guard. The other after a desperate struggle, succeeded in ravishing a young woman in the house in the presence of her father and grandfather.

Following the rape of a nine-year-old black girl by a group of his Union comrades, one white soldier wrote home from South Carolina: "While on picket guard I witnessed misdeeds that made me ashamed of America." In Hanover County, Virginia, another group of Union soldiers stopped five young black women and "cut their arms, legs, and backs with razors." White officers as well as enlisted men showed a disdain for black women and reinforced such sexual assaults. In his testimony before the Freedmen's Inquiry Commission, General Saxton claimed that "the colored women are proud to have illicit intercourse with white men."

The Fight for Equal Pay

African Americans did not accept discriminatory treatment without a fight. They soon protested against "the gross injustice." Black soldiers directed their greatest protests against unequal pay and neglect of their families. In June 1863, a black corporal, James Henry Gooding, wrote to President Lincoln: "Now your excellency, we have done a Soldier's duty. . . . Why can't we have a Soldier's pay?" When federal authorities rejected their claims, the men of the Massachusetts Fifty-Fourth fought without pay to protest the inequity. The state of Massachusetts offered to supplement their federal allowance, placing them on parity with white soldiers, but blacks rejected the offer. "In effect," they said, the offer "advertises us to the world as holding out for money and not from principle, that we sink our manhood in consideration of a few more dollars. . . . What false friend has been misrepresenting us to the Governor, to make him think that our necessities outweigh our self respect." From Jacksonville, Florida, a soldier in the Eighth U.S. Colored Troops wrote to officials for relief for his wife and children: "When we lie down to sleep, the pictures of our families are before us, asking for relief from their sufferings. How can men do their duty, with such agony in their minds?"

As black men faced increasing casualties on the field of battle, their patience wore thin and their demands for equal treatment intensified (see box). In a letter from the war front (around February 1864), Captain Bowditch of the Massachusetts Fifty-Fourth reported the contents of an anonymous letter sent to one of his commanders. The letter stated "that if we are not paid by the 1st of March, the men would stack arms and do no more duty, and that more than half the regiment were of that way of thinking." Later that year, a black soldier of the Fifty-Fifth was court-martialed and executed for his part in a "near mutiny." When they protested against injustice, authorities jailed twenty men of Rhode Island's Fourteenth Colored Heavy Artillery. At about the same time, military officials court-martialed and shot Sergeant William Walker of the Third South Carolina Volunteers. Walker had led his men to the captain's quarters and ordered them to lay down their arms and "re-

SOURCES FROM THE PAST
1863

Corporal
James Henry
Gooding
Writes to
President
Lincoln
Protesting
Unequal Pay
for Black
Soldiers

Morris Island [S.C.] Sept 28th 1863

Your Excelency will pardon the presumtion of an humble individual like myself, in addressing you. but the earnest Solicitation of my Comrades in Arms, besides the genuine interest felt by myself in the matter is my excuse, for placing before the Executive head of the Nation our Common Grievance: On the 6th of the last Month, the Paymaster of the department, informed us, that if we would decide to recieve the sum of $10 (ten dollars) per month, he would come and pay us that sum, but, that, on the sitting of Congress, the Regt would, in his opinion, be *allowed* the other 3 (three). He did not give us any guarantee that this would be, as he hoped, certainly *he* had no authority for making any such guarantee, and we can not supose him acting in any way interested. Now the main question is. Are we *Soldiers,* or are we LABOURERS. We are fully armed, and equipped, have done all the various Duties, pertaining to a Soldiers life, have conducted ourselves, to the complete satisfaction of General Officers, who, were if any, prejudiced *against* us, but who now accord us all the encouragement, and honour due us: have shared the perils, and Labour, of Reducing the first stronghold, that flaunted a Traitor Flag: and more, Mr President. Today, the Anglo Saxon Mother, Wife, or Sister, are not alone, in tears for departed Sons, Husbands, and Brothers. The patient Trusting Decendants of Africs Clime, have dyed the ground with blood, in defense of the Union, and Democracy. Men too your Excellency, who know in a measure, the cruelties of the Iron heel of oppression, which in years gone by, the very Power, their blood is now being spilled to maintain, ever ground them to the dust. But When the war trumpet sounded o'er the land, when men knew not the Friend from the Traitor, the Black man laid his life at the Altar of the Nation,—and he was refused. When the arms of the Union, were beaten, in the first year of the War, And the Executive called more food. for its ravaging maw, again the black man begged, the privelege of Aiding his Country in her need, to be again refused, And now, he is in the War: and how has he conducted himself? Let their dusky forms, rise up, out the mires of James Island, and give the answer. Let the rich mould around Wagners parapets be upturned, and there will be found an Eloquent answer. Obedient and patient, and Solid as a wall are they. all we lack, is a paler hue, and a better acquaintance with the Alphabet. Now Your Excellency, We have done a Soldiers Duty. Why cant we have a Soldiers pay?

Source: Ira Berlin et al., *Free at Last: A Documentary History of Slavery, Freedom, and the Civil War* (New York: New Press, 1992), pp. 461–463.

sign" from an army that failed to uphold its "contract" with the men. In the wake of such punitive decisions by military tribunals, African American soldiers added military justice to their list of grievances. In an anonymous letter to the *Liberator,* one black sergeant appealed for black commissioned officers and representation on military courts: "We want to be represented in court martial, where so many of us are liable to be tried and sentenced. We want to demonstrate our ability to rule, as we have demonstrated our willingness to obey. In short, we want simple justice."

On the home front, black servicemen gained the support of black leaders and their white allies. In Baltimore, the African Methodist Episcopal (AME) churchman Rev. J. P. Campbell supported the movement for equal pay based on the expectation of equal citizenship:

> We ask for equal pay and bounty, not because we set a greater value upon money than we do upon human liberty, . . . but we contend for equal pay and bounty upon the principle, that if we receive equal pay and bounty when we go into the war, we hope to receive equal rights and privileges when we come out of the war.

In April 1864, the AME *Christian Recorder* was even more direct. The paper linked pay equity to success on the battlefield:

> We, in the name of God and humanity . . . call upon Congress to at once pass a law, that these men shall at once be paid the same as all other soldiers are paid. . . . We ask that Congress will remember the words of the Lord God: "Thou shalt not muzzle the ox that treadeth out the corn." Will Congress violate that plain and positive language of the eternal Jehovah? We are frank to say, that God will not let us and our armies have success, until those who have it in their power to do right, do it.

On 15 June 1864, black soldiers finally prevailed. Congress enacted equal pay legislation, retroactive to 1 January 1864, for all black soldiers who had obtained their freedom on or before 19 April 1861. When this distinction between free men and freedmen caused friction over pay, several regiments instituted the "Quaker Oath," which allowed fugitives to claim their freedom by the "law of God" and receive retroactive pay for actual length of their service. Following receipt of this back pay, black soldiers celebrated, and morale soared. After eighteen months, as one officer of the Massachusetts Fifty-Fourth wrote: "Nine hundred men received their money; nine hundred stories rested on the faces of those men . . . now a petty carnival prevails. The fiddle and other music long neglected enlivens the tents day and night. Songs burst out everywhere; dancing is incessant." A sergeant in the Fifty-Fifth wrote simply: "We had a glorious celebration."

The Struggle for Full Citizenship

The "fight to fight" and the struggle for "equal pay" were deeply rooted in the fight for full citizenship for free blacks. Throughout the war years, free blacks intensified their battle against disfranchisement, segregation, and exclusion from the institutional, cultural, and political life of the nation. In February 1865, the *New Orleans Tribune* attacked segregated and unequal institutions: "The strength of the United States will require that the dictates of equity and justice be heeded. A country cannot be powerful unless the people be made one nation. We want to have one country; let us therefore have one law." Free blacks repeatedly assailed racial barriers in jury service, education, public accommodations, and especially voting. The struggle against exclusion from jury service emerged most forcefully in California, where the *Pacific Appeal,* edited by Philip Bell, kept the issue before the public and law makers. In an April 1862 editorial, the editor declared that "such laws are disgraceful to the statutes of our state, are relics of barbarism and slavery, retard the wheels of justice, degrade our manhood, and inflict irreparable damage on our rights and liberties." The editor also attacked the exclusion of blacks from testifying against whites. So long as such laws remained on the books, the editor concluded, "so long will we be fitting subjects for assaults on our persons and property, by knavish and brutal white men, who, knowing we have no protection in law, think they can rob and murder us with impunity." Under the leadership of John Jones, a free black businessman, Chicago blacks attacked the "black codes." In 1864, they formed the Repeal Association and soon secured some eleven thousand signatures on a petition urging the legislature to repeal the black codes. The petitioners charged the "black laws" with "our present degraded condition" and demanded, "in the name of the great republic," the same treatment as other citizens of the state.

In Philadelphia, blacks protested racial discrimination on the city's streetcars. During 1861 and 1862, the Philadelphian William Still circulated a petition requesting the Board of Presidents of the city railway company to "rescind the rules indiscriminately excluding colored persons from the inside of the cars." In short, the petition asked officials to stop forcing blacks to ride on the front platform outside streetcars:

> Riding on the platform of a bitter cold day like this I need not say is almost intolerable, but to compel persons to pay the same as those who enjoy comfortable seats inside by a good fire, seems quite atrocious. . . . Before I arrived at my destination it began to snow, which, as I was already thoroughly chilled with the cold, made the platform utterly intolerable.

African Americans waged perhaps their most vigorous fight against restrictions on the vote. In New York, blacks campaigned against the discriminatory property requirement for voting. Whereas white men had unrestricted access to the state's franchise, black New Yorkers had to demonstrate ownership of $250 worth of property. To repeal this restriction, New York blacks formed "suffrage committees" throughout the state. As early as 1860, the New York City and County Suffrage Committee of Colored Citizens urged voters to repeal the property law: "Principles of justice . . . to the state itself, require that the basis of voting should be equal to all." Three years later, Kansas blacks issued a similar appeal to the white citizens of the state:

> We ask you the right of suffrage. . . . This government was founded in the interest of Freedom . . . to deprive any portion of the native population of this country of so essential a right as that of suffrage, is to do violence to the genious of American institutions, and is a departure from the aims of the illustrious founders of the Republic.

Black soldiers fought in about 450 battles during the Civil War. In June 1863 African American soldiers turned back a Confederate assault at Milliken's Bend, located on the Mississippi River just above Vicksburg. *Corbis*

Similarly, in May 1864, five North Carolina free blacks traveled to the White House and delivered a petition to Lincoln. The petition urged the president "to finish the noble work" that he had started with the Emancipation Proclamation. More specifically, the petitioners asked the president to grant "that greatest of privileges . . . the right of suffrage, which will greatly extend our sphere of usefulness." In Louisiana, in September 1862, free blacks established a new bilingual French and English newspaper, *L'Union,* and appealed for full citizenship rights, including the vote. In its inaugural issue, the paper proclaimed "the Declaration of Independence as the basis of its platform" and the fight for "true republicanism, democracy, without shackles" as its primary goal.

Although internal class, color, and cultural conflicts did not disappear during the war years, they were less prominent than before. Louisiana blacks rejected an effort to enfranchise "light-skinned" blacks while leaving darker-skinned people of color "half-free." The *New Orleans Tribune* denounced the effort:

> Colored men desire political advancement and equal rights, but they do not desire the humbling of their brothers to serve as foot-walks for the attainment of privileges that are denied to the men of our race who are presently spilling their blood for the defense of the country.

In October 1864, black representatives from seven southern and eleven northern states met in Syracuse, New York. The convention called for "the elective franchise in all the states now in the Union, and the same in all such states as may come into the Union here after." To coordinate the day-to-day details of the campaign, the attendees also formed the National Equal Rights League.

Under the presidency of John Mercer Langston of Ohio, the Equal Rights League soon established state and local chapters across the country. Strong state units soon emerged in Ohio, Michigan, New York, Pennsylvania, Tennessee, and North Carolina. In early 1865, following a meeting of the Louisiana Equal Rights League, the *New Orleans Tribune* commented on the cross-class nature of the organization:

> There were seated side by side the rich and the poor, the literate and educated man, and the country laborer, hardly released from bondage, distinguished only by the natural gifts of the mind. There, the rich landowners, the opulent tradesmen, recorded motions offered by humble mechanics and freedmen. Ministers of the gospel, officers and privates of the U.S. Army, men who handle the sword or the pen, merchants and clerks, all classes of society were represented; and united in a common thought: the actual liberation from social and political bondage.

The End of the War

Although African Americans served against great odds, their homefront and battlefield activities helped to push the conflict into its final phases. After a brief but solid stand against Union forces, the Confederate army faced increasing reverses on the field of battle. Confederate officials like Secretary of State Judah Benjamin and leading Mississippi planters like J. L. Alcorn suggested the emancipation of enslaved blacks as a wartime measure, designed to secure Confederate independence. Such men expressed a preference for Confederate independence above the institution of slavery per se. As early as January 1864, rebel officers in the Tennessee area recommended the training and use of slaves as soldiers. In a report to their commanding officer, General Patrick R. Claiborne, the Confederate officers concluded: "As between the loss of independence and the loss of slavery, we assume that every patriot will freely give up the latter." Similarly, in a letter to a Confederate senator, General Robert E. Lee urged the government to train and enlist slave soldiers "without delay," even "if it ends in subverting slavery" and freeing the slaves. Thus, in February 1865, for example, under pressure from Robert E. Lee and other Confederate generals, the Confederate congress approved the recruitment of bondsmen into the southern army. The law stipulated that such men would be given their freedom in exchange for military service, but the Union defeated the Confederacy before the plan was put into effect.

The Confederacy degenerated rapidly after the fall of Atlanta to General William T. Sherman's army in September 1864. Sherman's troops marched across Georgia to the sea, taking Savannah and then moving on across South Carolina, exposing the Confederacy to some of its greatest losses of property and slaves as blacks deserted the plantations and followed Sherman's army. Partly out of desperation and partly out of hope, hundreds of blacks abandoned the land and joined Sherman's march. In his own words, Sherman reported that on his arrival "the negroes were simply frantic with joy. Whenever they heard my name, they clustered about my horse, shouted and prayed." As Sherman's troops stormed across the Deep South, Ulysses S. Grant, general in chief of the U.S. Army, pushed the Confederate general Robert E. Lee into the trenches of Petersburg and Richmond, which soon brought the war to a close at Appomattox Court House in April 1865. Over six hundred thousand soldiers had lost their lives in the conflict. When the war finally ended, African Americans had played a major role in their own liberation. By war's end, sixteen black men had received the Congressional Medal of Honor, including four for their services in the U.S. Navy. As Grant put it, "All that have [been] tried have fought bravely."

After Lee's surrender at Appomattox, word spread to enslaved blacks in different and uneven ways. Black soldiers, Freedmen's Bureau officials, army officers, and former slaveholders themselves all informed bondsmen and -women of their new legal status. Even before the end of 1864, Unionist governments in Arkansas, Louisiana, West Virginia, and Maryland had emancipated slaves. Tennessee and Missouri enacted similar measures in early 1865. In Texas, where black people still celebrate "Juneteenth" (June 19) as Emancipation Day, Confederates surrendered two months after Appomattox. In Delaware and Kentucky, loyalist slaveholders resisted emancipation until ratification of the Thirteenth Amendment (December 1865), which stated forthrightly: "Neither slavery nor involuntary servitude, except as a punishment for crime whereof the party shall have been duly convicted, shall exist within the United States, or any place subject to their jurisdiction."

The collapse of slavery also signaled the fall of certain restrictions on the rights of free blacks at the federal, state, and local levels. In March 1865, Congress repealed an early-nineteenth-century law that prohibited blacks from carrying the U.S. mail. In 1864, the United States lifted the ban on blacks testifying against whites in federal courts. In 1863, California repealed its law prohibiting blacks from giving testimony against whites in courts of law. Similarly, by early 1865, Illinois had repealed its black laws, which restricted black settlement in the state and limited their rights before the law. In March of the same year, the District of Columbia outlawed discrimination against blacks on its streetcars. Sojourner Truth, who now lived and worked among freedmen in Arlington, Virginia, soon tested the new law. According to her biographer and friend Olive Gilbert, when Sojourner entered the car,

> the angry conductor told her to go forward where the horses were, or he would put her out. Quietly seating herself, she informed him that she was a passenger. . . . She [also] told him that she was neither a Marylander nor a Virginian to fear his threats; but was from the Empire State of New York, and knew the laws as well as he did. . . . Sojourner rode farther than she needed to go. . . . She left the car feeling very happy.

REHEARSAL FOR RECONSTRUCTION

The Civil War not only resulted in the destruction of slavery and the expansion of civil rights but also set in motion the making of a free black proletariat and the rise of a free black yeomanry. The federal government, military officials, businessmen, churches, and benevolent societies mediated this transformation of enslaved people into free workers and landowners on the one hand, and that of slaveowners into employers and landlords on the other. It was a complicated process. Although northern whites hoped to impose capitalist notions of free, market-driven wage labor on the South, ex-slaveowners hoped to retain as many of the coercive features of bondage as possible. African Americans also had their own ideas about land and labor. They rejected not only slavery but also key features of capitalist ideas of wage labor and landownership. Specifically, they accepted the idea that they should be "free to contract" the terms of their own labor, but like many other workers, they rejected the idea that the "stick of hunger" and the "carrot of property" were sufficient to ensure social justice in the workplace, in the home, or in the community. Freedmen and -women also believed that land could help liberate them from slavery and dependence, but they did not believe that land was an "alienable commodity" subject to market forces. On the contrary, African Americans retained ideas about common uses of land rather than absolute rights of ownership and disposal. They believed that land derived its value from the labor and suffering of those who made it productive. Thus, rather than just any piece of land, blacks hoped to occupy the land of their birth that generations of their families and communities had made productive.

In March 1865, Lincoln signed congressional legislation establishing the Bureau of Refugees, Freedmen, and Abandoned Land (or Freedmen's Bureau) to oversee the transition from slavery to freedom. Although the government charged the agency with distributing food, clothing, and medical supplies to refugees—black and white—it failed to approve a budget for its operations. Consequently, the bureau had to rely on the resources of the War Department for its material base and even the latter's personnel to execute the bureau's mission, which also included support for the educational and religious pursuits of freed people and, above all, the resumption of plantation agriculture on the basis of free wage labor. In addition to the military and the Freedmen's Bureau, the U.S. Treasury Department and northern businessmen and philanthropic societies also played key roles in the transition of previously enslaved blacks into freedmen and -women.

The struggle over the terms of labor and landownership emerged most clearly in the "contraband camps" of the South Carolina Sea Islands and southern Louisiana. Since large numbers of Sea Island planters abandoned their land and slaves in the wake of Union invasion, bondsmen and -women gained extraordinary opportunities to cultivate the land on their own terms. Given the high demand for black men as soldiers and military laborers, black women greatly outnumbered men on some of these establishments. Rather than cultivating the established staple crops, however, black men and women focused on subsistence crops. Their decision displeased federal officials, northern businessmen, and white abolitionists, who hoped to reap private profit and public revenue while demonstrating the "superiority" of "free labor" over "slave labor." In early 1865, the *New York Times* editorialized that "white ingenuity and enterprise ought to direct black labor." More directly, however, the *Times* declared that the production of cotton required "the white brain employing the black labor."

In February 1862, Secretary of Treasury Salmon P. Chase appointed Edward L. Pierce, a Boston attorney, to supervise the cultivation of cotton with free black labor on the Sea Islands. Pierce enlisted the aid of freedmen's societies in New York, Philadelphia, and Boston and appointed some fifty special agents to supervise the plantations. These northerners soon instituted their own version of coerced labor. Instead of the lash, employers denied ex-slaves food, clothing, and other necessities of life. Since Confederates regularly raided the slave-run plantations, demolishing houses and destroying and/or stealing crops, household furnishings, and livestock, federal authorities relocated large numbers of blacks to islands near Port Royal Sound, where bondsmen and -women became dependent on direct government support for subsistence and protection. As enslaved people faced these difficult conditions, they gradually accepted wage labor under the supervision of northern capitalist, philanthropic, governmental, and military organizations.

The coercive features of the new labor system emerged even more clearly in southern Louisiana, where General Nathaniel Banks met with loyalist planters and placed black workers on free labor contracts. In exchange for planter loyalty, Banks promised to use the U.S. Army to discipline and regularize the black labor force. Rather than seeking the consent of blacks, he required all able-bodied men to enter contracts or risk arrest as vagrants. Although the contract specified a 5 percent share of the crop or a wage of $3 per month plus food, housing, and medical care, it also stipulated that blacks could not leave the plantations without the permission of their employers. Backed up by the force of the Union army, understandably, many slaveowners declared loyalty as a means of protecting and recovering their perceived "property right" in slaves. By war's end, some 474,000 blacks had participated in a variety of federally sponsored programs of free labor: in the Upper South, 203,000; in the Mississippi Valley, 125,000; in the South Carolina Sea Islands, the south Atlantic coast, and the Sherman Reserve, 48,000; and in southern Louisiana, 98,000.

Employers, military officials, and benevolent societies soon reported success with "free" black labor. They often compared blacks favorably with white workers. At Fortress Monroe, one supervisor described Irish workers as "crabbed" and willing to work "only so many hours a day," whereas blacks worked "night or anytime and do anything you want done." In the Mississippi Valley, an employer reported that "the lowest estimate is . . . that one negro is [worth] three [white] soldiers if they are decently paid." After a period of using free black labor, authorities like General Saxton of the Sea Islands reported that blacks successfully cultivated the cotton crop and proved that "the negroes will work cheerfully and willingly with a reasonable prospect of reward." Another general said that "the negro may be profitably employed by enterprising men."

Although the emergence of wage labor represented a cut above slavery, it was by no means an equitable arrangement. Under the threat of starvation and exposure to Confederate raids, African Americans reluctantly moved toward the production of traditional cash crops. Black plantation hands also made lower wages than military laborers or black soldiers. In 1863, whereas black soldiers could claim $10 per month, field hands earned from as low as $2 per month in the southern Louisiana district, to $6.50 in the Sea Islands, to a high of $7.00 in the Mississippi Valley. On the Sea Islands, federal authorities and their commercial allies also sought to transform the "task" system into "piece work" and to undercut the autonomy that bondsmen and -women had previously enjoyed under this arrangement. At the same time, in southern Louisiana and the Mississippi Valley, employers retained the "gang system" and employed overseers or foremen. The gang system reminded African Americans of the most detested aspects of chattel slavery. Thus, as part of the new arrangement, they insisted that the whip had to go. Indeed, some blacks assured federal officials that they would even work "without money," but they would not endure the whip, separation from their families, or work under "Secesh overseers." When these conditions were not met, according to one army provost marshal, blacks banned together and laid down "their own rules, as to when, and how long they will work etc. etc. and the overseer loses all control over them." In some cases, the bondsmen and -women drove off the overseers, stating that "they would make Laws for themselves."

Although enslaved blacks made the increasing transition to wage labor, they perceived wage labor as a temporary way station toward landownership. On 12 January 1865, Garrison Frazier, a spokesman for black freedmen in Savannah, declared that "the way we can best take care of ourselves . . . is to have land, and turn it and till it by our own labor . . . until we are able to buy it and make it our own." Although most Unionists resisted the allocation of planters' land to blacks, some northern whites believed that blacks should be compensated with land for their years of uncompensated toil. As one Methodist clergyman on the Sea Islands put it, blacks "had made [the land] what it was and . . . it belonged to them, and them only." In 1862, the U.S. government passed the Direct Tax Act, which provided for the confiscation of land on which owners failed to pay taxes and allowed federal officials to reallocate such land to blacks for lease or purchase. Under the provisions of this law, African Americans gained land in "contraband villages," including "Freedman's Village" in Washington, D.C., and "Point Lookout" on Maryland's western shore. On 31 December 1863, Lincoln authorized the direct tax commissioners "to permit loyal residents of Sea Islands to preempt forty-acre plots on any government-controlled land before it was put up for auction."

African Americans optimistically staked their claims. They invariably turned to land "on the old homestead, where they had been born, & had labored & suffered." As a result of opposition from some tax commissioners, however, the government soon revoked such claims and undercut the most promising avenue for landownership for ex-slaves. Still, compared with other areas of the Union-occupied South, blacks gained their greatest wartime opportunities for landownership on the Sea Islands, where over one hundred families gained estates designated for "charitable" purposes. Even more important, in January 1865, in his "march to the sea," General William T. Sherman enhanced black landownership when he issued Special Field Order #15, which allowed enslaved blacks to occupy and gain "possessory title" to forty-acre plots of land on the coastal islands and mainland rice plantations of South Carolina, Georgia, and parts of Florida. By war's end, some twenty thousand former enslaved blacks had settled on some one hundred thousand acres of land known as the Sherman Reserve.

At Davis Bend, Mississippi, blacks secured leases on six plantations during the Civil War years. Two of these plantations belonged to Jefferson Davis, president of the Confederacy, and a relative, Joe Davis. When Union forces took the area and confiscated the land, African Americans had already taken control of the place and were operating it on their own terms. Under General Grant's command, the federal government decided to transform the area into a refuge for the growing number of fugitives who had followed the Union forces there. The government not only leased parcels of land to groups of blacks but also provided "rations, mules, and tools," which the freedmen agreed to pay for out of the proceeds of their crops. Under the leadership of Benjamin Montgomery, a former bondsman, plantation manager, and store operator, African Americans soon raised nearly two thousand bales of cotton and realized a profit of $160,000 at Davis Bend. The settlement also had its own system of government, including elected judges and law enforcement officials.

Davis Bend demonstrated that African Americans were not uniformly hostile to the market economy. Rather, they were determined to enter freedom on their own terms. Independent black farmers also emerged in coastal North Carolina, parts of Arkansas, and Tidewater Virginia, where federal officials sanctioned the cultivation of land and use of the property "of Rebels in Arms against the Government." Landownership programs nonetheless benefited northern white migrants and ex-slaveowners far more than blacks. The direct tax provision resulted in the sale of nearly 90 percent of available property to northern whites. Although blacks gained substantial holdings in the Sherman Reserve, most of this land reverted to Confederate landowners during the final months of 1865. Moreover, even when the government permitted the confiscation of rebel property in the Confiscation Act of 17 July 1862, Congress amended the measure in accord with the constitutional prohibition of "bills of attainder." In other words, even in cases of forfeiture, on the death of primary offenders, property reverted to their heirs. The children of slaveholders would regain the property that formerly enslaved blacks occupied as a result of sales under the confiscation law. Thus, rather than a prelude to landownership and economic independence, the Civil War offered the most telling rehearsals for the postwar rise of inequitable wage labor and sharecropping systems.

ALTHOUGH WAGE LABOR PLACED SOME AFRICAN AMERICANS on a new economic footing, it was by no means an equitable process. Indeed, the government replaced the whip with the threat of starvation, homelessness, and exposure to Confederate attacks. At the same time, the government facilitated the transition of some blacks from wage earners to landowners, but this was the least successful aspect of the "rehearsal" for freedom. Federal authorities used land and labor policies to win the war, strengthen the Republican Party, and create loyal governments in Confederate territory. As we will see in Part IV, only briefly would blacks gain the franchise and enter the Republican coalition as partners. Thus, before African Americans could fully consolidate their position as workers and citizens, they would experience the onset of a new white supremacist regime. Jim Crow would not only restrict their participation in the polity but also undercut their thrust for landownership and economic independence.

PART IV

Emancipation and the First Generation of Freedom
1865–1915

Following the Civil War, some 4 million African Americans gained their free-dom and made the transition from "slave" to "citizen" and "free worker." Al-though African Americans had sacrificed their lives for emancipation and enabled the Union to triumph over the Confederacy, federal policies nonetheless hampered their passage from enslavement to freedom. President Abraham Lincoln and his successor Andrew Johnson enacted Reconstruction policies favorable to the defeated Confederate states. In rapid succession, southern states enacted the "black codes," which not only deprived blacks of the right to vote and aided and abetted the activities of terrorist groups like the Ku Klux Klan but also authorized the use of police power to coerce blacks into signing unjust labor contracts. African Amer-icans responded to postbellum restrictions on their rights by escalating their protest activities and building alliances with northern Republicans. Between 1867 and the early 1870s, partly as a way to defeat the Democratic Party in southern elections, northern Republicans enacted new legislation extending full citizenship rights to African Americans, including the right to vote, hold public office, and shape Re-construction policy in their own interests.

Although the demand for full citizenship rights gained the support of northern Republicans, the African American struggle for economic justice received less sup-port from white allies. Blacks believed that they were entitled to a portion of south-ern agricultural land as just compensation for years of enslavement, but both the Democratic and Republican Parties rejected their claims. Failure to ensure African Americans access to land weakened their position in the political economy and paved the way for the resurgence of the Democratic Party by the mid-1870s and the rise of the segregationist system by the 1890s and early 1900s.

As the promise of freedom faded, some African Americans moved to rural and urban settings outside the South, but most stayed put and intensified their institu-tion-building, cultural, political, economic, and civil rights activities on a national scale. Part IV discusses the economics and politics of emancipation; the rise of Jim Crow; and the emergence of a plethora of new African American strategies for so-cial change during the late nineteenth and early twentieth centuries.

269

CHAPTER 11

༄

The Politics of Emancipation: Winning and Losing the Franchise

After a bitter Civil War that claimed the lives of over six hundred thousand Americans, some four million African Americans gained their freedom. Blacks entered perhaps their most optimistic moment in the nation's history. For the first time since the arrival of Africans in the New World, the majority of blacks took the status of free people. Yet the transition from slavery to freedom was fraught with difficulties. From the outset of the emancipation era, a series of political, economic, and social decisions hampered the transformation of enslaved blacks into citizens and workers. Both President Abraham Lincoln and his successor, Andrew Johnson, defined Reconstruction policy as the prerogative of the executive branch of the federal government. They also proposed to reconstruct the nation on terms acceptable to southern whites. As such, their policies encouraged the disfranchisement of blacks, the rise of abusive labor practices, and the spread of racial violence. The emergence of white supremacist groups like the Ku Klux Klan and the passage of infamous "black codes" deprived blacks of their civil rights and set up a system of forced labor.

Although African Americans faced an exceedingly hostile socioeconomic and political environment during the first years of freedom, they did not take limits on their civil rights sitting down. They joined forces with a small group of white Republican allies to demand full citizenship rights, including the franchise and access to land. Their efforts led not only to the enfranchisement of black men with passage of the Fourteenth and Fifteenth Amendments but also to access to public offices, patronage positions, and state support for black education and social welfare services. Nonetheless, despite these achievements, radical Reconstruction governments failed to confiscate rebel land and redistribute it to ex-slaves. Moreover, Republican Party leaders soon turned away from blacks toward southern whites as the mainstay of the party's strength and helped to set the stage for the resurgence of the Democratic Party. The presidential election of 1876 symbolized the downfall of radical Reconstruction, the intensification of racial violence, and the subsequent disfranchisement of blacks through legal and extralegal means. By the early 1890s, African Americans faced a new and more hostile environment in the South and the nation. Accordingly, they would also search for new and more effective strategies for social change.

PRESIDENTIAL RECONSTRUCTION AND THE RADICAL CHALLENGE

From the initial announcement of emancipation in 1863 through the early postwar years, a variety of presidential decisions hampered the transition from slavery to freedom. Lincoln defined Reconstruction policy as the prerogative of the president. Except for certain high-ranking Confederate military and government officials, he pardoned and restored full citizenship rights to all southern whites who took an oath of "future loyalty" to the Union and pledged to abolish slavery. When the number of postwar loyalists amounted to at least 10 percent of the votes cast in the presidential election of 1860, he empowered the state to call a constitutional convention and establish a new government. By war's end, the president had approved the Reconstruction of the border states of West Virginia, Maryland, and Missouri. Although these newly reconstructed governments extended "freedom" to blacks, they denied African Americans full citizenship rights, including the right to vote. The law encouraged southern states to adopt measures toward blacks "consistent . . . with their present condition as a laboring, landless, and homeless class," rather than as free workers and citizens. Although Lincoln cautiously suggested the enfranchisement of the most educated, skilled, and even light-skinned blacks, southern states rejected the idea, and the president dropped the matter. In short, Lincoln hoped to reconstruct the South on terms acceptable to white southerners, ex-slaveholders and nonslaveholders alike.

Johnson and Early Reconstruction

Following Lincoln's assassination in April 1865, his successor, Andrew Johnson, gave even less consideration to African Americans. Johnson, a Tennessean and former owner of five bondsmen, entered politics as a champion of the white yeoman farmer. Early in his career, he had advocated a slave for every "white family" to perform the "drudgery and menial service." As a loyal Unionist, however, he accepted the emancipation of blacks but made his racial sentiments clear. "Damn the Negroes," he said to one Union general, "I am fighting those traitorous aristocrats, their masters." During the early Reconstruction years, Johnson declared his belief that "this is a country for white men, and by God, so long as I am president, it shall be government for white men." In his message to Congress in 1867, he took his disdain of African Americans a step further. He declared that blacks had "shown less capacity for government than any other race of people." Even more so than Lincoln, Johnson hoped to unify the white South against northern whites and free blacks alike. Within less than two years, he had pardoned over seven thousand high-ranking Confederates and property holders.

Beginning in mid-August 1865, southern states met in convention, adopted new constitutions, and regained their place in the Union. Loyalty to the "Lost Cause" and "white supremacy" defined the outcome of the first senatorial and congressional elections in North Carolina, South Carolina, Georgia, and Louisiana, where the Democratic Party advocated a government "for the exclusive benefit of the white race." Accordingly, legislators planned strategies and enacted laws designed to get things back "as near to slavery as possible." In 1865–1866, beginning with South Carolina and Mississippi, southern states enacted a plethora of new laws, called "black codes." Although these codes theoretically accepted the right of blacks to purchase and own property, marry, make contracts, and sue and be sued in courts of law, they identified the control of black labor as the linchpin of economic recovery and political influence for the postwar South. These laws permitted any white person to arrest blacks; authorized the removal of black children from the homes of poor families; and permitted whites to whip black children and adults as a measure of labor or social discipline.

As southern whites regained economic and political power, postbellum blacks joined forces to demand full citizenship rights. Newspapers, mass meetings, and the "Negro Convention Movement" articulated their position. As early as August 1865, the Nashville *Colored Tennesseean* proclaimed: "All we want is the rights of men. . . . We are Americans. . . . Deal justly with us. That's all we want. That we mean to have come what may!" In December of the same year, the black *New Orleans Tribune* urged Congress to end what the editor called the "conservative and exclusively white man loving administration" of Andrew Johnson. In Norfolk, Charleston, and Nashville, "Negro" conventions adopted the rhetoric of the Revolution and protested against "taxation without representation." As one resolution stated: "Representation and taxation go hand in hand and it is diametrically opposed to Republican institutions to tax us for the support and expense of the government, and deny us at the same time, the right of representation." In North Carolina, a group of blacks reminded President Johnson of their recent and past services in defense of the country:

> Some of us are soldiers and have had the privilege of fighting for our country in this war. . . . We want the privilege of voting. It seems to us that men who are willing, on the field of danger, to carry the muskets of Republics, in the days of peace ought to be permitted to carry its ballots; and certainly we cannot understand the justice of denying the elective franchise to men who have been fighting for the country, while it is freely given [to those who have been fighting against it].

Over and over again, such appeals also emphasized citizenship by birth and determination to stay in America and fight. The editor of one black newspaper was direct: "We do not intend leaving this country. . . . We were born here. Most of us will die here."

From the initial announcement of the Emancipation Proclamation in January 1863, African Americans regularly celebrated Emancipation Day. These occasions provided African Americans with not only an opportunity to join together for fellowship and thanksgiving for liberation but also a platform for protesting injustices and restrictions on their rights. Here are scenes from Emancipation Day celebrations in Charleston, South Carolina. *Black Charleston Photo Collection, College of Charleston*

"Radical" Republicans Strike Back

African Americans were not entirely alone in their early postbellum civil rights movement. They received support from the radical wing of the Republican Party: in the U.S. Senate, Charles Sumner of Massachusetts, Benjamin Wade of Ohio, and Henry Wilson of Massachusetts; in the U.S. House of Representatives, Thaddeus Stevens of Pennsylvania, George W. Julian of Indiana, and James M. Ashley of Ohio. Although some radicals hoped to pursue a punitive course, punishing ex-Confederates for treason, most envisioned a new nation where a strong national state would ensure "equality before the law" for all citizens. Henry Wilson stated, "I believe in equality among citizens—equality in the broadest and most comprehensive democratic sense." Although radicals like Sumner and Stevens supported black suffrage and rejected the dominant notion of "a white man's government," most Republicans were northern moderates and conservatives who

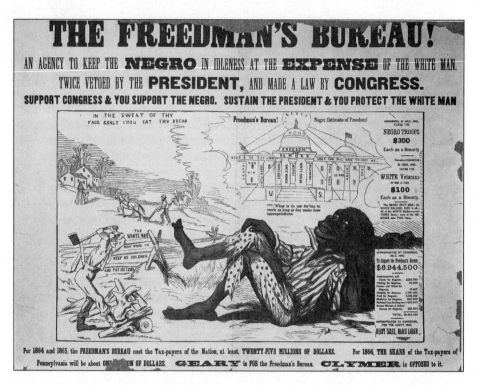

Andrew Johnson and the Democratic Party detested the Freedmen's Bureau and moved to abolish it, as shown in this campaign literature, but African Americans also gradually gained the support of white northern Republican allies such as Pennsylvania congressman Thaddeus Stevens (*opposite*). *Above and opposite: Library of Congress*

hoped to avoid or subordinate the black issue to their own economic and political concerns—that is, northern capitalists' penetration of the southern economy. Passage of the black codes, the growing use of violence, and black activism slowly turned most northern Republicans toward the position that presidential Reconstruction was "no reconstruction at all." By early 1866, radicals and moderates took the position that Congress had the authority to withhold national representation from the South until such states guaranteed the civil rights of freedmen. This position soon clashed with Johnson's idea of Reconstruction as a presidential prerogative and set the stage for the enfranchisement of southern black men as a political expedient. As during the Civil War, when Republicans needed blacks to win the war, they now turned toward blacks to help reconstruct the nation along industrial capitalist lines.

Beginning in early 1866, Congress took a series of steps that culminated in black manhood suffrage. First, in February, Republicans passed the Freedmen's Bureau and Civil Rights Bills. The former aimed to extend the life of the bureau, give it direct funding (that is, remove its reliance on the military budget), and expand the power of agents to judge cases involving black rights. (See the Documents section.) The Civil Rights Bill went even further. It conferred national citizenship on all persons (except Native Americans) born in the United States, without regard to race. Johnson vetoed both measures, describing the Freedmen's Bureau's provisions for black education as an "immense patronage" that gave more to blacks than it did "to our own [white] people." In his veto of the Civil Rights Bill, Johnson's racism was even clearer: "The distinction of race and color is by the bill made to operate . . . against the white race." In April, Congress overrode Johnson's veto and voted the Civil Rights Bill into law. Despite Johnson's opposition, Congress passed the Reconstruction Act of 1867, which divided the eleven Confederate states (except Tennessee, which early on cooperated with radical Republican plans for Reconstruction) into five military districts. Each district had a

Eng.'d by G.E.Perine & C.° N.York.

military commander with authority to use the army to ensure the protection of life and property. For national representation, southern states had to draft new constitutions, enfranchise black voters, and ratify the Fourteenth Amendment. The Fourteenth Amendment (approved in 1868) made it illegal for any state (1) to enforce or make any laws abridging the "privileges and immunities" of citizens; (2) to deny "equal protection of the law"; and/or (3) to deprive citizens of life, liberty, or property, without "due process of law." In a follow-up measure, Congress empowered military officials to register voters and organize and oversee elections. Still, the measure requiring black suffrage applied only to ex-Confederate states and not to the nation as a whole. Only in 1870, with passage of the Fifteenth Amendment, would all black men nationwide gain the right to vote.

Advocates of black suffrage had to overcome not only southern resistance but the opposition of white women, who vigorously pushed for the enfranchisement of women along with that of black men. During the Civil War years, northern white women had played a major role in the Union war effort. They had organized hundreds of freedmen's aid societies and fundraising efforts on behalf of Union soldiers. They had also curtailed their agitation for the suffrage. Many believed that their contributions to the abolition of slavery and preservation of the Union would also emancipate women and lead to their enfranchisement. Consequently, in the early postwar years, many white women regrouped their forces and pushed for woman suffrage. The Fifteenth Amendment angered woman suffragists, partly because the original draft inserted the word *male* into the Constitution for the first time, although the final version of the law was silent on sex or gender. As approved by the states, the Fifteenth Amendment outlawed the disfranchisement of men based on "race, color, or previous condition of servitude." White male supporters of black suffrage justified their position on the premise that this was the "Negro's hour," meaning black men.

When it appeared that black men might obtain the vote before white women, the woman suffrage movement split. Although some white suffragists like Lucy Stone supported black male suffrage as the right thing to do in the short run, others like Susan B. Anthony and Elizabeth Cady Stanton opposed black male suffrage. These women not only opposed black male suffrage but also joined the ranks of the Democratic Party and soon offered a racist rationale for their movement. Writing in the *Revolution*, a Democratic Party–supported organ, for example, Anthony declared:

> While the dominant party have with one hand lifted up TWO MILLION BLACK MEN and crowned them with the honor and dignity of citizenship . . . with the other they have dethroned FIFTEEN MILLION WHITE WOMEN— their own mothers and sisters, their own wives and daughters—and cast them under the heel of the lowest orders of manhood.

On another occasion, for her part, Stanton appealed to fears of interracial sexual relations between black men and white women. She charged that the vote would give black men a license to rape: "The Republican cry of 'Manhood Suffrage' creates an antagonism between black men and all [white] women that will culminate in fearful outrages on womanhood in the Southern states."

Black women desired the vote no less than white women, but most perceived their own interests in racial terms and supported black male suffrage. Frances Ellen Watkins Harper articulated their viewpoint. She argued that the primary obstacle in the path of black women was white racism rather than black men and sided with Frederick Douglass when he said that the defeat of black male suffrage would make black women less, rather than more, secure. Supporting Harper and Douglass were women like Caroline Remond Putnam and Lottie Rollin. Moreover, Douglass, Harper, and others agreed that black women suffered special forms of brutality and violations of their rights because they were black, not because they were women. In 1869, in his address to the American Equal Rights League, Douglass declared:

> When women, because they are women, are hunted down through the cities of New York and New Orleans, when they are dragged from their houses and hung upon lamp posts; when their children are torn from their arms, and their brains dashed upon the pavement; when they are objects of insult and outrage at every turn; when they are in danger of having their homes burnt down over their heads; when their children are not allowed to enter schools; then they will have an urgency to obtain the ballot equal to our own.

The fight for black male suffrage divided the predominantly white woman suffrage movement. It also created rifts within the black community. Not all black women supported black male suffrage over their own. Sojourner Truth, for example, joined Stanton and Anthony in opposing black manhood suffrage. As she put it, "If colored men get their rights, and not colored women theirs, you see the colored men will be masters over the women, and it will be just as bad as it was before." Supporting Truth were other black women like Mary Ann Shadd Cary and Hariett Forten Purvis. When the woman suffrage movement split, these women also supported the National Woman Suffrage Association, while Harper, Douglass, and others joined with the American Suffrage Association. Still, despite limitations, the acquisition of black manhood suffrage represented a fundamental break with the past. For the first time, most African American men gained citizenship rights on an equal legal footing with whites. They would soon use these new rights to transform their place in American politics and society.

FROM "RADICAL" TO "REDEEMER" REGIMES

Once African Americans achieved the right to vote, they wasted little time exercising their new power. Groups of blacks and their white Republican allies entered the black belt and set up Union Leagues, which spread the word of new political empowerment and the possible fruits that voting could bring. Contemporary observers frequently commented on the scope and spirit of early black political mobilization. The manager of one southern plantation declared: "You never saw a people more excited on the subject of politics than are the negroes of the South. They are perfectly wild." According to one observer, "It is the hardest thing in the world to keep a negro away from the polls . . . that is the one thing he will do, to vote." In the election of 1868, a northern reporter wrote from Alabama that blacks had defied "fatigue, hardship, hunger, and threats of employers" to stand in line in a "pitiless storm" to cast their votes. In another election, a Tennessee Valley Republican reported that "the negroes . . . voted their entire walking strength—no one staying at home that was able to come to the polls." During election times, southern planters would often declare, "Negroes all crazy on politics again." Recalling the initial impact of the franchise on blacks, one ex-slave later recalled that "politics got in our midst and our revival or religious work for a while began to wane." In some places, the Union League and offices of the Republican Party nearly displaced the black church as the principal communal gathering place.

Black Political Gains

Blacks used the franchise to augment and even to transcend their political strategies of the early emancipation years. Whereas African Americans were excluded from the presidential state conventions, they accounted for over a quarter (265) of the total delegates to the radical state constitutional conventions. They made up a majority of delegates at the Louisiana and South Carolina conventions; 40 percent in Florida; 20 percent in Georgia, Mississippi, Alabama, and Virginia; and 10 percent in Texas, North Carolina, and Arkansas. African Americans helped to draft new

A group portrait of the first African Americans to serve in the U.S. Senate and House of Representatives. Hiram Revels, seated on the far left, was elected to the Senate in 1870. He took the seat previously occupied by Jefferson Davis, president of the Confederacy. *The Granger Collection, New York, #E96.16*

constitutions that not only enfranchised ex-slaves but also initiated reforms that liberalized southern laws and improved the social welfare and legal position of poor whites. The new constitutions set up the South's first state-funded system of free public education, provided for the building of orphan homes, and established institutions for the mentally insane and the poor. Some states like Texas, Mississippi, Louisiana, and especially South Carolina also took limited steps to redistribute land to freedmen and poor whites, particularly up-country whites.

Following the enactment of the new constitutions, African Americans increased their influence on the political process. By the end of Reconstruction, sixteen blacks had served as U.S. congressmen; over six hundred as state legislators; eighteen as lieutenant governors, treasurers, superintendents of education, and/or secretaries of state; and hundreds of others as local justices of the peace, members of school boards, county commissioners, sheriffs, and aldermen. Some had served as mayors of small local municipalities like the towns of Donaldson, Louisiana, and Natchez, Mississippi. African Americans achieved their most impressive political gains in South Carolina. In 1870, blacks captured four of the state's eight executive offices, sent three of their numbers to the U.S. Congress, and elected Jonathan J. Wright to the state's Supreme Court. At the same time, they sent a majority to the state's House of Representatives (and Senate after 1873). Throughout the Reconstruction era, in South Carolina, the palmetto state, blacks controlled the legislature, including its principal committees. Moreover, after 1872, a black also served as Speaker of the House. In 1873, the racist journalist James S. Pike decried this show of black power: "Sambo . . . is already his own leader in the Legislature. . . . The Speaker is black, the clerk is black, the doorkeepers are black, the little pages are black."

Although the black majority states of South Carolina, Louisiana, and Mississippi accounted for the largest numbers of black public officials, Georgia, Florida, Alabama, and other southern states added to the total. Only Texas, Tennessee, and

Arkansas failed to send blacks to the U.S. Congress. As suggested earlier, these developments were closely intertwined with the rise of the Union Leagues, sponsored by the Republican Party. From the outset, the congressional headquarters of the leagues hired over eighty blacks as "itinerant lecturers," including men like William U. Sanders of Maryland, James H. Jones of Virginia, and James Lynch, editor of the African Methodist Episcopal (AME) *Christian Recorder*. These agents frequently received accolades for their ability to hold audiences of as large as three thousand freedmen "spellbound for hours at a time." Reinforcing the work of these paid agents were northern-born blacks like the Ohio-born Civil War veteran William N. Viney, who bought land in South Carolina and soon organized black political gatherings at his own expense. Tunis G. Campbell, a New Jersey–born black, achieved even greater results in McIntosh County, Georgia. More importantly, however, black political activism included growing numbers of ex-slaves. In Bolivar County, Mississippi, Blanche K. Bruce, an ex-slave, spearheaded the formation of a local political organization that enabled him to hold the office of sheriff, tax collector, and superintendent of education. It was this organization, patronage, and political base that allowed Bruce to enter the U.S. Senate in 1875. The former bondsman Henry Demas headed a similar Republican organization in St. John the Baptist Parish in Louisiana.

Each state soon produced its own coterie of grassroots black leaders. These included Alabama's James T. Alston, South Carolina's Alfred Wright, Florida's Calvin Rogers, and Georgia's Thomas Allen. Formerly enslaved blacks valued education and literacy as leadership qualities. A shoemaker, minister, and farmer, Thomas Allen explained the situation in rural Georgia: "In my county the colored people came to me for instructions, and I gave them the best instructions I could. I took the *New York Tribune* and other papers, and in that I found out a great deal, and I told them whatever I thought was right." Educated freeborn blacks and mulattoes took a disproportionate number of leadership positions. Although they made up only about 6 percent of the total black population, freeborn blacks and mulattoes accounted for an estimated 25 to 30 percent of all Reconstruction era black politicians. Few of these leaders claimed jobs as field hands or general laborers. In South Carolina, for example, nearly 85 percent of Reconstruction black politicians owned real or personal property, and 65 percent could read and write. Teachers, preachers, and artisans figured prominently among this group, but education and social standing on white terms did not fully determine former bondsmen's selection and evaluation of their leaders. They often articulated the belief "that what a man does, is no indication of what he is." Blacks frequently described their leaders as "thoroughgoing" men and "stump speakers" who tried to "excite the colored people to do the right thing."

Northern blacks also formed numerous Republican clubs and supported the Republican Party as the party of emancipation and citizenship. Black Republicans sometimes risked bodily harm and defied white Democratic opponents. During the 1880s, for example, a Cincinnati black challenged the illegal voting practices of the Democratic Party. "There upon," as one writer put it, "a gang of older hoodlums pounced upon the challenger, dragged him into the streets and beat him savagely." Other northern blacks also faced harassment and even death when they resolved to vote for the candidate of their choice. In 1871, when Philadelphia blacks promised to help the Republican Party oust the local Democratic machine, local police and the mayor's office fomented an attack on blacks designed to prevent them from voting. Rioting erupted in several wards of the city, and some four blacks lost their lives as a result. Among the dead was the activist school teacher Octavius V. Catto, who was a leader in the black community, an organizer for the Republican Party, and officer in the Pennsylvania Equal Rights League. *Harper's Weekly* later published a photo of Catto, commenting that he was "a worthy colored citizen of Philadelphia [whose murder was] entirely unprovoked."

Although disfranchised along with white women, black women also helped to mobilize the black electorate. They actively participated in political meetings, rallies, and parades. In some cases, they also voted on resolutions at mass meetings. On one occasion, for example, the *New York Times* reported that "the entire colored population [men and women] of Richmond" participated in the selection of black delegates. Moreover, during the state constitutional conventions themselves, black women joined men in the galleries and voiced their opinions during debates on the floor. Recent studies show that black women often accompanied men to the polls and helped to give broader family and communal meaning to the franchise. Along with men, they were also prepared for confrontations with hostile whites. One contemporary observer reported women carrying arms, axes, or hatchets, "their aprons or dresses half-concealing the weapons." These women justified the fight for black manhood suffrage as important to themselves, their families, and their communities.

African Americans expected and received greater consideration of their rights from black than from white elected officials. Whites often complained that black

Although black women were denied the vote along with white women, they were active participants in electoral politics, as depicted in this 1868 illustration. Harper's Weekly, *25 July 1868*

law officers prevented them from executing their usual labor and social practices. In Georgia, one overseer complained that if he proceeded as desired, "I should only get myself into trouble, and have the negro sheriff sent over by Campbell to arrest me." Moreover, when black voters placed whites into office, such recipients of black support also responded much better to the needs of their constituents than they would have otherwise. In North Carolina, one mayor remarked: "They look upon me as a protector . . . and not in vain. . . . The colored men placed me here and how could I do otherwise than to befriend them." In Alabama, one white newspaper reported in 1870 that "there is a vagrant law on our statute books . . . but it is a dead letter because those who are charged with its enforcement are indebted to the vagrant vote for their offices." Indeed, some black elected officials complained that black constituents often expected much more from them than they could reasonably hope to deliver. John R. Lynch said that blacks "magnified" his office of justice of the peace well beyond its importance or potential.

As we will see in Chapter 12, although radical state governments modified some of the harshest features of the black codes, they failed to establish blacks on their own land. At the national level, the government pursued policies that enriched capital over the needs of labor and permitted the proliferation of corrupt financial schemes. Such practices helped to rob the radical regimes of their legitimacy in the eyes of many northerners as well as southerners. Railroad land grants, tax policies, and state aid for a variety of projects entailed substantial fraud, bribery, and embezzlement of funds. To be sure, African Americans participated in these corrupt practices. In Texas, for example, railroad magnates bribed black legislators to enhance the disbursement of state monies for their projects. In other cases, black public officials like the lieutenant governor of Louisiana promoted projects that benefited their own business investments. Still, more often than not, corruption deprived rather than enriched black law makers and their constituents. In 1872, for example, when the South Carolina Republican Robert B. Elliott sought a U.S. Senate seat, his opponents offered him a bribe of $15,000 to withdraw from the race. When he refused, his opponents used money to destroy his campaign. Moreover, black schools suffered mightily from the theft of money earmarked for the education of black children. In Louisiana, for example, several parishes closed their schools because of insufficient funds.

Reaction and Backlash

Only slowly did radicals enact legislation guaranteeing blacks equal access to public accommodations. In 1875, Congress passed the Civil Rights Bill, which called for an end to racial discrimination in the selection of juries and in public accommodations, including theaters, restaurants, railroads, and hotels. Yet before Republicans passed the measure, they deleted the sections calling for an end to racial discrimination in churches, schools, and cemeteries. According to most radicals, the government had a responsibility to ensure blacks equal "political" and "civil" rights, but not "social" rights. As the Pennsylvanian Thaddeus Stevens put it, "Negro equality . . . does not mean that a negro shall sit on the same seat or eat at the same table with a white man. That is a matter of taste which every man must decide for himself." Moreover, Republican state governors often used their appointive powers and access to patronage to attract Democrats to the Republican fold. Such appointments displeased not only blacks but also southern white Unionists (scalawags) who had supported the Republican Party through the war years. In Louisiana, a group of loyalists protested that "it is a shame to erase a radical Republican off the School Board to take a dam rebel."

Republican efforts to woo rebel support failed. Blacks and their white Republican allies soon became the targets of new and more violent attempts to remove them from office, "redeem" the South for the Democratic Party, and promote the forces of white supremacy. As early as 1865, a visitor to Louisiana reported that whites governed "by the pistol and the rifle." As the principal cause, a white Tennessean stressed the postwar decline of a vested property interest in African Americans. As he said, black life was "cheap now. . . . Nobody like 'em enough to have any affair of the sort [murder] investigated." In his testimony, the former bondsman Henry Adams later recalled that whites killed more than two thousand blacks in the area near Shreveport, Louisiana, where he lived. According to Freedmen's Bureau officials, whites frequently shot blacks down "like wild beasts without provocation." In the Sabine River area of Texas, the ex-slave Susan Merritt recalled murdered blacks floating in the river and warned that whites would face numerous "souls crying" out against them on Judgment Day.

Between 1868 and 1871, blacks faced the onset of a new wave of violence. At least seven black members of the radical constitutional conventions were later murdered, and others faced intimidation and beatings. For his work on behalf of the Republican Party and the Georgia Equal Rights Association, Klansmen forced Abram Colby into the woods, stripped him naked, and beat him for nearly three hours. In Eutaw, Greene County, Alabama, a white mob attacked a Republican campaign rally, killing four blacks and wounding over fifty others. Following a loss at the polls of Laurens County, South Carolina, whites drove some 150 freedmen and their families from their homes, killing thirteen people, including a white judge who had gained election on the basis of black votes. As before, black women—mothers, wives, and daughters—not only witnessed these brutal beatings and murders of black men but also were victims. Indeed, some black women were beaten, raped, and murdered because their men "voted the radical ticket" (see box).

Organizations like the Ku Klux Klan, the Knights of the White Camellia, and the White Brotherhood proliferated. These organizations served as paramilitary support groups for the Democratic Party, which aimed to drive blacks and their white allies from office. Formed in Pulaski, Tennessee, in 1866, the Klan would soon become the most infamous of these terrorist groups. As violence escalated against blacks and their white allies, Congress passed the Ku Klux Klan and Enforcement Acts of 1871–1872. These laws empowered the president to appoint election supervisors to prevent intimidation of voters and/or fraudulent voting practices and made it easier for the U.S. district attorney to use federal courts to prosecute state officials as well as individuals for such violations. Prosecutions soon

1871

Harriet
Hernandez
Testifies
Before
Congress on
Ku Klux Klan
Violence

Spartanburg, South Carolina

WITNESS: HARRIET HERNANDEZ

Question How old are you?

Answer Going on thirty-four years.

Question Are you married or single?

Answer Married.

Question Did the Ku-Klux ever come to your house at any time?

Answer Yes, sir; twice.

Question Go on to the second time; you said it was two months afterwards?

Answer Two months from Saturday night last. They came in; I was lying in bed. Says he, "Come out here, sir; Come out here, sir!" They took me out of bed; they would not let me get out, but they took me up in their arms and toted me out—me and my daughter Lucy. He struck me on the forehead with a pistol, and here is the scar above my eye now. Says he, "Damn you, fall!" I fell. Says he, "Damn you, get up!" I got up. Says he, "Damn you, get over this fence!" and he kicked me over when I went to get over; and then he went to a brush pile, and they laid us right down there, both together. They laid us down twenty yards apart, I reckon. They had dragged and beat us along. They struck me right on the top of my head, and I thought they had killed me; and I said, "Lord o' mercy, don't don't kill my child!" He gave me a lick on the head, and it liked to have killed me; I saw stars. He threw my arm over my head so I could not do anything with it for three weeks, and there are great knots on my wrist now.

Question What did they say this was for?

Answer They said, "You can tell your husband that when we see him we are going to kill him."

Question Did they say why they wanted to kill him?

Answer They said, "He voted the radical ticket, didn't he?" I said, "Yes, that very way."

Question When did your husband get back after this whipping? He was not at home, was he?

Answer He was lying out; he couldn't stay at home, bless your soul! . . . He had been afraid ever since last October.

Question Is that the situation of the colored people down there to any extent?

Answer That is the way they all have to do—men and women both.

Question What are they afraid of?

Answer Of being killed or whipped to death.

Question What has made them afraid?

Answer Because men that voted radical tickets they took the spite out on the women when they could get at them.

Source: Excerpt from *U.S. Congressional Hearings on the KKK,* vol. 5, Gerder Lerner, ed., *Black Women in White America: A Documentary History* (New York: Random House, 1972), pp. 182–185.

took place in North Carolina, Mississippi, and South Carolina, where President Grant sent in the army and forced some two thousand Klansmen to flee the state, but violence continued in Louisiana, Alabama, and Mississippi, all of the so-called unredeemed states. Democratic rifle clubs took to the streets in broad daylight and traveled from place to place disrupting Republican Party meetings, beating and killing blacks. According to one black official, "It was the most violent time that ever we have seen." Encouraged by the surge of white supremacy, Virginia rejected radical Reconstruction and remained under military rule until Ulysses S. Grant took office in the spring of 1869. Only after Grant authorized a vote on the state's constitution, which enfranchised Confederate veterans, did Virginians approve a new constitution. The state then elected a Democratic governor and gave Democrats a majority in the legislature. At the same time, Georgia Republicans remained silent or voted with white Democrats to unseat duly elected black legislators. Democrats retained power in Delaware and regained control of Maryland in 1867; West Virginia in 1870; Georgia in 1870–1871; Alabama in 1874; Mississippi in 1875; and South Carolina, Louisiana, and Florida in 1876.

The so-called redeemer regimes soon worked to dismantle radical achievements. The governor of Georgia, James M. Smith, boasted that the southern states could "hold inviolate every law of the United States and still so legislate upon our labor system as to retain our old plantation system." After regaining the seats of power in the South, redeemers took a series of legislative steps to disfranchise black voters: poll tax requirements in Delaware and Tennessee; property qualifications in Maryland; poll tax and criminal conviction provisions in Virginia; and poll tax and residency requirements in Georgia. In Mississippi, Alabama, and elsewhere, the state instituted gerrymandering schemes that annulled the impact of black majority counties and districts. State and local officials also redefined certain offices from elective to appointive to accomplish the same aim. Moreover, as we will see in Chapters 12 and 13, redeemer governments reinforced ex-slaveholders' control over the black labor force by heightening vagrancy statutes, cutting social welfare and educational expenditures, and deepening the segregation of blacks and whites in the institutional, cultural, and social life of the region. In 1875, a southern newspaper captured the redeemers' intent when the editor declared that the Fourteenth and Fifteenth Amendments "may stand forever; but we intend . . . to make them dead letters on the statute-book."

The presidential election of 1876 symbolized the downfall of radical Reconstruction. In an election marked by violence throughout the South, the Democratic candidate, Samuel J. Tilden of New York, received nearly 4.3 million popular votes, compared with just over 4 million for his Republican opponent, Rutherford B. Hayes of Ohio. The election hinged on the outcome of 20 disputed electoral votes from the states of Oregon, Florida, Louisiana, and South Carolina. These states had sent in two sets of returns, one from the Democratic Party and the other from the Republicans. To resolve the dispute, which inflamed old hostilities growing out of the Civil War, Congress established an Electoral Commission, which consisted of seven Republicans and seven Democrats, plus five justices of the U.S. Supreme Court, one presumably independent (but who was in fact a Republican).

Consequently, the commission, which voted strictly along party lines, awarded all 20 votes to the Republican Rutherford B. Hayes, who won by an electoral vote of 185 to Tilden's 184.

Although the vote appeared strictly a partisan issue, it was more than that. It involved intense negotiations on racial and regional issues. At stake was the ability of the South to craft its own racial policies toward African Americans. Southerners accepted the decision, partly because Republicans and the new president promised a policy of noninterference in southern race relations. Shortly after his inauguration, Hayes ended radical Reconstruction by removing the remaining federal forces from the South and giving southerners a free hand in dealing with the black population. On removing the troops, Hayes declared: "I feel assured that no resort to violence is contemplated in any quarters, but that, on the contrary, the disputes in question are to be settled solely by such peaceful remedies as the Constitution and the laws of the State provide." From the perspective of blacks and their southern Republican white allies, however, the election of 1876 represented "a corrupt bargain" in which Hayes received the southern white vote in exchange for a northern promise of a future lenient hands-off policy regarding black-white relations in the South. The meaning of emancipation and Reconstruction became, and remains, one of the most contested areas in African American and American studies (see box).

LIMITS OF ELECTORAL POLITICS

Despite the downfall of Reconstruction, southern blacks continued to vote and hold public office through the turn of the century. African Americans served in every session of the Virginia Assembly through 1891; North Carolinians sent fifty-two blacks to the state's lower house from the election of 1876 through 1894; South Carolinians elected forty-eight blacks to the state's general assembly from about 1878 to 1902. Moreover, southern states sent ten blacks to the U.S. Congress after the settlement of 1876, the same number as elected before 1876. Blacks also continued to vote and hold office at the county and local levels, particularly in small enclaves like the "black second" congressional district of eastern North Carolina. Still, by 1890, the black vote dissipated in the violent climate of the post-Reconstruction South. Thus, when formal constitutional disfranchisement emerged during the 1890s, it sanctioned a practice that was already well under way in some places.

As redeemer regimes gained power in one southern state after another, blacks sought alternatives to the Republican Party. In 1872, Frederick Douglass, the foremost black Republican spokesperson of the period, had made his famous speech declaring the Republican Party the "deck" and all else "the seas." Now, in the 1880s, Douglass declared that he was "an uneasy Republican." Indeed, according to Douglass, "If the Republican party cannot stand a demand for justice and fair play . . . it ought to go down." In 1876, Senator Bruce of Mississippi criticized the

CHANGING HISTORICAL INTERPRETATIONS

The First Reconstruction

The historiography of slavery framed the first generation of scholarship on the meaning of emancipation in American and African American life. Writers took sides in the anti- and pro-slavery discussions of the antebellum and Civil War years. In 1874, for example, James S. Pike, formerly an antislavery journalist, published *The Prostrate South*. According to Pike, the emancipation and enfranchisement of some 4 million slaves empowered "a mass of black barbarism" and resulted in the rise of "the most ignorant democracy that mankind" ever saw. He emphasized the white South as victims of "Negro Rule," backed up by northern "carpetbag" and southern "scalawag" Republican allies. As such, he helped to set the tone for a "tragic" interpretation of Reconstruction. During the late nineteenth and early twentieth centuries, Columbia University professors John W. Burgess and William A. Dunning helped to perpetuate and popularize the racist view of the post–Civil War years. This perspective—emphasizing Reconstruction as a period of "corrupt," "ignorant," and "black" rule—culminated in the publication of historian Claude Bower's *The Tragic Era* (1927).

Like shifts in slavery studies, emancipation scholarship changed under the impact of the modern civil rights movement of the 1950s and 1960s. As African Americans and their white allies assaulted the bastions of the segregationist order, they also demanded a new look at the history of Reconstruction and the rise of Jim Crow. The new writers also emphasized the "tragic" nature of Reconstruction, but they turned the tables. In their view, Reconstruction was "tragic" for ex-slaves, not for ex-slaveholders and their descendants. It was "tragic" because it missed a unique opportunity to usher in a new multiracial democracy, sketched out by blacks and their white Republican allies. As W. E. B. Du Bois put it in his groundbreaking work of reinterpretation, *Black Reconstruction* (1935), "The unending tragedy of Reconstruction is the utter inability of the American mind to grasp its real significance, its national and worldwide implications. . . . The attempt to make black men American citizens was in a certain sense all a failure, but a splendid failure." Du Bois emphasized not only the failure to extend full citizenship rights to blacks in practice but also the failure to provide economic justice to ex-slaves in the form of land. "To have given each one of the million negro free families a forty acre freehold would have made a basis of real democracy in the United States that might easily have transformed the modern world." Instead, following emancipation, the nation crafted a new system of "white supremacy" under the legal rubric of "separate but equal." By the late 1960s, studies by historians John Hope Franklin, Kenneth Stampp, and Staughton Lynd elaborated on Du Bois's viewpoint.

In the wake of the Black Power movement and growing disappointment with the fruits of the civil rights movement during the mid- to late 1960s, a new generation of scholars highlighted the limitations of existing Reconstruction scholarship, which revolved increasingly around the "tragedy" of race relations and sidestepped important social and political issues. By the 1980s and 1990s, growing numbers of scholars advanced new studies of class formation and gender relations as keys to a fuller understanding of the early emancipation era. In 1987,

CONTINUED

for example, the late historian Armstead Robinson argued that the "Civil War origins of the post war labor system constitute the first line of inquiry that demands attention" in emancipation research. Studies by Thomas Holt, Peter Kolchin, Nell Painter, Gerald David Jaynes, and Julie Saville all emphasize in varying degrees the transition of enslaved blacks to free workers, sharecroppers, and members of a rural wage-earning proletariat. For their part, historians Evelyn Brooks Higginbottham, Tera Hunter, Leslie Schwalm, and Glenda Gilmore, among others, document the gendered as well as class and racial nature of African American life in the post–Civil War rural and urban South. They are sensitive to the ways that ex-slaves built on their cultural experiences in the slave community and influenced their own transformation from slaves into wage earners, commercial farmers, and sharecroppers. As the African Americans and the nation grapple with new labor and social policies in the early twenty-first century, the proliferation of scholarship on the emancipation era offers an extraordinary resource. This scholarship is replete with insights into the vagaries of culture, power, and economics.

Republican Party when the U.S. Senate failed to seat P. B. S. Pinchback of Louisiana. He even advised blacks to divide their vote between the two major parties to secure greater political concessions. In Mississippi and South Carolina, during the 1880s and 1890s, black Republicans affected a fusion arrangement with Democrats whereby they agreed to allow Democrats to obtain a certain number of positions in exchange for a seat in the legislature and a proportion of local offices.

Northern blacks also criticized the party of Lincoln. As early as 1883, George T. Downing, a well-to-do caterer of New York and Newport, Rhode Island, broke with the Republicans and supported the Democratic Party. He urged blacks to split their votes "because division would result in increased support from all quarters." At a convention in Pittsburgh in 1884, blacks refused to endorse either the Democrat or Republican candidate. In Massachusetts, James M. Trotter, a former officer in the state's famous Fifty-Fourth Regiment, deserted the Republican Party, resigned his patronage post, and supported the Democrat Grover Cleveland, who later appointed Trotter recorder of deeds for the District of Columbia. In New York, the Albany lawyer James C. Matthews, and the minister of the AME Bethel Church, T. McCants Stewart, led a group of blacks out of the Republican Party and into the Democratic Party. Black newspaper editors also increasingly criticized the Republican Party, although they did not make the break and join the Democratic Party. These included W. Calvin Chase of the *Washington Bee* and T. Thomas Fortune of the *New York Age*. In 1883, Chase described the Republican Party as "little, if anything, better than the hidebound slave-holding Democratic party." Similarly, Fortune, in 1886, encouraged blacks to split their votes under the motto "Race first: then party."

African Americans also supported independent movements like the Greenback Party, the Readjuster movement, and the Populist Party. In Virginia, for example, blacks supported the Readjuster movement against "redeemer" rule. The Readjusters advocated a partial repudiation of the state's debt to free funds for education and social services. In 1879, black voters helped Readjusters come to power in Virginia and soon gained recognition of black needs. Formed in 1875, the Greenback Party developed a program of "cheaper money and free silver coinage" that also appealed to black farmers. Moreover, some southern Greenbackers articulated a policy of interracial equity. In 1878, the Texas Greenback Labor Party held its first state convention, declaring that the party would "protect alike the rights of every individual in the union, irrespective of section, state, riches, poverty, race, color, or creed." Some seventy black groups claimed affiliation with the state's Greenbacks, comprising 482 local units. Two years later, the Texas Greenbackers denounced "the attempted disfranchisement of citizens as a crime, whether committed by Republicans in Massachusetts and Rhode Island or Bourbon Democrats in Texas."

Following the collapse of the Greenback Party by the mid-1880s, African American farmers gravitated to the emerging Farmers' Alliance movement. This movement coalesced around the national Farmers' Alliance and Industrial Union (called the Southern Alliance) and its northern and midwestern counterpart, the National Farmers' Alliance (called the Northern Alliance). Meeting in Houston, Texas, in 1886, African Americans formed a separate body, the Colored Farmers' Alliance and Cooperative Union (called the Colored Alliance). Although black and white alliance men cooperated on a series of educational, social, and economic programs, they soon parted ways over the question of disfranchisement and strategies for empowering black farm laborers. At its 1890 convention, the Colored Alliance supported the Lodge Federal Election Bill, designed to ensure black voting rights, but the white body staunchly opposed the measure. A year later, black alliance men called a strike of cotton pickers to improve the terms of their labor, but the white alliance men encouraged whites to break the strike of black farmers. Colonel Leonidas L. Polk, president of the Southern Alliance, declared that the strike would benefit blacks at the expense of white farmers. Moreover, the white alliance men hoped to strengthen their hand as owners of land and employers of labor, and avoid capital-labor confrontations and conflict. Predominantly tenants, sharecroppers, and farm laborers, blacks could not afford to take that position. Still, as the presidential campaign of 1892 unfolded, some black alliance men supported the formation of the Populist Party as their best hope for the future.

Although the Readjuster and Greenback movements gained modest support among blacks, the Populist Party emerged as the most promising alternative to southern racism during the 1890s. Tom Watson, the influential Georgia Populist, urged whites to overcome their racism and join forces with the black farmer. On one occasion, Watson declared that "the colored tenant . . . is in the same boat with the white tenant, the colored laborer with the white laborer." Moreover, Watson appealed directly to African Americans: "If you stand up for your rights and for your manhood, if you stand shoulder to shoulder with us in this fight, the people's party will wipe out the color line and put every man on his citizenship irrespective of color." When a white mob threatened to lynch the black Populist Anthony Wilson, who had made over sixty speeches supporting the Populist Party, white Populists responded to Watson's plea that they come to the man's defense as well as his own. Two thousand white farmers stood guard outside Watson's home for two nights. Still, except for parts of Texas and a few Upper South counties, where blacks made up a significant proportion of the electorate, the Populists failed to win over the bulk of black voters. Although Democrats continued to use terrorism against black voters, under the Populist threat they also launched underground appeals for blacks to go to the polls and vote the Democratic ticket. More importantly, however, Populists like Tom Watson soon succumbed to the onset of white supremacy and supported the constitutional disfranchisement of black voters.

Amidst the Populist upsurge of the late 1880s and early 1890s, southern states mobilized to remove the remaining vestiges of black political power. These states now adopted constitutional reforms to supplement the ongoing use of violence and legislative processes to deprive blacks of their civil rights. Mississippi launched the constitutional disfranchisement movement in 1890, followed by South Carolina in 1895 and Louisiana in 1898. By 1902, Alabama, Virginia, and North Carolina had amended their constitutions to disfranchise black citizens. In 1908, Georgia followed suit, and in 1910 Oklahoma became the last state to enact disfranchisement provisions by constitutional fiat. The Populist Tom Watson now took the position that "white men would have to unite before they could divide" along class lines. He now supported any Democratic candidate who would endorse black disfranchisement among other "Populist reforms." Some white conservatives like Alexander Caperton Braxton of Virginia hoped to eliminate poor blacks and some poor whites from the franchise while allowing some educated blacks to vote along with whites, but a new generation of radical white supremacists won the day. These included Governor, and later Senator, James K. Vardaman of Mississippi; Senators Benjamin Tillman of South Carolina, Braxton Cower Bragg of Alabama, and Charles Brantley Aycock of North Carolina; and Congressman Thomas W. Hardwick of Georgia. These men hoped to eliminate "all blacks" from the political process while including all white men.

Although the principal architects of white supremacy, racial violence, and disfranchisement were white men, they were joined by white women. One of the most articulate of these was Georgian Rebecca Latimer Felton, who later became the first woman to serve (although only briefly) in the U.S. Senate. In 1897, in a speech before the State Agricultural Society, she targeted enfranchised black men as a threat to white womanhood. She later recalled:

> I warned those representative men . . . of the terrible . . . corruption of the negro. . . . I told them that these crimes [rape] . . . would grow and increase with every election where white men equalized themselves at the polls with an inferior race.

Felton then justified the growing lynching of black men as a response to the alleged rape of white women. She even urged white men to lynch "a thousand a week if it becomes necessary." Felton was not the only southern white woman to advocate the lynching and disfranchisement of black men. Her ideas gained expression among white women across the South. Middle- and upper-class white women flooded the ranks of the United Daughters of the Confederacy and challenged white men to reclaim the control over black people that their fathers and grandfathers had gained over the slaves. In 1898, in North Carolina, white women joined the White Government Leagues and helped to mobilize votes against the interracial Populist movement. At one Democratic Party rally, a white woman urged white men to remove the "black vampire hovering over our beloved old North Carolina."

Although specific disfranchisement provisions varied somewhat from state to state, Mississippi and other southern states instituted what popular historian Lerone Bennett has described as "a wall with holes in it." Southerners barred blacks from voting by a wall of poll taxes, literacy tests, property qualifications, and moral stipulations, including prohibitions on persons convicted of major crimes like murder and arson, as well as lesser offenses like bribery, burglary, and theft. Even as such walls removed black voters, however, legislators punched holes in the wall for poor whites to qualify. The most famous of these provisions were the "grandfather," "understanding," and "good character" clauses. In other words, if literacy, property, or poll tax laws disqualified whites, they could nonetheless vote by claiming a grandfather who had voted in a previous election; an "understanding" of the contents of the Constitution or any other document that they might be required to read but could not; and/or "good character" despite possible prior criminal convictions. Other states—Florida, Texas, Arkansas, Kentucky, and Tennessee—continued to deprive blacks of the vote through the adoption of legislative mechanisms like the poll tax and the Australian secret ballot, which required a level of literacy that large numbers of blacks and whites lacked. In Louisiana, the number of black voters declined from over 130,300 in 1894 to less than 1,350 by 1900. The number of poor white voters also declined, but disfranchisement was fundamentally a racial movement, designed to remove black voters. Whites also later adopted the "white primary," whereby the Democratic Party allowed only whites to vote for the selection of candidates for public office. Thus, even where small numbers of blacks remained on the rolls, their influence was further diminished.

The disfranchisement movement precipitated a new wave of black activism. As early as September 1883, Frederick Douglass delivered his "Address to the People of the United States." In this speech, he justified "Negro" or "colored" conventions as a necessary step in the struggle for equal rights. As in the struggle against slavery, Douglass urged blacks to agitate for full citizenship rights:

> Until this nation shall make its practice accord with its Constitution and its righteous laws, it will not do to reproach the colored people of this country with keeping up the color line—for that people would prove themselves scarcely worthy of even theoretical freedom, to say nothing of practical freedom, if they settled down in silent, servile and cowardly submission to their wrongs, from fears of making their color visible. . . . Who would be free must strike the blow.

In 1890, black leaders staged several protest meetings in support of the Lodge Elections Bill, which aimed to eliminate racial discrimination in the exercise of the franchise.

In the same year, civil rights activities gained new strength with the formation of the Afro-American League. Formed in Chicago under the leadership of T. Thomas

Fortune, the organization elected the North Carolina educator J. C. Price as president and pushed to end all vestiges of racial discrimination. Later that same year, a group of blacks met in Washington, D.C., and formed the Citizens Equal Rights Association with goals similar to those of the Afro-American League. When these organizations became defunct, they gave way to the Afro-American Council in 1898, under the leadership of T. Thomas Fortune and Bishop Alexander Walters of the AME Zion church. The Afro-American Council retained the same ideological orientation as that of its predecessors but made little headway and gradually faded by 1908.

Despite vigorous protest activities, African Americans failed to stem the tide of white resistance and the weakening of the Republican alliance. From the election of Rutherford B. Hayes through the presidencies of Theodore Roosevelt and William Howard Taft during the early twentieth century, northern Republicans gradually turned their backs on southern blacks. In the *Civil Rights Cases* of 1883, the U.S. Supreme Court pronounced the Civil Rights Act of 1875 unconstitutional. It claimed that the federal government could protect citizens only against the discriminatory activities of the state rather than against the actions of its individual citizens. In the case of *Plessy v. Ferguson* (1896), the U.S. Supreme Court went a step further. It upheld the constitutionality of the "separate but equal" doctrine, accepted the notion of "white supremacy," and fomented the rise of Jim Crow. (See the Documents section.)

Such federal policies mirrored the transition of the Republican Party from what some historians call the "black-and-tan" racially mixed republicanism of the radical era to the "lily-white" republicanism of the 1890s. In the election of 1896, which placed the Republican William McKinley of Ohio in the president's office, the Republican Party sanctioned the separation of blacks and whites in the southern wing of the party and gradually excluded blacks from viable participation in the political arena. In 1901, George White of North Carolina left Washington. He was the last black southern congressman before the modern civil rights era. By 1910, however, some twelve white Republicans had entered Congress from the South, a product of black disfranchisement and exclusion from the political process.

During the early years following the downfall of Reconstruction, blacks had routinely gained key federal patronage positions. These included jobs in the postal service and as customs collectors at various ports. Theodore Roosevelt continued to make a few conspicuous black appointments in the South—Dr. William D. Crom as collector of customs at the port of Charleston, South Carolina, and a black woman as postmistress in Indianola, Mississippi, for example. For his part, although Taft retained black appointees in the capital city (particularly in the Treasury Department and the Office of the Recorder of Deeds) and in a few posts in the West and North, he replaced black appointees in the South with whites and also initiated the segregation of blacks and whites in federal buildings. When the Democrat Woodrow Wilson took office in 1912, he accelerated a process of segregation already set in motion by Republicans. The first southern president since the Civil War, Wilson also went a step further and required applicants for civil service jobs to submit photographs with their applications, which facilitated racial discrimination and the spread of segregation in the federal government.

The gradual disengagement of northern whites from support of black rights is vividly illustrated by the artist Thomas Nast's changing portrayal of blacks in his postbellum political sketches. Harper's Weekly, *5 August 1865 (left) and 14 March 1874 (right)*

THE TRANSFORMATION OF ENSLAVED BLACKS into citizens and workers was inextricably tied to the actions of the state. With the aid of black people as soldiers and civilians, the Union army had defeated the Confederacy on the battlefield. Blacks now expected to reap the full fruits of their labor. They wanted the federal government to use its authority to intervene, confiscate southern land, and help establish blacks on land of their own. Despite extraordinary efforts on their own behalf, blacks were soon disappointed—not only by the antiblack policies of presidential Reconstruction and the subsequent rise of the Democratic "redeemer" and Jim Crow regimes but also by the narrow class and racial policies of their Republican allies. Political Reconstruction failed to incorporate their hope for land and also frustrated their quest for full citizenship rights and opened the way for the violent resurgence of Confederates and ex-slaveowners to economic, social, and political power. Thus, as we will discuss in Chapter 12, the transition to freedom was complicated not only by the intensification of racist public policies but also by the rise of a new system of economic exploitation and unjust labor practices.

∼

Economic Emancipation, Land, and the Search for Industrial Opportunities

The struggle for political freedom was interwoven with the fight for land, employment, and economic opportunities. Postbellum employers and public officials not only instituted policies and practices that curtailed African American access to the franchise and full citizenship rights but also undermined their quest for economic independence. Planters sought to maintain old forms of labor control, including use of the whip, police, and military authority to force able-bodied men to work. At the same time, they happily transformed prior provisions to the enslaved—food, clothing, housing, medical care, and access to garden plots, hunting grounds, and fishing waters—into purchasable cash items for emancipated blacks. Only a thin line separated such southern labor practices from the free wage labor policies of northern employers and military and government officials. Northerners tied social welfare services and aid to the freedmen and their families to wage labor. They insisted that the freed people assume full responsibility for the care of their own sick, disabled, and indigent. In short, northerners enjoined African Americans to "work or starve." When the spur of hunger and need seemed insufficient, northerners, like southerners, also resorted to various forms of coercion, including the roundup and incarceration of vagrants without visible means of support. For their part, African Americans sided with free labor advocates against planters but resisted the exploitative and unjust practices of both. Formerly enslaved people advocated sharecropping over rural wage labor; landownership over sharecropping; and, increasingly, urban life and labor over work in the countryside. In other words, when the government failed to provide ex-slaves with land, black men and women pooled their resources and worked to protect and advance their own family, class, and racial interests.

RURAL WAGE LABOR AND NEW FORMS OF COERCION

Ex-slaveholders emerged from the Civil War with deep-seated notions about their right to command the labor of blacks. Planters detested the idea of treating ex-slaves as independent agents in the labor market, partly because of the racist heritage of slavery and partly because they lacked the money to pay sufficient wages to attract and retain a free black labor force. According to the *Augusta Transcript,* southern planters believed that the prosperity of the South and their own class interests depended on "one single condition—*the ability of the planter to command [black] labor.*" Over and over again, planters challenged northern victors with the question, Will the Negro work? Overwhelmingly, they concurred that blacks were "naturally lazy" and would not work under any incentive except the lash. In their view, high wages, opportunities for upward mobility, or even kindness would not compel blacks to work. One Louisiana sugar planter concluded in no uncertain terms that "the great secret of our success [as slaveholders] was the great motive power contained in that little instrument [the whip]." A Georgia newspaper made the same point, portraying blacks as "improvident and reckless of the future." Another Louisiana planter was even more direct: the "inborn nature of the negro . . . cannot be changed by the offer of more or less money." When one Alabama slaveowner returned to his plantation after the war, he reported that "Negroes will not work for pay, the *lash* is all I fear that will make them."

Northern employers shared much of the southern perspective on free black labor. Beginning during the war years, northerners purchased their own southern land, leased plantations from southern landowners, or entered partnerships with southern planters. Although northerners envisioned quick riches on cotton plantations "manned" by "cheap" free black labor, they couched their economic motives in a broader reform vision of "industrial progress." From their vantage point, they would bring "free labor" to a land suffering from stagnation and "backwardness" as a result of years of bondage. When blacks resisted the capitalist work regimen, northerners increasingly described black workers as "ignorant," "shiftless," and "unreliable." Harriet Beecher Stowe, who resided on a Florida plantation during the Reconstruction years, criticized the free people as "great conservatives" who failed to adopt northern suggestions for more efficient labor and farming techniques. Henry Lee Higginson, a northern investor in a Georgia cotton plantation, concluded: "It is discouraging to see how . . . much more hopeful they appear at a distance than near to." Other northerners expressed the view that slavery had destroyed the capacity of blacks for "self-directed labor" and advocated the restoration of corporal punishment. On one occasion, the *New York Times* suggested that perhaps freedmen and -women needed "new masters."

During the early post–Civil War years, military authorities, the Freedmen's Bureau, and state and local governments helped to underwrite a new system of coercion. In 1865–1866, military officials continued to aid planters by coercing black workers into signing contracts. When a Virginia couple resisted a whipping by their employer, an army provost marshal used the "wooden horse" to secure the desired result. In South Carolina, a planter expressed surprise when a Yankee officer punished two black men for loitering by hanging them by the thumbs. According to the planters, the men actually pleaded to be whipped instead. In Mississippi, a northern officer gave one black man "twenty lashes, and rubbed him down right smart with salt, for having no visible means of support." A Georgia minister and ex-slaveholder confided to his sister that the northern troops' discipline of black workers created "a remarkable quietude and order in all the region." Another planter was even more emphatic: he said that it is "good they are here."

Unlike the military, the Freedmen's Bureau initially protected black workers from the planters' efforts to reinstitute prewar forms of labor control. Bureau officials informed planters that the notion of "bodily coercion" had fallen with the destruction of slavery. Yet the bureau soon privileged the planters' labor demands over black workers' rights. Oliver O. Howard, bureau head, informed blacks that they must enter labor contracts with the landowners: "A man who can work has no right to support by government. No really respectable person wishes to be supported by others." A Mississippi agent of the bureau put it bluntly: "A man can scarcely be called free . . . who is the recipient of public charity." For its part, the Louisiana bureau not only eliminated the black orphan home and apprenticed black children to white employers but also ordered the arrest of all able-bodied persons without "written proof" of employment.

In their search for new modes of commanding black labor, planters adopted the contract labor agreement, enforceable by law. One planter said, "Let everything proceed as formerly . . . the contractual relation being substituted for that of master and slave." A Mississippi planter explained:

We go on like we always did . . . and I pol'em if they don't do right. This year I says to em, "Boys, I'm going to make a bargain with you. I'll roll out the ploughs and the mules and the feed, and you shall do the work; we'll make a crop of cotton and you shall have half. I'll provide for ye; give ye quarters, treat ye well, and when ye won't work, pole ye like I always have." They agreed to it and I put it into the contract that I was to whoop 'em when I pleased.

In North Carolina, the ex-slaveholder William L. DeRossett wrote to his brother regarding the newly emancipated woman Letitia:

Old Letitia is with me still on the old terms. . . . I notified her when I first saw the order freeing them, that she was, at liberty to go, but that if she staid with me it must be as she had before & if she misbehaved I would not hesitate to flog her. She acquiesced fully & I have had no trouble.

As suggested in Chapter 11, the black codes represented the pivot of southern efforts to coerce black labor. These codes revolved around southern states' definition and punishment of "vagrancy." The Mississippi law defined vagrancy broadly to include "idleness," "disorderly" conduct, and even those who "miss spend what they earn." Persons convicted of vagrancy faced punishment by fines and/or involuntary labor. By New Year's Day, the Mississippi code required blacks to show a written labor contract for the coming year. Law officers could arrest almost anyone without a job. Such persons could be arrested, jailed, fined, placed on a chain gang, or hired out to private employers. Under so-called false-pretense provisions, any workers who deserted their employment before the contract expired forfeited all wages owed up to that moment. For violation of the law, as during bondage, African Americans could also be arrested by any white citizen. Similarly, under "anti-enticement" statutes, any employer who

SOURCES FROM THE PAST

— 1865

The South Carolina Black Code Addresses Apprenticeship and Vagrancy

Husband and Wife

I. The relation of husband and wife amongst persons of color is established. . . .

Master and Apprentice

XV. A child over the age of two years, born of a colored parent, may be bound by the father, if he be living in the District, or in case of his death or absence from the District, by the mother, as an apprentice, to any respectable white or colored person, who is competent to make a contract—a male until he shall attain the age of twenty-one years and a female until she shall attain the age of eighteen years. . . .

XXII. The master or mistress shall teach the apprentice the business of husbandry, or some other useful trade or business, which shall be specified in the instrument of apprenticeship; . . .

XXIII. The master shall have authority to inflict moderate chastisement and impose reasonable restraint upon his apprentice, and to recapture him if he depart from his service.

XXIV. The master shall receive to his own use the profits of the labor of his apprentice. . . .

Contracts for Service

XXXV. All persons of color who make contracts for service or labor, shall be known as servants, and those with whom they contract shall be known as masters.

XXXVI. Contracts between masters and servants, for one month or more, shall be in writing, be attested by one white witness, and be approved by the Judge of the District Court, or by a Magistrate. . . .

Vagrancy and Idleness

XCV. These are public grievances, and must be punished as crimes.

XCVI. All persons who have not some fixed and known place of abode, and some lawful and reputable employment . . . shall be deemed vagrants, and be liable to the punishment hereinafter provided. . . .

XCVIII. The defendant, if sentenced to hard labor after conviction, may, by order of the District Judge, or Magistrate, before whom he was convicted, be hired for such wages as can be obtained for his services, to any owner or lessee of a farm, for the term of labor to which he was sentenced, or be hired for the same labor on the streets, public roads, or public buildings. The person receiving such vagrant shall have all the rights and remedies for enforcing good conduct and diligence at labor that are herein provided in the case of master and servant.

Source: Acts of the General Assembly of the State of South Carolina, 1864–1865, pp. 291–304.

offered work to a black person already under contract with another could be imprisoned for varying lengths of time and/or fined $500. With minor variations, other states erected similar statutes, including generous provisions for the removal of black children from their homes for apprenticeship with white families (see box).

Although some codes failed to single blacks out by name, everywhere it was understood that the labor contract and vagrancy provisions of southern laws referred primarily to blacks. Early postwar contracts entailed agreements between ex-slaveholders and "large groups" of freedmen. Some contracts provided for "standing wages" paid on an annual basis. This procedure enabled planters to extract the maximum amount of labor from the newly freed people, since workers forfeited their wages if they quit before the expiration of the contract. In reality, however, most contracts provided "share-wages." Because most planters had little cash following the Civil War, they offered former bondsmen a share of the crop as wages, which they often paid collectively to field hands, who then divided the crop among themselves. In these arrangements, planters continued to rely on antebellum methods of grading workers, whereby men as "full hands" received more than women and young workers, who were considered "half" to "three-quarter" hands. Rarely did workers receive as much as 20 percent of the produce. For their part, rural artisans—carpenters, coopers, blacksmiths—usually signed individual monthly wage contracts at higher rates of pay than their field hand brothers and sisters.

LANDOWNERSHIP AND RESISTANCE TO WAGE LABOR

Although some African Americans gave in to the new forms of coercion, most questioned the terms of their labor and frustrated efforts to place their work on an unequal wage basis. According to the editor of an Alabama newspaper, "We have land but can no longer control" the black workers; "hence we want Northern laborers, German laborers, to come down and take their places, to work our lands for ten dollars a month." The wife of one planter expressed the same view: "Give us five million of Chinese laborers in the Valley of the Mississippi . . . and we can furnish the world with cotton and teach the negro his proper place." Several southern states—South Carolina, Louisiana, Arkansas, Alabama, Tennessee, Mississippi, Texas, Virginia, and West Virginia—passed laws encouraging the recruitment of immigrant labor, but these efforts proved futile. European and Asian workers found southern working conditions and labor practices intolerable and thus moved on to other regions and jobs. The failure of these labor schemes forced southerners to recognize their long-term dependence on the labor of black freedmen.

Emancipated blacks knew very well the difference between their free present and their enslaved past. As two black leaders testified in July 1865, "They all knew they were their own men, and women." When asked, "Whose servant are you?" a South Carolina woman responded "that she was her own servant." When her ex-owner threatened to let her go if she refused to accept his terms, she replied, "I'll leave then," which she did. African Americans invariably asked questions about the precise nature of their employers' obligations as well as their own under contracts. Even before the war ended, African Americans on a Louisiana plantation asked: "When will our wages be paid?" "What clothing are we to have?" "What land are we allowed?" "Can we keep our pigs?" Soon after federal occupation of the Sea

Islands, one ex-slave made the point clearly: "I craves work, ma' am, if [I] gets a little pay, but if we don't gets pay, we . . . don't care to work." Frances Leigh, the daughter of the planter Pierce Butler, revealed how blacks responded to contract negotiations in a long description of contract time:

> For six mortal hours I rot in the office without once leaving my chair while the people poured in and poured out, each one with long explanations, objections, and demonstrations. . . . One wanted this altered in the contract, and another that. One was willing to work in the mill but not in the field. Several would not agree to sign unless I promised to give them the whole of Saturday for a holiday. Others . . . "would work for me till they died," but would not put their hand to no paper.

As suggested above, black women no less than men participated in demands for higher pay and better working conditions. According to one observer, Harriet Ware, a group of black women confronted the Boston plantation owner and manager Edward Philbrick:

> The women came up in a body to complain to Mr. Philbrick about their pay—a thing which has never happened before and shows the influence of very injudicious outside talk which has poisoned their minds against their truest friends. The best people were among them, and even old Grace chief spokeswoman.

Philbrick later leased his plantation to another white planter, but blacks soon confronted both men with demands for "a dollar a task: A dollar a task." This represented a substantial increase over their usual pay. On another occasion, Grace led a delegation of some twenty black women to Philbrick's door. She told Philbrick in no uncertain terms that the women were "done working for such agreement. I've done sir." Grace recounted her hard labor and the labor of her children in making two bales of cotton but receiving little in return: "I knows those two bales cotton fetch 'nought money, and I don't see what I'se got for 'em."

African Americans not only participated in individual or small group skirmishes with landowners but also organized statewide "labor conventions" between 1869 and 1871. In Georgia, South Carolina, and Alabama, African Americans called for "intermediary officers" to oversee the contracts and ensure equitable wages, hours, and conditions of labor. Although states largely rejected such proposals, blacks also used the conventions to form independent agricultural labor organizations. In some states, these farm labor organizations developed alongside the Union Leagues. Thus, even as they organized to influence public policy, black farmworkers took steps to set their own pay, hours, and conditions of work. As such, these efforts established precedents for the emergence of the Colored Farmers' Alliance, farmworkers' strikes, and the Populist movement of the late 1880s and 1890s (see Chapter 11).

Until the onset of World War I, African Americans resisted wage labor primarily through a relentless search for their own land. Blacks retained an abiding faith in the possibilities of landownership. On one South Carolina plantation, a black worker rejected wage labor with the comment: "I mean to own my own manhood . . . and I'm goin' on to my own land, just as soon as when I git dis crop in, an' I don't desire for to make any change until den." In Dublin County, North Carolina, a local police chief reported that some blacks, in their words, "intend to have lands, even if they shed blood to obtain them." Some of these North Carolina blacks also demanded "all of the crops" that they had raised on their former master's lands. On one occasion, General U. S. Grant complained that the ex-slaves' belief in landownership "is seriously interfering" with "their willingness . . . to make contracts for the coming years."

It is difficult to exaggerate the importance that ex-slaves attached to land, whether they owned it or rented it. After the Civil War, contemporary observers frequently commented on the enthusiasm of blacks working independently on their own or rented land. A Freedmen's Bureau official stated: "They appear to be willing to work but are decisive in their expressions to work for no one but themselves." One ex-slaveholder and planter had a reputation for treating his black wage laborers "with the utmost kindness." Yet even he reported that "they prefer to get a little patch [of land] where they can do as they choose." Some of this land was so poor that some employers claimed that blacks "could not raise a peck of corn to the acre." Another ex-slave wrote to Abraham Lincoln: "I had rather work for myself and raise my own cotton than work for a gentleman for wages."

Many African Americans believed that they should gain land as compensation for years of enslavement. As early as November 1861, the editor of the New York *Anglo-African,* a black newspaper, had advocated the redistribution of confiscated southern land to newly emancipated blacks:

> The government should immediately bestow these lands upon these freed men who know how to cultivate them, and will joyfully bring their brawn arms, their willing hearts, and their skilled hands to the glorious labor of cultivating as their own, the lands which they have bought and paid for by their own sweat and blood.

A Boston black rebuked the notion that former masters should be compensated:

> Why talk about compensating masters? Compensate them for what? What do we owe them? What does the slave owe them? What does society owe them? Compensate the masters? . . . It is the slave who should be compensated. The property of the South is by right the property of the slave. You talk of compensating the masters who has stolen enough to sink ten generations, and yet you do not prepare to restore even a part of that which has been [stolen from blacks].

In North Carolina, another black wrote that

> if the strict law of right and justice is to be observed, the country around about me, or the sunny South, is the entailed inheritance of the Americans of African

descent, purchased by the invaluable labor of our ancestors, through a life of tears and groans, under the lash and the yoke of tyranny.

The *New Orleans Tribune* also editorialized: "The land tillers are entitled by a paramount right to the possession of the soil they have so long cultivated. . . . Let us create a new class of landholders, who shall be interested in the permanent establishment of a new and truly republican system."

At war's end, the Freedmen's Bureau had embarked on its own land redistribution program for African Americans. In 1865, the bureau controlled some 850,000 acres of abandoned land. In addition to Oliver O. Howard, bureau head, officials like General Fisk in Tennessee, Lieutenant Thomas Conway in Louisiana, and General Rufus Saxton in South Carolina, Georgia, and Florida all worked to settle blacks on their own land as independent producers. In early summer 1865, Saxton initiated plans to settle blacks on forty-acre farms where they could work for themselves and "readily achieve an independence." Saxton expressed his firm belief that blacks could become successful commercial farmers: "Let the world see ere long the fields of South Carolina, Georgia and Florida white with [cotton]." By September 1865, President Johnson had not only ordered Howard and his agents to cease the allocation of land to ex-slaves but also ordered the restoration of all but a small fraction of the blacks' land to the former owners. By the early 1870s, only a few blacks held title to their small plots. In rapid succession, blacks lost land on the South Carolina Sea Islands, in the Sherman Reserve, on Davis Bend in Mississippi, and in southeastern Virginia, where the army evicted nearly twenty thousand blacks from confiscated and abandoned property.

Newly emancipated blacks resisted the reoccupancy of their land by ex-slaveholders. In Norfolk County, Virginia, armed blacks resisted sheriffs as well as federal officers sent to evict them. They even questioned the president's right to pardon the Confederate landowners. At a mass meeting of the group, one black leader, Richard Parker, declared: "We don't care for the President nor the Freedmen's Bureau. We have suffered long enough; let the white man suffer now." Only after a fierce battle with law officers did the blacks vacate the land. In South Carolina, Sea Island blacks also organized along military lines and fought repossession of land by former owners. According to a Bureau officer, "They [the former owners] . . . say openly, that none of them, will be permitted to live upon the Islands." When a group of planters arrived on John's Island in early 1866, African Americans disarmed the group and advised them to leave and never return. A similar force of blacks met and turned whites back on James Island. In the end, however, federal forces sided with ex-Confederates and helped them to recover the land.

Although northern and southern elites had clashed over efforts to liberate blacks and establish a free labor system, they agreed that the distribution of "free land" to ex-slaves violated the principle of "free enterprise" and "private property." They maintained that all "free people" could gain wealth and secure their well-being through industry, frugality, honesty, and ambition. Now that blacks were "free," they must prove themselves capable of functioning in a free society. Underneath the ideological opposition to land redistribution to blacks, as noted earlier, northern whites had their own plans for exploiting free black labor. Their plans were not limited to those who bought land in the South and hired black workers. They also included the designs of northern industrialists who hoped to employ southern blacks to help defeat the rising demands of the northern-based white labor movement. As early as 1866, for example, northern industrialists recruited southern blacks as strikebreakers. Indeed, northern and southern white elites feared that the distribution of land to blacks would disrupt class relations among whites. According to the *Nation*, a leading national publication during the period, "The division of rich men['s] lands among the landless . . . would give to our whole social and political system a shock from which it could hardly recover without the loss of liberty."

THE SHARECROPPING SYSTEM

As African Americans lost their struggle for landownership, particularly in the Deep South, they turned toward sharecropping as an alternative to rural wage labor. Since few blacks had access to capital, they placed a high premium on their labor. In exchange for their labor, African Americans insisted on access to small family plots. They hoped to cultivate this land independently, with their own family members, without strict day-to-day supervision under "overseers" or "foremen." African Americans believed that this arrangement would enable them to enter the landowning class much faster than wage labor. When planters repossessed the land of ex-slaves on James Island, South Carolina, one dispossessed black man remarked: "If I can't own de land, I'll hire or lease land, but I won't contract" (that is, work for wages). In addition to land, African Americans expected to receive access to tools, seed, and fertilizer, plus food, housing, supplies, and a substantial proportion of the final crop. Depending on how much they received from landowners upfront, crop shares might vary from one-third to one-half for the worker, with the remainder going to the landowner to cover supplies, rent, and debts to merchants and bankers.

As black families gained a footing on these small sharecropping units, black women now divided their labor more evenly between the field and household work. One Georgia plantation owner noted the change: "Gilbert will stay on his old terms, but withdrawn Fanny and puts Harry and Little Abram in her place and puts his son Gilbert out to a trade. Cook Kate wants to be relieved of the heavy burden of cooking for two and wait on her husband." On a Louisiana plantation, when planters tried to coerce black women into the field, black men responded that "whenever they wanted their wives to work they would tell them themselves; and if [they] could not rule [their] own domestic affairs on the place [they] would leave it." Although white elites viewed white women who stayed at home as the ideal of "true womanhood," they saw black women who did the same thing "as lazy" and even "ludicrous." Both northern and southern white elites ridiculed these black women as the "female aristocracy" or the people who "played the lady" by imitating white ideals. Although scholars have long noted the "withdrawal" of black women from "field labor" during the postbellum period, recent studies accent their reemployment in black household labor, alongside a persistent pattern of field labor as well. By 1870, although most women reported their occupation to the U.S. Census Bureau as "Keeping House," they were also consistent laborers in the cotton fields as well. Moreover, many women supplemented the family's income with household work for wages or in-kind payments. At the same time, children of various ages were an indispensable part of the family labor force.

The rise of radical Republican governments reinforced the expansion of the sharecropping system. In state after state, Republicans eliminated overt constraints on the free blacks' right to move from place to place; required parental consent before taking black children from their homes; and narrowed the scope of vagrancy laws, including prohibitions on the hiring out of blacks who could not pay fines to private employers. The radical governments also limited efforts to prohibit one employer from hiring workers employed by another. Perhaps most importantly, whereas the Johnson administration had permitted a creditor to place a lien on a planter's crop "superior to all other claims," including the black workers' right to a share of the crop, the new laws gave workers a lien on crops "superior to all other claims," including those of bankers and merchants who made loans or offered credit to landowners. As such, the law defined the sharecropper as "a partner" rather than an employee in the production process. Even in Mississippi, the new

African Americans continued to work on cotton plantations during the early emancipation years. *Valentine Museum*

radical laws instructed law enforcement officers to interpret the law "in the most liberal manner [for] the protection and encouragement of labor." By 1872, some planters complained that most southern states offered "ample protection" to the tenants and "very little" to landlords. By 1880, the total number of southern farms had increased to 1.1 million, but the average size had declined from 347 acres during the 1860s to 156 acres.

Before African Americans could secure their economic footing under radical governments, the Democratic Party replaced the radicals and reinstituted repressive labor legislation. By 1877, contemporary observers stated openly that the new racist governments would go as far as they could go "without actually reestablishing personal servitude." Calling themselves "redeemers" of southern society, southern Democrats strengthened the hand of the landowners and weakened the bargaining position of black workers. They extended or reinstituted the vagrancy, anti-enticement, and convict laws. The redeemer governments also reestablished the "superiority" of landlord and merchant claims to their proportion of the crop over the workers' share. State protection of landowners' rights gained perhaps its most extreme form in North Carolina's Landlord and Tenant Act of 1877. The Tar Heel state placed full authority over the crop and settlement in the hands of the planters. In effect, the state made the planter "court, sheriff, and jury." In short, courts of law redefined the sharecropper as a "wage earner only" rather than a "partner" in the production of the crop.

Whereas sharecropping had emerged as a hopeful alternative to wage labor, it now deteriorated into an exploitative system that undercut blacks' dreams of rising into the yeomanry. Planters regularly "fixed the books" at the end of the year and kept blacks in perpetual debt. Blacks could rarely break even. When they resisted this form of economic injustice by quitting, the vagrancy laws permitted the employment of convicts by private employers. This convict lease system, as it was called, rerouted black workers back into the plantation economy on even worse terms than before. By 1900, blacks owned a smaller percentage of land in the cotton belt than they had owned in 1877, but the amount of land owned by blacks had increased to an estimated 12 million acres. Nearly 80 percent of southern blacks worked as sharecroppers or cash tenants on land owned by whites. Between 1880 and 1910, the number of black sharecroppers increased from 429,000 to 673,000. Moreover, as the nation moved into the second decade of the twentieth century, the spread of the boll weevil increased the riskiness of cotton cultivation and intensified the difficulties of black farm families.

African Americans now sought a way out of the sharecropping system itself. Although the struggle for landownership continued, many blacks now pushed for "the fixed rent" over the "share crop" system. Since landlords invariably shortchanged them at the end of each growing season, they now hoped to pay a "fixed" amount in crops or cash up front for use of the land. Then, at the end of the year, they owned the entire yield and could market their produce as they saw fit. Moreover, they were not bound to the land through a system of debt. Once the rental period expired, they were free to move elsewhere. In 1900, nearly half of black tenants worked on "fixed" rather than share rents. By 1910, however, the percentage had dropped to nearly 43 percent.

Although sharecropping emerged as the dominant labor system in the postbellum cotton South and shaped patterns of black migration, it was by no means universal. Tobacco, sugar, and rice followed different patterns of production and generated different forms of resistance, with different levels of effectiveness. In Virginia and North Carolina, tobacco growers preferred wage labor and offered few opportunities for blacks to gain their own plots of land or work on shares. Only during the early twentieth century, as tobacco prices dropped and the industry declined, did sharecropping gradually spread among Upper South tobacco farmers. In short, compared with their counterparts in the cotton regions, tobacco workers experienced a greater continuity of wage labor throughout the emancipation era. On the other hand, in the sugar district of Louisiana, the centralized system of gang labor persisted well into the emancipation era. Northern capital poured into the sugar industry and enabled planters to concentrate production on a few large units by paying relatively high wages, which attracted black workers into the industry year round, but under strict, clocklike supervision. The sugar industry also lured black workers by the allotment of garden plots, which workers cultivated on their own time, for their own benefit. Still, sugar planters complained of labor shortages. Black workers placed a high priority on their own plots and used harvest time to bargain for higher wages. Consequently, sugar production lagged behind that for cotton and tobacco.

In the postbellum rice fields, landownership and independent production allowed ex-slaves to shape the terms of their labor more so than elsewhere. African Americans retained and strengthened the beneficial aspects of the antebellum "task" system, including access to small plots of land that they worked independently. One group of South Carolina freedmen declared that they hoped "to work just as we have always worked." Planters soon responded by letting rice growers work "as they choose without any overseer." During radical Reconstruction, rice planters also accepted a "two-day" system, whereby blacks agreed to give landowners two days of work per week, leaving the bulk of their time for work on their own land, which some received through the state land commission. Moreover, South Carolina's black majority exercised a great deal of political influence. According to one rice planter, black officials exerted authority at harvest times: "The Negro magistrate . . . tells them that no rice is to [be] shipped until it is all got out and divided according to law." South Carolina blacks also discouraged outside capitalist investments in the area and kept rice production relatively low. As one South Carolina ex-slave recalled, bondage provided "no rest, Massa all work, all de time; plenty to eat but no rest, no respose." Freedom, on the other hand, offered a "chance for [a] little comfort."

Whether blacks worked under a wage, sharecrop, or modified task system, they faced the brunt of economic exploitation in the postbellum South. To improve their position, black farmworkers not only regularly moved from one employer to another within their county of origin but also gradually moved westward. Despite legal restrictions on their movement from place to place, African Americans sought better opportunities on the newer cotton lands of the lower Mississippi Valley, including the states of Louisiana, Texas, Arkansas, and Mississippi. Defying anti-

This 1897 photo shows a group of migrant blacks waiting to board a Mississippi River boat to Kansas. *Library of Congress*

enticement laws, planters and labor recruiters entered the older black belt areas advertising higher wages and better working conditions in the West. As early as winter 1866, the U.S. Commissioner of Agriculture reported that every

> railroad train during this winter has been loaded with negroes going to the West under promise of increased wages. . . . It is estimated that twenty-five thousand negroes have left South Carolina this winter for Florida and the West and the number which have left Georgia is much greater, as for some time [the] average number passing through has been 1,000 daily. This depletion of labor still actively continues, and it is a matter of increasing importance to the planters. They offer ten to twelve dollars per month, besides food, house, firewood, and land for a garden, but the negroes are promised more in the West, and accordingly emigrate.

In 1877, the Civil War veteran and political organizer Henry Adams of Louisiana estimated that some sixty thousand black working people were prepared to leave the South. Adams described the South as an "impossible" place to live, with ex-slaveowners holding the power and enjoying "the right as they enjoy it." Under the leadership of Benjamin "Pap" Singleton, some six thousand blacks left the states of Louisiana, Mississippi, and Texas for Kansas in 1879. The "Kansas Exodus," as this movement was called, reflected the failure of Reconstruction to live up to its promise of citizenship and economic freedom. Although life in Kansas also proved disappointing and some blacks drifted back to the Deep South, most stayed and drew the line even more sharply between their slave past and the hope for a free future for themselves and their families. By 1910, blacks in southern counties with black majorities had dropped from 57 percent in 1880 to 45 percent of the total population.

Reinforcing the westward movement of postbellum blacks were black soldiers and cowhands. Although the federal government had quickly disbanded black units following the Civil War, the U.S. Army maintained four all-black units, the Twenty-Fourth and Twenty-Fifth Infantry and the Ninth and Tenth Cavalry. Some twenty-five thousand black men served in these units between 1866 and the beginning of World War I. Feared by Native Americans as "Buffalo Soldiers," presumably because of their black skin and woolly hair, these black units played a major role in the late-nineteenth-century wars that decimated the Native American population in the West. African American soldiers also participated in the last major U.S. military assault against Indians, the Ghost Dance campaign of 1890–1891, which culminated in the Battle of Wounded Knee Creek in South Dakota. In addition to helping to break Native American resistance, black soldiers also helped to suppress organized white labor in the silver mining strikes of Coeur d'Alene, Idaho. Although the earliest contingents of black soldiers were predominantly young single men or married men without their wives and children present, by the 1880s growing numbers of black soldiers brought their wives and children to western military outposts and facilitated the rise of black settlements in the West.

Along with the Buffalo Soldiers, some blacks entered the West as cowboys and herders in the cattle range industry. By the 1890s, blacks made up about 2 percent of the region's cowboys. They also spread widely throughout the western and southwestern states and territories of Texas, New Mexico, Arizona, Kansas, Wyoming, Montana, California, and the Dakotas, to name a few. Black range workers participated in longhorn cattle drives from central Texas north to railheads at towns like Abilene, Dodge City, Denver, and Cheyenne, among others. In his personal recollections of life as a cowboy, the Texas-born Daniel ("80 John") Wallace described how cowboys "slept on the ground in all kinds of weather with our blankets for a bed . . . a saddle for a pillow . . . and gun under his head." Moreover, Wallace later moved out of the rank of cowhand and became a rancher who owned his own cattle and over ten thousand acres of land in Mitchell County, Texas. Yet until the advent of the modern civil rights movement, African American cowboys and cattlemen were excluded from most popular and scholarly images and accounts of the West. Whether blacks lived in the rural South or on the western frontier, however, they found it exceedingly difficult to make ends meet. Consequently, they moved into the nation's cities in rising numbers before the onset of World War I.

URBANIZATION

From the outset of the emancipation era, blacks believed that "freedom was free-er" in the cities than in the countryside. In 1865, a group of eleven freedmen and -women and their children moved from the rural hinterlands to the outskirts of Macon, Georgia. When queried about their move, an old man spoke for the group: "I

wanted to be a free man . . . I likes ter be free man whar I's can go an' cum, an' nobody says not'ing." Another former bondsman made the same connection between
the city and freedom. Blacks, he said, wanted "to get closer to freedom, so they'd
know what it was—like it was a place or a city." In North Carolina, one man from
Warren County walked for miles to get to Raleigh, where he was determined "ter
find out I wuz really free." Another man spoke for a group of blacks who had left
rural Dinwiddie County, Virginia, for Richmond: "Thar a'n't no chance fo' people
o' my color in the country I came from." Rural Alabama blacks headed for Selma
"to be free." The belief that freedom was somehow "free-er" in the city persisted
through the early twentieth century. In 1908, for example, the scholar and activist
W. E. B. Du Bois wrote that the "country was peculiarly the seat of slavery . . . and
its blight still rests . . . heavily on the land . . . [but] in cities the negro has had his
chance."

Migration to Cities of the South, North, and West

The percentage of U.S. blacks living in cities increased from an estimated 5 to 7
percent in 1860 to over 25 percent in 1910. In the urban South, blacks averaged
about one-third of the total black and white population, whereas they rarely made
up more than 7 percent of the total in northern and western cities before the onset
of World War II. Between 1880 and 1910, Richmond's black population increased
from 27,800 to 46,700; Louisville's from 20,900 to 40,500; Savannah's from
15,700 to 33,200; and that of New Orleans from 57,600 to 89,700. For its part,
the black population of Washington, D.C., rose from only 11,000 in 1860, to
35,500 in 1870, to 95,000 in 1910, representing the second-largest black urban
population in the nation. Baltimore's black population also increased rapidly, rising
from about 28,000 during the 1860s to 85,000 in 1910. Moreover, as the nation
completed its interregional and national rail connections—particularly the Pennsylvania Railroad, the Illinois Central, and the Southern Pacific—black migrants,
who often worked on the rails, used these lines to seek better opportunities for
themselves and their families outside the South.

Between the Civil War and World War I, an estimated 400,000 blacks left the
South. The percentage of blacks living in the North and West increased from 7.8
percent in 1860 to about 11 percent in 1910. A few East Coast and Midwest cities
like Philadelphia, Chicago, Pittsburgh, and New York absorbed the bulk of these
newcomers, who came mainly from the Upper South and border states of Tennessee, Kentucky, Missouri, and Virginia. By 1910, New York's black population
had risen to 91,700, the largest urban concentration of blacks in the country.
Philadelphia's black population reached 84,500, the fifth-largest concentration of
blacks in the country, behind the District of Columbia, New Orleans, New York,
and Baltimore. Other black migrants gradually moved to West Coast and Pacific
Northwest cities like Los Angeles, Seattle, and San Francisco. Western cities attracted a more diverse black population than northern or southern ones. In San
Francisco, for example, the migrants included not only both northern- and southern-
born blacks but also a substantial number of foreign-born blacks: from Canada, the
Cape Verde Islands, and the West Indies, especially Jamaica. In short- and long-dis-

tance moves, blacks utilized established transportation, kin, and friendship networks. A Tennessee-born couple later recalled how they migrated to Los Angeles: "We came here in 1902. . . . We were doing pretty well, so we sent back and told cousins to come along. When the cousins got here, they sent for their cousins. Pretty soon the whole community was made up of Tennessee people."

Cities continued to attract disproportionately more women than men. By 1910, there were only 87 black males to every 100 black females in southern cities. The white sex ratio was nearly even. In cities like Nashville, Montgomery, and Charleston, the figure was less than 80 men to every 100 women. Even in the booming industrial city of Birmingham, with its huge demand for male iron- and steelworkers, there were slightly more women than men. Black women also dominated the migration flow to the older northeastern seaport cities of Philadelphia, Boston, and New York, where expanding domestic and personal service sectors offered relatively greater job opportunities for black women than for men. Conversely, young men dominated the migration stream to the newly expanding industrial cities of the Great Lakes. In 1910, for example, there were some 85 to 87 men to every 100 black women in New York and Philadelphia, compared with 105 to 108 men to every 100 women in Chicago, Detroit, Pittsburgh, and Cleveland.

Opposition and Exclusion

Despite the freed people's optimistic turn toward cities, contemporary whites viewed the rising black urban population with alarm. The ex-slaveholder Henry Ravenel of South Carolina lamented that "they all want to go to the cities, either Charleston or Augusta." Another South Carolinian remarked that "our beloved city has become Pandemonium." Freedmen's Bureau officials reinforced alarming images of migration. According to bureau reports, African Americans were "crowd[ing]," "flocking," "overrun[ning]," or "throng[ing]" the cities to "fearful excess." Referring to black urbanites as idle, immoral, criminal, and bearers of disease as well as "vice," public officials took steps to suppress the movement. In Richmond, New Orleans, Savannah, and other southern cities, authorities revived the antebellum pass system and regularly harassed old residents as well as newcomers. In Richmond, one observer complained that "all that is needed to restore Slavery in full is the auction block." In Galveston, Texas, the Union commander ordered blacks without a "home" or "master" to work on city streets or leave the city. The same commander urged the city council and mayor to enact a law punishing "all hired servants" who quit their jobs before the expiration of their contracts. In Mobile, Alabama, a group of freed people exclaimed that it was not the ex-Confederates that they feared, but Union soldiers.

In Meridian, Mississippi, authorities destroyed a black settlement on the edge of the city. Officials justified their actions on the pretext that it represented a public health hazard. Similarly, in Natchez, Mississippi, authorities removed blacks from their homes and destroyed the structures on the premise that they were contaminated with yellow fever. As late as 1900, George Washington Cable, the southern writer, observed that "there is a notion among Southern people . . . that it is highly important that the Negro should be kept on the plantation." In the North, too, whites expressed alarm at the possible in-migration of large numbers of southern blacks. In 1887, a journalist for an African American newspaper, the *New York Freeman,* complained that "the Northern white men knew practically nothing of the Negro; he is looked upon more as a problem than as a factor in the general weal, with the same desires, passions, hopes, ambitions as other human creatures." In 1906, Howard University professor Kelly Miller remarked that whites in New York and other northern cities displayed a "prevailing dread of overwhelming [black] influx from the South."

Southern and northern urbanites backed up their opposition to black settlement by violence. As lynching engulfed blacks in the countryside, urban whites adopted the race riot as their principal form of mob violence. Destructive race riots broke out in New Orleans and Memphis in 1866; in Philadelphia in 1871; in Danville, Virginia, in 1883; in Wilmington, North Carolina, in 1898; in New York in 1900; in Atlanta in 1906; and in Springfield, Illinois, in 1904 and 1908. White mobs entered black communities, destroyed property, and beat, killed, and injured scores of people, forcing many to flee for their lives. Invariably, local police joined the mobs in their attacks, while other officials, including mayors and governors, aided and abetted the violence by overt actions or by inaction as public servants responsible for ensuring public safety. Moreover, some of the violence involved outright lynchings. In Nashville, for example, brutal lynchings of blacks occurred in 1872, 1875, 1877, and 1890 (see Chapter 13).

Champions of white labor made it exceedingly difficult for blacks to make a living in the city. As early as 1865, the *Nashville Daily Press and Times* feared that freedmen and -women "would at once come into rivalry with white labor." Thus, the paper vigorously campaigned for the colonization of ex-slaves elsewhere. In Montgomery, Alabama, white mechanics criticized employers who hired blacks when whites were available "at the same price." In 1885, a racist columnist for the *Atlanta Constitution* protested the employment of blacks as brick masons and carpenters: "Darn this idea of getting indignant at shaking hands with the nigger when you're slapping the quarters and halves and dollars into that same paw." Even in household service, employers frequently advertised for white women over blacks. Southern daily newspapers lodged a growing battery of complaints against black women as workers. In such papers as the *Nashville Daily Press and Times*, the *Richmond Dispatch*, and the *Montgomery Daily Ledger*, employers criticized black women workers and advertised for white ones: "Wanted: a white girl to do general housework for a family of two persons. Irish or German preferred." Other ads stated simply: "Wanted a good white woman as a housekeeper." Although northern industrialists like the steel magnate Andrew Carnegie made generous contributions to black colleges and developed close relations with Booker T. Washington and other elites, they turned to Europeans and American-born whites to fill their labor needs. For their part, western employers often preferred Asian and white workers over blacks. African Americans lost out to Chinese in the railroad construction boom and to white workers of Irish, German, and other backgrounds in skilled trades and general labor jobs.

White workers barred blacks from their unions and reinforced the exclusionary practices of industrialists. According to one white steel unionist, compelling whites to work with black men "was itself cause sufficient to drive . . . [white workers] into open rebellion." The Sons of Vulcan, the Associated Brotherhood of Iron and Steel Heaters, the Iron and Steel Roll Hands Union, the Railroad Brotherhoods, the Boilermakers Union, the International Association of Machinists, and the Plumbers' Steamfitters' Union all restricted membership to white workers either formally or informally. Although the National Labor Union, formed in 1866, and the Knights of Labor (KOL), formed three years later, encouraged the inclusion of diverse ethnic and racial groups, they also permitted white locals to establish segregated bodies that discriminated against black workers. Similarly, when the American Federation of Labor supplanted the KOL after 1886, it initially organized black and white workers together but soon relinquished the fight for racial inclusion and permitted segregation and exclusionary practices.

Although black men had entered a variety of urban occupations as enslaved and free blacks, they now saw their occupational horizons shrinking. Black artisans, for example, were increasingly replaced by whites. On the eve of the Civil War, only about 17 and 21 percent of black men occupied bottom-rung jobs in New Orleans and Charleston, respectively. By 1880, however, nearly 50 percent of black men occupied such jobs in both cities. During the early 1880s, a visitor to Charleston reported that "the master mechanics, builders, carpenters, blacksmiths, etc. are white, while the journeymen and laborers are colured." Although exclusionary practices were less dramatic in the North than in the South, northern blacks also faced displacement from artisan jobs. In Cleveland, the percentage of black men who worked in jobs as blacksmiths, shoemakers, painters, and carpenters dropped from 31.7 percent in 1870 to only 11.1 percent forty years later. At about the same time, the percentage of black men in skilled trades declined from 15 percent to 1.1 percent in Philadelphia. White union members ensured the decline by barring young African Americans from training as craftsmen.

As blacks lost ground in the artisan field, they also faced exclusion from the rapidly expanding industrial sectors. In the postwar South, textile mills rapidly expanded, but employers largely excluded blacks from these new industrial enterprises. As early as 1881, a Nashville cotton manufacturer hired an all-white work force. Blacks, these employers often argued, were incapable of mastering work on machinery. Moreover, one employer argued, the whirring of the machines would put blacks to sleep. Although blacks continued to work in the iron and tobacco industries of Richmond, one of the most industrialized cities of the South, postwar employers narrowed their range of occupations according to certain stereotypes about black character. The Richmond Chamber of Commerce declared: "In temper he is tractable and can be easily taught . . . the negro in the heavier work . . . is a most valuable hand." Accordingly, new South iron and steel men employed blacks for the most difficult jobs in the rolling mills, whereas their tobacco counterparts employed blacks in the production of chewing tobacco. White workers took the more desirable, cleaner, cigar and cigarette production jobs, which utilized new machinery.

Growing numbers of urban black men and women worked as day laborers. By 1890, the percentage of black men in general labor, domestic, and personal service jobs stood at nearly 68 percent in Atlanta, 60 percent in Richmond, and 67 percent in Nashville. In the same cities, at the same time, 92, 81, and 90 percent, respectively, of the black female labor force worked in domestic and personal service occupations. Northern cities followed roughly the same pattern. In 1900, the percentage of black men in these positions exceeded 64 percent in Chicago, nearly 58 percent in New York, 68 percent in Detroit, and 60 percent in Cleveland. An estimated 80 to 90 percent of black women in these cities worked in domestic and personal service occupations. African American women washed, cleaned, and cooked, whereas black men dug ditches, built and repaired roads, and moved tons of freight in railroad yards and on the docks. Such jobs revolved around the arduous tasks of lifting, hauling, cleaning, and cooking, but they were carried out in a variety of settings: in private homes, hotels, factories, department stores, restaurants, theaters, train stations (and on trains), boat ports (and on boats), office buildings, hospitals, schools, churches, and clubhouses. Although some blacks worked in the newest and most fashionable hotels, offices, or bank buildings, with their spacious rooms, high ceilings, marble walls, and overhead fans, most labored in jobs and surroundings with long hours, few amenities, low pay, and close supervision of work routines. Certain descriptions of urban African American work emerged and persisted over the period: "It is the negroes who do the hard work. They handle goods on the levee, and at the railroad; drive drays and hacks; lay gas pipes and work on [and in] new buildings."

Although African Americans took jobs at the cellar of the urban economy, they nonetheless faced difficulties holding on to these positions. Under the impact of hard times, unemployment, technological change, and hardening racial attitudes, white workers coveted certain jobs in the service sector and moved to displace blacks. Black caterers, waiters, and barbers serving a white clientele faced increasing competition from European immigrants. In Louisville, as early as 1885, an Irishman not only exploited prevailing racist ideas about the benefits of racial separation but also reversed the rhetoric. Since black barbers retained wealthy white customers by serving blacks and whites on a segregated basis, the Irishman exclaimed: "It is nothing more or less than selling [their] birthright for a few dollars. If their barbers had race pride at heart they would step down and out of business." According to the black Cincinnati writer Wendell Dabney, African Americans were unprepared for the immigrant assault on their barbering stronghold:

> White men came into the barber business. The Negro barbers laughed. More white men came. Less laughing. The white man brought business methods. . . . He gave new names to old things. Sanitary and sterilized became his great words, the open sesame for the coming generation. . . . Old customers died and then their sons "who know not Joseph." . . . Negro barber shops for white patrons melted as snow before a July sun.

In Detroit, blacks dropped from 55 percent of all barbers serving a predominantly white clientele in 1870 to only 24 percent in 1890. Although blacks made up 17 percent of all barbers in Boston in 1870, by 1900 their percentage had plummeted to only 5 percent. Moreover, as Americans moved toward European-style (that is, modern or formal style) service in barbershops, catering, and restaurants, they increasingly emphasized qualifications, including literacy, training, and expertise, and replaced their black kitchen staffs with whites. In 1906, for example, Milwaukee's prestigious Plankinton House replaced its black waiters with Greeks and other European immigrants. As employers dismissed blacks from such service occupations, they often justified their actions in the language of efficiency as well as racism, suggesting that blacks "did not tend to business."

Opportunities in the New Industrial Economy

Although blacks found it exceedingly difficult to expand their footing in the urban economy, some gradually made inroads on new industrial jobs. In the South, except for textiles, they gained employment in companies producing cotton-related goods and services, such as the Nashville Cotton Seed Oil Company, the Dixie Oil Company, and the Alabama Compress and Storage Company in Montgomery. In South Carolina, some black workers moved from the rice fields into the phosphate pits of Charleston. As the city's phosphate industry developed and expanded after 1867, it employed a predominantly black labor force to dig rock from land-based pits as well as to collect rock from river beds by dredges. Black laborers also transported the rock to railroad lines, where it was then shipped to mills, crushed into fine powder, treated with acid, and transformed into fertilizer. These mill operations also employed a predominantly black work force.

In the rural industrial sectors of the economy, black men worked as coal, lumber, and railroad workers. Railroad expansion and rural industries like coal mining often went hand in hand. In parts of Virginia, West Virginia, and Ohio, for example, many blacks helped to build the Chesapeake and Ohio, Norfolk and Western, and Virginian Railroads. In each case, as they completed laying track, many black workers took jobs in the coal mining labor force of the central Appalachian region. Similarly, as the Birmingham coal and iron district expanded during the late nineteenth and early twentieth centuries, African Americans entered its labor force in growing numbers. Indeed, by the onset of World War I, blacks made up the majority of all coal miners in the Birmingham district. Yet they faced the abusive contract and convict labor systems, discriminatory wage scales that paid whites more than blacks for the same work, disfranchisement, and a brutal system of lynchings and racial violence. Although such labor conditions were more extreme in the Deep South than they were in the urban and industrial districts of the Upper South and border states, such socioeconomic and political conditions helped to prompt a growing number of blacks to seek a living farther north.

Northern blacks gained their most prominent opportunities in the steel, meatpacking, and other heavy industries. As European immigration fueled the rise of a new labor movement, employers reevaluated the potential of black workers. As early as 1881, the steel employers' *Iron Age* commented favorably on the skills of southern black boilers, heaters, and rollers. Less than ten years later, the magazine reported: "Wherever the Negro has had a chance to acquire the necessary skill . . . he has shown himself capable." In rapid succession, as white workers walked out on

African Americans responded to exclusion from white labor unions by forming their own all-black unions. Some of these unions developed affiliations with white bodies, as did this Charleston, South Carolina, bricklayers union (c. 1881). *Black Charleston Photo Collection, College of Charleston Library*

strike, industrial firms employed black strikebreakers. In the Pittsburgh district, steel companies employed black strikebreakers in 1875, 1887–1889, 1892, 1901, and 1909. As labor historians Sterling D. Spero and Abram L. Harris noted: "Almost every labor disturbance . . . saw Negroes used as strikebreakers. . . . In every instance the Negroes brought in were men trained in the mills of the South." Company officials would later refer to black workers as "strike insurance." In the Chicago stockyards strike of 1904 and again in the teamsters' strike of 1905, employers used nonunion black workers as strikebreakers. A mob of about two thousand to five thousand whites stoned about two hundred black workers who entered one plant under "police protection." White workers referred to blacks in derogatory terms as a "scab race" and as "big, ignorant, vicious Negroes, picked up from the criminal elements of the black belts of the country." In New York City, blacks served as strikebreakers in 1895, 1904, 1907, 1910, 1911, and 1912. In western cities, large numbers of Asians and Latino workers complicated the black industrial experience. In 1903, in Los Angeles, for example, nearly two thousand blacks gained jobs with the Southern Pacific Railroad when Mexican American workers walked out on strike. This development ushered in a set of interethnic conflicts that hampered the African American and Latino struggle for social justice.

Strikebreaking was not merely a consequence of employers dividing black and white workers. It also represented black workers' resistance to labor union discrimination. Moreover, in the iron and steel industry, where blacks were used most often and effectively to break the back of white labor, African Americans had developed deep antebellum work traditions that facilitated their responses to inequality in both racial and class terms. The Tredegar Iron Works in Richmond, Virginia, employed large numbers of blacks before the Civil War and nearly one thousand slaves during the war. Although whites stereotyped black workers as lazy, inefficient, and incapable of performing skilled work, black iron- and steelworkers mastered a variety of jobs, including skilled jobs as puddlers and iron and steel heaters. When U.S. Steel took over the Tennessee Coal and Iron Company in 1907, African Americans made up about 25 to 30 percent of the labor force in the Birmingham district of Alabama. Understandably, white workers in northern steel centers like western Pennsylvania feared African Americans as potential competitors.

Still, strikebreaking was not an entirely black affair. When African Americans gained steel industry jobs as strikebreakers, they were usually accompanied by small groups of immigrants and American-born white workers as well. In the Pittsburgh district, for example, when white puddlers struck one company, white heaters and rollers stayed on the job and later cooperated with black strikebreakers and ensured the return of the mills to full productivity. Nonetheless, unlike white immigrant workers who entered industrial jobs as strikebreakers and stayed, blacks often lost their jobs as whites returned to work. By 1910, Pittsburgh's iron and steel mills employed nearly 300,000 workers, but African Americans made up only about 3 percent of the total, compared with 29 percent for American-born whites and 68 percent for immigrants. At the same time, in Chicago, blacks made up fewer than 400 of the city's 16,367 packinghouse workers. Blacks made up an even smaller proportion of the city's steelworkers. In Cincinnati, African Americans made up an estimated 1 percent of the city's metal workers, while the black population in some small northern cities like Evansville, Indiana, either stagnated or declined as a result of limited job opportunities.

Although black workers used strikebreaking as one strategy for improving their economic position, they also gradually formed unions to fight for their rights and humanity as blacks and as workers. They knew that employers were no more likely to support their interests than were white workers. Thus, black workers sought to close ranks with organized white labor. They formed skilled unions of carpenters, barbers, and masons; semiskilled and common labor unions of teamsters, longshoremen, and bar, restaurant, and hotel employees, including bootblacks; and industrial unions of dock-, iron-, and steelworkers. As early as 1869, under the leadership of Isaac Myers of Baltimore, African Americans formed the black National Labor Union and pressed for higher wages, better working conditions, and recognition of their citizenship rights. In 1871, in Nashville, black dock workers went on strike for higher wages. In 1881, black boilers formed the Garfield Lodge No. 92 at the Black Diamond Steel Works in Pittsburgh. Complementing the

Pittsburgh local was the formation of Sumner Lodge No. 3 in Richmond, Virginia. When black workers struck the Black Diamond Works in 1881–1882, white union officials supported their search for work at other mills during the shutdown. When employers turned to Richmond for black strikebreakers, the Sumner Lodge foiled their effort. By gaining jobs in other mills, with the support of white workers and by joining hands with black workers in Richmond, African American workers demonstrated a resolve to organize across geographical as well as race lines, when possible.

When the American Federation of Labor (AFL) supplanted the Knights of Labor during the 1890s, black workers played a crucial role in the rise of the multiracial United Mine Workers of America (UMWA). Although the UMWA was a constituent of the racially exclusive AFL, it represented a radical departure from the parent body's discriminatory policies. Black coal miners became both members and officers of the UMWA. The coal miner Richard L. Davis of Ohio became the most renowned of the black office holders. In 1891, Davis was elected to the executive board of the UMWA District Six (Ohio). He held the Ohio post for six years, and in 1896 and again in 1897 he was elected to the national executive board, the highest position held by an African American in the UMWA. Although he consistently encouraged blacks to join the union (and, at times severely criticized them for their reluctance), he opposed exclusionary hiring practices, advocated the election of blacks to leadership positions in the union, and protested white miners' discriminatory

Black and white miners at Gary, McDowell County, West Virginia, c. 1900. Both black and white miners belonged to the United Mine Workers of America. *United Mine Workers of America Photo Archives*

attitudes and behavior toward black workers. Davis urged white workers to organize against corporate exploitation and confront those who gained unequal benefits from the "sweat and blood" of fellow workers. At a time when African Americans faced increasing restrictions on their civil rights, witnessed the meteoric rise of Booker T. Washington (the ex-slave and founder of the Tuskegee Institute), and turned increasingly toward the ideology of racial solidarity and self-help, black and white workers joined the United Mine Workers of America, an interracial union within the American Federation of Labor. Davis's life symbolized this complicated intertwining of black workers' class and racial identities at the turn of the twentieth century.

African American labor activism included black female household workers, who deployed a variety of strategies for changing the basis on which they lived and labored. Household workers regularly supplemented their meager income by taking food from their employers' cupboards, bringing loads of laundry home and refusing to return them, and quitting their jobs in the midst of their employers' plans to lavishly entertain and impress business and professional guests. Black women also organized collectively and launched strikes against exploitative employers. Black laundry women staged strikes in Jackson, Mississippi, in 1866; in Galveston, Texas, in 1877; and in Atlanta in 1881. The Atlanta strike became one of the most militant labor campaigns of the period. Black women formed the Association of Washer Women, established a strike fund of $300, and struck for higher wages. Within two weeks, the *Atlanta Constitution,* the city's leading newspaper, reported that the strike was "causing quite an inconvenience among our citizens." Only the combined activities of landlords, city council, and local police broke the strike. Before the strike ended, however, the women had defied municipal officials and encouraged the strike's spread to other sectors of the economy. According to a report in the city's leading newspaper, the *Atlanta Constitution,* "Not only washerwomen, but the cooks, house servants and nurses are asking an increase. The combinations are being managed by [the] laundry ladies."

EMERGENCE OF NEW BUSINESSES AND ENTREPRENEURS

As African American workers sought to improve their class position, their efforts coalesced with a rising race consciousness and helped to stimulate the growth of new entrepreneurial activities. As we will see in Chapter 13, these efforts were closely intertwined with a pattern of residential and institutional segregation in the larger community life of the city. From the outset of the emancipation era, blacks demonstrated a determination to accumulate capital, go into business, and create employment and necessary social services for themselves. As early as 1869, blacks from Baltimore, Wilmington, and Washington, D.C., formed the Chesapeake Marine and Dry Dock Company. Capitalized at $40,000, the company employed three hundred black mechanics, paid off its start-up loan in five years, and prospered through the next decade. At about the same time, other blacks placed their hope on the Freedmen's Savings Bank. Chartered in 1865, the Freedmen's bank failed during the economic depression of 1873. Thousands of ordinary blacks lost their life's savings during this crisis. Although many became discouraged and never quite trusted banks again, black banking and insurance institutions soon reemerged and expanded.

The Virginia Building and Savings Company symbolized nascent black capital accumulation and middle-class formation. In 1879, the company advertised that "in union there is strength!" It also made a special appeal to black workers as a cornerstone in black business development: "We desire to encourage and support our mechanics, and to supply capital and business for our merchants." In 1888, Richmond blacks formed the True Reformers Bank, while blacks in Washington, D.C., founded the Capital Savings Bank. In 1890, Alabama blacks formed the Penny Savings and Loan Company. By 1907, the Alabama bank had become the second-largest black bank in capital and deposits, behind the True Reformers. In Durham, North Carolina, considered by some scholars the capital of the black business world, blacks formed the North Carolina Mutual Life Insurance Company under the leadership of John Merrick, a former slave brickmason, hod carrier, and barber. By 1915, Merrick and his partners, Dr. Aaron McDuffie and the grocer Charles C. Spaulding, had not only opened offices in twelve states and the District of Columbia but also established two drugstores, a Mechanics and Farmers Bank, and a real estate company and were preparing to launch a textile mill employing black workers.

In 1900, under the leadership of Booker T. Washington, head of Tuskegee Institute in Alabama, African Americans formed the National Negro Business League (NNBL). The NNBL pledged to provide products, services, and jobs to the black community. Emphasizing self-help and racial solidarity, local chapters soon spread throughout the nation. According to league records, black enterprises in the United States increased by 100 percent between 1900 and World War I—from 20,000 to 40,000: banks increased from 4 to 51; funeral homes from 450 to 1,000; drugstores from 250 to nearly 700; and retail establishments from 10,000 to 25,000. Cosmetic firms also claimed a growing share of black business activities, which provided employment to black workers, particularly women. In Chicago, the Overton Hygienic Manufacturing Company, manufacturer of "High Brown Face Powder," was capitalized at $268,000, employed thirty-two people, and manufactured sixty-two different products, mainly serving the cosmetic needs of black people. By the early twentieth century, pioneering black beauty culturists and entrepreneurs like Annie Turbo Malone, Sarah Spencer Washington, and most notably Madame C. J. Walker successfully marketed skin, hair, and beauty products to black women. Born Sarah Breedlove to sharecropping parents in Delta, Louisiana, Madame Walker made the transition from St. Louis washerwoman to the foremost black female entrepreneur of the period. After working for a brief period for Annie Malone, Walker later moved to Denver and then to Indianapolis. Her cosmetics company employed an energetic black sales staff, which enabled large numbers of black women to escape domestic service. Until recently, Walker (see photo) was widely regarded as perhaps the first self-made African American female millionaire.

Madame C. J. Walker, born Sarah Breedlove, emerged as the most prominent African American businesswoman of the early twentieth century. She successfully marketed a variety of beauty projects designed to enhance the health and condition of black women's hair and skin. *Courtesy of A'Lelia Bundles/ Madame Walker Family Collection*

As we will see in Chapter 14, the black press both mirrored and promoted black business as a vehicle for self-employment and middle-class formation. The number of black weeklies increased from just over two dozen in 1880 to over 150 by the early 1900s. In addition to established papers like the *New York Globe,* the *Indianapolis Freeman,* and the Cleveland *Gazette,* new and more aggressive business-oriented black weeklies also moved to the fore during the early twentieth century—the *Chicago Defender, Pittsburgh Courier,* and *Norfolk Journal and Guide,* to name a few. One editor articulated a common view when he declared: "The men and women who are conducting business houses are worthy of our support. With our help they can develop into powerful institutions that will give employment to thousands of our boys and girls."

Some black business and professional people not only promoted black enterprise as a vehicle for black employment but also encouraged a radical critique of labor and race relations. As early as 1868, middle-class leaders supported the ship caulker Isaac Myers and the formation of the Colored National Labor Union. The labor convention of 1869 endorsed the call for government-funded forty-acre lots for ex-slaves, the right of workers to organize and bargain collectively, and the acquisition of full political and citizenship rights for formerly enslaved people. The convention concluded: "Our mottoes are liberty and labor, enfranchisement and education. The spelling-book and the hoe, the hammer and the vote, the opportunity to work and to rise . . . we ask for ourselves and our children." For their part, black leaders like Frederick Douglass, T. Thomas Fortune of the *New York Age,* and John R. Lynch of Mississippi criticized "wage slavery" and emphasized the unity of interest between black and white workers. During the 1880s, for example, Fortune adopted the "land monopoly" ideas of reformer Henry George and offered a radical class analysis of black life after emancipation. In his view, the same elite control of southern land that had given rise to chattel slavery now gave rise to "*industrial slavery*, a slavery more excruciating in its exactions, more irresponsible in its machinations than any other slavery." Fortune praised the Knights of Labor and urged black workers to join white labor against the "odious and unjust tyranny" of white capital. As Fortune put it, "Since we are largely of the laboring population, it is very natural that we should take sides with the labor forces in their fight for a juster distribution of the results of labor."

Cross-class responses to economic discrimination were by no means unproblematic. They produced tensions and conflicts within the black community even as they forged links across geographical, cultural, and class lines. As we will see in Chapter 14, middle-class and elite black business and professional people established their own institutions and articulated their own ideas and beliefs about the future of blacks in America. Their vision often clashed with the views of working-class and poor blacks. By the 1890s, black elites like Fortune had become disillusioned with the organized labor movement and stepped away from radical class analyses of black life and labor. As black elites abandoned the organized labor movement, some black workers like the coal miner Richard L. Davis sought to strengthen it.

More so than elites, black workers and the poor also retained an abiding interest in migration and possible emigration strategies for social change. Before moving to Kansas in 1879, for example, Henry Adams and others had anticipated emigration in the event the Kansas effort failed. African emigration associations developed throughout the South and even the West as African Americans moved outward. In 1891, the American Colonization Society (ACS) reported that the number of prospective emigrants had become "numerous and urgent." Some blacks expressed the view that "the colored man has no home in America." Two years after the election of 1876, a group of two hundred blacks left South Carolina for Liberia. In South Carolina, Reverend R. H. Cain and Martin R. Delany headed the South Carolina Liberian Exodus Association. Delany again reiterated his belief that Africa represented the best place "to seek new homes." By the 1890s, the African Methodist Episcopal bishop Henry McNeal Turner emerged as the leading advocate of emigration to Africa. A South Carolina–born black, Turner became the first black army chaplain in the U.S. Army during the Civil War. Following the war, he settled in Georgia and became one of the black members expelled from the state's legislature in 1868. By 1876, Turner had become a vice president of the ACS and advocated emigration through the 1890s. In 1892, he advocated Liberia as a place for black "manhood, freedom, and fullest liberty."

Other blacks rejected colonization overseas but sought a territory for an independent black state or nation within the United States. They considered New Mexico, Arizona, Nebraska, and Kansas, which (as noted earlier) soon emerged as a principal target of post-Reconstruction black migration. All-black towns proliferated during the late nineteenth and early twentieth centuries. Beginning with Nicodemus, Kansas (1877), black town building spread rapidly through the trans-Appalachian West: Mound Bayou, Mississippi (1887); Langston City, Oklahoma (1890); Boley, Oklahoma (1904); and Allensworth, California (1908). All-black towns emerged in northern, southern, and western states, including Alabama, Louisiana, Iowa, Illinois, Kansas, New Mexico, and especially Oklahoma, which contained over thirty all-black towns by World War I. Although African Americans provided the labor force of black towns, such towns usually included the investment of white as well as black capital. Some of the most well-known black founders included the northern freeborn black Edward P. McCabe, an early settler of Nicodemus, Langston City, and Liberty, Oklahoma; the former Mississippi bondsman Isaiah T. Montgomery of Mound Bayou; and Allen Allensworth, a formerly enslaved Kentuckian and the highest-ranking black soldier on his retirement from the U.S. Army in 1907. Although many poor and working-class blacks supported out-migration, members of the black upper and middle classes resisted out-migration for poor and working-class blacks. As political leaders, the former hoped to retain the latter as black constituents; as business and professional people, they hoped to retain them as clients; and as landowners and employers, they hoped to retain their labor. For their part, established northern and western black leaders also opposed the mass out-migration of southern blacks, hoping to hold on to the gains they believed small numbers brought to their communities.

∽

THROUGHOUT THE LATE NINETEENTH CENTURY, postbellum blacks retained a vision of landownership as the fundamental route to economic independence and political empowerment. They rejected both northern and southern white notions of wage labor. In their view, white visions of work robbed them of their birthright to a portion of the land that they had worked and enriched as bondsmen and -women. Consequently, they turned toward the sharecropping system as an alternative to rural wage labor. Sharecropping promised access to land, which they could work independently and avoid gang labor and the strict supervision of overseers. Yet the rise of new postwar forms of labor coercion—state laws regulating vagrancy, debt, and credit—compelled blacks to work under repressive conditions that rendered sharecropping far from free. Although blacks defied such restrictions and moved from place to place in search of better working and living conditions within the rural South, their responses also signaled a significant shift in their vision for social change.

Urban wage labor gradually expanded as a new and more promising alternative to both rural wage labor and sharecropping. By the eve of World War I, black men and women had not only engaged in strikebreaking as a means of gaining industrial jobs and counteracting the exclusionary practices of white unions but also formed their own all-black unions, walked out on strike, and challenged the unjust labor and social practices of their employers. At the same time, black workers gradually responded to the appeals of a new generation of black entrepreneurs who promised to help offset economic discrimination by employing black workers within black-owned and operated firms. These workplace struggles and entrepreneurial developments transcended the question of economic freedom. They were also closely related to the cultural, intellectual, and institutional dimensions of emancipation, the rise of Jim Crow, and the transformation of the larger African American community. These issues are examined in Chapters 13 and 14.

CHAPTER 13

◌

Freedom, Social Conditions, and the Rise of Jim Crow

B y late 1865, some 5 million blacks lived in the United States. About 90 percent of these had gained their freedom as a result of the Civil War. In the recent battle zones, many were refugees. They faced destitution, homelessness, hunger, and epidemics. Even on plantations where blacks had remained throughout the war, conditions had deteriorated by war's end. As a result of these conditions, coupled with racist perceptions of blacks as an improvident people, many whites predicted the rapid demise of the black population. In January 1866, the *Natchez Democrat* reported: "The child is already born who will behold the last negro in the state of Mississippi. . . . [I]ncompetent to provide for themselves, . . . they must surely and speedily perish." A Virginia planter made the same point: "[Within] less than a hundred years of freedom [we] will see the [black] race practically exterminated." On the contrary, by World War I, the black population had increased to 10 million, but the black percentage of the total population had dropped from 14 percent in 1860 to 11 percent in 1910 because the white population had increased at a faster rate under the impact of massive European immigration.

It was not simply a matter of whether blacks could survive and expand their numbers. It was also a matter of how they survived and under what conditions their population would grow. The late nineteenth and early twentieth centuries were years of extensive urbanization, technological change, industrial expansion, and intense socioeconomic and political exploitation of working people, blacks and whites alike. Yet by comparison, African Americans faced greater restrictions on where they could work, live, play, travel, lodge, and eat; educate their children; receive medical treatment; bury their dead; and gain fair treatment in courts of law, popular media, and scholarly publications. The postbellum years witnessed not only the political disfranchisement and economic subordination of African Americans but also their segregation within the housing, institutional, intellectual, and cultural life of the nation. As in other aspects of their lives during the postbellum

321

years, African Americans helped to transform their own housing, health, and living conditions under the onset of Jim Crow.*

HOUSING, EDUCATION, AND PUBLIC ACCOMMODATIONS

Whether they lived and labored in rural or urban America, postbellum blacks faced difficulties obtaining adequate housing, education, and social services. Partly because between 1865 and 1871 the Freedmen's Bureau offered assistance, planters not only eagerly relinquished responsibility for the physical well-being of free blacks but also now exaggerated their own previous provisions for enslaved people. As one Lowndes County, Alabama, planter explained to his former bondsmen and -women:

> Formerly, you were my slaves; you worked for me, and I provided for you. . . . But now all that is changed. Being free men, you assume the responsibilities of free men. You sell me your labor, I pay you money, and with that money you provide for yourselves.

A Virginian stated simply: "I do not like the negro as well free as I did as a slave. . . . Then, I was always thinking of how I could fix him comfortably. Now, I find myself driving a hard bargain with him for wages." In 1880, a U.S. Census Bureau report described rural black life as "destitute . . . many are in worse condition than they were during slavery." In 1910, a northern minister visited the South and declared that "the wretchedness is pathetic and the poverty colossal."

From Slave Quarters to Segregated Housing

African Americans inherited their housing stock from the antebellum regime. Some of these were sturdy frame structures, but most were small, one-room wooden houses with dirt floors, the fireplace serving as the only source of heat and light. Few of these homes had windows with glass panes or even wooden shutters. Moreover, cracks in the walls and holes in the ceilings exposed freedmen, -women, and their children to the rain and wind. As late as 1895–1896, the U.S. Department of Agriculture reported the persistence of poor housing among southern

---

*By the early twentieth century, the term *Jim Crow* characterized the emergence of a vicious system of legal and extralegal racial segregation in the American South, but the term had antebellum roots in both the North and South. In 1828, the minstrel man Thomas "Daddy" Rice observed the song-and-dance routine of an enslaved stableman in Louisville, Kentucky, who belonged to a Mr. Crow. Rice later blackened his face and performed stereotypical versions of the song and dance (under the title "Jump Jim Crow") for white audiences in the United States and Europe. Although the term soon gained wide currency as a comic depiction of black life and culture, abolitionists also used the term to denote the segregation of blacks and whites in public accommodations in the antebellum North. As such, they also foreshadowed use of the term to describe the racial order that undercut the fruits of emancipation in the American South by the 1890s.

Emancipation-era African Americans inherited their housing stock from the slave era. Here a black family occupies an antebellum structure near Eufala, Barbour County, Alabama. *Library of Congress*

blacks. In the Tuskegee region of Alabama, for example, little had changed since the days of bondage.

> Practically all the negroes live in cabins, generally built of logs, with only one, or at most two rooms. The spaces between the logs were either left open, admitting free passage of the wind in winter as well as in summer, or were chinked with earth or occasionally with pieces of board. The roofs were covered with coarse shingles or boards and were apt to be far from tight. The windows had no sash or glass, but instead, wooden blinds, which were kept open in all weather to admit the light.

In 1908, W. E. B. Du Bois described similar housing among the poorest rural blacks:

> [As] cooking, washing and sleeping go on in the same room an accumulation of stale sickly odors are [sic] manifest to every visitor. . . . A room so largely in use is with difficulty kept clean. The dish-water forms a pool beside the door; animals stray into the house; there are either no privies or bad ones; facilities for bathing even the face and hands are poor, and there is almost no provision for washing other parts of the body; the beds are filled with vermin. To be neat and tidy in such homes is almost impossible. Now and then one does find a tiny cabin

shining and clean, but this is not the rule. . . . The average country home leaks in the roof and is poorly protected against changes in the weather. A hard storm means the shutting out of all air and light; cold weather leads to overheating, draughts, or poor ventilation; hot weather breeds diseases. The conditions are aggravated in cases where the huge old-fashioned fireplace has been replaced by a poor smoky stove. . . . So far as actual sleeping space goes, the crowding of human beings together in the Black Belt is greater than in the tenement district of large cities like New York.

Despite the perception that freedom was "free-er" in cities, urban blacks inhabited the poorest, most segregated, and least healthy environments. In the early postbellum years, southern municipalities and military authorities restricted the settlement of urban blacks. In Montgomery, Alabama, the post adjutant general barred blacks from occupying "houses or tenements of any description" without careful scrutiny and authority from the "lawful owners" of such property. The *Montgomery Daily Ledger* complained that the rental or sale of property to blacks undermined the neighborhoods of "very worthy poor white families." During the 1880s, southern whites urged city councils to pass ordinances creating separate

When postbellum blacks moved into cities in growing numbers after the Civil War, they invariably found housing in the most crowded and dilapidated sections. This Lewis W. Hine photo shows African American housing in Washington, D.C., 1908. *George Eastman House. Gift of the Photo League of New York*

"colored districts." By World War I, Baltimore, Richmond, Louisville, Atlanta, and other southern cities had enacted housing segregation statutes, requiring the residential separation of blacks and whites. Northern cities accomplished similar goals through the use of legally binding restrictive housing covenants, which barred blacks from purchasing housing in certain areas. White property holders also formed watchdog organizations like New York's Harlem Property Owners Improvement Corporation and Chicago's Hyde Park Improvement Protective Club, which spurred the clustering of blacks in certain areas: Chicago's South and West Sides; Pittsburgh's Hill District; Cincinnati's old Bucktown and new West End; Los Angeles's Central Avenue; and New York City's Harlem.

Although black urbanites were more widely dispersed across the landscape in southern than in northern cities, they nonetheless clustered near cemeteries, industrial sites, railroads, and floodplains. Contemporary reports often remarked on flooded "bottoms," where "houses were set afloat, negroes were driven from the cabins to the streets, and poverty and distress were great." Moreover, almost everywhere, African Americans were the chief "shanty" and alley dwellers, occupying some of the most unsanitary and disease-infected areas of the city. These dwellings existed not only behind major hotels and places of commerce and business but also in some upper- and middle-class white neighborhoods where blacks worked as servants and handymen for white families. By the early twentieth century, municipal boards of health repeatedly described alley dwellings as "dilapidated shanties . . . [with] leaky roofs, broken and filthy ceilings, dilapidated floors . . . unfit for human habitation."

Poor nutrition and negligent social welfare policies reinforced the deleterious impact of poor housing on the black population. During the 1890s and early 1900s, the U.S. Department of Agriculture conducted dietary studies among blacks in several southern states and concluded that postbellum diets, like the earlier slave diets, were low in iron, calcium, vitamins, and proteins: "The only kind of meat which seemed to be in at all common use among the country people was fat pork. Whenever they spoke of meat they always meant fat pork. Some of them knew it by no other name." In addition to a plethora of diseases associated with their lives as bondsmen and -women—pneumonia, tuberculosis, and intestinal parasites or worms—African Americans confronted the ravages of two newly recognized though not entirely new diseases—pellagra and rickets, both nutrition-related illnesses. Even more so than in rural areas (where blacks had greater access to garden crops), black urbanites consumed diets deficient in fresh meats, milk, eggs, fruits, and vegetables. Moreover, from the outset of Reconstruction, southern municipal officials did little to help black families facing economic distress. In 1865, when federal officials asked Richmond authorities to aid two hundred poor freedmen and their families, officials responded a year later that they were "having trouble providing for the white poor." In Nashville, Montgomery, Atlanta, and other southern cities, municipal hospitals and poorhouses routinely excluded blacks or served them on a segregated and limited basis. When Redeemers (that is, southern Democrats and white supremacists) gained control of southern state and local governments, some closed public hospitals and eliminated systems of outdoor relief for the poor, claiming that radicals had used these services as a means of garnering the black vote.

It is difficult to estimate the number of blacks who suffered and died under the impact of poor housing and living conditions. White physicians, health officials, and the popular press used the poor health status of blacks to criticize emancipation. Citing mortality rates that were two to four times higher for blacks than for whites in cities like New Orleans, Savannah, Washington, D.C., and Richmond, they called emancipation a mistake and a detriment to the health of freedmen, -women, and their children. According to the *Montgomery Daily Ledger,* as slaves, black people "could be up early and late, labor hard, expose themselves in all kinds of weather and seldom complain or take to their beds. Now . . . the least exposure throws them." Such arguments ignored the destructive impact of human bondage in the past as well as the role of discriminatory social welfare policies in the wake of emancipation.

Despite exceedingly difficult times in the early postbellum years, African Americans took a hand in improving their own health, housing, and living conditions. As in the antebellum years, many blacks continued to supplement their diets with fresh garden vegetables—corn, turnips, collards, Irish potatoes, sweet potatoes, and cow peas. These vegetables helped to counteract certain vitamin deficiencies associated with the so-called three M's, "meal, meat, and molasses." Compared with the fare of most sharecroppers, however, the diets of renters and landowning families included more milk and milk products, eggs, and chickens. Even among sharecropping families, blacks with greater access to hunting grounds, fishing waters, and garden plots had more varied diets than others. Improved diets and living environments underlay the declining mortality rate and the slowly increasing life expectancy of blacks by 1910. Moreover, as growing numbers of rural southern blacks moved to the West and North, those who remained placed increasing pressure on landowners to improve the terms of their labor, including better housing and living conditions. In 1901, the Georgia commissioner of agriculture remarked:

> Landlords have been forced to build better tenant houses and provide them with modern systems that are adapted all around, in order to retain and keep the best labor. That is really the way that a great many of our best people succeed in keeping their labor, and the better class of labor, by making everything around them as comfortable as possible.

One Mississippi planter put it bluntly: "In the competition for laborers a steadily improving class of plantation houses is not the least of the inducements offered." Du Bois agreed that black farmworkers were often "induced to remain on farms by offers of higher wages and better houses."

By the early 1900s, travelers frequently commented on the passing of the earlier antebellum quarters. In 1901, on a trip from South Carolina to Washington, D.C., one traveler exaggerated the change: "I did not see but one log house . . . all the way through; the log cabin is disappearing." This traveler also said that "the dirt floor has disappeared entirely." In his turn-of-the-century study of black farm families in

Virginia, W. E. B. Du Bois not only noted the gradual passing of the log cabin and its dirt floor but also commented on the introduction of "glass windows . . . here and there." In his report before the U.S. Industrial Commission, a Georgia farm operator also contrasted the old and new housing among blacks:

> The original plantation houses of the South, I regret to say, were mostly 1-room affairs, 20 or 25 feet square, and those were mostly of logs. The modern house is a frame house, boarded and sheathed, with 3 rooms—a general family room, which is used only to put the family bed in, and then a separate bedroom, and a kitchen. The general modern tenant house now is a 3-room house.

The housing conditions of black landowners were even better. According to Robert Park, a friend and aide to Booker T. Washington, "Wherever one meets a little colony of Negro land owners and wherever one meets a Negro . . . farm manager, one invariably finds improvement in the character and condition of the Negro home."

The Challenge and Promise of Education

As with the quest for health and social services, African Americans found it exceedingly difficult to provide for the education of their children. Postbellum black schools became the targets of white resistance and numerous acts of terror (see box). According to James Atkins, the son of a Henry County, Georgia, planter, when his father established a school for blacks and employed a black teacher in 1865–1866, "His neighbors, as respectable men as I know, burned the school house so that he had to abandon the project of having colored schools." A southern white woman advised one northern missionary teacher, "I do assure you . . . you might as well try to teach your horse or mule to read, as to teach these niggers. They can't learn." Moreover, southern whites believed that education would ruin blacks for the jobs that they could do well. As one southern educator said, "The cook that must read the daily newspaper, will spoil your beef and your bread . . . [the black who] has to do his grammar and arithmetic, will leave your boots unblacked and your horse uncurried." In one Virginia county, a black man testified before a U.S. congressional committee that "down in my neighborhood they are afraid to be caught with a book."

In Magnolia, North Carolina, Amos McCallaugh, a black teacher, asked for federal protection to open a school. He eventually opened a school but closed it after one day: "Why? Because the house which I taught in was threatened of being burnt down." In 1871–1872, the U.S. district attorney for northern Alabama testified before the U.S. Congress that

> when reconstruction first took place, in most parts of the state where I was, it was dangerous to talk about even attempting to educate the negro at all. . . . They would hardly allow such a man as a teacher to go there. If he did he could not get board in a white man's house.

SOURCES FROM THE PAST

1871

The Ku Klux Klan Uses Violence to Prevent the Education of Ex-slaves

Atlanta, Georgia, October 21, 1871

WITNESS: CAROLINE SMITH (age: 35)

Question: What did you leave home for?

Answer: The Ku-Klux came there. . . .

Question: How many were there?

Answer: A great many of them, twenty-five or thirty, perhaps more; but ten of them whipped me.

Question: When was that?

Answer: Late in the night; I don't know what time. I sat up very late that night, for they had been there once before, and we never laid down early in the night all of us; some of us sat up the better part of the night. I was pretty nigh asleep when I heard them coming.

Question: How were they dressed?

Answer: They had on pants like anybody else, but they were put on their body like they made children's clothes. They had on some kind of false face. . . . They caught my husband and beat him as much as they wanted to, and then they came in and said, "Who is this?" I said, "Caroline." He said, "H'm, h'm, come out of here." I went out and they made me get down on my knees. . . . Felker then said, "Take off this," pointing to my dress, "and fasten it around you." They then made me fasten it to my waist. He whipped me some; and then he made me take my body off, which I wore under my dress. He gave me fifty more, and then said, "Go and get some water, and don't let's hear any big talk from you, and don't sass any white ladies." I said, "I don't do that. . . ."

Question: You say they made a general scattering of the darkies in March?

Answer: Yes, sir.

Question: What reason did they give for that?

Answer: They said we should not have any schools; and that white people should not countenance us, and they intended to whip the last one; that is what they said.

Question: Why did they not want you to have schools?

Answer: They would not let us have schools. They went to a colored man there, whose son had been teaching school, and they took every book they had and threw them into the fire; and they said they would dare any other nigger to have a book in his house. We allowed last fall that we would have a school-house in every district; and the colored men started them. But the Ku-Klux said they would whip every man who sent a scholar there. There is a school-house there, but no scholars. The colored people dare not dress up themselves and fix up, like they thought anything of themselves, for fear they would whip us. I have been humble and obedient to them, a heap more so than I was to my master, who raised me; and that is the way they serve us.

Source: Report of the Joint Select Committee to Inquire into the Condition of Affairs in the Late Insurrectionary States, 42nd Congress, 2nd Session, vol. 6 (Washington, D.C.: Government Printing Office, 1872), pp. 400–403.

At the height of Freedmen's Bureau educational activities, bureau schools enrolled only about 7 percent of school-age black children in the five major cotton states. In his reports and speeches on Freedmen's Bureau teachers in the South, O. O. Howard, bureau head, described the animosity that they encountered:

> It is difficult to describe the odium with which the excellent self-denying school teachers are met. Doubtless the treatment to which they are subjected arises in part from the feelings engendered by the war but it is mostly due to prejudices against educating the blacks and the belief that the teachers are fostering social equality.

By 1869–1870, the Freedmen's Bureau's educational effort had come to a virtual end.

Although African Americans would gradually gain access to segregated education, their schools and colleges remained far from equal in physical plants, pupil-teacher ratios, salaries, and teacher training. Between 1871 and 1880, the numbers of black and white school-age children were about the same in the major cotton states of Alabama, Georgia, and Mississippi, but white schools outnumbered black ones by over two to one. In the same states, the number of black children per school increased from 180 in 1871 to 576 in 1873, compared with an increase of from 77 to 164 for whites. By 1899, blacks made up nearly 32 percent of the southern school-age population, yet they received less than 13 percent of the expenditures for public education. In 1895, South Carolina spent $3.00 per white pupil and $1.05 per black student. In South Carolina and elsewhere, this disparity persisted from year to year over the next decade. In several Georgia counties, where blacks made up 75 percent of the total population, matters were even worse. They received less than 8 percent of the expenditures for public education. Moreover, in 1905, Georgia's white teachers received a monthly salary of nearly $43.00, whereas black teachers received less than $20.00. According to one ex-slave woman, when black children "did get to go to school dey wasn't lowed to use de old bluebook spellin' book 'cause white folks said it larn't them too much." In Mississippi, one public school teacher testified before a congressional hearing that black schools received teachers with far less formal training than their white counterparts. Similarly, between 1890 and 1910, the nationwide white illiteracy rate (for persons 10 years of age and over) dropped from 7.7 to 5.0 percent; the black illiteracy rate also declined but remained at about 30 percent.

Next to landownership and housing, African Americans looked to the school-house for liberation from the vestiges of slavery. Booker T. Washington later recalled how his mother explained to him the importance of education, emphasizing how whites considered education of blacks a dangerous thing: "At that moment . . . I resolved that I [would] never be satisfied until I learned what this dangerous practice was like." Washington also recalled that he had "the feeling that to get into a school house and study in this way would be about the same as getting into paradise." Ex-slaves also placed a growing premium on education because they now signed complicated labor contracts and hoped to avoid being cheated out of the fruits of their labor. They repeatedly stated that ex-slaveholders used "book larning" to cheat them out of their earnings. In Mississippi a black man said that he "gets almost discouraged" but he did want "to learn to cipher" so he "could do business." Education was also power. A black member of a South Carolina education society said that he considered the building of a school house "the first proof of their *independence*." In North Carolina, one missionary reported that blacks were prepared to "endure almost any penance" rather than be deprived of the privilege "of learning." In Virginia, a school official reported that blacks were not simply "anxious to learn"—"They are crazy to learn." In short, as with landlessness, ex-slave men and women often equated ignorance with bondage and education with freedom. Education and freedom, they believed, went hand in hand. To be "ignorant," they repeatedly stated, was to remain "in bondage." Even more telling, some African Americans ranked education second to "godliness" in their quest for family and community development.

Through their own determination and struggle, coupled with federal aid and philanthropic support, African Americans gradually made the transition from exclusion to segregation in the educational life of the South and the nation. Before its demise, the Freedmen's Bureau had spent over $5 million on black education, financed nearly 4,240 schools, employed some 9,300 teachers, and served an estimated 250,000 students. The early emancipation years also witnessed a wave of white philanthropic activities on behalf of black education. The Congregationalist American Missionary Association (AMA) became one of the most energetic of the missionary societies supporting the education of freedmen, -women, and children. As early as 1863, the AMA charged its people to go South, "take freed people by the hand," and "guide, counsel and instruct them in their new life, protect them from the abuses of the wicked, and direct their energies so as to make them useful to themselves, their families and their country." Aided by the Freedmen's Bureau and religious organizations like the AMA and the American Baptist Home Missionary Society, Reconstruction governments helped to establish over twenty black colleges by the early 1870s. These included Howard University (1866); Fisk (1866); Atlanta (1867); Morehouse (1867); and Hampton Institute (1868). During the 1890s and early 1900s, black self-help and white philanthropists had produced nearly a dozen hospitals and nursing training schools for African Americans. In addition to Freedmen's Hospital in Washington, D.C., established in 1870, these medical facilities included the Dixie Hospital Training School in Hampton, Virginia (1891); the Flint-Goodridge Hospital School of Nursing in New Orleans (1896); and the Hubbard Hospital and School of Nursing, Meharry Medical College, in Nashville (1900), to name a few. Similar hospitals and nursing schools emerged in Chicago (1891), New York (1896), and Philadelphia (1907). Along with northern white men and women, African American educators helped to staff these institutions.

As northern white missionary efforts gradually declined under the growing impact of Redeemer and white supremacist regimes, the philanthropic efforts of the new industrialists helped to fill the vacuum. The most important of these efforts included the contributions of northern financiers, merchants, and industrialists: George Peabody's Education Fund (1867); the Slater Fund (founded in 1882);

John D. Rockefeller's General Education Board (1902); the Anna T. Jeanes Fund (1905); the Julius Rosenwald Fund (1910); and the Caroline Phelps Stokes Fund (1910). The Rockefeller-funded General Education Board was especially insistent in its push for industrial education among blacks. Together, these philanthropic organizations sank millions of dollars into the education and social welfare of southern blacks. Whereas the earlier church-based denominational efforts sought to promote the ideas of the parent organization, as well as to assist blacks, the industrial philanthropies aimed to awaken a broader consciousness of unmet needs and to stimulate indigenous self-help initiatives among blacks themselves.

African Americans fought for every inch of their newly acquired access to public education. Baltimore, Maryland, offers an excellent example of this pattern. In June 1885, the black minister Harvey Johnson and five other black preachers organized the Mutual United Brotherhood of Liberty. Nearly three months later, the organization invited Frederick Douglass to speak at its first mass meeting. The group emphasized the issue of black teachers in public schools and the acquisition of equal facilities for black children. The brotherhood set up a committee on education and charged it with pressuring the school board, the mayor, and city council to allocate necessary funds for the expansion of black education. This committee in turn set up the Maryland Educational Union and pressed its demands at the state level as well. Within two years, the city council passed an ordinance authorizing the employment of black teachers. It also gradually expanded the number of schools available to black students. Partly as a result of such black activism, the number of schools for black students increased from less than a dozen during the early postwar years to twenty-seven in 1900, including a high school, which moved into new facilities in 1888.

African Americans also used their own resources to build schools and colleges. To help keep teachers in their area, they offered gifts of vegetables, fruits, and other produce from their garden plots and land. Missionary teachers often reported, as one Virginia teacher did, that black people "sent for tuition 5 eggs and a chicken." Other blacks vowed to work their fingers off to finance the education of their children. The withdrawal of children from the labor force to attend school represented a direct contribution to black education. More concretely, within five years after the war, free blacks had expended some $1 million on their own education. In 1867, a Selma, Alabama, resident expressed hope that the educational efforts of freedmen and -women on their own behalf would not be forgotten: "I trust the fact will never be ignored that Miss Lucy Lee, one of the emancipated, was the pioneer teacher of the colored children . . . without the aid of Northern societies."

Students and faculty also helped to build black educational institutions through curriculums of industrial education. By the early 1870s, schools like Hampton Institute in Virginia and Tougaloo College in Mississippi offered substantial programs of industrial education for African Americans. Booker T. Washington, the most renowned black proponent of industrial education, received his education at Hampton Institute. Founded by the white Civil War veteran and commander of black soldiers Samuel Chapman Armstrong, Hampton dramatically expanded its enrollments between its founding in 1868 and the early 1880s. By 1883, the school enrolled some five hundred students in its various departments: "the farm, saw mill,

Black families detested early postbellum apprenticeship laws, which deprived their children of an education. Symbolizing the increasing importance that blacks placed on educating their children is this graduating class at Avery Institute, South Carolina, 1880s. *Avery Research Center for African American History and Culture, College of Charleston*

machine shop, knitting, carpentering, harness making, tinsmithing, blacksmithing, shoe-making, wheelwri[gh]ting, tailoring, sewing, printing, etc." Through these various practical trades, black students and teachers literally helped to build their own schools brick by brick using skills learned in masonry and other building and construction classes. They also helped to supply their own food and clothing using skills learned in farm, sewing, and tailoring classes. As Washington himself later put it, "the idea of industrial education . . . beginning for our people at Hampton, has gradually spread until . . . it has permeated the whole race in every section of the country." Although early black schools associated with the American Missionary Association and the Freedmen's Bureau gained a reputation for the promotion of liberal arts education among blacks, they also played a key role in the early development of black industrial education.

Discrimination in Public Accommodations

Closely intertwined with efforts to improve health, education, and housing were efforts to improve access to public accommodations. From the outset of the emancipation years, blacks protested against discrimination on streetcars in New Orleans, Richmond, Nashville, Charleston, Atlanta, Mobile, and Savannah. In 1869, for example, when Savannah officials initiated segregated horse car service at the ratio of one car for blacks and three for whites, African Americans threatened to sue the company under federal civil rights legislation. Fearing a lawsuit, the company complied and integrated the system. Before blacks could take advantage of the new policy, groups of white men attacked black passengers, shoving them around, and even forcing them off the cars altogether. Rather than being intimidated, however, members of the all-black Lincoln Guards, a military unit, fought back, injuring eleven whites in a violent confrontation and forcing the case into federal court. Federal authorities ruled that the city could legally segregate the races so long as it provided "like and equal accommodations" for both groups. Following this decision, blacks left the courtroom and staged a boycott of the Street Railway Company. Within two months, the company dropped its segregation policies because of its "heavy pecuniary" loss. Blacks rode Savannah streetcars on a nonsegregated basis through the early 1900s.

Contemporary observers and later scholars often remarked on the integration of postbellum urban streetcars. In 1878, Sir Gregory Campbell of the British Parliament visited a large part of the South and concluded: "The humblest black rides with the proudest white on terms of perfect equality, and without the smallest symptom of malice or distance on either side. I was, I confess, surprised to see how completely this is the case; even an English radical is a little taken aback at first." In 1880, a Nashville newspaper reported that segregation existed in almost every sector of the city's life "but on the streetcars the races ride together without thought of it, or offensive-exhibition, or attempt to isolate the colored passenger." In 1890, when a rumor spread that a Richmond streetcar company intended to segregate blacks and whites on its lines, a black newspaper, the *Richmond Planet,* remarked that "we do not know of a city in the South in which discrimination is made on the street cars."

Despite the words of the *Planet,* African American access to public accommodations remained problematic. As African Americans moved from the platforms into the cars themselves, southern streetcar companies often designated certain seats for blacks and others for whites. In Mobile, the company divided black and white sections by an iron lattice. Several cities replaced their early horse-drawn streetcars with "dummy" steam-driven, and later electric, trolleys during the 1880s but reserved one car for blacks and one for whites in Montgomery (1886), Atlanta (1888), and Nashville (1888). During the 1890s and early 1900s, southern states and municipalities gradually codified emerging segregationist practices by passing laws mandating the separation of blacks and whites on public conveyances: Georgia (1891); North Carolina and Virginia (1901); Louisiana (1902); Arkansas, South Carolina, and Tennessee (1903); and most other southern states between 1903 and 1907. As noted in Chapter 11, the U.S. Supreme Court aided this process in the *Civil Rights Cases* of 1883, which annulled the Civil Rights Act of 1875, and in the *Plessy v. Ferguson* case of 1896, which sanctioned racially segregated institutions.

As southern states extended the color line through legal processes, northern states achieved the same results through extralegal means. From the outset of Reconstruction, northern states had passed a series of civil rights laws—Massachusetts in 1865, and New York and Kansas in 1874. Following the *Civil Rights Cases* of 1883, Ohio, Pennsylvania, Illinois, and other northern states followed suit. Although provisions varied somewhat from state to state, northern civil rights legislation prohibited racial discrimination in a broad range of public accommodations. The Illinois law stated, for example, that "all persons . . . shall be entitled to the full and equal enjoyment of the accommodations, advantages, facilities and privileges of inns, restaurants, eating houses, barber shops, theaters and public conveyances on land and water." Amendments to the law later added hotels, soda fountains, saloons, bathrooms, skating rinks, and concert halls. Persons convicted of violating the law faced a fine of up to $500 and imprisonment up to one year. Northern proprietors of hotels, theaters, restaurants, and places of public leisure and comfort routinely violated such statutes. They employed a variety of tactics for either excluding or segregating black patrons. Proprietors established separate seats for blacks in theater balconies, charged higher prices to black customers, and provided poor service to discourage their patronage. As these restrictions increased, northern and southern patterns of race relations converged, but southern states went a step further. They wrote such practices into law and backed them up with a more vicious system of violence and intimidation than existed elsewhere. As for so many other aspects of African American life in the post–Civil War years, historians have offered competing descriptions of and explanations for the rise of Jim Crow (see box).

LAW, JUSTICE, AND RACIST PUBLICATIONS

Although African Americans faced stiff discrimination in public accommodations and in health and educational institutions, they confronted the deepest, most painful, and most destructive forms of racial hostility in the criminal justice system. As noted in Chapters 11 and 12, intimidation and violence underlay race relations and undercut the citizenship rights and economic freedom of black people, but such violence spread well beyond the electoral arena and the workplace. In Pine Bluff, Arkansas, one year after the war, whites set fire to a black settlement and hanged some twenty-four black men, women, and children. In 1867, according to a Tennessee newspaper, white "regulators" rode about "whipping, maiming and killing all negroes" who did not "obey the order" of their erstwhile "masters." These group attacks revolved around the rise of Klan-type organizations—"regulators," "rangers," "reformers," and "moderators." Whether executed by individuals or groups, death came to formerly enslaved blacks for a variety of so-called offenses: efforts to save their children from the whipping post; attempts to peaceably assemble and determine the meaning of their freedom; and personal demeanor deemed "insolent" or "insubordinate."

Such violence was not limited to acts of the white working class and poor. Headed by the ex-Confederate general Nathan Bedford Forrest, commander during the Fort Pillow Massacre, organizations like the Ku Klux Klan included landowners, merchants, public officials, and ministers. Klansmen included editors of the *Raleigh Sentinel*, the *Tuscaloosa Monitor*, and the *Atlanta Constitution*, as well as men like John B. Gordon, Democratic candidate for governor of Georgia in 1868.

CHANGING HISTORICAL INTERPRETATIONS

The Origins of Segregation

The controversy over Reconstruction and the early emancipation years, discussed in Chapter 11, soon merged with the debate over the origins of segregation. In 1955, historian C. Vann Woodward produced his seminal study *The Strange Career of Jim Crow*. In this book, Woodward argued that racial separation as a rigid form of black-white relations did not appear with the end of slavery in 1865. Rather, in its most hostile legal and extralegal forms, segregation occurred during the last decade of the nineteenth century and the opening years of the twentieth century. Only then did southern states and localities enact statutes calling for the systematic separation of blacks and whites in virtually every aspect of social, cultural, and political life. Before this hostile pattern of racial segregation solidified, according to Woodward, there was a great deal of fluidity in race relations, including some support for a liberal, racially integrated society. By suggesting that patterns of black-white relations were malleable rather than fixed, the Woodward thesis buoyed the mid-twentieth-century struggle against the segregationist order.

Despite its timely appearance and social and political utility, the Woodward thesis underestimated the strength of white resistance to a multiracial democratic society. Partly because of white resistance to the contemporary civil rights struggle, a rising coterie of young scholars challenged the Woodward thesis. Historians Leon Litwack, Richard Wade, and Joel Williamson not only took issue with Woodward's optimistic view of race relations but also criticized his use of the law—that is, de jure segregation—as the key marker of black-white relations. According to these writers, a focus on the law ignored the prevalence of de facto, or customary, forms of racial separation, which had existed since the antebellum and early post–Civil War years in both the North and South. These scholars convincingly argued that the proliferation of Jim Crow laws during the 1890s and early 1900s often sanctioned social practices that were already well entrenched.

In the mid-1970s, as the civil rights movement gave way to the Black Power movement, the debate over the origins of segregation took a different turn. Viewing the era from a fresh perspective, historian Howard Rabinowitz argued that the Jim Crow debate—revolving as it did around the dichotomy of segregation versus integration—had obscured a third possibility: exclusion. According to Rabinowitz, parties to the segregation-integration debate erred by assuming that race relations necessarily flowed along "either/or" lines. Rabinowitz demonstrated that segregated institutions were partly the product of black power. African Americans often demanded separate institutions as a means to overcome previous patterns of exclusion from educational and social services. At the same time, such institutions reflected the limits of the black alliance with white Republicans, who resisted the integration of blacks and whites on an equal footing. As suggested by the debate over the First Reconstruction, discussed in Chapter 11, recent scholarship has moved well beyond efforts to conceptualize the emancipation years around dichotomous or even trichotomous notions like integration, separation, and exclusion. Yet, analyzed together, such scholarship sharpens our perspective on the choices open to African Americans, the South, and the nation during the first and second generations of freedom.

Ministers also sometimes administered the oaths to members of such organizations in their churches. According to the report of a Georgia Freedmen's Bureau agent, "The most respectable citizens are engaged in it." When one Alabama planter engaged in a dispute with a freedman over a horse, he later spoke for many when he reported that "I just put my Spencer to Sip's head, and told him if he pestered me any more about the horse, I'd kill him. He knew I was a man of my word, and he never pestered me any more." His white contemporaries described this planter as a "just and upright" man.

Racial Violence and Lynchings

It is impossible to know the precise numbers of black men, women, and children killed in the first two years of freedom. In areas where military authorities operated, whites took precautions to cover up their acts. According to the diary of Eliza Andrews, the daughter of a Georgia judge, "Over in Carolina, the men have a recipe for putting troublesome negroes out of the way . . . no one lets another know what he is going to do; and so, when mischievous negroes are found dead in the woods, nobody knows who killed them." A Georgia farmer corroborated the same point: "A heap of 'em [freedmen] out in my country get into the swamps and get lost. . . . I know four right here in Barnwell that have been drowned some way within the last two months. . . . By-and-bye they're seen floating down the river." Even if we knew the precise numbers, such statistics could never reveal what one historian has called

> the barbaric savagery and depravity that so frequently characterized the assaults made on freedmen in the name of restraining their savagery and depravity—the severed ears and entrails, the mutilated sex organs, the burnings at the stake, the forced drownings, the open display of skulls and severed limbs as trophies.

As suggested above, gender considerations did not preclude attacks on black women. On the contrary, their gender fueled such attacks as rape and retaliation for the alleged misdeeds of their men. Clara Barton, the white Civil War nurse, reported numerous cases of young black women being flogged in the streets of the postwar South. Shortly after the war, two white men attacked and killed a black woman near Washington, Georgia. They not only shot the woman but also broke her ribs and used a stone to crack her skull. The Kentucky Freedmen's Bureau reported several "cases of severe and inhuman beating and whipping" of black men and women: "three women assaulted and ravished; four women beaten; two women tied up and whipped until insensible; two men and their families beaten and driven from their homes, and their property destroyed; two instances of burning of dwellings, and one of the inmates shot." Black women and children were the principal victims of attacks on black homes, partly because white mobs often used such tactics to force men accused of certain offenses out of hiding.

Following the downfall of Radical Reconstruction, lynchings of African Americans escalated. This brutal form of mob law averaged 100 per year during the 1880s and 1890s, peaking at 161 in 1892. According to the leading authority on lynching statistics, Tuskegee Institute's annual *Negro Yearbook,* recorded lynchings reached

3,130 between 1882 and 1901; nearly 2,000 were blacks, including 40 black women out of a total of 63 women victims. Although the number of recorded lynchings gradually declined by 1910, the brutality of such atrocities intensified. Lynchings also became more social. With the blessings of the state, newspapers sometimes announced lynchings in advance. Families and communities planned festivities, celebrations, and picnics for the occasion. Lynchers burned, tortured, and dismembered their black victims while public officials and law enforcement officers aided and abetted the process, helping to cement white bonds of community at African Americans' expense, as suggested by the photo (page 338) of a Paris, Texas, lynching.

As lynchings spread through the countryside, urban riots swept through cities, leaving numerous deaths and injuries in their wake. White fears of rising black political influence, alleged rapes of white women, and confrontations between blacks and municipal police all fueled the violence. In 1866, a New Orleans mob killed some 48 black people and injured 166 others. A reporter for the *New Orleans Times* wrote that "to see the Negroes mutilated and literally beaten to death as they sought to escape, was one of the most horrid pictures it has ever been our ill fortune to witness." Both the U.S. Army stationed in New Orleans and the administration of Andrew Johnson ignored pleas for help, while the city's police actually participated in the attacks on blacks. In the same year, in Memphis, a similar event resulted in the deaths of 46 people and the rape of several black women. The Tennessee attorney general, the judge of the city's recorder's court, the mayor, and the police force all took a hand in inciting the violence. In the fall of 1898, a mob attacked the black community of Wilmington, North Carolina, killing 24 people and forcing hundreds to flee their homes. According to the scholar and activist W. E. B. Du Bois, "The Wilmington Riot alone sent a thousand negroes to Philadelphia." The Atlanta riot of 1906 started in the city's downtown area. White mobs beat a black shoeshine boy to death, stabbed another black man to death, and assaulted and killed nearly a dozen blacks in barbershops and streetcars and along city streets. The dead included two barbers, whose faces "were terribly mutilated [probably by their own razors], while the floor of the shop was wet with puddles of blood."

Racial violence also erupted in the urban North. In 1900, following the stabbing death of a policeman at the hands of an African American, New York police turned their anger on the black community. For nearly three days, according to an attorney for local blacks, "policemen stood by and made no effort to protect the Negroes who were assailed. They ran with the crowds in pursuit of their prey. . . . In many cases, they beat and clubbed men and women more brutally than the mob did." In 1904 and 1908, the most destructive northern riots flashed in Springfield, Illinois. In the first case, when a black man shot and killed a police officer, a mob of whites broke into the jail, removed the man, hanged him to a telegraph pole, and riddled his body with bullets. The mob then turned on the local black community, burning homes and physically attacking the fleeing residents. The second riot erupted when a white woman was allegedly raped by a black man. Although the woman later retracted her story, whites still insisted on lynching the accused. When authorities secretly removed the man from town, local whites attacked the black community, burning several homes, and lynching two black men. Only the arrival of some five thousand state militiamen put down the violence.

Recorded lynchings averaged about one hundred per year during the 1880s and early 1890s. A broad cross section of the white community turned out to witness the lynching of a black man in Paris, Texas, 1890. *Corbis*

In the North and South, blacks faced higher arrests, stiffer sentences, and incarceration rates than did whites for the same offenses. In 1890, blacks made up about 4 percent of Philadelphia's population but accounted for 22 percent of all new convicts for the period 1890–1895, and 20 to 22 percent of all children committed to the House of Refuge (a juvenile reformatory for youth under sixteen years of age) between 1860 and 1890. Although blacks made up about 30 percent of Richmond's total population in 1890, they accounted for over 50 percent of all arrests. Similar inequalities emerged in other northern and southern cities. In the South, however, the "chain gang"—chained groups of prisoners working on public and sometimes private projects under armed guard—soon emerged as a predominantly black penal institution. Richmond started its chain gang in 1866 with 12 blacks and 2 whites. By 1871, there were 230 blacks and 34 whites. In 1877, the figures jumped to 305 blacks and 40 whites. In Montgomery, for the year ending 30 April 1887, white men had worked 3,002 days on the chain gang, compared with 13,790 days for blacks. For their part, black women experienced arrests eight times those of their white counterparts and served 2,182 days on the chain gang, compared with only 92 days for whites. Indeed, white women could hire black men to take their places. Even pregnant black women worked on the chain gang and sometimes gave birth there.

Racist Publications and Black Responses

As the segregationist system intensified, white Americans used the principal organs of public opinion and knowledge to justify their actions. Scholarly and popular literature, newspapers, and journals reinforced social injustice. White writers produced a variety of racist works that denigrated African Americans: Frederick L. Hoffman's *Race Traits and Tendencies of the American Negro* (1896); Phillip Alexander Bruce's *The Plantation Negro as Freeman* (1889); Charles Carroll's *The Negro, A Beast* (1900); Robert W. Shufeldt's *The Negro, A Menace to American Civilization* (1907); and Thomas Dixon's *The Leopard's Spots* (1902) and *The Clansman: An Historical Romance of the Ku Klux Klan* (1905). D. W. Griffith later popularized Dixon's ideas in the racist film *The Birth of a Nation* (1915). Taken together, these writers took the view that different races had certain "fixed traits" that nature had ordained through "years of evolution." According to Dixon, blacks were an inferior species to whites, and nothing could be done to change that reality: "The Ethiopian can not change his skin or the leopard his spots." At the same time, according to these writers, freedom had produced a new generation of young blacks who had not known the discipline of slavery and were now retrogressing into a state of "heathenism and brutishness" that threatened not only the South but also the white republic. The black man as rapist and murderer emerged at the core of this racist portrait. Consequently, these writers articulated and justified white violence as a way to discipline the "unruly" black masses.

To be sure, a few southern whites supported the civil rights struggles of African Americans. In 1885, for example, the southern writer George Washington Cable wrote *The Silent South*, in which he argued that the South could not be entirely free without extending equal rights to all citizens, black and white, and supported racial equality in employment, in courts of law, and at the ballot box. In 1889, in a book entitled *The Prosperity of the South Dependent Upon the Elevation of the Negro* (1889), Lewis Harvie Blair of Virginia protested the spread of segregation in public accommodations and schools. Moreover, for a while, the Populists advocated the unity of poor black and white farmers against the exploitation of large landowners. Yet such efforts gained insufficient support to offset the spread of racial separation, hostility, and mob rule.

Although less rabid in their racist portrayals of blacks, northern journalists reinforced negative treatments of African Americans. Whereas they rarely identified whites involved in crime stories, they regularly identified blacks in such reports as "colored" or "negro," often using language designed to create animosity, such as "burly negro," "negro ruffian," "African Annie," "a Wild Western Negro," and even "colored cannibal." Moreover, in anecdotes, comics, cartoons, and short stories, northern papers regularly used such terms as "coon," "darky," "pickaninny," "uncle," and "nigger" or "nigah." During the height of southern lynchings of blacks, northern newspapers usually assumed the guilt of those lynched and justified such behavior. In 1883, the *Cincinnati Enquirer* reported one lynching as follows:

"Retribution—Jacob Nelling Lynched By A Mob—Red-Handed Murderer of Ada Atkinson Pays The Penalty For His Horrible Crime." In another case, later in the decade, the *Enquirer* reported that the alleged offender "Ought To Be Lynched." In 1886, the *Boston Evening Transcript* also assumed the guilt of the accused: "A Negro Desperado Lynched." Similarly, in 1900, the *New York Times* made the same assumption and failed to challenge the lynch atmosphere of the South: "Negro Murders A Citizen—Posses Are Looking For Him and He Will Be Lynched." Likewise, in the same year, the *Philadelphia North American* reported: "Armed Men Hunting Negro In Maryland—Man Who Brutally Attacked Pretty White Girl Will Be Lynched If Captured." Only gradually did northern papers adopt the language of "allegedly" rather than assuming the guilt of the accused.

Northern literary magazines also sanctioned the rising tide of white supremacy. *Harper's New Monthly Magazine, Scribner's* (renamed *Century* after 1881), *North American Review,* and *Atlantic Monthly* all depicted blacks in stereotypical terms. In fiction, cartoons, and poetry, these publications promoted the image of blacks as comic, inferior, dishonest, and good material for ridicule. Indeed, although northern-born whites edited most of these magazines, southerner Walter Hines Page edited the *Forum* between 1886 and 1895, but there was little difference in the treatment of African Americans during and after his tenure. Indeed, northern whites learned about blacks through a coterie of very influential white southern writers, most notably Thomas Nelson Page and Joel Chandler Harris. These writers not only regularly contributed to the leading literary journals of the North but also wrote volumes of short stories, poetry, and novels on black life and race relations in the South. According to one literary critic, these writers specialized in developing a set of stock stereotypes of black character, including "The Contented Slave, The Wretched Freedman, The Comic Negro, The Brute Negro, The Tragic Mulatto, The Local Color Negro and the Exotic Primitive." Joel Chandler Harris, considered by some contemporaries as a friend of blacks, produced these words for Uncle Remus: "Hit's [education is] de ruin ashum er dis country. . . . Put a spellin'-book in a nigger's han's, en right den en dar' you loozes a plow-hand." In his *Red Rock,* published in 1898, Thomas Nelson Page described the character Moses as "a hyena in a cage," "a reptile," "a species of worm," and "a wild beast."

African Americans responded to the spread of white supremacist ideas, violence, and the deprivation of their civil rights in a variety of ways. Some decided to "fight fire with fire." As early as November 1865, a Mississippi minister reported that "our negroes certainly have guns and are frequently shooting about." In the early postwar years, some black soldiers lynched whites for violating the rights of blacks. In Victoria, Texas, for example, when authorities jailed a white man accused of murdering a black, a group of black soldiers broke into the jail, took the accused outside, and lynched him. Similarly, in South Carolina, when an ex-Confederate white soldier killed a black sergeant, black troops exercised their own summary judgment and shot and buried the man. In 1871, a group of blacks lynched three whites in Arkansas for murdering a black lawyer.

Five years later, Charleston blacks protested the massacre of black militiamen at Hamburg, South Carolina. One spokesman reminded whites of black numbers and capacity for violence:

Remember that there are 80,000 black men in this State who can bear Winchester rifles and know how to use them, and that there are 200,000 women who can light a torch and use a knife, and that there are 100,000 boys and girls who have not known the lash of a white master, who have tasted freedom, once and forever, and that there is a deep determination never, so help them God, to submit to be shot down by lawless regulators for no crimes committed against society and law.

Although leaders like Frederick Douglass, T. Thomas Fortune, and others rejected violence as a strategy for social change, some blacks like the Albany, New York, journalist John Edward Bruce called for armed self-defense:

The Man who will not fight for the protection of his wife and children . . . is a *coward* and deserves to be ill treated. The man who takes his life in his hand and stands up for what he knows to be right will always command the respect of his enemy.

Bruce also went a step further and urged collective "organized resistance to organized resistance." As whites sought to disarm them, African Americans often retorted that they had "equal rights" with a white man to bear arms. On one occasion, a federal officer reported that blacks prized their guns "as their most valuable possessions next to their land."

African Americans faced extraordinary odds in the violent confrontations of the late nineteenth and early twentieth centuries. They faced not only southern whites but increasingly hostile federal forces. In the Spanish American War black troops helped to dismantle the Spanish empire and to bring large numbers of nonwhite peoples, including black ones, under U.S. colonial authority. Still, black soldiers met the same treatment as their civilian counterparts.

In 1906, the U.S. Army assigned the First Battalion of the Twenty-Fifth Infantry Regiment to Fort Brown, near Brownsville, Texas. The men faced repeated harassment from white civilians. One black soldier later recalled that the town displayed a sign stating: "No niggers and no dogs allowed." On more than one occasion, black soldiers were physically attacked for allegedly disrespecting whites. When an unidentified group of sixteen to twenty armed men shot into several buildings, killing a police officer and a bartender, military authorities assumed the guilt of black soldiers. Although a military investigation failed to identify the assailants, President Theodore Roosevelt discharged some 167 black soldiers, denying them back pay and pension benefits. Only during the civil rights movement of the 1960s and 1970s did the government admit to this injustice and restore the men to honorable discharges. The experiences of the Twenty-Fifth Infantry also underscored the limits of armed force even among blacks in the military. Following the president's decision, the segregationist senator Ben Tillman applauded the act as an "executive lynching." Only one man, Dorsey Willis, lived long enough to see his record cleared.

∼

THE RISE OF JIM CROW posed an extraordinary challenge to emancipated African Americans and their children. Segregated institutions represented the most visible manifestation of this challenge, but they were closely interwoven with the intensi-

Following the Civil War, the federal government quickly disbanded most black units. Yet at the outbreak of the Spanish American War, the U.S. Army included the all-black Twenty-Fourth and Twenty-Fifth Infantry and the Ninth and Tenth Calvary. These members of the Tenth Cavalry posed after the capture of San Juan Hill in July 1898. *National Archives*

fication of economic exploitation, disfranchisement, and violence against black people. Nonetheless, through their own energetic efforts, reinforced by federal aid and later by philanthropic support, African Americans gradually improved their social welfare, health, education, housing, and living conditions. Their strategies blurred the line between participation in the formal electoral process on the one hand and the exercise of influence through a variety of individual and collective forms of protests on the other. Although armed self-defense emerged as an important response to the most vicious aspects of class and racial proscription, African Americans soon recognized the limits of violent strategies for social change. Consequently, although they retained their arms and determined to defend themselves, they also turned inward, strengthened bonds of community, and devised alternative strategies for achieving their goals. As we will see in Chapter 14, African Americans would transform the processes of exclusion and segregation into new forms of culture, community, and power.

CHAPTER 14

~

Emancipation, Jim Crow, and New Forms of Community and Social Activism

D espite the onset of Jim Crow and the spread of white supremacist ideas and social practices, some whites rekindled their commitment to a broader multiracial democratic society, defying popular opinion to cooperate with blacks in the struggle for social justice. In 1909, their activities gained organized expression in the formation of the National Association for the Advancement of Colored People (NAACP). Such evidence of comity was nonetheless insufficient to remove barriers, offset the impact of segregation, and usher in a more equitable relationship between blacks and whites. Even as African Americans recruited white allies and pushed against the color line in the social, cultural, institutional, and intellectual life of the nation, they also pulled together, pooled their resources, built new institutions, and forged stronger and more cohesive communities. Although these efforts established the foundation for new and more effective strategies for social change, they also entailed numerous internal tensions and social conflicts. African American families, churches, fraternal orders, and social clubs—with deep roots in the changes of the early emancipation years—emerged at the vortex of these transformations.

FAMILY, CHURCH, AND FRATERNAL ORDER

During the first years of freedom, African Americans worked to strengthen their families and communities on the shifting terrain of political, economic, and institutional Reconstruction. They considered access to family and kin the most prized possessions of emancipation. According to one former bondsman, Charlie Barbour, the best thing about emancipation was the knowledge that he would not wake up some morning "and find my family . . . sold." Another ex-slave, Jacob Thomas, told a Works Progress Administration interviewer during the 1930s that he had thirteen

343

great-grandchildren and knew where each one lived. In slavery times, he said, they would have been on the auction block a "long time ago." As soon as they received word of emancipation, thousands of blacks took to the road looking for loved ones who had been sold away during the days of bondage or displaced by the ravages of war. According to a Freedmen's Bureau official, black men and women undertook these searches with "an ardor and faithfulness sufficient to vindicate the fidelity and affection of any race." Another bureau agent reported that "every mother's son among them seemed to be in search of his mother" and "every mother in search of her children." As this agent also put it, "In their eyes the work of emancipation was incomplete until the families which had been dispersed by slavery were reunited."

Searching for Family Members

The search for lost family members was an arduous, time-consuming, and painful task. Years had passed in many cases, and the physical attributes of loved ones had also changed. Moreover, the sheer distance that blacks had to travel, with few means of transportation beyond their feet, made their searches doubly difficult. Nonetheless, the tireless search for relatives continued into the 1870s and 1880s. In an extraordinary case, a northern journalist described a middle-aged black freedman in North Carolina who had traveled an estimated six hundred miles looking for his wife and children. The man plodded "along, staff in hand, and apparently very footsore and tired." Rebecca Grant remembered how she and her grandfather walked sixty-four miles to reunite with her family. In October 1866, Adam Plummer gave his son Henry permission to travel from Baltimore to New Orleans to locate his eldest sister, Sarah Miranda Plummer, who had been sold away during the Civil War. Fortunately, these family members had stayed in touch through a series of letters. On one occasion, Sarah had written to her mother from New Orleans:

> I hope that you will not forget that I am still alive; I send my love to you and to all my inquiring friends, remember me to my brother. . . . I write you much grief and my heart is full of sorrow, . . . but in the good providence of God I hope we will meet to part no more.

In addition to letters, aid from Freedmen's Bureau officials, and networks of friends and acquaintances, African Americans also used the same techniques that slaveholders had used to recover fugitives. They placed ads in newspapers and offered monetary rewards. In one advertisement, Ben and Flora East offered a $200 reward for the recovery of their daughter, Polly, and their son George Washington. In another ad, Samuel Dove sought "the whereabouts of his mother, Areno, his sisters Maria, Neziah, and Peggy, and his brother Edmond, who were owned by Geo. Dove, of Rockingham county, Shenandoah Valley, Va." Lucinda Lowery placed a detailed ad for her daughter, "who was sold from Nashville, Nov. 1st, 1862, by James Lumsden to Warwick (a trader in human beings), who carried her to Atlanta, Georgia, and she last heard of in the sale pen of Robert Clarke (human trader), from which she was sold."

Searches for family and friends produced joyful reunions. Ben and Betty Dodson reunited after twenty years of separation, and one mother found her eighteen-year-old daughter who had been sold away as an infant. When Mary Armstrong, a seventeen-year-old Missourian, found her mother in Texas, she later recalled the joy of reunion: "Law me, talk about cryin' and singin' and cryin' some more, we sure done it." When another woman met her husband after many years of separation, she later recalled the moment: "We threw ourselves into each other arms and cried." Near war's end, a Union officer also noted the joyful process of reunion: "Men are taking their wives and children, families which had been for a long time broken up are united and oh such happiness. I am glad I am here."

Although formerly enslaved people invariably recalled happy reunions with long-lost family members, some reunions were quite painful. On finding her daughter, separated from her at childhood, one mother cried: "See how they've done her bad. . . . See how they've cut her up. From her head to her feet she is scarred just as you see her face." Other reunions were painful because spouses had married and created new families. In such cases, some blacks decided against face-to-face reunions. Laura Spicer and her husband took this course. Believing that Laura had died, Spicer remarried, only to discover later that she was alive. On receiving this news, he wrote to her:

> I would come to see you but I know you could not bear it. I want to see you and I don't want to see you. I love you just as well as I did the last day I saw you; and it will not do for you and I to meet. I am married, and my wife have two children; and if you and I meet it would make a very dissatisfied family.

He urged Laura to remarry and also to send him some locks of the children's hair with their names attached.

Black men and women not only searched for lost loved ones but also remarried to give their unions the protection of the law. Many ex-slaves believed that their marriages required the laws and rituals of free people. One woman expressed the sentiment of many when she sought to reenact her marriage vows: "My husband and I have lived together fifteen years . . . and we wants to be married over again." Others recalled how they were bound by "broomstick" ceremonies during slavery but now "had a real sho' nuff weddin' wid a preacher. Dat cost a dollar." During the first years after bondage, however, many of these bondsmen and -women were wed in mass rather than individual ceremonies. Such marriage ceremonies frequently included fifty people or more. Nonetheless, newly emancipated blacks sought these unions as a means of strengthening their hold on their children, qualifying women to receive soldiers' pensions, and exercising their freedom and newly acquired civil rights.

As many ex-slaves strengthened their familial ties, others used their freedom to annul earlier relationships. In Washington, D.C., one man annulled his marriage of twenty-two years and returned to live with his first wife. Similarly, a woman on the Sea Islands left her husband when she learned that her first husband was alive. In her marriage to the second man, she stated: "I told him I never expects Martin to come back, but if he did he would be husband above all others." When a Louisiana man sought to remarry, his wife refused, saying that she could take care of herself and that she would simply not live with a man whom she did not love. Some women gained the poor end of these dilemmas. When Charlotte's husband returned from the war to the Sea Islands, he discovered that she had remarried and had three children, a daughter by the second man as well as his two sons. Unfortunately, both men claimed their children and left the woman "in a sore strait." One man whose wife had remarried reported to authorities:

> Things is powerfully mixed up. Last week I gets back and finds my wife all right an' powerful glad to see me. But she thought I was dead, an' so she's been married these ten years. . . . He's a drefful *ole* man; he can't skasely see. She wants me, and wants him to go away, he won't go.

The woman would not leave the old man unless she could take all her children, and the old man refused to relent and let her take the children. Authorities gave custody of the children to the woman and her first husband, but the old man remained in the family "as a sort of poor relation." Until 1883, when the U.S. Supreme Court officially upheld state legislation outlawing interracial marriages, emancipation also permitted some interracial couples to marry and give their relations the force of law. Some black mistresses of plantation owners insisted on marriage as a condition of their continuing the relationship.

Protecting the Nuclear Family

The nuclear family of father, mother, and children took on increasing significance among postbellum blacks. By 1880, according to available statistics, an estimated 90 percent of blacks "lived in households that had at their core two or more members of a black nuclear family: a husband and wife, two parents and their children, or a single parent (usually a mother) with one or more children." Both single-parent households as well as households composed of nonrelatives were rare among postbellum blacks. Although these patterns characterized both rural and urban black families, they were somewhat greater in rural than in urban areas. In short, there were few male-absent households among blacks, and some 66 to 75 percent of black children under age six lived with both a mother and father. Although the number of male-absent or female-headed households had increased by the early twentieth century, most blacks continued to live in double-headed families. This pattern prevailed for large northern as well as southern cities. In New York City, for example, despite the massive in-migration of southern blacks, by 1905 a husband or father was present in over 80 percent of black families. Fewer than 10 percent of the city's black women headed families or households without men.

As black men and women deepened their familial bonds, they also waged an aggressive effort to protect and provide for each other, their children, and their loved ones. During the early postwar years, against great odds, black men took steps to protect their women. Black men resented and protested the "old rule" that allowed white men to pinch or put an arm around a colored woman while shopping, or when she was on the street to stare at, make remarks to or about her of an insulting character, or, as was sometimes the case, openly invite an intrigue, and when resented by the lady, press it, by some course [coarse] speech or action.

In the postbellum South, scores of black men demanded "the same courteous treatment" for their wives, mothers, daughters, aunts, and nieces that white men claimed for white women. When such respect was not forthcoming, some men took heroic steps to protect the dignity of their women. In Richmond, Virginia, Jeannie Scott filed an affidavit detailing the insults and abuse that she faced at the hands of "two Reb boys with grey coats." Scott also described how her husband sought to protect her. When the couple met the white men on the street, they yielded the sidewalk, but one of them struck the woman across the breast with a stick.

> My husband told him I was his wife and asked what he had struck me for. He said I will strike her and you to, you damned nigger. My husband said no you won't strike her again I will strike you. They called me all kinds of bad names—I was frightened and ran off.

After the woman left, the white men gathered a mob, who beat and tortured the man.

In Georgia, a group of blacks formed an organization called the Sons of Benevolence. According to the diary of one white woman, Eliza Andrews, "the Negroes" were "frequently out very late at night, attending the meetings of a society they have formed . . . for the protection of [black] female virtue." In 1883, in Howard County, Arkansas, when a white man, Thomas Wyatt, assaulted and attempted to rape a young black woman, her father sought to bring her assailant to justice. When his efforts failed, he organized a group of black men to make a citizen's arrest and take the man to jail. Fighting broke out, and the armed blacks killed the accused. In the aftermath of this event, blacks faced brutal reprisals from local whites, within and outside the law. Although ten blacks were acquitted, forty-three received jail sentences, three received the death penalty, and one, Charles Wright, was actually executed on 25 April 1884. An estimated five thousand whites came out to witness Wright's death. Still, one of the participants in the battle that killed Wyatt defended his actions. He wrote to the *Arkansas Weekly Mansion,* a black newspaper:

> I want the public to know that if I am solicited to assist in bringing a brutish man to justice for outraging a woman I will do it every time. . . . If . . . we are also caught and hung, I say to the colored men that are left behind to stand firm and if our women are beaten and outraged [to] riddle the perpetrators of it with bullets, let the consequence be as it may.

Black men and women also took steps to protect their children from exploitation and abuse at the hands of ex-slaveholders. In Maryland, blacks protested against the state's apprenticeship laws, which permitted the forcible removal of black children from their homes for placement in the employ of white landowners. When one William Townsend took the children of Jane Kemper, she later reported how she took them back: "He locked up my children so I could not find them. I afterwards got my children by stealth and brought them to Baltimore. . . . My [former] master pursued me to the boat to get possession of my children but I hid them on the boat." Others were less successful. Julia Jandy was arrested three times for attempts to rescue her children. Black men also worked for the release of their children. When the state bound George Turner's son out to a white employer, he urged his son to escape, which he did. Another black man, a widower, took his three children and hid them at the home of an acquaintance, where they were arrested before they could make good on their escape. Still another black man found it difficult to free his daughter despite repeated efforts. "I went to Mr. Wilson's for her and he drove me from his house, and said I should not have her without authority." Black men and women repeatedly appealed to authorities for help in recovering their children. Such appeals invariably emphasized the parents' ability to provide for and protect their children. As one Maryland mother of two children reported: "I am able to provide for them and with the aid of my husband the father of them to protect them."

African American Familial Patterns

African Americans retained certain beliefs and practices that set their familial patterns apart from white elites. African American ideas about out-of-wedlock births continued to diverge from those of upper-class whites. In the postwar years, a Georgia woman, proprietor of a plantation, exclaimed that blacks "did not consider it wrong for a girl to have child before she married." After marriage, however, the woman stated, "blacks were extremely severe upon anything like infidelity on her part." Moreover, some black men resisted monogamy and sought legal support for two wives. Some of these men later recalled their reluctance to give up one or two of their wives. A Missouri man, Harry Quarls, had three wives, but recalled: "Dey wouldn't let me live with but one . . . I wants all three." Black preachers, missionaries, and government officials defined such relationships as "adulterous" and regularly preached against polygamy. A Freedmen's Bureau official, Clinton B. Fisk, told freedmen and -women that God would no longer tolerate "adultery and fornication" now that slavery's chains were broken. Black preachers reinforced the same point, instructing black men that it was "agin de law and de gospil" to marry a woman when they had "a lawful wife a libing." Indeed, some government officials gave black men and women little choice in the matter. As one Freedmen's Bureau official put it, "Whenever a negro appears before me with two or three wives who have equal claim upon him . . . I marry him to the woman who has the greatest number of helpless children who otherwise would become a charge on the Bureau."

Although most blacks continued to live in double-headed households, comprised of mother, father, and children, they also continued to house more extended kin and friends than did whites. Following the Civil War, large numbers of black families legally adopted the children of deceased or lost relatives and friends, hoping to avoid having such children become apprentices in former slaveholding households. Kinship ties extended well beyond the nuclear unit. Before war's end, Tom Mills and his mother were sold from their Alabama home to Texas. Following the war, it was Mills's uncle who came to Texas to find them. Similarly, when Sally Wroe's father left Texas for Mexico during the war, her cousin took care of her family until her father returned. Following the death of her father, Cornelius Holmes's mother took the ten-year-old to live with her grandfather in another South Carolina county. When Wylie Neal moved from Georgia to Arkansas, he joined his brothers and a nephew. As he later recalled, "We wanted to stay together . . . is why we all went—my brothers, my two brothers, and a nephew."

Despite the persistence of certain distinctive African American familial forms, emancipation witnessed the gradual transformation of family life. Whereas the antebellum family witnessed black men and women sharing responsibility for their families in a highly exploitative environment, black men now moved to the fore as the principal breadwinners and decision makers. "Abroad" marriages came to an end, and two-parent households increased. Southern planters soon complained that black women were no longer available to them. The editor of a farm journal, *The Plantation,* reported that black women no longer "pick cotton," which it described as "woman's work." Instead, according to the editor, all black women "mere[ly] take care of their own households and do but little or no work outdoors." Even black women who took household jobs now refused to live in, because, as one white Georgia up-country resident put it, "Every negro woman want to set up [her own] house keeping." The desire for black labor led one Georgia newspaper editor to decry the growing control that black men and women exercised over their own labor and the lives of their children: "The freedmen . . . have almost universally withdrawn their women and children from the fields, putting the first at housework and the latter at school." When a Tennessee employer requested the services of one woman, her husband rejected the offer: "When I married . . . I married her to wait on me and she has got all she can do right here for me and the children." According to Laura Town, a northern white teacher, black leaders often expressed the view that women held a higher place than their men in slavery: "It was the woman's house, the children were entirely hers, etc." Now they urged black men "to get women into their proper place—never to tell them anything of their concerns, etc., etc. and the notion of being bigger than women generally is just now inflating the conceit of the males to an amazing degree." A Deep South observer put the matter simply; she concluded that "the good old law of female submission to the husband's will on all points held good."

A variety of factors strengthened the role of men in the emancipation-era black family. First and perhaps most important, black men had served in the Union army and helped to win freedom for themselves, their families, and their communities. The war itself had been defined as an arena for the development of "manliness." Second, the Freedmen's Bureau identified men as the heads of household and insisted that men sign contracts for themselves and their families. When men defaulted on such contracts, unjust as they usually were, the entire family suffered eviction. Even the landownership provisions of the Freedmen's Bureau designated the "male" freedman or refugee for such benefits. Moreover, the enfranchisement of men and the lack of voting rights for all women reinforced the role of men as heads of families and their communities. Black political leaders repeatedly exhorted black women to shoulder the burden of the home sphere and make it "a place of peace and comfort" for themselves, their men, and children. Finally, black women supported an enlarged role for black men so long as it produced greater protection for themselves and their children, but they rejected physical abuse, adultery, and neglect. When black men failed to live up to their part of the bargain, some black women objected to their husbands' signing labor contracts on their behalf and demanded separate payment of wages and separate bills and debt obligations at the country stores. Although new forms of gender inequality took their toll on black family life, African American men and women forged strong familial bonds in the aftermath of slavery.

The Growth of Black Churches

Familial relations were deeply rooted in African American religious beliefs and social practices. Their faith not only underlay the search for loved ones and the effort to rebuild broken families but also fueled the quest for education, power, and a broader community. When asked why they pursued an education so diligently, elderly blacks often stated forthrightly: "Because I want to read de Word of de Lord." In Mississippi, one ex-slave wanted to read passages of the Bible that his old master and mistress had censored:

> Ole missus used to read de good book to us, black 'uns, on Sunday evenings, but she mostly read dem places whar it says, Saints obey your masters, an' didn't stop to splane it like de teachers, an' now we is free dar's heaps o' things in data ole book, we is jes' sufferin to larn.

Others expressed the belief that one could not be the "best Christian" that one could be without being able to read the Bible. Building on their prewar belief that they were "the chosen people," blacks also interpreted emancipation as the fulfillment of God's plan. In North Carolina, one black speaker referred to Chapters 2 and 4 of Joshua to describe the "full accomplishments of the principles and destiny of the race" and concluded that "the race have a destiny in view similar to the children of Israel." In 1866, a white army chaplain reported: "There is [no] part of the Bible with which they are so familiar as the story of the deliverance of the Children of Israel." In 1865, in their call for a political meeting, African Americans stated: "These are the times foretold by the Prophets when a nation shall be born in a day."

The church as an instrument of political liberation was inextricably linked to its spiritual role. Contemporary black and white observers regularly commented on the emotional style, content, and decorum of African American religious services, particularly in black Baptist and Methodist churches. A white visitor described

As it did during the antebellum years, the black church served as an instrument of both liberation and spirituality after the Civil War. Here African Americans conduct an evening prayer service.
Bettmann/Corbis

services in one church as "tearful," emotional, and communal as the preacher delivered his sermon and a preacher or deacon "read out, line by line" hymns, which the congregation sang together in a community of voices. In another case, a northern black minister reported:

> For fully ten minutes the preacher walked the pulpit, repeating in a loud incoherent manner, "And the angel will read from this letter." This created the wildest excitement, and not less than ten or fifteen were shouting in different parts of the house, while four or five were going from seat to seat shaking hands with the occupants of the pews. "Let an angel come right down n' red at letter," shouted a Sister, at the top of her voice. This was the signal for loud exclamations from various parts of the house. "Yes, yes, I want to hear the letter"; "Come, Jesus, come, or send an angel to read the letter"; "Lord, send us the power."

Although northern missionaries regularly condemned uneducated ministers, they sometimes recognized the commitment, knowledge, eloquence, and effectiveness of such preachers. In Beaufort, South Carolina, one African Methodist Episcopal (AME) missionary admitted that the effectiveness of one ex-slave minister made him "feel ashamed" of himself: "He talked about Christ and his salvation as one who understood what he said. . . . He was an unlearned man, one who could not read, telling of the love of Christ of Christian faith and duty in a way which I have not learned."

African Americans' quest for a broader community gained sharp expression in the institutional expansion of the black church. Postbellum blacks elaborated on established prewar churches; gave institutional form and visibility to the underground slave church; and increasingly severed their connections to antebellum white congregations, now called the "Old Slavery Church," and set up independent bodies. By 1890, the U.S. Census reported 1.3 million black Baptists in the United States. Nearly 1 million of these resided in the South. By World War I, the number of black Baptists reached 3 million, with about twenty-two thousand churches. There were, however, far more churches than ministers, who frequently pastored two to four churches, particularly in rural areas, on alternate Sundays. Since the Baptist church retained its decentralized structure and downplayed the role of formal training, it allowed greater lay access to the ministry and facilitated the rise of new churches.

The rapid growth of black churches entailed a complicated splintering process. Richmond's First African Baptist Church illustrates the pattern. Formed during the early 1800s, the First African Baptist Church had given rise to Ebenezer Baptist Church in 1858. During the Reconstruction years, however, members from First Baptist and Ebenezer formed two new churches: Shiloh Baptist (1867) and St. John's Baptist (1870). Similarly, by 1885, Raleigh's First Baptist Church had given rise to four different congregations. Even more telling, Atlanta's Mt. Zion Baptist Church gave birth to six additional black churches in the city. Splintering most often occurred when a deacon or minister became disenchanted (over doctrinal, financial, social status, or class disputes) and led his followers out of an established church and formed a new congregation. In Richmond, for example, Rev. William Troy led more than one schism, first when he left the pastorship of the Second Colored Baptist Church to found Sharon Baptist Church, and later when he left Sharon to found the Moore Street Baptist Church. Yet by the late nineteenth and early twentieth centuries, black Baptists had formed three national Baptist conventions—the Foreign Mission Convention of the U.S.A. (1880), the American National Baptist Convention (1886), and the Baptist Education Convention (1893)—and were moving toward greater centralization of their efforts. In 1895–1896, these three conventions merged and established the National Baptist Convention, U.S.A.

For its part, the AME church entered the emancipation years with its General Conference and retained its centralized structure. The organization emphasized expansion into the South. In addition to expanding its earlier Baltimore Conference, it opened up new conferences in South Carolina, Georgia, and Florida. In the South, AME membership increased from no more than 3,000–4,000 in 1865 to over 307,000 in 1890. By 1914, the denomination had an estimated membership of about 550,000 and some 6,600 churches north and south. At the same time, membership in the AME Zion and the Colored Methodist Episcopal (CME) churches, the third- and fourth-largest black denominations, rose to about 300,000, with about 2,700 and 2,600 churches, respectively.

The movement for black independence faced stiff resistance from white Presbyterians, Episcopalians, and Catholics. These denominations sought to maintain control of black congregations, arguing that such control was necessary to "stamp out" superstitious practices and beliefs among ex-slaves. Black membership in these churches steadily declined. One white Presbyterian church leader lamented: "We hardly know what to say, think, or hope, the [black Presbyterians] are disinclined to hear the word of God from us, and are led astray by superstitious leaders." Another noted: "Almost universally they [blacks] prefer separate organizations and preachers of their own color." Still, by World War I, where blacks remained in white churches, they made increasing demands for their own independent units. Black Catholics, for example, gradually formed their own churches: St. Benedict the Moor in Pittsburgh, St. Anne's in Cincinnati, and St. Augustine in Louisville, to name a few.

Postbellum black churches responded to the onset of the Jim Crow era by supplementing their programs of moral, spiritual, and emotional support with a growing range of social welfare, economic, political, and educational activities. By the early 1900s, the AME church operated twenty-five schools and colleges, including Allen University in Cokesbury, South Carolina; Morris Brown in Atlanta; and Wilberforce University in Ohio. At about the same time, the black Baptist denominations maintained fourteen institutions of higher education, and the CME congregations counted at least one college among their numerous educational activities. Some of these schools initially offered theological training as well as elementary, secondary, and college courses, later adding training in law and medicine to the curriculum. Black churches also launched their own publishing houses, including the AME Sunday School Union and the National Baptist Publishing Board, founded in 1896, and engaged in a variety of social welfare activities to aid orphans, the sick, the homeless, and the poor.

Black women played a pivotal role in the spiritual and social welfare activities of the church. They outnumbered men as members, built energetic church auxiliaries, and launched bold new social welfare programs. In 1900, under the leadership of Nannie Helen Burroughs, black women of the National Baptist Convention formed the Women's Convention. A year later, the convention founded the National Training School for Women in Washington, D.C., taking as their motto "We Specialize in the Wholly Impossible." The school received its first students in 1909 with an enrollment of thirty-one. By World War I, the facility trained growing numbers of young women at the high school and junior college levels. The curriculum included training in domestic science, clerical work, farming, and printing as well as missionary work. AME women also formed their own auxiliaries: the Women's Mite Missionary Society (1874) and the Women's Home and Foreign Missionary Society (1904). In both the AME and Baptist churches, black men slowly opened the doors to female auxiliaries but almost uniformly barred women from the pulpit. When these denominations did permit women to preach, they were limited. They could not head a church of their own, administer the sacraments, or perform marriages.

The Influence of Mutual Aid Societies

A growing number of mutual aid societies, benefit societies, and fraternal orders reinforced the educational and social welfare activities of the black church. Some of these orders took religious names: the Independent Order of St. Luke, the Mosaic Templars of America, the Nazarites, and the Galilean Fishermen. Others modeled themselves after leading white secret societies: the Masons (black, formed in 1787); Odd Fellows (black, formed in 1843); Knights of Pythias (black, formed in 1880); and Elks (black, formed in 1898). Although white and black organizations often had the same short name, the formal names were distinct. In the case of the Knights of Pythias, for example, the formal name of the white organization was Knights of Pythias of the World, whereas the black organization was the Knights of Pythias of North America, South America, Europe, Asia, and Africa—also referred to as the Colored Knights of Pythias. When a rival black Pythian society developed, it took the name Knights of Pythias of the Eastern and Western Hemispheres. Indeed, black fraternal orders established themselves against great odds. In 1909, for example, the Georgia state legislature barred black fraternal orders from using "the insignia," ritualistic words, handshakes, or "grips" of orders composed of whites. Despite such constraints, black fraternal orders continued to expand.

During the late nineteenth and early twentieth centuries, the Odd Fellows emerged as the largest of these societies. The organization increased from 89 lodges and an estimated 4,000 members in 1868 to some 1,000 lodges and nearly 37,000 members in 1886. The Odd Fellows lodges and membership continued to grow, rising to over 2,000 chapters and over 155,000 members by 1900. The Pythians, Masons, Elks, and Templars experienced similar, though less dramatic, growth. Among the nonsecret fraternal insurance societies were the United Order of True Reformers (founded in 1881) and the Independent Order of St. Luke (founded c. 1860), both originating in Virginia. Under the leadership of Rev. William Washington Brown, a former slave, school teacher, and temperance activist, the True Reformers claimed a membership of 100,000 by the early 1900s. Its bank, formed in 1888, reported 10,000 depositors just before its failure in 1910.

The Independent Order of St. Luke owed its success to the leadership of Maggie Lena Walker. The founder and owner of the St. Luke Penny Savings Bank of Richmond, Virginia, Walker became head of the organization around 1900. Under her leadership, the order increased its membership from about 1,000 to 20,000 in less than a decade. Like the other fraternal insurance societies, St. Luke also entered the real estate field, established retail stores, set up a printing facility, and launched a newspaper, the *St. Luke Herald,* which preached a vigorous brand of self-help and racial solidarity. On one occasion the paper asserted that racial discrimination in the social, economic, and political life of the nation would "sooner or later teach him [the Negro] the lesson of racial unity and cooperation." Despite ongoing obstacles to their survival, fraternal organizations not only served the social and cultural needs of members but also offered burial funds, aid to widows and children, sick benefits, and unemployment insurance. In short, these organizations played an important role in helping blacks to cushion the impact of economic hardships and disasters.

SOCIAL CLUBS, LEISURE TIME, AND CULTURAL CHANGE

Closely intertwined with the work of the fraternal orders were a variety of social clubs, especially women's clubs. Similar to fraternal orders, such clubs addressed not only the social and cultural concerns of members but issues of poverty, social welfare, and justice as well.

Black Clubs and Professional Organizations

Although black women's clubs emerged throughout the country, the most influential networks of clubs developed at black colleges and in the major urban centers. In 1895, Margaret Murray (Mrs. Booker T.) Washington and women at the Tuskegee Institute formed the Tuskegee Woman's Club. Lugenia Hope Burns, wife of Atlanta University president John Hope, spearheaded the formation of the Neighborhood Union in 1908. In 1912–1913, Fisk University women played a similar role in the development of the Nashville Urban League's Bethlehem House Settlement. Black college–based clubs were quite exclusive. As Margaret Washington stated: "Those who are acquainted with the nature of this club know that in certain ways it is an exclusive club, taking in as members only those connected with the faculty as teachers and those who are indirectly connected, that is, the wives of the gentlemen teachers." Similarly, Atlanta's Neighborhood Union accepted only "worthy" families residing within a delimited geographical boundary around Atlanta University.

In addition to college-based clubs, black women's clubs proliferated in cities like Philadelphia, Washington, D.C., New York, Boston, Chicago, and New Orleans. In 1892, under the leadership of women like Mary Church Terrell, black women formed the Colored Woman's League of Washington, D.C. At about the same time in New York, Victoria Earle Matthews, a frequent contributor to New York newspapers; Maritcha Lyons, a public school teacher; and the physician Susan Smith McKinney, among others, founded the Woman's Loyal League. A year later, Josephine St. Pierre Ruffin spearheaded the formation of Boston's Woman's Era Club, which also launched the *Woman's Era,* the first monthly magazine published by black women. By 1913, Chicago reported forty-one clubs, with a total of twelve hundred members. In 1896, two black women's organizations—the National League of Colored Women and the National Federation of Afro-American Women—closed ranks and formed the National Association of Colored Women (NACW). The organization selected Mary Church Terrell as its first president, adopted a motto of racial uplift, and launched an aggressive campaign to advance and protect the interests of black families, their communities, and the race. The

SOUTHERN HORRORS.

LYNCH LAW

IN ALL

ITS PHASES

Miss IDA B. WELLS,

Price, ·   ·   · Fifteen Cents.

THE NEW YORK AGE PRINT,
1892.

Ida Bell Wells Barnett, newspaper editor and leader of a vigorous antilynching campaign during the late nineteenth and early twentieth centuries. *Schomburg Center for Research in Black Culture, New York Public Library, Astor, Lenox and Tilden Foundation*

following year the women initiated a national publication called *National Notes*, published at Tuskegee Institute.

Whereas white women's clubs of the period emphasized individual self-improvement, the black women's clubs emphasized racial solidarity, uplift, and social justice. Under their motto, "Lifting as We Climb," these clubs developed nursery schools, orphanages, penny savings banks, homes for homeless young women and girls, and employment bureaus. According to the Chicago black clubwoman Fannie Barrier, the black women's club represented "the New Negro with new powers of self-help." Although most of these clubs strove to develop social welfare programs of direct material aid to black people, some pushed for equal rights and an end to Jim Crow laws and mob violence. In southern states like Louisiana and Tennessee, black women's clubs protested against Jim Crow statutes and worked for their repeal. Northern black women reinforced these efforts and vigorously supported the antilynching campaign waged under the leadership of Ida B. Wells (see page 369).

Women's clubs, fraternal orders, and churches did not exhaust the range of black institutions. African American institution-building activities cut across a broad spectrum of social and cultural concerns. Black medical, educational, and journalistic organizations not only expanded on the local and regional levels but also created national bodies to coordinate their work and extend their influence through annual conventions, speeches, professional papers, and publications. In 1895, black physicians formed the National Medical Association to combat racial discrimination in the white American Medical Association. Less than a decade later, black nurses formed their own National Association of Colored Graduate Nurses (1908). As early as 1880, editors of black religious, professional, and lay publications met in Louisville, Kentucky, and formed the Colored Press Association (CPA). By 1890, the CPA had changed its name to Afro-American Press Association, and in 1907, it became the Negro Press Association and continued to meet as a national organization that promoted the black press as a sharp alternative to the racist organs of public opinion.

Black Newspapers, Literature, and Scholarly Activities

Black weeklies increased from just over two dozen in 1880 to over 150 by the early 1900s. During the late nineteenth century, the most important black newspapers included the *New York Globe, New York Freeman, New York Age, Washington Bee, New Orleans Tribune,* and *Cleveland Gazette.* The New York papers had an average weekly circulation of six thousand, and the *Bee* reached numerous black households as well as members of the U.S. Congress. San Francisco's *Pacific Appeal* and the *Elevator* continued to serve blacks in the West. By World War I, other black newspapers also emerged in the urban North and South: the *Boston Guardian, Pittsburgh Courier, Chicago Defender, Baltimore Afro-American,* and *Norfolk Journal and Guide.* In January 1890, T. Thomas Fortune of the *New York Age* urged blacks to strengthen their separate communities because whites established the color line first. He urged blacks to "stand up" like men in their own organizations "where color will not be a brand of odium." By reporting on the day-to-day doings of African Americans, particularly their business, professional, religious, civic, and political leaders, black newspapers reinforced efforts to build unified black communities with strong regional and national linkages.

Along with the expansion of journalistic efforts, African American literary and scholarly activities enhanced the growth of black communities. As early as 1881, Washington, D.C., blacks formed their famous Bethel Literary and Historical Association of the Metropolitan AME Church. In 1897, African Americans initiated the American Negro Academy, which promoted African American achievement in literature, science, and the arts through advocacy of higher education, publication of scholarly works, and defense of the race against slanderous attacks from the white cultural establishment. Blacks also formed the Negro Historical Society of Philadelphia (1897); the Negro Society for Historical Research (1911); and, under the leadership of historian Carter G. Woodson, the Association for the Study of Negro Life and History (1915). Under the impetus of this organized cultural movement, blacks soon produced a new wave of novels, poems, and historical works.

Although black writers offered diverse styles, approaches, and perspectives, they articulated a shared set of ideas and beliefs that helped to combat the impact of white sources of culture, knowledge, and images of blacks. In 1882, the minister George Washington Williams wrote his two-volume *History of the Negro Race in America.* Like his antebellum counterparts, Williams emphasized the divine "unity of mankind": "one race," "one blood," and "one language." He also affirmed his belief in the Bible and concluded that in the "interpretation of *History* the plans of God must be discerned." Although Williams also acknowledged a growing belief in science, W. E. B. Du Bois, the first black to receive a Ph.D. degree from Harvard University, emerged as the most renowned of the new historians and social scientists. Du Bois's dissertation on the suppression of the African slave trade was the first work to appear in the Harvard Historical Studies series, and his *Philadelphia Negro,* published in 1899, gained recognition as the most comprehensive study of a black urban community.

Published in 1903, Du Bois's *The Souls of Black Folk* set the tone for the twentieth-century struggle of African Americans against the inequities of Jim Crow. In *The Souls of Black Folk,* Du Bois prophetically announced: "The problem of the twentieth century is the color line—the relation of the darker to the lighter races of men in Asia and Africa, in America and the islands of the sea." As the title suggests, *The Souls of Black Folk* also argued forcibly against the prevailing literature of the "Negro a Beast" by noting that blacks were people with "souls." As such, Du Bois also revealed how the first generation of black professional historians and social scientists aimed to bridge the gap between the academy's search for truth and the struggle for social justice in the larger society.

Black novelists and short-story writers also addressed key issues in the struggle of blacks during the rise of Jim Crow. The writings of Frances Ellen Harper, Paul Lawrence Dunbar, Charles Chestnut, and James Weldon Johnson, among others, supplanted the antebellum slave narratives with new perspectives on the emancipation experience. In 1892, Frances Ellen Harper wrote the first novel published by a black in the postbellum years. Entitled *Iola Leroy, or Shadows Uplifted,* Harper's book emphasized the lives of upper-class, well-educated, and "genteel" blacks. As such, it made a deliberate effort to counteract the prevailing white caricature of blacks as comical "plantation types." Paul Lawrence Dunbar, born in Dayton, Ohio, produced three novels, including *The Sport of the Gods;* two books of short stories, including *Folks from Dixie* and *Strength of Gideon;* and several volumes of poetry, including *Oak and Ivy, Lyrics of the Lowly Life,* and *Majors and Minors.* Dunbar gained prominence when the white writer William Dean Howells offered a favorable review of his *Majors and Minors,* published in 1895. Although Dunbar's writings adopted dialect form and reinforced aspects of the plantation stereotype of the contented "carefree slave," his skills as a writer offered evidence against prevailing notions of black inferiority. Moreover, his poem to Frederick Douglass and his "Ode to Ethiopia" demonstrated a keen race consciousness and protest against injustice.

Born in Cleveland, Ohio, Charles Chestnut spent most of his formative years in North Carolina. As a young man and writer, he returned to Cleveland, where he published several works of fiction: *The Conjure Woman* (1899), *The Wife of His Youth and Other Stories of the Color Line* (1899), *The House Behind the Cedars* (1900), and *The Marrow of Tradition* (1901). More so than Dunbar, however, Chestnut probed life behind the color line as well as interactions across the color line. He not only attacked the conventions of white supremacy by wielding the pen in an even more skillful manner than many of his white peers but also handled and interpreted serious subject matter in the lives of blacks, including unfair labor and selling practices, sharecropping and convict labor, and exorbitant legal fees. Chestnut's short stories utilized Uncle Julius almost as a counterpoint to Joel Chandler Harris's Uncle Remus. Unlike Remus, however, Julius dons a mask that allows him to indirectly critique the racial injustices of American society. In 1912, the Florida-born James Weldon Johnson produced his *Autobiography of an Ex-colored Man.* Although this novel focused on the phenomenon of "passing," it moved beyond the "genteel" order and probed the realities of black life at the bottom of New York

City's West End black class structure, thus anticipating certain themes that would gain prominence during the Harlem Renaissance.

Music and Dance

As in the antebellum era, music and dance emerged at the core of postbellum black artistic creations and leisure time activities. African Americans built on their past traditions to produce new music and dance forms in jook joints, honky-tonks, and after-hours places. The secular counterpart to the black church, jook joints first emerged in the rural plantation setting where blacks gathered to play cards, gamble, eat, drink, and dance. In the postbellum jook joints, communal or group dance and music forms gradually gave way to more individualized forms of expression. Solo singing moved toward center stage, with couples pairing off to dance with each other. The "shouts and hollers" work songs of the antebellum and early postbellum years gradually gave rise to the blues.

The blues revolved around the personal exploits and/or trials and tribulations of the singer, as suggested by the origins of the popular folk song "The Joe Turner Blues." During the 1890s and early 1900s, "Joe Turner" established a stylistic basis for the rapid spread of the blues. Based on the folk tale about Joe Turney, a white law officer who transported black men from Memphis to penitentiary labor in Nashville, the song got its lyrics from black women who lost their men to the penitentiary. When asked about their men, women replied:

Dey tell me Joe Turner's come and gone
Dey tell me Joe Turner's come and gone
Got my man an' gone
He come wid fo'ty links of chain Oh Lawdy
Come wid fo'ty links of chain Oh lawdy
Got my man an' gone

An intensely personal music form, the blues nonetheless resonated with the experiences of the group. Although enslaved blacks had used a variety of instruments in the pre–Civil War days, free blacks now expanded the range of instruments used. Black bluesmen turned increasingly toward the creative use of the guitar, which began to replace the banjo in the post–Civil War years. Bluesmen and -women adopted the guitar partly because it permitted the performer to accompany the music with lyrics and partly because the instrument could be made to imitate the human voice. W. C. Handy, considered the first person to popularize the blues, was inspired by a bluesman singing in a Mississippi train station. Handy published his "Memphis Blues" in 1912 and his famous "St. Louis Blues" two years later. White singers and entertainers like Mae West, Sophie Tucker, and Ann Pennington absorbed these cultural forms and carried them to white audiences throughout America and Europe.

In the meantime, the blues established the foundations for the rise of ragtime and later jazz, considered the American instrumental music most reflecting the influence of blacks. By World War I, the blues tradition had added the harmonica and European reed and brass instruments such as the clarinet, trombone, tuba, and trumpet. Although artists like Scott Joplin integrated postwar African American innovations on the piano with certain European musical forms to produce ragtime ("Maple Leaf Rag," 1899; "Frog Legs Rag," 1911; and "Climax Rag," 1914), Ferdinand "Jelly Roll" Morton became known as the "the first true jazz composer," mainly because he wrote his arrangements down in musical notation. In 1902, Morton composed his first tune, the "New Orleans Blues." Three years later, he published his jazz compositions as *Jelly Roll Blues.*

The popularization of black music and dance was deeply rooted in the rise of blacks on the commercial stage. A variety of black minstrel shows, traveling road shows, vaudeville productions, carnivals, and small circuses employed blues singers and blues bands. W. C. Handy remarked, "All the best [black] talent of that generation came down the same drain. The composers, the singers, the musicians, the speakers, the stage performers—the musical show got them all." As early as 1865–1866, Brooker and Clayton's Georgia Minstrels became a success in the Northeast. Advertising itself as "The Only Simon Pure Negro Troupe in the World," the Georgia Minstrels paved the way for the rise of black minstrelsy. By the early 1870s, however, the white tavern owner Charles Callender had established the Callender Minstrels, which soon became known as the best of the black minstrel shows. Blacks also established their own minstrel companies—with names like the Plantation Minstrel Slave Troupe (1875) and the Refined Colored Minstrels (1890)—but they found it difficult to compete with white companies and were usually short-lived.

The cakewalk epitomized the minstrel show's contribution to the spread of black dance to a wider white audience. The cakewalk mimicked the antebellum plantation dance, where enslaved blacks dressed in the castoff clothes of their owners and imitated European-style dances. White, and later black, minstrels carried these dance steps across the country and overseas. Culture critic Amiri Baraka raises a key question about the meaning of the cakewalk:

> If the cakewalk is a Negro dance caricaturing certain white customs, what is that dance when, say, a white theater company attempts to satirize it as a Negro dance? I find the idea of white minstrels in black-face satirizing a dance satirizing themselves a remarkable kind of irony.

The earliest and most widely known black male and female performers launched their careers on the minstrel stage. Billy Kersands and Wallace King emerged as two of the most well-known postbellum black minstrel stars, and James Bland became the most prolific songwriter for the black minstrel shows. Singers like Gertrude "Ma" Rainey, Jelly Roll Morton, and others facilitated the movement of black music and dance out of its indigenous settings into a broader arena. "Ma" Rainey became widely known when she joined the Rabbit Foot Minstrels and later mentored Bessie Smith, described as the most famous of all the classic blues singers. Although women dominated the classical blues styles that reached wider white audiences, black men dominated the earlier forms associated with country life, labor, and leisure, but these men would soon follow the women on recording labels of the emerging race record companies. The most highly paid black minstrels earned nearly as much as whites, but most received far less than their white counterparts. Moreover, although the emergence of small management agencies like the Theater Owners Booking Association (TOBA) arranged for black artists to perform before all-black audiences in the South and North, the returns were minimal, leading some black performers to dub the TOBA as "Tough on Black Artists." And although black performers like the comedian Bert Williams would make the transition to the predominantly white vaudeville circuits during the early twentieth century, most found their opportunities limited to predominantly black audiences.

Painters, Sculptors, and Sports Figures

In addition to dance, music, and literature, other blacks gained recognition as painters, sculptors, and professional sports figures. Mary Edmonia "Wildfire" Lewis became the first major sculptress of African American and Native American descent. Although she spent most of her professional life in Europe, the themes of slavery and racial oppression informed her accomplished marble works. In 1866, she produced *The Free Woman and Her Child* (1866), and a year later *Forever Free* (1867) at Howard University. Both reflect a preoccupation with the meaning of emancipation. The Philadelphia-born Meta Vaux Warrick Fuller became one of the nation's first studio sculptors. Although Fuller received part of her training in Paris (1899–1902) and initially focused on European themes, she gradually returned to African American topics and in 1907 won a gold medal for her diorama (150 figures) of progress at the black pavilion of the Jamestown Centennial Exposition. She also became the first black woman artist to receive a federal commission. The Pittsburgh-born painter Henry O. Tanner became a renowned artist after spending five years at the Julian Academy in Paris. Before embarking on his Paris studies, Tanner had produced works like *The Banjo Lesson* (1893), which promised to establish him as an artist of African American themes. In Paris, however, he turned to religious subjects, which included his famous *Resurrection of Lazarus, Christ on the Road to Bethany,* and *Christ at the Home of Mary and Martha.* For his achievements, Tanner received election to the National Academy of Design, suggesting that some whites recognized that artistic excellence was by no means limited by color.

African American artistic and cultural activities took on increasing symbolic significance as they aspired to compete on equal terms with their white counterparts. This process gained perhaps its most powerful expression in the sports world. Early black sports figures included Isaac Murphy, who had won the Kentucky Derby in 1884, 1890, and 1891. Murphy had also won the American Derby, the more prestigious event at the time, four out of five years between 1884 and 1888. During the early twentieth century, however, the boxing career of Jack Johnson took on the greatest symbolic importance. In 1908, Johnson became the first black heavyweight champion of the world when he defeated Tommy Burns in Sidney, Australia. Before some twenty-six thousand fans, Johnson also anticipated the late-twentieth-century

Jack Johnson became the first black heavyweight boxing champion of the world. Here Johnson (*right*) defends his crown against Jim Jeffries in Reno, Nevada, 1908. Race riots broke out after Johnson knocked out Jeffries in the twenty-fifth round. *Library of Congress*

style of Muhammad Ali by smiling and taunting his opponent. Following Johnson's victory, whites frantically searched for "a great white hope" to regain the crown. In the *New York Herald* and *Globe,* the novelist Jack London advocated the return of the retired undefeated champion Jim Jeffries to the ring. According to London, only Jeffries could beat Johnson and wipe "the Negro's golden smile" from his face.

Although Johnson was the reigning champion, Jeffries refused to fight him on an equal footing. Jeffries insisted on a 60-40 purse, with the black champion receiving the lower amount. On 4 July 1910, Johnson fought Jeffries in front of a sell-out crowd in Reno, Nevada. When Johnson knocked Jeffries out in the twenty-fifth round, riots broke out in Reno and across the country as blacks celebrated his victory and whites took offense. Although Johnson became a folk hero within the black community, whites despised him and conspired to bring him down. Johnson's open relationship with white women helped to fuel racial animosity toward him. Indeed, for his involvement with white women, Johnson was soon convicted and jailed under the federal Mann Act, ostensibly for transporting women across state lines for immoral purposes. After his release on bail, Johnson left the country for Canada and later for Europe but retained his heavyweight crown until 1915.

NEW IDEOLOGICAL, CLASS, AND SOCIAL STRUGGLES

Jack Johnson's victory not only symbolized the intensification of race consciousness and solidarity among African Americans. His independence and insistence on being his own man clashed with the moral sensibilities of large numbers of educated and middle-class African Americans who had hoped that Johnson would set a moral example for the race. Recent historians call black elites' preoccupation with moral example the "politics of respectability." Indeed, Johnson's career exposed intra- no less than interracial cleavages within African American society.

Class and Color Distinctions

Class, color, and status distinctions influenced virtually every aspect of African American institutional, cultural, and political life. By the late nineteenth and early twentieth centuries, for example, black elites had formed their own exclusive social clubs, which often restricted membership by color as well as class. Color distinctions took hold in Cleveland's Caterers Club (1903) and Euchre Club (1904); Chicago's Old Settler's Club (1902), Appomattox Club (1900), and Manasseh Society; and Detroit's Summer Club and Oak and Ivy Club (c. 1890s). At the same time, established AME and Baptist churches gradually moved into relatively imposing edifices, whereas the newer, smaller, and struggling working-class congregations took up residence in homes and low-rent storefronts. Although this process of differentiation proceeded further among the AME congregations—Bethel in Pittsburgh, Allen Temple in Cincinnati, and Quinn Chapel in Louisville, for example—than among the Baptists, the latter also exhibited growing class differentiation: Cincinnati's Union Baptist (formerly First Baptist), Fifth Street Baptist in Louisville, and Ebenezer Baptist in Pittsburgh. Established elite churches employed relatively well-educated ministers, whom they paid a substantial salary; erected new edifices; and expanded their social and religious programs. Members of Pittsburgh's Ebenezer Baptist Church paid their pastor, Reverend George Howard, an annual salary of $4,000 and contributed $16,000 per year toward maintenance of the edifice. In Cincinnati, Allen Temple purchased an edifice formerly owned by Sephardic Jews, replete with expensive carpets, several chandeliers (worth $1,000 each), pipe organs, and frescoes. The value of the property increased from $40,000 at the time of purchase in 1870 to $80,000 in the 1890s.

The formal services, language, dress, and decor of the elite AME and Baptist churches contrasted with the informal modes of worship at the predominantly working-class churches. In addition, the emotional services of black churches provoked increasing resistance and criticism from the young and educated members of the black community. One preacher lamented that some twenty-five black school teachers had deserted his church because so many ex-slaves worshipped there and dominated the services. Educated blacks increasingly articulated the belief that the young generation would need more than emotionalism to satisfy their religious needs. As one commentator put it, "With their enlarged intellectual life, they [young people] are naturally craving for a higher order of pulpit instruction. Their fathers were satisfied to be happy," but the children were "less emotional and excitable."

Black elite sensibilities were partly related to interactions with white philanthropists, benefactors, and/or missionaries. From the outset of emancipation, the American Missionary Association teachers set up Bible classes and campaigned against what they called "heathenish habits such as shouting" and other "un-Christian practices." Such teachers regularly reported on behavior that they deemed unfitting for Christians, including the way one funeral mourner "clapped her hands threw them over her head screaming 'glory to God' . . . dancing up and down in front of the pulpit." As such criticisms took hold, some African Americans turned away from spirituals, which they perceived as songs reflecting their slave past. Indeed, the spirituals gradually gave way to a new era of gospel music. Whereas earlier songs showed a preoccupation with rivers, the new songs gradually incorporated the railroad and other changes associated with freedom, industrialization, and the growing urbanization of the black population. Songs now included phrases like "getting on board the Gospel train" and "rumbling through the land." Moreover, the spirituals were increasingly sung by well-rehearsed professional choirs like the Fisk Jubilee Singers and similar groups at Hampton and other black colleges. Jubilee singers took the spirituals out of their communal setting and shared them with audiences across the United States and western Europe.

Black business and professional people regularly railed against dancing, drinking, gambling, and prostitution as detrimental to their efforts to build better race relations and improve the image of the race. In New York and other cities, these blacks frequently described the newcomers as a "hoodlum element," "rovers," "wanderers," "vagrants," and "criminals in search of the sporting life." In 1905, an editorial in the *New York Age* exclaimed: "Many of the worthless people of the race are making their way northward." In Milwaukee, one black newspaper editor called them "a floating, shiftless, and depraved element." The editor concluded on an antimigration note: "We do not . . . decry the Northern migration . . . but we would impress upon our Southern brethren and sisters to locate in the smaller towns and villages." Cities, these blacks believed, undercut the "morals, mind, and manners" of black workers and made them less productive and less law-abiding citizens than they could be. Consequently, middle-class blacks spearheaded a number of law and order societies: the Baltimore Colored Law and Order League, the Texas Law and Order League, the Michigan Co-operative League, and the Cincinnati National Negro Reform League and Criminal Elimination Society. In its statement of purpose, the Cincinnati organization defined old residents as the "better class" and newcomers as the "criminal class." More specifically, the organization aimed "to assist in the protection of the commonwealth from the criminal class of Negroes, to help the better class of Negroes distinguish itself from the bad citizens; to insure the arrest and conviction of lawbreakers and assist the innocent; and to protect young colored women."

Although poor and working-class blacks developed their own ethical standards, fought criminality, and moved to protect their women and children, they defied middle-class injunctions against their dance, music, and lifestyles. As black farmers and farm laborers moved into southern and northern cities in rising numbers, they elaborated on the rural "jook joint" by forming its urban variant, "the honky-tonk." These establishments proliferated in southern cities like New Orleans, Charleston, Memphis, Mobile, and Birmingham. According to contemporary black musicians like Jelly Roll Morton, the honky-tonks offered access to food, liquor, gambling, and prostitutes. Moreover, although these establishments attracted a mix of rural and urban people, patrons were predominantly wage-earning industrial workers—lumbermen, railroad laborers, and iron workers, among others. Born in 1893, the dancer Coot Grant later recalled her father's honky-tonk in turn-of-the-century Birmingham:

> I had already cut out a peephole in the wall so I could watch the dancers in the back room. They did everything. I remember the Slow Drag, of course, that was very popular—hanging on each other and just barely moving. Then they did the Fanny Bump, Buzzard Lope, Fish Tail, Eagle Rock, Itch, Shimmy, Squat, Grind, Moche, Funky Butt, and a million others. And I watched and imitated all of them.

By contrast, although the dances of black elites sometimes included a toned-down cakewalk, they invariably featured European-oriented music and dances—quadrilles, waltzes, polkas, cotillions, and schottisches.

By the early twentieth century, as municipalities imposed stricter licensing on dance halls and places of leisure, after-hours joints increasingly supplemented the honky-tonks and offered a similar range of music, dance, drinks, and food. The food usually included the staples that blacks brought from the farm: collard greens, cabbage, beans, chitlins (chitterlings—the small intestines of pigs), cornbread, fried fish, pigs' feet, and especially fried chicken. The blues, rag, jazz, and a variety of black dances emerged out of these settings and underlay the fame of well-known pioneers like W. C. Handy, Bessie Smith, "Ma" Rainey, and others. In New Orleans, class and color were especially prominent. The Creoles (light-skinned "downtown" blacks) played European-style instruments, but "uptown" dark-skinned blacks modified these instruments to fit the blues tradition. When segregationist ordinances hit the city in the 1890s, Creoles were expelled from white settings and forced to accommodate to the bluesmen and -women. New Orleans violinist Paul Dominguez explained:

> See, us Downtown people, we didn't think so much of this rough Uptown jazz until we couldn't make a living otherwise. . . . I don't know how they [poorly educated blues people] do it. But goddam, they'll do it. Can't tell you what's there on the paper, but just play the hell [out] of it.

The lives of black workers and poor remained deeply enmeshed in a rich oral culture. They carried the antebellum stories, anecdotes, and jokes forward into the postbellum era. The trickster animal tales persisted well into the twentieth century, but black oral folklore also changed under the shifting circumstances of freedom. In a Texas version of the trickster tale, the landowner became the "Bear," and the black sharecropper became "Brother Rabbit." When the landowner tried to trick the sharecropper out of his earnings, he found himself undone:

> De fust year I rents to de ole Rabbit, I makes de tops my sheer, en ole Rabbit planted 'taters; so I gits nothin' but vines. Den I rents ergin, en der Rabbit is to hab de tops, en I de bottoms, en ole Rabbit plants oats; so I gits nothin' but straw. But I sho is got dat ole Rabbit dis time. I gits both de tops en de bottoms, en de ole Rabbit gits only de middles. I'se bound ter git 'im dis time. Jes' den de old Bear come ter de field. He stopped. He look at hit. He shet up his fist. He cuss en he say, "Dat derned little scoundrel! He done went en planted dat fiel' in corn."

Whereas the trickster figure normally outwitted his opponents during the antebellum era, he now faced increasing difficulties. In one postbellum version of the "Brother Rabbit" tale, the Fox catches on to his tricks and delights in having a "Coon" carry Rabbit to the chopping block and cut his head off. Another postbellum version has Brother Rabbit losing out to the alligator: "Brother Gater went to work and run Brother Rabbit down an' grind up his bones."

At the same time that free blacks modified the old slave tales, they created new postbellum heroes and heroines. These stories often revolved around love, loyalty, and male-female relations as well as intragender relations. During the late nineteenth century, the story of Frankie and Johnny (also known as Frankie and Albert) gained widespread attention:

> First time she shot him, he staggered,
> Next time she shot him, he fell,
> Third time she shot him, O Lawdy,
> There was new man's face in hell.
> She killed her man,
> For doing her wrong.

At about the same time, but later in the nineteenth century, the bad man Stagolee emerged. Despite numerous versions of the tale, a gun battle between Stagolee and a gambling opponent made up the core. When his opponent won the game and the prize, a Stetson hat, Stagolee takes the man's life, despite the man's plea for mercy: "What do I care for yo' children / what do I care fo' yo' wife / You take my new Stetson hat / an' I'm goin' take yo' life." By the late nineteenth century, however, John Henry had become the most revered black hero. The use of large numbers of black workers on the Chesapeake and Ohio Railroad gave rise to the John Henry tale. Exslaves drilled through thick mountainous rock to create the Big Bend Tunnel. When completed in 1872, the Big Bend, a mile and a quarter long, was the longest tunnel in the United States. The John Henry songs not only elaborated on the man's legendary strength and even his sexual prowess but also symbolized the black man's heroic effort to counteract the impact of mechanization, particularly the steam-driven hammer, on his livelihood. As one version of the song puts it:

The man that invented the steam drill
He thought he was mighty fine.
John Henry sunk the steel fourteen feet
While the steam drill only made nine, O Lord,
While the steam drill only made nine.

Differences Among Black Leaders

The tensions between black workers and the black middle class were aggravated by the emergence of cleavages among black elites themselves. An old black economic and political elite with ties to a white clientele increasingly gave way to a new black elite with a predominantly black clientele. The two groups developed overlapping but contrasting strategies for social change. As suggested in Chapter 11, the rise of Jim Crow and the disfranchisement movement provoked a crisis in black leadership. As white Republican allies deserted the black cause, a new generation of black business and professional people increasingly challenged the ideas of the old leadership. Although Frederick Douglass symbolized the old leadership until his death in 1895, Booker T. Washington, a former bondsman, articulated the views of a rising new elite. In 1895, following his famous speech at the Atlanta Cotton Exposition, Booker T. Washington emerged as the chief spokesperson for the idea of economic self-help and racial solidarity. Washington urged blacks to put down their buckets where they were, cooperate with southern elites, eschew politics, and build a new independent institutional structure within the black community: "In all things purely social we [blacks and whites] can be as separate as the fingers, yet one as the hand in all things essential to mutual progress." Washington accented industrial education as a route out of sharecropping into the independent artisan class, and finally into the landowning class. Only then, he argued, by providing quality labor, services, and products, would blacks gain the "respect" and "power" necessary for demanding full citizenship rights.

Washington's ideas were by no means new. In 1873, the Episcopal minister Alexander Crummell of St. Luke's Church in Washington, D.C., returned to the United States after spending twenty years in Liberia. Crummell now rejected colonization in Africa, urging blacks to unite for industrial development, "for securing trades for youth, for joint-stock companies, for manufacturing, for the production of the great staples of the land, and . . . for mental and moral improvement." Two years later, black newspaper editors met in Cincinnati, Ohio, and advocated a strategy of self-help, racial solidarity, and landownership. In 1879, a Nashville convention recommended "to the youth of our race the observations of strict morality, temperate habits, and the practice of the acquisition of land, the acquiring of agriculture, of advancing to mercantile positions, and forcing their way into various productive channels of literature, art, science and mechanics." Educated at Hampton Institute, Washington later stated: "The idea of industrial education . . . beginning for our people at Hampton, has gradually spread until . . . it has permeated the whole race in every section of the country."

Booker T. Washington, a former slave and founder of the Tuskegee Institute in Alabama, emerged as the chief spokesperson for ideas of racial solidarity and economic "self-help." This statue stands on the Tuskegee campus. *Courtesy of the Tuskegee Institute*

Although few black leaders during the time took exception to the idea of industrial education for blacks, growing numbers rejected Washington's brand of leadership. By the turn of the twentieth century, the scholar and activist W. E. B. Du Bois, *Boston Guardian* editor William Monroe Trotter, and Harry C. Smith of the *Cleveland Gazette,* among others, offered powerful critiques of Washington's leadership. In *The Souls of Black Folk,* Du Bois exposed the limitations of Washington's philosophy in a chapter entitled "Of Mr. Booker T. Washington and Others." Du Bois decried Washington's willingness to forgo the franchise, downplay protest against civil rights violations, and elevate industrial over higher education. As Du Bois stated:

The question then comes. Is it probable that nine millions of men can make effective progress in economic lines if they are deprived of political rights, made a servile caste, and allowed only the most meager chance for developing their exceptional men? If history and reason give any distinct answer to these questions, it is an emphatic no.

Still, Du Bois urged blacks to oppose some but not all of Washington's ideas. Du Bois largely accepted Washington's ideas for the masses of poor and working-class blacks but opposed his stand on civil rights and education for a black "talented tenth":

> So far as Mr. Washington preaches Thrift, Patience, and Industrial Training for the masses, we must hold up his hands and strive with him. . . . But so far as Mr. Washington apologizes for injustice, North or South, does not rightly value the privilege and duty of voting, belittles the emasculating effects of caste distinctions, and oppose the higher training and ambition of our brighter minds—so far as he, the South, the Nation, does this—we must unceasingly and firmly oppose them.

In short, Du Bois urged blacks to maintain the struggle for equal rights, particularly the franchise and access to higher education. In his view, only by civil rights agitation could blacks hope to move out of laboring jobs and into the professions as educators, doctors, lawyers, and writers.

As Washington's critics gained adherents, they searched for new vehicles to give their ideas organized expression. In 1905, under the leadership of W. E. B. Du Bois, twenty-nine African Americans met at Fort Erie, Canada, and formed the Niagara movement. The group urged blacks "to complain, and to complain loudly and insistently" about racial inequality: "We refuse to allow the impression to remain that the Negro-American assents to inferiority, is submissive under oppression and apologetic before insults—the voice of protest of ten million Americans must never [cease] to assail the ears of their fellows so long as America is unjust." The Niagara movement convened in Harpers Ferry in 1906, Boston in 1907, and in Oberlin the following year. In 1909, most members of the Niagara movement, except William Monroe Trotter, answered the call of white activist William English Walling and formed the interracial National Association for the Advancement of Colored People (NAACP). Walling became the organization's first president, while Du Bois became editor of *Crisis* magazine, its radical organ of public and organizational opinion. Under its energetic leadership, the NAACP soon launched a vigorous antilynching campaign, opposed disfranchisement, and attacked Jim Crow.

Before the Niagara movement and formation of the NAACP, black women had taken a leading role in the antilynching crusade. Their efforts also fueled the rise of the Niagara movement and the NAACP. In 1889, Ida Bell Wells (later Barnett) became editor and part owner of the newspaper *Memphis Free Speech*. Her articles offered a sharp critique of southern injustice, particularly lynchings, and led to threats on her life and the burning and destruction of her newspaper office in 1892. Wells then moved to Chicago, where she continued her militant campaign against lynching and other forms of racial injustice in the South and the nation (see box). She later participated in the founding meetings of both the Niagara movement and the NAACP. Moreover, she linked her interest in racial justice with an equally diligent fight for woman's suffrage. Although other black women like Mary Church Terrell, a leader in the women's club movement, supported Washington's call for self-help, they soon rejected his plea to downplay politics and civil rights protests and reinforced the militant efforts of Ida Bell Wells.

Even as the influence of W. E. B. Du Bois, Ida Bell Wells, and other civil rights activists expanded, they did not eclipse the impact of Booker T. Washington. By the turn of the twentieth century, Washington had gained control of the Afro-American Council and helped to curtail its militant tactics, partly by covertly supporting voting rights, condemning mob violence, and taking "an active behind-the-scenes" role in opposing segregation on railroad cars and the exclusion of blacks from jury service. Washington's influence was also apparent in the work of the New York–based National Urban League, which aimed to assist migrants as they made the transition from farm to city. Formed in 1910 under the philanthropic efforts of Ruth Standish Baldwin, the widow of a New York railroad industrialist, and Dr. George E. Haynes, a black social work professional, the Urban League gained substantial assistance from philanthropist Julius Rosenwald, a Tuskegee Institute board

William Edward Burghardt Du Bois, the first black American to gain a Ph.D. in history from Harvard University. Du Bois also exposed the political and social limitations of Booker T. Washington's ideas and advocated militant protest for full citizenship rights. *Archives of the University of Massachusetts at Amherst*

SOURCES FROM THE PAST

1895

Ida Bell Wells Barnett Protests Lynchings

Not all or nearly all of the murders done by white men, during the past thirty years in the South, have come to light, but the statistics as gathered and preserved by white men, and which have not been questioned, show that during these years more than ten thousand Negroes have been killed in cold blood, without the formality of judicial trial and legal execution. And yet, as evidence of the absolute impunity with which the white man dares to kill a Negro, the same record shows that during all these years, and for all these murders only three white men have been tried, convicted, and executed. As no white man has been lynched for the murder of colored people, these three executions are the only instances of the death penalty being visited upon white men for murdering Negroes.

Naturally enough the commission of these crimes began to tell upon the public conscience, and the Southern white man, as a tribute to the nineteenth century civilization, was in a manner compelled to give excuses for his barbarism. His excuses have adapted themselves to the emergency, and are aptly outlined by that greatest of all Negroes, Frederick Douglass, in a article of recent date, in which he shows that there have been three distinct eras of Southern barbarism, to account for which three distinct excuses have been made.

The first excuse given to the civilized world for the murder of unoffending Negroes was the necessity of the white man to repress and stamp out alleged "race riots." . . .

From 1865 to 1872, hundreds of colored men and women were mercilessly murdered and the almost invariable reason assigned was that they met their death by being alleged participants in an insurrection or riot. But this story at last wore itself out. No insurrection ever materialized; no Negro rioter was ever apprehended and proven guilty, and no dynamite ever recorded the black man's protest against oppression and wrong. . . .

Then came the second excuse, which had its birth during the turbulent times of reconstruction. By an amendment to the Constitution the Negro was given the right of franchise, and, theoretically at least, his ballot became his invaluable emblem of citizenship. . . . "No Negro domination" became the new legend on the sanguinary banner of the sunny South, and under it rode the Ku Klux Klan, the Regulators, and the lawless mobs, which for any cause chose to murder one man or a dozen as suited their purpose best. It was a long, gory campaign. . . .

. . . With the Southern governments all subverted and the Negro actually eliminated from all participation in state and national elections, there could be no longer an excuse for killing Negroes to prevent "Negro Domination."

Brutality still continued; Negroes were whipped, scourged, exiled, shot and hung whenever and wherever it pleased the white man so to treat them, and as the civilized world with increasing persistency held the white people of the South to account for its outlawry, the murderers invented the third excuse—that Negroes had to be killed to avenge their assaults upon women. . . .

Humanity abhors the assailant of womanhood, and this charge upon the Negro at once placed him beyond the pale of human sympathy. . . .

Source: I. W. Barnett, *A Red Record* (Chicago, 1895), pp. 8–15.

member and friend of Booker T. Washington. Rosenwald helped to strengthen the link between the Urban League and the Tuskegee Institute by sponsoring annual trips to Tuskegee's graduation ceremonies.

ALTHOUGH AFRICAN AMERICANS PARTICIPATED in numerous multiclass ideological and social struggles, they also carved out their own specific class- and status-based responses to racial proscription. In addition to distinctions in modes of worship, music, dance, and leisure time activities, African Americans engaged in heated debates about appropriate strategies for social change. These debates were not limited to struggles over disfranchisement, segregated institutions, and racial violence. They were also related to issues of economic justice, as discussed in Chapter 12. Although growing numbers of poor and working-class blacks supported migration to urban centers, black business and professional people opposed mass migration strategies for social change. Black elites in the urban North and West also discouraged southern black migration. In their view, the onslaught of southern blacks would aggravate race relations and undermine their precarious status within the urban political economy. As African Americans transformed themselves into "New Negroes" during World War I and its aftermath, discussed in Part V, they would heighten as well as bridge these social cleavages.

PART V

Migration, Depression, and World Wars

1915–1945

Beginning gradually during the late nineteenth and early twentieth centuries, black population movement turned into the Great Migration during World Wars I and II. Although the Great Migration represented a massive protest against the injustices of the segregationist system, it was also closely intertwined with certain changes in the larger industrial economy and politics of the nation and the African American community itself. The dramatic curtailment of European immigration, the draft of large numbers of prime working-age men, the escalating overseas demand for American manufactured products during wartime, and the emergence of activist black communities and social networks in the urban North and West all helped to create new employment opportunities for black workers in the industrial sector of the nation's economy. For the first time, mass production industries like meatpacking, steel, and automobiles absorbed the bulk of black workers.

Although African Americans improved their lot by taking jobs in urban industries, they nonetheless entered the industrial economy at the lowest rungs of the occupational ladder. Moreover, as their numbers increased in northern and western cities, they faced growing restrictions on where they could find homes, educate their children, and gain access to essential social services and public accommodations. Partly because they anticipated a much better life in what many referred to as the "Promised Land," African Americans escalated their struggle against social injustice. Their activities included a variety of "New Negro" movements during the 1920s, participation in the Democratic party's New Deal coalition during the 1930s, and the March on Washington movement (MOWM) and the "Double V" campaign for victory at home and victory abroad during World War II.

Although the interwar struggle against inequality entailed substantial internal tensions and social conflicts, it formed the communal, institutional, and leadership foundation for the rise of the modern civil rights movement. Part V examines the impact of the Great Migration, the two world wars, and the Great Depression on the African American experience.

CHAPTER 15

∽

The Great Migration

World War I opened up new opportunities for African Americans in the nation's major industrial centers. As European nations mobilized for war, they heightened the demand for American manufactured products. At the same time, the European conflict disrupted established patterns of immigration to the United States and stimulated the search for national sources of labor. In 1917, when the United States declared war on Germany and initiated its own mobilization of young men for war, industrialists found it even more difficult to meet their wartime labor needs and turned to southern black workers. Moreover, after a brief economic downturn in the early postwar years, black migration resumed during the 1920s, when the U.S. government passed immigration restriction legislation and the urban economy dramatically expanded. For the first time in U.S. history, African Americans broke the agricultural and domestic "job ceiling" and moved into the industrial sector—iron, steel, automobile, meatpacking, and other mass production industries—in large numbers.

As the Great Migration accelerated, racial hostility intensified and undercut the upward mobility of African Americans. Compared with American-born whites, immigrants, and their children, African Americans occupied the lowest rungs of the industrial ladder and faced increasing discrimination in the social, institutional, cultural, and political life of the city. As earlier, however, African American urban life was not only shaped by the attitudes, policies, and practices of white industrialists, labor unions, and the state. It was also influenced by the political activities, culture, and consciousness of African Americans themselves. Although African Americans celebrated the Great Migration as an "escape from Egypt" and "a journey to the Promised Land," the increasing urbanization of the black population was by no means an unmixed blessing. It was fraught with a variety of inter- and intraracial class, cultural, and gender conflicts and forms of inequality.

AFRICAN AMERICANS AND WORLD WAR I

In April 1917, when President Woodrow Wilson asked Congress for a declaration of war against Germany to secure the "foundations" of "political liberty," African Americans rallied behind the nation's war effort. They believed that victory for Germany would spell "death to the aspirations of Negroes and all the darker races for equality, freedom and democracy." Lieutenant Colonel Charles Young, the highest-ranking black officer in the U.S. Army, exhorted blacks to fight now and take up "the cause" of social justice, then protest "when the storm is past." In a *Crisis* editorial, W. E. B. Du Bois urged African Americans to "close ranks," support the war, and forgo their own struggle for equal rights for the duration of the war:

> Let us, while this war lasts, forget our special grievances and close our ranks shoulder to shoulder with our white fellow citizens and the allied nations that are fighting for democracy. We make no ordinary sacrifice, but we make it gladly and willingly with our eyes lifted to the hills.

By war's end some 2.3 million black men had registered for the draft. An estimated 370,000 had served in the armed forces. This represented a 34 percent rate of acceptance for blacks, compared with a 24 percent rate of acceptance among whites. Some 540 officers and men of the Ninety-Third Division had received commendations for meritorious service and valor from either the French or the U.S. government. The 369th Infantry Regiment alone had lost 851 men in five days of heavy fighting. The unit's commander reported that the men had spent 191 days at the front, a record for regiments in the American Expeditionary Force. Called the "Hell Fighters," New York's 369th was the only regiment of the war allowed to fly a state flag; the only U.S. unit awarded the French command's highest mark of honor, the Croix de Guerre; and the regiment selected to lead the Allied march against the Germans to the Rhine River.

As blacks prepared for war and closed ranks with the nation, some whites expressed their gratitude by offering support for a different racial order after the war. When the 371st Infantry departed Camp Jackson, South Carolina, a Mississippi sergeant declared: "I'm done talking about niggers. These boys have been fine soldiers here, and if they ever get back from France, I'm big enough to lick any man who don't give 'em a square deal." But most whites determined that the war would not change the racial order. In New Orleans, a white man spoke for the vast majority of whites when he declared: "You niggers are wondering how you are going to be treated after the war. Well, I'll tell you, you are going to be treated exactly like you were before the war." Indeed, despite immense sacrifices on the battlefield and at home from the outset of hostilities (see map), African Americans faced a plethora of obstacles within and outside the military.

Although African Americans made up less than 10 percent of the population, they contributed nearly 13 percent of all draftees. Local draft boards routinely

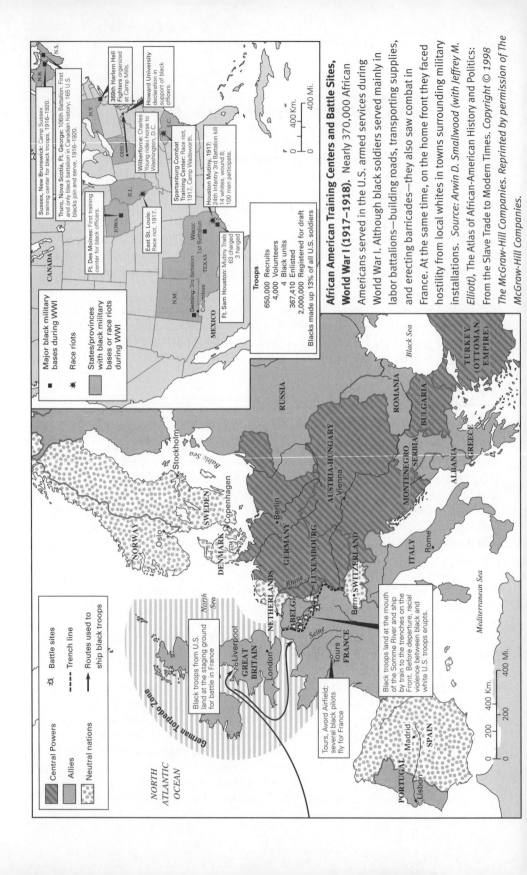

African American Training Centers and Battle Sites, World War I (1917–1918). Nearly 370,000 African Americans served in the U.S. armed services during World War I. Although black soldiers served mainly in labor battalions—building roads, transporting supplies, and erecting barricades—they also saw combat in France. At the same time, on the home front they faced hostility from local whites in towns surrounding military installations. *Source: Arwin D. Smallwood (with Jeffrey M. Elliott),* The Atlas of African-American History and Politics: From the Slave Trade to Modern Times. *Copyright © 1998 The McGraw-Hill Companies. Reprinted by permission of The McGraw-Hill Companies.*

Sussex, New Brunswick: Camp Sussex training center for black troops, 1916–1920.

Truro, Nova Scotia, Ft. George: 106th Battalion. First and only black battalion in Canadian history; 165 U.S. blacks join and serve, 1916–1920.

369th Harlem Hell Fighters organized at Camp Mills.

Howard University declaration in support of black officers.

Ft. Des Moines: First training center for black officers.

Wilberforce: Charles Young rides horse to Washington, D.C.

East St. Louis: Race riot, 1917.

Spartanburg Combat Training Center: Race riot, 1917, Camp Wadsworth.

Houston Mutiny, 1917: 24th Infantry 3rd Battalion kill 14 whites, wound 8; 100 men participate.

Deming: 3rd Battalion

Ft. Sam Houston: Mutiny Trials: 63 charged 3 hanged

Waco: 1st Battalion

Columbus

Troops

650,000 Recruits
4,000 Volunteers
4 Black units
367,410 Enlisted
2,000,000 Registered for draft
Blacks made up 13% of all U.S. soldiers

Major black military bases during WWI

Race riots

States/provinces with black military bases or race riots during WWI

Battle sites

Trench line

Routes used to ship black troops

Central Powers

Allies

Neutral nations

Black troops from U.S. land at the staging ground for battle in France

Tours, Avord Airfield; several black pilots fly for France

Black troops land at the mouth of the Somme River and ship by train to the trenches on the Front. Before departure, racial violence between black and white U.S. troops erupts.

German Torpedo Zone

NORTH ATLANTIC OCEAN

denied blacks exemptions from the draft while granting such exemptions to whites on the basis of dependents, medical disabilities, occupations, and even illiteracy. African Americans also served on a racially segregated and unequal basis. Secretary of War Newton D. Baker stated that the War Department would not disturb the established racial order. The army confined African American enlisted men to four all-black regiments, supplemented by several black National Guard units (notably the Illinois Eighth and the New York Fifteenth), and the all-black Ninety-Second and Ninety-Third Infantry Divisions. Moreover, as hostilities got under way, the War Department ordered the retirement of the highest-ranking black officer, Lieutenant Colonel Charles Young, on medical grounds. Young confided to W. E. B. Du Bois that his retirement was unjust and unwarranted: "No one in the regiment, either officer or [enlisted] man, believes me sick and no one save the doctors here at the hospital; not even the nurses." Although Young rode horseback from his home in Ohio to Washington, D.C., to prove his fitness, the army refused to reinstate him. Only under pressure from organizations like the NAACP did the government set up a black officer's training camp in Des Moines, Iowa. Still, although the army, and to some extent the navy, accepted large numbers of black enlisted men, the Army Air Corps, the Marine Corps, and the U.S. Army and Red Cross Nurses Corps excluded blacks. By war's end, only twenty-four black women had served in the nurses corps, compared with twenty-one thousand white nurses. Moreover, these black women had entered the corps just one month before the end of hostilities.

Although most African American soldiers served in segregated and poorly equipped labor regiments during World War I, some engaged in combat. These black troops are members of the 369th Infantry Regiment, near Maffrecourt, France, 1918. *National Archives*

On the home front, black enlisted men and officers faced a hostile environment on U.S. Army bases and in surrounding communities. White civilians and law enforcement officers regularly assaulted black servicemen and subjected them to verbal abuse. At Camp Logan in Houston, Texas, local whites harassed members of the all-black Third Battalion of the Twenty-Fourth Infantry. One white resident stated that "in Texas it costs twenty-five dollars to kill a buzzard and five dollars to kill a nigger." Policemen regularly targeted and arrested black soldiers for allegedly disobeying "Jim Crow signs." Racial tensions at Camp Logan intensified on 23 August 1917 when local police beat, shot at, and arrested Corporal Charles Baltimore, who had tried to investigate a police beating of a black soldier and a local black woman. Some one hundred black soldiers seized weapons, marched on the city, and confronted armed civilians and police. Four blacks lost their lives in the confrontation, and nearly sixteen whites died, four of them policemen. The War Department quickly disarmed the entire battalion and transferred the men to New Mexico. Thirteen of the men were soon tried, sentenced to death, and secretly hanged without a review of the proceedings by either the president or the War Department. By the trial's end, the military had hanged nineteen black men, sentenced sixty-three to life imprisonment, and handed down long prison terms to others. Only rising protests during the 1920s and 1930s would lead to the release of the incarcerated men.

Domestic patterns of race relations followed black men overseas. They traveled in the most poorly ventilated bottom holds of ships without mess facilities. On arrival, they worked long twelve- to sixteen-hour shifts, mainly as laborers—building roads, erecting barricades, and loading and unloading tons of cargo. Moreover, in addition to inadequate food, clothing, and shelter compared with their white counterparts, they faced racial hostility from white officers and enlisted men. On the arrival of black troops in France, U.S. officials issued a document entitled "Secret Information Concerning Black American Troops," which enjoined the French to isolate black soldiers: "We must not eat with them . . . must not shake hands with them or seek to talk or meet with them outside the requirements of military service." Most of all, the U.S. authorities urged the French to prohibit intimacy between black soldiers and white women. As the author of the document, Colonel Linard, put it, American opinion on the question was "unanimous" and did not permit "any discussion" of the matter. Even Du Bois soon cried out in the *Crisis* that "no land that loves to lynch 'niggers' can lead the hosts of almighty God."

MIGRATION TO THE NORTH, WEST, AND MIDWEST

Despite the nation's sorry response to black soldiers, World War I opened up new employment opportunities in northern industries and stimulated the Great Migration. Under the impact of World War I, an estimated 700,000 to 1 million blacks left the South for northern and western cities. Another 800,000 to 1 million departed during the 1920s. By 1930, an estimated 5.1 million blacks lived in cities, an increase from about 27 percent of all blacks in 1910 to over 43 percent as the

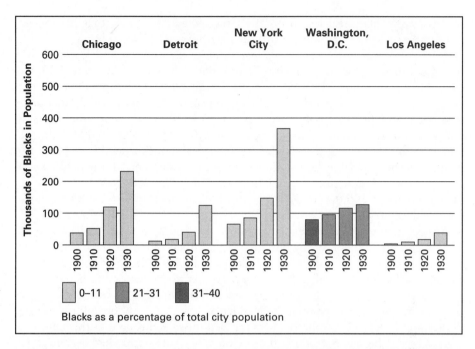

The Great Migration of African Americans from the South: Selected Northern and Western Cities, 1910–1930. An estimated 1.5 to 2 million blacks moved from the South to northern and western cities during World War I and the 1920s. Large cities such as Chicago, Detroit, New York, and Los Angeles absorbed the bulk of this black population growth.

Great Depression got under way. The editor of the *Atlanta Independent* articulated the views of black migrants:

> We will not hesitate to recite the fundamentals underlying the black movement North. In the first place, the Negro is a human being and citizen; [he] has aspirations, ambitions and intelligence in common with every other man. He knows that the . . . trend of legislation in every southern state has been to reduce the Negro to a serf, to unman him and to decitizenize him, to take from him every social, economic and political right enjoyed by other citizens.

In early 1916, in the *Biloxi Herald*, another writer urged Mississippians to make reforms: raise salaries, provide better educational facilities, offer fair treatment in the press, and by all means give blacks "an equal chance" in the courts of law. A Houston, Texas, writer made the same point, exhorting whites to "stop holding 'the Negro' up for ridicule." "[The Negro] dislikes and despises the terms 'nigger,' 'darky,' 'coon,' etc." In southern West Virginia, the editor of the black weekly *McDowell Times* enthusiastically supported black migration: "Let millions of Negroes leave the South. It will make conditions better for those who remain." A New York editor stated simply: "The real lesson of [the Great Migration] . . . is that [the South] must revise its whole attitude towards the Negro if it would keep him."

Blacks also moved to a broader range of cities in the West and Midwest than they did during the prewar years (see figure). Between World War I and 1930, Detroit's black population increased most dramatically. It rose by more than 600 percent during the war years and by another 200 percent during the 1920s, increasing from less than 6,000 in 1910 to over 120,000 in 1920. At the same time, the black population of Los Angeles jumped from under 8,000 to nearly 40,000. Nonetheless, as in the prewar era, New York City, Chicago, and Philadelphia continued to absorb disproportionately large numbers of black newcomers. Chicago's black population increased more than fivefold, from 44,000 to 234,000; New York City's trebled, from about 100,000 to 328,000; and Philadelphia's grew from 84,500 to an estimated 220,600.

Although white landowners referred to the South as "the Negro's Natural Home" and urged them to stay put, growing numbers of blacks voted for a greater measure of freedom with their feet. Under the editorship of Robert S. Abbott, the *Chicago Defender* emerged as the most vigorous promoter of black population movement (see the boxes on pages 381 and 383). During the war years, the *Defender* increased its reputation as a defender of "the race." Abbott built close relations with black Pullman porters, who traveled the rails throughout the nation. As early as September 1916, Abbott's promotion of black migration had become a crusade. In a front-page story, replete with a photograph of prospective black migrants crowding alongside a railroad track (see the photo on page 382), Abbott explained the exodus of black labor from the South: "The men tired of being kicked and cursed, are leaving by the thousands." In one editorial, the paper declared: "Anywhere in God's country is far better than the southland." Abbott encouraged southern blacks to move north even if they incurred an economic loss: "Every black man for the sake of his wife and daughters especially should leave even at a financial sacrifice every spot in the south where his worth is not appreciated enough to give him the standing of a man and a citizen in the community." The *Defender* portrayed the South in biblical terms as "the land of Egypt"—that is, the land of lynchings, disfranchisement, and economic exploitation—and the North as the "Promised Land" of hope, freedom, and citizenship. Abbott also appealed to the religious beliefs of prospective migrants by describing the journey north as "crossing Jordan."

Although a variety of socioeconomic, demographic, political, and cultural forces fueled black population movement, oppressive conditions in southern agriculture and the lure of higher wages in northern industries stood at the forefront of these forces. Most migrants came from the boll weevil–infested cotton regions of the Deep South, where African Americans captured the forces behind the migration in popular folklore:

Boll-weevil in de cotton
cut worm in de cotton
Debil in de white man
Wah's goin' on

SOURCES FROM THE PAST

1917

The Chicago Defender Advocates Black Migration to Northern Cities

To die from the bite of frost is far more glorious than at the hands of a mob. I beg you, my brother, to leave the benighted land. You are a free man. Show the world that you will not let false leaders lead you. Your neck has been in the yoke. Will you continue to keep it there because some "white folks' nigger" wants you to? Leave for all quarters of the globe. Get out of the South. Your being there in the numbers in which you are gives the southern politician too strong a hold on your progress. . . . So much has been said through the white papers in the South about the members of the race freezing to death in the North. They freeze to death down South when they don't take care of themselves. There is no reason for any human being staying in the Southland on this bugaboo handed out by the white press.

If you can freeze to death in the North and be free, why freeze to death in the South and be a slave, where your mother, sister and daughter are raped and burned at the stake; where your father, brother and sons are treated with contempt and hung to a pole, riddled with bullets at the least mention that he does not like the way he is treated. Come North then, all you folks, both good and bad. If you don't behave yourselves up here, the jails will certainly make you wish you had. For the hard-working man there is plenty of work—if you really want it. The *Defender* says come.

Source: In Emmett J. Scott, *Negro Migration During the War* (1920; reprint, New York: Arno Press, 1969), p. 31.

The states of Alabama, Mississippi, Louisiana, and Georgia gradually supplanted the Upper South and border state sources of black migrants. Moreover, unlike the prewar years, when economic growth favored the employment of female household workers, young men now outnumbered black women. In some northern industrial cities like Cleveland, Detroit, Buffalo, and Milwaukee, there were as many as 120 to 140 men (ages eighteen to forty-four) to every 100 women.

Wages in northern industries ranged from $3.00 to $5.00 per eight-hour day, compared with as little as 75 cents to $1.00 per day in southern agriculture. In southern industries, African Americans earned no more than $2.50 for a nine-hour day. In 1917, according to the Cincinnati Council of Social Agencies, nearly 75 percent of recent black newcomers reported that they came for better wages. Migrants invariably mentioned wages among other factors as a prime motivation for moving. A Shreveport, Louisiana, migrant desired to come north "to obtain better fre[e]dom and better pay." A Savannah, Georgia, migrant hoped "to find a good job where I can make a living as I cannot do here." Two Louisiana brothers, Matthew and William Malbrough, moved to the San Francisco Bay Area when they decided that they "could make more money and provide better" for their families in the Golden State than they could at home. On arriving in the North, higher wages

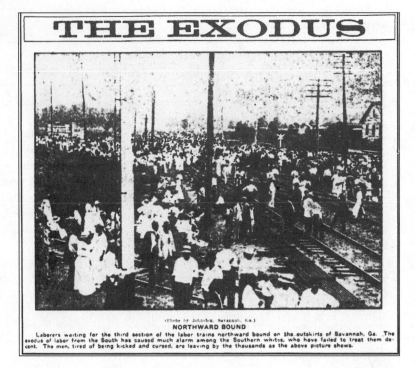

THE EXODUS

(Photo by Johnston, Savannah, Ga.)
NORTHWARD BOUND
Laborers waiting for the third section of the labor trains northward bound on the outskirts of Savannah, Ga. The exodus of labor from the South has caused much alarm among the Southern whites, who have failed to treat them decent. The men, tired of being kicked and cursed, are leaving by the thousands as the above picture shows.

The *Chicago Defender* depicts black migrants crowding alongside a railroad track. The editor explained, "The men, tired of being kicked and cursed, are leaving by the thousands."
Chicago Defender

prompted many southern blacks to write back home: "The (Col.) men are making good."

Despite the lure of higher wages in northern industry, migration north was a difficult and complicated undertaking. It involved the wartime labor policies of the federal government and industrial employers; northern black newspapers; and black kin, friend, and communal networks. The federal government encouraged the recruitment of southern black workers as a wartime emergency measure. On one day alone, 5 June 1917, the U.S. Selective Service processed for military service over 1.5 million young men of all nationalities between the ages of twenty-one and thirty. By war's end, nearly 4 million American men and a few women had joined the U.S. armed forces. At the same time, the number of immigrants from Europe had dropped from over 1 million in 1914 to only 198,000 in 1915, and to 141,000 in 1919.

As the draft of all young men escalated and European immigration plummeted, the U.S. Department of Labor helped northern industries recruit southern black workers. Although southern white employers and landowners resisted this practice, the Department of Labor concluded that black labor represented a valuable asset to the war effort. Near war's end, under pressure from African American civil rights groups, the government also created the Division of Negro Economics (DNE) in the Department of Labor. Under the direction of the black economist and sociologist George Edmund Haynes, the DNE enhanced black movement into the urban

SOURCES FROM THE PAST

1917

A Prospective Migrant Writes to the Chicago Defender

LUTCHER, LA., May 13, 1917.

Dear Sir: I have been reading the Chicago defender and seeing so many advertisements about the work in the north I thought to write you concerning my condition. I am working hard in the south and can hardly earn a living. I have a wife and one child and can hardly feed them. I thought to write and ask you for some information concerning how to get a pass for myself and family. I don't want to leave my family behind as I cant hardly make a living for them right here with them and I know they would fare hard if I would leave them. If there are any agents in the south there havent been any of them to Lutcher if they would come here they would get at least fifty men. Please sir let me hear from you as quick as possible. Now this is all. Please dont publish my letter, I was out in town today talking to some of the men and they say if they could get passes that 30 or 40 of them would come. But they havent got the money and they dont know how to come. But they are good strong and able working men. If you will instruct me I will instruct the other men how to come as they all want to work. Please dont publish this because we have to whisper this around among our selves because the white folks are angry now because the negroes are going north.

Source: "Letters of Negro Migrants," *Journal of Negro History,* 4 (July 1919): 296–297.

industrial sector of the nation's economy. Under the leadership of black clubwomen like Mary Church Terrell, black women also pushed for, but failed to obtain, a "Colored Women's Division" in the Women's Bureau of the Department of Labor.

Northern industrialists launched vigorous labor recruitment drives in the South. In the summer of 1916, the Pennsylvania and Erie Railroad recruited black labor for a variety of northern industries, including its own far-flung operations. Other railroad companies—the New York Central; the New Haven, Delaware and Hudson; and the Illinois Central—soon followed suit. Companies provided "free" transportation to black workers, who authorized the deduction of travel expenses from their paychecks. Although companies initially employed white labor agents, they gradually added black recruiters to the payrolls. Since southern states and municipalities had passed a variety of anti-enticement laws, which imposed huge fines for recruiting workers without a license, recruiters often had to work in secrecy. When the sociologist Charles S. Johnson toured Mississippi in 1917, he reported the activities of a black recruiter who "walk[ed] briskly down the street through a group of Negroes, and without turning his head would say in a low tone: 'Anybody want to go to Chicago, see me.'" In his portrait of black Cincinnati, the journalist William P. Dabney described the recruiting activities of Joseph L. Jones and Melvin J. Chisum. Dabney noted the dangers that they faced, as well as the tactics that they sometimes employed to escape harassment:

Upon Chisum devolved "the dirty work," that is, the job of going South to get the "goods." . . . He did an enormous business, ran a thousand risks. A price was set upon his life and liberty, but when cornered he would simulate a sweet simplicity, a servility that savored of the "good old days," as he talked with an unction and dialect that Uncle Tom would have envied. Thousands of Negroes were brought up by Chisum.

Ordinary poor and working-class black people debated the pros and cons of movement in a variety of settings—in barber and beauty shops; in poolrooms and grocery stores; in churches, lodge halls, and clubhouses; and in private homes, on front porches, and at a variety of work sites. Almost everywhere that they assembled, African Americans discussed, debated, and decided the merits and demerits of migration. Some turned to northern newspapers and social service agencies for assistance. In a letter to the *Defender,* a skilled worker from Mobile, Alabama, sought jobs for himself, his wife, and his brother-in-law:

> Dear Sir Bro . . . I am writeing to you for advice about comeing north. I am a brickmason and I can do cement work an stone work. . . . There is nothing here for the colored man but a hard time wich these southern crackers gives us. . . . My wife is a seamstress . . . my bro. in law want to get away to. He is a carpenter by trade.

In a letter to the Pittsburgh Urban League, one prospective migrant wrote for himself and seven other black men: "We Southern Negroes want to come to the north . . . they ain't giving a man nothing for what he do . . . they [white southerners] is trying to keep us down."

Married men often moved ahead of their families. They secured work and a place to stay before sending back or returning for kin and friends. A Burton, South Carolina, migrant was emphatic on this point: "I do not care to move family before I can locate myself, by coming and spend at least 6 months." In 1919, Joseph Griffin, a farmer from St. Landry Parish, Louisiana, moved his family to the San Francisco Bay Area city of Richmond, California. Shortly after arriving, Griffin purchased property, and his home soon became a magnet for other southern kin and friends. In his investigation of the Great Migration, the U.S. attorney for the Southern District of Alabama reported that at least 10 percent of those who had left had returned, but half of the returnees had come back for relatives and friends: "It is the returned negroes who carry others off." One South Carolina migrant recalled the impact that returnees had on his decision:

> I was plowin[g] in the field and it was real hot. And I stayed with some of the boys who would leave home and [come] back. . . . and would have money, and they had clothes. I didn't have that. We all grew up together. And I said, "Well, as long as I stay here I'm not going to get nowhere." And I tied that mule to a tree and caught a train.

Others pooled their money, bought tickets at reduced rates, and moved in groups. Since reduced railroad rates required groups of ten or more people, African Americans formed numerous migration clubs. Although most of these clubs were small, some were relatively large. In Hattiesburg, Mississippi, one *Defender* agent, barber, and church deacon organized a club of forty kin and friends, purchased tickets, and moved to Chicago. When one trainload of blacks crossed the Ohio River headed north, they knelt down to pray and sang the hymn "I done come out of the Land of Egypt with the Good News."

Although male employment dictated the direction of black migration, women shared decision making and sometimes determined the destination of their families. From South Carolina, a black woman wrote to a northern branch of the Urban League for her two sons: "[I have] two grown son[s] . . . we want to settle down somewhere north . . . wages are so cheap down here we can hardly live." In April 1917, a woman wrote from Biloxi, Mississippi, to a northern employer on behalf of her family:

Dear Sir . . . I am a good cook and can give good recommendation. . . . I could work my daughter a long with me. She is 21 years [old] and I have a husban all so and he is a fireman and want a positions. . . . I want to get out of this land of sufring I no there som thing that I can do—here there is nothing for me.

When her husband moved north in 1919, one black woman recalled her response and the final result:

I wrote him a letter back. My older sister had come to Pittsburgh, and I took her as a mother because I had lost my mother. And I wrote him back, and said, "I don't want to stay in Cincinnati. I want to go to Pittsburgh." Next letter I got, he had got a job in Pittsburgh and sent for me.

Black women also had their own specific reasons for leaving the South. In addition to working long hours at low pay, black domestics faced exploitation and verbal and physical abuse. Whereas freedom from lynch mobs figured prominently in the motives of black men and women, black women also sought freedom from sexual exploitation. Rape represented a distinctive form of violence for southern black women. According to one Deep South migrant woman, "Nobody was sent out before you was told to be careful of the white man or his sons. They'd tell you the stories of rape . . . no lies. You was to be told true, so you'd not get raped." Some women related abuse at the hands of black men as well as white. Sara Brooks, an Alabama migrant to Cleveland, Ohio, recalled how she left her husband for the third and final time:

When he hit me . . . I jumped outa the bed . . . I just ran. . . . I didn't have a gown to put on—I had on a slip and had on a short-sleeved sweater. I left the kids right there with him. . . . And I didn't go back.

Whereas black men often moved through a series of jobs in a variety of southern and northern cities before reaching their final destination, black women usually made one nonstop trip. Rather than traveling north alone, Sara Brooks traveled with a relative who came down from Cleveland to get her.

Despite increasing migration to northern and western cities, most blacks remained in the South. Fearing loss of their segregated clientele, some southern black business and professional people opposed mass migration. Robert R. Moton, head of Tuskegee Institute (later University), reinforced the views of his predecessor, Booker T. Washington, who had consistently argued that there was no "part of the world where . . . the masses of the Negro people would be better off than right here in these southern states." Moton celebrated the South as a land of "exceptional business opportunities" and "amazing progress" for the race. In December 1916, the black *Atlanta Independent* editorialized its position: "We are not in favor of wholesale migration. . . . We are going to stay in the South, for the reason it is our natural home and we have faith in its possibilities."

Between World War I and 1930, more black urbanites lived in southern than in northern and western cities. The number of blacks living in southern cities rose from 1.8 to nearly 3 million, about 1 million more than in northern and western cities combined. As one contemporary study of black migration noted, the mere fact that blacks had moved out of the rural South was no evidence that they had moved to a northern or western city. Southern cities like New Orleans, Jacksonville, Savannah, Memphis, and Birmingham "became concentration points" for blacks leaving outlying rural areas. They also served as major distribution points for blacks going north. Birmingham and Bessemer were the major launching points for blacks traveling north from Alabama. The Southern, Louisville, and Nashville Railroad; the St. Louis and San Francisco; and the Illinois Central all transported blacks northward from Birmingham and Bessemer. Cities like Columbus, Americus, and Albany served blacks leaving from west Georgia and east Alabama, while Valdosta, Waycross, Brunswick, and Savannah served a similar function for blacks leaving the counties of southern and eastern Georgia. Although most blacks remained in the South, growing numbers nonetheless devised ways to get out.

EXPANSION OF THE BLACK INDUSTRIAL WORKING CLASS

As blacks moved into northern cities in growing numbers, the black industrial working class dramatically expanded. Black men gained jobs in meatpacking, auto, steel, and other mass production industries. In Cleveland, Pittsburgh, Detroit, and Milwaukee, for example, the percentage of black men employed in industrial jobs increased from an estimated 10 to 20 percent of the black labor force in 1910 to about 60 to 70 percent in 1920 and 1930. In Cleveland, an official of the National Malleable Company reported: "In fact, there is no work in our shop that they cannot do and do well, [if] properly supervised."

As early as 1918, in western Pennsylvania, black steelworkers had increased from less than 3 percent of the total work force to 13 percent. Over 50 percent of these employees worked at Carnegie steel plants in Allegheny County and at Jones and Laughlin in Pittsburgh. The number of black workers in the meatpacking industries also dramatically expanded, rising from fewer than 6,000 blacks in 1910 to nearly 30,000 in 1920. The meatpacking centers of Kansas City, St. Louis, and Chicago attracted the bulk of these newcomers. In Detroit, as early as May 1917, the Packard Company had 1,100 blacks on the payroll, but the Ford Company soon outdistanced other automakers in the employment of African Americans. The number of blacks at Ford rose from only 50 in 1916 to 2,500 in 1920; to 5,000 in 1923; and to 10,000 in 1926. Ford also offered blacks a broader range of production and supervisory opportunities than did other companies. A reporter for the Associated Negro Press later recalled: "Back in those days [1920s and early 1930s] Negro Ford workers almost established class distinctions here. . . . The men began to feel themselves a little superior to workers in other plants. . . . 'I work for Henry Ford' was a boastful expression." In West Coast cities like Seattle, one black resident, Horace R. Cayton Jr., later recalled that World War I opened up "good jobs for negroes, in the shipyards and in many other places we had not worked before."

The rise of the black industrial working class was not limited to northern and western cities. Although the textile industry continued to exclude black workers, blacks represented a large percentage of workers in southern tobacco, lumber, railroad, and coal mining industries. With the exception of railroad employment, few northern and western blacks worked in these industries, which had strong connections with southern agriculture. The percentage of blacks in the tobacco industry increased from nearly 65 to 68 percent of the labor force between 1910 and 1930. The cities of Winston-Salem, Durham, Louisville, and Richmond were major centers of tobacco production. In southern cities like Norfolk, New Orleans, and Baltimore, blacks also gained jobs as longshoremen or stevedores. Although employment in southern sawmills and lumber camps gradually declined during World War I and its aftermath, the percentage of black lumber workers stabilized at about 25 percent of the total timber work force. In the bituminous coal mines of Alabama's Birmingham district and southern West Virginia, black workers made up a majority and nearly a quarter, respectively, of the total coal mining work force. Since coal mining, lumber camps, and much railroad labor were neither strictly urban nor strictly rural, these industries operated at the interface of the black agricultural experience on the one hand and the transition to a new urban industrial foundation on the other. In West Virginia, for example, the use of coal undercutting machines had increased from 45 percent of mines in 1910 to over 80 percent by the mid-1920s. Yet despite increasing mechanization, coal mining continued to unfold in highly rural and small-town settings.

Although their gains were less dramatic and less permanent than those of black men, black women also obtained access to industrial jobs during the labor shortages of World War I. They gained employment not only in jobs traditionally held

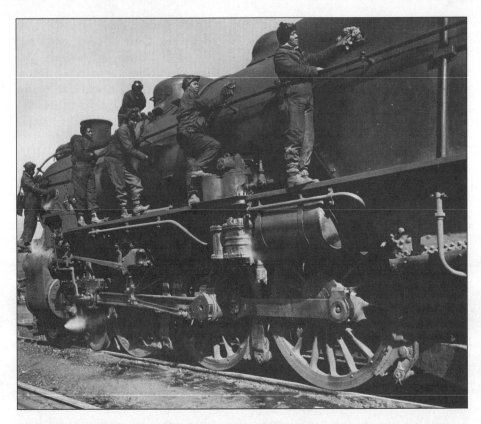

Black women worked in a wide range of industrial jobs during and after World War I. Here in 1918, employees of the Pennsylvania Railroad wash a locomotive engine. *National Archives*

by white women in textiles, clothing, and food production but also jobs in glass, leather, paper, iron, and steel manufacturing as well. In the postwar years, these jobs did not entirely disappear. In Louisville, Seattle, Pittsburgh, Philadelphia, New York, and Chicago, black women continued to work in a variety of industrial jobs. In 1922, the Women's Bureau of the U.S. Department of Labor surveyed the employment of black women in 150 plants in nine states and seventeen localities. Some 11,812 black women performed labor-intensive jobs in food processing, tobacco, clothing, glass, paper, iron, and steel plants. In Chicago, the number of black women classified in manufacturing trades increased from fewer than 1,000 in 1910 to over 3,000 in 1920. Industrial jobs now made up 15 percent of the black female labor force, compared with less than 7 percent in 1910. One woman wrote back from Chicago to her southern home: "I am well and thankful to say I am doing well. . . . I work in Swifts Packing Company." Prospective household employers now complained that black women wanted industrial wages: "Hundred of jobs go begging" at domestic pay.

Economic Inequality and Job Discrimination

As the black industrial work force expanded, African Americans faced new patterns of economic inequality. They worked in the most difficult, dangerous, dirty, and low-paying categories of industrial work. Between 1920 and 1930, an estimated 70 to 80 percent of black men and women worked in jobs defined by the U.S. Census as "unskilled labor." American-born white and immigrant men and women took the more highly skilled and better-paying jobs. In Milwaukee, Cleveland, and Detroit, white men had over 50 percent of their numbers in skilled and semiskilled jobs. For their part, white women had a similar concentration in education, clerical, health, and social welfare services. Moreover, despite the rise of mass production employment, large numbers of black men continued to work as longshoremen, elevator operators, porters, janitors, teamsters, chauffeurs, waiters, and "general laborers of all kinds." In the western cities of Seattle, San Francisco, and Los Angeles, such work accounted for the bulk of black male employment. Porters and janitors earned weekly wages of $15 to $18, compared with $23 to well over $40 for skilled molders, butchers, machinists, and electricians.

Southern blacks faced even greater constraints on their livelihood. In tobacco firms, most blacks labored in the difficult processing aspects of production. They were denied jobs in cigarette factories, where the introduction of machinery had revolutionized production and created cleaner and less arduous work. When they did work on machinery, they did so in a stifling atmosphere of dust particles, fumes, and humidity. Southern black workers also lost skilled jobs that they had previously occupied, especially on southern railroads. Before World War I, for example, African Americans made up 80 percent of the Southern Railway Company firemen, but their numbers declined to only 10 percent by the late 1920s. Moreover, southern employers paid blacks uniformly lower wages for performing the same jobs as whites. According to the Louisville Urban League (LUL), black tobacco workers made between $4 and $10 per week less than their white counterparts. As the LUL stated, "It is the low wage scale . . . that constitutes the basis for most of our industrial troubles."

Black workers repeatedly complained that their jobs entailed disproportionate exposure to debilitating heat, deadly fumes, disabling injuries, and even death. In the steel industry, African Americans worked in the hottest areas of the plants. They fed the blast furnaces and performed the most tedious operations that made rails for the railroads. As one black steelworker recalled, African American men "were limited, they only did the dirty work . . . jobs that even Poles didn't want." In packinghouses, few blacks worked in the butcher category, a skilled job requiring use of the knife. They unloaded trucks, slaughtered the animals, transported intestines, and generally cleaned the plants. Black tannery employees worked mainly in the beam houses. They placed dry hides into pits filled with lime to remove the hair. According to one black tannery worker, this job required rubber boots, rubber aprons, rubber gloves, "everything rubber because that lime would eat you up." For their part, coal miners reported low coal seams, excessive water, bad air, and rock.

Sometimes the circulation of air or no air would be so bad you'd have to wait sometimes up to two hours before you could get back in there and load any coal. . . . I have been sick and dizzy off of that smoke many times. . . . That deadly poison is there. . . . It would knock you out too, make you weak as water.

In New York, a black female garment worker complained: "Over where I work in the dye factory, they expect more from a colored girl if she is to keep her job. They won't give a colored girl a break." In Philadelphia and eastern Pennsylvania, employers presumably hired black women in glass factories, "where at times bits of broken glass were flying in all directions," because of "their ability to stand the heat without suffering."

African American men and women experienced disproportionate bouts of unemployment. They often averaged two to four months of unemployment per year, resulting in a working year of forty weeks or less and actual weekly earnings of about $18 per week. As a result of frequent periods of unemployment, some black workers "didn't worry about being promoted or getting a raise; you worried about keeping the job you had." Some blacks contemplated returning south—a consequence of such instability in the urban North. In a letter to his old employer, one migrant wrote: "I want you to save me my same place for me, for I am coming back home next year, and I want my same farm if you haven't nobody on it. . . . When I get home no one will never get me away any more." Although some migrants actually returned, most stayed but faced a severe economic downturn during the early postwar years of 1919–1922. Moreover, after a period of economic recovery during the mid-1920s, the National Urban League soon reported a deepening crisis for African American workers, their families, and their communities. More than a year before the stock market crash of 1929, the organization reported growing numbers of layoffs at industrial firms.

The discriminatory policies of employers, workers, and urban institutions made it exceedingly difficult for African Americans to improve their economic position. Whether employers hired or excluded blacks, they provided stereotypical, racist, and contradictory reasons for their choices. In Cincinnati, the Chamber of Commerce surveyed the conditions of black workers for the period 1925–1930. Employers who refused to employ black workers offered four major reasons:

1. Unable or unwilling to mix white and Negro workers
2. Skilled help required and Negroes lacked the proper training
3. White workers preferred
4. "Nature of business" (no further reason)

The next most commonly cited reasons included:

5. Lack of separate facilities for white and Negro workers
6. Union restrictions
7. No consideration ever given to use of Negro labor

8. Fear of public opinion if Negroes were introduced
9. Fear of disturbance from white workers

Similarly, in Milwaukee, employers perceived African Americans as unsteady and incapable of adapting to the requirements of factory employment: "The principal fault of the negro workmen is, they are slow and very hard to please. Not good on rapid moving machinery, have not had mechanical training; slow; not stable. Inclined to irregular in attendance to work. Very unsteady. Leave in summertime for road work." Conversely, even employers who hired black workers expressed a range of stereotypes about their pliability compared with white union or immigrant workers.

1. Loyalty and amiability
2. Willingness to do types of work white workers refuse to do or at less price
3. Better suited for hard and disagreeable work
4. Quick adaptability
5. Honesty

In Milwaukee, employers concluded: "They are superior to foreign labor because they readily understand what you try to tell them. Loyalty, willingness, cheerfulness. . . . Quicker, huskier, and can stand more heat than other workmen."

White workers and public officials shared the racism of employers and reinforced barriers to black employment. In the Great Steel Strike of 1919, the strike committee itself represented several decidedly hostile and racially exclusionary unions. The machinists and electrical workers barred African Americans altogether, whereas the blacksmiths relegated blacks to auxiliary lodges under the control of white locals. As a means of justifying their actions, white workers continued to refer to blacks as a "scab race." In August 1918, the NAACP protested the exclusion of black carpenters and bricklayers from the construction of U.S. Army cantonments. At Camp Lee in Petersburg, Virginia, authorities dismissed thirty-six black carpenters when white carpenters put down their tools and refused to work with African Americans. At the close of World War I, the U.S. Railroad Administration advised regional directors to restrict "the employment of Negro firemen, hostlers, switchmen, brakemen, etc. . . . upon any line or in any service where they have not heretofore been employed." Similarly, black carpenters, pipe fitters, riveters, and drillers repeatedly complained that they could not gain jobs in government-controlled shipyard jobs. In a letter to Charles Schwab, head of the United States Shipping Board, one black New Yorker wrote:

We are absolutely competent of earning a far better living at our trades which you refuse to give us. . . . If, Mr. Schwab, we are not fit to have a position as mechanics and officials then I contend that we are not good enough to fight for the country.

In another letter, a California worker made the same point:

> I or any of us may be called tomorrow, and how gladly would I give this life of
> mine if I knew, in giving life to make Democracy safe for the world I was making
> Democracy safe to give to my people. . . . We only ask an equal chance to take
> our part in the industrial world.

During the war years, the federal government also issued "work or fight" orders.
These orders soon generated a spate of state and local laws, especially in the South,
that required able-bodied men (up to forty-one years of age) to find gainful employment or face the draft. In Georgia, the small community of Wrightsville made
it "unlawful for any person from the ages of sixteen to fifty to reside in or upon the
streets of Wrightsville unless he is actively and assiduously engaged in useful employment fifty hours or more per week." The law also stipulated that such persons
had to carry an employment card showing their work history. The impact of compulsory "work or fight" laws was not limited to black men. In letters to President
Wilson, the NAACP reported several cases in which black women were forced out
of their homes into the work force. In Jackson, Mississippi, for example, when a
black woman quit her job as a cook for a white family, a police patrol wagon arrived
at her home. The officers informed her that she had a decision to make—return to
work or face arrest for vagrancy. In Vicksburg, Mississippi, two women were "tarred
and feathered" when they refused to work.

Resistance Strategies

From the outset of the Great Migration, black workers developed a variety of
strategies to combat economic discrimination. As in the prewar years, African
Americans frequently moved from one job to another to improve their working
conditions, increase wages, and gain greater recognition of their rights as workers
and citizens. In Cincinnati, the black social worker Theodore Berry noted that labor turnover was especially high "in certain industries where the disagreeable nature of the work and low pay combined to make jobs less attractive, and caused
workers to leave at the first opportunity." As one black tannery employee stated after working in the beam house, "I worked there one night and I quit." Coal, iron,
steel, and meatpacking workers regularly moved between jobs in the industrial centers of West Virginia, Ohio, Pennsylvania, Illinois, Wisconsin, and Michigan. During the war years, Milwaukee's Pfister-Vogel Tannery Company hired 300 black
workers to maintain a work force of 75 blacks. Similarly, in 1923, the A. M. Byer
Steel Company of Pittsburgh hired 1,048 black employees to maintain a work force
of 223 black men. Although employers, social welfare officials, and municipal authorities treated black turnover as evidence of unreliability, inconsistency, and
dearth of a solid work ethic, such behavior also revealed black workers' effort to
improve their status.

If black workers responded to discriminatory working conditions by quitting
and searching for better jobs elsewhere, they responded to the discriminatory poli-

cies of white workers by breaking their strikes and forming all-black labor unions. Southern black workers served as strikebreakers in a variety of industries during World War I and the 1920s: the East St. Louis aluminum strike (1917); coal mining strikes in Pennsylvania (1922, 1927), West Virginia (1925), and Ohio (1928); longshoremen strikes in Baltimore (1916), New Orleans (1923), and Boston (1929); meatpacking strikes in East St. Louis (1916), Chicago (1919), and a variety of meatpacking centers (1921); and the widespread steel strikes of 1919 and 1921. Although some managers skillfully implemented the use of black strikebreakers by supplementing their numbers with white strikebreakers, blacks had their own reasons for entering the work force as strikebreakers. They resented white workers' discriminatory practices and rhetoric, which referred to blacks as a "scab race."

Despite their resistance to discriminatory white unions, African Americans were by no means uniformly hostile to organized labor. When the First International Congress of Working Women met in Washington, D.C., in 1919, black women sought to influence the direction of the convention's work. Under the heading "Representative Negro women of the United States in behalf of Negro Women Laborers of the United States," Helen Burroughs, Elizabeth Ross Haynes, Mary Church Terrell, and other clubwomen urged the gathering to actively cooperate "in organizing the Negro Women workers of the United States into unions, that they may have a share in bringing about industrial democracy and social order in the world." Similarly, from the outset of the Great Steel Strike, the National Urban League urged William Z. Foster and the National Committee for Organizing Iron and Steel Workers to employ black organizers. Moreover, during the early postwar years, black and white workers sometimes cooperated in unions like the International Longshoremen's Association and especially the United Mine Workers of America. Although their efforts failed, black and white coal miners developed an amazing degree of unity across the color line. At the 1921 meeting of the national body, the black delegate Frank Ingham eloquently addressed the gathering on conditions in southern West Virginia:

> I will first say that I am happy to be permitted to speak, not for myself, but for Mingo county. . . . The real truth has never been told of Mingo county. It cannot be told. The language has not been coined to express the agonies the miners of Mingo county are enduring today. The world is under the impression that martial law exists there. That is not true. What exists in Mingo is partial law, because it is only brought to bear upon the miners that have joined the union.

African Americans also formed their own all-black labor organizations. In the spring of 1919, black delegates from twelve states and the District of Columbia formed the National Brotherhood Workers of America. Under the leadership of T. J. Free and R. T. Sims, two black unionists with ties to the radical Industrial Workers of the World, the organization aimed to organize "every Negro worker into industrial labor or trade unions in all skilled and unskilled occupations." Moreover, the organization urged black workers "to exact justice from both the employer and the white labor unions." In 1925, black communists H. A. Phillips and Levett Fort-Whitman formed the American Negro Labor Congress. In the same year, the black socialists Thomas J. Curtis and Frank L. Crosswaith spearheaded the formation of the Trade Union Committee for Organizing Negro Workers. Each of these unions represented the growing determination of black workers to fight discriminatory capital and labor; yet it was the formation of the Brotherhood of Sleeping Car Porters (BSCP) that emerged at the center of black workers' activism during the period.

Formed in 1925, the BSCP aimed to organize black porters and maids at the Chicago-based Pullman Company, the largest single employer of blacks in the nation. Under the leadership of the socialist Asa Philip Randolph, the organization adopted the motto "Service not Servitude" and launched a vigorous drive to organize the Pullman Company, increase wages, and improve the working conditions and treatment of black workers. According to a report in the *New Leader*, "The fight of the Pullman porters is the all absorbing topic wherever two or more Negroes gather in Harlem." The words of "the Marching Song of the Fighting Brotherhood" were widely known among porters and nonporters alike:

> We will sing one song of the meek and humble slave
> The horn-handed son of toil
> He's toiling hard from cradle to the grave
> But his masters reap the profit of his toil.
> Then we'll sing one song of our one Big Brotherhood
> The hope of the Porters and Maids
> It's coming fast it is sweeping sea and wood
> To the terror of the grafters and the slave.
>
> (chorus)
> Organize! Oh Porters come organize your might,
> Then we'll sing one song of our Big Brotherhood,
> Full of beauty, full of love and light.

Within six weeks of its formation, the wives and female relatives of sleeping car porters and maids formed "ladies' auxiliaries" and vigorously promoted the work of the organization. Beginning with the Hesperus Club of Harlem, women's auxiliaries soon spread to Philadelphia, Chicago, St. Louis, Los Angeles, and other cities. Under the leadership of women like Rosina Carrothers Tucker of Washington, D.C., Lucy Bledsoe Gilmore of St. Louis, and Mrs. Tinie Upton of Los Angeles, women directed the bulk of their efforts toward fundraising. They raised money to maintain union halls, pay the expenses of nationwide organizing campaigns, and publicize the grievances of the porters and maids within the larger community. Despite little success in changing the material conditions of black workers during the 1920s, the BSCP and other black labor organizations established the groundwork for a more vigorous labor movement during the New Deal era of the 1930s.

Beyond the activities of the Brotherhood of Sleeping Car Porters, black women forged their own forms of worker resistance. During the war years, they informally

If You are a Stranger in the City

If you want a job   If you want a place to live
If you are having trouble with your employer
If you want information or advice of any kind
CALL UPON

The CHICAGO LEAGUE ON URBAN
CONDITIONS AMONG NEGROES

3719 South State Street

Telephone Douglas 9098   T. ARNOLD HILL, Executive Secretary

No charges—no fees. We want to help YOU

The National Urban League provided professional social services for black migrants and their families, as suggested by this card distributed by the Chicago branch. *Special Collections, Chicago Urban League, University of Illinois at Chicago*

banded together to demand higher pay and better treatment in household service. In Gainesville, Georgia, one observer declared that black women "had formed an agreement as to the amount of work, number of hours, and the wages which they would agree upon with the whites." Some black women adopted the motto "W.W.T.K." (White Women to the Kitchen) and urged their sisters to leave domestic service employment for openings in the industrial sector. Domestics also adopted absenteeism, high turnover rates, and myriad day-to-day strategies for demanding better treatment and greater returns on their labor. In Rock Hill, South Carolina, a group of black women creatively referred to these activities as the work of "Fold-the-Arms Club[s]." By war's end, in Houston, Norfolk, and Washington, D.C., black women had formed domestic servants unions and wage earners associations and demanded higher pay and better working conditions. Although each of these efforts collapsed under the weight of brutal repression from municipal authorities and employers alike, they demonstrated that large numbers of black women as well as black men helped to establish a foundation for the growth of militant unionism during the 1930s. Moreover, the black woman carried out these activities within the context of work—washing, ironing, cooking, and tending children—within her own household.

Black workers not only developed their own independent class-based strategies for addressing economic inequality but also forged alliances with the black business and professional middle class and its small elite. The National Urban League (NUL) not only played a role in helping black workers find jobs but also helped to mediate grievances with white employers and labor unions. As noted above, during the steel strike of 1919, the NUL appealed to white unions to employ black organizers and bring black workers into the labor movement on an equal basis.

The activities of middle-class black women reinforced these efforts. Under the leadership of Mary Church Terrell, Jeanette Carter, and Julia Coleman, black women formed the Women Wage Earners Association in Washington, D.C. This organization aimed to aid black working-class women by advocating improved wages, working conditions, and adequate housing. Branches of the organization soon spread to other cities. In 1917, the Norfolk branch organized a variety of black women workers—oyster shuckers, tobacco stemmers, domestics, and waitresses—and staged a strike for higher pay. The Norfolk strike resulted in the arrest of black women as "slackers" under wartime "work or fight" rules, and the union declined. As noted above, middle-class black clubwomen also spoke out on behalf of their working-class counterparts at the First International Congress of Working Women in Washington, D.C.

Multiclass black churches also developed a variety of programs designed to aid newcomers. In Chicago, Cleveland, Detroit, and other sites of the Great Migration, black churches established a broad range of programs to meet the needs of migrants. Using Jane Addams's Hull House as a model, Chicago's Olivet Baptist Church, under the pastorship of Lacey Kirk Williams, set up health, recreational, and infant care facilities; an employment bureau; and housing and letter-writing services. Moreover, the church organized volunteers to meet migrants at the train station to assist them in finding housing and getting settled in their new homes. As a result of such services and the increasing numbers of black migrants in the city, Olivet's membership increased from an estimated four thousand in 1915 to nearly nine thousand in 1920. Similarly, Cleveland's Antioch Baptist Church became the city's largest black church and soon responded to the needs of migrants by forming youth clubs and setting up neighborhood-based recreation centers. In Detroit, Bethel AME Church created specialized social service, labor, and housing departments. As early as March 1917, the church's pastor, Rev. J. M. Evans, reported placing 197 men and 189 women in jobs with area firms.

An energetic roster of black women organized and executed the social welfare programs of black churches. Their activities were closely aligned with the work of such national organizations as the National Association of Colored Women (NACW) and the Woman's Baptist Convention (WBC), an auxiliary of the National Baptist Convention. Under the impact of World War I, the NACW intensified its development of multiservice centers, which offered housing, jobs, nursery, and emergency aid to migrant workers and their families; the WBC established new committees on child welfare and vital statistics. The WBC committees initiated social scientific studies designed to improve the health and life expectancy of African Americans as they made the transition from farm to city. At the annual meetings, black church and clubwomen from across the country exchanged ideas and shared information on the conditions, programs, and strategies for improving the social welfare of African Americans. One local Urban League official declared: "I wish all of the 10,000 [workers] who have been placed by us could have been secured through the churches because, from our experience, I believe they would have been diligent, regular and zealous in their work." Similarly, George E. Haynes, a National Urban League official, acknowledged "the industrial value of the church to the new-comers and to the community which benefits by their labor." As suggested by the brief review of the literature in the accompanying box, recent histori-

CHANGING HISTORICAL INTERPRETATIONS

African American Urban History

The urban-industrial transformation of African American life is a twentieth-century phenomenon. Thus, compared with scholarship on earlier periods in African American history, research on blacks in twentieth-century cities is a relatively recent occurrence. Although W. E. B. Du Bois, Charles S. Johnson, E. Franklin Frazier, St. Clair Drake, and Horace R. Cayton conducted sociological studies of black urban life during the late nineteenth and early twentieth centuries, detailed historical accounts did not emerge until the 1960s and 1970s. Focusing on the history of blacks in New York City, Chicago, and Cleveland, historians Gilbert Osofsky, Allan Spear, and Kenneth Kusmer, respectively, incorporated the insights of the earlier sociological studies and advanced a ghetto interpretation of black urban life. Writing at a time when the nation's cities literally exploded into violence, these scholars emphasized the rise of residential segregation and the growth of nearly all-black slumlike communities in the nation's major metropolitan areas. As blacks demanded an end to racial injustice in all areas of the nation's life, urban historians also hoped to awaken the nation's conscience and stimulate support for the expansion of social welfare programs. As such, the ghetto studies accented the "tragic" impact of racial discrimination on urban blacks but downplayed the corresponding impact of class inequality.

Struck by the slow pace of socioeconomic change under the impact of the Second Reconstruction, which ushered in new and powerful civil rights legislation, a new cohort of scholars responded to the insights as well as the limits of the ghetto model. By the mid- to late 1980s, studies by James Grossman, Richard Walter Thomas, Peter Gottlieb, Dennis Dickerson, and the author of this book advanced working-class- or proletarian-oriented approaches to black urban life. In our work, ghettoization remained an important development, but we accented the ways that black urbanites were also workers who made the increasing transition from rural occupations to new jobs in the industrial sector of the expanding urban economy. Moreover, whereas prior studies treated blacks as people "pushed and pulled" by forces beyond their control, working-class studies emphasized the role that southern migrants took in shaping their own experience. In these studies, southern migrants organized their kin, friend, and communal networks and shaped their own move from farm to city, from field to factory.

Despite the helpful insights of labor and working-class studies, a fresh wave of scholarship soon exposed crucial gender and cultural limitations of the proletarian approach. By the late 1980s and 1990s, scholars like Earl Lewis, Darlene Clark Hine, Elizabeth Clark Lewis, Robin D. G. Kelley, and Kimberley Phillips urged historians to pay closer attention to the role of working-class and elite women as well as men in the economics, politics, and culture of the black community. According to these scholars, working-class formation privileged the "point of production" and the experiences of black men while neglecting the role of women, gender, reproductive, and cultural issues. Like other bodies of scholarship on the African American experience, research on black life in the industrial age is another great resource for understanding and shaping the current reorientation of African American life and labor—from the manufacturing of durable goods to the provision of services in the computer and information age.

ans are moving the interplay of such cultural and economic issues to the fore of their research on urban blacks.

EXPANSION OF THE NEW BLACK MIDDLE CLASS

The increasing numbers of urban black workers, and their segregation within the city, established the foundation for the expansion of black business and professional enterprises. Growth of the black middle class was part of larger "New Negro" efforts to build the Black Metropolis—a city within the city that would serve the needs of African American families and their communities. The number of black-owned businesses increased from an estimated 40,000 before World War I to about 70,000 in 1930. The proliferation of black newspapers, mainly weeklies, both reflected and promoted this process in most of the major urban centers of the nation: the *St. Louis Argus, Pittsburgh Courier, Norfolk Journal and Guide, Afro-American* (Baltimore), *Atlanta Independent, Philadelphia Tribune, Dallas Express, Washington Tribune, Amsterdam News,* and *Chicago Defender.* The *Defender's* circulation increased from 33,000 in 1916 to 90,000 in 1917, to an estimated 160,000 to 250,000 by the mid-1920s. The paper's shipping manifest listed subscribers in over 1,500 towns and cities across the United States. Moreover, as noted above, Pullman porters influenced the paper's circulation well beyond its subscription lists.

Black newspapers and business advertisements vigorously promoted black enterprises as a means of providing employment to black workers. As the cosmetics industry (established during the prewar years by entrepreneurs such as Madame C. J. Walker) expanded during the 1920s, the newspaper columnist George Schuyler wrote that Madame Walker's business gave "dignified employment to thousands of women who would otherwise have had to make their living in domestic service." The editor of the *Wisconsin Enterprise Blade* believed that black business houses in Milwaukee could "develop into powerful institutions that will give employment to thousands of our boys and girls." In 1924, J. Willis Cole, editor of the *Louisville Leader,* celebrated the emergence of "two banks, four insurance companies, two hotels . . . two building and loan associations, six real estate companies, three drug stores, eight undertakers, two photographers, fifteen groceries, four newspapers, three architects . . . three movie houses and buildings for our business and professional men." In a laudatory article on black business in the city of Durham, North Carolina, the sociologist E. Franklin Frazier described Durham as the "capital of the Black Middle Class." According to Frazier,

> Durham . . . is not a place where men write and dream; but a place where black men calculate and work. No longer can men say that the Negro is lazy and shiftless and a consumer. He has gone to work. He is a producer. He is respectable. He has a middle class.

Although a variety of small cosmetic, personal service, restaurant, and rooming establishments continued to dominate the roster of black businesses, black urbanites also aimed to open avenues to white-collar employment by founding new banking, insurance, real estate, leisure, and sports firms. Despite stiff resistance from white companies and the discriminatory practices of state licensing agencies, in 1925–1926 the *Negro Yearbook* reported seventy-three black banks in nineteen states and the District of Columbia. The assets of these banks peaked at nearly $13 million before the onset of the Great Depression. In Chicago, Jesse Binga received a state charter for his bank in 1919. Formed in the prewar years as a private bank with close ties to Binga's real estate interests, the Binga State Bank emerged as a model of black banking institutions during the 1920s. When the state approved the bank's charter, the *Chicago Defender* enthusiastically described the Binga bank as "a house of rock-ribbed foundation."

Alongside banks, eleven new insurance companies emerged in southern cities. The so-called "Big Four" dominated the roster of black insurance firms: North Carolina Mutual, based in Durham; Atlanta Life; Standard Life (also in Atlanta); and National Benefit Life in Washington, D.C. The North Carolina Mutual's premium income rose from $405,000 at the outset of the war years to $1.2 million in 1919. The amount of insurance in force also increased from $4.9 million at the war's beginning to $42.8 million by the mid-1920s. The company not only expanded its operations into the Upper South cities of Washington, D.C., and Baltimore but also expanded into six new southern states: Tennessee, Florida, Mississippi, Arkansas, Alabama, and Oklahoma. In addition to North Carolina Mutual, Durham businessmen also formed the Bankers Fire Insurance Company in 1920 and the

Board of Directors, North Carolina Mutual Life Insurance Company, 1929. *Left to right:* E. R. Merrick, M. A. Goins, John Avery, W. D. Hill, W. J. Kennedy Jr., C. C. Spaulding, R. L. McDougald, George W. Cox, John L. Wheeler. *Courtesy of North Carolina Mutual Life Insurance Company*

National Negro Finance Corporation in 1924. In northern cities, African Americans formed the Victory Mutual Life Insurance Company in New York; the Liberty Life Insurance Company in Chicago; the Supreme Life and Casualty Company in Columbus; and the Northeastern Life Insurance Company in Newark, New Jersey.

Although professional baseball teams had roots in the prewar years, they were now organized into commercially successful "Negro Leagues." Professional black baseball teams included the Homestead Grays, the Pittsburgh Crawfords, the Kansas City Monarchs, the Birmingham Black Barons, and Chicago's American Giants. In 1920, under the leadership of Rube Foster of Chicago, managers of six midwestern baseball teams met in Kansas City and formed the National Negro Baseball League. Most clubs eventually built or purchased their own parks and paid players as much as $135 per week. In 1924, the Negro League held its first World Series. The Kansas City Monarchs played and beat the Hilldale Club of Philadelphia. The following year the two teams met again, with the Hilldale team claiming victory. Black baseball games sometimes attracted larger crowds than the white major leagues. As black businesses expanded and opportunities for self-employment increased, managers of one company enthusiastically exclaimed: "At last! At last! . . . The day of Negro enterprises of every kind has arrived."

African Americans also sought to counteract the racism of Hollywood producers by developing their own films and providing work for black actors and actresses. In an ill-fated venture, Booker T. Washington's personal secretary, Emmett Scott of Tuskegee Institute, sought to develop a film entitled *The Birth of a Race* (1915), an explicit response to D. W. Griffith's *The Birth of a Nation.* Although many blacks invested in the film, white producers gained control and produced a film that one critic called a "terrible waste" because of mismanagement of funds and poor shooting and editing. Nonetheless, numerous small black production companies developed during the war and early postwar years. The most significant and successful of these were the Lincoln Motion Picture Company and the Oscar Micheaux Corporation. Founded by brothers George P. and Noble Johnson in 1915, the Lincoln Company announced that it hoped "to picture the Negro as he is in his every day life, a human being with human inclination, and one of talent and intellect." Operating with a studio in Los Angeles and a booking office in Omaha, the Lincoln Company soon produced several films on black life, including *The Realization of a Negro's Ambition* (1915–1916); *The Trooper of Troop K* (1916); and *A Man's Duty* (1920–1921). Following the demise of the Lincoln Company, Oscar Micheaux became the most prolific black filmmaker, producing such films as *The Homesteaders* (1919); *Birthright* (1918); and *Body and Soul* (1925), starring Paul Robeson.

Reinforcing the growth of the black middle class was the expansion of black professional services. The number of African Americans engaged in professional service nearly doubled, rising from 68,400 in 1910 to 136,000 by the late 1920s. Although the number of black physicians and attorneys gradually increased as part of the black professional class, school teachers (about 50 percent), clergymen (18 percent), and musicians and teachers of music (about 8 percent) dominated the roster of black professionals. At the same time, African Americans gained increasing access to professional nursing and social work jobs. By the 1920s, the number of African American nurse training programs had increased from a handful at the turn of the century to thirty-six, with some 3,000 graduates. In 1910, the U.S. census of occupations reported 500 "semiprofessional" black religious and charity workers. Two decades later, there were over 1,000 "professional" black social workers (about 80 percent women), supplemented by another 1,200 "semiprofessional" religious and charity workers (also mostly women).

Formed in 1910, the National Urban League emerged at the forefront of training and job creation for black professional social workers. A major goal of the organization was "to secure and train Negro social workers." On the eve of World War I, the organization sponsored its first social work fellows and by 1919 maintained constant contact with black college women and men, encouraging them to study for a career in social work. By the mid-1920s, the league employed over 170 people at its New York headquarters and several others in some fifty-one branches in the North and parts of the South. The league's budget increased from an estimated $9,000 at the outset of World War I to $300,000 in 1923, when it also launched *Opportunity*, its monthly magazine. Although growing numbers of black women nurses, teachers, and social workers augmented the ranks of the black middle class, black men took the top managerial, executive director, and superintendent positions. The National Urban League invariably hired men as executive directors, while employing women as investigators or assistants. Moreover, black women specialists earned between $900 and $1,200 per year, compared with $1,200 to $1,500 per year for their male counterparts. Executive directors earned $1,500 to $2,000 per year. Still, within the constraints of the Jim Crow order, the Urban League offered African Americans an important outlet for their professional training and skills.

∼

ALTHOUGH WARTIME LABOR DEMANDS and the decline of European immigration opened up new economic opportunities in the nation's urban centers, African Americans faced an ongoing struggle to gain a viable footing in the industrial economy. White workers, employers, and the state developed policies that reinforced discrimination along racial as well as class lines. As such color and class lines hardened, African Americans deployed a range of informal day-to-day tactics, formed labor unions, and forged community-based alliances with the expanding black middle class and its small elite. Community-based alliances recognized the limits of workplace strategies for socioeconomic change and offered hope to African Americans that they could counteract discrimination by patronizing black enterprises, helping to build a Black Metropolis, and creating their own jobs, social services, and places to stay. As we will see in Chapter 16, however, efforts to build the Black Metropolis faced tremendous obstacles within and outside the black community.

Rise of the "New Negro"

W orld War I not only served as a catalyst for the rise of the black industrial working class but also precipitated the emergence of the "New Negro." A new generation of African Americans envisioned the growth of a Black Metropolis. Calling themselves "New Negroes," they hoped to build a city within a city and serve the needs of African Americans, their families, and their communities. At the same time, the New Negroes sought to reconcile the philosophy of economic self-help and racial solidarity with new demands for full citizenship rights. Their efforts reflected as well as stimulated the grassroots radicalization of the African American population. Black activism gained sharp articulation in the emergence of new and more diverse social, political, and cultural movements: Marcus Garvey and the Universal Negro Improvement Association; the Harlem Renaissance; and the accelerating demands of civil rights and political organizations like the National Association for the Advancement of Colored People (NAACP). African Americans demanded not only the fruits of their labor in the capitalist economy but also full citizenship rights and freedom of political and cultural expression within the democratic polity. To fully appreciate the scope and significance of this struggle, we must first examine the war and postwar disappointments of African Americans on the home front.

LEGACY OF WAR AND BROKEN PROMISES

African Americans faced not only inequality in the workplace and on the battlefield, as discussed in Chapter 15, but also hostility in the social, cultural, political, and institutional life of the larger war and postwar community. The war and early postwar years witnessed the intensification of racist portrayals of blacks in the popular media, the resurgence of "white supremacist" groups like the Ku Klux Klan, and the spread of residential segregation. At the same time, violent racial conflict escalated. Alongside the persistence of lynchings in the rural and small-town South, urban race riots emerged and spread across the urban North and South.

Racial Violence and the Growth of the New KKK

In the spring of 1915, D. W. Griffith's new movie *The Clansman* opened on the West Coast. It soon traveled to Washington, D.C., and then on to New York, where it received a new title, *The Birth of a Nation*. Film historians acknowledge the film as a technical cinematic triumph that "departed from short vignettes of former years and in a single stroke synthesized all of the devices and advances developed in the first generation of cinema." As noted in Chapter 14, *The Birth of a Nation* also represented the symbolic triumph of white supremacist thought and social practices. Like the novel on which it was based, it depicted the emancipation of enslaved blacks as a mistake and glorified violence to curtail African American freedom. Although such harsh and sharply drawn stereotypes would dissipate during the 1920s, they would not disappear. The emergence of radio supplemented and reinforced the racist portraits of movies and print media. In 1926, the white comedy team of Charles Correll and Freeman Gadsden created the characters that soon became known as Amos 'n' Andy. Although the *Amos 'n' Andy* show depicted a wider cast of black characters and revealed greater diversity within the black community than *The Birth of a Nation*, it nonetheless caricatured blacks as ignorant, lazy, and criminal. According to recent scholarship on the development of commercial radio, "Sales of radio sets soared during the months after *Amos 'n' Andy*'s debut, and the show became a powerful locomotive pulling commercial radio along behind it." In the meantime, before radio characterizations of blacks took hold, the rapid growth of the Ku Klux Klan reflected as well as heightened the spread of racial conflict.

On 3 March 1915, less than two weeks before *The Birth of a Nation* premiered in Atlanta, Georgia, sixteen men climbed Stone Mountain and revived the Ku Klux Klan, complete with Bible reading and cross burning. The Ku Klux Klan restricted membership to native-born white American citizens and directed its most vicious assaults on African Americans. Before its demise during the mid-1920s, the Klan made the shift from an earlier rural and predominantly southern setting to an urban organization with branches throughout the United States. By early 1921, the *New York World* estimated Klan membership at a half million. The organization had enrolled 3,000 members in Louisville; nearly 4,000 in Evansville; nearly 12,200 in Cincinnati; and an estimated 125,000 in western Pennsylvania, where branches opened in Pittsburgh, Homestead, Johnstown, and other towns along the three rivers. By 1921, the Klan had emerged in the western cities of Los Angeles, San Francisco, Seattle, Denver, and Portland. Although the Klan's influence on race relations varied from city to city, everywhere members of the "Invisible Empire" articulated their belief that the enemies of the republic were "non-Christians and colored people."

By the early 1920s, according to the *New York World*, the Klan had spearheaded more than 150 "outrages," including forty-one floggings, twenty-seven "tar and

MR. PRESIDENT, WHY NOT MAKE AMERICA SAFE FOR DEMOCRACY?

The New York *Evening Mail* decried the outbreak of racial violence against blacks in the East St. Louis riot of 1917. *Cartoon by Morris from New York Evening Mail*

feather" incidents, and four murders. According to NAACP records, lynchings of African Americans increased from fifty-eight in 1916, to sixty-three in 1918, to seventy-seven in 1919. During the early postwar years, another fifty-seven blacks were lynched. Most of these lynchings took place in southern rural areas and small towns. In 1916, in Waco, Texas, a mob lynched a seventeen-year-old black youth, Jesse Washington. Charged with assaulting and killing the wife of a white farmer for whom he worked, Washington faced a speedy and summary trial before an all-white jury. Nearly fifteen hundred whites crowded into the five-hundred-seat courtroom. The jury convicted the youth and called for the death penalty, but the mob took matters in their own hands, dragged the boy from the courtroom, and lynched him on the City Hall lawn before crowds of men, women, and children. A reporter for the *Waco Times Herald* described the brutal event:

Fingers, ears, pieces of clothing, toes and other parts of the Negro's body were cut off by members of the mob that had crowded to the scene. . . . Onlookers were hanging from the windows of the City Hall and every other building that commanded a sight of the burning, and as the Negro's body commenced to burn, shouts of delight went up from the thousands.

As lynchings increased in rural areas and small towns of the South, mob violence erupted in urban centers. With the exception of East St. Louis, Illinois (1917), and Tulsa, Oklahoma (1921), the most destructive of these riots broke out during the infamous "Red Summer" of 1919: Charleston, South Carolina; Elaine, Arkansas; Knoxville, Tennessee; Washington, D.C.; and Chicago, Illinois, to name a few. The eminent black historian Carter G. Woodson later described one scene in the nation's capital, as well as his own close scrape with death:

They had caught a Negro and deliberately held him as one would a beef for slaughter, and when they had conveniently adjusted him for lynching they shot him. I heard him groaning in his struggle as I hurried away as fast as I could without running, expecting every moment to be lynched myself.

In East St. Louis, when gangs of whites repeatedly attacked the black community under the cover of darkness, blacks armed to defend themselves. After blacks mistakenly fired on a police car and killed two white officers, armed whites escalated their attack on the black community, indiscriminately killing men, women, and children. The mob torched black houses and shot residents as they sought to flee. Some thirty-nine blacks and eleven whites lost their lives, and nearly $400,000 worth of property was destroyed. After observing the corpses of several black men, a writer for the *Post-Dispatch* reported: "I think everyone I saw had both hands above his head begging for mercy." Some of these blacks were hanged as members of the mob cried that "Southern niggers" deserved a "genuine lynching."

According to testimony before a congressional investigating committee, police and National Guardsmen "shared the lust of the mob for negro blood" and refused to arrest white rioters. When two blacks approached one officer and begged for help, the officer ordered them to "keep walking, you black ___." Both men were shot half a block away. In the same city, Charles F. Short, owner of a moving company, testified that a soldier shot a black man in an alley at Fourth and Broadway: "I ran to the back door and saw three militiamen. . . . I looked down and saw a Negro with his hands in the air . . . one man, I think in the middle, fired." Another militiaman fired into a group of "unoffending negroes . . . huddled together in fright" outside their burning homes. The U.S. congressional committee concluded:

> The conduct of the soldiers who were sent to East St. Louis to protect life and property puts a blot on that part of the Illinois militia that served under Colonel Tripp. . . . As a rule they fraternized with the mob, joked with them, and made no serious effort to restrain them.

On 27 July 1919, the Chicago riot erupted when a fight broke out between blacks and whites along the shore of Lake Michigan. A stone-throwing fight developed when whites tried to maintain a restricted area of the beach for whites only. During the confrontation, a black youth, Eugene Williams, drowned after being hit by a stone. Violence soon spread into the larger community when local police refused to arrest any whites for the drowning and instead tried to arrest blacks. For the next seven days, Chicago became the scene of intensive racial conflict as blacks fought members of white mobs and gangs or "athletic clubs"—"Ragen Colts," "Dirty Dozen," and "Our Flag." Although blacks fought back, the white mobs received police support and considerably outnumbered them. After some twenty-five whites dragged Joseph Scott from a streetcar and left him lying wounded in the street, a police officer approached the wounded man and inflicted additional wounds before arresting and shoving him roughly into a patrol wagon. None of the twenty-five whites were arrested for their attack on Scott. When the violence ceased, some twenty-three blacks and fifteen whites had lost their lives. Another five hundred persons, mostly blacks, received serious injuries. The riot also left a thousand persons homeless.

In May 1921, Tulsa, Oklahoma, witnessed one of the most destructive riots in the nation's history. The conflict emerged when a white female elevator operator accused a nineteen-year-old black man, Dick Rowland, of physically assaulting her and "tearing her clothes." When authorities arrested the man and took him to the county jail, a white mob soon gathered near the facility. Fearing a lynching, several armed blacks arrived on the scene and offered their services to the county sheriff. When members of the mob sought to disarm the blacks, violence broke out. For a while, some fifty to seventy-five blacks held their ground against an estimated fifteen hundred to two thousand whites, who soon forced blacks to retreat into their community, the Greenwood section of the city. Authorities deputized members of the mob, who assaulted, killed, jailed, and detained blacks en mass. Under martial law, Adjutant General Charles F. Barrett of the state National Guard disbanded the special deputies but continued the internment of some four thousand blacks at the city's jail, convention center, and fairgrounds. At the same time, the National Guard released all but a few whites to return to their homes. Whites burned and looted the black Greenwood District, destroying an estimated $500,000 in African American property, including the Gurley Hotel ($150,000); the Dreamland Theater and Williams Building ($100,000); and the Mount Zion Baptist Church ($85,000). Estimates of the number of dead and wounded ranged from twenty-seven to over two hundred and fifty, but contemporary accounts like the *Tulsa Tribune* and the *New York Times* reported that sixty-eight blacks and nine whites lost their lives.

Disproportionate arrests, incarceration, and police brutality were not limited to large-scale race riots. Such inequalities before the law were recurring phenomena during the war and postwar years. In Cincinnati, blacks accounted for 23 percent of recorded crimes although they made up only 7 percent of the population. In Evansville, blacks also made up about 7 percent of the total population but accounted for over 20 percent of persons arrested for petty theft, vagrancy, and drunkenness. In 1923, in Johnstown, Pennsylvania, when authorities charged a black migrant in a shooting incident with police, the mayor, chief of police, and other officials blamed black newcomers for stirring up trouble and ordered them "to pack up" and "go back from where you came." At about the same time, the city of Louisville launched a "drive on crime." Police raids on the black community resulted in wholesale arrests, especially for gambling and prostitution; white participants, however, were left unmolested. During the 1920s, according to one contemporary observer, Louisville police murdered no less than seventeen blacks, mostly black men who were unarmed and suspected or charged with petty crimes. Compounding such deaths were recurring cases of physical injury inflicted on blacks while in police custody. In 1926, Detroit's Mayor's Committee on Race Relations condemned police brutality:

> The assumption among many police officers that Negro criminals offer a special peril to the life of the officer and . . . justifies unusually precipitate action in firing upon Negro criminals is not borne out by the facts. This unjustified assumption has resulted in needless loss of life.

Housing and Institutional Segregation

Interracial violence and conflict heightened the spread of racially segregated neighborhoods. To be sure, some African Americans gained access to improved housing on the periphery of the expanding postwar black community, but real estate firms, homeowners, and municipal governments precipitated overcrowding and the rise of all-black areas in the North, West, and South. During the 1920s, the Cincinnati Real Estate Board instructed its employees that "no agent shall rent or sell property to colored people in an established white section or neighborhood and this inhibition shall be particularly applicable to the hill tops and suburban property." In Milwaukee, the city's leading daily, the *Milwaukee Journal,* reported that the city would have a "black belt . . . if the Real Estate Board can find ways to make it practicable." White property owners adopted the restrictive covenant (a legal agreement enforceable in courts of law) as the principal device for excluding blacks from their neighborhoods. In some cities, over 90 percent of the plats of land filed with municipal recorder of deeds offices contained restrictions prohibiting the sale of property to blacks (and often to Jews as well). White property owners' associations—notably New York's Harlem Property Owners' Improvement Corporation and Chicago's

As the black urban population increased, African Americans adapted to overcrowded conditions by renting small subdivided units in larger apartment buildings or houses. This black family shares an apartment in Harlem, c. 1915. *Brown Brothers*

Hyde Park Improvement Protective Club—monitored and resisted the movement of blacks into previously all-white areas. These organizations issued manifestos calling for concerted bans on the sale of real estate to blacks in certain areas. When such organized pressure failed, whites resorted to violence. In Chicago, for example, from July 1917 through February 1921, African Americans experienced some fifty-eight home bombings, which killed two persons, injured several others, and resulted in over $100,000 in property damage.

City zoning legislation reinforced residential segregation and housing exploitation. In Milwaukee, a 1920 ordinance zoned the entire southern half of the city's black district for commercial and light manufacturing. The law permitted no new residential construction in the area until World War II. In 1924, Cincinnati also passed a new comprehensive zoning law. The new legislation encouraged the building of single-family homes outside the black area while limiting new residential construction within. Although blacks in southern and western cities remained more dispersed than their northern counterparts, they also faced growing restrictions on their spatial mobility. In West Coast cities like Seattle, Los Angeles, and San Francisco, however, the large Asian and Latino populations created a more complicated pattern of housing competition and conflict. Restrictive housing covenants included Asian and Latino Americans as well as Jews and African Americans. As early as 1917, a Los Angeles resident described these covenants as "invisible walls of steel. The whites surrounded us and made it impossible for us to go beyond these walls."

Between World War I and 1930, the size and number of racially segregated neighborhoods increased. The index of dissimilarity (a statistical tool for measuring segregation, usually by city ward before 1940 and by block thereafter) rose from 67 to 85 percent in Chicago; from 61 to 85 percent in Cleveland; from 64 to 78 percent in Boston; and from 46 to 63 percent in Philadelphia. In Chicago, well over 35 percent of the city's blacks lived in census tracts that were over 75 percent black. Two-thirds of Manhattan's black population lived in Harlem, especially the area bordered by 126th Street on the south, 155th Street on the north, and Eighth Avenue on the west to Fifth Avenue on the east. In Cleveland, no census tract was more than 25 percent black in 1910. By 1930, 90 percent of the city's blacks lived in a restricted area bounded by Euclid Avenue on the north, East 105th Street on the east, Woodland Avenue on the south, and East 55th Street on the west. Likewise, although the black population of Milwaukee remained small by comparison with other cities, four wards contained over 93 percent of the city's 7,500 blacks. In Cincinnati, the West End absorbed the bulk of black newcomers. In western Pennsylvania, African Americans also found housing in carefully designated "colored areas": Port Perry in Braddock, Castle Garden in Duquesne, Rosedale in Johnstown, and the historic Hill District in Pittsburgh.

Southern blacks faced the most hostile municipal efforts to limit their space. As noted in Chapter 13, several southern cities—including Atlanta, Baltimore, Richmond, Norfolk, and Louisville—entered the war years with housing segregation statutes on the books. From the outset of the war, these cities moved to enforce their segregation ordinances. In Norfolk, Reverend Richard Bowling of the First

Baptist Church complained from the pulpit that the housing segregation law "hems the black brother in" and halts his "movement to the suburbs." At the outset of the period, Louisville police arrested two blacks for residing in white areas. State and local courts found the men guilty as charged, levied fines, and ordered them to move. Although the U.S. Supreme Court ruled housing segregation laws unconstitutional in 1917, it did little to halt the customary segregation of blacks in the city's housing market. Following the court's decision, for example, Louisville whites changed the names of several streets that housed black and white residents. They made certain that blacks knew where their neighborhood ended and the white began. Thirtieth Street represented the West End dividing line. Walnut Street changed to Michigan, Chestnut to River Park, Madison to Vermont, and Jefferson to Lockwood. At a West Side homeowners' association meeting, one speaker urged whites to make "a Negro living on the West End . . . as comfortable as if he was living in Hell." Likewise, few blacks moved into the East End. Those who did lived in a segregated "Smoketown."

Residential segregation entailed overcrowded, dilapidated, unsanitary, and overpriced housing for African Americans. Landlords took advantage of the desperate housing needs of black migrants, forcing them to pay higher rents for housing of substantially less quality than that of their white counterparts. Real estate speculators took over large mansions in older sections of cities, subdivided them into small one- or two-room apartments, and charged exorbitant rents. To pay rent, tenants took in large numbers of boarders, which led to overcrowding. In Chicago, one woman wrote home to her friend: "The people are rushing here by the thousands. . . . I know if you come and rent a big house you can get all the roomers you want." The Cincinnati Better Housing League reported cases of extreme overcrowding: twenty blacks inhabited one three-room flat, while another twelve-room tenement housed ninety-four blacks. Among urban blacks, heart disease, pneumonia, and tuberculosis represented the three most common causes of death, but tuberculosis continued to be the number one killer of African Americans nationally. In 1920, an estimated 202 blacks per 1,000 persons died from tuberculosis, compared with 86 whites. Although the average life expectancy of blacks increased by seven to eight years for men and women, compared with an increase of about five to six years for white men and women, African American life expectancy was fourteen years less than that of whites—forty-five years for blacks to fifty-nine years for whites in 1930. As housing and health conditions deteriorated for the urban black population, one public official exclaimed: "You could not produce a prize hog to show at the fair under conditions that you allow Negroes to live in this city."

"NEW" NEGROES IN THE MAKING

As suggested in Chapter 15, African Americans were determined to change the status quo. Even during the war years, when W. E. B. Du Bois urged blacks to close ranks, many questioned the efficacy of fighting in the war without guarantees of full citizenship and social justice. Black leaders like William Monroe Trotter, the Boston editor, and Washington, D.C.'s Archibald Grimké urged the federal government to end segregationist policies in exchange for black participation in the war. As Trotter put it, "We believe in democracy . . . but we hold that this nation should enter the lists with clean hands." Following the East St. Louis riot, an estimated ten thousand people joined the NAACP's "Silent Parade" to protest the violence. The organization issued a leaflet entitled "Why We March." "We march," it said, "because by the grace of God and the force of truth the dangerous, hampering wall of prejudice and inhuman injustices must fall." Men, women, and children silently marched through the streets, bearing signs such as "Thou Shalt Not Kill"; "MR. PRESIDENT, WHY NOT MAKE AMERICA SAFE FOR DEMOCRACY?"; and "YOUR HANDS ARE FULL OF BLOOD." In addition to protests over mob violence, NAACP branches staged protests against the showing of racially inflammatory films like *The Birth of a Nation*. They argued that such films fanned the flames of racial hatred and undercut the war effort.

African Americans also quietly pursued the struggle for social justice through the courts. In the case of *Guinn v. U.S.* (1917), the NAACP attacked Oklahoma's "grandfather clause," which the U.S. Supreme Court overturned on the grounds that it violated the Fifteenth Amendment guarantee of the right to vote. Similarly, in the case of *Buchanan v. Worley* (1917), the NAACP spearheaded the fight against residential segregation ordinances in Louisville, Baltimore, New Orleans, and other southern cities. NAACP lawyers Moorfield Storey and Clayton B. Blakey persuasively argued that segregation ordinances represented attempts "to deprive the [N]egro of the rights which belong to every citizen simply because white men consider him inferior by reason of his race and color. . . . A plainer case of racial discrimination could not well be imagined." The court agreed and struck down the residential segregation statutes.

Under the leadership of A. Philip Randolph and Chandler Owen, a small group of black socialists openly opposed the war. In their magazine, the *Messenger,* Randolph and Owen advised blacks to resist the draft and confine their fight to the home front. Described as "The Only Magazine of Scientific Radicalism in the World Published by Negroes," the *Messenger* accepted the socialist position that both war and racism emanated from the capitalist system. "When no profits are to be made," the editors believed, then no one would be interested in "stirring up race prejudice" and war. In one article, Owen invoked the lessons of history to support his antiwar position: "Did not the Negro fight in the Revolutionary War . . . the Spanish-American War. . . . And have not prejudice and rank hate grown . . . since 1898[?]" When the editors published the article, "Pro-Germanism Among Negroes," they received a jail sentence of two and one-half years, and the federal government suspended their mailing privileges. As noted in Chapter 15, the activities of A. Philip Randolph culminated in the formation of the Brotherhood of Sleeping Car Porters (BSCP) in 1925. Although it failed to achieve its principal aims, the BSCP soon engaged the Pullman Company in a protracted struggle for recognition.

Writers and commentators repeatedly contrasted the "Old" and "New" Negroes. They often expressed the contrast in gender terms, which exaggerated the quiescence of prewar blacks. Before the end of hostilities, Moorfield Storey, president of the NAACP, expressed the new mood among blacks: "The Negroes will come back feeling like men . . . and not disposed to accept the treatment to which they have been subjected." In Kansas City, a black weekly stated that the New Negro, unlike the Old Negro, "does not fear the face of day." The *Chicago Whip* believed "the Negro was breaking his shell and beginning to bask in the sunlight of real manhood." The militant *Crusader* declared: "The Old Negro goes. . . . His abject crawling and pleading have availed the cause nothing."

Edited by Cyril Briggs, the *Crusader* was the official organ of the African Blood Brotherhood (ABB). Formed in 1917 by West Indians and a few U.S.-born blacks, the ABB broke with the Harlem Section of the Socialist Party and demanded a more vigorous fight against colonialism abroad and racism at home. The ABB advocated "absolute race equality—political, economic, and social," by use of armed forces if necessary. Before its demise after 1921, the ABB claimed some 2,500 members in branches across the nation. Like Briggs, the West Indian socialist Hubert Harrison also broke from the Socialist Party and advanced a "Race First" form of socialism over the "color-blind" variety articulated by Randolph and Owen. Under the slogan "New Negro Manhood Movement," Harrison spearheaded the formation of the Liberty League and the short-lived magazine the *Voice*. When white socialists rejected his request for funds to start his own newspaper, Harrison joined the staff of Marcus Garvey's *Negro World* as contributing editor.

Adding to the nationalist ferment of the early postwar years was the NAACP's W. E. B. Du Bois. Although nationalists and socialists invariably cited the NAACP as part of the problem, Du Bois participated in the development of nationalist and internationalist consciousness within the African American community. In February 1919, he helped to organize a Pan-African Congress in the Grand Hotel in Paris, France. In addition to sixteen delegates from the United States, the Paris meeting attracted representatives from about sixteen African countries and colonies. As editor of the NAACP's *Crisis* magazine, Du Bois also captured the spirit of the New Negro's determination to fight. "We Soldiers of Democracy," he said, "return. . . . We return from fighting. We return fighting. Make way for Democracy. We saved it in France, and by the Great Jehovah, we will save it in the United States of America, or know the reason why."

THE GARVEY MOVEMENT

Postwar black militance and nationalism gained its most potent organizational expression in the rise of Marcus Garvey and the Universal Negro Improvement Association (UNIA). Born in Jamaica in 1887, Marcus Mosiah Garvey migrated to a variety of West Indian islands before spearheading the formation of the UNIA on August 1, 1914, the anniversary of British West Indian emancipation from slavery. The organization aimed to achieve two broad interlocking objectives: (1) to improve African American life in Jamaica by establishing Booker T. Washington–type

educational and industrial colleges, commercial and industrial leagues, and programs to strengthen "the bonds of brotherhood and unity among the races"; (2) to
promote "the spirit of race pride and love," create "a Universal Confraternity"
among blacks, promote "international commercial and industrial intercourse," and
support the independence struggles of African states. The organization adopted the
motto "ONE GOD! ONE AIM! ONE DESTINY!" Just before moving to the
United States in 1916, Garvey exhorted his West Indian brothers and sisters to

> cease the ignorance; unite your hands and hearts with the people of Africa. . . .
> Sons and daughters of Africa, I say to you arise, take on the toga of race pride,
> and throw off the brand of ignominy which has kept you back for so many cen-
> turies. . . . be a Negro in the light of the Pharaohs of Egypt, Simons of Cyrene,
> Hannibals of Carthage, L'Ouverture and Dessalines of Haiti, Blydens, Barclays
> and Johnsons of Liberia, Lewises of Sierra Leone, and Douglasses and Du Boises
> of America, who have made and are making history for the race.

On arrival in the United States, Garvey soon established headquarters in Harlem
and took his message to blacks across the nation and the world. Under the ringing
slogan of "Africa for Africans," Garvey repeatedly urged blacks to emulate their
own heroes, elevate their own women, take pride in blackness, build their own institutions, and strike blows for the liberation of the "motherland," Africa. "Black
men," he said, "you were once great, you shall be great again." Garvey called on
blacks to devote time, energy, and effort toward building racial unity. "If we must
have justice, we must be strong, if we must be strong . . . we must come together."
In unity, he believed, is strength. In the spirit of the New Negro, Garvey expected
black men to shoulder the burden of nation building. "We have come now to the
turning point of the Negro . . . we have changed from the cringing weakling, and
transformed into full-grown men, demanding our position as [men]." Accordingly,
the UNIA established the Universal African Legions, a paramilitary auxiliary, to
"prepare men for service by teaching them military skill and discipline and by reg-
istering them according to the various trades in which they have been trained."

The UNIA strove to transform blackness into a symbol of beauty, especially for
black women. Garvey idealized the black woman in poems like "The Black
Mother" and "The Black Woman," which referred to black women as "pure black
beauty"—"Black queen of beauty, thou hast given color to the world. Among other
women thou art royal and the fairest. . . . Nature's purest emblem." The UNIA also
canonized the Virgin Mary as a black Madonna and continually accented the purity theme as a way to counteract white stereotypes about the "leud" black woman.
As such, Garvey also reinforced the prevailing societal emphasis on the efficacy of
patriarchal, male-headed families.

Black women were not only principal targets of UNIA programs but also
shapers of its agenda. Black women made up about 50 percent of its membership
and served in influential state, local, and national posts. The UNIA divisions had a
male general president, who took charge of the organization as a whole, and a
woman president who directed and coordinated the work of the women members

and female auxiliaries, which included the Black Cross Nurses, the Ladies of the Royal Court of Ethiopia, and the Motor Corps. Black women also served on the board of UNIA enterprises like the Black Star Line and the *Negro World*. In addition to international organizer Henrietta Vinton Davis, both Amy Ashwood, Garvey's first wife, and Amy Jacques, his second wife, were instrumental in the UNIA's success. Amy Jacques-Garvey became the organization's "premier propagandist" when she edited the two-volume *Philosophy and Opinions of Marcus Garvey* (1923, 1925). In her preface to the volume, Jacques-Garvey wrote:

Born in Jamaica in 1887, Marcus Garvey founded the Universal Negro Improvement Association in 1914 and moved to the United States in 1916. His emphasis on black self-assertion, independence, and identity with Africa appealed to the masses of blacks who migrated to the nation's cities. *Library of Congress*

I decided to publish this volume in order to give the public an opportunity of studying and forming an opinion of him . . . from expressions of thoughts enunciated by him in defense of his oppressed and struggling race; so that by his own words he may be judged, and Negroes the world over may be informed and inspired, for truth, brought to light, forces conviction, and a state of conviction inspires action.

Although Garvey advanced the theme of African liberation, he advocated concrete steps to build black enterprises throughout the diaspora. In New York, the UNIA purchased a large auditorium, renamed it "Liberty Hall," and launched its own newspaper, the *Negro World;* the Black Star Line Shipping Company; and a plethora of grocery, restaurant, and laundry businesses. Garvey's appeal to "race pride" transcended material concerns, however. Under the leadership of West Indian Protestant Episcopal Church clergyman Rev. Alexander McGuire, the UNIA encouraged the formation of the African Orthodox Church. Rev. McGuire and other UNIA ministers exhorted blacks "to forget the white gods": "Erase the white gods from your hearts . . . go back to the native church, to our own true [black] God." Whether extolling the virtues of the African Orthodox Church, the African Legions, or the Black Cross Nurses, Garvey's oratory had a profound impact on his audiences. A Baltimore member, William L. Sherrill, later recalled his journey to Garveyism and the UNIA:

> One night on my way to a Show, I saw a huge crowd outside a Church, I went up and said, "what's going on in there?" A lady turned to me and said, "man alive, don't you know that Marcus Garvey is in there talking, yes, indeed, Garvey in person." "Shucks," I said, "I may as well see what he looks like." . . . I squeezed in, until I could get a good look at him; then suddenly he turned in my direction, and in a voice like thunder from Heaven he said, "men and women, what are you here for? To live unto yourself, until your body manures the earth, or to live God's Purpose to the fullest?" He continued to complete his thought in that compelling, yet pleading voice for nearly an hour. I stood there like one in a trance, every sentence ringing in my ears, and finding an echo in my heart. When I walked out of that Church, I was a different man—I knew my sacred obligations to my Creator, and my responsibilities to my fellow men, and so help me! I am still on the Garvey train.

Garvey was convicted of mail fraud in 1923, imprisoned in 1925, deported from the United States in 1927, and later died in England in 1940. Before the UNIA's demise, however, the organization played a key role in transforming the self-image of African Americans, instilling "race pride," and encouraging blacks to fight for the full recognition of their humanity. At Liberty Hall, Garvey held regular nightly meetings that attracted as many as six thousand listeners. The Garvey movement claimed 2 million members in 1918, nearly 4 million in 1920, and 6 million at its peak in 1923. Even conservative estimates placed peak membership at five hundred thousand or more. The organization represented the largest and broadest mass movement in African American history until the onset of the modern civil rights movement. It boasted seven hundred branches throughout the United States and another two hundred branches in the West Indies, Latin America, and Africa. The UNIA had also challenged European colonialism in Africa. From the outset of peace talks following World War I, the UNIA had sent commissioners to France to lobby for African or UNIA control of the ex-German colonies in Africa. Although without success, the UNIA regularly petitioned the League of Nations on behalf of African independence through the late 1920s.

Although Garvey and the UNIA surpassed earlier efforts to build a mass-based nationalist movement, the movement dissipated for a variety of internal and external reasons. Garvey paid greater attention to motivating the membership than he did to the financial operations of the organization. UNIA business enterprises were poorly managed and often mismanaged. They provided easy legal grounds for Garvey's conviction and imprisonment for mail fraud. Moreover, Garvey offered scathing criticisms of the black middle class and its small, integrationist-oriented elite. Friction between light- and dark-skinned blacks also hampered the organization's goal of racial unity, but the breaking point came when Garvey met with officials of white supremacist groups like the Ku Klux Klan and the Anglo-Saxon

League. Following Garvey's meeting with the Klan in 1922, a variety of media, civil rights, and labor leaders initiated a vigorous "Garvey Must Go Campaign." Anti-Garvey forces included not only officials of the NAACP and journalists like Robert Abbott of the *Chicago Defender* but also radical labor leaders like A. Philip Randolph and Chandler Owen. In its July 1922 issue, the *Messenger* claimed credit for "firing the opening gun in a campaign to drive Garvey and Garveyism . . . from the American soil."

Finally, and perhaps most importantly, the federal government feared the UNIA and placed Garvey under strict surveillance. U.S. officials believed that the UNIA's growing influence among the masses of black working people would undermine their loyalty to the nation and threaten national security. The American consul in Kingston, Jamaica, articulated the government's perspective when he declared that Garvey's "many references to fighting for negro rights . . . [tend] to alienate the loyalty of American and British negroes to his association." Shortly after his deportation to Jamaica, Garvey also accented the U.S. surveillance of his work: "The Great United States Government got men to investigate me; all manner of Secret Service people were set after me. . . . I must have cost the United States Government above five million dollars in ten years."

THE HARLEM RENAISSANCE

The spread of the Harlem Renaissance as a national movement gave literary and powerful cultural expression to the African American quest for liberation. The Great Migration transformed Harlem into the black cultural "capital of the world." The city's black population came mainly from the U.S. South, but immigrants from Africa and the West Indies made up nearly a quarter of the total. Plays, musical compositions, poems, and other artistic productions emerged from the creative interactions of African peoples from diverse regional and national backgrounds. Black artists produced some twenty-six novels, ten volumes of poems, five Broadway plays, and a plethora of short stories, essays, paintings, and sculpture. New Negro literary societies spread widely across the country: the Writer's Guild in New York; Black Opals in Philadelphia; the Saturday Evening Quill Club in Boston; the Ink and Slingers in Los Angeles; and the Book and Bench in Topeka, Kansas.

Leaders of the Renaissance

Helping black artists gain prominence was an influential core of black intellectuals and their white allies and patrons. Charles S. Johnson, editor of the National Urban League's *Opportunity* magazine; Alain Locke, a Howard University professor; and Jessie Fauset of the NAACP's *Crisis* magazine all helped to usher in the Harlem Renaissance. *Crisis* and *Opportunity* magazines sponsored literary contests, offered prizes to a variety of artists for their achievements, and arranged social events that brought artists, publishers, and white patrons together. Among these various architects of the Renaissance, Johnson was most influential.

Born in Bristol, Virginia, in 1893, Johnson obtained his undergraduate training at Virginia Union University and moved to Chicago in 1917. After completing an investigation of the Chicago race riot of 1919, he moved to New York, where he edited the National Urban League's new journal, *Opportunity*, between 1922 and 1928. Johnson used *Opportunity* to articulate his vision of the arts in the African American liberation struggle. In his view, the arts and letters represented the road of least resistance to black freedom. Johnson argued that white America would accept black participation in the arts much more readily than it would black equality in politics and economics. In other words, Johnson advocated opening the doors of Broadway, Carnegie Hall, and huge New York publishing houses to the products of black artists, even as the doors of corporate boardrooms, the ballot, and the highest echelons of government service and employment remained closed.

Along with Johnson and Locke, contemporary black artists also called Jessie Fauset a "midwife" of the Renaissance. Born in Camden, New Jersey, Fauset received her undergraduate education at Cornell University and later taught French and Latin at the M Street High School (later renamed Paul Laurence Dunbar High) in Washington, D.C. In 1919, she accepted the NAACP's offer to join the *Crisis* staff as literary editor. Under Fauset's leadership the *Crisis* soon became a centerpiece in the development of the Harlem Renaissance. Fauset's encouragement of young writers included the initiation of a children's publication, a monthly called *The Brownies' Book*. In her introduction to the magazine, Fauset said that she hoped to "teach Universal Love and Brotherhood for all little folks—black and brown, yellow and white."

Reinforcing the promotional activities of Fauset, Locke, and Johnson were entrepreneurs A'Lelia Walker, the daughter of the millionaire Madame C. J. Walker, and the wealthy West Indian–born numbers king Casper Holstein. When Madame Walker died in 1919, she left her daughter, A'Lelia, a fortune plus her hair-straightening business. A'Lelia entertained artists at her mother's Hudson River home, known as Villa Lewaro, as well as at other property that she owned in New York City. She also supported the arts through elaborate advertisements in magazines like *Crisis* and *Opportunity*. Although some intellectuals and members of the black elite decried support from illegal gambling enterprises, Holstein also regularly sponsored essay contests in the publications of both the NAACP and the National Urban League.

The African American artistic revival had fully emerged by the mid-1920s, when a special Harlem issue of the *Survey Graphic* magazine appeared. In March 1925, the *Survey Graphic* published its special edition of writings by Renaissance artists. Within a few months, the Albert and Charles Boni publishing company released an expanded book version of the anthology, entitled *The New Negro*. In his introduction to the volume, editor Alain Locke identified the social and psychological changes that gave rise to the new cultural movement:

The 1920s witnessed the fluorescence of African American literary and artistic expression. Harlem emerged as the most prolific center of the African American Renaissance in arts and letters, but it was a national and even international movement with centers in other cities across the United States and in Europe, particularly Paris. This photo (c. 1926) shows major figures of the Harlem Renaissance (*left to right*): Langston Hughes, Charles Johnson, E. Franklin Frazier, Rudolph Fisher, and Hubert Delaney. *Schomburg Center for Research in Black Culture, New York Public Library, Astor, Lenox and Tilden Foundation*

In the last decade something beyond the watch and guard of statistics has happened in the life of the American Negro. . . . For the younger generation is vibrant with a new psychology; the new spirit is awake in the masses, and under the very eyes of the professional observers—is transforming what has been a perennial problem into progressive phases of contemporary Negro life.

Locke also urged black artists to probe their own indigenous culture for inspiration, including their African heritage. He believed that African themes could revitalize and inspire black artists, especially those working as visual artists, sculptors, and painters. "If the forefathers could so adroitly master these mediums, why not we?" he asked.

Poets, Novelists, Short-Story Writers, and Artists

The most renowned Renaissance poets, novelists, short-story writers, and visual artists included Claude McKay, Jean Toomer, Countee Cullen, and Langston Hughes; Jessie Fauset, Nella Larsen, Georgia Douglas Johnson, and Zora Neale Hurston; Richmond Barthé, Sargent Johnson, Nancy Prophet, and Aaron Douglas, to name only a few. As early as 1921–1922, Claude McKay and Jean Toomer represented the advance guard of the new cultural explosion. Born in Clarendon Parish, Jamaica, McKay gave voice to the militant mood of black America in his poem "If We Must Die" (1919):

> If we must die, let it not be like hogs
> Hunted and penned in an inglorious spot . . .
> If we must die, O let us nobly die . . .
> Pressed to the wall, dying, but fighting back.

In 1922, McKay published his renowned collection of poems, *Harlem Shadows.* Recognized by growing numbers of whites and blacks alike as black America's leading poet, McKay nonetheless protested: "Must fifteen million blacks be gratified / that one of them can enter as a guest, / A fine white house—the rest of them denied / A place of decent sojourn and a rest?" A year later, the Washington, D.C.–born Jean Toomer (Nathan Eugene Toomer) released his novel *Cane,* an exploration of black life in rural and urban America. An *Opportunity* reviewer described *Cane* as "a book of gold and bronze, of dusk and flames, of ecstasy and pain." Toomer, the reviewer also declared, "is a bright morning star of a new day of the race in literature."

The New York–born Countee Cullen was undoubtedly elite Harlem's favorite black poet. During his undergraduate studies at New York University, Cullen won several poetry prizes and later received his master's degree from Harvard University. His poetry appeared not only in black publications like *Opportunity* but also in mainstream white publications like *Harper's Century* and *American Mercury.* Harper and Brothers published his first volume of poetry, *Color.* In the poem "Yet Do I Marvel," Cullen expresses amazement that whites continued to expect blacks to accommodate to racial inequality: "Yet do I marvel at this curious thing: To make a poet black, and bid him sing!"

If Cullen gained renown among Harlem's elite, Langston Hughes soon received recognition as the voice of ordinary black folk. Born in Joplin, Missouri, and raised in a variety of locales in Mexico and the Midwest, Hughes moved to New York in 1922–1923 and later sailed to Europe and Africa. In 1921, a year after Hughes graduated from Central High School in Cleveland, the *Crisis* published what would become his most widely known poem, "The Negro Speaks of Rivers," which he dedicated to W. E. B. Du Bois:

> I've known rivers:
> I've known rivers ancient as the world and older than the flow of
>   human blood in human veins.
> My soul has grown deep like the rivers.

I bathed in the Euphrates when dawns were young.
I built my hut near the Congo and it lulled me to sleep.
I looked upon the Nile and raised the pyramids above it.
I heard the singing of the Mississippi when Abe Lincoln went
    down to New Orleans, and I've seen its muddy bosom
    turn all golden in the sunset.
I've known the rivers.
Ancient, dusky rivers.
My soul has grown deep like the rivers.

Four years later, Alfred A. Knopf published Hughes's first collection of poems, *The Weary Blues* (1925). More so than other Renaissance poets, Hughes looked to the grassroots or "folk" for his inspiration. Even during his trip overseas, Hughes reported: "I got a little tired of palaces and churches and famous paintings and English tourists. And I began to wonder if there were no back alleys in Venice and no poor people and no slums." In *The Weary Blues,* he wrote:

Droning a drowsy syncopated tune,
Rocking back and forth to a mellow croon,
    I heard a Negro play.
Down on Lenox Avenue the other night
By the pale dull pallor of an old gas light
    He did a lazy sway. . . .
    He did a lazy sway. . . .
To the tune o' those Weary Blues.
With his ebony hands on each ivory key
He made that poor piano moan with melody.
    O Blues! Swaying to and fro on his rickety stool
He played that sad raggy tune like a musical fool.
    Sweet Blues!
Coming from a black man's soul.
    O Blues!

Zora Neale Hurston also looked to the grassroots for her inspiration. Born in Jacksonville, Florida, in 1891, she received her undergraduate training at Howard University before moving to New York City, where she earned a graduate degree from Barnard College. Hurston focused almost exclusively on intraracial rather than interracial themes in her first short stories in *Opportunity* magazine: "Drenched Light" (1924), "Spunk" (1925), and "Muttsy" (1926). During the 1930s, Hurston produced her best-known book, *Their Eyes Were Watching God.* Chicago-born Nella Larsen, who came to New York after graduating from Fisk University, also dealt with intraracial themes but accented conflicts along the color line, as well as issues of female sexuality, in her novels *Quicksand* (1928) and *Passing* (1929). In her volume of poetry, *Bronze: A Book of Verse* (1922), Georgia Douglas Johnson reluctantly addressed race and color themes, confiding privately that "if one can soar, he should soar, leaving his chains behind." For her part, Jessie

Aaron Douglas: *Rebirth*, 1927. Originally from Kansas City, Missouri, Douglas moved to New York in 1925 and soon became the most renowned visual artist of the Harlem Renaissance. His *Rebirth* appeared in Alain Locke's *The New Negro*. *Rebirth, 1927, by Aaron Douglas from* The New Negro, © *Charles Boni, 1925, ed. Alain Locke. Reprinted with permission of Scribner, an imprint of Simon & Schuster.*

Fauset's novels *There Is Confusion* (1924) and *Plum Bun* (1929) depicted elite blacks whose lives resembled those of their white counterparts (preoccupied with pedigree and manners) except for the color of their skin. The white civil rights activist Mary White Ovington was disappointed. She doubted that "such a colored world" existed. Whites, she said, just "don't expect Negroes to be like this."

Although Renaissance writers found substantial outlets for their work, African American visual artists only gradually gained recognition. As noted in Chapter 15, the filmmaker Oscar Micheaux produced several pioneering black films during the war and postwar years, but black sculptors and painters soon achieved greater renown. In 1928, Richmond Barthé won the Harmon Award for his sculpture *Flute Boy.* During the 1930s, he produced his most important bronze works, *African Dancer* and another dance figure, *Feral Benga.* The San Franciscan Sargent Johnson produced notable African-inspired terra cotta and porcelain figures. His lacquered-wood sculpture of a black woman, *Forever Free,* represents the successful integration of African motifs into his own vision of blacks in America. In 1930, the black artist Nancy Prophet received the Harmon Award for her sculpture *Head of a Negro.* Like her male counterparts, Prophet exhibited strong African influences.

Born in Topeka, Kansas, Aaron Douglas came to New York in 1925 and soon became the most well-known African American visual artist. Douglas studied under the widely regarded artist Winold Reiss. Among the various artists of the Renaissance era, Douglas responded most energetically to African themes. His African-inspired paintings appeared in publications like *Vanity Fair* and *Theatre Monthly* as well as *Opportunity* magazine and Alain Locke's *The New Negro.* Although visual artists emphasized connections between Africa and Afro-America, Renaissance writers downplayed African themes, as reflected in the tentative references to Africa in Langston Hughes's poem "Afro-American Fragment," with its refrain "so long, so far away is Africa."

The Mixed Blessings of White Supporters

The Harlem Renaissance both benefited and suffered from a coterie of white benefactors. The most influential of these included the publishers Boni and Liveright, Harper and Brothers, and Alfred and Blanche Knopf; Carl Van Vechten, the controversial author of the novel *Nigger Heaven;* and the wealthy philanthropist Charlotte Osgood Mason. White sponsors promoted the work of black artists by offering financial assistance, influential contacts, and encouragement. Both Van Vechten and Mason reflected the ideas of the so-called Lost Generation of white writers—F. Scott Fitzgerald and others—who rebelled against modern industrial society in the wake of World War I. Such writers and patrons perceived blacks as "primitive" people who lived close to nature, enjoyed an uninhibited sex life, and offered an alternative to what they saw as the destructive discipline and blandness of contemporary industrial society.

The ideas and expectations of white patrons produced diverse reactions among black artists. Take, for example, the relationship between several black writers and Charlotte Mason, who entertained black artists in her Park Avenue apartment "high above the streets of New York." Louise Thompson, a promising young writer, broke off the relationship early. She resented and resisted Mason's effort to reshape black artists into the "pagan savages" that she believed they were. On the other hand, Zora Neale Hurston put on the mask and feigned "the exuberant pagan that pleased her white friends." Louise Thompson recalled hearing Hurston talking on the phone to a white patron: "Here's your little darky and telling 'darky' stories, only to wink when she was through so as to show that she had tricked them again." For his part, Langston Hughes retained the relationship for as long as he could but gradually resisted Mason's effort to dictate and shape the content of his work. The final break came during the early years of the depression when Mason cut Hughes from her list of artists and denied him her friendship. Hughes later recalled the moment when "that beautiful room, that had been so full of light and help and understanding for me suddenly became like a trap closing in, faster and faster."

Whites not only supported black artists for their own profit and sense of philanthropy. They also increasingly turned to blacks as subject matter. As early as 1917, the white director Emily Hapgood produced three plays (with black casts) written by the white playwright Torrence Ridgely—*The Rider of Dreams, Simon the Cyrenian,* and *Granny Maumee.* During the 1920s, white writers using black materials included Eugene O'Neill, *Emperor Jones* (1921) and *All God's Chillun Got*

Wings (1924); Waldo Frank, *Holiday* (1923); Sherwood Anderson, *Dark Laughter* (1925); Du Bose Heyward, *Porgy* (1925) and *Mamba's Daughter* (1927); and Paul Green, the Pulitzer Prize–winning *In Abraham's Bosom* (1926). Black actors and actresses like Patrick Gilpin, Paul Robeson, and Rose McClendon took the lead role in these productions. Although white writers gradually moved away from stark racist images of blacks, they nonetheless reinforced older stereotypes, emphasizing the theme of "primitivism." As one analyst of the Renaissance notes, "Insofar as it idealizes simpler cultures, primitivism is a romantic retreat from the complexities of modern life. Reflecting the writings of Sigmund Freud, it exalts instinct over intellect, Id over Super Ego, and is thus a revolt against the Puritan spirit." In 1926, for example, Carl Van Vechten published his *Nigger Heaven* (1926). Although Van Vechten was a major supporter of the arts in Harlem, he catered to the white thirst for "primitive" themes in black culture. Du Bois called the book "a blow in the face" because it accented what Du Bois called "the squalor of Negro life, the vice of Negro life." Black literary critic George Schuyler complained that such writers believed that "it is only necessary to beat a tom tom or wave a rabbit's foot and the black man is ready to strip off" his Western suit, "grab a spear and ride off wide-eyed on the back of a crocodile."

Van Vechten's book exposed deep social cleavages within the Harlem Renaissance. A younger generation of artists perceived Van Vechten's portrait of black society as more realistic than some Renaissance promoters cared to admit. These writers included Wallace Thurman, Zora Neale Hurston, and Langston Hughes, among others. Under the leadership of Thurman and Richard Bruce Nugent, this disenchanted group launched a new literary magazine, *Fire!!* Described as a quarterly "Devoted to the Younger Negro Artists," *Fire!!* loudly announced its determination "to burn up a lot of the old, dead, conventional Negro ideas of the past." Specifically, it sought to sever the tie between the civil rights establishment (the NAACP and the Urban League) and the arts.

Fire!! advocated a more "truly Negroid note" and urged artists to turn toward the proletariat rather than the bourgeoisie for their creative materials. It hoped to appeal to blacks "who didn't dress properly, whose finger nails were dirty, and who didn't eat properly, and whose English was not good." Although some writers developed themes that pleased the white "primitivists"—as in Rudolph Fisher's *Walls of Jericho* (1928) and Claude McKay's *Home to Harlem* (1928)—they also took up issues of class relations. Fisher's novel clearly and forcefully portrayed class antagonisms among Harlem blacks. As his principal character and hero Joshua "Shine" Jones put it: "Dicties is evil—don' never trust no dickty." Conversely, however, McKay's principal character Jake is unfettered by any of the moral conventions of the day, proletarian or "dickty." Langston Hughes summed up what he believed was the cultural attitude and orientation of poor and working-class blacks when he said that the "low-down" folks

> do not particularly care whether they are like white folks or anybody else. Their joy runs, bang! into ecstasy. Their religion soars to a shout. Work maybe a little

today, rest a little tomorrow. Play awhile. Sing awhile. . . . These common people are not afraid of spirituals . . . and jazz is their child.

Still, *Fire!!* aspired to be a success in conventional artistic terms. Hughes later recalled that the volume "had to be on good paper. . . . It had to have beautiful type . . . so in the end it cost almost a thousand dollars, and nobody could pay the bills."

Jazz and Blues

Although *Fire!!* was a short-lived venture, it nonetheless revealed deep ideological fissures among Renaissance intellectuals and artists. Some Renaissance cultural and political elites eschewed jazz and blues as "low art" forms, but these forms of expression had far greater influence on European and white American culture than did most of the poems and novels of the principal Renaissance writers. Defined by musicologist and historian Eileen Southern as the "fusion of blues and ragtime with brass-band and syncopated dance music," jazz flourished during the 1920s. According to some musicologists, the music got its name from an itinerant black musician from the Mississippi Delta named Jazbo Brown. Brown was a frequent performer in honky-tonk cafes, where appreciative audiences would shout out, "More, Jazbo: More, Jaz, more!" In another origins story, jazz got its name from a sign announcing the appearance of bluesman Boisey James. The sign stated simply "Jas. Band," which became known as "Jas's music" and finally "Jazz."

The Great Migration and the city's closing of New Orleans' Storyville section sent black musicians up the Mississippi River to southern cities like Memphis and then to Kansas City and Chicago. The early Chicago jazz orchestras included migrants from New Orleans: Joseph "King" Oliver, Jelly Roll Morton, and Louis Armstrong. In New York, Fletcher Henderson helped to launch the "Big Band" movement of jazz musicians in 1923, and continued a tradition pioneered by James Reese Europe. The city's big bands soon proliferated under the direction of such black musicians as William "Chick" Webb, Jimmie Lunceford, Andy Kirk, and Duke Ellington. Big bandsmen also emerged in other cities—Erskine Tate in Chicago; Clarence Love in Omaha and Kansas City; Les Hite in Los Angeles; and George Morrison in Denver. Famous jazz pianists included Willie-the-Lion Smith, Lucky Roberts, James P. Johnson, Fats Waller, and Earl "Fatha" Hines.

During the Renaissance years, Harlem dance halls vied with Broadway in popularity. In 1921 and 1922, the African American musical *Shuffle Along* was the most popular musical in the city of New York, black or white. Although some white-owned establishments like the Cotton Club on Lenox Avenue and Connie's Inn on Seventh Avenue featured black performances for predominantly white audiences, others like the black-owned Small's Paradise served an interracial clientele. Opened in 1926, the white-owned but black-operated Savoy Ballroom symbolized the musical achievement of the Harlem Renaissance. Located at 140th and 141st Streets, the Savoy's ten-thousand-square-foot dance floor hosted some four thousand dancers nightly. Along with blacks, white musicians like Tommy Dorsey and Benny Goodman also occupied the Savoy's two bandstands.

Most working-class and poor blacks recreated themselves in numerous small dance halls, clubs, and private house parties. In these settings, they fused the older rural blues traditions with "the new learning" and produced the urban blues, but record companies turned to black female vaudeville singers for their first blues recordings. In 1920, Okeh Record Company released Mamie Smith's "Crazy Blues." Written by the black composer Perry Bradford, "Crazy Blues" was the nation's first commercial blues recording. When sales quickly rose to some 7,500 discs a week, rising numbers of companies added "race record" labels and catered to the expanding African American market. Bessie Smith emerged during the 1920s as the most renowned of the blues artists. Known as the "Empress of the Blues," she was a protégé of the older blueswoman Ma Rainey. Her songs combined elements of blues and jazz and appealed to a broad cross-section of the black community. Black musicians like Fletcher Henderson, Louis Armstrong, and James P. Johnson accompanied Smith. In addition to Rainey's numerous recordings, a film drama, *St. Louis Blues* (1929), captured her talents and contributions to U.S. and Afro-U.S. music. The blues singer Ethel Waters also launched her career during the 1920s. She gave the black-owned New York–based Pace Phonograph Company (formed in 1921) its first hit record with "Down Home Blues" and "O Daddy." Although black women dominated blues recordings during the 1920s, the singer Blind Lemon Jefferson set the pace for later black bluesmen, including Huddie "Leadbelly" Ledbetter and Josh White.

Closely related to its blind spot on class relations, the Harlem Renaissance overplayed its emphasis on art as an instrument for changing the material and political realities of black life. Although Du Bois produced his own artistic works and supported the arts in *Crisis* magazine, he rejected Charles S. Johnson's belief that artistic products could substitute for agitation, petitions, and marches on behalf of social justice. At a 1926 NAACP conference, Du Bois pointedly questioned the emphasis on art: "How is an organization like this . . . a group of radicals trying to bring new things into the world, a fighting organization . . . how is it that an organization of this kind can turn aside to talk about art?" Alain Locke would also later admit that there "is no cure or saving magic in poetry and art for . . . precarious marginal employment, high mortality rates, civic neglect." The selections in the box (pages 426–427) bring this important debate into sharper focus.

Ideological Fissures

Although jazz, blues, and the literary products of the Renaissance years cut across class lines within the black urban community, they were also shaped by internal social and cultural differences and conflicts. The black urban community not only expanded and consolidated but also stratified internally as the new black middle class slowly moved into better housing vacated by whites, leaving the black poor concentrated in certain sections. In his studies of Chicago and New York City, sociologist E. Franklin Frazier demonstrated the division of the black urban community along socioeconomic lines. In Chicago, poor and working-class blacks concentrated in the northernmost zones of the South Side black ghetto, while the higher socioeconomic groups lived on the extreme South Side. In Harlem, middle-, and upper-class blacks lived on the periphery, while working-class and poor blacks clustered in the center. More so than other urban neighborhoods, the black community contained interclass mixing, but poverty increasingly characterized specific sections of the ghetto.

Established black residents feared, resented, and sometimes resisted the influx of newcomers into their communities. Old residents believed that newcomers would endanger their relationship with local whites. Black migrants repeatedly shared stories about the cold treatment that they received in established churches. One black female newcomer complained, "Instead of the Colored Northern citizens trying to help lift up your [southern] colored neighbor . . . you run him down." Only in the churches with "down home" preaching and ways of greeting did many newcomers feel comfortable or at home. As one woman migrant put it, "The women, especially the older women—they were so friendly—they put their arms around me and made me feel so welcome." Another migrant said that he liked "the way they do, talk, and everything—so I joined."

Despite their helpful services (as discussed in Chapter 15), insurance companies, banks, real estate firms, and retail establishments paid close attention to their bottom lines. They frequently refused loans or canceled policies of delinquent clients. As C. C. Spaulding, head of the North Carolina Mutual, said: "Insurance is business. . . . It was this realization which caused our company to build upward from a small beginning until the present proportions have been reached." Throughout the 1920s, the company paid close attention to black actuarial tables. Indeed, President Spaulding noted that his policyholders had lower death rates than blacks insured by some white companies. According to Spaulding, the company owed its success to the "Negro agent's familiarity with colored risks . . . an understanding of distinctions among Negroes to which white men, through racial prejudice have blinded themselves." Black workers also paid attention to their own bottom line. One black customer of a retail store related: "I try to spend as much as I can with Negro stores but most of them don't have what you want, or they are too high. That may be our fault for not trading with them more, but we are poor and have to count pennies."

Poor and working-class people left their own imprint on African American cultural and community life. Their influence cut across the usual separation of the sacred and the secular. In Chicago, for example, migrants founded at least 5 new storefront or home-based Baptist churches between 1916 and 1919: Pilgrim, Progressive, Providence, Liberty, and Monumental. At the same time, other migrants initiated and sustained nearly 20 Holiness churches. In Harlem, a contemporary report (1926) identified 140 black churches in a 150-block area. An estimated two-thirds of these churches were storefront or home-based churches. One minister rented chairs from the local undertaker to seat the growing number of people who crowded into his home. On one occasion, neighbors sued a Harlem storefront for

SOURCES FROM THE PAST

1925–1926

Alain Locke and W. E. B. Du Bois Debate African American Art

Alain Locke Advocates Artistic Excellence as a Route to Black Liberation, 1925

As with the Jew, persecution is making the Negro international.

As a world phenomenon this wider race consciousness is a different thing from the much asserted rising tide of color. . . . With the American Negro, his new internationalism is primarily an effort to recapture contact with the scattered peoples of African derivation. Garveyism may be a transient, if spectacular, phenomenon, but the possible rôle of the American Negro in the future development of Africa is one of the most constructive and universally helpful missions that any modern people can lay claim to.

Constructive participation in such causes cannot help giving the Negro valuable group incentives, as well as increased prestige at home and abroad. Our greatest rehabilitation may possibly come through such channels, but for the present, more immediate hope rests in the revaluation by white and black alike of the Negro in terms of his artistic endowments and cultural contributions, past and prospective. It must be increasingly recognized that the Negro has already made very substantial contributions, not only in his folk-art, music especially, which has always found appreciation, but in larger, though humbler and less acknowledged ways. For generations the Negro has been the peasant matrix of that section of America which has most undervalued him, and here he has contributed not only materially in labor and in social patience, but spiritually as well. The South has unconsciously absorbed the gift of his folk-temperament. In less than half a generation it will be easier to recognize this, but the fact remains that a leaven of humor, sentiment, imagination and tropic nonchalance has gone into the making of the South from a humble, unacknowledged source. A second crop of the Negro's gifts promises still more largely. He now becomes a conscious contributor and lays aside the status of a beneficiary and ward for that of a collaborator and participant in American civilization. The great social gain in this is the releasing of our talented group from the arid fields of controversy and debate to the productive fields of creative expression. The especially cultural recognition they win should in turn prove the key to that revaluation of the Negro which must precede or accompany any considerable further betterment of race relationships. But whatever the general effect, the present generation will have added the motives of self-expression and spiritual development to the old and still unfinished task of making material headway and progress. No one who understandingly faces the situation with its substantial accomplishment or views the new scene with its still more abundant promise can be entirely without hope. And certainly, if in our lifetime the Negro should not be able to celebrate his full initiation into American democracy, he can at least, on the warrant of these things, celebrate the attainment of a significant and satisfying new phase of group development, and with it a spiritual Coming of Age.

W. E. B. Du Bois Underscores the Ongoing Need for Political Agitation and Protest, 1926

With the growing recognition of Negro artists in spite of the severe handicaps, one comforting thing is occurring to both white and black. They are whispering, "Here is a way out. Here is the real solution of the color problem. The recognition accorded Cullen, Hughes, Fauset, White and others shows there is no real color line. Keep quiet! Don't complain! Work! All will be well!"

I will not say that already this chorus amounts to a conspiracy. Perhaps I am naturally too suspicious. But I will say that there are today a surprising number of white people who are getting great satisfaction out of these younger Negro writers because they think it is going to stop agitation of the Negro question. They say, "What is the use of your fighting and complaining; do the great thing and the reward is there." And many colored people are all too eager to follow this advice; especially those who are weary of the eternal struggle along the color line, who are afraid to fight and to whom the money of philanthropists and the alluring publicity are subtle and deadly bribes. They say, "What is the use of fighting? Why not show simply what we deserve and let the reward come to us?"

And it is right here that the National Association for the Advancement of Colored People comes upon the field, comes with its great call to a new battle, a new fight and new things to fight before the old things are wholly won; and to say that the Beauty of Truth and Freedom which shall some day be our heritage and the heritage of all civilized men is not in our hands yet and that we ourselves must not fail to realize. . . .

Thus all Art is propaganda and ever must be, despite the wailing of the purists. I stand in utter shamelessness and say that whatever art I have for writing has been used always for propaganda for gaining the right of black folk to love and enjoy. I do not care a damn for any art that is not used for propaganda. But I do care when propaganda is confined to one side while the other is stripped and silent.

In New York we have two plays: "White Cargo" and "Congo." In "White Cargo" there is a fallen woman. She is black. In "Congo" the fallen woman is white. In "White Cargo" the black woman goes down further and further and in "Congo" the white woman begins with degradation but in the end is one of the angels of the Lord. . . .

Source: W. E. B. Du Bois, "Criteria of Negro Art," *Crisis* (1926). The publisher wishes to thank The Crisis Publishing Company, Inc., the publisher of the magazine of the National Association for the Advancement of Colored People, for the use of this work.

"conducting a public nuisance." They described the music, shouting, handclapping, and preaching as "weird sounds":

Are you ready-ee? Hah! For that great day, hah! When the moon shall drape her face in mourning, hah! And the sun drip down in blood, hah! When the stars, hah! Shall burst forth from their diamond sockets, hah! And the mountain shall skip like lambs, hah! Havoc will be there, my friends, hah! With her jaws wide open, hah! And the sinner-man, hah! And cry, Oh rocks! Hah! Hide me! Hah! Hide me from the face of an angry God, hah! Hide me, Ohhhhhh! . . . Can't hide, sinner, you can't hide.

Among the most successful of these storefront or home-based Holiness bodies were the ministries of Ida B. Robinson and Lucy Smith. Robinson moved to Philadelphia in 1917 and soon launched her career as a street evangelist. She initially affiliated with the United Holy Church of America. Two years later, she was ordained an elder and placed in charge of a small mission, Mount Olive Church. In 1924, she broke from the United Holy Church over limitations on female ministers and formed the Mount Sinai Holy Church of America. Mount Sinai held its first national convention in 1925 and later became one of the largest Pentecostal organizations in the country, with branches in the Caribbean. Likewise, in 1916, Elder Lucy Smith, a Georgia-born migrant, organized All Nations Pentecostal Church in a one-room prayer meeting in her house. For ten years, the church moved from storefront to storefront until Smith initiated the building of a new edifice. One contemporary observer, who misunderstood the intellectual genius of Elder Smith, described her as "a simple, ignorant, untrained woman with deep human sympathies, who believed absolutely in her own power to help and heal other people. Calm and serene in that faith, she has drawn together a following from the back streets of Chicago."

CIVIL RIGHTS AND POLITICAL STRUGGLES

The Harlem Renaissance, the Garvey movement, and the emergence of vibrant new forms of working-class black culture challenged established civil rights and political leadership. Under growing pressure from these alternative ways of thinking about black liberation, the NAACP intensified its fight against racial barriers. In 1920, James Weldon Johnson became the first black to occupy the top executive secretary's post of the NAACP. Under his leadership and that of assistant secretary Walter White, African Americans gradually gained control of the organization and set its agenda. The organization intensified its attack on the legal foundations of Jim Crow, disfranchisement, and mob violence. In 1923, the NAACP raised $50,000 to defend blacks in Philip County, Arkansas, where mobs had killed some twenty-five blacks and seventy-nine other blacks had received life imprisonment on trumped-up murder charges. When the case reached the Supreme Court, the organization persuasively argued that African Americans were the victims of mob law. The Court agreed and released the men. Justice Oliver Wendell Holmes explained the Court's decision: "If in fact a trial is dominated by a mob, so that there is an actual interference with the course of justice there is a departure from due process of law." In 1925, the NAACP defended Dr. Ossian Sweet and his family against murder charges when a member of a white mob lost his life in an attack on the Sweets's home. After two trials, the Sweets were cleared of all charges. The Court agreed that blacks had a right to use violence to defend their homes against mob attacks.

The campaign for a federal antilynching law emerged at the forefront of the NAACP's civil rights activities during the 1920s. In 1919, the organization mobilized support for the Dyer antilynching bill. Introduced by Senator Leonidas Dyer (R-Indiana) and Congressman Charles Curtis (R-Kansas), the Dyer Bill made it illegal for officials to aid and abet mob violence and provided penalties of five years' imprisonment and/or $5,000 in fines. The bill also provided for the prosecution of mob participants and barred persons associated with mobs from jury duty. In addition to the opposition of hostile southern Democrats, senior Republicans like Henry Cabot Lodge of Massachusetts, William Borah of Idaho, and James F. Watson of Indiana helped to defeat the measure in the Senate in 1921 and again in 1923.

As the campaign for a federal antilynching law stalled, the NAACP searched for ways to expand its legal victories. In 1930, the U.S. Supreme Court became the principal target of these efforts when President Hoover nominated North Carolina judge John J. Parker to the bench. The NAACP closely scrutinized Parker's record on race relations and found it wanting. In 1920, during his campaign for governor, Parker had opposed black suffrage: "The participation of the Negro in the political life of the South is harmful to him and to the community. . . . The Republican party of North Carolina does not desire him to participate in the politics of the state." When the NAACP wired Parker a telegram asking if he still retained such views, Parker ignored the correspondence. The national office then mobilized some 177 branches against Judge Parker's nomination. After a vigorous six-week campaign, the Senate defeated the Parker nomination by a vote of forty-one to thirty-nine. The Parker victory not only helped to transform the NAACP into a powerful national civil rights organization but also symbolized the growing significance of the black vote in American politics.

Closely aligned with the expanding civil rights and legal struggles of the NAACP, African Americans intensified their efforts to gain elective office and transform local, state, and national politics. Chicago symbolized the growing participation of blacks in electoral politics. The city's Second and Third Wards had become 80 percent black by 1930, and blacks had gradually established the organizational groundwork for winning elective offices. According to one contemporary political observer:

> The Negroes in Chicago have achieved relatively more in politics during this period than have the Negroes in other cities of the United States. They have been more aggressive along political lines than have the Negroes in New York City, they have been more experienced than the Negroes in Detroit, they have been more adventuresome than the Negroes in Cincinnati, and they have been more united than have the Negroes in St. Louis.

Under the leadership of men like Edward H. Wright, Oscar De Priest, and Robert R. Jackson, African Americans built a powerful political machine within the context of the larger Republican machine. They demanded a growing share of patronage positions, elective offices, and influential posts within the Republican Party itself. In 1919, they demanded and soon won control of the Second Ward Republican organization when Ed Wright replaced the white Republican committeeman. By the late 1920s, they had gained similar control over the Third Ward. As such, they controlled the Republican Party in the South Side "black belt." Ward, district, and precinct heads were black. Although legally disfranchised until 1920, black women nonetheless represented a major force in Chicago politics. In the prewar years, they had formed the Alpha Club and pushed for the inclusion of black women in the woman's suffrage campaign. When Oscar De Priest campaigned to become Chicago's first black alderman, he turned to the Alpha Club for assistance. Following his victory, De Priest thanked black women for contributing "some thousand votes toward his election!" In 1928, Chicago elected De Priest to the U.S. Congress and foreshadowed the resurgence of African American influence in national as well as state and local politics. The last black U.S. congressman, George L. White of North Carolina, had left office in 1901. On leaving office, he had predicted that "Phoenix-like" African Americans would "rise up someday and come again."

The acquisition of political office transcended symbolism, however. At the outset of the period, the mayor of Chicago appointed the Second Ward committeeman Ed Wright to a $100-a-day job with the State Traction Commission. The governor of Illinois later appointed Wright to a lucrative post with the Illinois Commerce Commission. When Oscar De Priest took his congressional post, black access to public service jobs dramatically expanded. One astute contemporary student of black urban politics, Ralph Bunche, summarized the economic benefits of black power in the city. According to Bunche, such public service jobs gradually transcended the lower-echelon sanitation positions and augmented the growth of Chicago's black middle class:

> These men are all entrusted with responsible positions. In illustration, in the office of the corporation council, a Negro, as assistant corporation counsel and trial lawyer in property damage litigation, represents the city in suits mounting to millions of dollars yearly. There are approximately twenty Negro investigators in the various legal departments. Additional appointments in the many city departments, as teachers, clerks, police, etc., run into hundreds.

By decade's end, blacks made up about 7 percent of the city's total population but accounted for some 25 percent of all postal service workers and over 6 percent of all civil service employees.

Electoral politics reinforced the larger civil rights struggle for social justice. Chicago's political leaders could no longer ignore protests against racial discrimination in various facets of the city's life. When a Republican candidate for governor set up headquarters in a hotel that discriminated against blacks, African Americans protested and the candidate agreed to relocate unless the hotel served blacks on a nondiscriminatory basis. African American city, state, and congressional leaders also secured a new state law that banned "the exhibition, manufacture, or sale of any lithograph, moving picture, book or drama which tends to entice race or religious prejudice." The state legislature also strengthened existing civil rights laws by making it illegal for places of public accommodation, realtors, and schools "to advertise a discriminatory policy."

Although the process was most pronounced in Chicago, the civil rights and political struggles of World War I and the 1920s signaled the dawn of a new day in black politics across the nation. Although most blacks continued to join the "Party of Lincoln," they pressed for more patronage, elective, and appointive positions. Despite the widespread disfranchisement of southern blacks, participation in electoral politics was not limited to the North. In some border and Upper South states, blacks retained the franchise and played an important role in the established political process. In 1918, unlike their counterparts in most southern states, for example, African Americans in West Virginia elected three of their numbers to the state legislature: the Charleston attorney T. G. Nutter; the Keystone attorney Harry J. Capehart; and the coal miner John V. Coleman of Fayette County. In 1927, when the black legislator E. Howard Harper died in office, his wife, Mrs. Minnie Buckingham Harper, served out his term and became "the first woman of the [N]egro race to become a member of a legislative body in the United States." Mountain state legislators also succeeded in obtaining a state antilynching statute and legislation barring the showing of racially inflammatory motion pictures like *The Birth of a Nation*.

Even in the heavily disfranchised states of the South, African Americans did not give up the fight for access to the mainstream political process. They used their small numbers on the voting roles to help revive the so-called Black and Tan alliances with white members of the Republican Party. It was an uphill and frustrating battle, however. At the national level, the Republican Party, after losing the presidency to the Democrat Woodrow Wilson in 1912 and again in 1916, accelerated its effort to build a "lily-white" constituency in the South. By decade's end, black political leaders from twenty-five states met in Washington, D.C., for the first convention of the National Non-Partisan League. They issued a variety of resolutions, one stating that the contrast between the Democrat and Republican Parties was fast "dwindling to the point of indistinction." Still, throughout the 1920s, blacks in southern states like Texas, Louisiana, Georgia, and Virginia challenged the seating of "lily-white" candidates at the party's national conventions. In the election of 1920, Texas "Black and Tans" reacted to their exclusion from the convention by nominating their own candidate for president. Louisiana blacks fought for representation by filing numerous lawsuits, whereas Georgia blacks allied with the lily-white organization in exchange for a specified share of patronage jobs. In southern cities, black influence in the electoral arena was sometimes considerable within the context of Jim Crow. In Memphis, for example, some thirty-five hundred blacks voted in municipal elections and played a key role in close elections between Democrats and Republicans. Despite lily-whiteism, the black businessman Robert Church retained a spot on the Republican state committee and helped to secure federal posts for African Americans.

Although African Americans routinely voted for the "party of Lincoln" in national elections, they exhibited substantial independence at the state and local levels. This phenomenon was perhaps most noticeable in New York, where the majority of blacks voted the Democratic ticket. As early as 1921, the Democratic candidate for mayor received nearly 75 percent of the black vote. A year later blacks gave their support to Alfred E. Smith, the state's gubernatorial candidate. By 1930, only three of the city's twenty-two black political clubs were Republican. Moreover, whereas the most influential black elected officials were Republican in other cities, they were members of the Democratic Party in New York. Consequently, Harlem foreshadowed the depression-era shift of black voters to the Democratic Party. This phenomenon was not entirely limited to the North. In Memphis, for example, when the incumbent Republican mayor Rowlett Paine reneged on promises to the city's black community and moved a garbage incinerator into the vicinity of a black high school and amusement park, African Americans defected from Republican ranks and supported the election of a Democratic mayor in 1928. In South Carolina, some blacks voted for the Democratic Party from the post-Reconstruction years through the 1930s. They represented the descendants of blacks who had allied with the so-called Redeemers when they wrested control of Reconstruction from the hands of the Republican Party. As we will see in Chapter 17, however, although some influential black intellectuals, labor leaders, and activists supported the Democratic Party and third-party movements like the Progressive, Socialist, and Communist Parties, most blacks confined their votes to the Republican Party until the onset of the Great Depression.

African American women played a key role in the political and civil rights struggles of the black community. Their efforts were closely interrelated with the struggle for woman's suffrage. They hoped to end gender as well as racial restrictions on the vote. White women like Alice Paul, head of the Woman's Party, repeatedly stated that "Negro men cannot vote in [the South] and therefore negro women could not [vote] if women were to vote in the nation." When white leaders of the woman's suffrage movement refused to support enfranchisement regardless of race, black women intensified their dual fight against color and sex limits on the franchise. To ensure the right of black women to vote in the South as well as the North, they insisted that Congress and not the states have enforcement powers. In an exchange with white suffragists, Elizabeth B. Carter, president of the Northeastern Federation of Women's Clubs, emphatically stated:

> The National Association of Colored Women is concerned most that women shall have the vote and that the word, women, shall include colored women without question or equivocation . . . in which the enforcement of the amendment shall be given to Congress and not to the states, either directly or by concurrent jurisdiction.

Black women gained a victory of sorts when Congress passed, and the states ratified, the Nineteenth Amendment, giving women the right to vote and Congress enforcement powers.

Following the enactment of the woman's suffrage amendment, black women escalated their participation in electoral politics. They used the suffrage department of the NAACP as well as their own local and national women's clubs to fight for the franchise. Despite disfranchisement laws, black women registered to vote in Deep

South states like Georgia and Louisiana as well as northern and Upper South states. In Birmingham, Alabama, a black school teacher, Indiana Little, led some one thousand black women and a few men downtown to demand the right to register and vote. Although authorities arrested Little on vagrancy charges and undermined the movement, the sight of large numbers of southern black women going to register inspired one black woman to pen a poem. The poem's refrain, "but still the colored women kept on coming," accented the ways that black women confronted one hurdle after another—long waiting lines, literacy tests, and police violence—but refused to give up. Following the election of 1920, black women confronted the Woman's Party and protested racial restrictions placed on black women. In the resolution to the party, spearheaded by NAACP field secretary Addie Hunton, black women demonstrated their resolve to fight: "Five million women in the United States can not be denied their rights without all the women of the United States feeling the effect of that denial. No women are free until all women are free."

UNDER THE IMPACT OF WORLD WAR I and its aftermath, African Americans redefined themselves as "New Negroes." They articulated their interests in militant racial terms and moved their struggle beyond the labor and housing markets, working to create unified cultural and political communities as well as economic and residential ones. Although African Americans struggled to reconcile their campaign for full citizenship rights and economic democracy with the imperatives of racial solidarity and self-help, their efforts confronted significant obstacles within the increasingly diversified African American community. Organizations like the African Blood Brotherhood, the Brotherhood of Sleeping Car Porters, and the Universal Negro Improvement Association challenged established civil rights and political organizations like the National Association for the Advancement of Colored People and Republican clubs to address the needs of the rapidly growing black industrial working class. African Americans would work hard to reconcile diverse nationalist, radical, and liberal strategies for social change but would increasingly coalesce around civil rights activism and electoral politics. As with other moments in African American history, however, before blacks could make good on their demands, the nation entered the Great Depression and put the needs of African Americans on the back burner, as we will see in Chapter 17.

~

The Old Deal Continues

Despite the vibrant socioeconomic, political, and cultural developments of the 1920s, the Great Depression undercut the position of black workers and revealed the precarious institutional foundation of the African American community. African American unemployment rapidly increased and remained at disproportionately high levels throughout the period. Blacks who retained their jobs faced increasing competition from unemployed white workers who demanded racial preferences in employment and layoff policies, which employers used to cut wages, speed up the work pace, and stiffen the discipline of the work force. Although urban blacks faced extraordinary difficulties, the depression took its greatest toll on blacks in the rural South, where the collapse of cotton prices and the growing use of mechanical devices reduced the demand for farm laborers. Neither the Republican administration of Herbert S. Hoover nor the early years of the Democratic regime of Franklin D. Roosevelt offered much hope. Although African Americans would continue to rely on their own familial- and community-based institutions for help, such responses were insufficient to address the mass suffering that they faced. Consequently, African Americans would deepen their political and civil rights struggles and demand greater access to government-supported social welfare programs. Only then would they make the transition from what they often called the same "Old Deal" to a "New Deal."

THE DEPRESSION, UNEMPLOYMENT, AND MASS SUFFERING

In the wake of the stock market crash of October 1929, the Great Depression spread rapidly throughout the country. National income dropped by nearly 50 percent, from $81 billion in 1929 to $40 billion in 1932; unemployment rose to an estimated 25 percent of the labor force; and nearly 20 million Americans turned to public and private relief agencies to prevent starvation and destitution. Such institutions were soon overwhelmed by the rapid spread of hunger and homelessness. In early 1932, a Chicago observer reported:

> You can ride across the lovely Michigan Avenue bridge at midnight [with] the lights all about making a dream city of incomparable beauty, while twenty feet below you, on a lower level of the same bridge, are 2,000 homeless decrepit, shivering and starving men, wrapping themselves in old newspapers to keep from freezing, and lying down in the manure dust to sleep.

In New York, the Council of the Unemployed reported thousands of men, women, and children "sleeping under the sky." Others found shelter in hallways, under steps, in cellars, and in public dance halls and poolrooms "until driven out." Still, African Americans suffered more than their white counterparts, received less from their government, and got what they called a "raw deal" rather than a "new deal."

Blacks in the rural South faced the most devastating impact of hard times. As cotton prices dropped from 18 cents per pound to less than 6 cents by early 1933, all categories of rural black labor—landowners, cash tenants, sharecroppers, and wage laborers—suffered from declining incomes. Mechanical devices had already reduced the number of workers needed for plowing, hoeing, and weeding, but planters now experimented with mechanical cotton pickers as well. The number of black sharecroppers dropped from nearly 392,000 in 1930 to under 300,000 as the depression spread. As one black woman stated, many jobs had "gone to machines, gone to white people or gone out of style." Black novelist Richard Wright reinforced the same point: "As plantation after plantation fails, the Bosses of the Buildings [northern industrialists] acquire control and send tractors upon the land, and still more of us are compelled to search for 'another place.'"

In their contracts with tenant farmers and sharecroppers, landlords drastically reduced or eliminated the provision of supplies. When one sharecropper despaired of getting an advance, he asked the landlord for just enough for "overalls"; the owner retorted that he needed "overalls" himself. Another tenant complained: "They don't give nothing now. Use to 'low us $10 provisions a month, but dey done cut us way down. The white folks say some of these banks done fell in; ain't no money to be got. That's all. Said this the suppression time." In Macon County, Alabama, when asked if her house leaked when it rained, a black woman said, "No, it don't leak in here, it just rains in here and leaks outdoors." Another cropper complained that the landlord refused to provide lumber for repairs: "All he's give us . . . is a few planks. . . . It's nothin' doin'. We just living outdoors." In her interview with the Works Projects Administration (WPA), Mary Brown of Charlotte, North Carolina, described how she tried to make ends meet and the abuse that she faced:

> I've been working from one place to the other; I don't make much. You see I jest room and always try to git me a job where I can git my meals. I work at a boardinghouse. . . . I wash dishes, dress fish and chickens and all kinder stuff. One lady I worked for didn't pay me at all, and when I asked her for it she grabbed a shovel

The depression took a heavy toll on the lives of all blacks, but particularly those who continued to sharecrop on southern farms. The sharecropper shown in this photo is plowing a field in Montgomery County, Alabama, 1937. *Library of Congress*

and come down on my head, she beat me so bad I had to leave. I ain't been back yet to see if she would pay me.

Although the depression took its toll on black men, women, and children, it was especially hard on elderly blacks, often ex-slaves, who had earlier experienced the ravages of human bondage as well as the most destructive aspects of the share-cropping system. In Macon, Georgia, poor health complicated the suffering of Lizzie Mercer, an unemployed widow. In her interview with the WPA, "She held up her . . . hands from which dry skin was peeling. 'Dat's pellagra,' she explained. . . . 'It comes out on my hands an feets but I'se sore all over my body. Lots of times I has to stay in bed . . . weak as a cat.'" In his interview with the WPA, ex-slave Charley Williams also accented the impact of poor health. "Iffen I could see better out'n my old eyes, and I had me something to work with and de feebleness in my back and head would let me 'lone, I would have me plenty to eat in de kitchen all de time, and plenty tobaccy in my pipe, too, bless God!"

Poor health and medical neglect represented an ongoing theme in African American history, but the 1930s produced one of the most callous race class–based medical experiments in the nation's history. In 1932, the U.S. Public Health Service initiated its infamous Tuskegee Study. In Macon County, Alabama, the government and medical establishment selected nearly four hundred black male subjects in an examination of the long-run effects of untreated syphilis. Treatment and relief from the ravages of the disease were outside the parameters of the study. Although the study highlighted what one scholar has called "racial medicine" in American society, it also underscored the precarious position of black health care professionals in the Jim Crow South. Black institutions, Tuskegee Institute and the Veterans Hospital of Tuskegee, hosted the experiment. The study offered poor black men free rides to the clinic, free physical examinations, hot meals on examination days, and a guaranteed burial stipend to their families, but it concealed its central aim—to permit a well-known disease to run its deadly course unhampered by medical intervention. Forty years later the study continued but would become a storm center of debate and protests over the confluence of race, class, law, and medicine in American society.

Since public and private relief efforts were virtually nonexistent in the rural South, black farm families continued their trek to the city, where they found it equally difficult to secure a position in the economy. The "last to be hired and first to be fired," urban black workers entered the depression earlier and stayed there longer than other racial and ethnic groups. Sociologists St. Clair Drake and Horace R. Cayton believed that the black community served as a "barometer sensitive to the approaching storm." Months before the stock market crash, the *Chicago Defender* warned: "Something is happening . . . and it should no longer go unnoticed. During the past three weeks hardly a day has ended that there has not been a report of another firm discharging its employees, many of whom have been faithful workers at these places for years." By 1931, 40 percent of the city's black men and 55 percent of black women were unemployed, compared with about 23 and 13 percent of their white counterparts. Black women continued to work mainly as maids, cooks, and laundresses, but the depression weakened their access to these jobs. Domestic employers expressed a growing preference for white women in their want ads. In a study of black female employment between 1929 and 1931, the U.S. Department of Labor reported that "the proportion of Negro women unemployed ordinarily was greater than their share in the total woman population."

As unemployment and destitution escalated, urban black women entered the notorious "slave market." Congregating on the sidewalks of major cities, these women offered their services to white women, who drove up in their cars seeking domestic help. Some of the employers, working-class women themselves, paid as little as $5 weekly for day laborers, who carried out a full regimen of housework. In their observations of the practice in the Bronx, New York, two black women, Ella Baker and Marvel Cooke, compared the practice to the treatment of slaves in *Uncle Tom's Cabin,* Harriet Beecher Stowe's 1832 novel:

> She who is fortunate (?) enough to please Mrs. Simon Legree's scrutinizing eye is led away to perform hours of multifarious household drudgeries. Under a rigid watch, she is permitted to scrub floors on her bended knees, to hang precariously from window sills, cleaning window after window, or to strain and sweat over steaming tubs of heavy blankets, spreads and furniture covers.

Another young woman, Millie Jones, offered a detailed description of her work for one family for $5 a week:

> Did I have to work? and how! For five bucks and car fare a week. . . . Each and every week, believe it or not, I had to wash every one of those windows [fifteen in a six-room apartment]. . . . There were two grown sons in the family and her

husband. That meant that I would have at least twenty-one shirts to do every week. Yeah, and ten sheets and at least two blankets, besides. They all had to be done just so, too. Gosh, she was a particular woman.

Making matters worse, many employers cheated the women out of their wages. As Baker and Cooke put it,

> Fortunate, indeed, is she who gets the full hourly rate promised. Often, her day's slavery is rewarded with a single dollar bill or whatever her unscrupulous employer pleases to pay. More often, the clock is set back for an hour or more. Too often she is sent away without any pay at all.

Household workers were not alone. Industrial workers who retained their jobs faced increasing speed-ups, wage cuts, and exploitation. In a New York commercial laundry, black women worked fifty hours each week. According to one employee, "It was speed up, speed up, eating lunch on the fly." Women working in the starching department stood on their feet for ten hours each day, "sticking their hands into almost boiling starch." When the employees complained, the boss threatened to fire and replace them with workers from the large pool of unemployed women. A Duquesne steelworker declared that the bosses gave black workers "a hard way to go. They . . . bawl you out and make you work fast." Some black steelworkers were fired when they refused to give kickbacks to the foreman for being permitted to keep their jobs. "I was just laid off—why? Because I wouldn't pay off the foreman. He knows us colored folks has to put up with everything to keep a job so he asks for two–three dollars anytime an' if you don't pay, you get a poor payin' job or a layoff." Other black workers expressed the same grievance.

> My division foreman charged me $20 one time for taking me back on, after he had laid me off; then asked me for $15 more after I had worked a while. I just got tired of that way of doin' and wouldn't pay him; now I'm out of a job.

In the urban South, blacks faced even greater difficulties than their northern kinfolk. In Atlanta, New Orleans, and other southern cities, white workers rallied around such slogans as "No Jobs for Niggers Until Every White Man Has a Job" and "Niggers, back to the cotton fields—city jobs are for white folks." By early 1933, the most violent efforts to displace black workers had occurred on southern railroads, where the white brotherhoods intimidated, attacked, and murdered nearly a dozen black firemen. One contemporary observer, Hilton Butler, offered a list of black firemen who lost their lives or were seriously injured:

> Gus Emera, Negro fireman at Durant, saw a closed car rush toward him as he stepped from an engine to a side track. He jumped back in time to miss the second shotgun load, but the first was sufficient to send him to the railroad hospital with serious wounds.—Cleve Sims, fireman also stationed at Durant, walked

1934

A White
Eyewitness
Describes the
Lynching of
Claude Neal

A Report of an Investigation Made for the National Association for the Advancement of Colored People, 69 Fifth Avenue, New York, by a White Southern College Professor into the Killing of Claude Neal by a Mob on October 26, 1934. . . .

According to a member of the mob with whom I talked, Claude Neal was lynched in a lonely spot about four miles from Greenwood, Florida, scene of the recent crime, and not in Alabama as it was first reported. After Neal was taken from the jail at Brewton, Alabama, he was driven approximately 200 miles over highway 231 leading into Marianna and from there to the woods near Greenwood, where he was subjected to the most brutal and savage torture imaginable.

Neal was taken from the Brewton jail between one and two o'clock Friday morning, October 26. He was in the hands of the smaller lynching group composed of approximately 100 men from then until he was left in the road in front of the Cannidy home late that same night. I was told by several people that Neal was tortured for ten or twelve hours. It is almost impossible to believe that a human being could stand such unspeakable torture for such a long period.

Due to the great excitement sweeping the entire northern section of Florida and southeastern Alabama and to the great number of people who wanted to participate in the lynching, the original mob which secured Neal from the jail at Brewton, evidently decided that if all the niceties of a modern Twentieth Century lynching were to be inflicted upon Neal that it would be unwise for a larger mob to handle the victim. They preferred that his last hours on earth be filled with the greatest possible humiliation and agony. However, the word was passed all over northeastern Florida and Southeastern Alabama that there was to be a "lynching party to which all white people are invited," near the Cannidy home Friday night. It is also reported that the information was broadcast from the radio station at Dothan, Alabama. I talked to at least three persons who confirmed this statement.

Source: Joe W. Trotter and Earl Lewis, eds., *African Americans in the Industrial Age: A Documentary History, 1915–1945* (Boston: Northeastern University Press, 1996), pp. 210–211. Copyright © 1996 by Joe W. Trotter and Earl Lewis. Reprinted with permission of Northeastern University Press.

into the yards at night to go to work. From behind a water tank a shotgun blazed, and Cleve fell badly wounded.

Butler concluded: "Dust had been blown from the shotgun, the whip, and the noose, and Ku Klux Klan practices were being resumed in the certainty that dead men not only tell no tales but create vacancies."

According to the *Negro Yearbook*, lynchings increased from twenty-four in 1928 to twenty-seven in 1929, to forty in 1930. The number declined during the early 1930s, but the brutality of such lynchings persisted. On 26 October 1934, a Marianna, Florida, mob lynched Claude Neal for allegedly murdering a twenty-year-old white woman (see box). The mob took Neal from a jail in Brewton, Alabama,

During the early years of the depression, lynchings of African Americans increased after having dropped significantly during the 1920s. When the National Crime Conference met in Washington, D.C., in 1934 and refused to place lynchings among its list of topics, Howard University students picketed the gathering. *Library of Congress*

and transported him nearly two hundred miles to the lynching site. Members of the mob tortured him for ten to twelve hours with knives, fire, and a hanging noose around his neck. "After several hours of this unspeakable torture, 'they decided just to kill him.'" Following Neal's death, the mob took his mutilated body and hung it on a tree in the courthouse square:

> Pictures were taken of the mutilated form and hundreds of photographs were sold for fifty cents each. . . . Fingers and toes from Neal's body [were] exhibited as souvenirs in Marianna, where one man offered to divide the finger which he had with a friend as "a special favor."

Yet the atmosphere of mob violence was not limited to the South. In August 1930, a twin lynching of two young black men took place in Marion, Indiana.

White hostility not only intensified black joblessness but undercut black access to much needed relief funds. In 1931, *Survey Graphic* magazine noted that southern cities like Richmond practiced "flagrant discrimination in the dispensing of relief to Negroes." In early 1933, the city of Norfolk set the daily allotment for black families at $1.25, compared with $2.00 for whites. At about the same time, in Houston, Texas, relief officials rejected the applications of African American and Latino residents. In Atlanta, blacks on relief received an average of $19.29 per month, compared with $32.66 for whites. In Jacksonville, Florida, about five thousand whites received 45 percent of the relief funds, while the fifteen thousand blacks on relief received the remaining 55 percent. Southern politicians and social welfare officials defended the practice, arguing that the low living standard of blacks enabled them to live on less than whites. By 1933, the U.S. Census of Unemployment Relief reported 18 percent of all black families on public relief, compared with 10 percent of whites. In urban areas the percentage was about the same for whites but over three times higher for blacks—33 percent in New York, Chicago, Philadelphia, and Detroit; 43 percent in Pittsburgh and Cleveland; 67 percent in Akron.

The depression not only took a toll on black families and reinforced an atmosphere of mob rule but also undermined the black middle class and community-based black institutions. Between 1929 and 1932, the earnings of Harlem's black business and professional people dropped by 44 and 37 percent, respectively. As E. Franklin Frazier observed:

The Negro professional and business man had prospered upon the earnings of the black masses in northern cities. . . . Then, suddenly, the purchasing power and savings of the masses began to melt. Doctors' and lawyers' fees dwindled and finally ceased, and the hothouse growth of Negro business behind the walls of segregation shriveled and died, often swallowing up the savings of the black masses.

As unemployment escalated, and black businesses and professional practices failed, membership in established churches, clubs, and fraternal orders dropped. Blacks frequently related the pain of this separation from friends and acquaintances. Their stories are well documented in Drake and Cayton's *Black Metropolis:*

"I used to belong to a Baptist church, but don't go there now. I can't go anywhere looking like this. . . ." "I don't attend church as often as I used to. You know I am not fixed like I want to be—haven't got the clothes I need."

Black women and men made similar comments about their club and lodge work. "I am interested but I don't belong to any clubs. I don't have the money to join clubs. I think clubs are for people who can afford to join them and pay dues." Similarly, a black man remarked: "I use to belong to the Knights of Pythias, but when times got hard I had to get out." Another black male made the same point: "I don't have any interest in any of those organizations now because I have no money to make the appearance and keep up the dues and what not." Moreover, although middle-class blacks held on to membership in the lodges longer than their working-class counterparts, they also gradually moved into business and professional organizations and further reduced membership in lodges and fraternal orders. In a survey of lodges and fraternal orders in twenty-two cities, the National Urban League reported that the lodges were declining among blacks and that young people "were showing less and less interest in them."

SOCIAL WELFARE AND RELIEF POLICIES

Neither the Republican administration of Herbert Hoover nor the first years of FDR's New Deal did much to relieve the mass suffering of African Americans.

Hoover's "Trickle Down" Approach

Hoover pursued a policy of indirect relief. He established agencies like the Reconstruction Finance Corporation, which provided loans to relieve the credit problems of huge corporations like railroads, banks, and insurance companies. By "priming the pump" of big business, Hoover believed that federal aid to corporations would stimulate production, create new jobs, and increase consumer spending—that is, "trickle down" to the rest of the economy and end the depression. An official of the Hoover administration testified before Congress: "My sober and considered judgment is that . . . federal aid would be a disservice to the unemployed."

Hoover not only provided little help to the unemployed, black or white, but also delayed important black patronage appointments, cut the size and appropriations for the all-black Tenth Cavalry, and permitted the abuse of black workers on projects with government contracts. The National Association for the Advancement of Colored People (NAACP) reported excessively long hours, low wages, unsanitary living conditions, and use of physical violence against black workers on the Boulder Dam in Colorado and the Mississippi flood control project under the supervision of the U.S. Army Corps of Engineers. Furthermore, just after his inauguration in 1929, Hoover had permitted the segregation of black Gold Star mothers—women who had lost sons overseas during World War I and traveled to Europe to visit battlegrounds and gravesites. Although white mothers traveled aboard U.S. Navy cruisers, black mothers traveled on poorly outfitted commercial ships—"cattle boats," as some black leaders called them.

African Americans nonetheless rallied to the slogan "Who but Hoover" in the presidential election of 1932. They gave the incumbent about 66 percent of their votes. Only in New York and Kansas City, Missouri, did the majority of blacks vote for Franklin Delano Roosevelt. The Republican Party was still the party of emancipation. Its role in the emancipation of slaves and the initial struggle for full citizenship rights represented a "long memory" for many black voters. Moreover, as discussed in Chapter 15, industrial expansion during the 1920s had opened up new opportunities for thousands of black workers. Most importantly, however, Roosevelt looked little better than Hoover. As assistant secretary of the navy, he had supported the racial segregation of the armed forces. Blacks also resented FDR's Haitian policy, one critic stating:

> Nothing could have condemned Roosevelt more . . . than the constitution—the treaty set-up for Haiti—which he wrote himself, he says when he was assistant secretary of Navy, and I don't see how any people could be treated worse than the Haitians were treated in their own territory.

FDR had also adopted Warm Springs, Georgia, as his home and accepted its system of racial segregation. Moreover, during its national convention, the Democratic Party rejected the NAACP's proposal for a civil rights plank calling for an end to racial discrimination.

Racial Discrimination During Roosevelt's Early Years

Following his election, FDR did little to build confidence among African Americans. Although he defined the depression as an economic disaster requiring massive federal aid and planning, he depended on southern segregationists to pass and implement his "New Deal" programs, mainly for big business, agriculture, and organized labor. Some African Americans hoped for equal consideration but received a "raw deal" during the first years of FDR's administration. Roosevelt opposed federal antilynching legislation, prevented black delegations from visiting the White House, and refused to make civil rights and racial equity a priority. FDR repeatedly justified his actions on the grounds that he needed southern white support for his economic relief and recovery programs. In a conversation with an NAACP official, he confided: "If I come out for the anti-lynching bill now, they will block every bill I ask Congress to pass to keep America from collapsing. I just can't take that risk." In short, African American rights were placed on hold.

Each piece of New Deal legislation failed to safeguard African Americans against racial discrimination. The National Recovery Administration (NRA), Agricultural Adjustment Administration (AAA), Works Progress Administration (WPA), Tennessee Valley Authority (TVA), Civilian Conservation Corps (CCC), and Federal Emergency Relief Administration (FERA) all left blacks vulnerable to discriminatory employers, agency officials, and local whites. Federal officials rejected proposals from African Americans and their white allies to make racial discrimination in New Deal social programs illegal. State, county, and municipal authorities gained a great deal of autonomy in the implementation of New Deal measures, and African Americans soon complained of discrimination in FERA relief efforts. In a nearly all-white Texas town, one woman recalled how they "would stand all day and wait and wait and wait. And get nothin' or if you did, [it] was spoiled meat." In a letter to the NAACP, a Louisiana man complained:

I have been deprived of work since Oct. 20th 1933. . . . Being denied of work so long I was forced to apply for direct relief and the woman Parrish director of the [F.]E.R.A. told me because I had quit a job in Sept. that only paid me $2.00 per week 10–14 hours per day and because I had written several letters to Washington reporting this office she said you will not get any direct relief here. I will show you that you cannot run this office [she said].

A letter from Alabama told the same tale:

N.A.A.C.P. Dear Sir— . . . I am one of families that is in very bad need of aid an up to this date have been denied. . . . It is a well known fact that one cannot live without food and clothes. . . . Will you see after this matter at once [for a friend and myself]. . . . Its awful bad to wait for someone who does not care to give you food.

From Georgia, a widow described and explained the abuse and violence that her seventeen-year-old son faced when he sought work relief:

The white peoples knocked him down run him out of town woulden let him com back to town . . . he went back to town in about 5 weaks they got after him agin about a hundred head of white mens with knives and they run him all over town they cout him they throwed him in back of a truck hog fashion he got out som way they put a Bulldog on him then he ran in a stor then som of the collord mens beg the cheef police to put him in jale to keep the mob from killing him the cheaff say let them kill him just so they dont mobb him heare in town . . . he had to leave town . . . if they see him enny more they will sure kill him he left in the night walking with no money. . . . that is my sun he is just 17 years old— . . . help me I am his mother. . . .

Along with the Federal Emergency Relief Administration, the Agricultural Adjustment Administration discriminated against blacks. The AAA paid farmers to withdraw cotton land from production, create a shortage, and drive up the price of cotton on the open market. Set up to administer the law at the local level, AAA county committees excluded African Americans from participation. After depriving African Americans of representation, landowners took government checks, plowed up cotton, and denied tenants a share of the government income. At the same time, the largest landowners turned increasingly toward scientific and mechanized farming. As the "thundering tractors and cotton picking machines" rendered black labor more and more dispensable, black sharecroppers earned a mean net income of $295 per year, compared with $417 for whites. White wage hands received $232 per year, compared with only $175 for blacks. A writer for the magazine the *New Republic* reported that some black farmers were near starvation:

Some of the men who are plowing are hungry. They don't have enough to eat. . . . And with hunger gnawing at their vitals they plow in earnest, because they are in a desperate situation and they exist in terrible anxiety. So they plow hard.

This cartoon shows Uncle Sam (the National Recovery Administration) mediating the interest of white workers and employers, but the NRA exempted domestic and general laborers from its provisions and provided little help to blacks. *Library of Congress*

If the AAA undercut the livelihood of rural blacks, the National Recovery Act had a similar impact on both urban and rural black wage earners. By exempting domestic service and unskilled laborers from its provisions, the NRA removed most blacks from its minimum wage and participatory requirements. Since over 60 percent of African Americans worked in the domestic and general labor sectors of the economy, the NRA did little to improve their lot. On the contrary, black workers in industries, plants, and jobs covered by the codes faced new pressures from employers and white workers. NRA legislation (particularly Section 7a, which gave workers the right to collective bargaining with employers) enabled labor unions to strengthen their hand at the expense of blacks in the North and South. When the U.S. Supreme Court declared the NRA unconstitutional in 1935, Congress quickly passed the Wagner Labor Relations Act and set up the National Labor Relations Board to protect the collective bargaining rights of workers. In 1938, Congress also passed the Fair Labor Standards Act (FLSA) to set minimum hours and wages designed to eliminate "labor conditions detrimental to the maintenance of the minimum standards of living necessary for health, efficiency and well-being of workers." Like the NRA, however, the FLSA and the Wagner Act omitted agricultural and domestic service employees from its provisions.

Although New Deal labor legislation enabled organized white workers to strengthen their hand in the struggle with employers, it also buttressed their efforts to exclude blacks. African American workers, the NAACP, and the National Urban League protested the exclusion of unskilled and semiskilled workers and proposed a nondiscrimination clause in the National Recovery Act, but white labor leaders defeated the measure. As late as 1935, organized white labor also blocked the inclusion of a nondiscrimination clause in the Wagner National Labor Relations Act. Sponsored by Senator Robert Wagner of New York, the new law gave workers and their unions extended protection in their effort to bargain collectively with management. According to Wagner's assistant Leon Kyserling, "The American Federation of Labor fought bitterly to eliminate this clause and much against his will Senator Wagner had to consent to elimination in order to prevent scuttling of the entire bill." AFL unions continued to use a variety of formal and informal procedures to exclude, segregate, or subordinate African Americans within the labor movement. At the 1934 national convention of the AFL, black workers escalated their fight against such discriminatory practices, their pickets and banners proclaiming, "Labor Cannot Be Free While Black Labor Is Enslaved."

When New Deal legislation did upgrade the status of black workers, white workers increased their efforts to squeeze them out. In 1934, the Urban League reported a strike at the Wehr Steel Foundry in Milwaukee. The chief aim of the strike, the league reported, was the "dismissal of Negroes from the plant." When black workers decided to cross the picket line, police joined strikers in attacks on them. In western Pennsylvania, the Allegheny Steel Company in Brackenridge replaced its black workers with whites, arguing that black workers' gambling, bootlegging, and disturbances justified the decision. Even on construction projects for black institutions, white workers rallied to bar African American carpenters and laborers. In St. Louis, for example, when the General Tile Company hired a black tile setter on the $2 million Homer Phillips Hospital for blacks, all the white AFL union men quit and delayed construction for two months. In Long Island and Manhattan, the Brotherhood of Electrical Workers and Building Service Employees' Union pursued similar practices.

In the South, textile firms reclassified African American jobs and removed them from the protection of the NRA codes. Such racial wage codes covered nearly one hundred southern industries employing some five hundred thousand black workers. In Forrest City, Arkansas, the Maid-Well Garment Company paid blacks (200 of its 450 employees) $6.16 a week, compared with $12.00 a week for white women. When one black worker filed a complaint with the Joint Committee on Economic Recovery (JCER), the company dismissed its entire black work force. In Montgomery County, Alabama, the Southland Manufacturing Company, a subsidiary of a Chicago-based textile manufacturing firm, also paid its black work force substantially below whites. When NRA officials rejected Southland's appeal for a lower wage for blacks than for whites, the company closed the plant and eliminated the jobs of some three hundred black employees. When NRA officials asked why Southland failed to operate at a profit, the company responded: "It must be on account of the characteristics of the people . . . their racial characteristics." In Atlanta, the Scripto Manufacturing Company justified its wage differential on the racist grounds of group efficiency. African Americans, the company argued, were 50 percent less efficient than white help in similar plants. It is no wonder that blacks frequently called the NRA the "Negro Run Around," "Negroes Ruined Again," or "Negro Rarely Allowed."

African Americans faced discrimination not only in industrial, agricultural, and relief programs but in federal housing, Social Security, regional planning, and youth programs as well. The Federal Housing Administration refused to guarantee mortgages in racially integrated neighborhoods; the Social Security Act excluded farm laborers and domestic service employees; and the TVA and CCC developed along segregationist and unequal lines. FDR promoted the Tennessee Valley Authority, established in 1933, as a model of social planning to improve the lives of millions of Americans. It covered seven states in the Tennessee River valley and aimed to stimulate economic development and reduce poverty by establishing a massive program of rural electrification at dramatically reduced rates. African Americans made up 11 percent of the 2 million residents of the region, and the project promised "nondiscrimination" in its official design. Yet the agency barred blacks from skilled and managerial positions; excluded them from vocational training programs; and reinforced patterns of residential segregation. Moreover, African Americans received inadequate benefits from the reduced rates for electrical power for their homes. In an essay on the "Plight of the Negro in the Tennessee Valley," the *Crisis* reported:

> For Negroes the introduction of cheaper electric rates into Lee County as [a] result of the TVA power policy has meant nothing. Landlords, whether of Negro slum dwellers in Tupelo or of Negro tenant farmers in the rural section of the county, have not found it to their advantage to wire their Negro tenants' homes at the cost of $15 to $25, when already they are squeezing all the rent possible from these tenants.

The Civilian Conservation Corps established camps to aid unemployed youth. The agency employed young men in the work of conservation, reforestation, and prevention of soil erosion, but it gave preference to young whites. Even where blacks constituted the majority of the total population—in certain counties of Mississippi and Alabama, for example—they were given less than 6 percent of CCC jobs. One contemporary observer reported that "the CCC has remained a white institution, with no more coloring than landownership, which tolerates the possession of one acre in twenty Negroes." When African Americans did gain employment on CCC projects, they were segregated and treated unfairly compared with whites. In New York, a young black man offered a vivid description of his induction into a CCC camp administered by the U.S. Army:

> We reached Camp Dix [New Jersey] about 7:30 that evening. When my record was taken at Pier I a "C" was placed on it. When the busloads were made up at Whitehall street an officer reported as follows: "35, 8 colored." . . . Before we left the bus the officer shouted emphatically: "Colored boys fall out in the rear." The colored from several buses were herded together, and stood in line until after the

white boys had been registered and taken to their tents. . . . This separation of the colored from the whites was complete and rigidly maintained at this camp. . . . Our officers who, of course, are white, are a captain, a first lieutenant, a doctor, and several sergeants.

African Americans had good reasons for calling the early years of the New Deal a "Raw Deal."

COPING WITH A "RAW DEAL"

Between the stock market crash of 1929 and the early years of the New Deal, the condition of African Americans deteriorated. Neither Hoover nor Roosevelt did much to alleviate the plight of African Americans. Only the Communist Party offered blacks an early prospect for an egalitarian interracial alliance against hard times. An unpopular minority, the Communist Party was especially eager to attract black members. Communists placed blacks in key leadership positions, condemned racial intolerance within its ranks, and conducted public mock trials to dramatize its stand against racism. Nearly fifteen thousand people attended the trial of August Yokinen. Accused of treating blacks with disdain, Yokinen was expelled from the party but given an opportunity for readmission by serving in the civil rights struggle of the black community. Although the party often used the race issue to foster its own specific ideological attacks on capitalist institutions, it nonetheless played a key role in publicizing racial injustice and placing civil rights before the nation. Although few blacks joined the Communist Party, its campaigns for racial justice—notably efforts to free the nine black Scottsboro, Alabama, boys from execution and their own black comrade Angelo Herndon from a Georgia chain gang—captured the attention of blacks and the nation.

The Communist Party and the Scottsboro Trial

During the depression years, blacks and whites routinely "hoboed" the nation's freight trains, traveling from place to place looking for work and the means to survive. In March 1931, a group of black and white youths boarded a freight train southbound from Chattanooga, Tennessee, to Alabama. A fight eventually broke out, and the blacks forced the whites off the train. One of the black young men later vividly recalled that day:

> Pretty quick the white boys began to lose in the fist fighting. We outmanned them in hand-to-hand scuffling. Some of them jumped off and some we put off. The train, picking up a little speed, that helped us do the job. A few wanted to put up a fight but they didn't have a chance. We had color anger on our side.

The young man insisted, however, that they had fought to defend themselves. White youth initiated the fight:

> The trouble began when three or four white boys crossed over the oil tanker that four of us colored fellows from Chattanooga were in. One of the white boys, he stepped on my hand liked to have knocked me off the train. I didn't say anything then, but the same guy, he brushed by me again and liked to have pushed me off the car. I caught hold of the side of the tanker to keep from falling off. I made a complaint about it and the white boy talked back—mean, serious, white folks Southern talk. That is how the Scottsboro case began . . . with a white foot on my black hand. . . . I don't argue with people. I show them. And I started to show those white boys. The other colored guys, they pitched in on these rock throwers too.

When the Scottsboro Boys (nine young black men accused of raping two white women) received summary trials and death sentences, the American Communist Party exposed the injustices of the case through an intense international publicity campaign and helped to save the men from execution. This photo shows the young men in a jail cell with their lawyer in Decatur, Alabama, c. 1931. *Brown Brothers*

When the white youth reported the incident to authorities near Scottsboro, Alabama, the local sheriff removed nine young black men and two white women from the train. Fearing arrest, the young women, Ruby Bates and Victoria Price, accused the black youths of rape at knifepoint. Although the black defendants pleaded "not guilty," the court failed to appoint proper legal representation for the young men. An all-white jury ignored the contradictory testimony of the women and found the defendants guilty of rape, and the court sentenced all but the youngest to death in the electric chair. The Communist Party described the sentence as a "legal lynching" and within a few days launched a national and international crusade to save the young men. Protest rallies emerged in major cities across the nation, and noncommunist organizations like the NAACP soon joined communists in demanding justice. At the same time, the party's International Labor Defense pressed the legal case through the Alabama Supreme Court, which upheld the convictions. On two separate occasions the party carried the case forward to the U.S. Supreme Court, which overturned the convictions and ordered retrials, which in turn led to new death sentences. Only after World War II was the last defendant released. The communists launched a similar defense of black party member Angelo Herndon, a coal miner. As in the Scottsboro case, the party used a complex combination of legal and mass protest strategies to secure Herndon's release from a Georgia chain gang. These cases established the party's usefulness in battling racial and class discrimination in American society.

A small number of blacks joined the Communist Party and played a role in its League of Struggle for Negro Rights (LSNR). In depression-era Alabama, blacks made up the majority of the party's membership during most of the period. The party's fight on behalf of the Scottsboro boys attracted local black steelworkers like Al Murphy and Hosea Hudson. Al Murphy was born in McRae, Georgia, in 1908; he grew up in a poor sharecropping family and moved to Birmingham, Alabama, in 1923. In Birmingham, he worked as a common laborer and attended night school. Unfortunately, as he recalled it, during the depression "I had to stop night school and join workers on breadlines." Shortly thereafter, he attended a Communist Party meeting for the unemployed. Impressed by what he saw and heard, he joined the party that same night, dedicated himself to party work, and soon recruited other black steelworkers for membership.

Born in a sharecropping family in Wilkes County, Georgia, in 1898, Hosea Hudson was among those that Al Murphy recruited. Hudson also belonged to a sharecropping family. As a youngster he had also worked hard on the land and in 1923 had moved to Birmingham and gained employment as an iron molder at a local foundry. Hudson later recalled that he always "resented injustice" and the way whites treated blacks. After failing to organize black workers independently, and after witnessing the communist campaign to free the Scottsboro boys, Hudson joined the Communist Party in September 1931. Hudson later recalled the social injustice that led him to the party: "Blacks are the last to be hired and the first to be fired. It was we, already existing on the crumbling edge of starvation, who suffered the highest death rate. If we had any medical care at all, it was just a whisper above being nothing." During the struggle to free Herndon, his black defense attorney, Benjamin Davis Jr., also joined the party. A graduate of Amherst College and Harvard Law School, Davis later explained his decision as "the only rational and realistic path to the freedom which burns in the breast of every Negro. It required only a moment to join but my whole lifetime as a Negro American prepared me for the moment."

The Communist Party not only staged demonstrations and legal actions to free blacks like Herndon and the Scottsboro boys but also carried out day-to-day activities designed to improve the economic status of African Americans. The party organized hunger marches, unemployed councils, farm labor unions, and rent strikes to aid unemployed and destitute workers. In Chicago, when families received eviction notices, mothers would sometimes "shout to the children, 'Run quick find the Reds!'" On one occasion, when communists attempted to prevent the eviction of a black family in Chicago, police shot and killed three African Americans. The Communist Party responded by distributing nearly five thousand leaflets, urging black and white workers to unite and demand justice for the deceased. Nearly fifty thousand people lined State Street for the funeral procession. Almost from the outset, when layoffs started and some companies cut wages, some black workers joined unemployment councils, sometimes spearheaded by the Communist Party, to gain necessary relief. Under the pressure of such councils, some companies issued food baskets but insisted that workers sign forms promising to repay on the return of good times.

In 1931, aided by the Communist Party, blacks in rural Alabama founded the Alabama Sharecroppers Union. The organization developed an underground network of communications that enabled them to maintain secrecy. Meetings took place in black churches, where their plans were disguised as religious undertakings. The union's membership increased to an estimated three thousand in 1934. Its efforts soon attracted the attention of local authorities, and violence broke out when law officers tried to confiscate the livestock of union members, who allegedly owed money to landowners. In 1932, Ned Cobb, referred to as Nate Shaw in the oral history of his life, joined the Sharecroppers Union and fought the system that oppressed him. As he recalled, he had to act because he had labored "under many rulins, just like the other Negro, that I knowed was injurious to man and displeasin to God and still I had to fall back." One cold morning in December 1932, Shaw refused to "fall back." When deputy sheriffs came to take his neighbor's livestock, he took part in a shootout with local law officers:

> I walked on in the door, stopped right in the hallway and looked back. . . . Run my hand in my pocket, snatched out my .32 Smith and Wesson and I commenced a shooting . . . and before I could reload my gun . . . [e]very one of them officers [four in all] outrun the devil away from there. I don't know how many people they might have thought was in that house, but that .32 Smith and Wesson was barkin too much for em to stand. They didn't see where the shots was comin from. . . .

The Socialist Party

Nate Shaw's action underscored the increasing militance of rural black workers as well as the role of the Communist Party in the lives of some southern blacks. Although less forcefully than the communists, the Socialist Party also campaigned against racial injustice. In 1929, the party established the United Colored Socialists of America (UCSA). U.S. Socialist Party head Norman Thomas appointed a special black organizer for the South and supported a resolution condemning racial discrimination by trade unions. By 1933, the Socialist Party endorsed federal anti-lynching and anti–poll tax legislation; organized sharecroppers' unions; and elevated blacks to leadership positions. Under the leadership of H. L. Mitchell, in 1934 the party launched the Southern Tenant Farmers Union (STFU). The STFU became the party's most prominent effort to organize workers across racial lines. As an eleven-year-old child, Mitchell witnessed the lynching of a black man and later credited this event with helping to shape his work as a labor radical. Founded near the town of Tyronza, Arkansas, the STFU resolved to organize black and white tenant farmers in the same union. A black farmer (probably cofounder Isaac Shaw) helped to inspire the organization when he spoke up at the initial meeting of the group:

> For a long time now the white folks and the colored folks have been fighting each other and both of us has been getting whipped all the time. We don't have nothing against one another but we got plenty against the landlord. The same chain that holds my people holds your people too. If we're chained together on the outside, ought to stay chained together in the union.

A white organizer for the STFU emphasized the futility of separate organizations and appealed to what he called "belly hunger" to help erase the color line among farmers:

> If we organize only a Union of Negro sharecroppers then the Negroes will be evicted and white sharecroppers from the hill country or the unemployed in Memphis will take their places. If on the other hand we organize only a Union of white sharecroppers then the white men will be evicted and Negro sharecroppers from Mississippi and the unemployed in Memphis will take their places.

Although the organization failed to bring landowners to the bargaining table, it demonstrated the growing importance of the American left in helping to create a "new deal." When white landowners evicted sharecroppers in Arkansas, the black STFU vice president, O. H. Whitfield, led some five hundred black and white farmers onto the main highway between Memphis and St. Louis and vowed to remain there until the federal government intervened. Although these radical actions produced few results, they highlighted the increasing activism of rural black workers in their own behalf. One skeptical black newspaper editor, William Kelley of the *Amsterdam News*, spoke for many when he concluded:

> A little less than a year ago . . . I was suspicious of these gift bearing Reds . . . lest they should rise to power on the backs of American Negroes and then leave them to their fate. Since that time, a lot of water has run under the bridge, enough to cause us to reevaluate the accomplishments of their movement in our cause . . . the fight that they are putting up . . . strikes forcefully at the fundamental wrongs suffered by the Negro today.

Kinship and Community Ties

Despite vigorous organizing by the Communist and Socialist Parties, African Americans continued their historic dependence on kinship- and community-based institutions. As novelist Richard Wright put it:

> There is nothing—no ownership or lust for power—that stands between us and our kin. And we reckon kin not as others do, but down to the ninth and tenth

cousin. And for a reason we cannot explain we are mighty proud when we meet a man, woman, or child who, in talking to us, reveals that the blood of our brood has somehow entered his veins.

As the "primary kinkeepers," black women creatively manipulated the family's resources and played a major role in helping their families remain intact. They took in boarders and cared for each other's children, the sick, and the elderly. Lizzie Mercer confirmed this process when she said: "I ain't got no health and I ain't got no money. I'se 'pendent on my chillen for my vituals an' my clothes an' a place to sleep." Although ill, elderly blacks insisted on doing what they could to make ends meet. In his interview, ex-slave Charley Williams exclaimed: "But I ant give up! Nothing like dat! On de days when I don't feel so feeble and trembly I jest keep patching 'round de place. I got to keep patching as so to keep it whar it will hold de winter out, in case I git to see another winter."

In rural (and to some extent urban) areas, African Americans maintained gardens, canned fruits and vegetables, fished, hunted, and gathered wild nuts and berries, which they bartered and shared. Willye Jeffries, a community activist, later recalled: "We divided whatever we had with each other." In Chicago, when one black couple got married and set up housekeeping in a basement room, the woman, Betty Lou, gained access to the kitchen of the building's janitor; in exchange, the janitor received a share of the food that she prepared. One woman recalled how her family were sharecroppers but were "able to make it 'cause I also worked people's homes, where they give old clothes and shoes." When the lady of the house turned poor blacks seeking aid away from their doors, black household workers would secretly aid them. As the domestic Emma Tiller recalled: "Sometimes we would hurry down the alley and holler at 'im: 'Hey, mister, come here!' And we'd say, 'Come back by after a while and I'll put some food in a box, and I'll set it down aside the garbage can so they won't see it!'" Black author Lofton Mitchell also recalled this pattern of sharing:

In this climate [Harlem] the cooking of chitterlings brought a curious neighbor to the door. "Mrs. Mitchell, you cooking chitterlings? I thought you might need a little cornbread to go with 'em." A moment later a West Indian neighbor appeared with rice and beans. Another neighbor followed with some beer to wash down the meal. What started as a family supper developed into a building party.

In Louise Meriwether's Harlem-based novel, *Daddy Was a Number Runner*, Francie, the protagonist, illuminated this communal system:

[Mother] gave me a weak cup of tea.
"We got any sugar?"
"Borrow some from Mrs. Caldwell."

> I got a chipped cup from the cupboard and going to the dining-room window, I knocked at our neighbor's window-pane. The Caldwells lived in the apartment next door and our dining rooms faced each other. . . . Maude came to the window.
>
> "Can I borrow a half cup of sugar?" I asked.
>
> She took the cup and disappeared, returning in a few minutes with it almost full.
>
> "Y'all got any bread?" she asked. "I need one more piece to make a sandwich."
>
> "Maude wants to borrow a piece a bread," I told Mother.
>
> "Give her two slices," Mother said.

Such support was both spiritual and material. As one woman put it, the black poor would "sit and tell us their hard luck story. Whether it was true or not we never questioned it. It's very important you learn people as people are." A Georgia relief official understood these creative responses to poverty:

> There is no dearth of resourcefulness. In their efforts to maintain existence, these people are catching and selling fish, reselling vegetables, sewing in exchange for

Elmer W. Brown: *Gandy Dancer's Gal*, 1943. African Americans devised creative ways to put food on the table and pay the rent during hard times of the 1930s. In this portrait, the artist captures a "rent party" in Cleveland, Ohio. *Courtesy of the Western Reserve Historical Society, Cleveland*

old clothes, letting out sleeping space, and doing odd jobs. They understand how to help each other. Stoves are used in common, wash boilers go their rounds, and garden crops are exchanged and shared.

Although some urban blacks turned to small gardens to aid in coping with hard times, many more turned to the "rent party" as a source of income to pay the rent. Sometimes described as "chitlin's struts," these parties had close connections to the rural South. "Down home" food—chitlins, cornbread, collard greens, hog-maws, pigs' feet, and so on—dance, and music characterized these parties. Sponsors charged a small admission fee and sometimes offered printed or handwritten tickets with rhymes to advertise the event:

> Shake it, break it, Hang it on the wall
> Sling it out the window and catch it before it falls
> Save your tears for a rainy day
> We are giving a party where you can play
> With red mammas and too bad Sheabas
> Who wear their dresses above their knees
> And mess around with whom they please

Rent parties became even more lucrative when sponsors added gambling and liquor to food, music, and dancing.

The "policy," or numbers game, was also an adaptation to poverty that African Americans brought to the city and used to help weather the storm during the depression years. A Harlem resident called numbers the black man's "stock market." Moreover, gambling establishments often represented a source of direct aid to the poor. As one interviewee stated, downplaying aid from black churches, "Well, the Christians would always give me good advice but that was all, so I just got so I wouldn't bother with them and whenever I wanted anything I used to make it [to] the gamblers." On the South Side of Chicago, one black resident tried to imagine a world without policy. It was so important to Chicago's black community that he believed that "7,000 people would be unemployed and business in general would be crippled, especially taverns and even groceries, shoestores, and many other business enterprises who depend on the buying power of the South Side." One numbers king, called by Drake and Cayton a "Gentleman Racketeer," articulated his vision for the community: "What good is a lot of money to a man if he doesn't put it to some use? If you pile it up just for the sake of piling money, you are selfish. Why not spread it out into business and continue to increase the possibility of employing more of your race?" Some black women not only gained clerical jobs in the numbers game but became runners or entrepreneurs as well. In New York, for example, Madam Stephanie St. Clair, wife of the political activist Sufi Abdul Hamid, operated a policy establishment until the police and the mob closed her down during the early 1930s. At the same time, black men also lost their footing in the policy game. In Harlem, the business of Casper Holstein, the "Bolito King," shrank to a fraction of its earlier size. White dealers in prohibition liquor and gambling either destroyed the existing black runners or absorbed them into their networks.

Like poor and working-class whites, some depression-era blacks also responded to hard times by prostitution, bootlegging, and theft. They stole coal off of slow-moving or sidetracked trains, demolished vacant houses for use as fuel, and altered gas pipes and electrical wiring to restore heat and light to their homes. The records of the Harlem police precinct frequently noted alterations or "tampering" with meters. Louise Meriwether's novel also captured this phenomenon:

> Our electricity had been cut off for months for nonpayment . . . [explained Francie] so Daddy had made the jumper. . . . I took the metal wire from behind the box where we hid it, and opening the box, I inserted the two prongs behind the fuse the way Daddy had showed me. . . . Daddy said almost everybody in Harlem used a jumper.

One woman reported to the UNIA that she had made ends meet by "manufacturing liquor," six gallons of 100 proof each week, until a raid closed her operation down; when relief officials refused her request for aid, she returned to making "hot stuff." Bootlegging, gambling, prostitution, and other illegal pursuits represented perilous choices that highlighted the precarious position of blacks during the depression years. Those who turned to the underground economy could and often did end up in the penitentiary or jail. Even so, some of the most destitute perceived incarceration as a way to alleviate homelessness. As one black man recalled:

> I have stole small things. I don't reckon I would care if I was turned-over to officers, because I would have a place to stay. You see I don't have any particular place to go and stay, so I could stay there. I'd just have a place to stay.

For most blacks, kin- and community-based relief efforts cushioned them against the most destructive aspects of the illegal economy. Despite the decline in membership at the outset of the depression, community-based black institutions weathered the storm and soon helped to relieve human suffering. In New Orleans alone, an estimated four hundred to five hundred mutual aid and benevolent associations continued to function during the 1930s. Moreover, by the mid-1930s, membership in black churches gradually recovered. At the outset of the depression, black churches reported an estimated 5.2 million members. By 1936, the figure stood at 5.6 million. Nearly 45 percent of blacks claimed church membership, compared with 42 percent for whites. Over 70 percent of these churches were Baptist (41 percent), Methodist (20 percent), and Pentecostal (11 percent) denominations.

Black churches developed their own relief efforts. In 1931, Harlem's Abyssinian Baptist Church launched a fundraising drive to help needy families. Rev. Adam Clayton Powell Sr., pastor of the church, declared: "The axe is laid at the root of the tree and this unemployed mass of black men, led by a hungry God, will come to the Negro churches looking for fruit and finding none, will say at it down and cast it into the fire." Before Powell finished delivering his sermon, members of the congregation rushed foward to put money on the table "to feed a hungry God." One woman donated her week's earnings and walked home. The church raised on that single day $2,500 in cash and pledges, including $1,000 from the pastor. Powell later reported that it was the most impressive response to a sermon that he ever witnessed.

The church soon provided clothing, fuel, and food, feeding two thousand persons daily in its soup kitchen. The city's prominent black church leaders also organized a cooperative Committee on Relief and Unemployment and aided some twenty thousand people with shelter and varying amounts of food, clothing, and health services. One Harlem minister later stated that "nothing in New York City in the way of feeding the unemployed was comparable to what the churches did for the Harlem people." Black churches in Chicago, Philadelphia, Boston, and elsewhere also established "welfare centers" and "employment agencies" to aid the black poor.

New religious movements increased their following, partly as a result of their success in feeding their parishioners. These religious movements included those spearheaded by Elder Lightfoot Solomon Michaux; Mother Rosa Artimus Horne; Bishop Charles Emmanuel Grace, or "Daddy Grace"; and Father Divine (George Baker). During the 1920s, "Daddy Grace" established the United House of Prayer of All People with headquarters in Washington, D.C. By the early 1930s, the organization had spread to more than twenty cities and promised thousands of people respite from hard times. Similarly, although Father Divine's Peace Mission movement started during the 1920s, it dramatically expanded during the depression. In 1932, Divine moved the mission from New Jersey to Harlem and gained credit for feeding the masses and offering hope in a time of widespread despair. He sometimes served well over six hundred people at special feasts like the Easter services. In 1932, Easter Sunday services included a parade of five thousand followers through the streets of Harlem and ended at the Rush Memorial Baptist Church, where a second church was opened to accommodate the crowd of over fifteen hundred. Father Divine did not simply run a soup kitchen. He served elaborate meals at his Holy Communion banquets. At one banquet, a contemporary account of the menu included tea, milk, rice, macaroni, potatoes, peas, baked beans, mashed turnips, corn, baked tomatoes, turkey, pork chops, cornbread, biscuits, graham bread, cake, pie, peaches, and salad.

Black women also built on their network of clubs and religious and social service organizations and launched new self-help organizations. In 1930, "a group of serious and determined" black women organized the Harlem Housewives League. Under the leadership of black women like Lucille Randolph, the wife of the head of the Brotherhood of Sleeping Car Porters, the group aimed to secure jobs for the city's black population by participating in a vigorous "Don't Buy Where You Can't Work" campaign. The Housewives League adopted the principles of economic nationalism and sought to harness the power of black consumers as a lever for creating jobs and helping blacks leave the unemployment and bread lines. The league soon claimed a membership of one thousand and visited the Atlantic and Pacific Tea Company (A&P), Woolworth's, and other chain stores conducting business in Harlem. They urged white-owned businesses to employ blacks or risk losing their business. Some businesses gradually added blacks to their list of employees. Inspired by the Harlem example, Fannie B. Peck and some fifty black women formed Detroit's Housewives League. League women believed that it was their duty "as women controlling 85 percent of the family budget to unlock through concentrated spending closed doors" to black employment. Housewives Leagues also spread to Chicago, Cleveland, Washington, D.C., and Baltimore. Together, the various leagues used the boycott to generate some "seventy-five thousand new jobs" for black people.

As helpful as African American kinship- and community-based responses were, they were insufficient to address the mass suffering that blacks faced. In 1930, the National Association of Colored Women (NACW) met in two days of executive sessions at Hot Springs, Arkansas. The financial difficulties of the organization dominated discussion, but the women failed to develop an aggressive response to the demands of the early depression years. Indeed, the national body did not meet again until 1933. Two years later, in 1935, the black clubwomen's movement split when Mary McLeod Bethune spearheaded the formation of the National Council of Negro Women (NCNW), which aimed to move beyond the earlier self-help tradition; to forge black women's organizations into a powerful coalition; and to make greater demands on government for social services. Under the leadership of Mary F. Waring of Chicago, the NACW continued to function, but its work as a self-help organization providing social services to the urban poor declined. In the meantime, under Bethune's leadership, the NCNW added established clubwomen like Charlotte Hawkins Brown, Mary Church Terrell, and Lucy D. Slowe to its roster of officers and moved black women into a new era of national and international organizing on behalf of black womanhood as well as the larger African American community.

Although African Americans turned inward to their own resources during the early years of the depression, they did not abandon efforts to gain access to public social welfare programs. In addition to the activities of the Communist and Socialist Parties, letters to civil rights organizations and New Deal officials, cited above, not only accented the nature of discrimination by relief agencies. They also revealed the growing determination of unemployed and poor blacks to gain access to government-funded programs of relief and recovery. In his memoir on life in Harlem, Lofton Mitchell recalled that blacks also confronted the depression years with a sense of humor:

> Though he complained of being broke, he never admitted his family was poor. "My old man puts all his dough in the bank," was the common complaint. "That's why I'm out here, stashed like a tramp." When the Harlemite stood on breadlines, he had a glib statement: "I'm here, picking up some food for some poor old lady next door to me." If he were seen in the relief office, he let you know he was there trying to get a poor neighbor on relief.

Although African Americans strove mightily to keep their spirit and sense of dignity intact, their good humor increasingly gave way to firm demands for equity.

Many blacks like Curtis Maggard of Birmingham, Alabama, took pride in their ability to get through the depression "without stealing or robbing." Yet Maggard also reached a breaking point in his tolerance of discriminatory social welfare agencies and made forceful demands for services. Maggard entered the welfare office with an empty "croker sack" and demanded food for his family:

> I said, "You been telling me that [a relief check is in the mail] for four weeks. . . . You got a grocery store up there, and here is a croker sack. When I get home, I'm going to have that croker sack full of food. . . . I'm going to send somebody to hell to get me something to eat."

Maggard got his food and a check.

~

BETWEEN THE STOCK MARKET CRASH of 1929 and the early years of the New Deal, the conditions of African Americans moved from bad to worse. Since neither the Republican nor the early Democratic regimes provided much relief to African Americans, kinship- and community-based institutions continued to play a major role in African American responses to hard times. Urban black families took in boarders, offered child care for working mothers, and staged house parties to pay their rent, while rural blacks hunted, fished, and raised their own food. Although membership in black churches, fraternal orders, and social clubs declined as unemployment escalated, such community-based institutions helped to relieve human suffering. African Americans, like many of their poor white counterparts, also participated in the underground economy of theft, gambling, and bootlegging. Yet such formal and informal kinship and communal responses proved inadequate to alleviate the widespread hunger, homelessness, and desperation brought on by the depression. Thus, as we will see in Chapter 18, African Americans would use their community-based institutions and social networks to mobilize their political resources, build broader interracial alliances, and demand a "New Deal" from their government and fellow citizens.

～

Emergence of a New Deal?

By the late 1930s, a variety of forces helped to usher in a New Deal for blacks. The growing significance of the black vote; the emergence of a new and more egalitarian labor movement; and the radicalization of the civil rights struggle all enabled African Americans to gain access to federal jobs, housing, and other social programs. In the presidential election of 1936, African Americans mobilized their resources and shifted their support from the Republican to the Democratic Party and increased their demands for equal access to federal aid. Their shifting electoral politics were closely intertwined with their movement into the "house of labor"; the impact of the Communist and Socialist Parties; and the reorientation of civil rights, artistic, and cultural developments toward the employment and relief needs of the black working class. Although these efforts helped many African Americans make the transition from an old to a new deal, the transition was nonetheless incomplete. In the late 1930s, disproportionately high levels of poverty and unemployment continued to affect the African American community. As white workers regained their footing in the economy, large numbers of African Americans continued to occupy the relief rolls and public works projects. African Americans would have to wait until the dramatic expansion of wartime production before they could put the Great Depression behind them.

LEAVING THE PARTY OF LINCOLN

Based on their expanding numbers and concentration in nearly all-black areas in cities, African Americans escalated their participation in electoral politics and left "the party of Lincoln." As early as 1932, Robert Vann, editor of the black weekly the *Pittsburgh Courier,* urged African Americans to change their political affiliation: "My friends, go turn Lincoln's picture to the wall . . . that debt has been paid in full." Vann became an active supporter of the Democratic Party in Pennsylvania and played an important role in the party's national effort to attract black voters. In the presidential election of 1936, African Americans voted for the Democratic Party in record numbers, giving Roosevelt 76 percent of the northern black vote. Although most blacks made the transition to the Democratic Party in 1936, New York had made the shift earlier (1932) and Chicago would change later (1940) than elsewhere. In Chicago, Republicans held the majority until the advent of Edward Kelley as mayor and Patrick J. Nash as chairman of the Cook County Democratic Central Committee. In 1934, however, the black belt elected the first black Democratic congressman, Arthur Mitchell, over the Republican Oscar De Priest. Four years later, the Republican William Dawson converted to the Democratic Party and soon gained control of the Second Ward Democratic committee, which enabled him to win election to the U.S. Congress during World War II.

The political shift to the Democratic Party was not limited to the urban North. Although largely disfranchised, southern blacks also joined the New Deal coalition. In Atlanta, Georgia, attorney A. T. Walden helped lead the movement of Georgia blacks into the Democratic column. Under Walden's leadership, some twenty-five thousand black voters merged their Democratic and Republican clubs into one organization called the Atlanta Negro Voters League. Walden also spearheaded the consolidation of all Democratic clubs in the state into the Associated Negro Democratic Clubs of Georgia. In Louisville, C. Eubanks Tucker, a lawyer and bishop in the African Methodist Episcopal Church, led the black transition to the Democratic Party. Joining Louisville's Democratic Party in 1933, he assisted Democrats in gaining control of municipal government for the first time since their ouster in the aftermath of World War I. Although Tucker ran for the state legislature on the Democratic ticket in the predominantly black Fifty-Eighth District, he lost to a black Republican, attorney Charles W. Anderson. Still, the black Democrat's challenge to the party of Lincoln encouraged white Republicans to endorse a black for elective office for the first time in the city's history. In Norfolk, Virginia, the predominantly black Twenty-First Precinct shifted its vote to Franklin Delano Roosevelt in the election of 1936. Formerly Republican political leaders like P. B. Young of the *Norfolk Journal and Guide* helped to engineer the shift by allying with the Citizen's Democratic League, which had close relations with the state's Democratic political machine. Under the leadership of Helen Dancy, a social worker and head of the women's auxiliary of the Colored Citizens' Democratic Club, black women played a key role in helping to realign black politics in Norfolk.

The role of black women in fueling the movement of blacks out of the Republican Party can also be seen in the career of Crystal Byrd Fauset of Philadelphia. Born in Maryland but raised in Boston and educated at the Teachers College of Columbia University, Fauset became the executive secretary of the Institute of Race Relations at Swarthmore College, outside of Philadelphia. In 1935, she was named director of the Negro women's division of the Democratic National Committee. As head of the party's work among black women, Fauset not only helped to recruit black women for the Democratic Party but in 1938 won a seat in the Pennsylvania House of Representatives from the Eighteenth District of Philadelphia. Although

Mrs. Minnie Buckingham Harper of West Virginia was the first black woman to serve in a U.S. state legislature, Fauset was the first to gain election to that post in her own right. Fauset served one term before resigning and taking a position as an assistant director with the Pennsylvania Works Progress Administration (WPA).

Black political activism helped to change federal policy toward a more helpful focus on the needs of African Americans. By 1939, African American income from New Deal work and relief programs nearly equaled their income from employment in agriculture and domestic service. African Americans occupied about one-third of all low-income Public Works Administration (PWA) housing units; were receiving a rising share of Farm Security Administration loans; and had obtained access to a variety of new WPA work, educational, and cultural programs, including nursery schools, adult education classes, vocational training, and school lunch programs. Partly because of increasing access to educational expenditures, black illiteracy dropped 10 percent during the 1930s. African American employment on Civilian Conservation Corps (CCC) projects increased from less than 6 percent in 1935 to 11 percent in 1939. African Americans increasingly hailed such New Deal social programs as "a godsend." Some even suggested that God "will lead me," but relief "will feed me." In Chapel Hill, North Carolina, Virgil Johnson, born just six years after the Civil War, applauded the New Deal. In an interview with the WPA, he said that the GOP ("Grand Old Party") "stands for the rich man. . . . Roosevelt is for all the poor folks, white and black. . . . If the Democrats keeps bein' friendly to the poor, there soon won't be one Republican in a thousand colored people." Because of disfranchisement, Johnson added, "I don't vote but I talk for him and I don't care if I do git scolded for it."

The changing relationship between blacks and the New Deal was closely related to the activities of FDR's "Black Cabinet." An informal network of black New Deal administrators, the "Black Cabinet" had roots in the political activism of a new generation of black political leaders, including Mary McLeod Bethune as well as Harvard-trained men like Robert W. Weaver, John P. Davis, Ralph Bunche, William Hastie, and Charles Hamilton Houston, dean of the Howard University Law School. In 1933, Weaver and Davis returned to their hometown of Washington, D.C., and set up the Negro Industrial League (NIL) to monitor the New Deal's impact on blacks, especially the National Recovery Administration (NRA). They regularly attended NRA code hearings and took Washington bureaucrats by surprise. As Weaver later recalled, "No one expected us, we were literate and we were contentious." Conditioned by the devastating impact of the depression on black communities across the nation, Weaver and Davis assailed the Republican machines for providing jobs for friends and relatives but doing little for the masses of black people. They also believed that the federal government could become a key lever in the struggle for economic and social justice. As Weaver stated: "This was the only way you were going to get meaningful activity because, of course, by this time all the states in the South had completely disfranchised blacks."

In September 1933, under the leadership of the NIL, a variety of civil rights groups launched the Joint Committee on National Recovery (JCNR). Participating groups included the National Association for the Advancement of Colored People (NAACP), the National Urban League (NUL), and thirteen other black

Members of the "Black Cabinet." This informal cluster of government advisers helped blacks gain greater access to New Deal programs. Mary McLeod Bethune (*center, first row*) was not only the sole female member of this stellar group but also its most influential member. *Library of Congress*

organizations. Under the leadership of John Davis, secretary, and Robert Weaver, director of research, the JCNR agitated for more jobs and representation in New Deal agencies. Realizing that his office now hinged on the strength of black votes, Roosevelt appointed increasing numbers of African Americans to federal posts. By the mid-1930s, nearly forty-five blacks had received appointments in various New Deal agencies and cabinet departments. The "Black Cabinet" included Robert L. Vann, editor of the *Pittsburgh Courier,* in the office of the attorney general; William H. Hastie, a civil rights attorney, in the Department of the Interior; Robert C. Weaver, an economist, also in the Department of the Interior; Lawrence A. Oxley, a social worker, in the Department of Labor; Edgar Brown, president of the United Government Employees, in the CCC; and Mary McLeod Bethune, founder of Bethune-Cookman College in Florida, as head of the Negro Division of the National Youth Administration (NYA).

Bethune became the most influential of the New Deal's black advisors. Bethune not only founded Bethune-Cookman College but also, as noted in Chapter 17, led grassroots black women's organizations during the 1920s and early 1930s. By the time she received appointment to the NYA in 1935, she was a widely known civil rights and political activist. As an NYA administrator, she organized two major conferences on "The Problems of the Negro and Negro Youth" (see box). Because of her growing efforts to address the problems of black people that cut across various departmental lines, Bethune helped to lay the groundwork for the development of the "Black Cabinet." Bethune believed firmly in the role of the state as a lever for social change, stating: "Our national life is largely directed by the legislation and other activities of our governmental units."

SOURCES FROM THE PAST

1937

Recommendations for Elimination of Racial Discrimination in Relief Programs

The stark reality of the present employment situation in the United States as it affects Negroes calls for a blunt recital of the disabilities under which they labor. Their social and economic existence is tragically at stake. Despite the tremendous efforts of the Governmental agencies during the past three or four years to rescue the country from the destroying effects of the depression, the mass Negro population of the United States still, at this time, January, 1937, is living on the lowest levels of existence, with attendant hunger and misery.

It is a matter of common knowledge that the Negro has not shared equitably in all the services the Government offers its citizens. We are mindful of the fact that during the past four years many benefits have come to him that before that time he did not have. But there still remain numerous instances of racial difference and inequality from which he suffers. While presenting specifically recommendations for action touching the Negro, we are not unmindful of the condition which faces the country, calling for the continuance of the policies and practices which have been in effect for the past four years.

We urge that in emergency relief and work programs care be exercised to secure Federal control and supervision of these programs in all their phases as opposed to the decentralization through reference to states and localities. We further urge that in all administration of these programs specific steps be made to eliminate racial discrimination. And finally, it is our urgent belief that not less than nine hundred million dollars ($900,000,000) must be appropriated for Federal emergency relief work for the period up to June 30, 1937 if the basic needs of the needy and indigent American population are to be met.

Source: "National Conference on the Problems of the Negro and Negro Youth," report, National Youth Administration, Division of Negro Affairs, January 1937, in Joe W. Trotter and Earl Lewis, eds., *African Americans in the Industrial Age: A Documentary History, 1915–1945* (Boston: Northeastern University Press, 1996), pp. 175–176.

Although First Lady Eleanor Roosevelt had little contact with the needs of African Americans before early 1933, she gradually increased her support of civil rights issues. Through her frequent interactions with black leaders, particularly Walter White of the NAACP and Mary McLeod Bethune, Eleanor Roosevelt endorsed legislation designed to abolish the poll tax, enact a federal antilynching law, and increase aid to black institutions, particularly schools. Mrs. Roosevelt also helped to change FDR's position on civil rights from one of caution and aloofness to one of significant support. FDR eventually took photographs with black leaders, conferred with civil rights delegations at the White House, and sent greetings to African American organizations.

As the White House seemed to escalate its support for social justice, other New Dealers took heart and advanced the cause of African Americans. The policies of Harold Ickes, secretary of the interior and administrator of the PWA; Harry Hopkins, head of the WPA; and a few others exemplified the growing support that African Americans received in some New Deal agencies. Before taking his post as secretary of the interior, Ickes had served as president of the Chicago chapter of the NAACP. On assuming his duties, he ended segregation in the department's restrooms and cafeteria. Although local whites often ignored his policies, Ickes advocated the employment of skilled and unskilled black laborers on PWA construction projects. The secretary insisted that all PWA contracts include "a clause specifying that the number of blacks hired and their percentage of the project payroll be equal to the proportion of Negroes in the 1930 occupational census." Under the leadership of Harry Hopkins, the WPA established policies making it illegal for any relief official to discriminate "on account of race, creed, or color." FDR had strengthened his hand by issuing Executive Order 7046, which mandated that the WPA would assign persons "qualified by training and experience" to work projects without discrimination "on any grounds whatsoever."

Under Hopkins's leadership, the WPA also promoted black adult education, hired unemployed black professionals, and stimulated the arts within the black community. The WPA education program employed over 5,000 blacks as leaders and supervisors, taught nearly 250,000 blacks to read and write, and trained many for skilled jobs. The Federal Music Project staged concerts involving the works of black composers; the Federal Art Project employed hundreds of black artists; and under the direction of Hallie Flanagan, the Federal Theater Project established an African American unit that employed about 500 blacks in New York, developed dramatic productions on African American life and history, and carried shows to black communities across the country. Supplementing the artistic work of the FTP was the Federal Writers Project. Young writers and scholars like St. Clair Drake, Horace R. Cayton, Richard Wright, and Ralph Ellison gained opportunities and early training on the Federal Writers Project.

Although most southern New Dealers resisted equal treatment for blacks, some southerners like Aubrey Willis Williams, Deputy WPA administrator and head of the NYA; Will Alexander, director of the Farm Security Administration; and Clark Foreman, "Special Adviser on the Economic Status of Negroes" in the Department of the Interior all supported efforts to improve the status of African Americans. According to Mary McLeod Bethune, Aubrey Williams was "one of America's foremost fighting liberals" and made "a very real contribution to the Negro's cause." Historians credit Williams with playing a role in moving both FDR and Eleanor Roosevelt to a more positive perspective on race. For his part, Will Alexander, founder and director of the Atlanta-based Commission on Interracial Cooperation, later recalled that he sensed "that Washington was going to become the center of the country and that perhaps" it could be used to hasten "the next [more cooperative] stage of race relations." Alexander's protégé Clark Foreman was even more supportive of a New Deal for blacks. Alexander worried that Foreman "leaned over backward to be on the liberal side and had a feeling that the way you got things done was to get at the billy-goat just butt right into them and keep butting until you're through." Although such statements exaggerate the extent to which white liberals would go to achieve results for blacks, they nonetheless underscore the interracial character of the New Deal.

Despite the New Deal's growing response to the needs of blacks, poverty, unemployment, and racial discrimination continued to affect the African American community. Even the most egalitarian programs experienced a huge gap in policy and practice. Although the WPA established regulations ending racial discrimination in its programs, southern whites continued to evade the rules and made it more difficult for blacks than whites to gain adequate public works jobs and relief. Moreover, southern officials often required black women to perform "men's jobs" at a time when white women received jobs defined as "clean" or "easy" work. In a South Carolina town, a local physician reported:

> The Beautification project appears to be "For Negro Women Only." This project is a type of work that should be assigned to men. Women are worked in "gangs" in connection with the City's dump pile incinerator. . . . Illnesses traced to such exposure as these women must face do not entitle them to medical aid at the expense of the WPA.

In Jackson, Mississippi, black women worked under the supervision of armed guards, and in Oklahoma, a WPA official closed the government project for black women to force them to pick "an abundant cotton crop which is in full picking flower." Equally important, African Americans repeatedly complained of the mistreatment that they received when applying for aid. As one black woman reported, "When I go to them for help they talk to me like I was a dog."

Although African Americans gained access to much needed low-income housing projects, such housing came at a tremendous cost. Under the "neighborhood composition rule," federal housing authorities mandated racial segregation and reinforced the residential segregation of blacks and whites in the urban environment. In Cincinnati, the city demolished over 1,160 residential structures housing over 3,500 families, disproportionately African Americans. Yet the city's redevelopment plan omitted the lower West End, which included census tract 5, over 95 percent black and locale of the worst housing, health, and sanitary conditions in the city. When Cincinnati finally constructed its public housing under the PWA, it allocated 1,400 units for white families and only 600 for black families. Making matters worse, when the city sought land to build black units, white resistance led to the redesignation of the proposed units as "all-white." Only black protests secured a portion of the units for African Americans on a segregated basis. When, under the Housing Act of 1937, the city finally established Lincoln Court, the project provided a net increase of 38 units for the displacement of 1,030 black families. A similar pattern of public housing emerged elsewhere in urban America.

ENTERING THE HOUSE OF LABOR

African Americans responded to the limits of New Deal work and relief programs by strengthening their ties with the labor movement. For the first time, they entered the predominantly white "house of labor." As the depression undercut the position of all workers, white labor leaders gradually opened their eyes to the need for a new and more egalitarian labor movement that addressed the needs of skilled and unskilled workers, black and white. Philip Murray, chairman of Steel Workers Organizing Committee, stated that black workers had

> the same ideals and aspirations and the same hopes beating within their breasts that beat within the breast of a white man. Their wives and children have the same feelings and emotions and they are entitled by the laws of nature itself to the same opportunity in the game of life as any white man.

As the organizing campaign escalated, white labor leaders broadened their efforts to reach blacks by linking labor organizing with civil rights. In a speech before the American Youth Congress, John L. Lewis, head of the United Mine Workers of America (UMWA), advocated the enfranchisement of all southern blacks, stating that the labor movement "stands for the preservation of civil liberties." In another speech, he said: "Labor's fight is the same as yours. . . . The problems of the Negro people are the problems of all American wage earners." In Memphis, Tennessee, the white riverboat worker W. E. "Red" Davis put the matter succinctly: "It was a question of self-interest on the part of whites. . . . I saw that and other white workers saw it too."

In 1935, the Committee for Industrial Organization (CIO) broke from the American Federation of Labor (AFL) and embarked on a vigorous organizing drive. Under the leadership of Lewis, the CIO (renamed the Congress of Industrial Organizations in 1938) pushed for a broader and more diverse labor movement. Building on the organizing experience of the UMWA, the CIO organized across craft and race lines, bringing blacks and whites, skilled and unskilled, together in one huge industrial organization. It targeted large mass production industries like transportation, steel, auto, rubber, and meat packing, which the AFL showed little interest in organizing.

Following the "UMWA formula," the CIO established the Steel Workers Organizing Committee (SWOC); the Packinghouse Workers Organizing Committee (PWOC); and the United Automobile Workers (UAW). The CIO appealed to black organizations like the NAACP and the National Urban League, employed black organizers, and placed African Americans in key union offices, but the day-to-day task of organizing black workers fell on the shoulders of black workers themselves. They faced entrenched and justified skepticism from many of their cohorts, who often responded to their efforts with statements like: "I've never seen a union mean anything to a Negro yet"; "the CIO wants black employees to join a union where we would be compelled to pay monthly dues and get absolutely nothing in return"; a closed CIO shop would mean "our race closed out"; or, the CIO "doesn't mean us any good." Despite such justified skepticism toward the labor movement, under the leadership of black organizers, growing numbers of black workers supported the new unions and helped to inaugurate a period of corporate recognition of organized labor.

In each industry, an energetic core of black organizers emerged in the foreground. Black organizers for the PWOC included Hank Johnson, Ercell Allen, and

As the Congress of Industrial Organizations sought to organize mass production workers, it faced stiff opposition from management. In Detroit, the Ford Motor Company employed both blacks and whites as guards to resist the organizing efforts of the United Automobile Workers. Here a black guard and a white guard chase a union leafleteer, 1937. *Archives of Labor and Urban Affairs, Wayne State University*

Philip Weightman, all of Chicago; LeRoy Johnson, Milwaukee; and James C. Harris, Omaha. Contemporaries remembered Hank Johnson, son of a black unionist from west Texas, as a "fantastic organizer" and a "powerful speaker." Similarly, an associate recalled Milwaukee's LeRoy Johnson as an "aggressive sort of guy and quite articulate." Ercell Allen later spoke of his commitment to the interracial organizing of blacks and whites together: "Once you become UPWA [United Packinghouse Workers of America], that's your sister, that's your brother . . . we did things together, black and white."

In the Detroit area, the UAW's black organizers included Paul Kirk, William Nowell, Frank Evans, Joseph Billups, and Walter Hardin. Hardin became an influential organizer at Ford's huge River Rouge complex. Later described by associates as a big, tall, muscular man with a big voice, Hardin was born in Tennessee and had worked in the steel industry before moving to Detroit. A fellow worker recalled Hardin as "a great speaker. . . . You could almost place him in the same category of an orator, he was so impressive. He could certainly shake an audience." Similarly, another associate described him as "the most convincing speaker I've ever seen in my life. He could move white union audiences because they respected his long fight for working people." In 1939, the *CIO News* featured Hardin in a story, concluding that his record had been "an inspiration to both his colored and white brothers."

SWOC's black organizers included Ernest McKinney, Ben Careathers, and Milford Peter Jackson, all in the Pittsburgh district. SWOC leaders welcomed socialist and communist organizers, who recruited Careathers and McKinney. During the early depression years, Ernest McKinney, the grandson of an active member of the UMWA, had joined a splinter group of the Communist Party and participated in demonstrations on behalf of unemployed workers in Pittsburgh. Originally from Chattanooga, Tennessee, Ben Careathers, another black communist, had migrated to Pittsburgh before World War I. In succession he worked as a janitor and helper on the railroads, opened an upholstery shop, and joined the Socialist and then the Communist Party by the early 1930s. He also participated in the Communist Party's unemployed councils and later gained credit for enrolling some two thousand black and a few white steelworkers into the union. In addition to black communists like Careathers and McKinney, black coal miners and UMWA organizers like Milford Peter Jackson also helped to bring black steelworkers into SWOC.

Black women were also instrumental in CIO organizing campaigns, especially in unions covering occupations with large numbers of black women workers. In the St. Louis area, for example, black women made up about 85 percent of nut pickers. Under the leadership of activist Connie Smith, they played a key role in organizing the Food Workers Industrial Union. Similarly, in Richmond, Virginia, black tobacco stemmer Louise "Mamma" Harris initiated walkouts and strike actions that led to the formation of the Tobacco Workers Organizing Committee in 1938. In an interview with the *New Republic,* Mamma Harris recalled her role in challenging the Export Tobacco Company. When the CIO launched its organizing efforts in the area, she attended a meeting and took sixty other black women:

> When they asked for volunteers to organize Export, I can't get to my feet quick enough. . . . And then on the first of August, 1938, we let 'em have it. We called our strike and closed up Export tight as a bass drum. The cops swooned down like ducks on a June bug . . . but we was ready for 'em. I was picket captain and there was five hundred on the line. And all five hundred was black and evil.

Even in unions where women were a small minority, they sometimes took important leadership posts. In Norfolk, Virginia, Lena Jarvis chaired the strike committee of the Veneer Box and Barrel Union. Although men made up 80 percent of the workers, they elected Jarvis "unanimously." Workers at Norfolk's M.F.G. Company referred to it as "one of the worst slave mills in Norfolk," operating at exceedingly low wages for skilled and unskilled work. In addition to low wages, the company had "no toilets or washrooms, no safety devices and no regular hours." Under Jarvis's leadership, workers struck the company in 1937.

CIO organizers encountered stiff resistance from employers, who often used plant police and hired hands to break the union. In Michigan, early in his organizing work, Walter Hardin was "kidnapped, taken to a desolate park outside Pontiac, undressed and then brutally whipped and forced to stagger 10 miles back into the city without shoes or stockings—in freezing weather." Other labor leaders in the Detroit area "were clubbed so viciously and their vital organs crushed so violently that they went insane shortly afterwards." The *CIO News* later reported the men as "inmates in a State asylum, a living testimonial of the terror that once stalked" the labor movement. In July 1937, *Crisis* magazine reported on the violence that union workers faced in the steel industry. Referring to the Memorial Day massacre, in which Chicago police fired into the backs of SWOC pickets at Republic Steel and killed ten people, *Crisis* concluded that the "little steel" industry had "the worst labor record of any great American industry." Independent steel companies, the NAACP organ said, are "conducting open warfare against labor." The NAACP also indicted the city of Chicago for allowing police to kill "its own citizens who do not happen to own factories and mills."

Interracial organizing confronted its greatest obstacles in the South, where entrenched patterns of racial segregation and hostility prevailed. Still, large numbers of southern white and black workers took steps to build the labor movement. In Memphis, Thomas Watkins emerged at the forefront of organizing among the city's black dock workers. Under Watkins's leadership, the AFL International Association of Longshoremen (ILA) locals cooperated with the CIO union—the Inland Boatmen's Union (IBU), an affiliate of the National Maritime Union (NMU). Their efforts culminated in the "Great Riverfront Strike of 1939" against the Federal Barge Line. During the strike, one dock owner told an FBI agent that "the entire labor disorder presently in force in Memphis could be laid to Tom Watkins, as he is a radical individual and apparently has aroused the colored longshoremen to rebel." One white riverboat worker later compared Watkins to leaders of antebellum slave rebellions: "He was like the slave revolt leader Denmark Vesey, absolutely fearless. . . . He figured he would not live long, but he decided to fight for the union anyway."

The strike resulted in the Federal Barge Line's recognition of the ILA and IBU as the sole collective bargaining agents in their companies. Following the strike, however, Watkins faced threats on his life from local police, employers, and white leaders of the AFL, who resented his cooperation with the CIO. According to Watkins, a white labor leader told him that "he was going to dig my grave and see me in it." A policeman told another black: "I have nothing against you, but that negro Tom Watkins is either going to get run out of town or get killed." The police, accompanied by dockworkers, took Watkins and his wife from their home at midnight. After suffering blows to the head, Watkins escaped, eluding bullets and jumping onto a barge in the Mississippi River. Union brothers eventually came to his aid and helped him and his wife leave the city.

Blacks faced similar organizing perils on the docks of New Orleans, Baton Rouge, Vicksburg, Mobile, and Helena, Arkansas. In the Birmingham coal, iron, and steel district of Alabama, CIO organizers faced similar resistance at the hands of employers. In 1936, when the Mine, Mill, and Smelter Union organized black and white workers in Bessemer, Alabama, black miners faced the brunt of violent antiunion attacks, which included severe beatings as well as shootings. The *Daily Worker* reported the shooting of Richard Holt, a black miner, who lived but remained in "serious condition." Similarly, another black miner, Pete Casey, "was severely beaten by company cops along the road leading to Wenonah mine." The McDuff National Detective Agency played an active role in the violence against union miners. Indeed, a federal mediator identified the "ambush shooting" of workers in the area "as the work of private detective agencies and mercenary thugs, bent on creating an atmosphere of terror in order to sell their 'protective service' to the Company."

Despite the perils of organizing that they faced, black workers helped usher in a new pattern of labor relations. Corporate America gradually recognized the influence of workers and their unions. In 1937, the Pullman Company signed a contract with the Brotherhood of Sleeping Car Porters (BSCP), ending twelve long years of struggle for official recognition by the union. Two years earlier, under the persistent prodding of A. Philip Randolph and growing competition from the industrial unions, the AFL had grudgingly approved a full international charter for the BSCP. This represented the first charter awarded to an all-black union, granting it sole jurisdiction over an important segment of the labor force.

On 12 March 1937, General Motors, the largest corporation in the world, signed a contract with the UAW. Five days later, Carnegie Illinois Steel signed a contract with SWOC. Jones and Laughlin and Crucible Steel soon followed. The new agreements increased wages and established an eight-hour day, a forty-hour week, and a week of paid vacation for black and white workers with five years' employment with the firm. In addition to establishing grievance procedures to address issues of unfair firing and other mistreatment, the contract stipulated that seniority rather than color would govern promotions and layoffs. Following the UAW's agreement with automakers, the *Pittsburgh Courier* enthusiastically reported benefits to black workers at Detroit's Budd Wheel Company, where they made up 70 percent of the firm's foundry workers:

> Today all workers enjoy seniority rights that enable them to be hired and laid off in accordance with their seniority. Throughout the shop steward system, all of the grievances of the workers are dealt with and adjusted. . . . Compare the wages before and after the Union came 18 months ago:
>
> Minimum wage per hour:
> 55 cents, after: 75 cents.
>
> Maximum wage per hour:
> 75 cents, after: $1.15
>
> Average wage per hour:
> 62 cents, after: 90 cents.
>
> Average weekly wage:
> $25, after: $38

By 1939, significant numbers of black workers believed that the union would curb the abuses of foremen and give them "the same job as the white man if they are qualified to do the work." The influence of black workers on the labor movement was not merely economic, however. African Americans also helped to shape the culture of union organizing. Black Southern Tenant Farmers' Union organizer John L. Handcox transposed the black gospel song "Roll the Chariot On" into the labor song "Roll the Union On." This song became a favorite of labor organizers in the South. A black woman, Hattie Walls, replaced the religious lyrics of "Gospel Train" with those of the "Union Train." Conversely, numerous black CIO leaders, especially those recruited from the Communist Party, credited the union with providing them with an education, including basic literacy. In 1934, for example, Alabama communist Hosea Hudson traveled to New York to participate in a ten-week course at the "Workers School." When he returned, he later recalled, he was a changed man: "I felt like I'm somebody. . . . I'm talking about political economy, about the society itself, how it automatically would breed war and fascism." Although they would face ongoing obstacles, African Americans had moved into the portals of the "house of labor."

THE CIVIL RIGHTS STRUGGLE

As black workers increased their organizing activities and gained access to the labor movement, they influenced the direction of the larger civil rights struggle. As the NAACP intensified its campaign against social injustices amidst increasing unemployment, hunger, and homelessness, a new generation argued that the organization had become "top heavy with white-collar interests and attitudes" and supported the call for programs designed to give the organization "some strength on the industrial side." At the organization's annual meetings, local branches increasingly urged the NAACP to "go to the masses." One delegate remarked, "We must share common ground with the Negro worker. When we call a meeting on discrimination we have nobody, but when we call a meeting on bread-and-butter matters, we have a full house." Abram Harris, the economist and NAACP board member, repeatedly made the same point:

> If the organization is to continue its effectiveness . . . it must go to the Negro workers and farmers with a program based on knowledge of what is happening in the present economy. . . . It will seek through practical lessons to show white and black working men that as contradictory as it may seem they have a real identity of common interests.

Accordingly, in the spring of 1933, the NAACP invited forty-three "young representatives of the colored race" to attend a three-day conference at Amenia, New York, the estate of Joel Spingarn, the association's president and board chairman.

The NAACP and the National Negro Congress

Under the leadership of W. E. B. Du Bois, the Amenia conference aimed to assess the current status of the association and discuss future directions. Roy Wilkins, assistant secretary, placed the issue in historical perspective: "In 1910 the Association's program was regarded as radical. . . . How is the program regarded today? How should the program be changed or enlarged or shifted?" Conference participants—including Bunche, Harris, and sociologist E. Franklin Frazier—discussed a variety of issues and strategies for social change. The gathering approved a program of cultural nationalism designed to mobilize the black vote but emphasized worker education and the need to make the black worker "conscious of his relation to white labor and the white worker conscious that the purpose of labor, immediate or ultimate, cannot be achieved without full participation from the Negro worker."

Following the Amenia conference, the NAACP increased its efforts on behalf of black workers. In 1934, under the chairmanship of Abram Harris, the organization established the Committee on the Future Plan and Program of the NAACP. The committee's report asked the organization to shift its focus on workers—from "an incidental phase" of its "civil liberty program" to a focused commitment to economic justice. Specifically, the Harris report urged the association to emphasize "the building of a labor movement, industrial in character, which will unite all labor, white and black, skilled and unskilled, agricultural and industrial." This work would take the form of (1) classes in "workers' education"; (2) political support for progressive labor legislation; (3) producer and consumer cooperatives; and (4) ongoing efforts to end job discrimination and segregated unions. The NAACP's board of directors approved the basic outline of the Harris report. Militant board members declared that the problems of black workers were "inextricably intertwined with those of white workers." Officials urged black workers to affiliate with labor unions as "the only means of changing low and unfavorable conditions of work imposed upon them." To facilitate these efforts, the NAACP formed a Committee on Economic Problems Affecting the Negro; invited representatives of the CIO to serve on its board; and worked with organized labor to gain housing, wages, hours, and Social Security benefits for black workers.

The National Urban League also facilitated the reorientation of the civil rights struggle toward organized labor. Early on, the Urban League had formed Emergency Advisory Councils and Negro Workers Councils. In major cities across the country, local branches played a major role in promoting closer ties between blacks and organized labor. Although the league had earlier supported black strikebreaking activities and emphasized amicable relations with employers, it now urged black workers to organize and "get into somebody's union and stay there."

The emergence of the National Negro Congress (NNC) symbolized the growing cross-class support for the labor movement. Formed in 1936, the NNC aimed to unite all existing African American organizations against the ravages of the depression. Representatives from some six hundred organizations selected A. Philip Randolph as president to spearhead this effort. Although the organization aimed to achieve a variety of goals in the struggle for citizenship and launched its own antilynching campaign, it emphasized economic democracy and the unionization of black workers as a principal goal. Shortly after the founding meeting, A. Philip Randolph traveled to Pittsburgh, where the local NNC and CIO sponsored a conference that included national leaders like T. Arnold Hill of the Urban League and Robert Vann, as well as Randolph. Vann captured growing middle-class endorsement of the labor movement when he "pledged the full support of the *Pittsburgh Courier* to the steel drive and declared that it would expose in its pages those Negroes who betrayed the best interests of their people by supporting the bosses."

"Don't Buy Where You Can't Work"

Although African American civil rights and political organizations urged black workers to affiliate with the predominantly white labor movement, they also launched new movements that reinforced earlier efforts to build a Black Metropolis. These efforts gained expression in the "Don't Buy Where You Can't Work" campaigns and Du Bois's call for the development of a separate economy. Aimed at white merchants who served the African American community but refused to employ blacks, the "Don't Buy Where You Can't Work" campaigns galvanized the black urban community perhaps even more so than the labor movement in some places. In New York, Chicago, Washington, D.C., and other cities, African Americans boycotted stores that refused to hire African Americans except in low-paying domestic and common laborer capacities.

New York launched its campaign under the leadership of the Reverend John H. Johnson, pastor of St. Martin's Protestant Episcopal Church. The black nationalist Sufi Abdul Hamid also played an important role in the New York boycott. When Harlem's white store owners refused to negotiate, blacks formed the Citizens League for Fair Play and later escalated their efforts. The Citizens League set up picket lines around Blumstein's Department Store, took pictures of blacks who crossed the line, and published photos in the black newspaper the *New York Age*. After six weeks, the store gave in and hired black clerical and professional staff. As a result of such actions, New York blacks obtained the nation's first black affirmative action plan. In 1938, the New York Uptown Chamber of Commerce negotiated with the Greater New York Coordinating Committee for Employment and agreed to grant African Americans one-third of all retail executive, clerical, and sales jobs. The businesses would not fire whites to make room for blacks but agreed to give blacks preference in all new openings.

After working on a "Don't Buy Where You Can't Work Campaign" in Chicago, Kiowa Costonie moved to Baltimore in 1933 and led a similar campaign. Under Costonie's leadership, blacks formed a citizens' committee and placed pickets around Baltimore's A&P stores. When A&P satisfied their demands and agreed to hire black clerks, the group moved their pickets to small retail stores on Pennsylvania Avenue, but Jewish merchants refused their demands and gained a court injunction against the boycotts. In April 1935, the Maryland Court of Appeals modified the injunction and allowed blacks to hold meetings and conduct a boycott of the offending establishments. In Washington, D.C., African Americans formed the New Negro Alliance. Assisted by attorney and Howard University law professor William Hastie, the alliance claimed the right to boycott businesses that refused to hire blacks under the same New Deal statutes that gave labor unions and workers the right to strike and picket their employers. After a boycott of A&P, the firm employed thirty-three black clerks. The Washington alliance also developed its own organ, *New Negro Opinion,* which defended the boycotts against charges of "racialism," arguing that it was appropriate to fight "segregation with segregation." When High's Ice Cream Stores and Kaufman's Department Stores, and later the Sanitary Grocery Company refused to cooperate and won injunctions against the boycotts, the alliance fought the issue and gained a hearing before the U.S. Supreme Court. On 28 March 1938, the Supreme Court reversed the lower court decisions and upheld the right of the alliance to picket establishments pursuing discriminatory employment policies. As Justice Owen Roberts said, the lower court's view that "the dispute was not a labor dispute . . . because it did not involve terms and conditions of employment [in] the sense of wages, hours, unionization, or betterment of working conditions is erroneous."

Although some civil rights leaders and labor activists rejected the idea of fighting "segregation with segregation," W. E. B. Du Bois applauded the "Don't Buy Where You Can't Work" campaigns as proof that "segregation without discrimination" could benefit African Americans. Following the Amenia conference of 1933, Du Bois rejected the singular focus on interracialism and urged the NAACP to promote the development of a separate black economy. The NAACP rejected Du Bois's distinction between "voluntary" and "involuntary" segregation and opposed his plan as a throwback to the accommodationist ideas of Booker T. Washington. In 1934, when he failed to convince the organization to endorse his ideas, Du Bois resigned from the NAACP, returned to his post at Atlanta University, and promoted his ideas independently. Before leaving the NAACP, however, he offered a vigorous defense of his call for economic nationalism. In his view, neither white workers, elites, nor the state offered much hope for ending racial inequality. Whereas he used to believe that a highly educated fraction of the black population could demonstrate the fallacy of racism and help elevate the group, he now believed that whites were as opposed to blacks of "education and culture, as any other kind, and perhaps more so." Thus he called on blacks of different class backgrounds to unite in developing a black "nation within the nation" and to "supply those things and those opportunities we lack because of segregation."

Du Bois insisted that his "Negro Nation Within the Nation" was not merely a throwback to Booker T. Washington. First, rather than advocating free competition and individual, private, and profit-making enterprises, he advocated "producer and consumer cooperatives" as key to the success of the black economy. Second, Du Bois argued that agitation for citizenship should continue despite his belief that such agitation would produce few results in the short run. Third, Du Bois forcefully argued that his plan would enable civil rights organizations like the NAACP to establish a firmer grassroots foundation for its work. Protests, as usually conceptualized by the NAACP, he claimed, attracted the attention of elites far more than the masses of working people. Moreover, he argued, some NAACP officials simply overplayed the efficacy of protests, believing that "the fight against segregation consists merely of one damned protest after another, that the technique is to protest and wail and protest again, and to keep this thing up until the gates of public opinion and the walls of segregation fall down."

Despite the force and logic of his arguments, Du Bois failed to convince either black workers or elites of the efficacy of his proposal. More so than ever before, black workers and their communities gained greater access to the labor movement and the fruits of New Deal social programs. As large industrial firms signed contracts with unions and established seniority rules rather than race to govern layoffs, some blacks hoped to benefit. Moreover, under the persistent and long-term campaign to end mob violence and bring about equality before the law, lynchings had gradually declined and some blacks had gained access to previously all-white institutions of higher education. Understandably, most African Americans were in no mood to compromise the fruits of full participation in the larger political economy. They were also less willing to tolerate the old order in any guise.

The Harlem Riot and Growing Internationalism

The Harlem riot of 1935 symbolized a significant shift in the mood and expectation of African Americans. Whereas earlier instances of group violence involved blacks as the principal victims, the Harlem conflict signaled a reversal of the process in northern cities. On 25 March 1935, a race riot broke out in Harlem when a rumor spread that a black youth had been brutally beaten and nearly killed by police. Flyers soon appeared: "Child Brutally Beaten—near death"; "One Hour Ago Negro Boy Was Brutally Beaten"; "The Boy Is Near Death." Although the youth in question had been released unharmed, outrage had already spread and African Americans smashed buildings and looted stores in a night of violence that resulted in at least one death, over fifty injuries, and thousands of dollars' worth of property damage. In his novel *Invisible Man*, Ralph Ellison later described the event:

> I could see a crowd rushing a store ... moving in, and a fusillade of canned goods, salami, liverwurst, hogs heads and chitterlings belching out to those outside ... as now out of the dark of the intersecting street two mounted policemen came at a gallop ... charging straight into the swarming mass. They came toward me as I ran, a crowd of men and women carrying cases of beer, cheese, chains of linked sausage, watermelons, sacks of sugar, hams, cornmeal, fuel lamps.

Along with the outbreak of violence in Harlem, African Americans expressed a growing internationalist consciousness. As the fascists mobilized to take power in Europe and extended their reach into Africa, African Americans expressed growing concern. When Mussolini invaded Ethiopia in 1935, New Yorkers set up the International Council of Friends of Ethiopia. Under the leadership of Willis N. Huggins, the council soon appeared before the League of Nations to plead the case of Ethiopia. African Americans also formed another organization, the United Aid to Ethiopia (later the Ethiopian World Federation) and strengthened their support for the beleaguered nation. For its part, the *Pittsburgh Courier* dispatched historian-journalist J. A. Rogers to the war front. Rogers later produced a booklet, *The Real Facts About Ethiopia,* and lectured to black and white audiences about the evils of Italian imperialism in Africa. When the U.S. government blocked participation in a volunteer army to help defend Ethiopia, other blacks expressed their internationalism by enrolling in the Abraham Lincoln Brigade and fighting to defend Spain from a German takeover. Some eighty black men and one woman joined the brigade. As one recruit put it, "I wanted to go to Ethiopia and fight Mussolini ... This Ain't Ethiopia, but it'll do."

The outbreak of urban violence and the growth of internationalist activities reinforced efforts to end mob rule and dismantle the Jim Crow system in the United States. In 1933, the NAACP had organized a Writers League Against Lynching and strengthened its nationwide movement to secure a federal antilynching law. Sponsored in the House of Representatives by Edward Costigan of Colorado and in the Senate by Robert Wagner of New York, the campaign for an antilynching law persisted through the 1930s. The campaign gained little support from FDR and failed when southern senators killed the measure in 1934, 1935, 1937, 1938, and 1940. Despite failure to pass the measure, the number of recorded lynchings dropped from eighteen in 1935 to two in 1939. Moreover, under the leadership of black attorneys William Hastie, Charles Hamilton Houston, and Thurgood Marshall, African Americans carefully planned an overall legal strategy that emphasized test cases with broad implications for dismantling the entire Jim Crow edifice. They focused on the admission of blacks to previously all-white law schools; selection of blacks to jury service; and greater access to employment, housing, and public accommodations.

Legal Challenges to Jim Crow Laws

Although legal change came only slowly, civil rights attorneys won significant decisions before the U.S. Supreme Court. In 1935, Charles Hamilton Houston became the first black attorney employed by the NAACP to argue a case before the U.S. Supreme Court. In the case of *Hollins v. State of Oklahoma,* the court accepted Houston's argument that a black accused of murdering a white and sentenced to death had been denied due process of law because blacks were illegally excluded from the jury. The court overturned the man's conviction. A year later, in the case of *Brown v. Mississippi* (1936), the U.S. Supreme Court overturned a 1908 ruling and declared that the federal Constitution does in fact offer protection against "compulsory self-incrimination in the courts of the States." In this case, law officers had brutally beaten the black defendants and coerced a confession to murder. The men showed up in court bearing the marks of physical brutality. In a unanimous decision, the court ruled: "It would be difficult to conceive of methods more revolting to the sense of justice than those taken to procure the confessions of these petitioners . . . the use of the confessions thus obtained [as evidence] . . . was a clear violation of due process." In a similar case, *Chambers v. Florida* (1940), the court issued the same ruling.

At the same time, the U.S. Supreme Court eroded the legal underpinnings of segregated institutions. In 1935, Donald Murray, a black graduate of Amherst College in Massachusetts, applied for admission to the University of Maryland Law School. When the school denied him admission based on his race, he took the case to court and challenged racial discrimination in graduate education. When Maryland, like most southern states, set up a tuition program to aid blacks seeking graduate and professional training elsewhere, the Maryland Court of Appeals ordered the University of Maryland to either set up a separate law school for blacks or admit them to the white one. Rather than contesting the court's decision, university officials quietly admitted blacks to the law school. In 1938, the U.S. Supreme Court reinforced the Maryland precedent by ruling that law schools in the various states had to admit blacks or establish separate law schools.

The U.S. Supreme Court also issued other rulings that gradually weakened the legitimacy of the segregationist order. On two occasions (1932, 1935), the U.S. Supreme Court overruled the Alabama Supreme Court in the Scottsboro case and insisted on due process of law for black defendants. In a Kentucky case (1938), the court noted the systematic exclusion of blacks from jury service and overturned the conviction of a black man accused of murder. Over the next three years, the U.S. Supreme Court also strengthened the economic position of African Americans. It upheld the right of African Americans to boycott businesses that discriminated in their employment practices; struck down a Georgia peonage law that sanctioned the virtual enslavement of blacks as sharecroppers; and upheld the elimination of unequal black and white teacher salaries in Norfolk, Virginia. In short, by 1939, the Court slowly undermined the historic *Plessy v. Ferguson* (1896) decision, which mandated a "separate but equal" society for blacks and whites.

CULTURAL DEVELOPMENTS

Reinforcing the lowering of legal barriers were new intellectual and cultural perspectives on race in American society. As black lawyers attacked the legal foundations of Jim Crow, black intellectuals, social scientists, and artists assaulted its intellectual underpinnings. Under the leadership of Carter G. Woodson, the Association for the Study of Negro Life and History (founded in 1915) continued to promote the study of African American history, emphasizing the role of blacks in the development of the nation. Although the organization continued to publish the scholarly *Journal of Negro History* (founded in 1916), it added the *Negro History Bulletin*—a publication designed for broader circulation—in 1933. Launched in 1926, Negro History Week also became a regular feature of African American community life across the country. Sociologist and Howard University professor E. Franklin Frazier conducted seminal studies of black community and family life, which culminated in the publication of his *The Negro Family in the United States* (1939). Although he underestimated the role that poor and working-class blacks played in shaping their own experience, Frazier emphasized environmental over racial factors in explaining poverty.

In his scholarship on African American history, W. E. B. Du Bois also called attention to the impact of class and racial discrimination in his massive reinterpretation of the emancipation period, *Black Reconstruction in America, 1860–1880* (1935). As the depression took its toll on the lives of black and white workers, Du Bois later recalled that he "began to awake and to see in the socialism of the New Deal, emancipation of all workers, and the labor problem, which included the Negro problem." According to Du Bois, black workers fueled the development of "modern industry" in Europe and the United States during the cotton revolution of the early nineteenth century. Du Bois also concluded that it was also the black worker "as founding stone of a new economic system" who brought the Civil War to America and ushered in "the finest effort to achieve democracy . . . this world has ever seen."

The intellectual assault on racism continued in 1937, when the Carnegie Corporation invited the Swedish economist Gunnar Myrdal to the United States to head "a comprehensive study of the Negro." The Myrdal study resulted in the publication of the monumental *An American Dilemma: The Negro Problem and Modern Democracy* (1944), which built on the scholarship of some thirty black scholars,

Richard Wright, author of *Native Son* (1940), at his typewriter in New York, 27 March 1945. Wright
hoped to use his art to facilitate the liberation of the masses of Americans, black and white.
When his book appeared, one critic opined that "American culture was changed forever."
AP/Wide World Photos

including young men like Charles S. Johnson, St. Clair Drake, Horace R. Cayton,
and Ralph Bunche. Defining the "Negro problem" as a problem of white racism,
immorality, and inequality, *An American Dilemma* concluded:

> The American Negro problem is in the heart of the [white] American. It is there
> that the interracial tension has its focus. It is there that the decisive struggle goes
> on. This is the central viewpoint of this treatise. Though our study includes eco-
> nomic, social, and political race relations, at bottom our problem is the moral
> dilemma of the American—the conflict between his moral valuations on various
> levels of consciousness and generality.

The Harlem Renaissance Continues

Intersecting with the work of black social scientists and historians were the contributions of black writers, artists, and musicians. In part, the Harlem Renaissance of
the 1920s persisted into the 1930s. Renaissance writers like Langston Hughes, Arna
Bontemps, Claude McKay, and Zora Neale Hurston were now joined by younger

writers—William Attaway, Richard Wright, Ralph Ellison, and Margaret Walker. Under the impact of the depression, black artists and writers returned to themes and issues raised by the literary magazine *Fire!!* They reassessed the meaning of the Renaissance and called for a more socially conscious art. Their ideas gained articulation in two new journals, *Challenge* (1934–1937) and the revised *New Challenge* (1937). Under the leadership of Dorothy West, a little-known Renaissance writer, and associate editor Richard Wright, *New Challenge* issued a manifesto to "all writers who realize the present need for the realistic depiction of life through the sharp focus of social consciousness." In his lead essay for the volume, "Blueprint for Negro Writing," Wright called for a Marxist orientation that would enable the black writer "to stand shoulder to shoulder with Negro workers in mood and outlook."

In 1938, Richard Wright won a WPA writing prize for his book *Uncle Tom's Children.* Two years later he published his most famous novel, *Native Son,* which emphasized the Great Migration of blacks to American cities and the destructive impact of racism on their lives. One observer later recalled that "the day *Native Son* appeared, American culture was changed forever." Wright's book set a sales record for Harper and Brothers and soon surpassed John Steinbeck's *The Grapes of Wrath* on the bestseller list. Born on a plantation near Natchez, Mississippi, in 1908, Wright later wrote that his head was "full of a hazy notion that life could be lived with dignity, that the personalities of others should not be violated." One literary historian later described the 1930s as the high-water mark of the black writers' turn to "proletarian art."

The themes of rebellion against exploitation gained further articulation in the novels of Arna Bontemps and William Attaway. Whereas Bontemps would take up issues familiar to Renaissance writers in his first novel, *God Send Sunday* (1931), he later took up the theme of rebellion in *Black Thunder* (1936) and *Drums of Dusk* (1939). In the former, Bontemps combed the Virginia court records dealing with slave rebellions and built his story around a heroic but aborted slave revolt. In the latter, he used the Haitian Revolution as the basis for his story of a successful slave rebellion. In his novel *Let Me Breathe Thunder* (1939), Attaway treated the lives of working people on a large interracial canvas. In *Blood on the Forge* (1941), however, he probed the specific process by which black sharecroppers left serflike conditions in rural Kentucky for the equally exploitative environment of the steel mills in western Pennsylvania.

As noted in Chapter 16, Zora Neale Hurston also produced her most important novels during the 1930s: *Jonah's Gourd Vine* (1934); *Mules and Men* (1935); *Tell My Horse* (1938); and *Moses, Man of the Mountain* (1939). Literary critics consider *Their Eyes Were Watching God* her masterpiece. Hurston insisted on portraying the black world in its own right, the struggle over self-definition taking on intense personal as well as collective meaning. In her novels, some of the most powerful confrontations and struggles involved black men, women, children, and families who came face to face with one another's strengths and weaknesses. In *Their Eyes Were Watching God,* Hurston highlights the impact of Jody's insistence on being "a big man with a big voice" on his relationship with his wife, Janie. On his deathbed, Janie tells him: "You wouldn't listen. You done lived wid me for twenty years and you don't half know me atall. . . . You wasn't satisfied wid me the way ah was. Naw!

1. Henry Ossawa Tanner, *The Resurrection of Lazarus* (1896). Born in Pittsburgh, Tanner became the most noted black artist of the late nineteenth century. After producing *The Banjo Lesson* (1893), he built his international reputation painting religious scenes like the one pictured here.

2. Archibald J. Motley Jr., *Tongues (Holy Rollers)* (1929). Motley studied at the School of the Art Institute of Chicago and became a stellar representative of the black Renaissance in the Midwest. He used portraiture to explore myriad dimensions of black life, mainly in urban settings, as shown in *Black Belt* (1934) and in the church scene here.

3. Allan Rohan Crite, *Harriet and Leon* (1941). Many lesser-known black artists documented ordinary, day-to-day events in black urban life, as in Crite's portrait of a black couple with two children looking on.

4. Robert Gwalthmey, *Hoeing Tobacco* (1947). Even as blacks made the transition from farm to city, agricultural labor retained a strong hold on the imagination of some black artists. Here Gwalthmey captures the persistence of black labor in the tobacco fields of the South.

5. Jacob Lawrence, *The Migrants Arrived in Great Numbers* (The Migration of the Negro Series, 1940–1941). A student of the depression-era Harlem Art Workshop and Harlem Community Art Center, Lawrence soon produced the most renowned paintings of the Great Migration of blacks from rural to urban America. This is one of sixty panels in the series.

6. Charles White, *The Contribution of the Negro to Democracy in America* (1943). Partly inspired by Mexican muralists such as Diego Rivera, White's mural at Hampton University sought to depict both the reality of black life in America and the way in which ordinary and extraordinary blacks from Crispus Attucks to Booker T. Washington had struggled to change it.

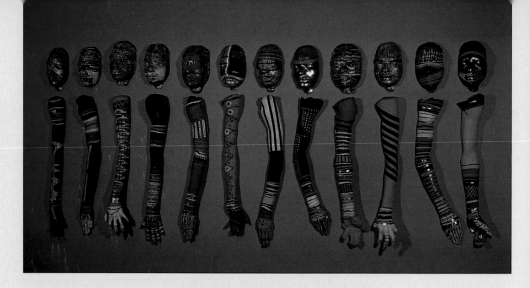

7. Ben Jones, *Black Face and Arm Unit* (1971). In his first exhibition at Harlem's Weusi Gallery, Jones underscored the Black Power movement's revival of African American interest in African aesthetics. Inspired by observations of ritual body paintings among black people during his travels to Africa, the Caribbean, and Brazil, Jones used his own face and arms to create colorful plaster casts.

8. Jean-Michel Basquiat, *Famous Moon King* (1984–1985). A product of New York's multinational hip-hop culture, Basquiat pioneered in moving graffiti art from the subways and streets into established art museums. His work also reflected the growing ethnic diversity of the African American population during the late twentieth century, as the number of blacks coming to America from Caribbean and African countries increased.

Mah own mind had tuh be squeezed and crowded out tuh make room for yours in me." Hurston's work demonstrates how black women writers confronted powerful male-centered gender conventions as well as class and racial ones. Other writers like Ralph Ellison and Margaret Walker were also schooled during the depression years, but their most important works would not appear until the postwar years.

Adding to the artistic portrayal of black life were the dramatic productions of black theater groups. As noted earlier, only the arrival of the Federal Theater Project enabled black actors to return to work in substantial numbers. For the first time, African Americans not only performed on stage but learned the techniques of stage production, including lighting and other technical aspects of production. Before the 1930s, white unions had barred blacks from participating in these aspects of production. White stagehands had previously demanded and obtained such jobs in black- as well as white-owned theaters. The Federal Theater Project stimulated black theater productions in cities across the country, including Chicago, Los Angeles, Cleveland, Seattle, and New York. The 1930s also witnessed the emergence of black theater groups like the Harlem Suitcase Theater, the Negro People's Theater, and the Rose McClendon Players. By 1940, African Americans had also formed the American Negro Theater and the Negro Playwrights Company. In New York, the Rose McClendon Players, founded in 1937, gave opportunities to young actors and actresses like Fred O'Neal, Helen Martin, and Ossie Davis and playwrights George Norford, Lofton Mitchell, and Abram Hill, who produced the popular Harlem comedy *On Strivers Row*.

Like their literary counterparts, black playwrights explored a variety of themes while turning to the hard times of the 1930s for material. Plays included H. F. V. Edward's *Job Hunters* (1931); Langston Hughes's *Don't You Want to Be Free* (1938); Theodore Ward's *Big White Fog* (1938); and Owen Dodson's *Divine Comedy* (1938). In 1970, Edward told an interviewer that his work in the New York State Employment Service inspired his play: "Half of my working time was spent in the field in an attempt to locate job vacancies, a discouraging task, but work in the dingy Harlem office on Lenox Avenue at 132nd Street was even more depressing." In his play, Edward warned that unrelieved suffering could spark violence and revolution. Langston Hughes merged the interests of black workers and business people by calling attention to white-owned stores that paid little attention to the needs of the black community but emphasized the utility of blacks and whites cooperating in the labor movement. Similarly, Owen Dodson addressed the multiclass character of the black community while urging blacks to find the God within themselves: "We need no miracles. . . . We are the miracle. . . . We are the earth itself." In *Big White Fog*, Ward compared the virtues of black nationalist strategies like the Garvey movement on the one hand with black capitalist strategies like the National Negro Business League on the other; he concluded that both were deficient and called for socialism/communism as the most appropriate vehicle for black liberation.

Although some black actors and actresses found employment in black theatrical productions, others gained much needed employment in plays directed and produced by whites for all-black or predominantly black casts, such as Marc Connelly's *Green Pastures* (1930); Paul Peters and George Sklar's *Stevedore* (1932); John Wexley and Workers Laboratory Theater's *Scottsboro!* (1932); and Du Bose and Dorothy Heyward's stage production of *Mamba* (1939), which featured Ethel Waters in the lead role. *Green Pastures* struck a deep chord within the black community. It drew on southern black religious culture (the Old Testament fall of man and the New Testament "redemption") and symbolically wrestled with the intraracial tensions between the "Old" and "New" Negroes. In a less overt way, it also addressed African Americans' ongoing struggle to combat racial subordination. The play ran on Broadway until its star Richard B. Harrison, the Canadian-born actor who played De Lawd, died in 1935. Harrison was sixty-five years old when he stepped on the Broadway stage to play De Lawd in 1930. He performed the part 1,568 times in consecutive performances, with a supporting black cast of nearly one hundred actors and singers. *Green Pastures* met increasing opposition as it toured the country, however, because white theaters invariably barred local blacks from the performance or forced them to view the show from segregated seats. *Mamba* also gained the favorable attention of black audiences by addressing the movement from plantation to city through the eyes of Mamba, her daughter, and granddaughter. The story also illuminated the lives of ordinary working people as well as the so-called "talented tenth." Despite their appeal to black audiences, plays like *Green Pastures* and *Mamba* attracted whites interested in racial stereotypes—that is, "exotic Negroes." Conversely, Wexley's *Scottsboro!* and Peters and Sklar's *Stevedore* reflected the imprint of 1930s labor radicalism. In his play, Wexley tried to convince whites to defend the Scottsboro defendants as part of their defense of themselves as workers: "Will you deliver your fellow workers to the capitalist murderers? Will you deliver yourselves to the capitalist murderers?" Peters and Sklar also reinforced the call for the unity of workers across racial lines but paid much more attention to the culture of African Americans.

Closely interrelated with the activities of the black theater, African American music continued to flourish and influence wide audiences. In 1932, Duke Ellington set the pace for 1930s-style "swing" jazz in his song "It Don't Mean a Thing If It Ain't Got That Swing." Originally from Washington, D.C., Ellington had little formal training except piano lessons, but he soon became a prolific composer with works such as "Creole Rhapsody" (1932), "Blue Harlem" (1934), and "Echoes of Harlem" (1935). Born in Redbank, New Jersey, William "Count" Basie had arrived in Kansas City during the late 1920s, but it was not until 1935 that he formed his renowned band, featuring blues singer Jimmy Rushing. Kansas City was an important center of blues, which influenced not only Basie but also such jazz pianists as Sammy Price, Pete Johnson, and Mary Lou Williams. In 1936, the Music Corporation of America took over the management of Basie's band and opened the door for Basie to play at Chicago's Grand Terrace Ballroom and New York's Roseland Ballroom and Famous Door Club.

At Carnegie Hall in New York, two John Henry Hammond productions showcased a wide variety of black music. Opening in December 1938, the first production, *From Spirituals to Swing* (dedicated to Bessie Smith), consisted of several sections—spirituals, holy roller hymns, and "soft swing"; harmonica, boogie-woogie piano, and blues; and New Orleans jazz and "swing." Performers included the gospel singer Sister Rosetta Tharpe, the blind bluesman Sonny Terry, Count Basie, and several Kansas City bands and blues singers. The second Carnegie Hall display of black musical talent took place in October 1939. Part of a week-long Jubilee Festival sponsored by the American Society of Composers, Authors and Publishers (ASCAP), the second night, *From Symphony to Swing,* featured black music. The program featured symphonies conducted by black composers like James P. Johnson, Charles L. Cooke, and William Grant Still, as well as a medley of black music from the minstrels of the nineteenth century through the music of the late 1930s. The event concluded with the music of bands led by Nobel Sissle, Louis Armstrong, Claude Hopkins, and Cab Calloway. Black music gained similar attention at the great world fairs of the period: the Chicago's Century of Progress International Exposition (1933–1934); San Francisco's Golden Gate International Exposition (1939–1940); and the New York World's Fair (1939–1940). Nineteenthirties concert artists included Roland Hays, Paul Robeson, Dorothy Maynor, Todd Duncan, and Lillian Evanti, who during the 1920s had become the first American black to sing operatic roles in Europe.

African Americans also gained greater access to mainstream radio and film and gradually used these media to project more positive images of themselves than before. After the production of *Hallelujah* (1929) and *Hearts of Dixie* (1929), black filmmaker Oscar Micheaux produced *Ten Minutes to Live* (1932), *Underworld* (c. 1938), and *Lying Lips* (1940). White filmmakers also produced all-black films— *The Emperor Jones* (1933), *Green Pastures* (1936), *The Spirit of Youth* (1937), and *Keep on Punching* (1939), to name a few. The latter two covered the careers of boxing champions Joe Louis and Henry Armstrong, respectively. African Americans also gained employment in predominantly white motion pictures dealing with black-white relations: *Arrowsmith* (1931), *Imitation of Life* (1934), *Showboat* (1936), and *Gone with the Wind* (1939), a screen adaptation of Margaret Mitchell's novel of the same name. Director David O. Selznick toned down some of the most blatant aspects of the novel's stereotypes of African Americans, giving black actresses like Hattie McDaniel an opportunity to portray more of the humanity and intelligence of bondsmen and -women than heretofore allowed onscreen. For her part as the maid, McDaniel became the first African American to receive an Oscar award. Blues singer Ethel Waters had her own radio show, and the concert singers Roland Hayes, Paul Robeson, and Marian Anderson frequently appeared onstage and on national radio broadcasts.

The Flowering of Black Visual Arts

Only weakly developed during the 1920s, black visual arts flowered during the 1930s. Under the aegis of the Federal Arts Project, black community-based art centers emerged in several cities: Chicago's Southside Community Art Center; Cleveland's Karamu House Artist Association; Detroit's Heritage House; and Harlem's Art Workshop and Community Art Center, to name a few. Augusta Savage, Richmond Barthe, Nancy E. Prophet, Sergeant Johnson, Aaron Johnson, Palmer Hayden, Hale Woodruff, Charles Alston, and Archibald Motley all produced striking sculptures and paintings of African American life. A younger generation of black artists—notably Jacob Lawrence and Romare Bearden—would also gain valuable training during the depression years and gradually produce their works during World War II and its aftermath. Lawrence's renowned *Migration of the Negro* series, consisting of sixty panels, appeared in 1940–1941.

Alain Locke continued to influence the direction of black art through his connection with the Harmon Foundation. In two new essays, "The African Legacy and the Negro Artist" (1931) and "The Negro Takes His Place in American Art" (1933), Locke intensified his emphasis on "the Negro theme and subject" as "a vital phase of the artistic expression of American life." He urged the black artist to offer "a vigorous and intimate document of Negro life itself." In 1930, Augusta

Inspired by James Weldon Johnson's "Lift Every Voice and Sing" (known as the Negro National Anthem), Augusta Savage produced *The Harp* (1939) for the New York World's Fair. The sixteen-foot-high plaster sculpture depicts black bodies in the shape of a stringed musical instrument. Here Savage is shown working on the figure in her Harlem studio, c. 1937–1938. *Schomburg Center for Research in Black Culture/New York Public Library*

Savage crafted her bronze statue of her nephew, Ellis Ford. A year earlier a plastic model of the same work had won her a Rosenwald Fellowship to study in France. When she returned to the United States in 1934, she became the first African American elected to the National Academy of Women Painters and Sculptors. In 1937, Savage was also the only African American to receive a commission to produce a work of art for the New York World's Fair. Inspired by James Weldon Johnson's "Lift Every Voice and Sing" (the black national anthem), she used her commission to produce *The Harp*, a sixteen-foot-high plaster monument, painted black and featuring black bodies in the shape of the string instrument.

Palmer Hayden and Archibald J. Motley also returned from Paris during the Great Depression and soon added to the artistic life of blacks during the period. In 1938, Hayden produced his most renowned painting, *Midsummer Night in Harlem.* Hayden's portrait of blacks occupying various spaces in their own environment captured the persistence of the idea of a black city within the city. Similarly, in 1935, Motley captured the inside of a dance club in his painting *Saturday Night.*

At the same time, inspired by the murals of Mexican artists like Diego Rivera, African American artists also turned toward the production of murals as part of the Federal Art Project, although Roosevelt complained that he did not want "a lot of young enthusiasts painting Lenin's head on the Justice Building." Black artists took the murals and tailored them to the African American experience. In 1934, Aaron Douglas produced his mural *Aspects of Negro Life in an African Setting* for the 135th Street branch of the New York Public Library. The mural featured African rituals and ceremonies as well as black life in the U.S. South and North. In 1937, Charles Alston completed two murals, *Modern Medicine* and *Magic and Medicine,* for Harlem Hospital. After returning from a trip to Mexico, where he assisted the Mexican artist Diego Rivera, Hale A. Woodruff produced the three-part mural *Meeting Aboard the Amistad* (1939). By depicting a successful slave revolt, this mural showed how the theme of resistance and liberation characterized black visual as well as literary culture during the period.

Music and Radio

African American artistic achievements were remarkable considering the conditions of the depression years, as well as the persistence of overt forms of discrimination. The problems of black artists were perhaps best symbolized in the barring of singer Marian Anderson from Constitution Hall in Washington, D.C. In 1939, the Daughters of the American Revolution (DAR), who owned Constitution Hall, barred Anderson from giving a concert there. African Americans and their white allies formed a committee of protest and got permission to hold the concert at the Lincoln Memorial. Nearly seventy-five thousand people stood in the cold open air to hear her sing, and millions more heard her on the radio. Born in Philadelphia in 1902, Anderson had pursued advanced musical training in Europe and had performed widely in the Scandinavian countries of Sweden, Norway, and Denmark. Following one concert, the famous European conductor Arturo Toscanini exclaimed: "What I heard today one is privileged to hear only once in a hundred

Marian Anderson, Lincoln Memorial concert, 10 April 1939. The open-air concert took place after the Daughters of the American Revolution barred Anderson from performing in Constitution Hall. Nearly 75,000 stood in the cold to hear the contralto singer. *Corbis*

years." As a result of her growing success in Europe, Anderson had returned to the United States in 1935. The *New York Times* reported that "Marian Anderson has returned to her native land one of the great singers of our time." Yet Constitution Hall remained closed to her despite the intervention of First Lady Eleanor Roosevelt, who resigned from the DAR over the affair. For their part, black actors and actresses faced competition from white artists who continued to gain employment impersonating blacks. The popular radio show *Amos 'n' Andy*, for example, not only portrayed blacks in stereotypical terms but also featured white actors who used black materials to make a living when few black artists could do so. Thus, in 1931, when the *Pittsburgh Courier* initiated a nationwide protest against the show, it underscored the issue of jobs as well as the negative portrayals of black men, women, and children. "These white men," the *Courier* lamented, "are commercializing certain types of American Negroes at a reputed salary of Six Thousand Dollars per week."

Despite persistent problems of racial discrimination that cut across all categories of black art, certain aspects of black culture continued to unfold along class lines.

Rent parties (discussed in Chapter 17) served not only as a mechanism for dealing with hard times but also as an incubator of working-class black culture and a training ground for the next generation of black blues artists—the bluesmen. As the recording studios recovered from the depression, the influence of bluesmen gradually eclipsed the classical blues recording artists like Mamie and Bessie Smith. LeRoy Carr, Jimmy Yancey, Cripple Clarence Lofton, Big Maceo Merriweather, Sonny Boy Williamson, and Big Bill Broonzy, among others, moved to the fore. Their lyrics were familiar to the house parties:

> I walked all night long, with my 32-20 in my hand
> I walked all night long, with my 32-20 in my hand
> Lookin' for my woman
> Well, I found her with another man

Closely intertwined with the spread of the blues were changes in black religious music. In 1932, the gospel pioneer Thomas Dorsey broke from his growing reputation as a blues pianist and dedicated himself to gospel song writing, which led to his most popular tune, "Precious Lord." Dorsey's songs eventually caught on and stirred "the entire world with their swinging, rocking rhythms and blueslike melodies." Over and over again, black blues artists would recall the church as the site of their first musical experience, but the blues, and especially the gospel, cut across class lines. By the early 1940s, nearly every storefront church had its own gospel choir, and the larger multiclass black Baptist and Methodist churches often had two or three. The names of black gospel singers like Sister Rosetta Tharpe, Clara Ward, and Mahalia Jackson would soon become household words as studios recorded and widely distributed their music.

Athletic Achievements

If certain aspects of black culture both united and divided blacks along class lines, others reinforced an unequivocal and firm sense of racial solidarity. All African Americans took pride in the athletic achievements of Olympic medalists Jesse Owens and Ralph Metcalfe. When blacks triumphed at the 1936 Olympic games, they symbolically smashed Hitler's notion of Aryan supremacy. Even more so than Owens and Metcalfe, the heavyweight boxing champion Joe Louis symbolized a common bond that united blacks from all walks of life. Louis was the most potent symbol of a common African American plight, kinship, and future. The exploits of Joe Louis helped to unify black people during the period and gave them hope that they could topple the segregationist system. When he lost they cried, as in his first fight against the German Max Schmeling in 1936. They were especially heartbroken because Hitler preached the doctrine of Aryan supremacy, which claimed the physical and intellectual superiority of all white people, and the German people in particular. As Maya Angelou recalls in her book *I Know Why the Caged Bird Sings*:

> It was our people falling. It was another lynching, yet another Black man hanging on a tree. One more woman ambushed and raped. A Black boy whipped and

maimed. It was hounds on the trail of a man running through slimy swamps. It was a white woman slapping her maid for being forgetful.

On the other hand, when Joe Louis won, black people celebrated. After he knocked out Max Schmeling in the first round of their rematch, black people everywhere applauded, celebrated, and danced in the streets. Similarly, when Joe Louis knocked out the Italian heavyweight Primo Carnera, black people were also elated and felt somewhat vindicated for Mussolini's invasion and bombing of Ethiopia in 1935. Following his fight with another opponent, black children created a rhyme that they sung as they bounced their balls and jumped rope: "I went downtown last Tuesday night / To see Joe Louis and Max Baer fight / When Joe Louis socked, Max Baer rocked." The singer Lena Horne offers a powerful statement on Joe Louis as a black folk hero: "Joe was the one invincible Negro, the one who stood up to the white man and beat him down with his fists. He in a sense carried so many of our hopes, maybe even dreams of vengeance." Lofton Mitchell also recalled the meaning of Joe Louis for African Americans:

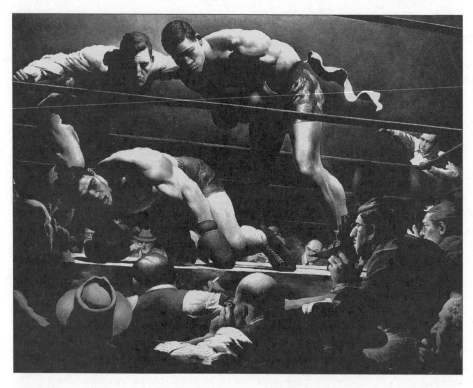

Heavyweight champion Joe Louis defeated the German fighter Max Schmeling in 1938. His victory symbolized for millions of African Americans the struggle against the racist ideas of both Adolf Hitler and proponents of Jim Crow in America. The black artist Robert Riggs captured the contest in *The Brown Bomber*, 1939. *Art Museum of Western Virginia, Roanoke, Virginia. Acquired with Funds Provided by the Horace G. Fralin Charitable Trust, 2000.003*

Our biggest celebrations were on nights when Joe Louis fought. The Brown Bomber, appearing in the darkness when Italy invaded Ethiopia and the Scottsboro Boys faced lynchings, became a black hero the history books could not ignore. It is for sociologists and psychologists to define what Joe meant to Negroes. Writers certainly have failed to do it. But, he was there, and I knew he was there, and he knew I was there. When he won a fight I went into the streets with other Negroes and I hollered until I was hoarse. Then, Joe would come to Harlem, to the Theresa, and he couldn't say what he felt when he saw us hollering at him. And he didn't have to. To paraphrase that old Negro expression: He didn't have to say a mumbling word!

Partly under the determined onslaught of black cultural, intellectual, and artistic developments, white scholars, artists, and the popular media gradually changed their views on race. Social scientists rejected the notion of the innate inferiority of races and developed a new consensus. Most intellectuals and social scientists agreed that African Americans were not inferior to whites; that racism injured its victims both psychologically and socially; and that racism itself was a mental illness that damaged the health of individual whites and the nation as a whole. These views had antecedents in the ongoing research of Columbia University anthropologist Franz Boas, his students, and his associates, who questioned the long-held assumption that racial and ethnic group differences were inherited through the genes. As Boas put it: "Where is the proof of the development of specialized hereditary capacities?" Boas and his associates challenged the racists to "prove" that African Americans' lower plane of living was due to their being intellectually inferior to their white counterparts. They urged the social scientific community, which prided itself on attending to the "facts," to recognize that it had little evidence to support some of its most cherished propositions. One contemporary scholar stated: "We do not yet know scientifically what the relative intellectual ability of the various races is. . . . Until we do know, probably the best thing is to *act* as if all races had equivalent mental ability."

∾

DURING THE YEARS OF THE GREAT DEPRESSION, African American politics, culture, and the struggle for economic freedom were closely intertwined. As African Americans mobilized their votes and intensified their civil rights struggle, they not only moved into the Democratic Party and the house of labor but also reoriented their intellectual, artistic, and cultural productions toward the liberation of black workers as well as their communities. Although these efforts would enable blacks to gain greater access to federal jobs and housing, cultural, and social programs, they nonetheless failed to lift African Americans out of the depression. Only during the escalation of wartime production and the intensification of the struggle for full citizenship and economic democracy would African Americans regain a footing in the private sector of the urban-industrial economy. This achievement would also enable African Americans to establish a stronger institutional foundation for a broader and more forceful fight against the segregationist system. Chapter 19 explores the wartime dimensions of this process.

CHAPTER 19

~

World War II

A s in World War I, African Americans gained new industrial opportunities during World War II. As the nation mobilized for war and called increasing numbers of draft-age men into the military, African Americans regained a foothold in the industrial economy and broke the unskilled "job ceiling." They now moved into semiskilled and skilled jobs in rising numbers. Although employers, labor unions, and government agencies discriminated against blacks and undermined their participation in the defense effort at home and abroad, African Americans nonetheless supported the nation's declaration of war against Germany and Japan. More so than in World War I, however, African Americans refused to simply "close ranks" and postpone their own struggle for full citizenship and recognition of their rights at home. Questioning why they should fight and die for democracy abroad while being denied it at home, blacks used the war emergency, as well as their growing influence in the Democratic Party and the new unions, to wage a "Double V" campaign—for victory at home as well as abroad. Their efforts coalesced around the militant March on Washington movement, which led to the federal Fair Employment Practices Committee (FEPC) and set the stage for the emergence of the modern civil rights movement.

AFRICAN AMERICANS, MILITARY POLICY, AND EARLY RESPONSES TO WAR

As early as 1937, the War Department had completed a study outlining its determination to maintain a Jim Crow armed forces. The military reiterated its old position that the army "would not be used as a sociological laboratory for effecting social change." In contrast to the discriminatory military policies of World War I, however, the government plan removed a ban prohibiting the induction of blacks as volunteers; increased the number of black recruits to their proportion in the population; and expanded the number of officer slots allotted to blacks in all-black units. Moreover, when Congress incorporated these policies into the Selective Service Training Act of 1940, it included two antidiscrimination measures: (1) it permitted "all men" eighteen to thirty-six years of age, regardless of race, to volunteer for service in the naval and ground forces; and (2) it prohibited racial and/or color discrimination in the selection and training of military personnel. However, since a third provision gave the War Department final authority to rule on the fitness of any candidates, it opened the door for state and local draft boards to reject black volunteers on the premise that they were illiterate or "inefficient."

The Marine Corps, Coast Guard, and Army Air Corps still barred blacks completely, and the Navy Department accepted them as messmen only. Rear Admiral Chester W. Nimitz defended the navy's position, emphasizing the need for an "efficient" naval force: "After many years of experience, the policy of not enlisting men of color for any branch of the naval service except as messmen's branch was adopted to meet the best interests of general ship efficiency." The First Army Headquarters (covering the states of Maine, Connecticut, Massachusetts, New Hampshire, Rhode Island, and Vermont) ordered draft boards to exclude blacks from induction altogether. African Americans who did volunteer their services, particularly in the South, received a hostile reception. In many cases they were told that "Negroes aren't wanted." In Charlotte, North Carolina, recruiting officers informed blacks that the recruiting station itself was for "whites only." In his diary, Secretary of War Henry L. Stimson later admitted that the army instituted rigid literacy requirements (as measured by the Army General Classification Test) "to keep down the number of colored troops" while at the same time pursuing policies designed to increase the number of illiterate white recruits. General Lewis B. Hershey, director of the U.S. Selective Service, stated: "What we are doing, of course, is simply transferring discrimination from everyday life into the army. Men who made up the army staff have the same ideas [about blacks] as they had before they went into the army."

When hostilities broke out on the European continent in 1939, African Americans invariably called it "a white man's war." The columnist George Schuyler wrote: "So far as the colored people of the earth are concerned . . . it is a toss-up between the democracies and the dictatorships. . . ." Another black journalist called the war a blessing. In his view, it was better that whites kill each other than "murder hundreds of thousands of Africans, East Indians and Chinese." As in the fighting editorials of the post–World War I years, the *Crisis* stated: "The hysterical cries of the preachers of democracy for Europe leave us cold. We want democracy in Alabama and Arkansas, in Mississippi and Michigan, in the District of Columbia—*in the Senate of the United States.*" A writer for the *Pittsburgh Courier* wrote: "Our war is not against Hitler in Europe, but against Hitler in America. Our war is not to defend democracy, but to get a democracy we have never had." When one woman quarreled with her employer in North Carolina, she expressed her frustration with southern injustice: "I hope Hitler does come, because if he does he will get you first." In Philadelphia, a black teamster told a uniformed black soldier that this is "a white man's government and war and it's no damned good." After the bombing of Pearl Harbor, a black sharecropper told one landowner that the Japanese "done declared war on you white folks."

As early as October 1937, African Americans rejected the War Department's segregationist guidelines. The special counsel for the National Association for the Advancement of Colored People (NAACP), Charles Hamilton Houston, urged Franklin Delano Roosevelt to issue an executive order ending racial discrimination in the armed forces. By 1940, African Americans called not only for nondiscrimination but for desegregation as well. Editor Percival L. Prattis, Robert L. Vann's successor at the *Pittsburgh Courier,* joined the NAACP counsel in demanding the integration of the armed services. Prattis urged blacks to "stop asking for more segregation even if there is a prospect of having complete Negro units in every branch of service; we must start fighting segregation sincerely." In a letter to FDR, Eugene K. Jones, executive secretary of the National Urban League (NUL), rejected the War Department's contention that segregation in the military had been a success and that changes "would produce situations destructive to morale." At its thirtieth annual convention, the NUL passed a resolution stating that "the National Urban League is unalterably opposed to the policy and practice of racial discrimination and segregation in the Army, Navy, Air Force, and Marine Corps of the United States." Another organization, the Citizens' Nonpartisan Committee for Equal Rights in National Defense, also called for both nondiscrimination and desegregation of the armed forces: "We want no discrimination or segregation . . . the need for national unity demands immediate revision of the stated policy." The NAACP emphasized the injustice of using black tax dollars to finance opportunities for whites while denying such opportunities to blacks:

> Our taxes help to keep up the Naval Academy at Annapolis where our boys may not attend. They help to maintain the numerous naval bases, navy yards, and naval air bases, from which we are excluded. . . . The training in numerous trades and skills which thousands of whites receive and use later in civilian life is not for us. The [health] care . . . the travel and education—all at the expense of the taxpayers—are for whites only. This is the price we pay for being classified as a race, as mess attendants only: At the same time we are supposed to be able to appreciate what our white fellow citizens declare to be the "vast difference" between American Democracy and Hitlerism.

The fight against discrimination in the military was not limited to male branches of the service. Under the leadership of Mabel K. Staupers, executive director of the National Association of Colored Graduate Nurses, African Americans waged a vigorous fight to integrate the Army and Navy Nurse Corps. The army established a discriminatory quota on the number of black women accepted for service, and the navy barred them altogether. In her campaign to end such discrimination, Staupers tried to enlist the support of white nurses' groups. In a letter to attorney William H. Hastie, a black appointee in the War Department, she explained her position:

> Although we know that pressure from Negro groups will mean something, nevertheless, I am spending all of my time contacting white groups, especially nursing groups. I have a feeling that if enough white nursing organizations can register a protest and enough white organizations of influence other than nurses

do the same, it will create in the minds of the people in the War Department the feeling that white people do not need protection in order to save themselves from being cared for by Negro personnel.

At the 1940 Democratic National Convention, held in Chicago, African Americans picketed the proceedings, demanding an end to the Jim Crow military. The signs that they carried mirrored their resolve: "Don't Jim Crow Army"; "We Demand an Executive Order Outlawing Military Segregation"; and "Prison Is Better Than Army Jimcrow Service."

Under increasing pressure from civil rights leaders and their white allies, the War Department took action. It appointed a black executive assistant, Major Campbell C. Johnson, to the Office of Selective Service; promoted Colonel Benjamin O. Davis to the rank of brigadier general; and appointed William Hastie to the post of civilian aide to the secretary of war. Hastie, nonetheless, made it clear that he did not accept segregation as a policy and would work to change it: "I have always been constantly opposed to any policy of discrimination or segregation in the Armed Forces of this country," he said. Following the attack on Pearl Harbor, a group of some sixty black leaders met at a leadership conference in New York City and passed a resolution, introduced by Hastie, that "colored people are not wholeheartedly and unreservedly all out in support of the present war effort," mainly because of discrimination and segregation in the military.

THE JIM CROW ARMED FORCES, TREATMENT, AND RESISTANCE

Despite vigorous protests against discriminatory military policies, the number of blacks selected for military service increased from 2,069 in 1940 to about 370,000 in 1942. By war's end, nearly 1 million black men and women had served in the armed forces, nearly three-quarters in the U.S. Army, followed in numbers by the U.S. Navy (and Coast Guard), Marine Corps, and a few blacks in the Air Corps (see map). Only the acute shortage of white nurses by early 1945 helped to end the army's quota system and break the bars on black women in the navy. About 500,000 blacks saw service overseas in the European, Mediterranean, and Pacific theaters of war (see map). In the Pacific theater, blacks made up the majority of laborers who cleared "some of the world's densest jungle" and built the Leda Road leading into China. In Europe, black troops not only manned the "Red Ball Express," a convoy of trucks that supplied the Allied ground forces in the Normandy campaign in 1944. They were also among the advance guard in the liberation of Jewish holocaust survivors in concentration camps like Dachau and Buchenwald (over 100,000 Jews had perished in Buchenwald). As one recent scholar notes, "When the survivors of the Buchenwald and Dachau concentration camps were liberated in 1944, the first faces they saw were African Americans" in all-black units like the 371st Tank Battalion. Many of these young African American soldiers received a presidential citation for their contributions to winning the war.

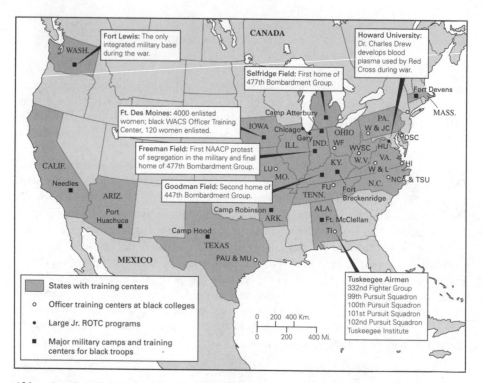

African American Training Centers, World War II (1941–1945). As in World War I, African Americans received military training in segregated facilities across the country. They also continued to face discrimination and harassment from white civilians in towns near military bases. *Source: Arwin D. Smallwood (with Jeffrey M. Elliott), The Atlas of African-American History and Politics: From the Slave Trade to Modern Times. Copyright © 1998 The McGraw-Hill Companies. Reprinted by permission of The McGraw-Hill Companies.*

The Air Corps awarded the Distinguished Flying Cross to eighty-two African American pilots, Their achievement was made possible by the training of black airmen at segregated institutions like Tuskegee Institute. Although some black leaders resisted the training of blacks in segregated facilities, others accepted the arrangement as an opportunity to expand their war- and peacetime opportunities. Tuskegee trained some six hundred black pilots who flew missions in Africa, France, Italy, Poland, Romania, and Germany. Colonel Benjamin O. Davis, a graduate of the U.S. Military Academy at West Point, became the highest-ranking black officer. He flew sixty missions and won several medals for distinguished service. According to one of his citations, Davis

led his group on a penetration escort attack in the Munich area June 9, 1944. The bomber formation was attacked by more than one hundred enemy fighters near Udine, Italy. Faced with the problem of protecting the large bomber formation

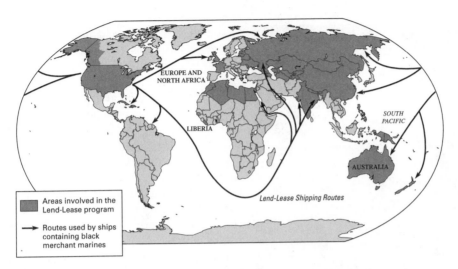

Countries Where Black Troops Were Deployed During World War II (1941–1945). Nearly one million black men and women served in the U.S. armed forces during World War II. Principally as part of the U.S. Army, blacks saw service in Europe, the Mediterranean, and the Pacific, where they built the famous Leda Road leading into China. *Source: Arwin D. Smallwood (with Jeffrey M. Elliott),* The Atlas of African-American History and Politics: From the Slave Trade to Modern Times. *Copyright © 1988 The McGraw-Hill Companies. Reprinted by permission of The McGraw-Hill Companies.*

with the comparatively few fighters under his control, Colonel Davis so skillfully disposed of his squadron that in spite of the large number of enemy fighters, the bomber formation suffered only a few losses.

The 761st Tank Battalion, which served in six European countries and fought in the Battle of the Bulge, also received commendations for its bravery on the battlefield. In the Mediterranean, the black Ninety-Second received at least two Distinguished Service Crosses, sixteen Legion of Merit Awards, ninety-five Silver Stars, and over 1,000 Purple Hearts. Several blacks received the Navy Cross. Messman Dorie Miller became perhaps the most renowned of these seamen: "Without previous experience [he] . . . manned a machine gun in the face of serious fire during the Japanese attack on Pearl Harbor, December 7, 1941, on the Battleship *Arizona* shooting down four enemy planes." Other African Americans received distinguished medals of honor from the governments of France, Yugoslavia, and the Soviet Union.

Discrimination and Barriers to Advancement

As in other wars throughout the nation's history, African Americans served against extraordinary odds. Even as their numbers in the military increased, they faced stiff barriers in the officer and specialist training schools. Specialist schools included pilot

"above and beyond the call of duty"

DORIE MILLER
Received the Navy Cross at Pearl Harbor, May 27, 1942

Dorie Miller symbolized the courage that African Americans displayed in the face of discriminatory practices in the armed forces during World War II. Although the navy limited black servicemen to the rank of messmen, Miller received the Distinguished Navy Cross for taking a machine gun and shooting down four planes during the Japanese attack on Pearl Harbor. *Library of Congress*

training, aviation, mechanics, foreign language, engineering, law, photography, and bomb disposal, among other highly skilled tasks. In a letter to Judge Hastie, Private Gilbert A. Cargill, an aviation pilot trainee, reported that he was not permitted to enter the training course at Maxwell Field in Alabama "solely because I was a Negro." When blacks did gain access to such training and positions, they confronted another round of barriers. Black volunteers for the Army Air Corps Enlistment Program (some twenty-five hundred black pilot trainees) were organized into separate aviation squadrons and assigned to army air fields where they were limited to labor and service work. Assistant Secretary of War Robert Patterson admitted that most of these men performed "labor and housekeeping jobs."

Blacks resented the limits placed on their service. In a letter to the *Pittsburgh Courier,* "A Lone Soldier" wrote: "The sad part about it that most of us are volunteers, but they didn't give us what we ask for, they gave us a pick . . . please report this to the President." Another soldier, private Aeron D. Bell, asked Hastie: "Why I WILL BE FORCED TO SHED MY BLOOD on democracy's battlefields as a Private, and am refused to volunteer as an officer candidate to fulfill the same job." In another letter, a black soldier reported: "We work at a very tiresome task [nine or ten hours daily], one that is unfit for even a dog. And yet the whites which are supposed to be labor battalion just sit down and watch us do their work." As Private Edgar B. Holt said, "After spending months in school being trained to do specific jobs we land in labor battalions while our skills go to waste." From Newport News, Virginia, Corporal Russell L. Banks wrote that he and fifteen enlisted men and one black officer had been "detailed to the city incinerator to burn army and city garbage." A college-educated private wrote to Truman K. Gibson Jr., an assistant civilian aide in the War Department, asking: "Should I be forced to continue . . . lugging five gallon cans of gasoline[?]" Another soldier spoke simply: "We are a group of permanent K.P.'s [kitchen police]."

By 1945, blacks made up less than 2 percent of all officers in the U.S. military. Yet they were assigned duties designed to reinforce a sense of racial subordination. In a letter to Gibson, Second Lieutenant Lowry G. Wright revealed the treatment of black officers at Camp Shelby in Mississippi: "In this battalion another colored officer and I have been provided with a latrine: 4 urinals (capacity 20+), 7 wash troughs (capacity 50+), 10 showers and 16 commodes. . . . The continuous little nasty items we are subjected to are quite disconcerting." In an anonymous letter to the *Atlanta Daily World,* one officer complained:

> Though we have some brilliant Negro officers they are never promoted. Some of these officers had degrees from the nation's outstanding universities, while white officers came from Ft. Benning, ignorant as the days are long. In a few months they are captains. The colored officer . . . is still a Second Lt.

Although they entered every branch of the military, blacks primarily staffed the Quartermaster Corps, the Corps of Engineers, and the Transportation Corps. As such, they worked in noncombat capacities as laborers, stevedores, and servants. They built bridges, dug ditches, cleaned latrines, peeled potatoes, cooked, washed laundry and dishes, collected and transported garbage, shined shoes, and drove trucks. Although they shared these responsibilities with white troops, this work symbolized limits on the mobility of blacks in the military. Whites could hope for greater advancement up the command chain. As suggested above, even blacks who scored highly on the army's General Classification Test received assignments in the labor division.

Black soldiers not only faced limits on their occupational classifications but also confronted discrimination in day-to-day treatment. On and off military bases, black service personnel found it difficult to secure courteous treatment and recognition of their human and civil rights. Soldiers regularly complained of limits on their freedom of movement and access to social and recreational services. From Camp Berkeley, Texas, "A Group of Soldiers" wrote to the *Pittsburgh Courier:*

> This is the [worst] camp we have ever been to. . . . There is a swimming pool here in the colored area and the colored use it on Mon. and Fri. only. They have a show [where] the colored go and you sit on the outside to see the picture if it rain[s] there isn't any picture. Most of the fellows we brought here with us like to play basketball we have no where to play but on the hard ground. They have a field house here and we can't even use it to practice to play basketball. . . . They have two buses for the colored. . . . The colored busses don't run on Mon. and Fri. and the white busses won't pick you up.

Even when black soldiers arranged their own recreation, white soldiers and officers often interfered. At Fort Meade, Florida, "A Negro Soldier" wrote to the *Baltimore Afro-American,* describing how the men were segregated at their own dance:

> We had a dance for the colored troops because Buddy Johnson's Band played and our girls came from Tallahassee, Florida, 57 miles from Camp to entertain our soldiers in the field house. There were about 30 lounging chairs for our guests to relax in but the white M.P. made them get out of them so that the officers and their wives could set in them and they were white, and it was our dance. So they

went out and got about 5 or 6 rows of benches and they were hard benches too, so that were the seats for our girls to sit on. Then, about a half hour later they got a rope and started roping our girls off like sheep, by that I mean they had given us one side and the white the other and then on the side we had they took half of that and put a rope around our women and they were herded up in a corner like a flock of sheep and the other half they gave it to white soldiers to have to sit down and where we had to stand and talk to our women. So practically most of us that came down here are from Balto., Washington, Phila., Pitts., and New York, with a couple of exceptions which I know you understand. We walked out of the dance and we demanded to see the Post Commanding Officer and see the reason why we were jim crowed in our own dance, but we never did see him. So that was the end of that.

In 1944, the army stationed a group of black Women's Army Corps (WACs) at Camp Forrest, Tennessee. The women, an all-black unit attached to the station hospital, reported ongoing cases of sexual harassment and assaults from white paratroopers on the base. In a letter to the editor of a black weekly, a black soldier shared their story, including letters one woman had written to him. In one letter the woman wrote:

Two paratroopers came into the barracks last night, downstairs where I sleep. When we woke up [one] was between my bed and other girls. He woke her up kissing her. She screamed and I jumped out of bed. The rest of them did the same. He and his buddy ran out so fast it was impossible to do anything about it.

Military and civilian authorities reinforced inequality by the regular use of intimidation, verbal abuse, and violence—on the streets, on public transportation facilities, and in places of amusement and business. In a Kentucky railroad station, white officers brutally assaulted three black WAC enlistees, allegedly because they did not "move along" fast enough when ordered to do so. In Durham, North Carolina, a white bus driver murdered a black soldier following an altercation on his route. According to one black officer, "To go to a nearby city is to invite trouble. Not only from civilian police but more often from the military police, who are upheld in any discourtesy, breach of discipline, arrogance and bodily assault they render the Negro officers." At Camp Livingston, Louisiana, Private James Pritchett reported that German prisoners of war exercised more "rights and freedom" than blacks. The poet Witter Bynner put the treatment of African Americans versus German POWs to verse:

On a train in Texas German prisoners eat
With white American soldiers, seat by seat,
While black American soldiers sit apart—
The white men eating meat, the black men heart.

Black soldiers frequently described their condition as "worse than hell itself." In a letter to the *Baltimore Afro-American*, one black soldier reported that "a U.S. army uniform to a colored man makes him about as free as a man in the Georgia chain gang and you know that's hell." At Camp Claiborne, Louisiana, a black soldier reported that "even little kids have 22 cal. rifles and B&B guns filled with anxiety to shoot a negro soldier." In correspondence to Secretary of War Stimson, dated 8 September 1941, Hastie cited a litany of violence and brutality that the War Department had failed to investigate and act upon—homicides at Fort Benning, Georgia; a shooting attack on barracks of blacks at Fort Jackson, South Carolina; murder of black troops at Fort Bragg, North Carolina; and the civilian police attack on black soldiers at Bastrop, Louisiana. As late as 1944, a black soldier appealed for help at Camp Rucker, Alabama. He compared the danger that the men faced to their recent service overseas and concluded that the dangers were greater in Alabama.

> We are now in Camp Rucker, Alabama; a name that shall live in the lives of the men that live to get out of here, just as much as the memories of Saipan, Tarawa, Pearl Harbor or any of the bloody battle fields of this war, live in the minds of the men who [fought] there. We are here on War Department orders. Not because we chose this theatre of war to serve in, without protection. It is the same if they had landed us on New Georgia without the support of the Navy and Air Force. Even with those great odds against us, we would rather be landed on New Georgia without protection than to be left here to die as "fatted pigs" at the mercy of the iron hearted people we are surrounded by, arms against our flesh. . . . Please take this call for mercy as the last whisper before we die.

Segregation and racial discrimination were not limited to southern bases. Black soldiers reported similar though less intense forms of inequality in the North and West. When Private Bert B. Babera left Camp Berkeley, Texas, for Camp Reynolds in Pennsylvania, he said that "leaving the south was like coming back to God's country," but he soon discovered that blacks could attend only one theater out of four on the post and could not use the post exchange of their choice. In Massachusetts, a white soldier wrote that a southern commander "from the land of hate" had initiated a "southern policy which is ruining the moral[e] of every soldier who reaches this camp. . . . Some of the fine colored soldiers go to some of the service clubs here on the post and are ordered out by the MP's." In the western camps—with smaller or no local black communities and institutions and few women—their lives were even worse than on southern bases. In a letter to the *Courier,* Corporal William D. Lee of Camp Adair, Oregon, declared:

> If we go up and start a conversation with the white ladies the MP's will chase you and press a charge against you . . . its worse out here than being way down South one thing sure they will have a camp some place where theirs plenty of colored ladies because they dont want you to bother theirs.

From Boise, Idaho, another black soldier wrote that "Jim Crowism" in this city was "terrible," because "there is 'not one' restaurant, beer garden, cafe or tavern which will serve a colored soldier." In Seattle's Camp George Jordan, black soldiers burned wood for fuel because there was a coal shortage, but white soldiers received coal that black soldiers delivered to their units. The soldiers decried this "undemocratic policy," among others, including greater restrictions on their passes than for whites. At Camp McCoy, Wisconsin, Major Samuel L. Ransom later recalled that there was "an inner tension growing among the men, they fel[t] they would just as soon be in the guard house as in this slave camp."

By insisting that blacks fight in segregated and unequal units, the War Department transported Jim Crow abroad. Black soldiers despised the racism and distorted views that white soldiers carried to civilian populations in Europe and the Pacific. Most damaging was the image of black men as "rapists, murderers, and thieves." Overseas, some blacks feared encounters with their white comrades more so than with the Germans. One soldier recalled his experience near Nuremberg, where the men of what he called "the Bloody I" would "kill you and throw you in the middle of the street. They didn't care anything about blacks at all." Although some soldiers recalled positive interactions with whites, most reported few such. As one black veteran recalled: "Everything was segregated then, everything—different water fountains, different bathrooms, different camps. . . . All your blacks over here, and all your whites over there." From the Pacific, "Negro Troops in India" wrote to black weeklies that "the first thing we encountered in India is segregation. [White] American, British, Indian, Chinese, and Negro troops, all attend the same show and Negroes are piled in a huddle right in the rear." This pattern conformed to wartime southern practices in the United States. When Japanese American soldiers arrived at Camp Shelby near Hattiesburg, Mississippi, local authorities classified them as white and sought to drive a wedge between them and blacks.

Resistance to Unjust Treatment

In letters to black newspapers, public officials, and civil rights organizations, black soldiers not only revealed their pain and victimization. They also protested and resisted inequality. For some historians, their letters represented "a literature of liberation." In these letters, soldiers repeatedly told the receivers to "kindly expose this statement in any issue of your paper"; "would appreciate it in the highest if you would make this a headline article in your next edition." Over and again they highlighted the discrepancy in fighting for the "four freedoms" abroad while being denied the same at home. (Roosevelt had said that the four freedoms—freedom of speech, freedom of worship, freedom from want, and freedom from fear—represented the cornerstone of American and world peace and "civilization.") From San Marcos, Texas, a black soldier urged blacks to first "fight for our rights in the United States—fight with our fists as weapons and brains which we have been attempting since the last war." Another soldier made the same point: "Democracy must, must be won at home—not on battlefields but through your bringing pressure to bear on Congress." In a letter to FDR, Private Charles Wilson called for the full integration of the armed forces:

Then and only then can your pronouncement of the war aims . . . mean to all that we "are fighting to make a world in which tyranny, and aggression cannot exist," a world based upon freedom, equality and justice; a world in which all persons, regardless of race, color and creed, may live in peace, honor, and dignity.

Black military men and women also developed ongoing day-to-day tactics for mitigating the impact of military injustice. On one stop in Alabama, black troops from Camp Lee in Virginia refused to drink coffee from an oil can: "The can was a lubricating oil can and coffee and oil don't look so good. Why it was so full of oil we raised cain and made them take it back." When white officers chained one AWOL black soldier to a tree, a black soldier told the *Pittsburgh Courier* that "the morale of the entire unit changed within just a few minutes and about five hundred soldiers stopped work and demanded the chains be taken off the soldier and use proper means to handle the case." At Camp Forrest, black WACs resolved to defend themselves against sexual harassment and attempted rape:

I've been telling you all along how the men have been coming into our barracks. Well last night about 25 paratroopers came in our area . . . and made a rush on our barracks again. This time we came out with knives and sticks, beat them off and alarmed the whole camp. They heard us down to the hospital. Well after that

Like African American men, black members of the Women's Army Corps faced racial discrimination at home and abroad, but unlike men they confronted sexual harassment and assaults as well. This photo shows a group of black WACs assigned to duty in England during the war. *Library of Congress*

round we stayed up all night, pile our foot-lockers to the door and stood guard until morning.

Court-martial records also reveal resistance to unjust military orders. In July 1944, the navy court-martialed fifty blacks when they failed to report to duty after an explosion that killed three hundred African American seamen in California's Port Chicago Ammunition Depot. Even in the late 1990s, some of the survivors continued to challenge the U.S. military's decision in the case. At Fort Devens, Massachusetts, the army court-martialed four African American WACs when they refused to perform the most demanding work at the base. And at Fort Bragg, Camp Davis, Fort Dix, and other military bases, racial violence erupted when black soldiers resisted maltreatment.

As black soldiers deepened their resistance to discrimination in the military, some black civilians refused to report for the draft. Although the government classified over two hundred blacks as conscientious objectors, it denied groups like the Nation of Islam such status and sentenced them and their leader, Elijah Muhammad, to varying jail terms. Whereas black Muslims refused service on religious grounds, other blacks refused on political and civil rights grounds. The most publicized of these were Winfred W. Lynn of New York and Edgar B. Keemer of Detroit. In June 1942, when Lynn's draft board classified him as 1-A, he responded:

> Gentlemen: . . . Please be informed that I am ready to serve in any unit of the armed forces of my country which is not segregated by race. Unless I am assured that I can serve in a mixed regiment and that I will not be compelled to serve in a unit undemocratically selected as a Negro group, I will refuse to report for induction.

When Lynn refused to report, he was arrested and indicted for draft evasion. Over a two-year period, a variety of lower courts heard his case. In 1944, it finally reached the U.S. Supreme Court, which refused to hear the case, stating in part that "if Congress had intended to prohibit separate white and Negro quotas and calls we believe it would have expressed such intention more definitely than by the general prohibition against discrimination." In Detroit, the black physician Edgar B. Keemer defied induction into the navy because the color line barred him from serving as a doctor.

DEFENSE INDUSTRIES, THE MOWM, AND THE "DOUBLE V" CAMPAIGN

The unequal treatment of blacks in the military fueled African American anger and resolve to combat social injustice at home. Rather than withhold their services, however, most blacks joined the "Double V" campaign and fought for democracy at home and abroad. Inspired by the *Pittsburgh Courier,* the "Double V" campaign had roots in the exclusion of African Americans from defense industry jobs in the private sector of the nation's economy. In 1940, blacks made up less than 2 percent of employees in the nation's expanding aircraft industry. Management officials clearly articulated their determination to keep blacks out. At the large North American Aviation firm, for example, the company's president reported that black applicants would be considered for general labor and service jobs only: "We will receive applications from both white and Negro workers. However, the Negroes will be considered only as janitors and in other similar capacities. . . . It is against the company policy to employ them as mechanics or aircraft workers." In none of its plants, the president clearly stated, would the company entertain the employment of skilled blacks, although it operated plants outside the South: "We use none except white workers in the plant . . . at Inglewood [California] and the plant in Dallas and we intend to maintain the same policy in Kansas City."

When black workers did seek employment on all-white jobs, some companies informed them that they simply did not "hire Negroes" because they "had no place for them, requiring only skilled white men." Other firms discouraged blacks even more directly, stating that they "never did and didn't intend to employ Negroes." Black women confronted even greater difficulties gaining defense jobs than black men. Employers expressed the belief that black women were peculiarly suited for domestic service, but not for industrial jobs. When black women applied for war industry jobs, some employers told them: "My wife needs a maid." Others said that their plants lacked segregated bathrooms for black and white women. Still others justified the exclusion of black women on the basis of maintaining harmony in the all-white workplace. In Detroit, for example, a personnel manager described a bomber plant as "nice and peaceful. [We] don't go around looking for trouble by putting colored people in."

Craft unions reinforced discrimination against black workers in defense work. Skilled black workers—plumbers, bricklayers, carpenters, electricians, cement finishers, and painters—faced exclusion from labor unions either by "constitutional" provision or by some form of "ritual." In a resolution introduced at the 1941 convention of the American Federation of Labor (AFL), the black labor leader A. Philip Randolph pinpointed labor union discrimination against black workers in a broad range of jobs in different parts of the country:

> Negro painters in Omaha cannot get into the painter's organization nor can they secure a charter. Plasterers and cement finishers in Kansas City, Missouri, cannot get into the organization nor can they get a charter. The A. F. of L. unions in shipbuilding yards in New Orleans refuse membership to Negro workers, although the company has expressed a willingness to employ them. . . . In St. Louis, Negro artisans cannot get work, but white workers come from outside St. Louis and are sent to work.

Randolph cited the International Association of Machinists (IAM) as the most conspicuous example of labor union discrimination against African Americans. Accepting only white members, the IAM reinforced the exclusion of blacks from the metal trades and the aircraft industry, including the huge Boeing Aircraft Corporation in Seattle.

Since many defense industry jobs required additional training for large numbers of white as well as black workers, the U.S. Office of Education financed such programs under the Vocational Education National Defense (VEND) Training Program. In his study of black labor during the period, economist and New Dealer Robert Weaver documented racial discrimination in the implementation of such programs. According to Weaver, such discrimination had deep roots in earlier patterns of discrimination in federal educational programs. During the 1930s, the federal government had already established a precedent for discrimination by awarding federal funds to whites at a rate of $8.00 per capita, compared with less than $4.75 per capita for blacks. When the government established VEND, it continued the same practices. As Weaver put it, "This discrimination was in reality a projection of past practices. Most vocational education officials at the national, state, and local levels were not prepared to champion new policies relative to minority groups' training." Vocational training programs reinforced a vicious cycle of black exclusion from defense jobs. When asked why blacks were not trained and employed in defense industry jobs, training school supervisors, unions, and employers conveniently passed the buck back and forth. On its July 1940 cover, the NAACP's *Crisis* underscored the exclusion of blacks from defense industry jobs. It featured an airplane factory marked "For Whites Only," with the caption "Warplanes—Negro Americans may not build them, repair them, or fly them, but they must help pay for them."

The African American quest for social justice gained its most potent expression in the emergence of the militant March on Washington movement (MOWM). Spearheaded by A. Philip Randolph of the Brotherhood of Sleeping Car Porters (BSCP), the MOWM was launched in 1941 following a meeting of civil rights groups in Chicago. The critical moment came when a black woman angrily addressed the chair:

> Mr. Chairman . . . we ought to throw 50,000 Negroes around the White House, bring them from all over the country, in jalopies, in trains and any way they can get there, and throw them around the White House and keep them there until we can get some action from the White House.

Randolph not only seconded the proposal but also offered himself and the BSCP as leaders: "I agree with the sister. I will be very happy to throw [in] my organization's resources and offer myself as a leader of such a movement" (see box).

By early June, the MOWM had established march headquarters in Harlem; Brooklyn; Washington, D.C.; Pittsburgh; Detroit; Chicago; St. Louis; and San Francisco. The movement spread through the major rail centers and soon joined forces with local NAACP and Urban League chapters, churches, and fraternal orders. *The Black Worker,* the official organ of the BSCP, became the official newspaper of the MOWM. The paper's May issue reprinted the official call to march:

> We call upon you to fight for jobs in National Defense. We call upon you to struggle for the integration of Negroes in the armed forces . . . of the Nation. . . . We call upon you to demonstrate for the abolition of Jim Crowism in all Government departments and defense employment. . . . The Federal Government

Call for African Americans to March on Washington

July 1, 1941

We call upon you to fight for jobs in National Defense.

We call upon you to struggle for the integration of Negroes in the armed forces, such as the Air Corps, Navy, Army and Marine Corps of the Nation.

We call upon you to demonstrate for the abolition of Jim-Crowism in all Government departments and defense employment.

This is an hour of crisis. It is a crisis of democracy. It is a crisis of minority groups. It is a crisis of Negro Americans.

What is this crisis?

To American Negroes, it is the denial of jobs in Government defense projects. It is racial discrimination in Government departments. It is widespread Jim-Crowism in the armed forces of the Nation. . . .

What shall we do?

What a dilemma!

What a runaround!

What a disgrace!

What a blow below the belt!

'Though dark, doubtful and discouraging, all is not lost, all is not hopeless. 'Though battered and bruised, we are not beaten, broken or bewildered. . . .

. . . Negroes, by the mobilization and coordination of their mass power, can cause PRESIDENT ROOSEVELT TO ISSUE AN EXECUTIVE ORDER ABOLISHING DISCRIMINATIONS IN ALL GOVERNMENT DEPARTMENTS, ARMY, NAVY, AIR CORPS AND NATIONAL DEFENSE JOBS.

Of course, the task is not easy. In very truth, it is big, tremendous and difficult.

It will cost money.

It will require sacrifice.

It will tax the Negroes' courage, determination and will to struggle. But we can, must and will triumph. . . .

In this period of power politics, nothing counts but pressure, more pressure, and still more pressure, through the tactic and strategy of broad, organized, aggressive mass action behind the vital and important issues of the Negro. To this end, we propose that ten thousand Negroes MARCH ON WASHINGTON FOR JOBS IN NATIONAL DEFENSE AND EQUAL INTEGRATION IN THE FIGHTING FORCES OF THE UNITED STATES.

An "all-out" thundering march on Washington, ending in a monster and huge demonstration at Lincoln's Monument will shake up white America.

It will shake up official Washington.

It will give encouragement to our white friends to fight all the harder by our side, with us, for our righteous cause.

It will gain respect for the Negro people.

It will create a new sense of self-respect among Negroes.

Source: A. Philip Randolph, *The Black Worker,* July 1941. Reprinted with permission.

cannot with clear conscience call upon private industry and labor unions to abolish discrimination based upon race and color so long as it practices discrimination itself against Negro Americans.

The MOWM helped to mobilize the masses of black working people as well as the middle and upper classes. According to Randolph:

It was apparent . . . that some unusual, bold and gigantic effort must be made to awaken the American people and the President of the Nation to the realization that the Negroes were the victims of sharp and unbearable oppression, and that the fires of resentment were flaming higher and higher.

Though the MOWM welcomed liberal white support, Randolph insisted that African Americans lead the movement. "[T]he March on Washington Movement is essentially a movement of the people. It is all Negro and pro-Negro, but not for that reason anti-white or anti-Semitic, or anti-Catholic, or anti-foreign, or anti-labor. Its major weapon is the non-violent demonstration of Negro mass power." Randolph was wary of the labor movement, the major political parties, and the growing communist influence in black organizations like the National Negro Congress (NNC), of which he was president. When the Communist Party gained control of the NNC in early 1940, Randolph resigned from the presidency and soon left the organization. In his departing speech, he urged blacks to pursue a more independent course in their struggle against racial subordination. According to Ralph Bunche, "He expressed the view that the Negro Congress should remain independent and non-partisan and that it should be built up by Negro effort alone."

Although Roosevelt resisted the movement as long as he could, the MOWM finally produced results. Roosevelt met with black leaders A. Philip Randolph and Walter White of the NAACP on 18 June 1941. A week later, 24 June 1941, FDR issued Executive Order 8802, which banned racial discrimination in government employment, defense industries, and training programs. The order also established the Fair Employment Practices Committee (FEPC) to implement its provisions. The FEPC was empowered to receive, investigate, and address complaints of racial discrimination in the defense program. Randolph recalled the details of the initial meeting with FDR. The turning point came when FDR turned to White and asked, "How many people will really march?"

White's eyes did not blink. He said, "One hundred thousand, Mr. President." . . .
    "You can't bring 100,000 Negroes to Washington," Roosevelt said. "Somebody might get killed."
    Randolph said that that was unlikely, especially if the President himself came out and addressed the gathering.
    Roosevelt was not amused. "Call it off," he said curtly, "and we'll talk again."
    Randolph replied, "I shall have to stand by the pledge I've made to the people."

It was Mayor La Guardia who broke the impasse. "Gentlemen," he said, "it is clear that Mr. Randolph is not going to call off the march, and I suggest we all begin to seek a formula."

African Americans soon used the FEPC to broaden their participation in the war effort, but it was a slow process. Although an estimated 118,000 blacks were trained for industrial, professional, and clerical jobs in 1941, by the end of 1942 only a small percentage had obtained employment in defense industries. Black women complained that white women received work, whereas they remained unemployed. "When there is so much defense work," one Cincinnati woman asked, "how is it I cannot have a chance to work?" When they did gain jobs, they occupied the least desirable slots. In a letter to P. T. Fagan, area director of the Labor Manpower Commission, George E. Denmar, secretary of the Pittsburgh Urban League, complained of discrimination against black women at the American Bridge Company:

White women by the hundreds have entered training and the employ of the company, as welders and burners. . . . But in all, only five Negro women have been hired to clean the lavatories. . . . These Negro women have come to realize that advertisements for help . . . as proclaimed over the radio and through the press do not mean Negroes, particularly women.

Similarly, in a letter to FDR, a Pittsburgh woman wrote: "There are two plants close by. . . . They will hire the white girls but when the colored girls go there they always refuse them." In Cincinnati, one light-skinned woman advanced further along in the interview process before she was stopped cold:

Well, after I filled out the application, the young man came to the door of the office and asked me what I wanted, so I told him . . . the job of inspector training. I asked him if he had such a job and he said yes. . . . In speaking he glanced down at my application and he said, "Oh, you are a Negro." I said, "Yes." At this point, the interview stopped.

Industrial firms in the North and South dragged their feet on the implementation of fair employment practices. In January 1942, the FEPC cited five Milwaukee firms for racial discrimination against the city's black workers and directed them "to give written notice" that they would end such practices. Shipyard companies in Houston, Galveston, Mobile, New Orleans, and Tampa widely advertised for white women and boys to pursue training as welders to fill labor shortages in those areas, but they resisted the FEPC's push to place black welders. Southern colleges also barred blacks from training programs supported by federal money, forcing African Americans to travel to a limited number of black training centers. In Mobile, when the FEPC pressured the Alabama Drydock and Shipbuilders Company to upgrade some black workers to the job of welder, the company supported the walkout and a riot of some twenty thousand white workers, who quit in protest against the

employment of black workers. In 1940, with the support of the National Media-
tion Board, the southeastern railroads and the exclusively white unions signed the
notorious "Washington Agreement," designed to eliminate black firemen from employment. Black workers soon challenged the Washington Agreement under the
new FEPC guidelines. The FEPC ordered the companies and unions to adjust their
policies "so that all needed workers shall be hired and all company employees shall
be promoted without regard to race, creed, color or national origin." When the
roads and unions defied the order, African Americans took their case to court, but
it took until 1944 for a ruling by the U.S. Supreme Court to uphold their claims—
in *Bester William Steele v. The Louisville and Nashville Company, Brotherhood of Locomotive Firemen and Engineers.*

In 1942, according to the report of the Pennsylvania Temporary Commission on
the Urban Conditions among Negroes, 50 percent of Pittsburgh firms barred
blacks from employment or relegated them to the lowest rungs of their employment ladder. By war's end, nearly 40 percent of all Allegheny County employers
continued to bar black applicants. Some of the firms included metal industries. After Superior, Columbia, Bethlehem, and other area steel plants turned down black
applicants in 1942, the Pittsburgh Urban League lamented that "there are still
plants in this area which refuse to hire Negroes even at common labor." In Cincinnati, FEPC investigators cited the Crossley Radio Corporation, the Formica Insu-
lation Company, the American Can Company (which produced machine gun
shells during the war), Victor Electronics, the Baldwin Company, and the Steit-
mann Biscuit Company (which packed food for the military), among others, for
racial discrimination in their employment practices. On completing his survey of
Cincinnati firms in 1943, investigator Ernest E. Trimble concluded that "on the
whole, it seems clear that the defense industries in the Cincinnati area have rather
generally refused to employ colored people equally with whites."

Some companies admitted that they barred black men and women from employment but justified their practices by arguing that white employees would not
work with blacks. Indeed, rank-and-file white workers as well as AFL and some
Congress of Industrial Organizations (CIO) unions reinforced job discrimination
during World War II. When asked if white workers would strike if the company
hired blacks, a white worker at Cincinnati's Victor Electronics, which barred blacks
entirely, exclaimed: "They certainly would . . . just send one [black] out there and
the whole place would empty in five minutes. No union, no guards, no management will hold them." Fred Ross, president of the International Brotherhood of
Electrical Workers (IBEW), corroborated the claim. Ross not only confirmed that
white workers would strike to bar blacks but also expressed the view that the war
aimed "to preserve the American way of life" and to keep black people "in their
places."

Cincinnati's white workers conducted a series of "hate strikes" against the employment of black workers. An estimated fifteen thousand white workers walked off the
job at the city's Wright Aeronautical Corporation when managers sought to hire
blacks in the machine shop in June 1944. As late as 1945, white workers at Delco
Products and the Lunkenheimer Company also walked out to protest the employment of black workers. When the Lodge and Shipley Company hired blacks under

pressure from the FEPC, it did so on a segregated basis—employing blacks in Plant #2 but barring them from Plant #1. One personnel manager argued, "The sudden influx might cause considerable troubles in our plant, so that we have gone on the slow, sure method of doing it gradually, getting the other employees used to seeing them around." Complaints of racial discrimination became so numerous near war's end that federal officials opened a subregional FEPC office in Cincinnati and made plans to open one in Pittsburgh. Every year, at the annual meetings of the AFL, A. Philip Randolph exhorted white workers to end racial bias. He repeatedly stated:

> It won't do for the trade union movement, which ought to be the bulwark of democracy and which ought to maintain the tradition of democracy, to say "no, you cannot participate in our organization, because you are not competent, because you are not worthwhile, because you are colored, because you are not white."

Despite the persistence of discrimination and stiff resistance, Executive Order 8802 proved to be a turning point in African American history. It linked the struggle of African Americans even more closely to the Democratic Party and helped to transform the federal government into a significant ally. Blacks in war production increased from less than 3 percent in March 1942 to over 8 percent in 1944. In contrast to World War I, substantial numbers now moved into semiskilled and skilled positions. As St. Clair Drake and Horace R. Cayton noted in their study of Chicago during the period:

> The Second World War broke the ceiling at the level of semiskilled work and integrated thousands of Negroes as skilled laborers in the electrical and light manufacturing industries, from which they had been barred by custom, and in the vast new airplane-engine factories. . . . They also began to filter into minor managerial and clerical positions in increasing numbers.

Although the AFL unions and the railroad brotherhoods did much to hamper this process, the unions of the CIO often supported the FEPC claims of black workers and helped them to break the job ceiling. At its annual convention in 1941, for example, the CIO denounced racially discriminatory hiring policies as a "direct attack against our nation's policy to build democracy in our fight against Hitlerism." A year later, the organization established its own Committee to Abolish Racial Discrimination and urged its affiliates to support national policy against discrimination: "When a decision to employ minority group workers is made, the union must be prepared to stand behind it."

WARTIME HOUSING AND COMMUNITY CONFLICT

As defense industry jobs expanded, African Americans nonetheless found it difficult to expand their footing in the larger community life of American cities. Nearly

1.6 million blacks left the South during the 1940s. The percentage of blacks living in urban areas rose from less than 50 percent in 1940 to nearly 60 percent in 1945. Western cities like Los Angeles, San Francisco, and Seattle now joined established northern and southern cities as major centers of black urban population growth. In addition to the persistence of castelike social relations in the South, race relations deteriorated and violence broke out in several northern and western cities. A contemporary observer described wartime patterns of urban race relations as "a growing subterranean war." An NAACP official warned: "White people are sitting on a powder keg . . . blind to what is developing. I expect to see race riots flare up all over the country unless something is done to give the Negro a real opportunity in this war effort." African Americans purportedly formed "Eleanor Clubs" and "Pushing Clubs" and challenged whites in public spaces. Some of the violence took focus in the "Zoot Suit" riots. In Los Angeles, San Diego, Long Beach, Chicago, Detroit, and Philadelphia, white sailors and/or civilians attacked African American and Latino youth who wore the "Zoot Suit"—broad felt hats, pegged trousers, and pocket knives on gold chains. The young men were targeted because of their color as well as their dress, but wartime racial violence went well beyond the "Zoot Suit" confrontations.

The most violent conflicts occurred over wartime housing, public accommodations, and police brutality. In a survey of black wartime opinion in Cincinnati and Baltimore, the Office of War Information reported growing dissatisfaction and militancy among black workers. African Americans in the two cities highlighted police brutality as a major grievance that they hoped to rectify:

> One thing they could stop—the white cops from arresting colored people and beating them with their guns. You could just turn around and chop their heads off. . . . The other day they run a black boy in here—they knew that they had him. After they had him they took their guns and beat him. . . . If I'd had a bomb I would have tried my best to blow them to hell.

In 1943, a policeman shot a black soldier and touched off the Harlem riot, which resulted in at least five deaths, five hundred injuries, hundreds of arrests, and $5 million in property damage. The actor Sidney Poitier later recalled his experience of the riot:

> In a restaurant downtown where I was working I heard that there was trouble in Harlem. After work I took a train uptown, came up out of the subway, and there was chaos everywhere—cops, guns, debris and broken glass all over the street. Many stores had been set on fire, and the commercial district on 125th Street looked as if it had been bombed.

An investigative reporter for the New York newspaper *PM* also reported on the riot: "Harlem yesterday morning . . . resembled a bombed-out city wherein destruction miraculously stopped at the first story. Virtually every show window along the main shopping districts was shattered, their contents cleaned out or in disorder."

In Detroit, on 20 June 1943, over 100,000 people crowded the city's Belle Isle Amusement Park. Beginning at the park's casino, ferry dock, playgrounds, and bus

White men and boys converge on two streetcars during the Detroit riot of 1943. Black men and women are being attacked as they seek to exit the cars. *Corbis/Bettmann*

stops, violence soon spilled over into the black Paradise Valley area. At a local club, a patron took the microphone and announced: "There's a riot at Belle Isle! The whites have killed a colored lady and her baby. Thrown them over a bridge. Everybody come on! There's free transportation outside!" By early morning African Americans had smashed windows and looted numerous white-owned stores on Hastings Avenue. Only the arrival of federal troops put down the violence, which resulted in 34 deaths, 675 injuries, nearly 1,900 arrests, and an estimated $2 million in property damage. In both the Harlem and Detroit riots, most of the deaths, injuries, and arrests involved blacks, whereas the damaged property belonged almost exclusively to whites.

Racial violence was intertwined with the growing residential segregation of African Americans in the urban environment. In June 1944, when two black families occupied their home in the Mt. Adams area of Cincinnati, a mob of some fifty to one hundred men and boys stoned the home, destroying all the doors and windows. Described as the "first Negro residents" on the street, the family had to vacate their home and flee for their lives. When a white female neighbor publicly criticized whites for their actions, several hundred whites marched to her home and hung an effigy of the woman. Federal housing policy reinforced patterns of residential segregation and racial conflict. Federal housing authorities, influenced by powerful southern Democrats, insisted on racial segregation in federally funded units. Such housing policies, along with restrictive employment practices, aggra-vated black-white relations; in the city of Detroit, they also fueled the underlying forces leading to the 1943 race riot. In 1941, the Federal Public Housing Author-ity (FPHA) had approved the city's Sojourner Truth Housing Project. Named for the black abolitionist leader and designated for black occupancy, the project was lo-cated in a predominantly white working-class neighborhood. When local residents protested, federal authorities rescinded their decision and handed the project over to whites. Only the vigorous protests of the black community secured the project for African Americans. On the other hand, the federal government established an all-white project at the Ford Motor Company's new Willow Run facility. Although blacks fought to integrate the units, the FPHA opposed the movement and main-tained the separation of blacks and whites.

Closely linked to the MOWM, a variety of old and new civil rights and political organizations staged protests and lodged legal actions against racial segregation and inequality. Compared with the depression years, however, the interracial character of this struggle dissipated. Following the Nazi Germany nonaggression pact, signed in June 1941, blacks lost communists as vigorous defenders of equal rights. Rather than urging blacks to plunge forward with their "Double V," the Communist Party now asked African Americans to forgo their agitation, defend the nation, and save democracy abroad. Under the growing recognition of this change in communist thinking and politics, the *Negro Digest* published a special issue devoted to the ques-tion, "Have the communists quit fighting for Negro rights?" Formerly militant CIO unions now organized southern plants that retained a systematic racial wage scale, in which blacks were paid uniformly less than whites. Thus, despite its commitment to abolish discrimination, the CIO left the color line intact both on shop floors and in the union halls of southern cities and towns. Communist youth organizations like the Southern Negro Youth Congress and the National Youth Congress were now transformed into "Negro Labor Victory Committees" with a focus on winning the war abroad rather than at home. As Communist Party radicalism declined, so did black communist-inspired organizations like the National Negro Congress.

Whereas civil rights organizations like the NAACP had lost prestige in the context of the 1930s Communist Party's fight for the Scottsboro boys, they now reclaimed the initiative on behalf of African American rights. The NAACP rapidly expanded under the impact of wartime mobilization. The number of branches increased from 355 in 1940 to over 1,000 by war's end. The number of members rose from over 50,600 to over 500,000. The organization continued to work through the courts to end lynchings, the poll tax, the white primary, and inequality in teachers' salaries. Similarly, the National Urban League also struggled to aid wartime blacks. The or-ganization continued and even intensified its professional social work orientation.

The wartime activities of civil rights organizations culminated in several war and early postwar victories. In the case of *Smith v. Allwright* (1944), the U.S. Supreme Court outlawed the Texas white primary. The court reversed *Grovey v. Townsend* (1935), arguing that primaries were "conducted by the party under state authority," which made it "an agency of the State in so far as it determines the participants in primary elections." The Court denied states the right to erect "legal fictions" as a means of depriving blacks of their constitutional rights. Similarly, in *Morgan v. Virginia* (1946), the Court used the "commerce clause" to attack segregation in interstate commerce as a violation of equal protection of the law. In so doing, the Court undermined the ruling of *Plessy v. Ferguson* (1896) and strengthened the hand of civil rights attorneys. In *Shelley v. Kramer* (1948), the Court struck down restrictive covenants in St. Louis, Detroit, and Washington, D.C. The Court held that these were cases in which the states had "made available to individuals the full coercive power of government" to deny people, "on the grounds of race or color, the enjoyment of property rights."

As the NAACP deepened its legal challenge to Jim Crow, new organizations adopted direct nonviolent action as their principal mode of organizing the black community and confronting social injustice. In 1943, the Congress of Racial Equality (CORE) emerged and staged demonstrations to desegregate places of public accommodation in north-

African Americans not only gave their lives and labor on the battlefield but also volunteered their service to organizations such as the United Service Organization and the Red Cross. Lena Horne performed at Fort Huachuca, Arizona, in 1943. *Courtesy of the Fort Huachuca Museum*

ern and border cities. Under the leadership of James Farmer and Bayard Rustin, CORE developed from a merger of the Chicago committee of the Fellowship of Reconciliation (FOR) and the national body of FOR. Using the nonviolence tactics of the Indian Nationalist Mahatma Gandhi as well as the CIO's sit-down strike, CORE helped to establish precedents for later postwar civil rights organizations. It helped to integrate white-only restaurants in Chicago's downtown Loop and in Cincinnati, Ohio. Although the organization had some wartime successes, it would not launch its first freedom rides until 1946. Along with the emergence of the MOWM, CORE not only reinforced the wartime political mobilization of African Americans but also helped to plant the seeds of the modern civil rights movement.

Even as blacks intensified their struggle for equal rights at home, they did their part to achieve victory abroad. When making their case for victory at home, they

repeatedly reminded the nation of "our boys" in the "fighting forces" of the country. Moreover, neither black men nor black women uniformly despised life in the
military. They often expressed pride in their accomplishments. A Laurel, Mississippi, WAC recalled that she "enjoyed every minute of it." As she put it, black
women gained "opportunities to do things" that they "never would have done" outside the army. Others, like Nathan Harris of the Mississippi Delta, recalled the
army as a place that helped to build pride and "self-esteem." As Harris said, "The
army built me up and made me proud of myself. It sounds stupid. But that's the
way it was. And I've still got it in me." Another black soldier reinforced the same
point: "I'm about the only black that I know was in the infantry. . . . The biggest
pride I ever had in my life [was] when the guy put that combat infantry badge on
me." According to veteran Dabney Hammer, "When you're in combat those folks
forget that you're black. When the shells start, incoming mail—Boom—your
Whole self is shaking. [Color] don't make no difference." Another black veteran recalled the Battle of the Bulge: "That was the first time . . . that I was an American
soldier. For those six, maybe eight days there was no black or white soldiers. . . . We
was soldiers."

African Americans not only gave their lives and labor on the fields of battle but
also pooled their meager financial resources to contribute to a variety of voluntary
war support activities. They organized war bond–purchasing campaigns in their
churches, schools, and community organizations. They also cooperated with the
government's food conservation program and staffed United Service Organization
(USO) facilities to boost the morale of black servicemen and -women. The USO
coordinated the social service activities of a wide range of organizations, including
the Young Women's Christian Association (YWCA), the Young Men's Christian Association (YMCA), and the Salvation Army, to name a few. In addition, African
Americans served as nurse's aides, drivers in motor corps, and other voluntary but
vital jobs in the Red Cross.

Volunteer service was not easy. Like other organizations within and outside the
military, war support groups like the USO and Red Cross initially resisted the services of black volunteers. Take the American Red Cross and the work of the black
physician Dr. Charles Drew, for example. At Presbyterian Hospital in New York,
Drew pioneered in the development of a system for preserving blood plasma. In
1940, the British employed Drew to establish a mass-volume blood plasma project,
which became a model for blood banks throughout the United Kingdom and Europe. In 1941, the United States hired Drew to develop a similar system for American enlisted men. Despite Drew's important contributions to the war effort and
medical science, the American Red Cross at first refused to accept the blood of
black donors. When it did, it did so on a segregated basis. Nonetheless, all segments
of the African American community took part in volunteer activities. These included ordinary working-class and poor blacks as well as numerous well-known individuals—W. E. B. Du Bois, A. Philip Randolph, Father Divine, Paul Robeson,
Joe Louis, and Hattie McDaniel. Historian Arvarh Strickland recently recalled
growing up in Hattiesburg, Mississippi, and participating in the conservation effort
by "collecting scrap iron" from his customers on his paper route. One columnist

During the war years, black artists often performed to raise money for the war effort. Duke Ellington gave benefit performances at a variety of clubs in New York City. This photo shows Ellington and his band in the Columbia Pictures production of *Reveille with Beverly* (1943). *Bettmann/Corbis*

wrote that "the more we put in . . . the more [we] have a right to claim." Another columnist, Joseph Bibb, opined that "war may be hell for some . . . but it bids fair to open up the portals of heaven to us."

African Americans' sense of intense sacrifice on behalf of the nation fueled their demand for full participation in the postwar social order. When black soldiers witnessed the skeleton-like remains of Jews in Hitler's Buchenwald concentration camp, they were even more determined to defeat American racism. According to Luella Newsome, a black Woman's Army Corps veteran, African Americans returned from the war determined that they "wouldn't take it anymore. . . . It had to change . . . because we're not going to have it this way anymore." Mississippi veteran Wilson Ashford declared that the war "changed a great deal of things. . . . It changed the individual." Ashford judged his experience against his prewar predicament. "That [military service] was the first step in change, where you would feel that you could do it. . . . [Whites] they'd always tell the negative side. Nothing positive. From that standpoint it gave you an opportunity to see things in a different light." Furthermore, Ashford said that he "believed" whites were "wrong all the time," but after he got out of the army he "knew" they were wrong. Another soldier remembered thinking, "Now its going to be difficult to get me back to total darkness. That was my attitude. Deep within me I made up my mind I've got to move out of the situation that I'm in to something better." In his wartime collection of essays, *What the Negro Wants* (1944), historian Rayford Logan offered a firm statement that the Jim Crow system had to go. Black conservatives, liberals, and radicals wanted "the same rights, opportunities and privileges that are vouchsafed to all other Americans and to fulfill" the same obligations.

~

FOLLOWING A DECADE OF UNEMPLOYMENT, relief, and public service work, World War II enabled African Americans to regain and strengthen their foothold in the industrial economy. Wartime production helped to break the job ceiling above the general labor and domestic categories of work. African Americans now claimed the CIO, the Democratic Party, and the federal government as important allies in their struggle for social change and freedom. Yet it was a fragile alliance. Organized labor, employers, and the government modified but did not abandon racially discriminatory policies and social practices. Only the organizational and political activities of African Americans in their own behalf ensured access to industrial jobs and a larger measure of freedom and civil rights. They had learned that "closing ranks" in support of the nation did not preclude the continuation of their own struggle for equity and fair play. The "Double V" campaign for victory at home and abroad, the March on Washington movement, and the growing use of the federal government to secure their aims all helped to write a new chapter in the history of African Americans. World War II represented the seedtime of the postwar black revolution. Part VI examines the rise of the modern civil rights and Black Power movements and their aftermath.

PART VI

Civil Rights, Black Power, and Deindustrialization
1945–2000

Building on their wartime militancy, during the 1950s and 1960s African Americans moved their struggle to the streets. The modern civil rights movement adopted nonviolent direct action strategies for social change, destroyed the legal foundations of the segregationist system, and established a Second Reconstruction with passage of the Civil Rights Acts of 1964, 1965, and 1968. The movement gained the support of white allies in federal agencies and in diverse peace and freedom organizations, but it was deeply rooted in African American grassroots, community-based organizations as well as in new regional and national organizations like the Southern Christian Leadership Conference and the Student Nonviolent Coordinating Committee. Although the civil rights movement demolished the legal underpinnings of Jim Crow, the slow pace of change precipitated a search for new and more effective modes of struggle.

Following Martin Luther King Jr.'s assassination in 1968, growing numbers of African Americans adopted Black Power as an alternative to nonviolent direct action. They advocated black control of black communities, armed self-defense, black pride, and identification with a unique African American heritage. The Black Panther Party (formed in 1966) soon emerged as the most potent symbol of the Black Power movement. However, after federal authorities launched a highly coordinated assault on the party's headquarters across the nation, the Black Power movement fragmented and dissipated in the early 1970s. Together, the decline of the civil rights and Black Power movements exposed the African American community not only to rising resistance to the gains of the Second Reconstruction but also to the most destructive impact of deindustrialization and the loss of jobs to mechanization and low-wage overseas locations. Part VI analyzes the rise of the modern civil rights and Black Power movements during the 1950s and 1960s, the decline of the Second Reconstruction during the 1970s and 1980s, and the African American effort to launch new movements for social change during the 1990s.

CHAPTER 20

~

The Modern Civil Rights Movement

African American life during the Great Depression and World War II established the framework for the emergence of the modern civil rights movement as a grassroots struggle for social change. Designed to dismantle both legal and extralegal forms of racial discrimination and segregation in American society, the civil rights movement was deeply rooted in the continuing transformation of rural blacks into urban workers. It was also intertwined with the corresponding growth of the black middle class, the expansion of community-based institutions, and key legal victories over Jim Crow in federal courts. Moreover, African Americans would skillfully harness a variety of national and international social and political changes to their cause. These included the new visual media of television, the worldwide decolonization movement, and the nation's moral claims to leadership of the "free world" during the Cold War era. The civil rights movement emerged from a variety of local grassroots initiatives, but African Americans also formed new organizations and transformed local and regional developments into a broader national, and increasingly international, campaign. Although their efforts encountered ongoing and violent white resistance and profound internal conflicts, they gradually gained the support of an influential core of white allies within and outside the federal government and advanced the project of citizenship begun nearly one hundred years earlier. In short, the modern civil rights movement would give rise to the Second Reconstruction.

SOCIAL CHANGE AND EARLY POSTWAR LEGAL BATTLES

Following World War II, a variety of technological and social changes continued to transform the southern countryside and stimulate the movement of blacks into cities. Thanks partly to federal assistance, large southern landowners increased their use of labor-saving technologies—including tractors, flamethrowers, herbicides, and mechanical cotton pickers—and dramatically reduced the demand for black workers. A single cotton-picking machine performed the work of fifty farm hands and drove the cost of production down from over $39 per bale by hand to under $6 per bale by machine. In his poignant photographic essay *12 Million Black Voices,* novelist Richard Wright captured the meaning of this transformation for thousands of displaced black farmworkers: "How can we win this race with death when our thin blood is set against the potency of gasoline, when our weak flesh is pitted against the strength of steel, when our loose muscles must vie with the power of tractors?" Black sharecropper Ned Cobb (Nate Shaw) underscored the same point in his autobiography: "I knowed as much about mule farmin' as ary man in this country. But when they brought in tractors, that lost me." At the same time, blacks in the southern Appalachian coalfields of West Virginia, Virginia, Kentucky, Tennessee, and Alabama faced the rapid spread of the mechanical coal-loading machine, which nearly destroyed the black coal mining proletariat. In West Virginia alone, machine-loaded coal increased by nearly 5,000 percent between the late 1930s and early 1950s. Although all coal miners lost ground and increasingly left the area, the number of black coal miners plummeted more drastically than that of their white counterparts, from nearly thirty-five thousand during the 1940s to less than nine thousand in 1960. By 1970, only three thousand black coal miners worked in the region, a drop from nearly 16 percent to less than 7 percent of the total work force.

African Americans adapted to such changes by continuing their trek to the nation's major metropolitan areas. The percentage of blacks living in cities increased from less than 50 percent in 1940 to over 80 percent in 1970. African Americans were now spread almost equally between the urban North and West on the one hand and the urban South on the other. Building on the gains of the war years, they slowly expanded their numbers in new industries, including aircraft, electronics, and chemicals. Indeed, during the early postwar years, the wages and salaries of black men increased from 54 percent of those of white males in 1947 to 64 percent in 1951; the labor force participation rate of black men in their twenties rose to over 90 percent; and the unemployment rate of black men and women reached a postwar low of 4.4 and 3.7 percent, respectively. At the same time, seniority provisions in labor contracts in the major mass production industries enabled some blacks to maintain their jobs during layoffs. Moreover, as we will see later, the percentage of black men and women in middle-class professional, clerical, and sales jobs gradually increased, especially in the case of black women. In other words, the postwar economic position of blacks was not entirely bleak. Yet all was not well for African Americans in the postwar urban economy.

As African Americans became a predominantly urban people, their opportunities for employment in mass production industries decreased over the long run. Although seniority provisions in labor contracts provided some protection for older industrial workers, young black workers remained the "last hired and first fired" in the wake of new labor-saving technologies and plant relocations to low-priced suburban land. Between 1947 and the late 1960s, manufacturing in the nation's central cities declined from about 66 percent to about 40 percent of the total. Even seniority provisions failed to fully protect the jobs of veteran black workers and union men, who had gained seniority in a narrow range of jobs, often in segregated general labor departments. Thus, when mechanization eliminated their jobs, they could not take jobs in other departments, where young white workers with less seniority gained and retained jobs over black workers with more seniority. Black women gradually improved their position during the period but faced stiff competition from white women, who entered the postwar labor force in rising numbers. Although the labor force participation rate of black women remained relatively stable at about 44 percent, the rate for white women increased from 30 percent in 1948 to nearly 40 percent during the 1960s. In his report on racial progress in the steel industry, the recording secretary of one local described a general pattern when he bluntly reported: "I wish to express with regret that the range of jobs now open to minority groups has not changed one bit since our plant organized. In fact, the negroes are worse off now, in some respects, than they were before the plant was organized."

Blacks faced even greater difficulties with the rise of Cold War politics. When the United States and the Soviet Union parted ways over the postwar peace settlement in Europe, their actions provoked a vigorous reaction against radical ideas on class and race in American economics, politics, and culture. In 1948, the U.S. attorney general warned that "those who do not believe in the ideology of the United States, shall not be allowed to stay in the United States." Legislators and public policy makers allowed the wartime Fair Employment Practices Committee to expire, leaving blacks vulnerable to the resurgence of racial discrimination in industrial jobs; enacted the antilabor Taft-Hartley Act; and took steps to eliminate communists from labor and civil rights organizations. In 1950, federal officials revoked the passport of artist and activist Paul Robeson when he made speeches praising the Soviet Union as a defender of human rights and "full human dignity" for black people. A year later, the government also withheld W. E. B. Du Bois's passport and indicted him as an "agent" of a foreign power, citing his work with the Peace Information Center in New York as evidence. Although a federal judge later dismissed the charges for lack of evidence, thousands of public libraries, colleges, and universities prohibited the acquisition and display of Du Bois's scholarship and political writings.

Although the experiences of blacks like Robeson and Du Bois symbolized restrictions on black militancy, the career of Ralph Bunche symbolized the efforts of other blacks to work within the constraints of the Cold War order. During the war and early postwar years, for example, Bunche became the first black to hold a high-ranking position in the U.S. State Department when he served as a specialist on African and Far Eastern Affairs and then as associate chief of the Division of Dependent Area Affairs, responsible for areas of Africa and Asia then under European colonial rule. In 1947, two years after the formation of the United Nations, Bunche was appointed head of the organization's Trusteeship Division, where he played a major role in negotiating agreements leading to the collapse of European colonialism and the rise of new independent nations in Africa and Asia. Three years later, Bunche became the first black person to win the Nobel Peace Prize for his role in negotiating a Middle East peace settlement between the Jews and Arabs. A *Newsweek* reporter described him as "the foremost Negro of his generation—the distinguished symbol of how far a black man could rise in the Establishment." In 1955, Bunche became the undersecretary of the United Nations and went on to oversee a variety of UN projects, including the establishment of a peacekeeping force in the Suez Canal zone between 1956 and 1967.

Although some individuals like Ralph Bunche thrived in the Cold War atmosphere of the 1950s, government repression of political and social activists set the stage for the emergence of more conservative labor and civil rights movements. By the early 1950s, organizations like the National Association for the Advancement of Colored People (NAACP), the Congress of Racial Equality (CORE), and the Congress of Industrial Organizations (CIO) had purged communists from their ranks and paved the way for the merger of the American Federation of Labor (AFL) and the CIO in 1955. The new AFL-CIO admitted racially exclusionary unions like the Brotherhood of Locomotive Firemen and the Brotherhood of Railroad Trainmen, which barred blacks from membership by constitutional provisions. The AFL had exhibited little interest in the welfare of black workers compared with CIO bodies, but it nonetheless received over 75 percent of the executive council positions in the merger. African Americans would face an uphill battle seeking to desegregate constituent unions and remove racial bars. In the meantime, southern states took advantage of the Taft-Hartley Act and passed a variety of antiunion "right to work" statutes, and some fifteen northern, southern, and western states enacted new "antisubversion laws" making it a crime to espouse revolutionary ideology.

African Americans responded to the repressive climate of the early postwar years by intensifying their use of legal machinery to secure their rights. As noted in Chapters 18 and 19, the U.S. Supreme Court had already chipped away at the legal foundations of Jim Crow during the 1930s and 1940s. Following World War II, civil rights organizations heightened their challenges and gained additional legal concessions. Between 1946 and 1948, President Harry S. Truman established a series of interracial committees to study the issue of civil rights in American society. The resulting committee reports, including "To Secure These Rights" and "Freedom to Serve," recommended the eradication of discrimination and segregation "based on race, color, creed, or national origin" from all facets of American life. The Defense Department desegregated the armed forces during the Korean War; the U.S. Supreme Court and the Interstate Commerce Commission outlawed racial segregation in interstate travel; and President Truman issued an executive order banning discrimination in federal employment. Moreover, by 1953, African Americans attended some ten predominantly white public colleges and twenty-three graduate schools within the South.

Under the leadership of the NAACP, early postwar legal actions culminated in the U.S. Supreme Court's landmark decision in *Brown v. Board of Education* (1954). In the *Brown* case—including black school children and their parents in Kansas, Virginia, Delaware, South Carolina, and Washington, D.C.—the Supreme Court ruled that "in the field of public education the doctrine of 'separate but equal' has no place. Separate educational facilities are inherently unequal." (See the Documents section.) In this ruling, the Court struck down the "separate but equal" ruling of *Plessy v. Ferguson* (1896) and dismantled the key legal underpinning of the entire segregationist order. Shortly after delivering its decision, the Court also ordered boards of education to implement desegregation plans "with all deliberate speed."

In 1954, the U.S. Supreme Court delivered its famous *Brown v. Board of Education*. The *Brown* decision struck down the principle of "separate but equal" in public education and symbolized the growing civil rights assault on segregation in American society. After the Court's momentous decision, Thurgood Marshall (*center*), chief counsel for the NAACP's Legal Defense and Education Fund, posed with desegregation leaders George E. C. Hayes (*left*) and James M. Nabrit (*right*) on the steps of the Supreme Court. *AP/Wide World Photos*

Three years later, Congress passed the Civil Rights Act of 1957. The first federal civil rights legislation since the fall of the Reconstruction governments during the 1870s, the Civil Rights Act of 1957 established the U.S. Civil Rights Commission and empowered it to investigate civil rights violations and seek remedies. Three years later, the Civil Rights Act of 1960 strengthened civil rights protection by empowering federal judges to oversee or "referee" and punish persons using violent and unlawful means to interfere with desegregation orders and the right of blacks to vote.

Intellectual currents in U.S. social science and historical scholarship supported the desegregation movement. Influential white scholars and intellectuals now accepted the antiracist arguments of pioneering black historians like W. E. B. Du Bois and Carter G. Woodson and their younger contemporary counterparts like Kenneth and Mamie Clark. In their explanation of poor socioeconomic and edu-

cational conditions within the black community, increasing numbers of white intellectuals and shapers of public opinion rejected racist interpretations, which accented notions of innate biological, cultural, and social characteristics. They now
emphasized the destructive impact of racial discrimination and state-mandated segregation on the black population, particularly unequal access to employment and
educational opportunities. As noted in Chapters 8 and 13, these ideas also gained
increasing scholarly treatment in studies of antebellum bondage and postbellum
emancipation by Kenneth Stampp, Stanley Elkins, John Hope Franklin, and
C. Vann Woodward. Such studies, which culminated in Daniel Patrick Moynihan's
The Negro Family: The Case for National Action (1965), largely ignored the very
positive role that poor and working-class blacks played in shaping their own experience in the past and present but nonetheless supported the use of federal funds to
address the destructive impact of racial inequality in American society.

Although changes in the intellectual and legal context of the civil rights movement stimulated progress, real change was exceedingly slow. To be sure, the Upper
South; the border states of Maryland, West Virginia, and Delaware; and the
District of Columbia moved swiftly to desegregate their schools. By May 1955,
some 350 school boards in nine southern states had quietly desegregated their
schools with only minor public opposition. When the city of Louisville quickly established a voluntary and peaceful plan of desegregation, the *New York Times* reported enthusiastically: "Yesterday as schools opened there were no mobs, no
pickets, no need for calling the Guard to put out fires." Two years later, the number of desegregated southern school districts had doubled and now included more
than three hundred thousand students. Despite substantial compliance with the
school desegregation ruling in the Upper South, border states, and Washington,
D.C., some 3,000 local school boards opposed the desegregation order and dragged
their feet. An estimated 2.5 million black children continued to attend segregated
schools.

Arkansas emerged at the center of the school desegregation campaign in the
wake of the *Brown* decision. Under the leadership of Daisy Bates, head of the local
branch of the NAACP, blacks in Little Rock, Arkansas, urged the city to move
swiftly to integrate its schools, particularly Central High School. By the fall of
1956, the city had developed a plan to integrate its schools, but the state's Supreme
Court rejected the plan and blocked the admission of black students to previously
all-white facilities. When a federal court overruled the Arkansas Supreme Court
and ordered desegregation to go forward, Governor Orval E. Faubus defied the order. He sent the Arkansas National Guard to Central High School to block the enrollment of nine black students. Along with the efforts of the state National Guard,
angry white students, parents, and members of the larger white community threw
bricks, hurled racist epithets, and pushed and shoved the black students as they
tried to enter the school. Faced with this blatant challenge to federal authority,
President Eisenhower dispatched units of the U.S. Army to Little Rock and federalized the Arkansas National Guard. Arkansas authorities nonetheless eventually
closed Little Rock public schools for two years before they were reopened on a desegregated basis. Other school districts closed their schools for an even longer period before opening their doors to African American students.

NONVIOLENT DIRECT ACTION, THE YOUTH CHALLENGE, AND WHITE RESISTANCE

Dissatisfied with the slow pace of change, African Americans developed a variety of local grassroots movements to speed the desegregation process. Unlike their early postwar efforts, they now adopted massive nonviolent direct action techniques and fearlessly engaged the system of Jim Crow head on.

The Nonviolent Direct Action Movement

As early as 1953, African Americans in Baton Rouge, Louisiana, launched a boycott of the state capital's segregated buses. Although the bus company owed two-thirds of its revenue to black passengers, it served blacks on a segregated and unequal basis. Bus drivers daily harassed and mistreated black passengers. Although buses allotted a certain number of seats in the back for blacks and others in the front for whites, during rush hour blacks were routinely forced to relinquish their seats to whites; some were even forced to leave the bus before reaching their destination. Moreover, drivers often took fares and then pulled off before passengers could securely seat themselves. According to Rev. T. J. Jemison, pastor of Mt. Zion Baptist Church and leader of the boycott, blacks initiated the boycott because "the Negro passenger had been molested and insulted and intimidated and all Negroes at that time were tired of segregation and mistreatment and injustice."

Under Jemison's leadership, African Americans formed a new mass, church-based, direct action organization, the United Defense League (UDL). This organization developed desegregation strategies and tactics that foreshadowed the activities of the later and more renowned Montgomery bus boycott. The UDL held nightly mass meetings (first in the churches and then in the city's all-black high school auditorium); organized private carpools to ensure that black workers reached their jobs in a timely manner; and set up a boycott fund to finance the work of coordination and implementation. The Baton Rouge boycott was nearly 100 percent effective. March leaders reported that "nobody rode the bus during our strike. . . . For ten days not a Negro rode the bus." The boycott cost the city nearly $1,600 daily. Finally, on the sixth day of the boycott, city officials offered a compromise. They agreed to reserve a few seats for blacks and whites but offered the remainder on a first-come, first-serve basis. Although some blacks wanted to "stay off, stay off . . . Walk, Walk" until the bus company provided all seats on a nonsegregated first-come, first-serve basis, most voted to accept the compromise as a victory and end the boycott.

Baton Rouge offered an inspiring example of black activism, but the Montgomery bus boycott became the pivotal event in the rise of the modern civil rights movement. Unlike the Baton Rouge protest, which left segregated transportation intact, the Montgomery bus boycott built on the courageous stand of the seamstress Mrs. Rosa Parks, lasted for more than a year, and resulted in the successful desegregation of the municipal buses. Although Rosa Parks had defied segregationist rules before, her actions on 1 December 1955 touched off a citywide boycott that reverberated throughout the South and the nation. She later described her actions on that day: "When the driver saw me sitting, he asked if I was going to stand up and I said, 'No, I'm not.' And he said, 'Well, if you don't stand up, I'm going to call the police and have you arrested.' I said, 'You may do that.'" After nearly a year of walking and carpooling to get to and from work, school, and places of business, Montgomery blacks achieved a major victory on 13 November 1956, when the U.S. Supreme Court ruled that segregation on the city's buses was unconstitutional. Initially, however, like Baton Rouge blacks, boycott leaders had called not for an end to segregation, but for a more humane version of the segregationist system. Only after authorities rejected their appeal did they demand the abolition of segregation itself.

The Montgomery bus boycott and Rosa Parks's arrest symbolized the growing willingness of African Americans to confront arrest and go to jail rather than endure the indignities of Jim Crow. Like blacks in Baton Rouge, African Americans

In December 1955 seamstress Rosa Parks helped to spark the Montgomery bus boycott when she refused to relinquish her seat to a white passenger. She was later fingerprinted by the Montgomery police. *AP Photo/Gene Herrick*

in Montgomery formed a new grassroots nonviolent direct action organization, the Montgomery Improvement Association (recalling Garvey's Universal Negro Improvement Association of the 1920s). The MIA held regular church-based mass meetings to boost morale for the struggle, established effective carpools, and launched a plethora of fund-raising activities. The Pullman porter and unionist E. D. Nixon not only spearheaded the effort by gaining the support of local black ministers like Rev. Ralph David Abernathy but also persuaded Martin Luther King Jr., the recent seminary graduate and new minister in town, to lead the boycott. As Nixon later recalled, King was an ideal candidate to lead the march. As a new minister in town, he was not a partisan in ongoing ideological and political conflicts within the local black community, and, most importantly, he had not been in the city "long enough for the [white] city fathers to put their hand on him." As Nixon recalled, "Usually, you come to town and you start wanting to do this and do that, and the city fathers get their hand on you . . . and it ends up you're on their side."

A graduate of Morehouse College in Atlanta and the Boston University Theological Seminary, Martin Luther King Jr. accepted the pastorship of Montgomery's Dexter Avenue Baptist Church in April 1954. Drawing on his seminary training as well as his experience in the black church, he emphasized the roots of the civil rights struggle in the black Christian faith, inspired and intensified by the methods of the Indian nationalist Mahatma Gandhi:

> From the beginning a basic philosophy guided the movement. This guiding principle has since been referred to variously as nonviolent resistance, noncooperation, and passive resistance. But in the first days of the protest none of these expressions was mentioned; the phrase most often heard was "Christian love." . . . As the days unfolded, however, the inspiration of Mahatma Gandhi began to exert its influence. I had come to see early that the Christian doctrine of love operating through the Gandhian method of nonviolence was one of the most potent weapons available to the Negro in his struggle for freedom.

At a mass meeting following the first day of protest, King articulated even more clearly the resolve of Montgomery blacks: "You know, my friends, there comes a time when people get tired of being trampled over by the iron fist of oppression. . . . And we are determined here in Montgomery to work and fight until justice runs down like water and righteousness like a mighty stream." The following day, a Montgomery journalist wrote an editorial describing the boycott as "a flame that would go across America."

Key to the success of the boycott were the grassroots organizing activities of black women like Jo Ann Robinson, an English teacher and head of the city's Women's Political Council. From the outset of the postwar years, black women had formed the Women's Political Council to fight the arrest of dozens of black people on the buses for allegedly violating the segregation ordinance. In March 1955, the organization had witnessed the arrest and conviction of Claudette Colvin, "a 15-year-old . . . 'A' student, quiet, well-mannered . . . and deeply religious," for refusing to give up her seat in the black section of a city bus to a white passenger. Thus, when the boycott commenced, black women were prepared to act. As Robinson recalled, "We had members in every elementary, junior high, and senior high school, and in federal, state, and local jobs. Wherever there were more than ten blacks employed, we had a member there. We were prepared to the point that we knew that in a matter of hours, we could corral the whole city." On the night of Rosa Parks's arrest, Robinson stayed up until 4:00 A.M. copying protest leaflets encouraging blacks to stay off the buses. Assisted by two student volunteers, she delivered some fifty thousand leaflets to schools, businesses, barbershops, poolrooms, and factories by early afternoon. As a result of such diligent work, on the first day of the boycott, Coretta Scott King enthusiastically observed that the first bus was

> empty! . . . This first bus was usually filled with domestic workers going to their jobs. . . . Eagerly we waited for the next bus. In fifteen minutes it rolled down the street, and, like the first, it was empty. A third bus appeared, and it too was empty of all but two white passengers. . . . It was becoming apparent that we had reached almost 100 percent.

As the nonviolent direct action movement spread throughout the South, African Americans formed new organizations to advance their efforts on a national and increasingly international scale. In 1957, senior civil rights leaders met at the church of Rev. Martin Luther King Sr. in Atlanta and formed the Southern Christian Leadership Conference (SCLC) to coordinate the multiplying centers of black activism. The organization selected Martin Luther King Jr. to serve as president, while local movement leaders, mostly ministers, took other influential posts—Rev. C. K. Steele of Tallahassee, first vice president; Rev. T. J. Jemison of Baton Rouge, secretary; Rev. Fred Shuttlesworth of Montgomery, corresponding secretary; and Rev. Ralph Abernathy of Montgomery, treasurer. The stimulus for the formation of SCLC came partly from the growing support that the movement gained from white allies in the North and South. The most prominent centers of support were the Highlander Folk School in Monteagle, Tennessee; the Southern Conference Educational Fund; the northern-based Fellowship of Reconciliation; and the New York–based "In Friendship" committee. The idea for SCLC grew out of discussions between black activist Ella Baker, labor leader Bayard Rustin, and white attorney Stanley Levison of the "In Friendship" committee, but it was Martin Luther King Jr. and other southern black activists who took the initiative to transform the idea into a reality.

Student Activists

By the early 1960s, the emergence of the nonviolent direct action movement had given rise to a new generation of black college students who increasingly challenged established leaders to intensify the struggle. Student activists were moved to act not only by the heroic deeds of their elders but also by their own precarious place within the Jim Crow system. Southern whites ignored age distinctions in their defense of white supremacy. In 1955, the brutal lynching of fourteen-year-old Emmett Till in Money, Mississippi, underscored this point. Till, on a visit from Chicago, was killed for allegedly making sexual advances toward a white woman. When authorities recovered his water-soaked and badly brutalized body from a river, his mother insisted on an open-casket funeral and encouraged the wide dissemination of photographs showing the world what they had done to her son. Mrs. Mamie Till Bradley Mobley later recalled:

> After the body arrived I knew that I had to look and see and make sure it was Emmett. That was when I decided that I wanted the whole world to see what I had seen. There was no way I could describe what was in that box. No way. And I just wanted the world to see.

Although eyewitnesses identified Till's abductors, an all-white jury acquitted the defendants, and higher courts refused to review the case. As civil rights historians note, Till's murder served as an important catalyst for the spread of the modern civil rights movement, but it was especially significant from the vantage point of young people. In Louisville, Kentucky, the fifteen-year-old future heavyweight champion of the world, Cassius Marcellus Clay (Muhammad Ali), and his friends expressed their anger at the Till murder by going out one night and derailing a train engine. This same kind of anger propelled other young blacks to the front lines of the freedom struggle.

Under the impact of student activists, African Americans deepened their movement for social justice. Students were deeply enmeshed in the grassroots activities of black churches and civil rights organizations like SCLC, CORE, and the NAACP youth councils. Beginning in the fall of 1959, the black Methodist minister James Lawson, a student at the Vanderbilt University Divinity School and southern field secretary for the Fellowship of Reconciliation, regularly conducted nonviolent workshops for SCLC and student activists. He helped to train a stellar roster of young civil rights leaders from Fisk, Meharry, Tennessee State, and the American Baptist Theological Seminary in the Nashville, Tennessee, area. These student activists included Diane Nash, James Bevel, Marion Barry, Bernard Lafayette, and John Lewis, among others. According to the student activist Rev. Kelley Miller Smith:

> John Lewis, Bernard [Lafayette] and myself were the major participants in the seminary. All of us were like the top student leaders in our schools. I think John at the time was the president of the Student Council. I was a member of the Student Council. I was one of the editors of the yearbook. So all of us were like the top leaders in our school.

In his workshops, Lawson emphasized one fundamental lesson:

> Ordinary people who acted on conscience and took terrible risks were no longer ordinary people. They were by their very actions transformed. They would be heroes, men and women who had been abused and arrested for seeking the most elemental of human rights. The city officials in the end would involuntarily and unconsciously help in their recruiting. That was what Jesus had done in his time, and that was what Gandhi had done.

For his increasing involvement in the freedom struggle, Lawson was expelled from the Vanderbilt Divinity School in March 1960.

Although Lawson helped to train a solid core of young nonviolent direct action-ists in Nashville, the bold stand of young blacks in Greensboro, North Carolina, first captured the attention of the nation and the world. On 1 February 1960, black students at the North Carolina Agricultural and Technical College initiated the sit-in movement at the "white" lunch counter of the city's Woolworth Department Store. The huge sixty-seat counter was the largest single profit-making establish-ment in the city's downtown business district. African Americans could patronize every department in the store except the "white" eating counter. Leading this move-ment were four college students—Joseph McNeil, David Richmond, Franklin Mc-Cain, and Izell Blair. As McNeil later recalled, "Woolworth seemed logical because it was national in scope and somehow we had hoped to get sympathies from with-out as well as from within." Like their Nashville counterparts, Greensboro students had close ties to black grassroots organizations. Nearly a dozen black colleges ex-isted within a ten-mile radius of Greensboro. Students made up such a large part of the membership that some black churches were called "college churches." More-over, McNeil, Richmond, McCain, and Blair had been members of active NAACP youth councils in the area and were familiar with sit-in demonstrations designed to desegregate nearby Durham, North Carolina, between 1957 and 1960.

McNeil, Richmond, McCain, and Blair carefully selected their target as well as their strategy of engagement. When the four students entered the store, they estab-lished themselves as paying customers by purchasing sundry items before taking their seats at the counter and requesting, "Coffee please." Rather than ousting the young protesters, company and town officials allowed them to sit but ignored their requests for service. On the second day of protests, twenty other A & T students joined the young men, and the sit-in movement spread rapidly to other towns and cities of the Upper and Lower South, including Nashville, Montgomery, and At-lanta. Within a one-month period between 1 February and 1 March 1960, sit-in protests hit eleven cities in North Carolina, seven in Virginia, four in South Car-olina, and from one to three cities in Florida, Tennessee, Alabama, Kentucky, and Maryland. Less than six months after sit-ins started, black students formed the Stu-dent Nonviolent Coordinating Committee (SNCC) to direct their activities on a national scale. Marion Barry, a veteran of the Nashville struggle, became SNCC's first president. When reporters asked the Greensboro students how long they had been planning the demonstrations, they responded, "All our lives."

SCLC and SNCC challenged established civil rights organizations to intensify their fight against Jim Crow. In May 1961, under the leadership of veteran organ-izer James Farmer, CORE sent "freedom riders" into the South to force compliance with federal orders to desegregate interstate transportation—buses, terminals, wait-ing rooms, and services. With support from both SCLC and leading branches of the NAACP, an interracial team of thirteen volunteers left Washington, D.C., on two buses headed for cities in Alabama and Mississippi. After nearly a year and a half of protests, violence, and growing pressure from the federal government, southern officials gradually relented and removed the segregationist signs from bus terminals engaged in interstate commerce. By the end of 1962, CORE announced

Students at North Carolina Agricultural and Technical College—Joseph McNeil, David Richmond, Franklin McCain, and Izell Blair—stage a sit-in at the "white" lunch counter of Greensboro's Woolworth Department Store in 1961. Their actions also challenged black employees in segregated establishments, such as the man behind the counter here. *Bettmann/Corbis*

that Jim Crow had collapsed in most interstate travel. Coterminous with the freedom rides, a coalition of civil rights organizations—SCLC, SNCC, and the NAACP—launched a vigorous desegregation campaign in Albany, Georgia, but local authorities stymied the movement by massive arrests and jail sentences, coupled with a public display of restraint in the use of physical force. When officers arrested Martin Luther King Jr. and Ralph David Abernathy for staging an illegal protest, city officials quickly released them before public sympathy and support could build up on their behalf. On his release, Abernathy quipped somewhat disappointedly: "I've been thrown out of lots of places in my day but never before have I been thrown out of jail." Unlike other law officers, Sheriff Laurie Pritchett also anticipated massive jail sentences for followers and brought an almost inexhaustible supply of jails throughout the region into use. One young civil rights activist recalled: "We were naive enough to think we could fill up the jails. Pritchett was hep to the fact that we couldn't. We ran out of people before he ran out of jails." Pritchett later boasted that "We . . . met 'nonviolence' with 'nonviolence.'" Nonetheless, Pritchett permitted gross violations of civil rights off-camera. When some local blacks reacted to off-camera police brutality by hurling bricks at police officers in the black section of Albany, Pritchett urged reporters to go there and record "them nonviolent bricks" in a shrewd effort to discredit the nonviolent tenets of the movement. The following year, after a largely aborted campaign in Albany, Georgia, the center of civil rights activism shifted to Birmingham, Alabama.

The Southern Christian Leadership Conference targeted Birmingham as the site of a highly organized, massive, and deliberate desegregation campaign. As one recent sociologist puts it, Birmingham represented "a planned exercise in mass disruption." It was a city of pivotal significance to the success of the civil rights movement. Birmingham's vicious record of police brutality and commitment to the segregationist system made it a highly respected model among segregationists. Thus, movement strategists argued that a successful attack on the citadel of segregation in Alabama would weaken confidence in the system throughout the South. To paraphrase the saying at the time, "as Birmingham goes, so goes the South." More so than any other single campaign, Project-C, as the Birmingham movement was called, highlighted the diverse components of the larger civil rights struggle. First, African Americans demanded not only desegregation of lunch counters and stores but access to jobs in white-owned establishments above the usual domestic and general laborer categories of work. Second, the Birmingham movement transformed the nation's Cold War hysteria, fear of communism, and claim to leadership of the "free world" into a forceful demand for freedom in America. Third, African Americans seized the media, especially the growing popularity of television, and skillfully used it to awaken the consciousness of the nation and generate support for their cause. Under the constant prodding of civil rights activists like Andrew Young, the freedom struggle added television to its repertoire of strategies, adapting a phrase attributed to the theologian Benjamin E. Mays of Morehouse College: "One tiny little minute / just sixty seconds in it / I dare not abuse it / It's up to me to use it."

On 2 May 1963, Rev. James Bevel led a march of six thousand black children ages six to sixteen to downtown Birmingham. Public officials soon upheld the city's reputation as a violently antiblack place to live, work, and advocate for African American rights. The city's police not only arrested over one thousand black youths but also met them with a barrage of police dogs, high-powered water hoses, and clubs as they knelt down to pray. Fearing the deleterious impact of extensive media coverage on foreign policy initiatives, President John F. Kennedy threatened to send federal troops into the city to secure a desegregation agreement. Only then did Birmingham officials relent and sign an accord with civil rights leaders. The agreement toppled the city's Jim Crow laws. The signs designating "Colored" and "White" came down from places of public accommodation and business; merchants desegregated lunch counters and hired blacks for positions above the usual domestic and general laborer categories of work; and municipal officials opened the city's libraries, golf courses, public buildings, and schools to African Americans. Pleased with the outcome, Rev. Fred Shuttlesworth described the fall of Jim Crow as a victory for "human supremacy."

White Resistance to the Civil Rights Movement

Although the civil rights struggle culminated in a series of local and regional victories, it was an incomplete and exceedingly costly achievement. Resistance to the civil rights movement intensified as African Americans escalated their struggle. In addition to resuscitating old-line white supremacist organizations like the Ku Klux Klan, southern whites formed new citizens' councils to overturn *Brown*. Although the white citizens' councils comprised the middle- and upper-class members of the white community and presented an aura of legitimacy that transcended the brutal tactics of the KKK, the two modes of white resistance reinforced each other. The bus boycotts, student sit-ins, and freedom rides produced a recurring pattern of arrests, jailings, bombings, beatings, and killings. During the Montgomery bus boycott, the city developed a "get tough" policy that resulted not only in the arrest and regular harassment of movement leaders and participants but also in the bombing of Martin Luther King Jr.'s home, although members of the King family escaped injury.

Between late 1961 and early 1963, some twenty thousand men, women, and children were arrested for participating in civil rights protests. In 1963 alone, fifteen thousand persons were imprisoned as some one thousand desegregation campaigns broke out in more than one hundred cities. When the Freedom Riders arrived in the Deep South, law officers stood by while mobs brutally beat protesters and overturned, stoned, and burned buses. One police commissioner promised the Ku Klux Klan fifteen minutes to attack the riders until "it looked like a bulldog got hold of them." Authorities did step in, but they arrested twenty-six freedom riders for violating the Jim Crow laws and sentenced them to sixty-seven-day jail terms for sitting in the whites-only section of the city's bus terminal. During the Birmingham confrontation, terrorists bombed both the A. G. Gaston Hotel, headquarters of King and SCLC, and the home of King's brother, Rev. A. D. King. Senator Wayne Morse of Oregon told the Senate that the spectacle "would disgrace a Union of South Africa or a Portuguese Angola," and the *New York Times* compared Birmingham's white resistance to Nazi Germany and Fascist Italy.

Local officials and vigilantes received the firm support of their various state and federal officials. On 12 March 1956, North Carolina senator Sam Ervin Jr. issued a "Southern Manifesto," pledging to resist desegregation by using the legal machinery of the federal government. Over one hundred members of Congress from the former Confederate states signed Ervin's manifesto, and state legislators in Mississippi, Georgia, South Carolina, Louisiana, and Alabama passed a new round of segregationist laws. At the same time, southern states like South Carolina and Louisiana defined the NAACP as a "subversive organization" and ordered it to cease its work. In 1961, violence erupted when a federal court of appeals ordered the University of Mississippi to admit black students. When its first black student, James Meredith, approached the registrar's office, Governor Ross Barnett personally blocked Meredith from enrolling in the institution. Barnett also announced that any federal officials who arrived in Mississippi to assist Meredith would be arrested by state militia. When President John F. Kennedy dispatched some 320 federal marshals to the scene to escort Meredith into his dormitory room, several thousand whites attacked the marshals with guns, clubs, and homemade bombs, and touched off the so-called Battle of Oxford. Only the arrival of 2,500 federal troops brought the mob under control. The conflict resulted in two deaths, over three hundred injuries, and several thousand dollars worth of property damage. In addition, the federal government stationed three hundred soldiers at the University of Mississippi for another year to ensure order.

After losing his bid for governor of Alabama in 1958, circuit judge George C. Wallace exclaimed that his opponent had catered to the basest of white racism and "out-niggered" him. Wallace vowed that "they'll never do it again." In the gubernatorial election of 1960, Wallace won and became a public spokesmen for the segregationist status quo. In his inaugural address for governor, Wallace exclaimed, "I draw the line in the dust . . . and I say, Segregation now! Segregation tomorrow! Segregation forever!" In Birmingham, eight of the city's "moderate" white ministers reinforced the stand of public officials when they issued a public statement criticizing King for what they viewed as his impatience and disruptive tactics, while praising Sheriff Bull Connor for using "restraint in maintaining order." Their criticism stung King and prompted his now classic "Letter from Birmingham Jail":

> While confined here in the Birmingham city jail, I came across your recent statement calling my present activities "unwise and untimely." . . . You deplore the demonstrations . . . but your statement, I am sorry to say, fails to express a similar concern for the conditions that brought about the demonstrations. . . . For years now I have heard the word "Wait!" . . . This "Wait" has almost always meant "Never." We must come to see, with one of our distinguished jurists, that "justice too long delayed is justice denied."

Partly because of the persistent dangers, risks of imprisonment, ostracism, and promise of a better life for the group, activism had a profound effect on its participants. Over and over again, participants expressed the sense of empowerment that they felt as a result of putting their lives on the line for a noble cause. Jo Ann Robinson recalled a feeling of empowerment and self-respect that African Americans felt during and after the Montgomery bus boycott. "We had won self-respect. We had won a feeling that we had achieved, had accomplished. We felt that we were somebody, that somebody had to listen to us, that we had forced the white man to give us a part of our own citizenship." In the Little Rock school desegregation case, Ernest Green recalled the political as well as personal triumph that he experienced on graduating as part of the first integrated class at Central High School: "I knew that once I . . . received the diploma, that I had cracked the wall."

In the sit-ins at lunch counters, one black youth described his participation as one of elation: "It was like a fever. Everyone wanted to go. We were so happy." Franklin McCain, one of the original four sit-in students in Greensboro, later explained that their activism gave them "the confidence, my goodness, of a Mack truck." Another youth activist, Cleveland Sellers, recalled that word of the boycott itself hit him "like a shot of adrenaline" and gave him "a burning desire to get involved." Doris Smith, a student at Spellman College, carefully followed the televised coverage of the Greensboro boycott and was encouraged to join similar efforts in Atlanta. Another Atlanta activist, Julian Bond, said that their arrest and brief period in jail transformed them into "heroes" and gave them a stature on campus usually reserved for the football players and other sports stars. When authorities arrested young SNCC activist John Lewis during the Nashville sit-in, he described going to jail as a "badge of honor" and "like being involved in a holy crusade. . . . I felt very good, in the sense of righteous indignation, about being arrested, but at the same time I felt the commitment and dedication on the part of the students." Similarly, another Nashville activist, Diane Nash, recalled how the movement emboldened its participants: "The movement had a way of reaching inside of you and bringing out things that even you didn't know were there. Such as courage. When it was time to go to jail, I was much too busy to be afraid." (See box.)

Through such courageous and ongoing challenges to the status quo, the civil rights movement developed its own movement culture and reinforced solidarity among its participants. Using the "Old Negro spirituals" as materials, participants updated and transformed such songs as "Walking for Freedom," "Fight On," and "I'll Be All Right." The latter song became the movement's anthem, "We Shall Overcome." Participants repeatedly commented on the spiritual nature of the movement. Donie Jones, a household worker, described the first mass meeting of the Montgomery bus boycott: "The church was so full, there were so many people. It was like a revival starting. That's what it was like." Similarly, Joe Azbell, the sympathetic white journalist of the *Montgomery Advertiser,* described the same meeting: "I was the first white person there. The preachers were preaching as I came in, and that audience was so on fire. . . . There was a spirit there that no one could ever capture again in a movie or anything else, because it was so powerful."

FEDERAL ACTION, INTERNAL CONFLICTS, AND THE LIMITS OF NONVIOLENCE

Spurred by the successes as well as limitations of their local and regional struggles, African Americans focused increasingly on the nation's capital. They demanded a Second Reconstruction—that is, sweeping federal legislation designed to end all vestiges of the segregationist order once and for all. Their efforts culminated in the March on Washington for Jobs and Freedom in August 1963. Convened at the Lincoln Memorial, the March on Washington attracted some 250,000 people from around the world, including some 60,000 whites. Martin Luther King Jr.'s "I Have a Dream" speech accented the African American quest for a world that transcended color as a criteria for denying black people access to economic and political democracy:

I have a dream that one day this nation will rise up and live out the true meaning of its creed: "We hold these truths to be self-evident—that all men are created equal." . . . When we let freedom ring, when we let it ring from every village and every hamlet, from every state and every city, we will be able to speed up that day when all of God's children, black men and white men, Jews and Gentiles, Protestants and Catholics, will be able to join hands and sing in the words of the old Negro spiritual, "Free at last! Free at last! Thank God almighty, we are free at last!"

Florida Student Patricia Stephens Writes from Jail in Tallahassee

I am writing this in Leon County Jail. My sister Priscilla and I, five other A & M students and one high school student are serving 60-day sentences for our participation in the sit-ins. We could be out on appeal but we all strongly believe that Martin Luther King was right when he said: "We've got to fill the jails in order to win our equal rights." Priscilla and I both explained this to our parents when they visited us the other day. Priscilla is supposed to be on a special diet and mother was worried about her. We did our best to dispel her worries. We made it clear that we want to serve-out our full time.

Students who saw the inside of the county jail before I did and were released on bond, reported that conditions were miserable. They did not exaggerate. It is dank and cold. We are in what is called a "bull tank" with four cells. Each cell has four bunks, a commode and a small sink. Some of the cells have running water, but ours does not. Breakfast, if you can call it that, is served at 6:30. Another meal is served at 12:30 and in the evening, "sweet" bread and watery coffee. At first I found it difficult to eat this food. . . .

. . . It is almost six months since Priscilla and I were first introduced to CORE at a workshop in Miami. Upon our return we helped to establish a Tallahassee CORE group, whose initial meeting took place last October. Among our first projects was a test sit-in at Sear's and McCrory's. So, we were not totally unprepared when the south-wide protest movement started in early February.

Our first action in Tallahassee was on Feb. 13th. At 11 A.M. we sat down at the Woolworth lunch counter. When the waitress approached, Charles Steele, who was next to me, ordered a slice of cake for each of us. She said: "I'm sorry: I can't serve you" and moved on down the counter repeating this to the other participants. We all said we would wait, took out our books and started reading—or at least, we tried.

The regular customers continued to eat. When one man finished, the waitress said: "Thank you for staying and eating in all this indecency." The man replied: "What did you expect me to do? I paid for it."

One man stopped behind Bill Carpenter briefly and said: "I think you're doing a fine job: just sit right there." . . .

The second sit-in at Woolworth's occurred a week later. . . .

At about 3:30 P.M. a squad of policemen led by a man in civilian clothes entered the store. Someone directed him to Priscilla, who had been chosen our spokesman for this sit-in. "As Mayor of Tallahassee, I am asking you to leave," said the man in civilian clothes.

"If we don't leave, would we be committing a crime?" Priscilla asked. The mayor simply repeated his original statement. Then he came over to me, pointed to the "closed" sign and asked: "Can you read?" I advised him to direct all his comments to our elected spokesman. He looked as though his official vanity was wounded but turned to Priscilla. We did too, reiterating our determination to stay. He ordered our arrest.

Two policemen "escorted" each of the eleven of us to the station. I use quotes because their handling of us was not exactly gentle nor were their remarks courteous. At 4:45 we entered the police station. Until recently the building had housed a savings and loan company, so I was not surprised to observe that our cell was a renovated bank vault. One by one, we were fingerprinted. . . .

Source: Gilbert Osofsky, *The Burden of Race: A Documentary History of Negro-White Relations in America* (New York: Harper Torchbooks, Harper and Row, 1967), pp. 527–531.

The March on Washington not only symbolized the maturation of the modern civil rights movement as an interracial phenomenon but also accented the growing merger of civil rights and workplace struggles. The march demanded a vigorous federal civil rights program that would include "Jobs and Freedom." Marchers demanded equal employment opportunities, job training programs, open housing policies, and voting rights for all U.S. citizens regardless of race or color. A. Philip Randolph and Bayard Rustin hoped to use the march as a platform for articulating the demands of the black working class for economic democracy. They urged "the black laboring masses" to "speak! . . . ARISE and MARCH." In his opening address to the marchers, Randolph declared:

> Demonstrations are the hallmark of every revolution since the birth of civilization. . . . And there is no way . . . to stem these demonstrations until the cause is removed; and the cause is racial bias, the cause is exploitation and oppression, the cause is second-class citizenship in a first-class nation.

A year later, Randolph made the same point: "We will continue our boycotts, sit-ins, and civil disobedience until grievances are completely redressed. . . . We are in the midst of a full-dress revolution. We demand, we do not beg or plead, fundamental economic changes."

Civil Rights Legislation

Although President Kennedy refused to appear at the March on Washington, he supported its demands for new civil rights legislation designed to redress years of racial inequality in the economic, political, and social life of the nation. Nearly two months earlier, in June, Kennedy had proposed comprehensive civil rights legislation designed to end the segregationist system. In nationally televised and radio messages to the public, he described the struggle over desegregation as "a moral crisis" that had deep roots in the failure of the nation to include blacks under the protection of the Constitution. As such, he said, its resolution could not be met by repressive police actions, demonstrations in the streets, or "token moves or talk." He urged Americans to act in federal, state, and local legislative bodies "and, above all, in all of our daily lives." Accordingly, Kennedy asked Congress for a "commitment it has not fully made in this century to the proposition that race has no place in American life or law." Within weeks after the March on Washington, terrorists had bombed the Sixteenth Street Baptist Church in Birmingham, killing five young girls attending a Sunday school class. The bombing of the Sixteenth Street Baptist Church underscored the urgency of Kennedy's proposed civil rights legislation and the crisis facing blacks and the nation.

Kennedy's new civil rights initiative promised to fully usher in the Second Reconstruction "to secure blacks their full rights" as citizens. Kennedy acted not only because of direct pressure from the civil rights movement. He also responded to growing pressure from corporate and business leaders who sensed dwindling profit lines under the steady onslaught of black protests. It was the South's white businessmen who invariably expressed alarm over the economic impact of the boycotts and marches and pushed for a favorable resolution of the crisis. In Nashville, as Rev. C. T. Vivian noted, "Nobody came downtown. Blacks wouldn't come downtown, whites were afraid to come downtown, so . . . the businessmen began to lose money and they began to ask for a change." Moreover, some southern businesses were branches of northern firms that faced additional pressure from northern sympathizers with the freedom struggle. Before Kennedy could steer his legislation through Congress, an assassin's bullet took his life during a visit to Dallas, Texas, in November 1963.

Following Kennedy's assassination, African Americans expressed little faith that his successor, Lyndon Baines Johnson, would become an advocate for their cause. Despite Kennedy's own slow and halting record on civil rights issues, his death in the wake of unveiling his civil rights agenda enhanced his stature as a friend of the movement. As Coretta Scott King recalled, "We felt that President Kennedy had been a friend of the Cause and that with him as President we could continue to move forward. We watched and prayed for him. Then it was announced that the President was dead." In his address to the nation a few days later, Johnson sought to allay fears that he would allow Kennedy's civil rights agenda to lapse. Johnson urged lawmakers to continue the course charted by Kennedy. As he put it, the "ideas and the ideals" that Kennedy "so nobly represented must and will be translated into effective action." Congress quickly passed the Civil Rights Act of 1964, which outlawed discrimination by race in hotels, stores, restaurants, and other public accommodations; prohibited school segregation; and banned job discrimination by public and private employers (including public schools and local governments after 1972). (See the Documents section.) The Civil Rights Act of 1964 also created the Equal Employment Opportunity Commission (EEOC), an independent regulatory body similar to the National Labor Relations Board, to address issues of race and sex discrimination by all private employers (except those with few employees). To deal with discrimination by firms receiving government contracts or financial assistance, the Civil Rights Act of 1964 also established the Office of Federal Contract Compliance (OFCC) in the Department of Labor. Similar oversight agencies were created in the Departments of Health, Education, and Welfare; Defense; Housing and Urban Development; and Transportation. Although the Civil Rights Act outlawed discrimination in jobs, education, and employment, African Americans faced an uphill battle translating the provisions of the new legislation into reality.

Southerners continued to use a variety of legal and extralegal measures to prevent blacks from voting. In 1964, only 2 million of the South's 5 million voting-age blacks were registered to vote. The proportion of blacks on the voting rolls stood at 32 percent in Louisiana, 19 percent in Alabama, and 6 percent in Mississippi. As early as 1961, SNCC had initiated a voter registration campaign in McComb, Mississippi, described by blacks as the most violent city in the state. A year later, a coalition of civil rights organizations, including SNCC, SCLC, and the NAACP, formed the Voter Education Project (VEP). Funded by the Council of Federated Organizations, VEP registered over a half million southern black voters over the next two years. Most of this growth occurred in urban rather than rural areas, where intimidation and even death continued to confront prospective black voters in cities like McComb, Mississippi, and Selma, Alabama. In 1964, VEP launched the Mississippi Freedom Summer Project and stepped up its efforts to register black voters in the rural South.

Under the leadership of Bob Moses, a former high school teacher and Harvard graduate student, young black and white volunteers poured into rural Mississippi. They set up "freedom schools" for the children of black sharecroppers and enrolled thousands of blacks in the Mississippi Freedom Democratic Party (MFDP), a democratically and openly elected alternative to the state's all-white Democratic Party. The organization selected Aaron Henry as president and Fannie Lou Hamer as vice president. The MFDP vigorously challenged the state's regular Democratic Party at the Democratic National Convention in August. Although the Kennedy administration had supported the voter registration campaign as good for the Democratic Party, it refused to protect volunteers from police and citizen brutality. For his part, Johnson uniformly opposed the work of the MFDP and offered even less protection to civil rights workers. Indeed, his policies opened the door for the escalation of violence against organizers during the Freedom Summer Project. From the out-

Martin Luther King and Ralph David Abernathy at a rally in Selma, Alabama, likely in March 1965. After the Mississippi Freedom Summer Project, the civil rights movement focused on Selma and the campaign for federal voting rights legislation. *Flip Schulke/Black Star*

set of the Mississippi campaign, organizers faced stubborn and violent resistance. In Winona, Mississippi, police brutally beat and imprisoned civil rights activist Fannie Lou Hamer and others. In Jackson, Mississippi, a gunman assassinated the head of the Mississippi NAACP, Medgar Evers, at the front entrance to his home. In Philadelphia, Mississippi, a deputy sheriff arranged for a mob to lynch three "Freedom Summer" volunteers—Michael Schwerner, James Chaney, and Andrew Goodman. The decomposed bodies of the three men were later recovered from a grave near Philadelphia, Mississippi.

Following the Mississippi Freedom Summer Project and the election of 1964, the voter registration campaign turned toward Selma, Alabama. Blacks constituted a majority of the city's population but had only 3 percent of their numbers on the voting lists. As with Mississippi's voter registration drive, organizers faced stiff and violent resistance from law officers under the direction of Sheriff Jim Clark. On 7 March 1965, when activists planned a march from Selma to Montgomery to demand the franchise, helmeted state troopers and local police wearing gas masks met some six hundred nonviolent marchers on Selma's Pettus Bridge. Law officers brutally clubbed, beat, and gassed the marchers, forcing them back across the bridge into the black community. "Bloody Sunday," as activists called the encounter, resulted in the hospitalization of some seventy marchers. After a second aborted effort to march from Selma to the Alabama state capital, a third march finally succeeded. The five-day march reached Montgomery on March 25 without violence, partly because Johnson had federalized the Alabama National Guard and convinced Governor Wallace that he would not hesitate to send in federal troops if necessary to protect the marchers. It also rained heavily. *Ebony* photographer Moneta Sleet later recalled: "I remember vividly the fifty-mile march from Selma to Montgomery. Half of it was spent in the rain, with the military jeeps on one side, helicopters overhead and soldiers all around us."

In the wake of the Selma-to-Montgomery march, movement leaders focused on the passage of a federal Voting Rights Act. In proposing the act in the aftermath of growing violence in Selma, Johnson described the civil rights cause as the cause of the entire nation, "because it is not just Negroes, but really all of us who must overcome the crippling legacy of bigotry and injustice." Johnson concluded his address by using the rhetoric of the movement itself—"we shall overcome." Johnson's rhetoric partly reflected concern for the growing number of white casualties among the civil rights forces. During the Mississippi Freedom Summer Project, white volunteers Michael Schwerner and Andrew Goodman were murdered in Philadelphia, Mississippi, along with their fellow black activist James Chaney, who unlike his white counterparts suffered severe beatings and torture as well as gunshot wounds. Following the second aborted effort to march from Selma to Montgomery, vigilantes attacked four white Unitarian ministers who had arrived in town to join the march. One of the men, Rev. James J. Reeb of Boston, died two days later from his wounds. On a lonely stretch of Highway 80 in Alabama, four Klansmen shot and killed Viola Liuzzo, a Detroit housewife, in the aftermath of the successful march from Selma to Montgomery.

The House passed the Voting Rights Act on August 3, and the Senate followed suit the next day. Two days later, Johnson signed the measure into law at a

Selma-to-Montgomery march. After law enforcement officials violently turned back two attempts to march from Selma to Montgomery on behalf of voting rights, African Americans and their white allies finally completed a five-day march and reached the Alabama state capital on 25 March 1965. *Dan Budnik/Woodfin Camp & Associates*

ceremony in the same room where Lincoln had signed emancipation legislation nearly one hundred years earlier. The Voting Rights Act of 1965 aimed to enforce the Fifteenth Amendment by authorizing the use of federal examiners to register voters and oversee the political process. The civil rights movement also served as a catalyst for passage of the Economic Opportunity Act of 1964, which created the Office of Economic Opportunity and launched Johnson's "War on Poverty" programs—including the Job Corps, Head Start, Medicare, and Medicaid—and community action programs that provided legal aid to poor people and enabled inner-city neighborhoods to democratically elect representatives to local antipoverty boards and help determine the distribution of federal poverty funds (see box).

Organizational and Ideological Conflicts

The civil rights movement not only swept across America and stimulated changes in class and race relations. It also created great tensions and conflicts within African American families and communities. Unlike their parents, who repeatedly extolled

---

CHANGING HISTORICAL INTERPRETATIONS

The Second Reconstruction

As with other facets of the African American experience, the post–World War II years are the subject of considerable scholarly debate. Key to the opening phases of this debate was the question of change or continuity in the civil rights struggle. Did the modern civil rights movement represent a dramatic break with the past or did it represent a continuation of prior developments? In the wake of the nonviolent direct action campaigns of the 1950s and 1960s, scholars initially emphasized a dramatic break with the past—that is, the emergence of a Second Reconstruction. They showed how African Americans and their white allies returned to the unfinished project of citizenship that had begun and faltered following the Civil War years. Until the mid-1960s, these scholars invariably pinpointed important legal precedents like the *Brown v. Board of Education* decision of 1954; President Harry S. Truman's executive order desegregating the armed forces; President Dwight Eisenhower's establishment of the U.S. Civil Rights Commission in 1957; and the dramatic outpouring of new civil rights legislation during the 1960s. Then in 1968, Richard Dalfiume, influenced by the ideas of Gunnar Myrdal, E. Franklin Frazier, and James Baldwin, among others, published his essay "The 'Forgotten Years' of the Negro Revolution" in the *Journal of American History.* Although governmental edicts and court decisions were important, Dalfiume argued that "the seeds" of the black revolution were sown in the "mass militancy and race consciousness" of the World War II years, particularly the March on Washington movement and the "Double V" campaign for victory at home and abroad.

Although subsequent studies treated World War II as the genesis of the modern civil rights movement, research soon moved well beyond questions of origins, continuity, and discontinuity in the civil rights struggle. During the 1980s and 1990s, scholarship shifted from a focus on legislative and judicial decisions (and the top tier of civil rights leaders and their white allies) to highly sensitive local, community, and organizational grassroots studies. Such research offers new generational, class, and gender perspectives. Illuminating these changes are studies by Clayborne Carson (*In Struggle: SNCC and the Black Awakening of the 1960s,* 1981); Aldon D. Morris (*The Origins of the Civil Rights Movement,* 1984); Robert Korstad and Nelson Lichtenstein, *Opportunities Found and Lost* (1988); Michael Honey (*Black Workers Remember,* 1999); Chana Lee (*For Freedom's Sake: The Life of Fannie Lou Hamer,* 1999); and Charles Payne (*I've Got the Light of Freedom,* 1995), among many others. According to Payne, scholars do not yet fully understand "how to use what we know about the past to shape a more just present," but civil rights scholarship can illuminate how "ordinary, flawed, everyday sorts of human beings frequently manage to make extraordinary contributions to social change."

---

the virtues of hard work and personal sacrifice to get ahead, postwar black youth proposed to engage the system of racial inequality, level the playing field, and increase their chances of success. Some parents reacted to the decision of their children with extreme measures. When two young women decided to join the Mississippi Freedom Summer Project, their parents warned them: "If you go to Mississippi with these people [SNCC organizers], you can consider yourself homeless!" Hollis

Watkins of Mississippi related a similar tale of family ostracism when he participated in a sit-in at a local Woolworth store: "My relatives would see me walking down the street and then they would pass over to the other side rather than meet me on the street. . . . This is aunts, uncles, first cousins, and, you know, close relatives." Similar to the families, when black students sat in at lunch counters, some of the first faces that they encountered were often blacks, mainly cooks, dishwashers, and other general laborers in establishments that served whites only. Black kitchen help often responded to the sit-in students with fear that they would produce trouble and cause workers to lose their jobs. In Greensboro, North Carolina, a black female employee told the youth that they were "rabble-rousers" and "troublemakers" who made it difficult for blacks to "get anyplace today." Moreover, although some college administrators encouraged the students, others expelled or punished them at the behest of white public officials. At Southern University in Baton Rouge, Louisiana, President Felton Grandison Clark screened out student activists by technically expelling the entire student body and requiring everyone to reapply for admission.

Organizational and ideological conflicts and turf battles also took their toll on the freedom struggle. When southern civil rights activists proposed to organize SCLC, the NAACP opposed the effort, fearing distraction from its own historic role in the freedom struggle. According to the files of the SCLC, "persons in the top echelon" of the NAACP "sowed seeds of dissension" designed to undermine the work of the organization. Accordingly, Martin Luther King moved swiftly to clear up misunderstanding by holding "a conference with Roy Wilkins and other NAACP staff members." Similarly, when students formed their own national organization (SNCC), SCLC, CORE, and the NAACP all urged affiliation with their own respective bodies. Ella Baker, the executive director of SCLC, dissented from these appeals, sided with student activists, and encouraged them to maintain their independence. Diane Nash later praised Baker as a stellar senior supporter of the student movement: "Ella Baker saw how important it was to recognize the fact that the students should set the goals and directions and maintain control of the student movement." Although SNCC favored the activities of SCLC over the slow legal maneuvers of the NAACP, it rejected SCLC's effort to determine strategy and direct the overall campaign. Efforts to desegregate Albany, Georgia, brought organizational competition and conflicts into sharp focus. According to Wyatt T. Walker, SCLC strategist, SNCC needed the legal and financial resources of the NAACP and "wanted the international and national attention that Martin Luther King's presence would generate, but they did not want the input of his organization."

The rift between young SNCC activists and their elder counterparts nearly undermined the March on Washington. As early as 1963, amidst plans for the March on Washington, CORE chapters took an increasingly militant stance toward the segregationist system. Local units established firm deadlines for white businesses to employ blacks and announced plans to escalate the use of disruptive tactics designed to tie up commerce and force the dismantling of discriminatory practices. By late 1963, SNCC also moved toward a more aggressive posture toward the injustices of capitalist institutions. In his proposed speech for the March on Washington, SNCC president John Lewis sounded a militant, impatient, and radical note, which he reluctantly modified for the sake of unity. One section of his speech, which he changed, particularly worried other members of the march coalition:

> We will march through the South, through the heart of Dixie, the way Sherman did. We shall pursue our own "scorched earth" policy and burn Jim Crow to the ground, nonviolently. We shall crack the South into a thousand pieces and put them back together in the image of democracy.

From the beginning of his organizational work for SNCC, Stokely Carmichael distanced himself from the religious and nonviolent tenets of the civil rights movement. Although he participated in nonviolent campaigns and went to jail over twenty-five times for the cause, he nonetheless armed himself with a loaded pistol and retained his right to violent self-defense if necessary. At the same time, by the mid-1960s, SNCC and CORE opposed U.S. involvement in Vietnam, urging black people to resist the war "for the white man's freedom, until all the Negro people are free in Mississippi." As we will see in Chapter 22, SCLC would also eventually take a similar antiwar stand.

The cleavage among civil rights organizations also entailed different interpretations and approaches to class and gender as well as racial dimensions of the black experience. During the 1950s, the National Urban League distanced itself from the nonviolent direct action struggles that raged across the land. It also deemphasized its historic focus on helping black workers gain access to industrial jobs. It now developed its "Pilot Placement Program," designed to showcase the employment of black individuals in highly skilled, white-collar, clerical, and managerial positions previously closed to them. As late as 1958, Whitney Young, dean of the Atlanta School of Social Work, urged the annual conference of the Urban League to avoid "protest, civil rights or civil liberties" groups. In 1961, however, when Young took the executive director's post, he gradually moved the organization toward the objectives of the modern civil rights movement. Under Young's leadership, the Urban League placed increasing pressure on employers and government bureaucracies to increase the numbers and upgrade black employees. At the same time, the organization increased pressure on the federal government to provide aid for the revitalization of central city black communities. By the mid-1960s, the organization had initiated its National Skills Bank for the unemployed or underemployed; on-the-job training for unskilled workers in private industry; and specialized programs for blacks seeking employment in radio, television, and clerical services. Unlike its earlier pilot program, the National Skills Bank placed some ninety-six hundred blacks in jobs in a single year. When a hesitant staff member told Young, "We don't work this fast," he replied, "From now on, we will. We have to, or we'll be left behind."

Although most civil rights organizations concentrated on blacks in the major urban centers with substantial numbers of black professional and business people as well as industrial workers, SNCC reached the most dispossessed blacks in small southern towns and rural areas. Contrasting responses to issues of class were apparent in the struggles of the Mississippi Freedom Democratic Party (MFDP). Describing themselves as the only democratically elected group of representatives from the state of Mississippi, the MFDP challenged the all-white Mississippi Democratic Party at the Democratic National Convention in 1964. When Lyndon

Baines Johnson and white national party leaders opposed the group in favor of the state's all-white party, the principal civil rights and labor leaders—Bayard Rustin, Martin Luther King Jr., and CORE's James Farmer—endorsed a compromise that undermined the hard work of SNCC and the Mississippi delegation. Rustin's address urging compromise particularly chagrined Stokely Carmichael, who openly questioned Rustin's so-called liberal white labor "friends." Under the leadership of rural and small-town delegates like Fannie Lou Hamer, the MFDP delegation held its own and rejected the compromise.

In addition to tensions along class lines, the rising number of white volunteers precipitated internal gender and racial conflicts. As whites increased their participation, they took a disproportionate share of leadership positions. From the beginning, well-educated white men had taken the key leadership positions in CORE. By the early 1960s, however, Roy Innis and other black members of CORE formed a black caucus and demanded leadership posts. In 1964, for the first time in its history, CORE became a predominantly black organization. During the Mississippi Freedom Summer Project, white student volunteers from elite institutions like Stanford and Harvard Universities also increased their influence in SNCC. However, under pressure from activists like Stokely Carmichael, who became a full-time organizer in 1964, SNCC quickly curtailed its reliance on white volunteers. Although Carmichael was acutely sensitive to race and class biases, he was less sensitive to gender inequities. During the Freedom Summer Project, for example, he stated that women were most valued for their sexual rather than their political and intellectual capacities. Accordingly, when SNCC later elected Ruby Doris Smith executive secretary in 1966, men refused to cooperate. James Forman later recalled: "She endured vicious attacks from the SNCC leadership. They also embodied chauvinism in fighting her attempts as executive secretary to impose a sense of organizational responsibility and self-discipline, trying to justify themselves by the fact that their critic was a woman." According to Kathleen Neal Cleaver, a SNCC activist and later member of the Black Panther Party, the constant struggle with notions of male dominance and the need to juggle family and movement responsibilities killed Smith at the young age of twenty-six: "What killed Ruby Doris was the constant outpouring of work, work, work, work with being married, having a child, the constant conflicts, the constant struggles that she was subjected to because she was a woman. She was destroyed by the movement." Black women activists also decried the apparent ease with which black men entered sexual liaisons with white women and sharply condemned similar relations between white men and black women. Such relations produced long and heated debates that ultimately undermined the day-to-day work of the movement.

Despite a variety of internal conflicts, the civil rights movement ushered in a new era of socioeconomic and political progress for African Americans. Aside from the legal triumphs over de jure segregation, African Americans gradually improved their economic position. The black middle class experienced its greatest gains during the 1960s. In 1960, only 13 percent of all African Americans occupied middle-class positions. Ten years later, the percentage had nearly doubled, rising to nearly 26 percent. Unlike the earlier black middle class, which existed mainly behind the walls of segregation, this one pushed outward into jobs and sectors of the economy formally occupied by whites only. Middle-class and elite blacks not only occupied earlier jobs as teachers, ministers, social workers, physicians, dentists, and attorneys but also took a larger share of jobs as accountants, sales managers, scientists, architects, and engineers in predominantly white firms. Although the old middle class and its children benefited from these changes, the new black middle class of the civil rights era was recruited mainly from among the "sons and daughters of garbage collectors, assembly line workers, domestics, waiters, taxicab drivers, and farmers." Thus, as one contemporary sociologist notes, the new middle class had roots that stretched "far down into the neighborhoods and homes" of the urban working class. At the same time, although black businesses continued to serve a predominantly black clientele, they reached out into the larger white market. As we will see in Chapter 21, Detroit's Motown Industries symbolized these changes. Formed in 1959, Motown Industries reached both black and white consumers with the music of leading rhythm and blues artists.

$\sim$

BETWEEN THE END OF WORLD WAR II and the mid-1960s, African Americans launched the largest and most successful mass movement for civil and human rights in the nation's history. They moved their struggle from courts, presidential edicts, and congressional legislation to the streets. In rapid succession, they initiated boycotts, sit-ins, freedom rides, and voter education projects across the South. Although their actions were deeply rooted in local community-based institutions and organizations, they transformed such struggles into a broader national, and increasingly international, movement. Inspired by independence movements in Africa and Asia as well as their own history, culture, and social struggles, African Americans used America's Cold War advocacy of democratic freedoms abroad to demand a Second Reconstruction. Supported by a growing core of white allies in federal agencies and diverse peace and freedom organizations, the modern civil rights movement demolished the legal pillars of the segregationist system and established a new and more promising framework for social change. Still, in addition to ongoing white resistance, a variety of internal conflicts limited the achievements of nonviolent direct action strategies. Chapter 21 discusses how divergent approaches to the struggle for freedom would gain their sharpest and most militant articulation in the urban North and West.

~

The Civil Rights Struggle in the Urban North and West

The segregationist system and the rise of the modern civil rights movement were not limited to the South. In its de facto form, Jim Crow limited the civil rights, economic opportunities, and channels of self-expression of African Americans in the urban North and West as well. Consequently, like their southern brothers and sisters, northern and western blacks also turned toward non-violent direct action strategies for social change. Unlike their southern counterparts, however, northern and western blacks exhibited less faith in the long-run efficacy of nonviolent strategies and tactics. By the mid-1960s, their impatience with the slow pace of change would fuel the rise of the Nation of Islam; the eruption of urban revolts; and, with southern blacks, the transformation of African American intellectual, artistic, and cultural life. Northern and western blacks would help reorient the black freedom struggle toward the Black Power movement, which justified the use of defensive violence; toward separate organizations; and toward pride in blackness over assimilationist tendencies. Before reorienting their priorities, however, African Americans in the urban North and West tested the possibilities of nonviolent direct action strategies.

THE FIGHT FOR JOBS, HOUSING, AND PUBLIC ACCOMMODATIONS

Following World War II, civil rights campaigns emerged in a variety of northern and western cities. As early as 1948–1953, civil rights organizations and student activists boycotted and desegregated downtown restaurants, lunch counters, theaters, and places of amusement in Albuquerque, Wichita, and Oklahoma City; San Francisco, Berkeley, and Los Angeles; and Philadelphia, Chicago, New York, Indianapolis, and Cincinnati. The NAACP encouraged these efforts by taking violators to court under existing civil rights laws, but the Congress of Racial Equality (CORE) and grassroots black activists emerged at the forefront of militant postwar efforts to desegregate the urban North and West. An interracial organization with a predominantly white membership until the early 1960s, CORE expanded from thirteen local affiliates in 1947–1948 to twenty in 1950. Although the number of chapters dropped to about a dozen in the late 1950s, grassroots black activists revitalized the organization during the early 1960s.

From the outset, working-class blacks provided the backbone of the numerous civil rights engagements. St. Louis machine operator and laborer Ivory Perry is a stellar example. In a photo exhibit of social protest movements in the city of St. Louis, Ivory Perry appeared in over half of the selections:

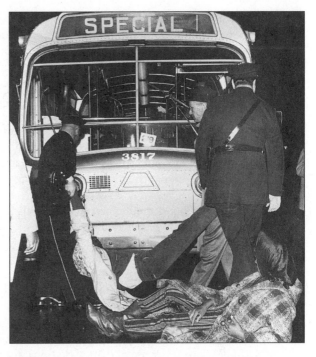

Police officers remove the St. Louis activist Ivory Perry from beneath a bus during a 1963 demonstration against the city's Jefferson Bank. *Collections of the St. Louis Mercantile Library Association*

In one picture, he lay sprawled under the wheels of a car, blocking traffic to call attention to complaints against police brutality. In another, he chained shut the doors of an office building to dramatize charges that the company headquartered there discriminated against black job applicants. A third photograph presented Perry outside the editorial offices of a daily newspaper, protesting the paper's treatment of racial issues by holding a match to a copy of that morning's edition and setting it on fire.

As one contemporary observer who knew Perry recalled, "The interesting thing about Ivory Perry was that he didn't shoot for the limelight. You'd always see him in a secondary role getting the job done. Ivory was always there, and I always understood that." Marian Oldham, a CORE activist, recalled tersely: "Ivory as far as I perceived him was a very nice, sincere, dedicated, really hard worker."

St. Louis emerged as perhaps the most militant and energetic center of civil rights activism outside the South during the early postwar years. The St. Louis chapter of CORE, founded under the leadership of Bernice Fisher in 1948, had a strong labor union and working-class orientation although the membership was predominantly middle class. For the first six years, blacks in St. Louis concentrated on a variety of downtown establishments, including the cafeterias of the YMCA and the YWCA; the Stix, Baer, and Fuller Department Store; Woolworth; Sears

Roebuck; the Greyhound Bus terminal; and the Fox Theater. CORE members and supporters like Perry distributed leaflets, sat in, and picketed these establishments, sometimes for several months or even years before they opened their doors to black patrons. Although small five-and-ten-cent stores proved most vulnerable and often opened their doors to blacks after only a few encounters with protesters, others put up stiff and sometimes protracted resistance. Only gradually did the Fox Theater open its doors to blacks; initially, it accepted only couples and imposed a dress code of jacket and tie for black men. It took three years before Sears Roebuck and the Greyhound Bus terminal served blacks and whites on an equal basis. The firm of Stix, Baer, and Fuller held out for six years. As activist Billie Ames observed, "Little did we know when we started that campaign that it would take six years to complete."

As proprietors of public accommodations like restaurants, theaters, and lunch counters gradually eliminated segregation in the urban North and West, African Americans turned toward the desegregation of public pools and amusement parks. As early as 1946, blacks in Chicago protested and ended segregation at the White City Roller Rink on the South Side. In 1948, members of the Los Angeles CORE protested discrimination at the Bimini Baths. Four years later, the Cleveland chapter carried out a similar protest against the city's Skateland Roller Rink. New Jersey blacks and their white allies conducted "stand-ins" at the state's Palisades Amusement Park swimming pool. In Cincinnati, it took local branches of CORE and the NAACP nearly a decade of demonstrations, litigation, and the arrest of nearly two dozen protesters before officials fully desegregated the city's Coney Island amusement park. During the first two years of demonstrations, Cincinnati park officials agreed to "a quiet opening" of the park but refused to desegregate the park's swimming pool and dance hall. Only after five more years of intermittent demonstrations and court cases did park officials desegregate "all facilities" at Coney Island in 1961. In Indianapolis, African Americans launched an equally long but less successful struggle against the city's privately owned Riverside Park, which instituted a "Negro Day" and displayed a huge sign, "White Patronage Only Solicited," through the early 1960s.

Northern and western blacks not only fought to desegregate public accommodations. They also waged equally vigorous campaigns against the discriminatory policies of employers and labor unions. As early as 1948–1950, CORE chapters boycotted northern California's Lucky's grocery chain (now Albertson's); Wichita's Safeway stores; and Chicago's Goldblatt's Department Store. In Omaha, Nebraska, students at Creighton University launched successful boycotts and pickets of the local Coca-Cola plant as well as local laundromats, a dairy, and a chain of ice cream parlors.

In 1951, black workers formed the National Negro Labor Council (NNLC) and strengthened demonstrations against employment discrimination. Under the leadership of William R. Hood, the NNLC not only initiated strikes and boycotts against discriminatory employers but also demanded black representation in a broad range of leadership positions in the labor movement. When the NNLC declined during the mid-1950s, black trade unionists formed the American Negro Labor Council (ANLC) in 1959. The ANLC heightened the connection between the labor and civil rights movements, emphasizing the utility of nonviolent direct action strategies for social change. As noted in Chapter 20, labor leaders A. Philip Randolph and Bayard Rustin played key roles in this process. According to Randolph, "Even Jesus Christ participated in civil disobedience."

After dissipating somewhat during the mid- to late 1950s, the campaign for equal employment resurfaced and became even more militant during the early 1960s. Activists now moved well beyond local retail outlets and food chains and targeted such diverse companies as Bank of America, Bell Telephone, the Western Electric Company, and the building and construction trades. Beginning in 1963, activists demonstrated against the building and construction trades in such cities as Philadelphia, Newark, and New York. On several occasions, protests forced public officials to postpone construction and negotiate with activists over the hiring of black workers. In New York, the mayor stopped work on the city's Municipal Services Building when the NAACP and CORE threatened the escalation of demonstrations. In the mayor's view, the protests made municipal officials "fear another Birmingham." Other protests emerged at the sites of hospitals, public schools, apartment complexes, and university expansion projects. Activists in Brooklyn, Manhattan, and Queens lay in muddy streets of construction sites, locked arms, and obstructed the work of cement mixers, cranes, and supply trucks. At one site, four protesters climbed to the top of a crane some sixty feet above the ground, chained themselves to the machinery, and defied work crews to operate the equipment.

In the spring and summer of 1964, the California chapters of CORE coordinated a statewide campaign against the discriminatory policies of the Bank of America. The organization picketed branch offices in San Francisco, Los Angeles, and San Diego, where CORE members were arrested for defying a court injunction and CORE chairman Harold Brown served a sixty-day jail sentence. A year earlier, the St. Louis chapter of CORE had carried out a similar demonstration at the downtown Jefferson Bank building. Authorities arrested fifteen demonstrators and sentenced them to sixty days in jail for blocking the bank's main entrance as well as the windows of the bank tellers. In Newark, New Jersey, CORE not only picketed the offices of the Western Electric Company but also initiated a massive "phone-in" campaign, which created a crisis by jamming telephone switchboards. When the Newark branch of CORE threatened similar actions against Bell Telephone Company, management agreed to improve employment opportunities for black workers at the firm, including the employment of linemen and installers as well as female telephone operators. In the meantime, African Americans and their white allies launched protests against Sheraton hotels, Howard Johnson's restaurant chain, Safeway, A&P, Sears Roebuck, beer manufacturers, car dealerships like Lincoln-Mercury and Chrysler, and commercial advertising agencies. Such gains were nonetheless insufficient and small in numbers. Thus, when blacks and their white allies gathered for the historic March on Washington for Jobs and Freedom, discussed in Chapter 20, they aimed to eliminate discriminatory practices within the labor movement, corporate personnel offices, and the larger institutional life of the North, South, and West.

Although protests against discrimination in public accommodations and jobs took center stage in the early postwar northern and western freedom struggle, housing and public education gained increasing attention in the early 1960s. In 1961, activists in New York and Brooklyn staged sit-ins at the LeFrak Realty Company and the Ira Management Corporation. Protesters carried sleeping mats and pieces of furniture into one apartment and occupied it for seventeen days. Calling their actions a "dwell-in," activists demanded the rental of units to black tenants. In New Haven, Blyden Jackson, a young black factory worker, spearheaded a "sit-out" to protest the displacement of black families by urban renewal. Hundreds of blacks sat out on the sidewalks to demonstrate their demand for a local fair housing ordinance that would allow them to move into previously all-white neighborhoods. When city officials defeated the bill, demonstrators sat in at City Hall and blocked corridors until they were arrested by local police. At the same time, others picketed and sat in at the offices and homes of "slum lords" in Philadelphia, Boston, New York, and New Haven.

Along with housing demonstrations, African Americans launched school desegregation campaigns. Efforts to desegregate schools quickly escalated into some of the most intense encounters between northern and western blacks and public authorities. St. Louis activists blocked buses carrying students to segregated schools and staged mass marches on the offices of the Board of Education. In Los Angeles, a coalition of seventy-six organizations conducted sit-ins, study-ins, and sing-ins at the Board of Education, demanding an end to racially segregated schools. Chicago police arrested nearly two hundred protesters when they conducted a week-long sit-in at the office of the city's school board president, demanding the dismantling of segregated mobile classrooms within the black community. Several demonstrators and policemen were injured as the protests escalated. In the meantime, school boycotts also emerged in Boston, Kansas City, New York, and Milwaukee.

The fight against education and housing discrimination was closely intertwined with grievances against the building and construction trades. By the early 1960s, blacks often protested urban renewal policies and segregated schools by confronting work crews at construction sites. In the summer of 1963, Syracuse activists blocked bulldozers, sat on cranes, obstructed demolition work, and refused to budge when arrested by police. Officers had to physically carry large numbers of demonstrators from the scene of protests to squad cars. Chicago protesters also marched on segregated school construction sites, chained themselves to construction equipment, and conducted a "lay-down" in front of moving trucks, bulldozers, and squad cars. A year later, the vice chairman of the Cleveland chapter of CORE was accidentally killed when a bulldozer rolled backward and crushed him as he lay behind it. An all-black school was nonetheless soon erected on the same site.

Vigorous protests against school and residential segregation emerged, but they were far less successful than the campaigns for access to public accommodations and certain inner-city jobs. Whites vehemently opposed residential desegregation movements, partly because such movements promised to break down segregation in schools and jobs in the segregated suburban periphery, where federal transportation, housing, and urban renewal projects reinforced patterns of residential segregation along racial lines. In 1947 and again in 1956, Congress provided for the construction of more than eighty thousand miles of highway and facilitated the spread of all-white communities. Expenditures for highway construction increased to over $2 billion in 1949; $3 billion in 1953; and to over $4 billion in 1955. The Interstate Highway Act of 1956 provided another $60 billion for highway construction nationwide. At the same time, the Federal Housing Administration and the Veterans' Administration underwrote the spread of white families in new suburban homes. Before World War II, private lending agencies customarily required families to place 50 percent down payments on homeowner loans and set short ten-year limits on repayment of the loan in full. The government eased the burden on white homeowners by allowing low 5- to 10-percent down payments and up to thirty years to repay loans at low 2- to 3-percent interest rates. Suburban real estate developers rushed to the fore to build housing for expanding postwar white baby boomer families. The builder Arthur Levitt of Long Island, New York, revolutionized the housing market by applying mass production techniques to home construction. Levitt built model planned communities in Pennsylvania, New Jersey, and New York. His so-called Levittowns required that such settlements house "members of the Caucasian Race" only. Such restrictions persisted informally through the 1950s and only gradually diminished during the 1960s.

Urban renewal programs included funds for new public housing projects for the working class and poor, but such programs failed to offset the destruction of existing housing defined as "slum," "blighted," or unfit for human habitation. In Pittsburgh, for example, the city's urban renewal project resulted in the destruction of the Lower Hill District, where the largest proportion of the city's black population resided. Under the rubric of Renaissance I, urban renewal displaced some fifteen hundred black families to make room for the new Civic Arena and luxury apartments. Displaced families crowded into available public housing projects and into emerging black neighborhoods in other parts of the city, including the Upper Hill, the Homewood-Brushton area, and East Liberty. Similarly, according to a report of the Chicago Urban League, urban renewal forced "new slums" to develop in place of those it cleared and forced blacks to "double-up in areas of transition"—that is, the previously all-white neighborhoods of Oakland, Kenwood, Hyde Park, and Woodlawn in the Cottage Grove Avenue area to the east; Park Manor and Englewood to the south and southwest; and North Lawndale on the west side, which became the second largest black community within the Chicago metropolitan area. In New York, federal housing policies not only encouraged the continuing concentration of African Americans in Harlem, Brooklyn's Bedford-Stuyvesant, and the Bronx's Morrisania–Mott Haven section but also helped to fuel the movement of blacks into the South Jamaica–St. Albans area in southern Queens, where the black population doubled between 1940 and 1950 and increased by another 125 percent by 1960. Cincinnati's urban redevelopment policies underlay the transformation of the city's Avondale-Corryville section, near the University of Cincinnati, into the so-called second ghetto. Within less than three decades the black population had increased from a minority in the area to over 80 percent. In the urban West, African Americans constituted the majority of public housing residents in the Bay Area cities of Oakland, Richmond, Vallejo, and Berkeley, whereas working-class whites moved increasingly into industrial suburbs like Milpitas, Fremont, and San Leandro.

Housing-related violence regularly erupted on the edges of expanding black urban communities. Out of nearly five hundred racial incidents reported by the Chicago Commission on Human Relations between 1945 and 1950, over 70 percent related to housing or residential property. In 1947, when a few black veterans gained access to the Fernwood Park Homes, a Chicago Housing Authority project in the midst of a white neighborhood, some fifteen hundred whites surrounded the facility. They threatened to destroy it rather than permit its occupancy by black veterans and their families. For three nights, police guarded the unit against mobs, who then attacked black motorists, pedestrians, and patrons of nearby streetcars. The city stationed some seven hundred officers on duty around the clock for nearly two weeks to quash the riot. Two years later, a similar riot broke out in the Englewood District when whites mobilized to block what they feared would be the sale of a home to a black family. In 1951, in the city's working-class suburb of Cicero, a mob of some two thousand to five thousand whites attacked an apartment building housing a single black family among its twenty tenants. For several nights, mobs set fire to the building. Only the mobilization of 450 National Guardsmen along with the local police and sheriff's department brought the crowd under control. Unlike many local incidents of this nature, this one attracted worldwide attention, including coverage in newspapers in Pakistan and Singapore. Fifteen years later, when Martin Luther King Jr. and the Southern Christian Leadership Conference (SCLC) targeted Chicago for protests to break down housing segregation, white residents met the marchers with racist epithets, bricks, bottles, knives, and Confederate flags. In one march into the city's Marquette Park neighborhood, King was hit in the head by a brick and knocked to the ground. Following the march, the Nobel Laureate reported: "I've never seen anything like it. I've been in many demonstrations all across the south, but I can say that I have never seen—even in Mississippi and Alabama—mobs as hostile and as hate-filled as I've seen in Chicago."

In Detroit, white homeowners formed over 190 associations designed to prevent blacks from moving into their neighborhoods. Such associations targeted what they called the "colored," "Negro," "undesirable," or "Nigger" problem and "Property Values." They regularly held "emergency meetings" to discuss resistance to black occupancy by any legal or extralegal means available. In April 1955, the family of autoworker Easby Wilson purchased a new home in a predominantly white neighborhood at 18199 Riopelle Street. Before they could occupy the premises, someone broke into the house, damaged the walls and floors, stopped up the drains, turned the water faucets on, and splattered black paint all over the place. Undaunted, the Wilsons nonetheless moved in but suffered an escalation of harassment—threatening phone calls; snakes in the basement; egg-, paint-, and rock-throwing incidents; and recurring mobs of as many as four hundred people who yelled, jeered, and hurled obscenities at the family. Although the Wilsons eventually moved out, other blacks continued to insist on their right to live in previously all-white neighborhoods. Such incidents would continue through the 1950s and early 1960s. In 1963 alone, the Detroit Commission on Community Relations reported over sixty violent incidents involving blacks and housing in predominantly white areas.

Similar incidents occurred in Seattle, Brooklyn, and Cincinnati. In 1956, when a black family purchased a home in a predominantly white community, the head of a Seattle neighborhood association appeared on the family's front lawn. He told the family that the association wanted to "buy you people out." "The neighbors," he threatened, "won't stand for this [that is, black occupancy]." At about the same time, in south Brooklyn, whites stoned the home of a black woman, verbally taunted members of the family, and piled refuse on the lot next door and menacingly set it afire. Black families in other sections of the city—Canarsie, Park Slope, and East Flatbush—faced similar threats, including window smashing and arson. When the Cincinnati Metropolitan Housing Authority proposed a project for poor and black residents in one area, white residents formed homeowners' associations, asking their neighbors, "Do you want Niggers in your backyard?" Some African American families would later recall the dangers that they encountered in such pioneering efforts to open up previously closed neighborhoods to black occupancy. Ethel Johnson, a Chicagoan, remembered how her family "barricaded the doors with furniture and put a mattress behind it." She also described how the family "crawled around" on "hands and knees when the missiles started coming through the windows. . . . Then they [the mobs] started to throw gasoline-soaked rags stuck in pop bottles. They also threw flares and torches. The crowds didn't leave . . . until daybreak."

African Americans in the urban North and West increasingly described their struggle for equal rights in the language of the southern freedom movement. At a march and protest rally in San Francisco, one banner explicitly linked the civil rights struggle across regional lines: "We March in Unity for Freedom in Birmingham and Equality of Opportunity in San Francisco." In New York City, a Corona resident explained the local fight against school segregation: "Some of us felt that we should march across Junction Boulevard into Jackson Heights just like King and them did at the [Edmund] Pettus Bridge in Alabama. Because, you see, Junction Boulevard was our Mason-Dixon line. There was no difference." A CORE officer reinforced the point, declaring that New York City's mounted police were "no different than police dogs in Birmingham." In 1966, when Martin Luther King Jr. and SCLC moved the civil rights campaign to Chicago, they symbolized the merger of both the image and the reality of the southern, northern, and western movements for social change. As white resistance escalated nationwide, northern and western blacks increasingly lost faith in the efficacy of nonviolent direct action. Their search for alternative strategies underlay the spread of the Nation of Islam and the outbreak of urban violence.

THE NATION OF ISLAM, MALCOLM X, AND URBAN REBELLIONS

Although northern and western blacks adopted nonviolent direct action techniques to achieve their goals, they were less philosophically and ideologically committed to such methods than their southern counterparts. By the mid-1960s, their impatience with nonviolent direct action gained clear expression in the growing appeal of the Nation of Islam and the outbreak of violence in inner-city black communities. As noted in previous chapters, the Nation of Islam had its beginnings during the early 1930s, when the Georgia-born Elijah Muhammad (formerly Robert Poole) established the order. Muhammad followed the lead of W. D. Fard, the group's initial founder, who claimed that he had come to America from the Holy City of Mecca to secure "freedom, justice, and equality" for blacks living in the "wilderness of North America, surrounded and robbed" by "satan," the white man, or the "caucasian devil."

As noted in Chapter 19, Muhammad and several of his followers went to jail rather than register for the draft during World War II. During his prison term between 1942 and 1946, Muhammad discovered that the mainline black Christian churches largely neglected incarcerated blacks. Following his release from prison, he directed the Nation of Islam's energy toward proselytizing among the black urban poor, with a particular focus on the prison population. With only four Muslim temples in 1945—in Detroit, Chicago, Milwaukee, and Washington, D.C.—the order had added eleven new temples by 1955; by the early 1960s, it had fifty temples in over twenty-eight cities in twenty-two states and the District of Columbia. At the same time, membership soared from an estimated one thousand to ten thousand registered Muslims.

Malcolm X

The rising influence of the Nation of Islam took increasing focus in the activities of Malcolm X, the order's most energetic postwar spokesperson. Born in Omaha, Nebraska, Malcolm Little converted to Islam while serving a prison sentence for robbery between 1946 and 1952. Shortly after his conversion, Malcolm Little became Malcolm X. After his release from prison, he soon became the Nation of Islam's most articulate and influential young minister. Although the organization launched vigorous membership campaigns in black urban communities, it eschewed the nonviolent direct action movement to desegregate American institutions. Malcolm denounced the civil rights movement as an exercise in "self-hatred" because it risked black lives in an effort to gain access to the households of white supremacists. Malcolm repeatedly challenged Martin Luther King Jr., Roy Wilkins, Bayard Rustin, Whitney Young, and other civil rights leaders to justify their pursuit of integrationist goals in the face of mob rule.

As an alternative to the nonviolent direct action movement, Malcolm advocated armed self-defense and separatism, but he forcefully countered efforts to label his position as "fascist," "violent," or "racist." He repeatedly declared that "for the white man to ask the black man if he hates him is just like the rapist asking the raped, or the wolf asking the sheep, 'Do you hate me?' The white man is in no moral position to accuse anyone else of hate." As Malcolm's influence increased, however, he came into increasing conflict with Elijah Muhammad. In 1963, Malcolm permanently broke with the Nation of Islam when Muhammad silenced him,

Nation of Islam minister Malcolm X speaks to reporters in Washington, D.C., in May 1963, shortly after black children were sent to the frontlines of the civil rights struggle in Birmingham, Alabama. *AP/Wide World Photos*

ostensibly for commenting on the assassination of President Kennedy. Malcolm had said to a reporter that Kennedy's death represented an example of "the chickens coming home to roost . . . that the hate in white men had not stopped with killing of defenseless black people, but that hate, allowed to spread unchecked, finally had struck down this country's Chief of State."

Malcolm faced increasing difficulties within the Nation of Islam partly because he sought ways to involve the order in the rapidly accelerating freedom struggle of black people. Despite its potent rhetoric of nation building, self-determination, and the right to use violence in self-defense, the Nation of Islam refused to participate in direct action campaigns, including the March on Washington. As Malcolm sought to extend the Nation of Islam's reach deeper into the black community, the organization's disengagement from the civil rights struggle struck him as increasingly untenable. As Malcolm debated civil rights leaders in a variety of public forums, he received accolades for dissecting and enunciating the problems of blacks in America, but the Nation of Islam's stand on the struggle exposed important weaknesses in his position. On one occasion, CORE's James Farmer pressed

SOURCES FROM THE PAST

1963

Malcolm X Defines Revolution and Black Nationalism

I would like to make a few comments concerning the difference between the black revolution and the Negro revolution. . . . First, what is a revolution? . . .

Look at the American Revolution in 1776. That revolution was for what? For land. Why did they want land? Independence. How was it carried out? Bloodshed. . . . The French Revolution—what was it based on? The landless against the landlord. What was it for? Land. How did they get it? Bloodshed. Was no love lost, was no compromise, was no negotiation. . . .

The Russian Revolution—what was it based on? Land; the landless against the landlord. How did they bring it about? Bloodshed. You haven't got a revolution that doesn't involve bloodshed. And you're afraid to bleed. . . .

If violence is wrong in America, violence is wrong abroad. If it is wrong to be violent defending black women and black children and black babies and black men, then it is wrong for America to draft us and make us violent abroad in defense of her. And if it is right for America to draft us, and teach us how to be violent in defense of her, then it is right for you and me to do whatever is necessary to defend our own people right here in this country. . . .

So I cite these various revolutions, brothers and sisters, to show you that you don't have a peaceful revolution. You don't have a turn-the-other-cheek revolution. There's no such thing as a nonviolent revolution. The only kind of revolution that is nonviolent is the Negro revolution. The only revolution in which the goal is loving your enemy is the Negro revolution. It's the only revolution in which the goal is a desegregated lunch counter, a desegregated theater, a desegregated park, and a desegregated public toilet; you can sit down next to white folks—on the toilet. That's no revolution. Revolution is based on land. Land is the basis of all independence. Land is the basis of freedom, justice, and equality.

The white man knows what a revolution is. He knows that the black revolution is worldwide in scope and in nature. The black revolution is sweeping Asia, is sweeping Africa, is rearing its head in Latin America. The Cuban Revolution—that's a revolution. They overturned the system. Revolution is in Asia, revolution is in Africa, and the white man is screaming because he sees revolution in Latin America. How do you think he'll react to you when you learn what a real revolution is? You don't know what a revolution is. If you did, you wouldn't use that word. . . .

. . . A revolutionary wants land so he can set up his own nation, an independent nation. These Negroes aren't asking for any nation—they're trying to crawl back on the plantation.

When you want a nation, that's called nationalism. . . . All the revolutions that are going on in Asia and Africa today are based on what?—black nationalism. A revolutionary is a black nationalist. He wants a nation. . . . If you're afraid of black nationalism, you're afraid of revolution. And if you love revolution, you love black nationalism.

Source: Clayborne Carson, David J. Garrow, Gerald Gill, Vincent Harding, and Darlene Clark Hine, eds., *The Eyes on the Prize Civil Rights Reader: Documents, Speeches, and Firsthand Accounts from the Black Freedom Struggle, 1954–1990* (New York: Viking Penguin, 1991), pp. 251–254. Copyright © 1965, 1989 by Betty Shabazz and Pathfinder Press. Reprinted by permission.

Malcolm with the statement: "Brother Malcolm, don't tell us any more about the disease—that is clear in our minds. Now, tell us, physician, what is thy cure?" In bars and on the streets, poor and working-class blacks also raised similar concerns: "All he's ever done was talk, CORE and SNCC and some of them people of Dr. King's are out getting beat over the head."

After leaving the Nation of Islam, Malcolm soon responded to his critics. Following his pilgrimage to Mecca, he returned to the United States as El-Hajj-Malik El-Shabazz and set up the Muslim Mosque, Inc., in March 1964. A few months later, he launched the nondenominational political Organization of African American Unity (OAAU), modeled after the Organization of African Unity. After initiating these organizations, Malcolm announced that he was now "prepared to cooperate in local civil rights actions in the South and elsewhere and shall do so because every campaign for specific objectives can only heighten the political consciousness of the Negroes and intensify their identification against white society." He clearly articulated a philosophy of black nationalism (see box), emphasizing black control of their own community—its economy, culture, and politics, including the police forces. In the meantime, Malcolm urged activists to create "rifle clubs" and defend the black community from terrorist attacks. Although Malcolm continued to emphasize black nationalism, he now held out hope for an interracial alliance with progressive white activists. He told photographer Gordon Parks that his Muslim period with Elijah Muhammad "was a bad scene. . . . The sickness and madness of those days—I'm glad to be free of them."

Before Malcolm gained the necessary support for his new nationalist initiative, an assassin's bullet ended his life during a meeting of the OAAU at the Audubon Ballroom in New York City on 21 February 1965. Existing evidence suggests that the FBI and members of the Nation of Islam were responsible for his death. Shortly after embarking on his new and broader engagement with the freedom struggle, Malcolm had said: "It's a time for martyrs now. And if I'm going to be one, it will be in the cause of brotherhood. That's the only thing that can save this country." Though short-lived, Malcolm's efforts struck a deep chord within a broad cross-section of the African American community. Although African Americans would later reevaluate the gender implications of Malcolm's message (as we will see in Chapter 22), few disagreed at the time with the eloquent words of Malcolm's eulogist, actor Ossie Davis:

> Malcolm was our manhood, our living, black manhood! This was his meaning to his people. And, in honoring him, we honor the best in ourselves, then for what he was and is—a Prince—our own black shining Prince!—who didn't hesitate to die, because he loved us so.

Violence in the Cities

Although Malcolm's message would gradually influence a broad cross-section of the black community, it especially resonated among blacks in the inner cities of the urban North and West. Poor and working-class blacks expressed growing impatience

Selected Urban Riots/Revolts, 1964–1967					
Year	City	Deaths	Injuries	Arrests	Property Loss
1964	Harlem	1	140	500	$1,000s
1965	Los Angeles	34	1,032	3,952	$40 million
1966	Chicago	2	1,004	400	$1,000s
1967	Newark	26	1,100	1,600	$15 million
1967	Detroit	43	2,000	5,000	$500 million

with the slow pace of change by attacking white-owned property and other symbols of authority within the black urban community. During the mid-1960s, violence erupted in New York's Harlem (1964); Los Angeles (1965); Chicago (1966); Cleveland (1966); Newark (1967); Detroit (1967); and in the wake of Martin Luther King Jr.'s assassination in 1968, virtually every major city in the United States, including the nation's capital (see table). Thousands of African Americans poured into the streets. They smashed windows, looted, and burned white-owned stores; attacked, overturned, and burned automobiles carrying white motorists; shot at policemen; and prevented firemen from extinguishing flames that spread from building to building. Numerous arrests, injuries, and deaths, mostly involving blacks, soon resulted from the violence.

In the summer of 1966 alone, federal officials reported some forty "civil disorders" in American cities. Two years later, within a week after King's assassination, violence broke out in over one hundred cities. Government reports placed the death toll at forty-one blacks and five whites, along with thousands of arrests and millions of dollars in property damage. The most violent episode occurred in the nation's capital. In Washington, D.C., over a three-day period, thousands of black men, women, and children entered the streets, setting over twenty-six hundred fires, smashing storefront windows, and looting white-owned places of business. Only after the city had mobilized some 130,000 policemen and National Guardsmen did the violence cease, with the arrest of some twenty thousand participants. Property damage amounted to an estimated $100 million. One young participant declared that "almost everyone" participated: "I'm talking about women and children as well as [old] adult males and also young adult males." Between the outbreak of violence in Harlem in 1964 and the four years following Martin Luther King's death, inner-city explosions resulted in an estimated sixty thousand arrests, ten thousand serious injuries, 250 deaths, and billions of dollars in property damage.

Although each outbreak of violence exhibited aspects of spontaneous "riots," they also displayed crucial elements of "rebellion" or "revolt." They were deeply rooted in specific social conditions and forms of racial and class inequality at the local level. They were also fueled partly by the bitter opposition that African Americans faced in the southern freedom struggle. Some members of the crowds could be heard saying, "We've got no rights at all—it's just like Selma!" as well as "Burn, baby, burn!" and "Long live Malcolm X." Participants attacked and looted white-owned property and stores of white merchants who paid low wages and set exorbitant prices for their goods. Some participants explained their behavior as a form of "reclaiming property taken through low wages and high prices." Black merchants as well as some whites hastily posted signs in their store windows declaring: "Soul Brother," "Negro Owned," or "Owned by a Brother." In Washington, D.C., one participant and observer noted that participants did not need such signs in any case: "The brothers know who owns the joint." A popular black restaurant, Mama San's, survived, although "she didn't have 'soul sister' up there. She wasn't even there!"

The elements of revolt were perhaps most acute in Detroit (August 1967), the site of the most destructive outbreak of violence before spring 1968. Although a police raid on a "blind pig" (an after-hours entertainment and gambling spot that usually sold alcoholic beverages illegally) precipitated the violence, the underlying causes were much deeper. Detroit policemen had routinely raided such establishments, but this time crowds gathered and soon challenged police procedures. As the deputy superintendent of the Detroit police force later recalled, "The crowd just increased and increased and increased. . . . the rioters mobilized faster than the police did." According to Ron Scott, a twenty-two-year-old autoworker:

> Inside of most black people there was a time bomb. There was a pot that was about to overflow, and there was rage that was about to come out. And the rebellion just provided an opportunity for that. I mean, why else would people get so upset, cops raiding a blind pig. They'd done that numerous times before. But people just got tired, people just got tired of it. And it just exploded.

Detroit congressman John Conyers came to a similar conclusion:

> People were letting feelings out that had never been let out before, that had been bottled up. It really wasn't that they were that mad about an after-hours place being raided and some people being beat up as a result of the closing down of that place. It was the whole desperate situation of being black in Detroit and now, all of a sudden, there was no supervening force. There was nobody on top of you.

Bookstore owner Edward Vaughn, made the same point: "We were not surprised that the riot came, because we knew that the unrest was there—it was seething, it had always been there, and we were not surprised that it happened."

Despite deep-seated grievances underlying the eruption of violence, the explosion elicited a range of reactions from black residents. For some youths, it was a festive occasion. Albert Wilson, a thirteen-year-old at the time, recalled:

> It was kind of like a carnival, a parade, a party, because everybody that was there was laughing. No one was crying or worried. If you saw me running down the street, you saw me running with a smile on my face. I saw people running from

stores with televisions but with a smile on their face. Everybody was happy. That's about it. Everybody was happy that day.

Other African Americans vividly recalled the burning, the flames, the warlike atmosphere. Daisey Nunley, a homeowner, recalled:

Everywhere I looked I could see flames burning. I looked towards Twelfth Street and over St. Agnes Church. I could see the flames just burning. Twelfth Street was just burning, all you could see was just flames, and in the air you could see the ash just fluttering down. The smell of char, that burning smell, was in the air, and it was just smoky, the whole area.

Other blacks like bookstore owner Edward Vaughn believed that the hoped-for revolution had finally arrived but expressed great ambivalence: "It felt like the revolution was here. But it also felt like we were going to lose the revolution, because I knew that you could not defeat tanks with bricks."

In each community, existing social conditions—unemployment, residential crowding, police brutality, and inadequate access to essential social services—underlay the frustrations that fueled the violence. In the Watts District of Los Angeles, where the riot of 1965 took thirty-four lives and resulted in nearly four thousand arrests and $40 million in property damage, over 250,000 African Americans occupied a space that represented four times more people per square block than the city as a whole. Unemployment stood at 34 percent among adult black males (compared with about 6 percent for all the city's adult men), and two-thirds of the residents received some form of public assistance. The city's streets and sanitation departments offered irregular service, allowing garbage and broken glass to take over the streets. Although Watts was 98 percent black, all but 5 of its 205 policemen were white. In Cleveland, the black unemployment rate was four times the city's average; only thirteen blacks worked in the city's construction trades; and blacks comprised fewer than 4 percent of apprentices on federally funded job training programs. Moreover, the city's power structure, including the mayor and the chief of police, regularly ignored the requests of local blacks for hearings to voice their grievances. Blacks in Harlem, Newark, Detroit, San Francisco, Chicago, and other major metropolitan areas told similar tales of tight space, disproportionately high levels of unemployment and poverty, inadequate sanitation services, predominantly white police forces, and insensitive municipal officials.

Although the urban revolts were fundamentally driven by deep-seated grievances over existing social conditions, they were also partly driven by what sociologists and psychologists called the "rising expectations" for a better life that the civil rights movement had generated. As noted in Chapter 20, the postwar economic position of blacks was not entirely pessimistic. African Americans not only slowly expanded their numbers into new industries but also gained access to a broader range of jobs in the middle class. In Chicago, when young blacks booed Martin Luther King Jr.'s call for a "Freedom Sunday March" to City Hall, King later admitted that the civil rights movement itself had generated a level of expectation that

Ironic, things beginning to get better, worse riots.

it had not met. According to King, large numbers of poor and working-class blacks were justifiably upset with the slow pace of change:

> For twelve years I, and others like me, had held out radiant promises of progress. I had preached to them about my dream . . . "all, here and now." I had urged them to have faith in America and in white society. Their hopes had soared. They were now booing because they felt that we were unable to deliver on our promises.

Coupled with new civil rights legislation and the widely articulated "dream" that King expressed during the March on Washington, Johnson's "War on Poverty" promised to eliminate want and suffering from the land, both rural and urban. Yet congressional appropriations remained too low for the program to meet its loudly proclaimed goals. According to a former assistant director of the Office of Economic Opportunity, most poor people had no contact with the War on Poverty "except to hear the promises of a better life to come." Dashed hopes for a better future certainly helped to foment rebellion.

Although local, state, and federal officials quickly mobilized their military and police forces and put down the urban revolts, some participants nonetheless claimed victory for their side. In the aftermath of the Watts riots, for example, one black youth exclaimed: "We won!" When asked how he could draw that conclusion in the face of so many deaths, massive property damage in the black neighborhood, and thousands of arrests and injuries, he replied: "We won . . . because we made them pay attention to us." In some respects, he was right. Social, civic, and philanthropic organizations and public officials hastily set up study commissions to determine what had occurred and to make recommendations for reforms, mainly to restore order and ensure peace in the future. Following the Watts rebellion, California governor Jerry Brown appointed a commission to "prepare an accurate chronology and description of the riots and attempt to draw any lessons which may be learned from retrospective study of these events." Under the chairmanship of businessman John McCone, the McCone Commission released its report, *Violence in the City—An End or a Beginning?* in December 1965. The report largely exonerated public, civic, and business leaders of blame for the events of August but recommended improvements in educational, employment, and health services for the African American community. President Lyndon Baines Johnson established the National Advisory Commission on Civil Disorders on 28 July 1967. He charged the commission, under the chairmanship of former governor Otto Kerner of Illinois, to answer three basic questions about the spread of racial violence in urban America: "What happened? Why did it happen? What can be done to prevent it from happening again?"

In less than a year, the commission released its report, declaring that the perilous state of race relations required swift action. The commission concluded: "Our Nation is moving toward two societies, one black, one white—separate and unequal." The report nonetheless maintained that the continuing polarization of American society was not inevitable. Accordingly, the commission recommended "a commitment to national action—compassionate, massive, and sustained, backed by the resources of the most powerful and the richest nation on this earth. From every American it will require new attitudes, new understanding, and, above all, new will." The commission recommended that the federal legislature enact "a comprehensive and enforceable federal open housing law to cover the sale or rental of all housing, including single family homes," along with "new and vigorous action to remove artificial barriers" to employment and educational opportunities. Congress soon passed the Civil Rights Act of 1968, which outlawed racial discrimination in both the sale and rental of privately owned housing.

Along with governmental responses to urban violence, civil rights organizations also sharpened their focus on the needs of the black working class and poor. As noted in Chapter 20, the National Urban League initiated new programs to deal with social service and employment issues. Similarly, SCLC launched economic assistance programs and protest activities like Operation Breadbasket. Symbolic of these changes in orientation was the work of Martin Luther King Jr. on the eve of his assassination (4 April 1968) in Memphis, Tennessee. King was assassinated during a campaign to help striking sanitation workers in the city. William Rutherford, a former executive director of SCLC, later explained King's shift to economic improvement of the poor as a priority in the civil rights movement:

> Dr. King . . . said, "Fine, we now have the right to vote. Fine. We can now go to any restaurant, any hotel, anyplace we want to in America, but we don't have the means. So what good does it do for people to go to any restaurant in the world if you don't have the money to pay for a meal?" So, he says, we've got to attack the whole issue of poverty and economic deprivation.

In early December 1967, King announced that in April 1968, SCLC would bring poor people from around the nation to Washington, D.C., to "stay until America responds."

After King's death, his successor, Ralph David Abernathy, organized the Poor People's Campaign. Within a month of King's murder, poor people from across the nation headed for Washington, D.C. The SCLC contingent gathered in Memphis for the trip. At the outset of the march, Abernathy told the gathering: "We have business on the road to freedom. . . . We must prove to white America that you can kill the leader [the dreamer] but you cannot kill the dream." On May 13, Abernathy welcomed poor people from across the nation to "Resurrection City," a makeshift camp on the National Mall near the Lincoln Memorial, where the March on Washington had taken place five years earlier. But times had changed. This time the federal government and the nation had turned away from the civil rights agenda.

On 24 June 1968, the capital city police evicted the marchers from their encampment using tear gas. Jesse Jackson, the unofficial mayor of Resurrection City, later recalled that day: "The dreamer had been killed in Memphis and there was an attempt now to kill the dream itself, which was to feed the hungry, which was to bring the people together. . . . They drove us out with tear gas." Following their

In spring 1968, a group of Atlanta, Georgia, marchers head for Washington, D.C., where they would help to erect "Resurrection City" as part of the Poor People's Campaign. *James L. Amos/Corbis*

eviction from the mall, the campers expressed "an awful sense of betrayal and abandonment," but Jackson urged them "to keep the struggle moving—if you will, to keep hope alive." Before charting the ways that blacks moved beyond Resurrection City, however, we must turn first to the ways that the modern civil rights movement and the urban revolts helped to reorient black creative energies toward the freedom struggle.

INTELLECTUAL, ARTISTIC, AND CULTURAL DEVELOPMENTS

In the wake of the modern civil rights movement, black artists underscored their hope for the desegregation of American society. Unlike novelist Richard Wright, who sought to harness art to the class struggle and the revolutionary transformation of capitalist institutions, postwar writers hoped to transcend what they saw as the limits of "race" or "protest art," but they nonetheless confirmed their commitment to the political aims of the modern freedom struggle in the long run.

Black Writers

Ralph Waldo Ellison, a protégé of Richard Wright, and James Baldwin best captured the emerging mood of the civil rights generation. In 1947, Ellison produced his classic work, the novel *Invisible Man*. Born in Oklahoma City in 1914, Ellison attended Tuskegee Institute during the early 1930s but left for New York City before graduating. In New York, as noted in Chapter 18, he worked on the Federal Writers Project, where he met Richard Wright. After serving time in the U.S. Merchant Marine during World War II, Ellison returned to New York, where he soon received a grant from the Julius Rosenwald Fund. Partly with funding from the Rosenwald Foundation, he initiated and completed *Invisible Man*, his first novel and the only one to be published during his lifetime. Based partly on Ellison's own journey from the South to New York City, *Invisible Man* carefully probed both inter- and intraracial relations. But literary critics gave Ellison most credit for probing the color line in a new way in his use of symbolic rather than naturalistic language to explore the black-white encounter. In the opening lines of the book, his principal character declared:

> I AM AN invisible man. . . . I am invisible, understand, simply because people refuse to see me . . . you're constantly being bumped against by those of poor vision. You wonder whether you aren't simply a phantom in other people's minds. . . . It's when you feel like this that, out of resentment, you begin to bump back. And, let me confess, you feel that way most of the time.

For his part, within a ten-year period, James Baldwin published three collections of essays, a play, and three novels: *Go Tell It on the Mountain* (1953), *Giovanni's Room* (1956), and *Another Country* (1962). Although the latter two works reflected Baldwin's effort to address the complicated issues of sexuality as well as race, the former best expressed his engagement with the issues of race, class, and social change during the period. Baldwin, a World War II veteran and former minister, set *Go Tell It on the Mountain* within the urban North but used the South to help explain the choices that confronted black people in the postwar years, and the part that they would play in shaping their own future.

Some postwar black writers tested the limits of the desegregation movement by placing the lives of whites, rather than blacks, at the center of their stories. In *Seraph of the Suwanee* (1948), Zora Neale Hurston explored the lives of whites in the rural South. Similarly, although Chester Himes explored the problematic relationship between black and white workers, the labor movement, and the Communist Party in his second novel, *Lonely Crusade* (1947), he moved white characters to the forefront of his postwar novel, *Cast the First Stone* (1952), a story about white prison inmates. Young writers like Willard Motley, Ann Petry, and William Gardner Smith also produced works on white subjects, but the popular novelist Frank Yerby was perhaps most well known. Yerby produced a series of historical novels that appealed to the masses of whites in Europe and America: *The Foxes of Harrow* (1946), *The Vixens* (1947), *The Golden Hawk* (1948), and *The Saracen Blade* (1952). Each of these books was also adapted to Hollywood film. At the same time, as certain black writers moved across the color line and wrote about whites or ostensibly nonblack subjects, white writers also continued to mine black materials: William Demky, Arthur Gordon, Loren Wahl, Truman Nelson, and Robert Penn Warren in his New Orleans–based novel *Band of Angels* (1955).

Although some black writers took advantage of cracks in the segregationist system and appealed to white audiences on their own terms, others addressed the unfinished work of the freedom struggle. In 1950, the poet Gwendolyn Brooks became the first African American to win the Pulitzer Prize for poetry, for her volume *Annie Allen* (1949). Although Brooks urged young poets to "polish" their technique because they had "a duty to words," she also confirmed the claims of the freedom movement on her art: "Grant me that I am human, that I hurt / Not that I now ask alms, in shame gone hollow. / Nor cringe outside the loud and sumptuous gate. / *Admit me to our mutual estate* [my italics]." In her poem "Fight fight. Then fiddle" (1963), Brooks declared:

> Be deaf to music and to beauty blind.
> Win war. Rise bloody, maybe not too late
> For having first to civilize a space
> Wherein to lay your violin with grace.

The poet and playwright LeRoi Jones (later Amiri Baraka) expressed similar sentiments. Although his first collection of poems, *Preface to a Twenty-Volume Suicide Note* (1961), emerged from the rebellious intellectual world of Greenwich Village rather than the expanding civil rights struggle, Baraka upheld Richard Wright's legacy. As he put it, "A writer must have a point of view, or he cannot be a good writer. He must be standing somewhere in the world, or else he is not one of us, and his commentary is of little value." As we will see in Chapter 22, Baraka would lead a strong resurgence of interest in Richard Wright's approach to art, politics, and society during the Black Power movement.

As poets articulated the aspirations of postwar blacks in verse, black playwrights used the stage to express similar ideas. In 1959, Lorraine Hansberry's *Raisin in the Sun* received the prestigious New York Drama Critics Circle Award. Set on the South Side of Chicago, Hansberry's *Raisin in the Sun* offers a compelling look at the rising aspirations of northern blacks. When the play's central character Walter Younger's business venture fails, it jeopardizes the family's plans to buy a house in the suburbs, using dear funds from the proceeds of an insurance policy, paid to Younger's mother on the death of her husband. The play shows how such strivings placed tremendous strain on black families, particularly on male-female relationships, including those between wives and husbands as well as mothers and sons. Other postwar black playwrights included Theodore Ward, Louis Peterson, Lofton Mitchell, Ossie David, Douglas Turner Ward, James Baldwin, and Amiri Baraka. In 1964, Baraka staged his play *Dutchman*, which probed the growing volatility of black-white relations as blacks increasingly realized that playing by the rules of middle-class respectability did not insulate them from racial discrimination.

Black Visual Artists

Compared with poets and playwrights, black visual artists took a more ambiguous journey to the expanding freedom struggle. Like some of their literary counterparts, some hoped to transcend the limits of what they perceived as "race art." Providing a vehicle for their effort was the growing popularity of abstraction in the visual arts. Since this art form downplayed recognizable objects in favor of "nonobjective" or "nonrepresentational" paintings and sculpture, the social backgrounds of the artist, as well as the subject matter of the art, were less easily identifiable than they were in the works of earlier black artists like Archibald Motley, Palmer Hayden, and Augusta Savage, to name a few. In 1947, for example, a group of black artists and art scholars—Hale Woodruff, Richmond Barthé James V. Herring, and Romare Bearden—urged the International Business Machine (IBM) Corporation to drop all references to the racial identity of artists featured in its catalogue of art collections. Woodruff said, "In light of the Negro artist's present achievements in the general framework of American art today . . . there does not exist the necessity to continue all Negro exhibitions which tend to isolate him and segregate him from other American artists."

The largely self-taught artist Romare Bearden became the most widely known black abstractionist. As early as 1945, Bearden produced his series of abstract watercolor and oil paintings entitled *The Passion of Christ,* which included *He Is Risen.* The art community enthusiastically received Bearden's work as a work of "spiritual integrity" and "nobility of theme." According to Bearden, he selected the life of Christ as a symbol of universality:

> The concept supersedes reality and the usual conformist interpretations. The power of the Christ story, its universal recognition, make it unnecessary to dwell on its literary aspects . . . my concern is with those universals that must be digested by the mind and cannot be merely seen by the eye.

Yet Bearden's work was considered too "foreign" for many in the U.S. art community and too conservative for the avant-garde of New York and Paris. Consequently, for a while, Bearden turned away from painting, producing little before his painting *Blue Is the Smoke of War, White the Bones of Men* (c. 1960). Other postwar black abstractionists were the sculptor Richard Hunt (*Arachne,* 1956) and the painters Richard Charleston (*The Family,* 1955), Herbert Gentry (*Untitled Figures,* 1958), and Edward Clark (*Wasted Landscape,* 1961).

Although some black artists used the abstract form to subvert the segregationist system, others used it to broaden their artistic reach without losing touch with the history and culture of black people. The blues informed the New York artist Rose Piper's painting *Slow Down Freight Train* (1946), which she produced after traveling through the South on a Rosenwald Fellowship. A variety of themes from African American life and history shaped Hale Woodruff's *Art of the Negro* (1950–1951). A six-panel mural prepared for the Trevor-Arnett Library of Clark Atlanta University (formerly Atlanta University), the *Art of the Negro* provided a visual history of African Americans from their African background through their New World enslavement and emancipation. Artist Norman Lewis not only produced comments on the perils of the nuclear age in paintings like *Every Atom Glows: Electrons in Luminous Vibrations* (1951) but also created works like *Harlem Court Yard* (1954) and *Harlem Turns White* (1955). Together, these paintings were informed not only by the rhythms of the African American blues and jazz forms but also by consciousness of the rise of predominantly black communities in spaces formerly occupied by whites. Supplementing the work of black painters and sculptors was a growing roster of professional photographers. Gordon Parks's photos for *Life* magazine; Roy DeCarvara's collaborative work with Langston Hughes in *The Sweet Flypaper of Life* (1955); Robert Frank's photos in *The Americans* (1958); and Ernest C. Withers's *Complete Photo Story of Till Murder Case* (1955) all turned photography into a weapon of social struggle. Withers's photographs on the Till murder were featured in the Johnson Publishing Company's *Jet* magazine, sold widely throughout the black community, and helped to intensify the struggle for civil and human rights in the 1950s.

Even as some black artists experimented with different ways of portraying the black condition, others portrayed the stark social reality of poverty in postwar black America. In the early aftermath of World War II, painter Eldzier Cortor produced his *Americana* (1947), featuring a nude black woman stepping from a wooden bathtub onto a chipped linoleum-covered floor in a room with newspapers and magazine covers serving as wallpaper. Before producing the work, Cortor had traveled widely in the Sea Islands of Georgia and South Carolina under a grant from the Rosenwald Fund. Cortor's protest against poverty touched a raw nerve in white consciousness. When the painting reached the exhibit area at the Carnegie Institute of Art in 1947, it became the target of vandalism. Working-class culture was also the theme of Robert Gwathmey's painting *Work Song* (1946), depicting a woman and two men, one strumming a guitar. In her *Negro Woman Series* (1946–1947), Elizabeth Catlett documented the ongoing difficulties that black people faced under the Jim Crow system. In one of the images from the series, *I Have a Special Fear for My Loved Ones* (1946), she depicted the lynching of a black man. Charles White, Catlett's former husband, produced similar works, his *O' Mary, Don't You Weep* (1956) showing two working-class black women overcome with grief.

The Influence of African American Music

The civil rights movement also precipitated changes in music, leisure, entertainment, and sports. Even more so than in the past, African Americans influenced the music of the nation. During the 1940s, a group of black jazz musicians, including trumpeter Dizzy Gillespie, saxophonist Charlie Parker, and pianist Thelonious Monk, used Harlem's Minton's Playhouse and other after-hours clubs to develop new music forms. They modified the big swing band sound of the period and helped to usher in small-band music that became known by jazz fans as "rebop," "bebop," or simply "bop." This music differed from earlier swing and band music by its commitment to improvisational sounds that made it much more listening than dance music. Under the influence of such jazz musicians as trumpeter Miles Davis, bebop gave rise to "cool jazz" during the 1950s. Davis signaled this change with his album *Birth of the Cool* (1949). Another cohort of jazz musicians—saxophonists Ornette Coleman and John Coltrane and bassist Charles Mingus—helped usher in "modern jazz" during the late 1950s and early 1960s. In the meantime, before these new forms of jazz could fully gain their bearings, musicians like Thelonious Monk, Art Blakey, Edwin "Cannonball" Adderley, and Jimmy Smith, among others, spearheaded a strong opposition movement. They protested that jazz was losing touch with its roots in African American blues, spirituals, and gospel traditions and themselves turned back to the basics, emphasizing what musicologists call "hard bop" or "soul jazz."

Although jazz expanded and picked up a broad following among blacks and whites in the postwar years, rhythm and blues best captured the cultural impact of the desegregation movement. As early as 1949, *Billboard* magazine changed the name of its black pop-music chart from "race" records to "rhythm & blues." Five years earlier, Louis Jordan and his band, Tympani Five, had helped pave the way for the transition with the release of some nineteen pop hits, including the million-copy sellers "Is You Is or Is You Ain't My Baby?" (1944) and "Choo Cho Ch'Boogie" (1946). Pivotal to the transition of black music from big swing bands to rhythm and blues, however, was the emergence of independent record companies, black urban radio stations, and popular disc jockeys. In 1947, *Ebony* magazine reported only sixteen black DJs in the entire country; by 1955, there were over five hundred. Some of the most popular DJs appeared on such stations as WXLW, St. Louis; WOKJ, Jackson; KVET, Austin; WMBM, Miami; WDIA, Memphis; WLAC, Nashville; WLOU, Louisville; and the black-owned WERD in Atlanta. DJ Jack Gibson later recalled his experience in launching Atlanta's first black radio station: "I'm proud to have been the jock who flipped the switch October morning in 1949 and greeted the day with a hearty 'Good morning, Atlanta! We are here!'"

Aided by black DJs and radio stations, independent record companies played a major role in the production and dissemination of black music. These companies included Savoy, Apollo, Four Star, Philco-Aladdin, Mercury, Atlantic, and the black-owned Vee Jay and Motown, among others. With five independent recording companies at the end of World War II, Los Angeles had more independent companies recording black music than any other city. Independent record companies also sprang up in Memphis, Houston, Nashville, Chicago, and particularly New York. In 1949, New York's Atlantic Records had its first hit with Sticks McGee's "Drinkin' Wine Spo-dee-o-dee," but its most significant star was Ruth Brown, who released her first hit, "So Long," in 1949. Over the next five years, she produced ten more hits, including "Teardrops from My Eyes" (1950), "Mama, He Treats Your Daughter Mean" (1953), and "Oh What a Dream" (1954). Because of her lucrative hits for the company, some fans called Atlantic Records "the house that Ruth built." Other performers on the Atlantic label included Big Joe Turner, LaVern Baker, Ray Charles, and the Drifters.

By the mid-1950s, rhythm and blues had increasingly crossed over to the pop charts and had given birth to a new musical genre called rock 'n' roll, America's most popular music during the period. White record companies initially adopted the term *rock 'n' roll* to camouflage the music's roots in rhythm and blues. To peddle their own ostensibly less threatening version of black music to white audiences, record companies groomed white singers to remake hits first made popular on the black charts. The executive of one white record company declared: "If I could find a white man who had the Negro sound and the Negro feel, I could make a billion dollars." White rock 'n' roll singers Elvis Presley and Bill Haley and His Comets answered the call for black-sounding white artists, but young whites increasingly demanded the "real thing"—that is, the songs released by black artists themselves. White DJs like Alan Freed of Cleveland and later New York facilitated this process by playing music by black and white artists on their popular radio shows.

Despite substantial efforts to censor the movement, a growing number of black rhythm and blues artists had hits on both black and white charts. Solo artists like Chuck Berry, Bo Diddley, Ray Charles, and Little Richard not only had crossover hits but also appeared on the *Ed Sullivan Show* and *American Bandstand*. Such appearances made it increasingly difficult for white critics of black music to divorce rock 'n' roll from its roots in, and continuing links to, rhythm and blues. Formed under the proprietorship of the former prizefighter Berry Gordy in 1959, Motown became a major producer of crossover artists like Martha Reeves and the Vandellas, Mary Wells, Marvin Gaye, the Supremes, the Temptations, and numerous others

Sidney Poitier embraces Claudia McNeil, playing his mother in *A Raisin in the Sun* (1961). To Poitier's left and right, respectively, are co-stars Diana Sands and Ruby Dee. *Bettmann/Corbis*

by the mid-1960s. As indicated by the career of rhythm and blues, in significant ways, black music was desegregated earlier than housing, schools, and public accommodations.

Even as black music reached growing numbers of whites and black performers became household names in America, commercial movies and now television continued to present stereotypical images of black people. Such TV shows as *Beulah* and *Amos 'n' Andy* adhered closely to such formats. Still, in the postwar years, blacks gradually gained access to better roles. Ethel Waters, Dorothy Dandridge, and Sidney Poitier took leading roles in such films as *Member of the Wedding* (Waters, 1952); *Carmen Jones* (Dandridge, 1954); and *Edge of the City* (1957), *The Defiant Ones* (1958), and the film version of Lorraine Hansberry's *Raisin in the Sun* (1961), all starring Poitier. Waters (as Berenice the cook) and Dandridge (as the "tragic mulatto") took stereotypical roles for black women and transformed them into positive statements about the ability of blacks to bring expertise and professionalism to the stage. Poitier's movies shifted the image of black men from improvident to diligent and hard-working men, as in his portrayal of Tommy the stevedore in *Edge of the City.* Poitier also pioneered in the portrayal of black men with serious aspirations for middle-class status, as in his role as Walter Younger in *A Raisin in the Sun.* In 1963, Sidney Poitier became the first black to win the Oscar for best actor for his role in *Lilies of the Field.*

Desegregation of Sports

Symbolizing changes in the world of sports were the careers of professional baseball player Jackie Robinson and professional prizefighter Cassius Clay (later Muhammad Ali). On 9 April 1947, a terse press release heralded the desegregation of major league baseball: "Brooklyn [Dodgers] announces the purchase of the contract of Jack Roosevelt Robinson from Montreal." To short-circuit white resistance, the Brooklyn Dodgers organization deliberately downplayed the significance of its actions. Robinson was the first black to play major league baseball since the 1880s. Although he faced extraordinary harassment and insults from white fans and opposing players alike, Robinson soon fought back and went on to win accolades as Rookie of the Year (1947) and Most Valuable Player (1949), as well as induction into the Baseball Hall of Fame (1962). He also appeared on the cover of *Life* magazine (1950) and received the NAACP's prestigious Spingarn Medal (1956). Although Robinson was soon joined by other black players—notably Willie Mays of the New York Giants, Ernie Banks of the Chicago Cubs, and Hank Aaron of the Milwaukee Braves—the recruitment of black players into the major leagues was a slow process, mostly within the National rather than the American League. It was not until 1959 that the Boston Red Sox signed their first black player.

The desegregation of audiences for black baseball was not an unmixed blessing. As a result of the growing recruitment of blacks for professional baseball teams, the Negro leagues gradually declined and then disappeared. The Negro National League closed after its 1948 season. Although the Negro American League (NAL) continued to play, the number of teams in the league had dwindled to only four in

Jackie Robinson swings a bat in spring training in Sanford, Florida, March 1946. A year later Robinson became the first black to play in the major leagues since the 1880s. *AP/Wide World Photos*

1953, and, in 1960, the NAL played its final game. In the meantime, African American attendance at major league games increased dramatically. During the first season with Robinson in the lineup, the Dodgers set season attendance records. At Brooklyn's Ebbets Field, black attendance increased by 400 percent. In effect, the Dodgers became black America's team and replenished box offices wherever the team played. As the numbers of blacks attending big-league games rose, the Negro leagues declined. One manager lamented, "We couldn't draw flies."

Despite its downside, the desegregation of major league baseball helped to fuel the desegregation of other sports. Tennis player Althea Gibson became the first black to be admitted to competition in the National Tennis Championship (1950). A year later she became the first black athlete to play at Wimbledon, which she won in both the singles and doubles in 1957. In 1963, Arthur Ashe became the first black named to the U.S. Davis Cup tennis team. Five years later, he would become the first African American to win the U.S. Open singles championship. In 1950, the National Basketball Association (NBA) signed its first black player, Charles "Chuck" Cooper, although Earl Lloyd was the first black to play in a regularly scheduled NBA game. Subsequently, Don Barksdale became the first black to play in an NBA All-Star game (1953); Bill Russell of the Boston Celtics was voted Most Valuable Player (1958); and Wilt Chamberlain of the Philadelphia 76ers scored his first one-hundred-point game against the New York Knickerbockers (1962). In the meantime, on the gridiron, Jim Brown of the Cleveland Browns won the National Football League's rushing title and held that distinction each year between 1957 and 1965.

Prizefighting continued to hold great symbolic value for the black community, and black boxers continued to dominate the heavyweight division. In nearly unbroken succession, blacks retained the heavyweight crown—Joe Louis, Jersey Joe Wolcott, Ezzard Charles, Floyd Patterson, Sonny Liston, and Cassius Marcellus Clay (later Muhammad Ali). In 1960, Ali won the Golden Gloves at the Olympic games in Rome. Four years later he knocked out Sonny Liston and won the heavyweight championship of the world. Ali also enlivened the boxing game by predicting the round in which his opponent would fall and boasting, "I am the greatest!" Following his victory over Liston, he exerted his independence and rejected the usual efforts of promoters to control the personal and professional lives of fighters. He announced his conversion to Islam and changed his name from Cassius Marcellus Clay to Muhammad Ali. As we will see in Chapter 22, Ali would best symbolize the growing transition of the black freedom struggle from nonviolent direct action to black power.

∼

AS SUGGESTED BY THE EXPERIENCES of blacks in the urban North and West, the modern civil rights movement was a national phenomenon. The northern and western struggles were most successful in breaking down barriers to public accommodations; somewhat successful in opening certain inner-city jobs; and least successful in breaking down barriers to housing and education in all-white neighborhoods. Most important, the modern freedom struggle helped to transform the intellectual, cultural, and social life of African Americans and the nation. Although some creative artists initially hoped to maintain their independence and distance from the unfolding political struggles of black people, they gradually embraced the modern civil rights movement and used their creative talents and energies to help ensure its success. At the same time, the desegregation of professional sports and the rapid spread of jazz and rhythm and blues influenced the cultural life of the nation. Spearheaded by small independent record companies, black radio stations, and DJs, rhythm and blues gave rise to rock 'n' roll, which became the music of choice for the masses of white youth. Some critics of the black freedom struggle would use these important cultural achievements to mask the slow pace of economic change in American society, but the rise of the Black Power movement would pinpoint persistent patterns of class and racial inequality and challenge activists, intellectuals, and artists alike with a new set of aesthetic demands, political strategies, and visions for the future of blacks in America. The Black Power movement is the subject of Chapter 22.

~

The Black Power Movement

A variety of forces underlay the emergence of the Black Power movement during the late 1960s and early 1970s. First, the outbreak of violence in the urban North and West heightened the debate over nonviolent versus violent strategies for social change and split the ranks of the civil rights movement. One faction retained allegiance to nonviolent direct action, whereas another expanding cadre of young activists sought alternatives to the old way. Second, passage of the Civil Rights Acts of 1964, 1965, and 1968 exposed weaknesses in the freedom struggle that the focus on de jure segregation and formal patterns of disfranchisement had camouflaged. Now the civil rights movement faced the hard job of translating legal victories into real change, something that northern and western blacks had confronted much earlier. Third, the assassination of Martin Luther King Jr. removed a key symbol and source of unity in the overall freedom struggle. According to one activist, King was "the one man of our race that this country's older generations, the militants, and the revolutionaries and the masses of black people would still listen to."

Following King's death, Stokely Carmichael of the Student Nonviolent Coordinating Committee (SNCC) told black people: "[We must] stand up on our feet and die like men. . . . If that's our only act of manhood, we're going to die." Black women activists were equally determined, but somewhat more optimistic. In her "Poem for Black Boys," Nikki Giovanni exhorted:

DO NOT SIT IN DO NOT FOLLOW KING
GO DIRECTLY TO THE STREETS
This is a game you can win.

In 1966, the debate over strategies came to a head when pioneer James Meredith, who integrated the University of Mississippi, was shot down during a one-man freedom march through hostile southern territory. Thereafter, the Black Power movement gained increasing momentum, but it soon fragmented under the weight of government repression and contrasting ideas about the precise meaning of black power within the African American community itself. Although black power advocates agreed on its potential to transform African American culture, identity, and beliefs, some emphasized armed struggle, whereas others turned toward black capitalism and conventional electoral politics.

REVOLUTIONARY BLACK NATIONALISM, ANTIWAR SENTIMENT, AND REPRESSION

In the spring of 1966, James Meredith proposed a one-man march from Memphis, Tennessee, to Jackson, Mississippi, hoping to demonstrate that the Second Reconstruction had arrived. In Meredith's mind, African Americans had a right to freedom of movement throughout the South and the nation without fear of intimidation or mob violence. However, Meredith had traveled only a short distance on his nationally publicized journey when gunshots brought him down on June 6, cutting his trip short. Police quickly arrested a thirty-year-old Klansman, who proudly confessed to the shooting. Meredith survived the attack, but civil rights leaders converged on the spot where he was shot, pledging to complete the march. This symbolic effort resulted in a turning point in the black freedom struggle. Martin Luther King Jr. of the Southern Christian Leadership Conference (SCLC) and Floyd McKissick of the Congress of Racial Equality (CORE) could not contain the militant demands of young SNCC activists like Stokely Carmichael, elected chairman just one month earlier, and Willie Ricks, who had joined the freedom struggle as a high school student in Chattanooga, Tennessee. SNCC leaders proposed to limit white participation in the march and vigorously asserted the right of marchers to defend themselves against physical attacks. Under the forceful demands of young blacks like Ricks and Carmichael, King and McKissick reluctantly accepted the services of an organization called the Deacons of Defense, a Louisiana-based black paramilitary organization. Although whites did participate in the march, they were far less visible on the road to Jackson than in other marches of the early to mid-1960s.

Beginnings of the Black Power Movement

Young activists not only sharpened the focus on self-defense. They also took control of the rallying rhetoric of the movement. At a freedom rally in Greenwood, Mississippi, where several SNCC activists were arrested and detained for a short period, Carmichael announced that he had been to jail twenty-seven times and did not intend to return. He then told the crowd: "What we gonna start saying now is 'black power.'" Willie Ricks (who first impressed the term on Carmichael) took up the phrase and repeatedly urged rural and small-town black southerners to join in: "What do you want?" The crowds repeatedly and resoundingly replied: "Black Power." When the march from Memphis to Jackson closed at a rally on June 26, "Black Power!" increasingly displaced "We Shall Overcome" and "Freedom Now!" as the rallying cry of the black freedom struggle.

On 6 June 1966, James Meredith pulls himself off Highway 51 in Hernando, Mississippi, after being shot during his one-man march from Memphis to Jackson, Mississippi. The attempt on Meredith's life helped to spark the Black Power movement. *AP Photo/Jack Thornell*

Following the march from Memphis to Jackson, "black power" became a dividing line between those who looked backward to the old nonviolent direct action movement and those who looked forward to a new day of militant, independent black self-assertion. CORE and SNCC emerged at the forefront of the new movement. Floyd McKissick, CORE's head, declared that 1966 would be remembered "as the year we left our imposed status of Negroes and became Black Men." In McKissick's view, the march from Memphis to Jackson marked the moment when black men realized their full worth, dignity, beauty, and, most of all, "their power" in American society. At its 1966 convention one month after the march, CORE invited Carmichael to speak. Carmichael told the gathering: "We don't need white liberals. . . . We have to make integration irrelevant." The CORE audience responded positively to Carmichael's words, repudiated nonviolent direct action as a philosophy for social change, and informed white members that they were no longer welcome. In short, the CORE convention endorsed black power, declaring in its official resolution that "racial co-existence through Black Power" represented "the only meaningful way to total equality" (see box). At an exceedingly acrimonious staff meeting in December 1966, by a narrow vote, SNCC also excluded whites from the organization.

Symbolizing the new departure was SNCC's militant organizing activities in predominantly black Lowndes County, Alabama. Encouraged by the organizing

SOURCES FROM THE PAST

1966

SNCC
Chairman
Stokely
Carmichael
Defines Black
Power

One of the tragedies of the struggle against racism is that up to now there has been no national organization which could speak to the growing militancy of young black people in the urban ghetto. There has been only a civil rights movement, whose tone of voice was adapted to an audience of liberal whites. It served as a sort of buffer zone between them and angry young blacks. None of its so-called leaders could go into a rioting community and be listened to. In a sense, I blame ourselves—together with the mass media—for what has happened in Watts, Harlem, Chicago, Cleveland, Omaha. Each time the people in those cities saw Martin Luther King get slapped, they became angry; when they saw four little black girls bombed to death, they were angrier; and when nothing happened, they were steaming. We had nothing to offer that they could see, except to go out and be beaten again. We helped to build their frustration. . . .

An organization which claims to speak for the needs of a community—as does the Student Nonviolent Coordinating Committee—must speak in the tone of that community, not as somebody else's buffer zone. This is the significance of black power as a slogan. For once, black people are going to use the words they want to use—not just the words whites want to hear. And they will do this no matter how often the press tries to stop the use of the slogan by equating it with racism or separatism. . . .

. . . Where Negroes lack a majority, black power means proper representation and sharing of control. It means the creation of power bases from which black people can work to change statewide or nationwide patterns of oppression through pressure from strength—instead of weakness. Politically, black power means what it has always meant to SNCC: the coming-together of black people to elect representatives and *to force those representatives to speak to their needs*. It does not mean merely putting black faces into office. A man or woman who is black and from the slums cannot be automatically expected to speak to the needs of black people. Most of the black politicians we see around the country today are not what SNCC means by black power. The power must be that of a community, and emanate from there. . . .

Black people do not want to "take over" this country. They don't want to "get whitey"; they just want to get him off their backs, as the saying goes. . . .

Source: New York Review of Books, 7, no. 4 (September 22, 1966), pp. 5, 6, 8.

activities of SNCC, African Americans formed the Lowndes County Freedom Organization (LCFO) and pushed for control of the county. Unlike the Mississippi Freedom Democratic Party, formed nearly three years earlier, LCFO selected an all-black rather than an interracial slate of candidates for public office; adopted the black panther as its symbol; and expressed a willingness to defend itself against white violence. Because of the ongoing violence that blacks faced, Carmichael defended the use of arms in the Alabama campaign by local blacks and activists alike.

In describing the organization's actions in the region, he explained: "We are not King or SCLC. . . . They don't do the kind of work we do nor do they live in the areas we live in. They don't ride the highways at night." In the fall 1966 elections, Lowndes County blacks posted their own armed guards to protect themselves, defied local authorities, and voted in record numbers. Because they failed to discourage blacks from voting, white election officials adopted openly fraudulent ballot counting measures to win the county.

The black power advocacy of CORE and SNCC helped to unleash a torrent of organizing activities on college campuses. At Indiana University, a sophomore captured the tone of the campus movement when he declared:

> I don't think that honkies should be in anything Black. The only thing that crackers can do for us is give us the money and other stuff that we need to do our thing. Anything else they have, they can keep—their sympathy, their ideas, and their damn advice.

Between 1967 and the early 1970s, at predominantly white university and college campuses across the country, black students formed all-black student organizations and demanded increases in the number of black students, faculty, and courses dealing with the black experience. In varying degrees of intensity, these protests shook such universities as Northwestern, Cornell, Columbia, and Wisconsin, to name a few. In presenting their demands, African American students emphasized the necessity of swift and positive responses. At the University of Massachusetts, student leader Robert Henderson reflected a recurring pattern when he informed university officials: "We will expect a yes decision on all of these points by twelve o'clock Monday. If not, we will be back Tuesday." In short, blacks described their requests as "non-negotiable demands."

In some cases, black students nearly placed institutions of higher education under siege. In California, officials closed San Francisco State College when black students boycotted classes, picketed classrooms and administrative offices, and engaged in diverse acts of civil disobedience. At Duke University in Durham, a group of about thirty demonstrators followed up their demands by occupying the central administration building. In Wisconsin State–Oshkosh, some ninety students were arrested, jailed, and later expelled for ransacking the president's offices after delivering a set of demands. At Cornell, black students carried out a variety of actions— but, notably, they left a two-day occupation of one building dressed in military uniform and carrying rifles and shotguns. Although the most militant demonstrations occurred on predominantly white northern and western campuses, black students also organized and advanced similar demands for change at predominantly white southern universities like the University of Mississippi and at predominantly black institutions like Howard University. Moreover, such demonstrations touched small public and private college campuses across the nation. In 1968, for example, at Carthage College, a small Lutheran School in Kenosha, Wisconsin, a handful of black students gathered in the wake of King's assassination and formed the Afro-American Society (later changed to the Black Student Union) and soon demanded an increase in the number of black students, faculty, and courses on African American history and culture.

The black student movements produced substantial results. The number of black students, faculty, and courses dramatically increased; African American studies programs and departments emerged at most major institutions of higher education; and black community-based colleges proliferated. These included Malcolm X College in Chicago; Federal City College in Washington, D.C.; Malcolm X Liberation University in Durham; and Nairobi College in East Palo Alto, California. Charles G. Hurst Jr., president of Malcolm X and a leading spokesman of the black community college idea, argued that such colleges would "serve as a catalytic agent to synthesize the varied components of the community into a viable force for liberation." The rise of black studies programs and community-based black colleges reinforced the scholarly reinterpretation of African American history, life, and culture. Under the impact of the Black Power movement, scholars now moved well beyond the victimization approach to research on the black experience (see Chapters 11, 13, and 15).

Although SNCC, CORE, and campus-based organizers emerged as the early vanguard of the Black Power movement, the Black Panther Party soon took center stage by shifting the movement deep into the African American community. In 1966, Huey P. Newton and Bobby Seale, students at Merritt College in Oakland, California, formed the Black Panther Party for Self Defense. Inspired by SNCC's militant Lowndes County Freedom Organization (also known as the Black Panther Party), the Oakland party adopted the black panther as its symbol and advanced a "ten-point program" of action (see box). The "ten-point program" emphasized black control of the black community. As point number one stated, "We want freedom. We want power to determine the destiny of our Black Community." Subsequent points spelled out the same determination vis à vis employment, businesses, housing, education, military service, police forces, and courts of law. Recruiting mainly among poor and working-class urbanites, the party established liberation schools, free health clinics, and free breakfast programs. The party also launched armed community patrols to monitor and protect African Americans from police brutality. Black Panthers arrived on the scene of arrests with law books and rifles; reported on police conduct; informed blacks of their constitutional rights; and helped to curb the incidence of police brutality and arbitrary arrests and jailings.

In early 1967, the Black Panther Party gained national attention when it protested a proposed California gun control law. An armed contingent of Panthers arrived at the state capitol in Sacramento. They demonstrated their right to bear arms and protested the recent killing of a black youth, Denzil Dowell, by the Richmond, California, police. As Bobby Seale later recalled:

> We arrived, all these black men and women—twenty-four males and six females—with guns, and Ronald Reagan, then the governor, was on the lawn with two hundred future leaders of America. You know, twelve- and thirteen- and fourteen-year-old kids. And these kids are leaving his session on the lawn and coming to see us.

The Black
Panther Party
States Its
Platform

1. *We want freedom. We want power to determine the destiny of our Black Community.*

We believe that black people will not be free until we are able to determine our destiny.

2. *We want full employment for our people. . . .*

3. *We want an end to the robbery by the white man of our Black Community. . . .*

4. *We want decent housing, fit for shelter of human beings. . . .*

5. *We want education for our people that exposes the true nature of this decadent American society. We want education that teaches us our true history and our role in the present-day society. . . .*

6. *We want all black men to be exempt from military service.*

We believe that black people should not be forced to fight in the military service to defend a racist government that does not protect us. . . .

7. *We want an immediate end to POLICE BRUTALITY and MURDER of black people. . . .*

8. *We want freedom for all black men held in federal, state, county and city prisons and jails. . . .*

9. *We want all black people when brought to trial to be tried in court by a jury of their peer group or people from their black communities, as defined by the Constitution of the United States. . . .*

10. *We want land, bread, housing, education, clothing, justice and peace. And as our major political objective, a United Nations–supervised plebiscite to be held throughout the black colony in which only black colonial subjects will be allowed to participate, for the purpose of determining the will of black people as to their national destiny.*

When, in the course of human events, it becomes necessary for one people to dissolve the political bands which have connected them with another, and to assume, among the powers of the earth, the separate and equal station to which the laws of nature and nature's God entitle them, a decent respect to the opinions of mankind requires that they should declare the causes which impel them to the separation.

We hold these truths to be self-evident, that all men are created equal; that they are endowed by their Creator with certain unalienable rights; that among these are life, liberty, and the pursuit of happiness. *That, to secure these rights, governments are instituted among men, deriving their just powers from the consent of the governed; that, whenever any form of government becomes destructive of these ends, it is the right of the people to alter or to abolish it, and to institute a new government, laying its foundation on such principles, and organizing its powers in such form, as to them shall seem most likely to effect their safety and happiness.* Prudence, indeed, will dictate that governments long established should not be changed for light and transient causes; and accordingly, all experience hath shown, that mankind are more disposed to suffer, while evils are sufferable, than to right themselves by abolishing the forms to which they are accustomed. *But, when a long train of abuses and usurpations pursuing invariably the same object, evinces a design to reduce them under absolute despotism, it is their right, it is their duty, to throw off such government, and to provide new guards for their future security.*

Source: Deirdre Mullane, ed., *Crossing the Danger Water: Three Hundred Years of African-American Writing* (New York: Doubleday, 1993), pp. 683–685. Reprinted by permission of Bobby Seale, founding chairman and national organizer of the Black Panther Party, 1966–1974.

After reading a statement outside the capitol, the party asked directions to the spectator section of the legislative chambers, but reporters (seeking a controversial news story) directed the Panthers onto the actual floor of the California legislature. News media flashed photos of the scene across the country and around the world. Following this dramatic episode, the Black Panther Party's membership soared. Within three years, the organization had grown to over forty chapters and five thousand members in the major metropolitan areas of the nation.

As the Black Panther Party recruited new members, it moved beyond its initial community-based nationalism to revolutionary black nationalism. Largely under the leadership of Eldridge Cleaver, its minister of information, the party adopted a notion of revolution based on the so-called lumpenproletariat—the unemployed and workers in the underground economy of drugs, prostitution, theft, and gambling. In announcing the party's new direction, Cleaver declared Huey P. Newton as Malcolm's successor:

> For the revolutionary youth today, time starts with Malcolm. . . . Before Malcolm, time stands still. . . . Malcolm prophesied the coming of the gun to the black liberation struggle. Huey P. Newton picked up the gun and pulled the trigger, freeing the genie of black revolutionary violence in Babylon.

Embedded in the Panther ideology and mode of organizing, however, was an acceptance of alliances with revolutionary white socialists, although the organization insisted that blacks serve as "the vanguard." In the presidential election of 1968, the Black Panther Party joined forces with the predominantly white Peace and Freedom Party. At a founding convention in Richmond, California, the Peace and Freedom Party endorsed the ten-point program of the Black Panther Party and, in accord with the Panthers' insistence that blacks serve as the vanguard of the revolution, selected Eldridge Cleaver as its presidential candidate. The party's antiwar plank supported a ban on "all aggressive wars and immediate withdrawal from Vietnam."

Although the Panthers' emphasis on interracial alliances discouraged some black nationalists, by taking such bold steps as armed self-defense and organizing among the poorest black urbanites, the party soon attracted several influential SNCC activists into its ranks. These included for varying periods Kathleen Neal (later Kathleen Cleaver); Stokely Carmichael; and Hubert (H. "Rap") Brown, Carmichael's successor as chairman of SNCC. Cleaver described Carmichael as a leading example of black intellectuals "who have thrown off the shackles of the slave and are willing to put their talents and genius selflessly to work for the masses." For his part, Carmichael saw the Black Panther Party as a vehicle for the transition of SNCC from a rural-based movement to one with an increasing focus on the volatile urban centers of the nation. Moreover, SNCC staff member James Forman and others believed that affiliation with the Panthers would enable SNCC to overcome some of its history of class-biased reliance on college students as organizers: "The emphasis on recruiting street brothers, young people from the 'ghettos,' rather than college students, gave it a large base and eliminated some of the class tensions which we had experienced."

Black Panther Party chairman Bobby Seale and minister of defense Huey P. Newton bear arms outside the party's headquarters in Oakland, California, 1967. *AP Photo/S.F. Examiner*

Although the concept of a lumpen-based movement deemphasized the centrality of workplace struggles as the locus of black people's power, a variety of militant black workers' unions emerged between 1967 and the early 1970s. Workers, particularly young workers, in the auto industry led the way. In 1967, a coterie of revolutionary black nationalists and Marxists formed the *Inner City Voice*, a Detroit-based newspaper. Under the leadership of attorney Ken Cockrel, Mike Hamlin, General Baker, John Watson, and John Williams, the *Inner City Voice* forged a strong relationship with Detroit's black working class. In 1968, black workers and radical black intellectuals formed the Dodge Revolutionary Union movement (DRUM). The organization not only launched "wildcat strikes" against the company but also criticized the United Auto Workers for failing to address the issue of black workers in the union's struggle with management. According to DRUM's statement of priorities, "Our sole objective . . . is to break the bonds of white racist control over the lives and destiny of black workers." One black worker accented the need for black supervisors, remarking: "Everywhere I look there sits some honky looking down on me." By the end of 1969, the revolutionary union movement had spread widely throughout the Detroit region and the nation, including such groups as the Ford Revolutionary Union Movement (FRUM); the Harvester Revolutionary Union Movement (HARUM); the General Motors Revolutionary Union Movement (GRUM); and the Black Panther Caucus of Fremont, California. Representatives from these diverse groups soon met and formed the League of Revolutionary Black Workers to coordinate their activities on a national scale.

Under the growing impact of the Black Power movement, some black ministers embraced the concept and reinforced the thrust of revolutionary black nationalism. As early as July 1966, a group of forty-eight black clergymen took out a full-page ad in the *New York Times* endorsing black power. The ministers countered the notion that "white people are justified in getting what they want through the use of power, but that Negro Americans must, either by nature or by circumstances, make their appeal only through conscience." As noted in Chapter 20, large numbers of blacks had already gravitated toward an activist and liberation theology within the context of the civil rights movement. Now, however, some black ministers and their congregants challenged the growing appeal of Islam with a new black nationalist Christian theology. Leading the way toward a systematic articulation of a black nationalist Christianity were theologian James Cone and Rev. Albert Cleage Jr. of Detroit. Cone, in his books *Black Theology and Black Power* (1969) and *Black Theology of Liberation* (1970), revamped the symbols of color, identified much that was good and righteous with blackness, and unflinchingly called for "the destruction of whiteness," which he identified as "the source of human misery in the world." Cleage, pastor of the Shrine of the Black Madonna, sketched a framework for black liberation theology in two books, *Black Christian Nationalism* and *The Black Messiah,* in which he forcefully argued that a black spiritual perspective was necessary to complement political black nationalism. Closely intertwined with the influence of Rev. Cleage was the caucus of black theologians within the predominantly white Unitarian Universalist Church. Both Cleage and his Unitarian counterparts reinterpreted the life of Christ as a black Messiah and supreme liberator of humankind. Although liberation theologians and ministers expressed a preference for peaceful social change, they argued that violence could not be ruled out in the face of an unjust status quo, thereby reinforcing the right of revolutionary black power advocates to bear arms.

As black ministers and theologians crafted a liberation theology, black parents and educators advocated community control of schools. Their efforts gained national attention in Brooklyn's Ocean Hill–Brownsville District. By the mid-1960s, the struggle to integrate the city's schools had failed. Even the state commissioner of education bluntly reported: "We must conclude that nothing undertaken by the New York City Board of Education . . . has contributed or will contribute in any meaningful degree to desegregating the public schools in this city." In December 1966, African Americans and their Puerto Rican allies staged three days of sit-ins at the office of the board of education. Calling themselves the Peoples Board of Education, the protesters demanded that the system give local parents and community groups effective control over the education of their children. The following year, the city responded by setting up three "experimental school districts"—one in Harlem, one on the Lower East Side, and the final one at Ocean Hill–Brownsville—to test the efficacy of community control. The community elected an eleven-member governing board that included only one white member and selected the black New York public school teacher Rhody McCoy as district superintendent. Under McCoy's leadership and with broad-based grassroots support, the governing board soon fired nineteen school teachers (seventeen white, one black, and one Puerto Rican), explaining that the fired teachers failed to cooperate with the community control mission of the district.

The firing of teachers touched off a heated dispute between the governing board and the United Federation of Teachers, who demanded the reinstatement of the teachers. When the board refused to reinstate the fired teachers, 350 union teachers struck in support of their colleagues. Undaunted, the governing board kept the schools open by using community volunteers and replacement teachers. The Ocean Hill–Brownsville schools also remained open despite three separate citywide sympathy strikes, which involved a million students and nearly 60,000 teachers across the city. Community activists and parents kept control of the schools until the state legislature abolished the three demonstration districts at the end of the 1968–1969 academic year. Despite the dismantling of community control, Rhody McCoy declared the short-lived struggle a victory for black power:

> You've got to understand that the members of the community board were community people who were disenfranchised with the system, who were nameless and faceless, who had never been incorporated and included, even though their children were mandated to go to school. For them to take on that responsibility was tremendous. And they did a herculean job.

Opposition to the Vietnam War

Integral to the rise of black nationalist ideology was the emergence of antiwar sentiment within the black community. As the Vietnam War escalated from 25,000 U.S. troops in early 1965 to 184,000 in 1966, and to over a half million by decade's end, it took a heavy and disproportionate toll on the black community. The war not only undercut efforts to generate resources for rebuilding black urban communities ravaged by urban violence and social and economic exploitation but also offered few opportunities for African Americans to rise in the ranks of the military. Although blacks now fought in desegregated armed forces, their percentage of officers fell far below their proportion of enlisted men in each branch of the armed services. In the Marines, they made up nearly 10 percent of all enlisted men, but less than 1 percent of the officers. In the army, blacks made up nearly 14 percent of all enlisted men, but only about 3 percent of officers. African Americans served mainly in combat units and faced disproportionately higher casualties than their white counterparts. In 1966, for example, blacks made up over 20 percent of army casualties.

Although SNCC and CORE had officially opposed the war as early as 1965 (discussed in Chapter 20), antiwar sentiment intensified with the rise of the Black Panther Party and the spread of revolutionary black nationalism. In 1965, Martin Luther King Jr. had also expressed antiwar sentiment, but only in 1966 did he and SCLC formally declare opposition to the war. The following year, in a speech at New York City's Riverside Church, King succinctly stated his antiwar position: "It would be very inconsistent for me to teach and preach nonviolence in this situation and then applaud violence when thousands and thousands of people, both adults and children, are being maimed and mutilated and many killed in this war." As suggested in Chapter 21, King's antiwar activities were inextricably interwoven with his and SCLC's growing efforts on behalf of black poor and working people. In an interview with the *New York Times,* King declared: "In a real sense, the Great Society has been shot down on the battlefields of Vietnam." Although established civil rights and labor leaders like Roy Wilkins, Whitney Young, and Bayard Rustin vehemently opposed King's stand, some black elected officials and intellectuals supported his position, notably Julian Bond of the Georgia House of Representatives; Ronald Dellums, U.S. congressman from California; and renowned author James Baldwin. According to Baldwin, "A racist society can't but fight a racist war—this is the bitter truth. The assumptions acted on at home are also acted on abroad, and every American Negro knows this, for he, after the American Indian, was the first Viet Cong victim."

Government Reaction

The spread of antiwar sentiment heightened federal, state, and local surveillance of civil rights leaders and organizations. Early on, the FBI had placed members of SNCC, SCLC, CORE, and the Nation of Islam under close surveillance. During the rise of black power, however, surveillance became a violent campaign to eradicate the Black Panther Party and similar radical black organizations. During the summer of 1967, in the wake of widespread urban violence, FBI head J. Edgar Hoover launched an extensive campaign to infiltrate and disrupt militant black power organizations. Under its COINTELPRO, or Counter Intelligence Program, the FBI defined the Black Panther Party as the "greatest threat" to the internal security of the country. Federal authorities took extreme steps to "prevent a coalition of militant black nationalist groups from coalescing and giving rise to a 'messiah' who could articulate the needs of the masses of working class and poor blacks."

The FBI, federal marshals, and local police officers launched over 230 separate assaults against the Black Panther Party, including armed raids on local Panther headquarters in cities across the nation. In 1969 alone, nearly 30 Black Panther Party members were killed, and nearly 750 were jailed or arrested. In the trial of Bobby Seale and several white radicals accused of disrupting the 1968 Democratic National Convention in Chicago, a federal judge silenced Black Panther Bobby Seale by having him bound and gagged in the courtroom. As the decade ended in December 1969, Chicago police raided the Panthers' headquarters and killed its leaders, Mark Clark and Fred Hampton. According to the report of a federal grand jury, police had fired over eighty shots into the apartment, but only one shot had emerged from inside the unit.

Federal attacks on the headquarters of revolutionary black nationalist organizations spread beyond the Black Panther Party. In August 1971, federal officers raided the Jackson, Mississippi, headquarters of the Republic of New Africa (RNA), an organization devoted to the development of an independent black nation in five black belt states of the Deep South. Within less than a month, the FBI launched a similar raid on the Detroit office of the RNA. Two years later, the head of the Republic of New Africa, Imari Obadele (formerly Richard Henry) and six other party members were jailed on charges of conspiracy to assault federal officers, assault, and the use of firearms to commit a felony. Other prominent examples of conflict between police, the FBI, and black power advocates included the cases of Rev. Ben Chavis and the "Wilmington [North Carolina] Ten," jailed for allegedly setting fire to a local grocery store to protest discrimination against black children in the public schools; and, most notably, the UCLA professor, activist, and Communist Party member Angela Davis.

In 1969, Angela Davis became an assistant professor of philosophy at the University of California—Los Angeles, but the board of regents refused to renew her contract for a second year, ostensibly because she had not received a doctorate degree. Most importantly, however, Davis's membership in the Communist Party and outspoken activism displeased the regents. The following year, Davis increased her activism on behalf of the "Soledad Brothers," W. L. Nolen and George Jackson. When George Jackson's young brother Jonathan and others sought to take hostages at a California courthouse and dramatize the plight of the Soledad prisoners, a shootout erupted and left four people dead—two prisoners, a judge, and Jonathan. Following this incident, the FBI placed Davis on its list of ten most wanted criminals, for allegedly planning the escape and precipitating the deaths of four people. Rather than face arrest, Davis went underground for nearly two months before being arrested in New York and extradited to stand trial in California. She was charged with kidnapping, conspiracy, and murder, but a mass-based "Free Angela" movement soon developed nationwide. Demands for her release appeared on bumper stickers, urban walls, and T-shirts, and in countless newspapers and magazine publications. The soul singer Aretha Franklin publicly offered to pay her bail, explaining, "I'm going to set Angela free . . . not because I believe in communism but because she's a Black woman who wants freedom for all Black people." Davis had become a folk hero for large numbers of African Americans and radical activists across the color line. After spending sixteen months in jail, Davis was acquitted of all charges. She then helped to transmute the Free Angela movement (that is, the Free Angela Committee) into a new organization, the National Alliance Against Racism and Political Repression, and became its cochair.

Although authorities eventually released Angela Davis and the "Wilmington Ten," San Quentin prison guards killed George Jackson on 21 August 1971. Jackson's death helped spark a radical prison movement that culminated in the Attica, New York, prison revolt of 9 September 1973. Some thirteen hundred inmates from different ethnic and racial backgrounds (predominantly black but also white and Puerto Rican) took over the facility, demanding better treatment, food, clothing, and shelter. State and federal authorities responded by mobilizing the National Guard, as well as state and local police, and attacking the facility, killing twenty-nine prisoners and ten prison guards who had been taken hostage. In the process of retaking the prison, police and National Guardsmen left in their wake a string of racist epithets scrawled on prison walls, including phrases like "Black blood will flow freely." In the aftermath of Attica, sixty prisoners faced trial for murder, kidnapping, and other felony charges. In the meantime, the government's repression of radical movements had nearly destroyed the Black Panther Party. Most of the party's leaders, to paraphrase one observer, were either dead, in jail, or in exile.

Encouraging attacks on black social movements was the resurgence of the Republican Party and the disintegration of the old New Deal coalition of liberal Democrats. The white working class increasingly abandoned the Democratic Party and joined middle- and upper-class whites in a wave of conservative reactions against the civil rights and Black Power movements. In the presidential election of 1968, Republican Richard Nixon won over Democrat Hubert Humphrey, but the white supremacist candidate for president, George C. Wallace of Alabama, received 13 percent of the popular vote and between an estimated 25 and 40 percent of the working-class white vote in southern cities like Little Rock, Nashville, Jacksonville, and Greensboro. This trend continued during the election of 1972, when nearly two-thirds of white workers voted to reelect Richard M. Nixon, who campaigned against open housing and busing to achieve racial balance in public schools. Nixon took over 60 percent of the popular vote and thoroughly defeated Democrat senator George M. McGovern, who not only opposed the Vietnam War but also supported civil rights legislation for minorities and women. The leadership of the AFL-CIO encouraged the Nixon landslide by declaring its "neutrality" in the contest and facilitating the drift of white workers to the right.

During Nixon's second term, resistance to the civil rights agenda stiffened. Symbolic of this resistance was the outbreak of violence over court-ordered busing in Boston. In 1974, U.S. district court judge W. Arthur Garrity Jr. declared the city of Boston guilty of violating the constitutional rights of black children by maintaining racially segregated schools. The judge ordered the integration of two schools—one in the predominantly black Roxbury section and the other in the predominantly Irish-American South Boston. Shortly thereafter, some eight thousand whites from all over the city staged a mass protest to thwart the court's order. Spearheaded by the antibusing group called ROAR (Restore Our Alienated Rights), the rally helped create a climate of hostility that soon resulted in violent attacks on black students during the first day of busing. In South Boston, some five hundred demonstrators hurled stones, rotten eggs, and tomatoes at buses and shouted racial epithets at black students brought into the area. By day's end, nine children were injured and eighteen buses damaged. Violence persisted over the next two years. In the meantime, white parents increasingly removed their children from the public school system and rapidly transformed it into a predominantly black institution. Resistance to school integration and the exit of whites from the public school system would repeat itself across urban America.

CRISIS OF RADICALISM, THE NEW POLITICS, AND BLACK CAPITALISM

Coupled with local, state, and federal attacks on revolutionary black power, popular white resistance exposed and aggravated divisions within the black freedom struggle. From the outset, activists had defined the term *black power* loosely enough to encompass a wide range of specific ideological positions and strategies, but now they sharpened their definitions and charted more precise directions for the movement.

Defining "Black Power"

Some black power activists, like Stokely Carmichael, left the Black Panther Party and launched a new Pan African movement, which accented the cultural unity of black peoples around the globe. When Carmichael left the party in July 1969, he publicly condemned the Panthers for their alliance with white radicals. Carmichael's rejection of interracial alliances gained support among outspoken black nationalists like Ron Karenga, head of the Los Angeles–based organization US; Ronald Daniels, chair of the National Black Political Assembly; political scientist Ronald Walters; and poet Haki Madhubuti (Don L. Lee). In early 1969, the clash between members of US and the Black Panther Party led to violence on the UCLA campus, where US members killed two members of the Black Panther Party, although FBI files suggest that these conflicts were encouraged by government agents.

By the early 1970s, other activists blended Pan Africanism's focus on race with Marxian emphasis on class analysis. Reflecting these efforts were the African Liberation Support Committee (ALSC), under the leadership of Owusu Sadaukai (Howard Fuller), and the Students Organized for Black Unity (SOBU) and the "Peoples College," both under the leadership of Abd-al Hakimu Ibn Alkalimat (Gerald McWorter), professor at Fisk University in Nashville. Amiri Baraka and Ron Karenga also gravitated toward Marxist-Leninist ideas and linked the black liberation struggle to issues of class as well as race during an era of imperialism, the highest stage of capitalist development. In his play, *The Motion of History*, Baraka gave his faith in class-based interracial movements dramatic form.

At the Sixth Pan African Congress, held in Tanzania in 1974, these contrasting ideas gained even sharper focus and divided the Black Power movement between black nationalists emphasizing the primacy of race and those emphasizing the salience of class as well as racial conflict. In his address before the congress, President Sekou Touré of Guinea urged the gathering to fight a narrow race-based definition of the global freedom struggle. According to Touré, "skin color, be it black, white, yellow or bronzed, does not indicate anything about social class, the ideology, the nature of behaviorism, or the qualities and skill of man or people." In his view, "the reclamation of Pan-Africanist identity" required "a fight against racist, segregationist and Zionist movements and any attempts to encapsulate the movement in a particularistic identity, for these are retrograde tendencies."

Whereas Pan Africanists like Karenga, Baraka, Alkalimat, and Sadaukai emphasized class as well as racial conflict, black nationalists like Daniels, Walters, and Madhubuti accented race. According to Madhubuti:

The ideology of white supremacy precedes the economic structure of capitalism and imperialism, the latter of which are falsely stated as the cause of racism. . . .

As far as we are concerned communism and capitalism are the left and right arms in the same white body. And the highest state of white supremacy is imperialism whether it's communist or capitalist.

As black nationalists struggled over the precise meaning of black power, other blacks used the notion to gain influence through the established channels of electoral politics. In his earliest articulation of black nationalist ideas in such publications as the *New York Review of Books* and the *Massachusetts Review,* Stokely Carmichael emphasized its potential for reform rather than revolution. In 1967, Carmichael's reformist notions of black power gained their most articulate expression in his *Black Power: The Politics of Liberation,* a book coauthored with political scientist Charles V. Hamilton. Carmichael and Hamilton argued that black power offered America its "last reasonable opportunity" to reform itself without "prolonged and destructive guerrilla warfare." In their view, the notion of black power would enable blacks to gain control over their lives politically, economically, and "psychically" within the context of existing capitalist institutions. In short, as formulated by Carmichael and Hamilton, black power offered a vehicle for blacks to take control of elective offices, businesses, and cultural institutions within the black community. As Carmichael embraced revolutionary black power and then the Pan African movement, others turned toward the electoral arena to build a new black politics.

Mobilizing Black Political Power

Between 1967 and 1974, the movement for elective office took focus in a series of Black Power conferences. Designed to mobilize the black electorate and take control of central cities through conventional means, these conferences were held in such cities as Newark, Philadelphia, Gary, and Little Rock. Educated black professionals, businessmen, and public officials dominated these gatherings. The first meeting convened in Newark, New Jersey, and the last one in Little Rock, Arkansas, but the most significant convention took place in Gary, Indiana (1972). Held in the wake of heavy government repression of the revolutionary Black Power movement, the Gary convention emerged from the collaborative efforts of black elected officials and leading black nationalists. As early as 1969, under the leadership of Charles Diggs of Detroit, nine black congressmen had formed the Democratic Select Committee to resist the conservative public policies of the Nixon administration. In 1971, the Select Committee evolved into the Congressional Black Caucus, which voiced African American policy concerns and served as a center for mobilizing black voters. Black nationalists like Amiri Baraka and black elected officials like Richard Hatcher, Ronald Dellums, and Charles Diggs came together to coordinate a strategy for empowering black people in the major metropolises of the nation. Convened at Northlake, Illinois, in September 1971, this initial meeting made plans for a black independent political convention, to be held in Gary, Indiana, in March 1972.

The Gary convention attracted some three thousand official delegates. Representing a broad cross-section of integrationist and black nationalist thought, the convention resulted in the formation of the National Black Political Assembly, designed to coordinate poor and working-class constituencies to elect blacks to public office at all levels of government—local, county, state, and federal. Although additional black power conferences convened until 1974, they failed to attract the mass-based support evident at the Gary meeting. As historian Manning Marable concludes:

> Gary represented, in retrospect, the zenith not only of black nationalism, but of the entire black movement during the Second Reconstruction. The collective vision of the convention represented a desire to seize electoral control of America's major cities, to move the black masses from the politics of desegregation to the politics of real empowerment, ultimately to create their own independent black political party.

Black Power conferences facilitated the expansion of black representation at all levels of government. Primarily members of the Democratic Party, the number of black elected officials rose from about 100 in 1965; to nearly 1,200 in 1969; to about 3,500 (2,969 men and 530 women) in 1975. Spread almost evenly across the South on the one hand and the North and West on the other, black elected officials included 18 U.S. congressmen and -women; 281 state legislators or executives; 135 mayors of cities, towns, or municipalities; 305 county executives; 387 judges and elected law enforcement officials; 939 elected members of city or county boards of education; and 1,438 other elected municipal government officials. Some black public officials owed their success to significant white support—most notably Georgia state senator Julian Bond; Fayette mayor Charles Evers; U.S. congressman Ronald Dellums of California; and Republican senator Edward Brooks of Massachusetts, the first black U.S. senator since the First Reconstruction. Most black public officials were indebted to blacks voting along racial lines. In 1967, for example, when Cleveland elected Carl Stokes the first black mayor of a major American city, African Americans gave Stokes nearly 95 percent of their votes, compared with less than 25 percent of whites. In the same year, when Gary, Indiana, a predominantly black city, elected Richard Hatcher as the second black mayor of a major U.S. city, nearly all African Americans voted for Hatcher, whereas whites voted almost unanimously for his opponent.

Three years later, aided by poet, playwright, and political activist Amiri Baraka, Kenneth Gibson became the first black mayor of Newark, also a city with a black majority. Gibson owed his victory to the organizational activities of Baraka and the United Brothers of Newark (UBN). In 1973, African Americans also helped fuel the election of black mayors in other northern and western cities: Coleman Young in Detroit; Maynard Jackson in Atlanta; and, though to a lesser degree, Thomas Bradley in Los Angeles. In 1970, black public officials strengthened their ranks by forming the National Black Caucus of Elected Officials (NBCLEO), which not only assisted the Congressional Black Caucus but also pressed its own demands at the meetings of the predominantly white National League of Cities and its kindred organization, the

U.S. Conference of Mayors. Carl Stokes of Cleveland and Kenneth Gibson of Newark soon gained seats on the executive councils of the predominantly white bodies.

The growing politicization of blacks inspired the presidential bid of Democratic congresswoman Shirley Chisholm of New York. In 1972, Chisholm became the first woman as well as the first black to seek the presidential nomination of a major party. Four years earlier, she had become the first black woman to receive election to the U.S. House of Representatives. Campaigning under the slogan "Unbought and Unbossed," Chisholm took outspoken stands on issues not only of racial equality but of gender equity as well. She was an early member of the National Organization of Women, a founding member of the National Women's Political Caucus, and a spokesperson for the National Abortion Rights Action League. Yet she received little support from white feminists or African Americans, particularly black men. Still, Chisholm carried her bid for the presidential nomination to the convention floor and received 150 votes on the first ballot.

By strengthening their position in established centers of power, blacks not only inspired Chisholm's bid for the presidential nomination but also increased their impact on public policy. Under the escalating political demands of African Americans, the federal government gradually adopted "color conscious" modes of making

Shirley Chisholm, the first black woman elected to the U.S. House of Representatives and the first woman to seek the presidential nomination of a major political party. *Ted Streshinsky/Corbis*

equal education and employment opportunities a reality. In a series of cases, the U.S. Supreme Court declared the "color-blind" principle unfair in its impact on black students and workers. In *Green v. County Board of New Kent County* (1968) and *Swann v. Charlotte–Mecklenberg County Board of Education* (1971), the Court ordered widespread busing of public school children to achieve racial balance. In *Griggs v. Duke Power Company* (1971), the U.S. Supreme Court upheld the "color conscious" affirmative action principles of the Philadelphia Plan, which sought proportional representation of blacks in skilled and white-collar jobs commensurate with their numbers in the metropolitan work force. The plan also required construction firms with government contracts and grant-in-aid money (for building bridges, hospitals, schools, libraries, and government buildings) to prepare specific hiring schedules designed to integrate minorities into their work forces. By 1972, Congress and the courts extended the plan's coverage beyond the construction industry to more than three hundred thousand firms conducting business with the government. The Nixon administration also added the Office of Minority Business Enterprise (OMBE) in the Department of Commerce and a Voting Rights Division in the Justice Department.

At the local level, blacks gained greater access to municipal services and employment opportunities than they had had under the largely Democratic white regimes. In Gary, when Hatcher took office, no new public housing had been built in a decade. Beginning in 1968, the city constructed over one thousand low-income housing units. Although less successful than Gary, the city of Cleveland added fifty-two hundred new public housing units within the first two years of Stokes's tenure. Gibson was even less successful than Stokes in providing public housing for his low-income constituents. Yet by 1975, Newark had launched a new multibillion-dollar program of new and rehabilitated housing. Although uneven, the employment of blacks in municipal jobs also gradually improved, particularly in the professional and technical services areas. Following Maynard Jackson's election, for example, Atlanta's municipal work force increased from about 40 percent black in 1972 to about 50 percent black by the end of Jackson's first term. At the same time, the municipal contracts held by Atlanta blacks rose from 2 to 13 percent.

Despite their electoral successes, however, African Americans made up less than 0.5 percent of all elected officers. Moreover, they inherited cities that were in some ways "hollow prizes." In Gary, Newark, and Cleveland, black mayors and other local public officials faced a plethora of difficulties from the old regimes. As noted in Chapter 21, urban industries increasingly relocated to suburban locations or moved to the Sun Belt cities of the South and West. As industry relocated, so did the city's middle and working classes, which left the older central cities with a declining tax base and a rising public debt. From the end of World War II through the mid-1970s, municipal debts rose several times faster than income. Even as blacks took over the mayoralty of municipal governments and gained parity or majorities on city councils, whites continued to occupy the most highly paid slots as policemen, firemen, and various administrators, whereas blacks filled the lower-rung service, clerical, and support positions as park, recreation, transportation, and sanitation workers.

Black elected officials also faced the rise of new fiscally conservative Republican regimes. The resurgence of the Republican Party resulted in deep cuts in public spending at the national and state levels. Such cuts deprived municipalities of resources for much-needed social welfare programs. Supplementing its coercive and harsh policies toward welfare recipients on the one hand and militant advocates of black power on the other, the Republican Party used its enormous economic resources, power, and influence to build a conservative black constituency. From the vantage point of the Republican Party, certain affirmative action programs served a dual purpose. Even lukewarm endorsement of the Philadelphia Plan would strain the civil rights–labor alliance, whereas set-asides for black entrepreneurs promised to drive a wedge between the radical nationalist and integrationist wings of the black freedom movement. As early as March 1968, Richard Nixon foreshadowed the Republican strategy of fragmenting the black freedom struggle by seeking to redefine black power in conservative terms:

> Much of the black militant talk these days is actually in terms far closer to the doctrines of free enterprise than to those of the welfarist thirties terms of "pride," "ownership," "capital," "self-assurance," "self-respect." . . . What most of the militants are asking is not separation, but to be included in not as supplicants, but as owners, as entrepreneurs to have a share of the wealth and a piece of the action . . . yes, black power.

Black Capitalism and Entrepreneurship

Black capitalism was by no means invented by the Nixon administration during the late 1960s and early 1970s. As noted in previous chapters of this book, the concept of black entrepreneurship had deep roots in African American history. At the turn of the twentieth century, African Americans formed the Negro Business League under Booker T. Washington's leadership. During the 1920s, black enterprises proliferated with the upsurge of the "New Negro," the Garvey movement, and the cultural renaissance. Similarly, with the advent of the Black Power movement, some blacks accented entrepreneurial development as a form of black power. The Nation of Islam, for example, represented a great deal of continuity with past efforts to build a black economy within the larger context of the U.S. economy. By the early 1970s, the Nation of Islam had 250,000 dues-paying members; maintained 120 temples; and held property valued at $80 million. In addition to owning its own farmland in Georgia, Alabama, and Michigan, the organization owned its own clothing stores, bakeries, restaurants, dry cleaners, and food stores at its headquarters in Chicago, as well as in cities across the country. Moreover, the Nation of Islam operated a multimillion-dollar printing business that published its official organ, *Muhammad Speaks* (later the *Balalian News*). In one headline during the early 1970s, the paper declared: "Muslim Businesses Prosper While [U.S.] Economy Fails."

Following Nixon's endorsement of economic black nationalism (coupled with the government's violent repression of revolutionary black nationalism), black capitalism gained additional but quite diverse support within the African American community. Pioneer black nationalists and CORE activists Roy Innis and Floyd McKissick emerged as leading proponents of black capitalism. Innis soon articulated the view that "Black Power is Black Business," whereas McKissick adopted the tenets of black capitalism in his proposed Soul City, a new town to be carved out of rural North Carolina. Under the auspices of McKissick Enterprises, Soul City aimed to provide "a means for Black people to become a part of the American capitalist system and thereby achieve social and economic parity with the white community." Another version of black capitalist development emerged under the leadership of James Forman, former executive director of SNCC. In his "Black Manifesto to the White Christian Churches and the Jewish Synagogues of America, and All Other Racist Institutions," Forman rejected black capitalism as an ideology in favor of revolutionary socialism but nonetheless demanded $500 million in reparations from white institutions as partial payment for past discrimination against African Americans. Endorsed by the Black Economic Development Conference (held in Detroit in 1969), such reparations payments would be used to support a southern land bank for black farmers, small businesses for urban blacks, and a mass communications industry to counteract white racist propaganda.

After heading SCLC's Operation Breadbasket for four years, Rev. Jesse Jackson broke from the parent body in 1971 and formed a new organization, People United to Save Humanity (PUSH—later changed to People United to Serve Humanity). PUSH launched a variety of community-based social welfare and educational programs "to keep hope alive." Programs like PUSH-Excel encouraged young blacks to turn away from drugs, gangs, and street life and take responsibility for their own education and future. Jackson repeatedly told young blacks: "Up with Hope. Down with Dope." Yet from the outset, PUSH also encouraged the development of black capitalism. Under Jackson's leadership, PUSH negotiated economic "covenants" with major corporations, including General Foods, Avon Products, Schlitz and Miller Brewing Companies, and Quaker Oats, to name a few. The agreement with General Foods, for example, promised blacks not only some 360 new jobs at all levels of the firm but also a $500,000 increase in deposits in black banks; $20 million of business to black insurance companies; increased advertisements in the black press; and the use of black construction firms in the work of renovating General Foods plants.

Black economists also promoted various forms of black capitalism. As early as 1968, economist Andrew Brimmer, member of the Federal Reserve Board, exhorted blacks to forgo traditional definitions of black capitalism (which emphasized community-based black-owned businesses); to take jobs in established white corporations; and to create a new class of black managers, consultants, and chief executive officers. In his view, although the desegregation movement had removed the protective walls of segregation that had enabled black enterprises to thrive in the past, it had opened up new and more expansive opportunities in corporate America. Other black economists and their white allies advocated government and philanthropic support to help build a black capitalist class. Using a million-dollar philanthropic gift, economist Robert S. Browne spearheaded efforts to create a black economic research center, an emergency land fund, and an investment corporation. In his 1972–1973 report, Browne expressed the view that blacks would eventually break free of dependence on white support "at some far off day [when] there will have developed an array of financially independent black institutions which can fund the needs of the black community without reliance on sympathetic whites or on special government programs."

Under the impact of black capitalism, black enterprises expanded during the late 1960s and early 1970s. The number of black businesses increased from an estimated 32,000 in 1960; to 187,000 in 1972; to 231,200 in 1977. Between 1972 and 1977, black enterprises increased by 12 percent, with gross receipts rising by 47 percent. Manufacturing and wholesale firms showed the most significant increases in gross receipts (69 and 104 percent, respectively), but food stores and auto dealers/service stations reported the largest total amount of business ($786 million and $1.1 billion, respectively). Among the one hundred largest black-owned businesses by sales, the top three were the entertainment firm Motown Industries; the petroleum company Wallace and Wallace Enterprises; and the Johnson Publishing Company, which included cosmetics manufacturing and broadcasting networks. As a group, however, black insurance firms remained the oldest and most lucrative black-owned businesses. North Carolina Mutual of Durham had assets of $129 million; Atlanta Life Insurance, $80 million; and Golden State Mutual of Los Angeles, $44 million. Under pressure from black customers and civil rights organizations, IBM shifted a large portion of its group life coverage from Prudential to North Carolina Mutual, and the Ford Motor Company moved part of its group life coverage from John Hancock Insurance to Golden State Mutual.

Despite substantial growth, black enterprises did not reach their full potential. The poor economic position of blacks in the U.S. economy weakened black businesses, but it was not the full story. In dollar amount, the black consumer market was about the ninth largest in the world (about $70 billion in 1973). As the desegregation movement proceeded apace, large corporations launched new market research projects designed to tap the African American market. These firms minutely studied the consumer behavior of blacks, hired African American market specialists, and peddled their wares to targeted black consumers. Pepsi-Cola, Pillsbury, Procter & Gamble, and a plethora of alcohol and tobacco firms aggressively advertised in black publications and various outlets within the black community. When Procter & Gamble learned that large numbers of black households (22 percent, compared with 3 percent of white households) used Tide as a dishwashing as well as a laundry detergent, it tailored its marketing strategy to blacks. In the white-oriented media, the company's advertisement referred to Tide as a laundry detergent only, but in the black media, Tide became "an all-purpose detergent for dishes, in the bath, for washing fine fabrics, and in the laundry." In short, coupled with the ongoing difficulties that black workers and the poor faced in the changing urban economy, the aggressive campaigns of large corporations cut into the prospective market of black business people and made black capitalism a limited route of upward mobility for African Americans.

THE SECOND BLACK RENAISSANCE: CULTURAL AND INTELLECTUAL LIFE

As suggested earlier, the Black Power movement took a variety of forms. It gained expression in the resurgence of black capitalism, the expansion of electoral politics, and the growth of revolutionary black nationalism. Yet it had its most far-reaching impact on the development of black culture and consciousness. From the outset, some activists emphasized cultural black nationalism as the first step along the road to revolution. As a preparatory step to picking up the gun and informing its use, cultural nationalists emphasized the need to lay claim to the minds of African Americans. They rejected European and Euro-American models of culture, economics, and society and called for a thorough revamping of African American thought and social practices—through a deeper appreciation of African and African American history and culture. Symbolic of this change, cultural nationalists urged blacks to abandon "slave names" and adopt Swahili-, Islamic-, or African-based names at the individual level and to transform their collective self-designation from "colored" or "Negro" to "black," "Afro-American," or "African American." Ron Karenga stated, "We're fighting a revolution to win the minds of black people . . . for race pride and the pursuit of blackness. . . . The issue is racism, not economics; not a class struggle but a global struggle against racism."

Black Cultural Nationalism

Cultural nationalists not only encouraged African Americans to look back to a glorious African past before the slave trade but also acknowledged the struggles, beauty, dignity, and courage of black people within America itself. They accented elements of continuity between enslavement, Jim Crow, and contemporary black culture. Accordingly, cultural nationalists adopted the slogan "Black Is Beautiful" and coined the term *soul* as a distinguishing feature of African American identity. Such terminology linked African Americans to each other and to all peoples of African descent and encouraged African-inspired aesthetics and tastes—hairstyles such as "the natural" (or even shaved heads) over artificially straightened or processed hair; clothing such as the dashiki over conventional European forms of dress; the music of such artists as James Brown ("Soul Brother No. 1") and Aretha Franklin (the "Queen of Soul"); and the staples of African American cuisine: chitterlings, hogmaws, black-eyed peas, collard greens, and cornbread, among other dishes.

Under the leadership of Ron Karenga and the Los Angeles–based group US, black cultural nationalism gained organized and disciplined expression. Formed in the wake of the Watts rebellion, US aimed to rebuild African American culture around Afrocentric rather than Eurocentric ideas. US required members to learn Swahili, adopt Afro-Swahili names, shave their heads, wear African-style clothes, and adopt the Kwaida's ("black value system") seven principles: unity, self-determination, collective work and responsibility, cooperative economics, purpose, creativity, and

Aretha Franklin *(above)*, called the "First Lady of Soul" and the "Queen of Soul," and James Brown *(opposite)*, called the "Godfather of Soul" and "Soul Brother No. 1," pioneered the transition of black music from rhythm and blues to soul. *Neal Preston/Corbis*

faith. Amiri Baraka became the most important convert to Karenga's ideas. A graduate of Howard University in Washington, D.C., and author of numerous poems and plays, Baraka aimed to develop a black aesthetic that highlighted the gulf between African American and Euro-American culture. As early as 1964, partly with funds from the Office of Economic Opportunity's War on Poverty program, Jones founded the Black Arts Repertory Theatre in Harlem. The increasing radicalization of his plays soon provoked poverty officials to cancel his funding. In 1966, he moved to Newark, New Jersey, where he founded the Spirit House Temple of Kwaida (community center and school of spiritual values); established the journal *Newark* and Jihad Publications; and helped to launch the united-front Congress of African Peoples in 1970. In a collection of essays called *Home* (1966), Baraka signaled his gradual return to his roots as a black man. He now criticized his earlier lifestyle among the white "beat generation." As he put it, "The rebels among us have become merely people like myself who grow beards and will not participate in politics. Drugs . . . complete isolation from the vapid mores of the country, a few current ways out." Baraka soon abandoned LeRoi Jones, his "slave name," and adopted Imamu ("leader") Amiri ("warrior") Baraka ("blessing"); divorced his white wife; married a black woman; and embarked on a vigorous effort to transform U.S. society and the place of blacks within it. In the poem "For Tom Postell, Dead Black Poet," Baraka expressed regret for ignoring his black past: "You told me, you told me a thousand years ago. And the white man thing you screamed on me, all true. . . . I strode with them, played with them, thought myself one with them."

Baraka emphasized the use of poems and plays as vehicles for black revolutionary struggle. He called for "poems that kill / Assassin poems, poems that shoot guns." At one point, he even declared a moratorium on love poems: "Let there be no love poems written / until love can exist freely and / cleanly." Nonetheless, in the poems "Nation Time" (1970) and "In Our Terribleness" (1970), he urged black men and women to build the black nation through love, family, and revolutionary struggle: "Man woman child in a house is a nation." Along with poems, Baraka believed that the central mission of the black playwright was to create a drama that responded to the contemporary needs of black people. Such drama would be performed in black communities, where black audiences would provide critical feedback and shape the artists' creative work itself. In rapid succession, Baraka wrote and produced plays that addressed issues of black nationalism, revolution, and social struggle: *A Black Mass; Great Goodness of Life; Madheart;* and, most

notably, *Slave Ship,* which reminded African Americans of the pain and suffering of their enslavement and encouraged resistance in the present.

The Black Arts Movement

Amiri Baraka both reflected and influenced the fluorescence of the Second Renaissance, or Black Arts movement (BAM). Growing numbers of black creative artists contributed to the emergence of the Second Renaissance. Such artists sought an explicit relationship with the expanding freedom struggle; a more positive identification with their blackness; a sense of brotherhood and sisterhood with Africa; and a willingness to encourage armed struggle if necessary to secure their freedom. No less forceful than Baraka in their call for poems of liberation were poets Sonia Sanchez, Don L. Lee (Haki Madhubuti), and Nikki Giovanni, among others. As noted in Chapter 21, Giovanni asked, "Nigger / Can you kill . . . kill a honkie." In "Poem for Black Boys," mentioned earlier, she also encouraged young black males to "GO DIRECTLY TO THE STREETS / This is a game you can win." Addressing black women, she wrote: "What can I, a poor Black woman, do to destroy America?" Her answer was also equally potent: "Blessed be machine guns in Black hands . . . that destroy our oppressor / Peace Peace, Black Peace at all costs."

Reinforcing the ideas of black poets were the works of black novelists, playwrights, and visual artists. Novelist John Oliver Killens succeeded his integrationist *Youngblood* (1954) with his militant *And Then We Heard the Thunder* (1968), which accented the need for black unity in the fight for social justice. Similarly, novelist William Melvin Kelley followed his *A Different Drummer* (1962), a treatment of black migration as a symbol of resistance to Jim Crow, with two condemnations of northern whites in *Dem* (1967) and *Dunsford Travels Everywheres*

(1970). In *Dunsford Travels Everywheres,* Kelley's principal character discovered the language of the black working class and poor as a resource for resisting the racist assumptions of his white friends. When Dunsford refused to join in patriotic singing and celebration of white power, his white friend asked: " 'Well, didn't you feel like singing?' . . . 'No, motherfucker!' 'Where on earth,' Dunsford asks himself, 'had those words come from.' . . . [After all, he was the son of middle-class parents.] He smiled, laughed behind closed lips at the street-words that had waited inside him all these years to jump out at Lane's face." Black theater flourished under the leadership of artists like Barbara Ann Teer, founder of the National Black Theater (1968); Fred Hudson, founder of the Frederick Douglass Creative Arts Center (an outgrowth of the Watts Writers Workshop) in Los Angeles; and the playwright Ed Bullen, founder of the Black Arts West in San Francisco. Bullen's plays included *Death List, Night of the Beast,* and *Gentleman Caller.* The latter featured the transformation of a maid into a revolutionary black nationalist who urged "Black people to come together in unity, brotherhood and Black spirituality to form a nation that will rise from our enslaved mass and meet the oppressor. DEATH TO THE ENEMIES OF BLACK PEOPLE!"

Visual artists strengthened the spread of black nationalism. By the mid-1960s, the painter Romare Bearden had moved away from abstraction and focused explicitly on scenes from contemporary black life. In 1966, Bearden organized the showing of "Art of the American Negro" in New York. Two years later, the American Greetings Gallery in New York City exhibited "New Voices: Fifteen Black Artists." In 1969, the New York Metropolitan Museum featured the photographs of James Van Der Zee in its "Harlem on My Mind" exhibit. In 1971, the Whitney Museum of American Art also sponsored an exhibit, entitled "Contemporary Black American Art." As early as 1962, under the leadership of Jeff Donaldson, Wadsworth Jarrell, and Barbara Jones-Hogu, African Americans formed the Organization of Black American Culture (OBAC) artists' workshop. In 1967, the group painted *The Wall of Respect* on Chicago's South Side, featuring the images of black leaders, mainly men like King, Malcolm X, and Du Bois. Two years later, the group produced *The Wall of Truth.* Located across the street from the first mural, this one reinforced the message of empowerment and cultural kinship among blacks. In the meantime, OBAC had changed its name to Coalition of Black Revolutionary Artists (COBRA); it later adopted another name, the African Commune of Bad Relevant Artists (AfriCOBRA). In the 1970s, the group staged an exhibit entitled "Ten in Search of a Nation," first at the black-owned Weusi Gallery and later at the Studio Museum in Harlem. Jeff Donaldson, a founding member of the group, explained: "We strive for images inspired by African people/experience and images which African people can relate to directly without formal art training and/or experience. Art [is] for people and not for critics."

The rise of cultural black nationalism was by no means unproblematic. Some artists rejected the call for an engaged black arts movement. Douglas Turner Ward, founder of the Negro Ensemble Company in 1967, hoped to keep black theater flexible enough to accommodate white participants "if they found inspiration in its purpose." Playwright Lonne Elder, author of the widely staged *Ceremonies in Dark Old Men,* took a pragmatic position. Although he looked forward to a time when blacks could produce independently of white support, he believed that it was necessary for blacks to tailor their offerings to white audiences. In the pamphlet *Black Is a Color* (1968), San Francisco Bay Area painter Raymond Saunders attacked the black arts movement as too narrowly focused on the racial issue. For their part, black women accented the need for a more gender-conscious black arts movement. In 1969, sculptor Barbara Chase-Riboud affirmed her commitment to the Black Power movement in her *Monument to Malcolm X,* which aimed to "embody the idea of Malcolm rather than to make monuments to a dead man." Three years later, however, she produced *Confessions,* a black bronze sculpture of a female figure draped in a wool-like garment from head to foot, symbolizing Chase-Riboud's growing gender consciousness. In 1970, author/poet/playwright Maya Angelou wrote *I Know Why the Caged Bird Sings.* The first part of a four-volume autobiographical work, *Caged Bird* focuses on the difficulties of a young black girl growing up in Arkansas, Missouri, and California. When an interviewer later asked Angelou if she envisioned "young Maya as a symbolic character for

The author, playwright, and poet Maya Angelou became the first black woman to have a screenplay produced when her first book, *I Know Why the Caged Bird Sings* (1970), was made into a film. *AP/Wide World Photos*

every black girl growing up in America," she replied, "Yes, after a while I did." In 1974, Ntozake Shange crafted her choreopoem *for coloured girls who have considered suicide when the rainbow is enuf,* which appeared on Broadway two years later. Shange emphasized the ability of diverse black women to surmount rejection and verbal and physical abuse and move forward with strength and dignity; she also expressed a commitment to fighting class and racial inequality by helping to strengthen linkages between black men and women.

The writings of Toni Morrison, Alice Walker, and Margaret Walker are perhaps most emblematic of the difficulties and triumphs of black women artists during the period of black power and shifting African American definitions of themselves as a people. In the 1970s, Toni Morrison produced the first and second of her several novels: *The Bluest Eye* (1970) and *Song of Solomon* (1974). In *The Bluest Eye,* she explored the obstacles facing young black girls entering puberty. Sexual assaults from within and outside the family threatened to destroy their lives before they embarked on adulthood, and the pain that Pecola suffered drove her into a pathetic yearning for the blue eyes of a white girl. Morrison concludes by indicting the social system that closed channels to Pecola's realization of her full human potential:

"This soil is bad for certain kinds of flowers. Certain seeds it will not nurture, certain fruit it will not bear, and when the land kills of its own volition, we acquiesce and say the victim had no right to live." In *The Third Life of Grange Copeland* (1970), Alice Walker details the difficulties that a father and son face in white America and the ways that they turn their anger on the women in their lives. Such men prove incapable of showing the love that both the civil rights and the Black Power movement advocated. Margaret Walker's *Jubilee* (1966), a fictionalized biography of Elvira Ware Brown (Vyry, Walker's great-grandmother), expressed faith in the ability of people to maintain their humanity against the odds. Forty years in the making, Walker's *Jubilee* is also a key illustration of the difficulties that faced black women writers, compared with those of their male counterparts, before the 1970s and 1980s. Walker later described these difficulties in two separate publications, *How I Wrote Jubilee* and *Why I Wrote Jubilee*. Speaking of Walker's long career and difficulties with publishers and the public, one recent critic concluded that a "sense of alienation, of being embattled, of feeling betrayed, is a significant part of the experience of Black women writers."

Under the impact of the Black Power movement, African Americans also revamped their music and changed the nature of their participation in American popular culture. Black filmmakers like Melvin Van Peebles, Gordon Parks Sr., and Gordon Parks Jr. produced films emphasizing an urban world of drugs, prostitution, theft, and violence: *Sweet Sweetback's Bad-Ass Song* (1971), *Shaft* (1971), and *Superfly* (1972). Understandably, critics soon referred to this genre as "blaxploitation films." Yet in the hands of black directors and writers, these films portrayed blacks resisting and even defeating previous white exploiters of the black community, including the Mafia as well as corrupt mainstream public officials like policemen and other representatives of city government. As such, these films reflected the influence of the Black Power movement. Other black films of the period cut against the grain of the blaxploitation genre: *The Landlord*, starring Diana Sands and Louis Gossett Jr. (1970); *Sounder*, with Cicely Tyson and Paul Winfield (1972); and *Lady Sings the Blues*, with Diana Ross and Billy Dee Williams (1972). Although the big screen offered some diversity in its portrayal of blacks, comedies dominated the roster of television shows about blacks: *Julia* (1968), *Sanford and Son* (1971), *Good Times* (1973), and *The Jeffersons* (1974). Nonetheless, by portraying a wider and more diverse cast of characters within the black community, the new comedies often underscored a strong work ethic and intelligence among African Americans and transcended earlier stereotypes.

More so than the movies or television, music captured the impact of the Black Power movement as rhythm and blues increasingly gave way to "soul" during the late 1960s and early 1970s. Defined as a fusion of rhythm, blues, spiritual, and gospel elements, soul gained its most powerful expression in the music of Aretha Franklin and James Brown. Both James Brown, called the "Godfather of Soul" and "Soul Brother No. 1," and Aretha Franklin, called the "First Lady of Soul" and the "Queen of Soul," produced gospel-inspired rhythm and blues with an emotional intensity that appealed to the masses of African Americans. In addition to numerous songs exploring personal relationships, soul artists emphasized black pride and called for African American unity in the struggle for empowerment and full recognition of their human and civil rights. In a series of songs, for example, James Brown reiterated these themes: "Say It Loud—I'm Black and I'm Proud" (1968); "I Don't Want Nobody to Give Me Nothing (Open Up the Door I'll Get It Myself" (1969); and "Get Up, Get Into It and Get Involved" (1970). In 1968, *Time* magazine carried a cover story on Aretha Franklin under the headline "The Sound of Soul. Singer Aretha." The magazine entitled its feature article "Lady Soul Singing It Like It Is." Franklin's signature song, "Respect" (1967), not only resonated as a rallying cry for the freedom struggle of black men and women but crossed over and reached the top of the white-oriented pop music chart as well. In 1969, precisely twenty years after *Billboard* recognized the arrival of rhythm and blues and changed its "Race Record" chart, the magazine now changed its "Rhythm & Blues" label to "Soul." As musicologist Portia Maultsby concludes, "These two events signaled a victory for the Black Power Movement because both magazines used a term that was first coined and used by African Americans to describe a new and distinctive black musical genre."

As the Black Power movement faced the repressive apparatus of the state, coupled with dashed expectations for upward mobility for large numbers of poor and working-class blacks, soul music underwent a metamorphosis into "funk." Rooted deeply in the rhythm, blues, and soul sounds of Aretha Franklin, James Brown, and others, funk gradually surfaced by the mid-1970s with such groups as Earth, Wind, and Fire; Cool and the Gang; the Isley Brothers; and, most notably, George Clinton and the P(ure)-Funk groups like Parliament-Funkadelic. Somewhat emblematic of the transition to funk was James Brown's changing relationship with Richard Nixon. Before 1972, Brown told *Rolling Stone Magazine* that he and Nixon "did not get along. . . . He asked me to go to Memphis with him in the campaign. I don't want to be his bullet proof vest. I didn't want to protect him from my people, deceive them. Make them think he is with me and I'm with him." In 1972, however, following his endorsement of Nixon, some of Brown's most scathing critics now substituted "Sold Brother No. 1" for "Soul Brother No. 1." Brown would later lament his choice in the song "Funky President (People It's Bad)," but it was George Clinton who produced some of the most telling social commentary on early to mid-1970s class and race relations in his albums *Chocolate City* (1975) and *Mothership Connection* (1975). Although the Black Power movement and black nationalist thinking informed the music of artists like Clinton, African American music retained its place in leisure time activities, dance, and the pursuit of "a good time." Artists Kool and the Gang and Graham Central Station, with "Let the Music Take Your Mind" (1974), "Release Yourself" (1974), and "It's Alright" (1975), helped to set the stage for the rise of the music dubbed "disco" during the late 1970s.

Black Power in the Sports World

In professional sports, Cassius Clay best captured the growing influence of the Black Power movement. During the early 1960s, he had won the heavyweight boxing championship of the world, joined the Nation of Islam, and changed his name

Muhammad Ali knocking out Floyd Patterson, December 1965. By changing his name from Cassius Clay to Muhammad Ali and refusing induction into the U.S. Army because of his religious beliefs, Ali symbolized the growing assertiveness of African Americans during the Black Power movement. *Archive Photos*

to Muhammad Ali. In his subsequent fight with former heavyweight champion Floyd Patterson in 1966, whites perceived Ali as a dangerous symbol of revolt and loudly proclaimed their support of his opponent; Ali won the match, and his reputation as a skilled prizefighter soared. He now became an even greater symbol of black power and resistance. He not only opposed the persistence of racial inequality in the United States and urged blacks to help build their own nation but also denounced the war in Vietnam, arguing that the Viet Cong were not the enemy of black people. When ordered to appear for induction into the U.S. Army, he refused to step forward. As a result of these actions, the U.S. government stripped him of his boxing crown and forbade him to fight in the United States.

Muhammad Ali's actions, coupled with the rapid spread of the Black Power movement, helped to bring increasing numbers of black athletes into the liberation struggle. Under the leadership of Harry Edwards, a black sociology professor at San Jose State College in California, several black athletes supported a movement to boycott the 1968 Olympic games. Boycott leaders outlined a list of several demands: reinstatement of Muhammad Ali's crown; exclusion of apartheid South African and Rhodesian teams from the event; the hiring of black coaches for the U.S. teams; and the desegregation of the New York Athletic Club (NYAC). At its

100th Anniversary Track and Field Games scheduled for Madison Square Garden, the NYAC planned to showcase prospective athletes for the 1968 Olympic games. The protest succeeded when the Soviet Union refused to participate, and most blacks and some of their white supporters refused to compete.

Although some black athletes like UCLA's basketball star Lew Alcindor (later Kareem Abdul-Jabbar) boycotted the games in Mexico City, others participated in the 1968 games but voiced their solidarity with the movement by staging their own protests. The most prominent of these were gold medal sprinter Tommie Smith and bronze medalist John Carlos. At the 1968 games, the two men mounted the victory stand, and while the National Anthem played and the American flag waved, they bowed their heads and raised their gloved, clenched fists high in the air, giving the Black Power salute. As with the U.S. Boxing Commission's response to Ali, the U.S. Olympic Committee swiftly removed Smith and Carlos from the U.S. team, confiscated their medals, and demanded that they leave Mexico City within forty-eight hours. The actions of Smith and Carlos provided one of the most potent symbols of black dissatisfaction with the slow pace of change and the shift from nonviolent direct action to black power in the black freedom struggle. In the wake of Mexico City, black athletes launched protests on campuses across the nation and increasingly joined forces with the larger Black Power movement. They demanded the hiring of black coaches at predominantly white institutions; freedom to express their cultural beliefs; and an end to various forms of harassment from coaches, teammates, and members of the wider university and college towns in which they lived, played, and studied.

～

DURING THE LATE 1960S AND EARLY 1970S, the Black Power movement offered a revolutionary alternative to the nonviolent direct action strategies of the modern civil rights movement. Emphasizing black pride, independent self-assertion, and the right to armed self-defense, a generation of college students and community-based activists built new secular organizations designed to complement and even supplant the church as the organizing base for social change. For a brief moment, SNCC, CORE, the Black Panther Party, US, and a series of Black Power conferences constituted the organizational centers of the black liberation movement. Partly because revolutionary black nationalism emphasized the mass mobilization of poor and working-class blacks and encouraged opposition to the Vietnam War, it came under the combined assault of federal, state, and local authorities. Such repressive tactics exposed and intensified deep divisions within the ranks of the Black Power movement and precipitated a search for more precise definitions of the term. Whereas some activists focused on armed struggle, others emphasized black power as a vehicle for gaining influence through established channels while at the same time affirming the beauty, struggles, dignity, and courage of black people in Africa and the diaspora. As we will see in Chapter 23, these unresolved issues precipitated a movement to redefine the boundaries of black culture, politics, and economics during the closing decades of the twentieth century.

CHAPTER 23

~

Redefining the Boundaries of Black Culture and Politics

During the final quarter of the twentieth century, African Americans continued to struggle and achieve within the context of rapid socioeconomic and
technological changes. The nation's transition from a durable-goods to a
service-providing economy nearly destroyed the urban industrial working class
without fully integrating blacks into the new knowledge-intensive industries or
white-collar jobs. These changes were not simply the result of large-scale structural
changes influencing the U.S. working class as a whole. They also reflected the impact of new patterns of labor, housing, and institutional discrimination that gained
expression in the resurgence of racism and popular attacks on affirmative action
and social welfare programs. Although both Republicans and Democrats would occupy the White House during the period, the Republican regime of President
Ronald Reagan would set the tone for social welfare and affirmative action policies.

As deindustrialization and conservative reactions against the gains of the modern civil rights and Black Power movements gained momentum, African Americans
faced deep and troubling social relations at home. Black urban communities increasingly fragmented along class and, to some extent, gender lines. The benefici-
aries of affirmative action programs—middle-class blacks and better-educated
members of the black working class—experienced a degree of upward mobility and
migrated into outlying urban and suburban neighborhoods. They left working-
class and poor blacks, disproportionately single women with children, concentrated in the central cities, where violence, drug addiction, and class-stratified social
spaces intensified, causing acute tensions in day-to-day intraracial as well as interracial relations. Like so many past eras in black history, this one challenged African
Americans to develop strategies for coping with the harsh realities of life in the
postindustrial city. Although their responses were inadequate to fully address the
enormous difficulties that they faced, African Americans were able to redefine
the boundaries of black politics and culture and give direction to their own lives as
the nation neared the new millennium.

DEINDUSTRIALIZATION AND COMMUNITY FRAGMENTATION

Deindustrialization resulted in the increasing movement of jobs to the suburbs, the Sun Belt, South America, and other parts of the world. Globalization, as one economist described these changes, was "the intensification of worldwide social relations which link distant localities in such a way that local happenings are shaped by events occurring many miles away and vice versa." Between 1983 and 1988, U.S. workers lost nearly 10 million jobs through plant closings, movement of companies overseas, or the adoption of new labor-displacing technologies. Whereas nearly 33 percent of all U.S. workers held manufacturing jobs before 1960, by 1980 that figure had shrunk to 20 percent; by 1990 it was down to 10 to14 percent, and government economists were predicting a drop to under 5 percent by the turn of the century.

Although economic inequality affected all American workers, African Americans bore the brunt of hardship and suffering caused by the transition to a new information-producing and service economy. The vast majority of African Americans continued to work, but their prospects for a decent living wage decreased. Between 1973 and 1987, the number of black men twenty to twenty-nine years of age in manufacturing jobs declined from about three of every eight to about one in five. African Americans regularly accented the destructive impact of the machine and technological change on their lives. On the South Side of Chicago, for example, a janitor spoke for many of his black counterparts when he described how a machine destroyed his old job at a printing company:

> The machines are putting a lot of people out of jobs. I worked for *Time* magazine for seven years on a videograph printer and they come along with the Abedic printer, it cost them half a million dollars: they did what we did in half the time, eliminated two shifts.

Although the share of such men in retail trade and service jobs increased, wages were 25 to 30 percent lower than those in industrial jobs. The number of unemployed and discouraged black workers (prime working-age adults who were not in school, not working, and not looking for work for even a single week in a particular year) also increased from less than 10 percent before 1975 to over 13 percent of the black work force for most of the 1980s. The number of discouraged white workers also increased, but the black figure was double that of whites. Moreover, although some blacks continued to gain access to middle-class professional, clerical, and managerial occupations, such jobs were insufficient to offset the loss of industrial jobs.

In retrospect, the old industrial order seemed like a golden age of job opportunities and neighborhood cohesion. An unemployed industrial worker recalled:

> You could walk out of the house and get a job. Maybe not what you want but you could get a job. Now, you can't find anything. A lot of people in this neighborhood,

they want to work but they can't get work. A few, but a very few, they just don't want to work. The vast majority they want to work but they can't find work.

In frustration and having few alternatives, many turned to crime and drugs and ended up in jail or dead at an early age. In a North Philadelphia neighborhood, social anthropologist Elijah Anderson reported drug dealers and users as young as ten years old. One of his interviewees lamented the decline of neighborhood oversight of the young:

> Ten years old? Man, that freaked me right out. . . . Ten years old, smoking a joint, had over $300 worth of clothes on . . . you should have seen him sitting like this [pretends to roll a joint], rolled that shit like a pro, two hands and tongue in it. I said, Jesus, Oh, my God[!]

In her interview with the anthropologist John Langston Gwaltney, one black woman related the painful death of a drug addict with whom she had grown up: "Every time he got caught [for illegal substances] they'd just give him a little time and then send him back here to worry and rob and cut and shoot up! . . . He used to be the finest person you would ever want to meet." Living conditions grew worse as well. In Chicago's Robert Taylor Homes, a public housing project, over 90 percent of the families with children were headed by women (most on Aid to Families with Dependent Children), and 47 percent of the population were unemployed. One resident of the Robert Taylor Homes complained: "We live stacked on top of one another with no elbow room. Danger is all around. There is little privacy or peace and no quiet. And the world looks on all of us as project rats, living on a reservation, like untouchables."

Demographics of Inner-City Black Communities

Even more so than black workers and the poor themselves, scholars, policymakers, journalists, and activists underscored a grim reality for large numbers of African Americans and their families. Inner-city black communities included disproportionately high rates of poverty, homelessness, single-parent households, crime, drug addiction, and deteriorating health conditions. The average life expectancy of black men and women continued to lag five to eight years behind that of their white counterparts. The proportion of blacks living in metropolitan ghetto poverty areas rose from about 33 percent in 1970 to nearly 50 percent in 1990. By 1982 homelessness had increased so rapidly that analysts treated it as an increasingly distinct social category. Five years later, blacks made up 40 to 47 percent of the single homeless men and women and 56 percent of all homeless women and children.

Out-of-wedlock black births (particularly teenage births) and families headed by women increased from 25 percent in the mid-1960s to well over 60 and 40 percent, respectively, by the late 1980s. Heroin and cocaine addiction reached epidemic proportions during the early 1980s when street-level drug dealers transformed the more expensive white powder into small but potent "nuggets that could be smoked—crack." In 1991, the National Institute of Drug Abuse household survey

The city of Chicago, with the South Side's Robert Taylor Homes in the foreground. As the nation's industrial economy collapsed, life in public housing projects symbolized the increasing fragmentation of the African American community along gender and class lines. *AP Photo/Beth A. Keiser*

reported nearly a half million crack users in the United States: 39 percent black, 14 percent Hispanic, and the remainder white. At the same time, the AIDS epidemic was taking its toll. According to the Atlanta-based Center for Disease Control, African Americans made up nearly 27 percent of all AIDS cases, but African American and Latino women made up nearly 90 percent of all women and children reported with AIDS. Medical studies also showed that blacks with AIDS died nearly five times as rapidly as their white counterparts.

Poverty and crime were disproportionately concentrated in black public housing projects. In 1983, nearly twenty-five thousand families with children lived in Chicago's public housing projects, but only 8 percent were married-couple families, and nearly 80 percent of married couples received Aid for Families with Dependent Children. The Robert Taylor Homes, the city's single largest housing project, housed only 0.5 percent of the city's total population but accounted for 9 percent of rapes, 10 percent of aggravated assaults, and 11 percent of the city's reported murders. With an estimated 12 percent of the nation's total population, black men made up over 50 percent of prison inmates—mostly young men under age thirty by 1990. The black incarceration rate was seven-fold that of whites, making African Americans the most heavily incarcerated population in the world.

Federal policies exacerbated the problems of violence, drug use, and incarceration within the black community. In 1988, the Reagan administration enacted the Omnibus Anti–Drug Abuse Act, which required a mandatory sentence for anyone possessing five grams of crack cocaine. In contrast, the law allowed possessors of five grams of the more expensive powdered cocaine to escape any minimum sentence and often permitted offenders to go free on probation when caught and convicted. Moreover, the law required the possession of five hundred grams of powdered cocaine before a sentence of five years' incarceration could be imposed. Consequently, although powdered cocaine users exceeded crack cocaine users, the latter accounted for the bulk of arrests, convictions, and incarceration. In 1992,

African Americans, mainly young men, accounted for over 90 percent of all federal crack cocaine offenders. In contrast to the crackdown on street users, however, drug enforcement policies ignored the powerful international suppliers of drugs, partly for foreign policy reasons. In 1988, the U.S. Senate Subcommittee on Terrorism, Narcotics, and International Operations reported that the U.S. State Department regularly dealt with drug dealers. A former military official was even more direct: "The fact is, if you want to go into the subversion business, collect intelligence, and move arms, you deal with drug movers."

As part of the growing harshness of criminal procedures, many states abandoned "indeterminate sentencing" and established "mandatory sentences" for certain crimes. Critics of the new approach to criminal justice increasingly complained that the new trend emphasized "warehousing and punishment" rather than "rehabilitation, which is the professed goal of state prisons." The return of chain gangs and the death penalty to the nation's criminal justice system underscored the harsh conditions facing young blacks in the post–civil rights era. In May 1996, after a thirty-year hiatus, Alabama reestablished the chain gang, placing male prisoners on state-sponsored road-building, forestry, and gravel-making projects. Florida and Arizona soon followed suit, and northern states like Wisconsin seriously considered instituting similar measures. After disappearing in 1972, the death penalty for certain crimes returned in 1977 when Utah became the first state to carry out the death penalty since 1967. In 1986, the U.S. Supreme Court sanctioned the death penalty, despite widespread evidence of racial bias in such sentencing. Two years later, the Court also sanctioned death sentences for juveniles and mentally retarded offenders. Between1967 and 1996, the states executed some 313 people, and another 3,000 occupied death row. African Americans and Latinos made up over 45 percent of all new capital deaths, mainly for crimes against whites. Among the 32 juveniles put to death, 56 percent were minorities—again, executed mainly for crimes against whites. A *New York Times* journalist denounced such decisions as "a mockery" of the nation's "pretensions to be the leading proponent of human rights!" When DNA tests exonerated some black death-row inmates, the unequal administration of capital punishment was confirmed.

Migration to the Suburbs and the South

Motivated by deteriorating social conditions in the inner cities and the prospects for a better life on the periphery, the number of blacks moving to the suburbs nearly doubled during the 1980s. Since suburban blacks had higher average incomes, rates of homeownership, and education than inner-city blacks, some contemporary analysts celebrated this movement as the harbinger of a new and more viable black middle class. As one demographic study put it, the trend toward suburbanization promised to give more blacks "the opportunity to build equity in a home" and thus "help to secure middle-class status and transmission of that status across generations." The percentage of blacks living in suburban areas nationwide increased from less than 10 percent during the 1960s and early 1970s to 23 percent in 1980. Partly as a result of suburbanization, between 1970 and 1980, the residential segregation index (based on census tract data within cities, not including suburbs) dropped slightly in Chicago, New York, Detroit, Milwaukee, Los Angeles, Atlanta, and Oakland.

As some northern and western blacks moved out of the central cities to the surrounding suburbs, still others moved back south. Beginning in the 1970s and accelerating during the 1980s and early 1990s, more blacks moved from the North and West to the South than vice versa. Before the 1970s, only a small group of about fifteen thousand people who had moved north returned south each year. Thereafter, the return migration of blacks increased to about fifty thousand annually. And whereas young adult men and women had dominated earlier streams of migration, now young children often led the way, suggesting that northern and western blacks sent children south to protect them from the growing dangers of the urban environment of their birth. When the civil rights activist Bernard LaFayette took a job as principal of Tuskegee High School in Tuskegee, Alabama, he discovered that many of his young students

> had been raised in the ghettos of the North and the West, in New York or Chicago or Detroit or Los Angeles, more often than not in single-parent homes. Their parents, barely able to manage their own lives, had eventually shipped them back home to be with their grandparents in the presumably gentler, less predatory, and less violent atmosphere of the small-town South.

When elderly southern-born adults returned, they came to retire or to work. One returnee stated, "You go back to your proving ground, the place where you had your first cry, gave that first punch you had to throw in order to survive." For their part, young working-age adults hoped to carve out a life for themselves in an economy that promised more than their deindustrializing home. In 1978, for the first time, the black monthly magazine *Ebony* listed five southern cities among the "ten best cities for blacks" seeking upward mobility in the U.S. economy. In the past, northern and western cities had predominated, with few or no southern cities on the list. By 1990, some five hundred thousand blacks had returned south, and the U.S. Census Bureau predicted a continuation of the trend through the 1990s.

Migration from the frost belt to the Sun Belt was not easy for some young migrants. Take the experience of Massillon, Ohio's Z-Band, for example. During the mid-1980s, three young brothers—Donnie, Bruce, and Greg Harris—and their friends set out to advance their music career. Members of a local group, the Z-Band (including Rodney Wisdom, Bobby Birdsong, and Tim Cousins), they had gained substantial recognition for their music in the Massillon-Canton, Ohio, area. Their music provided hope and helped to lift the spirit of a community in the throes of deindustrialization. As one out-of-town visitor recalled, "Man, they could play and sing!" But now it was time to move on and try their luck in Atlanta via a short stay in Los Angeles, California. After hearing a promoter describe opportunities in Atlanta, the group moved to this Sun Belt metropolis, but opportunities to gain jobs in the music field failed to materialize. The band ran out of money and members took to sleeping in their cars while working part-time jobs to make ends meet.

After they secured a small apartment together, the resulting tensions from living in close quarters tested their endurance.

Along with suburbanization and return migration, there was a parallel movement of middle-class and affluent whites from the suburbs, now in decline, to the central cities. These young urban professionals, or "yuppies," claimed large areas of living space in renovated Victorian homes previously occupied by poor and working-class blacks in the central cities. This process of "gentrification" enabled whites to reclaim prime urban real estate, drove up costs, and forced increasing numbers of the black poor and working class to disperse to other poor areas of the city, leave for the South, or migrate to deteriorating sections of white working-class and lower-middle-class suburbs on the periphery of cities as diverse as Boston, San Francisco, Philadelphia, Savannah, Charleston, and Baltimore. In Charleston, young urban professional and business people converted former slave quarters into expensive apartments. In Washington, D.C., alley dwellings formerly occupied by the city's poorest residents now housed U.S. senators and congressmen, among other urban elites.

At the same time, growing numbers of Asian, Latino, and Caribbean immigrants occupied neighborhoods adjacent to, or formerly occupied by, blacks. By 1990, nearly 25 percent of the nation's total population were people of Asian, Latino, Native American, and African descent (including thousands of people from the English-speaking Caribbean and Africa). Such diversity added a new and more complex dimension to race and class relations.

As these diverse groups entered the nation's cities, competition and friction emerged between them and African Americans. When numerous Koreans established grocery stores in African American and Latino areas, the resulting conflicts culminated in the killing of several African Americans and some Koreans. The most well-known case involved the killing of fifteen-year-old Latasha Harlins in Los Angeles by Korean grocer Soon Ja Du. Blacks launched widespread boycotts of Korean businesses, and their resentment was heightened when a local judge placed Du on five years' probation and levied a fine of $500 rather than imposing a prison sentence.

Although diversity among nonwhite ethnic and nationality groups heightened multiple lines of racial conflict, the black-white divide retained prominence. Despite the passage of open-housing legislation in 1968 and the increasing suburbanization of the black population, whites had over 70 percent of their numbers in outlying metropolitan suburbs, compared with just over 20 percent for blacks. The most outstanding examples of black suburbanization were in Birmingham; Norfolk; Memphis; East St. Louis; Camden, New Jersey; and to some extent, Pittsburgh, where blacks experienced substantial segregation in areas that resembled the central city in unemployment and poverty rates. Residential segregation along black-white lines persisted for a variety of reasons: weak enforcement of the laws; costly and time-consuming litigation required to break down remaining highly informal but stiff barriers; and the inability of government to withhold property from the market until claims of discriminatory real estate practices could be investigated and resolved. Moreover, municipal zoning laws and discriminatory lot sizes for single-family homes continued to restrict the housing options of African Americans.

OPPOSING THE SECOND RECONSTRUCTION

African Americans confronted not only rising unemployment, poverty, and residential segregation but also overt attacks on the gains of the civil rights and Black Power movements. Although there were significant differences between and among Republican and Democratic administrations on these issues, they were linked by a thread of resistance to social welfare and affirmative action programs.

Resistance to Social Welfare and Affirmative Action Programs

In 1976, Jimmy Carter's election rested on almost unanimous black support, but he soon took public policy positions that dissatisfied his black constituents. As early as May 1977, Carter announced that his administration would not initiate new social welfare, health, and education programs. Black colleges and universities had received about 75 percent of their support from federal spending under Title III of the Civil Rights Act of 1964, but Carter reduced such support to nearly 50 percent in 1977 and to 18 percent in 1980. Although he promised to reduce the defense budget, the military's budget increased to a historic $111.8 billion. In the meantime, the U.S. Supreme Court gradually chipped away at the legal underpinnings of affirmative action programs and minority set-asides. In *University of California Regents v. Bakke* (1978), the Court ruled that a quota-based admission policy violated white student Allan Bakke's right to equal access to educational opportunities and ordered his admission to the University of California medical school at Davis. Although the Court upheld the validity of using race as part of an admissions policy designed to increase the diversity of the student body, the ruling had the effect of dampening institutional incentives to pursue vigorous affirmative action plans.

Under pressure from civil rights organizations and dissatisfied black constituents, the Carter administration nonetheless retained affirmative action and minority set-aside programs. In 1977, Congress passed the Public Works Employment Act, which set aside 10 percent of each grant for "minority enterprises," including those of white women. In 1982, when Congress passed the Surface Transportation Act, it required that 10 percent of all federal highway expenditures go to disadvantaged-group enterprises. Similarly, the 1987 National Defense Authorization Act set a 5 percent minority goal for procurement and research and development grants and contracts. By 1990, minority set-aside programs had spread widely throughout the federal government and represented some $8.6 billion in contracts. In a series of cases during the 1970s and 1980s, the U.S. Supreme Court upheld the constitutionality of such affirmative action and set-aside programs. In *United Steelworkers of America v. Weber* (1979), the Court upheld affirmative action hiring and training programs for minorities. Although Brian Weber's race (white) prevented him from joining a minority job training program, the Court held that his rights were not violated. In its craftsman training program in Gramercy, Louisiana, the Kaiser Aluminum Company admitted blacks and whites on a one-to-one ratio until blacks in craft jobs reached their proportion in the local work force. The Court also held that Kaiser's program was private and voluntary and that past discrimination against blacks justified its existence. A year later, the Court ordered the Alabama Department of Public Safety to hire black and white state troopers at a ratio of one to one until blacks reached 25 percent of all patrolmen. Blacks made up over 26 percent of the state's total population but had no state troopers before taking the matter to court. In *Fullilove v. Klutznick* (1980), the U.S. Supreme Court upheld the constitutionality of federal set-aside programs. Strengthened by congressional and judiciary support for affirmative action, states, counties, and municipalities instituted their own affirmative action procedures during the 1980s. By 1990, over 230 state and local jurisdictions had set up set-aside programs of various types.

Even as federal courts, states, and municipalities strengthened affirmative action programs, both Reagan and Bush cut the affirmative action enforcement powers of the Office of Federal Contract Compliance (OFCC) and the Equal Employment Opportunity Commission (EEOC) and reduced expenditures for social welfare services. Whereas Carter had initiated seventeen civil rights violation suits and Nixon twenty-four during their first six months in office, Reagan's civil rights division lodged only five. In 1983, Reagan fired three liberal members of the U.S. Civil Rights Commission and engineered its reconstitution with a conservative majority. However, Commissioner Mary Frances Berry, a civil rights activist, attorney, and scholar, fought back and won reinstatement. She not only filed a lawsuit but also kept the issue before the public through an extensive press campaign exposing the injustice of Reagan's actions. Despite Berry's heroic actions on behalf of civil rights, thereafter the U.S. Civil Rights Commission hampered the enforcement of civil rights legislation, abetted by Reagan's reduction of its budget by nearly $4 billion. Whereas Carter required federal contractors with 50 or more employees to file affirmative action plans, Reagan restricted such requirements to firms with 250 or more employees. The Reagan administration also eliminated the Guaranteed Student Loan program and reduced the level of support for food stamps and Aid to Families with Dependent Children.

Following Reagan's reelection in 1984, the Supreme Court took an even more aggressive stand against affirmative action. During his second term, Reagan took advantage of vacancies on the high bench and made appointments that shifted the balance of power from the liberal to the conservative end of the political spectrum. Subsequent court rulings reversed support for affirmative action by tightening the rules of evidence. In the *City of Richmond v. Croson* (1989), the high court held that the city's set-aside program violated the Fourteenth Amendment's equal protection clause. According to Justice Sandra Day O'Connor, writing for the majority, there was "no evidence" that "qualified minority contractors" had been passed over for contracts or subcontracts because of race "either as a group or in any individual case." O'Connor and the Court held that blacks would have to meet a strict "disparity impact" test—that is, they would have to prove case by case the impact of current discrimination rather than broad societal discrimination or past evidence of discrimination. As a result of this decision, within two years state and local governments spent nearly $13 million on "disparity impact" studies designed to prove the extent of past and present discrimination and to justify their set-aside programs. Following the Court's increasingly restrictive decisions in civil rights cases, Associate Justice Thurgood Marshall declared that such decisions represented nothing less than "the product" of "deliberate retrenching of the civil rights agenda."

In comparison to Reagan, Bush announced a "kinder and gentler" set of policies. Although he reinforced the policies of his predecessor on the core issues of social welfare, employment, and urban poverty, Bush opened the White House to more meetings with black leaders; increased the budget of the EEOC; and signed the Civil Rights Act of 1991, a modified version of a 1990 measure that he had vetoed. Nonetheless, by the early 1990s, popular white support for the civil rights agenda had nearly disappeared. In 1990, a survey conducted by the Times-Mirror Corporation showed that nearly 81 percent of white men and women alike disagreed that the nation should make "every possible effort to improve the position of blacks and other minorities, even if it means giving them preferential treatment." Such sentiment cut across party lines and pushed the Democratic Party toward the right on civil rights and social welfare issues.

In their presidential bid, William Jefferson Clinton and his running mate, Al Gore, penned a book, *Putting People First* (1992), that stated their goals for the nation. Key to the Clinton-Gore campaign was a pledge to "end welfare as we know it." Clinton and Gore declared, "It's time to honor and reward people who play by the rules. This means ending welfare as we know it. . . . No one who can work should be able to stay on welfare forever." Clinton also disappointed prospective black voters when he approved the execution of a severely retarded black death row inmate as part of a deliberate strategy to undercut Republican charges that Democrats were soft on crime. Jesse Jackson made a special plea on behalf of the condemned man on "moral" and "humanitarian" grounds, but to no avail. One New York political analyst remarked that Clinton "had someone put to death who had only part of a brain. You can't find them any tougher than that."

On assuming office, Clinton established a working group on welfare reform and proposed to Congress his "Work and Responsibility Act of 1994." At issue were several interrelated programs—Supplemental Security Income, Food Stamps, Medicare, Medicaid, and especially Aid to Families with Dependent Children (AFDC). The established AFDC programs included a work component entitled JOBS (Job Opportunities and Basic Skills Training), but critics argued that few recipients actually worked or received basic skills training under the program. Single women with children made up about 90 percent of all AFDC recipients. Since the federal government worked closely with states and guaranteed that money would be available to meet needs despite fluctuations in the economy, these programs were considered "entitlements." To move current welfare recipients into the work force, the measure proposed to limit unrestricted cash payments under public assistance programs to a maximum of two years but made exceptions for mothers of infants and disabled children. Although the plan's shortcomings were criticized by Democratic supporters, congressional Republicans killed the measure and substituted their own, harsher, "Personal Responsibility Act of 1995." The Republican bill set up the Temporary Assistance to Needy Families program, provided single block grants to states, and revised the notion of "entitlements" to "funds based on need." Emboldened by their so-called Contract with America, a document signed by numerous Republican leaders pledging a balanced budget and an end to the welfare state, a number of newly elected Republican congressmen insisted on eliminating the old New Deal social welfare arrangement. The Republican measure restricted recipients to a lifetime limit of sixty months on public assistance programs and eliminated exemptions for mothers of infants and disabled children, as well as the elderly.

On 22 August 1996, President Clinton signed the Republican Personal Responsibility and Work Opportunity Reconciliation Act, or "welfare to work," legislation into law. Only by proving that he was not soft on welfare, Clinton believed, could he win reelection in November 1996. At the same time, the federal government extended grants in aid to large corporations. In 1994, for example, spending for social welfare programs reached about $75 billion, whereas corporate aid was over $100 billion. In March 1994, the *Washington Post* reported that "ending welfare as we know it" should mean cutting off not only unwed mothers but "indolent corporations that have grown fat at the public trough." Although a cross-section of liberal and conservative constituents formed the Stop Corporate Welfare Coalition in August 1996, efforts to curtail federal aid to corporations produced few results.

Anti–social welfare and anti–affirmative action policies were deeply rooted in popular white resistance to the gains of the civil rights and Black Power movements. The state of California helped to lead the way. In 1978, white workers and middle-class property owners joined forces and passed Proposition 13, which cut taxes that supported social welfare services. During the 1980s, the so-called tax revolt spread across the country. In 1996, California voters approved Proposition 209. Known as the California Civil Rights Initiative, Proposition 209 mandated an end to affirmative action and set-aside programs in educational, public service, and any other agency supported by government funds. In the wake of Proposition 209, anti–affirmative action movements spread rapidly to other states, including Arizona, Colorado, Florida, Washington State, Ohio, and Michigan, where a federal court challenge to the conservative reaction to affirmative action in higher education was pending as of mid-2000.

"Color-Blind" Approaches and Genetic Theories

Some conservative intellectuals justified the emerging racial order on the basis of "color-blind" ideology, or meritocracy. They argued that racial categories should be discarded as things of the past, emphasizing individuals rather than groups as the core constituents of postmodern society. As one recent analyst noted, "The view that race is not biological . . . appears at first blush as progressive, but in fact, color blindness as advocated in the mainstream attempts to neutralize . . . the social power of race." In short, as the legal scholar Kimberle Crenshaw notes, "Neutral functions here as a euphemism for white." Unlike their "color-blind" contemporaries, however, social theorists like Charles Murray and his late colleague Richard J. Herrenstein turned to older genetic arguments to support the dismantling of the Second Reconstruction. In their book *The Bell Curve* (1994), they argued that

African Americans occupied the lower rungs of the political economy not only because of cultural conditions but because of "inherited racial characteristics." Although both Murray and Dinesh D'Souza, another late-twentieth-century conservative intellectual, initially emphasized cultural explanations, Murray and Herrenstein now adopted explicitly genetic or biological explanations of racial disparities.

Intimidation and Violence

The spread of extralegal forms of intimidation and violence reinforced the conservative agenda. During the 1980s and 1990s, the Ku Klux Klan and neo-Nazi groups experienced a revival. The Klan nearly tripled its national membership and staged massive rallies across the country. White vigilantes shot, beat, and killed blacks in northern, southern, and western states and cities. Victims included men and women, young and old, middle-class and poor blacks, political activists and nonactivists. In November 1979, Klansmen and Nazis killed five protesters at an antiracist rally in Greensboro, North Carolina. An all-white jury acquitted the accused despite the preponderance of evidence pointing to their guilt. A year later, a gunman shot Vernon Jordan, director of the National Urban League, in Fort Wayne, Indiana. Although Jordan's assailant, Joseph Franklin, admitted that he hated blacks, an all-white jury exonerated him of attempted murder charges. In 1980 alone, some twelve blacks were lynched in Mississippi. In Atlanta, twenty-eight black youths were murdered between 1979 and 1982. Although authorities linked two of the murders to a black man, Wayne B. Williams, the FBI showed a disregard for black families by failing to pursue evidence leading to possible convictions in the other cases. In 1989, a white mob killed a sixteen-year-old black youth, Yusuf Hawkins, in a predominantly white neighborhood in Brooklyn.

Police brutality and injustice before the law reinforced the wave of extralegal violence that blacks faced during the period. Between 1976 and 1981, police killed and/or maimed black suspects in Philadelphia, Detroit, New Orleans, and Oakland. In New Orleans, police killed four young black men in retaliation for the death of a white police officer, allegedly killed by an African American. In 1979 alone, Oakland police killed nine black males. In February 1989, Tampa, Florida's black community erupted into violence when police killed Edgar Allen Price, a black man suspected of drug dealing. And on 31 March 1992, a Los Angeles resident and amateur photographer filmed the brutal police beating of black motorist Rodney King. Officers had given chase to King's automobile, which they reported as speeding. After catching up to King, and stopping and cornering his automobile, they ordered him out of the car. According to officers, King resisted arrest, which justified the excessive force used to subdue him, but the film that flashed across national and international television portrayed several policemen mercilessly flailing the man with nightsticks after he had fallen to the ground. As we will see later, after courts found the offending officers not guilty, the South Central Los Angeles community exploded into violence.

California was also the site of the explosive murder trial of O. J. Simpson, the black professional football star, movie actor, and commentator on ABC's popular

Monday Night Football. In June 1994, Simpson was charged with the murder of his white ex-wife, Nicole Brown Simpson, and her friend Ronald Goldman in Los Angeles. The ensuing televised trial lasted for eight months and attracted some 150 million viewers, who took highly emotional positions on the presumed guilt or innocence of the accused. A jury of nine blacks, two whites, and one Latino acquitted Simpson, arguing that the state (which included black as well as white prosecuting attorneys) did not prove its case. The turning point in the trial came when Simpson's team of defense lawyers, headed by the able black attorney Johnnie Cochran, revealed that one of the white police officers had manufactured evidence and covered up his own racist attitude, language, and actions designed to ensure Simpson's conviction. In the wake of Simpson's acquittal, in February 1997, a jury of nine whites, one Latino, one Asian, and a person of mixed African American/Asian ancestry exposed the depth of the racial divide over the case. It found Simpson responsible for the deaths and ordered him to pay the aggrieved families $25 million in damages.

Defense attorney Johnnie Cochran delivers closing arguments in O. J. Simpson's double-murder trial. Cochran effectively used the portrait (*right*) of Simpson and his young daughter Sydney to reinforce his case for acquittal. *AP Photo/Sam Miorcovich, Pool*

The Ebonics Controversy

Given California's growing reputation as a site of racial tensions, it is not surprising that the Ebonics controversy also erupted in California. On 21 December 1996, the Oakland Board of Education unanimously approved the so-called Ebonics resolution, which required all schools in the district to participate in the Standard English Proficiency (SEP) program and acknowledge Black English as a unique language with its own "systematic, rule-governed" structure. Teachers were then exhorted to learn and respect the linguistic structure of Black English as a foundation for helping young blacks make the transition to Standard English in reading and writing. Specifically, the resolution charged "the Superintendent in conjunction with her staff" to

> immediately devise and implement the best possible academic program for imparting instruction to African-American students in their primary language for the combined purposes of maintaining the legitimacy and richness of such language whether it is known as "Ebonics," "African Language Systems," "Pan-African Communication Behaviors" or other description, and to facilitate their acquisition and mastery of English language skills.

In the volatile racial context of the mid- to late 1990s, however, this program of language education generated widespread opposition from African Americans nationwide—including such diverse groups and leaders as Jesse Jackson of People United to Serve Humanity (PUSH), Kwesi Mfume of the National Association for the Advancement of Colored People (NAACP), and writer Maya Angelou, to name a few. Part of the difficulty was embedded in the resolution itself. The task force asserted in the second section of its resolution that "African Language Systems" were "genetically based," which dovetailed with emergent "bell curve" ideas about the inferiority of blacks in the minds of many whites. As we will see below, stripped of its genetic notions, the idea of a unique African American language was quite consonant with the resurgence of black consciousness during the late 1980s and early 1990s. As articulated in the mainstream media and with the problematic use of "genetic," however, most African Americans perceived Ebonics as a call for resegregation and a denial of equal educational opportunities to black children. Thus, for large numbers of blacks, resistance to Ebonics became part of a larger struggle to defend the gains of the Second Reconstruction.

DEFENDING THE SECOND RECONSTRUCTION

In the wake of rising racial conflict and conservative reactions against the gains of the civil rights and Black Power movements, African Americans aimed first and foremost to preserve the benefits of the Second Reconstruction and to transform urban spaces into healthy and safe places to live, work, and play. More so than ever, established civil rights organizations—the NAACP, the National Urban League, and PUSH—needed grassroots support to carry the struggle forward. Reagan budget cuts, coupled with downturns in the economy, forced civil rights organizations to lay off personnel and curtail their social services. Take the case of PUSH, for example. In 1976, PUSH-Excel, a program designed to encourage poor black youngsters to take responsibility for their own education, received its first Health, Education, and Welfare grant of $45,000. Over the next four years, PUSH received some $4.5 million in government and foundation aid for its various programs, like PUSH-Excel, which expanded to some thirty-five cities nationwide. With the advent of the Reagan administration, however, not only did funding dry up but also, on the basis of a report conducted by Charles Murray (later author of *The Bell Curve*), the government ordered PUSH to pay back over $56,000. The NAACP, National Urban League, and PUSH all soon attacked "Reaganomics" as detrimental to the interests of African Americans.

Grassroots Organizations

Key to the social struggles of the 1980s and 1990s were the activities of poor and working-class blacks, especially black women. According to Vernon Jordan, head of the National Urban League, the black community now had a broader leadership structure—one that expanded well beyond the major civil rights organizations. Although the new leaders included black business and professional people, Jordan acknowledged the critical importance of "the new community people" who came out of "the Model Cities program, the antipoverty programs, and all those Great Society programs that required that poor people be brought into the decision making." The National Welfare Rights Union (successor to the National Welfare Rights Organization, formed in 1973) both reflected and encouraged the proliferation of poor people's organizations. By the early 1990s, a variety of local welfare rights organizations had emerged in cities across the country: the Coalition for Basic Human Need in Boston; the Welfare Warriors in Milwaukee; Empower in Rochester; Women for Economic Security in Chicago; and the Women's Economic Agenda in Oakland. In their local organizations, black women invariably expanded their concerns to a broad range of community issues as well as matters of cutbacks in social welfare spending. In 1992, for example, Theresa Allison of Los Angeles spearheaded the formation of Mothers Reclaiming Our Children, which challenged the mistreatment of black youth by the criminal justice system. As she explained it:

> We formed Mothers ROC . . . to ensure that our children would no longer face the lawyers, judges and courts alone. Our aim is to be the voice of the tens of thousands of young men and women who are locked away in the rapidly growing prison system.

Within five years, Mothers ROC had spread throughout the country with over one hundred chapters and a growing membership base.

Marian Wright Edelman, attorney, civil rights leader, and children's advocate. As head of the Children's Defense Fund, Edelman played a key role fighting for humane social welfare reforms during the 1980s and 1990s. Here she speaks at the Lincoln Memorial during the Stand for Children rally, June 1996. *AP Photo/Robert Giroux*

In the welfare debates of the 1980s and 1990s, poor black women and their middle-class and intellectual supporters were among the most vocal defenders of black families. Inspired by the grassroots activism of welfare recipients, black women scholars and activists pinpointed and counteracted public distortions of poor black women's lives. The scholar Wahneema Lubiano summarized the issue:

> Read the newspapers, watch television, or simply listen to people talk; among other things, welfare queens are held responsible for the crack trade and crack babies.... She is [depicted as] the agent of destruction, the creator of ... crack dealers, addicts, muggers, and rapists.

Similarly, historians Barbara Ransby and Tracye Matthews rebutted the "regular attacks on our black women in the media, most often disguised as an attack on the admittedly inadequate welfare system." Under the leadership of Marian Wright Edelman, the Children's Defense Fund championed the welfare rights of children. Formed in 1973, the organization regularly carried out careful assessments of the needs of poor children and developed forceful policy positions in *Portrait of Inequality: Black and White Children in America* (1980) and *Families in Peril: An Agenda for Social Change* (1987). The CDF lamented that "the federal government no longer will be the protector of last resort for hungry, disabled, poor, abused, and neglected boys and girls. It will pass the buck to 50 states with 40 billion fewer dollars. And states are making no promises about how children will be protected." CDF regularly recommended employment, education, and training opportunities, along with child care, health care, and other support services for women with children.

Political Gains

African Americans also defended the Second Reconstruction by intensifying their efforts to elect blacks to influential public offices. They enabled Douglas Wilder to become the first black governor of Virginia (1990) and the only black governor of a state since the First Reconstruction; and Carole Mosely Braun to become the first black female U.S. senator (1992) and the first black Democratic U.S. senator. In addition, African Americans elected black mayors in Philadelphia (Wilson Goode, 1983); Chicago (Harold Washington, 1983); and New York City (David Dinkins, 1989). Most importantly, African Americans fueled Rev. Jesse Jackson's bid to gain the Democratic Party's nomination for president in 1984 and 1988. Under Jackson's leadership, African Americans formed the Rainbow Coalition and gained the support of grassroots religious and nationalist groups like the National Baptist Convention, the Nation of Islam, and the Black United Front. Substantial numbers of Latino, Puerto Rican, and white left-wing organizations also supported the Jackson campaign, which included a call for a reduction in military spending and an increase in federal spending for social welfare, job creation, and training programs. Jackson said he hoped to answer the "empty materialism" of the Reagan years with a program for "humanizing this society and our policies" at home and "around the world" (see box). In the Democratic primary of 1984, Jackson received 3.5 million popular votes. Four years later, Jackson increased his total to 7 million (3 million of whom were whites and nonwhite minorities) and became the party's second most popular choice for president.

Despite Jackson's impressive showing, white presidential contender Michael Dukakis passed him over as a possible vice presidential running mate. This slight angered and alienated the huge constituency that Jackson's campaign had helped to mobilize. Understandably, African Americans were unenthusiastic voters in the 1988 presidential election. Partly for this reason, Republican George Bush defeated his Democratic contender. Still, as a result of Jackson's impressive showing, his campaign manager, Ronald Brown, became head of the Democratic Party's National Committee. Under Brown's leadership, William Jefferson Clinton regained the White House for the Democrats in the presidential election of 1992. During his first term, Clinton appointed Vernon Jordan, former director of the National Urban League, as the chairperson of his transition team. He also appointed several blacks to high-level administrative posts: Ron Brown as Secretary of Commerce; Hazel O'Leary as Secretary of Energy; and Joycelyn Elders as Surgeon General.

As local black elected and appointed officials increased, they strengthened the hand of the Congressional Black Caucus (CBC). The CBC repeatedly urged Congress to pass welfare reforms and economic legislation that provided "job creation, meaningful job training, and more money" for the African American community, particularly poor inner-city neighborhoods. The CBC supported the Full Employment and Balanced Growth Act of 1978, although the final version of the act (sponsored by black California legislator Augustus Hawkins in the House and Hubert Humphrey of Minnesota in the Senate) was considerably weaker than the original. In 1993, the CBC opposed Clinton's North American Free Trade Agreement

1984

Presidential Candidate Jesse Jackson Addresses the Democratic National Convention, San Francisco

Tonight we come together bound by our faith, in a mighty God, with genuine respect for our country, and inheriting the legacy of a great party—a Democratic party—which is the best hope for redirecting our nation on a more humane, just and peaceful course.

This is not a perfect party. We are not perfect people. Yet, we are called to a perfect mission: our mission, to feed the hungry, to clothe the naked, to house the homeless, to teach the illiterate, to provide jobs for the jobless, and to choose the human race over the nuclear race.

We are gathered here this week to nominate a candidate and write a platform which will expand, unify, direct and inspire our party and the nation to fulfill this mission.

My constituency is the damned, disinherited, disrespected and the despised.

They are restless and seek relief. They've voted in record numbers. They have invested the faith, hope and trust that they have in us. The Democratic Party must send them a signal that we care. I pledge my best not to let them down.

There is the call of conscience: redemption, expansion, healing and unity. Leadership must heed the call of conscience, redemption, expansion, healing and unity, for they are the key to achieving our mission.

Time is neutral and does not change things.

With courage and initiative leaders change things. No generation can choose the age or circumstances in which it is born, but through leadership it can choose to make the age in which it is born an age of enlightenment—an age of jobs, and peace, and justice.

Only leadership—that intangible combination of gifts, discipline, information, circumstance, courage, timing, will and divine inspiration—can lead us out of the crisis in which we find ourselves.

Leadership can mitigate the misery of our nation. Leadership can part the waters and lead our nation in the direction of the Promised Land. Leadership can lift the boats stuck at the bottom.

I have had the rare opportunity to watch seven men, and then two, pour out their souls, offer their service and heed the call of duty to direct the course of our nation.

There is a proper season for everything. There is a time to sow and a time to reap. There is a time to compete, and a time to cooperate.

I ask for your vote on the first ballot as a vote for a new direction for this party and this nation; a vote for conviction, a vote for conscience. . . .

Our flag is red, white and blue, but our nation is rainbow—red, yellow, brown, black and white—we're all precious in God's sight. America is not like a blanket—one piece of unbroken cloth, the same color, the same texture, the same size. America is more like a quilt—many patches, many pieces, many colors, many sizes, all woven and held together by a common thread.

CONTINUED

The white, the Hispanic, the black, the Arab, the Jew, the woman, the Native American, the small farmer, the businessperson, the environmentalist, the peace activist, the young, the old, the lesbian, the gay, and the disabled make up the American quilt. . . .

Our time has come. Suffering breeds character. Character breeds faith. And in the end, faith will not disappoint.

Our time has come. Our faith, hope and dreams will prevail. Our time has come. Weeping has endured for the night. And, now joy cometh in the morning. . . .

Our time has come. No graves can hold our body down.

Our time has come. No lie can live forever.

Our time has come. We must leave racial battleground and come to economic common ground and moral higher ground. America, our time has come.

We've come from disgrace to Amazing Grace, our time has come.

Give me your tired, give me your poor, your huddled masses who yearn to breathe free and come November, there will be a change because our time has come.

Thank you and God bless you.

Source: Deirdre Mullane, ed., *Crossing the Danger Water: Three Hundred Years of African-American Writing* (New York: Doubleday, 1993), pp. 734–740.

(NAFTA), which established free trade between Mexico, Canada, and the United States. Clinton repeatedly argued that NAFTA would help all American workers, including blacks. As he put it, a "rising tide would lift all boats," but the CBC and working-class black constituents were not convinced. In its statement on NAFTA, the CBC argued that "those who lose jobs because of import competition do not climb up the job ladder, but fall back to lower wages or fall off the job ladder into unemployment." In the wake of Republican victories in the 1994 congressional elections, the CBC created the Working Group for a New Agenda for New Times and opposed the Republican Personal Responsibility Act as a harsh and punitive measure that would disproportionately harm the black poor. In 1996, black elected officials encouraged opposition to California's Proposition 209, which aimed to eliminate the state's affirmative action programs.

The Struggle at Home and Abroad

The struggle for social justice was not limited to the United States. African Americans launched a vigorous movement to end apartheid in South Africa. In 1984, under the leadership of Randall Robinson, head of Transafrica, African Americans staged demonstrations at the South African Embassy in Washington, D.C. When police arrested a small group of demonstrators in front of the South African Embassy, similar demonstrations erupted at South African consulates in Chicago, Boston, Houston, and Salt Lake City. African Americans also pressured the Democratic Party to demand the release of Nelson Mandela, the imprisoned leader of the

Rev. Jesse Jackson addresses the 1984 Democratic National Convention. Jackson, founder of People United to Serve Humanity, was a contender for the Democratic Party's presidential nomination in 1984 and again in 1988, when he received the second highest number of popular votes in the primaries. *AP/Wide World Photos*

African National Congress. The movement to topple apartheid also gained widespread support on college and university campuses, where black students, faculty, staffs, and their white allies protested against university, government, and corporate investments in South Africa. As a result of such protests, growing numbers of universities, corporations, and state and local governments ordered divestment from firms doing business in South Africa. These developments not only helped to speed the release of Mandela from prison but also hastened the arrival of Democratic rule in South Africa during the early 1990s.

African Americans also questioned U.S. involvement in the Persian Gulf War. To be sure, African Americans took pride in the accomplishments of General Colin Powell, who not only was the first African American to become chairman of the U.S. Joint Chiefs of Staff but also, at age fifty-two, was the youngest man to hold that position. In 1991, Powell convinced President Bush to wage the war and later directed the U.S. invasion of Iraq in Operation Desert Storm, as the Persian Gulf War was called. The United States soon declared victory in the forty-two-day war, which many believed finally put the ghost of defeat in Vietnam to rest. President Bush later remarked: "By God, we've kicked the Vietnam Syndrome once and for all." Yet despite Powell's role in this turn of U.S. fortunes in foreign policy, a careful poll of black opinion showed that nearly 50 percent of African Americans opposed the war. Moreover, black congressional representatives unanimously voted against Operation Desert Storm. Still, as in the Vietnam War, black fighting men and women made up a disproportionately large percentage of the armed forces (about 25 percent of the U.S. troops) in the Persian Gulf. Their presence again underscored the historic willingness of African Americans to fight for their country even as they struggled against injustice at home.

In addition to addressing the problems of interracial political and social relations at home and abroad, African Americans aimed to transform relations within the black community. Symbolic of these efforts was the Million Man March on Washington (MMM), the largest grassroots demonstration of the late twentieth century. On 16 October 1994, over 1 million black men (and a few women) answered the call of minister Louis Farrakhan, head of the Nation of Islam. As head of the Nation of Islam, Farrakhan defined the march as a "Holy Day of Atonement and Reconciliation." He urged black men to apologize to black women for past irresponsible and even abusive behavior, to make a resolution to take charge of their own lives, and to become viable providers and defenders of their families and their communities. Motivated partly by the increasing numbers of poor female-headed families, the growing incidence of drugs, and black youth violence, the Million Man March attracted a broad cross-section of African Americans across class, political, religious, and (despite its emphasis on men) gender lines. The march gained the support of such diverse Christian and black nationalist organizations and spokespersons as Jesse Jackson of the Rainbow Coalition/People United to Serve Humanity; Dorothy Height of the National Council of Negro Women; poet Maya Angelou; minister and scholar Cornel West of Princeton University; and former NAACP executive director Rev. Benjamin Chavis, who helped to coordinate the event. Shortly after the march, Chavis converted to Islam and became Benjamin Chavis Muhammad and continued his activities on behalf of the Million Man March movement. The historic march not only gave African American discontent a spirited expression but also demonstrated that African American spiritual and political unity could coalesce around Islamic as well as Christian leadership.

Conflicts and Fragmentation Within

African Americans were by no means of one mind on the various issues that they faced. A variety of old and new points of conflict undermined their quest for solidarity. By the early 1980s, a highly vocal black conservative voice emerged on topics like affirmative action. Like their white counterparts, black conservatives decried affirmative action programs and blamed poverty on the welfare system. Among the most influential of these black conservatives were economist Thomas Sowell of the Hoover Institution at Stanford University; economist Walter E. Williams of George Mason University; Glenn Loury of Harvard University; Republican Party leader J. A. Y. Parker; and Robert Woodson, president of the National Center for Neighborhood Enterprise. Conservatives argued that the current welfare system "helped destroy many black families by taking wage-earning fathers out of the home and replacing them with a monthly government check." In Cali-

Minister Louis Farrakhan helped to rebuild the Nation of Islam following the death of Elijah Muhammad. Here Farrakhan speaks at the Million Man March in Washington, D.C., October 1995. *AP Photo/Doug Mills*

fornia, black University of California Board of Regents member Ward Connerly maintained that the effort to end affirmative action was consistent with the civil rights movement's dream of a "color-blind" society and blamed black people for "fighting it with every fiber of their being."

In 1991, black conservatism became a storm center of controversy when President Bush appointed Clarence Thomas to fill the U.S. Supreme Court seat vacated by retiring black justice Thurgood Marshall. Televised nationwide on CNN, Thomas's confirmation hearings faced a crisis when Anita Hill, a black attorney and former employee, testified that the nominee had subjected her to sexual harassment during her tenure under his supervision at the Equal Employment Opportunity Commission. A law school professor at the University of Oklahoma at the time of the hearings, Hill offered compelling testimony that received the support of numerous women's groups. But Thomas helped to turn the tide in his favor by charging his accuser and her supporters with executing a "high-tech lynching" of a black man, whose record, he argued, warranted confirmation to the high bench. Thomas received the firm and vociferous support of leading Republicans and gained confirmation. The Thomas confirmation hearings and Hill's testimony revealed both the growth of conservative politics within the black community and the deep cleavages that existed over issues of male-female relations within black and white America.

Along with the Thomas-Hill testimony, the Million Man March focused attention on gender relations within the black community. One well-known scholar-activist later reported that he stayed away from the march because of what he called "the exclusion (and diminishing) of women explicit and inherent in the call." In

March 1998, black women staged their own Million Woman March in Philadelphia. They called attention to the centrality of women in any movement designed to liberate the contemporary black community, particularly poor and working-class blacks. Khadijah Farrakhan, wife of minister Louis Farrakhan, stated in her speech before the gathering: "A nation can rise no higher than its women. We focus on women but cannot lose sight that we must rise as a family. Men, women and children." In her address, congresswoman Maxine Waters of California told the women: "After today, we will never be the same. . . . America, please be placed on notice: We know who we are. We know what kind of power we have. We will act on that power." Winnie Mandela of South Africa linked the destiny of black women in the United States with that of African women on the continent: "We have a shared destiny, a shared responsibility, to save the world from those who would destroy it." Although the event accented the particular interests of black women, some black men were also present. Indeed, men from the Nation of Islam provided security around the stage area.

The Million Man March also exposed issues of sexuality within the freedom struggle. Black gay and lesbian activists criticized the MMM movement for what they called "its sexist and patriarchal tone and the homophobic comments made by march organizers." Yet the National Black Gay and Lesbian Leadership Forum urged its male members to attend the event as a symbolic statement that they "will no longer allow outsiders to dictate who is welcome at the black family table or divide African Americans by sexual orientation or by gender." In addition to its stand on sexual orientation and gender, others criticized the march for its "theocratic" and individualistic rather than collective democratic vision for social change. Designed to create an ongoing vehicle for black self-determination and empowerment at the grassroots level, the MMM movement emphasized the virtues of hard work and self-help, reminiscent of Booker T. Washington's philosophy at the turn of the twentieth century. In contrast with the March on Washington for Freedom and Jobs some thirty years earlier, this one did not direct its demands to public policy makers or the state.

Although cleavages along gender, sexuality, and ideological lines were significant, the class divide continued to represent the major fault line of conflict within the black struggle for social justice. The masses of working-class and poor blacks joined their middle-class and elite counterparts in voting for black elected officials, but the results were invariably disappointing. To get reelected, some black leaders gradually distanced themselves from grassroots issues. In Atlanta, for example, Andrew Young won election to the mayor's office in 1982 and 1985 partly by embracing a conservative economic agenda. As federal funds to cities declined, his black predecessor, Maynard Jackson, had done likewise. In 1977, when nearly one thousand sanitation workers (mainly blacks) struck over frozen pay scales over the previous three-year period, Jackson dismissed them. The men lost their jobs although they were members of the American Federation of State, County, and Municipal Employees union (AFSCME) and had supported Jackson's candidacy as mayor. In Detroit, Coleman Young also gained the support of black workers but later formed an alliance with corporate leaders like automaker Henry Ford; he then slashed the city's services and social welfare programs while lowering corporate property taxes. Similarly, in his bid for governor of Virginia, Wilder reversed his earlier pro-union and anti–death penalty positions and wooed the conservative white vote.

The most disappointing exercise of power by a black public official occurred in Philadelphia. In 1985, Mayor Wilson Goode authorized the fire bombing of MOVE, a black nationalist organization located on the city's West Side. When neighbors complained that MOVE's African-inspired communal practices constituted "a public nuisance," city officials launched a concerted effort to eliminate the group. On 13 May 1985, police arrived at the row houses occupied by group members and used a bullhorn to call out arrest warrants for occupants. When occupants refused to surrender, authorities sprayed tear gas through the walls, fired thousands of rounds of ammunition at the buildings, and dropped deadly explosives from a helicopter onto the settlement. This attack on the MOVE quarters resulted in the deaths of six adults and five children. The fire also consumed sixty-two houses and left hundreds of residents homeless. A member of a citizens' fact-finding committee later reported: "This was a military attack on a low-income, African-American, working class neighborhood. . . . The equipment used, the munitions, the legal requirements for use, . . . all show it. They made war on us." Only after eleven years of legal battles on behalf of MOVE victims did a federal civil court finally award nearly $2 million in damages to Ramona Africa, the sole survivor of the blaze, and the families of other victims of the fire. Still, the courts failed to sustain charges against any public officials involved in ordering the military-like attack on a civilian neighborhood.

As black mayors proved unable or unwilling to press the interests of black poor and working people, the class fragmentation of the black community deepened, and the explosive ingredients for urban revolt remained. In May 1980, for example, the outbreak of racial violence in Liberty City and other black neighborhoods in Miami, Florida, symbolized the deep and ongoing resentment that poor and working-class blacks harbored toward the injustices of the changing social order. The violence represented the most destructive urban explosion since Martin Luther King Jr.'s death in 1968. Five incidents—involving police brutality and injustice before an all-white jury—provided the immediate spark for the violence. Before some thirty-six hundred National Guardsmen restored order, the violence resulted in the loss of some $50 million to $100 million worth of property, over twelve hundred arrests, four hundred injuries, and eighteen deaths. In 1992, when a jury of ten whites, one Asian American, and one Latino American acquitted all of the police officers of wrongdoing in the Rodney King police brutality case, African Americans and large numbers of Latino residents poured into the streets of South Central Los Angeles, looting and burning buildings as well as attacking white passengers of automobiles trapped in the riot zone. Fifty-two people died, mostly blacks, and another 2,383 received serious injuries. Participants set some five hundred fires, which resulted in $1 billion in property damage (see box). As suggested above, unlike the outbreak of urban violence in the past, this conflict was in effect what some scholars call a "multicultural" revolt. Some observers suggested that 60 percent of the participants were Latino, 25 percent black, and 13 percent white. Moreover, Latino and African American participants also targeted community-based Korean grocers for

Although the Los Angeles riot of 1992 was a multicultural revolt of diverse nationality groups, African American participants interpreted the event through the lens of their own history and struggle against inequality. In this photo, a young black man gives the Black Power salute as South Central L.A. burns in the background. *Peter Turnley/Corbis*

destruction. Although urban violence did not reach the levels of the 1960s, the conditions for such responses remained and made the project of racial solidarity all the more precarious.

REDEFINING THE BOUNDARIES OF BLACK CULTURE

The changing parameters of black politics were closely intertwined with the struggle to redefine African American culture. As African Americans confronted a variety of internal conflicts and revamped their politics, artists and intellectuals worked to broaden the boundaries of black culture, ideas, and beliefs. In the aural, visual, and literary arts, racial solidarity portraits increasingly gave way to emphases on the diversity of black experiences along lines of class, color, gender, nationality, sexuality, and even individuality. Visual artists like Lyle Ashton Harris, Alison Sarr, Martin Puryear, and especially Jean-Michel Basquiat all emphasized the plurality of the black experience. Assisting in this project was the adoption of so-called postmodernist concepts (which accented the notion of multiple rather than single meanings in artistic works).

Born in New York to Haitian and Puerto Rican parents, Jean-Michel Basquiat took his subject matter from a broad range of themes in African American, African,

Rep. Maxine Waters Testifies Before Congress on the Underlying Causes of the Los Angeles Riots

Mr. Chairman, members of the committee, it is a privilege to be here today. The riots in Los Angeles and in other cities shocked the world. They shouldn't have. Many of us have watched our country—including our government—neglect the problems, indeed the people, of our inner-cities for years—even as matters reached a crisis stage.

The verdict in the Rodney King case did not cause what happened in Los Angeles. It was only the most recent injustice—piled upon many other injustices—suffered by the poor, minorities and the hopeless people living in this nation's cities. For years, they have been crying out for help. For years, their cries have not been heard.

I recently came across a statement made more than 25 years ago by Robert Kennedy, just two months before his violent death. He was talking about the violence that had erupted in cities across America. His words were wise and thoughtful: "There is another kind of violence in America, slower but just as deadly, destructive as the shot or bomb in the night. . . . This is the violence of institutions; indifference and inaction and slow decay. This is the violence that afflicts the poor, that poisons relations between men and women because their skin is different colors. This is the slow destruction of a child by hunger, and schools without books and homes without heat in the winter."

What a tragedy it is that America has still, in 1992, not learned such an important lesson.

I have represented the people of South Central Los Angeles in the U.S. Congress and the California state Assembly for close to 20 years. I have seen our community continually and systematically ravaged by banks who would not lend to us, by governments which abandoned us or punished us for our poverty, and by big businesses who exported our jobs to Third-World countries for cheap labor.

In LA, between 40 and 50 percent of all African-American men are unemployed. The poverty rate is 32.9 percent. According to the most recent census, 40,000 teenagers—that is 20 percent of the city's 16 to 19 year olds—are both out of school and unemployed.

An estimated 40,000 additional jobs were just lost as a result of the civil unrest the last two weeks. The LA Chamber of Commerce has said that at least 15,000 of these job losses will be permanent. This represents another 10 to 20 percent of South-Central LA's entire workforce permanently unemployed. Keep in mind, our region had one of the country's highest unemployment rates before the recent unrest. It is hard to imagine how our community will cope with the additional devastation.

We have created in many areas of this country a breeding ground for hopelessness, anger and despair. All the traditional mechanisms for empowerment, opportunity and self-improvement have been closed. . . .

Is it any wonder our children have no hope?

The systems are failing us. I could go on and on. All we can hope for is that the President, his Cabinet and Congress understand what is happening. We simply cannot afford the continued terror and oppression of benign neglect—the type of inaction that has characterized the federal government's response to the cities since the late 1970s.

Source: Deirdre Mullane, ed., *Crossing the Danger Water: Three Hundred Years of African-American Writing* (New York: Doubleday, 1993), pp. 749–752.

Caribbean, Hispanic, and pre-Columbian history, culture, and politics. Along with an accent on multinationality, Basquiat's art also reflected efforts to broaden the parameters of black culture downward in the class structure. Basquiat came to maturity within the context of New York's multiethnic hip-hop culture, where he became a young graffiti artist, spray painting both words and images on subway cars and walls, and signing his name, or "tag," as SAMO. Beginning with his first solo shows in Italy (1981) and the United States (1982), by the time of his death at age twenty-nine, Basquiat had become a prolific painter who pioneered in moving the streets of the deindustrializing city to mainstream art museums (see his *Famous Moon King* series, 1984/1985).

Black Writers Accentuate Themes of Gender, Sexuality, Family, and Afrocentrism

Some of the most salient portraits of difference within the black community focused on questions of gender and sexuality. Reflecting as well as helping to sharpen the debate over gender and sexuality was Michele Wallace's *Black Macho and the Myth of the Superwoman* (1980). Wallace offered a scathing critique of sexism in the black freedom struggle, particularly its black power phase. In Wallace's view, the black male's racial subordination was secondary to his role in a gender-stratified society where both black and white men shared dominion over women. Although Wallace underestimated the role of race in the subordination of black men and women, her book helped to force the issue of gender inequality to the forefront of discussions within the black community. Yet it was black activists and scholars like bell hooks (Gloria Watkins), Angela Davis, and Patricia Hill Collins who offered the most probing critiques of both white feminist racism and black male chauvinism. At the same time, black radical lesbian critics like Barbara Smith, June Jordan, and Audre Lorde pushed the critique of African American culture forward into the realm of sexual identification as well as gender differences. Smith edited the collection *Home Girls: A Black Feminist Anthology* (1983) and coedited *All the Women Are White, All the Blacks Are Men, But Some of Us Are Brave: Black Women's Studies* (1982).

Black women writers placed issues of gender inequities and sexuality at the forefront of their creative works. Toni Morrison produced several novels during the late twentieth century: *Song of Solomon* (1977), *Tar Baby* (1981), *Beloved* (1987), and *Jazz* (1992). For *Beloved* Morrison received the 1988 Pulitzer Prize in literature and the Robert F. Kennedy Award. In 1993, following publication of *Jazz,* she received the prestigious Nobel Prize in literature. During the 1980s and 1990s, Alice Walker also produced her novels: *The Color Purple* (1982), *The Temple of My Familiar* (1989), and *Possessing the Secret of Joy* (1992). *The Color Purple,* her most widely acclaimed work, broke new ground in the black novel by exploring not only black-on-black oppression but also incest and lesbianism within the black community. In an edited collection of her essays, *In Search of Our Mothers' Garden* (1983), Walker defined a distinctive black female stance as "womanism" or "womanist" consciousness. In her view, a womanist was a black feminist who expressed a commitment "to survival and wholeness of entire people, male and female." Although Toni Morri-

The novelist Toni Morrison won the Pulitzer Prize in 1988 and the Nobel Prize for literature in 1993. *AP/Wide World Photos*

son also wrote against the grain of a presumed black art or aesthetics and accented the special conditions that faced black women within African American culture, her works retained a close link with the idea of community within the black experience. In her novels she demonstrated an abiding interest in the ways that white racial restrictions interacted with certain black cultural traditions and shaped the experiences of black men, women, and children. As one critic of *Tar Baby* noted: "The novels may focus on individual characters . . . but . . . it is the strength and continuity of the black cultural heritage as a whole which is at stake and being tested."

Even more so than black novelists and fiction writers, poets and playwrights built on the achievements of the black arts movement and accented themes of resistance, family, and community formation. For her volume of poems about her grandparents, *Thomas and Beulah* (1987), poet Rita Dove received the Pulitzer Prize and became Poet Laureate of the United States between 1993 and 1995. August Wilson became perhaps the most renowned U.S. playwright of the period, winning a Tony Award and two Pulitzer Prizes for his work. In rapid succession Wilson produced a variety of well-crafted urban-based plays set during the era of the Great Migration: *Ma Rainey's Black Bottom* (1988); *Joe Turner's Come and Gone* (1992); *Two Trains Running* (1993); *Fences* (1995); and *Seven Guitars* (1997). Through his plays, Wilson told the story of black life in the twentieth-century transition from farm to city and highlighted the impact of deindustrialization on black urban communities for contemporary audiences. In 1991, Wilson articulated his notion of a black vision of art when he insisted that an African American direct the film version of *Fences,* even though a white director had taken charge of the New York stage version. Wilson articulated his desire to obtain a black director who shared what he called "the cultural responsibilities of the characters." Although he agreed that blacks and whites shared certain cultural beliefs, he emphasized that there were "specific ideas and attitudes" that were not shared "on the same cultural ground." Thus, he explained, he rejected a white director on the basis of culture and "not on the basis of race." Wilson also articulated a firm desire to gain "control over our own culture and its products." He stated, "Therein lies the crux of the matter as it relates to Paramount [the movie company] and the film *Fences.*"

Wilson's artistic decision on the filming of *Fences* dovetailed with the cresting of a new Afrocentric movement in African American life. The Afrocentric movement opposed Eurocentric theories that "dislocated" blacks to the periphery of human thought and actions. These ideas gained their most forceful articulation in a series of books by Temple University professor Molefi Asante: *The Afrocentric Idea* (1987); *Afrocentricity* (1988); and *Kemet, Afrocentricity, and Knowledge* (1990). Reinforcing the Afrocentric idea were several professional associations and journals, including the *Journal of Black Studies* and the *Afrocentric Scholar*. Although Temple University became the principal center of Afrocentric studies, Afrocentric scholars also taught on the faculties of Hunter College in New York, Ohio State University, and the campuses of the California State University system, which included the pioneer Maulana Karenga. By the late 1980s, Rev. Jesse Jackson of PUSH helped to symbolize and heighten the appeal of Afrocentrism when he endorsed the call for black people to substitute "African American" for "black" as their group designation of choice. Jackson explained, "We are a hybrid people. . . . We are of African roots, with a little Irish, German, Indian. We are made up of America's many waters. Which makes us a new people, a true [African] American people."

Black Influences on Popular Culture and Entertainment

Even as black creative artists sought to affirm their distinctiveness as a black people, they continued to penetrate and even dominate aspects of U.S. popular culture and entertainment. In 1978, Muhammad Ali became the first heavyweight champion to regain the world crown for a third time. Two years later, Larry Holmes defeated Ali, and a succession of black boxers held the heavyweight crown through the remainder of the twentieth century, although the title shifted overseas when black Englishman Lennox Lewis defeated Evander Holyfield in 1999. In 1977, Reginald "Reggie" Martinez Jackson of the New York Yankees became the first baseball player to hit three home runs in a single World Series game. When Jackson retired in 1987 as a member of the California Angels, he had the highest batting average in World Series history. Five years later, he was inducted into the National Baseball Hall of Fame. In basketball, a variety of black players compiled outstanding records: Kareem Abdul-Jabbar of the Los Angeles Lakers; Earvin "Magic" Johnson, also of the Lakers; Julius "Dr. J" Erving of the Philadelphia 76ers; and Michael Jordan of the Chicago Bulls. Sparked by the extraordinary performance of Jordan, the Chicago Bulls became the first team in over thirty years to win three straight National Basketball Association titles. After retiring for nearly two seasons, Jordan returned to the game and enabled the Bulls to win three more successive NBA championships before retiring at the end of the 1997–1998 season. In the meantime, Jordan had also become the most sought-after player for endorsements by global corporations like the sportswear manufacturer Nike; Nike's Air Jordan shoes boosted the firm's sales by $28 million during their first year (1985) and exceeded $500 million in sales in 1990.

By century's end, African Americans had gradually entered new areas of sports, most notably figure skating, tennis, and golf. In 1986, ice skater Debi Thomas won first place in the World Figure Skating Championship. Track and field star Jackie Joyner-Kersee won the gold medal in the heptathlon at the 1988 Olympic games in Los Angeles and again in 1992. In April 1997, Eldrick "Tiger" Woods became the first African American (and Asian American) to win a major golf tournament when at age twenty-one he won the prestigious U.S. Masters championship in Augusta, Georgia. The son of an African American father and an Asian mother (originally from Thailand), Woods was also the youngest golfer to win a major tournament since the end of World War II. That same year, Woods went on to win three more Professional Golf Association (PGA) Tour games and also received the PGA's Player of the Year Award. In 1999, Serena Williams defeated Martina Hingis in the U.S. Open tennis championship and became the first African American woman to win a Grand Slam title since Althea Gibson in 1958. During the same year, with her sister Venus, Serena also won the doubles titles at the U.S. and French Opens.

In music during the 1980s, Michael Jackson emerged as the most successful black "crossover" artist. In 1979, Jackson released his album *Off the Wall.* Produced in collaboration with award-winning composer Quincy Jones, *Off the Wall* resulted in four top-ten singles and sold multiplatinum. Four years later, *Thriller* became the number one album for thirty-seven weeks and generated a record seven top-ten singles. The album also won eight Grammy Awards for Jackson and another four for Jones. As one music scholar stated: "Thriller was a musical *tour de force.* . . . Its songs and arrangements were well crafted, its production was crisp and

Eldrick "Tiger" Woods, the first person of African- and Asian American descent to win the U.S. Masters Tournament and the Player of the Year Award. In this photo, Woods reacts to a hole-in-one during the final round of the Greater Milwaukee Open, September 1996. *AP Photo/Morry Gash*

uncluttered, its dance grooves were positively infectious, and Jackson's vocals were flawless." For his musical achievements, Jackson gained the accolade "King of Pop." Jackson also helped break the color line on MTV with his videos of "Billie Jean," "Beat It," and finally "Thriller," which became the third best-selling video for 1984. In the meantime, artists like Prince, Janet Jackson, Tina Turner, and Whitney Houston ascended the charts as artists with wide interracial crossover appeal. At the same time, Donna Summer emerged as the "Queen of Disco" following release of her "Love to Love You Baby" (1976). Summer went on to produce three number one albums and eight top-ten singles in a row, including "Hot Stuff" and "Bad Girls." For her music, Summer won four Grammies before turning away from disco and becoming a born-again Christian during the early 1980s.

Despite the successes of certain black artists, black and white music continued to diverge quite sharply. In 1983, for example, of the fourteen records that reached number one on the black chart, only one reached the top ten of the pop chart, and that was Donna Summer's "She Works Hard for the Money." Major songs by Aretha Franklin, Gladys Knight and the Pips, and George Clinton reached only number forty or lower on the pop chart. As black music continued to diverge from the white mainstream in significant ways, a young generation of black artists pioneered in the creation of a new musical form, "rap" or "hip hop." As one commentator put it, "Hip Hop is to funk what bebop was to jazz . . . a new strain of an old form, stripped down and revved up, rejuvenated." Beginning with DJs in the South Bronx, Brooklyn, Harlem, and Queens, early rap artists built on the oral style of the older radio personality DJs. The verbal dexterity of DJs like D. J. Hollywood, Kool Herc, Afrika Bambaataa, and Grandmaster Flash influenced a generation of black youth to develop a "rap" style. One observer noted: "Since nobody in New York City, America, or the rest of the world wanted to know about the black so-called ghettos—the unmentionable areas of extreme urban deprivation—the style was allowed to flourish as a genuine street movement."

Rap music was also technologically and musically innovative. Some artists combined and remixed selections from existing records, whereas others incorporated record-scratching and backspinning techniques—that is, they repeated key lyrics and rhythms by manipulating the record with the sound system turned on. In 1979, rap gradually entered the mainstream when the Sugar Hill Gang, a group of three black teenagers from New Jersey, released its single "Rapper's Delight." The Sugar Hill Gang's record reached the top five in Canada and the top ten in Europe and was later named the black single of the year by the National Association of Retail Merchandisers. Five years later, the rap group Run-D.M.C. produced the first gold rap album and signaled the movement of rap from its provenance in black neighborhoods into the music of choice for blacks and growing numbers of youth in America and around the world.

African Americans also made new inroads on the large and small screens. In addition to serious shows like *Roots* (1977), *Roots—The Next Generation* (1978), and Gloria Naylor's *Women of Brewster Place* (1989), television produced several popular situation comedies and talk shows: *The Cosby Show* (1984–1992); *The Oprah Winfrey Show* (1986–); and *The Arsenio Hall Show* (1989). *The Cosby Show,* starring

Bill Cosby and Phylicia Ayers-Allen (later Rashad), became the most popular "situation comedy" on TV during the late 1980s and early 1990s. Oprah Winfrey transformed a local talk show opposite the popular white host Phil Donahue into a nationally syndicated show in 1986. Beginning with a sensationalist approach to subject matter, Winfrey later purchased the rights to all her shows, changed the format, and appealed to the diverse social and intellectual needs of her audiences, including establishing a book club that soon influenced the sale of books by popular and scholarly writers alike.

Although Hollywood continued to produce racially stereotypical popular entertainment films, it also released important black culture and history films, such as *The Color Purple* (1985), *Glory* (1990), and *Amistad* (1997). More important, independent black filmmakers expanded the range of black topics treated cinematically: John Singleton, in *Boyz N the Hood* (1992); Julie Dash, in *Daughters of the Dust* (1991); and, most notably, Spike Lee, in *She's Gotta Have It* (1986), *School Daze* (1988), *Do the Right Thing* (1989), and *Malcolm X* (1992). Julie Dash's film was the first by a black woman to have a national release; Singleton became the first black American director to be nominated for an Academy Award; and *Malcolm X* earned actor Denzel Washington an Academy Award nomination for best actor and established Spike Lee as one of the most creative artists of the late twentieth century.

Born in Atlanta, Georgia, in 1957, Spike Lee moved to Brooklyn, New York, as a child. The son of a jazz musician and a school teacher, Lee attended Brooklyn's John Dewey High School, earned his undergraduate degree from Morehouse College, and received his graduate degree in film studies at New York University. As a student at NYU, Lee won a prestigious Student Academy Award for his project "Joe's Bed-Stuy Barbershop: We Cut Heads" (1982). Lee also initiated his own production company, Forty Acres and a Mule, symbolizing the ongoing quest of blacks for economic independence. In his film *Malcolm X,* Spike Lee not only affirmed the significance of Malcolm X in African American history but also underscored the importance of the Black Power movement of the late 1960s and early 1970s in African American popular culture.

At the same time, some aspects of black popular culture fractured the black community along generational, gender, and class lines. Some rappers soon came under fire for the content of their songs, including references to violence and the sexual exploitation of women. Sexist lyrics gained their most pungent articulation in the works of the Miami-based 2 Live Crew, such as "Move Somethin'" (1988) and "As Nasty As They Wanna Be" (1989). To be sure, some scholars like the literary critic Henry Louis Gates defended rappers against government efforts to censure their music. In 1990, for example, a federal court declared "As Nasty As They Wanna Be" obscene (and local law enforcement officers arrested members of the group as well as a Fort Lauderdale record store owner for selling the records). When the case reached a federal appellate court in 1993, Gates testified on behalf of the artists. According to Gates, as offensive as they may have seemed to contemporary adults, rap lyrics were part of a long oral tradition within the black community, where working-class and poor blacks "signified" (or "loud-talked" each other), played the "dozens," and offered exaggerated claims to machismo.

When the federal appellate court reversed the censure decision and the U.S. Supreme Court allowed the ruling to stand, several established civil rights and political groups waged a vigorous campaign to remove the music from retail outlets. These organizations included the National Political Congress of Black Women; the National Council of Negro Women; the National Association for the Advancement of Colored People; and the Rainbow Coalition. In 1994, their efforts resulted in U.S. House and Senate hearings on gangsta rap. The first persons called to testify in the Senate hearings, headed by the newly elected black senator Carole Mosely Braun, were such leaders as Jesse Jackson and Dr. C. Delores Tucker, who had spearheaded the campaign as chair of the National Political Congress of Black Women. Although most of the testimony emphasized the conditions that gave rise to rap rather than simply condemning the lyrics, the U.S. Senate and House hearings underscored the existence of deep generational cleavages within the black urban community. Those divisions surfaced in a nationally televised talk show, *Rivera Live,* on 2 March 1994. Middle-class black leaders like C. Delores Tucker, Congressman Charles Rangel of New York, and Joseph Madison of the NAACP national board confronted rap artists and DJs like Schooly D, called by some "The Father of Gangsta Rap"; Luther Campbell of the group 2 Live Crew; and the cohosts of *Yo, MTV Raps,* Ed Lover and Doctor Dre. Although black leaders tried to separate their opposition to gangsta rap from what they considered to be other "more positive" forms of rap, the line remained blurred. Lover captured the dividing line between the young artists and the older civil rights generation when he declared:

> I have a lot of respect for the brother from the NAACP, I have a lot of respect for Dr. Tucker, I have more respect for Luther Campbell than I . . . can mention right here on this show, and I have a lot of respect for Freddie Foxxx and Schooly D and everybody that's on this panel. But they [the black leaders] are using gangsta rap as an escapegoat for their lack of being on the ground level and the grass roots of this community. We look for our black leaders every day, and where do we see them? Up in Washington tap-dancing in front of some white man. You're never in the projects, you're never in the hood.

Intra- and Interracial Diversity

If African Americans appeared fragmented as the century came to a close, it was partly because they inhabited a complicated world of opportunity and restrictions on their upward mobility and self-expression. For example, although the O. J. Simpson case by no means symbolized the plight of ordinary black men and women before the law, his trial and exoneration did highlight the shifting legal status of blacks in late-twentieth-century America. Under the impact of the modern civil rights and Black Power movements, African Americans were now highly visible on all sides of the law—as jurors and as defense and prosecuting attorneys as well as the accused. In addition to changes in their legal status, African Americans also experienced significant changes in their economic and social conditions. By the mid-1990s, the racial gap in median years of schooling had nearly disappeared, and the percentage of blacks completing college degrees had risen from 1.5 percent during the early 1950s to 13 percent in 1995 (although whites had a 25 percent college graduation rate). At the same time, as African Americans diversified and expanded their numbers in middle-class occupations, the earnings gap gradually decreased for married-couple black families and for single men and women who worked full-time year round. According to income data for 1995, African Americans in the middle class (36 percent) exceeded those below the poverty line (about 30 percent).

Changes in black-white relations were attitudinal as well as material. Even as racial attitudes hardened, most white Americans avoided expressing overtly racist attitudes toward blacks. In a 1991 *Times Mirror* poll of racial attitudes, only 13 percent of white Americans expressed "dislike" for the black minority. (A similar poll in European countries ranged from 20 to over 45 percent expressing dislike for racial and ethnic minorities.) In 1999, the *National Catholic Reporter* launched a contest to update the image of Christ for the new millennium. From the various submissions the magazine selected a painting entitled *Jesus of the People,* a dark-skinned multiracial image, for its December issue closing the twentieth century. The judges for the contest expressed the belief that "the era of the blond, blue-eyed Jesus is over," stating that "this work of art may be prophetic of where and how Christianity will flourish in the next millennium or two."

As suggested by antiracist attitudes among whites, there was substantial room for interracial alliances as the century came to a close. In 1997, a group of white members of Congress proposed that the U.S. government issue an official apology to African Americans for the enslavement of their ancestors. Although few public officials responded positively to the call, during the same year President Clinton launched his "Race Initiative." Under the chairmanship of the eminent historian John Hope Franklin, the Race Initiative aimed to achieve five major goals: (1) to articulate the chief executive's "vision of racial reconciliation"; (2) to educate the American people on the "facts surrounding the issue of race"; (3) to promote "constructive dialogue" about race; (4) to help develop leadership "to help bridge racial divides"; and (5) to advance solutions to deal with problems in contemporary race relations. Asian American board member Angela Ho quickly challenged the board to move beyond the black-white definition of race in America, but the board emphasized the centrality of black-white conflict as the most crucial ethnic and racial dividing line in late-twentieth-century U.S. history. In the spring of 1999, the advisory board issued its report, *One America in the 21st Century: Forging a New Future.* The report concluded that "the greatest challenge facing Americans is to accept and take pride in defining ourselves as a multi-racial democracy." To enhance this goal the report recommended the establishment of a President's Council for One America, whose "main function would be to coordinate and monitor the implementation of policies designed to increase opportunity and eliminate racial disparities."

The prospects for interracial cooperation included not only the mainstream political parties but the struggling white socialist and communist left as well. In the aftermath of the Cold War and the collapse of socialist and communist states during the 1990s, American radicals turned increasingly toward interracial organizing to end the death penalty. This movement gained its most potent expression in the effort to free Mumia Abu-Jamal. A Philadelphia journalist and former member of the Black Panther Party, Jamal was convicted of killing a Philadelphia policeman in 1981 and sentenced to die by lethal injection the following year. Jamal's attorneys and defenders not only cited a series of irregularities in the proceedings of the original trial, including the exclusion of all but one black from the jury and the contradictory and even coerced statements of witnesses. They also accented the disproportionate numbers of blacks on death row from the Philadelphia area. African Americans accounted for nearly 85 percent of all death row cases from Philadelphia, where they faced the death sentence nearly four times more often than their white counterparts. After the publication of Jamal's book *Live From Death Row* in 1996, his case became an international cause celebre and gained the support of a broad cross-section of academics and activists across the country and around the world. Yet even as blacks welcomed the prospects of diverse interracial alliances, they also built on their own history of social struggles and entered such alliances from a position of strength and confidence in their ability to forge fresh strategies for addressing inequality in U.S. society.

∾

CHANGES IN THE U.S. AND WORLD ECONOMY framed African American life during the late twentieth and early twenty-first centuries. Deindustrialization resulted not only in the movement of jobs to the suburbs and the Sun Belt but also in the growing export of industrial production to overseas locations, where workers continued to produce durable goods at low costs. Although this process weakened the position of all U.S. workers, African Americans also faced the persistence of racially discriminatory labor markets; barriers to training programs for the new economy; and popular white movements to roll back the gains of the civil rights and Black Power movements. Unemployment, poverty, incarceration, and homelessness remained disproportionately higher for blacks than for their white counterparts, whereas African American rates of college graduation, homeownership, and life expectancy remained lower. On the other hand, compared with the pre–civil rights and Black Power eras, African Americans nearly closed the black-white gap in high school graduation rates and gradually narrowed the wage gap for married-couple black families. At the same time, African Americans broadened the scope of black culture and politics to include class, color, nationality, gender, and sexual diversity while accenting threads of unity and cohesion based on a shared history. As in the past, these important achievements were the products of both multiclass and interracial movements for social change, but the lives of poor and working-class blacks represented the greatest promise and limits of American and African American family, community, and nation building in an increasingly global age.

PART I	The African American Experience in Global Perspective: Prelude to a New World (Chapters 1–2)
3000–2850 B.C.	Upper and Lower Egypt unite into a single kingdom, forming one of the earliest recorded cultures in human history.
1000 B.C.	South of Egypt, the Nubians develop an independent state, known by the Egyptians as Kush.
730 B.C.	Kush invades Egypt and establishes the 25th, or Ethiopian, Dynasty.
146 B.C.	The Romans conquer Carthage, renaming it "Africa," a name that will eventually refer to the entire continent.
A.D. 711	The Arabs gain control of North Africa and Egypt; the Islamic faith gains increasing influence.
A.D. 1000–1591	In succession, the great West African kingdoms of Ghana, Mali, and Songhay reach their peak and gradually decline.
1200–1400	Europeans initiate sugar plantations on the islands of Cyprus and Sicily, and in southern Spain and Portugal, using enslaved European, Arab, and African labor.
1444	The Portuguese reach the Senegal River and establish a fort at El Mina and sugar plantations on the islands of Madeira, Príncipe, and São Tomé.
1492	Christopher Columbus makes his first voyage to the New World. (Some scholars believe that African presence in the New World predates the arrival of Columbus.)

1494	The Treaty of Tordesillas gives to Spain most land in the Americas and to Portugal the territory of West Africa.
1502	Spain imports the first Africans to work on sugar plantations in Hispaniola (later Saint-Domingue, then Haiti).
1516	The king of Benin restricts and later bans slave trade.
1522	The earliest recorded revolt of African captives in the Americas takes place in Hispaniola.
1556	The Angolans defeat the king of Kongo with Portuguese assistance; slave raiding escalates.
1595	The Spanish government gives Portugal a monopolistic license, *asciento,* to provide slaves to Spain's New World colonies.

PART II	**Enslavement, Revolution, and the New Republic, 1619– 1820** (Chapters 3–6)
1526	Africans accompany Lucas Vásquez de Ayllón to the future site of South Carolina, where they staged the earliest recorded slave rebellion in North America.
1565	Enslaved Africans help the Spanish establish St. Augustine, Florida, the first permanent non-Indian settlement in North America.
1607	The British establish their first permanent settlement, at Jamestown, Virginia.
1619	The first Africans enter British America at Jamestown, Virginia, via a ship engaged in piracy against Spanish colonies in the Caribbean.
1624	John Phillip, described as "a negro Christened in *England* 2 years since," testifies in the Virginia court against a white man.
1626	The Dutch initiate African bondage in the North, importing blacks from the Dutch West Indian colony of Curaçao.
1630	The Virginia court sentences a white man, Hugh Davis, to a sound whipping "for . . . defiling his body in lying with a negro."
1639	Maryland statute declares: "All the inhabitants of the province of Christian standing (slaves excepted) to enjoy full liberties and rights of Englishmen."
1640	The Virginia court sentences a black runaway to a lifetime of servitude but gives two white runaways only one additional year of service. In Virginia, a white man has "to do penance in church according to the laws of England, for getting a negroe woman with child and the woman whipt."

1641	Massachusetts sanctions the institution of slavery and indentured servitude for blacks and whites in its Body of Liberties.
1656	New England prescribes the death penalty for any slaveowner who "willfully killed his servant or slave."
1661	The Virginia assembly passes a statute mandating the enslavement of Africans *durante vita*—for life.
1662	Chesapeake slave codes redefine offspring by the status of the mother rather than the status of the father.
1664	The Maryland assembly passes a statute pronouncing Africans "slaves for life."
1669	Virginia approves a law permitting masters to kill slaves as a disciplinary measure.
1670	Virginia prohibits blacks from importing white servants. The first Africans enter the colony of South Carolina with planters from the Caribbean island of Barbados.
1676	Enslaved African Americans help lower- and middle-class whites challenge the unjust authority of colonial elites in Bacon's Rebellion in Virginia.
1688	Germantown, Pennsylvania, Mennonites issue their protest against the African slave trade.
1712	New York slaves and some Native Americans set fire to buildings and kill nine whites before authorities put down the revolt.
1718	A French company under the direction of Scotsman John Law lays out the city of New Orleans and encourages the importation of blacks into Louisiana.
1727	Pennsylvania iron masters express their dependence on black labor by petitioning the colonial legislature to reduce tariff duties on slaves.
1728	Boston prohibits blacks from carrying a stick or cane or "any other thing of that nature" that might "be fit for quarrelling or fighting."
1730	Connecticut enacts a law permitting the whipping of blacks for "attempting to strike" a white person.
1733	Spanish officials promise freedom to blacks who desert the plantations of British North America.
1734	South Carolina officials accuse Charleston blacks of cornering the market on certain products through legal and illegal trade.
1735	South Carolina's Negro Act restricts clothing blacks may wear, arguing that slaves wear clothes "much above" their condition.

1735	The First Great Awakening, a new brand of Christianity, attracts the attention of growing numbers of slaves and poor whites.
1750	The British Parliament reverses its prohibition of slave labor in the colony of Georgia.
1754	New Jersey Quaker John Woolman writes antislavery pamphlet *Some Considerations on the Keeping of Negroes.*
1755	Two white Baptists initiate the first evangelical mission among blacks, on William Byrd's plantation in Mechlenburg County, Virginia.
1760	New York slave Jupiter Hammon writes "An Evening Thought," the earliest known poem by an American-born black.
1766	Philadelphia school teacher Anthony Benezet publishes the anti-slavery pamphlet *A Caution and Warning to Great Britain and Her Colonies.*
1767	In Boston, Senegal-born slave Phillis Wheatley writes "Address to the Atheist," expressing her firm commitment to Christianity.
1770	Runaway slave and sailor Crispus Attucks is the first of four colonials to die in the Boston Massacre.
1772	In the Somerset case, the English Supreme Court declares that the free "law of England" overrules the institution of slavery elsewhere on English soil. Phillis Wheatley writes a poem expressing the hope that the earl of Dartmouth, the king's representative in North America, will fight tyranny.
1773	The *Pennsylvania Gazette* urges colonists to reconcile the contradiction between their fight against England and the continuing enslavement of Africans. A group of Virginia slaves holds a secret meeting to select a leader to guide their participation in the growing conflict between England and the colonies.
1774	The Continental Congress votes to outlaw African slave trade and sanctions a boycott against those who continue the practice. In St. Andrew Parish, Georgia, six black men and four women revolt against their owner and neighboring planters.
1775	Abolitionists form the Society for the Relief of Free Negroes Unlawfully Held in Bondage (April). British officer Lord Dunmore declares freedom for "all indentured servants and negroes" in exchange for taking up arms against the rebel forces (November).
1776	The colonies issue their Declaration of Independence but delete Jefferson's clause condemning England for slave trade and slavery (July 4).

1777	The Connecticut legislature enlists able-bodied soldiers without regard to "color or status." Most northern states pass similar legislation by 1781.
1779	The Continental Congress approves the use of black troops, slave and free.
	The British issue the Philipsburg Proclamation, extending freedom to slaves in exchange for military service.
1781	Maryland authorizes enlistment of slave and free blacks; Virginia bars enlistment of slave blacks but admits free blacks.
	South Carolina and Georgia bar both slave and free blacks from military service but offer slaves as bounties to encourage enlistment of whites.
1782	Black New York minister and writer Jupiter Hammon publishes *A Winter Piece*, a sermon reinforcing the quest for freedom.
1783	The Revolutionary War officially ends with the signing of the Treaty of Paris.
	By war's end, some 5,000 blacks have served in the revolutionary army.
	The Massachusetts Supreme Court concludes in the Quok Walker case that slavery is "inconsistent with our own conduct and constitution."
1785	The Second Great Awakening emerges in the James River, Virginia, area and merges antislavery religious traditions with new revolutionary ideology.
1786	Some blacks join white farmers in Shays's Rebellion; others volunteer to help put down the revolt.
1787	The Articles of Confederation government passes the Northwest Ordinance, which prohibits slavery in the territory north of the Ohio River.
	African Americans gain an English charter for a black Masonic order.
1789	The U.S. Constitution guarantees the extension of slavery until 1807 and mandates the return of fugitives who escape across state lines.
1791	Benjamin Banneker is appointed "scientific assistant" to Major Andrew Ellicott, the presidential appointee to survey the District of Columbia as the location of the nation's capital.
1792	The outbreak of Haitian Revolution sends growing numbers of free black émigrés to the United States.
1793	Congress passes the Fugitive Slave Act, authorizing slaveowners to enter free territory and apprehend runaways.

1794	Under the leadership of Richard Allen, blacks found the Bethel African Methodist Episcopal Church of Philadelphia. Eli Whitney invents his cotton gin, resulting in the dramatic expansion of cotton production.
1800	Boston invokes a state law against free blacks and orders the deportation of 240 free blacks from the city. Gabriel Prosser and a group of enslaved artisans plan a revolt in Richmond, Virginia.
1804	Beginning with Pennsylvania in 1780, all northern states pass gradual abolition laws; southern states allow manumission by will or deed.
1811	A large slave rebellion erupts in St. John the Baptist Parish in Louisiana; free blacks volunteer to help put down the revolt.
1812–1814	During the War of 1812, free blacks play an important role in the navy and in the defense of New Orleans.
1814	Andrew Jackson's frontier army attacks the Creek nation and forces concessions that enable the expansion of slavery into the southwest.
1817	Influential whites form the American Colonization Society to push resettlement of free blacks on African soil.

PART III — **The Antebellum Era, Expansion of Cotton Culture, and Civil War, 1820–1865** (Chapters 7–10)

1820	Northern and southern states approve the Missouri Compromise, which violates the Northwest Ordinance by extending slavery northwest of the Ohio River.
1821	New York black businessman Allen Royce opens the African Grove, billed as America's first black theater.
1822	Free black carpenter Denmark Vesey plots a rebellion against slaveholders in Charleston, South Carolina.
1823	The U.S. Supreme Court declares unconstitutional the incarceration of free black seamen who enter southern ports; southern states defy the ruling.
1827	Presbyterian minister Samuel Cornish and Jamaican-born teacher John Russwurm found *Freedom's Journal*, the nation's first black newspaper, in New York.
1829	Free black North Carolina carpenter David Walker issues his famous antislavery pamphlet, *Walker's Appeal*.
1830	African Americans hold the first National Negro Convention at Bethel AME Church in Philadelphia, with representatives from eight states.

1831	Slave preacher, carpenter, and carriage driver Nat Turner leads the most renowned slave rebellion in rural Virginia.
	In Boston, William Lloyd Garrison launches the abolitionist newspaper *Liberator*.
1832	The New England Anti-Slavery Society (later renamed the Massachusetts Anti-Slavery Society) is formed in Boston.
1833	The American Anti-Slavery Society is formed in Philadelphia by black and white abolitionists.
	A white mob destroys a school for young black women in Canterbury, Connecticut.
1836	Samuel Cornish, Philip Bell, and Charles B. Ray launch the *Colored American* (originally the *Weekly Advocate*), the longest-running antebellum black publication.
	Washington, D.C., prohibits free blacks or their agents from keeping "any tavern, ordinary, shop, porter cellar, refectory, or eating house of any kind, for profit or gain."
1838	Frederick Douglass escapes from his Maryland owner and moves to New Bedford, Massachusetts.
	Abolitionist David Ruggle initiates the first black magazine, the *Mirror of Liberty*, in New York.
1839	Led by Cinque, 53 enslaved Africans overpower the Cuban slaver *Amistad* and sail into Long Island Sound; they are later freed by the U.S. Supreme Court.
1840	The American and Foreign Anti-Slavery Society is formed, partly as a protest against the women's rights stand of the American Anti-Slavery Society.
1841	One of the most destructive antebellum race riots breaks out in Cincinnati.
	Rev. J. W. C. Pennington writes *A Text Book of the Origin and History of the Colored People*.
1843	Isabella Baumfree changes her name to Sojourner Truth and later becomes one of the most renowned itinerant ministers, antislavery activists, and women's rights advocates.
	At the National Convention of Colored Men in Buffalo, Henry Highland Garnet delivers "An Address to Slaves of the United States."
1845	Frederick Douglass, under pressure from white abolitionists, publishes his *Narrative of the Life of Frederick Douglass*.
	Harriet Jacobs (Linda Brent) escapes from slavery and later publishes her *Incidents in the Life of a Slave Girl: Written by Herself* (1861).

1846	The U.S. Senate rejects the Wilmot Proviso, which calls for a ban on slavery in any territory gained as a result of military conquest.
1847	Richmond's Tredegar Iron Works hires a predominantly slave work force after white workers walk out to protest the training of slaves for skilled jobs.
1848	Frederick Douglass launches a new organ of abolitionism, the *North Star*, which aims to increase the role of blacks in their own liberation.
1849–1850	Harriet Tubman escapes from her master on the eastern shore of Maryland and later makes nearly twenty trips into slave territory to aid fugitives.
1850	The Fugitive Slave Act outlaws the slave trade in Washington, D.C., but strengthens the hand of slave catchers in the free states.
	New York City blacks form the American League of Colored Laborers to organize skilled black workers and stimulate the growth of black business.
1851	In Christiana, Pennsylvania, abolitionists kill one slave catcher and mortally wound another. Participants are later acquitted of treason and murder.
	At the Akron, Ohio, Woman's Rights Convention, Sojourner Truth delivers an address that later becomes famous as the "And Ar'n't I a Woman?" speech.
1852	Harriet Beecher Stowe publishes her influential antislavery novel, *Uncle Tom's Cabin*.
	Martin R. Delany publishes *The Condition, Elevation, Emigration and Destiny of the Colored People of the United States*.
1853	William Wells Brown publishes *Clotel, or, The President's Daughter*, the first novel by an African American.
	Solomon Northrup publishes *Twelve Years a Slave: Narrative of Solomon Northrup, a Citizen of New York*.
1854	The Kansas-Nebraska Act violates the provisions of the Missouri Compromise of 1820 and helps set the stage for the Civil War.
	A national Emigration Convention meets in Cleveland, Ohio, and endorses a plan of African American resettlement in Africa.
1857	The U.S. Supreme Court rules in the Dred Scott case that blacks "were not intended to be included under the word 'citizens' in the constitution."
1859	The *Clothilde*, the last known slave ship to dock in a U.S. port, transports 130 Africans to Mobile, Alabama.
	Harriet E. Wilson writes *Our Nig, or, Sketches from the Life of a Free Black*, the first novel by an African American woman.

1859	John Brown, a white abolitionist minister from Kansas, leads an attack on the federal arsenal at Harpers Ferry, Virginia.
1860	Abraham Lincoln is elected president on the Republican Party ticket, which promises to uphold slavery where it already exists but to block its expansion into the new territories.
1861	Eleven southern states secede from the Union and establish the Confederate States of America. Congress passes the First Confiscation Act, which defines slaves as "contraband" of war (August).
1862	General David Hunter defies War Department orders and recruits the First Regiment of South Carolina Volunteers (May). Congress passes the Second Confiscation Act, which proclaims all slaves owned by southern rebels "forever free" (July).
1863	President Lincoln's Emancipation Proclamation declares all slaves free, except those in loyal territory (January). The New York draft riot results in violent attacks on the black community (July). Mary Ann Shadd Cary, a black journalist and antislavery activist, becomes the first official woman recruiter for the Union Army (August). Black soldiers of the Massachusetts Fifty-Fourth decide to fight without pay to protest racial inequality between black and white soldiers (September).
1864	Confederate troops massacre black soldiers after they surrender at Fort Pillow on the Mississippi River (April). Congress passes legislation equalizing the pay of black and white soldiers (June). Blacks from southern and northern states form the National Equal Rights League to protest racial discrimination (October).
1865	Congress establishes the Bureau of Freedmen, Refugees, and Abandoned Land (Freedmen's Bureau) to oversee the transition from slavery to freedom (March). The Civil War ends when Confederate general Robert E. Lee surrenders at Appomattox Court House in Virginia (April). Abraham Lincoln is assassinated; Andrew Johnson succeeds him as president (April). The Thirteenth Amendment outlaws slavery (December).

PART IV	Emancipation and the First Generation of Freedom, 1865–1915 (Chapters 11–14)
1865–1866	Beginning with South Carolina and Mississippi, southern states pass "black codes," which deny blacks full citizenship rights.
1866	Veterans of the Confederate army form the Ku Klux Klan in Pulaski, Tennessee. The Freedmen's Bureau and northern philanthropic and missionary societies establish Fisk (1866), Howard (1866), and Atlanta (1867) Universities.
1867	Radical Republicans pass the Reconstruction Act of 1867 and make Reconstruction a prerogative of Congress rather than the president.
1868	The Fourteenth Amendment provides blacks full citizenship rights under the law.
1869	African Americans form their own National Labor Union under the leadership of Isaac Meyers of Baltimore.
1870	The Fifteenth Amendment enfranchises all men regardless of race, color, or previous condition of servitude.
1871	Congress passes the first of several Ku Klux Klan and Enforcement Acts, outlawing the use of violence to deprive citizens of the right to vote.
1873	The Freedmen's Bureau Bank, chartered in 1865, fails during an economic depression.
1875	Congress passes the Civil Rights Act of 1875, which calls for an end to racial discrimination in public accommodations like theaters, hotels, and restaurants.

1876	The presidential election of Republican Rutherford B. Hayes symbolizes the downfall of Radical Reconstruction.
1879	Some 6,000 blacks leave the Deep South states of Texas, Louisiana, and Mississippi for Kansas.
1880	African Americans form the Knights of Pythias, followed by the United Order of True Reformers (1881) and the Mosaic Templars of America (1882).
1882	Historian and minister George Washington Williams publishes *History of the Negro Race in America: From 1619 to 1880.*
1883	The U.S. Supreme Court strikes down the Civil Rights Act of 1875 and limits federal protection to the activities of states rather than those of individual citizens.
1884	Blacks in Washington, D.C., form the Medico-Chirurgical Society, the earliest black medical society.
1890	Numerous black farmers join whites in the Populist movement, designed to address the issues of class inequality.
	Mississippi initiates the movement for the constitutional disfranchisement of black voters; other southern states soon follow suit.
1891	Black labor leader Richard L. Davis is elected to the Executive Board of the United Mine Workers of America District Six (Ohio).
1892	The number of recorded lynchings peaks at about 160.
	Frances Ellen Harper publishes *Iola Leroy, or Shadows Lifted,* the first novel by a postbellum black writer.
1895	Booker T. Washington delivers his famous "Atlanta Compromise" address, urging blacks to push for economic and institutional improvements rather than political rights.
1895–1896	African Americans form the National Medical Association; the National Baptist Convention, U.S.A.; and the National Association of Colored Women.
1898	Four all-black units fight with the U.S. Army in the Spanish-American War.
1899	Charles Chestnut publishes *The Conjure Woman* and the *Wife of His Youth and Other Stories of the Color Line.*
1900	The National Negro Business League is formed under the leadership of Booker T. Washington.
1902	Gertrude "Ma" Rainey, considered the earliest professional black singer, tours Missouri (with the Rabbit Foot Minstrels), where she first hears the blues.
1903	W. E. B. Du Bois publishes *Souls of Black Folk* and becomes Booker T. Washington's leading critic.

1903	Under the leadership of W. E. B. Du Bois, 29 African Americans form the Niagara movement "to complain, and to complain loudly and insistently about racial discrimination."
1905	St. Louis laundress Madame C. J. Walker works for beauty manufacturer Annie Malone before producing her own renowned skin and hair care products for black women. Ferdinand "Jelly Roll" Morton, known as the first true jazz composer, publishes his jazz compositions as *Jelly Roll Blues*.
1906	President Theodore Roosevelt unjustly discharges some 167 black soldiers of the Twenty-Fifth Infantry Regiment.
1908	In his bout with Tommy Burns in Sydney, Australia, Jack Johnson becomes the first black heavyweight champion of the world.
1909–1910	African Americans and their white allies form the National Association for the Advancement of Colored People and the National Urban League. Race riots break out when Jack Johnson knocks out "great white hope" Jim Jeffries to retain his crown as heavyweight champion of the world.
1911	Black women form the Negro Women's Equal Franchise Federation and push for the right to vote.
1912	Woodrow Wilson, the first southern president since the Civil War, takes office and escalates the segregation of blacks and whites in the federal government. W. C. Handy, considered the first person to popularize the blues, publishes his *Memphis Blues*.

PART V — Migration, Depression, and World Wars, 1915–1945 (Chapters 15–19)

1915	The Lincoln Motion Picture Company produces the film *The Realization of a Negro's Ambition* to counteract the racist film *Birth of a Nation*. The Ku Klux Klan is revived on Stone Mountain in Georgia.
1916	Marcus M. Garvey moves the Universal Negro Improvement Association from Jamaica to New York and soon builds the largest mass movement in African American history.
1917	The United States declares war against Germany (April). Robert Abbott, editor of the *Chicago Defender*, emerges as a major champion of black migration to the urban North and West. The East St. Louis, Illinois, race riot claims the lives of 39 blacks and 11 whites.

1917	*Buchanan v. Worley* and *Guinn v. U.S.*, respectively, overrule housing segregation statutes and pronounce the grandfather clause unconstitutional.
	Socialists A. Philip Randolph and Chandler Owens found the *Messenger* magazine and urge blacks to oppose the war.
1918	The U.S. government establishes the Division of Negro Economics in the Department of Labor.
	Nearly 2.3 million black men register for the draft, and an estimated 370,000 serve in the armed forces.
	Oscar Micheaux, the most prolific of the early black filmmakers, produces the film *Birthright*.
1919	Black delegates from twelve states and the District of Columbia form the National Brotherhood Workers of America.
	The Chicago race riot claims the lives of 25 blacks and 15 whites.
	Claude McKay publishes his militant poem "If We Must Die."
1920	The United States ratifies the Nineteenth Amendment, giving women the right to vote, but black women confront southern disfranchisement laws along with black men.
	The Okeh Record Company launches the race record movement with its release of Mamie Smith's "Crazy Blues."
	The National Negro Baseball League is formed in Kansas City under the leadership of Rube Foster of Chicago.
1921	Singer Ethel Waters gives the black-owned Pace Phonograph Company its first hit record, "Down Home Blues."
	The Tulsa, Oklahoma, race riot claims the lives of 68 blacks and 9 whites.
1923	The National Urban League forms its magazine, *Opportunity*, and helps promote the Harlem Renaissance.
	Marcus Garvey is convicted on mail fraud charges.
	Jazzman Fletcher Henderson forms his New York band and helps launch the "Big Band" movement.
1924	The National Negro Baseball League holds its first World Series.
1925	The Brotherhood of Sleeping Car Porters is formed under the leadership of A. Philip Randolph.
	Marcus Garvey is imprisoned at a federal penitentiary in Atlanta, Georgia.
	The publication of Alain Locke's *The New Negro* signals the emergence of the Harlem Renaissance.
1926	Wallace Thurman and a group of rebellious Harlem Renaissance writers launch a new magazine, *Fire!!*

1927	Marcus Garvey is deported from the United States.
1928	Oscar De Priest is elected to the U.S. Congress from Chicago, the first black to serve in that position since 1901.
1929	The stock market crash signals the arrival of the Great Depression.
1930	Following the NAACP's vigorous anticonfirmation campaign, the U.S. Senate rejects Judge John J. Parker's nomination to the U.S. Supreme Court.
1931	The Communist Party mounts a vigorous and effective international defense of nine black youths sentenced to death for allegedly raping two white women near Scottsboro, Alabama. Elijah Muhammad (born Elijah Poole) founds the Nation of Islam in Detroit before moving its headquarters to Chicago.
1932	Franklin D. Roosevelt is elected president and soon initiates his New Deal social programs. Blacks escalate "Don't Buy Where You Can't Work" campaigns in Washington, D.C.; New York; Baltimore; and Chicago.
1933	Civil rights organizations form the Joint Committee on National Recovery (JCNR) to oversee New Deal programs on behalf of blacks. The NAACP strengthens its nationwide movement for a federal antilynching law, but efforts fail in 1934, 1935, 1937, 1938, and 1940.
1934	Arthur Mitchell of Chicago defeats Oscar De Priest to become the first black Democratic U.S. congressman. W. E. B. Du Bois resigns from the NAACP when the organization rejects his proposal for reaching out to the masses. Zora Neale Hurston produces her most important novels, *Jonah's Gourd Vine* (1934), *Mules and Men* (1935), and *Their Eyes Were Watching God* (1937).
1935	The National Council of Negro Women forms after a split within the National Association of Colored Women. The "Black Cabinet," an informal group of black employees in government agencies, emerges in Washington, D.C. The Committee for Industrial Organization (renamed the Congress of Industrial Organizations in 1938) forms a new union along industrial rather than craft lines and appeals to workers of all colors. The American Federation of Labor grants an international charter to the Brotherhood of Sleeping Car Porters.
1936	For the first time, African Americans give the majority of their votes to a Democrat, Franklin D. Roosevelt, in a presidential election. The National Negro Congress forms in Chicago, with A. Philip Randolph as president.

1936	At the Olympic games in Berlin, Jesse Owens wins four gold medals; ten other black athletes win thirteen medals.
1937	Joe Louis becomes the first black heavyweight champion of the world in twenty-two years when he knocks out the German Max Schmeling in the first round.
1938	The U.S. Supreme Court upholds the legality of the "Don't Buy Where You Can't Work" campaigns under New Deal labor legislation.
	Crystal Byrd Fauset of Pennsylvania becomes the first black woman elected to a state legislative body.
1939	Actress Hattie McDaniel becomes the first African American to receive an Academy Award, for her role in *Gone with the Wind*.
	Singer Marian Anderson performs at an outdoor concert at the Lincoln Memorial when the DAR bars her from Constitution Hall on the basis of her color.
1940	The Selective Service Training Act prohibits racial or color discrimination in the selection and training of military personnel.
	Richard Wright publishes his most famous novel, *Native Son*.
	Marcus Garvey dies in London.
1941	The *Pittsburgh Courier* popularizes the African American "Double V" campaign (victory at home and victory abroad).
	Led by A. Philip Randolph, African Americans organize the March on Washington movement to end racial discrimination in defense industries.
	President Franklin D. Roosevelt issues Executive Order 8802, which sets up the Fair Employment Practices Committee.
	Beginning in 1941, "Zoot Suit" riots break out in northern and western cities.
1941–1945	The Air Corps awards the Distinguished Flying Cross to 82 African American pilots.
	The Ninety-Second Regiment, stationed in the Mediterranean, receives 2 Distinguished Service Crosses, 16 Legion of Merit Awards, 95 Silver Stars, and over 1,100 Purple Hearts.
1943	The Detroit riot results in 34 deaths, 675 injuries, and an estimated $2 million in property damage.
	The Congress of Racial Equality is formed in Chicago and launches nonviolent direct action campaigns to desegregate public accommodations.
1944	Swedish economist Gunnar Myrdal publishes his monumental study *An American Dilemma: The Negro Problem and Modern Democracy*.
	Smith v. Allwright outlaws the Texas white primary.

PART VI	Civil Rights, Black Power, and Deindustrialization, 1945–2000 (Chapters 20–23)
1945–1948	Two Truman presidential committee reports, "To Secure These Rights" and "Freedom to Serve," recommend the eradication of discrimination and segregation from all facets of American life. Blacks stage boycotts to protest discrimination in employment and public accommodations in northern and western cities from San Francisco to New York.
1946	Louis Jordan and his band, the Tympani Five, release "Choo Cho Ch'Boogie," spurring the development of rhythm and blues.
1947	Ralph Ellison publishes his highly acclaimed novel, *Invisible Man.* Jackie Robinson becomes the first black to play professional baseball since the 1880s.
1949	*Billboard* magazine recognizes the shift in black musical styles, changing the name of its "Race Records" chart to "Rhythm & Blues." Trumpeter Miles Davis pioneers a new form of jazz with his album *Birth of the Cool.*
1950	Poet Gwendolyn Brooks becomes the first African American to win the Pulitzer Prize for poetry, for her volume *Annie Allen.* The National Basketball Association signs its first black player, Charles "Chuck" Cooper, although Earl Lloyd is the first black to play in an NBA game. Black workers form the National Negro Labor Council.
1953	African Americans successfully boycott city buses in Baton Rouge, Louisiana, but their goals are limited to improvements within the segregationist system. James Baldwin publishes his first novel, *Go Tell It on the Mountain.*
1954	The U.S. Supreme Court outlaws segregated public schools in the landmark *Brown v. Board of Education* case. Martin Luther King Jr. becomes pastor of Montgomery's Dexter Avenue Baptist Church and soon emerges as the principal spokesman in the Montgomery bus boycott.
1955	The new AFL-CIO accepts racially exclusionary unions, weakening the position of blacks in the labor movement. Fourteen-year-old Chicago-born Emmett Till is lynched in Money, Mississippi, for allegedly saying "Bye, baby" to a white woman.
1955–1956	African Americans conduct a year-long boycott of buses in Montgomery, Alabama, when seamstress Rosa Parks refuses to give up her seat to a white passenger.

1957	The struggle to desegregate schools in Little Rock, Arkansas, precipitates stiff white resistance and the use of federal troops.
	Congress passes the Civil Rights Act of 1957, which sets up the U.S. Civil Rights Commission and spurs the beginning of the Second Reconstruction.
	Civil rights leaders meet in Atlanta, Georgia, and form the Southern Christian Leadership Conference with Martin Luther King Jr. as its first president.
1959	Berry Gordy founds Motown Records in Detroit and soon produces music that appeals to both black and white markets.
	Black workers form the American Negro Labor Council.
	Lorraine Hansberry receives the prestigious New York Drama Critics Circle Award for *Raisin in the Sun*.
1960	Four black North Carolina A&T students begin a nationwide sit-in movement when they demand service at Greensboro's segregated Woolworth Department Store.
	Black college students form SNCC and elect Marion Barry its first president.
1961	CORE sends "freedom riders" into the South to force compliance with federal orders to desegregate interstate transportation facilities.
	Violence erupts on the campus of the University of Mississippi when a federal court orders the admission of its first black student, James Meredith.
1963	Birmingham, Alabama, becomes the site of SCLC's highly organized and deliberate desegregation campaign involving hundreds of black children, massive arrests, and intense police brutality.
	African Americans stage the March on Washington for Jobs and Freedom, where Martin Luther King Jr. delivers his famous "I Have a Dream" speech.
	President Kennedy is assassinated in Dallas, Texas, before he can steer his recently proposed civil rights legislation through Congress.
1964	The Civil Rights Act of 1964 outlaws discrimination in public accommodations and employment.
	The Economic Opportunity Act establishes "War on Poverty" programs.
	The Voter Education Project launches its Mississippi Freedom Summer campaign.
	African Americans form the Mississippi Freedom Democratic Party and challenge the exclusionary policies of the regular party.
	Muslim minister Malcolm X forms the Muslim Mosque, Inc., and the Organization of African American Unity.

1964	Muhammad Ali (Cassius Clay) wins the heavyweight boxing championship from Sonny Liston.
1964–1967	Violence breaks out in numerous cities where blacks face rising unemployment, police brutality, and overcrowded and deteriorating housing conditions.
1965	The U.S. Department of Labor issues Daniel Patrick Moynihan's *The Negro Family: The Case for National Action.*
	Helmeted state troopers use tear gas and billy clubs to stop civil rights marchers in Selma, Alabama.
	Congress passes the Voting Rights Act of 1965, authorizing the use of federal examiners to register voters and oversee the political process.
	Muslim minister and black nationalist leader Malcolm X is assassinated during a mass meeting at the Audubon Ballroom in New York.
1966	Martin Luther King Jr. and other marchers face violence as they march to desegregate all-white neighborhoods in Chicago.
	James Meredith is shot by a white gunman during a one-man march from Memphis, Tennessee, to Jackson, Mississippi.
	The Black Power movement emerges as civil rights leaders converge on Memphis and continue Meredith's march to Jackson.
	Muhammad Ali refuses induction into the U.S. Army, stimulating support for the antiwar movement.
	The Black Panther Party is formed in Oakland, California, under the leadership of Merritt College students Huey P. Newton and Bobby Seale.
1967	The FBI launches its COINTELPRO, or Counter Intelligence Program, against a variety of civil rights and Black Power organizations.
	In Cleveland, Ohio, Carl Stokes becomes the first black mayor of a major American city; Richard Hatcher of Gary, Indiana, quickly becomes the second.
1968	The president's National Advisory Commission on Civil Disorders releases its report, concluding that America is "moving toward two societies, one black, one white—separate and unequal."
	Violence breaks out in over 100 cities following Martin Luther King Jr.'s assassination in Memphis, Tennessee, on April 4.
	SCLC's Poor People's Campaign erects a "Resurrection City" on the mall of the nation's capital; police use tear gas to evict the occupants.
	Green v. Board of New Kent County endorses the idea of goals and timetables for achieving racial balance in public schools, thus paving the way for busing.

1968	Olympic gold medalist Tommie Smith and bronze medalist John Carlos mount the victory stand and give the Black Power salute to dramatize racial injustice in the United States.
1969	Black artists like Amiri Baraka, Barbara Ann Teer, and Ed Mullen spearhead the Black Arts movement, or Second Renaissance.
	Billboard magazine acknowledges the impact of the Black Power movement when it changes the name of its black music chart from "Rhythm & Blues" to "Soul."
1971	Rev. Jesse Jackson breaks from SCLC and forms People United to Save Humanity (later changed to People United to Serve Humanity).
	Swann v. Charlotte-Mecklenberg County Board of Education and *Griggs v. Duke Power Company* declare the "color-blind" principle of affirmative action unfair in its impact on black students and workers.
	African Americans initiate a series of Black Power conferences designed to increase the number of black elected officials.
1972	The most successful Black Power conference takes place in Gary, Indiana.
1974	Leading black nationalists seek to internationalize the Black Power movement at the Sixth Pan African Congress in Tanzania.
	White resistance to busing erupts into violence in Boston.
1976	Ntozake Shange's choreopoem *for colored girls who have considered suicide when the rainbow is enuf* (1974) reaches Broadway.
1977	The death penalty returns after disappearing in 1972.
1978	The U.S. Supreme Court weakens affirmative action in *University of California Regents v. Bakke* but later supports employment and business set-aside programs in *United Steelworkers of America v. Weber* (1979) and *Fullilove v. Kluznick* (1980).
1979	Following the release of his first album, *Off the Wall,* Michael Jackson gains the accolade "King of Pop" with a string of hit songs and videos like *Billie Jean, Beat It,* and *Thriller.*
	The Sugar Hill Gang releases their hit single "Rapper's Delight," foreshadowing the rise of rap as a new musical genre.
1980	The worst outbreak of urban violence since the 1960s occurs in Miami's Liberty City neighborhood following a series of police brutality incidents.
	The Children's Defense Fund issues its study *Portrait of Inequality: Black and White Children in America.*

1982	Alice Walker publishes *The Color Purple,* which wins the Pulitzer Prize and becomes a motion picture in 1985.
1984	Rev. Jesse Jackson spearheads the formation of the Rainbow Coalition and launches a spirited campaign to gain the Democratic nomination for president.
	Led by Randall Robinson, head of Transafrica, blacks escalate their protests against South African apartheid.
	The Cosby Show, starring Bill Cosby and Phylicia Rashad, premieres and soon becomes the nation's most popular "situation comedy."
1985	Philadelphia authorities launch a fire-bomb attack on the black nationalist organization MOVE, leaving six adults and five children dead.
1986	Oprah Winfrey becomes the nation's favorite television talk show host when her show is syndicated and shown on TV stations across the country.
	The Children's Defense Fund issues a follow-up report, *Families in Peril: An Agenda for Social Change.*
1987	Rita Dove receives the Pulitzer Prize for her volume of poems, *Thomas and Beulah.*
1988	Jesse Jackson and the Rainbow Coalition again mount a vigorous campaign to win the Democratic party's nomination for president.
	Congress passes the Omnibus Anti–Drug Abuse Act, which appoints a "drug czar" and exacerbates the problem of drug use and incarceration for young black men.
	Toni Morrison receives the Pulitzer Prize for *Beloved.*
1989	Queen Latifah emerges as a prominent female rap artist with her first album, *All Hail to the Queen.*
1990–1991	General Colin Powell, the first African American chairman of the U.S. Joint Chiefs of Staff, directs the U.S. invasion of Iraq in the Persian Gulf War.
	The nomination of conservative jurist Clarence Thomas to the U.S. Supreme Court is challenged when former employee Anita Hill charges Thomas with sexual harassment during his tenure as head of the EEOC. Thomas is nevertheless confirmed.
1992	A multiracial riot breaks out in South Central Los Angeles when a predominantly white jury acquits police officers in the Rodney King police brutality case.
	Filmmaker Spike Lee's *Malcolm X* earns actor Denzel Washington an Academy Award nomination and establishes Lee as one of the most creative artists of the late twentieth century.
1993	Toni Morrison receives the Nobel Prize for literature.
	Rita Dove becomes poet laureate of the United States.

1994	Led by Muslim minister Louis Farrakhan, over a million black men participate in the Million Man March on Washington, D.C.
	The U.S. House of Representatives and Senate open hearings to investigate the social implications of gangsta rap as a music form.
1995	After an eight-month trial, a predominantly black jury finds O. J. Simpson, the professional football star and actor, not guilty of murdering his ex-wife and her friend.
1996	California voters approve Proposition 209, which abolishes affirmative action for minorities and women in state-funded programs.
	The Oakland, California, School Board touches off a nationwide controversy when it accepts Black English as a tool for teaching black youngsters Standard English.
1997	President Bill Clinton announces his new "Race Initiative" and selects John Hope Franklin, the eminent historian, to chair the project.
	August Wilson releases his play *Seven Guitars.*
	Eldrick "Tiger" Woods becomes the first African American and the first Asian American to win the U.S. Masters golf tournament.
1998	Black women stage a Million Woman March in Philadelphia to demonstrate the centrality of women in movements for social change.
1999	Serena Williams defeats Martina Hingis and becomes the first African American woman to win a Grand Slam tennis title since Althea Gibson in 1957.
	The President's Advisory Board on Race issues its report, *One America in the 21st Century: Forging a Future*, which concludes that the greatest challenge facing the nation is the creation of "a multi-racial democracy."
	In a contest to update the image of Christ, the *National Catholic Reporter* selects the painting *Jesus of the People,* a dark-skinned multiracial image.
2000	Multinational and multiracial groups protest the acquittal of four New York City policemen in the shooting death of West African immigrant Amadou Diallo (February).
	An NAACP-led national boycott of South Carolina results in the removal of the Confederate flag from the dome of the state capitol (May).
	Colin L. Powell, former chairman of the Joint Chiefs of Staff, addresses the Republican National Convention and criticizes the party for opposing affirmative action for the poor while supporting it for "special interests" (July).
	Rev. Jesse Jackson addresses the Democratic National Convention and urges the party to "make room for protesters and turn their idealism into progress" (August).

DOCUMENTS AND TABLES

THE BLACK POPULATION IN COLONIAL AMERICA, 1630–1780

	1630	1640	1650	1660	1670	1680	1690	1700
North	10	427	880	1,162	1,125	1,895	3,340	5,206
South	50	170	720	1,758	3,410	5,076	13,389	22,611
Total	60	597	1,600	2,920	4,535	6,971	16,729	27,817

	1710	1720	1730	1740	1750	1760	1770	1780
North	8,303	14,091	17,323	23,958	30,222	40,033	48,460	56,796
South	36,563	54,748	73,698	126,066	206,198	285,773	411,362	518,624
Total	44,866	68,839	91,021	150,024	236,420	325,806	459,822	575,420

THE ENSLAVED AND FREE BLACK POPULATION IN THE NEW REPUBLIC, 1790–1860

	1790	1800	1810	1820
Slave	697,624	893,602	1,191,362	1,538,022
Free	59,557	108,435	186,446	233,634
Total	757,181	1,002,037	1,377,808	1,771,656

	1830	1840	1850	1860
Slave	2,009,043	2,487,355	3,204,313	3,953,760
Free	319,599	386,293	434,495	488,070
Total	2,328,642	2,873,648	3,638,808	4,441,830

Source: Both tables from Harry A. Ploski and James Williams, eds., *The Negro Almanac: A Reference Work on the Afro-American,* 4th ed. (New York: John Wiley and Sons, 1983), p. 457.

THE AFRICAN AMERICAN POPULATION AS A PERCENTAGE OF THE TOTAL U.S. POPULATION, 1790–1860

Year	Total Population	Black Population	Percentage
1790	3,929,214	757,208	19.3
1800	5,308,483	1,002,037	18.9
1810	7,239,881	1,377,808	19.0
1820	9,638,453	1,771,656	18.4
1830	12,866,020	2,328,642	18.1
1840	17,069,453	2,873,648	16.8
1850	23,191,876	3,638,808	15.7
1860	31,443,321	4,441,830	14.1

Source: Kenneth Estell, ed., *The African American Almanac,* 6th ed. (Detroit: Gale Research, Inc., 1994), p. 635. Used by permission.

THE DECLARATION OF INDEPENDENCE: THE DELETED SECTION

Thomas Jefferson's original draft of the Declaration of Independence sharply denounced the slave trade. The document also blamed British king George III for the horrors of human bondage, but the founding fathers eliminated this section from the final draft.

He (George III) has incited treasonable insurrections of our fellow citizens, with the allurements of forfeiture and confiscation of our property.

He has waged cruel war against human nature itself, violating its most sacred rights of life and liberty in the persons of a distant people who never offended him, captivating and carrying them into slavery in another hemisphere, or to incur miserable death in their transportation thither. This piratical warfare, the opprobrium of INFIDEL powers, is the warfare of the CHRISTIAN King of Great-Britain. Determined to keep open a market where MEN should be bought and sold, he has prostituted his negative for suppressing every legislative attempt to prohibit or to restrain this execrable commerce. And that this assemblage of horrors might want no fact of distinguished die, he is now exciting those very people to rise in arms among us, and to purchase that liberty of which he has deprived them, by murdering the people on whom he also obtruded them: thus paying off former crimes committed against the LIBERTIES of one people with crimes which he urges them to commit against the LIVES of another.

THE CONSTITUTION OF THE UNITED STATES (1788) COMPARED WITH THE CONSTITUTION OF THE CONFEDERATE STATES (1861)

When the southern states seceded from the Union in 1861, they adopted the provisions of the U.S. Constitution nearly verbatim. Unlike the U.S. Constitution, which referred to blacks in code language such as "three fifths of all other persons," the Confederate Constitution explicitly named blacks as "negroes," "Africans," and "slaves."

THE CONSTITUTION OF THE UNITED STATES	THE CONSTITUTION OF THE CONFEDERATE STATES OF AMERICA
Article I	**Article I**

SEC. 2. . . . Clause 3. Representatives and direct taxes shall be apportioned among the several States which may be included within this Union, according to their respective numbers, which shall be determined by adding to the whole number of free persons, including those bound to service for a term of years, and excluding Indians not taxed, three fifths of all other persons. The actual enumeration shall be made within three years after the first meeting of the Congress of the United States, and within every subsequent term of ten years, in such manner as they shall by law direct. The number of Representatives shall not exceed one for every thirty thousand, but each State shall have at least one Representative; and until such enumeration shall be made, the State of *New Hampshire* shall be entitled to choose three, *Massachusetts* eight, *Rhode Island and Providence Plantations* one, *Connecticut* five, *New York* six, *New Jersey* four, *Pennsylvania* eight, *Delaware* one, *Maryland* six, *Virginia* ten, *North Carolina* five, *South Carolina* five, and *Georgia* three. . . .

SEC. 9. Clause 1. The migration or importation of such persons as any of the States now existing shall think proper to admit shall not be prohibited by the Congress prior to the year one thousand eight hundred and eight, but a tax or duty may be imposed on such importation, not exceeding ten dollars for each person. . . .

SEC. 2. . . . (3) Representatives and direct taxes shall be apportioned among the several States which may be included within this Confederacy according to their respective numbers, which shall be determined by adding to the whole number of free persons, including those bound to service for a term of years, and excluding Indians not taxed, three-fifths of all slaves. The actual enumeration shall be made within three years after the first meeting of the Congress of the Confederate States, and within every subsequent term of ten years, in such manner as they shall by law direct. The number of Representatives shall not exceed one for every fifty thousand, but each State shall have at least one Representative; and until such enumeration shall be made, the State of South Carolina shall be entitled to choose six; the State of Georgia ten; the State of Alabama nine; the State of Florida two; the State of Mississippi seven; the State of Louisiana six; and the State of Texas six. . .

SEC. 9. (1) The importation of negroes of the African race, from any foreign country, other than the slaveholding States or Territories of the United States of America, is hereby forbidden; and Congress is required to pass such laws as shall effectually prevent the same. . . .

THE FUGITIVE SLAVE ACT (1793)

In its first official legislation designed to enable slaveholders to recover fugitives, the U.S. Congress followed the lead of the U.S. Constitution and avoided use of the term SLAVE.

An act respecting fugitives from justice, and persons escaping from the service of their masters

SECTION 1. *Be it enacted by the Senate and House of Representatives of the United States of America in Congress assembled,* That whenever the executive authority of any state in the Union, or of either of the territories northwest or south of the river Ohio, shall demand any person as a fugitive from justice, of the executive authority of any such state or territory to which such person shall have fled, and shall moreover produce the copy of an indictment found, or an affidavit made before a magistrate of any state or territory as aforesaid, charging the person so demanded, with having committed treason, felony, or other crime, certified as authentic by the governor or chief magistrate of the state or territory from whence the person so charged fled, it shall be the duty of the executive authority of the state or territory to which such person shall have fled, to cause him or her to be arrested and secured, and notice of the arrest to be given to the executive authority making such demand, or to the agent of such authority appointed to receive the fugitive, and to cause the fugitive to be delivered to such agent when he shall appear: But if no such agent shall appear within six months from the time of the arrest, the prisoner may be discharged. And all costs or expenses incurred in the apprehending, securing, and transmitting such fugitive to the state or territory making such demand, shall be paid by such state or territory.

SEC. 2. *And be it further enacted,* That any agent, appointed as aforesaid, who shall receive the fugitive into his custody, shall be empowered to transport him or her to the state or territory from which he or she shall have fled. And if any person or persons shall by force set at liberty, or rescue the fugitive from such agent while transporting, as aforesaid, the person or persons so offending shall, on conviction, be fined not exceeding five hundred dollars, and be imprisoned not exceeding one year. . . .

AN ACT TO PROHIBIT THE IMPORTATION OF SLAVES (1807)

In this act outlawing the international slave trade, Congress used the words "negro, mulatto, or person of colour" interchangeably with "slave."

An act to prohibit the importation of slaves into any port or place within the jurisdiction of the United States, from and after the first day of January, in the year of our Lord one thousand eight hundred and eight

Be it enacted by the Senate and House of Representatives of the United States of America in Congress assembled, That from and after the first day of January, one thousand eight hundred and eight, it shall not be lawful to import or bring into the United States or the territories thereof from any foreign kingdom, place, or country, any negro, mulatto, or person of colour, with intent to hold, sell, or dispose of such negro, mulatto, or person of colour, as a slave, or to be held to service or labour. . . .

THE *DRED SCOTT* CASE (1857)

During the late 1830s and early 1840s, Dred Scott, a Missouri slave, spent several years with his owner in the free territories of Illinois and Minnesota. In 1847, when his owner returned him to Missouri and to enslavement, Scott (aided by white supporters) sued for his freedom. The Circuit Court of St. Louis County granted him his freedom, but the Missouri State Supreme Court reversed the decision. The U.S. Supreme Court upheld the ruling of the state court. Chief Justice Roger B. Taney wrote the Court's majority opinion.

The question is simply this: Can a negro, whose ancestors were imported into this country, and sold as slaves, become a member of the political community formed and brought into existence by the Constitution of the United States, and as such become entitled to all the rights, and privileges, and immunities, guaranteed by that instrument to the citizen? One of which rights is the privilege of suing in a court of the United States in the cases specified in the Constitution. . . .

It is difficult at this day to realize the state of public opinion in relation to that unfortunate race, which prevailed in the civilized and enlightened portions of the world at the time of the Declaration of Independence, and when the Constitution of the United States was framed and adopted. But the public history of every European nation displays it in a manner too plain to be mistaken.

They had for more than a century before been regarded as beings of an inferior order, and altogether unfit to associate with the white race, either in social or political relations; and so far inferior, that they had no rights which the white man was bound to respect; and that the negro might justly and lawfully be reduced to slavery for his benefit. . . .

And upon a full and careful consideration of the subject, the court is of opinion, that, upon the facts stated in the plea in abatement, Dred Scott was not a citizen of Missouri within the meaning of the Constitution of the United States, and not entitled as such to sue in its courts; and, consequently, that the Circuit Court had no jurisdiction of the case, and that the judgment on the plea in abatement is erroneous. . . .

. . . Its judgment for the defendant must, consequently, be reversed, and a mandate issued, directing the suit to be dismissed for want of jurisdiction.

THE EMANCIPATION PROCLAMATION (1 JANUARY 1863)

On New Year's Day 1863, President Abraham Lincoln issued his famous Emancipation Proclamation. Although this document symbolized the gradual transformation of the Civil War into a war for the emancipation of slaves, it excluded slaveholding Unionists from its provisions.

Whereas, on the twenty-second day of September, in the year of our Lord one thousand eight hundred and sixty-two, a Proclamation was issued by the President of the United States, containing among other things the following, to wit:

"That on the First Day of January, in the Year of our Lord One Thousand Eight Hundred and Sixty-three, all persons held as Slaves within any State, or designated part of a State, the people whereof shall there be in rebellion against the United States, shall be then thenceforth and FOREVER FREE, and the Executive Government of the United States, including the Military and Naval authority thereof, will recognize and maintain the freedom of such persons, and will do no act or acts to repress such persons, or any of them, in any effort they may make for their actual freedom. . . ."

THE FREEDMEN'S BUREAU ACT (1865)

The short-lived Bureau of Refugees, Freedmen, and Abandoned Lands (1865–1872) provided much-needed emergency food, clothing, health, and education services for black and white victims of war. It also promised blacks a mechanism for purchasing their own land, specifying forty acres as an upper limit.

An act to establish a bureau for the relief of freedmen and refugees

Be it enacted by the Senate and House of Representatives of the United States of America in Congress assembled, That there is hereby established in the War Department, to continue during the present war of rebellion, and for one year thereafter, a bureau of refugees, freedmen, and abandoned lands, to which shall be committed, as hereinafter provided, the supervision and management of all abandoned lands, and the control of all subjects relating to refugees and freedmen from rebel states, or from any district of country within the territory embraced in the operations of the army, under such rules and regulations as may be prescribed by the head of the bureau and approved by the President. The said bureau shall be under the management and control of a commissioner to be appointed by the President, by and with the advice and consent of the Senate, whose compensation shall be three thousand dollars per annum, and such number of clerks as may be assigned to him by the Secretary of War, not exceeding one chief clerk, two of the fourth class, two of the third class, and five of the first class. . . .

SEC. 2. *And be it further enacted,* That the Secretary of War may direct such issues of provisions, clothing, and fuel, as he may deem needful for the immediate and temporary shelter and supply of destitute and suffering refugees and freedmen and their wives and children, under such rules and regulations as he may direct.

SEC. 3. *And be it further enacted,* That the President may, by and with the advice and consent of the Senate, appoint an assistant commissioner for each of the states declared to be in insurrection, not exceeding ten in number, who shall, under the direction of the commissioner, aid in the execution of the provisions of this act; . . .

SEC. 4. *And be it further enacted,* That the commissioner, under the direction of the President, shall have authority to set apart, for the use of loyal refugees and freedmen, such tracts of land within the insurrectionary states as shall have been abandoned, or to which the United States shall have acquired title by confiscation or sale, or otherwise, and to every male citizen, whether refugee or freedman, as aforesaid, there shall be assigned not more than forty acres of such land, and the person to whom it was so assigned shall be protected in the use and enjoyment of the land. . . .

APPROVED, March 3, 1865.

THE THIRTEENTH AMENDMENT (1865)

Shortly after the Confederate army was defeated, the Thirteenth Amendment to the Constitution declared an end to the system of human bondage throughout the nation.

SEC. 1. Neither slavery nor involuntary servitude, except as a punishment for crime whereof the party shall have been duly convicted, shall exist within the United States, or any place subject to their jurisdiction.

SEC. 2. Congress shall have power to enforce this article by appropriate legislation.

THE FOURTEENTH AMENDMENT (1868)

Before southern states could regain their full and legitimate place in the Union, Radicals insisted that they approve the Fourteenth Amendment to the U.S. Constitution, which offered African Americans full citizenship rights and equal protection of the laws.

SEC. 1. All persons born or naturalized in the United States, and subject to the jurisdiction thereof, are citizens of the United States and of the State wherein they reside. No State shall make or enforce any law which shall abridge the privileges or immunities of citizens of the United States; nor shall any State deprive any person of life, liberty, or property, without due process of law; nor deny to any person within its jurisdiction the equal protection of the laws. . . .

THE FIFTEENTH AMENDMENT (1870)

Despite the enactment of the Fourteenth Amendment, southern states continued to obstruct African American access to full citizenship rights. The Fifteenth Amendment dispelled any uncertainty that black men were entitled to vote.

SEC. 1. The right of citizens of the United States to vote shall not be denied or abridged by the United States or by any State on account of race, color, or previous condition of servitude.

SEC. 2. The Congress shall have power to enforce this article by appropriate legislation.

THE AFRICAN AMERICAN POPULATION AS A PERCENTAGE OF THE TOTAL U.S. POPULATION, 1870–2000

Year	Total Population	Black Population	Percentage
1870[1]	39,818,449	5,392,172	13.5
1880	50,155,783	6,580,793	13.1
1890	62,947,714	7,488,676	11.9
1900	75,994,575	8,833,994	11.6
1910	91,972,266	9,827,763	10.7
1920	105,710,620	10,463,131	9.9
1930	122,775,046	11,891,143	9.7
1940	131,669,275	12,865,518	9.8
1950	151,325,798	15,044,937	9.9
1960[2]	179,323,175	18,871,831	10.5
1970	203,211,926	22,580,289	11.1
1980	226,545,805	26,495,025	11.7
1990	248,709,873	29,986,060	12.1
2000 (est.)	273,482,000	35,456,000	12.9

1. Revised to include adjustments for under enumeration in the southern states.
2. Denotes first year for which figures include Alaska and Hawaii.

DISTRIBUTION OF THE BLACK POPULATION BY REGION, 1870–2000

Year	Percentage of Blacks Living in:			
	Northeast	North Central	South	West
1870	3.7	5.6	90.6	0.1
1880	3.5	5.9	90.5	0.2
1890	3.6	5.8	90.3	0.4
1900	4.4	5.6	89.7	0.3
1910	4.9	5.5	89.0	0.5
1920	6.5	7.6	85.2	0.8
1930	9.6	10.6	78.7	1.0
1940	10.6	11.0	77.0	1.3
1950	13.4	14.8	68.0	3.8
1960	16.0	18.3	59.9	5.8
1970	19.2	20.2	53.0	7.5
1980	18.3	20.1	53.0	8.5
1990	18.7	19.1	52.8	9.4
2000 (est.)	18.7	18.4	54.6	8.5

PERCENTAGE OF AFRICAN AMERICANS LIVING IN CITIES, 1880–2000

Year	Total Population	Blacks	Whites
1880[1]	26.3	12.9	28.3
1890[1]	32.9	17.6	35.1
1900[1]	37.3	20.5	39.7
1910	46.3	27.4	48.7
1920	51.4	34.0	53.4
1930	56.2	43.7	57.6
1940	56.5	48.6	57.5
1950	64.0	62.4	64.3
1960[2]	69.9	73.2	69.5
1970	73.5	81.3	72.4
1980	73.7	85.3	71.3
1990	75.2	87.2	71.9
2000 (est.)	80.8	86.1	77.5

1. Definition modified to exclude population in incorporated places and New England towns in the 2,500–3,999 size range.
2. Denotes first year for which figures include Alaska and Hawaii.

Source: Three tables from Kenneth Estell, ed., *The African American Almanac,* 6th ed. (Detroit: Gale Research, Inc., 1994), pp. 635, 632, 634. Estimated data for 2000 from www.census.gov. Used by permission.

THE *CIVIL RIGHTS CASES* OF 1883

Following the Civil War, Congress enacted many new civil rights laws. This legislation peaked with passage of the Civil Rights Act of 1875, which outlawed racial discrimination in public accommodations. Eight years later, the U.S. Supreme Court declared the Civil Rights Act of 1875 unconstitutional. Justice Joseph Bradley delivered the opinion of the Court, arguing that the federal government could protect citizens against the actions of state governments but was helpless in protecting them against the actions of institutions and individuals within the various states. Justice John Marshall Harlan, a former Kentucky slaveowner, wrote an eloquent dissenting opinion, decrying the denial of blacks equal protection under the laws.

Mr. Justice Bradley delivered the opinion of the court. After stating the facts . . . he continued:

The first section of the Fourteenth Amendment (which is the one relied on), after declaring who shall be citizens of the United States, and of the several States, is prohibitory in its character, and prohibitory upon the States. . . .

It is State action of a particular character that is prohibited. Individual invasion of individual rights is not the subject-matter of the amendment. It has a deeper and broader scope. It nullifies and makes void all State legislation, and State action of every kind, which impairs the privileges and immunities of citizens of the United States, or which injures them in life, liberty or property without due process of law, or which denies to any of them the equal protection of the laws. . . .

On the whole we are of opinion, that no countenance of authority for the passage of the law in question can be found in either the Thirteenth or Fourteenth Amendment of the Constitution; and no other ground of authority for its passage being suggested, it must necessarily be declared void, at least so far as its operation in the several States is concerned. . . . *And it is so ordered.*

M r. Justice Harlan dissenting.
     The opinion in these cases proceeds, it seems to me, upon grounds entirely too narrow and artificial. I cannot resist the conclusion that the substance and spirit of the recent amendments of the Constitution have been sacrificed by a subtle and ingenious verbal criticism. . . .

I am of the opinion that such discrimination practised by corporations and individuals in the exercise of their public or quasi-public functions is a badge of servitude the imposition of which Congress may prevent under its power, by appropriate legislation, to enforce the Thirteenth Amendment; and, consequently, without reference to its enlarged power under the Fourteenth Amendment, the act of March 1, 1875, is not, in my judgment, repugnant to the Constitution.

. . . To-day, it is the colored race which is denied, by corporations and individuals wielding public authority, rights fundamental in their freedom and citizenship. At some future time, it may be that some other race will fall under the ban of race discrimination. . . .

For the reasons stated I feel constrained to withhold my assent to the opinion of the court.

PLESSY V. FERGUSON (1896)

The movement to segregate blacks and whites in the institutional life of the South culminated in the U.S. Supreme Court's "separate but equal" decision in the Plessy *case. Justice Henry Brown wrote the majority opinion, while Justice John Marshall Harlan dissented—calling the Court's ruling "as pernicious" as its decision in the* Dred Scott *case.*

M r. Justice Brown, after stating the case, delivered the opinion of the court.
     This case turns upon the constitutionality of an act of the General Assembly of the State of Louisiana, passed in 1890, providing for separate railway carriages for the white and colored races. Acts 1890, No. 111, p. 152. . . .

The constitutionality of this act is attacked upon the ground that it conflicts both with the Thirteenth Amendment of the Constitution, abolishing slavery, and the Fourteenth Amendment, which prohibits certain restrictive legislation on the part of the States. . . .

A statute which implies merely a legal distinction between the white and colored races— a distinction which is founded in the color of the two races, and which must always exist so long as white men are distinguished from the other race by color—has no tendency to destroy the legal equality of the two races, or reëstablish a state of involuntary servitude. Indeed, we do not understand that the Thirteenth Amendment is strenuously relied upon by the plaintiff in error in this connection. . . .

The object of the [Fourteenth] amendment was undoubtedly to enforce the absolute equality of the two races before the law, but in the nature of things it could not have been intended to abolish distinctions based upon color, or to enforce social, as distinguished from political equality, or a commingling of the two races upon terms unsatisfactory to either. Laws permitting, and even requiring, their separation in places where they are liable to be brought into contact do not necessarily imply the inferiority of either race to the other, and have been generally, if not universally, recognized as within the competency of the state legislatures in the exercise of their police power. The most common instance of this is connected with the establishment of separate schools for white and colored children, which has been held to be a valid exercise of the legislative power even by courts of States where the political rights of the colored race have been longest and most earnestly enforced. . . .

. . . Legislation is powerless to eradicate racial instincts or to abolish distinctions based upon physical differences, and the attempt to do so can only result in accentuating the difficulties of the present situation. If the civil and political rights of both races be equal one cannot be inferior to the other civilly or politically. If one race be inferior to the other socially, the Constitution of the United States cannot put them upon the same plane. . . .

Affirmed.

Mr. Justice Harlan dissenting.
. . . However apparent the injustice of such legislation may be, we have only to consider whether it is consistent with the Constitution of the United States. . . .

I am of opinion that the statute of Louisiana is inconsistent with the personal liberty of citizens, white and black, in that State, and hostile to both the spirit and letter of the Constitution of the United States. If laws of like character should be enacted in the several States of the Union, the effect would be in the highest degree mischievous. Slavery, as an institution tolerated by law would, it is true, have disappeared from our country, but there would remain a power in the States, by sinister legislation, to interfere with the full enjoyment of the blessings of freedom; to regulate civil rights, common to all citizens, upon the basis of race; and to place in a condition of legal inferiority a large body of American citizens, now constituting a part of the political community called the People of the United States, for whom, and by whom through representatives, our government is administered. Such a system is inconsistent with the guarantee given by the Constitution to each State of a republican form of government, and may be stricken down by Congressional action, or by the courts in the discharge of their solemn duty to maintain the supreme law of the land, anything in the constitution or laws of any State to the contrary notwithstanding.

For the reasons stated, I am constrained to withhold my assent from the opinion and judgment of the majority.

EXECUTIVE ORDER 8802 (25 JUNE 1941)

Under pressure from the March on Washington movement, President Franklin D. Roosevelt established the Fair Employment Practices Committee and facilitated the movement of blacks into industrial jobs above the general labor and semiskilled levels.

Reaffirming Policy of Full Participation in the Defense Program by All Persons, Regardless of Race, Creed, Color, or National Origin, and Directing Certain Action in Furtherance of Said Policy

Whereas it is the policy of the United States to encourage full participation in the national defense program by all citizens of the United States, regardless of race, creed, color, or national origin, . . . the Nation can be defended successfully only with the help and support of all groups within its borders. . . .

. . . I do hereby reaffirm the policy of the United States that there shall be no discrimination in the employment of workers in defense industries or government because of race, creed, color, or national origin, and I do hereby declare that it is the duty of employers and of labor organizations, in furtherance of said policy and of this order, to provide for the full and equitable participation of all workers in defense industries, without discrimination because of race, creed, color, or national origin;

And it is hereby ordered as follows: . . .

. . . There is established in the Office of Production Management a Committee on Fair Employment Practice, which shall consist of a chairman and four other members to be appointed by the President. The Chairman and members of the Committee shall serve as such without compensation but shall be entitled to actual and necessary transportation, subsistence and other expenses incidental to performance of their duties. The Committee shall receive and investigate complaints of discrimination in violation of the provisions of this order and shall take appropriate steps to redress grievances which it finds to be valid. The Committee shall also recommend to the several departments and agencies of the Government of the United States and to the President all measures which may be deemed by it necessary or proper to effectuate the provisions of this order.

Franklin D. Roosevelt
The White House
June 25, 1941

BROWN V. BOARD OF EDUCATION OF TOPEKA (1954)

After a series of NAACP challenges to segregation in public education, the U.S. Supreme Court struck down the "separate but equal" doctrine of the Plessy *case.*

Mr. Chief Justice Warren delivered the opinion of the Court.

These cases come to us from the States of Kansas, South Carolina, Virginia, and Delaware. They are premised on different facts and different local conditions, but a common legal question justifies their consideration together in this consolidated opinion. . . .

Today, education is perhaps the most important function of state and local governments. Compulsory school attendance laws and the great expenditures for education both demonstrate our recognition of the importance of education to our democratic society. It is required in the performance of our most basic public responsibilities, even service in the armed forces. It is the very foundation of good citizenship. Today it is a principal instrument in awakening the child to cultural values, in preparing him for later professional training, and in helping him to adjust normally to his environment. In these days, it is doubtful that any child may reasonably be expected to succeed in life if he is denied the opportunity of an education. Such an opportunity, where the state has undertaken to provide it, is a right which must be made available to all on equal terms.

We come then to the question presented: Does segregation of children in public schools solely on the basis of race, even though the physical facilities and other "tangible" factors may be equal, deprive the children of the minority group of equal education opportunities? We believe that it does. . . .

We conclude that in the field of public education the doctrine of "separate but equal" has no place. Separate educational facilities are inherently unequal. Therefore, we hold that the plaintiffs and others similarly situated for whom the actions have been brought are, by reason of the segregation complained of, deprived of the equal protection of the laws guaranteed by the Fourteenth Amendment. . . .

THE CIVIL RIGHTS ACT OF 1964

The Civil Rights Act of 1964 set up precise mechanisms for counteracting discrimination in voting, public accommodations, public education, federally funded programs, and employment. Perhaps more than any single piece of legislation, this law symbolized the promise of the Second Reconstruction.

An act to enforce the constitutional right to vote, to confer jurisdiction upon the district courts of the United States to provide injunctive relief against discrimination in public accommodations, to authorize the Attorney General to institute suits to protect constitutional rights in public facilities and public education, to extend the Commission on Civil Rights, to prevent discrimination in federally assisted programs, to establish a Commission on Equal Employment Opportunity, and for other purposes

Be it enacted by the Senate and House of Representatives of the United States of America in Congress assembled, That this Act may be cited as the "Civil Rights Act of 1964."

Title I—Voting Rights . . .

SEC. 101. . . . "(2) No person acting under color of law shall—

"(A) in determining whether any individual is qualified under State law or laws to vote in any Federal election, apply any standard, practice, or procedure different from the standards, practices, or procedures applied under such law or laws to other individuals within the same county, parish, or similar political subdivision who have been found by State officials to be qualified to vote; . . ."

Title II—Injunctive Relief Against Discrimination in Places of Public Accommodation

SEC. 201. (a)   All persons shall be entitled to the full and equal enjoyment of the goods, services, facilities, privileges, advantages, and accommodations of any place of public accommodation, as defined in this section, without discrimination or segregation on the ground of race, color, religion, or national origin. . . .

Title III—Desegregation of Public Facilities

SEC. 301. (a)   Whenever the Attorney General receives a complaint in writing signed by an individual to the effect that he is being deprived of or threatened with the loss of his right to the equal protection of the laws, on account of his race, color, religion, or national origin, by being denied equal utilization of any public facility which is owned, operated, or managed by or on behalf of any State or subdivision thereof, other than a public school or public college as defined in section 401 of title IV hereof, . . . the Attorney General is authorized to institute for or in the name of the United States a civil action in any appropriate district court of the United States against such parties and for such relief as may be appropriate, and such court shall have and shall exercise jurisdiction of proceedings instituted pursuant to this section. The Attorney General may implead as defendants such additional parties as are or become necessary to the grant of effective relief hereunder. . . .

Title IV—Desegregation of Public Education

DEFINITIONS

SEC. 401.   As used in this title—

(a) "Commissioner" means the Commissioner of Education.

(b) "Desegregation" means the assignment of students to public schools and within such schools without regard to their race, color, religion, or national origin, but "desegregation" shall not mean the assignment of students to public schools in order to overcome racial imbalance.

(c) "Public school" means any elementary or secondary educational institution, and "public college" means any institution of higher education or any technical or vocational school above the secondary school level, provided that such public school or public college is operated by a State, subdivision of a State, or governmental agency within a State, or operated wholly or predominantly from or through the use of governmental funds or property, or funds or property derived from a governmental source.

(d) "School board" means any agency or agencies which administer a system of one or more public schools and any other agency which is responsible for the assignment of students to or within such system. . . .

Title V—Commission on Civil Rights

. . . DUTIES OF THE COMMISSION

"SEC. 104. (a)   The Commission shall—

"(1) investigate allegations in writing under oath or affirmation that certain citizens of the United States are being deprived of their right to vote and have that vote counted by reason of their color, race, religion, or national origin; which writing, under oath or affirmation, shall set forth the facts upon which such belief or beliefs are based;

"(2) study and collect information concerning legal developments constituting a denial of equal protection of the laws under the Constitution because of race, color, religion or national origin or in the administration of justice;

"(3) appraise the laws and policies of the Federal Government with respect to denials of equal protection of the laws under the Constitution because of race, color, religion or national origin or in the administration of justice;

"(4) serve as a national clearinghouse for information in respect to denials of equal protection of the laws because of race, color, religion or national origin, including but not limited to the fields of voting, education, housing, employment, the use of public facilities, and transportation, or in the administration of justice;

"(5) investigate allegations, made in writing and under oath or affirmation, that citizens of the United States are unlawfully being accorded or denied the right to vote, or to have their votes properly counted, in any election of presidential electors, Members of the United States Senate, or of the House of Representatives, as a result of any patterns or practice of fraud or discrimination in the conduct of such election; . . ."

Title VI—Nondiscrimination in Federally Assisted Programs

SEC. 601.   No person in the United States shall, on the ground of race, color, or national origin, be excluded from participation in, be denied the benefits of, or be subjected to discrimination under any program or activity receiving Federal financial assistance. . . .

Title VII—Equal Employment Opportunity

DISCRIMINATION BECAUSE OF RACE, COLOR, RELIGION, SEX, OR NATIONAL ORIGIN

SEC. 703. (a)   It shall be an unlawful employment practice for an employer—

(1) to fail or refuse to hire or to discharge any individual, or otherwise to discriminate against any individual with respect to his compensation, terms, conditions, or privileges of employment, because of such individual's race, color, religion, sex, or national origin; or

(2) to limit, segregate, or classify his employees in any way which would deprive or tend to deprive any individual of employment opportunities or otherwise adversely affect his status as an employee, because of such individual's race, color, religion, sex, or national origin. . . .

EQUAL EMPLOYMENT OPPORTUNITY COMMISSION

SEC. 705 (a)   There is hereby created a Commission to be known as the Equal Employment Opportunity Commission, which shall be composed of five members, not more than three of whom shall be members of the same political party, who shall be appointed by the President by and with the advice and consent of the Senate. . . .

(g) The Commission shall have power—

(1) to cooperate with and, with their consent, utilize regional, State, local, and other agencies, both public and private, and individuals;

(2) to pay to witnesses whose depositions are taken or who are summoned before the Commission or any of its agents the same witness and mileage fees as are paid to witnesses in the courts of the United States;

(3) to furnish to persons subject to this title such technical assistance as they may request to further their compliance with this title or an order issued thereunder;

(4) upon the request of (i) any employer, whose employees or some of them, or (ii) any labor organization, whose members or some of them, refuse or threaten to refuse to cooperate in effectuating the provisions of this title, to assist in such effectuation by conciliation or such other remedial action as is provided by this title;

(5) to make such technical studies as are appropriate to effectuate the purposes and policies of this title and to make the results of such studies available to the public;

(6) to refer matters to the Attorney General with recommendations for intervention in a civil action brought by an aggrieved party under section 706, or for the institution of a civil action by the Attorney General under section 707, and to advise, consult, and assist the Attorney General on such matters. . . .

EXECUTIVE ORDER 13050 (13 JUNE 1997)

Executive Order 13050 created President Bill Clinton's Initiative on Race. Clinton established a seven-member advisory board under the chairmanship of the well-known historian John Hope Franklin. The advisory board's report concluded that perhaps the greatest challenge facing the nation is to see "our history, ourselves . . . through the eyes of others."

By the authority vested in me as President by the Constitution and the laws of the United States of America, including the Federal Advisory Committee Act, as amended (5 U.S.C. App.), and in order to establish a President's Advisory Board on Race, it is hereby ordered as follows:

SECTION 1. Establishment. (a) There is established the President's Advisory Board on Race. The Advisory Board shall comprise 7 members from outside the Federal Government to be appointed by the President. Members shall each have substantial experience and expertise in the areas to be considered by the Advisory Board. Members shall be representative of the diverse perspectives in the areas to be considered by the Advisory Board.

(b) The President shall designate a Chairperson from among the members of the Advisory Board.

SEC. 2. Functions. (a) The Advisory Board shall advise the President on matters involving race and racial reconciliation, including ways in which the President can:

(1) Promote a constructive national dialogue to confront and work through challenging issues that surround race;

(2) Increase the Nation's understanding of our recent history of race relations and the course our Nation is charting on issues of race relations and racial diversity;

(3) Bridge racial divides by encouraging leaders in communities throughout the Nation to develop and implement innovative approaches to calming racial tensions;

(4) Identify, develop, and implement solutions to problems in areas in which race has a substantial impact, such as education, economic opportunity, housing, health care, and the administration of justice. . . .

(b) The Advisory Board also shall advise on such other matters as from time to time the President may refer to the Board.

(c) In carrying out its functions, the Advisory Board shall coordinate with the staff of the President's Initiative on Race.

SEC. 3. Administration. (a) To the extent permitted by law and subject to the availability of appropriations, the Department of Justice shall provide the financial and administrative support for the Advisory Board.

(b) The heads of executive agencies shall, to the extent permitted by law, provide to the Advisory Board such information as it may require for the purpose of carrying out its functions.

(c) The Chairperson may, from time to time, invite experts to submit information to the Advisory Board and may form subcommittees or working groups within the Advisory Board to review specific matters.

(d) Members of the Advisory Board shall serve without compensation but shall be allowed travel expenses, including per diem in lieu of subsistence, as authorized by law for persons serving intermittently in the Government service (5 U.S.C. 5701-5707).

SEC. 4. General. (a) Notwithstanding any other Executive order, the functions of the President under the Federal Advisory Committee Act, as amended, except that of reporting to the Congress, that are applicable to the Advisory Board shall be performed by the Attorney General, or his or her designee, in accordance with guidelines that have been issued by the Administrator of General Services.

(b) The Advisory Board shall terminate on September 30, 1998, unless extended by the President prior to such date.

William J. Clinton
The White House
June 13, 1997.

BIBLIOGRAPHY

Research Guides, General Studies, and Document Collections

Reference Guides and Historiography

Gates, Henry Louis, et al. *Harvard Guide to African American Research*. Cambridge: Harvard University Press, forthcoming.

Goings, Kenneth W., and Raymond A. Mohl, eds. *The New African American Urban History*. Thousand Oaks, Calif.: Sage Publications, 1996.

Ham, Debra Newman, ed. *The African American Mosaic: A Library of Congress Resource Guide for the Study of Black History and Culture*. Washington, D.C.: U.S. Government Printing Office, 1993.

Hine, Darlene Clark. *Hine Sight: Black Women and the Re-Construction of American History*. Brooklyn, N.Y.: Carlson, 1994.

————. *The State of Afro-American History: Past, Present, and Future*. Baton Rouge: Louisiana State University, 1986.

Jewsiewicki, Bogumil, and David S. Newbury, eds. *African Historiographies: What History for Which Africa?* Beverly Hills, Calif.: Sage, 1986.

McPherson, James M., et al., eds. *Blacks in America: Bibliographical Essays*. Garden City, N.Y.: Anchor Books, 1971.

Meier, August, and Elliott Rudwick. *Black History and the Historical Profession*. Urbana: University of Illinois Press, 1986.

Neale, Caroline. *Writing "Independent" History: African Historiography, 1960–1980*. Westport, Conn.: Greenwood Press, 1985.

Norton, Mary Beth, and Pamela Girardi, eds. *The AHA's Guide to Historical Literature*. Vols. 1 and 2. 3rd ed. New York: Oxford University Press, 1995.

Walker, Clarence E. *Deromanticizing Black History: Critical Essays and Reappraisals*. Knoxville: University of Tennessee Press, 1991.

Weinberg, Meyer, ed. *Racism in the United States: A Comprehensive Classified Bibliography*. New York: Greenwood Press, 1990.

Documentary Volumes and Anthologies

Adero, Mulaika, ed. *Up South: Stories, Studies, and Letters of This Century's Black Migra-tions.* New York: W. W. Norton, 1993.

Adler, Mortimer A., Charles Van Doren, and George Ducas, eds. *Great Documents in Black American History.* Chicago: Encyclopedia Britannica Educational Corporation, 1969.

Andrews, William, Frances Smith Foster, and Trudier Harris, eds. *The Oxford Companion to African American Literature.* New York: Oxford University Press, 1997.

Bardolph, Richard, ed. *The Civil Rights Record: Black Americans and the Law, 1849–1970.* New York: Thomas Y. Crowell, 1970.

Berlin, Ira, et al. *Free At Last: A Documentary History of Slavery, Freedom and the Civil War.* New York: New Press, 1992.

Blassingame, John. *The Frederick Douglass Papers.* Vol. 1. New Haven: Yale University Press, 1979.

————. *Slave Testimony: Two Centuries of Letters, Speeches, Interviews, and Autobiographies.* Baton Rouge: Louisiana State University Press, 1977.

Blaustein, Albert P., and Robert L. Zangrando. *Civil Rights and African Americans: A Documentary History.* Evanston, Ill.: Northwestern University Press, 1968.

Carson, Claybourne, et al., eds. *The Papers of Martin Luther King, Jr.* Berkeley: University of California Press, 1992.

Emanuel, James A., and Theodore L. Gross, eds. *Dark Symphony: Negro Literature in America.* New York: Free Press, 1968.

Fishel, Leslie H., Jr., and Benjamin Quarles. *The Black American: A Documentary History.* 3rd ed. Glenview, Ill.: Scott, Foresman, 1976.

Foner, Philip Sheldon, and Ronald L. Lewis, eds. *The Black Worker: A Documentary History from Colonial Times to the Present.* Vols. 1–8. Philadelphia: Temple University Press, 1978–1984.

Frazier, Thomas R., Jr. *Afro-American History: Primary Sources 1970.* Rev. ed. Chicago: Dorsey Press, 1988.

Genovese, Eugene. *In Red and Black: Marxian Explorations in Southern and Afro-American History.* 1971. Reprint, Knoxville: University of Tennessee Press, 1984.

Goodheart, Lawrence B., Richard D. Brown, and Stephen G. Rabe, eds. *Slavery in American Society.* 3rd ed. Lexington: D. C. Heath, 1993.

Hampton, Henry, and Steve Fayer. *Voices of Freedom: An Oral History of the Civil Rights Movement from the 1950s Through the 1980s.* New York: Bantam, 1990.

Harlan, Louis, and Raymond M. Smock, eds. *The Booker T. Washington Papers.* Urbana: University of Illinois Press, 1972.

Hatch, James V., and Ted Shine. *Black Theater, U.S.A.: Forty-Five Plays by Black Ameri-cans, 1847–1974.* New York: Free Press, 1974.

Hayes, Floyd W., III. *Turbulent Voyage: Readings in African American Studies.* San Diego: Collegiate Press, 1992.

Hill, Patricia Liggins, ed. *Call and Response: The Anthology of the African American Literary Tradition.* Boston: Houghton Mifflin, 1998.

Hill, Robert, ed. *The Marcus Garvey and University Negro Improvement Association Papers.* Berkeley: University of California Press, 1983–1987.

Holt, Thomas C., and Elsa Barkley Brown, eds. *Major Problems in African-American History.* Vol. 1, *From Slavery to Freedom, 1619–1877.* Boston: Houghton Mifflin Company, 2000.

Kousser, J. Morgan, and James M. McPherson, eds. *Region, Race, and Reconstruction: Essays in Honor of C. Vann Woodward.* New York: Oxford University Press, 1982.

Kusmer, Kenneth L. *Black Communities and Urban Development in America, 1720–1990.* Vols.1–9. New York: Garland, 1991.

Lerner, Gerda. *Black Women in White America: A Documentary History.* New York: Vintage Books, 1973.

Lowenberg, Bert J., and Ruth Bogin, eds. *Black Women in Nineteenth Century American Life: Their Words, Their Thoughts, Their Feelings.* University Park: Pennsylvania State University Press, 1976.

Meier, August, Elliott Rudwick, and Francis L. Broderick, eds. *Black Protest Thought in the Twentieth Century.* Indianapolis and New York: Bobbs-Merrill, 1971.

Meltzer, Milton, ed. *In Their Own Words: A History of the American Negro, 1619–1865.* New York: Thomas Y. Crowell Company, 1964.

Mullane, Deirdre, ed. *Crossing the Danger Water: Three Hundred Years of African-American Writing.* New York: Doubleday, 1993.

Nichols, Charles H. *Many Thousands Gone: The Ex-Slaves' Account of Their Bondage and Freedom.* Bloomington: Indiana University Press, 1963.

Osofsky, Gilbert. *The Burden of Race: A Documentary History of Negro-White Relations in America.* New York: Harper & Row/Harper Torchbooks, 1967.

Rawick, George P., ed. *The American Slave: A Composite Autobiography.* Westport, Conn.: Greenwood Press, 1972–1979.

Ripley, C. Peter. *The Black Abolitionist Papers.* Chapel Hill: University of North Carolina Press, 1985.

Rose, Willie Lee, ed. *A Documentary History of Slavery in North America.* New York: Oxford University Press, 1976.

Sterling, Dorothy. *We Are Your Sisters: Black Women in the Nineteenth Century.* New York: W. W. Norton, 1984.

Weinstein, Allen, and Frank Otto Gatell, eds. *American Negro Slavery: A Modern Reader.* 2nd ed. New York: Oxford University Press, 1973.

General Studies

Asante, Molefi Kete. *African American History: A Journey of Liberation.* Maywood, N.J.: Peoples Publishing Group, 1995.

Bennett, Lerone, Jr. *Before the Mayflower: A History of Black America.* 5th ed. New York: Penguin Books, 1982.

Berry, Mary Frances, and John W. Blassingame. *Long Memory: The Black Experience in America.* New York: Oxford University Press, 1982.

Christian, Charles M. *Black Saga: The African American Experience.* Boston: Houghton Mifflin, 1995.

Cowan, Tom, and Jack Maguire. *Timelines of African American History: 500 Years of Black Achievement.* New York: Roundtable Press, 1994.

Davis, F. James. *Who Is Black? One Nation's Definition.* University Park: Pennsylvania State University Press, 1991.

Foner, Philip Sheldon. *Organized Labor and the Black Worker, 1619–1982.* 2nd ed. New York: International Publishers, 1982.

Forbes, Jack. *Black Africans and Native Americans: Color, Race, and Caste in the Evolution of Red-Black Peoples.* New York: Basil Blackwell, 1988.

Franklin, John Hope, and Alfred A. Moss Jr. *From Slavery to Freedom: A History of African Americans.* 8th ed. New York: McGraw-Hill, 2000.

Giddings, Paula. *When and Where I Enter: The Impact of Black Women on Race and Sex in America.* New York: Morrow, 1984.

Harley, Sharon. *The Timetables of African-American History: A Chronology of the Most Important People and Events in African-American History.* New York: Simon & Schuster, 1995.

Hine, Darlene Clark, Elsa Barkley Brown, and Rosalyn Terborg-Penn, eds. *Black Women in America: An Historical Encyclopedia.* 2 vols. Brooklyn, N.Y.: Carlson, 1993.

Hine, Darlene Clark, William C. Hine, and Stanley Harrold. *The African-American Odyssey.* Upper Saddle River, N.J.: Prentice Hall, 2000.

Hine, Darlene Clark, and Kathleen Thompson. *A Shining Thread of Hope: The History of Black Women in America.* New York: Broadway Books, 1998.

Horton, James Oliver, and Lois E. Horton, eds. *A History of the African People: The History, Traditions & Culture of African Americans.* London: Salamander Books, 1995.

Huggins, Nathan I., Martin Kilson, and Daniel M. Fox, eds. *Key Issues in the Afro-American Experience.* Vols. 1 and 2. New York: Harcourt Brace Jovanovich, 1971.

Hull, Gloria T., Patricia Bell Scott, and Barbara Smith. *But Some of Us Are Brave: Black Women's Studies.* Old Westbury, N.Y.: Feminist Press, 1982.

Jones, Jacqueline. *American Work: Four Centuries of Black and White Labor.* New York: W. W. Norton, 1998.

———. *Labor of Love, Labor of Sorrow: Black Women, Work, and the Family from Slavery to the Present.* New York: Basic Books, 1985.

Kelley, Robin D. G., and Earl Lewis, eds. *To Make Our World Anew: A History of African Americans.* New York: Oxford University Press, 2000.

Marable, Manning. *How Capitalism Underdeveloped Black America: Problems in Race, Political Economy and Society.* Boston: South End Press, 1983.

Meier, August, and Elliott Rudwick. *Black History and the Historical Profession.* Urbana: University of Illinois Press, 1986.

———. *From Plantation to Ghetto.* 3rd ed. New York: Hill and Wang, 1976.

Palmer, Colin A. *Passageways: An Interpretive History of Black America.* Vols. 1 and 2. Ft. Worth: Harcourt Brace, 1998.

Smallwood, Arwin D., and Jeffrey M. Elliot. *The Atlas of African-American History and Politics: From the Slave Trade to Modern Times.* New York: McGraw-Hill, 1998.

Smith, Jessie Carney. *Black Firsts: 2,000 Years of Extraordinary Achievements.* Detroit: Visible Ink Press, 1994.

Taylor, Quintard. *In Search of the Racial Frontier: African Americans in the American West, 1528–1990.* New York: W. W. Norton, 1998.

Walker, Juliet E. K. *The History of Black Business in America: Capitalism, Race, Entrepreneurship.* New York: Macmillan Library Reference, 1998.

Walton, Hanes, Jr. *Black Politics: A Theoretical and Structural Analysis.* Philadelphia: J. B. Lippincott, 1972.

PART I: The African American Experience in Global Perspective: Prelude to a New World (Chapters 1–2)

North and East Africa

Abun-Nasr, Jamil M. *A History of the Maghrib in the Islamic Period.* Cambridge: Cambridge University Press, 1987.

Adams, William Yewdale. *Nubia: Corridor to Africa.* 1977. Reprint, Princeton: Princeton University Press, 1984.

Bagnall, Roger S. *Egypt in Late Antiquity.* Princeton: Princeton University Press, 1993.

Bernal, Martin. *Black Athena: The Afroasiatic Roots of Classical Civilization.* Vol. 1. New Brunswick, N.J.: Rutgers University Press, 1987.

Breasted, James Henry. *A History of Egypt: From the Earliest Times to the Persian Conquest.* 1912. Reprint, New York: Scribner's, 1967.

Drake, St. Clair. *Black Folk Here and There: An Essay in History and Anthropology.* 1987. Reprint, Los Angeles: Center for Afro-American Studies, UCLA, 1990.

Grimal, Nicolas. *A History of Ancient Egypt.* Cambridge, Mass.: Blackwell, 1992.

Hodgson, Marshall G. S. *The Classical Age of Islam.* Vol. 1. Chicago: University of Chicago Press, 1974.

———. *The Expansion of Islam in the Middle Period.* Vol. 2. Chicago: University of Chicago Press, 1974.

Levine, Molly Myerowitz. "The Use and Abuse of Black Athena." *American Historical Review* 97, no. 2 (1992): 440–460.

Lewis, Bernard. *The Arabs in History.* 6th ed. New York: Oxford University Press, 1993.

Trigger, Bruce G., et al., eds. *Ancient Egypt: A Social History.* New York: Cambridge University Press, 1983.

West Africa

Connah, Graham. *African Civilizations: Precolonial Cities and States in Tropical Africa: An Archaeological Perspective.* New York: Cambridge University Press, 1987.

Conrad, David C. "Islam in the Oral Traditions of Mali: Bilali and Surakata." *Journal of African History* 26, no. 1 (1985): 33–50.

Dunn, Ross E. *The Adventures of Ibn Battuta, a Muslim Traveler of the Fourteenth Century.* Berkeley: University of California Press, 1986.

Hopkins, A. G. *An Economic History of West Africa.* New York: Columbia University Press, 1973.

Law, Robin C. C. *The Horse in West African History: The Role of the Horse in the Societies of Pre-Colonial West Africa.* Oxford: Oxford University Press and the International African Institute, 1980.

———. *The Oyo Empire, c. 1600–c. 1836: A West African Imperialism in the Era of the Atlantic Slave Trade.* Oxford: Clarendon, 1977.

Levtzion, Nehemia. *Ancient Ghana and Mali.* London: Methuen, 1973.

Lewis, Bernard. *Race and Color in Islam.* New York: Harper & Row, 1971.

Mbiti, John S. *African Religions and Philosophy.* Garden City, N.Y.: Doubleday/Anchor, 1970.

Paulme, Denise. *African Sculpture.* New York: Viking, 1962.

Phillips, William D., Jr. *Slavery from Roman Times to the Early Transatlantic Trade.* Minneapolis: University of Minnesota Press, 1985.

Saad, Elias. *Social History of Timbuktu: The Role of Muslim Scholars and Notables, 1400–1900.* Cambridge: Cambridge University Press, 1983.

Sanneh, Lamin O. *West African Christianity: The Religious Impact.* Maryknoll, N.Y.: Orbis, 1983.

Smith, Robert S. *Kingdoms of the Yoruba.* 3rd ed. Madison: University of Wisconsin Press, 1988.

Verger, Pierre. *Trade Relations Between the Bight of Benin and Bahia from the Seventeenth to Nineteenth Century.* Ibadan, Nigeria: Ibadan University Press, 1976.

Vogel, Susan, ed. *For Spirits and Kings: African Art from Paul and Ruth Tishman Collection.* New York: Harry N. Abrams, 1981.

Vogt, John. *Portuguese Rule on the Gold Coast, 1469–1682.* Athens: University of Georgia Press, 1979.

Slave Trade and Slavery

Curtin, Philip D., ed. *Africa Remembered: Narratives by West Africans from the Era of the Slave Trade.* Madison: University of Wisconsin Press, 1967.

————. *The Atlantic Slave Trade: A Census.* Madison: University of Wisconsin Press, 1969.

Davidson, Basil. *The African Slave Trade.* Rev. ed. Boston: Little, Brown, 1970.

Davis, David Brion. *The Problem of Slavery in Western Culture.* New York: Oxford University Press, 1966.

Ewald, Janet. "Slavery in Africa and the Slave Trades from Africa." *American Historical Review* 97, no. 2 (1992).

Inikori, Joseph E., and Stanley L. Engerman, eds. *The Atlantic Slave Trade: Effects on Economies, Societies, and Peoples in Africa, the Americas, and Europe.* Durham: Duke University Press, 1992.

————. *Forced Migration: The Impact of the Export Slave Trade on African Societies.* New York: Africana, 1982.

Miers, Suzanne, and Igor Kopytoff, eds. *Slavery in Africa: Historical and Anthropological Perspectives.* Madison: University of Wisconsin Press, 1977.

Patterson, Orlando. *Slavery and Social Death: A Comparative Study.* Cambridge: Harvard University Press, 1982.

Robertson, Claire C., and Martin A. Klein, eds. *Women and Slavery in Africa.* Madison: University of Wisconsin Press, 1983.

Rodney, Walter. *How Europe Underdeveloped Africa.* Rev. ed. Washington, D.C.: Howard University Press, 1982.

Thomas, Hugh. *The Slave Trade: The Story of the Atlantic Slave Trade: 1440–1870.* New York: Simon & Schuster, 1997.

Thornton, John. *Africa and Africans in the Making of the Atlantic World, 1400–1680.* Cambridge: Cambridge University Press, 1992.

Latin America and the Caribbean

Beckles, Hilary McD. *White Servitude and Black Slavery in Barbados, 1627–1715.* Knoxville: University of Tennessee Press, 1989.

Berlin, Ira, and Philip D. Morgan, eds. *Cultivation and Culture: Labor and the Shaping of Slave Life in the Americas.* Charlottesville: University Press of Virginia, 1993.

Blakely, Allison. *Blacks in the Dutch World: The Evolution of Racial Imagery in a Modern Society.* Bloomington: Indiana University Press, 1993.

Bovill, E. W. *The Golden Trade of the Moors.* 1963. Reprint, with additional material by Robin Hallet, ed., London: Oxford University Press, 1968.

Bush, Barbara. *Slave Women in Caribbean Society, 1650–1838.* Bloomington: Indiana University Press, 1990.

Conrad, Robert. *The Destruction of Brazilian Slavery, 1850–1888.* Berkeley: University of California Press, 1972.

Cox, Edward L. *Free Coloreds in the Slave Societies of St. Kitts and Grenada, 1763–1833.* Knoxville: University of Tennessee Press, 1984.

Craton, Michael. *Sinews of Empire: A Short History of British Slavery.* Garden City, N.Y.: Anchor, 1974.

Degler, Carl N. *Neither Black Nor White: Slavery and Race Relations in Brazil and the United States.* New York: Macmillan, 1971.

De Montillano, Bernard Ortiz, et al. "They Were Not Here Before Columbus." *Ethnohistory* 44 (Spring 1997).

De Queirós Mattoso, Katia M. *To Be a Slave in Brazil, 1550–1888.* New Brunswick, N.J.: Rutgers University Press, 1986.

Foner, Laura, and Eugene D. Genovese, eds. *Slavery in the New World: A Reader in Comparative History.* Englewood Cliffs, N.J.: Prentice Hall, 1969.

Gaspar, David Barry, and Darlene Clark Hine, eds. *More Than Chattel: Black Women and Slavery in the Americas.* Bloomington: Indiana University Press, 1996.

Genovese, Eugene. *From Rebellion to Revolution: Afro-American Slave Revolts in the Making of the Modern World.* Baton Rouge: Louisiana State University Press, 1979.

Herskovits, Melville J. *The Myth of the Negro Past.* Boston: Beacon Press, 1958.

Hoetink, H. *Slavery and Race Relations in the Americas: Comparative Notes on Their Nature and Nexus.* New York: Harper & Row, 1973.

Klein, Herbert. *African Slavery in Latin America and the Caribbean.* New York: Oxford University Press, 1986.

Knight, Franklin W. *Slave Society in Cuba During the Nineteenth Century.* Madison: University of Wisconsin Press, 1970.

Lockhart, James, and Stuart Schwartz. *Early Latin America: A History of Colonial Spanish America and Brazil.* Cambridge: Cambridge University Press, 1983.

Mintz, Sidney. *Sweetness and Power: The Place of Sugar in Modern History.* New York: Viking, 1985.

Mintz, Sidney W., and Richard Price. *The Birth of African-American Culture: An Anthropological Perspective.* Boston: Beacon, 1992.

Palmer, Colin A. *Slaves of the White God: Blacks in Mexico, 1570–1650.* Cambridge: Harvard University Press, 1976.

Palmié, Stephan, ed. *Slave Cultures and the Cultures of Slavery.* Knoxville: University of Tennessee Press, 1995.

Price, Richard, ed. *Maroon Societies: Rebel Slave Communities in the Americas.* Garden City, N.Y.: Anchor Books, Doubleday, 1973.

Rout, Leslie B., Jr. *The African Experience in Spanish America, 1502 to the Present Day.* Cambridge: Cambridge University Press, 1976.

Schwartz, Stuart B. *Slaves, Peasants, and Rebels: Reconsidering Brazilian Slavery.* Urbana: University of Illinois Press, 1992.

Stein, Stanley J. *Vassouras: A Brazilian Coffee County, 1850–1900.* 1957. Reprint, Princeton: Princeton University Press, 1985.

Thompson, Vincent Bakpetu. *The Making of the African Diaspora in the Americas, 1441–1900.* New York: Longman, 1987.

Van Sertima, Ivan. *They Came Before Columbus: The African Presence in Ancient America.* New York: Random House, 1976.

General Studies

Ajayi, J. F. Ade, and Michael Crowder, eds. *History of West Africa.* Vol. 1. 2nd ed. New York: Columbia University Press, 1976.

Collins, Robert O. *African History: Text and Readings.* 1971. Reprint, New York: M. Wiener, 1999.

Curtin, Philip D., et al. *African History.* Boston: Little, Brown, 1978.

Fage, J. D., and Roland Anthony Oliver, eds. *The Cambridge History of Africa.* Vol. 2, *From c. 500 B.C. to A.D. 1050.* New York: Cambridge University Press, 1977.

July, Robert W. *A History of the African People.* 5th ed. Prospect Heights, Ill.: Waveland Press, 1998.

Shillington, Kevin. *History of Africa.* London: Macmillan, 1995.

PART II: Enslavement, Revolution, and the New Republic, 1619–1820
(Chapters 3–6)

The Colonial South and North

Berlin, Ira, and Philip D. Morgan, eds. *The Slave's Economy: Independent Production by Slaves in the Americas.* London: Frank Cass, 1991.

Breen, T. H., and Stephen Innes. *"Myne Owne Ground": Race and Freedom on Virginia's Eastern Shore, 1640–1676.* New York: Oxford University Press, 1980.

Corkran, David H. *The Cherokee Frontier: Conflict and Survival, 1740–62.* 1962. Reprint, Norman: University of Oklahoma Press, 1966.

———. *The Creek Frontier, 1540–1783.* Norman: University of Oklahoma Press, 1967.

Craven, Wesley Frank. *White, Red, and Black: The Seventeenth-Century Virginian.* New York: W. W. Norton, 1977.

Greene, Lorenzo Johnston. *The Negro in Colonial New England, 1620–1776.* 1942, Reprint, New York: Atheneum, 1968.

Hall, Gwendolyn Midlo. *Africans in Colonial Louisiana: The Development of Afro-Creole Culture in the Eighteenth Century.* Baton Rouge: Louisiana State University Press, 1992.

Hatley, M. Thomas. *The Dividing Paths: Cherokees and South Carolinians Through the Era of Revolution.* New York: Oxford University Press, 1993.

Jordan, Winthrop D. *White Over Black: American Attitudes Toward the Negro, 1550–1812.* Chapel Hill: University of North Carolina Press, 1968.

Klein, Herbert S. *Slavery in the Americas: A Comparative Study of Virginia and Cuba.* Chicago: University of Chicago Press, 1967.

Kulikoff, Allan. *Tobacco and Slaves: The Development of Southern Cultures in the Chesapeake, 1680–1800.* Chapel Hill: University of North Carolina Press, 1986.

Landers, Jane. *Black Society in Spanish Florida.* Urbana: University of Illinois Press, 1999.

Littlefield, Daniel C. *Rice and Slaves: Ethnicity and the Slave Trade in Colonial South Carolina.* 1981. Reprint, Urbana: University of Illinois Press, 1991.

Menard, Russell R. "The Maryland Slave Population, 1658 to 1730: A Demographic Profile of Blacks in Four Counties." *William and Mary Quarterly* 1, no. 32 (1975): 29–54.

Morgan, Edmund S. *American Slavery, American Freedom: The Ordeal of Colonial Virginia.* New York: W. W. Norton, 1975.

Piersen, William D. *Black Yankees: The Development of an Afro-American Subculture in Eighteenth-Century New England.* Amherst: University of Massachusetts Press, 1988.

Silver, Timothy. *A New Face on the Countryside: Indians, Colonists, and Slaves in South Atlantic Forests, 1500-1800.* New York: University of Cambridge Press, 1990.

Tate, Thad W. *The Negro in Eighteenth-Century Williamsburg.* 1965. Reprint, Williamsburg, Va.: Colonial Williamsburg Foundation for the University Press of Virginia, 1985.

Usner, Daniel H., Jr. *Indians, Settlers, and Slaves in a Frontier Exchange Economy: The Lower Mississippi Valley Before 1783.* Chapel Hill: University of North Carolina Press for the Institute of Early American History and Culture, 1992.

Wood, Betty. *Slavery in Colonial Georgia, 1730–1775.* Athens: University of Georgia Press, 1984.

Culture, Resistance, and Abolitionism

Andrews, William L. *To Tell a Free Story: The First Century of Afro-American Autobiography, 1760–1865*. Urbana: University of Illinois Press, 1986.

Aptheker, Herbert. *Negro Slave Revolts in the United States, 1526–1860*. New York: Columbia University Press, 1943.

Creel, Margaret Washington. *A Peculiar People: Slave Religion and Community-Culture Among the Gullahs*. New York: New York University Press, 1988.

Davis, Thomas J. *A Rumor of Revolt: The "Great Negro Plot" in Colonial New York*. Amherst: University of Massachusetts Press, 1990.

Equiano, Olaudah. *The Life of Olaudah Equiano, or, Gustavus Vassa, the African*. 1837. Reprint, edited by Paul Edwards, New York: Negro Universities Press, 1969.

Essig, James D. *The Bonds of Wickedness: American Evangelicals Against Slavery, 1770–1808*. Philadelphia: Temple University Press, 1982.

Frey, Sylvia R. *Water from the Rock: Black Resistance in a Revolutionary Age*. Princeton: Princeton University Press, 1991.

Gomez, Michael A. *Exchanging Our Country Marks: The Transformation of African Identities in the Colonial and Antebellum South*. Chapel Hill: University of North Carolina Press, 1998.

Hine, Darlene Clark, and Earnestine Jenkins, eds. *A Question of Manhood: A Reader in U.S. Black Men's History and Masculinity, 1750–1870*. Vol. 1. Bloomington: Indiana University Press, 1999.

Lampe, Gregory P. *Frederick Douglass: Freedom's Voice, 1818–1845*. East Lansing: Michigan State University Press, 1998.

McManus, Edgar J. *Black Bondage in the North*. Syracuse: Syracuse University Press, 1973.

Melish, Joanne Pope. *Disowning Slavery: Gradual Emancipation and "Race" in New England, 1780–1860*. Ithaca: Cornell University Press, 1998.

Mullin, Michael (Gerald W.) *Africa in America: Slave Acculturation and Resistance in the American South and the British Caribbean, 1736–1831*. Urbana: University of Illinois Press, 1992.

———. *Flight and Rebellion; Slave Resistance in Eighteenth-Century Virginia*. New York: Oxford University Press, 1972, 1979.

Nash, Gary B. *Forging Freedom: The Formation of Philadelphia's Black Community, 1720–1840*. 1988. Reprint, Cambridge: Harvard University Press, 1991.

Sobel, Mechal. *Trabelin' On: The Slave Journey to an Afro-Baptist Faith*. Princeton: Princeton University Press, 1988.

Soderlund, Jean R. *Quakers and Slavery: A Divided Spirit*. Princeton: Princeton University Press, 1985.

White, Shane. *Somewhat More Independent: The End of Slavery in New York City, 1770–1810*. Athens: University of Georgia Press, 1991.

Zilversmit, Arthur. *The First Emancipation: The Abolition of Slavery in the North*. Chicago: University of Chicago Press, 1967.

Revolutionary and Early National Era

Berlin, Ira, and Ronald Hoffman, eds. *Slavery and Freedom in the Age of the American Revolution*. 1983. Reprint, Urbana: University of Illinois Press and the United States Capitol Historical Society, 1986.

Davis, David Brion. *The Problem of Slavery in the Age of Revolution, 1770–1823*. Ithaca: Cornell University Press, 1975.

Hoffman, Ronald, and Peter J. Albert, eds. *The Transforming Hand of Revolution: Reconsidering the American Revolution as a Social Movement.* Charlottesville: University Press of Virginia, 1996.

Johnston, James Hugo. *Race Relations in Virginia and Miscegenation in the South, 1776–1860.* Amherst: University of Massachusetts Press, 1970.

Lynd, Staughton. *Class Conflict, Slavery, and the United States Constitution: Ten Essays.* 1967. Reprint, Indianapolis: Bobbs-Merrill, 1968.

Macleod, Duncan J. *Slavery, Race, and the American Revolution.* London: Cambridge University Press, 1974.

McColley, Robert. *Slavery and Jeffersonian Virginia.* 2d ed. Urbana: University of Illinois Press, 1973.

McDonald, Roderick A. *The Economy and Material Culture of Slaves: Goods and Chattels on the Sugar Plantations of Jamaica and Louisiana.* Baton Rouge: Louisiana State University Press, 1993.

Mellon, Matthew T. *Early American Views on Negro Slavery: From the Letters and Papers of the Founders of the Republic.* 1934. Reprint, New York: Bergman, 1969.

Quarles, Benjamin. *The Negro in the American Revolution.* 1961. Reprint, New York: W. W. Norton, 1973.

Robinson, Donald L. *Slavery in the Structure of American Politics, 1765–1820.* 1970. Reprint, New York: W. W. Norton, 1979.

Walker, James W. St. G. *The Black Loyalists: The Search for a Promised Land in Nova Scotia and Sierra Leone, 1783-1870.* 1976. Reprint, Toronto: University of Toronto Press, 1992.

Wiecek, William M. *The Sources of Antislavery Constitutionalism in America, 1760–1848.* Ithaca: Cornell University Press, 1977.

Wright, Donald R. *African Americans in the Early Republic, 1789–1831.* Arlington Heights, Ill.: Harlan Davidson, 1993.

General Studies

Berlin, Ira. *Many Thousands Gone: The First Two Centuries of Slavery in North America.* Cambridge: Harvard University Press, 1998.

Boles, John B. *Black Southerners, 1619–1869.* Lexington: University of Kentucky Press, 1984.

Duignan, Peter, and Clarence Clendenen. *The United States and the African Slave Trade, 1619–1862.* California: Stanford University Press, 1963.

Ferguson, Leland. *Uncommon Ground: Archaeology and Early African America, 1650–1800.* Washington, D.C.: Smithsonian Institution Press, 1992.

Higginbotham, A. Leon, Jr. *In the Matter of Color: Race and the American Legal Process.* New York: Oxford University Press, 1978.

Huggins, Nathan Irvin. *Black Odyssey: The Afro-American Ordeal in Slavery.* New York: Vintage Books, 1977.

Kolchin, Peter. *American Slavery, 1619–1877.* New York: Hill and Wang, 1993.

Morton, Patricia, ed. *Discovering the Women in Slavery: Emancipating Perspectives on the American Past.* Athens: University of Georgia Press, 1996.

Scherer, Lester B. *Slavery and the Churches in Early America, 1619–1819.* Grand Rapids: Eerdmans, 1975.

Williams, Eric. *Capitalism & Slavery.* Chapel Hill: University of North Carolina Press, 1944.

Williams, William Henry. *Slavery and Freedom in Delaware, 1639–1865.* Wilmington: SR Books, 1996.

PART III: The Antebellum Era, Expansion of Cotton Culture, and Civil War, 1820–1865 (Chapters 7–10)

Social Conditions, Culture, and Community Life

Abrahams, Roger D. *Singing the Master: The Emergence of African American Culture in the Plantation South.* New York: Pantheon, 1992.

Bay, Mia. *The White Image in the Black Mind: African-American Ideas About White People, 1830–1925.* New York: Oxford University Press, 2000.

Blassingame, John W. *The Slave Community: Plantation Life in the Antebellum South.* Rev. ed. New York: Oxford University Press, 1979.

Botkin, B. A. *Lay My Burden Down: A Folk History of Slavery.* Chicago: University of Chicago Press, 1945.

Cornelius, Janet Duitsman. *"When I Can Read My Title Clear": Literacy, Slavery, and Religion in the Antebellum South.* Columbia: University of South Carolina Press, 1991.

Escott, Paul D. *Slavery Remembered: A Record of Twentieth-Century Slave Narratives.* Chapel Hill: University of North Carolina Press, 1979.

Frazier, E. Franklin. *The Negro Church in America.* New York: Schocken, 1974.

———. *The Negro Family in the United States.* 1939. Reprint, Chicago: University of Chicago Press, 1966.

Fredrickson, George M. *The Arrogance of Race: Historical Perspectives on Slavery, Racism, and Social Inequality.* Middletown, Conn.: Wesleyan University Press, 1988.

———. *The Black Image in the White Mind: The Debate on Afro-American Character and Destiny, 1817–1914.* 1972. Reprint, Middletown, Conn.: Wesleyan University Press, 1987.

Genovese, Elizabeth Fox. *Within the Plantation Household: Black and White Women of the Old South.* Chapel Hill: University of North Carolina Press, 1988.

Gutman, Herbert G. *The Black Family in Slavery and Freedom, 1750–1925.* New York: Vintage Books, 1977.

Harris, J. William, ed. *Society and Culture in the Slave South.* London: Routledge, 1992.

Joyner, Charles. *Down by the Riverside: A South Carolina Slave Community.* Urbana: University of Illinois Press, 1984.

King, Wilma. *Stolen Childhood: Slave Youth in Nineteenth-Century America.* Bloomington: Indiana University Press, 1995.

Levine, Lawrence W. *Black Culture and Black Consciousness: Afro-American Folk Thought from Slavery to Freedom.* New York: Oxford University Press, 1977.

Lincoln, C. Eric. *The Black Church Since Frazier.* New York: Schocken Books, 1974.

Malone, Ann Patton. *Sweet Chariot: Slave Family and Household Structure in Nineteenth-Century Louisiana.* Chapel Hill: University of North Carolina Press, 1992.

Mintz, Steven, ed. *African American Voices: The Life Cycle of Slavery.* St. James, N.Y.: Brandywine Press, 1993.

Owens, Leslie Howard. *This Species of Property: Slave Life and Culture in the Old South.* New York: Oxford University Press, 1976.

Painter, Nell Irvin. *Sojourner Truth: A Life, A Symbol.* New York: W. W. Norton, 1996.

Perdue, Theda. *Slavery and the Evolution of Cherokee Society.* Knoxville: University of Tennessee Press, 1979.

Raboteau, Albert J. *A Fire in the Bones: Reflections on African-American Religious History.* Boston: Beacon Press, 1995.

———. *Slave Religion: The "Invisible Institution" in the Antebellum South.* New York: Oxford University Press, 1978.

Salvatore, Nick. *We All Got History: The Memory Books of Amos Webber.* New York: Random House, 1996.

Savitt, Todd L. *Medicine and Slavery: The Diseases and Health Care of Blacks in Antebellum Virginia.* Urbana: University of Illinois Press, 1978.

Savitt, Todd L., and Ronald L. Numbers, eds. *Science and Medicine in the Old South.* Baton Rouge: Louisiana State University Press, 1989.

Scarborough, William K. *The Overseer: Plantation Management in the Old South.* 1966. Reprint, Athens: University of Georgia Press, 1984.

Schwarz, Philip J. *Twice Condemned: Slaves and the Criminal Laws of Virginia, 1705–1865.* Baton Rouge: Louisiana State University Press, 1988.

Stuckey, Sterling. *Slave Culture: Nationalist Theory and the Foundations of Black America.* New York: Oxford University Press, 1987.

Tadman, Michael. *Speculators and Slaves: Masters, Traders, and Slaves in the Old South.* Madison: University of Wisconsin Press, 1989.

Van Deburg, William L. *The Slave Drivers: Black Agricultural Labor Supervisors in the Antebellum South.* 1979. Reprint, New York: Oxford University Press, 1988.

Webber, Thomas L. *Deep Like the Rivers: Education in the Slave-Quarter Community, 1831–1865.* New York: W. W. Norton, 1978.

Weiner, Marli F. *Mistresses and Slaves: Plantation Women in South Carolina, 1830–80.* Urbana: University of Illinois Press, 1998.

White, Deborah Gray. *Ar'n't I a Woman? Female Slaves in the Plantation South.* New York: W. W. Norton, 1985.

Woodson, Carter G. *The History of the Negro Church.* 1921. Reprint, Washington, D.C.: Associated Publishers, 1985.

Resistance, Abolitionism, and the Law

Barnes, Gilbert Hobbs. *The Antislavery Impulse, 1830–1844.* 1933. Reprint, Gloucester, Mass.: P. Smith, 1973.

Belz, Herman. *Abraham Lincoln, Constitutionalism, and Equal Rights in the Civil War Era.* New York: Fordham University Press, 1998.

Bracey, John H., Jr., August Meier, and Elliott Rudwick, eds. *American Slavery: The Question of Resistance.* Belmont, Calif.: Wadsworth Publishing, 1971.

Campbell, Stanley W. *The Slave Catchers: Enforcement of the Fugitive Slave Law, 1850–1860.* Chapel Hill: University of North Carolina Press, 1970.

Cheek, William F., and Aimee Lee Cheek. *John Mercer Langston and the Fight for Black Freedom, 1829–1865.* Urbana: University of Illinois Press, 1989.

Dillon, Merton L. *Slavery Attacked: Southern Slaves and Their Allies, 1619–1865.* Baton Rouge: Louisiana State University Press, 1990.

Douglass, Frederick. *Narrative of the Life of Frederick Douglass: An American Slave.* Edited by Houston A. Baker. New York: Penguin, 1982.

Fehrenbacher, Don E. *Slavery, Law, & Politics: The Dred Scott Case in Historical Perspective.* New York: Oxford University Press, 1981.

Finkelman, Paul. *Dred Scott v. Sandford: A Brief History with Documents.* Boston: Bedford Books, 1997.

———. *An Imperfect Union: Slavery, Federalism, and Comity.* Chapel Hill: University of North Carolina Press, 1981.

Fladeland, Betty. *Abolitionists and Working-Class Problems in the Age of Industrialization.* Baton Rouge: Louisiana State University Press, 1984.

Friedman, Lawrence J. *Gregarious Saints: Self and Community in American Abolitionism, 1830–1870.* New York: Cambridge University Press, 1982.

———. *The Inner Civil War: Northern Intellectuals and the Crisis of the Union.* 1965. Reprint, New York: Harper & Row, 1968.

Harrold, Stanley. *The Abolitionists & the South, 1831–1861.* Lexington: University Press of Kentucky, 1995.

Jacobs, Harriet A. [Linda Brent]. *Incidents in the Life of a Slave Girl: Written by Herself.* Edited by Jean Fagan Yellin. Cambridge: Harvard University Press, 1987.

Jones, Norrece T. *Born a Child of Freedom, Yet a Slave: Mechanisms of Control and Strategies of Resistance in Antebellum South Carolina.* Middletown, Conn.: Wesleyan University Press, 1990.

Kraditor, Aileen S. *Means and Ends in American Abolitionism: Garrison and His Critics on Strategy and Tactics, 1834–1850.* 1969. Reprint, Chicago: Dee, 1989.

Lofton, John L. *Denmark Vesey's Revolt: The Slave Plot That Lit a Fuse to Fort Sumter.* Rev. ed. Kent, Ohio: Kent State University Press, 1983.

McFeely, William S. *Frederick Douglass.* New York: W. W. Norton, 1991.

McKivigan, John R. *The War Against Proslavery Religion: Abolitionism and the Northern Churches, 1830–1865.* Ithaca: Cornell University Press, 1984.

McLaurin, Melton Alonza. *Celia, a Slave.* Athens: University of Georgia Press, 1991.

McPherson, James M. *The Struggle for Equality: Abolitionists and the Negro in the Civil War and Reconstruction.* Princeton: Princeton University Press, 1964.

Oates, Stephen B. *The Fires of Jubilee: Nat Turner's Fierce Rebellion.* 1975. Reprint, New York: Harper & Row, 1990.

———. *To Purge This Land With Blood: A Biography of John Brown.* 1970. Reprint, Amherst: University of Massachusetts Press, 1984.

Pease, William Henry, and Jane H. Pease. *They Who Would Be Free: Blacks' Search for Freedom, 1830–1861.* 1974. Reprint, Urbana: University of Illinois Press, 1990.

Quarles, Benjamin. *Black Abolitionists.* New York: Oxford University Press, 1969.

Richards, Leonard L. *Gentlemen of Property and Standing: Anti-Abolition Mobs in Jacksonian America.* New York: Oxford University Press, 1970.

Starobin, Robert S. *Denmark Vesey: The Slave Conspiracy of 1822.* Englewood Cliffs, N.J.: Prentice Hall, 1970.

Ullman, Victor. *Martin R. Delany: The Beginning of Black Nationalism.* Boston: Beacon, 1971.

Walters, Ronald G. *The Antislavery Appeal: American Abolitionism After 1830.* 1978. Reprint, New York: W. W. Norton, 1984.

Yellin, Jean Fagan. *Women and Sisters: The Antislavery Feminists in American Culture.* New Haven: Yale University Press, 1989.

Free Blacks and Urban and Industrial Bondage

Alexander, Adele Logan. *Ambiguous Lives: Free Women of Color in Rural Georgia, 1789–1879.* Fayetteville: University of Arkansas Press, 1991.

Berlin, Ira. *Slaves Without Masters: The Free Negro in the Antebellum South.* New York: Oxford University Press, 1974.

Brown, Letitia W. *Free Negroes in the District of Columbia, 1790–1846.* New York: Oxford University Press, 1972.

Curry, Leonard P. *The Free Black in Urban America, 1800–1850: The Shadow of the Dream.* Chicago: University of Chicago Press, 1981.

Finkelman, Paul. *Free Blacks in a Slave Society.* Vol. 17. New York: Garland Publishing, Inc., 1989.

Franklin, John Hope. *The Free Negro in North Carolina, 1790–1860.* 1943. Reprint, New York: W. W. Norton, 1971.

Goldin, Claudia D. *Urban Slavery in the American South, 1820-1860: A Quantitative History.* Chicago: University of Chicago Press, 1976.

Horton, James Oliver. *Free People of Color: Inside the African American Community.* Washington, D.C.: Smithsonian Institution Press, 1993.

Jackson, Luther P. *Free Negro Labor and Property Holding in Virginia, 1830–1860.* 1942. Reprint, New York: Russell & Russell, 1971.

Johnson, Michael P., and James L. Roark. *Black Masters: A Free Family of Color in the Old South.* New York: W. W. Norton, 1984.

———. *No Chariot Let Down: Charleston's Free People of Color on the Eve of the Civil War.* New York: W. W. Norton, 1994.

Johnson, Whittington B. *Black Savannah, 1788–1864.* Fayetteville: University of Arkansas Press, 1996.

Landers, Jane G. *Against the Odds: Free Blacks in the Slave Societies of the Americas.* Portland: Cass, 1996.

Lebsock, Suzanne. *The Free Women of Petersburg: Status and Culture in a Southern Town, 1784–1860.* New York: W. W. Norton, 1984.

Lewis, Ronald L. *Coal, Iron, and Slaves: Industrial Slavery in Maryland and Virginia, 1715–1865.* Westport, Conn.: Greenwood Press, 1979.

Litwack, Leon F. *North of Slavery: The Negro in the Free States, 1790–1860.* Chicago: University of Chicago Press, 1961.

Phillips, Christopher. *Freedom's Port: The African American Community of Baltimore, 1790–1860.* Urbana: University of Illinois Press, 1997.

Powers, Bernard E., Jr. *Black Charlestonians: A Social History, 1822–1885.* Fayetteville: University of Arkansas Press, 1994.

Starobin, Robert. *Industrial Slavery in the Old South.* New York: Oxford University Press, 1970.

Taylor, Henry Louis, Jr., ed. *Race and the City: Work, Community, and Protest in Cincinnati, 1820–1970.* Urbana: University of Illinois Press, 1993.

Trotter, Joe W., Jr. *River Jordan: African American Urban Life in the Ohio Valley.* Lexington: University Press of Kentucky, 1998.

Wade, Richard C. *Slavery in the Cities: The South, 1820–1860.* New York: Oxford University Press, 1964.

Wikramanayake, Marina. *A World in Shadow: The Free Black in Antebellum South Carolina.* Columbia: University of South Carolina Press, 1973.

Civil War and Early Emancipation

Berlin, Ira, Joseph P. Reidy, and Leslie S. Rowland, eds. *The Black Military Experience.* New York: Cambridge University Press, 1982.

Berlin, Ira, et al., eds. *The Destruction of Slavery.* New York: Cambridge University Press, 1985.

———. *The Wartime Genesis of Free Labor: The Lower South.* New York: Cambridge University Press, 1990.

Bernstein, Iver. *The New York City Draft Riots: Their Significance in American Society and Politics in the Age of the Civil War.* New York: Oxford University Press, 1990.

Cox, LaWanda. *Lincoln and Black Freedom: A Study in Presidential Leadership.* 1981. Reprint, Urbana: University of Illinois Press, 1985.

Crofts, Daniel W. *Reluctant Confederates: Upper South Unionists in the Secession Crisis.* Chapel Hill: University of North Carolina Press, 1989.

Faust, Drew Gilpin. *The Creation of Confederate Nationalism: Ideology and Identity in the Civil War South.* Baton Rouge: Louisiana State University Press, 1988.

Glatthaar, Joseph T. *Forged in Battle: The Civil War Alliance of Black Soldiers and White Officers.* New York: Free Press, 1990.

McPherson, James M. *Battle Cry of Freedom: The Civil War Era.* New York: Oxford University Press, 1988.

———. *The Negro's Civil War.* New York: Random House, 1965.

Quarles, Benjamin. *The Negro in the Civil War.* 1953. Reprint, New York: Da Capo, 1989.

Rose, Willie Lee, ed. *Rehearsal for Reconstruction: The Port Royal Experiment.* 1964. Reprint, New York: Oxford University Press, 1976.

Savage, Kirk. *Standing Soldiers, Kneeling Slaves: Race, War, and Monument in Nineteenth-Century America.* Princeton: Princeton University Press, 1997.

State, Regional, and General Studies

Berwanger, Eugene H. *The Frontier Against Slavery: Western Anti-Negro Prejudice and the Slavery Extension Controversy.* Urbana: University of Illinois Press, 1967.

Campbell, Randolph B. *An Empire for Slavery: The Peculiar Institution in Texas, 1821–1865.* Baton Rouge: Louisiana State University Press, 1989.

David, Paul A., et al. *Reckoning With Slavery: A Critical Study in the Quantitative History of American Negro Slavery.* New York: Oxford University Press, 1976.

Elkins, Stanley. *Slavery: A Problem in American Institutional and Intellectual Life.* 1959. 3rd ed. Chicago: University of Chicago Press, 1976.

Fields, Barbara J. *Slavery and Freedom on the Middle Ground: Maryland During the Nineteenth Century.* New Haven: Yale University Press, 1985.

Fogel, Robert W. *Without Consent or Contract: The Rise and Fall of American Slavery.* New York: W. W. Norton, 1989.

Fogel, Robert W., and Stanley L. Engerman. *Time on the Cross: The Economics of American Negro Slavery.* 1974. Reprint, New York: W. W. Norton, 1989.

Foner, Jack D. *Blacks and the Military in American History.* New York: Praeger, 1974.

Genovese, Eugene. *Roll, Jordan, Roll: The World the Slaves Made.* 1974. Reprint, New York: Vintage Books, 1976.

Harding, Vincent. *There Is a River: The Black Struggle for Freedom in America.* New York: Vintage Books, 1983.

Kolchin, Peter. *Unfree Labor: American Slavery and Russian Serfdom.* Cambridge: Harvard University Press/Belknap Press, 1987.

Lane, Ann J., ed. *The Debate Over Slavery; Stanley Elkins and His Critics.* Urbana: University of Illinois Press, 1971.

Moore, John Hebron. *The Emergence of the Cotton Kingdom in the Old Southwest: Mississippi, 1770–1860.* Baton Rouge: Louisiana State University Press, 1988.

Oakes, James. *The Ruling Race: A History of American Slaveholders.* New York: Vintage Books, 1983.

———. *Slavery and Freedom: An Interpretation of the Old South.* New York: Alfred A. Knopf, 1990.

Rose, Willie Lee, ed. *Slavery and Freedom.* New York: Oxford University Press, 1982.

Smith, Julia Floyd. *Slavery and Plantation Growth in Antebellum Florida, 1821–1860.* Gainsville: University of Florida Press, 1973.

————. *Slavery and Rice Culture in Low Country Georgia, 1750–1860*. Knoxville: University of Tennessee Press, 1985.

Stampp, Kenneth M. *The Peculiar Institution: Slavery in the Ante-bellum South*. 1956. Reprint, New York: Vintage Books, 1989.

Woodward, C. Vann. *American Counterpoint: Slavery and Racism in the North-South Dialogue*. 1971. Reprint, New York: Oxford University Press, 1983.

PART IV: Emancipation and the First Generation of Freedom, 1865–1915
(Chapters 11–14)

Institutions, Culture, and Politics

Abbott, Richard H. *The Republican Party and the South, 1855–1877: The First Southern Strategy*. Chapel Hill: University of North Carolina Press, 1986.

Anderson, James D. *The Education of Blacks in the South, 1860–1935*. Chapel Hill: University of North Carolina Press, 1988.

Blackett, R. J. M. *Beating Against the Barriers: Biographical Essays in Nineteenth-Century Afro-American History*. Baton Rouge: Louisiana State University Press, 1986.

Bowen, David Warren. *Andrew Johnson and the Negro*. Knoxville: University of Tennessee Press, 1989.

Brodie, Fawn M. *Thaddeus Stevens: Scourge of the South*. 1959. Reprint, New York: W. W. Norton, 1966.

Brown, Elsa Barkley. "'What Has Happened Here': The Politics of Difference in Women's History and Feminist Politics." *Feminist Studies* 18 (Summer 1992).

Current, Richard N. *Those Terrible Carpetbaggers*. New York: Oxford University Press, 1988.

Donald, David. *Charles Sumner and the Rights of Man*. New York: Knopf, 1970.

Du Bois, W. E. B. *The Autobiography of W. E. B. Du Bois: A Soliloquy on Viewing My Life from the Last Decade of Its First Century*. New York: International Publishers, 1968.

————. *Darkwater: Voices from Within the Veil*. 1920. Reprint, New York: Schocken, 1969.

Duster, Alfreda M., ed. *Crusade for Justice: The Autobiography of Ida B. Wells*. Chicago, Ill.: University of Chicago Press, 1970.

Dvorak, Katherine L. *An African-American Exodus: The Segregation of the Southern Churches*. Brooklyn: Carlson, 1991.

Fields, Mamie Garvin, and Karen Fields. *Lemon Swamp and Other Places: A Carolina Memoir*. New York: Free Press, 1983.

Fierce, Milfred C. *The Pan-African Idea in the United States, 1900–1919: African-American Interest in Africa and Interaction with West Africa*. New York: Garland, 1993.

Fitzgerald, Michael W. *The Union League Movement in the Deep South: Politics and Agricultural Change During Reconstruction*. Baton Rouge: Louisiana State University Press, 1989.

Gaines, Kevin K. *Uplifting the Race: Black Leadership, Politics, and Culture in the Twentieth Century*. Chapel Hill: University of North Carolina Press, 1996.

Gatewood, Willard B. *Aristocrats of Color: The Black Elite, 1880–1920*. Bloomington: Indiana University Press, 1993.

Gilmore, Glenda Elizabeth. *Gender and Jim Crow: Women and the Politics of White Su-*

premacy in North Carolina, 1896–1920. North Carolina: University of North Carolina Press, 1996.

Harlan, Louis R. *Booker T. Washington: The Making of a Black Leader, 1856–1901*. New York: Oxford University Press, 1972.

———. *Booker T. Washington: The Wizard of Tuskegee, 1901–1915*. New York: Oxford University Press, 1983.

Henderson, Alexa Benson. *Atlanta Life Insurance Company: Guardian of Black Economic Dignity*. Tuscaloosa: University of Alabama Press, 1990.

Higginbotham, Evelyn Brooks. *Righteous Discontent: The Women's Movement in the Black Baptist Church, 1880–1920*. Cambridge: Harvard University Press, 1993.

Holt, Thomas. *Black Over White: Negro Political Leadership in South Carolina During Reconstruction*. Urbana: University of Illinois Press, 1977.

Jones, Jacqueline. *Soldiers of Light and Love: Northern Teachers and Georgia Blacks, 1865–1873*. 1980. Reprint, Athens: University of Georgia Press, 1992.

Kaczorowski, Robert. *The Politics of Judicial Interpretation: The Federal Courts, Department of Justice, and Civil Rights, 1866–1876*. Dobbs Ferry, N.Y.: Oceana Publications, 1985.

Lewinson, Paul. *Race, Class, & Party: A History of Negro Suffrage and White Politics in the South*. New York: Grosset and Dunlap, 1965.

Lewis, David Levering. *W. E. B. Du Bois: Biography of a Race, 1868–1919*. New York: Henry Holt, 1993.

McFeely, William S. *Yankee Stepfather: General O. O. Howard and the Freedmen*. New Haven: Yale University Press, 1968.

McMurry, Linda O. *George Washington Carver: Scientist and Symbol*. New York: Oxford University Press, 1981.

Meier, August. *Negro Thought in America, 1880–1915: Racial Ideologies in the Age of Booker T. Washington*. Ann Arbor: University of Michigan Press, 1963.

Montgomery, David. *Beyond Equality: Labor and the Radical Republicans, 1862–1872; with a Bibliographical Afterward*. 1967. Reprint, Urbana: University of Illinois Press, 1981.

Moses, Wilson Jeremiah. *Alexander Crummell: A Study of Civilization and Discontent*. New York: Oxford University Press, 1989.

Neverdon-Morton, Cynthia. *Afro-American Women of the South and the Advancement of the Race, 1895–1925*. Knoxville: University of Tennessee Press, 1989.

Nieman, Donald G. *To Set the Law in Motion: The Freedmen's Bureau and the Legal Rights of Blacks, 1865–1868*. Millwood, N.Y.: KTO, 1979.

Ovington, Mary White. *Black and White Sat Down Together: The Reminiscences of an NAACP Founder*. New York: The Feminist Press at the City University of New York, 1995.

Perman, Michael. *Reunion Without Compromise: The South and Reconstruction, 1865–1868*. Cambridge: Cambridge University Press, 1973.

———. *The Road to Redemption: Southern Politics, 1869–1879*. Chapel Hill: University of North Carolina Press, 1984.

Redkey, Edwin S. *Black Exodus: Black Nationalist and Back-to-Africa Movements, 1890–1910*. New Haven: Yale University Press, 1969.

Render, Sylvia Lyons, ed. *The Short Fiction of Charles W. Chesnutt*. Washington, D.C.: Howard University Press, 1981.

Ripley, C. Peter. *Witness for Freedom: African American Voices on Race, Slavery, and Emancipation*. Chapel Hill: University of North Carolina Press, 1993.

Roberts, John W. *From Trickster to Badman: The Black Folk Hero in Slavery and Freedom.* Philadelphia: University of Pennsylvania Press, 1989.

Robinson, Cedric J. *Black Marxism: The Making of the Black Radical Tradition.* Atlantic Highlands, N.J.: Zed Books, 1983.

Rudwick, Elliott. *W. E. B. Du Bois: Voice of the Black Protest Movement.* Urbana University of Illinois Press, 1982.

Singletary, Otis A. *Negro Militia and Reconstruction.* 1957. Reprint, New York: McGraw-Hill, 1969.

Smith, Gerald L. *A Black Educator in the Segregated South: Kentucky's Rufus B. Atwood.* Lexington: University Press of Kentucky, 1994.

Smith, J. Clay, Jr. *Emancipation: The Making of the Black Lawyer, 1844–1944.* Philadelphia: University of Pennsylvania Press, 1993.

Stepto, Robert B. *From Behind the Veil: A Study of Afro-American Narrative.* 2nd ed. Urbana: University of Illinois Press, 1991.

Stuckey, Sterling. *Going Through the Storm: The Influence of African American Art in History.* New York: Oxford University Press, 1994.

Terborg-Penn, Rosalyn. *African American Women in the Struggle for the Vote, 1850–1920.* Bloomington: Indiana University Press, 1998.

Thornbrough, Emma Lou. *T. Thomas Fortune: Militant Journalist.* Chicago: University of Chicago Press, 1972.

Toll, Robert C. *Blacking Up: The Minstrel Show in Nineteenth-Century America.* New York: Oxford University Press, 1974.

Walker, Clarence E. *A Rock in a Weary Land: The African Methodist Episcopal Church During the Civil War and Reconstruction.* Baton Rouge: Louisiana State University Press, 1982.

Wells-Barnett, Ida B. *Crusade for Justice: The Autobiography of Ida B. Wells.* Chicago: University of Chicago Press, 1972.

Wheeler, Edward L. *Uplifting the Race: The Black Minister in the New South, 1865–1902.* New York: University Press of America, 1986.

White, John. *Black Leadership in America from Booker T. Washington to Jesse Jackson.* 2nd ed. New York: Longman, 1990.

Woodson, Carter G. *The Mis-Education of the Negro.* New York: Associated Publishers, 1977.

Economic Emancipation and the Sharecropping System

Cohen, William. *At Freedom's Edge: Black Mobility and the Southern White Quest for Racial Control, 1861–1915.* Baton Rouge: Louisiana State University, 1991.

Glymph, Thavolia, and John J. Kushma, eds. *Essays on the Postbellum Southern Economy.* College Station: Texas A&M University Press for University of Texas at Arlington, 1985.

Higgs, Robert. *Competition and Coercion: Blacks in the American Economy, 1865–1914.* New York: Cambridge University Press, 1977.

Jaynes, Gerald David. *Branches Without Roots: Genesis of the Black Working Class in the American South, 1862–1882.* New York: Oxford University Press, 1986.

Magdol, Edward. *A Right to the Land: Essays on the Freedmen's Community.* Westport, Conn.: Greenwood Press, 1977.

Mandle, Jay R. *Not Slave, Not Free: The African American Economic Experience Since the Civil War.* Durham: Duke University Press, 1992.

Oubre, Claude F. *Forty Acres and a Mule: The Freedmen's Bureau and Black Land Owner-ship.* Baton Rouge: Louisiana State University Press, 1978.

Powell, Lawrence N. *New Masters: Northern Planters During the Civil War and Reconstruc-tion.* New Haven: Yale University Press, 1980.

Ransom, Roger L., and Richard Sutch. *One Kind of Freedom: The Economic Consequences of Emancipation.* Cambridge: Cambridge University Press, 1977.

Saville, Julie. *The Work of Reconstruction: From Slave to Wage Laborers in South Carolina, 1860–1870.* Cambridge: University of Cambridge Press, 1994.

Schwalm, Leslie A. *A Hard Fight for We: Women's Transition from Slavery to Freedom in South Carolina.* Urbana: University of Illinois Press, 1997.

Schweninger, Loren C. *Black Property Owners in the South, 1790–1915.* Urbana: University of Illinois Press, 1990.

Migration, Cities, and Wage Labor

Arnesen, Eric. *Waterfront Workers of New Orleans: Race, Class and Politics, 1863–1923.* New York: Oxford University Press, 1991.

Crew, Spencer R. *Black Life in Secondary Cities: A Comparative Analysis of the Black Com-munities of Camden and Elizabeth, N.J., 1860–1920.* New York: Garland, 1993.

Daniels, Douglas Henry. *Pioneer Urbanites: A Social and Cultural History of Black San Francisco.* Philadelphia: Temple University Press, 1980.

Du Bois, W. E. B. *The Philadelphia Negro: A Social Study.* 1899. Reprint, Philadelphia: University of Pennsylvania Press, 1996.

Fink, Gary, and Merl E. Reed. *Race, Class, and Community in Southern Labor History.* Tuscaloosa: University of Alabama Press, 1994.

Hamilton, Kenneth Marvin. *Black Towns and Profit: Promotion and Development in the Trans-Appalachian West, 1877–1915.* Urbana: University of Illinois Press, 1991.

Hunter, Tera W. *To 'Joy My Freedom: Southern Black Women's Lives and Labors After the Civil War.* Cambridge: Harvard University Press, 1997.

Johnson, Whittington B. *Black Savannah, 1788–1864.* Fayetteville: University of Arkansas Press, 1996.

Katz, Michael B., and Thomas J. Sugrue, eds. *W. E. B. Du Bois, Race, and the City: The Philadelphia Negro and Its Legacy.* Philadelphia: University of Pennsylvania Press, 1998.

Katzman, David M. *Seven Days a Week: Women and Domestic Service in Industrializing America.* New York: Oxford University Press, 1978.

Letwin, Daniel. *The Challenge of Interracial Unionism: Alabama Coal Miners, 1878–1921.* Chapel Hill: University of North Carolina Press, 1998.

Painter, Nell Irvin. *Exodusters: Black Migration to Kansas after Reconstruction.* Kansas: University Press of Kansas, 1976.

Rabinowitz, Howard N. *Race Relations in the Urban South, 1865–1890.* Urbana: University of Illinois Press, 1980.

Rachleff, Peter J. *Black Labor in the South: Richmond, Virginia, 1865–1890.* Philadelphia: Temple University Press, 1984.

Tripp, Steven Elliott. *Yankee Town, Southern City: Race and Class Relations in Civil War Lynchburg.* New York: New York University Press, 1997.

Weare, Walter B. *Black Business in the New South: A Social History of the North Carolina Mutual Life Insurance Company.* Urbana: University of Illinois Press, 1973.

Wright, George C. *Life Behind a Veil: Blacks in Louisville, Kentucky, 1865–1930.* Baton Rouge: Louisiana State University Press, 1985.

Social Conditions, Lynchings, and Race Riots

Brundage, W. Fitzhugh, ed. *Under Sentence of Death: Lynching in the South.* Chapel Hill: University of North Carolina Press, 1997.

Downey, Dennis B., and Raymond M. Hyser. *No Crooked Death: Coatesville, Pennsylvania, and the Lynching of Zachariah Walker.* Urbana: University of Illinois Press, 1991.

Ingalls, Robert P. *Urban Vigilantes in the New South: Tampa, 1882–1936.* Knoxville: University of Tennessee Press, 1988.

Lane, Roger. *Roots of Violence in Black Philadelphia, 1860–1900.* Cambridge: Harvard University Press, 1986.

Royster, Jacqueline Jones, ed. *Southern Horrors and Other Writings: The Anti-Lynching Campaign of Ida B. Wells, 1892–1900.* Boston, Mass.: Bedford, 1997.

Trelease, Allen W. *White Terror: The Ku Klux Klan Conspiracy and Southern Reconstruction.* Westport: Greenwood Press, 1979.

State, Regional, and General Studies

Ayers, Edward L. *The Promise of the New South: Life After Reconstruction.* New York: Oxford University Press, 1992.

Berwanger, Eugene H. *The West and Reconstruction.* Urbana: University of Illinois Press, 1981.

Cobb, James G. *The Most Southern Place on Earth: The Mississippi Delta and the Roots of Regional Identity.* New York: Oxford University Press, 1992.

Dittmer, John. *Black Georgia in the Progressive Era, 1900–1920.* Urbana: University of Illinois Press, 1977.

Du Bois, W. E. B. *Black Reconstruction in America.* 1935. Reprint, New York: Atheneum, 1992.

Foner, Eric. *Nothing but Freedom: Emancipation and Its Legacy.* Baton Rouge: Louisiana State University Press, 1983.

———. *Reconstruction: America's Unfinished Revolution, 1863–1877.* New York: Harper & Row, 1988.

Franklin, Jimmie Lewis. *Journey Toward Hope: A History of Blacks in Oklahoma.* Norman: University of Oklahoma Press, 1982.

Franklin, John Hope. *Reconstruction After the Civil War.* Chicago: University of Chicago Press, 1961.

Kolchin, Peter. *First Freedom: The Response of Alabama's Blacks to Emancipation and Reconstruction.* Westport, Conn.: Greenwood Press, 1972.

Litwack, Leon F. *Been in the Storm So Long.* 1979. Reprint, New York: Vintage Books, 1980.

———. *Trouble in Mind: Black Southerners in the Age of Jim Crow.* New York: Vintage Books, 1998.

Logan, Rayford W. *The Betrayal of the Negro: From Rutherford B. Hayes to Woodrow Wilson.* New York: Collier, 1965.

McMillen, Neil R. *Dark Journey: Black Mississippians in the Age of Jim Crow.* Urbana: University of Illinois Press, 1990.

Savage, W. Sherman. *Blacks in the West.* Westport: Greenwood Press, 1976.

Stampp, Kenneth M. *The Era of Reconstruction, 1865–1877.* 1965. Reprint, New York: Vintage Books, 1967.

Williamson, Joel. *The Crucible of Race: Black-White Relations in the American South Since Emancipation.* New York: Oxford University Press, 1984.

Woodward, C. Vann. *Reunion and Reaction: The Compromise of 1877 and the End of Reconstruction.* 1951. Reprint, New York: Oxford University Press, 1991.

———. *The Strange Career of Jim Crow.* 1955. 2nd ed. rev. New York: Oxford University Press, 1966.

Wright, Gavin. *Old South/New South: Revolutions in the Southern Economy Since the Civil War.* New York: Basic Books, 1986.

PART V: Migration, Depression, and World Wars, 1915–1945
(Chapters 15–19)

Migration, Work, and Urban Community Formation

Anderson, Jervis. *A. Philip Randolph: A Biographical Portrait.* Berkeley: University of California Press, 1986.

Ballard, Allen B. *One More Day's Journey: The Making of Black Philadelphia.* Philadelphia: ISHI Publications, Institute for the Study of Human Issues, 1987.

Beardsley, Edward H. *A History of Neglect: Health Care for Blacks and Mill Workers in the Twentieth-Century South.* Knoxville: University of Tennessee Press, 1987.

Bethel, Elizabeth Rauh. *Promiseland: A Century of Life in a Negro Community.* Philadelphia: Temple University Press, 1981.

Bigham, Darrel E. *We Ask Only a Fair Trial: A History of the Black Community of Evansville, Indiana.* Bloomington: Indiana University Press, 1987.

Bodnar, John, Roger Simon, and Michael P. Weber. *Lives of Their Own: Blacks, Italians, and Poles in Pittsburgh, 1900–1960.* Urbana: University of Illinois Press, 1982.

Borchert, James. *Alley Life in Washington: Family, Community, Religion, and Folklife in the City, 1850–1970.* Urbana: University of Illinois Press, 1980.

Bracey, John H., Jr., August Meier, and Elliott Rudwick, eds. *The Rise of the Ghetto.* Belmont, Calif.: Wadsworth, 1971.

Broussard, Albert S. *Black San Francisco: The Struggle for Racial Equality in the West, 1900–1954.* Lawrence: University Press of Kansas, 1993.

Clarke, John Henrik, ed. *Harlem: A Community in Transition.* New York: Citadel Press, 1969.

Connolly, Harold X. *A Ghetto Grows in Brooklyn.* New York: New York University Press, 1977.

Drake, St. Clair, and Horace R. Cayton. *Black Metropolis: A Study of Negro Life in a Northern City.* Vols. 1 & 2. New York: Harcourt, Brace and World, 1945.

Gottlieb, Peter. *Making Their Own Way: Southern Blacks' Migration to Pittsburgh, 1916–30.* Urbana: University of Illinois Press, 1987.

Greenberg, Cheryl Lynn. *Or Does It Explode?: Black Harlem in the Great Depression.* New York: Oxford University Press, 1991.

Griffin, Farah Jasmine. *"Who Set You Flowin'?": The African-American Migration Narrative.* New York: Oxford University Press, 1995.

Grossman, James R. *Land of Hope: Chicago, Black Southerners, and the Great Migration.* Chicago: University of Chicago Press, 1989.

Harrison, Alferdteen, ed. *Black Exodus: The Great Migration from the American South.* Jackson: University Press of Mississippi, 1991.

Henri, Florette. *Black Migration: Movement North, 1900–1920.* Garden City, N.Y.: Doubleday/Anchor, 1975.

Kusmer, Kenneth L. *A Ghetto Takes Shape: Black Cleveland, 1870–1930.* Urbana: University of Illinois Press, 1976.

Lemke-Santangelo, Gretchen. *Abiding Courage: African American Migrant Women and the East Bay Community.* Chapel Hill: University of North Carolina Press, 1996.

Lewis, Earl. *In Their Own Interests: Race, Class, and Power in Twentieth-Century Norfolk, Virginia.* Berkeley: University of California Press, 1991.

Marks, Carole. *Farewell—We're Good and Gone: The Great Black Migration.* Bloomington: Indiana University Press, 1989.

Moore, Shirley Ann. *To Place Our Deeds: The African American Community in Richmond, California, 1910–1963.* Berkeley: University of California Press, 2000.

Osofsky, Gilbert. *Harlem: The Making of a Ghetto, Negro New York, 1890–1930.* 1963. 2nd ed. New York: Harper & Row, 1971.

Phillips, Kimberley L. *Alabama North: African-American Migrants, Community, and Working-Class Activism in Cleveland, 1915–45.* Urbana: University of Illinois Press, 1999.

Sernett, Milton C. *Bound for the Promised Land: African American Religion and the Great Migration.* Durham: Duke University Press, 1997.

Spear, Allan H. *Black Chicago: The Making of a Negro Ghetto, 1890–1920.* Chicago: University of Chicago Press, 1967.

Taylor, Quintard. *The Forging of a Black Community: Seattle's Central District from 1870 Through the Civil Rights Era.* Seattle: University of Washington Press, 1994.

Thomas, Richard W. *Life for Us Is What We Make It: Building Black Community in Detroit, 1915–1945.* Bloomington: Indiana University Press, 1992.

Trotter, Joe W., Jr. *Black Milwaukee: The Making of an Industrial Proletariat, 1915–45.* Urbana: University of Illinois Press, 1985.

Watkins-Owens, Irma. *Blood Relations: Caribbean Immigrants and the Harlem Community, 1900–1930.* Bloomington: Indiana University Press, 1996.

Williams, Lillian Serece. *The Development of a Black Community: Buffalo, New York, 1900–1940.* Bloomington: Indiana University Press, 1999.

Race, Class, and Labor Relations

Blee, Kathleen M. *Women of the Klan: Racism and Gender in the 1920s.* Berkeley: University of California Press, 1991.

Bracey, John H., Jr., August Meier, and Elliott Rudwick, eds. *Black Workers and Organized Labor.* Belmont, Calif.: Wadsworth, 1971.

Capeci, Dominic J., Jr., and Martha Wilkerson. *Layered Violence: The Detroit Rioters of 1943.* Jackson: University of Mississippi Press, 1991.

Carter, Dan T. *Scottsboro: A Tragedy of the American South.* Rev. ed. Baton Rouge: Louisiana State University Press, 1979.

Cayton, Horace R., and George S. Mitchell. *Black Workers and the New Unions.* Chapel Hill: University of North Carolina Press, 1939.

Clark-Lewis, Elizabeth. *Living In, Living Out: African American Domestics in Washington, D.C., 1910–1940.* Washington, D.C.: Smithsonian Institution Press, 1994.

Dickerson, Dennis C. *Out of the Crucible: Black Steelworkers in Western Pennsylvania, 1875–1980.* New York: State University of New York Press, 1986.

Ellsworth, Scott. *Death in a Promised Land: The Tulsa Race Riot of 1921.* Baton Rouge: Louisiana State University Press, 1982.

Harris, William H. *Keeping the Faith: A. Philip Randolph, Milton P. Webster, and the Brotherhood of Sleeping Car Porters, 1925–37.* Urbana, Ill.: University of Illinois Press, 1977.

Honey, Michael K. *Southern Labor and Black Civil Rights: Organizing Memphis Workers.* Urbana: University of Illinois Press, 1993.

Jackson, Kenneth T. *The Ku Klux Klan in the City, 1915–1930.* New York, Oxford University Press, 1967.

Jacobson, Julius, ed. *The Negro and the American Labor Movement.* Garden City: Doubleday, 1968.

Jones, James H. *Bad Blood: The Tuskegee Syphilis Experiment—a Tragedy of Race and Medicine.* New York: Free Press, 1981.

Lamon, Lester C. *Black Tennesseans, 1900–1930.* Knoxville: University of Tennessee Press, 1977.

McGuire, Phillip, ed. *Taps for a Jim Crow Army: Letters from Black Soldiers in World War II.* 1983. Reprint, Lexington: University Press of Kentucky, 1993.

McKiven, Henry M., Jr. *Iron and Steel: Class, Race, and Community in Birmingham, Alabama, 1875–1920.* Chapel Hill: University of North Carolina Press, 1995.

McMillen, Neil R. *Dark Journey: Black Mississippians in the Age of Jim Crow.* Urbana: University of Illinois Press, 1990.

Meier, August, and Elliott Rudwick. *Black Detroit and the Rise of the UAW.* New York: Oxford University Press, 1979.

Naison, Mark. *Communists in Harlem During the Depression.* Urbana: University of Illinois Press, 1983.

O'Brien, Gail Williams. *The Color of Law: Race, Violence, and Justice in the Post–World War II South.* Chapel Hill: University of North Carolina Press, 1999.

Painter, Nell Irvin. *The Narrative of Hosea Hudson: His Life as a Communist.* Cambridge: Harvard University Press, 1979.

Pfeffer, Paula F. *A. Philip Randolph, Pioneer of the Civil Rights Movement.* Baton Rouge: Louisiana State University Press, 1990.

Reed, Linda. *Simple Decency and Common Sense: The Southern Conference Movement 1938–1963.* Bloomington: Indiana University Press, 1991.

Rosenberg, Daniel. *New Orleans Dockworkers: Race, Labor, and Unionism, 1892–1923.* New York: State University of New York Press, 1988.

Rosengarten, Theodore. *All God's Dangers: The Life of Nate Shaw.* New York: Avon Books, 1974.

Ross, Arthur M., and Herbert Hill, eds. *Employment, Race, and Poverty: A Critical Study of the Disadvantaged Status of Negro Workers from 1865 to 1965.* New York: Harcourt, Brace and World, 1967.

Rouse, Jacqueline Anne. *Lugenia Burns Hope: Black Southern Reformer.* Athens: University of Georgia Press, 1989.

Rudwick, Elliott. *Race Riot at East St. Louis, July 2, 1917.* Urbana: University of Illinois Press, 1982.

Santino, Jack. *Miles of Smiles, Years of Struggle: Stories of Black Pullman Porters.* Urbana: University of Illinois Press, 1989.

Shapiro, Herbert. *White Violence and Black Response: From Reconstruction to Montgomery.* Amherst: University of Massachusetts Press, 1988.

Spero, Sterling D., and Abram L. Harris. *The Black Worker: The Negro and the Labor Movement.* New York: Atheneum, 1968.

Trotter, Joe W., Jr. *Coal, Class, and Color: Blacks in Southern West Virginia, 1915–32.* Urbana: University of Illinois Press, 1990.

Tuttle, William M., Jr. *Race Riot: Chicago in the Red Summer of 1919.* New York: Atheneum, 1984.

Culture, Politics, and Institutions

Anderson, Jervis. *This Was Harlem: A Cultural Portrait, 1900–1950.* New York: Farrar, Straus & Giroux, 1982.

Broderick, Francis L., and August Meier, eds. *Negro Protest Thought in the Twentieth Century.* New York: Bobbs-Merrill, 1965.

Burkett, Randall K. *Black Redemption: Churchmen Speak for the Garvey Movement.* Philadelphia: Temple University Press, 1978.

Collier-Thomas, Bettye. *Daughters of Thunder: Black Women Preachers and Their Sermons, 1850–1979.* San Francisco: Jossey-Bass, 1998.

Cooper, Wayne F. *Claude McKay: Rebel Sojourner in the Harlem Renaissance: A Biography.* New York: Schocken Books, 1987.

Cripps, Thomas. *Slow Fade to Black: The Negro in American Film, 1900–1942.* New York: Oxford University Press, 1993.

Dalfiume, Richard M. *Desegregation of the U.S. Armed Forces: Fighting on Two Fronts, 1939–1953.* Columbia: University of Missouri Press, 1969.

Egerton, John. *Speak Now Against the Day: The Generation Before the Civil Rights Movement in the South.* Chapel Hill: University of North Carolina Press, 1994.

Ely, Melvin Patrick. *The Adventures of Amos 'n' Andy: A Social History of an American Phenomenon.* New York: Free Press, 1991.

Essien-Udom, E. U. *Black Nationalism: A Search for an Identity in America.* New York: Dell, 1964.

Franklin, Vincent P. *The Education of Black Philadelphia: The Social and Educational History of a Minority Community, 1900–1950.* Philadelphia: University of Pennsylvania Press, 1979.

Frazier, E. Franklin. *Black Bourgeoisie: The Rise of a New Middle Class in the United States.* New York: Collier Books, 1957.

Goings, Kenneth W. *The NAACP Comes of Age: The Defeat of Judge John J. Parker.* Bloomington: Indiana University Press, 1990.

Gregg, Robert. *Sparks from the Anvil of Oppression: Philadelphia's African Methodists and Southern Migrants, 1890–1940.* Philadelphia: Temple University Press, 1993.

Hill, Robert A., ed. *The Marcus Garvey and Universal Negro Improvement Association Papers.* Berkeley: University of California, 1983–1986.

Huggins, Nathan Irvin. *Harlem Renaissance.* New York: Oxford University Press, 1971.

Hughes, Langston. *The Big Sea: An Autobiography.* 1940. Reprint, New York: Thunder's Mouth Press, 1986.

Hughes, Langston, and Milton Meltzer. *Black Magic: A Pictorial History of the Negro in American Entertainment.* Englewood Cliffs, N.J.: Prentice Hall, 1967.

Hutchinson, George. *The Harlem Renaissance in Black and White.* Cambridge: Harvard University Press, 1995.

Johnson, James Weldon. *Black Manhattan.* 1930. Reprint, New York: Atheneum, 1968.

Keil, Charles. *Urban Blues.* Chicago, Ill.: University of Chicago Press, 1966.

Kelley, Robin D. G. *Hammer and Hoe: Alabama Communists During the Great Depression.* Chapel Hill: University of North Carolina Press, 1990.

Kellogg, Charles Flint. *NAACP: A History of the National Association for the Advancement of Colored People.* Baltimore: Johns Hopkins University Press, 1967.

Kneebone, John T. *Southern Liberal Journalists and the Issue of Race, 1920–1944.* Chapel Hill: University of North Carolina Press, 1985.

Levy, Eugene. *James Weldon Johnson: Black Leader, Black Voice.* Chicago: University of Chicago, 1973.

Lewis, David Levering. *When Harlem Was in Vogue*. New York: Oxford University Press, 1981.

Lisio, Donald J. *Hoover, Blacks, and Lily-Whites: A Study of Southern Strategies*. Chapel Hill: University of North Carolina Press, 1985.

Locke, Alain, ed. *The New Negro: Voices of the Harlem Renaissance*. 1925. Reprint, New York: Atheneum, 1992.

Martin, Tony. *Race First: The Ideological and Organizational Struggles of Marcus Garvey and the Universal Negro Improvement Association*. 1976. Reprint, Dover, Mass.: Majority Press, 1986.

Meier, August, and Elliott Rudwick. *CORE: A Study in the Civil Rights Movement, 1942–1968*. Urbana: University of Illinois Press, 1973.

Mohraz, Judy Jolley. *The Separate Problem: Case Studies of Black Education in the North, 1900–1930*. Westport, Conn.: Greenwood Press, 1979.

Natanson, Nicholas. *The Black Image in the New Deal: The Politics of FSA Photography*. Knoxville: University of Tennessee Press, 1992.

Patton, Sharon F. *African-American Art*. New York: Oxford University Press, 1998.

Pinderhughes, Dianne M. *Race and Ethnicity in Chicago Politics: A Reexamination of Pluralist Theory*. Urbana: University of Illinois Press, 1987.

Rampersad, Arnold. *The Life of Langston Hughes*. Vol. 1, *1902–1941: I, Too, Sing America*. New York: Oxford University Press, 1986.

Reed, Chrisopher Robert. *The Chicago NAACP and the Rise of Black Professional Leadership, 1910–1966*. Bloomington: Indiana University Press, 1997.

Rooks, Noliwe M. *Hair Raising: Beauty, Culture, and African American Women*. New Brunswick: Rutgers University Press, 1996.

Ruck, Rob. *Sandlot Seasons: Sport in Black Pittsburgh*. Urbana: University of Illinois Press, 1993.

Rudwick, Elliott. *W. E. B. Du Bois: Voice of the Black Protest Movement*. Urbana: University of Illinois Press, 1982.

Shaw, Stephanie J. *What a Woman Ought to Be and to Do: Black Professional Women Workers During the Jim Crow Era*. Chicago: University of Chicago Press, 1996.

Smith, Susan L. *Sick and Tired of Being Sick and Tired: Black Women's Health Activism in America, 1890–1950*. Philadelphia: University of Pennsylvania Press, 1995.

Stearns, Marshall W. *The Story of Jazz*. New York: Oxford University Press, 1956.

Turner, W. Burghardt, and Joyce Moore Turner, eds. *Richard B. Moore, Caribbean Militant in Harlem: Collected Writings, 1920–1972*. Bloomington: Indiana University Press, 1988.

Tushnet, Mark V. *The NAACP's Legal Strategy Against Segregated Education, 1925–1950*. Chapel Hill: University of North Carolina Press, 1987.

Wall, Cheryl A. *Women of the Harlem Renaissance*. Bloomington: Indiana University Press, 1995.

Watts, Jill. *God, Harlem U.S.A.: The Father Divine Story*. Berkeley: University of California Press, 1992.

Weiss, Nancy Joan. *Farewell to the Party of Lincoln: Black Politics in the Age of FDR*. Princeton: Princeton University Press, 1983.

White, Deborah Gray. *Too Heavy a Load: Black Women in Defense of Themselves, 1894–1994*. New York: W. W. Norton, 1999.

Williams, Vernon J., Jr. *From a Caste to a Minority: Changing Attitudes of American Sociologists Toward Afro-Americans, 1896–1945*. New York: Greenwood Press, 1989.

Zangrando, Robert L. *The NAACP Crusade Against Lynching, 1909–1950*. Philadelphia: Temple University Press, 1980.

General Studies

Buchanan, Albert Russell. *Black Americans in World War II*. Santa Barbara: Clio, 1977.

Jackson, Walter A. *Gunnar Myrdal and America's Conscience: Social Engineering and Racial Liberalism, 1938–1987*. Chapel Hill: University of North Carolina Press, 1990.

Kirby, John B. *Black Americans in the Roosevelt Era: Liberalism and Race*. Knoxville: University of Tennessee Press, 1980.

McMillen, Neil R., ed. *Remaking Dixie: The Impact of World War II on the American South*. Jackson: University Press of Mississippi, 1997.

Myrdal, Gunnar. *An American Dilemma: The Negro Problem and Modern Democracy*. Vols. 1 and 2. 1944. Reprint, New York: Pantheon Books, Random House, 1962.

Sullivan, Patricia. *Days of Hope: Race and Democracy in the New Deal Era*. Chapel Hill: University of North Carolina Press, 1996.

Wolters, Raymond. *Negroes and the Great Depression: The Problem of Economic Recovery*. Westport, Conn.: Greenwood Press, 1970.

Wynn, Neil A. *The Afro-American and the Second World War*. New York: Holmes & Meier, 1976.

PART VI: Civil Rights, Black Power, and Deindustrialization, 1945–2000 (Chapters 20–23)

Nonviolent Direct Action Campaigns

Abernathy, Ralph David. *And the Walls Came Tumbling Down: An Autobiography*. New York: Harper & Row, 1989.

Bartley, Numan V. *The Rise of Massive Resistance: Race and Politics in the South During the 1950s*. Baton Rouge: Louisiana University Press, 1969.

Bloom, Jack M. *Class, Race, and the Civil Rights Movement*. Bloomington: Indiana University Press, 1987.

Branch, Taylor. *Parting the Waters: America in the King Years, 1954–63*. New York: Simon & Schuster, 1988.

Burner, Eric R. *And Gently He Shall Lead Them: Robert Parris Moses and Civil Rights in Mississippi*. New York: New York University Press, 1994.

Carson, Clayborne. *In Struggle: SNCC and the Black Awakening of the 1960s*. Cambridge: Harvard University Press, 1980.

Chafe, William H. *Civilities and Civil Rights: Greensboro, North Carolina, and the Black Struggle for Freedom*. New York: Oxford University Press, 1981.

Chappell, David L. *Inside Agitators: White Southerners in the Civil Rights Movement*. Baltimore: Johns Hopkins University Press, 1994.

Chestnut, J. L., Jr., and Julia Cass. *Black in Selma: The Uncommon Life of J. L. Chestnut, Jr. Politics and Power in a Small American Town*. New York: Farrar, Straus & Giroux, 1990.

Collins, Donald E. *When the Church Bell Rang Racist: The Methodist Church and the Civil Rights Movement in Alabama*. Macon: Mercer University Press, 1998.

Crawford, Vicki L., Jacqueline Anne Rouse, and Barbara Woods, eds. *Women in the Civil Rights Movement: Trailblazers and Torchbearers 1941–1965*. Bloomington: Indiana University Press, 1993.

Dittmer, John. *Local People: The Struggle for Civil Rights in Mississippi.* Urbana: University of Illinois Press, 1994.

Eskew, Glenn T. *But for Birmingham: The Local and National Movements in the Civil Rights Struggle.* Chapel Hill: University of North Carolina Press, 1997.

Evans, Sara. *Personal Politics: The Roots of Women's Liberation in the Civil Rights Movement and the New Left.* New York: Vintage Books, 1979.

Fairclough, Adam. *To Redeem the Soul of America: The Southern Christian Leadership Conference and Martin Luther King., Jr.* Athens: University of Georgia Press, 1987.

Farmer, James. *Lay Bare the Heart: An Autobiography of the Civil Rights Movement.* New York: New American Library, 1985.

Garrow, David J. *Bearing the Cross: Martin Luther King, Jr., and the Southern Christian Leadership Conference.* New York: Vintage Books, 1988.

———. *The FBI and Martin Luther King, Jr.: From "Solo" to Memphis.* New York: Penguin Books, 1981.

———. *Protest at Selma: Martin Luther King, Jr., and the Voting Rights Act of 1965.* New Haven: Yale University Press, 1978.

Hampton, Henry, and Steve Fayer, with Sarah Flynn. *Voices of Freedom: An Oral History of the Civil Rights Movement from the 1950s Through the 1980s.* New York: Bantam Books, 1990.

Lawson, Steven F., and Charles Payne. *Debating the Civil Rights Movement, 1945–1968.* Lanham, Md.: Rowman & Littlefield, 1998.

Lee, Chana Kai. *For Freedom's Sake: The Life of Fannie Lou Hamer.* Urbana: University of Illinois Press, 1999.

McAdam, Doug. *Freedom Summer.* New York: Oxford University Press, 1988.

Meier, August, and Elliott Rudwick. *CORE: A Study in the Civil Rights Movement, 1942–1968.* Urbana: University of Illinois Press, 1973.

Morris, Aldon D. *The Origins of the Civil Rights Movement: Black Communities Organizing for Change.* New York: Free Press, 1984.

Norrell, Robert J. *Reaping the Whirl-Wind: The Civil Rights Movement in Tuskegee.* New York: Knopf, 1985.

Payne, Charles M. *I've Got the Light of Freedom: The Organizing Tradition and the Mississippi Freedom Struggle.* Berkeley: University of California Press, 1995.

Raines, Howell. *My Soul Is Rested: Movement Days in the Deep South Remembered.* New York: Penguin Books, 1983.

Robinson, Jo Ann Gibson. *The Montgomery Bus Boycott and the Women Who Started It: The Memoir of Jo Ann Gibson Robinson.* Knoxville: University of Tennessee Press, 1987.

Whitfield, Stephen J. *A Death in the Delta: The Story of Emmett Till.* New York: Free Press, 1988.

Black Power, Urban Violence, and the Law

Blair, Thomas L. *Retreat to the Ghetto: The End of a Dream?* New York: Hill & Wang, 1977.

Chang, Edward T., and Russell C. Leong. *Los Angeles—Struggles Toward Multiethnic Community: Asian American, African American, and Latino Perspectives.* Seattle: University of Washington Press, 1994.

Cross, Theodore. *The Black Power Imperative: Racial Inequality and the Politics of Nonviolence.* New York: Faulkner, 1984.

Fine, Sidney. *Violence in the Model City: The Cavanagh Administration, Race Relations, and the Detroit Riot of 1967.* Ann Arbor: University of Michigan Press, 1989.

Fleming, Cynthia Griggs. *Soon We Will Not Cry: The Liberation of Ruby Doris Smith Robinson.* Lanham: Rowman & Littlefield, 1998.

Fogelson, Robert M. *Violence as Protest: A Study of Riots and Ghettoes.* 1971. Reprint, Westport, Conn: Greenwood Press, 1980.

Harry, Margot. *Attention, Move! This is America!* Chicago: Banner, 1987.

Kerner Commission, ed. *The Kerner Report: The 1968 Report of the National Advisory Commission on Civil Disorders, 1968.* New York: Pantheon, 1988.

Madhubuti, Haki R., ed. *Why L.A. Happened: Implications of the '92 Los Angeles Rebellion.* Chicago: Third World Press, 1993.

O'Brien, Gail Williams. *The Color of Law: Race, Violence, and Justice in the Post–World War II South.* Chapel Hill: University of North Carolina Press, 1999.

Wagner-Pacifici, Robin Erica. *Discourse and Destruction: The City of Philadelphia Versus MOVE.* Chicago: University of Chicago Press, 1994.

Urban Social Change and Deindustrialization

Abbott, Carl. *The New Urban America: Growth and Politics in Sunbelt Cities.* Rev. ed. Chapel Hill: University of North Carolina Press, 1987.

Anderson, Elijah. *Street Wise: Race, Class, and Change in an Urban Community.* Chicago: University of Chicago Press, 1990.

Bayor, Ronald H. *Race and the Shaping of Twentieth-Century Atlanta.* Chapel Hill: University of North Carolina Press, 1996.

Bluestone, Barry, and Bennett Harrison. *The Deindustrialization of America: Plant Closings, Community Abandonment, and the Dismantling of Basic Industry.* New York: Basic Books, 1982.

Bullard, Robert D., ed. *In Search of the New South: The Black Urban Experience in the 1970s and 1980s.* Tuscaloosa: University of Alabama Press, 1989.

Darity, William A., Jr., et al. *The Black Underclass: Critical Essays on Race and Unwantedness.* New York: Garland, 1994.

Davis, Mike. *City of Quartz: Excavating the Future in Los Angeles.* New York: Vintage Books, 1990.

Farley, Reynolds, and Walter R. Allen. *The Color Line and the Quality of Life in America.* New York: Oxford University Press, 1989.

Fink, Leon, and Brian Greenberg. *Upheaval in the Quiet Zone: A History of Hospital Workers' Union, Local 1199.* Urbana: University of Illinois Press, 1989.

Goldfield, David R. *Black, White and Southern: Race Relations and Southern Culture, 1940 to the Present.* Baton Rouge: Louisiana State University Press, 1990.

Greer, Edward. *Big Steel: Black Politics and Corporate Power in Gary, Indiana.* New York: Monthly Review Press, 1979.

Gregory, Steven. *Black Corona: Race and the Politics of Place in an Urban Community.* Princeton: Princeton University Press, 1998.

Katz, Michael B., ed. *The "Underclass" Debate: Views From History.* Princeton: Princeton University Press, 1993.

Lemann, Nicholas. *The Promised Land: The Great Black Migration and How It Changed America.* New York: Knopf, 1991.

Lembcke, Jerry, and Ray Hutchison, eds. *Race, Class, and Urban Change.* Greenwich, Conn.: JAI, 1989.

Massey, Douglas S., and Nancy A. Denton. *American Apartheid: Segregation and the Making of the Underclass.* Cambridge: Harvard University Press, 1993.

Miller, Randall M., and George E. Pozzetta, eds. *Shades of the Sunbelt: Essays on Ethnicity, Race, and the Urban South.* Westport, Conn.: Greenwood Press, 1988.

Nightingale, Carl Husemoller. *On the Edge: A History of Poor Black Children and Their American Dream.* New York: Basic Books, 1993.

Oliver, Melvin, and Thomas M. Shapiro. *Black Wealth/White Wealth: A New Perspective on Racial Inequality.* New York: Routledge, 1997.

Stack, Carol B. *All Our Kin: Strategies for Survival in a Black Community.* New York: Harper & Row, 1974.

———. *Call to Home: African Americans Reclaim the Rural South.* New York: Basic Books, 1996.

Sugrue, Thomas J. *The Origins of the Urban Crisis: Race and Inequality in Postwar Detroit.* Princeton: Princeton University Press, 1996.

Sullivan, L. Mercer. *Getting Paid: Youth Crime and Work in the Inner City.* Ithaca: Cornell University Press, 1989.

Terkel, Studs. *Race: How Blacks and Whites Think and Feel About the American Obsession.* New York: Anchor, 1992.

Wallace, Phyllis A. *Black Women in the Labor Force.* Cambridge: MIT Press, 1982.

Wilhelm, Sidney M. *Who Needs the Negro?* Garden City, N.Y.: Doubleday, 1971.

Wilson, William Julius. *The Declining Significance of Race: Blacks and Changing American Institutions.* Chicago: University of Chicago Press, 1978.

———. *The Truly Disadvantaged: The Inner City, the Underclass, and Public Policy.* Chicago: University of Chicago Press, 1987.

———. *When Work Disappears: The World of the New Urban Poor.* New York: Knopf, 1996.

Politics, Culture, and Identity

Baker, Houston A., Jr., and Patricia Redmond, eds. *Afro-American Literary Study in the 1990s.* Chicago: University of Chicago Press, 1989.

Barker, Lucius, and Mack Jones. *African Americans and the American Political System.* 3rd ed. Englewood Cliffs, N.J.: Prentice Hall, 1994.

Barlow, William. *Voice Over: The Making of Black Radio.* Philadelphia: Temple University Press, 1999.

Bell, Derrick. *And We Are Not Saved: The Elusive Quest for Racial Justice.* New York: Basic Books, 1979.

Bogle, Donald. *A Separate Cinema: Fifty Years of Black Cast Posters.* New York: Noonday, 1992.

Burk, Robert Fredrick. *The Eisenhower Administration and Black Civil Rights.* Knoxville: University of Tennessee Press, 1984.

Carbado, Devon W. *Black Men on Race, Gender, and Sexuality: A Critical Reader.* New York: New York University Press, 1999.

Carson, Clayborne. *Malcolm X: The FBI File.* New York: Carroll & Graf, 1991.

———, ed. *The Autobiography of Martin Luther King, Jr.* New York: Warner Books, 1998.

Christian, Barbara. *Black Women Novelists: The Development of a Tradition, 1892–1976.* Westport: Greenwood Press, 1980.

Collins, Patricia Hill. *Black Feminist Thought: Knowledge, Consciousness, and the Politics of Empowerment.* New York: Routledge, Chapman & Hall, Inc., 1991.

Cripps, Thomas. *Making Movies Black: The Hollywood Message Movie from World War II to the Civil Rights Era.* New York: Oxford University Press, 1993.

Davis, Angela Y. *Women, Culture, and Politics.* New York: Vintage Books, 1990.

DeVeaux, Scott. *The Birth of Bebop: A Social and Musical History.* Berkeley: University of California Press, 1997.

Dickerson, Dennis C. *Militant Mediator: Whitney M. Young, Jr.* Lexington: University Press of Kentucky, 1998.

Duneier, Mitchell. *Slim's Table: Race, Respectability, and Masculinity.* Chicago: University of Chicago Press, 1992.

Dyson, Michael Eric. *Between God and Gangsta Rap: Bearing Witness to Black Culture.* New York: Oxford University Press, 1996.

———. *Making Malcolm: The Myth and Meaning of Malcolm X.* New York: Oxford University Press, 1995.

Elliot, Jeffrey M. *Black Voices in American Politics.* Orlando: Harcourt Brace Jovanovich, 1986.

Evans, Mari., ed. *Black Women Writers (1950–1980): A Critical Evaluation.* Garden City, N.Y.: Doubleday/Anchor, 1994.

Frady, Marshall. *Jesse: The Life and Pilgrimage of Jesse Jackson.* New York: Random House, 1977.

Franklin, John Hope, and August Meier, eds. *Black Leaders of the Twentieth Century.* Urbana: University of Illinois Press, 1982.

Gates, Henry Louis, Jr., and Cornel West. *The Future of the Race.* New York: Vintage Books, 1997.

Gayle, Addison, Jr. *Black Expression: Essays By and About Black Americans in the Creative Arts.* New York: Weybright & Talley, 1969.

George, Nelson. *The Death of Rhythm and Blues.* New York: Plume, 1988.

Graham, Lawrence Otis. *Our Kind of People: Inside America's Black Upper Class.* New York: HarperCollins, 1999.

Gwaltney, John Langston. *Drylongso: A Self-Portrait of Black America.* New York: Vintage Books, 1981.

Haines, Herbert H. *Black Radicals and the Civil Rights Mainstream, 1954–1970.* Knoxville: University of Tennessee Press, 1988.

Henry, Charles P. *Culture and African American Politics.* Bloomington: Indiana University Press, 1990.

Higginbotham, A. Leon, Jr. *Shades of Freedom: Racial Politics and Presumptions of the American Legal Process.* New York: Oxford University Press, 1996.

Hill, Anita. *Anita Hill: Speaking Truth to Power.* New York: Doubleday, 1997.

hooks, bell. *Black Looks: Race and Representation.* Boston: South End Press, 1992.

James, Joy. *Transcending the Talented Tenth: Black Leaders and American Intellectuals.* New York: Routledge, 1997.

Johnson, Charles. *Being and Race: Black Writing Since 1970.* Bloomington: Indiana University Press, 1990.

Johnson, Charles, and John McCluskey, Jr., eds. *Black Men Speaking.* Bloomington: Indiana University Press, 1997.

Kelley, Robin D. G. *Race Rebels: Culture, Politics, and the Black Working Class.* New York: Free Press, 1996.

———. *Yo' Mama's Disfunktional!: Fighting the Culture Wars in Urban America.* Boston: Beacon Press, 1997.

Keppel, Ben. *The Work of Democracy: Ralph Bunche, Kenneth B. Clark, Lorraine Hansberry, and the Cultural Politics of Race.* Cambridge: Cambridge University Press, 1995.

Kleppner, Paul. *Chicago Divided: The Making of a Black Mayor.* DeKalb: Northern Illinois University Press, 1985.

Kousser, J. Morgan. *Colorblind Injustice: Minority Voting Rights and the Undoing of the Second Reconstruction.* Chapel Hill: University of North Carolina Press, 1999.

Landry, Bart. *The New Black Middle Class.* Berkeley: University of California Press, 1987.

Lawson, Steven F. *Black Ballots: Voting Rights in the South, 1944–1969.* New York: Columbia University Press, 1976.

―――. *In Pursuit of Power: Southern Blacks and Electoral Politics, 1965–1982.* New York: Columbia University Press, 1985.

Lipsitz, George. *A Life in the Struggle: Ivory Perry and the Culture of Opposition.* Philadelphia: Temple University Press, 1988.

McAdam, Doug. *Political Process and the Development of Black Insurgency, 1930–1970.* Chicago: University of Chicago Press, 1982.

McBride, David. *Integrating the City of Medicine: Blacks in Philadelphia Health Care, 1910–1965.* Philadelphia: Temple University Press, 1989.

McCloud, Aminah Beverly. *African American Islam.* 1995. New York: Routledge.

McDowell, Deborah E. *Leaving Pipe Shop: Memories of Kin.* New York: Scribner, 1996.

Maultsby, Portia. "African-American Music." Forthcoming in *The New Grove Dictionary of Music and Musicians.* London: Macmillan Publishers.

Mufwene, Salikoko, et al., eds. *African-American English: Structure, History, and Use.* New York: Routledge, 1998.

Panish, Jon. *The Color of Jazz: Race and Representation in Postwar American Culture.* Jackson: University Press of Mississippi, 1997.

Perkins, Eric, ed. *Droppin' Science: Critical Essays on Rap Music and Hip Hop Culture.* Philadelphia: Temple University Press, 1996.

Perry, Bruce. *Malcolm: The Life of the Man Who Changed Black America.* Barytown, N.Y.: Station Hill Press, 1991.

Perry, Theresa, and Lisa Delpit, eds. *The Real Ebonics Debate: Power, Language, and the Education of African-American Children.* Boston: Beacon Press, 1998.

Poplack, Shana, ed. *The English History of African American English.* Oxford: Blackwell Publishers, 1999.

Posnock, Ross. *Color and Culture: Black Writers and the Making of the Modern Intellectual.* Cambridge: Harvard University Press, 1998.

Reed, Ishmael, ed. *MultiAmerican: Essays on Cultural Wars and Cultural Peace.* New York: Penguin Books, 1997.

Smith, Robert C. *Racism in the Post–Civil Rights Era: Now You See It, Now You Don't.* Albany: State University of New York Press, 1995.

Smith, Robert C., and Richard Seltzer. *Race, Class, and Culture: A Study in Afro-American Mass Opinion.* New York: State University of New York Press, 1992.

Stanley, Lawrence, ed. *Rap: The Lyrics.* New York: Penguin Books, 1992.

Stewart, Jeffrey C., ed. *Paul Robeson: Artist and Citizen.* New Brunswick: Rutgers University Press, 1998.

Tate, Claudia, ed. *Black Women Writers at Work.* New York: Continuum, 1998.

Tygiel, Jules. *Baseball's Great Experiment: Jackie Robinson and His Legacy.* New York: Vintage Books, 1983.

Wailoo, Keith. *Drawing Blood: Technology and Disease Identity in Twentieth-Century America.* Baltimore: Johns Hopkins University Press, 1997.

Watts, Jerry Gafio. *Heroism and the Black Intellectual: Ralph Ellison, Politics, and Afro-American Intellectual Life.* Chapel Hill: University of North Carolina Press, 1994.

Weiss, Nancy Joan. *Whitney M. Young, Jr., and the Struggle for Civil Rights.* Princeton: Princeton University Press, 1989.

Werner, Craig. *A Change Is Gonna Come: Music, Race and the Soul of America.* New York: Plume, 1998.

Race and Federal Policy

Anderson, Martin. *The Federal Bulldozer.* Cambridge: MIT Press, 1964.

Belz, Herman. *Equality Transformed: A Quarter-Century of Affirmative Action.* New Brunswick: Transaction, 1991.

Burstein, Paul. *Discrimination, Jobs, and Politics: The Struggle for Equal Employment Opportunity in the United States Since the New Deal.* Chicago: University of Chicago Press, 1985.

Clark, E. Culpper. *The School House Door: Segregation's Last Stand at the University of Alabama.* New York: Oxford University Press, 1995.

Clark, Kenneth B. *Dark Ghetto: Dilemmas of Social Power.* New York: Harper & Row, Publishers, 1965.

Conant, James B. *Slums and Suburbs.* New York: James Bryant, 1961.

Eley, Lynn W., and Thomas W. Casstevens, eds. *The Politics of Fair-Housing Legislation: State and Local Case Studies.* San Francisco: Chandler, 1968.

Formisano, Ronald P. *Boston Against Busing: Race, Class and Ethnicity in the 1960s and 1970s.* Chapel Hill: University of North Carolina Press, 1991.

Hirsch, Arnold. *Making the Second Ghetto: Race and Housing in Chicago, 1940–1960.* Cambridge: Cambridge University Press, 1983.

King, Desmond, *Separate and Unequal: Black Americans and the US Federal Government.* New York: Oxford University Press, 1995.

Kluger, Richard. *Simple Justice: The History of Brown v. the Board of Education and Black America's Struggle for Equality.* New York: Vintage Books, 1975.

Lukas, J. Anthony. *Common Ground: A Turbulent Decade in the Lives of Three American Families.* New York: Vintage Books, 1985.

Mershon, Sherie, and Steven Schlossman. *Foxholes and Color Lines: Desegregating the U.S. Armed Forces.* Baltimore: Johns Hopkins University Press, 1998.

Moreno, Paul D. *From Direct Action to Affirmative Action: Fair Employment Law and Policy in America, 1933–1972.* Baton Rouge: Louisiana State University Press, 1997.

Orser, W. Edward. *Blockbusting in Baltimore: The Edmondson Village Story.* Lexington: University Press of Kentucky, 1994.

Rainwater, Lee, and William L. Yancey. *The Moynihan Report and the Politics of Controversy.* Cambridge: M.I.T. Press, 1967.

Scott, Daryl Michael. *Contempt and Pity: Social Policy and the Image of the Damaged Black Psyche, 1880–1996.* Chapel Hill: University of North Carolina Press, 1997.

Skrentny, John David. *The Ironies of Affirmative Action: Politics, Culture, and Justice in America.* Chicago: University of Chicago Press, 1996.

Wilkinson, J. Harvie, III. *From Brown to Bakke: The Supreme Court and School Integration: 1954–1978.* New York: Oxford University Press, 1979.

Wolters, Raymond. *The Burden of Brown: Thirty Years of School Desegregation.* Knoxville: University of Tennessee Press, 1984.

General Studies

Graham, Hugh Davis. *Civil Rights in the United States.* University Park: Pennsylvania State University Press, 1994.

Hacker, Andrew. *Two Nations: Black and White, Separate, Hostile, Unequal.* New York: Ballantine Books, 1992.

Higham, John, ed. *Civil Rights and Social Wrongs: Black-White Relations Since World War II.* University Park: Pennsylvania State University Press, 1997.

Jaynes, Gerald David, and Robin M. Williams, Jr., eds. *A Common Destiny: Blacks and American Society.* Washington, D.C.: National Academy Press, 1989.

Lawson, Steven F. *Running for Freedom: Civil Rights and Black Politics in America Since 1941.* Philadelphia: Temple University Press, 1991.

Lusane, Clarence. *Race in the Global Era: African Americans at the Millennium.* Boston: South End Press, 1997.

Marable, Manning. *The Crisis of Color and Democracy: Essays on Race, Class and Power.* Monroe, Maine: Common Courage Press, 1992.

———. *Race, Reform, and Rebellion: The Second Reconstruction in Black America, 1945–1990.* Jackson: University of Mississippi Press, 1991.

Newman, Dorothy K., ed. *Protest, Politics, and Prosperity: Black Americans and White Institutions, 1940–1975.* New York: Pantheon, 1978.

Omi, Michael, and Howard Winant. *Racial Formation in the United States from the 1960s to the 1990s.* New York: Routledge, 1994.

Patterson, Orlando. *The Ordeal of Integration: Progress and Resentment in America's "Racial" Crisis.* Washington, D.C.: Civitas Counterpoint, 1997.

Sitkoff, Harvard. *The Struggle for Black Equality, 1954–1980.* New York: Hill & Wang, 1981.

Weisbrot, Robert. *Freedom Bound: A History of America's Civil Rights Movement.* New York: W. W. Norton, 1990.

TEXT CREDITS

INDEX

Aaron, Hank, 570
Abbott, Robert S., 380
Abdul-Jabbar, Kareem, 632
Abernathy, Ralph, 526, 527, 530, 538(illus.)
Abolitionism, 111–112, 227–232; slavery in North and, 73; among women, 111–112, 253–255; during Revolution, 114; decline in South, 139; underground railroad and, 229–231; solidarity in, 231–232
Abraham Lincoln Brigade, 476
"Abroad" marriages, 349
Abu Bakr, 14
Abuse: by overseers, 161–162; of children, 347–348. *See also* Sexual abuse
Abyssinian Baptist Church (Harlem), 456–457
ACS, *see* American Colonization Society (ACS)
Activism, 290–292, 402; during New Deal, 462; student, 527–531, 535; conflict among approaches, 542–543; direct action techniques, 553–563; gay and lesbian, 626. *See also* Abolitionism; Civil rights struggle; Protests
Actors and actresses, *see* Movies; specific individuals
Adams, Henry, 282, 305, 319

Addams, Jane, 396
Adderley, Edwin "Cannon-ball," 568
Aesthetics, 91. *See also* Art(s)
Affirmative action, 591; Republican Party and, 592; resistance to, 611–614
AFL, *see* American Federation of Labor (AFL)
AFL-CIO, segregated unions in, 521
Africa: kingdoms in, 1; West, 1, 9, 11–25; ancient, 2; Northeast, 2–8; precolonial, 2–25; vegetation zones in, 4(illus.); North, 6, 8–9; naming of, 8; societies of, 8; Arabs in, 8–9; Northwest, 8–11; regional differences in, 25; plantation system in, 28; migration to, 136, 220–221, 234–235, 319; family life ideas from, 184–188; cultural roots in, 188; religious roots in, 192–193
African Americans: culture of, 48–49; organizations of, 50–51; separation from whites, 61–62; differences based on African or American birth, 101–102; exclusion from military, 112–113; recruitment during Revolution, 113–114; family life of,

131–133; limits of democracy and, 134–140; religious beliefs and practices of, 189–193; slave ownership by, 217; color, class, gender, and ideological differences among, 232–235; Civil War and, 236–268; enfranchisement of, 270; as voters, 277; at Reconstruction constitutional conventions, 277–278; discrimination against in South, 290; enthusiasm for work on own land, 299; evictions from land, 300; response to World War I, 375–378; refusal to employ, 390–391; anthropological studies and, 489; Persian Gulf War and, 624; conflicts and fragmentation among, 624–628, 628(illus.). *See also* Africans; Free blacks
African Blood Brotherhood (ABB), 411
African Civilization Society, 234–235
African Commune of Bad Relevant Artists (Afri-COBRA), 598
African Episcopal churches, 143, 146(illus.)
African Free School, 231
African Grove (theater), 225

I-1